Other books in the BYU New Testament Commentary series:

The Testimony of Luke by S. Kent Brown

The Revelation of John the Apostle
  by Richard D. Draper and Michael D. Rhodes

Paul's First Epistle to the Corinthians
  by Richard D. Draper and Michael D. Rhodes

The Gospel according to Mark

BRIGHAM YOUNG UNIVERSITY
NEW TESTAMENT COMMENTARY

Julie M. Smith

BYU Studies
Provo, Utah

BYU New Testament Commentary Series Board of Editors

JOHN A. WIDTSOE
———— ❧ ————
FOUNDATION

Significant support from the John A. Widtsoe Foundation in Los Angeles, California, as the Publication Sponsor for this Commentary Series is gratefully acknowledged.
http://www.widtsoefoundation.org/

This Commentary Series is made possible by a generous gift from John S. and Unita W. Welch.

Published by BYU Studies. To contact any member of the board of editors or BYU Studies, write to 1063 JFSB, Brigham Young University, Provo, Utah, 84602, or visit http://byustudies.byu.edu or http://www.byunewtestamentcommentary.com.

Cover images (left to right):

Panel painting of a woman in a blue mantle; Roman period, AD 54–68; Egypt; encaustic on wood; height 38 cm, width 22.3 cm; Director's Fund, 2013; Metropolitan Museum of Art, New York; accession number 2013.438. Image reversed.

Sea of Galilee; photographed by John W. Welch, 2012.

Glass alabastron (perfume bottle); Greek period, 2nd–mid-1st century; eastern Mediterranean; glass; height 11.5 cm, diameter 3.8 cm; Bequest of Walter C. Baker, 1971; Metropolitan Museum of Art, New York; accession number 1972.118.183.

Scripture quotations marked SBLGNT are from the SBL Greek New Testament. Copyright © 2010 Society of Biblical Literature http://www.sbl-site.org and Logos Bible Software http://www.logos.com.

First time in print. Substantive corrections, additions, questions, or comments may be sent to byu_studies@byu.edu.

Library of Congress Cataloging-in-Publication Data

Names: Smith, Julie M., author.
Title: The Gospel according to Mark / Julie M. Smith.
Description: Provo, Utah : BYU Studies, 2018. | Series: Brigham Young University New Testament commentary series | Includes bibliographical references and index.
Identifiers: LCCN 2017053522| ISBN 9781942161530 (hardcover) | ISBN 9781942161547 (ebook)
Subjects: LCSH: Bible. Mark--Commentaries. | Church of Jesus Christ of Latter-day Saints--Doctrines. | Mormon Church--Doctrines.
Classification: LCC BS2585.53 .S65 2018 | DDC 226.3/077--dc23
LC record available at https://lccn.loc.gov/2017053522

Printed in the United States of America
10 9 8 7 6 5 4 3 2 1

About the Brigham Young University New Testament Commentary Series

Welcome to the BYU New Testament Commentary, a project by a group of Latter-day Saint specialists offering to readers a careful, new look at the biblical records that witness the life and ministry of Jesus Christ and the first generation of his church. The commentary series seeks to make the New Testament more accessible to Latter-day Saint general readers and scholars by employing much of current biblical scholarship while reflecting important LDS insights. At the same time, this effort may also be helpful to interested readers of other faiths who want to learn how a group of Latter-day Saint scholars understands the Bible. A fundamental article of faith for Latter-day Saints (Mormons) affirms the Bible "to be the word of God" while adding, understandably, that it needs to be "translated correctly" in order for it to be accurately comprehendible to modern language speakers.

These objectives have helped shape the purposes and parameters of this commentary series. Serious LDS readers of the Bible search the scriptures, looking for depth and breadth in passages whose meanings and mandates may ultimately be plain but not shallow. Such readers and interpreters are served by treatments that unite faith and research, reason and revelation, in prayerfully confronting profound and difficult issues that arise in the texts and affect one's path of progression. The New Testament has served as an influential guide to western civilization for centuries. As such, its records have long been studied by lay people and scholars alike, resulting in a rich reservoir of information that illuminates the New Testament era culturally, historically, and linguistically. Selectively, the BYUNTC builds upon this vast body of knowledge, resting on the Greek texts of the New Testament and connecting helpful elements of linguistic, literary, histori-cal, and cultural research and traditional scholarship together with LDS scriptures and doctrinal perspectives. The combination of all these features distinguishes the BYUNTC from other commentaries, which are readily available elsewhere and which readers may also want to consult for more encyclopedic or specialized discussions.

The tone of the BYUNTC aims to be informative rather than hortatory, and suggestive rather than definitive in its interpretation. The opinions expressed in this series are the views of its contributors and should not necessarily be attributed to The Church of Jesus Christ of Latter-day Saints; Brigham Young University, where many of those involved here are headquartered; or anyone else, though these works have benefitted from input and guidance from a number of colleagues, advisors, editors, and peer reviewers.

Each volume in this series sets in two parallel columns the King James Version (KJV) and a new working translation of the New Testament. Calling this a new "rendition" clarifies that it does not seek to replace the authorized KJV adopted by the LDS Church as its official English text. Rather, it aims to enhance readers' understanding conceptually and spiritually by rendering the Greek texts into modern English with LDS sensitivities in mind. Comparing and explaining the New Rendition in light of the KJV then serves as one important purpose for each volume's notes, comments, analyses, and summaries. This effort responds in modest ways to the desire President J. Reuben Clark Jr. expressed in his diary in 1956 that someday "qualified scholars [would provide] . . . a translation of the New Testament that will give us an accurate translation that shall be pregnant with the great principles of the Restored Gospel."

Depending on their personal skills and interests, the authors of these volumes approach their scholarly sources and LDS materials differently but always with careful exposition and engaging perspectives. In several ways, they employ various interpretive tools, including semantic considerations of Greek vocabulary; cultural, historical, critical, literary, and structural analyses; and intertextual comparisons with other biblical passages, the Book of Mormon, and other scriptural works including the Joseph Smith Translation of the Bible. Observations are also proffered about the doctrinal and spiritual reception of New Testament teachings and practices in the broad LDS religious tradition.

The format also varies moderately from volume to volume regarding introductory materials and the style of commentary. Throughout, Greek and Hebrew terms appear in transliterated form in conformity with standards adopted by the Society of Biblical Literature. In some cases, a volume reproduces the Greek New Testament text based on the Greek text published by the Society of Biblical Literature (2010) or draws upon the twenty-eighth edition of the Nestle-Aland text in *Novum Testamentum Graece* (2012).

Contents

Acknowledgments

I am deeply grateful to friends and colleagues who sacrificed their time to assist me with this endeavor. Kevin Barney generously read and commented on the New Rendition. My sounding board included Craig Harline, Keith Lane, Jennifer Lane, Rico Martinez, Ben Peters, Mike Pope, Joseph Spencer, Thomas Wayment, Mark Wright, and Walker Wright. Kim Berkey, Erica Eastley, Ellen Ellsworth North, Emily Page, and Jenny Webb read early versions of the book; Dave LeFevre read a later version. Lauri and Jeremy Baird, Mary Ann and Rob McFarland, Matt and Scharman Grimmer, Richard and Angela Ross, Carol Armga, and Jeannie Welch made my work easier. Jack Welch and Eric D. Huntsman provided exemplary leadership and support. The volume would not have reached its full potential without Marny K. Parkin and Jennifer Hurlbut.

Working with the BYUNTC 2016 Summer Seminar was one of the highlights of the project; I thank Philip Abbott, Chris Brockman, Andrea Brunken, Andy Mickelson, Joshua Matson, Nathaniel Pribil, Jacob Rennaker, Ben Spackman, Nataliya Tunytska, Elicia Cheney, and Avram Shannon. Brent Schmidt, Kent Brown, and Gaye Strathearn also provided valuable feedback. Andy Mickelson's aid was greatly appreciated. And, of course, I thank Derrick, Simon, Nathan, and Truman.

List of Abbreviations

BCE and CE   Before the Common Era and Common Era[1]

D&C   The Doctrine and Covenants

ESV   English Standard Version

HB   Hebrew Bible[2]

JST   The Joseph Smith Translation[3]

KJV   King James Version

LXX   The Septuagint[4]

NET   The New English Translation

NIV   The New International Version

NRSV   The New Revised Standard Version

NT   New Testament

---

1. These terms replace "BC" and "AD"; they are used to conform to current academic convention.

2. While the term "Old Testament" is more common for the general reader, I have chosen to use the term "Hebrew Bible" in deference to current academic convention and out of respect for those who find the idea of referring to their sacred text as "old" dismissive. But there is controversy surrounding the terminology here; Amy-Jill Levine (a Jewish scholar of the NT) has argued against the use of "Hebrew Bible." See Amy-Jill Levine, *The Misunderstood Jew* (San Francisco: HarperSanFrancisco, 2006), 193–99.

3. See appendix I: "The Joseph Smith Translation."

4. The Septuagint is the ancient Greek translation of the HB/Old Testament. It was the version of the Bible known to Mark's community. As with all translations, it differs in some respects from its source text. In some cases, the numbering of the Psalms differs from the KJV to the LXX; the commentary indicates both to avoid confusion.

Introduction

The four Gospels have been compared to the facets of a diamond; each one reflects the light of Christ in a distinct manner.[1] For me, as a believing Latter-day Saint scholar, it is Mark whose shine most attracts my gaze—partially because its light is so often ignored. The Jesus presented in Mark's Gospel is a man of action and few words. He is witty, warm, and wise. He's also the Son of God. He has power which leaves people in awe, and he uses that power to help people whom most people don't like. He hugs little kids. He listens to and learns from women. He banishes demons and reminds parents to feed their children. He doesn't know everything, but he knows how to end chaos. This Jesus is betrayed and abandoned and alone and humiliated, but he still chooses God's will over his own—even though he didn't want to. Mark tells an amazing story.

Mark—at least from the vantage point of a twenty-first-century Latter-day Saint audience—is virtually unknown. Following broader trends in Christian history, Latter-day Saints have privileged John's and Matthew's Gospels.[2] Mark's Gospel gets very little attention, and when it does, it is

---

1. Roger R. Keller, "Mark and Luke: Two Facets of a Diamond," in *Sperry Symposium Classics: The New Testament*, ed. Frank F. Judd Jr. and Gaye Strathearn (Provo, Utah: Religious Studies Center, Brigham Young University; Salt Lake City: Deseret Book, 2006), 92–107.

2. According to the LDS Scripture Citation Index (which includes general conference addresses from 1942 to the present as well as the *Journal of Discourses* and similar sources; see Stephen W. Liddle and Richard Galbraith, LDS Scripture Citation Index, scriptures. byu.edu), citations of the four Gospels are as follows as of July 2018: Matthew: 9,855 citations; Mark: 1,420 citations; Luke: 4,135 citations; and John: 6,799 citations. The current seminary manual is similarly disproportionate (28 lessons on Matthew, 9 on Mark, 17 on Luke, and 21 on John). Even accounting for the varying lengths of the Gospels, this is quite a disparity. The preference for the other Gospels likely stems from the traditional (but inaccurate) belief that Mark is an abbreviation of Matthew's Gospel. And because

usually read through the lenses of the other Gospels, and thus Mark's distinctive voice is muted. So it is truly a gem hidden in plain sight. My overriding goal in this commentary is to recover Mark's distinct, unique voice.

The Approach of This Commentary

Despite its hefty page count, this commentary is extremely narrow. There is simply no way that one volume could adequately cover all one might want to examine in the Gospel of Mark, and so I've chosen just a few areas on which to comment and left the rest to other interpreters.

The primary question that this commentary seeks to answer is this: What would this story have meant to Mark's earliest audiences? Because this is the guiding question, the following interpretive approaches—although indubitably important and valuable—were not employed:

1. *Source Criticism* (Where did Mark get the stories about Jesus?).[3] It is clear that Mark's Gospel is not an entirely new creation but includes underlying sources, oral and perhaps written. Many interpreters have done fine work in teasing out which portions of the story were more likely to have been written by Mark and which are more likely to have predated the text, but this commentary does not explore this issue. It is extremely unlikely that Mark's early audiences would have listened to the story with an ear to which parts were new and which were traditional, and so a source critical approach does not help answer the guiding question of the commentary.

2. *The Quest for the Historical Jesus* (How closely does the story relate to the actual life of Jesus?). For over a century, scholars have labored mightily to determine which of the words and deeds recorded in the NT originate with Jesus and which are later additions. This is an important question for better understanding Jesus, but it is not the focus of this commentary because it is tangential to the guiding question. Mark's earliest audiences would have heard the narrative as a story; they would have been unlikely to ponder which parts of that story stemmed from Jesus and which from later storytellers. So this commentary does not explore the question of how close or loose the relationship is between Mark's Gospel and Jesus' actual life story,

---

Mark is often read through the lens of Matthew and Luke's retelling of the stories, students sometimes assume they are familiar with Mark's Gospel when they have not considered it in its own right.

3. As used in biblical interpretation, the word "criticism" does not carry the common meaning of being critical. Rather, it simply suggests a close analysis. Hence, this term refers not to being critical of Mark's sources but rather of analyzing them carefully.

although there is at least some distance between the two. Some interpreters acknowledge this distance by referring to "Mark's Jesus" instead of to "Jesus"; the gain in precision created by this usage did not, for me, outweigh the pedantry of the phrasing, so I have not used it. Nonetheless, given that the first Gospel is written about forty years after Jesus died and in a language that he did not speak, there is no doubt that the text contains at least some materials that do not reflect his mortal life (see, for example, the Notes on 7:19). So references herein to "Jesus" are not necessarily to the historical figure but more specifically to the character in Mark's story, and the question of how much overlap there is between the historical Jesus and the Markan Jesus is a question for another volume. As a matter of my personal faith, I think that Mark's Jesus is a fairly close but not perfect approximation of the historical Jesus, but I recognize that this question cannot be settled by analysis of the text. S. Kent Brown has written that Mark's Gospel is recognized as being the closest "both in time and in tone"[4] to the ministry of Jesus, which amply justifies a close study of Mark's story.

3. *Reception History* (How have various people or groups interpreted this story?). This includes:

   a. *Matthew and Luke.* It is fairly common practice to solve interpretive problems in Mark's Gospel by turning to the other Gospels, particularly Matthew and Luke. However, Mark's earliest audiences would not have had access to these writings because they postdate Mark.[5] But even if they had those texts, there is good reason to be suspicious about the practice of using them to interpret Mark. For example, in 3:13, the text permits two possible readings: (1) Jesus leads a large group up the mountain and chooses the Twelve from that group or (2) Jesus takes only the Twelve up the mountain and then ordains them. It is understandable that an interpreter would want to erase the ambiguity by consulting Matthew's and Luke's accounts. Matthew 10:1–2 clarifies that Jesus took only the Twelve with him, but Luke 6:12–13 clarifies that Jesus took a larger group. This example shows why Mark should not be interpreted with reference to the other Gospels: they do not always agree with each other.[6]

---

4. S. Kent Brown, "The Testimony of Mark," in *Studies in Scripture, Volume Five: The Gospels,* ed. Kent P. Jackson and Robert L. Millet (Salt Lake City: Deseret Book, 1986), 61.

5. There is ample evidence that Mark's Gospel was written first and that, when Matthew and Luke wrote their Gospels, they had access to the Gospel of Mark. For an explanation of the relationship between Mark and the other Gospels, see Craig A. Evans, *Mark 8:27–16:20* (Nashville: Thomas Nelson Publishers, 2001), xliii–lviii.

6. For an exploration of Mark's relationship to the other Gospels, see Robert H. Stein, *Mark* (Grand Rapids, Mich.: Baker Academic, 2008), 17–18; Adela Yarbro Collins, *Mark: A Commentary* (Minneapolis, Minn.: Fortress Press, 2007), 94–95; and Ben Witherington III, *The Gospel of Mark: A Socio-rhetorical Commentary* (Grand Rapids, Mich.: William B. Eerdmans Publishing, 2001), 18–19.

b. *Christian History.* Because it was believed for most of history that Mark was an abbreviation of Matthew, very little attention was paid to the Gospel of Mark. This commentary does not engage with what little interpretation there is.[7] Again, while interesting in its own right, how later Christians interpreted Mark does not necessarily shed light on how Mark's first audiences would have understood the text.

c. *Latter-day Saint History.* There has been very little in the Latter-day Saint tradition that speaks specifically to the Gospel of Mark. This commentary does not focus on what there is because (1) it is either already known—or at least accessible—to most Latter-day Saint readers and (2) it does not speak to the question of how Mark's first audiences would have interpreted the text. For example, Latter-day Saint readers normally interpret the scene on the Mount of Transfiguration as including the bestowal of priesthood keys. From a Restoration perspective, that is certainly possible (see the Notes on 9:2–13). But there is nothing in Mark's text that would have led its first audiences to conclude that the story of Jesus' Transfiguration involved the transmission of priesthood keys, so this idea is not germane to the guiding question of this commentary. (This is not to conclude that keys were not given on the Mount of Transfiguration; it is merely to say that this is not part of Mark's story.) Readers may be surprised to find that there are virtually no quotations from Latter-day Saint authorities in this book; while these leaders have been given authority to determine doctrine and practice for the current Church, this generally does not involve commenting on how Mark's first audiences interpreted this text. Hence, while their comments are properly and importantly the concern of Church members seeking to understand doctrine, they are not germane to understanding what Mark's early audiences thought about Mark's story of Jesus. The Joseph Smith Translation (JST) presents a special case since in some instances it may restore the text to how it originally read; the JST is treated in appendix I. (Readers may wonder in what sense this is a Latter-day Saint commentary if it does not cite Latter-day Saint authorities; it is a Latter-day Saint commentary in the sense that it is directed to a Latter-day Saint audience and speaks to Latter-day Saint concerns.)

4. *Doctrinal* (What is the correct doctrine?). In other Christian traditions, where doctrine is determined solely by the text of scripture, a commentary on scripture would be, in effect, a doctrinal commentary. But this is not the case for the Latter-day Saint tradition, which gives place to prophetic revelation alongside scripture in determining doctrine. So it would not be possible for any

---

7. For a good basic history of the interpretation of the Gospel of Mark, see Janice Capel Anderson and Stephen D. Moore, "Introduction: The Lives of Mark," in *Mark and Method: New Approaches in Biblical Studies,* 2d ed., ed. Janice Capel Anderson and Stephen D. Moore (Minneapolis: Fortress Press, 2008).

Latter-day Saint scripture commentary to declare doctrine based exclusively on the text, but in the case of this commentary in particular, its focus is on the topics enumerated in the next section and not doctrine per se. This commentary attempts to describe Mark's Gospel without inferring that it should always be normative for modern Latter-day Saint belief and practice. (See, for example, the Notes on 10:1–12, where Mark's account of Jesus' teachings on divorce does not mesh precisely with modern Latter-day Saint policies.)

5. *Devotional Application* (What impact should this story have in my life?). It should go without saying that personal application of the scriptures is important. Nonetheless, this commentary does not explicitly draw out ways in which readers might do that, despite my fervent hope that they will. Latter-day Saint readers are generally well-versed in applying texts to themselves, so, given space constraints, it didn't make sense to devote attention to that topic, despite its importance. Instead, I used the limited space for the part of the interpretive task that readers might not be prepared to undertake themselves: to survey, present, and assess the text using the methodologies described below.

Again, all of the above approaches are valid and important, but because they aren't germane to the guiding question of this book, they are generally not treated herein. (There are a few instances where these questions are pertinent to understanding the text and so are briefly treated.[8]) Answering the guiding question led me to focus on five areas:

1. *Textual Variants and Translation Issues.* Mark's first audiences did not, obviously, have the King James Version of the Bible. The first copies of Mark's Gospel were written in common Greek. There are many ancient fragments and complete copies of Mark, and they do not agree in every detail. So this commentary considers variants in ancient manuscripts that might better reflect the story as the early audiences would have heard it.[9] Tricky translation issues are also discussed (see also the section on the New Rendition below).

2. *Basic Cultural Knowledge.* There are things Mark's audiences would have known that modern readers may not. This includes items such as the relative size of a mustard seed (see the Notes on 4:31) and divorce customs (see the Notes on 10:2). This background knowledge would have informed how Mark's first audiences approached the text and so is necessary for modern readers. This commentary makes use of rabbinic sources—which are a crucial tool for understanding the Jewish background to Jesus' life and to Mark's text— while simultaneously recognizing that these sources are problematic in some

---

8. See, for example, the section "Does Mark 4:10–20 Stem from Jesus' Ministry or from the Early Church" after the Notes on 4:12, or "The Transfiguration in Restoration Thought" after the Notes on 9:8.

9. See, for example, the Notes on 1:41 and, especially, appendix D: "Mark 16:9–20."

ways since they post-date Jesus and are the product of a different environment. I assume that most of the readers of this book are Latter-day Saints, and so I address assumptions that they are likely to bring to their reading of the text.

3. *Biblical Allusions.* It may be an exaggeration to say that every verse of Mark's Gospel alludes to the Hebrew Bible (abbreviated as HB[10]), but it isn't much of one. Because modern readers may be unaware of these allusions, echoes, and quotations that Mark's first audiences could have recognized, one of the focal points of this commentary is careful attention to biblical allusions. For example, the enigmatic scene where the partially healed blind man announces that he sees men as trees walking can be better understood in light of similar texts in Jeremiah 1:11–13; Zechariah 4:1–6; Judges 9:7–15; and Isaiah 6:9.[11] For Mark, that Bible is the Septuagint (abbreviated as LXX), which is the Greek translation of Jewish scripture. As with all translations, it is not identical to its source text; the Notes will discuss passages where the Septuagint differs from the Hebrew text.[12] This commentary leaves open the question of whether (1) specific HB texts prophesied of Jesus and are thus fulfilled in Mark, (2) Jesus himself deliberately modeled his ministry to match these HB texts, (3) Mark shaped the accounts of Jesus' life to echo HB texts, or (4) there is no intentional relationship between the texts, but the reader might nonetheless learn from comparing them. Which situation occurs with each allusion is left for the reader to determine for herself. This commentary seeks to be inclusive instead of selective in the presentation of possible intertexts; this means that some possibilities are included that have less claim than others do for being important echoes of HB texts; it is up to the reader to examine the evidence.

4. *Literary Interpretation.* In the 1980s, biblical studies took a turn toward literary approaches to scripture. Tools common in the analysis of literature—plot, structure, characterization, repetition, and many others—were deployed in the interpretation of biblical texts with insightful results. Because these tools are so very helpful in interpreting Mark's text, much of this commentary focuses on literary approaches to the text. For example, much of the power of 5:21–43 derives from the way in which Mark has structured the plot so that one story interrupts the other.[13] Similarly, the recognition that Jesus prophesies of his coming death three times—and that each time that teaching is followed by a misunderstanding by the disciples and then by Jesus' paradoxical

---

10. Latter-day Saints customarily use the term "Old Testament" to describe this portion of scripture. Out of deference to Jewish sensibilities, most modern biblical scholarship uses the term "Hebrew Bible," and so it is used in this commentary.

11. See the Notes on 8:24.

12. See particularly the commentary on the use of the title "Son of Man" in the Notes on 2:10.

13. See "The Relationship between the Bleeding Woman and Jairus's Daughter" after the Notes on 5:43.

teachings about discipleship—is a crucial insight into Mark's narrative strategy.[14] Recent research suggesting that Mark's Gospel was primarily an oral performance (with the written text being secondary, much as sheet music is a tool for the performer and not the primary vehicle for communication with the audience) will be closely considered and its many implications explored throughout the commentary.

5. *Nonandrocentric Interpretation.*[15] For most of its history, the Bible has been interpreted only by men. It is, therefore, no surprise that most interpretations have been unconsciously androcentric. Yet a text that contains a story with menstruation as its focal point (5:25–34), a woman who anoints Jesus (14:3–9), and female disciples as the sole witnesses to Jesus' death, burial, and Resurrection (15:40–41, 47; 16:1–8) clearly displays a focus on women. This commentary seeks to correct the historical imbalance by paying close attention to women's stories and concerns.

I selected these five areas for emphasis because I felt that they had the largest potential return on investment—they are the most helpful for understanding Mark but the least well explored. Other areas that surely deserve more attention than I could provide include a deeper consideration of the Hellenistic cultural background of the text and a fuller linguistic focus on the Greek text. Within the constraints of this commentary, I was only able to touch on these important considerations.[16]

An unusual feature of this commentary is its inclusion of multiple options for interpretation, presented in the form of a list. For example, the Notes on 1:10—when the Spirit descends like a dove at Jesus' baptism—includes seven options for the symbolism of the dove. I tried to collate all of the reasonable interpretive options and present them along with any significant strengths, weaknesses, and implications of each position. (I also hope that the lists will make a long and dense volume a bit more user friendly by making it easier to focus on information that is or is not of interest to the reader.) In many cases, the options are not mutually exclusive.

---

14. See the Analysis of 10:32–45.

15. I prefer the term "nonandrocentric" to "feminist" in this context because it suggests avoiding the bias—namely, an androcentric (male-focused) bias—common to virtually all interpretations of biblical texts, as opposed to the perception that the word "feminist" can have of imposing an agenda that advances certain modern concerns that may be foreign to the text. I intend for my version of nonandrocentric interpretation to be an uncovering and a restoration and not an external imposition on the text.

16. Readers interested in a fuller treatment of the Hellenistic cultural background should consult Collins, *Mark.* A good source for a linguistic focus on the Greek text is Rodney J. Decker, *Mark 1–8: A Handbook on the Greek Text* and *Mark 9–16: A Handbook on the Greek Text* (Baylor: Baylor University Press, 2014).

Some readers may be disappointed in this lack of certainty, but I feel that it best reflects the reality of biblical interpretation: in many instances, we simply cannot determine from this historical distance which interpretation is best. These lists might be useful to those teaching the Gospel of Mark, since they can promote active class discussion.

This approach of presenting the reader with options to ponder takes its cue from the Gospel of Mark itself. A common occurrence in Mark is for a story to include a thought-provoking question so that the audience will reflect and reach their own conclusions (for example, 4:41; 6:2; 8:17–21, 29). Mark frequently poses questions and provides the tools with which to answer the questions but does not explicitly provide the answers. This volume often does the same.

While this approach is unusual, I think it can be defended as a legitimate model for a Latter-day Saint commentary due to the openness that a Latter-day Saint reader should have to entertaining many options. While Latter-day Saint readers might worry that commentaries will be in error (and this is certainly possible), I worry more that commentaries will close down discussion. Presenting options and encouraging thoughtful consideration of them is, as I see it, a way to empower readers, to avoid the temptation to advance one's own authority, and to reinforce the idea that texts can have more than one meaning, and thus the reader should be open to new possibilities. This is especially important in a text that probably was originally presented as an oral performance,[17] which means that various storytellers might have presented the story quite differently.

I feel strongly that this kind of pondering of multiple options can lead to personal revelation. As President Dallin H. Oaks has written, "One trouble with commentaries is that their authors sometimes focus on only one meaning, to the exclusion of others. As a result, commentaries, if not used with great care, may illuminate the author's chosen and correct meaning but close our eyes and restrict our horizons to other possible meanings. Sometimes those other, less obvious meanings can be the ones most valuable and useful to us as we seek to understand our own dispensation and to obtain answers to our own questions. This is why the teaching of the Holy Ghost is a better guide to scriptural interpretation than even the best commentary."[18] Where many commentaries might present only one

---

17. See the subheading "Was the Gospel of Mark Originally a Written Text or an Oral Performance?" in appendix A.

18. Dallin H. Oaks, "Scripture Reading and Revelation," *Ensign* 25 (January 1995): 9.

option, I felt that it was important to present all reasonable options to the reader and leave her to reach her own conclusions. In that sense, this is a thoroughly Latter-day Saint commentary in that it leaves the reader to the guidance of the Spirit to interpret the text. The lists are not presented as an end in themselves but rather as an invitation to the reader to continue thinking about the text. For example, in the discussion of 2:8, Jesus perceived that his audience was reasoning within themselves after he announced that a man's sins had been forgiven, and so Jesus asked them, "Why reason ye these things in your hearts?" The commentary points out that there are three different ways to understand Jesus' concern:

1. They were *reasoning* (when the situation called for something else, perhaps faith).

2. They were reasoning *within themselves* (instead of asking Jesus for more understanding).

3. They were reasoning *in their hearts* (instead of, perhaps, in their spirits).

This is a fine opportunity for pondering and self-reflection; it presents an occasion for readers to consider instances where their own behavior might not meet the standard that Jesus is setting here. I suspect that different readers would be led to focus on different interpretations of this verse.

The lists also make explicit that any reader must make a nearly infinite number of interpretive decisions while reading; hopefully, the lists will make the process of making those choices more deliberate and intentional and will also open up to the reader options that were not previously realized. Early readers of this volume were sometimes disappointed that the lists are not normally followed by my opinion of which option is most likely. Indeed, the options are rarely all equally likely. But I felt that, in general, it was better to present options and leave the interpretation to my reader. (Readers interested in my own approach will find it in the Analysis sections, where I sometimes assume one of the options from a previous list.) The lists are not ordered by likelihood.

There are some topics related to the Gospel of Mark that are not treated as lists of options because they are not debatable or ambiguous in Mark's text: Mark very clearly presents Jesus as the Son of God, who called disciples, performed miracles, suffered, died, and was raised from the dead.

The commentary contains the following sections for each portion of Mark's text:

1. *Greek Text.* The NT was written in Greek. While the original texts are no longer extant, scholars examine the existing ancient manuscripts and fragments and attempt to determine which variants most likely reflect the earliest texts

of Mark. The Greek text used in this volume, the Society for Biblical Literature's Greek New Testament, is a product of that process.[19]

2. *King James Version.* This is the official English-language Bible for Latter-day Saints.

3. *The New Rendition.* This is a new rendition of the text; see the section on it below for more information.

4. *Notes.* These exegetical notes proceed phrase by phrase through Mark's Gospel and provide textual, background, and interpretive comments. It is important to also read the Analysis section and not just the exegetical notes in order to get a full picture of the meaning of the text.

5. *Additional Information.* As needed, supplemental comments, marked by lines, provide additional information about the passage. Most of these explore the relationship between a text in Mark and an HB text.

6. *Analysis.* This section summarizes and analyzes the passage and calls attention to important implications of the passage.

While this commentary covers many different themes in Mark's Gospel, three predominate and so will be briefly introduced here: discipleship, women's roles, and the nature of Jesus.

Discipleship in Mark's Gospel

Perhaps the most distinctive feature of Mark's Gospel is its comprehensive focus on the theme of discipleship. This theme permeates every scene in Mark—even those that might not seem to focus on it. For example, Mark's Gethsemane scene does not emphasize Jesus' experience of suffering to the same extent as it focuses on Jesus' directions to his disciples and their response. This discipleship focus explains the inclusion of scenes in Mark that might at first appear to have little to do with Jesus: the lengthy account of the death of John the Baptist is a story about being a firm disciple in the face of persecution, and that theme is emphasized by the way in which that story is placed between material concerning the mission of the Twelve. Similarly, Peter's denial of Jesus—the only other scene in Mark of any length that does not include Jesus—is an exploration of a moment of failed discipleship.

---

19. For more information about this text, including downloadable copies of it, see the Society of Biblical Literature Greek New Testament, http://sblgnt.com.

Mark's story requires the audience to think about discipleship in countercultural ways. Mark shows Jesus' disciples making significant mistakes: they don't understand the parables (4:13; this material is not found in the other Gospels), they don't understand what Jesus teaches (8:14–21), they rebuke Jesus for his teachings (8:32–33), they fail when they try to perform miracles (9:14–29), they argue about who is best (9:33–34), they ask for positions of honor (10:35–40), they turn Jesus in to the authorities (14:10–11, 18–21, 41–46), they fall asleep when Jesus asked them to watch (13:34–41), they deny that they know Jesus (14:9–21, 66–72), and they all flee when Jesus is arrested (14:50–52). In the Gospel of Mark, Jesus' disciples are far from flawless; instead, they are learners who repeatedly stumble: "the very fact that Mark's story is being told suggests that Mark views failure as part of continuing discipleship."[20] The failures of the disciples—and Jesus' patience in continuing to teach them—become a subtle testimony of the power of the Atonement to bridge the gap between human inadequacy and the demands of discipleship. The note that Judas would betray Jesus—presented at the very first reference to Judas in the story—primes Mark's audience for the idea that the Twelve are not presented as perfected models of discipleship to emulate but rather as students of Jesus. Their primary role is as learners; the audience is implicitly invited to learn along with the Twelve. The audience would have concluded that their own discipleship—however muddled and inadequate—would be acceptable to Jesus as long as they were willing to continue to follow him. Because Jesus does not reject his fumbling disciples, the audience learns that those who struggle while attempting to follow Jesus are not to be cast aside but rather to be welcomed to continue despite their inadequacies.

In contrast to the Twelve, it is the minor characters—people such as Jairus, the Greek woman, and Bartimaeus—who are presented as model disciples. In Mark, the exemplary disciples are not the leaders. This is doctrinally significant: one need not be a leader to be an exemplary disciple. Mark teaches that just because they occupied part of Jesus' inner circle does not mean that the Twelve are to be emulated (at least not as they were during Jesus' mortal life).

Part of Mark's concept of discipleship is that it is not viewed in exclusive terms. This is apparent in Mark's treatment of the authority to exorcise: early on, Jesus gave the Twelve authority to cast out demons, so it is not

---

20. Joanna Dewey, "Women in the Gospel of Mark," *Word & World* 26 (Winter 2006): 29.

surprising when the Twelve complain to Jesus that others were casting out demons. But Jesus teaches that anyone who wants to follow him has access to that power, and the point is driven home by the fact that the Twelve had themselves been unable to cast out demons. Given this portrayal, it is unlikely that Mark's audience would have viewed the Twelve as members of an exclusive inner circle. Rather, their callings would have been seen as Jesus' effort to symbolically restore the twelve tribes of Israel.

The inadequacy of the Twelve peaks when they flee from Jesus at his arrest. This is a picture of failed discipleship, but it is not the final word on discipleship in Mark. When the young man at the tomb tells the women to tell the disciples and Peter that Jesus will go before them to Galilee, he is extending the opportunity for them to resume their discipleship. The point of the narrative is that the Resurrection creates an opportunity for renewed discipleship, even after catastrophic failure. This would have been a most reassuring message for Mark's audience—not to mention the modern student of Mark's Gospel.

This picture of the Twelve might puzzle Latter-day Saint readers, who are likely to think of Mark's Twelve in light of the modern Quorum of the Twelve. But Mark presents the Twelve only during Jesus' mortal ministry—not after the Resurrection, not after the Day of Pentecost, not after they had grown and matured in their discipleship. Many Latter-day Saints are familiar with the story of discouraged young missionary Gordon B. Hinckley writing home to his father that he was wasting time and money.[21] When they read it, they understands that this is not an attitude for the modern reader to emulate but rather a youthful experience from which the young Elder Hinckley learned an important lesson and from which the modern audience should learn as well. Unfortunately, many readers assume that what the disciples do is a model to emulate, but, especially in Mark's Gospel, the audience is seeing something more akin to a young elder than to a church president and should approach the stories accordingly.

Modern readers are accustomed to glossing over the imperfections of the disciples in Mark, but if they do, they lose the power of the tomb scene: the young man's command to the women to tell the disciples and Peter that they will meet Jesus in Galilee is a powerful witness to the reality of Jesus' continuing invitation to the disciples to follow him despite their abandonment of him, but this invitation is drained of its power if

---

21. Sheri L. Dew, *Go Forward with Faith: The Biography of Gordon B. Hinckley* (Salt Lake City: Deseret Book Company, 1996), 64.

the audience treats the Twelve as if they were still in full fellowship with Jesus. That invitation is drenched with the power of mercy, forgiveness, and the reality of the Atonement. So reading Mark's Twelve through the understanding of the role of the modern Twelve is akin to trying to better understand an acorn by thinking about an oak tree: it is a useful exercise inasmuch as it suggests the potential of the acorn despite its current appearance, but it can also be extremely misleading if one treats an acorn as if it were a mature tree.

Mark presents women as disciples. Simon's mother-in-law is healed, and her story is told in such a way that it might be considered a call story (see the Notes on 1:29–31). Throughout Jesus' ministry, women follow him and thus are disciples. And yet it is not until after Jesus dies that Mark specifically describes their ministry (see the Notes on 15:40–41). There appears to be a contrast between male and female disciples, with the women presented as better models for the audience to follow, while the inner circle of male disciples shows, by way of example, what not to do when following Jesus. Significantly, women are at the cross, burial, and tomb; they function as the sole witnesses after all of the male disciples have fled.

Jesus teaches directly about the concept of discipleship throughout Mark's story. In 8:34, Jesus says, "Whosoever will come after me, let him deny himself, and take up his cross, and follow me." Jesus is emphasizing the costs—not the benefits—of discipleship here. Jesus explains to them that being a disciple means self-sacrifice and persecution. In 10:29–31, Jesus teaches that discipleship brings blessings, but "many that are first shall be last; and the last first." Similarly, in 9:35, Jesus says, "If any man desire to be first, the same shall be last of all, and servant of all." This word for "servant" (Greek: *diakonos,* root of the English word "deacon" and with some similarities to modern Latter-day Saint practice) finds its root in the idea of performing simple, menial, physical acts of service. Jesus is not promising them status or power—he's asking them to wait tables and tend to other physical needs. Even the highest-status males are expected to do the kind of work that was typically the sole domain of low-status females: "The Twelve are called to do women's work."[22] Similarly, women in this Gospel are invited to join in work normally restricted to men: theological discussions (see 7:24–30), the ritual of anointing (see 14:3–9), and following a teacher (see 15:40).[23]

---

22. Dewey, "Women in the Gospel of Mark," 25.

23. Note that women are still expected to engage in traditional acts of service; see 1:31.

Mark's message about discipleship is interwoven with the concepts of "insiders" and "outsiders." Surprisingly, it is those who should be insiders—the religious and political leaders, Jesus' family, Jesus' chosen male disciples—who act like outsiders again and again. The picture is nuanced by the righteous Jairus (5:21–43), the good scribe (12:28–34), Joseph of Arimathea (15:43), and, most significantly, the centurion at the cross (15:39), but the point remains that most members of these groups are opposed to Jesus. Those who seem to be outsiders—a woman with a hemorrhage of blood (5:25–34), a Greek woman (7:24–30), a poor widow (12:41–44)—show faith and devotion to Jesus that results in their insider status. (This is a theme developed throughout the commentary, but see especially the discussion on 3:31–35.) Paradoxically, the insiders have the harder time figuring out who Jesus is while outsiders are more easily able to comprehend his identity and mission.[24] It is significant that Jesus' own biological family is, at least at one point, opposed to his mission (see the Notes on 3:21). For Mark, being family does not grant one insider status. As Jesus explains, even his own family will need to choose to follow him. Interestingly, "home" and "family" seem to be separate and distinct categories in Mark: private homes are often the site of special instruction to insiders in Mark's Gospel, but there is no benefit to simply being family. Rather, Jesus teaches in 10:28–31 that living in the kingdom of God means being part of a new family of disciples, which may not overlap with one's biological family.

Significantly, despite Jesus' mighty powers and his willingness to use them to benefit all people, there is not one instance in Mark where Jesus forces someone to believe in or to follow him. Jesus will force demons but not humans. Part of Mark's portrait of discipleship, then, is an emphasis on its voluntary nature.

If the immediate setting for Mark's Gospel is either the persecution that followed the fire in Rome or the Jewish War,[25] then the audience might have been particularly concerned about what it meant to be a true disciple in a time of intense trial as well as what might happen to those who experience setbacks and personal failures as disciples. Mark's message on discipleship would have been intensely comforting to those willing to follow Jesus.

---

24. Werner H. Kelber, *Mark's Story of Jesus* (Philadelphia: Fortress Press, 1979), 56.
25. See appendix A: "Authorship and Date."

WOMEN IN MARK'S GOSPEL

Traditionally, Luke has been thought to be the Gospel with a special concern for women. But as feminist awareness has increased in recent decades, some scholars have taken a closer look at Mark's Gospel, not only because as the oldest Gospel it is the one closest to Jesus' lifetime, but also because of an increased recognition that Luke's Gospel tends to showcase women in stereotypically female roles[26] while Mark's Gospel tends to have a more expansive view of women. For example, one of the first miracles that Jesus performs is to heal Peter's mother-in-law from a fever (see 1:30–31). At the end of this brief account, Mark relates that she "ministered" to Jesus and the disciples. While the word used for "ministered" can mean simple, menial service, it is also the paradigm for the kind of service that disciples offer, and it is the same Greek word used in 1:13 to describe the action of the angels. She serves as the prototypical disciple in a text that is very concerned with that topic and features repeated failures by the leading (male) disciples. Women definitely are included as "disciples" in Mark: "they are described as 'following' Jesus and 'serving' him, both words used to define discipleship in Mark (8:34; 9:35; 10:43)."[27] In general, the female disciples in Mark are more successful than the male disciples.

Throughout the Gospel, women interact with Jesus in ways that were not culturally appropriate. From the woman who touches Jesus' clothing seeking healing (which would not have been socially acceptable because she would have transmitted her impurity to him), to the Syrophenician woman who disagrees with Jesus and is blessed for it, to the woman who interrupts a dinner party to anoint Jesus, there are many women in this narrative who occupy space normally restricted to men.

Mark's clever use of sandwiches—where a story is explicated based on the material that surrounds it—can convey an additional layer of meaning when compared with the other Gospels, even when they both include the same story. For example, Mark and Matthew recount the story of a woman who is healed when she touches the edge of Jesus' clothing. In both

---

26. For example, Elizabeth becomes a mother (Luke 1), Mary's story is focused on her motherhood (Luke 2), a widow has her son restored to her (Luke 7:11–15), and a woman in a parable cleans her home (Luke 15:8–10).

27. Dewey, "Women in the Gospel of Mark," 28.

narratives, that story is surrounded by references to the death and raising of the daughter of a ruler of a synagogue. But Mark includes details that serve to emphasize the links between the stories while Matthew omits a detail crucial to Mark's telling: that the daughter was twelve years old. Both Matthew and Mark note that the woman had had a hemorrhage of blood for twelve years, but only in Mark's account does this detail link the woman to the little girl. Twelve was a symbolic number, carrying associations of leadership from the idea of the twelve tribes of Israel. Mark associates both the woman and the girl with Israel, but the girl is a daughter of the synagogue in a literal sense while the woman becomes, in effect, a daughter of Jesus (see 5:34) when Jesus refers to her as his daughter. In Mark, the woman and the girl serve as a commentary on what it means to be a daughter of the synagogue or a daughter of Jesus: the daughter of the synagogue is passive and is only healed through the intervention of her father; the daughter of Jesus is active (in socially inappropriate ways) and speaks for herself. The status of women in Jesus' movement is more independent than their status in the synagogues. So in Mark's account, this is more than just two healing miracles; the audience is encouraged to compare the stories and learn yet another lesson from the comparison.

Similarly, while the anointing story (see 14:3–9) occupies roughly the same location in Mark's Gospel as it does in Matthew's, Matthew omits the story of the widow's mites, which eliminates the arrangement of the text that encourages the audience to compare the widow and the anointer. When compared, these stories position both women's stories as commentary on the teachings in the Olivet Discourse (chapter 13/Matthew 24–25), an arrangement which makes the anointing story in Mark's Gospel much more meaningful. Matthew also avoids having Jesus use the word "anointed" to describe what the woman had done (14:8; contrast Matt. 26:12); this may have been because of discomfort with the idea of a woman anointing Jesus. Given how close the stories are verbally, it is striking how differently the anointing story functions in Matthew's Gospel.

There is quite a bit of indirect evidence for the presence of women at the Last Supper. It was Jewish tradition for women to take part in Passover, and so to break from that tradition would have been worthy of mention in itself. Since in all recorded cases, Jesus is as open to women's participation as (if not more than) his surrounding culture, it would have been doubly worthy of attention if his celebration of Passover excluded women. Additionally, referring to "one of the Twelve" in 14:20 suggests that there were others present (see also 14:16 and 17). And 15:41 indicates that women came up with Jesus to Jerusalem; his purpose in going to Jerusalem was to celebrate the Passover. Also, 14:28 points out that Jesus said at the Last Supper that he would go before his disciples to Galilee. At the tomb, the young man says, "He goeth before you into Galilee: there shall ye see him, as he said unto you." So the most logical reading is that these women were at the Last Supper and had heard this prophecy. In sum, there is very good evidence in Mark's Gospel for thinking that women were present at the Last Supper.

In Mark's Gospel, women are central to the stories of Jesus' ministry, and they take on roles that are surprisingly expansive given the first-century context. Women in Mark's Gospel have three key roles: as examples of what it means to serve, as anointers (both in 14:3–9 and in 16:1–8), and as witnesses to Jesus' life, death, and Resurrection.[28] Given the very close overlap between these three concepts and Mark's key concerns as a writer, it is no exaggeration to claim that women are central to this Gospel narrative and occupy important space in it as they model what it means to be a disciple of Jesus Christ.

CHRISTOLOGY: MARK'S PORTRAIT OF JESUS

Each of the Gospel writers has a somewhat different way of describing Jesus and his ministry (the technical term for this is Christology). Mark is known for having a "low" Christology, meaning that Jesus' human aspects are more on display than they are in the other Gospels. (For example, it is difficult to imagine John, who has the "highest" Christology, featuring a miracle that required more than one step for completion; compare 8:22–25.) The question of Jesus' identity is a large concern in this Gospel, and it is frequently explicitly commented on within the text itself.[29]

Many scholars turn to the titles attributed to Jesus in Mark's Gospel in order to determine Mark's message about Jesus (see appendix F, "Titles for

---

28. Susan Miller, *Women in Mark's Gospel* (New York: T&T Clark International, 2004), 193–98.

29. The question of Jesus' true identity is raised in 1:27; 2:7; 4:41; 6:2–3; 8:27–29; 11:28; 14:61; and 15:2.

Jesus in Mark"). Perhaps it is part of Mark's extensive use of irony that many of the most exalted titles applied to Jesus are done so either by demons or in mockery; these titles illustrate the problem of naming in the Gospel. Some of the most compelling titles come from the unclean spirits (1:24; 3:11; 5:7). Similarly, the fact that Peter can correctly label Jesus "the Christ" but then immediately show his lack of understanding of Jesus' mission suggests the limitations of titles in this text: "to reconstruct the history of titles as if this were the study of Christology is like trying to understand the windows of Chartres cathedral by studying the history of coloured glass."[30] The Christology of Mark's Gospel must therefore consider not only the names given to Jesus but also the stories about him.

For example, Jesus preached extensively about the "kingdom of God."[31] While this preaching doesn't give a title to Jesus, knowing that his ministry was focused on teaching people what the kingdom of God would be like does indeed reveal a lot about him. He is a teacher but not because of a title but rather because he does in fact teach. Additionally, there are frequent references in Mark's Gospel to the idea that Jesus taught "with authority."[32] It tells a lot about Jesus to say that he had God's authority. While a concept of priesthood congruent with modern Latter-day Saint thought is not specifically articulated in the Gospel of Mark, the idea that people around Jesus were aware of the authority that he held becomes a starting point for thinking about priesthood in this text, especially since Jesus shares that authority with his followers.[33] The audience learns more about who Jesus is when he is shown repeatedly victorious as he engages in controversial discussions,[34] and there is an entirely different side of his personality explored as he experiences a range of human emotions.[35] These

---

30. Leander E. Keck, "Toward the Renewal of NT Christology," *New Testament Studies* 32 (1986): 362–77.

31. Jesus preaches about the kingdom of God in 1:14–15; 4:11, 26, 30; 9:1, 47; 10:14–15, 23–25; 12:34; and 14:25. The kingdom of God is also mentioned in 15:43. Contrast 3:24; 6:23; and 13:8.

32. References to Jesus' authority occur in 1:21–27; 2:10–11, 28; 4:39–41; and 11:27–33.

33. References to Jesus sharing authority occur in 3:14–15; 6:7; and 13:34 (in parable form).

34. Verbal controversies occur in 2:1–3:6; 11:15–19, 27–33; and 12:1–44.

35. References to Jesus' emotions in Mark's Gospel include 1:41 (compassion or anger, depending on the textual variant); 1:43 (displeasure); 3:5 (anger and grief); 6:6 (amazement); 6:34 (compassion); 8:12 (precise emotion not stated, but he "sighs deeply"); 10:14 (displeasure); 10:21 (love); and 14:34 (sorrow). While Mark shows Jesus experiencing a wide range of emotions, Matthew and Luke will frequently omit these references.

incidents reveal who he is and do so more fully than any title could. But perhaps the most significant part of Mark's narrative Christology is the fact that Jesus consistently and repeatedly prophesies that he will suffer and die.[36] This is some of the most important Christological material in the Gospel precisely because it was so difficult for his disciples to understand. The common expectation in first-century Judaism was that the Messiah would liberate the people from Roman rule and then reign victoriously; the idea that the Messiah would suffer and die was not generally expected.[37] Jesus' predictions that he will suffer and die thus can be seen as a key part of Mark's Christology.

A more strictly narrative-based Christology can also seek to understand Jesus based on what he actually does: heal people, dispute religious authorities, and teach about God's kingdom. Perhaps the most fruitful avenue for considering the Christology of Mark's Gospel is a close analysis of 14:3–9, where an unnamed woman anoints Jesus. Because the act is presented as at once a burial anointing and a royal anointing, these different aspects of what it means to be "the Christ" (or, to translate instead of transliterate into English, "the anointed") are simultaneously encapsulated in her single prophetic act. Jesus' statement that her act will be recounted wherever the gospel is preached hints at the supreme significance of this anointing. It is only through recognition of the priestly aspects of Jesus' ministry, the need for him to suffer and die, and his royal nature that the audience can understand what it means to say that he is "the Christ."

Jesus is presented as a healer, teacher, leader, authority figure, crowd gatherer, and debate winner. But he is also presented as someone who is humble, patient, caring, and attentive to marginal people and who willingly suffers and dies a humiliating and painful death. The distinctiveness of Jesus in Mark's Gospel is that he combined the two seemingly contradictory ideas of suffering and glory. His suffering is highlighted by his ability, as the Son of God, to have avoided pain had he wanted to; his glory is highlighted by the choice he made to set aside that glory for the benefit of humankind.

---

36. Prophecies of Jesus' suffering and death include 8:31; 9:12, 31; 10:33–34; 12:1–12 (in parable form); 14:24–25, and 14:36.

37. The biblical passages that Christian (including Latter-day Saint) readers usually understand to suggest that the Messiah would suffer and die—including especially the "suffering servant" passages in Isaiah (see Isa. 42:1–4; 49:1–6; 50:4–9; and especially Isa. 53)—were generally not understood to apply to the Messiah, but perhaps to Israel as a corporate body.

The majority of NT scholars find that Mark shows the lowest Christology of the four canonized Gospels. Evidence for this position comes from the many instances where Mark highlights the very human aspects of Jesus' identity and ministry, in contrast with the other Gospel writers who frequently elide this material in favor of a more magisterial portrait of Jesus. However, a close examination of the way in which Mark's story of Jesus echoes stories from the HB suggests that, in many instances, Mark's Christology is extremely high since Jesus is frequently identified with the God of the Bible. Thus, Mark's Christology is neither low nor high but rather full (see appendix G: "Mark's Christology").

OUTLINE

Outlining the Gospel of Mark is more art than science; there is no consensus on the outline, and proposals other than the one below merit consideration. Any effort to outline or create titles is itself an act of interpretation.[38] It is not neutral or objective but rather nudges readers toward emphasizing or de-emphasizing certain aspects of the text.

Some parts of the outline have a stronger case to being intrinsic and intentional to the Gospel than others do. For example, it is highly likely that 2:1–3:6 is a discrete section of text consisting of five similar stories that show increasing hostility to Jesus. On the other hand, there are various ways one might organize 6:32–8:21. So this outline is more of a pragmatic, if subjective, aid to organizing the commentary than a definitive statement about Mark's original organization. Since the Gospel was almost certainly a primarily oral production, efforts at outlining will necessarily flounder to some extent since oral presentations tend to be more recursive and less linear and logical than written compositions.

There are three primary divisions, and they are geographical, not chronological. Within those geographical divisions, material is presented by type instead of chronologically in the first third, so that, for example, 2:1–3:6 consists of stories where people dispute with Jesus, while 4:1–34

---

38. As Robert J. Matthews has noted, even the chapter headings in the Latter-day Saint Bible are, in a sense, commentary. Robert J. Matthews, "The JST: Retrospect and Prospect—a Panel," in *The Joseph Smith Translation: The Restoration of Plain and Precious Truths*, ed. Monte S. Nyman and Robert L. Millet (Provo, Utah: Religious Studies Center, Brigham Young University, 1985), 291–305.

concerns parables, and 4:35–5:43 contains miracle stories. Thus it is highly unlikely that Mark reflects the chronology of Jesus' ministry since this material is ordered by topic. By contrast, the material in the third and final section is demarcated by time notations and thus is presented with more attention to chronology. The final third of the Gospel covers only one week of Jesus' life and thus emphasizes the events of that final week.

1. Galilee (1:1–8:21)
   a. Mark 1: Beginnings
      i. Mark 1:1–8: Jesus Is Introduced
      ii. Mark 1:9–15: Jesus Is Baptized
      iii. Mark 1:16–20: Jesus Calls Disciples
      iv. Mark 1:21–28: Jesus Exorcises a Demon
      v. Mark 1:29–39: Jesus Performs Many Miracles
      vi. Mark 1:40–45: Jesus Heals a Leper
   b. Mark 2:1–3:6: Controversies
      i. Mark 2:1–12: Jesus Heals a Lame Man
      ii. Mark 2:13–17: Jesus Eats with Sinners
      iii. Mark 2:18–22: Jesus Teaches about Fasting
      iv. Mark 2:23–28: Jesus Teaches about the Sabbath
      v. Mark 3:1–6: Jesus Heals on the Sabbath
   c. Mark 3:7–35: Reactions
      i. Mark 3:7–12: Jesus' Ministry Summarized
      ii. Mark 3:13–19: Jesus Calls Disciples
      iii. Mark 3:20–35: Jesus' Family and the Scribes Respond
   d. Mark 4:1–34: Parables
      i. Mark 4:1–9: The Parable of the Soil
      ii. Mark 4:10–20: Jesus Teaches about Parables
      iii. Mark 4:21–34: Jesus Shares More Parables
   e. Mark 4:35–5:43: Miracles
      i. Mark 4:35–41: Jesus Stills the Sea
      ii. Mark 5:1–20: Jesus Exorcises Demons
      iii. Mark 5:21–43: Jesus Heals a Woman and Raises a Girl
   f. Mark 6:1–31: Mission and Rejection
      i. Mark 6:1–6: Jesus Is Rejected
      ii. Mark 6:7–13: Jesus Sends Out the Twelve
      iii. Mark 6:14–31: John the Baptist Is Killed

g. Mark 6:32–8:21: Food and Gentiles

    i. Mark 6:32–44: Jesus Feeds Five Thousand Men

    ii. Mark 6:45–52: Jesus Walks on Water

    iii. Mark 6:53–56: Jesus' Ministry Summarized

    iv. Mark 7:1–23: Jesus Teaches about Food Traditions

    v. Mark 7:24–30: Jesus and the Greek Woman

    vi. Mark 7:31–37: Jesus Heals a Disabled Man

    vii. Mark 8:1–10: Jesus Feeds Four Thousand People

    viii. Mark 8:11–21: Jesus Reviews the Feeding Miracles

2. On the Way (8:22–10:52)

    a. Mark 8:22–26: Jesus Heals a Blind Man

    b. Mark 8:27–9:1: A First Prediction of Death

    c. Mark 9:2–13: Jesus Is Transfigured

    d. Mark 9:14–29: The Disciples Fail to Heal

    e. Mark 9:30–37: A Second Prediction of Death

    f. Mark 9:38–50: The Disciples Fail to Welcome

    g. Mark 10:1–12: Jesus Teaches about Divorce

    h. Mark 10:13–16: Jesus Teaches about Children

    i. Mark 10:17–31: Jesus Teaches about Wealth

    j. Mark 10:32–45: A Third Prediction of Death

    k. Mark 10:46–52: Jesus Heals Another Blind Man

3. Jerusalem (11:1–16:8)

    a. Mark 11:1–13:37: The Temple

        i. Mark 11:1–11: Jesus Enters Jerusalem

        ii. Mark 11:12–26: The Fig Tree and the Temple

        iii. Mark 11:27–12:12: Jesus Questioned about His Authority

        iv. Mark 12:13–17: Jesus Questioned about Paying Taxes

        v. Mark 12:18–27: Jesus Questioned about Resurrection

        vi. Mark 12:28–34: Jesus Questioned about the Commandments

        vii. Mark 12:35–37: Jesus Questions the Scribes

        viii. Mark 12:38–44: Jesus Praises the Widow

        ix. Mark 13:1–4: Jesus Prophesies about the Temple

        x. Mark 13:5–31: Jesus Teaches about the Destruction of the Temple

        xi. Mark 13:32–37: Jesus Teaches about the Future

    b. Mark 14: Approaching Death

        i. Mark 14:1–11: Jesus Is Anointed

    ii. Mark 14:12–25: Jesus Observes Passover

    iii. Mark 14:26–31: Jesus Prophesies Betrayal

    iv. Mark 14:32–42: Jesus Prays

    v. Mark 14:43–52: Jesus Is Arrested

    vi. Mark 14:53–65: Jesus Is Questioned by Jewish Leaders

    vii. Mark 14:66–72: Jesus Is Denied by Peter

  c. Mark 15–16: Death and Resurrection

    i. Mark 15:1–15: Jesus before Pilate

    ii. Mark 15:16–32: Jesus Is Crucified

    iii. Mark 15:33–41: Jesus Dies

    iv. Mark 15:42–47: Jesus Is Buried

    v. Mark 16:1–8: Jesus' Resurrection Is Announced

THE NEW RENDITION

English-speaking Latter-day Saint readers normally use the King James Version (KJV), which is the official Bible for the Church in English.[39] This commentary includes the Greek text, the KJV, and a new English version that is called the New Rendition. John W. Welch has noted that calling this project a "rendition" is an appropriate title for two reasons. First, because much like a rendition of a song, it implies a framework where one person's unique stamp is put on a project while acknowledging that others would create a very different interpretation. Second, to "rend" implies to "open up" and thus suggests one of the goals of the New Rendition: to open up the Greek text to a new perspective.[40]

---

39. For a defense of the use of the KJV, see J. Reuben Clark, *Why the King James Version* (Salt Lake City: Deseret Book, 1956). Note that President David O. McKay disagreed with Clark's position; see Philip L. Barlow, *Mormons and the Bible: The Place of the Latter-day Saints in American Religion* (New York: Oxford University Press, 1991), 169–70. See also Ben Spackman, "Why Bible Translations Differ: A Guide for the Perplexed," *Religious Educator* 15, no. 1 (2014): 31–65. This commentary interacts with the KJV—since that is the version most familiar to English-speaking Latter-day Saint readers—in ways that most modern bible commentaries do not, but it also addresses textual variants, translation issues, and other difficulties with the KJV.

40. John W. Welch, in "Panel Discussion of *The Revelation of John the Apostle,*" BYU New Testament Commentary conference, Provo, Utah, May 14, 2014, video, at 1:05:21, http://www.byunewtestamentcommentary.com/conferences/may-2014/conference-videos/.

Translating any text into another language can be a vexing prospect; translating a sacred and ancient text even more so. There is no such thing as perfect translation, even theoretically. The New Rendition reflects the deliberate choice to translate as woodenly and literally as possible in order to aid the reader in appreciating the literary features of Mark's text, which include repetition, awkward constructions, intentional word choice, and similar features. One exception to the principle of strictly literal translation is that the idioms in Mark are translated with comparable English idioms (see, for example, the Notes on 1:24). A second exception is for culturally specific referents, so that "the fourth watch" is translated as "when night was ending" (6:48) and "over three hundred denarii" is rendered as "over a year's wages" (14:5). But aside from these two exceptions, literalism was the overriding concern—even at the cost of smoothness and elegance. There is no doubt that the New Rendition will strike the reader as infelicitous. But conforming to the source text outweighs, at least in this context, the benefits of attempting to improve the source.

The New Rendition will sound foreign to Latter-day Saint readers accustomed to the distinctive register of the KJV—which strikes the modern reader as elegant, formal, and magisterial—but the New Rendition more closely reflects the tone of Mark's text, which would not have sounded antiquated, lofty, or reverent but rather common and plain. Readers may well be disgruntled by the awkwardness of the New Rendition, but the goal was not to produce a translation that reads smoothly; the goal was to hew as closely as possible to the Greek text—which is often awkward and sometimes even ungrammatical (see the Notes on 16:6). As Philip L. Barlow has written, "One can hear no King James–like cathedral bells ringing in the background when one reads the Gospel of Mark in koine Greek. Mark's writing is raw, fresh, breathless, primitive. The lordly prose of the KJV, as it is heard by twenty-first-century ears, is for many texts an external imposition, shifting the locus of authority away from the power of the story itself and toward an authority spawned by the partially artificial literary holiness suffusing our culturally created notion of scripture."[41]

The First Presidency of The Church of Jesus Christ of Latter-day Saints has articulated a policy regarding scripture translation that states, "Only translations which very precisely reproduce the words, phrases, and sentence constructions, as well as the expressions and style of the author of

---

41. Melissa, "12 Answers from Philip Barlow: Part 1," *Times and Seasons* (blog), March 6, 2005, http://timesandseasons.org/index.php/2005/03/12-answers-from -philip-barlow-part-1/.

the original, can transmit impartially the sense of what the Lord revealed in the language of the original. . . . The translation must contain the recurring expressions and also awkward sentence constructions. No attempt may be made to paraphrase in an explanatory way, to make alterations, or indeed to improve the literary ability and knowledge as expressed in the current English text versions."[42] With the two exceptions noted above, the New Rendition of Mark attempts to follow these guidelines.

One of the distinctive characteristics of the Gospel of Mark is its use of a verb tense known as the historical present, used when events that happened in the past are recounted using a present tense verb (for example, 1:44: "and he says to him"). Most modern translations change these verbs to the past tense ("and he said to him"), but I have chosen not to do that, partially to preserve Mark's original sense but also because the historical present tense was probably used deliberately in order to create the sense that the audience was party to a story unfolding in that very moment.

The New Rendition also avoids technical religious terms where possible (for example, "gospel" for good news) and, when faced with two equally plausible options for translation, uses the less common one since there is benefit in exposing the reader to a new way to perceive the text. So, for example, the KJV's "repent and believe the gospel" in 1:5 is rendered "change your life and trust the good news." "Repent and believe" is a perfectly adequate translation, but "change your life and trust" is as well, and the unfamiliarity of the latter recommends its use in a commentary designed to expose the reader to new insights into the text. Similarly, while either "ordain" or "make" might be used to describe what Jesus does to the Twelve (see the Notes on 3:14), the New Rendition uses "make" because it is unfamiliar to Latter-day Saint readers and because it suggests a link to God's creative actions and Moses' selection of leaders. There is value in disorientation and novelty; I did not let that concern control the New Rendition, but I did permit it to be a tie breaker in certain cases.

The New Rendition is included within the commentary and is also included below in its entirety. As mentioned above, Mark's earliest audiences would have experienced his story of Jesus as just that: a fast-paced, engaging story that was likely performed in one sitting. In contrast, modern

---

42. First Presidency and Quorum of the Twelve Apostles, "Guidelines for Translation of the Standard Works," April 17, 1980, quoted in Marcellus S. Snow, "The Challenge of Theological Translation: New German Versions of the Standard Works," *Dialogue: A Journal of Mormon Thought* 17 (1984): 136. Although articulated a generation ago, this is still the current policy.

readers of scripture usually read only short sections at a time, interacting with a written text divided into chapters and verses. In order to help modern readers experience Mark as a story, I have formatted the New Rendition text below with paragraphs divided by narrative transitions. Readers may benefit from reading the entire text of the New Rendition in one sitting in order to experience its narrative impact.

According to Mark

1:1 The Beginning of the Good News of Jesus, the Anointed One, Son of God
2 As it is written in Isaiah the prophet,
"See! I send my messenger ahead of you,
who will prepare your way.
3 A voice shouting in the desert:
'Make ready the way of the Lord—
straighten his paths.'"
4 John appeared, baptizing in the desert, proclaiming a baptism of repentance for forgiveness of sins. 5 And all the Judean region and all those of Jerusalem were going out to him; all were being baptized by him in the Jordan River, as they were confessing their sins. 6 And John wore clothing made of camel's hair and a leather belt around his waist, and he was eating grasshoppers and wild honey. 7 And he proclaimed, saying, "One who is more powerful than I comes following me, of whom I am not worthy to stoop to untie the strap of his sandals. 8 I baptized you with water, but he will baptize you with the Holy Spirit."
9 And it happened in those days that Jesus came from Nazareth in Galilee and was baptized in the Jordan by John. 10 And immediately as he was coming up out of the water, he saw heaven being torn open and the Spirit as a dove coming down into him. 11 And a voice out of heaven: "You are my beloved son in whom I take joy." 12 And immediately the Spirit drives him into the desert. 13 And he was in the desert for forty days, being tested by Satan, and he was with the animals, and the angels were serving him. 14 But after John was arrested, Jesus went into Galilee, proclaiming the good news of God. 15 And saying, "The time is filled, and the reign of God has drawn near. Change your life and trust the good news."
16 And walking beside the Sea of Galilee, he saw Simon and Andrew— the brother of Simon—casting a net in the sea, for they were fishers. 17 And Jesus said to them, "Come follow me and I will make you into fishers of people." 18 And immediately, having left their nets, they followed him. 19 And having gone on a little, he saw Jacob, Zebedee's son, and his brother

John. And they were in a boat preparing the nets. 20 And immediately he invited them. And having left their father Zebedee in the boat with the laborers, they followed him.

21 And they went into Capernaum. And immediately on the Sabbath he taught in the synagogue. 22 And they were amazed at his teaching, for he was teaching as one having power/authority and not like the scriptorians. 23 And immediately there was in their synagogue a man with an unclean spirit. And he exclaimed, 24 saying, "Mind your own business, Jesus of Nazareth! Have you come to destroy us? I know who you are: God's Holy One!" 25 And Jesus stopped him, saying, "Silence! And come out of him." 26 And convulsing him and crying out with a loud voice, the unclean spirit came out of him. 27 And all were astonished, so they questioned, saying, "What is this new teaching with power/authority? And he even commands the unclean spirits and they obey him." 28 And immediately news about him went out everywhere, in all the region of Galilee.

29 And immediately, having come out of the synagogue, they came into the house of Simon and Andrew with Jacob and John. 30 But Simon's mother-in-law was lying down sick with a fever, and immediately they speak to him about her. 31 And having come to her, he raised her up, having grasped her hand. And the fever left her, and she ministered to them.

32 When it was evening, after sunset, they kept bringing to him all who were sick and who were demon-possessed. 33 And all the city was gathered at the door. 34 And he healed many who were sick with various diseases, and he cast out many demons. But he did not allow the demons to speak because they knew him.

35 And very early, having risen up while it was still night, he went out and departed into a deserted place and was praying there. 36 And Simon and those with him searched for him. 37 And having found him, they say to him, "Everyone is looking for you!" 38 And he says to them, "Let's go somewhere else, into the nearby villages, that I might proclaim there also, because this is why I came." 39 And he went proclaiming in their synagogues in all of Galilee and casting out demons.

40 And a leper comes to him, begging and kneeling and saying to him, "If you are willing, you can make me clean." 41 And having become angry, he stretched out his hand, touched him, and he says to him, "I am willing. Be made clean." 42 And immediately the leprosy left him, and he was clean. 43 And having sternly warned him, he immediately drove him away. 44 And he says to him, "See that you say nothing to anyone, but go, show yourself to the priest and offer, because of your cleaning, what Moses

commanded for a testimony to them." 45 And having gone out, he began to preach much and to spread the word, so that he was no longer able to enter a town openly, but he was out in deserted places and they were coming to him from everywhere.

2:1 And having entered again into Capernaum after some days, it was reported that he is at home. 2 And many were gathered, so there was no more room, not even near the door. And he spoke about the word to them. 3 And they come, bringing to him a man who could not walk, carried by four people. 4 And not being able to come near him because of the crowd, they removed the roof where he was. And having torn it off, they lowered the mat on which the lame man was lying. 5 And Jesus, having seen their trust, says to the lame man, "Child, your sins are forgiven." 6 But there were some scriptorians there, sitting and questioning in their minds, 7 "Why does this one speak this way? He blasphemes! Who is able to forgive sins except one, God?" 8 And immediately Jesus, recognizing in his spirit that they are questioning within themselves this way, he says to them, "Why are you questioning about these things in your minds? 9 What is easier: to say to the lame man, 'Your sins have been forgiven,' or to say, 'Rise and take your mat and walk'? 10 But so you may know that the son of man has authority to forgive sins on earth—" He says to the lame man, 11 "I say to you: Rise. Take up your mat and go into your home." 12 And immediately he rose, and having taken up the mat, went in front of all of them, so that all were amazed and honored God, saying, "We never saw this before!"

13 And he went forth again by the sea, and all the crowd was coming to him, and he was teaching them. 14 And passing by, he saw Levi, the son of Alphaeus, sitting at the tax booth, and he says to him, "Follow me." And, having risen, he followed him. 15 And it comes to pass that, as he ate at his house, many tax collectors and sinners were eating with Jesus and his disciples. Indeed, they were many, and they followed him. 16 And the scriptorians of the Pharisees, having seen him eating with sinners and tax collectors, said to his disciples, "Why does he eat with tax collectors and sinners?" 17 And having heard, Jesus says to them, "The healthy do not have need of a doctor, but those who are sick. I did not come to call the righteous, but sinners."

18 And John's disciples and the Pharisees were fasting. And people come and say to him, "Why do John's disciples and the Pharisees' disciples fast, but your disciples do not fast?" 19 And Jesus said to them, "The wedding guests can't fast when the groom is with them, can they? As long as the groom is with them, they cannot fast. 20 But the days will come when

the groom is taken away from them, and on that day they will fast. 21 No one sews a patch of unprepared cloth onto an old cloak; otherwise, the patch takes away part of the cloak—the new from the old—and a worse tear results. 22 And no one pours new wine into old wineskins; otherwise, the wine bursts the skins and the wine is destroyed, as is the skin. But new wine is for new wineskins."

23 And it happened on the Sabbath that he went through the grain fields. And his disciples began to make their way, plucking the grain. 24 And the Pharisees said to him, "Look, why do they do on the Sabbath that which is against the law?" 25 And he says to them, "Did you never read what David did, when he had need and was hungry, him and those with him, 26 how he went in to the house of God in the time of Abiathar, the high priest, and ate the consecrated bread—which is unlawful for any to eat except the priests—and he gave some to those who were with him?" 27 And he said to them, "The Sabbath was made for the sake of people, and not people for the Sabbath." 28 So the son of man is even master of the Sabbath.

3:1 And again he entered into the synagogue. And there was a man with a deformed hand. 2 And they were watching him closely, whether he would heal him on the Sabbath, so they could accuse him. 3 And he says to the man who had the deformed hand, "Stand in the middle." 4 And he says to them, "Is it legal on the Sabbath to do good or to do evil? To save life or to kill?" But they were silent. 5 And having looked around at them with anger, being grieved at the hardness of their hearts, he says to the man, "Stretch out your hand." And he stretched it out, and his hand was restored. 6 And having gone out, the Pharisees immediately conspired with the Herodians against him, how they could destroy him.

7 And Jesus, with his disciples, went away to the sea. And a large crowd from Galilee followed, and from Judea, 8 and from Jerusalem, and from Idumea, and from beyond the Jordan River, and from around Tyre and Sidon. A large crowd, having heard how much he was doing, came to him. 9 And he told his disciples to get a boat ready for him, because of the masses of people, so that they would not crowd him. 10 For he had healed many people, so they pushed toward him in order to touch him, as many as had diseases. 11 And the unclean spirits, whenever they saw him, fell down before him, and cried out, saying, "You are the Son of God." 12 And he sternly ordered them that they should not reveal him.

13 And he goes up into the mountain and calls to him those he wanted, and they went to him. 14 And he made Twelve whom he also named apostles, that they might be with him and that he might send them out

to proclaim 15 and to have power/authority to cast out demons. 16 So he made the Twelve: Simon (whom he named Peter), 17 and Jacob the son of Zebedee, and John the brother of Jacob (whom he named Boanerges, which means "sons of thunder"), 18 and Andrew, and Philip, and Bartholomew, and Matthew, and Thomas, and Jacob the son of Alphaeus, and Thaddaeus, and Simon the Zealot, 19 and Judas Iscariot, who even delivered him up.

20 And they went home. And again a crowd came together, so that they were not even able to eat. 21 And his family having heard about it, they went out to seize him, for they said, "He is out of his mind."

22 And the scriptorians, the ones who came down from Jerusalem, were saying, "He is possessed by Beelzebul" and "By the ruler of demons he casts out demons." 23 And having called them to him, in parables he said to them, "How can Satan cast out Satan? 24 And if a kingdom is divided against itself, that kingdom cannot endure. 25 And if a family is divided against itself, that family cannot endure. 26 And if Satan has risen up against himself and is divided, he cannot endure but has an end. 27 But no one can enter into the strong man's house to steal his possessions unless first he ties up the strong man, and then he can rob his house. 28 Amen, I say to you that all will be forgiven the people, the sins and the blasphemies, as much as they shall have blasphemed. 29 But whoever blasphemes against the Holy Spirit never has forgiveness in the eternities but will be guilty of eternal sin." 30 Because they were saying, "He has an unclean spirit."

31 And his mother and his siblings come. And standing outside, they sent to him, calling him. 32 And a crowd sat around him, and they say to him, "Look, your mother and your siblings are outside asking for you." 33 And having answered them, he says, "Who is my mother and my siblings?" 34 And having looked around at those sitting in a circle around him, he says, "Look! My mother and my siblings. 35 For whoever does the will of God is my brother and my sister and my mother."

4:1 And again he began to teach beside the sea. And a large crowd was gathered to him, so having gotten into a boat, he sat in it in the sea, and all the crowd was beside the sea on the land. 2 And he taught them in parables many things and said to them in his teachings, 3 "Listen! Look! A planter went out to plant. 4 And it came to pass that as he planted, some indeed fell by the [path]way, and the birds came and ate it. 5 And other seed fell on rocky land, where it did not have much soil. And immediately it sprouted because there was no depth to the soil. 6 But after the sun rose, it was burned. And since it did not have root, it withered away. 7 And other seed fell into the thorns. And the thorns came up and choked it, and it produced no crop. 8 But other seeds fell into the good soil and produced a crop, coming up and increasing, and bore thirty times and sixty times and one hundred times as much." 9 And he said, "Whoever has ears to hear, hear!"

10 And when he was alone, those around him and the Twelve were asking him about the parables. 11 And he said to them, "To you the secret of the kingdom of God has been given. But to those who are outside, all things come in parables. 12 So that

'they might see but not perceive,
and hear but not understand,
to prevent them from ever returning and being forgiven.'"

13 And he says to them, "You don't understand this parable? Then how will you understand all of the parables? 14 The planter plants the word. 15 These are the ones along the pathway where the word is planted: and when they hear, Satan immediately comes and takes away the word that has been planted in them. 16 And, similarly, these are the ones who are planted in rocky places: who, when they hear the word, immediately receive it with joy, 17 and they do not have any root in themselves but are temporary; then when trouble or persecution comes because of the word, they immediately stumble. 18 And others are the ones who are planted among the thorns: these are the ones who, having heard the word, 19 the anxieties of this life, the lure of wealth, and the desires for other things enter in, choke the word, and it becomes fruitless. 20 And these are the ones planted on the good soil: they hear the word and accept it and produce a crop, one thirty times, and one sixty times, and one a hundred times as much."

21 And he was saying to them, "The lamp doesn't come so that it might be placed under the bowl or under the cot, does it? Doesn't it come in order that it might be placed on a lampstand? 22 For nothing is hidden that will not be revealed, nor is there any secret that will not come to light. 23 Whoever has ears to hear, hear!" 24 And he was saying to them, "Look closely at what you hear; by what measure you measure, it will be measured to you, and more will be added to you. 25 Indeed, whoever has will be given more, but whoever does not have, even what he has will be taken from him."

26 And he was saying, "So is the kingdom of God like a person who scatters seed upon the ground 27 and sleeps and rises, night and day, and the seed sprouts and grows, but he does not know how. 28 By itself the ground

produces the crop: first a stalk, then a head, then the full grain in the head. 29 But when the crop is ready, he immediately sends in the sickle, because the harvest has come."

30 And he was saying, "To what should we compare the kingdom of God? Or, with what parable could we describe it? 31 It is like a mustard seed that, when it has been planted in the ground, is the smallest of all of the seeds that are in the ground. 32 But when it has been planted, it rises and becomes taller than all of the shrubs and produces large branches so that the birds are able to nest in its shade."

33 And with many such parables, he was speaking the word to them, as they were able to hear. 34 He was not speaking to them without a parable. But privately, alone with his own disciples, he was explaining all things.

35 And he says to them on that day, when the evening had come, "Let's go across to the other side." 36 And leaving the crowd, they take him with them in the boat, just as he was, and other boats were with him. 37 And a great wind storm comes, and the waves beat into the boat, so that the boat is already being filled up with water. 38 And he was in the stern, sleeping on the cushion. And they wake him and say to him, "Teacher, don't you care that we are being destroyed?" 39 And awakening, he commanded the wind and said to the sea, "Be quiet! Be calm!" And the wind stopped, and there was a great calm. 40 And he said to them, "Why are you so afraid? Do you not yet have trust?" 41 And they were completely terrified and were saying to one another, "Who, then, is this? Even the wind and the sea obey him!"

5:1 And they came to the other side of the sea, to the region of the Gerasenes. 2 And having gone forth out of the boat, he immediately met a man from the tombs with an unclean spirit, 3 who lived in the tombs. And not even with a chain was anyone able to confine him anymore. 4 For he had often been bound with leg chains and handcuffs, but the cuffs had been wrenched apart by him, and the chains were shattered, and no one was strong enough to control him. 5 And constantly—all night and all day—in the tombs and in the mountains, he was shouting and cutting/bruising himself with rocks. 6 And having seen Jesus from a distance, he ran and knelt in front of him. 7 And having shouted with a loud voice, he says, "Mind your own business, Jesus, son of the Most High God! I urge you by God not to torture me." 8 For he was saying to him, "Come out of the man, unclean spirit!" 9 And Jesus asked him, "What is your name?" And he says, answering, "Legion is my name, because we are many." 10 And he begged him repeatedly that he would not send them out of the region. 11 Near the mountain there was a great herd of hogs feeding. 12 And they begged him, saying,

"Send us into the hogs, that we might enter into them." 13 And he permitted them. And having gone out of the man, the unclean spirits entered into the hogs and rushed the herd, numbering about two thousand, down the cliff into the sea. And they were drowned in the sea.

14 And those who fed the hogs fled and told it in the city and in the countryside. And the people came to see what it is that has happened. 15 And they come to Jesus and see the demon-possessed man sitting, clothed and sane—the same one who had had the legion—and they were afraid. 16 And those who saw it related to them what happened to the demon-possessed man and about the hogs. 17 And they began to beg him to leave their region. 18 And as he was getting into the boat, the man who had been possessed by demons begged that he might go with him. 19 But he did not permit him to, but he says to him, "Go into your home, to your own people, and proclaim to them how much the Lord did for you and had mercy on you." 20 And he departed and began to proclaim in the Decapolis how much Jesus had done for him, and everyone was amazed.

21 And Jesus having crossed over in the boat again to the other side, a great crowd was gathered to him, and he was by the sea. 22 And one of the synagogue leaders, named Jairus, comes and, having seen him, falls at his feet. 23 And he begged him urgently, saying, "My little daughter is about to die. Come, place hands on her so that she may be cured/saved and live." 24 And he went with him.

And a large crowd followed him and clustered around him. 25 And a woman having a flow of blood for twelve years, 26 suffering many things under many doctors, spending all that she had, not improving but getting worse, 27 hearing stories about Jesus, and coming after him in the crowd, touched his clothes. 28 For she said, "If I should touch even just his clothes, I shall be cured/saved." 29 And immediately her flow of blood was dried up, and she knew in her body that she had been healed of her illness. 30 Jesus, having known in himself immediately that power had gone out of him, having turned to the crowd, said, "Who touched my clothes?" 31 And his disciples said to him, "You see the crowd clustered around you, and yet you say, 'Who touched me?'" 32 And he looked around to see who had done this. 33 And the woman, having been frightened and trembling, knowing what had been done to her, came and fell down in front of him and told him the whole truth. 34 And he said to her, "Daughter, your trust has cured/saved you. Go in peace, and be whole from your disease."

35 While he was speaking, people come from the synagogue leader's house, saying, "Your daughter is dead. Why are you still bothering the

teacher?" 36 And Jesus, ignoring/overhearing what was said, says to the synagogue leader, "Don't fear—only trust." 37 And he allowed no one to follow him, except for Peter, Jacob, and John, the brother of Jacob. 38 And they come to the synagogue ruler's house, and he sees a commotion and people crying and lamenting loudly. 39 And having entered the house, he says to them, "Why are you making this commotion and crying? The child is not dead but sleeps." 40 And they were laughing at him. But he threw them all outside, keeping with him the father of the child and the mother and those with him, and he enters into where the child was. 41 And having taken the child's hand, he says to her, "Talitha koum," which is translated, "Young girl, I say to you: stand up!" 42 And immediately the girl stood up and walked, for she was twelve years old. And immediately they were amazed with great amazement. 43 And he sternly directed them that no one should know about this. And he told them to give her something to eat.

6:1 And he went out from there and came to his hometown. And his disciples follow him. 2 And the Sabbath having come, he began to teach in the synagogue. And many hearing him were astonished, saying, "Where did this one get these things? And what is this wisdom that has been given to him? What miracles are done by his hands? 3 Isn't this the builder? Mary's son, and the brother of Jacob, Joses, Judas, and Simon? And aren't his sisters here with us?" And they did not respect him. 4 And Jesus said to them, "A prophet is not without honor except in his hometown and among his relatives and in his own household." 5 And he wasn't able to perform any miracle there, except on a few sick people: having laid on hands, he healed them. 6 And he was amazed at their lack of belief.

And he went around among the villages teaching. 7 And he calls the Twelve to him and began to send them out two by two and gave them power/authority over unclean spirits. 8 He instructed them that they should take nothing for the way except for a staff only—no bread, no satchel, no money in their belts— 9 "but wear sandals and don't wear two tunics." 10 And he said to them, "Wherever you enter a house, stay there until you leave that area. 11 And if any place will not accept you or hear you, depart from there and shake the dirt off of your feet as a testimony to/against them." 12 And having gone out, they proclaimed that people should change their minds. 13 And they drove out many demons and anointed many sick people with oil and healed them.

14 And King Herod heard of him, for indeed his name became known. And some said, "John the Baptizer has been raised from the dead—because of this, miraculous powers are at work in him." 15 But others said, "He

is Elijah." And others said, "He is a prophet like one of the prophets of old." 16 But Herod having heard, said, "John—whom I beheaded—has been raised!" 17 For Herod himself had John arrested and bound in prison because of Herodias, his brother Philip's wife, because Herod had married her. 18 For John had been telling Herod, "It is not lawful for you to have your brother's wife." 19 And Herodias had a grudge against him and wanted to kill him, but she could not 20 because Herod revered John, knowing him to be a righteous and holy man, and so protected him. And having heard him, he, Herod, was greatly perplexed but heard him gladly. 21 And an opportunity came when Herod on his birthday hosted a banquet for the court officials, the military officers, and the prominent people of Galilee. 22 And his daughter Herodias, having come in and danced, delighted Herod and those dining with him. And the king said to the girl, "Ask me for whatever you want, and I will give it to you." 23 And he swore to her, "Whatever you ask me, I will give it to you, up to half of my kingdom." 24 And having gone out, she asked her mother, "What should I ask?" She said, "the head of John the Baptizer." 25 And having entered immediately—with haste—to the king, she asked, saying, "I want you to give me at once upon a plate the head of John the Baptizer." 26 And the king was very sorrowful, but because of his oath and because of those dining with him, he would not refuse her. 27 And immediately having sent for an executioner, he commanded that John's head be brought. And having gone, he cut off his head in the cell 28 and brought the head upon a plate and gave it to the girl, and the girl gave it to her mother. 29 And having heard about it, his disciples came and took his body and placed it in a grave.

30 And the apostles are gathered to Jesus. And they told him everything—what they had done and what they had taught. 31 And he says to them, "Come by yourselves into a deserted place and rest a little." For there were so many people coming and going that they did not even have enough time to eat.

32 And they went in the boat into a deserted place by themselves. 33 And many saw them going and recognized them, and they ran together there by land from all the towns and arrived before them. 34 And having gone out [of the boat], he saw a large crowd and was filled with compassion toward them because they were like sheep not having a shepherd. And he began to teach them many things. 35 And already the hour was late, having come to him, his disciples were saying to him, "This is a deserted place, and already the hour is late. 36 Send them away, so that having gone into the surrounding countryside and towns, they might buy themselves something to eat." 37 But

answering, he said to them, "You give them something to eat." And they say
to him, "Having gone out, should we buy two hundred days' wages worth of
bread and give it to them to eat?" 38 And he says to them, "How many loaves
of bread do you have? Go and see." And having found out, they say, "Five,
and two fish." 39 And he commanded them to make everyone in groups on
the green grass. 40 And they sat down in rows, by hundreds and by fifties.
41 And having taken the five loaves and the two fish, having looked up into/
to heaven, he blessed and broke the loaves and gave them to his disciples
so that they might present them to the people. And the two fish he divided
among them all. 42 And they all ate and were filled. 43 And they picked up
twelve basketfuls of scraps [of bread] and of the fish. 44 And those having
eaten of the loaves were five thousand males.

45 And immediately he required his disciples to enter into the boat
and to go on ahead to the other side, to Bethsaida, while he dismisses the
crowd. 46 And having left them, he went to the mountain to pray. 47 And
evening having come, the boat was in the middle of the sea, and he was
alone on the land. 48 And having seen them straining at rowing, for the
wind was against them, as the night was ending, he comes to them walking
on the sea and intending to pass by them. 49 And having seen him walking on the sea, they thought that it is a ghost and screamed. 50 For all saw
him and were terrified. And immediately he spoke with them and says to
them, "Have courage. I am [here]. Do not fear." 51 And he went up into
the boat to them, and the wind stopped. And they were extremely, utterly
amazed. 52 For they did not understand about the loaves, but their heart
was hardened.

53 And having crossed over to the land, they came to Gennesaret and
anchored there. 54 And having come out of the boat, Jesus was immediately recognized. 55 They were running through all of that region, and they
began to carry on mats those who were sick to wherever they were hearing
that he is. 56 And wherever he entered—into villages or into towns or into
the countryside—they laid down those who were sick in the marketplaces,
and they were begging him that they might touch just the fringe of his
clothing. And as many as touched him were cured/saved.

7:1 And the Pharisees and some of the scriptorians, having come from
Jerusalem, gather to him. 2 And having seen some of his disciples who with
impure hands (that is, unwashed [hands]) are eating the loaves— 3 (For
the Pharisees, and all the Jews, if they do not ritually wash the hands, they
do not eat, keeping to the tradition of the ancestors. 4 And coming from
the market, if they do not ritually immerse, they do not eat. And there are

many other things that they received to keep, the ritual immersion of cups and pots and kettles.) 5 And the Pharisees and the scriptorians asked him, "Why don't your disciples live according to the tradition of the ancestors, but with impure hands they eat the loaf?" 6 But he said to them, "Isaiah correctly prophesied about you pretenders. It stands written,

'This people honors me with their lips,
but their heart is very far away from me.
7 They worship me uselessly,
teaching human rules as doctrines.'

8 "Abandoning the commandment of God, you keep the human tradition."

9 And he was saying to them, "'Correctly' you set aside the commandment of God so that you can observe your tradition. 10 For Moses said, 'Honor your father and your mother' and 'The one who speaks evil of father or mother must be put to death.' 11 But you say, 'If a person says to the father or the mother, "It is korban (that is, a gift [for God]), whatever you might otherwise have gotten from me,"' 12 so you don't permit him or her to do anything for the father or the mother, 13 canceling the word of God for your tradition that you have handed down. And you do many similar things."

14 And having called the crowd to him again, he was saying to them, "All of you hear me and understand. 15 There is nothing outside of a person that has the power to defile him or her by entering in. But the things coming out of the person are the things defiling the person." [16]

17 And when he went into a house away from the crowd, his disciples asked him about the parable. 18 And he says to them, "So you also lack understanding? You don't realize that everything from the outside entering into a person cannot defile him or her 19 because it does not enter into his or her heart but into the stomach and goes out into the latrine?" (He was declaring clean all food.) 20 And he was saying, "What comes out of a person—that defiles the person. 21 For from within, out of the human heart, evil ideas go out: sexual immoralities, thefts, murders, adulteries, 22 covetings, wickedness, deceit, indecency, envy/malice, slander, pride, and foolishness. 23 All of these evils from within go out and defile the person."

24 From there, having risen up, he went away into the region of Tyre. And having entered into a house, he wanted no one to know, but he was not able to be hidden. 25 But immediately, a woman, having heard about him and having a little daughter with an unclean spirit, having come, fell

at his feet. 26 But the woman was a Greek, a Syrophenician by origin, and she was asking him to cast the demon out of her daughter. 27 And he was saying to her, "First let the children be filled. For it is not right to take the children's loaf and throw it to the dogs." 28 And she answered and says to him, "Sir/Lord, but the dogs under the table eat the children's crumbs." 29 And he said to her, "For this answer, go. The demon has gone out of your daughter." 30 And having gone away to her home, she found the child lying on the bed and the demon having gone out.

31 And again having departed from the region of Tyre, he came through Sidon, to the sea of Galilee through the middle of the region of the Decapolis. 32 And they bring him a man who was deaf and who couldn't speak well, and they begged him that he would place a hand on him. 33 And having taken him aside from the crowd privately, he put his fingers into the man's ears. And having spit, he touched his tongue. 34 And having looked up to heaven, he groaned and says to him, "Ephphatha" (that is, be opened). 35 And his ears were opened, the bond of his tongue was loosened, and he spoke clearly. 36 And he instructed them that they should tell no one. But as much as he instructed them, they proclaimed it even more zealously. 37 And they were completely astonished, saying, "He has done all things well—he makes the deaf to hear and the mute to speak."

8:1 In those days, again, the crowd being large and not having anything they might eat, having called to him the disciples, Jesus says to them, 2 "I have empathy for the crowd because they have continued with me for three days and have had nothing that they might eat. 3 And if I send them away hungry to their homes, they will collapse on the way. For some of them are come from far away." 4 And his disciples answered him, "From where could anyone satisfy these people with loaves of bread in this desert?" 5 And he was asking them, "How many loaves do you have?" And they said, "Seven." 6 And he commands the crowd to sit on the ground. And having taken the seven loaves and having given thanks, he broke them and gave them to his disciples so that they might set it before them. And they set it before the crowd. 7 And they had a few small fish. And having blessed them, he also wanted these to be set before them. 8 And they ate and were satisfied. And they picked up the leftover pieces, seven baskets. 9 And there were about four thousand people. And he sent them away. 10 And immediately having entered into the boat with his disciples, he came into the district of Dalmanutha.

11 And the Pharisees went out and began to argue with him, seeking a sign from heaven from him, testing him. 12 And having sighed deeply in his

spirit, he says, "Why does this generation seek a sign? Amen, I say to you, [may God's judgment come upon me] if a sign will be given to this generation." 13 And having left them, again having entered the boat, he went away to the other side. 14 And they forgot to take loaves, except they did have one loaf with them in the boat. 15 And he ordered them, saying, "Watch out! Beware of the leaven of the Pharisees and of the leaven of Herod." 16 And they were discussing with one another, because they did not have loaves. 17 And having known it, he says to them, "Why are you discussing that you do not have loaves? Do you not yet perceive or understand? Have your hearts been hardened? 18 Having eyes, do you not see? And having ears, do you not hear? And do you not remember? 19 When I broke the five loaves for the five thousand, how many baskets full of pieces did you collect?" They say to him, "Twelve." 20 "And when I broke the seven to the four thousand, how many baskets full of pieces did you collect?" And they say, "Seven." 21 And he said to them, "Do you still not understand?"

22 And they come to Bethsaida, and they bring him a blind man and begged him to touch him. 23 And having taken hold of the blind man's hand, he led him out of the village. And having spit upon his eyes, having laid hands on him, he asked him, "Do you see anything?" 24 And having looked up [or: gaining his sight], he said, "I see people; as trees I see them walking." 25 Then again he laid hands upon his eyes, and he opened his eyes, and he was restored, and he saw everything clearly. 26 And he sent him to his home saying, "Do not even go into the village."

27 And Jesus and his disciples went out into the villages of Caesarea Philippi. And on the way, he was questioning his disciples, saying to them, "Who do people say I am?" 28 And they told him, saying, "John the Baptizer, and others [say] Elijah, but others [say] one of the prophets." 29 And he questioned them, "But [all of] you—who do you say I am?" Answering, Peter says to him, "You are the anointed one." 30 And he rebuked them that they should tell no one about him.

31 And he began to teach them that it is necessary for the son of man to suffer many things and to be rejected by the elders and the chief priests and the scriptorians and to be killed and after three days to rise again. 32 And he spoke the word openly. And Peter, having taken him aside, began to rebuke him. 33 And [Jesus] having turned and having seen his disciples, he rebuked Peter and says, "Follow me, Satan! For you are not on God's side, but the side of people."

34 And having called the crowd to him, along with his disciples, he said to them, "If anyone wants to come follow me, they must deny themselves

and take up their crosses and follow me. 35 For whoever wants to save their souls/lives will destroy them. But whoever destroys their souls/lives for me and for the good news will save them. 36 For what good does it do them to gain the entire world and to lose their souls/lives? 37 For what should they give in exchange for their souls/lives? 38 For if anyone is ashamed of me and my words in this adulterous and sinful generation, the son of man will be ashamed of him or her, when he shall come in the glory of his father, with the holy angels." 9:1 And he was saying to them, "Amen, I say to you: there are some standing here who will not die before they see the kingdom of God having come in power."

2 And after six days, Jesus takes with him Peter and Jacob and John and leads them up apart into a high mountain themselves alone. And he was changed in appearance in their presence. 3 And his clothing became intensely, brilliantly white, as no launderer on the earth is able to whiten it. 4 And Elijah with Moses appeared to them, and they were talking with Jesus. 5 And interjecting, Peter says to Jesus, "Rabbi, it is good for us to be here. And let us make three shelters—one for you and one for Moses and one for Elijah." 6 For he did not know what he should say, for they were terrified. 7 And a cloud came, covering them, and a voice came out of the cloud: "This is my son, the beloved one. Listen to him." 8 And suddenly, having looked around, they no longer saw anyone except Jesus alone with them.

9 And as they were descending from the mountain, he instructed them that they should tell no one what they had seen, not until after the son of man had risen from the dead. 10 And they kept that matter to themselves, questioning what it is to rise from the dead. 11 And they were asking him, saying, "Why do the scriptorians say that it is necessary for Elijah to come first?" 12 And he was saying to them, "Does Elijah indeed, having come first, restore everything? And why is it written of the son of man that he should suffer many things and be scorned? 13 But I say to you that Elijah has come, and they did to him whatever they wanted, as it has been written of him."

14 And having come to the disciples, they saw a large crowd around them and scriptorians arguing with them. 15 And immediately all the crowd, having seen him, were stunned and, running to him, greeted him. 16 And he asked them, "What are you arguing about with them?" 17 And one out of the crowd answered him, "Teacher, I brought you my son, who is possessed by a spirit that makes him mute. 18 And when it seizes him, it throws him down, and he foams [at the mouth] and grinds his teeth and becomes rigid. And I spoke to your disciples, if they might cast it out, and they did not have the power to do it." 19 And answering them, he says, "You faithless

generation! How long must I be with you? How much longer do I have to put up with you? Bring him to me." 20 And they brought him to him. And having seen him, the spirit immediately caused the boy to go into spasms. And having fallen upon the ground, he rolled around, foaming at the mouth. 21 And he asked his father, "How long has he been like this?" And he said, "From childhood, 22 and it often throws him into the fire and into the water, so that it might destroy him. But if you can do anything, help us and have compassion on us!" 23 And Jesus said to him, "'If you can do anything'? All things can be done for one who trusts." 24 Immediately having cried out, the father of the child was saying, "I trust you! Help my lack of trust!" 25 Jesus, having seen that a crowd was gathering, rebuked the unclean spirit, saying to it, "Mute and deaf spirit, I command you: come out of him and never enter him again." 26 And having cried out and having caused many spasms, it came out, and he became as if dead, so that most were saying, "He is dead." 27 And Jesus, having taken him by the hand, raised him, and he arose. 28 And having entered into a house, his disciples asked him privately, "Why were we not able to cast it out?" 29 And he said to them, "This kind cannot be cast out except by prayer."

30 Having gone out from there, they passed through Galilee, and he did not want anyone to know it. 31 For he was teaching his disciples and was saying to them, "The son of man is delivered into the hands of humans, and they will kill him. And having been killed, after three days, he will arise." 32 But they did not understand the statement, and they were afraid to ask him.

33 And they came to Capernaum. And when he was in the house, he asked them, "What were you discussing on the way?" 34 But they were silent, for on the way they had been discussing with one another who was the greatest. 35 And having sat down, he called the Twelve, and he says to them, "If anyone wants to be first, he or she must be last of all and servant of all." 36 And having taken a child, he put him/her in the middle of them, and hugging him/her, he said to them, 37 "Whoever welcomes one of these children in my name welcomes me. And whoever will welcome me does not welcome me, but the one having sent me."

38 John was saying to him, "Teacher, we saw someone casting out demons in your name. And we tried to stop him because he was not following us." 39 And Jesus said, "Do not stop him. For there is no one who will do a miracle in my name who will be able soon after to revile me. 40 For whoever is not against us is for us. 41 For whoever should give you a cup of water because you are the anointed one's—amen, I say to you—that person will not destroy his/her reward. 42 And whoever causes one of these little

ones who trusts me to stumble, it would be better for them if a large mill-stone were put around their neck and they were cast into the sea. 43 And if your hand should cause you to stumble, cut it off. It is better for you to enter into life maimed instead of going away into hell with two hands, into the unquenchable fire. [44] 45 And if your foot should cause you to stumble, cut it off. It is better for you to enter into life maimed instead of having two feet [and] being cast into hell. [46] 47 And if your eye causes you to stumble, cast it out. It is better for you to enter into the kingdom of God with one eye rather than having two eyes and having to be cast into hell, 48 where their worm does not die and the fire is not quenched. 49 For everyone will be salted with fire. 50 Salt is good, but if the salt becomes unsalty, how could you season it? Have salt in yourselves, and be at peace with one another."

10:1 And having risen up from there, he comes through the region of Judea and beyond the Jordan. And the crowds again come together to him, and as again, as was his habit, he was teaching them. 2 And having come to him, they demanded of him, "Is it lawful for a husband to divorce his wife?" testing him. 3 But answering he said to them, "What did Moses command you?" 4 And they said, "Moses permitted [a man] to write a divorce decree and to send her away." 5 But Jesus said to them, "Because of the hardness of your heart, he wrote this commandment for you. 6 But from the beginning of creation he 'made them male and female.' 7 'Because of this, a man will leave his father and mother, 8 and the two will be one flesh,' so that they are no longer two but one flesh. 9 Therefore, what God has united together, let no one separate." 10 And in the house the disciples were asking him, once again, about this. 11 And he says to them, "Whoever divorces his wife and marries another commits adultery against her. 12 And if a woman divorces her husband and marries another, she commits adultery."

13 And they were bringing little children to him, so that he might touch them. But the disciples rebuked them. 14 But having seen this, Jesus was angry and said to them, "Let the little children come to me—don't stop them. The kingdom of God belongs to such as these. 15 Amen, I say to you, whoever will not receive the kingdom of God like a little child will never enter into it." 16 And having hugged them, he was blessing them, having laid hands on them.

17 Now as he went forth on the way, a man having run up to him and having knelt down, asked him, "Good teacher, what should I do so that I might inherit eternal life?" 18 But Jesus said to him, "Why do you call me good? No one is good except God alone. 19 You know the commandments:

'Do not commit adultery. Do not murder. Do not steal. Do not give false testimony. Do not defraud. Respect your father and mother.'" 20 But he said to him, "Teacher, all of these I have strictly obeyed from my youth." 21 But Jesus, having looked at him, loved him, and said to him, "One thing of yours is lacking: go, as much as you have—sell, and give [the money] to the poor, and you will have treasure in heaven. And come, follow me." 22 But he, his face falling at this saying, went away grieving, for he was one who had many possessions.

23 And having looked around, Jesus says to his disciples, "How hard it is for those having riches to enter into the kingdom of God!" 24 But the disciples were astonished at his words. But Jesus again answering says to them, "Children, how hard it is to enter the kingdom of God. 25 It is easier for a camel to go through the eye of a needle than for a rich person to enter into the kingdom of heaven." 26 But they were extremely astonished, saying to him, "Then who can be saved?" 27 Jesus, having looked at them, says, "With mortals it is impossible, but not with God. Indeed, all things are possible with God."

28 Peter began to say to him, "Look, we have left all things and are following you." 29 Jesus said, "Amen, I say to you, there is no one who has left home or brothers or sisters or mother or father or children or land for my sake and for the good news 30 who will not take a hundred times as much now in this time—homes and brothers and sisters and mothers and children and land, with persecution—and in the age which is coming, eternal life. 31 But many who are first will be last, and the last first."

32 They were on the way, going up to Jerusalem. And Jesus was going before them, and they were astonished. And those following were afraid. And having taken to him the Twelve again, he began to tell about the things that were going to happen to him. 33 "Look, we are going up to Jerusalem, and the son of man will be handed over to the chief priests and the scriptorians. And they will condemn him to death, and they will hand him over to the Gentiles. 34 And they will mock him and spit on him and whip him and kill him, and after three days he will rise again."

35 And Jacob and John, the sons of Zebedee, come up to him, saying to him, "Teacher, we want you to do for us whatever we ask you." 36 But he said to them, "What do you want me to do for you?" 37 And they said to him, "Grant us that one of us will sit at your right hand and one at your left hand, in your glory." 38 But Jesus said to them, "You do not know what you are asking for. Can you drink the cup that I drink and be baptized with the baptism that I am baptized with?" 39 But they said to him, "We can!" But

Jesus said to them, "The cup that I drink, you will drink. And the baptism that I am baptized with, you will be baptized with. 40 But to sit at my right hand or at my left hand is not mine to give but [is] for those for whom it has been prepared." 41 And having heard this, the ten began to be angry with Jacob and John. 42 And having called them to him, Jesus says to them, "You know that those recognized to rule over the Gentiles exercise lordship over them, and their great ones exercise authority/power over them. 43 But it is not this way among you. Whoever wants to become great among you will be your servant, 44 and whoever wants to be first among you will be the slave of all. 45 For even the son of man did not come to be served but to serve and to give his life for the release of many."

46 And they come to Jericho. And as he was going out of Jericho with his disciples and a large crowd, the son of Timaeus, Bartimaeus, a blind beggar, was sitting beside the way. 47 And having heard that it is Jesus of Nazareth, he began to shout and to say, "Son of David, Jesus, have mercy on me!" 48 And many were rebuking him that he should be silent, but he shouted all the more, "Son of David, have mercy on me!" 49 And having stopped, Jesus commanded, "Call him." And they call the blind man, saying to him, "Have courage—rise up! He is calling you." 50 And having thrown off his cloak, having jumped up, he came to Jesus. 51 And answering him, Jesus says, "What do you want me to do for you?" And the blind man said to him, "Rabbi, that I may see." 52 And Jesus said to him, "Go. Your trust has healed/saved you. And immediately he could see and followed him on the way."

11:1 And when they are coming near to Jerusalem, to Bethphage and Bethany, near the Mount of Olives, he sends two of his disciples. 2 And he says to them, "Go into the village ahead of you and immediately entering into it, you will find a colt having been tied up, upon which no one has ever sat. Untie it and bring it. 3 And if anyone says to you, 'Why are you doing this?' say, 'The master has need of it, and he will send it back here immediately.'" 4 And they left and found a colt having been tied at the door, out in the road, and they untied it. 5 And some of those who were standing there were saying to them, "What are you doing untying the colt?" 6 But they spoke to them as Jesus had commande,d and they allowed them [to go]. 7 And they lead the colt to Jesus. And they threw their cloaks on it, and he sat on it. 8 And many spread their cloaks on the way, but others cut leafy branches from the fields. 9 And those going in front and those going behind were shouting, "Hosanna! Blessed is the one coming in the name of the Lord! 10 Blessed [is] the coming kingdom of our father David! Hosanna in the highest!" 11 And he entered into Jerusalem, into the temple.

And having looked around at everything, the hour already being late, he went to Bethany with the Twelve.

12 And on the next day, as they went out from Bethany, he was hungry. 13 And having seen in the distance a fig tree having leaves, he went [to see] if perhaps he would find any [figs] on it. And having come to it, he found nothing but leaves, for it was not fig season. 14 And answering, he said to it, "May no one ever again eat your fruit." And his disciples heard.

15 And they come to Jerusalem. And having entered into the temple, he began to cast out those selling and those buying in the temple. And he toppled the moneychangers' tables and the chairs of those selling the doves. 16 And he didn't permit anyone to carry any goods through the temple. 17 And he was teaching and was saying to them, "Has it not been written 'My house will be called a house of prayer for all the nations'? But you have made it 'a hideout for robbers.'" 18 And the chief priests and the scriptorians heard [it], and they sought how they could destroy him because they feared him because all of the crowd was astonished at his teaching. 19 And when evening came, they went out of the city.

20 And passing by in the morning, they saw the fig tree, withered from the roots. 21 And having remembered, Peter says to him, "Rabbi, look, the fig tree that you cursed has withered." 22 And answering, Jesus says to them, "Have trust in God. 23 Amen, I say to you, if you say to this mountain, 'Be lifted and thrown into the sea,' and you do not waver in your heart, but trust that what you say will happen, it will happen for you. 24 Therefore I say to you, all things you pray and ask for, trust that you have received it, and it will be yours. 25 And whenever you stand praying, forgive anything you have against anyone, so that your father who is in the heavens will forgive your sins." [26]

27 And they come again to Jerusalem. And as he is walking in the temple, the chief priests and the scriptorians and the elders come to him. 28 And they were saying to him, "By what authority are you doing these things? Or, who gave you this authority, that you should do these things?" 29 But Jesus was saying to them, "I will ask you one thing, and if you answer me, then I will tell you by what authority I do these things. 30 The baptism of John: was it from heaven, or from humans? Answer me." 31 And they were reasoning with each other, saying, "If we say from heaven, he will say, 'Then why did you not trust him?' 32 But if we should say from humans . . .'"— they feared the crowd, for all held that John indeed was a prophet. 33 And answering Jesus, they say, "We do not know." And Jesus says to them, "Neither will I tell you by what authority I do these things."

12:1 And he began to say to them in parables, "A man planted a vineyard and placed around it a wall and dug a pit for the winepress and built a watchtower and rented it to tenant farmers and went on a journey. 2 And he sent a slave to the tenant farmers at the right time, so that he might receive the fruits of the vineyard from the tenant farmers. 3 But seizing him, they beat him and sent him away with nothing. 4 And again he sent another slave to them; this one they beat on the head and treated shamefully. 5 And he sent another, and this one they killed. And many others, beating some and killing others. 6 Yet having one beloved son, he sent him to them last, saying, 'They will have respect for my son.' 7 But those tenant farmers said to one another, 'This is the heir. Come, let's kill him, and the inheritance will be ours.' 8 And seizing him, they killed him and cast him out of the vineyard. 9 So what will the owner of the vineyard do? He will come and will destroy the tenants and will give the vineyard to others. 10 Have you not even read this scripture:

'The stone the builders rejected
has become the cornerstone.
11 This was from the Lord,
and it is wonderful in our eyes'?"

12 And they wanted to arrest him—but they feared the crowd—for they knew that he had spoken the parable against them. And having left him, they went away.

13 And they send to him some of the Pharisees and the Herodians, so that they might trap him in his words. 14 And having come, they say to him, "Teacher, we know that you are truthful and do not cater to anyone, for you are impartial, but with truth you teach the way of God. Is it right to pay taxes to Caesar or not? Should we pay or not pay?" 15 And knowing of their pretending, he said to them, "Why do you test me? Bring me a coin, so that I might see it." 16 And they brought it. And he says to them, "Whose image is this? And the inscription?" And they said to him, "Caesar's." 17 And Jesus said to them, "The things of Caesar you give to Caesar, and the things of God [you give] to God." And they were amazed at him.

18 And Sadducees—who say there is no resurrection—come to him. And they were questioning him, saying, 19 "Teacher, Moses wrote for us, 'If a man's brother should die and leave behind a wife and not leave children, he should marry his brother's wife, and he should raise children for his brother.' 20 There were seven brothers, and the first took a wife and, dying, left no children. 21 And the second took her and died, not having left children, and the third, the same. 22 And none of the seven had children. And

last of all, the woman died. 23 In the resurrection whose wife will she be? For the seven had her as a wife." 24 Jesus said to them, "Aren't you mistaken because you do not know the scriptures or the power of God? 25 For when they rise from the dead, they do not marry nor are they given in marriage but are like angels in heaven. 26 Now as for the dead—that they are raised— have you not read in the book of Moses, in the passage about the [burning] bush, how God spoke to him, saying, 'I am the God of Abraham and the God of Isaac and the God of Jacob?' 27 He is not the God of the dead but of the living. [So] you are very mistaken."

28 And having come up, one of the scriptorians having heard them rea- soning together, having known that he answered them well, he asked him, "Which is the first commandment of all?" 29 Jesus answered, "The first is, 'Listen, Israel: The Lord our God, the Lord is one. 30 And love the Lord your God, with all your heart and with all your soul and with all your mind and with all your strength.' 31 The second is this: 'Love your neighbor as yourself.' There is no other commandment greater than these." 32 And the scriptorian said to him, "Right, teacher, you have spoken truthfully that 'he is one and there is no one else besides him.' 33 And to love him with all the heart, and with all the understanding, and with all the strength, and to love a neighbor as oneself is more important than all the burnt offerings and sacrifices." 34 And Jesus, having seen that he answered wisely, said to him, "You are not far from the kingdom of God." And no one dared any longer to question him.

35 While teaching in the temple, answering, Jesus said, "Why do the scriptorians say that the anointed one is a son of David? 36 David himself said by the Holy Spirit,

'The Lord said to my Lord,
"Sit at my right hand
until I place your enemies under your feet."'

37 "David himself calls him Lord. So how is he his son?" And the large crowd happily heard him.

38 And in his teaching, he said, "Watch out for the scriptorians who like walking around in long robes and greetings in the markets, 39 the first seats in the synagogues and the first places at banquets, 40 the ones consuming the property of widows and, on a pretext, [making] long prayers. These will be more harshly punished." 41 And having sat down opposite the tem- ple treasury, he watched the crowd put money into the treasury, and many rich people were putting in much. 42 And having come, one poor widow put in two coins, which equals less than a penny. 43 And having called his

disciples to him, he says to them, "Amen, I say to you that this poor widow has put in more than all of those [who are] putting in to the treasury, 44 for they put in out of their abundance. However, she put in out of her poverty as much as she had—her whole life."

13:1 And as he is leaving the temple, one of his disciples says to him, "Teacher, look! What [impressive] stones and what [impressive] buildings!" 2 And Jesus said to him, "You are watching these great buildings? There will not be left one stone upon [another] stone here that shall not be thrown down." 3 And while he is sitting upon the Mount of Olives—opposite the temple—Peter, Jacob, John, and Andrew asked him privately, 4 "Tell us when these things will be. And what will be the sign when these things are all going to happen?"

5 But Jesus began to say to them, "Watch, so that no one misleads you. 6 Many will come in my name, saying, 'I am [he],' and they will mislead many people. 7 And when you hear of wars and reports of wars, do not be alarmed—it must be. But the end is not yet. 8 For nation will rise up against nation, and kingdom against kingdom. There will be earthquakes in [various] places. There will be famines. These are the beginning of labor pains.

9 "But watch yourselves: they will hand you over to courts and in synagogue councils. You will be beaten. And you will be brought before governors and kings because of me, for a witness to them. 10 And first, the good news must be proclaimed to all nations. 11 And when they lead you away, handing you over, do not worry ahead of time about what you should say, but say what is given you at that time—for you are not speaking, but the Holy Spirit. 12 And sibling will hand over sibling to death, and a father his child. And children will rise up against parents and will put them to death. 13 And you will be hated by all because of my name. But the one having persevered to the end will be saved.

14 "But when you observe 'the detestable [thing] causing desolation' standing where he should not (let the one reading understand), then those people in Judea should flee into the mountains. 15 But the one on the roof must not come down to go inside to take anything out of the house. 16 And the one in the field should not return to the things left behind to take clothing. 17 But alas to those who are pregnant and to those who are breastfeeding in those days! 18 And pray that it may not be during the winter. 19 For there will be suffering in those days such as there has never been from the beginning of creation, which God created, until now and never shall be [again]. 20 And if the Lord had not limited the days, no one would have been saved. But on account of the elect whom he chose, he has limited

the days. 21 And if anyone says to you, 'Look! Here is the anointed one!' or 'Look! There!' you should not trust it. 22 For there will arise fake anointed ones and fake prophets, and they will give signs and wonders to deceive, if possible, the elect. 23 But you—watch! I have told you all things ahead of time.

24 "But in those days, after that suffering, the sun will be darkened, and the moon will not give its light. 25 And the stars will be falling out of the sky/heaven, and the powers that are in the skies/heavens will be shaken. 26 And then they will see 'the son of man coming in clouds,' with great power and glory. 27 And then he will send the angels/messengers, and he will gather together his elect from the four winds—from the end of earth to the end of the sky/heaven.

28 "But you know the parable of the fig tree: when the branch is already tender and has put out its leaves, you know that summer is near. 29 So when you see these things happen, know that it/he is near, at the door. 30 Amen, I say to you, this generation will not pass away until these things all have taken place. 31 The sky/heaven and the earth will pass away, but my words will not pass away.

32 "But of the day or the hour no one knows—not even the angels in the sky/heaven, nor the Son—except the Father. 33 Watch; keep alert, for you do not know when the appointed time is. 34 It is like a person going on a journey, having left his house, having given his slaves authority, [assigning] to each his work. And he commanded the doorkeeper to be on guard. 35 Therefore, be on guard, for you do not know when the master of the house will come—in the evening or at midnight or when the rooster crows or in the morning—36 or else, having come suddenly, he should find you sleeping. 37 And what I say to you, I say to all: be on guard!"

14:1 It would be the Passover, and the feast of unleavened bread, after two days. And the chief priests and the scriptorians were looking for a way that they might kill him [after] having taken him by stealth. 2 For they were saying, "Not during the feast, or there will be a riot by the people."

3 And being in Bethany, in the house of Simon the leper, being reclined [at the table], there came a woman having an alabaster flask of expensive ointment of pure nard; having broken the alabaster flask, she poured it on his head. 4 But some were angry among themselves: "Why was this ointment wasted? 5 For this ointment could have been sold for more than a year's wages and [the money] have been given to the poor." And they were scolding her. 6 But Jesus said, "Leave her alone. Why do you bother her? She did a good work in me. 7 For 'you always have the poor with you,' and

whenever you want to, you are able to do them good. But me you do not always have. 8 She did what she could: she came before the fact to anoint my body for burial. 9 Amen, I say to you: wherever the good news is proclaimed in the whole world, what she has done will also be told in memory of her."

10 And Judas Iscariot, the one of the Twelve, went away to the chief priests that he might betray Jesus to them. 11 But having heard, they rejoiced and promised to give him money. And he was looking for a good opportunity to betray him.

12 And on the first day of [the feast of] unleavened bread, when the Passover lamb was being sacrificed, his disciples say to him, "Where do you want us to go to prepare for you to eat the Passover meal?" 13 And he sends out two of his disciples and says to them, "Go into the city and a man carrying a jar of water will meet you. Follow him. 14 And wherever he enters, say to the owner of the house, 'The teacher says, "Where is my guest room, where I might eat the Passover with my disciples?"' 15 And he will show you a big room upstairs, furnished and ready. Prepare for us there." 16 And the disciples left and came into the city. And they found things just as he had said to them. And they prepared the Passover.

17 And when it was evening, he comes with the Twelve. 18 And as they were reclining and as they were eating, Jesus said, "Amen, I say to you: one of you will betray me, the one who is eating with me." 19 They began to be distressed and to say to him, one by one, "Not me, right?" 20 But he said to them, "[It is] one of the Twelve, who is dipping [his hand] in the bowl with me. 21 For the son of man goes, as it has been written about him, but woe to the man who betrays the son of man! It would have been better for that man had he never been born."

22 And while they were eating, having taken bread, [and] having blessed, he broke [it] and gave [it] to them and said, "Take [it]. This is my body." 23 And having taken a cup, having given thanks, he gave [it] to them, and they all drank of it. 24 And he said to them, "This is my blood of the covenant being poured out for many. 25 Amen, I say to you that I will never drink of the fruit of the vine until the day when I drink it new in the kingdom of God."

26 And having sung a hymn, they went out to the Mount of Olives. 27 And Jesus says to them, "All of you will desert me, for it has been written, 'I will strike down the shepherd, and the sheep will be scattered.' 28 But after I am raised, I will go ahead of you into Galilee." 29 But Peter said to him, "Even if everyone deserts you, I will not!" 30 And Jesus says to him,

"Amen, I say to you: today—this very night—before the rooster crows twice, you will deny me three times." 31 But he was insisting, "Even if I have to die with you, I will never deny you!" And they all said the same thing.

32 And they come to a place that is called Gethsemane. And he says to his disciples, "Sit here while I pray." 33 And he takes Peter, Jacob, and John with him. And he began to be stunned and deeply distressed. 34 And he says to them, "My soul is greatly grieved—even to death. Stay here and watch." 35 And having moved forward a little, he threw himself on the ground and prayed that, if it is possible, the hour might pass from him. 36 And he was saying, "Abba, Father, all things are possible for you. Take away this cup from me. But not what I want, but what you want." 37 And he comes and finds them sleeping. And he says to Peter, "Simon, are you asleep? Were you not strong enough to watch for one hour? 38 Watch and pray so that you don't enter into temptation. The spirit is willing, but the flesh is weak." 39 And having gone away again, he prayed, having said the same words. 40 And having returned again, he found them sleeping—because they could not keep their eyes open. And they didn't know what to tell him. 41 And he comes the third time, and he says to them, "Are you still sleeping and resting? Enough. The hour has come. Look: the son of man is delivered into the hands of sinners. 42 Rise up, let's go. Look: the one who is betraying me is approaching."

43 And immediately—while Jesus was still speaking—Judas, one of the Twelve, arrives. And a crowd [was] with him, with swords and clubs, [sent] from the chief priests and the scriptorians and the elders. 44 The one who was betraying him had given a signal to them, saying, "Whomever I kiss is he. Arrest him and securely lead him away." 45 And having arrived, immediately having come up to him, he says, "Rabbi." And he kissed him. 46 And they took hold of him and arrested him. 47 But one who was standing there, having drawn his sword, struck the high priest's slave and cut off his ear. 48 And answering, Jesus said to them, "Are you come out, as [if] against a bandit, with swords and clubs to capture me? 49 Every day I was with you in the temple teaching—and you did not arrest me. But the scriptures must be fulfilled." 50 And having deserted him, they all fled.

51 And a certain young man was following him, wearing a linen cloth on his naked body. And they seize him. 52 But having left behind the linen cloth, he fled naked.

53 And they led Jesus to the high priest. And all of the chief priests, elders, and scriptorians assembled. 54 And Peter followed him from a distance, up to the high priest's courtyard. And he was sitting with the guards and warming himself at the fire. 55 But the chief priests and the whole Sanhedrin were

seeking testimony against Jesus, to put him to death, but they were not finding any. 56 For many were falsely testifying against him, but their testimonies were not consistent. 57 And some, having risen up, falsely testified against him, saying, 58 "We heard him saying, 'I will destroy this temple, the one made with hands, and in three days another one—not made with hands—I will build.'" 59 And thus their testimony did not agree. 60 And having stood up in the middle, the high priest questioned Jesus, saying, "Do you have no answer? What is it that these people testify against you?" 61 But he was being silent and did not answer at all. Again the high priest was questioning him and says to him, "Are you the anointed one, the son of the Blessed One?" 62 And Jesus said, "I am. And you will see the son of man 'sitting at the right hand' of the Power and 'coming with the clouds of heaven.'" 63 But the high priest, having torn his clothing, says, "Why do we still need witnesses? 64 You heard the blasphemy. What do you decide?" And all judged him to be deserving of death. 65 And some began to spit on him and to cover his face and hit him and to say to him, "Prophesy!" And the guards slapped him.

66 And while Peter was below, in the courtyard, one of the female servants of the high priest comes. 67 And having seen Peter warming himself, having looked at him, she says, "And you were with the Nazarene, Jesus." 68 But he denied it, saying, "I don't know, or even understand, what you say." And he went out onto the entryway. 69 And the servant, having seen him, began again to say to those nearby, "This is one of them!" 70 But again he was denying it. And after a little while, again those nearby were saying to Peter, "Surely you are with them. For you are definitely a Galilean." 71 But he began to curse and to swear [an oath]: "I don't know this man you are talking about!" 72 And immediately, a rooster crowed the second time. And Peter remembered what Jesus had said to him: "Before the rooster crows twice, you will deny me three times." And having broken down, he cried.

15:1 And immediately, in the morning, having held a hearing, the chief priests, with the elders and scriptorians and all the Sanhedrin, having bound Jesus, led him away and handed him over to Pilate. 2 And Pilate questioned him: "Are you the king of the Jews?" And answering him, he says: "You say so." 3 And the chief priests were repeatedly accusing him. 4 And again Pilate questioned him, saying, "You do not answer? Look, they accuse you of many things!" 5 But Jesus answered nothing, so that Pilate was amazed.

6 And at the feast, he used to release to them one prisoner whom they were requesting. 7 And there was one called Barabbas having been bound with the rebels who in the uprising had committed murder. 8 And having

come up, the crowd began to ask him to do as he usually did for them. 9 But Pilate answered them, saying, "Do you want me to release the king of the Jews to you?" 10 (For he knew that it was because of envy that the chief priests had handed him over.) 11 And the chief priests incited the crowd, so that he might release Barabbas to them instead. 12 Again answering, Pilate was saying to them, "Then what do you want me to do to him that you call the King of the Jews?" 13 And again they shouted, "Crucify him!" 14 And Pilate was saying to them, "Why? What has he done wrong?" But they shouted all the more: "Crucify him!" 15 But Pilate, desiring to do what the crowd wanted, released Barabbas to them and handed over Jesus, having whipped him, that he might be crucified.

16 And the soldiers led him away into the courtyard of the governor's house, and they called the entire band of soldiers together. 17 And they put a purple cloak on him and placed on him a thorn crown, having woven it. 18 And they began to salute him: "Hail, King of the Jews!" 19 And they hit his head with a staff, and they spit on him. And, kneeling down, they paid homage to him. 20 And when they had ridiculed him, they took the purple cloak off of him and put his own clothes on him and led him out to crucify him.

21 And they forced a passerby, Simon of Cyrene—the father of Alexander and Rufus—who was coming from the fields, to carry his cross. 22 And they bring him to a place called Golgotha (which means "the place of a skull"). 23 And they gave him wine mixed with myrrh, but he did not take it. 24 And having crucified him, "they divided his clothes, throwing dice for them" [to see] who should take what.

25 And it was about nine in the morning when they crucified him. 26 And the inscription of the charge against him read, "The King of the Jews." 27 And they crucified two outlaws with him, one on the right side and one on his left. [28] 29 And those passing by blasphemed him, shaking their heads and saying, "Ha! The one destroying the temple and building it in three days 30 save yourself by coming down from the cross!" 31 In the same way, the chief priests were mocking, together with the scriptorians, [and] saying among themselves, "He saved/healed others, but he does not have the power to save/heal himself. 32 Let the anointed one, the King of Israel, come down now from the cross so that we might see and trust!" And those being crucified with him insulted him.

33 And at about noon, darkness came over all the land until about three o'clock. 34 And at around three o'clock, Jesus screamed with a loud voice, "Eloi, Eloi, lema sabachthani?"—which means, "'My God, my God, why have you abandoned me?'" 35 And some of those standing by, having heard,

were saying, "Look, he calls Elijah." 36 But someone, having run, and having filled a sponge with wine, having put it on a stick, was giving him a drink, saying, "Leave him be! Let's see if Elijah comes to take him down." 37 And Jesus, having uttered a loud cry, breathed his last breath. 38 And the temple veil was torn in two—from top to bottom. 39 But the centurion, standing against him, having seen that he breathed his last breath, said, "Truly this man was God's son!"

40 There were also women looking on from a distance, including Mary of Magdala and Mary the mother of Jacob the Younger and the mother of Joses and Salome, 41 who, when he was in Galilee, followed him and ministered to him. And many other women, those having come up with him to Jerusalem, [were there].

42 And already evening had arrived. Since it was the day for preparation (that is, the day before the Sabbath), 43 Joseph of Arimathea, a prominent member of the council who also himself was looking forward to the kingdom of God, having come with boldness, went to Pilate and asked for Jesus' body. 44 And Pilate wondered if Jesus was already dead. And having summoned the centurion, he asked him if Jesus was now dead. 45 And learning [that Jesus was dead] from the centurion, he gave the body to Joseph. 46 And having bought a linen cloth, having taken him down, he wrapped him in the linen cloth and placed him in a tomb, which was cut out of a rock. And he rolled a stone across the entrance to the tomb. 47 And Mary Magdalene and Mary the mother of Joses saw where he was placed.

16:1 And the Sabbath having passed, Mary of Magdala, and Mary [the mother] of Jacob, and Salome bought spices so that they might go and anoint him. 2 And very early on the first day of the week, the sun having risen, they come to the tomb. 3 And they were saying to each other, "Who will roll away for us the stone from the entrance to the tomb?" 4 And having looked up, they see that the stone had been rolled away—it was extremely large indeed! 5 And having entered into the tomb, they saw a young man sitting on the right, wearing a white robe, and they were really stunned. 6 But he says to them, "Don't be stunned. You seek Jesus the Nazarene—the one who was crucified. He has been raised. He is not here. Look! [This is] the place where they laid him. 7 But go. Say to his disciples and to Peter that he goes before you into Galilee. There you will see him, as he said to you." 8 And having gone out, they fled from the tomb, trembling and amazement having taken hold of them, and they said nothing to anyone because they were awestruck.

PART 1: GALILEE (1:1–8:21)

The Gospel of Mark cleaves into three parts, organized geographically. The first third of the Gospel focuses on Galilee (1:1–8:21), the middle third recounts the journey to Jerusalem (8:22–10:52), and the final third occurs in and around Jerusalem (11:1–16:8).

It is not only geography that distinguishes these sections, however. The emphasis of Jesus' ministry is different in each part: the Galilean ministry is focused on miracles and authority, the time "on the way" highlights discipleship, and the story set in Jerusalem emphasizes Jesus' suffering and death. Time notations are also different in each section: in the first third, Mark uses the word "immediately" (Greek: *euthys*) with incredible frequency, but this word fades in the middle and final sections. There are no concrete time references in the first or second sections, but by the third section, Jesus' time is demarcated by days and then hours.[1]

This first third of the text, set in Galilee, focuses on Jesus' ministry and authority and provides a glimpse of what life is like in the kingdom of God: "In the kingdom there will be no demons, and so Jesus casts out demons; in the kingdom there will be no disease, and so Jesus heals the sick; in the kingdom there will be no more death, and so Jesus raises the dead. The kingdom of God could already be seen in Jesus' own ministry and that of his followers (6:7–13). That is the point of many of Jesus' parables in Mark: the kingdom has a small, even hidden, appearance in the activities of Jesus, but it will

---

1. Dean B. Deppe, *The Theological Intentions of Mark's Literary Devices: Markan Intercalations, Frames, Allusionary Repetitions, Narrative Surprises, and Three Types of Mirroring* (Eugene, Ore.: Wipf and Stock, 2015), 106.

appear in a big way at the end."[2] Given that Jerusalem was regarded as the religious center point and Galilee was thought of as an irrelevant backwater, it is significant that Jesus' early ministry is in Galilee.

Mark ends with an admonition to return to Galilee (16:7): Jesus' story does not end in Jerusalem with his suffering and death. Rather, the audience is invited to return to the beginning of the text, but this time with a deeper appreciation for Jesus' identity and message.

2. Bart D. Ehrman, *Jesus, Interrupted: Revealing the Hidden Contradictions in the Bible (and Why We Don't Know about Them)* (New York: HarperOne, 2009), 78–79.

Beginnings
(Chapter 1)

TITLE

Greek Text

KATA MAPKON [SBLGNT]

King James Version	New Rendition
The Gospel According to St Mark	According to Mark

Notes

the gospel: It is difficult to determine precisely what is meant by the word "gospel" (Greek: *euangelion*) because the word underwent two shifts in meaning in the first century:

1. Before the time of Christianity, the word "gospel" meant "the good news" of, for example, a military victory,[3] the birth or ascension of the emperor,[4] or the festival held on the emperor's birthday.[5] In the LXX, "gospel" refers to the announcement of good news, often without any religious connotation.[6] If "gospel" refers to good news, either in the title or in subsequent uses in Mark's Gospel (see 1:14; 8:35; 13:10; 14:9; 16:15), it is theologically significant that

---

3. See Ched Myers, *Binding the Strong Man: A Political Reading of Mark's Story of Jesus* (Maryknoll, N.Y.: Orbis Books, 1995), 123.

4. See C. E. B. Cranfield, *The Gospel according to St Mark* (New York: Cambridge University Press, 1959), 36.

5. Witherington, *Gospel of Mark,* 70.

6. For example, 1 Kgs. 1:42 (KJV: "good tidings"); Jer. 20:15 (KJV: "tidings"); and Isa. 40:9 (KJV: "good tidings").

this good news is not a military victory or a new earthly king, but rather the ministry of a plain man from Nazareth. "Gospel" may have led the audience to expect the dramatic tale of the ruler of an empire or an impressive battlefield performance, but instead they will find miracles performed to benefit people who live on the margins of society; it is the good news of an entirely different kind of victory.

2. Later, in the time of the writing of the earliest NT texts, "gospel" would describe the teachings about Jesus Christ that were transmitted by word of mouth (see, for example, 1 Cor. 9:14; Gal. 1:11; Eph. 1:13). This seems to be the way that this word is used in Paul's letters (for example, in Rom. 15:19; 1 Cor. 15:1). It is possible that Mark (unintentionally) coined this meaning of the term, although it is more likely that this usage began with Paul.

3. Still later, "gospel" would refer to the genre of texts recounting the life of Jesus Christ. This definition would have been in use only after Mark's Gospel was written, so while this meaning might apply to the title of Mark (assuming the title was written sometime after the text; see appendix A: "Authorship and Date"), it probably does not apply to instances of the word within the text itself.

It is worth remembering that the Gospel of Mark is intended to be *the good news,* even though it will recount Jesus being shunned by family and friends, tortured, mocked, and killed.

Some ancient manuscripts omit the words "The Gospel" so that the title is simply "According to Mark." Both versions have a plausible claim to being the earlier title: the shorter title because the tendency was for titles to expand over time and the longer title because the shorter title could have been an abbreviation of it.[7]

according to: The phrase "according to" may sound unwieldy to modern readers, but it implies that there is only one gospel (that is, only one good news story about Jesus Christ), and this is Mark's rendition of it.

St: The addition of "St" (the abbreviation for "Saint") came about much later than the Gospel's writing and reflects the practice of canonizing people by conferring sainthood upon them.

Mark: See appendix A: "Authorship and Date" for a discussion of what is known about the author.

Analysis

It is likely that the first copy of the Gospel of Mark had no title at all since, in the first century, titles were more likely to be created by the audience

---

7. Collins, *Mark,* 129.

than the author.[8] A title would not have been necessary until the Gospel circulated beyond its original location or until there were other written Gospels from which it needed to be distinguished.

Overview of Chapter 1. Mark begins with a prologue, but it is debated whether that prologue ends

1. after 1:3, which would bracket the HB prophecies from the main text, which makes little reference to fulfillment of HB prophecies.

2. after 1:8, which would bracket John's ministry from the main text, which is concerned with Jesus' ministry.

3. after 1:11, which would bracket Jesus' baptism from the main text, which is concerned with Jesus' active ministry.

4. after 1:13, which would bracket the temptations from the main text; because geography is an important narrative marker in this text, the move from the wilderness to Galilee in 1:14 supports ending the prologue here. Additionally, 1:1–13 has a "heavenly perspective" on Jesus' ministry—with HB prophecy, a vision, and temptations known only to Jesus—but in 1:14, there is a shift to a human perspective on events.

5. after 1:15, since the word "gospel" appears in both 1:1 and 1:15, which bookends this section of text and emphasizes its main theme. References to John the Baptist at the beginning (1:4) and end (1:14) of the passage also function as bookends, highlighting the role of John the Baptist in the prologue.

Mark 1:21–45 can be understood as a "typical day" in Jesus' ministry, showcasing the usual events of a day in Capernaum: teaching, exorcism, healing, and preaching. It is more likely to be a composite presentation than the report of any actual twenty-four-hour day.

Jesus Is Introduced (1:1–8)

Greek Text

1 Ἀρχὴ τοῦ εὐαγγελίου Ἰησοῦ χριστοῦ. 2 Καθὼς γέγραπται ἐν τῷ Ἠσαΐᾳ τῷ προφήτῃ· Ἰδοὺ ἀποστέλλω τὸν ἄγγελόν μου πρὸ προσώπου σου, ὃς κατασκευάσει τὴν ὁδόν σου· 3 φωνὴ βοῶντος ἐν τῇ ἐρήμῳ· Ἑτοιμάσατε τὴν ὁδὸν κυρίου, εὐθείας ποιεῖτε τὰς τρίβους αὐτοῦ, 4 ἐγένετο Ἰωάννης ὁ βαπτίζων ἐν τῇ ἐρήμῳ κηρύσσων

---

8. Collins, *Mark,* 129.

βάπτισμα μετανοίας εἰς ἄφεσιν ἁμαρτιῶν. 5 καὶ ἐξεπορεύετο πρὸς αὐτὸν πᾶσα ἡ Ἰουδαία χώρα καὶ οἱ Ἱεροσολυμῖται πάντες, καὶ ἐβαπτίζοντο ὑπ' αὐτοῦ ἐν τῷ Ἰορδάνῃ ποταμῷ ἐξομολογούμενοι τὰς ἁμαρτίας αὐτῶν. 6 καὶ ἦν ὁ Ἰωάννης ἐνδεδυμένος τρίχας καμήλου καὶ ζώνην δερματίνην περὶ τὴν ὀσφὺν αὐτοῦ, καὶ ἔσθων ἀκρίδας καὶ μέλι ἄγριον. 7 καὶ ἐκήρυσσεν λέγων· Ἔρχεται ὁ ἰσχυρότερός μου ὀπίσω μου, οὗ οὐκ εἰμὶ ἱκανὸς κύψας λῦσαι τὸν ἱμάντα τῶν ὑποδημάτων αὐτοῦ· 8 ἐγὼ ἐβάπτισα ὑμᾶς ὕδατι, αὐτὸς δὲ βαπτίσει ὑμᾶς ἐν πνεύματι ἁγίῳ. [SBLGNT]

King James Version

1 The beginning of the gospel of Jesus Christ, the Son of God; 2 As it is written in the prophets, Behold, I send my messenger before thy face, which shall prepare thy way before thee. 3 The voice of one crying in the wilderness, Prepare ye the way of the Lord, make his paths straight. 4 John did baptize in the wilderness, and preach the baptism of repentance for the remission of sins. 5 And there went out unto him all the land of Judaea, and they of Jerusalem, and were all baptized of him in the river of Jordan, confessing their sins. 6 And John was clothed with camel's hair, and with a girdle of a skin about his loins; and he did eat locusts and wild honey; 7 And preached, saying, There cometh one mightier than I after me, the latchet of whose shoes I am not worthy to stoop down and unloose. 8 I indeed have baptized you with water: but he shall baptize you with the Holy Ghost.

New Rendition

1 The Beginning of the Good News of Jesus, the Anointed One, Son of God

2 As it is written in Isaiah the prophet,
"See! I send my messenger
    ahead of you,
who will prepare your way.
3 A voice shouting in the desert:
'Make ready the way of the Lord—
straighten his paths.'"

4 John appeared, baptizing in the desert, proclaiming a baptism of repentance for forgiveness of sins. 5 And all the Judean region and all those of Jerusalem were going out to him; all were being baptized by him in the Jordan River, as they were confessing their sins. 6 And John wore clothing made of camel's hair and a leather belt around his waist, and he was eating grasshoppers and wild honey. 7 And he proclaimed, saying, "One who is more powerful than I comes following me, of whom I am not worthy to stoop to untie the strap of his sandals. 8 I baptized you with water, but he will baptize you with the Holy Spirit."

Notes

1:1 *The beginning of the gospel:* The word "the" is lacking in the Greek text, perhaps indicating that this verse functioned as a title or heading.[9]

---

9. However, because 1:2 begins with the word "as" (Greek: *kathōs*), 1:1 may not be entirely independent of the rest of the text. (See the Notes on 1:2 below.)

"Beginning" can mean

1. *a moment in time.* This use would then indicate the moment in time when the gospel began. The three other uses of "beginning" in Mark's Gospel (see 10:6; 13:8; and 13:19) use "beginning" in this sense.

2. *fundamentals.* The Gospel of Mark would then be presenting the basic story and message of the life of Jesus.

3. *first exposure.*[10] The Gospel of Mark would thus be the first presentation of the life of Jesus for an audience.

4. *rule or norm.* Jesus' life would thus be presented as a pattern for the audience to follow.

of Jesus Christ: This "of" can be understood in two different ways: the gospel is proclaimed *by* Jesus Christ or the gospel is *about* Jesus Christ. It may encompass both meanings ("the good news by and about Jesus Christ").

"Jesus" is the Greek form of the Hebrew name "Joshua" and was one of the most common names for first-century Jewish men.[11] It is perhaps ironic that Jesus had such a common name when he lived a singular life.

"Christ" is the Greek equivalent of the Hebrew word "Messiah" and can be translated into English as "the anointed one," which reflects the underlying meaning of the Hebrew term. It was initially a title ("Jesus the Messiah" or "Jesus the Anointed One") and only later functioned as a proper name ("Jesus Christ"). It is possible that by the time the Gospel of Mark was written, it already would have been considered a proper name, but it may still have been a title. This verse is the only time that the phrase "Jesus Christ" appears in Mark's Gospel.

the Son of God: Whether this phrase was in the earliest copies of Mark is disputed since some ancient manuscripts omit the words "the Son of God" here.[12] There are two possibilities for what has happened:

---

10. In Philip. 4:15, the phrase "the beginning of the gospel" refers to the beginning of preaching the gospel in a specific geographical area.

11. R. T. France, *The Gospel of Mark: A Commentary on the Greek Text* (Grand Rapids, Mich.: William B. Eerdmans Publishing, 2002), 49 n. 1.

12. Bruce M. Metzger, *A Textual Commentary on the Greek New Testament: A Companion Volume to the United Bible Societies' Greek New Testament (Second Edition)* (Stuttgart: United Bible Societies, 2001), 62; Philip W. Comfort, *New Testament Text and Translation Commentary: Commentary on the Variant Readings of the Ancient New Testament Manuscripts and How They Relate to the Major English Translations* (Carol Stream, Ill.: Tyndale House Publishers, 2008), 92.

1. The phrase was originally in the text, but a scribe's eye skipped from the word "Christ" to the word "God" (since both words end with the same two letters in Greek), and so it was accidentally omitted.

2. "The Son of God" was not originally in the text but was added later for one of these reasons:

   a. This verse seems to have functioned as a title, and there is a trend for expanding the titles of texts.[13]

   b. There is also a tendency to elaborate titles for Christ. In fact, some later manuscripts read "Christ, the Son of the living God" here.[14]

   c. The phrase may have been added later to counter the belief that Jesus was not the Son of God until his baptism by noting that he was called "the Son of God" even before he was baptized.[15]

The theme of Jesus as God's son is an important one to Mark, and the Gospel will have a lot to say about it: the title "Son of God" will appear again, and at crucial junctures, in Mark's Gospel (see 1:11; 3:11; 5:7; 9:7; 12:6–8; 14:61–62; 15:39). While it is well established in Mark's Gospel that Jesus Christ is the Son of God, that does not necessarily mean that this phrase was originally in this particular verse. But if it was included here, it serves as an important identity marker for Jesus since Mark's early audiences would have understood that calling Jesus "the Son of God" implied his "preexistence and deity";[16] other interpreters reject this association, pointing out that the HB uses it for mortal kings.[17] There may be a distinction here based on audience, with Jews thinking that a mortal could be God's son but Gentiles thinking that "Son of God" implied a divine status.[18]

This verse does not contain a verb, perhaps indicating that it functioned as a heading, either for the entire text or for part of it (that is, just for the "beginning" of the gospel). The meaning would differ based on what exactly it is introducing:

---

13. Metzger, *Textual Commentary*, 62.

14. Collins, *Mark*, 396 note b.

15. Bart D. Ehrman, "The Text of Mark in the Hands of the Orthodox," *Lutheran Quarterly*, n.s., 5, no. 2 (1991): 146–49. But Gundry thinks this is much too subtle a way to defend this belief; see Robert H. Gundry, *Mark: A Commentary on His Apology for the Cross* (Grand Rapids, Mich.: William B. Eerdmans Publishing, 1993), 39n.

16. Stein, *Mark*, 41.

17. See 2 Sam. 7:14 and Ps. 2:7 for examples that might involve the Lord naming regular mortals as "son." See Gundry, *Mark*, 34.

18. Gundry, *Mark*, 34.

1. If it introduces 1:2–3, it means that "the beginning of the gospel of Jesus Christ" consists of the prophecies of HB prophets. This would suggest that the gospel began with the HB prophets.

2. If "the beginning" extends to 1:8, then John's ministry is the beginning of the gospel. Reading John's ministry this way is intriguing because of the possibility (see the Notes on 1:7) that Jesus was John's disciple.

3. If it includes 1:11, then Jesus' baptism is part of the beginning. This would frame Jesus' baptism as well as the practice of baptism as part of "the beginning."

4. If it includes 1:13, then the temptations in the wilderness are part of the beginning of the gospel. Because the temptations are dissimilar to any other event in Jesus' life, it makes sense to bracket it as being part of the introduction.

5. If it includes 1:15, then it contains the summary of Jesus' preaching. Thus the beginning of the gospel includes all of the preparatory events as well as an overview of Jesus' message.

6. If it introduces the entire Gospel, then the first half (1:2–8:29) explains how Jesus is the Christ and climaxes with Peter's statement "Thou art the Christ" (8:29), and the second half (8:30–16:8) explains how Jesus is the Son of God and climaxes with the centurion's statement "Truly this man was the Son of God" (15:39). While this is possible, it is less likely since Mark's story seems to be divided into thirds—not into halves (see the overview above).

It is possible that this verse was not originally part of the Gospel of Mark (although it is included in the extant manuscripts) because

1. it does not contain a verb, suggesting that it functioned as a title; titles were not usually written by the author.

2. it is not included in either Matthew's or Luke's texts, and, since both wrote their Gospels with Mark's text in hand, it is likely that this verse was not included in their copies of Mark.

3. there are many variants in the wording of this verse in the various ancient manuscripts; often, variants arise when the text is unsure or was deemed in some way defective.

4. it seems to use a meaning of "gospel" (written text) that postdates Mark.

5. it uses "Jesus Christ" as a proper name, which is not done elsewhere in Mark and probably postdates Mark.

6. the "as" in 1:2 normally follows other material and is a subordinate clause lacking a main clause, so a scribe might have wanted to insert text to give it something to follow. It is possible that there was other material, later lost, at the beginning of the gospel, leaving the inadequate "as" in 1:2 and leading a scribe to compose 1:1 to fill the gap.

7. it simply indicates "here begins the Gospel of Mark," inserted to distinguish it from the Gospel before it when the Gospels were collected into one written text.[19]

1:2 *As it is written in the prophets:* The verb tense may indicate how Mark thought about scripture: "the Greek perfect tense ('has been written'), which implies a past action with permanent results, is particularly appropriate for such a formula, since it suggests that the ancient writing is not just a dead letter but a living force in the present."[20]

This is the standard formula used in the NT to introduce biblical quotations. What is unusual about Mark's usage is that this is the only time Mark uses this formula and the formula normally follows after a story and shows how it fulfills HB prophecy.[21]

There is an intriguing tension between the idea of Jesus' life as "new" and the idea that it was prophesied of hundreds of years in advance.

Instead of "in the prophets," many of the earliest Greek texts read "in Isaiah the prophet." There are several possibilities for what has happened here:

1. The phrase was originally "in Isaiah the prophet," but given that the quotation that follows is a combination of Exodus 23:20, Malachi 3:1, and Isaiah 40:3, later scribes—realizing the referent was incorrect—changed it to "in the prophets."[22] From a Latter-day Saint perspective, there is no problem viewing "in Isaiah the prophet" as an example of the "mistakes of men"[23] that might be found in a text.

2. Ancient texts can have multiple iterations (compare Mal. 4; 3 Ne. 25; D&C 98:16–17; and especially JS–H 1:36–39); it is theoretically possible that Mark had access to a copy of Isaiah that did indeed contain all of the material quoted in this verse, which would make "in Isaiah the prophet" a correct description of the quotation and "in the prophets" an inaccurate "correction" made by a later hand.

3. Mark's Gospel as originally written only included the quotation from Isaiah, and a later copyist inserted the quotations from Exodus and Malachi.

---

19. N. Clayton Croy, "Where the Gospel Text Begins: A Non-theological Interpretation of Mark 1:1," *Novum Testamentum* 43, no. 2 (2001): 105–27.

20. Joel Marcus, *Mark 1–8: A New Translation with Introduction and Commentary.* Vol. 27 of the Anchor Yale Bible. New Haven, Conn.: Yale University Press, 2005), 147.

21. But consider the discussion on 16:8, where it appears that Mark's Gospel ended with a word that is not normally used to end a text; perhaps Mark is making a point about the eternal nature of the story of Jesus Christ by beginning with a word not used for beginnings and ending with a word not used for endings.

22. Metzger, *Textual Commentary,* 62.

23. Title Page of the Book of Mormon.

4. Mark was following a customary practice of naming only the most important of his sources and not all of them;[24] Isaiah was much better known than Malachi.

5. Isaiah is named here because he was the source of the majority of the quotation.

6. The idea of being "written in Isaiah" refers more generally to the themes in 1:1–15 and not to the quote here in particular. Many themes from Isaiah play out throughout Mark in general and in this first section of text in particular.

Behold, I send my messenger before thy face: The purpose of the word "behold" is to focus the audience's attention on the coming material. It could be translated as "pay attention."[25]

The "I" here refers to God.

"Messenger" is the same word (Greek: *angelos*) that is translated as "angel" (for example, 1:13; 12:25; 13:32). There are several possibilities for the identity of the messenger:

1. In Exodus 23:20, which might be quoted here, the messenger is an angel sent from God to lead the people to the promised land.

2. The messenger from Malachi 3:1 (which also may be quoted here) is identified as Elijah (Mal. 4:5), whose job it is to prepare the earth so it will not be cursed when the Lord returns. Because Elijah did not die but was taken up to heaven (2 Kgs. 2:11), his return was expected.

3. The messenger might be John, who prepares the way of Jesus Christ, as the context of Mark's first chapter suggests.

4. The messenger might be Jesus, preparing the way for God's reign.

It is also possible that more than one meaning was intended. In that case, Mark is relying on the multiple possible meanings of this verse in order to encourage his audience to see the prophecy fulfilled in more than one manner.

Many modern translations read "ahead of you" (NIV and NRSV) here instead of "before thy face"; "thy face" is probably an overly literal translation of an idiom meaning "in your presence." The word "thy" could refer either to Jesus (which makes sense grammatically since he was named in 1:1) or to the nation of Israel (which is the meaning in the context of Ex. 23:20). Perhaps both meanings are intended, which has the effect of making Jesus Christ the personified nation of Israel—an idea that might also be present at

---

24. Stein, *Mark,* 42.

25. C. S. Mann, *Mark: A New Translation with Introduction and Commentary* (Garden City, N.Y.: Doubleday, 1986), 195.

Jesus' baptism (see the Analysis of 1:9–15). Once again, the multiple possible layers of meaning allow Mark to convey multiple messages to the audience.

The New Rendition presents this quotation from Isaiah as poetry (that is, written in lines instead of in paragraph form) to better reflect Isaiah's writing style.

which shall prepare thy way before thee: The type of "preparation" envisioned here depends on who is doing the preparing and for whom they are doing it:

1. In the Exodus 23:20 context, an angel prepares the way for the people.
2. In Malachi 3:1, the messenger prepares for the return of the Lord.
3. Mark may be borrowing scriptural language but applying it to a different context.

The customary interpretation of this text is that John the Baptist is preparing the way for Jesus. Support for this reading comes from 9:11–13, where Elijah and John the Baptist are linked. This preparation would involve preparing people, through repentance and baptism, for Jesus' ministry. It is also possible that John's ministry and martyrdom prepared the way for Jesus in the sense of showing Jesus (or others) the pattern for Jesus' own life.

"Thy" can refer to:

1. In Exodus 23:20, the people's way is being prepared, so "the people" would be the referent for "thy."
2. This text quotes Malachi 3:1, but where Malachi has "my way," Mark has "thy way." The likely purpose of this shift is to associate Jesus with the Lord of the HB, which would have been a startling idea to those new to the Christian message.

But again, Mark may be borrowing the language but changing the referents or relying on the possibility that the language can carry multiple referents.

There are two options for understanding the meaning of "way":

1. "Way" is a physical road. It is uncertain if in the HB this was intended literally or metaphorically, but in Mark a more metaphorical usage is intended.
2. "The Way" is a name for the early Christian movement;[26] it is difficult to know if this meaning existed when Mark was writing and so could have been intended here, or if it was only used later.

---

26. See Acts 9:2 ("belonged to the Way," NRSV); 19:9 ("spoke evil of the Way," NRSV); 19:23 ("concerning the Way," NRSV); 22:4 ("persecuted this Way," NRSV); 24:14 ("according to the Way," NRSV); and 24:22 ("about the Way," NRSV).

The best Greek manuscripts lack the phrase "before thee"; it seems to have been added later to harmonize with the accounts in Matthew 11:10 and Luke 7:27.[27]

Relationship to Malachi 3:1 and Exodus 23:20. Mark quotes Malachi 3:1 ("Behold, I will send my messenger, and he shall prepare the way before me"). The rest of Malachi 3:1 reads, "and the Lord, whom ye seek, shall suddenly come to his temple, even the messenger of the covenant, whom ye delight in: behold, he shall come, saith the Lord of hosts." Mark omits the reference to the temple; there are several possible reasons for this:

1. The temple was not particularly relevant to Mark's audience—either because of their location, their lack of ties to Judaism, or because the temple had been destroyed—so Mark de-emphasizes its role.

2. Mark wants to emphasize that John is offering forgiveness independent of the temple rituals and therefore sees no need to mention it. It is even possible that the lack of reference to it where it would have been expected was meant to convey that the temple was, in effect, deliberately missing from the story.

3. In chapters 11–13, the corruptness of the temple leadership will take center stage; Mark lays the groundwork for that theme here by de-emphasizing the temple.

4. While it is not quoted, Mark does intend for the audience to apply the prophecy that the Lord will come to the temple; this prophecy will be fulfilled when Jesus enters the temple (11:15). In this case, the omission would not be because Mark is downplaying the role of the temple, but rather it would be evidence of an allusive writing style.

Malachi was generally regarded by first-century Jews as the last of the prophets, so it would have been appropriate to use his words to introduce God's new messengers, John and Jesus. Malachi's message, as taken up by Mark, is clear: God is about to begin acting in history again.

It is possible that Exodus 23:20 (KJV: "Behold, I send an angel before thee, to keep thee in the way, and to bring thee into the place which I have prepared") is quoted here as well.

As indicated above, there are various ways to interpret whom Mark intends to fill each role:

1. I (God) send my messenger (John) before your (Jesus') face. This reading features God speaking to Jesus and making promises to him, making this quite an important moment. The audience for Mark's Gospel would enjoy a privileged position as they "overheard" this statement.

---

27. Comfort, *New Testament Text and Translation Commentary,* 93.

2. I (God) send my messenger (Jesus) to go before your (the audience's) face. This reading makes sense of Jesus going before the disciples (10:32), crying out on the cross (15:34), and going before the disciples to Galilee (14:28; 16:7). In this view, this HB quotation becomes a summation for Jesus' entire mortal ministry.

3. I (God) send my messenger (Mark) before your (the audience's) face who makes a path (writing the gospel) for you.[28] In this reading, the audience is invited to see themselves as playing a role foretold in scripture.

While the first reading is traditional, the other two are also possible; perhaps more than one level of meaning was implied.

1:3 *The voice of one crying in the wilderness:* The verb "crying" does not mean "weeping" but rather shouting or proclaiming.

In LXX Isaiah 40:3 (which is quoted here), the phrase "in the wilderness" modifies the previous phrase ("the voice in the wilderness"), but in the Hebrew text of Isaiah 40:3, it modifies the following phrase ("prepare in the wilderness").

Contra the modern Western impression of "the wilderness" as a forest, in the Bible it was a desert: "an extraordinarily barren and arid area riven by canyons between cliffs filled with caves, rocky and sun-blasted."[29] While it is possible that the wilderness—barren, harsh, and dangerous—was considered a terrifying place filled with demons, it is more likely a positive symbol since it was there that the Lord met and guided the people of Israel (in what is the prime Jewish association with wilderness), and it was prophesied to be where God would make a new beginning with the covenant people (Isa. 40:3–5; 41:18–19; 43:19–21; Ezek. 20:35–38; Hosea 2:14–15), a theme particularly appropriate to the context of chapter 1. The Essene community established themselves at Qumran (which is in the wilderness of Judea) precisely in order to fulfill this expectation; they thought that God would visit them there and would support their stances against the corruption in Jerusalem.[30] It was only later in Christian thought that the wilderness became a symbol for hostile forces. Interestingly, despite the multiple references to the wilderness in chapter 1, there are only two references to it in the rest of the Gospel, in chapter 6.

---

28. Myers, *Binding the Strong Man*, 124–25.

29. Marcus Borg, *Jesus: Uncovering the Life, Teachings, and Relevance of a Religious Revolutionary* (San Francisco: HarperSanFrancisco, 1989), 122.

30. Shemaryahu Talmon, "The 'Desert Motif' in the Bible and in Qumran Literature," in *Biblical Motifs: Origins and Transformations,* ed. Alexander Altmann (Cambridge: Harvard University Press, 1966), 60–63.

Prepare ye the way of the Lord: This phrase does not use the same Greek word that was translated as "prepare" in 1:2.[31] This verb is plural, indicating that more than one person is expected to prepare. Repeating the idea of "preparation" from the previous verse (even using a different word) implies that John prepares the way for Jesus by urging other people to prepare.

The "of" here means "the path that the Lord will use," not "the path that the Lord owns" or "the path that the Lord prepared."

This text is presented as poetry in the New Rendition since the Isaiah text that it is quoting is poetry.

make his paths straight: This phrase suggests that everything possible is done to make his way easy, since a straight path would be easier to follow.

Relationship to Isaiah 40:3. Mark 1:3 quotes Isaiah 40:3 ("The voice of him that crieth in the wilderness, Prepare ye the way of the Lord, make straight in the desert a highway for our God"), in a version closer to the LXX than to the Hebrew.

The "way" in Isaiah 40:3 is not how the Lord wants people to walk, but the way that the Lord himself will walk: "his triumphant march through the wilderness and into the holy city as he leads his people back from exile in a magnificent demonstration of saving power."[32]

Both the Hebrew and the LXX of Isaiah 40:3 read "our God" where Mark has "his" in reference to the "path." The change from "God" to "his" (which presumably refers to Jesus) in Mark makes a link between Jesus and God. So not only is Mark quoting HB scriptures about preparation here, he is also teaching about Jesus' relationship to the God of the HB.

Both the Exodus/Malachi scripture in the previous verse and the Isaiah scripture in this verse are about a figure sent to lead an exodus through the wilderness. By quoting both,[33] Mark strongly emphasizes that theme as the introduction to the story of Jesus. But there is quite a contrast between the Exodus/Malachi quotation and the Isaiah quotation: the Isaiah material strikes a hopeful note and envisions a positive event, while the context in Malachi is one of judgment and punishment. So by combining them, there is a balance of the positive (hope) and negative (judgment).

---

31. Mark 1:2: *kataskeuazō,* but this verse: *hetoimazō.*

32. Marcus, *Mark 1–8,* 148.

33. There is some evidence that the three texts quoted here had been previously combined by others and that Mark is using a pre-existing "scripture chain."

The reference to Isaiah in 1:2 and the quote from Isaiah in 1:3 form book-ends around the Exodus/Malachi quotation; if this structure was intentional, then it highlights the idea of Isaiah as a prophetic witness to the gospel story.

Jesus' Identity. While these verses might initially seem to be about the role of John the Baptist, it is also possible to read them with an eye to what they convey about Jesus:[34]

1. They suggest that his ministry was prophesied of in the HB.
2. They equate him with the God of the HB.
3. They introduce his ministry as nested within John's ministry and within HB expectations.

These are very important theological principles and are quite the introduction to Jesus, especially considering that Jesus has not yet appeared in the text.

1:4 *John did baptize in the wilderness:* Mark presents no introduction to John here (except the HB quotations), either because Mark's audience already knew who John was[35] or because his background would not have fit Mark's narrative purposes, which emphasize discipleship over lineage. This abrupt introduction presents John as the prophesied voice in the wilderness who, in the HB sources, is not given a background either. So the lack of background, ironically, becomes a background: it strengthens the association between John and the voice crying in the wilderness that had been prophesied in the HB. Perhaps Mark thought that any other information about John would have diluted that message.

Before the NT, the verb "baptize" meant to dip or to plunge. Only in the NT does it take on a technical meaning with reference to a religious ritual. The precedent[36] for John's baptism is debated:

---

34. Stein, *Mark,* 44.

35. In the past, it was thought that John was associated with the Qumran community (the group that probably produced the Dead Sea Scrolls), but lately that idea has fallen out of fashion; it is perhaps more accurate to say that both the group at Qumran and John independently emphasized similar themes (such as the need for renewal, asceticism, wilderness, fulfillment, and the coming one). If John had been a part of that community, he has clearly moved physically and doctrinally away from them by this point. See Witherington, *Gospel of Mark,* 73.

36. Latter-day scripture contains numerous references to baptism before the time of John the Baptist (see, for example, Moses 6:64–66; D&C 84:27–28; and Mosiah 18:8–17), but it is unclear whether John the Baptist and/or Mark were aware of this practice.

1. In the HB, priests washed themselves before participating in temple rituals, as did regular worshipers if they had become impure (which would have happened regularly),[37] but there are some differences between this practice and John's baptism:

    a. In the HB, one immersed oneself—no one performed the action for them.

    b. The washings were required repeatedly, not just once.

    c. There was no connotation of changing one's mind (the Greek word that the KJV translates as "repentance" connotes changing one's mind).

2. A ritual bath became one of the requirements for conversion to Judaism, but the date of this practice is unknown and perhaps only occurred after John's time. This practice differed from John's baptism in that:

    a. People apparently immersed themselves.

    b. It was only for Gentiles who were converting, not Jews.

3. In Qumran, a baptism associated with repentance was performed as a ritual immersion in a desert locale[38] (although it is possible that this was metaphorical and not a literal practice). This differed from John's practice because the baptism was repeated, not done only once.

Given what was likely known to John and his audience (and to Mark and the Gospel's audience) about practices similar to John's baptism, the following innovations are important:

1. If the HB practice of purity washings is in view, then the suggestion is that purity doesn't have to do with ritual status but rather with internal moral condition. The focus of John's baptism is on repentance, not ritual purity. This would be a profound shift, particularly given Mark's emphasis on the idea that John's ministry prepared the way for the Lord.

2. If convert baptism is in view, then John is making quite a claim to suggest that the covenant people required something akin to a conversion in order to be forgiven of their sins.

3. Under the Mosaic law, forgiveness of sins was to be found in the performance of sacrificial temple rituals. So John's suggestion that remission of sins could be found *without* performing temple sacrifices was a radical and innovative idea.

---

37. For example, see Lev. 13, 16; Num. 19; see also Collins, *Mark,* 138–39.

38. Stephen J. Pfann, "The Essene Yearly Renewal Ceremony and the Baptism of Repentance," in *The Provo International Conference on the Dead Sea Scrolls: Technological Innovations, New Texts, and Reformulated Issues,* ed. Donald W. Parry and Eugene Ulrich (Leiden: Brill, 1999), 337–52.

4. If John is introducing the idea that baptism requires someone else to perform it against a backdrop where people were used to performing their own ritual purifications, then that is quite the innovation. While specifically Latter-day Saint ideas of authority and ordinances are not explored in this text, John's practice would be a profound commentary on the need for an authorized person to perform an ordinance. This innovation may make sense of why it is that John needs to baptize Jesus: it emphasizes that Christian baptism is not something that one does for oneself, but rather something that someone else—someone with authority—does. It might even begin to hint at the idea of an atonement, where someone else performs something one cannot do for oneself.

5. There is no suggestion that John would baptize people more than once; this appears to be a one-time-only ritual. Given the contrast to the washings under the law of Moses, there may be a hint of a final "great and last sacrifice" (Alma 34:14) in the idea that rituals (sacrifices for forgiveness, washings for purity) that were repeated many times were no longer needed.

Perhaps the (perceived) novelty of the baptism that he offered explains why John is one of the rare persons in scripture known by a title such as "the Baptist" (there is no "Moses the Anointer" or "Elijah the Sealer," but see also 1 Chr. 29:29).

The fact that John is pictured baptizing in the wilderness requires consideration, as it is not the most logical place to draw a crowd. The purpose of baptizing "in the wilderness" is likely more theological than practical:

1. John's ministry is associated with the time of trial and learning that Israel spent in the wilderness.

2. John's ministry is associated with messianic movements, which were often located in the wilderness.

3. John fulfilled the HB prophecies that Mark has just referenced that envisioned a preparer in the wilderness.

John fulfilled a general theme in the HB regarding the wilderness: "essential to the prophetic concern with repentance in Hosea, Amos and Isaiah is the concept of Israel's time in the wilderness as the period of true sonship to God, a status into which the Lord is going to lead his people once again in a future time."[39]

and preach the baptism of repentance for the remission of sins: In modern English, "preach" can have a negative connotation[40] which can be avoided by translating "proclaim" here.

---

39. William L. Lane, *The Gospel according to Mark* (Grand Rapids, Mich.: William B. Eerdmans Publishing, 1974), 49–50.

40. "Preachy" is not a compliment.

"Repentance" means "to change one's mind." The word is used not only in religious contexts but also more generally in the extant literature. Possible meanings here include the following:

1. Baptism was an effort to get God to "repent" (change the mind) about judging the people as wicked: "there is a biblical tradition that God's decisions regarding punishments and blessings are conditional and may be altered."[41]

2. Outside of the Bible, "repent" meant "regret for individual acts."[42] This is similar to the modern Latter-day Saint usage of the word. So those seeking John's baptism may have been expressing contrition over their actions.

3. "To repent" can be understood as "to return," a common idea in the HB where a wayward people are frequently pictured as being invited by prophets to return to God. Compared with option 2, this is a more community-oriented approach to repentance. This reading makes sense of the idea of a "path" or "way" being prepared, although there is a bit of irony in the fact that it is God who uses the way to return to the people and not the people who use it to return to God.

The word "remission" is used for the release of debts or, more generally, sending something away. It is perhaps misleading to modern English speakers who normally associate it with a disease that is under control but not cured; that meaning would be inaccurate here since forgiveness conveys the idea that the sin has been completely eradicated.

There are several possibilities[43] for understanding how the terms baptism, repentance, and remission relate to each other:

1. The relationship is chronological: first baptism, then repentance, then the remission of sins.

2. Baptism itself could have the effect of remitting sins.

3. Baptism could be evidence of remitted sins.

4. Baptism could be a symbol that one is seeking remission of sins.

5. Repentance causes the remission of sins.

6. The reference to repentance ensures that baptism isn't viewed as a sort of magical act that washes away sins by itself (which would be one possible reading of #2 above), but rather as the outward sign of an inward commitment, with remission of sins as the result.

7. The "of" describes *what kind* of baptism this was—not for membership in a community or for ritual purification, but rather a "repentance baptism."

---

41. Collins, *Mark,* 140. See also Jer. 18:7–10; Joel 2:13; Amos 7:3, 6; and Jonah 3:9–10.
42. Marcus, *Mark 1–8,* 150.
43. Marcus, *Mark 1–8,* 155.

There are at least three ways to understand the relationship between 1:2–3 (the HB references) and 1:4 (the description of John's ministry):

1. John's ministry—focused on repentance and baptism—prepared the way of the Lord by priming the people to hear the gospel message.

2. Those who repented and were baptized were ready to learn about and from Jesus—they were prepared for the Lord.

3. John's ministry prepared the way of the Lord by setting the stage for Jesus' own baptism.

Regardless of which option best explains the relationship between the HB prophecies and John's ministry, the fulfillment of the HB prophecies is something other than strictly literal. (That is, John did not create a road in the desert for Jesus to walk upon, but he did engage in the very real action of preparing the "way" for the Lord.) If more than one of these options is thought to be reasonable, then not only is the fulfillment not strictly literal, but it is also multilayered; this suggests a certain approach to HB prophecy that sees the fulfillment of those prophecies as very real but not literal.

Relationship to Ezekiel 36:25–28. This text from Ezekiel has the following similarities to Mark's presentation of John's ministry:

1. A water ritual for purification.

2. Reference to the role of the Spirit.

3. Covenant language.

4. Prophecy of a future action of the Lord.

If Mark understood John's ministry to be the fulfillment of this prophecy, then it suggests that Mark wanted to emphasize the idea of a new covenant, which is the main theme of the passage in Ezekiel.

1:5 *And there went out unto him all the land of Judæa, and they of Jerusalem:* The imperfect verb tense (new Rendition: "were going out") implies a stream of people over a period of time, not a one-time event.

Because Jerusalem was in Judea, the phrasing here is unusual. Mark's point may have been to emphasize the "reverse exodus" of people from Jerusalem into the wilderness or to make a connection to Zechariah 13:1.

and were all baptized of him in the river of Jordan: It is virtually certain that not "all" of Judea or Jerusalem were baptized by John, so this statement requires a bit of probing:

1. Josephus notes that many people sought out John,[44] so this may be hyperbole, but it is not fabrication. As hyperbole, it emphasizes John's popularity. And if

---

44. See Josephus, *Antiquities* 18:5:2.

John is incredibly popular, that casts John's statement about his unworthiness relative to Jesus as all the more powerful. Reading the "all" as an instance of Mark's penchant for hyperbole is the most common reading of this passage.

2. The focus is on the repentance and baptism of the entire community, not on the proportion of individuals who were baptized.

3. The "all" could refer to people from a variety of classes—it would then not be hyperbole but literally true that people from all walks of life sought John's baptism.

4. There may be an allusion to
    a. Zechariah 13:1, where all the people of Jerusalem will be washed in a future day to become ritually pure. As background, this would again illustrate that John's ministry is a fulfillment of prophecy.
    b. Jonah 3:5, where the entire city of Nineveh repents. If this is the allusion that Mark has in mind, it is a powerful indictment of Jerusalem to associate them with wicked Nineveh.

"Of him" emphasizes that John performed the baptisms. This might seem like a mundane observation to modern readers, but it actually implies quite a departure from standard practice on John's part.

The fact that they are baptized in a river and that Jesus is described as coming up out of the water implies that this was baptism by immersion.

While not apparent in the KJV, the Greek text has a small chiastic structure with references to all, Judea, Jerusalem, and then "all" again. This pattern emphasizes the idea that "all" people went out to be baptized by John.

confessing their sins: It is likely too wooden a reading to see the baptism as happening at precisely the same time as the confession, but the Greek text does link the two events. There are several different ways to understand how the confession worked here:

1. They confess their sins to themselves, perhaps literally at the moment of baptism.

2. They confess to John; this would be another indication of John's authority.

3. They confess their sins to God. This would be an interesting inversion of what happens at Jesus' baptism: the people speak to God when they are baptized, but when Jesus is baptized, God speaks to him.

4. The act of baptism itself was considered a confession of sins; no other confession is envisioned.

Relationship to 2 Kings 5:1–19. Naaman is invited by the prophet Elisha to bathe in the Jordan River to heal his leprosy. Mark 1 echoes that story through references to water, the Jordan River, purification, and the presence of a prophetic figure. But there is also a critical edge to the comparison: Naaman is a Gentile, so the people coming "out of Jerusalem" to be baptized are filling the narrative role of a Gentile, something that would have been shocking to most first-century Jewish sensibilities. The association between the stories also positions John as a prophet, as Elisha was, asking the people to do something apparently simple that would have profound results.

Theme: A Reverse Exodus. "Went out" (Greek: *ekporeuomai*) is the same word used to describe the Exodus (Ex. 13:4, 8; Deut. 23:5; Josh. 2:10), so there might be Exodus imagery here.[45] But since the people are going out *from* Jerusalem *into* the wilderness, it reverses the original Exodus journey: Jerusalem has become the new Egypt from which the covenant people need to flee. Being baptized may be, at least symbolically, akin to crossing the Red Sea in the Exodus narrative, especially since "the Jordan River also has symbolic significance as the site of the miraculous entrance of the tribes of Israel into the promised land, an event analogous to the miraculous crossing of the Red Sea."[46] The sequence of motion from Jerusalem, into the wilderness, and (symbolically) across the water suggests a move backwards in history, returning to the "old" relationship with God. But at the same time, the reversal of direction suggests something new, creating a compelling tension between the old and the new.

1:6 *And John was clothed with camel's hair, and with a girdle of a skin about his loins:* Some ancient manuscripts lack the phrase "with a girdle of a skin about his loins."[47] Perhaps this phrase was added by a copyist, but it is also possible that it was originally present and was omitted when a scribe's eye accidentally skipped from one word to a similar one.

A "girdle of a skin about his loins" refers to a leather belt worn around the waist. The belt could have held money or other items—in 6:8, the same word (Greek: *zōnē*) is translated as "purse"—and would have been used to tuck in the robe (in this case, it was made out of camel hair, which would have been roughly woven and coarse) for ease of movement.

Because John has already been introduced and the story has moved on to the baptism of the people, this description of John's clothing seems awkwardly placed, but it calls attention to his clothing in a way that mentioning it when he was first introduced would not have. His clothing has rich symbolic associations (see the section "Relationship to 2 Kings 1:1–8" below).

---

45. For a contrasting opinion, see Gundry, *Mark,* 43.
46. Collins, *Mark,* 142.
47. Collins, *Mark,* 133 note e.

and he did eat locusts and wild honey: These were typical foods for the wilderness. There may be a symbolic element to John's diet, as there is with his clothing:

1. John has, at least metaphorically, escaped Adam's curse by not having to work by the sweat of his brow in order to eat; he eats what is freely available. This would emphasize the theme of a new creation in chapter 1.

2. John has rejected human community and only eats what he can get for himself. This would emphasize the wickedness and corruptness of society.

3. Because these foods would have been easily accessible in the wilderness, John would have been able to focus on his ministry. The simple food may indicate that John was an ascetic.

4. A diet of locusts and wild honey would have made observance of purity laws simple for John since these foods "would not have been handled by anyone else, and wild honey would not be subject to tithing."[48]

5. The HB links wild honey to God's care for Israel (for example, Ex. 3:8; Deut. 32:13; and Ps. 81:16). Perhaps John's diet, like his clothes, is one of the ways that he preaches. The clothing sends a message about John's identity, while the diet sends a message about God's provision for the covenant people.

6. These typical wilderness foods strengthen the association between John and the HB prophecies about the wilderness that opened the text.

7. While John dresses like Elijah, he does not eat like Elijah: Elijah was fed by ravens (1 Kgs. 17:6). Maybe John's diet teaches that while John fulfills the role of Elijah, he is not literally Elijah.

Relationship to 2 Kings 1:1–8. In this text, the messengers of King Ahaziah encounter a man who gives them a prophetic message. When the king later asks them to identify the man, they describe a hairy man with a leather belt. The king instantly knows that this must have been Elijah. In other words, Elijah was identifiable by his appearance; a leather belt and camel's hair were not normal clothing in the wilderness. So when John dresses as Elijah (substituting camel's hair for natural hairiness), he becomes instantly identifiable as Elijah, almost as if he were wearing a costume. The association between a prophet and hairy clothing [KJV: "rough garment"] is also made in Zechariah 13:4.

Why would John have done this?[49] Perhaps to encourage the association between his own ministry and that of Elijah's:

1. Elijah preaches repentance (1 Kgs. 18:21).

---

48. Collins, *Mark,* 145.

49. From a Latter-day Saint perspective, it would likely be assumed that John had been inspired to act this way. The question then becomes: Why was John inspired to do this?

2. Elijah is linked to the wilderness (1 Kgs. 17:3; 19:3–18).

3. Elijah's ministry is linked to the Jordan (2 Kgs. 2:4–11).

4. Elijah's ministry ends as his successor, Elisha, receives a "double portion" of the prophetic spirit (2 Kgs. 2:4–11); this is similar to the ending of John's ministry as well as the idea taught by John that Jesus would be "mightier" than he was.

Because they believed that Elijah would return (Mal. 4:5), the audience would have been primed to see John in the role of Elijah.[50] The stage has been set for God to act in history and for ancient prophecies to be fulfilled. There is a compelling tension between the fact that Mark has promised the audience "good news" while the texts that speak of Elijah's return (Mal. 4:5) speak of the end times.

1:7 *And preached, saying, There cometh one mightier than I after me:* Through this preaching, John is the voice crying in the wilderness known from the HB prophecies. The syntax here suggests something about the preaching: "The emphatic position of this futuristic present (ἔρχεται, *erchetai*) should be noted. Placed first in the sentence, it underscores the urgency of John's message."[51]

The oblique phrasing of "one mightier than I" may suggest that John himself was not entirely sure of the identity of the coming one (Would it be God? The Messiah? The Son of Man?) at this point;[52] he only knew that someone was coming and that that person had more strength (or authority) than he had. It might also imply that John is aware of some lack in his own authority—a lack that the coming one will fill. Once again, while modern Latter-day Saint notions of the priesthood are not present in the Gospel of Mark, this does not imply that similar themes are not explored.

This statement combines with the three HB quotations above to emphasize that someone important is coming. Given that John is presented as the fulfillment of HB prophecies and as someone so popular that "all" of Judea

---

50. Interestingly, if John the Baptist is fulfilling the Elijah role and the prophecies that Elijah would return but is not literally Elijah, then the text is advocating a view of scriptural fulfillment that is something other than strictly literal.

51. Stein, *Mark,* 49.

52. Matt. 11:3 and Luke 7:19 suggest that John wasn't sure if Jesus was the stronger one. (Of course, the Gospel writers do not always share precisely the same understanding of events.) Also, if the vague reference to a greater one means that John was not entirely clear on the identity of who was coming, this then supports the historical accuracy of Mark: one would assume a later writer with a free hand could have interjected into John's mouth a precise identification of who was coming based on later understanding.

went to him, the fact that he is preaching that someone who is stronger than even he is coming is quite extraordinary and sets up very high expectations for who this coming person will be. Because this prophecy will be fulfilled almost instantly (1:9), it adds to the audience's ability to trust John.

The word "after" can have two different meanings:

1. Time (that is, "he will come at a later time"). In Mark's Gospel, there seems to be a deliberate structuring of the text to imply that Jesus' public ministry happens only after John the Baptist is imprisoned (1:14).

2. Position (that is, "following behind me") with the sense of following as a disciple (1:17, 20; 8:34) and perhaps even as a technical term for discipleship. Thus Jesus would be John's disciple. While this concept might initially seem unusual, several ideas recommend it:

    a. It is consistent with the idea that Jesus grew in wisdom (Luke 2:40, but note that Mark does not have a parallel text).

    b. It emphasizes Jesus' humility.

    c. The reference to Jesus as John's disciple is made in the context of pointing out that John knows that Jesus will be greater than he is, instantly eliminating any sense that John was greater than Jesus just because Jesus was John's disciple.

    d. Filling the role of disciple would be part of Jesus setting an example for all people.

    e. Having been a disciple himself, Jesus would then be able to have disciples of his own while still showing humility. He would thus be following the pattern John set of having disciples while still being humble.

    f. It illustrates how John prepared the way of the Lord by being his teacher and letting Jesus be his disciple.

    g. The metaphor about untying sandals (see the Notes on 1:7 below) may by itself indicate that Jesus was John's disciple. This metaphor also makes it clear that the disciple will surpass the teacher.

    h. The fact that Jesus sought out John for baptism might itself be evidence that Jesus was John's disciple.

the latchet of whose shoes I am not worthy to stoop down and unloose:
The thong (KJV: "latchet") of the sandals (KJV: "shoes") was a length of leather that bound the sandal to the foot.

Some manuscripts lack the phrase "to stoop down," probably under the influence of the parallel accounts in Luke 3:16 and John 1:27.[53] But if that phrase was in the earliest texts of Mark, note that John doesn't only say

---

53. Collins, *Mark,* 133 note f.

that he is unworthy to untie Jesus' sandal but also that he is unworthy to stoop down to do it; perhaps there is a connection to Malachi 3:2 (a text close to the HB quotations that began Mark's Gospel), which asks who will be able to "stand" when the Lord comes. If this is the case, John is making the point that not only will he not "stand," he won't even be worthy to stoop.

In rabbinic teaching, a disciple should perform for the teacher every task that a slave would for his master except untying his sandals;[54] the disciple was exempted from this particular task because it was thought to be too demeaning. In some expressions of Jewish tradition, a Hebrew slave was not obligated to attend to his master's shoes.[55] If these customs are the background to John's statement, then he is saying that he is not only unworthy to be Jesus' disciple, but he is also unworthy to be his slave. Given the efforts Mark has taken to make John appear prominent (as the fulfillment of HB prophecies) and popular (as one who draws enormous crowds), John's statement of his unworthiness relative to Jesus is very powerful. Given that these are John's first spoken words in the text, the fact that they so powerfully attest to Jesus' superiority over him signals both his own humility and Jesus' high status.

John's statement might also explain why Jesus would have sought out what has been identified as a "baptism of repentance": John's expression of his unworthiness relative to Jesus would ensure that his audience (and Mark's audience) did not regard Jesus as in need of baptism.

John is a Moses figure who leads the people—but not all the way—into the promised land. Jesus, like Joshua (with whom he shares a name since "Jesus" is the Greek form of the Hebrew "Joshua"), finishes the journey with the people. This reading makes sense of John's baptism as preparatory.

1:8 *I indeed have baptized you with water:* "Indeed" is not present in the Greek text as a separate word but was probably included in the KJV to indicate that the "I" is emphasized in Greek. The point of John's statement is thus more about the contrast between John and Jesus (which is also the point of the previous verse) than the difference between water and Holy Spirit baptism. The emphasis on John as baptizer is also significant

---

54. Babylonian Talmud, Seder Nashim II, Ketubbot 96a.

55. Tractate Neziqin, chapter 1, in Jacob Z. Lauterbach, trans., *Mekhilta de-Rabbi Ishmael: A Critical Edition, Based on the Manuscripts and Early Editions, with an English Translation, Introduction, and Notes,* 2d ed., 2 vols. (Philadelphia: Jewish Publication Society, 2004), 2:358.

given that most rituals similar to his baptism (ritual washings, etc.) were self-administered; here, John calls attention to the fact that he performed baptisms.

The word translated as "have baptized" is in the perfect tense, which could imply one of the following:

1. John has just baptized the people to whom he is speaking. His words might be understood differently if they were addressed to people who have already been baptized: perhaps learning about Jesus (as the coming one who is mightier than John) and about baptism of the Holy Spirit are restricted to those who have been baptized.

2. John recognizes that his ministry is now functionally over (at least in the narrative of Mark's Gospel) and that he will no longer be baptizing. The work of ministry will pass to Jesus, as 1:14 will indicate.

3. The tense used here might not be particularly significant.

but he shall baptize you with the Holy Ghost: While neither the KJV nor the vast majority of ancient manuscripts include the phrase "and with fire" in this verse, there are some manuscripts that do include it.[56] Because the phrase occurs in only a few late manuscripts, it is highly unlikely to have been there originally but was probably added to conform with Matthew 3:11 and Luke 3:16.

There is no place in Mark's Gospel where Jesus does something that Mark specifically refers to as baptizing with the Holy Spirit. While modern Latter-day Saint readers would likely understand this as a reference to the gift of the Holy Spirit bestowed upon those who have recently been baptized, it is not certain that this is John's meaning here; there are several possibilities for what John meant:

1. In Acts 2, on the Day of Pentecost, the disciples received an outpouring of the Holy Spirit. Perhaps John is prophesying of that event. Given that Jesus has already ascended into heaven at that point in Acts, however, it is somewhat awkward to describe Jesus baptizing in the Holy Spirit on the Day of Pentecost. Furthermore, it is unclear why John would use the word "baptize" to describe that experience with the Spirit—where its use would be metaphorical—but then contrast it with his own baptism, which is most literal.

2. In Greek, the phrases "in water" and "in spirit" are grammatically similar, so it is possible to understand the Spirit as a substance in which one is baptized.[57]

---

56. Kevin L. Barney, "The Joseph Smith Translation and Ancient Texts of the Bible," *Dialogue* 19, no. 3 (1986), 95.

57. The idea of the spirit as a substance has interesting resonances with D&C 131:7–8, but one cannot determine if John and/or Mark were aware of these ideas.

Perhaps John is thinking about the Spirit as being of a substance more like a liquid or as "a cleansing agent parallel to water-baptism."[58] In this reading, baptism of the Spirit would happen when the Spirit descends on Jesus after his water baptism. Yet this theory would not entirely explain John's meaning, since he didn't say that Jesus would be baptized in the Spirit but rather that Jesus would baptize others in the Spirit—something that does not happen (at least in any obvious way) in this text.

3. In Joel 3:28–29, Joel prophesied of a future time when the Spirit would be "poured out" like water. Perhaps John was alluding to this connection between water and Spirit and implying that Jesus would be instrumental in the fulfillment of this prophecy. This association is not perfect, however, since in Joel the Spirit is "poured out," which is not quite the same thing as being immersed in the Spirit, as one is in a water baptism.

4. In the HB, only God gives the Spirit to people. So regardless of specifically how the baptism in Spirit is understood, the point of John's statement is to equate Jesus with the God of the HB or, at the very least, as sharing a power normally possessed only by God.

5. Acts 19:1–6 addresses the difference between the baptism that John offered and receiving the Holy Spirit: Paul baptizes people in the name of Jesus (after they had already been baptized by John) and then lays his hands on their heads, which causes the Holy Spirit to come upon them. This has a strong parallel to 1:8 (as well as to modern Latter-day Saint practice), but it must be noted that there is no way to be sure that John and/or Mark shared this understanding. Further, Paul—not Jesus—is the person performing the baptisms, although he does do it in the name of Jesus.

6. John may be alluding to Ezekiel 36:25–28, which also mentions purification by water and the granting of the Spirit. In that passage, it is God granting the Spirit to those who are purified by water, and so this would link Jesus and God in the minds of those who heard John. This parallel is not perfect, however, because Ezekiel doesn't seem to envision a separate water baptism and spirit baptism.

7. Some HB passages were understood to teach that the Messiah possessed the Spirit (see 2 Sam. 23:1–2; Isa. 11:1–2; 61:1). If John is alluding to that idea, then he is identifying Jesus with the Messiah and teaching that not only will the Messiah have God's Spirit, but the Messiah will share it with others. (But it is also possible that there is no precedent for the idea of the Messiah bestowing the Spirit on others.)

---

58. Robert A. Guelich, *Mark 1–8:26,* vol. 34A of Word Biblical Commentary (Dallas: Word Books, 1989), 25.

8. Isaiah 32:15 states that desolation will continue "until a spirit from on high is poured out on us, and the wilderness becomes a fruitful field, and the fruitful field is deemed a forest" (NRSV). Perhaps if John had this passage in mind, his wilderness location would be functioning as a metaphor for the spiritually arid state of the people until they receive the Spirit. In this view, the "Spirit baptism" that Jesus provides is a metaphor suggesting his ability to share the Spirit with the people; a specific ordinance would not be in view.

9. Ezekiel 39:29 reads, "I will never again hide my face from them, when I pour out my spirit upon the house of Israel, says the Lord God" (NRSV). If John had this passage in mind, then he is identifying Jesus with the God of the HB and proclaiming that Jesus will be present with his people through the Spirit.

10. Isaiah 63:11 envisions a trek through the wilderness under the guidance of the Spirit, suggesting ample parallels with John's ministry. This verse features Moses leading the people through the water and being given the Spirit. If John had this verse in mind, it would suggest not that he is differentiating his ministry from Jesus', but rather that he is suggesting a unity between the two ministries, since in the Isaiah reference, Moses is responsible for both the water and the Spirit.

11. There is no article before "holy spirit" in the Greek text, perhaps suggesting that this is not a reference to what modern Latter-day Saints would call the third member of the Godhead but rather a generic idea of Jesus baptizing them in the Spirit (contrasted with water); this Spirit is identified as "holy" to preempt the scribal charge that Jesus is working through an unclean spirit.

12. Perhaps the stronger one who is coming refers to God, since Jesus does not baptize with the Holy Spirit in Mark, but the Holy Spirit comes from heaven (God's realm) at Jesus' baptism.[59] (One weakness of this interpretation is that the saying about loosening the sandal tie makes less sense as a reference to God than it does to Jesus.)

13. Given the parallels between 1:7 and 1:8, it may be better to focus on the idea that Jesus' ministry will be superior to John's ministry, without pushing the meaning of spirit baptism to any specific meaning.

14. John may be making a metaphorical comparison: he will immerse them in the water (in a literal way), but Jesus will immerse them in the spirit (metaphorically, through a ministry guided by and filled with the spirit).[60]

---

59. Herman C. Waetjen, *A Reordering of Power* (Minneapolis, Minn.: Fortress Press, 1989), 66–67.

60. John Paul Heil, *The Gospel of Mark as a Model for Action: A Reader-Response Commentary* (New York: Paulist Press, 1992), 33.

There is a chiastic structure as the reference to John baptizing (1:5–6) is surrounded by references to John preaching (1:4; 1:7–8). This implies a tight link between the preaching and the baptism.

Analysis

Chapter 1 is a rushing narrative that covers much ground in an amazingly short amount of time. And yet Mark is able to provide a nuanced introduction to who Jesus really is in this short text.

Mark's Gospel begins with John the Baptist's ministry—not with Jesus' premortal life (as John's Gospel does), his genealogy (Matthew), or his mother's and aunt's experiences (Luke). Given that discipleship will be the signal theme in the Gospel of Mark, this is the logical place for Mark to begin Jesus' story.

John's baptismal practice was, in its context, innovative in many ways. And by linking baptism and repentance, John is denying the exclusive ability of temple sacrifices to provide forgiveness, which was a challenge to the temple leadership. Additionally, John's clothing and lifestyle portray him as one who rejects many social conventions. Jesus' ministry will continue this theme of innovation.

Generally, Mark is much less concerned with showing how Jesus fulfilled HB prophecies than the other Gospel writers, especially Matthew. So it is even more striking that there are several HB references in the crucial introductory words of the text. The biblical quotations in Mark's text do three things:

1. God promises Jesus a preparer of his way.[61] The role of this preparer was important enough to have been prophesied in the HB. The inclusion of those texts also allows Mark's audience to "overhear" God speaking to Jesus. It suggests a very close relationship between God and Jesus.

2. There is a description of the preparer, as one crying in the wilderness.

3. There is a summary of the preparer's message: do everything you can to make the paths accessible.[62]

The introduction creates a sense of "this is the one you have been waiting for!"

---

61. This promise of help makes an interesting contrast with Jesus' cry of desolation on the cross (15:34).

62. This list is adapted from Marcus, *Mark 1–8*, 145.

Jesus does not appear in the first eight verses of the text, but Mark has introduced him through biblical prophecies and John's description of the coming one. There are three comparisons that John makes between himself and Jesus: Jesus is stronger, John is not worthy to be Jesus' slave, and Jesus offers a baptism of spirit instead of water. These three items serve to emphasize Jesus' superiority to John, although they do not deny the possibility that Jesus was one of John's disciples for a time. In fact, it is possible to read the prologue of Mark not as a description of John's ministry but as an introduction to Jesus; this way of introducing Jesus makes sense in light of Mark's emphasis on discipleship, especially if Jesus was a disciple of John's.

If Jesus was John's disciple, then the prologue has some very interesting things to say about discipleship. While the idea of Jesus being a disciple might initially seem unusual, it fits with Mark's focus on discipleship to have Jesus introduced to the audience as a disciple. This positions him as an exemplar of discipleship for the audience. Nowhere in Mark's Gospel does Jesus command anyone to be baptized or to baptize anyone. However, Jesus does tell people to follow him, and part of his own path was being baptized by John. It makes sense to see baptism as part of the pattern of discipleship.

The audience learns from the prologue something about Mark's style. First, it is drenched in HB allusions, from actual quotations to specific allusions (mentioning John's clothing to evoke Elijah) to thematic allusions (the idea of a reverse exodus or Jesus as the new creation or new Israel). These HB allusions prime Mark's audience to see that the HB promises are fulfilled in the life and ministry of Jesus—but not in a literal or expected manner. John the Baptist does not build an actual road nor is he literally Elijah. Thus, Mark wants his audience to take the HB seriously but not literally. Mark is also allusive rather than pedantic; he presents John the Baptist dressed as Elijah instead of merely telling the audience that John was similar to Elijah. As will be shown throughout this commentary, Mark's style is a very subtle one—more likely to leave clues for the perceptive listener than to make proclamations.[63]

---

63. There is an interesting contrast with Nephi, who delighted in plainness (see 2 Ne. 25:4).

JESUS IS BAPTIZED
(1:9–15)

Greek Text

9 Καὶ ἐγένετο ἐν ἐκείναις ταῖς ἡμέραις ἦλθεν Ἰησοῦς ἀπὸ Ναζαρὲτ τῆς Γαλιλαίας καὶ ἐβαπτίσθη εἰς τὸν Ἰορδάνην ὑπὸ Ἰωάννου. 10 καὶ εὐθὺς ἀναβαίνων ἐκ τοῦ ὕδατος εἶδεν σχιζομένους τοὺς οὐρανοὺς καὶ τὸ πνεῦμα ὡς περιστερὰν καταβαῖνον εἰς αὐτόν· 11 καὶ φωνὴ ἐγένετο ἐκ τῶν οὐρανῶν· Σὺ εἶ ὁ υἱός μου ὁ ἀγαπητός, ἐν σοὶ εὐδόκησα.

12 Καὶ εὐθὺς τὸ πνεῦμα αὐτὸν ἐκβάλλει εἰς τὴν ἔρημον. 13 καὶ ἦν ἐν τῇ ἐρήμῳ τεσσεράκοντα ἡμέρας πειραζόμενος ὑπὸ τοῦ Σατανᾶ, καὶ ἦν μετὰ τῶν θηρίων, καὶ οἱ ἄγγελοι διηκόνουν αὐτῷ.

14 Καὶ μετὰ τὸ παραδοθῆναι τὸν Ἰωάννην ἦλθεν ὁ Ἰησοῦς εἰς τὴν Γαλιλαίαν κηρύσσων τὸ εὐαγγέλιον τοῦ θεοῦ 15 καὶ λέγων ὅτι Πεπλήρωται ὁ καιρὸς καὶ ἤγγικεν ἡ βασιλεία τοῦ θεοῦ· μετανοεῖτε καὶ πιστεύετε ἐν τῷ εὐαγγελίῳ. [SBLGNT]

King James Version

9 And it came to pass in those days, that Jesus came from Nazareth of Galilee, and was baptized of John in Jordan. 10 And straightway coming up out of the water, he saw the heavens opened, and the Spirit like a dove descending upon him: 11 And there came a voice from heaven, saying, Thou art my beloved Son, in whom I am well pleased. 12 And immediately the Spirit driveth him into the wilderness. 13 And he was there in the wilderness forty days, tempted of Satan; and was with the wild beasts; and the angels ministered unto him. 14 Now after that John was put in prison, Jesus came into Galilee, preaching the gospel of the kingdom of God, 15 And saying, The time is fulfilled, and the kingdom of God is at hand: repent ye, and believe the gospel.

New Rendition

9 And it happened in those days that Jesus came from Nazareth in Galilee and was baptized in the Jordan by John. 10 And immediately as he was coming up out of the water, he saw heaven being torn open and the Spirit as a dove coming down into him. 11 And a voice out of heaven: "You are my beloved son in whom I take joy." 12 And immediately the Spirit drives him into the desert. 13 And he was in the desert for forty days, being tested by Satan, and he was with the animals, and the angels were serving him. 14 But after John was arrested, Jesus went into Galilee, proclaiming the good news of God. 15 And saying, "The time is filled, and the reign of God has drawn near. Change your life and trust the good news."

Notes

1:9 *And it came to pass in those days:* There are three different ways to understand this time reference:

1. "Those days" links 1:9 to "the beginning of the gospel" (1:1) since both happened "in those days," implying that Jesus' baptism is (a part of) the beginning of the gospel.

2. "And it came to pass" is a Hebrew idiom used to impart a biblical flavor to the text.[64] It does not imply anything about the specific timing of the story. Rather, since "came" but not "and it came to pass" was used to introduce John the Baptist (1:4),[65] the language here suggests some similarity between John and Jesus, but also lends a more authoritative and important note to the introduction to Jesus through the use of a biblical-sounding phrase.

3. "And it came to pass" signals a change in time, implying that there is not necessarily anyone but John and Jesus present at his baptism (that is, the crowds who were baptized are no longer present).

that Jesus came from Nazareth of Galilee: Nazareth had a few hundred residents; no public buildings have been found there, presumably because it was too small to have any. Nazareth is never mentioned in the HB, Josephus, or the Talmud, and this silence speaks to its obscurity. Mark probably included the phrase "of Galilee" because Nazareth would otherwise not have been identifiable to the audience. This introduction is akin to saying that Jesus was "from Nowheresville."[66]

Hostility to Galilean Jews was a trait shared by many Jews from Judea (see 14:70; John 1:46; 7:41, 52), "particularly when any religious issue was at stake,"[67] suggesting that the typical audience member would not have anticipated Jesus to be a religious figure with authority based on this introduction.

Mark presents no other background for Jesus. This may be because

1. the audience was already familiar with Jesus' background, and Mark wanted to use the limited time to focus on other topics.

2. Mark may have been unfamiliar with Jesus' earlier life.

---

64. This phrase is not known in Greek outside of the NT, suggesting that it was used to imitate the language of the LXX. France, *Gospel of Mark,* 75.

65. The same word for "came" (Greek: *ginomai*) is used in both verses, although this is not obvious in the KJV.

66. Myers, *Binding the Strong Man,* 128.

67. France, *Gospel of Mark,* 75. See also John 1:46; 7:40–52.

3. Mark wanted to emphasize the theme of discipleship, which would neither require nor be advanced by an exploration of Jesus' birth and youth; rather, introducing Jesus at his baptism (and, if he was in fact John's disciple,[68] introducing him in relation to his teacher) emphasizes the theme of discipleship.

4. Mark may be alluding to Genesis 14:18 (which presents Melchizedek as an important figure with no background) and/or 1 Kings 17:1 (which presents Elijah as a great prophet with no background).

and was baptized of John in Jordan: The idea that Jesus would be baptized is surprising in this context given that Mark has presented this ritual as being "for the remission of sins."[69] There are several different ways to explain why Jesus would have sought out this baptism:

1. Jesus had sinned and therefore sought repentance. While this idea does not cohere with Latter-day Saint theology, it is not explicitly denied in the text and is perhaps what some of Mark's audience would have assumed.

2. Jesus, while sinless himself, was identifying himself with sinners (compare Isa. 53:12) and taking their sins upon him. Therefore, he required baptism. This reading coheres with the presentation of masses from the south converging on John for baptism while one figure from the north meets John for baptism: Jesus is standing in for "all" people. Jesus' baptism would prefigure the Atonement, where Jesus took upon him other people's sins. This view is supported by the fact that in the only other reference that Jesus makes to baptism in Mark's Gospel,[70] Jesus uses "baptism" as a metaphor for his death. Perhaps Jesus understood his baptism as, in some sense, foreshadowing his own death or preparatory for his death.

3. Modern Christian (including Latter-day Saint) theologies often interpret Jesus' baptism as showing an example or pattern for everyone else to follow. However, it does not appear to be used this way in Mark's Gospel.

4. Immediately following Jesus' baptism in this text, he has a visionary experience. Because these events are linked in the text, the baptism was in some sense a preparation for the vision.

5. Jesus, while sinless, did not realize that he was sinless and therefore sought out baptism.

6. Jesus was baptized to identify himself with John's ministry and as a follower of John, despite the fact that Jesus did not have sins that required remittance. Jesus is willing to associate himself with self-professed sinners, even to be mistaken for one of them, in his act of baptism; this is an expression of his humility.

---

68. See the discussion on 1:7–8.

69. Notice how Matt. 3:14 addresses this tension.

70. See 10:38. (Mark 16:16 is not considered here, since it likely was not originally part of Mark's text. See appendix D: "Mark 16:9–20.")

7. Later in this verse, when Jesus is baptized "in Jordan," a different preposition is used than when the masses were baptized "in Jordan."[71] This may be a meaningless distinction, but it might imply that there is some sense in which Jesus' baptism is different from the other baptisms that John performed (as the heavenly vision that follows it indicates). If this is the case, then the text may be hinting at Jesus' sinlessness through the different nature of his baptism.

8. Mark seems to delight in violating the audience's expectations. Surely the HB prophecies and John's talk of a coming one who would baptize in the spirit led them to expect a strong figure. To see Jesus then appear as a lone man from an out-of-the-way place and seek baptism is a profound inversion of the audience's expectations. Perhaps the point of Jesus' baptism is to emphasize his humility; the juxtaposition of Jesus' humility and his regal status will be a theme throughout Mark's Gospel.

9. The ways in which Jesus' baptism and the masses' baptisms are contrasted are many (all/one, south/north, Jerusalem/Nazareth), and climax when, at the moment when the audience would have expected Jesus to confess his sins, he instead has a vision. The vision therefore can be taken as a confirmation of his sinlessness: presumably the approving voice from heaven would not have come had Jesus had sins that needed confessing. If this is the best reading, it confirms the fact that Mark often teaches subtly what the other Gospel writers teach explicitly and plainly.

10. The baptism is preceded by John's prophecy that Jesus will baptize with the Spirit and followed by the Spirit's descent upon Jesus from heaven; it is possible to see the baptism as the ritual that made the receipt of the Spirit possible for Jesus and thus commissioned him. Jesus performs no miracles, calls no disciples, and engages in no ministry before his baptismal experience. So while Jesus' baptism did not remit any sins, it was a necessary part of his preparation.

11. The focus should not be on the baptism per se but on the visionary experience that immediately followed it and was similar to the prophetic call stories found in Isaiah 6, Jeremiah 1, and Ezekiel 1–2.

12. Some ancient Christian thinkers argued that Jesus "needed no purifying rites himself—his purpose was to hallow water."[72] While that may initially sound excessively apologetic or poetic, a similar dynamic does exist in the stories where Jesus' touching a leper or an unclean woman does not have the expected effect of making him unclean but rather of cleansing the other person (1:42; 5:30). This reading also aligns with the viewpoint that Jesus'

---

71. Mark 1:5 has *en* (generally: "in") while 1:9 has *eis* (generally: "into").

72. Thomas C. Oden and Christopher A. Hall, eds., *Mark,* vol. 2 of Ancient Christian Commentary on Scripture, New Testament (Downers Grove, Ill.: InterVarsity Press, 1998), 11, 15.

baptism is part of a "reverse exodus," and so his immersion in the water has a miraculous effect similar to the parting of the Red Sea and therefore consecrates the water.

Mark did not feel that this issue needed clarification; whether that was because the solution was obvious or because it was unimportant is not knowable. While it is difficult to determine which reading is best,[73] one thing is certain: there is a broad consensus that Jesus' baptism is one of the most historically likely events in Jesus' life because no one would have concocted a story where Jesus was baptized "for a remission of sins." The idea that the vision stands in for the confession of sin (option 9 above) has much to recommend it.

The idea that a ritual immersion would not be self-administered appears to have been an innovation—at least in this time and place—on John's part. The fact that Jesus sought out John to baptize him (instead of Jesus baptizing himself) indicates that Jesus approves of John's innovation and affirms the idea that baptism required someone to perform it. Once again, Latter-day Saint notions of authority and ordinances are not directly taught in the text, but their underpinnings are supported.

1:10 *And straightway coming up out of the water:* This verse contains the first occurrence of "straightway," a word used with incredible frequency in Mark. There are three theories offered for the frequent use of this word:

1. It creates a sense of things happening very quickly and gives a rushing sense to the narrative. This is the most likely reason for the word's frequent use.

2. It is simply a way to move along the narrative (and so perhaps should be translated as "then" or "next").

3. Because it was "used in the LXX to [translate] the common HB formula 'wehinneh' ("and behold"'),"[74] Mark uses it to make the text sound scriptural.

Here "straightway" modifies "then the heavens opened," not "coming up out of the water" so it closely links the baptism to the vision.

"Coming up out of the water" presumes that Jesus had previously gone down into the water, so baptism by immersion is pictured here.

he saw the heavens opened: It is possible that the antecedent of "he" is John, but it is more likely that it is Jesus since Jesus was the subject of 1:9 and will be addressed in 1:11.

---

73. See 2 Ne. 31:4–7, but the understanding reflected in that chapter may differ from Mark's understanding of the meaning of Jesus' baptism.

74. Marcus, *Mark 1–8,* 159.

The wording "he saw" implies that only Jesus saw the heavens open and the dove descend. Of course, the audience of Mark's Gospel is also privy to this information; this is one of many times that the audience enjoys "insider" status in this Gospel.

"The heavens" could be translated as "sky," which may be preferable so as not to give the impression that heaven was destroyed as it was torn open. It is likely that the heavens/sky here was understood to be the firmament (Gen. 1:6–8) that separated humans from heaven, so its tearing open would then be symbolic of increased access between humans and God. Because the firmament is part of the created order in Genesis 1, tearing the firmament may feed the new creation theme in this chapter.

"Opened" is too tame a translation for the Greek word *schizō*,[75] which means "tear," "rip," or "shred," with "the idea of violence ... present in the verb."[76]

and the Spirit like a dove descending upon him: "Holy" does not modify Spirit here; Mark may be simply abbreviating since there was just a reference to the Holy Spirit. In the HB, the Spirit has the following functions:

1. making prophesying possible (Num. 11:25; 1 Sam. 10:6, 10)
2. providing physical strength (Judg. 14:6, 19)
3. physically transporting someone to a different location (1 Kgs. 18:12; 2 Kgs. 2:16; Ezek. 3:12, 14)
4. providing leadership ability (Judg. 3:10)
5. providing courage (Micah 3:8)
6. providing wisdom (Isa. 11:2)

The most relevant reference for understanding the role of the Spirit here is Isaiah 61:1–2, where the Spirit from God endows the chosen leader with the ability to perform a task.

This bestowal of the Spirit upon Jesus might be understood as a prerequisite to Jesus' own ability to baptize in the Spirit, as John has just mentioned.

There are several possibilities for what "like a dove" would have conveyed to Mark's early audiences. The first consideration is: What does the phrase "like a dove" describe?

---

75. Note that both Matt. 3:16 and Luke 3:21 change it to the typical word for "open" (Greek: *anoigō*).

76. Robert G. Bratcher and Eugene A. Nida, *A Translator's Handbook on the Gospel of Mark* (Leiden: E. J. Brill, 1961), 27, 28.

1. It describes the appearance of the Spirit. Given that Jesus sees the Spirit descend, the Spirit had a physical manifestation and so looked like a dove. Some Restoration scriptures seem to support this view, indicating that the Holy Ghost descended in the "form" of a dove (1 Ne. 11:27; 2 Ne. 31:8; D&C 93:15).

2. It describes the manner of the Spirit's descent, which leads to the question: What does it mean to descend like a dove? Does it suggest gentleness, slowness, rapidity, precision, or something else?[77]

Joseph Smith taught that, from before the Creation, the dove was a "sign" for the Holy Spirit,[78] leading some Latter-day Saint thinkers to conclude that "the dove was not literally [presumably: physically?] present."[79] Possible symbolic resonances for the dove include the following:

1. In Genesis 1:2, the Spirit "hovers" (KJV: "moved") over the waters, using a verb that can describe the motion of a bird (see Deut. 32:11). While the verb used in LXX Genesis 1:2 does not have the connotation of a hovering bird, in later Jewish tradition the "hovering" would be identified with a dove.[80] If this image is in Mark's mind, then Jesus' baptism is associated with the Creation (with links also to be found in the references to water and the heavens), and Jesus' baptism might even be understood as a new creation.

2. After the flood, the dove serves as a sign to Noah that the crisis is over (Gen. 8:11). In this reading, Jesus' body is paralleled with Noah's ark, implying that it is a vehicle for salvation for those who choose to join with him.

3. In Greek mythology and the Greek tradition generally, the entrance of a bird into a human signified that the person had divine status or was a god in human form. So "members of the audience familiar with Greek mythology would understand v. 10 to mean that the earthly Jesus, from the time of his baptism, was a divine being walking the earth."[81]

---

77. These are arbitrary suggestions for what "like a dove" would have implied about the manner of descent, as there are no uses of this metaphor in extant ancient literature that would explain what this phrase would have conveyed to Mark's audience.

78. "Journal, December 1842–June 1844; Book 1, 21 December 1842–10 March 1843," 155, Church History Library, available online at Church Historian's Press, The Joseph Smith Papers, http://www.josephsmithpapers.org/paper-summary/journal-december -1842-june-1844-book-1-21-december-1842-10-march-1843/163; published in Andrew H. Hedges, Alex D. Smith, and Richard Lloyd Anderson, eds., *Journals, Volume 2: December 1841–April 1843,* vol. 2 of the Journals series of *The Joseph Smith Papers,* ed. Dean C. Jessee, Ronald K. Esplin, and Richard Lyman Bushman (Salt Lake City: Church Historian's Press, 2011), 251.

79. Robert L. Marrott, "Dove, Sign of the," in *Encyclopedia of Mormonism,* ed. Daniel H. Ludlow, 4 vols. (New York: Macmillan, 1992), 1:428.

80. Babylonian Talmud, Seder Mo'ed IV, Hagigah 15a.

81. Collins, *Mark,* 149.

4. In Matthew 10:16 the dove suggests innocence, so its use in Mark would be an indirect way of emphasizing Jesus' sinlessness at precisely the moment in the narrative where the audience had been led to expect Jesus to confess his sins.

5. The dove was sometimes a symbol for Israel. If that association was already present in Mark's time, then Jesus is viewed as a symbol for Israel, an idea that nicely aligns with the metaphor of Jesus as a New Israel or new creation. It also fits with the reverse Exodus theme.

6. The dove could be used in the HB sacrifices (Lev. 1:14), so perhaps its presence at Jesus' baptism is meant to emphasize the idea of holiness and sanctification.

7. Given that John's baptismal practice is innovative, perhaps the dove is as well, and efforts to find a precise analogue to explain its meaning are fruitless.

Because this detail is found in all four Gospels—which is rare—it is possible that it was part of a widespread, well-known tradition that Mark felt obligated to include despite not having any interest in developing the imagery; this would explain why it is so enigmatic.

After the baptism, Jesus was ascending (Greek: *anabainō*) from the water; here the dove is descending (Greek: *katabainō*; this word is similar to "ascending"). This inversion heightens the sense that the bestowal of the Spirit is one of the results of Jesus' choice to be baptized.

Some manuscripts read "to/into him," and others read "upon him" here.[82] It is likely that "to/into" was the earlier reading, with the change to "upon"[83] made either to parallel the other Gospels (Matt. 3:16; Luke 3:22; John 1:32) or because it was considered important to the theological debates about the nature of Jesus' identity that were raging when the text was copied to have the Spirit rest "upon" him instead of "in" him.[84]

---

82. Collins, *Mark,* 133–34 note h.

83. Restoration scripture, when it speaks of Jesus' baptism, uses "upon" (see 1 Ne. 11:27; 2 Ne. 31:8; D&C 93:15). It may be that scripture translated by or revelation received by Joseph Smith used "upon" because that was the language he was familiar with from the NT, or it may weigh in favor of reading "upon" in Mark. Note that the difference between the two variants implies a choice between the Holy Ghost being "upon" a person or "in" a person, but Restoration scripture suggests that no choice is really necessary; 3 Ne. 19:13 uses both concepts: "the Holy Ghost did fall upon them, and they were filled with the Holy Ghost." Generally, the Book of Mormon describes people as being "filled" with the Holy Ghost (see Alma 8:30; 36:24; 3 Ne. 26:17; and D&C 84:27; 107:56).

84. Ehrman, "Text of Mark," 148.

HB Allusions. The idea of the heavens being ripped apart may allude to Isaiah 64:1, where the prophet prays for the ripping open of the heavens and a victory for the Lord. Similarly, in Ezekiel 1:1, the heavens open immediately before a prophet receives a vision calling him to a certain task. These associations help the audience understand that the opening is not so much novel or destructive as it is an allusive manner of suggesting that the Lord is present in a new and real way and is acting in history.

Jesus' Baptism and Death Compared. The only other use of the verb translated as "opened" (Greek: *schizō*) in Mark's Gospel is in 15:38, where immediately after Jesus' death the temple veil is ripped open from top to bottom. There are about a half dozen other verbal and thematic similarities between these two stories, suggesting that Mark wants the audience to interpret Jesus' death in light of his baptism. (See the Notes on 15:38 for a fuller discussion of these parallels and their implications.)

1:11 *And there came a voice from heaven, saying:* "Came" is the same verb used in "came to pass" in 1:9.

Some ancient manuscripts read "and a voice was heard from the heavens,"[85] although this is less likely to be original. Some ancient manuscripts omit "and there came" (either accidentally or to harmonize with Matt. 3:17),[86] leaving "and a voice from the heavens: Thou art . . ."[87] The variant preferred here does not seem to impact the interpretation of the passage, but the shortest reading does have a certain dramatic appeal and perhaps underscores the suddenness of the event. As the italics in the KJV indicate, the word "saying" was not part of the Greek text from which they were translating but was added so the verse would read more smoothly in English.

Thou art my beloved son, in whom I am well pleased: As a description of Jesus that comes straight from heaven, this sentence is extremely important. The word "you" is given emphasis in Greek. There are two significant translation options here:

---

85. Collins, *Mark,* 134 note i.

86. Metzger, *Textual Commentary,* 63.

87. D&C 93:15 reads, "And I, John, bear record, and lo, the heavens were opened, and the Holy Ghost descended upon him in the form of a dove, and sat upon him, and there came a voice out of heaven saying: This is my beloved Son." But it is difficult to determine whether that wording reflects Joseph Smith's familiarity with the NT or is itself an independent witness to the idea.

1. "Beloved" could be translated as "only," which might make sense in this context, given that Mark sets up a contrast between the masses who come to John from the south for baptism and the single person, Jesus, who comes from the north. It would also emphasize the idea that Jesus has a unique relationship with God.

2. "Beloved/only" could be translated as a title: "You are my son, the Beloved One" or "You are my son, the Only One."

There are two different ways that the relationship between the two phrases ("Thou art . . ." and "in whom . . .") can be understood:

1. Regardless of whether it is translated as "beloved" or "only," that phrase speaks to Jesus himself, while "in whom I am well pleased" speaks to Jesus' choices and actions. In other words, Jesus is loved just for being who he is but also brings pleasure to God because of his actions. There are some interesting theological implications here for how the audience understands God's love and pleasure.

2. Perhaps "in whom I am well pleased" should have a "therefore" before it, which would mean that God is pleased because Jesus is his son, not because of any particular actions that Jesus has taken.

See also the Notes on 9:7, where a voice from heaven will make a very similar pronouncement.

Relationship to Psalm 2, Isaiah 42, and Genesis 22. The statement from heaven is a combination of two (or three) texts:

1. LXX Psalm 2:7 (KJV: "Thou art my son") but with three changes:

   a. Mark omits "this day have I begotten thee." There are two different ways to understand this omission:

      i. It was left out because that phrase was not relevant to Jesus' situation.[88]

      ii. It was left out, but its presence should be assumed by the audience, so there is some sense in which Jesus was "begotten" at his baptism.

   b. Psalm 2:7 doesn't include the word "beloved/only." Perhaps "beloved/only" is imported from the story of the near-sacrifice of Isaac (LXX Gen. 22:2, 12, 16); this would be the third HB text quoted here. If so, it is an "ominous note"[89] that foreshadows Jesus' sacrificial death by associating it with Isaac's story.

---

88. Compare Acts 13:33, where the entire sentence is quoted, but note that that is in reference to Jesus' Resurrection, not his baptism.

89. Sharyn Dowd, *Reading Mark: A Literary and Theological Commentary on the Second Gospel* (Macon, Ga.: Smyth and Helwys, 2000), 12.

c. In Psalm 2:7, in both Hebrew and Greek, there is no definite article and "my son" is the first phrase, meaning that "a son of mine [are] you" is a reasonable translation. But "Mark puts . . . 'you' in first position to accent the identification of Jesus as God's Son."[90] This change emphasizes Jesus' relationship to God.

The material in Psalm 2 undergirds what the voice from heaven is teaching about Jesus and his identity and mission: this psalm is considered a royal enthronement psalm, meaning that its setting is the coronation of a new king, and it may have been used at royal coronations.[91] But not only is it about the crowning of a new king, it is also about the identity of the king. Psalm 2:6 reads, "Yet have I set my king upon my holy hill of Zion," and Psalm 2:8–9 promises this son an inheritance of all that the Lord has and great power. Further, it makes a contrast between earthly rulers and the chosen ruler described in the psalm; this distinction, if behind the reference in Mark, suggests that Jesus is different from earthly kings. To members of Mark's audience familiar with this psalm, the use of a line from it by the voice from heaven would have emphasized Jesus' unique relationship and powers.

2. Isaiah 42:1 describes the servant "in whom my soul delighteth." Isaiah 42:1–7 is an important text in terms of understanding Jesus' mission: it points to Jesus' care for those on the margins of society (Isa. 42:3, 7), his role as mediator of the covenant (Isa. 42:4), and his eventual success despite obstacles (Isa. 42:4). The reference to "spirit" (Isa. 42:1) is another link to the present context. As one scholar explained, "The servant of Yahweh portrayed in Isaiah 42:1–4 is a nonviolent figure who achieves justice for the nations by patient faithfulness, under the direction of the Spirit of Yahweh."[92]

3. The reference to the "only/beloved" may come from Genesis 22, where it is used repeatedly to describe Isaac. This may be a hint of Jesus' eventual death.

Relationship to Isaiah 61:1–3. While not directly quoted by the voice from heaven, Isaiah 61:1–3 may be alluded to, as there are several points of connection between that text and chapter 1:

1. The role of the Spirit, which comes upon Jesus in Mark and is explained in the Isaiah passage.

2. Isaiah 61:1 refers to "good tidings," using a form of the Greek word translated as "gospel" in 1:1.

3. Isaiah 61:1 refers to the anointed one, using a form of the Greek word translated as "Christ" in 1:1.

---

90. Gundry, *Mark,* 49.
91. Collins, *Mark,* 150.
92. France, *Gospel of Mark,* 81.

4. The healing and release of captives in Isaiah may be understood as a way of describing the exorcism that will happen near the beginning of Jesus' ministry (1:23).

5. Isaiah's "year of the Lord" (Isa. 61:2) is conceptually similar to the summary statement of Jesus' preaching: "the time is fulfilled" (1:15).

If Mark is encouraging the audience to associate that text from Isaiah with the inauguration of Jesus' ministry, then there is encouragement to see Jesus' mission as a fulfillment of HB prophecy that is focused on blessing those on the margins of society and preaching a message of hope.

1:12 *And immediately the Spirit driveth him into the wilderness:* Mark's use of "immediately" reinforces the fast-paced nature of the narrative. It suggests an association between this passage and Jesus' baptism: being driven into the wilderness is a direct result of being baptized.

The audience would have expected the Spirit to give Jesus power to perform some mighty act or deliver some impressive teaching, so it is most surprising that the first action of the Spirit, after descending upon Jesus at his baptism, is to drive Jesus into the wilderness. It is not clear whether the purpose of the Spirit sending Jesus into the wilderness was so Jesus could be tempted, or if there was some other purpose and then the temptation followed. It is possible that, much as God tested Israel in the wilderness, God's spirit will here test Jesus in the wilderness.

There are three references to the Spirit in this first section of the Gospel of Mark (1:8, 10, 12), but only three more throughout the entire rest of the text (3:29; 12:36; 13:11).[93] It may be that much as "the Word" is a key concept in the beginning of the Gospel of John, the Spirit is a key concept in the beginning of the Gospel of Mark. In the HB, the presence of the Spirit was associated with the end of days (for example, Isa. 32:15; Ezek. 36:26–27; and Joel 2:28–29). So perhaps the cluster of references to the Spirit at the beginning of Mark's Gospel is meant to emphasize the idea that the beginning of the end was near.

"Driveth" is in the historical present tense,[94] which means that events in the past are narrated in the present tense. This form might have been particularly appropriate to an oral presentation as it draws the listener in by portraying the story as if it were happening in the current moment.

---

93. The word "spirit" [Greek: *pneuma*] is used in other contexts, most frequently "unclean spirit."

94. Stein, *Mark,* 62. This is the first of 151 verbs in the historical present tense in Mark; by way of contrast, Matthew has 78 and Luke has only 6. See Stein, *Mark,* 62.

The word translated as "driveth" can connote "moral compulsion,"[95] force, and, sometimes, violence; this is the same word used by Mark to describe demons being cast out (for example, in 1:34, 39). It is surprising to imagine Jesus being forced by the Spirit; perhaps the point is that Jesus does not resist the Spirit. In the HB, a common function of the Spirit is to move a person from place to place (see the Notes on 1:10), which suggests that the action is not as unusual as it might strike the modern reader.

Soon, Mark will introduce a man controlled by an "unclean spirit" (1:23); perhaps this story presents the opposite, where Jesus here is under the control of a Holy Spirit. While Latter-day Saints don't speak of Jesus being "possessed" by the Holy Spirit, the idea that Jesus submitted to God's will in all things is well understood, and, while the language here is different, the concept is the same.

On a literal level, "into the wilderness" is confusing since Jesus was just baptized by John "in the wilderness." But Mark's purpose here is more theological than geographical: the point is that Jesus will have a "wilderness" experience as he is tempted. The wilderness can typify the dwelling place of chaos and evil; others have understood it as the place where God is most likely to visit (for example, Isa. 32:14–20); in this passage, both views could be harmonized with the idea that God visits the people after a time of testing.

1:13 ***And he was there in the wilderness forty days:*** Because "in the wilderness" was used at the end of the previous verse, Mark is either redundant or deliberate. The latter is more likely; Mark is emphasizing Jesus' wilderness location because of its metaphorical significance.

In the HB, numbers are sometimes used symbolically, and forty is often a symbol for trial, testing, or learning.[96] While Mark does not specifically mention that Jesus fasted in the wilderness, the times of testing in the HB associated with the number forty normally include references to fasting and/or food, so it is possible that Mark assumed it.[97]

tempted of Satan: "Tempted" can have a full spectrum of nuances:

1. *Positive* ("determine one's mettle"). Focusing on the Spirit's role in delivering Jesus into the wilderness implies that a positive meaning was intended.

---

95. Cranfield, *Gospel According to St Mark*, 56.

96. For example, Gen. 7:12 (the flood), Ex. 34:28 (Moses), Deut. 2:7 (Israel), 1 Kgs. 19:8 (Elijah), Jonah 3:4 (Nineveh).

97. It is also possible that Mark did not intend to convey that Jesus was fasting, but that Matthew and Luke inferred it from Mark's account and made it explicit (Matt. 4:2 and Luke 4:2).

2. *Neutral* ("test"). Given that both the Spirit and Satan have a role in Jesus' tempting, a neutral reading might be appropriate,[98] especially since this verb in its other uses in Mark's Gospel[99] involves (mortal) opponents of Jesus where "test" is probably a better translation than "tempt."

3. *Negative* ("tempt"). Focusing on Satan's role suggests a negative meaning, with Satan encouraging Jesus to violate God's commandments.

While Matthew and Luke mention three temptations, Mark does not give a number; it is possible that more than three temptations are implied here. Many readers assume that, after this passage, Jesus' mortal temptations ended since they are not mentioned again (save for, as mentioned above, the human opponents who test Jesus), but there is no reason to assume that Jesus was not tempted throughout his entire mortal life. It is possible to read Jesus' mortal ministry as bookended by temptations—in the wilderness and in Gethsemane. This suggests that Jesus' life was literally surrounded by temptation and suffering.

and was with the wild beasts: "Wild beasts" has a negative connotation in English that is absent from the Greek text, which might be translated as, simply, "animals." But still their role is not clear.[100] Options include:

1. In Greek thought, wild beasts were associated with demons.[101] In this reading, the wild beasts would be part of the temptations.

2. In the HB, the absence of wild beasts is often linked with God's protection,[102] and the presence of wild animals is sometimes associated with God's judgment or punishment (for example, Num. 21:6; Isa. 34:14), so the presence of the beasts here could either

   a. indicate that God is not protecting Jesus during this experience. This could be particularly relevant to Mark's audience, whose persecution might have included being literally thrown to the lions.

   b. indicate that, because the beasts do not harm Jesus, God is protecting Jesus during this experience.

3. The beasts might allude to the story of Daniel in the lions' den (Dan. 6:10–28), with the expectation that the animals would harm Jesus, but divine protection

---

98. In the LXX, this word is used for "testing" but not "tempting."

99. See 8:11; 10:2; and 12:15. A noun from the same root is used in 14:38, where "tempt" seems more appropriate to the context than "test."

100. Perhaps this is why Matthew and Luke omit this detail from their accounts of Jesus' temptations, in one of the rare instances where a detail included in the Gospel of Mark is not included elsewhere in the record.

101. Collins, *Mark,* 152–53.

102. Deut. 32:10 (where "howling" implies the presence of dangerous animals); Isa. 35:9 (which mentions not just beasts but also "way" and "wilderness"); and Ezek. 34:25.

prohibited that outcome. In this reading, the animals become a symbol of Jesus' ability to overcome challenges and the divine protection that he enjoys.

4. The animals could represent the "natural" dangers of the fallen world, which Jesus must experience along with the supernatural temptations represented by Satan. Thus, both physical and spiritual forces test his resolve to be faithful to God.

5. Wild beasts are often presented in the HB as evidence of desolation (for example, Deut. 8:15; Isa. 13:21–22; 34:11), so here they would contribute to the "wilderness" theme or magnify Jesus' temptations.

6. In Daniel's vision (Dan. 7:3–7) and in the book of Revelation, animals are symbols for political entities; perhaps there is a subtle nod to the political themes that will be more prominent later in Mark's Gospel.

7. The animals are part of the post-temptation scene showing that Jesus has overcome the temptations: perhaps the beasts, like the angels, are serving Jesus.

8. In Isaiah 43:19–21, God promises to do something new: after making a way in the wilderness (compare to 1:2–3), the righteous and animals will be able to live in peace. In this view, the animals are part of the post-temptation scene and fulfill HB prophecy (see Isa. 11:6–9; 65:25; and Hosea 2:18).

9. The *Testament of Naphtali,* an apocryphal book, refers to the devil, wild beasts, and angels and describes the wild beasts as "afraid" of the righteous one. This is a compelling parallel to 1:13, but it may have been written (or edited) under the influence of the accounts of Jesus' temptations, which would negate its value as an independent witness to the symbolic meaning of the wild beasts in this story.

Most of these theories fall into two groups, based on whether the presence of the wild beasts is negative (part of the temptation) or positive (evidence of overcoming the temptation). The inability to determine which is correct is largely due to the inability to determine whether the animals are present during or after the temptation.

and the angels ministered unto him: "Angels" is the same word used in 1:2 (KJV: "messenger"), so it is possible to read this incident as (part of) the fulfillment of that scriptural promise.

It is not clear what "ministered" means in this passage, partially because under the influence of Christian thought and practice, the meaning of this word transitioned. The two main options are:

1. Physical, often menial, service, such as serving food. Perhaps the angels minister to Jesus by protecting him from the animals or providing him with food or otherwise attending to his physical needs.

2. Spiritual, in the modern sense of being a minister, such as providing spiritual aid, counsel, and/or comfort.

The ministering of the angels can be understood to have several different rhetorical functions:

1. It connotes that the angels are subservient to Jesus, perhaps specifically because of his success in overcoming temptation.

2. The need for Jesus to be aided by others shows the limits that mortality places upon him.

3. The fact that John the Baptist had to procure his own food (locusts and wild honey)—but Jesus does not—illustrates John's teaching that Jesus would be "mightier" than he was.

4. In 1 Kings 19:4–8, an angelic messenger provides Elijah with food that strengthens him for his journey. If Mark had that text in mind, perhaps these angels are, similarly, feeding Jesus to equip him for the opening phase of his ministry. Further, Jesus is associated with Elijah as a prophet.

5. If Jesus is understood as "the new Israel," then the angels are providing his "manna" during his time in the wilderness.

Relationship to Genesis. The introductory section of Mark has several possible echoes of Genesis 1–3, including:

1. Genesis 1:1 starts with "in the beginning," which in the LXX uses the same word for "beginning" (Greek: *archē*) as 1:1.[103] Perhaps Mark alluded to that text in order to suggest that Jesus' story was as much a new beginning for humankind as the creation of the world.

2. When Mark mentions the voice crying in the wilderness, the idea of a "voice" calling a new situation into being may allude to the voice of God causing the Creation in Genesis 1. If this allusion was intentional, then it serves to suggest that Jesus' ministry offers a new beginning for the world.

3. The voice from heaven pronouncing Jesus a beloved son might be paralleled with God's voice in Genesis 1, announcing that each phase of the Creation is good. This would align with other elements of new creation imagery in Mark 1, including the "hovering" dove, the opened firmament, and the water. If Jesus is the "new creation," then this might explain and account for his sinlessness.

4. When the Spirit drives Jesus into the wilderness after his baptism, the word "driveth" (Greek: *ekballō*) is the same word used in LXX Genesis 3:24 when Adam and Eve are removed from the garden after the Fall. There may be a useful contrast to be made between Jesus and Adam:

---

103. Compare Matt. 1:1, where "the book of the generation" is also reminiscent of Genesis (KJV's "generation" is *genesis* in Greek), and John 1:1 ("in the beginning"), where the link to Genesis 1 is even stronger.

a. If Mark had the story of the Fall in mind, then history is running backwards, as Jesus is driven out, then tested, then has an experience with animals. (By contrast, in Genesis, Adam names the animals, is tested, and is then driven out.)

b. The fact that Jesus did not merit his driving out through disobedience may hint at Mark's Atonement theology here, as Jesus is suffering a punishment that he did not deserve.

c. If Jesus is the new Adam, then the angels' service is an inversion of the role of the cherubim, who keep Adam from the tree of life: Jesus' angels provide food while Adam's cherubim kept him away from food. This difference emphasizes Jesus' sinlessness.

d. Animals are hostile to humans after the Fall; the fact that Jesus is here shown at peace with animals implies that a new paradisaical state has been created, perhaps specifically as a result of his ability to withstand temptation.

The overall effect of these echoes of Genesis 1–3 in chapter 1 is to imply that a new creation is occurring in the ministry of Jesus.

Relationship to Elijah. Like Jesus in this story, Elijah spends time in a wilderness area, is associated with the number forty, and is helped by angels (1 Kgs. 19:4–8). But in that story, Elijah is very discouraged; perhaps there is a contrast with Jesus, who does not seem to be discouraged by his difficult circumstances.

The prologue featured comparisons between John the Baptist and Elijah, but the association here between Jesus and Elijah may be designed to help the audience recognize that John was not the only representation of Elijah; Jesus had some things in common with Elijah as well.

Relationship to Job. As in the story of Job, where the adversary tests a righteous man, Jesus is tested in Mark's story. Both temptations come immediately after God has praised the faithfulness of the man (1:11; Job 1:8). The difference, however, is that in Job, the real dispute is between God and Satan, but in Mark's story, the dispute is between Jesus and Satan, which suggests by analogy Jesus' divine status.[104]

---

104. Note that this is the traditional reading of the book of Job, which would have been common in the first century and thus to Mark and his audience, but is disputed by modern scholars, who do not necessarily identify the adversary with Satan.

Relationship to Psalm 91. Mark seems to be alluding to Psalm 91,[105] with its references to the support of angels (Ps. 91:11) and the control of threatening animals (Ps. 91:13). The larger context of that psalm is one of trust and faith in God by the psalmist, so an allusion would emphasize that Jesus was able to be victorious in the wilderness because he trusted God to deliver him from all threats.

In Jewish tradition, Psalm 91 was sometimes associated with exorcism and protection from evil spirits,[106] and so this psalm might be a bridge from the baptism to the exorcism in 1:21–28. It also emphasizes that Jesus' success in fighting off temptation is related to his understanding of its evil root.

Psalm 91:14 ("Because he hath set his love upon me, therefore will I deliver him: I will set him on high, because he hath known my name") is particularly significant as a recap of the baptismal scene, emphasizing God's love for and acknowledgment of Jesus' special status. Recognizing the allusions to Psalm 91 allows the audience to see that Mark is using this scene as a commentary on Jesus' relationship with God.

Relationship to Isaiah's Prophecy. Isaiah 35:8–10 speaks of a "highway" (compare the references in the prologue) that the righteous will travel where no beast will be present and where the redeemed and ransomed will return in the Lord in a future time. There are plenty of echoes between this passage in Isaiah and this section in Mark's Gospel; they imply that the time of which Isaiah had prophesied has come.

The following themes from Isaiah can be identified in chapter 1 of Mark:

1. wilderness
2. proclaiming forgiveness
3. tearing of the heavens
4. descent of the Spirit
5. heavenly voice
6. animals
7. "good news"

105. Matt. 4:6 and Luke 4:10 quote this psalm in relation to the temptations directly, but Mark does not.

106. Babylonian Talmud, Seder Nezikin IV, Shebu'oth 15b. See also Brennan Breed, "The Reception of the Psalms: The Example of Psalm 91," in *The Oxford Handbook of the Psalms,* ed. William P. Brown (Oxford: Oxford University Press, 2014), 297–303.

These associations, as well as the (possibly inaccurate) reference to Isaiah in 1:2, may suggest that Mark deliberately structured this section of the Gospel to evoke Isaiah's message.

1:14 *Now after that John was put in prison:* Some of the ancient manuscripts have "but" (Greek: *de*) instead of "and" (Greek: *kai*; translated as "now" in the KJV).[107] The "but" heightens the contrast between 1:13 and this verse; perhaps those who arrested John are foils for the angels who served Jesus in the wilderness.

This verse does not use the standard verb for "put" but rather a verb sometimes translated as "delivered up" (Greek: *paradidōmai*); it emphasizes the parallels between John's arrest and Jesus' arrest later, where the same verb is used.[108] Perhaps part of John's task to prepare the way for the Lord (or John's role as teacher for Jesus, if indeed Jesus was John's disciple) was to show Jesus the way by being "delivered up" first. Jesus makes the comparison between John's experience and his own experience explicit in 9:12–13. The reference to John being put in prison is a bit of foreshadowing: if Jesus is John's follower and John goes to prison, then Jesus' fate will be similar.

This verse implies that John and Jesus did not have active ministries at the same time. (It is also possible to understand this verse as saying that Jesus did preach before John was arrested, just not in Galilee.[109]) It seems that Mark's concern was "more theological than chronological."[110] One of the themes of 2:1–3:6 is the incompatibility of the "old" and the "new." Perhaps as a result of this teaching, Mark thought it would not do to have John and Jesus preaching at the same time[111] in light of the idea that John had preached that a "mightier one" was coming; the lack of a concurrent ministry emphasizes John's role as someone who prepared the way for Jesus. Once the preparation is made, there is a theological necessity in Mark for John to step off of the stage. Mark will say more about John in chapter 6— not because it is chronologically appropriate there, but rather because it allows Mark to make a contrast between John's disciples and Jesus' disciples.

---

107. Marcus, *Mark 1–8*, 171.
108. For example, 9:31 (KJV: "delivered") and 14:21 (KJV: "betrayed").
109. Witherington, *Gospel of Mark*, 79.
110. Guelich, *Mark 1–8:26*, 42.
111. John 3:22–24 describes a concurrent ministry, but in Mark, people wondering if Jesus was John raised from the dead (6:14) only makes sense if they were not publicly active at the same time.

Jesus came into Galilee: John went out into the wilderness, but Jesus preaches in areas where people live. Perhaps "the geographical contrast [between the wilderness and Galilee] suggests a thematic and qualitative distinction between the time of repentance and asceticism in the wilderness and the time of good news, fulfillment and trust in Galilee."[112]

preaching the gospel of the kingdom of God: Some ancient manuscripts read "the gospel of God" instead of "the gospel of the kingdom of God" here.[113] The phrase "the kingdom of" was probably added by scribes because:

1. It makes the summary of Jesus' teachings in this verse align more closely with the report of Jesus' teachings in the next verse.
2. The phrase "the kingdom of God" is more common in the NT. "The gospel of God" is much less common (it is not otherwise used in Mark's Gospel and is used only a few times in the rest of the NT), perhaps making it sound odd to the copyists.

There are two ways to interpret "of God" in this verse:

1. "The good news about God"
2. "The good news that God delivers"

This is the same word (Greek: *kēryssō*) used in 1:4 to describe John's preaching, so it emphasizes the continuity between the two of them. Yet there is a distinction in that John preached about the coming one, and Jesus preaches about the kingdom of God.

This verse can be viewed as an important moment of transition within the text, with everything before it giving a divine perspective on who Jesus is (something no one in the story has), while this verse shifts to the perspective of a mortal and what she or he would have been able to observe of Jesus' ministry.

1:15 *And saying, The time is fulfilled:* The idea here is that a certain period of time has reached its end; the perfect verb tense indicates that the time has already been fulfilled. This is presumably a divine passive, indicating that God is the understood subject and thus the one who has fulfilled the time. In other words, this time was prophesied about and now is here. The idea of time being fulfilled may come from Daniel 7:22, which prophesies of a coming time when "the saints [will possess] the kingdom." By making a statement such as this, Jesus is acting like a prophet who functions as a herald, bringing the news (see, for example, Isa. 56:1).

---

112. Collins, *Mark,* 154.
113. Metzger, *Textual Commentary,* 64.

and the kingdom of God is at hand: There is great debate[114] as to the better interpretation of "at hand" in this verse:

1. "At hand" means "here" ("the kingdom of God is here"). Support for this reading comes from

    a. 2:21–22, which indicates that the "old" and the "new" cannot be mixed.

    b. the fact that John the Baptist was in prison before Jesus began to preach, suggesting a break with the old order of things.

2. "At hand" means "near" ("the kingdom of God is near"). Mark 13:28 lends support to the idea of the kingdom being near but not yet present. Further, it is possible to view "the kingdom of God" as coming in a special sense with the mortal life of Jesus Christ and/or his Atonement and Resurrection.

3. "At hand" is ambiguous, possibly encompassing both "here" and "near."

Which of these options the reader finds most persuasive depends to some extent on how "the kingdom of God" is defined:

1. The Davidic kingdom
2. The spiritual reign of God in the human heart
3. The end of history with final judgment
4. The rule of God now, but with more to come in the future (in other words, the beginning of the rule of God)
5. The obligation humans owe to God as subjects[115]

What is at stake here is whether Jesus is preaching that the kingdom of God had already arrived or was about to arrive. If he is saying that it was about to arrive, then the kingdom of God would, presumably, have reference to his Atonement and Resurrection and perhaps his establishment of a community of believers. If he is saying that it had arrived, then presumably the kingdom of God was tied primarily to his incarnation.

Because this verse is parallel to the previous verse, consideration of the parallel might help determine the meaning, but there are still two options:

1. The kingdom of God is "here," yielding synonymous parallelism with "has been fulfilled."

2. The kingdom of God is "at hand," to provide a heightening of the parallelism with "has been fulfilled."

In either case, "at hand" may be related to the repetition of "immediately" previously in the chapter as a way to emphasize the closeness of

---

114. Gundry, *Mark,* 64–65. The Latter-day Saint Bible has a footnote on 1:15 that reads, "[Greek] has arrived," but this is debatable.

115. Stein, *Mark,* 72.

the appointed time. (See also the Notes on 9:1, which contains a similar teaching.)

repent ye, and believe the gospel: "Repent" is plural, as is "believe" below. "Repent" carried the implication of change, as in changing one's mind; it might be more similar to the way modern Latter-day Saints use the term "convert" and could be understood as a call to turn away from the previous way of life. In an HB context, similar language usually implies "returning [to God]."[116]

This reference to the gospel may form a bookend with the reference in 1:1, framing 1:1–15 as the prologue or "beginning" of the gospel. Here, "believe" probably has the connotation of trust rather than of offering intellectual assent to a proposition. Therefore, it "denotes not only an intellectual acceptance that the 'news' is true, but a response of acceptance and commitment."[117] So it is possible to translate this verse, which contains a summary of the core of Jesus' preaching mission, as a call to

1. change your mind and trust the good news.
2. convert and trust the good news.
3. convert and believe in the gospel.

Regardless of the preferred translation here, there is a compelling parallel in this short statement of Jesus' teachings, with two perfect tense indicative verbs (the time "had been fulfilled" and the kingdom of God "has come near") balanced by two imperatives ("repent" and "believe"). "Repent" could encapsulate one's relationship to the past, and "believe" would express one's relationship to the future. The two declarations lead to two actions, suggesting a tight link between action and response.

Analysis

After hearing the HB prophecies and John's multiple declarations about the superiority of the "coming one," the audience is primed for the arrival of an extremely important person. Through his preaching about the coming mightier one—one so important that John is unworthy to be his slave, let alone his disciple—John creates the expectation of the arrival of a truly spectacular person. Mark then toys with the audience's expectations by presenting a man with no pedigree, coming from the least important place imaginable, seeking baptism "for the remission of sins." Mark thus teaches that Jesus will simultaneously conform to and violate expectations of what

---

116. Guelich, *Mark 1–8:26*, 45.
117. France, *Gospel of Mark*, 94.

the Coming One should be. In another instance of violated expectations, the biblical quotes that Mark has placed in the introduction have the Coming One going to Jerusalem (Isa. 40:1–5) and the temple,[118] but Mark introduces Jesus in the wilderness. So Jesus would not have seemed to be the "coming one" that the audience was led to expect. But then the voice from heaven, placed in the narrative precisely where the audience had been led to expect a confession of sins, affirms that God is pleased with Jesus. Mark has begun to teach what will become a theme in this Gospel: Jesus is the Coming One, but he is likely not what has been expected—he simultaneously meets and denies expectations. Mark's style—characterized by subtlety and allusion— is on full display here.

Jesus' baptism is narrated in a minimalistic way, and the emphasis of the passage is really on the postbaptismal experience of the Spirit and the voice from heaven; Mark seems more concerned with the latter event. Several aspects of Jesus' baptism suggest that Jesus fulfills the role of the "New Israel." First, John baptized masses ("all") of people who came to him from the south; by contrast, Jesus is one person coming to John from the north. This suggests that Jesus in himself is somehow equated with those masses of people; Mark may intend to portray Jesus here as Israel personified. This association sets the stage for understanding Jesus' ability to atone for the sins of all people.

The combination of quotations from Isaiah 42:1 and Psalm 2:7 in the statement made by the voice from heaven shapes the perception of Jesus' identity. The royal setting and themes of the psalm present Jesus as someone who is regal and exalted, while the Isaiah text presents a servant of the Lord who must suffer. The hint of Genesis 22 points to Jesus' death. But Genesis 22 concerns Abraham's commitment to God, while in Mark's context, the issue is God's commitment to humans;[119] while subtle, this is an evocative way for Mark's audience to think about Jesus' death. So the juxtaposition of these two texts conveys a paradoxical and crucial principle about Jesus' ministry. This is a perfect introduction to Jesus as it presents him as the "paradox of a suffering, unrecognized Messiah."[120] The same paradox is found in the form of the text, as Jesus is introduced by both a

---

118. See Mal. 3:35; the temple setting is assumed because of the reference to purification rituals.

119. Sharyn Dowd and Elizabeth Struthers Malbon, "The Significance of Jesus' Death in Mark: Narrative Context and Authorial Audience," *Journal of Biblical Literature* 125, no. 2 (2006): 273–74.

120. France, *Gospel of Mark*, 81.

very humble voice (John's, saying that he is unworthy to be Jesus' slave) and a mighty voice (God's, announcing pleasure with the beloved son).

Immediately after Jesus is baptized, he sees and hears something that apparently no one else in the story can. There are several different ways to understand what purpose this experience served:

1. Some early Christian thinkers read this story as Jesus' "adoption" as God's son, implying that Jesus had no special status before this experience. This is not consonant with Latter-day Saint thought. However, Latter-day Saints understand that Jesus increased in knowledge, and it is possible that this experience was the first time he became aware of his special status.

2. While the idea that Jesus was God's beloved Son was not new to Jesus, this vision could have been a restatement or confirmation of it or a sign that it was time to begin his ministry.

3. Similar to prophetic call narratives (see Isa. 6; Jer. 1; Ezek. 1; 1 Ne. 1), this story is Jesus' call to ministry.

4. The vision expresses God's approval of Jesus' decision to be baptized.

For Mark's audience, the vision could have clarified that Jesus was not baptized "for the remission of sins" because at precisely the point in the narrative where the audience would have expected him to confess his sins, he has an entirely different experience, one that includes divine approval for his actions.

Immediately after Jesus chooses to be baptized, the Spirit descends, and, immediately after that, Jesus is cast out into the wilderness where he is tempted. The repetition of the word "immediately" suggests a tight link between the decision to be baptized and Jesus' wilderness temptations. God's pleasure with Jesus stems from Jesus' willingness to be baptized, which is linked to his willingness to suffer temptations. (Later in Mark, in the only time that he speaks about baptism, Jesus will use baptism as a metaphor for his own death.) In this light, there is a parallel to the Atonement, where Jesus' willingness to do what is right leads to his suffering. This parallel is particularly compelling if Jesus was baptized in behalf of all Israel. There is a sense in which this is a foreshadowing of the Atonement, where Jesus will take on the sins of all people. Perhaps the combination of spiritual testing (by Satan) and physical testing (by the presence of threatening animals and the wilderness setting) foreshadows the spiritual and physical aspects of the Atonement.

The prologue emphasizes "the way of the Lord" (1:3) and John's role in preparing it; the role of the Spirit is also emphasized. Perhaps the last thing the audience would have expected would be that that "way" and that Spirit would lead Jesus to be tempted by Satan in the wilderness. It is

a prime example of Mark's irony: the audience expects that John will prepare Jesus' path—the path that Isaiah indicates is like the path of a glorious,
conquering army (Isa. 40:3–4). Instead, Jesus' path is shown not to be one
of glory but one of temptation and even suffering. There is also irony in the
compelling tension between continuity with Israel's past (references to
Isaiah and Elijah) and a radical departure from it (baptism for remission of
sins instead of temple sacrifice and the invitation to "change your life and
believe the good news").

Mark 1:1–8 focuss on John while 1:9–15 focus on Jesus. Both sections
identify the person, locate him in the wilderness, note his preaching, and
describe the preaching. Thus Jesus is "following" John (either in the sense
of coming after him or in the sense of being his disciple), and the HB
prophecies about "preparing the way" are being fulfilled as Jesus acts in a
manner similar to John. Yet there are significant differences as well, since
the content of Jesus' preaching is different: John preaches about the coming one and Jesus preaches about the kingdom of God.

Several parallels can be found between the experiences of Israel and
Jesus (the wilderness, the Red Sea/baptism, temptation, caretaking angels),
but in Jesus' case, unlike in Israel's case, there is no yielding to temptation.
While the Gospel of Mark never explicitly teaches that Jesus is without sin,
the presentation of Jesus as the "new Israel" who resists temptation would
convey that idea in a subtle manner. With this comparison, there is a sense
in which time is moving backwards: John's baptism features people leaving the promised land to go into the wilderness, an inversion of the Exodus journey. They are baptized, which is perhaps analogous to the journey
through the Red Sea. Continuing with the backwards march of time, Jesus
is tempted and then surrounded by animals and angels. It is as if the fallen
world has been reversed in Jesus' story, which is a powerful background to
Mark's Atonement theology.

Throughout the rest of Mark's Gospel, neither Jesus' friends nor his
adversaries are aware of his identity and his authority as it has been
described here. But Mark's audience has heard the prologue, and this puts
them in a different position from the people within the text. They already
know who Jesus is, and they bring that knowledge to each story in the text
as they observe the other characters discover (or refuse to discover) this
knowledge for themselves.[121]

---

121. Francis J. Moloney, *Mark: Storyteller, Interpreter, Evangelist* (Peabody, Mass.:
Hendrickson Publishers, 2004), 62.

In the first fifteen verses, Mark has had HB prophets, a contemporary prophet (John the Baptist), a voice from heaven, Satan (indirectly), beasts (whether their purpose is helpful or harmful), and angels all attest to Jesus' special status. This is quite the introduction to Jesus.

JESUS CALLS DISCIPLES (1:16–20)

Greek Text

16 Καὶ παράγων παρὰ τὴν θάλασσαν τῆς Γαλιλαίας εἶδεν Σίμωνα καὶ Ἀνδρέαν τὸν ἀδελφὸν Σίμωνος ἀμφιβάλλοντας ἐν τῇ θαλάσσῃ, ἦσαν γὰρ ἁλιεῖς· 17 καὶ εἶπεν αὐτοῖς ὁ Ἰησοῦς· Δεῦτε ὀπίσω μου, καὶ ποιήσω ὑμᾶς γενέσθαι ἁλιεῖς ἀνθρώπων. 18 καὶ εὐθὺς ἀφέντες τὰ δίκτυα ἠκολούθησαν αὐτῷ. 19 καὶ προβὰς ὀλίγον εἶδεν Ἰάκωβον τὸν τοῦ Ζεβεδαίου καὶ Ἰωάννην τὸν ἀδελφὸν αὐτοῦ, καὶ αὐτοὺς ἐν τῷ πλοίῳ καταρτίζοντας τὰ δίκτυα, 20 καὶ εὐθὺς ἐκάλεσεν αὐτούς. καὶ ἀφέντες τὸν πατέρα αὐτῶν Ζεβεδαῖον ἐν τῷ πλοίῳ μετὰ τῶν μισθωτῶν ἀπῆλθον ὀπίσω αὐτοῦ. [SBLGNT]

King James Version

16 Now as he walked by the sea of Galilee, he saw Simon and Andrew his brother casting a net into the sea: for they were fishers. 17 And Jesus said unto them, Come ye after me, and I will make you to become fishers of men. 18 And straightway they forsook their nets, and followed him. 19 And when he had gone a little further thence, he saw James the son of Zebedee, and John his brother, who also were in the ship mending their nets. 20 And straightway he called them: and they left their father Zebedee in the ship with the hired servants, and went after him.

New Rendition

16 And walking beside the Sea of Galilee, he saw Simon and Andrew—the brother of Simon—casting a net in the sea, for they were fishers. 17 And Jesus said to them, "Come follow me and I will make you into fishers of people." 18 And immediately, having left their nets, they followed him. 19 And having gone on a little, he saw Jacob, Zebedee's son, and his brother John. And they were in a boat preparing the nets. 20 And immediately he invited them. And having left their father Zebedee in the boat with the laborers, they followed him.

Notes

1:16 *Now as he walked by the sea of Galilee:* This sea is also called the Sea of Tiberias (John 6:1), the Sea of Gennesar, the Lake of Gennesaret (Luke 5:1), and the Sea of Chinnereth (Num. 34:11). As a freshwater, inland body, the best English term would be "lake," but most translations use "sea" since it is customary.

he saw Simon and Andrew his brother: The idea that Jesus saw Simon and Andrew may be a mundane note, or it may reflect something more: perhaps Jesus is "seeing" (in a visionary sense) the future potential of these disciples.[122] Because the only other previous reference in Mark to Jesus "seeing" was the visionary experience immediately after his baptism, the audience is primed to find something more than normal sight here. Much as Jesus "saw" his true identity as God's beloved son after his baptism, perhaps he here sees the true potential of these fishermen. If so, this brief phrase is an important component of Mark's picture of discipleship: the disciples frequently make mistakes, yet Jesus continues to patiently teach them, perhaps because of the vision of their potential that immediately preceded their call.

casting a net into the sea: for they were fishers: Some manuscripts lack "a net" here.[123]

The net would have been circular, probably ten to fifteen feet in diameter, with stones (as weights) along the edges. There would have been a rope attached and it would have been pulled after the net was thrown into the water, trapping whatever fish were underneath. This type of fishing required a great deal of physical strength since it meant repeatedly throwing this large net weighed with stones either from a boat or while wading in the water.

The presence of the phrase "for they were fishers" is puzzling: who else would be casting a net in the water besides fishermen? Possible reasons for the inclusion of this phrase include the following:

1. Because the verb translated as "casting a net" is so unusual (in fact, this is its only use in the NT except for the parallel story in Matt. 4:18), Mark may have added this phrase to explain it to the audience. Of course, this raises the question of why Mark would use an unfamiliar verb and then explain it instead of using a more familiar verb.

2. Mark's audience, more urban than the Galilean setting of this story, required some clarification.

3. Mark wanted to introduce the word "fisher" to set up the connection to the next verse, where the same word is used and likely has a symbolic dimension.

---

122. Marcus, *Mark 1–8,* 183.
123. Collins, *Mark,* 156 note a.

1:17 *And Jesus said unto them, Come ye after me:* "After me" is a technical term meaning "be my disciple."

Standard practice was for students to choose which teacher to follow, so Jesus upsets expectations here by calling disciples: "Jesus' peremptory summons, with its expectation of radical renunciation even of family ties, goes far beyond anything they would be familiar with in normal society. It marks him as a prophet rather than a rabbi."[124] Jesus acts not like a rabbi or a philosopher but like the God of the HB, who calls Abraham (Gen. 12:1–4).

This calling is an important piece of the puzzle of discipleship in Mark: the disciples will make many mistakes as they learn how to follow Jesus; undergirding the portrayal of the disciples, however, is the knowledge that Jesus chose them—they did not choose to follow him. Each instance of misunderstanding on the part of the disciples does not so much make them look inadequate but rather points to Jesus' design in having chosen them to follow him.

Mark does not discuss what motivated them to follow Jesus; perhaps omitting the motivation speaks to Jesus' authority to call them. (In other words, they followed him because he told them to, not because of their own assessment of Jesus' worth as a teacher.) Perhaps Simon and Andrew had a prior association with Jesus, or perhaps this is the first time that they see him; the text permits either reading. Either scenario is powerful in its own way: in the first, it is time for them to give up their "day jobs" for full-time discipleship, and they are willing and able to do this because of what they have seen of Jesus. In the latter scenario, there is something so compelling about Jesus' brief words that they abandon all to follow him.

and I will make you to become fishers of men: The future tense "I will make" indicates that Jesus will make them into fishers in the future and perhaps envisions a period of training before that time.

Jesus' language is reminiscent of the covenant formula in the HB as he promises to do something for the disciples if they honor their part of the contract. If the idea of being "fishers of men" is primarily associated with acting as God does, then Jesus is offering to make the disciples godlike.

The perception of fishing as a hobby requiring great patience, little movement, quiet, and minimal physical effort would not apply here: the kind of fishing Peter and Andrew are engaged in required extensive and sustained effort. It was physically demanding, so the image of being "fishers of men" should include this element of hard labor.

---

124. France, *Gospel of Mark*, 96.

There are many possibilities for the symbolism of being fishers of men:[125]

1. In Greco-Roman tradition, a teacher is a "fisher," which would emphasize the disciples' teaching role. It would also be ironic because Jesus is "fishing" for disciples himself in this passage, suggesting that the disciples are supposed to do what he is doing.

2. In the Qumran texts, one possible reading is that Satan (called Belial) catches people in nets (although this reading is tentative). In Jesus' usage, the disciples would be fishers who remove people from Satan's grasp and put them into God's net. Perhaps this meaning is linked to the frequent concern with demonic possession in this text, pictured as rescuing people from Satan's grasp.

3. The closest HB parallel to this text is Jeremiah 16:16, which is an end-time gathering of people in the context of the judgment of the wicked. Either Jesus is ignoring the context of Jeremiah (because these disciples will bring good news and not catch people for judgment) or he is implying that these disciples will be focused on bringing people to judgment.[126] In the HB, it is God who fishes for people in judgment (Jer. 16:16), so Jesus is inviting these disciples to be godlike.

4. In the HB, water is a symbol for chaos, so the fishing that the disciples do will liberate people from chaos.

5. Because fishing was their livelihood, perhaps Jesus is suggesting that, in one sense, they will be doing what they have always done, but in another sense, they will be doing something entirely different if they follow him. Perhaps the point is that their occupations prepared them for discipleship.

6. In Ezekiel 47:8–10, the fish can be interpreted as a symbol for redeemed souls living in an area previously barren but now teeming with life. Perhaps this links to the recent imagery of the wilderness to suggest that the disciples will save souls from a barren land.

Perhaps more significant than the precise meaning of "fishers" is what Jesus did not call them to be: they are not to be students of the law or scribes or experts. The focus will not be on their own knowledge or attainments but on their relationship to others and the heavy labor that they will expend in their calling.

1:18 *And straightway they forsook their nets, and followed him:* Mark's favorite term ("straightway") is put to good use here emphasizing the quick obedience of Simon and Andrew.

---

125. Marcus, *Mark 1–8*, 184.

126. D&C 29:12 suggests that the Twelve will have a role in judgment.

Some manuscripts have "all things" instead of "their nets."[127] The latter is probably the earlier reading, likely changed to make the text more relevant to later Christians.

This call story differs in significant ways from what would have been common in this culture, where it would have been expected for disciples to maintain their trade and to devote time to study. So Mark's early audiences would have seen this as a surprising departure from the standard practice.

It is somewhat common for interpreters to understand "leaving their nets" as an abandonment of their occupation and wealth, but 1:29 shows Simon and Andrew back in their home, so that interpretation seems to be a misreading. (But see the Analysis on 1:38 for a possible second call to discipleship that would have involved a further break with home and possessions.)

"Followed" can have a literal meaning (physically follow) as well as a metaphorical one (follow as a disciple); in reference to leaving the nets, both meanings seem to be intended here. The abrupt and devoted response of Simon and Andrew is evidence of Jesus' power: "it is, presumably, a mark of the [authority] of Jesus that he could make an outrageous demand without explanation and receive instant obedience."[128]

1:19 *And when he had gone a little further thence, he saw James the son of Zebedee, and John his brother, who also were in the ship mending their nets:* The word "preparing" would probably be a better translation than "mending," as it reflects the verb's basic meaning of "to put in order."[129] Because fishing was done at night and mending/preparing was done during the day, either some time has passed since Simon and Andrew were called or Mark is taking a small liberty with the chronology, probably to make the contrast between the two callings more vivid.

The New Rendition uses the name "Jacob" instead of "James." This translation choice is uncommon but justifiable. The name rendered as "James"[130]

---

127. Collins, *Mark,* 156 note b.

128. France, *Gospel of Mark,* 97.

129. Marcus, *Mark 1–8,* 181.

130. There are actually two versions of the Greek word in the NT; one reflects the way the name is rendered in the LXX. Since the earliest English translation of the NT, translators have maintained the distinction between these two different Greek forms by rendering *Iakōb* as "Jacob" (such as in 12:26) and *Iakōbos* as "James." Note that there is no difference in meaning or referent between the two. John Painter, "James, Brother of Jesus," in *Encyclopedia of the Bible and Its Reception,* 14 vols. to date (Berlin: De Gruyter, 2009–), 13:714.

is a Greek form of the Hebrew name normally translated as "Jacob." While the English name "James" can be traced back to "Jacob,"[131] modern English speakers are generally unaware of this, and thus the name's connection to the HB is lost. This would not have been the case with Mark's original audience: just as names like "Simon" would have brought to mind figures from Israel's past, so "Jacob" would have conjured memories of Abraham's grandson. Thus, in order to better reflect the Jewish roots of the text and the experience of Mark's early audiences, the New Rendition uses "Jacob" instead of "James."

1:20 *And straightway he called them: and they left their father Zebedee in the ship with the hired servants, and went after him:* Because of the seriousness with which the command to honor father and mother was taken, their actions here would have likely been regarded as a dereliction of duty.

HB Allusions. In 1 Kings 19, Elijah calls Elisha to follow him. Elisha leaves his occupation but asks for—and receives—permission to say goodbye to his parents before following Elijah. If this story was on Mark's mind, then Jesus, like Elijah, is a prophet acquiring disciples. But there is also a significant difference in that Jesus' disciples do not ask for (and do not receive and are not expected to have) permission to say goodbye to their parents before following Jesus, which suggests that following Jesus requires an even greater level of devotion and obedience than following an HB prophet.

These stories of calling disciples are also similar to Exodus 3:1–2, where Moses is called as he works as a shepherd, and Judges 6:11–12, where Gideon is called as he threshes grain. These parallels would emphasize Jesus' role as an authorized messenger from God and the disciples' role as being called from their daily work.

The Two Call Stories Compared. The two stories of Jesus calling disciples are very similar; each contains the following elements:

1. a participle that shows Jesus' movement

2. the verb "he saw"

3. a phrase describing the future disciples going about their daily occupation

---

131. "Jacob" underwent several phonetic shifts while passing through Latin and French. See *Oxford English Dictionary,* online ed., s.v. "James," http://www.oed.com/view/Entry/100704.

4. Jesus' call
5. the disciples follow
6. a mention of leaving their occupation[132]

Given how similar these stories are and how brief they are, it is perhaps surprising that Mark did not collapse them into one story. Thus their presentation as two separate stories is likely significant; it seems that Mark intended the audience to compare the two.

One major difference between the two stories stands out: Simon and Andrew are in the water with a net—no boat, no hired hands.[133] James and John, on the other hand, are much more prosperous, with a boat and servants. It appears that an important part of Mark's message is that Jesus called his disciples from a variety of socioeconomic positions.

Another difference between the two stories is timing, since fishing was done at night but mending/preparing the nets was done during the day. Perhaps the point of this contrast is to emphasize the universality of Jesus' call or the fact that, unlike his disciples, Jesus was busy with his "fishing" (for disciples) both day and night.

There is also some heightening from the first call to the second: Simon and Andrew leave only nets, but James and John leave more prosperous circumstances, not to mention their own father.

Analysis

Given Mark's emphasis on discipleship, it is no accident that the first story of Jesus' ministry shows Jesus calling disciples. And considering the close proximity of this call story to the note that John the Baptist has been arrested, there is some foreshadowing of the challenges that the disciples will face. The view of discipleship presented in this brief call story is one of instant obedience, even at great personal cost, to a command issued with authority. The socioeconomic contrast between the two calls also hints at themes that will be later developed in Mark more fully.

The summary of Jesus' teachings in 1:14–15, with its talk of the appointed time and the kingdom of God, leads the audience to expect something absolutely momentous to happen next, but instead, in a classic example of Mark's irony, Jesus asks four rather ordinary men to follow him. This

---

132. See Marcus, *Mark 1–8*, 182.

133. It is possible to read 1:19 as implying that, like James and John, Simon and Andrew were in a boat (compare Luke 5:3).

surprising turn of events encourages a reexamination of what exactly the kingdom of God means: its coming is not a dramatic event but rather will be manifested through seemingly ordinary actions. Calling disciples as the inaugural act of Jesus' ministry is an illustration of the parable of the mustard seed (4:31) as "the kingdom of God comes not with fanfare but through the gradual gathering of a group of socially insignificant people in an unnoticed corner of provincial Galilee."[134]

Coming so soon after two other instances where the audience's expectations were dashed (when John preaches of a coming "strong one" but instead a seemingly unimpressive man shows up for baptism, and when the gift of the Holy Spirit doesn't lead to great displays of power but rather a wilderness temptation), Mark continues to show that Jesus will not meet the prevailing expectations.

In other stories from the ancient world where disciples choose to follow a teacher, the story normally emphasizes the disciples' reasons for choosing the teacher (such as seeing him perform a miracle). The conspicuous absence of the disciples' reasons for following Jesus emphasizes that Jesus' brief words were filled with power and authority. His authority is also emphasized by the fact that, contrary to normal practice, he chose his disciples; they did not choose him. While the issue of Jesus' authority is not explicitly raised in this story, it will be in the next one; Mark is doing a bit of foreshadowing and slowly developing this theme.

One of the most common literary techniques used in the Gospel of Mark is sandwiching,[135] where one story (the "meat") is surrounded by two similar stories (the two pieces of bread), with the purpose of calling attention to the way that the two relate to each other. In this case, the story of the calling of these four disciples is sandwiched by references to Satan and an unclean spirit. Mark may have been hinting that the process of calling disciples and/or accepting a call to discipleship would be surrounded by satanic efforts. Another signal characteristic of Mark is the use of irony; it is present in this story in the sense that Jesus is "fishing" for disciples as he calls them to abandon their fishing to become fishers of humans.

---

134. France, *Gospel of Mark,* 94.

135. The technical term for this is *inclusio,* but a refreshingly large portion of the literature uses "sandwich" instead.

Jesus Exorcises a Demon (1:21–28)

Greek Text

21 Καὶ εἰσπορεύονται εἰς Καφαρναούμ. καὶ εὐθὺς τοῖς σάββασιν ἐδίδασκεν εἰς τὴν συναγωγήν. 22 καὶ ἐξεπλήσσοντο ἐπὶ τῇ διδαχῇ αὐτοῦ, ἦν γὰρ διδάσκων αὐτοὺς ὡς ἐξουσίαν ἔχων καὶ οὐχ ὡς οἱ γραμματεῖς. 23 καὶ εὐθὺς ἦν ἐν τῇ συναγωγῇ αὐτῶν ἄνθρωπος ἐν πνεύματι ἀκαθάρτῳ καὶ ἀνέκραξεν 24 λέγων· Τί ἡμῖν καὶ σοί, Ἰησοῦ Ναζαρηνέ; ἦλθες ἀπολέσαι ἡμᾶς; οἶδά σε τίς εἶ, ὁ ἅγιος τοῦ θεοῦ. 25 καὶ ἐπετίμησεν αὐτῷ ὁ Ἰησοῦς λέγων· Φιμώθητι καὶ ἔξελθε ἐξ αὐτοῦ. 26 καὶ σπαράξαν αὐτὸν τὸ πνεῦμα τὸ ἀκάθαρτον καὶ φωνῆσαν φωνῇ μεγάλῃ ἐξῆλθεν ἐξ αὐτοῦ. 27 καὶ ἐθαμβήθησαν ἅπαντες, ὥστε συζητεῖν πρὸς ἑαυτοὺς λέγοντας· Τί ἐστιν τοῦτο; διδαχὴ καινή· κατ᾽ ἐξουσίαν καὶ τοῖς πνεύμασι τοῖς ἀκαθάρτοις ἐπιτάσσει, καὶ ὑπακούουσιν αὐτῷ. 28 καὶ ἐξῆλθεν ἡ ἀκοὴ αὐτοῦ εὐθὺς πανταχοῦ εἰς ὅλην τὴν περίχωρον τῆς Γαλιλαίας. [SBLGNT]

King James Version

21 And they went into Capernaum; and straightway on the sabbath day he entered into the synagogue, and taught. 22 And they were astonished at his doctrine: for he taught them as one that had authority, and not as the scribes. 23 And there was in their synagogue a man with an unclean spirit; and he cried out, 24 Saying, Let us alone; what have we to do with thee, thou Jesus of Nazareth? art thou come to destroy us? I know thee who thou art, the Holy One of God. 25 And Jesus rebuked him, saying, Hold thy peace, and come out of him. 26 And when the unclean spirit had torn him, and cried with a loud voice, he came out of him. 27 And they were all amazed, insomuch that they questioned among themselves, saying, What thing is this? what new doctrine is this? for with authority commandeth he even the unclean spirits, and they do obey him. 28 And immediately his fame spread abroad throughout all the region round about Galilee.

New Rendition

21 And they went into Capernaum. And immediately on the Sabbath he taught in the synagogue. 22 And they were amazed at his teaching, for he was teaching as one having power/authority and not like the scriptorians. 23 And immediately there was in their synagogue a man with an unclean spirit. And he exclaimed, 24 saying, "Mind your own business, Jesus of Nazareth! Have you come to destroy us? I know who you are: God's Holy One!" 25 And Jesus stopped him, saying, "Silence! And come out of him." 26 And convulsing him and crying out with a loud voice, the unclean spirit came out of him. 27 And all were astonished, so they questioned, saying, "What is this new teaching with power/authority? And he even commands the unclean spirits and they obey him." 28 And immediately news about him went out everywhere, in all the region of Galilee.

Notes

1:21 *And they went into Capernaum:* "They" presumably refers to Jesus and the four disciples who were just called.

Capernaum was on the north side of the Sea of Galilee; studies suggest that it had between a thousand inhabitants[136] and ten times that figure.[137]

and straightway on the sabbath day he entered into the synagogue, and taught: It is unclear whether "he entered" should be included in the text; some ancient manuscripts omit it.[138] The Jewish Sabbath is on Saturday. "Sabbath" is plural here, which leads to two different interpretations:

1. Jesus taught on more than one Sabbath.
2. This is just a customary usage meaning one Sabbath that should not be translated as a plural.

If there is a new creation theme in the beginning of chapter 1, then this verse is the Sabbath of the Creation week. Perhaps ironically, this is a very busy day of work for Jesus.

There are remains of a third-century synagogue in Capernaum, but there is dispute as to whether that synagogue was built on top of the remains of an earlier synagogue (which likely would have dated to the time of Jesus) or on a private home.

Synagogue worship was led by a layperson (not a priest, whose responsibilities were tied to the temple, and not by rabbis, who did not yet have a formalized role) with some familiarity with the scripture, such as a scribe. If a scribe normally led the service in this synagogue, it might explain why the people thought to compare Jesus' teaching style to that of the scribes.

This verse, despite its sparseness, is telling: "[the wording] might suggest that this unknown man of Nazareth took the initiative in imposing himself on the congregation, but the right to teach in the synagogue was controlled by its leaders (Acts 13:15), and the fact that Jesus was invited or allowed to do so suggests that, despite the role of this [story] in Mark's narrative as Jesus' first public appearance, he had already been active in the area long enough to be known and respected."[139]

---

136. Matthew J. Grey, "Simon Peter in Capernaum: An Archaeological Survey of the First Century Village," in *The Ministry of Peter the Chief Apostle: The 43rd Annual Brigham Young University Sperry Symposium,* ed. Frank F. Judd Jr., Eric D Huntsman, and Shon D. Hopkin (Provo, Utah: Religious Studies Center; Salt Lake City: Deseret Book, 2014), 31.

137. Stein, *Mark,* 84.

138. Collins, *Mark,* 161 note b.

139. France, *Gospel of Mark,* 101.

It might seem odd to be told that Jesus taught without providing the content of his teaching, but this highlights Jesus' authority by removing the potential distraction of the content of his teaching.[140]

There has been a narrowing focus of geographical references: from Galilee (1:14), to near the sea of Galilee (1:16), to the village of Capernaum (1:21), to a synagogue (1:21).[141] This structure, if intentional, might exist in order to

1. focus the audience's attention by zeroing in on one specific locale.

2. call attention to the idea of a synagogue as sacred space, which makes the presence of the unclean spirit all the more ironic.

3. mirror the text's move from general statements about Jesus' ministry to a specific incident.

1:22 *And they were astonished at his doctrine: for he taught them as one that had authority:* Their astonishment likely has a negative cast: "the response to Jesus' words and deeds has overtones of fear and alarm; it reflects an awareness of the disturbing character of his presence."[142]

The noun for "doctrine" (Greek: *didachē*) has the same root as the verb translated as "taught" in the previous verse, in this verse, and in the next verse. "Teaching" would probably be a better translation here, both to emphasize the similarities between these four words and to avoid implying that certain concepts ("doctrine") were taught, especially since the exorcism itself might be the teaching.

"Authority" can also be translated as "power."

and not as the scribes: Scribes were associated with three main tasks: interpreting the law of Moses, teaching the law of Moses, and acting as judges.

The common perception was that scribes had no real authority of their own but rather enjoyed an expertise related to sacred texts; they would have been considered religious authorities of a fairly low level. Most scribes were associated with the Pharisees, although it was possible for a scribe to be part of any or no Jewish sect.

Because scribes were seen as teachers of the tradition, they are frequently contrasted with Jesus, who teaches not from tradition but from his own authority/power, which sometimes contradicts the tradition.

---

140. Unless the "teaching" is not a sermon, but the exorcism itself—a possibility that will be discussed in the Analysis of 1:21–28.

141. Collins, *Mark,* 162.

142. Lane, *Gospel according to Mark,* 72 n. 110.

Whether all scribes were united in opposition to Jesus or whether it just seems that way because Mark included stories of oppositional scribes[143] is difficult to determine.

Determining an appropriate translation for "scribe" is very difficult; no one English word quite captures the right nuance:

1. "Scribe" is not an ideal choice because it implies someone who simply copies texts.

2. "Lawyer" is inadequate because it suggests secular and commercial concerns.

3. "Biblical scholar" suggests something too modern and academic.[144]

4. "Scholar" lacks the sense of religious authority.

5. "Scripturalist" is inadequate because it means "one who follows the scriptures."

The New Rendition uses "scriptorian," a word perhaps unique to the Latter-day Saint tradition. Its use in Latter-day Saint discourse is generally positive and so has the same unexpected effect as the reference to scribes would have had for Mark's early audience.

1:23 *And there was in their synagogue:* The Greek text, but not the KJV, contains the word "immediately" (Greek: *euthys*) in this verse; it links closely the issue of Jesus' authority (from the previous verse) to the conflict with the unclean spirit.

a man with an unclean spirit; and he cried out: Instead of "with" (Greek: *meta*), this verse has "in" (Greek: *en*), so it could be translated as "a man in an unclean spirit," leading to the following possibilities:

1. The unclean spirit should be understood as something like a jacket that one might put on or take off.

2. The man is completely contained "in" the demon; it has, in effect, swallowed him whole.

3. Because Greek prepositions are often imprecise, the use of "in" instead of "with" may not be significant here.

In any case, the unclean spirit would have made the man ritually unclean[145] (see appendix E: "Demonology in Mark's Gospel"). And its presence in a synagogue may be a criticism of the prevailing religious system, with its scribes wedded to tradition. Perhaps the demon is summoned by Jesus' novel teaching or simply by his presence as one who teaches with authority

---

143. But see 12:28–34 for an exception to the pattern.

144. Not to mention how it would offend those doing the translation.

145. Witherington, *Gospel of Mark,* 90.

or more generally because he is the Son of God. Regardless, the unclean spirit is an inadvertent but powerful witness to the authority that Jesus holds and the threat that he presents to evil powers.

1:24 *Saying, Let us alone; what have we to do with thee:* The phrase "what have we to do with thee" would literally be translated as "what to us and to you?" but it is an idiom. Possible English translations include:

1. What do we have to do with each other?
2. You don't/shouldn't have anything to do with us.
3. What do we have in common?
4. Why are you bothering us?
5. Why are you interfering with us?
6. Go away and leave me alone![146]
7. Mind your own business!

This same idiom is used in the LXX, with two slightly different meanings:

1. Why is there hatred between us?[147]
2. What do we have in common?[148]

The translation here uses "mind your own business" as it is idiomatic and conveys a similar meaning, but the Greek text is a question (so the unclean spirit asks two questions in this verse).

Three things stand out about the unclean spirit's statement:

1. It is quoting scripture by using an idiom from the LXX. Especially given the reference to the scribes and the synagogue setting, it may be significant that the demon is quoting scripture; the point would be that ability to quote scripture is no guarantee of righteousness.
2. It initiates the conversation with Jesus only to accuse Jesus of meddling with him. This is best understood as interpreting Jesus' authoritative teaching as meddling with the ability of evil to prevail. The unclean spirit has interpreted that teaching as an existential threat: "the demon seems to be suggesting that by his teaching there, Jesus had invaded the territory of this spirit."[149]

---

146. France, *Gospel of Mark*, 103.

147. Judg. 11:12 (KJV: "What hast thou to do with me?"); 2 Sam. 16:10 (KJV: "What have I to do with you?"); 2 Sam. 19:22 (KJV: "What have I to do with you?"); 1 Kgs. 17:18 (KJV: "What have I to do with thee?"); and 2 Chr. 35:21 (KJV: "What have I to do with thee?").

148. 2 Kgs. 3:13 (KJV: "What have I to do with thee?"); and Hosea 14:8 (KJV: "What have I to do any more with . . . ?").

149. Witherington, *Gospel of Mark*, 91.

3. The use of "us" in the statement. There are three ways this could be interpreted:

   a. It refers to the man and the unclean spirit.

   b. It refers to all unclean spirits; this spirit is speaking on their behalf.

   c. It refers, at least metaphorically, to the scribes—those most likely to see Jesus' authoritative teaching as meddling. This would be a subtle allusion, but it makes sense of the juxtaposition of 1:22 and 1:23, where immediately after Jesus is compared with the scribes, the unclean spirit accuses Jesus with a comparative idiom.

Because the spirit asks to be left alone, Mark may be conveying that evil forces make what can seem to be reasonable requests to be ignored, but this request is incompatible with Jesus' ministry; Jesus takes the position that evil cannot be left alone. There is also some irony or even hypocrisy since the demon requests to be left alone but is the one who isn't leaving Jesus alone but rather initiating a conversation with him.

thou Jesus of Nazareth: Several theories are offered to explain why the unclean spirit calls Jesus "Jesus of Nazareth" and why Mark would have included this detail:

1. The demon is making a pun on the similarity between Nazareth and Nazarene.

2. The fact that Jesus is currently in Capernaum implies that the unclean spirit knows things about Jesus that are not otherwise obvious and thus suggests its powers.

3. "In ancient magical texts the magician often invokes the name of a god or demon and uses 'I know you' or a similar formula in order to gain control over it."[150] (Most scholars accept the idea of naming someone in order to control them, but a minority do not.[151]) So the naming of Jesus by the demon may be an effort by the demon to gain control over Jesus.

art thou come to destroy us: This sentence can be read two different ways:

1. As a statement ("you have come to destroy us"), which would clarify the charge of interference from the previous statement.

2. As a question (as the KJV takes it), paralleled with the previous question.

"Come" could mean "come to Capernaum" or "come to earth." If the latter, then this question (or statement) is part of the demon's ability to recognize who Jesus is.

Given that the other statements the demon makes about Jesus ("Jesus of Nazareth," "the Holy One of God") are accurate, perhaps this statement

---

150. Marcus, *Mark 1–8,* 187.
151. Guelich, *Mark 1–8:26,* 57.

is accurate as well, and the audience should conclude that destroying evil spirits was an important component of Jesus' earthly mission.

I know thee who thou art: The demon doesn't just announce who Jesus is, but announces first that it knows who Jesus is. This is important to Mark's picture of discipleship: being able to identify Jesus is obviously not enough to be a disciple—even the demons can do that (James 2:19). And when Jesus calls disciples, he doesn't call them to learn his identity; rather, he calls them to do what he does and to follow him.

the Holy One of God: "The" indicates a special status here, one not shared with others. This phrase could mean "the holy one who comes from God" or "the holy one who belongs to God."

It is possible that this statement should be read as a title: "I know who you are, you Holy One of God."[152] In that case, there would be a good parallel to the previous sentence, where the unclean spirit identifies Jesus as "Jesus of Nazareth" after making a statement about him.

"Holy One of God" is a rare title, not used elsewhere in Mark, with only one other NT use,[153] and it "does not occur in ancient Jewish literature as a messianic title,"[154] although the phrase "holy one" does occur frequently in the Bible.

Because of the double naming and the outburst, "at this point a Hellenistic audience think[s] that the unclean spirit has gained the upper hand and is going to adjure Jesus not to torment it."[155] Once again, Mark creates expectations only to dash them and, in so doing, teaches that Jesus is not what people expect him to be.

Relationship to 2 Kings 4:9. In 2 Kings 4:9, Elisha is called a holy man of God; perhaps the demon's outburst here serves to make a connection in the minds of the audience between Elisha and Jesus and thus emphasize Jesus' nature as a prophet. As a prophet, the contrast between Jesus and the scribes, mentioned earlier in this passage, is emphasized since Jesus is teaching with prophetic authority and not simply as a transmitter of tradition.

---

152. Bratcher and Nida, *Translator's Handbook,* 50.

153. John 6:69 (KJV: "Son of the Living God"); it is also in the parallel story in Luke 4:34.

154. Gundry, *Mark,* 82.

155. Gundry, *Mark,* 76.

1:25 *And Jesus rebuked him, saying:* There are two different ways to understand the word "rebuke" here:

1. As a technical term for an exorcism.
2. Not a technical term but rather as related to the HB word used for God's "subjugating word" against his enemies.[156]

Hold thy peace, and come out of him: The KJV translation is far too tame; the verb here (Greek: *phimoō*) is literally "be muzzled" and "the effect is slangy and rude, like our 'Shut up!'"[157]

Why does Jesus command the demon to be silent when it is accurately identifying him?

1. Perhaps Jesus did not want the demon to be seen as trying to control him by naming him.
2. Perhaps Jesus did not want people to learn about his actual identity from a dubious source.

1:26 *And when the unclean spirit had torn him:* "Torn" probably has the sense of "convulsing."[158] It is not clear whether convulsing is a necessary part of the flight of the unclean spirit or if this is a multistep healing (compare 8:23–25), or it is simply one more insult that the demon can inflict on the man without violating Jesus' command to be silent.

and cried with a loud voice, he came out of him: "Cried" here is neuter, unlike "saying" (1:24, which was masculine). This grammatical shift likely indicates that the spirit is now speaking for itself, as opposed to speaking through the man. So this cry from the demon—not the man—is evidence that Jesus' word is being obeyed, as the demon is no longer speaking through the man.

1:27 *And they were all amazed:* While a different verb was used in 1:22 (Greek: *ekplēssō*; this verse has *thambeō*), the sentiment is the same, and so the exorcism is sandwiched by references to the amazement of the audience. The amazement is focused on the issue of Jesus' authority as manifested by his power over unclean spirits. As was the case in 1:22, there is a bit of a negative tinge to this verb, suggesting that they are in a panic at the prospect of Jesus' power and authority. Their fear may be focused on the demands

---

156. France, *Gospel of Mark,* 104.
157. Marcus, *Mark 1–8,* 189.
158. France, *Gospel of Mark,* 105. "Literally to 'tear,' but sometimes used medically of convulsions."

that Jesus could make of them or on the likelihood that his presence will attract other evil spirits.

The "all" may be another instance of Mark's hyperbole or it might be technically accurate, given that the audience would have been a relatively small group of people in the synagogue.

insomuch that they questioned among themselves, saying, What thing is this?: "Questioned" has the sense of "discussed," possibly with the negative connotation of "disputed."

There is irony in their inability to determine what happened as compared with the demon's ability to recognize Jesus.

what new doctrine is this: This phrase (along with the ones before and after it) could be translated as "What is this? A new teaching with authority."[159]

Because exorcisms were not unknown, their amazement is probably because Jesus performs this exorcism without ritual words or props; in fact, this might be the "new doctrine" that so amazed them: "what makes Jesus unique is not just that he exorcised demons but also how he did this. He did not use special incantations of adjurations. He did not scream or yell. He made no special physical manipulation or appeal to God. His exorcisms were based not on technique or knowledge but on who he is."[160] There may be a link here to the Creation account in Genesis 1, where God creates using simple verbal commands; the people would be amazed if there was someone in their midst acting as God acted.

for with authority commandeth he even the unclean spirits, and they do obey him: "Authority" can be translated as "power," which may be a preferable translation if the audience is reacting to the power shown in the exorcism.

"For with authority" might modify either "doctrine" before it or "commandeth" after it.

Ironically, their question about Jesus' teaching has already been answered: just a few verses ago, the demon told them that Jesus of Nazareth was the Holy One of God, and this explains why the demons obey him. Mark may be critiquing the amazed audience since they seem to be more impressed by the demon's obedience than by the knowledge of Jesus' identity. They have misplaced their focus and thus don't recognize that the question they are asking has already been answered.

---

159. Lane, *Gospel according to Mark,* 70 n. 106.
160. Stein, *Mark,* 90.

Both this verse and 1:22 contain references to authority/power, teaching, and amazement. It is likely Mark intended these paired references to bookend this section of text and to emphasize certain themes in the story of the exorcism. These parallels imply that Mark's focus is not on the exorcism itself but rather on what it implies about Jesus' authority and what kind of teacher he is. The note of amazement in the audience can seem positive, but it also has a sinister edge that might hint at the opposition to Jesus that will become a major theme in 2:1–3:6.

1:28 *And immediately his fame spread abroad throughout all the region round about Galilee:* The word translated as "spread abroad" does not have the connotation of a foreign country as it would in English; in this context, it means throughout all of Galilee.

The spread of Jesus' fame is ironic, given the efforts that he took to keep the unclean spirit quiet. Perhaps the point of the secretiveness was to emphasize Jesus' humility: it is clear from the text that Jesus did not release the man from the grip of the unclean spirit for self-serving reasons.

The word "all" is likely another example of Mark's penchant for hyperbole. This could mean the region of Galilee or the region surrounding Galilee, but the former is more likely.

Relationship to Zechariah 13:2. In this text, a future day when the Lord will remove unclean spirits from the land is prophesied; perhaps Jesus' action in the synagogue is the fulfillment of that prophecy. Zechariah 13:1 can be read as an allusion to Jesus' baptism and Zechariah 13:4 to the end of John the Baptist's ministry, which strengthens the connections between that text and Mark 1.

Role of the Holy Spirit. If Jesus was "possessed" by the Holy Spirit, in contrast with this man who is possessed by an unclean spirit, then comparing the two situations might be instructive. First, Jesus made a choice that led to his "possession": he chose to be baptized, which led directly (through Mark's use of "immediately") to the Spirit entering his body. By the same token, it is possible that the man with the unclean spirit at some point made a decision (or perhaps a series of decisions) that led to the unclean spirit entering his body. Next, comparing the stories suggests that the influence of neither the Holy nor the unclean spirit is irresistible, but rather that as one becomes accustomed to listening, it becomes easier to listen to it. And, ultimately, the conflict between the unclean spirit and Jesus shows that the Holy Spirit is more powerful than unclean spirits.

Analysis

Throughout the entire Gospel of Mark, Jesus' disciples will have a very difficult time understanding who he is (8:31–33). But here, at the very beginning of Jesus' ministry, an unclean spirit is able to correctly identify Jesus. Of course, this demon is not understood as a disciple but as the epitome of evil. So the message is clear: correct verbal identification of Jesus is neither a necessary nor a sufficient condition for true discipleship. The unclean spirit offers two different titles for Jesus: "Jesus of Nazareth" and "the Holy One of God." The juxtaposition of these titles is instructive because they span the range from the most earthly and mundane (identifying Jesus by his first name and town) to the most vaunted (identifying Jesus as special to God). Thus the demon recognizes the full range of Jesus' nature and its paradoxical components.

Because the audience knows that the first title is accurate, they would likely take the second title as correct as well; so, oddly, the demon becomes a source of correct information for the audience. But in the world of Mark's text, this means that a full spectrum of sources—from HB prophets, to John, to a voice from heaven, to Satan, beasts, and angels, and now even the unclean spirits—recognize who Jesus really is. The only groups that have a difficult time recognizing Jesus are his opponents—and his disciples.

Because the audience hears this exclamation concerning Jesus' identity and understands it to be accurate, they gain a position as "insiders" who understand things that the disciples do not. This might have been an important idea to Mark's community (and maybe Mark himself) who may have felt that they had missed out by not knowing Jesus during his mortal life. Perhaps part of Mark's message is that a personal association with the mortal Jesus was not necessarily more useful or important than knowing who he really is.

In the Gospels, healing miracles usually contain evidence that the person returned to their normal activities; the absence of that note after the exorcism implies that Mark's concern was elsewhere, likely on the issue of Jesus' authority and not the exorcism per se. The idea of Jesus' authority is key in this narrative. Interestingly, it is not Jesus nor the disciples—but rather the audience in the synagogue—who teaches Mark's audience about Jesus' authority. Given the comparison between Jesus' teaching and the teaching of the scribes, it is likely that the "teaching" of Jesus is the performance of the exorcism, something that scribes did not do and that showed he had authority and wasn't simply teaching about the tradition. In Mark's

Gospel, Jesus does not deliver lengthy sermons—there is no Sermon on the Mount or Farewell Discourse. But this does not mean that he does not teach. In this story, his teaching is through the performance of the exorcism.

JESUS PERFORMS MANY MIRACLES (1:29–39)

Greek Text

29 Καὶ εὐθὺς ἐκ τῆς συναγωγῆς ἐξελθόντες ἦλθον εἰς τὴν οἰκίαν Σίμωνος καὶ Ἀνδρέου μετὰ Ἰακώβου καὶ Ἰωάννου. 30 ἡ δὲ πενθερὰ Σίμωνος κατέκειτο πυρέσσουσα, καὶ εὐθὺς λέγουσιν αὐτῷ περὶ αὐτῆς. 31 καὶ προσελθὼν ἤγειρεν αὐτὴν κρατήσας τῆς χειρός· καὶ ἀφῆκεν αὐτὴν ὁ πυρετός, καὶ διηκόνει αὐτοῖς.

32 Ὀψίας δὲ γενομένης, ὅτε ἔδυ ὁ ἥλιος, ἔφερον πρὸς αὐτὸν πάντας τοὺς κακῶς ἔχοντας καὶ τοὺς δαιμονιζομένους· 33 καὶ ἦν ὅλη ἡ πόλις ἐπισυνηγμένη πρὸς τὴν θύραν. 34 καὶ ἐθεράπευσεν πολλοὺς κακῶς ἔχοντας ποικίλαις νόσοις, καὶ δαιμόνια πολλὰ ἐξέβαλεν, καὶ οὐκ ἤφιεν λαλεῖν τὰ δαιμόνια, ὅτι ᾔδεισαν αὐτόν.

35 Καὶ πρωῒ ἔννυχα λίαν ἀναστὰς ἐξῆλθεν καὶ ἀπῆλθεν εἰς ἔρημον τόπον κἀκεῖ προσηύχετο. 36 καὶ κατεδίωξεν αὐτὸν Σίμων καὶ οἱ μετ' αὐτοῦ, 37 καὶ εὗρον αὐτὸν καὶ λέγουσιν αὐτῷ ὅτι Πάντες ζητοῦσίν σε. 38 καὶ λέγει αὐτοῖς· Ἄγωμεν ἀλλαχοῦ εἰς τὰς ἐχομένας κωμοπόλεις, ἵνα καὶ ἐκεῖ κηρύξω, εἰς τοῦτο γὰρ ἐξῆλθον. 39 καὶ ἦλθεν κηρύσσων εἰς τὰς συναγωγὰς αὐτῶν εἰς ὅλην τὴν Γαλιλαίαν καὶ τὰ δαιμόνια ἐκβάλλων. [SBLGNT]

King James Version

29 And forthwith, when they were come out of the synagogue, they entered into the house of Simon and Andrew, with James and John. 30 But Simon's wife's mother lay sick of a fever, and anon they tell him of her. 31 And he came and took her by the hand, and lifted her up; and immediately the fever left her, and she ministered unto them. 32 And at even, when the sun did set, they brought unto him all that were diseased, and them that were possessed with devils. 33 And all the city was gathered together at the door. 34 And

New Rendition

29 And immediately, having come out of the synagogue, they came into the house of Simon and Andrew with Jacob and John. 30 But Simon's mother-in-law was lying down sick with a fever, and immediately they speak to him about her. 31 And having come to her, he raised her up, having grasped her hand. And the fever left her, and she ministered to them.

32 When it was evening, after sunset, they kept bringing to him all who were sick and who were demon-possessed. 33 And all the city was gathered at the

he healed many that were sick of divers diseases, and cast out many devils; and suffered not the devils to speak, because they knew him. 35 And in the morning, rising up a great while before day, he went out, and departed into a solitary place, and there prayed. 36 And Simon and they that were with him followed after him. 37 And when they had found him, they said unto him, All men seek for thee. 38 And he said unto them, Let us go into the next towns, that I may preach there also: for therefore came I forth. 39 And he preached in their synagogues throughout all Galilee, and cast out devils.

door. 34 And he healed many who were sick with various diseases, and he cast out many demons. But he did not allow the demons to speak because they knew him.

35 And very early, having risen up while it was still night, he went out and departed into a deserted place and was praying there. 36 And Simon and those with him searched for him. 37 And having found him, they say to him, "Everyone is looking for you!" 38 And he says to them, "Let's go somewhere else, into the nearby villages, that I might proclaim there also, because this is why I came." 39 And he went proclaiming in their synagogues in all of Galilee and casting out demons.

Notes

1:29 *And forthwith, when they were come out of the synagogue, they entered into the house of Simon and Andrew, with James and John:* "Forthwith" in this context can

1. be a simple narrative marker meaning "and next" or "and then."
2. mean "immediately" and thus
   a. imply a link between the story of the man with the unclean spirit and this story.
   b. imply a sense of a rushing narrative.
3. indicate distance. While it is uncertain, there is some archaeological evidence suggesting that Peter's home was only a few yards away from the synagogue in Capernaum,[161] so there could be a quite literal element to the idea that they went immediately from the synagogue to the house.
4. indicate the speed with which Jesus moved: he did not loiter around the synagogue, basking in his new fame, but instead moved immediately to the next opportunity to spread the good news.

Some manuscripts have "he came out" instead of "they came out" here.[162]

---

161. Marcus, *Mark 1–8*, 196.
162. Metzger, *Textual Commentary*, 64.

"With James and John" modifies "they entered" not "the house of." In other words, there is no indication that James[163] and John co-own this house; rather, the group entering the house consisted of Jesus and four named disciples (and perhaps others).

1:30 *but Simon's wife's mother lay sick of a fever:* Healing stories do not normally identify the person healed beyond their gender; perhaps this referent was included since the woman was related to a disciple. Normally, a woman would have been identified by her husband, so the fact that she is called Simon's mother-in-law[164] may imply that her husband has died. If she were a widow, then the HB's outsized concern for the needs of widows and orphans—who were considered the most vulnerable members of society since they lacked anyone to advocate for their needs and care for them—may be in view here; Jesus and his disciples are shown to share this concern.

This is the only use of "fever" in the NT;[165] its root is the same as the Greek word for "fire." A fever was usually considered an illness in its own right and not a symptom of an underlying illness.

and anon they tell him of her: "Anon" means "immediately."

It is not clear whether "they" refers to the four disciples named in the previous verse or whether it refers to other people already in the house. This line is another instance of the historical present tense, likely used to draw the audience into the story by emphasizing its immediacy. It is possible that they are telling Jesus about her by way of apology for the fact that no one is available to serve him, but it is more likely that this is an implicit request for a healing.

1:31 *And he came and took her by the hand, and lifted her up:* "Came" might indicate that Jesus entered the room or that he came closer to the woman.

For Jesus to touch a woman to whom he was not related was an offense against the prevailing interpretation of the law; there are no stories involving rabbis taking a woman by the hand. The offense is compounded by the fact that Jesus is healing her on the Sabbath (although that is not made an issue in this story). It was common practice for Jesus to touch those whom he healed (for example, 5:41; 6:5; 7:32–33; 8:23–25).

---

163. See the Notes on 1:19.

164. Simon's wife is not mentioned in this story. 1 Cor. 9:5 refers to Peter's wife and possibly to her going on a missionary journey with him. (But had Peter been a remarried widower by the time of 1 Corinthians, that wife might not be the daughter of the woman mentioned in Mark.)

165. Except for the parallel story in Matt. 8:15.

In Greek, the word order is not what might be expected: first Jesus raised her, and only after that does he take her by the hand. It is possible that Mark structured the text this way to emphasize the fact that he touched her.

and immediately the fever left her, and she ministered unto them: While "immediately" is in some of the ancient manuscripts, others do not include it.[166]

Healing stories traditionally include a note at the end showing the healed person engaging in their normal life activities to demonstrate that they are fully healed.

"Ministered" can mean simple menial labor or Christian servant-leadership (see the Notes on 1:13). So this may be simple household service, with no indication of discipleship or ministering, or her "ministering" may be very significant (see the Notes on 10:43–45, where Jesus defines greatness as the willingness to serve).

Once again, it is unclear whether "them" refers to Jesus and the four named disciples or to a broader group, including people who may have already been in the house when they arrived.

Relationship to Deuteronomy 5:15. This text has several points of contact with the healing here in Mark: serving, a change in state caused by the Lord, taking by the hand, raising, and a link to the Sabbath day. If Mark had this passage in mind, then the parallels heighten the Sabbath setting but, more importantly, attest to the idea that Jesus is the Lord of the HB.

Relationship to 1 Kings 17. There are many similarities between the healing of Simon's mother-in-law and the experience of the widow of Zarephath:

1. Jesus and Elijah are introduced with minimal background information (1:9; 1 Kgs. 17:1).

2. The woman of Zarephath is a widow; Simon's spouse is perhaps deceased as well, since no wife is mentioned in the text when it would have been logical for her to have had a role in the household.

3. Because of a famine, Elijah had been in desert-like conditions near Jordan; because of the temptations, Jesus had been in the desert near Jordan.

4. Ravens fed Elijah in the desert, and later, a widow takes over the role; angels fed Jesus in the wilderness, and later, Simon's mother-in-law takes over this role as she ministers/serves Jesus.

5. The widow is going about her daily tasks when Elijah interrupts with a call to serve him; Simon was going about his daily tasks when Jesus interrupts with

---

166. Bratcher and Nida, *Translator's Handbook,* 57.

a call to serve him; in Greek, both texts use the word *opisō* ("follow (after),"
not in the KJV of 1 Kgs. 17).

6. The widow's son dies in her home; Simon's mother-in-law is sick with a fever
(whcih was sometimes thought to be fatal) in his home.

7. In LXX 1 Kings 17:18, the same Greek idiom ("What do we have to do with
each other?") used by the unclean spirit in the previous story is used by the
widow when she feels that Elijah has brought trouble to her home.

8. Elijah and Jesus have physical contact with the person who is healed.

These extensive parallels lead to the following conclusions:

1. Jesus is to be viewed as a prophet like Elijah.

2. Simon is in the role of a poor gentile widow. This may have been shocking to
early audiences of Mark's Gospel, who would not have expected to see a male
chosen by Jesus compared with a defenseless, poverty-stricken woman who
is outside of the covenant line. The fact that, in the story, the widow grows
into a person of great faith (Luke 4:25–26) suggests that while Peter's starting place might be ever-so-humble, he too has the potential to grow into a
mature spirituality.

3. Simon's mother-in-law is compared with the widow's son. This is also surprising: sons, especially of widows, had an important economic and social
role as providers for their mothers. Simon's mother-in-law would have been
on the receiving end of that caretaking. Restoring the son to life is a way of
ensuring the future protection of the widow to the extent that, the way the
story is written, the raising from the dead seems to be more about meeting
the needs of the mother than the son.[167] So making a parallel to Simon's
mother-in-law is a powerful statement about the worth of a woman who
would likely have been viewed as a liability, not an asset, to the household.
The fact that the healing story ends with a note about her "ministering" to the
household emphasizes this important point. To show her life as worthy of
renewing is a powerful commentary on Jesus' views on the value of economi-
cally "useless" women.

4. The raising of the widow's son is the first raising from the dead in the HB, so
the parallel would also have been a bit of foreshadowing for Mark's audience
because Jesus, here paralleled to Elijah, will also soon raise the dead. In fact,
the idea that Jesus does not need to do what Elijah did—repeat words three
times and stretch himself out over the boy—hints that he has even greater
power than Elijah.

---

167. Elijah's words after the raising from the dead seem to indicate that this story is
more concerned with the widow's life than the boy's. See 1 Kgs. 17:23.

Parallels with 1:23–28. The summary statement in 1:32–34 indicates that these two stories should be compared. The stories have the following points of contact:

1. In neither story does Jesus enter the building (synagogue or house) for the purpose of performing the miracle; he enters for another reason and then only performs the miracle when the need arises. This may imply something about the role of miracles in Jesus' ministry: he did not go searching for opportunities to perform them but did so only as warranted.

2. The stories suggest a parallel between the synagogue and the home; this association may have been particularly meaningful to Mark's early audiences, who would have not had dedicated buildings in which to meet but would have met in private homes. It also suggests that homes, the primary domain of women, were to be considered sacred space alongside synagogues, where a certain number of men (but not women) were needed to constitute the required number for prayer.

3. The exorcism is dramatic (with a speaking demon identifying Jesus and with astonished crowds in a public setting), but the healing is very understated (no one speaks during the healing, no one reacts with astonishment, and it happens in a private home); perhaps this is a commentary on Jesus' ability and desire to react to both dramatic and ordinary situations.

4. There is a pattern in Mark of moving from public teaching to private teaching.[168] Thus the synagogue exorcism was the public teaching (teaching was a theme in that story), and this at-home healing is the private teaching.

Simon's Mother-in-Law as a Type of Christ. There are several parallels between this woman's story and Jesus' story:

1. The word in 1:31 translated as "took" (Greek: *krateō*) is the same word used to describe efforts to seize or arrest Jesus.[169]

2. The word in 1:31 translated as "lifted up" (Greek: *egeirō*) is used to describe Jesus' Resurrection in 14:28 (KJV: "risen") and 16:6 (KJV: "risen").

3. Jesus describes the role of the Son of Man as being "to minister" (10:45), using the same word (Greek: *diakoneō*) that describes the woman's actions in 1:31. Because this verb is used rarely in Mark's Gospel, it suggests a connection between this woman's actions and Jesus' own ministry.

---

168. See 7:1–16 to 7:17–23; 9:14–27 to 9:28–29; and 10:1–9 to 10:11–12. See also Miller, *Women in Mark's Gospel*, 25.

169. See 12:12 (KJV: "lay hold"); 14:1 (KJV: "take him"); 14:44 (KJV: "lead him away"); and 14:46 (KJV: "took").

4. Isaiah 42:6–7 reads, "I the Lord have called thee in righteousness, and will hold thine hand, and will keep thee, and give thee for a covenant of the people, for a light of the Gentiles; To open the blind eyes, to bring out the prisoners from the prison, and them that sit in darkness out of the prison house." The LXX uses the same verb for "hold" as is used for Jesus' taking the woman's hand here, perhaps suggesting a ritual element associated with being a chosen one and making a link between Jesus and the woman.

1:32 *And at even, when the sun did set, they brought unto him all that were diseased, and them that were possessed with devils:* If chapter 1 is understood to be a stereotypical day in Jesus' ministry, then this time reference indicates that that day is now over (since the Jews considered days to end at sunset).

There are two possible reasons for the doubled time references ("at even" and "when the sun did set") here:

1. Mark has a penchant for doubled time references (1:35; 4:35; 13:24; 14:1, 12; 15:42; 16:2), so perhaps this is just an issue of style.

2. Mark wanted to emphasize that it was no longer the Sabbath. Jeremiah 17:21–22 was interpreted to mean that one couldn't carry anything on the Sabbath (perhaps with an exception when life was at risk), so carrying a sick person to be healed would have been considered a Sabbath violation.

The "all" is likely Mark's hyperbole; the purpose would be to emphasize Jesus' popularity. It may also link to earlier in the chapter when "all" of Judea went to John for baptism.

1:33 *And all the city was gathered together at the door:* The city is Capernaum, which likely had at least one thousand people[170] and perhaps ten times that amount, so this is almost certainly hyperbole.

1:34 *And he healed many that were sick of divers diseases:* There is a contrast between "all" in the previous verse and "many" here; there are a few ways to understand the difference:

1. Jesus did not heal all of those who sought healing but only a subset.

2. Mark was not concerned with precision, and the distinction makes no difference: "many" here is equivalent to "all" in the previous verse.

3. Jesus did not have time to heal all of them (especially if the numbers were close to "all" ten thousand residents of Capernaum); this would explain why they will seek him out in 1:37.

4. While "all" were gathered, only some (the "many") required healing.

---

170. Jonathan L. Reed, *Archaeology and the Galilean Jesus: A Re-examination of the Evidence* (Harrisburg, Pa.: Trinity Press International, 2000), 83.

and cast out many devils; and suffered not the devils to speak, because they knew him: A different word is used for "devils" here (Greek: *daimonion*) than for "unclean spirit" in 1:23, but it is likely that Mark used these words interchangeably.

In the previous exorcism story, it appeared that Jesus did not allow the demon to speak because it knew his identity, but this was not specified in the story; here, however, Mark does specify the reason for the command for silence. It is perhaps significant that this is the detail—the only detail—that is included from the exorcism story in this summary statement. It suggests that the key point of that exorcism is the role of the demon in identifying Jesus.

_____

Narrative Structure. These verses serve as a summary statement,[171] indicating that the stories related in 1:21–28 and 1:29–34 were not the only exorcisms and healings that Jesus performed, but the only ones that Mark recounted in depth. Why were those particular stories shared? Theories include:

1. These were "textbook cases," illustrating Jesus' exorcism and healing practice.
2. These were unusual cases for one reason or another (perhaps the link to Jesus' authority for the exorcism and the healing of a disciple's family member? Or perhaps for symbolic reasons?) and therefore included for their novelty.
3. These were the only stories that Mark knew in detail.

While the question of why these stories were included is not answerable with any certainty, the position that the interpreter chooses will have a large impact on how the stories are understood.

_____

The Sabbath. Jesus performed healings and exorcisms on the Sabbath earlier in this chapter, but it appears that many of the people of Capernaum did not feel that it was acceptable to bring the afflicted to Jesus until after the Sabbath was over. There are three different ways that this might be understood:

1. While the theme of Sabbath healings is not explored here, it will become central in the next chapter, so Mark is doing a bit of foreshadowing in anticipation of the key themes of chapter 2.
2. Private healing events (in a synagogue or a home), but not public ones, were considered appropriate on the Sabbath—or at least less likely to cause problems for Jesus with the authorities.
3. Perhaps Peter's family was less orthodox in their observance of the Sabbath than many of their neighbors.

_____

171. Other summary statements in Mark may include 1:39; 3:10–12; and 6:53–56.

1:35 *And in the morning, rising up a great while before day, he went out, and departed into a solitary place, and there prayed:* This would have been between 3 am and 6 am.

The text is not clear as to whether Jesus is departing from the house or from Capernaum; it may be the former since the verb here is normally used when Jesus leaves enclosed spaces.

While "solitary" is the same word translated as "wilderness" in 1:3, 4, and 13, here it describes not a desert but an area near Capernaum, presumably consisting of cultivated land, that would have been free of people. The word "deserted" captures the link to the references to the wilderness in the prologue and suggests that Jesus is staying true to the pattern of John's wilderness ministry. Jesus may even be deliberately reorienting his ministry back to the wilderness (in a thematic or theological sense, if not a literal sense) and away from the crush of people in the city. Given the important role of the Spirit in the wilderness, perhaps the implication of this section is that Jesus was seeking the Spirit to know what he should do next.

Given that there are three separate references (in the morning, before day, and in a solitary place) that point to Jesus' efforts to be alone, it appears that Mark wanted to emphasize this idea, especially since, between three and six in the morning, Jesus could presumably have stayed in the house and prayed without interruption. There are several possible ways to understand the triple emphasis on Jesus' solitude in this story:

1. If the last section of text is read as a typical day of ministry, then—despite having just finished a day filled with healings and exorcism—Jesus is once again awake and active very early.

2. Perhaps Jesus had to get up this early to avoid crowds; the point of these extreme time references is to highlight Jesus' popularity and illustrate how persistent the crowds were.

3. It wasn't ultimately possible for Jesus to be left alone since his disciples interrupt him. Perhaps Mark is commenting on Jesus' lack of omnipotence: as a mortal he had limitations and wasn't willing (or able?) to override Simon's agency in his efforts to find Jesus.

4. This story contains the first real action or speech of the disciples after their decision to follow Jesus, and it is clearly contrary to Jesus' wishes. Throughout the text, Mark will present the disciples as willing to follow Jesus but not entirely clear on how best to do that. It is possible that Jesus' efforts here were to put some space between him and his own disciples.

Mark does not include the content of the prayer, thus focusing on the fact of the prayer as opposed to its subject matter. There are two schools of thought regarding this prayer:

1. This is a routine prayer: early morning prayer "was a characteristic of Jewish piety."[172]

2. This is a special prayer, included in the record because, at a key moment in Jesus' ministry, he sought special guidance for the next phase of his mission. The discussion in the next verses about Jesus' purposes for "coming" and his plans to move to nearby towns supports this understanding of the prayer. Jesus' ministry is bookended by this prayer and the prayer in Gethsemane; if there is a parallel between the two, then it is possible that Jesus no more wanted to leave Capernaum than he wanted to drink the bitter cup, but he did both out of obedience. And there is an intriguing difference between the two prayers: in Gethsemane, Jesus wanted his disciples to "watch" (but they couldn't) while here, Jesus has apparently tried to put some distance between himself and his disciples (but he couldn't). This difference might emphasize the inability of the disciples to follow Jesus at key moments in his ministry and thus contrast his perfect obedience with their limited efforts.

1:36 *And Simon and they that were with him followed after him:* The people with Simon are likely the other three named disciples, but it is also possible that others have joined him, perhaps members of Simon's household who have witnessed Jesus' teaching and miracles.[173]

The verb does not imply that they literally followed Jesus as he left but rather that they later realized he was gone and went looking for him. "Followed" is not translating the same Greek word that is used to describe discipleship in Mark's Gospel: here, "followed" has the connotation of hunted, searched, or tracked down. It is the same verb used in LXX Genesis 31:36, which the KJV translates as "hotly pursued"; this is the only NT use of this verb.

There may be some irony here: the disciples are supposed to be "following" Jesus, but they are doing it in an inappropriate way that has more in common with hunting him down. Jesus has taken great pains to be alone, but the disciples foil his plans.

1:37 *And when they had found him, they said unto him, All men seek for thee:* Because they were able to find him, Jesus was likely in a place where he normally went to pray.

"Said" is an example of Mark's use of the historical present tense.

The "all" is likely more Markan hyperbole.

---

172. Stein, *Mark,* 100.

173. Thomas A. Wayment and Richard Neitzel Holzapfel, *Making Sense of the New Testament* (Salt Lake City: Deseret Book, 2010), 39.

1:38 ***And he said unto them, Let us go into the next towns:*** There are several different ways to interpret what Jesus is saying here:

1. Notice the first-person plural ("let us")—Jesus is inviting the disciples along with him. The point of the exchange is to extend an invitation to the disciples to follow him.

2. Jesus' statement may be a direct response to Simon's words that everyone is seeking for him:

   a. Perhaps Jesus feels that they are seeking him for the wrong reasons and thus he wants to move on. The reference to preaching in the next phrase—combined with the assumption that people were not as interested in a preacher as a miracle worker—may support this view.

   b. Perhaps Jesus feels that if people are seeking him, his work is done and it is time to move on; now that interest in his ministry has been generated, others can continue to teach the gospel (including, perhaps, Simon's mother-in-law, who "ministers").

3. Perhaps Jesus' response should be interpreted ironically or even humorously: Simon says, "Everyone is looking for you!" and Jesus responds (in effect), "Then let's leave!" The point would be that Jesus' ministry was not about pleasing people but about doing what God wanted him to do (and the early morning prayer for guidance had revealed that God wanted him to move on).

4. Jesus may be suggesting that the size or tenor of the crowd was such that continuing in Capernaum was not possible for logistical reasons—and if he can't pray privately in the middle of the night without people interrupting him, that certainly seems to be true.

that I may preach there also: for therefore came I forth: This phrase could refer to:

1. Why Jesus left Capernaum that morning to pray: he wanted guidance for his ministry and received the inspiration that it was time to move on.

2. Why Jesus came to earth: he came to preach to many and therefore couldn't spend all of his time in Capernaum. This statement may serve to take the sting out of his departure from Capernaum—it is nothing personal (perhaps Simon's words could be interpreted as taking it personally, and it is likely that some of the people seeking Jesus were friends and family of the disciples) but rather a sad fact of his ministry.

3. It could be ambiguous, suggesting both Capernaum and earth.

1:39 ***And he preached in their synagogues throughout all Galilee:*** The same two verbs that Jesus used to describe his mission at the end of the last verse (KJV: "preach" and "came") are used in this verse (KJV: "preached"; "came" is left untranslated), which emphasizes that Jesus did exactly as he planned to do and was faithful to his mission.

and cast out devils: Preaching in the synagogues and casting out devils is what Jesus did in Capernaum, but he also healed people although healings are not mentioned here. There are several explanations for this omission:

1. He didn't heal elsewhere.
2. He did heal, and Mark wants the audience to assume that based on the pattern.
3. He did heal, but Mark doesn't know any of the stories about those healings, so he doesn't mention them.
4. The lack of reference to healing is not particularly significant.

Analysis

Mark begins Jesus' ministry with the exorcism of a man and the healing of a woman; this is an important early indication of the prominence of women in Mark's Gospel.[174] The healing of Peter's mother-in-law is the shortest healing miracle in the Gospel of Mark. Given Mark's penchant for lengthy stories (at least relative to the other evangelists), the very brevity of this account might be noteworthy. Perhaps Mark has whittled the account down to the scantest of details in order to emphasize what has been included: in this case, that Jesus touches a woman—contra social norms—and that she ministers to them. The concept of ministering is crucial to this story, although it is difficult to pin down the precise meaning of the word. But even if "ministered" here means menial table service, it anticipates 9:33–37 and 10:43–45, where the essence of Christian discipleship will be ministering, with the same root word used there. It will be this term that Jesus uses to describe his own ministry.

Discipleship is a key concern in Mark's Gospel, and it is associated with women more than with men, at least in terms of the concept of ministering and the ability to be model disciples. The male disciples whom Jesus has called will struggle throughout the story with what it means to minister (10:35–45); in Mark's Gospel, only Jesus, angels, and women minister. Simon's mother-in-law can be viewed as a model disciple: one healed by Jesus who responds to his loving care by serving/ministering to others. And if ministering implies that one is a disciple, then this story recounts the call of a disciple: Simon's mother-in-law. (It might seem odd to call a disciple and not mention her or him again, but the same thing happens with Levi in the next chapter.)

---

174. Kelber, *Mark's Story of Jesus*, 21–22.

The word "forthwith" at the beginning of this story implies that the healing happens on the Sabbath (something that the note about crowds bringing the sick to Jesus after the sun sets in 1:32 further emphasizes). While Sabbath controversies will become a concern in the next chapter, there is no such controversy here.

Because of the idea of Sabbath rest as a part of the coming kingdom of God, Jesus' healings on the Sabbath "should be seen as a deliberate attempt to bring in that final Sabbath rest, a time when creation would be relieved not just of the toil and turmoil of a fallen world but of disease, decay, and death as well. From this perspective, there was no better time to heal a person than on the Sabbath as an indicator that the ultimate Sabbath was coming."[175]

Her healing fills out the meaning of discipleship in another way: while the story of the calling of the disciples (1:16–20) is often understood to mean that the disciples were leaving everything to follow Jesus, this story features Simon back in his home, where he has at least one person dependent on him. Perhaps it would be better to view Simon as having consecrated (instead of abandoned) his home, since Jesus seems to be using it as a base of operations. This story may also imply that Jesus will now care for those who were under Simon's care, since Simon has chosen to follow Jesus.

In Mark's narrative, 1:37 contains the very first word or deed from the disciples after they have decided to follow Jesus. It illustrates two things, each central to how Mark treats the role of the disciples: on the one hand, they are trying their best; on the other hand, they often do precisely the wrong thing. In this case, they think they know what Jesus should be doing better than Jesus does. In fact, this statement can be read as comic relief, or at least irony: because Jesus has gone to great lengths to get away from the crowds, it was already obvious to him that "all" people were seeking for him. His response was to go seek a moment alone—a moment that his disciples have now interrupted in order to tell him something that he already knew! Mark suggests that the disciples do not yet know how to follow Jesus; they will need to follow him in order to figure out how to do it better. The text highlights their willingness to follow, their initial bumbling, and Jesus' unfailing patience with them.

Now that Jesus is moving his ministry beyond the disciples' own town, they will have to decide if they are willing to leave not just occupation but also home and family to follow Jesus. These verses can thus be read as their plea for Jesus to return to Capernaum so that they will not have to leave

---

175. Witherington, *Gospel of Mark*, 100.

their homes. Jesus explains that this is not the plan, creating the moment when the disciples have to decide if they really will leave everything to follow Jesus. In this sense, this becomes a second call story that invites the audience to a more profound level of discipleship. If the better understanding of the first call story is that they had no previous association with Jesus but followed only based on his command, now that they have seen him teach and perform miracles, they are being called to sacrifice more to follow him, in step with their increasing understanding of his work. One way to understand the first call story is that it is relatively easy to follow Jesus if he asks the disciples to take a break from work to watch him perform miracles. It is harder to follow Jesus when that requires getting out of bed at 3 am, going against the will of the crowd (which wants Jesus to stick around and which likely includes friends and family members), and traveling away from home and family. Fortunately, it is possible to understand the healing and ministering of Simon's mother-in-law as a sign to the disciples that all matters—physical and spiritual—at home will be tended to in their absence.

Jesus Heals a Leper (1:40–45)

Greek Text

40 Καὶ ἔρχεται πρὸς αὐτὸν λεπρὸς παρακαλῶν αὐτὸν καὶ γονυπετῶν λέγων αὐτῷ ὅτι Ἐὰν θέλῃς δύνασαί με καθαρίσαι. 41 καὶ ὀργισθεὶς ἐκτείνας τὴν χεῖρα αὐτοῦ ἥψατο καὶ λέγει αὐτῷ· Θέλω, καθαρίσθητι· 42 καὶ εὐθὺς ἀπῆλθεν ἀπ' αὐτοῦ ἡ λέπρα, καὶ ἐκαθαρίσθη. 43 καὶ ἐμβριμησάμενος αὐτῷ εὐθὺς ἐξέβαλεν αὐτόν, 44 καὶ λέγει αὐτῷ· Ὅρα μηδενὶ μηδὲν εἴπῃς, ἀλλὰ ὕπαγε σεαυτὸν δεῖξον τῷ ἱερεῖ καὶ προσένεγκε περὶ τοῦ καθαρισμοῦ σου ἃ προσέταξεν Μωϋσῆς εἰς μαρτύριον αὐτοῖς. 45 ὁ δὲ ἐξελθὼν ἤρξατο κηρύσσειν πολλὰ καὶ διαφημίζειν τὸν λόγον, ὥστε μηκέτι αὐτὸν δύνασθαι φανερῶς εἰς πόλιν εἰσελθεῖν, ἀλλὰ ἔξω ἐπ' ἐρήμοις τόποις ἦν· καὶ ἤρχοντο πρὸς αὐτὸν πάντοθεν. [SBLGNT]

King James Version

40 And there came a leper to him, beseeching him, and kneeling down to him, and saying unto him, If thou wilt, thou canst make me clean. 41 And Jesus, moved with compassion, put forth his hand, and touched him, and saith unto

New Rendition

40 And a leper comes to him, begging and kneeling and saying to him, "If you are willing, you can make me clean." 41 And having become angry, he stretched out his hand, touched him, and he says to him, "I am willing.

him, I will; be thou clean. 42 And as soon as he had spoken, immediately the leprosy departed from him, and he was cleansed. 43 And he straitly charged him, and forthwith sent him away; 44 And saith unto him, See thou say nothing to any man: but go thy way, shew thyself to the priest, and offer for thy cleansing those things which Moses commanded, for a testimony unto them. 45 But he went out, and began to publish it much, and to blaze abroad the matter, insomuch that Jesus could no more openly enter into the city, but was without in desert places: and they came to him from every quarter.

Be made clean." 42 And immediately the leprosy left him, and he was clean. 43 And having sternly warned him, he immediately drove him away. 44 And he says to him, "See that you say nothing to anyone, but go, show yourself to the priest and offer, because of your cleaning, what Moses commanded for a testimony to them." 45 And having gone out, he began to preach much and to spread the word, so that he was no longer able to enter a town openly, but he was out in deserted places and they were coming to him from everywhere.

Notes

1:40 *And there came a leper to him:* It is debated whether leprosy (now known as Hansen's disease) existed in first-century Palestine; if it did, it was likely only one of many skin conditions included in the biblical term "leprosy." Regardless of precisely which medical conditions are pictured here, leprosy was associated with sin.[176] Under the law of Moses, a leper was considered ritually unclean, and there was quite a social stigma surrounding it as well. Lepers were supposed to keep their distance and warn others of their presence.

beseeching him, and kneeling down to him: Some manuscripts omit "and kneeling."[177] Determining whether it was originally present is difficult:

1. It may have been there originally and was omitted accidentally because a scribe's eye skipped between similar word endings.

2. It may not have been there originally but was added in order to make the account parallel to Matthew 8:2 and Luke 5:12 (but those verses use different verbs for "kneeling"). The fact that Matthew and Luke have "kneeling" but with different verbs suggests that the copies of Mark that they had contained a reference to kneeling, but for some reason they found the verb unacceptable and so replaced it; this unacceptability may explain why later scribes

---

176. Hence the need to make a sin offering (Lev. 14:10–32) and leprosy as a punishment for sins (Num. 12:4–12).

177. Metzger, *Textual Commentary*, 65.

removed the phrase from Mark. But one can only speculate as to what they would have found unpalatable about Mark's verb choice.

and saying unto him, If thou wilt, thou canst make me clean: The verb used here for "wilt" indicates that the leper is wondering about Jesus' willingness, not his ability, to make him clean.

The meaning of "make clean" is disputed:

1. It could refer to physically healing the man's skin condition.
2. It could mean to declare the man clean under the law of Moses (without curing the man's skin condition). The verb here is the one used in LXX Leviticus 14:2, 4 for "proclaiming clean."[178]
3. It might be ambiguous: the verb could carry either meaning, so there is no way to determine what precisely the leper was seeking.

It is difficult to determine which meaning is best here, and its meaning impacts how one thinks about other aspects of the story. Unfortunately, this is the first in a long line of interpretive conundrums in 1:40–45.

1:41 *And Jesus, moved with compassion:* Some of the Greek manuscripts read "being angry" instead of "moved with compassion" here;[179] this is one of the more significant textual variants in the Gospel of Mark.

One of the main—although admittedly counterintuitive—principles used to determine which reading was earlier is that the reading that makes *less* sense is likely to have been earlier: one can imagine a scribe changing a less-likely reading to a more-likely reading, but it is harder to imagine a scribe changing a more-likely reading to a less-likely reading.[180] Using that principle, "being angry" is likely to have been the earlier wording because one can imagine a scribe's confusion leading to a change to "moved with compassion" far more easily than one can imagine confusion over "moved with compassion" leading a scribe to change the text to "being angry." In fact, there is a very plausible reason why scribes would have wanted to change "being angry" to "compassion": fear that "pagan opponents of Christianity, like Celsus, who were known to be perusing the Gospels for incriminating evidence against the divine founder of the faith, might find here ammunition for their charges"[181] if Jesus were thought to have been angry.

---

178. Collins, *Mark,* 179.

179. Metzger, *Textual Commentary,* 65.

180. The technical term for this principle is *lectio difficilior,* Latin for "the harder reading."

181. Bruce M. Metzger and Bart D. Ehrman, *The Text of the New Testament: Its Transmission, Corruption, and Restoration,* 4th ed. (New York: Oxford University Press, 2005), 292.

Further evidence for preferring "being angry" comes from how Matthew and Luke write about this story: both of them omit any reference to anger or compassion (Matt. 8:3; Luke 5:13), likely because they were uncomfortable with Jesus' anger and therefore omitted the reference entirely. It is much more difficult to explain why they both would have omitted a reference to Jesus' compassion; another instance in Mark's Gospel where Jesus feels angry (3:5) is omitted by Matthew and Luke as well, but there is no other time in Mark's Gospel where Jesus is said to feel compassion and Matthew or Luke omit the reference.

Why, then, might the text originally have referred to Jesus' anger? There are various theories:

1. The strict warning that Jesus gives in 1:43–44 is tied to Jesus' anger as it reflects his strong emotions about the importance of keeping the matter private.

2. The doubt that the man expressed in 1:40 about Jesus' ability or willingness to heal the leper caused Jesus to be angry (but compare 9:24–25: in that passage, Jesus is not angered by a supplicant's doubt, but see also the variant reading on 9:23). Jesus is angry that anyone would doubt his willingness to decrease human suffering.

3. The story may imply that the man has already been to the priests, but they were unwilling or unable to cleanse the man.[182] Thus, Jesus' anger is addressed not at the man but at the priests who had not healed him.

4. Jesus was angry with Satan's power to cause suffering.

5. Mark 3:5 might shine light on this text: in that story, a healing is preceded with reference to Jesus' anger, which is due to the reaction of those who were watching Jesus to see if he would violate the Sabbath by performing a healing. Perhaps a similar dynamic is implied here (although this is not the Sabbath, and no opponents are present).

6. If the leper were requesting that Jesus pronounce him pure, perhaps Jesus' anger is directed at the man

   a. because he should have asked for a physical healing.

   b. because he is asking Jesus to assume the rights of a priest.

   c. because he is just asking for a shortcut—a pronouncement from Jesus that saves the trouble and expense of a trip to the temple. (This would make sense of Jesus' statement after the healing asking the leper to go to the priest and make the offering.)

   However, this theory doesn't mesh well with the fact that Jesus accedes to the man's request.

---

182. Myers, *Binding the Strong Man*, 153.

7. Jesus' anger is related to the previous story, where he decided to leave Capernaum to preach after he became very popular there. Perhaps Jesus feels that this healing will interfere with his ability to preach. (Again, it is hard to understand why Jesus would have agreed to heal the man.)

8. Jesus is angry that the leper violated the law of Moses in approaching him. (Although, again, this does not explain why Jesus would have healed the man.)

9. It is possible to interpret the anger more generically as a strong emotion; it was common for miracle workers to become physically worked up before performing miracles.[183]

10. Jesus is angry that the leper has made him unclean. (But Jesus is made unclean many times in Mark without becoming angry.)

11. It is grammatically possible that the one who is angry is the leper and not Jesus, leading to the following possibilities:

   a. The anger might be at his condition or the response of others to his condition.

   b. The leper is not angry but just strongly emotional (see #9 above).

   c. His emotional state is mentioned to justify his unclean touch.[184]

12. When Jesus performs the cleansing, he uses the divine passive ("be clean"; see the Notes on 1:42), which assumes that God is the actor. Perhaps Jesus does not support the leper's assumption that Jesus himself could heal when in fact it was God who was performing the healing. (Again, it is hard to explain why Jesus would have healed the man without correcting him if this were the case.)

13. Because only God could heal lepers, the leper is, in effect, recognizing Jesus' divinity. Jesus may therefore be angry at this inappropriate revelation of his identity.

While compassion is the most frequently mentioned emotion that Jesus feels in the Gospels, he does experience a range of feelings, including anger.[185] (See also the Notes on 1:43.)

It is also possible that "moved with compassion" is the better reading here; this may explain why, despite many possible explanations for Jesus' anger, none has commanded a consensus, and all have shortcomings. Supporters of reading "moved with compassion" note that "being angry" appears in only a few ancient manuscripts and that copyists did not feel the

---

183. See 3:5; 6:34; 7:34; and 8:2 for possible parallels.

184. Kirsopp Lake, "Εμβριμησαμενος and Ὀργισθεις, Mark 1, 40–43," *Harvard Theological Review* 16, no. 2 (1923): 197–98.

185. Restoration scripture includes references to the Lord's anger in Alma 8:29; D&C 63:32; 59:21; all three of those passages tie the Lord's anger to disobedience.

need to correct the text when Jesus is described as being angry in 3:5 and 10:14. It is also possible that the confusion came about because in Aramaic (the language Jesus spoke), the words for "pity" and "rage" are very similar.[186] It is therefore difficult to determine whether a reference to "anger" or "compassion" is more likely to have been original.

put forth his hand, and touched him, and saith unto him, I will; be thou clean: Given that the next phrase is "and touched him," "put forth his hand" is not strictly necessary. Its presence heightens the drama of the physical contact between Jesus and the leper.

Touching the leper would, under the law of Moses, have made Jesus unclean.[187] Because Jesus could heal people without touching them, the act of touch here is all the more significant. It also contrasts sharply with 2 Kings 5:1–14, where a prophet heals a leper at a distance.

In the HB, leprosy was like death, and so cleansing a leper was roughly the equivalent of raising someone from the dead.

There are two ways to understand who actually performs the healing: First, "be clean" is a divine passive, indicating that it is God who is doing the actual healing, but the name of God is not mentioned out of reverence. It was thought that only God could heal leprosy.[188] Second, Jesus uses God's power to heal the man.

1:42 *And as soon as he had spoken, immediately the leprosy departed from him, and he was cleansed:* "As soon as he had spoken" is not present in most of the ancient manuscripts.[189] The inclusion of Mark's favorite word ("immediately") emphasizes Jesus' power; the immediate healing of the leper would have been most miraculous. It also links Jesus' words to his act of healing, pointing to the power manifest in his words.

This would have been an incredible spectacle for anyone who saw it since leprosy had an obvious visible component (whether it was Hansen's disease or some other skin condition).

When Jesus touched the leper, he should have been made unclean under the law of Moses. Instead, Jesus' touch does not make Jesus unclean but makes the leper clean.

1:43 *And he straitly charged him, and forthwith sent him away:* Jesus did not literally send him away immediately—he still has more to say to him in the next verse!

---

186. Metzger, *Textual Commentary*, 65.

187. Compare 2 Kgs. 5:1–14, where the absence of physical contact is conspicuous.

188. Dowd, *Reading Mark*, 19.

189. Bratcher and Nida, *Translator's Handbook*, 67.

"Sent" is the word used for casting out demons (for example 1:34, 39; 3:15; 7:26).

"Straitly charged" is somewhat difficult to translate. Its root means "to snort like a horse," and it suggests not only an emotion but also its expression. In its only other usage in Mark (14:5), it is a statement of disapproval (KJV: "murmur"); in the only other NT usage,[190] it is an expression of deep emotion (KJV: "groan") that is not necessarily negative. It could be defined as "to express indignation by an explosive expulsion of breath."[191] It could be translated as "growling at him"[192] or "being enraged."[193]

It is difficult to determine the motive behind Jesus' apparently strong emotional expression here; any of the theories offered to explain Jesus' anger in 1:41 (see the list above) could be marshaled here as well, but all will suffer from the same problem: they cannot explain how Jesus transitions from anger at the leper, to a willingness to heal the leper, and then back to a negative emotion in the space of a few words and without any explanation. While the verb can be interpreted as forceful but not negative, it is still difficult to explain Jesus' forcefulness here.

1:44 *And saith unto him, See thou say nothing to any man:* There is a double negative[194] here ("say nothing to no one"), emphasizing the prohibition. At the same time, this command isn't absolute—the next phrase will present an exception to the rule.

It is difficult to know what to make of this prohibition. There are comparable restrictions in 5:43 and 7:36, both after spectacular healings; in all three situations, however, the audience is left to wonder how Jesus thinks it would have been possible for the news not to spread: Wouldn't the neighbors have noticed the healed leper or the girl raised from the dead? Would they not have figured out what had happened? Oddly, the demons and disciples stay quiet, but the healed people don't follow the injunction to silence. Further, in the very next story, Jesus will heal a lame man and pronounce his sins forgiven in front of a hostile crowd, making it difficult to imagine that, in this story, Jesus intended to keep his healing ability private. One way to resolve this problem (at least in this story, if not the others) is to see the command to silence as temporary: the leper is not to tell anyone

---

190. Aside from the parallel story in Matthew; see John 11:33, 38.

191. Marcus, *Mark 1–8,* 206.

192. Marcus, *Mark 1–8,* 205.

193. Witherington, *Gospel of Mark,* 99.

194. Double negatives are not considered errors in Greek usage as they would be in English; rather, they are used for emphasis.

about the healing until he has spoken to the priest and, presumably, had the priest declare him ritually clean. Perhaps the concern is that the priest will withhold the declaration of cleanness if he hears rumors that the man was healed by Jesus; maybe Jesus wants the priest's declaration to affirm the validity of his miracle.

go thy way, shew thyself to the priest: This may be a local priest or a priest at the temple in Jerusalem.

Jesus conforms to the law of Moses by sending the man to the priest to be pronounced clean. Because the next section of the text (2:1–3:6) will include controversies over Jesus' adherence to the law of Moses, this story may be a bit of scene-setting on Mark's part to show an instance when Jesus supported the requirements of the law. At the same time, it is hard to reconcile the idea that Jesus would want to conform to the law of Moses with the fact that he has just touched a leper. Perhaps the point of this saying is to emphasize, by way of contrast, that Jesus did not need to visit the priest to be pronounced clean.

Leprosy would have destroyed the man's ability to interact normally with family and friends, so Jesus is here telling him how to restore those relationships; thus Jesus is providing both physical and social/emotional healing.

offer for thy cleansing those things which Moses commanded: These offerings are explained in Leviticus 14:1–32.

for a testimony unto them: This phrase presents several interpretive challenges. First, who is "them": the priests or the people in general? Second, what does "a testimony unto them" mean?

1. Parallel language in 6:11 and 13:9 suggests the translation "a testimony against them," which could imply that:

    a. Jesus wants to showcase the priests' unwillingness to accept him, despite his confirmed ability to perform miracles.

    b. Jesus wants to point out the limitations of the sacrificial system, which is unable to provide healing and only able to provide declarations after healing has occurred naturally.

    c. In light of the controversies in 2:1–3:6 related to Jesus' observance of the law, Mark wanted to establish that not only did Jesus keep the law but also encouraged others to do so as well.

    d. Malachi 3:3–5 (which should be on the minds of Mark's audience since the text immediately before it was quoted in the prologue) explains that the Lord will "purify the sons of Levi" and will witness against the corruption of the temple leadership. Jesus' actions here might be understood as a fulfillment of that scripture.

e. Perhaps the text is designed to explain why no objective observers from Jesus' time could confirm his miraculous powers: this text would show that Jesus made an effort to have independent witnesses but was thwarted by the actions of the healed ones.

2. This is a positive testimony, designed to encourage the temple priests (and those who later hear about the miracle and the priest's de facto ratification of it) to have a testimony of Jesus' healing powers.

Left unnarrated is whether the leper actually goes to the priest or whether he disobeys Jesus (but see below for how the first word of the next verse might hint at the answer to this question).

1:45 *But he:* There are two different ways to translate "but":

1. It can have an adversarial force ("however"), which would imply that the leper did not obey Jesus' command from the previous verse.

2. It can have a sense of continuance ("and" or "now"), which would imply that the leper's actions in this verse harmonize with and follow naturally from the command in the previous verse.

Does "he" refer to the leper or to Jesus?

1. The more common interpretation is that it refers to the leper, who disobeys Jesus' command to say nothing, which complicates Jesus' plans. Support for this reading comes from the fact that the language here is always used to indicate a new subject,[195] so that would make the first "he" in this verse a reference to the leper (unless the pattern were being violated). It is also possible that one should assume that the leper went to the priest, was pronounced clean, and then became a disciple, preaching the gospel. This would see the leper as keeping the command that Jesus made (if that command were understood to be temporary).

2. It is possible that "he" refers to Jesus, so this verse refers to Jesus' going out and preaching now that the story of the leper is over. Support for this reading includes:

    a. The word "word" (Greek: *logos*) normally means "the [whole] message" (for example, 2:2; 4:14–20) of the gospel and not just one incident.

    b. "Publish" (Greek: *kēryssō*) is often translated as "preach" or "proclaim," which is Jesus' mission.

    c. If the "but" at the beginning of the verse had an adversarial force, then it makes sense of the contrast: the *leper* wasn't supposed to say anything to anyone, but *Jesus'* ministry is to preach the gospel.

---

195. Bratcher and Nida, *Translator's Handbook,* 70.

went out, and began to publish it much: It is not clear whether "went out" refers to leaving a house or a town.

"Publish" is normally translated as "preach." It is even possible to translate it as "spread the word." This would suggest that the topic of the preaching was not the healing of the leper but, more broadly, the entire gospel message. In other uses, "preaching" is always positive, and so perhaps it should be viewed that way here as well.

If the leper is the subject, he is either being shown as a model disciple, or the account drips with irony as words normally used for the spread of the gospel are used for an act of disobedience. If the latter is the case, there is more to Mark's irony: as a leper, he was not permitted to approach people, but because Jesus healed him, he is now able to interact with them—and violate Jesus' command to him. In that reading, there is an interesting comparison between this story and the last one: both show Jesus going to extraordinary lengths (to be alone, to get the leper to stay quiet) that are not successful. This surprising parallel indicates Jesus' respect for human autonomy: he'll do everything (within typical mortal powers) to encourage compliance, but he won't force it.

and to blaze abroad the matter: if the leper is the subject, then perhaps he thought that this local preaching might have been an adequate substitute for the lengthy journey to the temple and costly offering.

insomuch that Jesus could no more openly enter into the city but was without in desert places: and they came to him from every quarter: While this turn of events might seem negative, it is important to remember that it is a fairly standard response to Jesus' ministry.

The fact that 2:1 presents Jesus in Capernaum presents an apparent conflict; there are several ways that it might be resolved:

1. This phrase is to be understood symbolically: Jesus, now unable to enter cities, has in effect traded places with the leper (who would not have been allowed to be near people), and thus the factual difference with 2:1 would not be a problem.

2. This phrase is hyperbole, a hallmark of Mark's writing style.

3. The disjunction is evidence that Mark's Gospel was not written in order; perhaps the healing of the leper occurred at a different point in Jesus' ministry.

4. Enough time passes between the end of chapter 1 and the beginning of chapter 2 for the situation to change.

5. The operative word here is "openly"; 2:1 can be read to say that Jesus did not "openly" enter the city, but did so quietly or privately, and it was only after some days that people became aware that he was there.

Did the leper obey Jesus? This question is difficult to answer:

1. It depends on whether Jesus or the leper is the subject of the beginning of 1:45.
2. It depends on whether the command to "say nothing to anyone" was temporary or permanent.
3. It depends on whether the leper did or did not go to the priest.

Another option is to call the leper's actions "laudable disobedience";[196] he is technically disobedient, but only out of an overabundance of enthusiasm for the gospel message.

Analysis

The story of the leper is rather difficult to interpret due to the textual variant (was Jesus compassionate or angry?) and the ambiguity of some key terms. Nonetheless, the story showcases Jesus' miraculous healing ability and his unexpected relationship to the law of Moses.

There are several layers of irony in this story: touching a leper should make Jesus unclean, but instead it cleanses the leper. And yet the result is that Jesus, like a leper, cannot enter into any cities. And yet the people come out to him in the wilderness.

Jesus' spreading fame, despite his efforts to forestall it, is a theme throughout chapter 1. Perhaps Mark emphasized this idea in order to set the stage for 2:1–3:6, where controversies surround Jesus; chapter 1 would then contain not just healing miracles but veritable double-edged swords for Jesus since each act of healing increases the threat against his ministry and, ultimately, his life. There seems to be some ambiguity in how Mark presents miracles: on the one hand, they are evidence of Jesus' powers and often teach symbolically. On the other hand, they generate crowds that interfere with Jesus' ministry and perhaps encourage people to follow him for the wrong reasons. Depending on how the healing of the leper is interpreted, the leper's reaction to Jesus can be seen as an example of the negative outcomes of healing miracles. Regardless, there is a very real sense in which the healings that Jesus performs in chapter 1 represent an exchange of his own physical safety for that of the people he heals.

While only specifically articulated during the exorcism, Jesus' authority is a theme that undergirds all of chapter 1. From the HB prophecies of his coming, to the visionary experience after his baptism, to the calling of the

---

196. Guelich, *Mark 1–8:26,* 79.

disciples and their instant response, to the exorcism, to the two healing miracles, Jesus is presented in chapter 1 as someone with the power/authority to do extraordinary things. Jesus is someone greater than the audience could possibly have anticipated and yet in many ways more humble and unremarkable. In this rushing narrative, one thing is clear: the heavens have opened for Jesus.

Controversies
(2:1–3:6)

OVERVIEW

Mark 2:1–3:6 is a distinct section of text, containing five stories of conflict arranged in a deliberate structure. (See the end of this chapter for a discussion of the structure and its implications.) There is no reason to think that these events happened sequentially in Jesus' ministry; instead, Mark (or Mark's source) grouped them together in the same way that healing miracles are grouped in chapter 1 and parables are grouped in chapter 4.

JESUS HEALS A LAME MAN
(2:1–12)

Greek Text

1 Καὶ εἰσελθὼν πάλιν εἰς Καφαρναοὺμ δι᾽ ἡμερῶν ἠκούσθη ὅτι ἐν οἴκῳ ἐστίν· 2 καὶ συνήχθησαν πολλοὶ ὥστε μηκέτι χωρεῖν μηδὲ τὰ πρὸς τὴν θύραν, καὶ ἐλάλει αὐτοῖς τὸν λόγον. 3 καὶ ἔρχονται φέροντες πρὸς αὐτὸν παραλυτικὸν αἰρόμενον ὑπὸ τεσσάρων. 4 καὶ μὴ δυνάμενοι προσενέγκαι αὐτῷ διὰ τὸν ὄχλον ἀπεστέγασαν τὴν στέγην ὅπου ἦν, καὶ ἐξορύξαντες χαλῶσι τὸν κράβαττον ὅπου ὁ παραλυτικὸς κατέκειτο. 5 καὶ ἰδὼν ὁ Ἰησοῦς τὴν πίστιν αὐτῶν λέγει τῷ παραλυτικῷ· Τέκνον, ἀφίενταί σου αἱ ἁμαρτίαι. 6 ἦσαν δέ τινες τῶν γραμματέων ἐκεῖ καθήμενοι καὶ διαλογιζόμενοι ἐν ταῖς καρδίαις αὐτῶν· 7 Τί οὗτος οὕτως λαλεῖ; βλασφημεῖ· τίς δύναται ἀφιέναι ἁμαρτίας εἰ μὴ εἷς ὁ θεός; 8 καὶ εὐθὺς ἐπιγνοὺς ὁ Ἰησοῦς τῷ πνεύματι αὐτοῦ ὅτι οὕτως διαλογίζονται ἐν ἑαυτοῖς λέγει αὐτοῖς· Τί ταῦτα διαλογίζεσθε ἐν ταῖς καρδίαις ὑμῶν; 9 τί ἐστιν εὐκοπώτερον, εἰπεῖν τῷ παραλυτικῷ· Ἀφίενταί σου αἱ ἁμαρτίαι, ἢ εἰπεῖν· Ἔγειρε καὶ ἆρον τὸν κράβαττόν σου καὶ περιπάτει; 10 ἵνα

δὲ εἰδῆτε ὅτι ἐξουσίαν ἔχει ὁ υἱὸς τοῦ ἀνθρώπου ἐπὶ τῆς γῆς ἀφιέναι ἁμαρτίας—λέγει τῷ παραλυτικῷ· 11 Σοὶ λέγω, ἔγειρε ἆρον τὸν κράβαττόν σου καὶ ὕπαγε εἰς τὸν οἶκόν σου. 12 καὶ ἠγέρθη καὶ εὐθὺς ἄρας τὸν κράβαττον ἐξῆλθεν ἔμπροσθεν πάντων, ὥστε ἐξίστασθαι πάντας καὶ δοξάζειν τὸν θεὸν λέγοντας ὅτι Οὕτως οὐδέποτε εἴδομεν. [SBLGNT]

King James Version

1 And again he entered into Capernaum after some days; and it was noised that he was in the house. 2 And straightway many were gathered together, insomuch that there was no room to receive them, no, not so much as about the door: and he preached the word unto them. 3 And they come unto him, bringing one sick of the palsy, which was borne of four. 4 And when they could not come nigh unto him for the press, they uncovered the roof where he was: and when they had broken it up, they let down the bed wherein the sick of the palsy lay. 5 When Jesus saw their faith, he said unto the sick of the palsy, Son, thy sins be forgiven thee. 6 But there were certain of the scribes sitting there, and reasoning in their hearts, 7 Why doth this man thus speak blasphemies? who can forgive sins but God only? 8 And immediately when Jesus perceived in his spirit that they so reasoned within themselves, he said unto them, Why reason ye these things in your hearts? 9 Whether is it easier to say to the sick of the palsy, Thy sins be forgiven thee; or to say, Arise, and take up thy bed, and walk? 10 But that ye may know that the Son of man hath power on earth to forgive sins, (he saith to the sick of the palsy,) 11 I say unto thee, Arise, and take up thy bed, and go thy way into thine house. 12 And immediately he arose, took up the bed, and

New Rendition

1 And having entered again into Capernaum after some days, it was reported that he is at home. 2 And many were gathered, so there was no more room, not even near the door. And he spoke about the word to them. 3 And they come, bringing to him a man who could not walk, carried by four people. 4 And not being able to come near him because of the crowd, they removed the roof where he was. And having torn it off, they lowered the mat on which the lame man was lying. 5 And Jesus, having seen their trust, says to the lame man, "Child, your sins are forgiven." 6 But there were some scriptorians there, sitting and questioning in their minds, 7 "Why does this one speak this way? He blasphemes! Who is able to forgive sins except one, God?" 8 And immediately Jesus, recognizing in his spirit that they are questioning within themselves this way, he says to them, "Why are you questioning about these things in your minds? 9 What is easier: to say to the lame man, 'Your sins have been forgiven,' or to say, 'Rise and take your mat and walk'? 10 But so you may know that the son of man has authority to forgive sins on earth—" He says to the lame man, 11 "I say to you: Rise. Take up your mat and go into your home." 12 And immediately he rose, and having taken up the mat, went in front of all of them, so that all were

went forth before them all; insomuch that they were all amazed, and glorified God, saying, We never saw it on this fashion.

amazed and honored God, saying, "We never saw this before!"

Notes

2:1 *And again he entered into Capernaum after some days:* It is unclear whether "after some days" modifies "entered" (he entered after some days) or "noised" (his presence was not widely known until some days after he entered). Either way, the phrase prevents a conflict with 1:45 (where Jesus couldn't enter into the towns), either by indicating that enough time had passed so that the crowd had died down (if it modifies "enters") or that Jesus entered the town quietly so that no crowd gathered (if it modifies "noised").

and it was noised that he was in the house: The "that" (Greek: *hoti*) can indicate direct speech, so this part of the verse could be translated as, "It was said, 'He was in the house.'" The house could be

1. Peter's house, since that was the last house mentioned (1:29).
2. any (unspecified) house.
3. Jesus' own home.[1]

2:2 *And straightway:* Most ancient manuscripts do not include "straight-way" (Greek: *euthys*) here.[2]

many were gathered together insomuch that there was no room to receive them, no, not so much as about the door: This phrase emphasizes Jesus' popularity in two ways:

1. A double negative in the Greek emphasizes that there was not enough room for everyone who wanted to be near Jesus.
2. This phrase implies that even outside of the house (KJV: "about the door") there was not enough space. Because the phrase "about the door" was used in 1:33, where there was room outside the door (even for the entire city of ten thousand people!), this verse suggests a magnification of Jesus' popularity.

and he preached the word unto them: In early Christianity, "the word" (Greek: *logos*) was a technical term for the basic message about Jesus Christ. This reference to "the word" links to the story of the healing of the

---

1. Stein, *Mark,* 116.
2. Comfort, *New Testament Text and Translation Commentary,* 99.

leper (1:45), where the leper (or Jesus—see the Notes on 1:45) preached "the word" (KJV: "the story").

Mark is about to narrate a healing story, but this reference to preaching keeps the preaching and healing aspects of Jesus' ministry woven together.

2:3 *And they come unto him:* "They" may refer to the four people carrying the man, or it could refer to other people who accompanied them.

bringing one sick of the palsy: The word "palsy" (Greek: *paralytikos*) indicates that the man could not walk but is no more specific than that. He might have had a stroke, broken legs that were not properly set, arthritis, or a head injury.[3] However, it is unlikely that he was a paraplegic or a quadriplegic because these conditions were fatal before modern medical care.[4]

which was borne of four: That he had to be carried emphasizes his incapacity.

2:4 *And when they could not come nigh unto him for the press, they uncovered the roof where he was:* "Uncovered the roof" is literally "they unroofed the roof."

The house probably had one story with external stairs leading up to a flat roof that would have been used as additional living space. The "roof would be replaced every year after the rainy season."[5]

and when they had broken it up: The roof was most likely made of wooden beams covered with mud and branches, leading some translations to say, accurately, that they were "digging through" the roof. One wonders what the owner of the house thought as his roof was destroyed and whether Jesus continued teaching as bits of mud and wood fell on him.

they let down the bed wherein the sick of the palsy lay: "Bed" (Greek: *krabbatos*) might be translated as "mat" or "pallet"; it refers to the kind of bed that a poor person would have used.

Relationship to Psalm 7:15. There may be an allusion here to Psalm 7:15, where wicked men dig a pit and then fall "into the pit they have made" (NIV). There are two different ways this psalm could be related to Mark's story:

---

3. Dwight N. Peterson, "Translating παραλυτικός in Mark 2:1–12: A Proposal," *Bulletin for Biblical Research* 16, no. 2 (2006): 261–72. (Interestingly, Mr. Peterson himself is paralyzed.)

4. Peterson, "Translating παραλυτικός," 261–72.

5. Elizabeth Struthers Malbon, *Hearing Mark: A Listener's Guide* (Harrisburg, Pa.: Trinity Press International, 2002), 21.

1. The friends who bring the paralytic are the opposite of the wicked person in the psalm: instead of digging a pit in wickedness and falling into it themselves, they "dig" a pit (in the roof) to save a friend.

2. The paralytic is like the wicked man (see the Notes on 2:5 on the link between sickness and sin) from the psalm, but the faith of his friends and Jesus' intervention changes the pit (in the roof) from a further source of injury to something that saves him.

2:5 *When Jesus saw their faith:* Faith is not normally thought of as something one can physically see; what Jesus actually saw were clumps of dirt falling. The friends do not say a word in Mark's account, but their faith is nonetheless evident, and Jesus chose to see the faith that motivated their actions.

"Their" is plural; it may refer to any combination of the following:

1. The people who came with the paralyzed man.
2. The four people who carried him.
3. The man himself.

Perhaps Mark is making a point about the importance of community: the paralyzed man would not have been able to enter Jesus' presence without the help of his friends.

The word "faith," which occurs only four other times in Mark's Gospel, (4:40; 5:34; 10:52; 11:22) is related to "actions taken to receive Jesus' help"[6] and not, as the word is often used in modern English, to mean agreement with certain theological beliefs, hence the New Rendition's translation of "trust." And because the Greek word for "faith" (Greek: *pistis*) is very similar to the verb "believe" (Greek: *pisteuō*) that was used to describe Jesus' ministry in 1:15, Mark's audience likely would have made a connection between Jesus' call for people to believe/trust him and the action that Jesus sees in this verse.

Contrary to what was expected in healing stories in the Greek world, this story shows faith *before* the miracle and not as a result of the healing.

he said unto the sick of the palsy, Son: While it is possible that the paralyzed person was literally a child, "son" (Greek: *teknon*; this is not the same Greek word found in the phrases "Son of God" or "Son of Man") is likely metaphorical. It might have expressed affection or reflected the fact that the man was stuck in a childlike state because of his dependence on others. "Child" may be a more appropriate translation than "son," given that the

---

6. Guelich, *Mark 1–8:26*, 85.

paralytic's gender does not seem to be a focal point of the story. There is debate as to how the word "son" was used in antiquity:

1. It was an uncommon method of address, and so Jesus' use of it here is a profound statement of his "adoption" of this poor, ill man.

2. It was regularly used by teachers when addressing pupils, which means that Jesus is treating this man as if he were a disciple.

thy sins be forgiven thee: There is a textual variant here: some texts read "are forgiven" (in this moment) while others read "have been forgiven"[7] (in the past). If the sins are being forgiven as Jesus speaks, it is more likely that his words are causing the forgiveness to happen, much as his words cause the healing to happen.

It may seem odd that Jesus introduces the topic of forgiveness when what the man and his friends were seeking was physical healing. But in the HB there is often a link between sin and sickness,[8] so this would not have seemed unusual to Jesus' audience; only in modern times would healing and forgiveness be considered two separate issues. Nonetheless, it was not Jesus' normal practice to address the issue of sin when performing a healing, so there is still reason to consider why Jesus links forgiveness and healing; options for explaining the link include:

1. Soon, Jesus will know the unexpressed thoughts of the scribes (2:8); perhaps he also knows what is in the crippled man's mind, and so he mentions forgiveness because the condition was due to sin. It is even possible that the man has experienced somatization (the manifestation of physical ailments based on psychological causes) related to some sin he had committed, and his lameness is the result of his sinful state. The contrast with other healings—where no reference to sin is made—suggests that some illnesses are a result of sin but others are not.

2. Perhaps the man thought (incorrectly) that his condition was due to sin, so Jesus forgave him to reassure him.

3. Jesus forgives the sins primarily as a "teaching moment" for the scribes; the man is no more or less guilty of sin than any other person.

There are three different ways to understand Jesus' actions:

1. Jesus is announcing that God has forgiven the man's sins, as suggested by the passive voice: this is an example of the divine passive, used when God

---

7. Witherington, *Gospel of Mark*, 115.

8. Deut. 28:27; Ps. 38:3 (NRSV: "there is no health in my bones because of my sin"); Ps. 41:3–4; and Micah 6:13. The association between sin and sickness occurs in some NT passages (John 5:14) but is denied in others (Luke 13:1–5; John 9:2–3).

is the subject of the verb. In support of this reading is the possibility that the phrase "on earth" (2:10) implies that Jesus is just announcing on earth something that was already a reality in heaven. The problem with this reading is that it is difficult to understand why the scribes object if Jesus was only announcing that God had forgiven the man's sins, since there is precedent for a prophet proclaiming that God had forgiven sins (2 Sam. 12:13). (If they had thought Jesus was announcing forgiveness that God had granted, they might have accused him of presuming to be a prophet but not of blasphemy.) While it has been suggested that the scribes thought Jesus was forgiving sins but Jesus meant that God was forgiving the sins, this reading seems unlikely because one presumes that Jesus would have corrected their mistaken impression, particularly since the story emphasizes his ability to understand their thoughts (see also the Notes on 2:10).

2. Jesus himself is forgiving the man's sins. The reference to the Son of Man in 2:10 supports this reading, as does Jesus' statement that he will heal the man in order to show the Son of Man's authority to forgive sins. Given the problems with #1 above, this seems to be the better reading. The power and authority to forgive sin is quite a claim, as the internal thoughts of the scribes make clear, because it means that Jesus is exercising a right that only God has. This is a significant moment for Jesus' ministry since performing exorcisms, enacting healings, touching lepers, and calling disciples might have been unexpected, but they would not have been regarded as blasphemy.

3. Perhaps Jesus' statement was ambiguous as to who was actually forgiving the sins.

2:6 *But there were certain of the scribes sitting there:* The "but" at the beginning of this verse positions the scribes as antagonistic to Jesus, and their sitting contrasts with the physical activity of the four friends who showed faith.

and reasoning in their hearts: The verb here (Greek: *dialogizomai*) "is almost always used in a negative sense in the NT."[9] In the biblical world, the heart is a metaphor for what now would be called the mind. (Moderns consider the heart the seat of emotions, but in the NT the bowels were, so the scribes are thinking about what has happened; there is no implication that they are being emotional.) They are not speaking out loud.

It is tempting to accuse the scribes of having more concern with being correct than with being merciful, but it is also true that blasphemy was a serious crime that they felt obligated to address.

2:7 *Why doth this man thus speak:* The wording "this man" is probably filled with contempt. It is ironic that while Jesus is in the very act of forgiving sins and healing infirmities, they refer to him in this rude manner.

---

9. Marcus, *Mark 1–8*, 216.

blasphemies?: Here, "blasphemies" can be translated as an adverb ("he speaks blasphemously") or as a verb ("he speaks . . . he blasphemes"). It could be punctuated as a question ("Does he speak blasphemously?" or "Is he blaspheming?") but one with a very hostile edge.

The blasphemy here would not be speaking ill of God but rather assuming a privilege (in this case, forgiving sins) that is limited to God alone.

Under the law of Moses, blasphemy merited a death sentence (Lev. 24:16), so there may be a bit of foreshadowing here since that charge will ultimately be leveled against Jesus (14:64).

who can forgive sins but God only?: The phrasing here suggests that they are alluding to Deuteronomy 6:4 (commonly known as the Shema), with its reference to God being "one" (KJV: "only"). The idea that God—and only God—could forgive sins is well-established in the HB (Ex. 34:6–7; 1 Kgs. 8:39; Isa. 43:25; 44:3).

2:8 *And immediately when Jesus:* The word "immediately" probably indicates that Jesus used a miraculous capacity to understand what they were thinking; he didn't need time to, for example, ponder their body language. Mark underplays the fact that a miracle happens here as Jesus is able to read their thoughts. (But some scholars think this phrase reflects common discernment and no miracle.[10]) In the HB, God (and only God) can know what is in people's hearts (1 Kgs. 8:39), so this phrase identifies Jesus with the God of the HB. It is ironic that at the very same moment when the scribes are questioning Jesus' authority, he is exercising miraculous powers to understand their thoughts.

perceived in his spirit that they so reasoned within themselves: This does not seem to be a reference to the Holy Spirit but rather to Jesus' own spirit. There may be a contrast between Jesus' spirit and the hearts (minds) of the scribes.

he said unto them, Why reason ye these things in your hearts?: By responding to a question with a question, Jesus was using a common rabbinic teaching style, which encouraged reflection and pondering among Jesus' audience as well as Mark's. It required work on their part and a willingness to learn.

There are three different ways to understand precisely what it is that Jesus is objecting to:

1. They were *reasoning* about these things. The situation called for something other than reason (perhaps faith?).

---

10. Mann, *Mark*, 224.

2. They were reasoning *within themselves* (instead of asking Jesus a question). The objection is that they are not being open about their questions or seeking information from the person who could address their concerns but limiting themselves to what they already know.

3. They were reasoning about these things *in their hearts.* Perhaps there is an opposition between heart (mind) and spirit, especially since the previous phrase showed Jesus gaining knowledge by perceiving in his spirit.

2:9 ***Whether is it easier to say to the sick of the palsy, Thy sins be forgiven thee; or to say, Arise and take up thy bed, and walk?:*** Jesus' question is somewhat tricky to interpret:

1. On the one hand, healing is easier than forgiving sins: prophets (and others) can heal, but only God can forgive sins.

2. On the other hand, *saying* that one could forgive sins would have been easier than healing because it would have been simple to verify whether someone had been healed, but there is no way to (dis)prove that sins had been forgiven. Because Jesus heals the man in order to demonstrate his authority to forgive sins, this meaning is more likely.

3. If the proper backdrop to this story is a belief in the link between sin and illness (see the Notes on 2:5), then the answer to the question is that the two cannot be separated.[11]

The next verse will offer one solution to this conundrum: Jesus will do both, and so there will be no doubts about his authority.

Relationship to Psalm 103. In Psalm 103:3, the very structure of the verse parallels forgiving sins with healing. Because the psalmist was speaking to the Lord, the allusion between that text and Mark associates Jesus with the God of the HB.

2:10 ***But that ye may know:*** Normally in Mark, an explanatory clause like this would come after the main clause, but here it is placed at the beginning of the sentence in order to emphasize that what is most at stake is the issue of Jesus' authority. "Know" may contrast with the reasoning of the scribes and imply a difference between reasoning and knowing.

Jesus implies that his audience can know something because of what they see—they will see a healing, and that will illustrate that Jesus has authority to forgive sins. Perhaps this phrase echoes Jesus' seeing their faith when they brought the lame man to him: the people will know what

---

11. Frederick J. Gaiser, "'Your Sins Are Forgiven. . . . Stand Up and Walk': A Theological Reading of Mark 2:1–12 in the Light of Psalm 103," *Ex Auditu* 21 (2005): 74.

is true based on what they see, just as Jesus knew they had faith based on what he could see.

Relationship to Exodus 7–10. When Moses appeared before Pharaoh, he spoke of what Pharaoh should know—namely, who the Lord is and what his powers are (Ex. 7:17; 8:10, 22; 9:14; 10:2). That is, the plagues were not ultimately about frogs or punishment but rather about the identity and power of the Lord. This makes a compelling parallel to this healing in Mark because it suggests that this text is not primarily about forgiveness or healing but rather about Jesus' identity—what his audience should know is who the Lord is and what his powers are. The allusion would also imply that Jesus, like Moses, is a spiritual figure in front of earthly authorities and that he will use his miraculous powers to give the leaders an opportunity to repent. But the parallel also suggests that, like Pharaoh, they will not accept this offer and will suffer the consequences. So the allusion turns the scribes into the functional equivalent of Pharaoh—a stinging indictment of those who should be religious leaders.

One distinction between the stories is significant: instead of the destructive signs that Moses performed, Jesus' sign is a positive, healing one. This implies the superiority of Jesus over Moses.

---

that the Son of man: See the section on "Son of Man" in appendix F: "Titles for Jesus in Mark." Because "Son of Man" can be a modest way to refer to oneself, it may be particularly (if ironically) appropriate here, where Jesus is claiming a great power. The link of the title to Daniel 7:13 might suggest Jesus' unique authority. It is also possible that "Son of Man" refers not just to Jesus but to any human being,[12] which would mean that all people have authority to forgive sins. While that reading might seem unlikely, two facts make it less so:

1. The qualifier "on earth" could imply one person granting forgiveness for another person's sins in the earthly sphere; heavenly or eternal forgiveness would still be God's prerogative.

2. Matthew 9:8 implies that Matthew understood the story to mean that more than one person on earth (hence "men," which is plural) had authority to forgive sins.[13]

---

12. This seems to be the sense in 3:28, but note that it is plural ("sons of men") there.

13. There are other ways to read Matt. 9:8; perhaps the crowd misunderstood what had happened, although presumably Jesus or Matthew would have corrected them in that case.

hath power: "Power" can be translated as "authority." (English makes a distinction between power [the ability to do something] and authority [the right to do something], but Greek does not in this case.) Significantly, "there is no evidence in other Jewish literature that any man, whether prophet, priest, king, or Messiah, had such authority to forgive sins."[14] So this would have been one way in which Jesus would have violated expectations.

on earth: There are many possibilities for what "on earth" modifies:

1. "Sins." So the Son of Man has authority to forgive sins that are committed on earth. This implies the possibility of sinning after (and before?) this life; it would be interesting to speculate as to why the Son of Man did not (at this time) have authority to forgive those sins.

2. "To forgive." The idea that Jesus has the authority to forgive on earth can be understood in several different ways:

   a. The forgiveness that the Son of Man extends applies on earth only. (This implies a different forgiveness on earth than in heaven.) If the idea is that God has delegated some power to Jesus to exercise on earth only, there might be some interesting implications here for Latter-day Saint thought regarding authority and delegation of authority.

   b. Jesus' authority to forgive sins covers the entire earth and is not limited to the house of Israel.

   c. Jesus' ability to forgive sins is not tied to the sacrificial rituals performed in the temple but extends throughout the entire earth.

3. "The Son of Man." This would imply that the Son of Man, while on earth, can forgive sins. Perhaps this just means that he can offer forgiveness because he is physically present. Or it might mean that, contrary to the past (when authority to forgive sins resided only in heaven), that authority is now on earth with Jesus.

4. In some manuscripts, the phrase is omitted,[15] implying that the Son of Man's authority to forgive sins is not limited to earth.

Regardless of which option is chosen, the scribes had thought that only God (who is in heaven) could forgive sins, but Jesus' statement declares that God's power now functions on earth in new ways. This authority may be the result of the baptismal vision, where Jesus saw the heavens ripped open and the Spirit descending, symbolically representing the commissioning of Jesus to forgive sins. The reference to the earth might also link this statement to Daniel 7 (which is likely already in the audience's minds

---

14. Stein, *Mark,* 121.
15. Marcus, *Mark 1–8,* 218.

due to the reference to the Son of Man), since in that text the Son of Man is given power to rule the nations on earth and since that power comes from heaven.

Ironically, Jesus actually does answer the scribes' question: they asked who had authority to forgive sins and Jesus says that the Son of Man does.

to forgive sins: Unlike the reference to forgiving sins in 2:5, this reference is not passive. So it should be obvious by this point (even if it was not before) that the issue is not Jesus' ability to announce that God has forgiven sins, but rather Jesus' own practice of forgiving sins.

Notice that Jesus (or Mark) does not actually finish this sentence; at least, not with words. This is a rhetorically clever move that Mark has preserved: the way that they know that Jesus has authority to forgive sins is not that he reasons them into believing it but rather that he acts in a way that demonstrates that it is true.

(he saith to the sick of the palsy): In mid-sentence, Jesus (or Mark) shifts from addressing the audience to addressing the man. This phrase was probably included to make clear that he wasn't telling the scribes to rise.

It is possible to read 2:10 not as Jesus' words but as Mark's aside to the audience. In this reading, the "ye" is Mark's audience. Support for this reading includes:

1. The "Son of Man" reference seems misplaced since all other references to the Son of Man are in the second half of Mark's Gospel.

2. It makes sense of the rather direct statement about Jesus' authority, which is atypical for his ministry and so perhaps more likely to be Mark's statement.

Direct address to the audience adds an immediacy to the text that draws them into the story. The aside also explains that this was not just another healing miracle but rather proof that Jesus can forgive sins.[16]

Relationship to Daniel 7. The reference to the Son of Man likely alludes to Daniel 7. In that text, the Son of Man is pictured as judging sin, so when Jesus says that the Son of Man has the authority to forgive sins, he's identifying with the Son of Man but also inverting the audience's expectations for what the Son of Man will do.

2:11 *I say unto thee, Arise:* Because this is the word (Greek: *egeirō*) that will be used for Jesus' rising from the dead (14:28), there may be a bit of foreshadowing of the Resurrection here.

---

16. George H. Boobyer, "Mark II, 10a and the Interpretation of the Healing of the Paralytic," *Harvard Theological Review* 47 (April 1954): 115–20.

and take up thy bed: The verb for "take up" (Greek: *airō*) is the same one used when the man was being carried (2:3, where it was passive). There is a moving irony here since he is carrying what used to carry him; as Peter Chrysologus, a fifth-century Christian bishop, described it, "Take up your bed. Carry the very mat that once carried you. Change places, so that what was the proof of your sickness may now give testimony to your soundness. Your bed of pain becomes the sign of healing, its very weight the measure of the strength that has been restored to you."[17]

and go thy way into thine house: As is often the case, Jesus performs a healing by commanding the person to do something that presumes that she has been healed. So the healing requires a display of faith on the part of the person healed—they must act as if the healing has already occurred in order for the healing to happen.

2:12 *And immediately:* "Immediately" emphasizes the fact that Jesus' command is instantly followed.

he arose, took up the bed, and went forth: This language is very similar to the previous verse, implying that Jesus' words are instantly and completely enacted; this highlights his authority.

before them all: Notice that the parallelism with the previous verse is broken here by the reference to "before them all" instead of "home." This departure emphasizes that the audience witnesses what has happened and therefore should now understand that Jesus has authority to forgive sins.

insomuch that they were all amazed: There are two different ways to interpret "all" here:

1. It is not literal but rather an example of Mark's hyperbole; the scribes were neither amazed nor glorified God.

2. The "all" is taken at face value, meaning that it would include the questioning scribes[18] as well as the crowd, the paralytic, and his friends. This would emphasize Jesus' healing and forgiving power. It is possible that some scribes became followers of Jesus; it is also possible that they were amazed at the miracle but failed to apply the larger message of the healing as evidence of Jesus' ability to forgive sins.

and glorified God: They did not glorify Jesus. This illustrates that Jesus' words were not blasphemous; Jesus' ministry does not harm God's name but increases its glorification.

---

17. Oden and Hall, *Mark,* 29.

18. While the scribes are usually opposed to Jesus, this is not universally the case in Mark; see 12:28–34.

saying, We never saw it on this fashion: There are two different ways to interpret their exclamation:

1. The "it" refers to the healing of the man. One weakness of this reading is that they likely had seen a healing before, either by Jesus or another healer. (It is possible that this is an entirely different Capernaum crowd than the one that saw the leper healed and the demon exorcised, but it is also possible that it consists of some of the same people.)

2. The "it" refers to forgiveness of sins, which they believe that they have witnessed because they accept Jesus' statement that healing illustrates power to forgive sins.

Narrative Structure. This story can be understood chiastically:

    A introduction (2:1–2)
        B spiritual healing (forgiveness) (2:3–5)
            C Jesus' power to forgive (2:6–10a)
        B' physical healing (2:10b–12a)
    A' conclusion (2:12b)[19]

If this structure was deliberate, it suggests an interesting parallel between physical and spiritual healing, as well as the idea that spiritual healing should precede (or must precede) physical healing. And the central point of the story is neither the controversy per se nor Jesus' ability to heal but rather his authority to forgive, which is the center point of the structure.

Relationship to Isaiah. In Isaiah 35:4–6, there is a prophecy of a future time when "the lame shall leap like a deer" (NRSV). This story in Mark may be a fulfillment of that prophecy as the man takes up his bed and walks.

In Isaiah 64:4, the speaker expresses amazement at acts that have never been seen before, perhaps making a link to the similar exclamation in the present text. In Isaiah, it is God who is performing the new acts, suggesting a link between Jesus and the God of the HB.

Analysis

There has only been one previous reference to the scribes in Mark's Gospel: in 1:22, the people marvel that Jesus' authority makes his teaching very different from the scribes'. So it is perhaps not surprising that in this story, the scribes are also concerned with Jesus' authority and whether he

---

19. Marcus, *Mark 1–8*, 219.

is exercising a power—to forgive sins—to which he is not entitled. While modern Latter-day Saint notions of priesthood are not overtly explored in Mark's Gospel, it is nonetheless true that proper authority is a major concern, and the issue of Jesus' authority is raised again and again. The idea that specific authority is required to perform certain acts has already been affirmed at the baptism (where Jesus sought out John), in Jesus' teachings in the synagogue (which were, unlike the scribes, "with authority"), and in Jesus' authority to forgive sins. It is worth mentioning the obvious: the point of this story is that Jesus has authority to forgive sins. Prophecies about the Messiah do not state that the Messiah will forgive sins,[20] so for Jesus to announce that the man's sins were forgiven is to challenge the prevailing expectations for what the Messiah would be and to claim a power that was regarded as belonging to God alone. This is a profound statement about Jesus' identity.

The audience learns something else about Jesus as well, something about his character. Jesus could have chosen to focus on the fact that the roof was destroyed and his preaching was interrupted by falling debris, not to mention the spectacle of a man being lowered to him. But instead of "seeing" the disruption, Jesus chose to "see" their faith. There is a lesson here about what he chose to focus on.

The actions of the lame man's friends are technically unnecessary. Because Jesus can heal from a distance, there was no need to destroy the roof or to disturb the sermon to bring the man into Jesus' presence. (In fact, their actions show a *lack* of faith since they do not understand that Jesus can heal from a distance.) They even could have waited outside until Jesus left the house—presumably he wasn't going to stay inside forever. But Jesus does not focus on their shortcomings; he focuses on their faith.

Jesus is accused of blasphemy, but there is another objection that could have been raised to Jesus' actions: under the law of Moses, it is only the priest who can perform the atoning ritual by which sins are forgiven (Lev. 4:26), and "although there is no explicit statement that such atonement rituals were accompanied by the priest's declarations of divine forgiveness, it can be assumed that they were."[21] By offering forgiveness in this story, Jesus implicitly teaches that forgiveness can be granted outside of those

---

20. Lane, *Gospel according to Mark,* 95. (It is possible that there were prophecies that were lost, but from what is extant, there was no expectation that the Messiah would be able to forgive sins.)

21. Marcus, *Mark 1–8,* 216.

sacrificial rituals. While the issue is not directly addressed in the story, there is an undercurrent of Atonement theology here, since faith makes forgiveness possible through Jesus.

This story contains several intriguing observations about seeing and knowing. For example, Jesus is able to see the faith of the friends who carry the man, although faith is not something one can normally see. Jesus is able to perceive the thoughts of his opponents, which is also atypical. And Jesus expects his audience to see a miracle and thus conclude that he can forgive sins. In effect, the healing becomes a sign of Jesus' ability to forgive, just as the carrying of the man was a sign of their faith. Thus the story implies that seeing can transcend normal bounds and that knowledge can come from seeing.

The four people who bring the paralyzed man to Jesus can be contrasted with the scribes, especially in terms of faith and (in)action. Given that whether it is easier to do or to say is a theme in this story, the contrast between the friends who do something and the scribes who just think is compelling. The friends are willing to destroy a roof and risk the wrath of the homeowner; they are willing to take risks in order to see their friend enter Jesus' presence and have access to his power. The scribes, in contrast, neither do nor say anything. Neither the friends nor the scribes speak: the friends act, and the scribes reason in their hearts. The contrast in the characterization of the two groups leads to the conclusion that action, loyalty, community, and faith are needed to achieve forgiveness of sins.

This story also contains a subtle commentary on the relationship between words and deeds. Not only does Jesus ask whether it is easier to do something or to say something, but Jesus apparently breaks off in mid-sentence in order to do something. This is a brilliant move on the literary level: it implies that words are not capable of conveying information as well as deeds are, which was also the case earlier in the story when Jesus saw—not heard—the friends' faith.

Since Jesus interweaves healing and forgiveness in this story, sickness can be understood as an analogy for sin. Just as illness had paralyzed this man, making it impossible for him to perform even the most basic tasks for himself, sin is similar: it makes it impossible to function and requires an intermediary to overcome its effects. The story conceives of sin, like illness, as a limiting condition. Just as Jesus' healing is to be a sign of his ability to forgive sins, perhaps the illness is a sign of a sinful state. Repentance and resumption of normal life are pictured as rising and taking up one's bed; the forgiven sinner is just as different from the sinner as a paralytic is from a man walking and carrying his bed.

It is likely that there were people in Mark's audience with horrible illnesses and no hope for recovery, as was the case for many in the ancient world. This story would have provided them with two types of hope: first, that the power that Jesus held could heal their condition and, second, that Jesus could forgive sins. While they might not have expected physical healing in their lifetimes, they could have developed faith that their sins could be forgiven.

In this story, the association between Jesus and God is strong since Jesus is aware of unspoken thoughts, an ability shown only by God in the HB (1 Sam. 16:7; 1 Kgs. 8:39; Ps. 7:9; Jer. 11:20). Forgiving sins, also a prerogative of God alone, points to a theology of Atonement that is worked out in actions, not words, in Mark's Gospel. Because "a person doing the sorts of things Jesus was doing, in not merely a Jewish environment but in a milieu in which a holiness reformation was in progress (led by the Pharisees), could reasonably expect a premature death,"[22] this story is about more than the forgiveness of sins. Jesus is setting in motion a chain of events that he would know (even without inspiration) would lead to his own death; in a very real sense, Jesus is willingly trading his own life for the man's wholeness.

JESUS EATS WITH SINNERS (2:13–17)

Greek Text

13 Καὶ ἐξῆλθεν πάλιν παρὰ τὴν θάλασσαν· καὶ πᾶς ὁ ὄχλος ἤρχετο πρὸς αὐτόν, καὶ ἐδίδασκεν αὐτούς. 14 καὶ παράγων εἶδεν Λευὶν τὸν τοῦ Ἀλφαίου καθήμενον ἐπὶ τὸ τελώνιον, καὶ λέγει αὐτῷ· Ἀκολούθει μοι. καὶ ἀναστὰς ἠκολούθησεν αὐτῷ.

15 Καὶ γίνεται κατακεῖσθαι αὐτὸν ἐν τῇ οἰκίᾳ αὐτοῦ, καὶ πολλοὶ τελῶναι καὶ ἁμαρτωλοὶ συνανέκειντο τῷ Ἰησοῦ καὶ τοῖς μαθηταῖς αὐτοῦ, ἦσαν γὰρ πολλοὶ καὶ ἠκολούθουν αὐτῷ. 16 καὶ οἱ γραμματεῖς τῶν Φαρισαίων ἰδόντες ὅτι ἐσθίει μετὰ τῶν ἁμαρτωλῶν καὶ τελωνῶν ἔλεγον τοῖς μαθηταῖς αὐτοῦ· Ὅτι μετὰ τῶν τελωνῶν καὶ ἁμαρτωλῶν ἐσθίει; 17 καὶ ἀκούσας ὁ Ἰησοῦς λέγει αὐτοῖς ὅτι Οὐ χρείαν ἔχουσιν οἱ ἰσχύοντες ἰατροῦ ἀλλ᾽ οἱ κακῶς ἔχοντες· οὐκ ἦλθον καλέσαι δικαίους ἀλλὰ ἁμαρτωλούς. [SBLGNT]

---

22. Witherington, *Gospel of Mark*, 114.

King James Version

13 And he went forth again by the sea side; and all the multitude resorted unto him, and he taught them. 14 And as he passed by, he saw Levi the son of Alphæus sitting at the receipt of custom, and said unto him, Follow me. And he arose and followed him. 15 And it came to pass, that, as Jesus sat at meat in his house, many publicans and sinners sat also together with Jesus and his disciples: for there were many, and they followed him. 16 And when the scribes and Pharisees saw him eat with publicans and sinners, they said unto his disciples, How is it that he eateth and drinketh with publicans and sinners? 17 When Jesus heard it, he saith unto them, They that are whole have no need of the physician, but they that are sick: I came not to call the righteous, but sinners to repentance.

New Rendition

13 And he went forth again by the sea, and all the crowd was coming to him, and he was teaching them. 14 And passing by, he saw Levi, the son of Alphaeus, sitting at the tax booth, and he says to him, "Follow me." And, having risen, he followed him. 15 And it comes to pass that, as he ate at his house, many tax collectors and sinners were eating with Jesus and his disciples. Indeed, they were many, and they followed him. 16 And the scriptorians of the Pharisees, having seen him eating with sinners and tax collectors, said to his disciples, "Why does he eat with tax collectors and sinners?" 17 And having heard, Jesus says to them, "The healthy do not have need of a doctor, but those who are sick. I did not come to call the righteous, but sinners."

Notes

2:13 *And he went forth again:* "Again" may refer to the last time Jesus walked along the Sea of Galilee (1:16), which is appropriate because he called disciples then, as he will here. There is a compelling mix of continuity and contrast between this calling story and the last one.

by the sea side: Presumably this is the Sea of Galilee, although that is not specified.

and all the multitude resorted unto him: Because imperfect verbs are used here for "resorted" and in the next phrase for "taught," repeated action is implied—this is not a one-time event.

and he taught them: The content of the teaching is not mentioned, which puts the emphasis on the authority by which he taught as opposed to what was taught; presumably it is the same teachings as 1:15.

2:14 *And as he passed by, he saw Levi the son of Alphæus:* When a relationship is mentioned ("son of Alphaeus"), it is normally either because:

1. The relative (in this case, Alphaeus) was known to Mark's audience.

2. Mark wants to distinguish the person from others with the same name. (While there is no other Levi in Mark's Gospel, there could have been another Levi known to Mark's audience.)

Either way, this phrase presents a bit of a puzzle since Levi is not mentioned elsewhere in the NT (save the parallel account in Luke 5:27) and since there is no Levi in other lists of the Twelve (3:16–18). There are several possibilities for what has happened here:

1. Mark 3:18 refers to James[23] as the son of Alphaeus, so:

   a. Levi might be the brother of James (which is a helpful data point, but doesn't solve the problem).

   b. Levi might be another name for James. (Some manuscripts read James instead of Levi here, but that is almost certainly a later reading.[24]) It was not uncommon for people to be known by more than one name; Jesus himself renamed a disciple on at least one occasion, although unlike with Simon Peter, there is no story in the text describing a renaming of Levi.

   c. It is possible that this might not even be the same Alphaeus; there could be no relationship whatsoever between Levi and James.

2. The reason that Levi is not mentioned on any of the lists of the Twelve is because Levi was not one of the Twelve. (The same verb will not be used by Jesus to call Levi as was used in 1:17 when Jesus called the others.) This story states that Jesus called Levi to follow him but does not mention a specific calling; it is certainly possible that Jesus called Levi to a different role (compare Luke 10:1).

3. Matthew 9:9–13, which is parallel to this story, has a toll collector named Matthew (although he is not called the son of Alphaeus). Because the name Matthew appears on the apostolic lists and because he was also a publican, perhaps Levi was another name for Matthew. (This seems to be how the Gospel of Matthew understands this story, but this does not necessarily mean that Mark understood the situation in the same way.)

4. "Levi" could be a tribal marker ("the Levite") and not a proper name. The idea of a Levite tax collector would be most ironic since tax collectors were regarded as particularly unclean, while Levites needed to be clean to perform the temple rituals. But most scholars do not accept reading "Levite" here since it would be odd for Jesus to call someone without his name being included in the story. (Although perhaps this was the case with Simon's mother-in-law; see the Notes on 1:29–31.)

---

23. See the Notes on 1:19.
24. Metzger, *Textual Commentary,* 66.

Regardless, the emphasis here is not on Levi's identity but on the fact that he was a tax collector.

sitting at the receipt of custom, and said unto him, Follow me. And he arose and followed him: The "receipt of custom" was a booth for collecting taxes. Levi was likely working along the Via Maris, an important trade route; he would have collected a customs tax on goods going through (or to) Capernaum. His employer would have bid for the right to collect taxes at this location and was allowed to keep whatever money he collected after paying his bid; he was thus motivated to collect as much revenue as possible.

Tax collectors were considered unclean because they handled coins with human images and pagan symbols on them, had many dealings with Gentiles (and their unclean merchandise), and were likely to be exploitative. Many Jews considered them traitors collaborating with an occupying enemy—and making the occupation profitable at the expense of their countrymen. It is thus no surprise that they were classed with thieves and murderers in the Talmud, especially in cases where they collected more than was their due.[25] Thus, "when a Jew entered the customs service he was regarded as an outcast from society: he was disqualified as a judge or a witness in a court session, was excommunicated from the synagogue, and in the eyes of the community his disgrace extended to his family."[26] The people around Jesus and in Mark's audience would have been surprised at the selection "of someone perceived as a corrupt toady of a hated imperial presence."[27] But Jewish sources indicate that tax collectors are permitted to resume fellowship if they abandon tax collecting,[28] so Jesus' call of Levi can be understood in that framework as calling back one of the lost sheep.

Mark noted that Levi was by the shore, a location more typical of fishermen than tax collectors. It is possible that he was by the sea in order to collect customs from trade by boat, but it is also possible that Mark paints an other-than-literal picture in order to link this story to the calling of the four disciples in 1:16–20.

Comparison with 1:16–20. There are many similarities between Levi's call and the two call stories in chapter 1: the seaside setting, the description

25. Babylonian Talmud, Seder Nashim III, Nedarim 27b.
26. Lane, *Gospel according to Mark*, 101–2.
27. Marcus, *Mark 1–8*, 229.
28. Tosefta Demai 3:4.

of the future disciple going about his daily tasks, Jesus' abrupt command to follow, and the disciple's instant obedience. Much as Jesus "fished" for Peter, Andrew, James, and John, he "collects" Levi. There are no similar call stories after this one; either all disciples received similar calls but Mark saw no need to record them after the pattern was established, or perhaps others were not called as Simon, Andrew, James, John, and Levi were.

Levi has a very different occupation and social role than the four fishermen. While Jesus was able to make symbolic allusions to the HB by calling fishermen, calling a tax collector was a shocking thing to do: it made him look sympathetic to the Romans and would have offended Jewish sensibilities. In fact, this story isn't so much about the call of Levi per se as it is about who Jesus thinks is fit to be a disciple—and his answer would likely have stunned just about everyone.

It is possible that Levi knew the four fishermen and had collected taxes on their catch (and kept some as his own payment). If so, one can only imagine the dynamics among the disciples as Levi is welcomed into the circle of brotherhood.

In a sense, the call of Levi represents a heightening of the previous call stories: while it would have been possible for the fishermen to return to their fishing, either occasionally or full time, it would not have been possible for Levi to resume his post after abandoning it.

2:15 *And it came to pass, that:* Mark likely used this phrase to give a biblical sound to his writing. It may also suggest that some time had passed between the calling of Levi and this story.

as Jesus sat at meat in his house: The word "Jesus" is not in the Greek text (it reads "he"), but it is likely that Jesus is in fact eating in Levi's house;[29] perhaps Levi is hosting this banquet to celebrate his calling in particular or Jesus' ministry in general. Jesus would have been considered ritually impure after eating in Levi's home because he would touch items that Levi, himself unclean because of his work as a tax collector, had made unclean.

"Sat" is the translation of a word (Greek: *katakeimai*) that reflects the Greco-Roman custom of eating while reclining on one's side. It is debated whether reclining or sitting (which was the common Jewish eating style) was typical in Galilee at this time; perhaps one sat at normal meals but reclined at banquets.

---

29. This is how Luke 5:29 understands this passage, but it is not clear if Mark shared that understanding.

many publicans and sinners sat also together: "Publicans" are tax collectors. It seems that Levi's call has resulted in other tax collectors joining Jesus. "Sinners" has several possible meanings:

1. Those who did not observe the Pharisees' interpretation of the law of Moses and so were, according to that interpretation, often unclean; these would have been "common people who possessed neither time nor inclination to regulate their conduct by Pharisaic standards."[30] (The majority of Jews would not have affiliated with Pharisees, Sadducees, or other similar groups.) It is possible to consider "sinners" to connote "nonobservant Jews."[31] As will soon be clear, the Pharisaical view of what constitutes a sinner does not agree with Mark's view.

2. Holders of certain occupations (such as leather workers) who were rendered unclean by their work.

3. Those guilty of moral sins.

4. People Jesus had healed: because illness was associated with sin, if healed people followed Jesus, they could have been regarded as sinners because of their previous illnesses.

There is no indication here that these people had repented, although perhaps Mark assumes that. Because the Pharisees were trying to increase holiness (by having purity laws apply all of the time and not just when someone was entering the temple), eating with sinners runs contrary to that impulse. The HB condemns associating with sinners (for example, Ps. 141:4; Prov. 10:30).

It has been proposed that "Jesus' eating with such people serves as a visual declaration of the offer of forgiveness such as he pronounced in 2:5,"[32] so the objection is not primarily that Jesus is eating with them but rather that he is implicitly offering forgiveness to them.

with Jesus and his disciples: This is the first reference to "disciples" (Greek: *mathētēs*) in Mark; the Twelve have not yet been called.

for there were many: There are three possible referents for this phrase:

1. The disciples. This would be an aside to the audience, appropriate for the first use of the word "disciple" in the text, explaining that the disciples include a group larger than the Twelve.

2. The sinners who followed Jesus. The purpose is to explain why, in the next verse, the scribes object: perhaps early in Jesus' ministry, when there were only a few "sinners" following Jesus, the scribes ignored them, but now they

---

30. Lane, *Gospel according to Mark*, 103.
31. France, *Gospel of Mark*, 133, quoting Mann.
32. Stein, *Mark*, 128.

feel obligated to act as Jesus' following increases. It is possible that the story of Levi's call is placed here to show that these people were not just following Jesus around (something that he presumably would have had little control over) but rather that the "sinners" were following him at his invitation. Perhaps the reference to "many" suggests that it is not just Levi the "publican and sinner" who is following Jesus, but many other sinners as well; if this reading is correct, it implies that Jesus also called other publicans and sinners to follow him.

3. The scribes (who will be mentioned in the next verse, which means that the next phrase about following Jesus must also apply to the scribes). The point would be to show that Jesus had many opponents who followed him, waiting for a reason to accuse him.

and they followed him: This phrase might apply to

1. The disciples, which would clarify that it is not just the four fishermen and Levi who have been mentioned by name, but many others who were following Jesus.

2. The sinners, which would suggest that eating with Jesus was related to following him. The association between following and eating is strengthened by the fact that "were following" and "were reclining" (KJV: "sat") are paralleled in form and location. This, in turn, implies that the eating is not just a meal but rather has symbolic connotations, perhaps even to the "messianic banquet" spoken of in HB prophecies (for example, Isa. 25:6–8) or at least as an occasion for Jesus to teach.

3. The scribes and Pharisees (who will be mentioned in the next verse). Presumably, they were following Jesus, looking for an occasion to accuse him. (Weighing against this reading is the fact the "following" is otherwise always used in a positive sense [following as a disciple] in Mark.)

2:16 ***And when the scribes and Pharisees:*** Many ancient Greek texts read "scribes of the Pharisees" instead of "scribes and Pharisees." Scribes could have been affiliated with the Pharisees, with another Jewish sect, or with no sect at all. So "scribes of the Pharisees" would mean scribes who were also Pharisees. It is likely that later scribes changed "of" to "and" since scribes and Pharisees were later understood as separate groups.

While it has been suggested that the word "Pharisee" derives from the word "Persian" (and thus points to the foreign nature of their beliefs) or from "interpreter"[33] (and thus emphasizes their role in interpreting the law of Moses), it probably comes from "to separate"[34] and thus reflects

---

33. Cranfield, *Gospel according to St Mark*, 104.
34. Bratcher and Nida, *Translator's Handbook*, 88.

their desire to separate themselves from corrupting influences (particularly Hellenistic culture), which led to their emphasis on strict observance of the purity rules. With a focus on purity, eating rules were crucial to them. The Pharisees were the largest Jewish sectarian group at Jesus' time, and they would rise to even greater prominence after the destruction of the temple since their focus on personal purity was an attractive rallying point when temple rituals were no longer available. (Because they maintained the temple, the Sadducees experienced a decline after the destruction of the temple.)

saw him eat with publicans and sinners: Presumably, these scribes were not in the house (which would have made them unclean) but rather were observing from outside; it may have been normal for nonparticipants to observe feasts. Eating a meal together was a symbol of social acceptability and identification, so they aren't just observing Jesus eating with the sinners but also observing him accepting and identifying with them.

These scribes "saw" Jesus eating, just as Jesus "saw" Levi as a potential disciple. There might be a subtle commentary here on what one chooses to see: the scribes see Levi as a source of impurity, but Jesus sees him as a future follower.

they said unto his disciples: There are several possible reasons why they spoke to the disciples and not to Jesus directly:

1. They are trying to avoid a direct confrontation with Jesus.

2. Because Jesus is inside the house and they are outside, they cannot access Jesus but can only speak to the disciples. (This reading cannot easily explain how Jesus hears and answers them, but perhaps Mark has abbreviated the story.)

3. They speak to the disciples because their goal is to convince the disciples to stop following Jesus.

How is it that he eateth and drinketh with publicans and sinners?: Many ancient manuscripts omit "and drinketh" here.[35] Either way, this phrase can be read as a question or as an (outraged) statement.

The objection here is that Jesus would have been violating the purity laws by eating impure foods and/or eating with impure people. (Tax collectors would have been ritually unclean; see the Notes on 2:14.)

2:17 *When Jesus heard it, he saith unto them:* Jesus is answering a question that was directed not to him but to his disciples.

---

35. Metzger, *Textual Commentary,* 66.

There may be a contrast between the scribes who see and Jesus who hears: the scribes are reacting to Jesus' actions, but Jesus is reacting to their words. Later in Mark, the distinction between words and deeds will become more pronounced.

They that are whole have no need of the physician, but they that are sick: Because a similar sentiment can be found in other ancient writings, it is likely that Jesus is quoting a proverb here.

Jesus' statement not only permits eating with sinners but casts it as a requirement of his ministry: "It is ridiculous to imagine a doctor who refuses to meet his patients; so any effective 'healer' must expect to get his hands dirty."[36]

Relationship to Exodus 15:26. In that passage, the Lord announces, "I am the Lord that healeth thee." If that text is alluded to here, then it is an important piece of self-revelation as Jesus identifies with the God of the HB.

I came not to call the righteous, but sinners to repentance: "To repentance" is missing from the oldest manuscripts.[37] It may have been added to harmonize with Luke 5:32; Luke may have added it to explain why Jesus did not call the righteous.

"I came" probably does not refer to Jesus' presence near the Sea of Galilee but rather to his mortal mission; even some non-Latter-day Saint scholars think that it points to Jesus' awareness of and teaching about the preexistence.[38]

There are at least two ways to understand Jesus' statement that he did not come to call the righteous:

1. Jesus is doing the ancient equivalent of putting air quotes around "the righteous," meaning that he is not claiming that there is a group of people who can be called righteous but rather gently mocking the scribes' (incorrect) use of the word. Jesus' statement "satirizes the Pharisees' claim to have achieved righteousness by separation from sin."[39] It is even possible to translate this word as "self-righteous." So this would not imply that there were people to whom Jesus offered nothing but rather that there were people who did not respond to his call because they considered themselves to be righteous. This statement is a subtle but provocative way for Jesus to get his audience to consider whether they are completely righteous.

---

36. France, *Gospel of Mark,* 135.

37. Comfort, *New Testament Text and Translation Commentary,* 101.

38. Cranfield, *Gospel according to St Mark,* 106.

39. Marcus, *Mark 1–8,* 231.

2. The statement can be read as dialectical negation, which is a form of speech meant to emphasize the positive half of the statement. Thus no great emphasis should be placed on whether Jesus was calling the righteous; the point is that his ministry gives more emphasis to sinners.

While the previous verse has multiple references to publicans and sinners, "publican" drops out of Jesus' statement here. This breach of the pattern may be Jesus' subtle commentary that the tax collectors were not sinners of a special class but rather were no different from any other sinner.

The HB develops the idea of the messianic banquet, a future time of harmony and celebration between God and humans that is symbolized by a feast. It is possible to see this meal as a foreshadowing of the messianic banquet, which makes the presence of "sinners" all the more meaningful because it teaches that they also have a seat at God's table.

Analysis

After the four fishermen were called in 1:16–20, Jesus entered their home and performed a healing. Here, after Levi is called, Jesus again enters the home of the recently called disciple and discusses his role as a healer. The extensive parallels between the fishermen's calls and Levi's call emphasize the idea that Jesus treated Levi, a despised tax collector, precisely the same as he did his other disciples. The structure of the text speaks to Jesus' inclusion of Levi in the full scope and fellowship of his ministry. The choice of a tax collector as a disciple would have been stunning and challenging to Jesus' audience—and to Mark's.

Jesus uses a proverb about physicians to teach several important truths. He is teaching that sin in another person is not a reason to separate from that person. Because everyone sins, a separatist mindset would either require withdrawing from all human society or ignoring some sins. The Pharisees' focus is on what effect the sinners will have on Jesus; Jesus' focus is on what effect he will have on the sinners. The proverb also suggests an analogy between sin and sickness; this is part of a theology of the Atonement that develops gradually throughout the Gospel. The analogy subtly teaches that forgiveness for sins is outside the reach of any human; it points to the need for a mediator (a doctor, one who can atone). The proverb puts an entirely different spin on the calling of the disciples: they were called not because they were already knowledgeable or competent but because Jesus called the sick who needed him to heal them so that they could mature into discipleship.

In 2:1–12, the audience learned that Jesus had authority to forgive sins. In this story, the opportunity to have sins forgiven is extended not just to those who, like the paralyzed man, suffer innocently, but also to those who are deemed culpable for their sins.

JESUS TEACHES ABOUT FASTING (2:18–22)

Greek Text

18 Καὶ ἦσαν οἱ μαθηταὶ Ἰωάννου καὶ οἱ Φαρισαῖοι νηστεύοντες. Καὶ ἔρχονται καὶ λέγουσιν αὐτῷ· Διὰ τί οἱ μαθηταὶ Ἰωάννου καὶ οἱ μαθηταὶ τῶν Φαρισαίων νηστεύ-ουσιν, οἱ δὲ σοὶ μαθηταὶ οὐ νηστεύουσιν; 19 καὶ εἶπεν αὐτοῖς ὁ Ἰησοῦς· Μὴ δύνα-νται οἱ υἱοὶ τοῦ νυμφῶνος ἐν ᾧ ὁ νυμφίος μετ᾽ αὐτῶν ἐστιν νηστεύειν; ὅσον χρόνον ἔχουσιν τὸν νυμφίον μετ᾽ αὐτῶν οὐ δύνανται νηστεύειν· 20 ἐλεύσονται δὲ ἡμέραι ὅταν ἀπαρθῇ ἀπ᾽ αὐτῶν ὁ νυμφίος, καὶ τότε νηστεύσουσιν ἐν ἐκείνῃ τῇ ἡμέρᾳ.

21 Οὐδεὶς ἐπίβλημα ῥάκους ἀγνάφου ἐπιράπτει ἐπὶ ἱμάτιον παλαιόν· εἰ δὲ μή, αἴρει τὸ πλήρωμα ἀπ᾽ αὐτοῦ τὸ καινὸν τοῦ παλαιοῦ, καὶ χεῖρον σχίσμα γίνεται. 22 καὶ οὐδεὶς βάλλει οἶνον νέον εἰς ἀσκοὺς παλαιούς· εἰ δὲ μή, ῥήξει ὁ οἶνος τοὺς ἀσκούς, καὶ ὁ οἶνος ἀπόλλυται καὶ οἱ ἀσκοί. ἀλλὰ οἶνον νέον εἰς ἀσκοὺς καινούς. [SBLGNT]

King James Version	**New Rendition**
18 And the disciples of John and of the Pharisees used to fast: and they come and say unto him, Why do the disciples of John and of the Pharisees fast, but thy disciples fast not? 19 And Jesus said unto them, Can the children of the bride-chamber fast, while the bridegroom is with them? as long as they have the bridegroom with them, they cannot fast. 20 But the days will come, when the bridegroom shall be taken away from them, and then shall they fast in those days. 21 No man also seweth a piece of new cloth on an old garment: else the new piece that filled it up taketh away from the old, and the rent is made	18 And John's disciples and the Phari-sees were fasting. And people come and say to him, "Why do John's dis-ciples and the Pharisees' disciples fast, but your disciples do not fast?" 19 And Jesus said to them, "The wedding guests can't fast when the groom is with them, can they? As long as the groom is with them, they cannot fast. 20 But the days will come when the groom is taken away from them, and on that day they will fast. 21 No one sews a patch of unprepared cloth onto an old cloak; otherwise, the patch takes away part of the cloak—the new from the old—and a worse tear results. 22 And no one pours

worse. 22 And no man putteth new wine into old bottles: else the new wine doth burst the bottles, and the wine is spilled, and the bottles will be marred: but new wine must be put into new bottles.

new wine into old wineskins; otherwise, the wine bursts the skins and the wine is destroyed, as is the skin. But new wine is for new wineskins."

Notes

2:18 *And the disciples of John:* Not all disciples of John became disciples of Jesus (6:29; Matt. 11:2–3; Acts 18:25; 19:1–7), so there would have still been disciples of John at this point. This controversy comes immediately after the audience is introduced to the disciples of Jesus; Mark may have arranged the material to show the difference between Jesus' disciples and the disciples of John and the Pharisees: while Jesus' disciples were known for eating with people considered socially unacceptable, John's disciples were known for the self-denial of their fasting practices (compare Matt. 11:18–19).

and of the Pharisees: The idea of "disciples of the Pharisees" is unusual; there are two different ways to understand it:

1. One either was or was not a Pharisee and so there was no such thing as a disciple of the Pharisees, but Mark is more concerned with creating a parallel between "disciples of John" and "disciples of the Pharisees" than with literal accuracy.

2. It is possible that some people may have followed the Pharisees' rules but did not consider themselves to be Pharisees, and thus might have been considered disciples of the Pharisees.

used to fast: Fasting had the following contexts in Jesus' time:

1. Under the law of Moses, fasting was only required on the Day of Atonement.[40] Thus, it was understood as an act of repentance.

2. In the HB, fasting is an expression of mourning (1 Sam. 31:13; 2 Sam. 1:12; 3:35).

3. Fasting was an effort to seek God's favor (2 Sam. 12:15–23).

4. Zechariah 7:1–17 describes a yearly fast to commemorate the destruction of the temple. Later developments in Judaism added more fasts,[41] and the Pharisees fasted twice per week (Luke 18:12).

---

40. Lev. 16:29; the command "ye shall afflict your souls" was interpreted to mean that fasting was required.

41. Zech. 8:19 shows four annual fasts; Esth. 9:31 adds one more to the total. Luke 2:37 suggests additional, individual fasts.

This verse implies that Mark—but not his audience—was familiar with the customs of John's disciples and the Pharisees. It is material such as this—which explains customs—that leads some interpreters to believe that Mark's Gospel was written for an audience that was not very familiar with Palestine and its customs.

and they come and say unto him: It is unlikely that "they" refers to the disciples of John and the Pharisees (as it would be rather awkward for them to refer to themselves in the third person later in this verse); it is more likely that it refers to some (unspecified) others who wondered why Jesus' disciples' practice was different from what they saw other groups doing.

Why do the disciples of John and of the Pharisees fast: This description implies that other Jews did not fast in the same way.

but thy disciples fast not?: This question may be read as informational— a genuine question as to why his religious practice was different—or as hostile—criticizing them for improper behavior. It may seem odd that they are asking Jesus about the behavior of his disciples, but it was assumed that a disciple's behavior was the responsibility of his teacher. Thus, the question may have more to do with Jesus' authority to teach his disciples not to fast than with fasting per se. The fact that John's fasting practice was more like the Pharisees than like Jesus might imply that John lacked the authority to change the common fasting practice—an authority that Jesus does possess.

It is possible that this story is completely separate from the one before it, but it is also possible that the meal described in 2:15 occurred on one of the Pharisees' designated fast days and thus raised the question of why Jesus' disciples were eating when others were fasting; this would explain how they knew that Jesus' disciples did not fast.

2:19 *And Jesus said unto them, Can the children of the bridechamber fast:* In Greek, the form of the question indicates that the expected answer is no. (The words "can they?" were added to the end of the question in the New Rendition—despite the fact that there is no such phrase in the Greek text—in order to convey that Jesus expected a negative answer to his question.)

"Children of the bridechamber" is a very literal rendering of a Greek idiom (actually, of the Greek form of a Semitic idiom) whose meaning is either

1. Wedding guests. This meaning might better fit the context since in 2:13–17, the role of the disciples at the dinner seems closer to that of guests than of attendants.

2. Wedding attendants. This meaning might better fit the context since, in general, Jesus' disciples are more like wedding attendants than they are mere guests (3:9).

Either meaning points to a celebratory aspect to Jesus' ministry. While the end of the verse acknowledges a future time of mourning, Jesus' statement makes clear that future mourning does not abrogate the current celebration.

The wedding metaphor is a logical one to explain why Jesus' disciples did not need to fast because under Jewish law "wedding guests were freed from certain religious obligations that were deemed to be incompatible with the joy of the occasion."[42] Jesus' ministry should be a celebratory time since he is proclaiming the good news of the kingdom of God.

while the bridegroom is with them?: In the HB, there is no link between the coming Messiah and the bridegroom, but there is between the God of Israel and the bridegroom, which means that Jesus is implicitly identifying himself with the God of the HB (Isa. 54:5; 61:10; 62:4–5; Jer. 2:2; Ezek. 16; Hosea 2:19–20). So this story is not just about fasting but about Jesus' identity.

as long as they have the bridegroom with them: The subtext here is that being Jesus' disciple should be as joyous as attending a wedding. Given that Jesus will teach his disciples about his coming suffering and death—as well as the persecution and suffering that they will experience—this picture of joy forms an important counterpoint to the more somber aspects of his message.

they cannot fast: Of course, the disciples could fast—the point is that it would not be appropriate. Fasting was often a sign of mourning, and so they would not want to fast on a happy occasion.

It is important to interpret this statement in the context of the Pharisees' twice-per-week fast, since they were choosing to go well beyond (103 times beyond!) what the law of Moses required of them. Jesus is not denying the importance of fasting but rather releasing his disciples from the Pharisees' interpretation of the tradition.

2:20 *But the days will come when the bridegroom shall be taken away from them:* The idea of the groom being taken away would have struck the audience as most unexpected since "in Jewish wedding custom the guests leave rather than the bridegroom."[43]

The verb "taken away" suggests the use of force. Violently taking away the groom would suggest an attack, even a death and thus a funeral—where mourning and thus fasting would be appropriate—and hence a complete

---

42. Marcus, *Mark 1–8*, 233.
43. Guelich, *Mark 1–8:26*, 112.

reversal of the joyous wedding scene. There is the suggestion in this verse that what has happened to John will also happen to Jesus, thus emphasizing the theme established in the prologue that Jesus would follow John.

While subtle, this is Jesus' first reference to his own death in the Gospel of Mark.

and then shall they fast in those days: The "then" is emphatic in Greek, focusing attention on the contrast between the two times.

2:21 *No man also seweth a piece of new cloth:* "New" refers to cloth that had not been combed, bleached, and cleaned of impurities such as oils and gums. This treatment would shrink the cloth, so new cloth would contract substantially the first time that it was washed.

on an old garment: This analogy would have been particularly relevant to poorer people, who would have more experience than the wealthy with mending old clothes.

Relationship to Psalm 102. In Psalm 102:26–28, the world is compared to an old garment; in Hebrews 1:10–12, a similar comparison is made. So it is possible to read this text in Mark as suggesting that "Christ rolls up this old world-garment and unfurls the new cosmos."[44] Thus, Jesus is not here to "patch up" the old world but to reveal a new one.

---

else the new piece that filled it up: The word "piece" (Greek: *plērōma*) in this phrase is not the same word translated as "piece" (Greek: *epiblēma*) earlier in this verse; this may be a variation for stylistic reasons, but given that the word translated as "piece" in the second occurrence is the same word sometimes translated as "fullness" (John 1:16; Rom. 15:29), it may suggest that the new piece represents the "fullness" (of the gospel, of authority) that Jesus brings. If the cloth symbolizes the world, then the idea of Jesus bringing fullness to the world is particularly appropriate.

taketh away from the old: The Greek verb here is a compound form of the same verb used in 2:20 for the groom being taken away, which implies an association between Jesus and the patch: much as a new patch tears away, Jesus will be torn away. This in turn would suggest that Jesus is new and that he and his ministry are incompatible with the old order of things.

and the rent is made worse: New fabric sewn onto old fabric would, on the first washing, not only rip away from the old fabric but cause the old to tear even more.

---

44. Marcus, *Mark 1–8,* 234.

2:22 And no man putteth new wine into old bottles: else the new wine doth burst the bottles, and the wine is spilled: New wine was still fermenting and therefore still expanding. New skins (the KJV's "bottles" is misleading for the modern reader since Mark is describing a leather pouch) were soft and pliable but once aged would be stretched out and no longer able to expand. So new wine would cause old wineskins to tear apart.

and the bottles will be marred: Once again, Jesus emphasizes that not only would the new thing be harmed by the attempt to mix old and new but the old item would be harmed as well.

but new wine must be put into new bottles: It is possible to read this line as something akin to a slogan:[45] "new wine into new wineskins!"

Comparing 2:21 with 2:22. There are obvious similarities between these two examples since both involve mixing old and new and causing the destruction of both. Why, then, would Jesus have described both the patch and the wine instead of using just one example?

1. As a teaching technique, repetition allows for emphasis and an increased opportunity for the audience to understand the message.

2. With analogies or parables, there is always the danger that the audience will focus on the wrong aspect of the comparison and miss the message; combining two analogies decreases the likelihood of a mistake. (In this case, the point is that the new and old don't mix and destroy both; by contrast, the fact that the problem with the patch is shrinkage but with the wine is expansion suggests that neither shrinking nor expanding is the key part of the analogy.)

3. Multiple examples allow for more audience members to relate to the topic from their own experiences. In this case, the poor and the women in the audience would feel that Jesus was teaching in a way that was instantly understandable to them and that recognized their own experiences.

4. Multiple examples also allow for contrast. In this case, wine goes inside of a wineskin, but a patch goes on the outside of a garment, suggesting, perhaps, that both inward and outward observances are important.

Analysis

In this controversy, Jesus teaches that his disciples will fast—but not on the Pharisees' timetable. With this comment, Jesus makes clear that he is not rejecting the practice of fasting altogether but only in certain situations.[46]

---

45. Marcus, *Mark 1–8*, 238.

46. In the modern Church of Jesus Christ, pregnant women, nursing mothers, the elderly, small children, and those with certain medical conditions are not expected to

Because Mark records very little about church organization and practice, this one brief reference to fasting in Jesus' absence takes on an even greater significance as a guide for Christian practice. Whether his disciples should fast is not determined by laws or traditions but rather by Jesus' presence or absence. In other words, his body becomes the substitute for the traditions; his presence changes things. Because the appropriate time for fasting is determined by Jesus' own death, a link is made between his death and the only legally mandated fast, the Day of Atonement. Thus Jesus ties his own death to the concept of the Atonement.

While the obvious similarity in structure between 2:21 and 2:22 encourages their comparison, it might be better to think of Jesus as offering three separate analogies: the wedding, the new patch, and the new wine. These examples are linked by the fact that "a wedding requires good clothes on the part of the guests and an ample supply of wine on the part of the host."[47] Preparation for the wedding involves not fasting, but also not ruining the clothes or the wine. The inability of the guests to fast in the presence of the groom is similar to the inability of the new patch to work on an old cloak or new wine in old bottles. The problem isn't fasting, untreated patches, or new wine per se, but rather their presence at an inappropriate place and time. With both the wine and the patch, not only will the new item be ruined by mixing it with the old, but Jesus points out that the old will be ruined as well, resulting in a complete loss. So not only would fasting at the wrong time "destroy" the message of Jesus, but it would harm the practice of fasting as well.

Jesus' teachings about the old and the new suggest not only a contrast between his practice and that of the Pharisees but also between his teachings and that of John's. While John's ministry was appropriate for its time, even John himself recognized that a stronger one was coming (1:7). Jesus' teachings also emphasize the idea that the old and the new cannot simply be combined—one cannot just add Jesus' teachings on top of a base of others' beliefs and practices. (Jesus is not advocating a complete abandonment of the old: the very next story will show him using the HB as a guide to correct behavior.)

In a commentary designed to help translators determine how best to translate the Gospel of Mark into languages that had not yet had a NT

---

fast. While most Latter-day Saints understand this exception to be based on physical considerations, it is also true that "all things unto me are spiritual" (D&C 29:34), and so it is worth considering whether people in these situations enjoy a special presence of Jesus Christ, somewhat akin to his mortal ministry, that makes fasting inappropriate for them.

47. Gundry, *Mark*, 133–34.

translation, the authors recommend that "the best way to find the appropriate vocabulary [for sewing and patches] is to spend time observing proficient seamstresses, and finding out how they would describe such processes as sewing, ripping, shrinking, etc."[48] This advice acknowledges that sewing is normally women's work in traditional societies, which means Jesus is requiring his audience to identify with the labor and concerns of women. Thus one area to which Jesus' teachings about the old and the new can be applied is that he is requiring his audience to relate to the lives of women and the poor. Comprehending this saying would likely have required women to step into a teaching role to help men understand what it meant; this would have been revolutionary.

As the center point of the five controversy stories, the sayings about not mixing old and new cast a shadow over all of the other stories, whether the issue is forgiveness of sins, acceptable dinner guests, fasting, plucking grain on the Sabbath, or healing on the Sabbath. Each story can be understood as a time when Jesus is offering something entirely new, but critics are attempting to limit Jesus to the old ways of doing things: "Attempts to contain Jesus with these constraints have already proved futile, and his followers must be prepared to break free."[49]

JESUS TEACHES ABOUT THE SABBATH (2:23–28)

Greek Text

23 Καὶ ἐγένετο αὐτὸν ἐν τοῖς σάββασιν παραπορεύεσθαι διὰ τῶν σπορίμων, καὶ οἱ μαθηταὶ αὐτοῦ ἤρξαντο ὁδὸν ποιεῖν τίλλοντες τοὺς στάχυας. 24 καὶ οἱ Φαρισαῖοι ἔλεγον αὐτῷ· Ἴδε τί ποιοῦσιν τοῖς σάββασιν ὃ οὐκ ἔξεστιν; 25 καὶ λέγει αὐτοῖς· Οὐδέποτε ἀνέγνωτε τί ἐποίησεν Δαυὶδ ὅτε χρείαν ἔσχεν καὶ ἐπείνασεν αὐτὸς καὶ οἱ μετ' αὐτοῦ; 26 πῶς εἰσῆλθεν εἰς τὸν οἶκον τοῦ θεοῦ ἐπὶ Ἀβιαθὰρ ἀρχιερέως καὶ τοὺς ἄρτους τῆς προθέσεως ἔφαγεν, οὓς οὐκ ἔξεστιν φαγεῖν εἰ μὴ τοὺς ἱερεῖς, καὶ ἔδωκεν καὶ τοῖς σὺν αὐτῷ οὖσιν; 27 καὶ ἔλεγεν αὐτοῖς· Τὸ σάββατον διὰ τὸν ἄνθρωπον ἐγένετο καὶ οὐχ ὁ ἄνθρωπος διὰ τὸ σάββατον· 28 ὥστε κύριός ἐστιν ὁ υἱὸς τοῦ ἀνθρώπου καὶ τοῦ σαββάτου. [SBLGNT]

---

48. Bratcher and Nida, *Translator's Handbook,* 94.
49. France, *Gospel of Mark,* 142.

King James Version

23 And it came to pass, that he went through the corn fields on the sabbath day; and his disciples began, as they went, to pluck the ears of corn. 24 And the Pharisees said unto him, Behold, why do they on the sabbath day that which is not lawful? 25 And he said unto them, Have ye never read what David did, when he had need, and was an hungred, he, and they that were with him? 26 How he went into the house of God in the days of Abiathar the high priest, and did eat the shewbread, which is not lawful to eat but for the priests, and gave also to them which were with him? 27 And he said unto them, The sabbath was made for man, and not man for the sabbath: 28 Therefore the Son of man is Lord also of the sabbath.

New Rendition

23 And it happened on the Sabbath that he went through the grain fields. And his disciples began to make their way, plucking the grain. 24 And the Pharisees said to him, "Look, why do they do on the Sabbath that which is against the law?" 25 And he says to them, "Did you never read what David did, when he had need and was hungry, him and those with him, 26 how he went into the house of God in the time of Abiathar, the high priest, and ate the consecrated bread—which is unlawful for any to eat except the priests—and he gave some to those who were with him?" 27 And he said to them, "The Sabbath was made for the sake of people, and not people for the Sabbath." 28 So the son of man is even master of the Sabbath.

Notes

2:23 *And it came to pass:* It is likely that Mark used this phrase to create a biblical sound in the text, making it another example of Mark's irony: "a passage in which Jesus' disciples are to be accused of violating a biblical law begins with the Old Testament formula 'and it came to pass.'"[50] For the perceptive reader or listener, this phrase would contribute to the redefinition of what it means to be scriptural.

that he went through the corn fields: The KJV's "corn" is likely misleading to American readers since the grain would have been wheat or barley and not maize, which is a New World crop and was therefore unknown to the biblical world.

on the sabbath day; and his disciples began, as they went: It is debated whether "began" describes making their way (KJV: "as they went") or "plucking."[51]

---

50. Marcus, *Mark 1–8,* 244.
51. Bratcher and Nida, *Translator's Handbook,* 97.

The normal practice would have been for Jesus, as the teacher, to walk in front of his disciples. While it is possible that the passage conforms to that custom, it is more likely that the text pictures the disciples walking ahead of Jesus.

to pluck the ears of corn: There is a textual variant here: this passage probably first read that they began "to make a way by plucking,"[52] meaning that the purpose of plucking the grain was to clear a path through which they could walk. It appears that some later manuscripts changed it to "to pluck," probably because there seemed to be a discrepancy between what they were doing (plucking to clear a path) and Jesus' explanation (plucking to eat because of hunger).

They are not plucking "ears of corn" but heads of grain. A modern reader might wonder if this was considered theft. It was not, since the law of Moses permitted people to pluck what they could gather just with their hands—not with a sickle—from a field (Deut. 23:25). There are three possible reasons for why they were plucking the grain:

1. They were making a path for Jesus. Evidence for this reading includes:

   a. In 2:23, the grammatical emphasis seems to be on making a way, not on eating.

   b. The phrase "as they went" can mean "to create a road."[53]

   c. No one is described as eating, and the story does not say that they were hungry.

   d. Jesus himself apparently does not pluck the grain, just the disciples. Making a way would be the role of the disciples.

   e. This reading fulfills the Isaiah prophecy quoted in 1:3 ("Prepare ye the way of the Lord, make his paths straight"). Ironically, the Pharisees miss this important moment because they are focused on (their interpretation of) the Sabbath rules.

   f. A Jewish tradition that may have been extant in Jesus' lifetime (although there is no written record of it until later) grants kings the right to make a road through any property.[54] If this practice were on Mark's mind, it would suggest an element of royal imagery in the story.

   g. If the disciples were walking in front of Jesus, then it emphasizes his "royal authority, since royal visits were often prepared for by roadworks."[55]

---

52. Collins, *Mark*, 200.

53. Marcus, *Mark 1–8*, 239.

54. Collins, *Mark*, 205.

55. Marcus, *Mark 1–8*, 239.

h. It makes better sense of the David story, which is not about activity prohibited on the Sabbath but rather about the special prerogatives of kings.
The point of the David story is that very special circumstances justify violation of the law; it is probably easier to locate similar circumstances in the
need to further Jesus' ministry than in the physical desire to eat.

2. They were hungry. Evidence for this reading includes:

a. In the David story, his men are hungry, not creating a path through a field;
by analogy, that reading would be more likely here.

b. In Matthew's and Luke's uses of the story (Matt. 12:1; Luke 6:1), the disciples' hunger (Matthew) and the eating of the grain (Luke) is specifically
mentioned. (Of course, it is possible that they understood this story differently than Mark did.)

c. The idea of plucking grain to make a path does not make sense on a logical
level since removing the heads of grain would not create a path; the stalks
would need to be removed as well.

3. It is possible that there are two layers of meaning here—a literal level of hunger and a more symbolic level (perhaps created by or expanded upon by
Mark) of making a path.

2:24 *And the Pharisees said unto him:* It is possible that the presence
of Pharisees in the middle of a field is another example of Mark's irony if
they are thought to be violating the Sabbath. But it is also possible that the
Pharisees' behavior is within their interpretation of the law if they were
neither picking grain nor walking farther than was permitted.

It is likely that they directed the question to Jesus (and not to the disciples) because a teacher was considered responsible for the behavior of
his students.

Behold, why do they on the sabbath day that which is not lawful?:
The law of Moses prohibited work, including reaping, on the Sabbath (Ex.
34:21). If the disciples were creating a path, that also would have been
forbidden and may have further offended the Pharisees by its equation of
Jesus with the royal one who had been promised by the prophets.

The HB mandated death for Sabbath violations (Ex. 31:14–15); later Jewish tradition required a warning before that penalty was imposed.[56] It is
possible to read this question—which is not a simple request for information but rather an attack phrased as a question—as the warning tradition
required. (See also the Notes on 3:2 and 3:6.)

---

56. Bavli Sanhedrin 8b.

2:25 *And he said unto them, Have ye never read:* The Greek form of this question presumes an affirmative answer. Of course the Pharisees would have read this story; the point behind Jesus' question is that they had not understood or applied what they had read.

what David did, when he had need, and was an hungred, he, and they that were with him?: See 1 Samuel 21:1–6.

2:26 *How he went into the house of God:* At this time, the "house of God" would have been the tabernacle. David, who was not a priest, should not have entered into it.

in the days of Abiathar the high priest: Many manuscripts omit this phrase, presumably because in 1 Samuel 21, the priest in question was Ahimelech and not Abiathar. (Some variant readings state that it was during the lifetime of, not during the high priesthood of, Abiathar.[57]) There are many theories to explain the reference to "Abiathar" in this text:

1. It did not refer to the time of the high priest but rather to the section of the scroll where the story about the bread could be found.

2. The phrase meant "in the lifetime of Abiathar."

3. It originally read "the father of Abiathar" but "the father of" dropped out because the beginning of the words "father" and "Abiathar" were similar. (But why would Jesus refer to "the father of Abiathar"?)

4. The whole phrase is a later addition. Perhaps the most puzzling aspect of the text is that it is difficult to understand why Jesus would have made reference to any high priest, as it is not relevant to the story. So perhaps this phrase was an early (and incorrect) gloss. This would explain why the line is missing from Matthew and Luke: it was not included in their copies of the Gospel of Mark.

5. The earlier reading, referring to Abiathar, is a textbook example of "the mistakes of men"[58] that can occur in a record: either Mark (or a source) erred in naming Abiathar here.[59] Because Abiathar was associated with David as the high priest during his reign, it is an understandable mistake.

It is likely that the text is in error; the other theories come mostly from those committed to the inerrancy of scripture. While the error is not terribly significant, it does raise an interesting question: Does the mistaken referent stem from Jesus or from Mark (or a source)? If it was Mark's or a

---

57. Metzger, *Textual Commentary,* 68.
58. Title Page of the Book of Mormon.
59. Note that both Matthew and Luke omit any reference to the high priest.

source's error, then this is an instance where Mark did not correctly record Jesus' words. If it was Jesus' error—an option most Latter-day Saints would not find acceptable, although perhaps some readings of Luke 2:52 ("and Jesus increased in wisdom") would permit such a position—then that speaks to the nature of his mortal limitations.

and did eat the shewbread: On each Sabbath, twelve loaves of bread (KJV: "shewbread") were placed on a table in the tabernacle (and, later, in the temple). At the end of the week, the old loaves were given to the priests (Lev. 24:5–9).

which is not lawful to eat but for the priests: There are two different ways to understand this phrase:

1. It is Mark's aside to the audience to explain an unfamiliar Jewish custom or to emphasize the key element of the story.

2. It is part of what Jesus says to the Pharisees, who would have been well aware that it was not lawful for the laity to eat this bread; Jesus would not have been providing new information but rather highlighting the point of the story.

Either way, the phrase concedes the point that it was unlawful for the disciples to pluck the grain—the issue is not what constitutes a violation of the law but rather whether this situation justified violating it.

The main issue here is not what is or is not done on the Sabbath but rather Jesus' authority: if David was allowed to do something contrary to the rules, then how much more should Jesus be allowed to since, as will soon be seen, he is the Lord of the Sabbath.

and gave also to them which were with him?: This statement creates something of a conundrum because, contrary to these words, it does not seem that David's men were in fact with him, and there is no record in 1 Samuel of him actually sharing the bread with them.

Relationship to 1 Samuel 21:2–6. It is likely that Jesus is referring in 2:25–26 to 1 Samuel 21:2–6. However, there are a few differences between that story and what Mark has preserved in Jesus' retelling of it:

1. David refers to having men with him (1 Sam. 21:2), but this seems to be more of a ruse than a fact.

2. In 1 Samuel 21:4, the priest's objection is not that David is not a priest, but rather his answer implies that David and his men can eat the bread as long as they are ritually pure. Both Leviticus 24:9 and Mark's text imply that the bread is restricted to priests only.

3. Jesus' story refers to Abiathar, but the priest in 1 Samuel 21 is Ahimelech.

There are several possible ways to reconcile these discrepancies:

1. Jesus was recounting a different story, one with many similarities to 1 Samuel 21, but nonetheless a different incident. There are many pairs of stories in the HB where two different events are narrated with significant overlap between the stories. In this case, Jesus would be relating a story not otherwise preserved in the HB.

2. Jesus was familiar with a version of 1 Samuel 21 that was quite a bit different from the extant record (although the same historical incident was behind his account and 1 Samuel 21).

3. Jesus was shaping the details of 1 Samuel 21 to fit his purposes. While this seems improper to modern readers, ancient interpreters of scripture did not have the same expectation. (The fact that Jesus' use of the text is meant to convince the Pharisees may weigh against this theory, since they would have to accept his retelling.)

2:27 *And he said unto them:* Sometimes Mark uses this phrase to introduce a completely separate saying, so it is possible that this material was included here not because Jesus said this immediately after what he said in 2:26 but because Mark felt it fit in with the theme of Sabbath observance.

The sabbath was made for man: Jesus' statement contains an important insight about the Sabbath: the Sabbath was created. It is perhaps unusual to think of the Sabbath as a created entity, but this language, as well as the Creation account in Genesis 1–2, encourages this view of the Sabbath. God's powers extend not only to the creation of objects but to sacred time.

and not man for the sabbath: This phrase is probably best read as another example of dialectical negation,[60] meaning that the negative term is not completely negated but the positive term is emphasized.

2:28 *Therefore the Son of man:* There are two different ways to understand this verse:

1. The "therefore" implies that Jesus is still speaking, and this verse is the conclusion he draws from his statement in the previous verse.

2. The "therefore" signals that this is the conclusion that Mark is drawing from Jesus' words. So Mark, and not Jesus, is the speaker here; Mark felt the need to explain to his audience what conclusion they should draw from Jesus' statement in the previous verse.

There are also two ways to interpret the phrase "Son of Man":

1. "Son of Man" refers to any human being. Because the Sabbath was created for man, each person is therefore lord (or master) of the Sabbath, with the right

---

60. See the Notes on 2:17.

to determine what is or is not appropriate on the Sabbath. Support for this reading includes:

  a. The question is the behavior of Jesus' disciples—not Jesus himself—on the Sabbath; thus, the issue is the privileges of the disciples. In that context, it makes more sense to see this passage as suggesting that all disciples—and not just Jesus—are masters of the Sabbath.

  b. Because Jesus uses a story rooted in David's special prerogatives as king to justify his disciples' behavior on the Sabbath, the implication is that Jesus' followers have the same rights as kings and priests.

2. "Son of Man" refers to Jesus. In this verse, Jesus (or Mark) is explaining that he has the authority to determine what is proper Sabbath observance. Support for this reading includes the following:

  a. Mark usually uses the phrase "Son of Man" in the context of Daniel 7 (2:10), which refers to one special figure who is given authority, not to humans in general.

  b. "Son of Man" probably would not have had an article ("the Son of Man" versus "a son of man") if it meant any human.[61] Because it has the article in this case, it refers to Jesus.

  c. In Jesus' own time, "Son of Man" could have referred to any human, but by the time of the Gospel of Mark and its audience, it is a title for Jesus. Therefore, the Gospel would have needed to provide some explanation if it intended to refer to a particular person.

is Lord also of the sabbath: "Lord" is an acceptable translation here, but so is "lord" (lowercase and thus not a reference to Jesus but to anyone acting in a ruling capacity) or "master," which may be preferable in this context, since the idea is that the Son of Man is the master of the Sabbath.

In the HB, "God is the Lord of the Sabbath because he instituted and consecrated it."[62] Once again, Jesus is subtly identifying himself with the God of the HB.

Jesus' Three Answers. When presented with a question about plucking grain on the Sabbath, Jesus offers three separate answers: David's story, the saying about the Sabbath being made for man, and the statement about the Son of Man being the Lord of the Sabbath. (It is also possible to parse this as two answers instead of three, with the "Lord of the Sabbath" saying as the conclusion drawn from the fact that the Sabbath was created for man and therefore part of that saying.) Why did Jesus offer more than one response?

61. Marcus, *Mark 1–8,* 246.
62. Stein, *Mark,* 149.

1. The David story was an incomplete answer and therefore required more explanation.
2. The David story is an argument from scripture, while the two other answers are logical explanations.
3. It is likely that Mark's material is not in chronological order; it is therefore possible that the second or third answers were delivered at other points in Jesus' ministry but were placed here because they fit the theme of Sabbath observance.

Relationship to 2:13–17. There is likely a chiastic arrangement in this group of five controversy stories, which means that this story should be compared with 2:13–17. Both stories concern discipleship, eating, and the observance of the law. Both imply that Jesus' authority permits his disciples to behave in ways contrary to expectations. The chiastic structure thus emphasizes the issue of Jesus' authority.

Relationship to 2:18–22. There is a compelling tension between this story and the previous one: here, Jesus uses an example from the HB as a guide to proper behavior. In the last story, he taught that the "old" and the "new" should not be mixed. Clearly, he did not consider the HB part of the old; perhaps Mark juxtaposed these stories to make precisely that point.

Analysis

When confronted about his disciples' behavior, Jesus compares himself to David and thus alludes to his role as the Davidic Messiah. Jesus implies that he has the same status as David because of his similar ability to be exempt from a law as special circumstances require. If the purpose of plucking grain was to make a path, then royal themes are emphasized and Jesus is pictured as the king for whose royal visit a road is made.

In 1 Samuel 21, David is taking on the role of the priest by eating something that only the priest should eat, so David is acting as both priest and king. This dual role might explain why Jesus chose this story despite the fact that the incident is not a perfect parallel to his situation.

In a sense, the real issue here is not Sabbath observance but Jesus' authority to determine what constitutes appropriate Sabbath observance. The emphasis on Jesus' authority is heightened by the fact that the story does not portray Jesus himself plucking or eating but permitting his disciples to do so and then defending them when they do.

JESUS HEALS ON THE SABBATH (3:1–6)

Greek Text

1 Καὶ εἰσῆλθεν πάλιν εἰς συναγωγήν, καὶ ἦν ἐκεῖ ἄνθρωπος ἐξηραμμένην ἔχων τὴν χεῖρα. 2 καὶ παρετήρουν αὐτὸν εἰ τοῖς σάββασιν θεραπεύσει αὐτόν, ἵνα κατηγορήσωσιν αὐτοῦ. 3 καὶ λέγει τῷ ἀνθρώπῳ τῷ τὴν χεῖρα ἔχοντι ξηράν· Ἔγειρε εἰς τὸ μέσον. 4 καὶ λέγει αὐτοῖς· Ἔξεστιν τοῖς σάββασιν ἀγαθοποιῆσαι ἢ κακοποιῆσαι, ψυχὴν σῶσαι ἢ ἀποκτεῖναι; οἱ δὲ ἐσιώπων. 5 καὶ περιβλεψάμενος αὐτοὺς μετ᾽ ὀργῆς, συλλυπούμενος ἐπὶ τῇ πωρώσει τῆς καρδίας αὐτῶν, λέγει τῷ ἀνθρώπῳ· Ἔκτεινον τὴν χεῖρα· καὶ ἐξέτεινεν, καὶ ἀπεκατεστάθη ἡ χεὶρ αὐτοῦ. 6 καὶ ἐξελθόντες οἱ Φαρισαῖοι εὐθὺς μετὰ τῶν Ἡρῳδιανῶν συμβούλιον ἐδίδουν κατ᾽ αὐτοῦ ὅπως αὐτὸν ἀπολέσωσιν. [SBLGNT]

King James Version

1 And he entered again into the synagogue; and there was a man there which had a withered hand. 2 And they watched him, whether he would heal him on the sabbath day; that they might accuse him. 3 And he saith unto the man which had the withered hand, Stand forth. 4 And he saith unto them, Is it lawful to do good on the sabbath days, or to do evil? to save life, or to kill? But they held their peace. 5 And when he had looked round about on them with anger, being grieved for the hardness of their hearts, he saith unto the man, Stretch forth thine hand. And he stretched it out: and his hand was restored whole as the other. 6 And the Pharisees went forth, and straightway took counsel with the Herodians against him, how they might destroy him.

New Rendition

1 And again he entered into the synagogue. And there was a man with a deformed hand. 2 And they were watching him closely, whether he would heal him on the Sabbath, so they could accuse him. 3 And he says to the man who had the deformed hand, "Stand in the middle." 4 And he says to them, "Is it legal on the Sabbath to do good or to do evil? To save life or to kill?" But they were silent. 5 And having looked around at them with anger, being grieved at the hardness of their hearts, he says to the man, "Stretch out your hand." And he stretched it out, and his hand was restored. 6 And having gone out, the Pharisees immediately conspired with the Herodians against him, how they could destroy him.

Notes

3:1 *And he entered again into the synagogue:* This seems to be the same synagogue as in 2:1 (hence the "again"), although this is not explicitly stated.

The wording "and he entered again" is very similar to "and again he entered" in 2:1, so Mark is drawing attention to the chiastic structure of the five controversy stories by locating the first and last stories in the synagogue and introducing them with similar wording.

and there was a man there which had a withered hand: "Withered" is a figurative expression (literally: "dried up"); it is not clear from the Greek text what precisely was wrong with his hand, but the point is that he cannot use it.

"A man" echoes the previous story, which stated that the Sabbath was made for "man" and not man for the Sabbath. The question here is: How does one observe the Sabbath in the presence of this man?

3:2 And they watched him: The precise identity of the "they" is not explained here, but see 3:6.

"Watched" has the connotation of "to lie in wait"; it is not disinterested observation but watching with negative intent and anticipating a specific outcome. This is the same verb used elsewhere in the NT for close observance of the law (Gal. 4:10); Mark is ironically showing the Pharisees directing the attention that they should be devoting to following the law to Jesus instead. (Which is ironic on multiple levels: first, because the Pharisees would claim that they were focused on watching the law and not Jesus and, secondly, because Mark would approve of a focus on Jesus instead of the law.)

whether he would heal him on the sabbath day: They are not doubting his ability to heal—just the propriety of doing so on the Sabbath—so this is an indirect testimony of his ability to heal.

Observance of the Sabbath was a key marker for Jewish identity; it was not just one rule among many but rather the rule that marked them as a distinct people. The previous story announced that Jesus was Lord of the Sabbath; this story will show how the Lord of the Sabbath acts on the Sabbath.

that they might accuse him: "Accuse" is a technical term for bringing legal charges against someone.[63]

As mentioned above, Sabbath violations merited a death penalty, but the law was interpreted to require a warning first. It appears that the encounter over plucking grain on the Sabbath was Jesus' warning, and now they are watching him closely for a second Sabbath violation so they can pursue a death penalty, presumably before a local court. The story portrays their single-minded focus on watching for a violation; they are not paying attention to the specifics of the situation—in this case, that Jesus intends to heal and therefore do good.

---

63. Bratcher and Nida, *Translator's Handbook,* 104.

Relationship to Psalm 37:12. The verb used here for "watch" is the same verb found in LXX Psalm 36:12 (KJV Psalm 37:12, "plotteth") where sinners are watching and planning to slay a good person; the irony of the allusion is that it casts the Pharisees in the role of the sinners. Further, while they think they are getting ready to entrap Jesus, Jesus ends up entrapping them by asking a question that points to the contradictions of their position (since they will seek to kill on the Sabbath) and shows how they are the ones who are truly violating the Sabbath. The echo of Psalm 37:12 points the careful listener to the ways in which this text in Mark is the opposite of what it might initially seem to be.

3:3 *And he saith unto the man which had the withered hand, Stand forth:* The synagogue likely had benches around the perimeter and mats on the floor. The Greek text reads literally "arise in the middle," so Jesus is inviting the man from the periphery to the center of the room, where all could see him. There are two possible (and not mutually exclusive) reasons for this:

1. Jesus hopes to kindle some compassion for the man from the crowd once they see him close up.

2. Because they are watching Jesus closely (as if they expect Jesus to hide his actions), Jesus goes out of his way to perform the miracle in the most public way possible. This would be another example of the inversion of expectations and irony in this story.

3:4 *And he saith unto them, Is it lawful to do good on the sabbath days, or to do evil?:* No one has said anything; Jesus has either read their thoughts or is aware that they have been watching him for a second Sabbath violation.

Normally, Sabbath observance was framed in terms of doing something versus not doing something, so Jesus is changing the classification scheme from "do" or "don't do" to "do good" or "do evil." The implication is that, in some cases, refraining from action can itself be evil. It is debated whether "evil" refers to moral evil or to harm here. The Pharisees' rules privilege inaction, but Jesus teaches that inaction is a choice with consequences.[64]

to save life, or to kill?: Jewish tradition permitted breaking the Sabbath in order to save a life,[65] so the Pharisees would have readily agreed that one can save a life on the Sabbath no matter what rules have to be broken to do

---

64. One potential weakness of this interpretation is that it appears to do away with the idea of the Sabbath as a special time if one can do anything that is "good." (In other words, if that were the case, what would be left to distinguish the Sabbath from any other day?)

65. Babylonian Talmud, Seder Mo'ed III, Yoma 83b–84a.

so. But the man's hand is unlikely to cause his death that day, which raises questions about how this saying would apply here and leads to several different interpretations of Jesus' statement:

1. Jesus is alluding to Deuteronomy 30:14–19 (where the Lord sets out two paths, one of life and the other of death), which implies that this situation has two paths: one where the man's full life, including temple worship, is possible, and one with a wooden examination for Sabbath violations, ending with the goal of killing Jesus. Because the Deuteronomy text mentions cursings, Jesus is suggesting that the Pharisees have chosen to curse themselves by choosing (Jesus') death over (the man's) life. Jesus' allusion makes clear that the Pharisees are on the side of the wicked—a truly remarkable accusation. LXX Deuteronomy 30:14 mentions the mouth, heart, hands, and doing, all four of which are also mentioned in this story in Mark.[66] In the HB text, references to the hand are prominent in the context of the violation of covenants as a result of failing to act; if this is paralleled to Mark's text, it implies that the man with the withered hand is literally suffering the consequences of the curses of inaction, from which Jesus rescues him by his own action.

2. The passage implies that withholding healing is a form of killing: "Jesus makes withholding the cure of the man's paralyzed hand, even for a few hours, tantamount to killing him, and performing the cure immediately tantamount to saving his life. For Mark's Jesus, the [last days] war is already raging, and on that battlefield every human action either strikes a blow for life or wields one for death; the cautious middle ground, upon which one might wait a few minutes before doing good, has disappeared."[67]

3. Jewish tradition held that if there is any doubt concerning whether life is in danger, it is acceptable to heal on the Sabbath, even for an illness as minor as a sore throat. Since there is at least a hypothetical chance that the withered hand could cause the man's death before the Sabbath is over and it would show callous disregard for the man's life to take the risk, healing him constitutes saving a life. And the objectors' actions are all the more venal since Jesus' healing was permitted under the law.

4. "Life" is to be understood as "quality of life." The man's withered hand would have prevented him from participating in temple worship (Lev. 21:16–23). So Jesus is not merely restoring a hand but also restoring his ability to engage in temple worship. This reading links this story to 2:1–12, since restoring the man's hand makes worshiping possible, just as the forgiveness in 2:1–12 restores the man's spiritual wholeness.

---

66. Kurt Queller, "'Stretch Out Your Hand!': Echo and Metalepsis in Mark's Sabbath Healing Controversy," *Journal of Biblical Literature* 129, no. 4 (2010): 744. The parallel to "doing" is found in the man's action of stretching out his hand.

67. Marcus, *Mark 1–8*, 252.

5. "Save" can have a theological meaning in Mark (5:34; 10:26; 13:13). This would imply that Jesus' miracle will increase the man's faith and therefore "save" his soul—an action most appropriate to the Sabbath. This reading creates a nice link to this controversy story's chiastic partner (2:1–12), where the issue is forgiveness of sins.

6. This statement is an example of exaggeration to make a point.

Regardless of which interpretation is correct, Jesus' reference to taking a life applies to the plot against his own life (see 3:6). Obviously it is a violation to kill someone on any day of the week, and yet the Pharisees are closely watching Jesus so they can level an accusation that will result in his death. In this sense, the contrast between his actions and theirs is clear: to any extent that Jesus is guilty of violating the Sabbath, they are guilty of much, much worse.

One implication of Jesus' statement is that the categories that they have adopted ("do" and "don't do") create horrifying outcomes, since the man can be left disabled on the Sabbath, but it is permissible to plan a murder.

But they held their peace: Because the obvious retort—that the man's withered hand did not endanger his life—is not voiced, it appears that they understood that Jesus was referring to their plot to kill him. There might also be an allusion here to how Jesus silences demons.

Any number of theories could be offered for their silence, but the next verse states that Jesus attributed it to their hardness of heart.

3:5 *And when he had looked round about on them with anger:* "Looking around" seems to be in anticipation of an answer to his question; when none is forthcoming, Jesus' anger changes to grief.

being grieved for the hardness of their hearts: Having hard hearts implied being set in their ways and unwilling to learn something new or to think differently. Because Israel often responded to the prophets with hard-heartedness (Deut. 29:18; Jer. 7:24; 9:13; 13:10), Mark is portraying Jesus as the rejected prophet and the Pharisees as unrepentant Israel. Additionally, several key texts show Pharaoh to be hard-hearted (Ex. 7:3, 13), thus linking the Pharisees to Pharaoh, a link enhanced by the fact that in Greek both words are quite similar. Since Pharaoh was the archetypal enemy of God's people, this is quite a stinging indictment of the Pharisees.

There are two references to Jesus' emotional state here: he is angry and grieved. There are several possible reasons for Mark to mention this:

1. The focus on Jesus' emotions delays the narration of the healing and thus increases the tension and drama in the story.

2. There was an expectation in the Roman world that healers would show some sort of emotionally heightened state before performing a healing; perhaps Jesus was conforming to this cultural convention.

3. The references show that Jesus was not only concerned with the man but also with his opponents, for whom he grieves.

he saith unto the man, Stretch forth thine hand: Despite the emotions directed at the Pharisees, Jesus does not speak to them; his words are addressed to the man.

Unlike many of his other healing miracles, Jesus does not touch the man. This raises the question of whether Jesus could be accused of performing work on the Sabbath:

1. Because speaking was not defined as work,[68] Jesus had not violated the Sabbath laws. This makes the plot to kill him (see 3:6) all the more insidious, since he has not broken any law.

2. There is evidence from ancient Jewish tradition indicating that it was not an act per se but rather the intent for which it was performed that determined whether the Sabbath was violated: "it is the intention of healing and the performance of any activity for the purpose of healing that are forbidden on the Sabbath. The issue does not seem to be whether what one does is otherwise defined as work or not, since the same activity is permitted if it is not done with the intention of healing. In other words, anything done with the intention of healing is defined as work, even if the same activity done without the intention of healing would not be classified as work."[69] Thus, Jesus did in fact work on the Sabbath and violated (the Pharisees' interpretation of) the law.

It is likely that a withered hand could not be stretched out, so Jesus is commanding him to do something that requires him to have been healed in order to do it. (Compare 2:1–12, where Jesus' command to the man to take up his bed and walk requires that he be healed in order to do so.)

And he stretched it out: and his hand was restored whole as the other: "Whole as the other" does not appear in the best ancient manuscripts,[70] but even without this phrase, the text presumes that his hand was restored to the same state as his other hand.

"Restored" (Greek: *apokathistēmi*) is the same word used in 9:12, in the context that Elijah will "restore" all things. This suggests a metaphorical aspect to the restoration, particularly if the man's withered hand was regarded as evidence of sin.

---

68. Witherington, *Gospel of Mark*, 136.
69. Collins, *Mark,* 207.
70. Comfort, *New Testament Text and Translation Commentary*, 103.

Relationship to Exodus 14. The following points of contact between this story and Exodus 14 have been identified:[71]

1. "Stretch out your hand" is the same phrase as in LXX Exodus 14:16. This parallel puts the man with the withered hand in the role of Moses and Jesus in the role of the God of the HB. In Exodus, the stretched hand introduces plagues, but in Mark's story, it ends one; this inversion speaks to Jesus' power to right wrongs and perhaps even subtly alludes to the Atonement. Much as the plagues were a witness to Pharaoh, the ending of the man's plague should be a witness to the Pharisees of Jesus' power. (One of the most remarkable—and yet rarely remarked upon—aspects of Mark's story is that the scribes seem completely unaffected by witnessing a miracle.) Just as Moses and Aaron stretch forth their hands to enact plagues that condemn Pharaoh, the man's stretching out of his hand seems like it will condemn Jesus (to the death plot) but, ironically, ends up condemning the Pharisees.

2. The word for "restored" (Greek: *apokathistēmi*) is the same word used in LXX Exodus 14:27, where the waters are "restored." There are two possible ways to understand this parallel:

   a. Much as the restoring of the water resulted in the death of the Egyptian army, the restoring of the man's hand results in Jesus' death (as a result of the Pharisees' plot). Unlike Pharaoh's army, however, Jesus is innocent of wrongdoing, a fact which encourages the audience to draw some conclusions here about the Atonement, mainly that Jesus' suffering is unjustified.

   b. The restoring of the waters is what made it possible for the children of Israel to be free. Similarly, the restoring of the man's hand frees him to fully participate in life and worship. (And in a typical example of Mark's irony, it has precisely the opposite effect on Jesus since it will ultimately lead to his death.)

3. "In the midst of the sea" (LXX Ex. 14:16, 22, and 23) might explain the odd phrasing in 3:3 inviting the man to appear in the middle. Much as the focus in Exodus 14 is on the miraculous action that affects the sea, the focus in Mark's story should not be on the watching Pharisees or the death plot but on the miracle that happens to the man.

4. The reference to hardness of heart parallels Pharaoh's hardness of heart (despite the fact that the LXX uses different language to describe it).

5. The "withered" (dried out) hand might allude to the Red Sea, which also becomes "dried out," although the same word is not used. In both cases, the "restoration" points to miraculous powers and divine care.

---

71. Queller, "'Stretch Out Your Hand!'" 739–41.

6. Just as Pharaoh's plot to enslave the Hebrews failed because of divine intervention, the Pharisees' plot to kill Jesus will ultimately fail because of the Resurrection.

Relationship to Isaiah 56:1–8. Isaiah 56:1–8 has several resonances with 3:1–5, including references to the Sabbath, the hand, and being dried up. If Mark wrote with that story in mind, it suggests the following:

1. In the Isaiah passage, the main concern is the exclusion of a physically imperfect man (a eunuch) from being counted among the people of the Lord. In Mark's passage, the man with the withered hand would have been excluded from temple worship. So the topic at hand is not so much working on the Sabbath but the inclusion or exclusion of people from the house of God. Mark's story makes the point that restoring this man to the blessings of full participation in the house of Israel was a most appropriate act for the Sabbath. Isaiah 56:3 emphasizes that the Lord's ministry will not and must not exclude anyone, so by analogy, Mark's story implies that Jesus will not allow this man to be excluded from the blessings of full participation.

2. The Isaiah text is focused on the will and actions of the Lord, who is the one who restores the eunuch. Thus, Mark's text focuses attention on Jesus as the Lord who reveals righteousness (see Isa. 56:1).

3. Immediately after issuing the command to promote justice (Isa. 56:1), the Lord commands the people to keep the Sabbath. This parallel ensures that Mark's story is not interpreted as encouraging lawlessness but rather as promoting honoring the Sabbath by saving a life.

The Isaiah passage ends with a reference to the Lord gathering all people who will follow him. In the Markan context, the withered man is one of those people (at least literarily if not literally). The position of the Pharisees is that it is acceptable to exclude this man; Jesus' position is that including this man supersedes the need to follow the Sabbath rules. Because the prevailing interpretation of Sabbath rules permitted violations when life was at stake, Jesus' point here is that exclusion from the temple rituals constitutes a sort of living death.

3:6 *And the Pharisees went forth:* In 3:2, Jesus' opponents were mentioned but not by name (they were called "they"); here, they are called Pharisees. It is odd that Mark would identify them here but not at the beginning of the story; this verse may suggest that their identity is, in a sense, revealed by their actions.

The verb "went forth" (Greek: *exerchomai*) is not required to advance the narrative, so it may be here to emphasize the Pharisees' act of leaving the synagogue. The story began with Jesus entering the synagogue, so Jesus is aligned with the place of worship, but the Pharisees abandon that place.

and straightway took counsel with the Herodians against him: "Immediately" (KJV: "straightway") makes clear that the healing leads directly to the plot against Jesus. It is amazing that their reaction to a miracle is not awe but rather vengeance. The "immediately" also makes clear that they are plotting Jesus' death on the Sabbath. Mark exposes them as the rankest hypocrites for accusing Jesus of breaking the Sabbath by healing, while they are willing to violate the Sabbath by planning to kill Jesus. Jesus' comment about killing on the Sabbath (3:4) indicates that he anticipated their actions.

There is some debate as to who exactly the Herodians were; possible meanings include:

1. a group that thought Herod was the Messiah
2. a (religious) group favoring (or favored by) Herod
3. the Essenes
4. the Sadducees
5. a political group
6. people from Herod's household
7. Jews who disliked Roman rule
8. a Roman group
9. Jews who lived in certain geographic areas
10. tax collectors
11. the scribes
12. a local government council[72]
13. some combination of the above groups that had formed an alliance
14. there was no group called "Herodians"; it is Mark's creation, meant to link Jesus' fate to John's since Herod had John killed.[73]

Regardless of who the Herodians actually were, it is not clear which "Herod" is referenced since "Herod" was the name of a dynasty.[74] Because

---

72. Collins, *Mark,* 210.

73. List adapted from John P. Meier, "The Historical Jesus and the Historical Herodians," *Journal of Biblical Literature* 119, no. 4 (2000): 741.

74. Meier, "Historical Jesus and the Historical Herodians," 742.

there are very few references to this group in the NT,[75] little is known about them. But there is evidence that Herod disagreed with the Pharisees, so the idea of the Pharisees and the Herodians working together is puzzling. Perhaps the Pharisees and Herodians put aside their antipathy in order to silence Jesus. Since the Pharisees would have needed cooperation from local Roman rulers in order to put Jesus to death, this would have encouraged the Pharisees to work with them despite disagreeing on other matters.

how they might destroy him: "Destroy" is the same verb used in 1:24, where the demons asked if Jesus had come to destroy them. So by attempting to destroy Jesus, the Pharisees have aligned themselves with the demons.

While death was the penalty for Sabbath violations, it was not normally enforced, so seeking it here as a reaction to a healing is a most disproportionate response.

Mark 2:24 can be read as Jesus' warning for a Sabbath violation and 3:2 as the Pharisees watching him for a second violation. Mark 3:6 reflects their conclusion that Jesus has violated the Sabbath twice, and so they feel justified in seeking the death penalty for him. While many controversy stories show Jesus silencing his opponents through his words and deeds, in this case, they are not persuaded by him. Perhaps this explains why he grieves.

Relationship to Deuteronomy 15. In this passage, the Lord teaches that the law requires them to lend money to benefit the poor. The passage denounces those who refuse to lend because the year of release (when debts would be canceled) is approaching. So righteousness requires acting, even with the expectation that the loan won't be repaid. Jesus makes a similar argument in Mark when he categorizes Sabbath rules not according to the prevailing norm of "do" or "don't do" but rather according to whether the action "saves a life" or "kills." If Jesus' words echo Deuteronomy 15, it might explain the somewhat puzzling line about "saving a life," since not lending money to a poor person could result in starvation or enslavement and death; thus the allusion teaches that sometimes inactivity can be tantamount to causing a death. Deuteronomy 15 has several references to stretched out hands, hearts, and secret plans that further align it with this story in Mark.[76] Jesus' Sabbath healing is like releasing the man from debt, which is precisely what

---

75. When Matthew tells this story, he drops the reference to the Herodians (Matt. 12:14). The only other reference in Mark is 12:13 (interestingly, Matthew maintains that reference; Matt. 22:16).

76. Queller, "'Stretch Out Your Hand!'" 749.

the law required Jesus to do; the Pharisees are compared to those who refuse to lend money because the Sabbath year is approaching.

Relationship to Deuteronomy 29:18–20. The passage in Deuteronomy warns those who imagine that they can keep their evil plans secret that they will be met with the Lord's anger. The parallel to the Mark story (where Jesus is aware—even beforehand—of the secret plot to kill him) provides a context for Jesus' anger here and aligns him with the God of the HB. It also shows that the Pharisees—not Jesus—are the ones who are truly violating the law.

Relationship to 1 Kings 13:1–6. In 1 Kings 13:1–6, Jeroboam's hand withers after he attempts to arrest a prophet. He pleads with the prophet to heal his hand, which he does. If this story is part of the background to 3:1–6, it identifies Jesus as a prophet.

Relationship to 2:1–12. Mark 3:1–6 has many similarities to 2:1–12, which is to be expected since these texts bookend the group of five controversy stories. The similarities include:

1. Both stories feature healing miracles (unlike the other three controversies). This distinction helps clarify that these controversies bracket this section of the text.

2. The issue of Jesus' authority is raised—in the first story overtly and in this one more subtly. And since forgiving sins and defining the Sabbath were seen as God's prerogatives, both identify Jesus with the God of the HB.

3. The first story starts and finishes with references to a pleased crowd; this one begins and ends with references to the opposition that Jesus faced. Thus the framing indicates progression from general acceptance to general condemnation.

4. Both stories are set in the synagogue.

5. In neither story is the challenge to Jesus verbalized. This points to what today might be called the passive-aggressive nature of his opponents as well as to Jesus' own miraculous powers to discern thoughts.

6. The issue of what is in Jesus' opponents' hearts is raised. (In the first story, Jesus knows what is in their hearts, and in this story, Jesus knows that they are hard-hearted.) In both cases, Jesus' knowledge emphasizes his power and authority.

7. Jesus tells the person being healed to rise (Greek: *egeirō,* 2:9 and 3:3).

8. Both charges—blasphemy and a (second) Sabbath violation—carried a penalty of death.

9. Jesus responds to an unspoken objection with a question in both stories.

Analysis

This healing story not only showcases Jesus' miraculous powers but also emphasizes the increasing hostility to his ministry, culminating in a plot to kill him.

This story emphasizes Jesus' blamelessness in several ways: he does not perform work on the Sabbath, he saves a life, he knows his opponent's thoughts, he knows the future, and he is clearly more righteous than his accusers (who seek his death on the Sabbath). And despite this blamelessness, the story ends with Jesus' death being plotted. Clearly, Jesus knows that healing this man will lead to his own death, and yet he chooses to do so anyway. Thus Jesus is pictured as innocent but willing to die in order to save other people.

Jesus could have healed the man on the next day or in private.[77] The fact that Jesus chose to heal the man in public (even inviting him to stand "in the middle" where no one could possibly miss what was happening) and on the Sabbath (when the man does not, at least according to this story, even seek healing), combined with the emphasis on Jesus' innocence, implies that Jesus is doing something very deliberate here: there is a very real sense in which Jesus intentionally trades his own life for the "restoration" of the man in this story.

The Controversy Stories (2:1–3:6). This section of Mark's Gospel appears carefully composed: not only does each story teach something about Jesus, but the order and arrangement of the stories is also instructive:

1. The stories show an increasing level of hostility to Jesus: first silent accusation (2:6–7), then questioning his disciples (2:16), then neutral parties asking Jesus a question (2:18), then adversaries asking Jesus a question (2:24), and, finally, plotting to kill him (3:6). The fact that Jesus willingly perseveres in the face of this hostility shows his commitment to his mission.

2. The second and fourth stories have compelling parallels since the story of David procuring food for his men is similar to Jesus permitting food to his disciples, both in situations contrary to the law. Both stories use the same phrase ("have need" in 2:17 and 2:25) for David's need for food and the sick person's need for a physician. And both stories end with a proverb and a saying about Jesus' identity.[78]

---

77. In 1:29–31, Jesus heals Simon's mother-in-law on the Sabbath, but, presumably because of the private setting, there is no outcry.

78. Joanna Dewey, "Literary Structure of the Controversy Stories in Mark 2:1–3:6," *Journal of Biblical Literature* 92, no. 3 (1973): 396.

3. The center point of the entire structure is the subtle reference to Jesus' death (as the bridegroom taken away in 2:20). This suggests that the point of this section is not primarily the opposition to Jesus or the various issues (eating, fasting, the Sabbath) but rather the (literal) centrality of Jesus' death to the gospel message.

4. It is possible to interpret chapter 1 as concerning Jesus' relationship with demons and disease and 2:1–3:6 as concerning Jesus' relationship with other humans. In that light, the escalation of hostilities over the course of these five stories suggests that Jesus' interactions with religious and political leaders are only going to get worse as the story progresses.

5. In some way, each story concerns Jesus' authority. Instead of seeing the controversial elements as primary, it may be preferable to view the issue of Jesus' authority as central. These are not debates over how best to interpret the law; these stories are ultimately about Jesus' authority to act.

6. These five stories are surrounded by framing references: in 1:45 and 3:7–8, people flock to Jesus. Surrounding the controversies with references to Jesus' popularity places them in a different light: the opposition to Jesus comes from religious and political leaders, not from the people in general, and the controversies do not impede Jesus' increasing popularity.

7. Each story comments on Jesus' identity: he has authority to forgive sins, he is the great physician, he is the bridegroom, he is like David, and he acts as the Lord of the Sabbath.

8. The second story enacts the forgiveness of sins that the first story mentioned. The fifth story enacts the rights of the Lord of the Sabbath that the fourth story mentioned.[79]

9. There is the following interwoven pattern in these stories:[80]

$$
\text{sin}\begin{cases} \text{Healing the paralytic (2:1–12)} \\ \text{Eating with sinners (2:13–17)} \end{cases}
$$
$$
\text{Fasting (2:18–22)} \quad \Big\} \text{ eating}
$$
$$
\text{Sabbath}\begin{cases} \text{Grain on the Sabbath (2:23–28)} \\ \text{Healing on the Sabbath (3:1–6)} \end{cases}
$$

The central story, with Jesus' statement that the old and new cannot mix, serves as a key to understanding the entire section, as the audience sees in each story that Jesus' "new" ministry cannot mix with the "old" order.

---

79. Dewey, "Literary Structure," 396.
80. This chart is adapted from Marcus, *Mark 1–8*, 214.

Reactions
(3:7–35)

OVERVIEW

Mark 2:1–3:6, which forms a distinct section of text with a tight internal structure, can be read as a digression with the main thread of the narrative from 1:45 resumed in 3:7. In fact, 3:7 can be understood as the logical continuation of 1:45. Mark 1:45 and 3:7 also serve as bookends to 2:1–3:6 since both refer to the incredible response of the crowds to Jesus.

Unlike 2:1–3:6, the material in 3:7–35 is not so tightly organized. It is treated here as a section of text mostly because the material before it (2:1–3:6, the controversies) and after it (4:1–34, the parables) form discrete sections. If there is a unifying theme to 3:7–35, it is the various reactions of different groups to Jesus: the crowds, the demons, the disciples, the scribes, and Jesus' family respond to Jesus in different ways.

This section can also be understood chiastically:

A calling the Twelve (3:13–19)
    B family (3:20–21)
        C conflict with scribes (3:22–30)
    B' family (3:31–32)
A' new family (3:33–35)[1]

One tweak to this structure would be to expand the section on the conflict with the scribes so that the parable of the strong man is the center point and is surrounded by the two charges of demonic possession.[2] The calling of the Twelve, which presents many names that are new to Mark's

---

1. Austin Busch, "Questioning and Conviction: Double-Voiced Discourse in Mark 3:22–30," *Journal of Biblical Literature* 125, no. 3 (2006): 80.
2. Marcus, *Mark 1–8,* 278.

text, is, in effect, the creation of a new group and therefore parallels the new family at the end of the chapter. In both A and A', outsiders become insiders. The scribes, who as religious leaders from Jerusalem should be the ultimate insiders, are shown to be outsiders, to the extent of (possibly) being beyond forgiveness.

JESUS' MINISTRY SUMMARIZED (3:7–12)

Greek Text

7 Καὶ ὁ Ἰησοῦς μετὰ τῶν μαθητῶν αὐτοῦ ἀνεχώρησεν πρὸς τὴν θάλασσαν· καὶ πολὺ πλῆθος ἀπὸ τῆς Γαλιλαίας ἠκολούθησεν, καὶ ἀπὸ τῆς Ἰουδαίας 8 καὶ ἀπὸ Ἱεροσολύμων καὶ ἀπὸ τῆς Ἰδουμαίας καὶ πέραν τοῦ Ἰορδάνου καὶ περὶ Τύρον καὶ Σιδῶνα, πλῆθος πολύ, ἀκούοντες ὅσα ἐποίει ἦλθον πρὸς αὐτόν. 9 καὶ εἶπεν τοῖς μαθηταῖς αὐτοῦ ἵνα πλοιάριον προσκαρτερῇ αὐτῷ διὰ τὸν ὄχλον ἵνα μὴ θλίβωσιν αὐτόν· 10 πολλοὺς γὰρ ἐθεράπευσεν, ὥστε ἐπιπίπτειν αὐτῷ ἵνα αὐτοῦ ἅψωνται ὅσοι εἶχον μάστιγας. 11 καὶ τὰ πνεύματα τὰ ἀκάθαρτα, ὅταν αὐτὸν ἐθεώρουν, προσέπιπτον αὐτῷ καὶ ἔκραζον λέγοντα ὅτι Σὺ εἶ ὁ υἱὸς τοῦ θεοῦ. 12 καὶ πολλὰ ἐπετίμα αὐτοῖς ἵνα μὴ αὐτὸν φανερὸν ποιήσωσιν. [SBLGNT]

King James Version

7 But Jesus withdrew himself with his disciples to the sea: and a great multitude from Galilee followed him, and from Judæa, 8 And from Jerusalem, and from Idumæa, and from beyond the Jordan; and they about Tyre and Sidon, a great multitude, when they had heard what great things he did, came unto him. 9 And he spake to his disciples, that a small ship should wait on him because of the multitude, lest they should throng him. 10 For he had healed many; insomuch that they pressed upon him for to touch him, as many as had plagues. 11 And unclean spirits, when they saw him, fell down before him, and cried, saying, Thou

New Rendition

7 And Jesus, with his disciples, went away to the sea. And a large crowd from Galilee followed, and from Judea, 8 and from Jerusalem, and from Idumea, and from beyond the Jordan River, and from around Tyre and Sidon. A large crowd, having heard how much he was doing, came to him. 9 And he told his disciples to get a boat ready for him, because of the masses of people, so that they would not crowd him. 10 For he had healed many people, so they pushed toward him in order to touch him, as many as had diseases. 11 And the unclean spirits, whenever they saw him, fell down before him, and cried out, saying, "You are the Son of God." 12 And he sternly

art the Son of God. 12 And he straitly charged them that they should not make him known.

ordered them that they should not reveal him.

Notes

3:7 *But Jesus withdrew himself with his disciples:* This is the only occurrence of the word "withdrew" (Greek: *anachōreō*) in Mark's Gospel; it implies taking refuge or fleeing (although it lacks the note of fear that "fleeing" can carry in English). There are three different (and not mutually exclusive) reasons why Jesus might have withdrawn:

1. He wanted to avoid the crowds. If this was his goal, he did not accomplish it, as the end of this verse explains.
2. In the last verse, people were plotting Jesus' death; here, he is trying to get away from them.
3. Jesus wanted to spend some time in a peaceful place (compare 1:35), perhaps to refocus his ministry after the string of conflicts in the previous section of text.

to the sea: This presumably refers to the Sea of Galilee. In the HB, the sea is normally a symbol for chaos; it may not be symbolic here, but if it is, Jesus has inverted the symbolism by treating it as a place of safety. This would imply that he possesses the power to tame chaos.

The previous two scenes at the seaside both featured Jesus calling disciples (1:16–20; 2:13–14); the pattern seems to be broken here as great crowds follow Jesus without him asking them to follow him.

and a great multitude from Galilee followed him, and from Judæa: "Multitude" (Greek: *plēthos*) is not Mark's usual word (Greek: *ochlos*) for a crowd.[3] Mark may have chosen this word to emphasize the size of the crowd, which is also underlined by the use of the word "great." (It might be the very size of the crowd that prompts Jesus to call the Twelve later in this chapter to assist him with his ministry.)

Throughout Mark's Gospel, there is a contrast between the multitude who follow Jesus and the religious and political leaders who are opposed to him; this distinction is important to keep in mind since it is not "the Jews" who were opposed to Jesus.

---

3. *Plethos* is only used in 3:7 and 8 (which has led to the suggestion that perhaps this material was originally written by someone other than Mark); *ochlos* is used three dozen times in Mark.

"Followed" can be understood literally ("walked behind") or metaphorically ("were disciples"); either meaning is possible and appropriate here.

3:8 *And from Jerusalem:* Given that Jerusalem is within Judea and Judea was already mentioned in the previous verse, this reference is a little awkward on the literal level. Mark may have mentioned Jerusalem because:

1. He wanted to emphasize that even the sophisticates from the city followed Jesus.

2. Mark is reminding the audience of John's ministry, where he also mentioned Jerusalem and Judea (1:5) as the source of followers. But while John's ministry drew only from Judea, the rest of this verse will show that Jesus attracts followers from a greater area, reflecting his "mightier" (1:7) ministry.

and from Idumæa: "Idumea" is not otherwise mentioned in the NT (although the term is used for "Edom" in the LXX). In the first century, it referred to the area south of Judea. It was considered "at best part-Jewish"[4] because its settlers had been forced to convert to Judaism.

and from beyond Jordan: This is a stock phrase that refers to the area east of the Jordan River and is otherwise called Perea (the Greek word *peran* means "beyond"). This area was southeast of Galilee.

and they about Tyre and Sidon: This is the first time that Mark recounts Jesus' impact spreading beyond Galilee: Tyre and Sidon are north of Galilee and regarded as pagan, although they did have a tiny Jewish population. So this phrase could describe either followers of Jesus who were Gentiles or who were part of the small Jewish population in those areas.

The only areas of Palestine not mentioned here are Samaria and the Decapolis. The reason for this is not known, although it might be because those areas did not have large Jewish populations and/or were not Christian strongholds in Mark's time (but compare 5:20 and 7:31).

a great multitude: Given the similar phrase in 3:7, "a great multitude" is probably repetition for emphasis. It also frames the names of the seven specific places and thus further emphasizes the idea that large numbers of people wanted to be with Jesus. (It also sets the stage to stress, by way of contrast, Jesus' abandonment on the cross.)

when they had heard what great things he did: There may be a negative edge to Mark's statement here, since the people are attracted by Jesus' deeds and not necessarily to his teachings—and some of the people who are hearing about what Jesus did include adversarial scribes.

---

4. France, *Gospel of Mark*, 154.

This phrase assumes that some people were telling other people about Jesus' "great things," which might be considered an early, if uncoordinated, form of missionary work.

came unto him: It is possible that "came" implies something different than "followed" in 3:7, but it is also possible that it is variation for stylistic reasons. If the difference is significant, it probably implies that these people were not disciples (followers).

3:9 *And he spake to his disciples, that a small ship should wait on him:* While not specified, this may have been Zebedee's boat (1:19–20). The imperfect tense of "should wait" implies continual action and thus perhaps explains why Jesus doesn't actually use a boat in this chapter (although he will almost a dozen times in the next few chapters). But it is still somewhat uncertain why Mark mentions the boat here when it is not needed:

1. It is included to preempt the accusation from Jesus' family in 3:21 that he is unable to protect himself from the crowds.
2. The reference might emphasize the size and power of the crowd that surrounds him.
3. Later, the boat will be the means by which Jesus crosses from Jewish to gentile territory (4:35–36); it is referenced here because the mention of people from Tyre and Sidon hearing of Jesus anticipates the need for Jesus to travel to gentile lands.

because of the multitude, lest they should throng him: "Throng" can have a literal meaning of "press against" or a more metaphorical meaning of "oppress"; it is used elsewhere in the NT to describe the persecution of Christians (for example, 2 Cor. 1:6 [KJV: "afflicted"] or Heb. 11:37 [KJV: "afflicted"]).

When read in concert with 3:8, 3:9 further emphasizes Jesus' popularity: not only did people come to him from all points of the compass, but they also came in great numbers and with great fervor.

3:10 *For he had healed many:* This verse explains why the people mobbed Jesus; they have heard of his healing ability.

insomuch that they pressed upon him for to touch him: These people believe that just touching Jesus is sufficient to heal them; Mark neither confirms nor denies this belief, although the idea will be explored again later (5:28; 6:56; see also Acts 5:15; 19:11–12).

The word translated as "pressed" (Greek: *epipiptō*) "can also be used for a disease attacking a person . . . ; those who have been attacked and lashed by disease in their turn attack Jesus in their eagerness to be healed."[5]

---

5. Marcus, *Mark 1–8*, 258.

as many as had plagues: The word "plagues" can mean different things in addition to a simple illness:

1. It can refer to the lashes that a criminal would receive as a punishment. (And while they may have been criminals in the eyes of Rome, they may have considered themselves to be politically oppressed innocents.)

2. It can refer "metaphorically to the affliction God brings in judgment."[6]

3. It could refer to afflictions caused by the unclean spirits in 3:11. This interpretation would make sense of the fact that 3:11 doesn't show the unclean spirits being exorcised; the exorcisms would have happened in 3:10.

3:11 *And unclean spirits, when they saw him, fell down before him:* The word translated "fell down" (Greek: *prospiptō*) is similar to the word translated as "pressed" (Greek: *epipiptō*) in 3:10, perhaps suggesting that the crowds and the unclean spirits have somewhat similar reactions to Jesus despite their different motivations.

and cried, saying, Thou art the Son of God: The Greek verb tenses imply that this was not a one-time event but rather something that happened repeatedly. This proclamation can be understood as an effort by the unclean spirits to gain control over Jesus by naming him. It is most ironic that these unclean spirits are saying precisely the same thing about Jesus as the voice from heaven (1:11; see also 9:7).

3:12 *And he straitly charged them:* Again, the verb tense indicates that this happened on more than one occasion.

that they should not make him known: The phrasing of "they should not make him known" presumes that what they have said is true. One of the puzzles in Mark's Gospel is the so-called messianic secret,[7] which seeks to consider why Jesus frequently tries to limit information about him. There are various theories offered to explain this phenomenon that might be relevant to this passage:

1. For Mark's audience (if not Jesus' audience), the unclean spirits have in fact made it known who Jesus is. So, clearly, it was not Mark's intention that people never know that Jesus is the Son of God—Mark has just made that information available to the audience. This suggests that Jesus commands the demons to be silent because it was not the appropriate time to reveal his identity, although it would be after his death.

2. Perhaps Jesus does not want information about his identity to spread because it would have increased opposition to his ministry before the appointed

---

6. Stein, *Mark*, 164.
7. See appendix H: "The 'Messianic Secret' in Mark."

time. (One weakness of this reading is that he did not avoid other events that increased opposition, such as plucking grain and healing on the Sabbath.)

3. The title "Son of God" would have had political connotations and Jesus did not want people confused about the nature of his ministry.

4. If the demons are trying to name Jesus in order to exercise power over him, then Jesus would silence them in order to stop them from so doing.

5. The problem was not the message but the messengers: the information is accurate, but it is not the role of unclean spirits to deliver it. They attempt to usurp God's role—the role of the voice from heaven that announces that Jesus is God's son. This reading has two important implications:

   a. It makes sense of the link between this story and the next, where the Twelve are called. The implicit question raised here is: Who can testify of Jesus if the unclean spirits cannot? The calling of the Twelve provides the answer to that question.

   b. This story teaches something about Satan's tactics since he is delivering correct information through unauthorized channels in order to confuse the audience.

6. One of Mark's strategies here is to suggest that Jesus was killed not because of people's messianic expectations of him (which Jesus prevented by silencing the demons and not preaching about that himself) but rather from the jealousy of the political and religious leaders.

Narrative Structure. Mark 3:7–12 is a summary statement (compare 1:14–15); there are three different ways to interpret it:

1. It is a backward-looking summary of what has already happened, focused on chapter 1, with the controversy stories (2:1–3:6) as an aside and this passage functioning as a reorientation to the main thread of the narrative.

2. It is forward-looking and summarizes the next stage of Jesus' ministry, which will be described in more detail as chapter 3 progresses.

3. It is a bridge between the past and the future, summarizing chapters 1 and 3.

Because 3:7–12 mirrors 1:45 with its reference to the crowds, it frames the five controversy stories and literally surrounds them with the idea of Jesus' increased popularity. It positions the controversies with religious leaders as secondary to Jesus' growing popularity with the common people. Because the end of chapter 1 only mentioned Galilee but this passage shows people following Jesus from a broader area, it implies an extension of his ministry. The expansion is a significant commentary on the controversy stories: some leaders may have used them as an excuse to plot Jesus' death, but the events—perhaps especially the healing miracles—also led to Jesus' increased popularity.

Analysis

With the south (Judea, Idumea), the east (the other side of Jordan), and the north (Tyre and Sidon) all represented, this passage shows people coming to Jesus from all directions. There are various levels of religiosity associated with each of these locales, with a decreasing level of "Jewishness" for each place named: Judea and Jerusalem are the central Jewish areas, Idumea is an area of forced Jewish conversion, the Transjordan is part of the biblical inheritance but currently controlled by Gentiles, and Tyre and Sidon are outside the realm of Jewish lands (but contain a Jewish minority). So Mark is suggesting that all sorts of people followed Jesus. And if Mark was thinking in terms of symbolic numbers, the fact that seven (which was a symbol for completeness) places are named suggests Jesus' universal appeal. Further, "the places mentioned are the furthest boundaries of King David's kingdom,"[8] which implies that Jesus is as great as Israel's greatest king.

Mark 3:1–6 ends with a plot against Jesus' life as a result of his healing ministry; 3:7–10 shows the opposite reaction to Jesus, with people who are desperate to follow him and touch him. The contrast highlights the fact that, while religious and political leaders were increasingly hostile, the common people were drawn to Jesus. It also showcases the wide range of responses to Jesus' ministry, and this, in turn, sets the groundwork for the parables in the next chapter that explore different reactions to the gospel message. Ironically, both the very positive and very negative reactions to Jesus have the same effect on him: they endanger his life. This passage shows that one of the results of Jesus' ministry is a threat to his physical safety—not only from those who plot to kill him but also from well-meaning crowds who want to be near him. There might be a subtle foreshadowing of the Atonement here as Jesus' ministry leads to his death. Ill people in this Gospel "trade places" with Jesus as they are healed. In this case, they are pressing upon him just as their diseases had pressed upon them. A pillar of Mark's Atonement theology is that sickness is a metaphor for sin; here sickness is, in effect, transferred to Jesus much as, through the Atonement, the effects of sin will be transferred to Jesus.

The fact that the unclean spirits can say the right words about Jesus is one way that Mark conveys the importance of teaching about Jesus through stories instead of through titles. The demons get the title correct here, but they

---

8. Malbon, *Hearing Mark*, 25.

are not role models because they do not follow Jesus. (On the other hand, the Twelve will have a very difficult time correctly naming Jesus, but they are ultimately still disciples because of their willingness to follow Jesus and to continue to learn from him.)

JESUS CALLS DISCIPLES (3:13–19)

Greek Text

13 Καὶ ἀναβαίνει εἰς τὸ ὄρος καὶ προσκαλεῖται οὓς ἤθελεν αὐτός, καὶ ἀπῆλθον πρὸς αὐτόν. 14 καὶ ἐποίησεν δώδεκα, ἵνα ὦσιν μετ᾽ αὐτοῦ καὶ ἵνα ἀποστέλλῃ αὐτοὺς κηρύσσειν 15 καὶ ἔχειν ἐξουσίαν ἐκβάλλειν τὰ δαιμόνια· 16 καὶ ἐποίησεν τοὺς δώδεκα, καὶ ἐπέθηκεν ὄνομα τῷ Σίμωνι Πέτρον, 17 καὶ Ἰάκωβον τὸν τοῦ Ζεβεδαίου καὶ Ἰωάννην τὸν ἀδελφὸν τοῦ Ἰακώβου (καὶ ἐπέθηκεν αὐτοῖς ὀνόματα Βοανηργές, ὅ ἐστιν Υἱοὶ Βροντῆς), 18 καὶ Ἀνδρέαν καὶ Φίλιππον καὶ Βαρθολομαῖον καὶ Μαθθαῖον καὶ Θωμᾶν καὶ Ἰάκωβον τὸν τοῦ Ἁλφαίου καὶ Θαδδαῖον καὶ Σίμωνα τὸν Καναναῖον 19 καὶ Ἰούδαν Ἰσκαριώθ, ὃς καὶ παρέδωκεν αὐτόν. [SBLGNT]

King James Version

13 And he goeth up into a mountain, and calleth unto him whom he would: and they came unto him. 14 And he ordained twelve, that they should be with him, and that he might send them forth to preach, 15 And to have power to heal sicknesses, and to cast out devils: 16 And Simon he surnamed Peter; 17 And James the son of Zebedee, and John the brother of James; and he surnamed them Boanerges, which is, The sons of thunder: 18 And Andrew, and Philip, and Bartholomew, and Matthew, and Thomas, and James the son of Alphæus, and Thaddæus, and Simon the Canaanite, 19 And Judas Iscariot, which also betrayed him: and they went into an house.

New Rendition

13 And he goes up into the mountain and calls to him those he wanted, and they went to him. 14 And he made Twelve whom he also named apostles, that they might be with him and that he might send them out to proclaim 15 and to have power/authority to cast out demons. 16 So he made the Twelve: Simon (whom he named Peter), 17 and Jacob the son of Zebedee, and John the brother of Jacob (whom he named Boanerges, which means "sons of thunder"), 18 and Andrew, and Philip, and Bartholomew, and Matthew, and Thomas, and Jacob the son of Alphaeus, and Thaddaeus, and Simon the Zealot, 19 and Judas Iscariot, who even delivered him up.

Notes

3:13 *And he goeth up into a mountain:* The Greek text has an article before "mountain" (so "the mountain," not "a mountain"), which implies that a specific mountain is in mind. But since no mountain has been previously mentioned in Mark, this is probably symbolic space. In the HB, mountains can be symbolic spaces where humans encounter God, most notably in the case of Moses on Mount Sinai (Ex. 19; see also Ex. 34; Num. 27:12; and Deut. 9–10). God's role is filled by Jesus in Mark, while the prophet's role will be filled by the Twelve. Because only Moses is allowed up the mountain into God's presence, yet Jesus invites the Twelve (and perhaps others; see the Notes on 3:14) with him, it implies that God's presence is extended through Jesus' work. This theme will come to fruition in the scene at the foot of the cross. This story could even be seen as the fulfillment of Moses' wish that all the Lord's people be prophets (Num. 11:29), as more than one person is called in a way similar to how Moses was called. Moses will also go up a mountain (Ex. 24:4) with a group of priests and put up pillars that symbolize the twelve tribes. Jesus' calling of the Twelve constitutes new "pillars," once again symbolizing the twelve tribes.

and calleth unto him whom he would: Because "he" (Greek: *autos*) is not required in Greek, it is emphatic, indicating that these were people Jesus himself had chosen. This is important for several reasons:

1. The defining characteristic of those called is not ancestry (the original twelve tribes were led by biological brothers) but the fact that Jesus has chosen them. Mark teaches that Jesus' act of choice substitutes for and supersedes biology, a message that will be reexplored in different terms at the end of the chapter.

2. Because Jesus' choice is the defining characteristic, it emphasizes his authority.

3. That these disciples will struggle to understand Jesus makes the fact that Jesus had personally chosen them all the more important: Jesus did not require them to have a perfect knowledge in order to be his disciples. By emphasizing that Jesus has chosen them, Mark makes clear that the slow learning of the disciples was expected by Jesus.

4. There may also be a contrast here between the crowds who mobbed Jesus by the seashore and the people Jesus chose to follow him up the mountain.

5. Once again, Jesus is countercultural in that he is choosing people to follow him, when the standard practice was for a student to choose which teacher/rabbi to follow.

"Whom he would" is ambiguous: it could refer to the Twelve or to a larger group from which the Twelve will be chosen.

and they came unto him: This phrase implies that the people who had been called came up the mountain to Jesus. It might have a metaphorical element: "literally, [the verb 'came'] means 'to come away,' 'to depart' and connotes one's leaving one's former way of life."[9]

3:14 *And he ordained twelve:* The word that the KJV translates as "ordain" (Greek: *poieō*) is somewhat difficult to translate for a Latter-day Saint audience, since in Latter-day Saint usage "ordain" implies a very specific ritual: hands laid upon heads as a new calling is conferred through priesthood power. The Greek verb here does not prohibit that meaning, but it doesn't require it either. There are two main meanings for this word in the LXX:

1. It is the same word used when Moses selects rulers of thousands, hundreds, fifties, and tens, an action quite similar to the calling of the Twelve in Mark (Ex. 18:25 [KJV: "made"]; see also 1 Sam. 12:6 [KJV: "advanced"]).

2. The underlying meaning of the word is "to create," and it is found frequently in the Creation account in Genesis 1 (see also Ex. 36:1 [KJV: "wrought"]). It is interesting to think about the Twelve as a creation of Jesus.

So while "ordain" does not necessarily carry all of the connotations here that it would in Latter-day Saint usage, it does point to the creation and appointment of the Twelve as a key moment in Jesus' ministry and as an instance of Jesus' authority.

As mentioned above, 3:13–14 can be read in two different ways:

1. Jesus first calls a (larger) group to him in 3:13 and then, out of that group, calls the Twelve in this verse. In 4:10, which is the next reference to the Twelve, there is a larger group with them, perhaps supporting the idea that a larger group was called here. (Luke 6:12–13 probably reflects this understanding of events.)

2. Jesus calls twelve men to come up the mountain in 3:13, and then he makes them into "the Twelve" as an organized group in this verse. The fact that there is no definite article before "twelve" encourages this reading. (Matt. 10:1–2 probably follows this understanding.)

The number twelve is not coincidental but symbolic; calling the Twelve can be understood as a "parabolic act."[10] It extends the HB associations begun with the mountain setting in 3:13 and alludes to the twelve tribes of Israel as the leadership core.

In Jesus' day, there were not twelve tribes—ten had been lost to deportation and then assimilation by the Assyrians (2 Kgs. 17:6, but compare

---

9. Guelich, *Mark 1–8:26*, 157.
10. Stein, *Mark*, 169.

Luke 2:36)—and the tribal structure was inoperative, but there was great hope for their restoration.[11] So Jesus' calling of the Twelve is not so much a replication of the twelve tribes as it is their restoration. As mentioned above, the defining characteristic of this Twelve, unlike the original twelve, is not biology but Jesus' choice in calling them.

[whom he also named apostles]: Some ancient manuscripts include the phrase "whom he also named apostles." There are two possibilities for what has happened to the text here:

1. This phrase was not original to Mark but was added to harmonize with Luke 6:13 and Matthew 10:1–4.[12] Mark normally prefers the terms "the Twelve" (used twelve times) or "the disciples" (used fifty-two times)[13] instead of "apostles" (used only one other time), suggesting that this phrase was not likely original to Mark.

2. The phrase was initially present and was accidentally omitted.[14] It is present in many ancient manuscripts and Mark's other use of "apostle" (6:30), which comes without any explanation, would be awkward if there had not been a previous reference to the apostles. This phrase might imply that Jesus is giving the Twelve, as a group, a new name: they are now apostles.

that they should be with him: It is significant that the first purpose given for this calling is that they will "be with" Jesus, presumably to learn from him.

and that he might send them forth to preach: "Send forth" (Greek: *apostellō*) is the verb form corresponding to the noun "apostle."

There are two purposes given ("that they should be with him" and "that he might send them forth") for Jesus calling the Twelve. While these purposes can sound as if they contradict each other, there are several different ways to understand this tension:

1. A contradiction was Mark's intention, and the aim was for a bit of irony here.

2. Mark is describing a sequence: they are called to, first, be with Jesus so they can learn from him and then, second, to go forth and preach at a later point. They will in fact leave to preach later (6:7), which means that the text between

---

11. Isa. 11:11–12; 27:12–13; 49:5–6; Jer. 31:7–9; Ezek. 45:8. Note that if the calling of the Twelve is the fulfillment of the long-anticipated restoration of the twelve tribes, then the restoration was symbolic, not literal (as there is no indication that the Twelve Jesus called came from each of the twelve original tribes). This fact might guide the interpretation of texts such as Isaiah and Jeremiah by suggesting that while one should anticipate their fulfillment, it may not be a literal fulfillment.

12. Metzger, *Textual Commentary,* 69.

13. Christopher W. Skinner, "'Whom He also Names Apostles': A Textual Problem in Mark 3:14," *Bibliotheca Sacra* 161 (July–September 2004): 324 note 7.

14. Skinner, "'Whom He also Names Apostles,'" 325.

this verse and their leaving could be read as the training period for the Twelve. Because they are called first to be with Jesus and then to preach, the implication is that they will preach about what they have witnessed during their time with Jesus. In other words, they prepare to become special witnesses of Jesus by being with him.

3. They will be with Jesus during his mortal life, and then they will be sent out to preach about him after he is resurrected.

Contrast 1:38 ("let us go . . . that I may preach"), noting that the disciples were with Jesus but not preaching; here, the idea of the Twelve preaching is introduced. Now that Jesus has established a pattern for his ministry, he is inviting the Twelve to follow that pattern.

If the phrase "whom he also named apostles" was originally in the text, then this verse shows this group of disciples being given two names (the Twelve, apostles) and two tasks (being with him, being sent out). Given the verbal similarity between "apostles" and "sent out," Mark may also intend for the audience to find a thematic similarity between "the Twelve" and "being with him."

3:15 *And to have power to heal sicknesses:* Some ancient manuscripts omit the reference to healing sickness[15] so that this verse reads, "and to have power to cast out devils." It is likely that the material about healing sickness was added later to parallel Matthew 10:1 and Luke 9:1. From a Latter-day Saint perspective, specific authority is not necessary to heal,[16] so there might be a theological preference to read the verse without this phrase. (In 6:12–13, the Twelve do in fact heal.)

"Power" (Greek: *exousia*) can also be translated as "authority." Their authority/power comes from Jesus. There is a parallel with the previous verse: the Twelve are being called "to preach" and to "have power/authority."

---

15. Collins, *Mark,* 214 note c.

16. Joseph Smith taught that it was acceptable for all church members, including women, to offer blessings for healing: "Respecting the female laying on hands, he further remark'd, there could be no devil in it if God gave his sanction by healing—that there could be no more sin in any female laying hands on the sick than in wetting the face with water—that it is no sin for any body to do it that has faith, or if the sick has faith to be heal'd by the administration." Joseph Smith, discourse, April 28, 1842, recorded in "A Book of Records, Containing the Proceedings of the Female Relief Society of Nauvoo," 6, CHL, available online as "Nauvoo Female Relief Society Minute Book," Church Historian's Press, The Joseph Smith Papers, http://www.josephsmithpapers.org/paper-summary/nauvoo-relief-society-minute-book/33. See also Jonathan A. Stapley and Kristine Wright, "Female Ritual Healing in Mormonism," *Journal of Mormon History* 37 (Winter 2011): 1–85.

and to cast out devils: Since the passage before this one summarized Jesus' ministry of casting out unclean spirits, the Twelve are now being called to do what Jesus does. The fact that Jesus can send others out to exercise his power points to how great that power is but also indicates his willingness to share it. In just a few verses, Jesus will be accused of casting out demons using Satan's power; by calling the Twelve to cast out demons, Jesus is also inviting them to be misunderstood and persecuted. This passage could create the impression that only the Twelve are permitted to cast out demons, but 9:38–41 will show that this is not the case.

At this point, there is no mention of them having authority over the community of disciples; their authority is over the demons only.

Relationship to Exodus 18. Moses, overwhelmed by his administrative burdens, follows his father-in-law's counsel to commission others to help him govern the people. Both the similarities and the contrasts with this passage in Mark are instructive. Jesus, too, appoints others to assist in his work, but Mark indicates Jesus' superiority to Moses by showing that the initiative for the callings comes from Jesus himself.

3:16 *[So he made/ordained the twelve]:* While not in the KJV, these words are found in some ancient manuscripts.[17] It is common for Mark to have a reorienting comment after a digression, so perhaps Mark thought that it was necessary to return to the train of thought from the beginning of 3:14. Scribes may have omitted the phrase because, given how short the digression was, it may have seemed redundant. It is difficult to imagine why scribes would have added this phrase to the text unless it was accidentally copied from 3:14. If original, it would function to bookend the calling of the Twelve with references to the Twelve.

And Simon he surnamed Peter: There are two (not mutually exclusive) explanations for the renaming of Simon here:

1. In the biblical tradition, new names are given to reflect a new status (Gen. 17:5, 15; 32:28; Judg. 8:31; 2 Kgs. 24:17; Dan. 1:7; Rev. 3:12), and they were "viewed as the external sign of an important change in the life or role of the bearer";[18] the practice derives from the custom of a king taking a new name when enthroned. The fact that the next two members of the Twelve, but none of the others, also get new names supports this reading. This name change happens when Peter is called to the Twelve, not when he was called to follow

---

17. Metzger, *Textual Commentary*, 69.
18. Collins, *Mark*, 219.

Jesus in chapter 1. Not only is Simon Peter named first in the list of the Twelve, but his name is presented in a different grammatical form than the rest of the names.[19] Both of these factors (as well as his renaming, which happens to only a few others) suggest that his status is different from the others.

2. Because "Simon" is one of the most common names in this time and place, the renaming was necessary to distinguish him from others with the same name.

There are two ways to interpret this passage:

1. It is during the calling of the Twelve that this new name was given to Peter.
2. The name was given earlier, but this is the point in the narrative when Mark recorded that it had (previously) happened.[20]

Because there is no extant reference to Peter as a proper name,[21] Mark's audience likely would have perceived this as more of a nickname: "The Rock" or "Rocky." There are several reasons why this particular name might have been chosen:[22]

1. The customary interpretation is that Peter is the foundation of the church— the rock upon which it was built. This interpretation derives from Matthew 16:18 but not from Mark's text and, as will be shown throughout this commentary, is not consonant with Mark's portrayal of this stage of Peter's ministry. Mark shows Peter as a work in progress, learning as he follows Jesus. This is an important component of Mark's picture of discipleship, and it would have been very encouraging to the audience to realize that mistakes were part of being a disciple. But in Mark's Gospel, Peter is not presented as the foundation of the church but rather as a learner. (See the section on discipleship in the Introduction.)

2. The name links Peter to the "rocky" soil mentioned in 4:16.[23] While this sounds harsh, it is true that in this Gospel, Peter's response to Jesus fits the pattern of the rocky soil: he is initially zealous but later betrays Jesus under pressure (14:66–72). This nickname could have served as a warning to Peter. Since

---

19. "Simon" is written in the dative case while the accusative case (which is the case that would have normally been used) is used for all of the other members of the Twelve.

20. John 1:42 has the renaming occur when Simon first meets Jesus, but Matt. 16:18 places it much later.

21. Margaret H. Williams, *Jews in a Graeco-Roman Environment* (Tübingen: Mohr Siebeck, 2013), 309.

22. Unlike Matthew (Matt. 16:18), Mark does not explain the name. The fact that Matthew does explain it might imply that Matthew did not like Mark's presumed explanation of the name or that Matthew thought Mark's use of the name was ambiguous.

23. Mary Ann Tolbert, *Sowing the Gospel: Mark's World in Literary-Historical Perspective* (Minneapolis: Fortress Press, 1989), 145.

Mark's audience likely knew that Peter ended up leading the church, they would have understood that his "rockiness" was not a permanent condition.

3. The nickname points "to Peter's 'tough' character."[24]

4. The name is ironic: Peter will be anything but rock-like in his discipleship (8:32; 14:37, 66–72).

These options need not be mutually exclusive. Mark has always used "Simon" up to this point and will always use "Peter" hereafter, with the exception of 14:37, which is significant as the one and only time that Jesus directly addresses him by name.

Relationship to Abraham. Simon is renamed Peter much as Abram is renamed Abraham (Gen. 17:5). Peter's story is similar to Abraham's: the overriding issue in Abraham's story is whether he will get his promised posterity; the question in Peter's is whether he will bear fruit as a disciple. In Isaiah 51:1–2, Abraham is called a rock—the rock that is the source of God's people. This is a good metaphor for Peter as the leading member of the Twelve.

Relationship to Isaiah 45:4. Isaiah 45:4 concerns the renaming of Jacob as Israel. If Mark was thinking of this passage and/or if the renaming of Peter is a fulfillment of the promise in the Isaiah verse, then the renaming is significant for two reasons:

1. In Isaiah 45:4, it is the Lord who performs the renaming, emphasizing Jesus' identification as the Lord of the HB.

2. The ending of Isaiah 45:4 ("I have surnamed thee, though thou hast not known me") foreshadows a theme that will be developed later in Mark's Gospel: the inability of the disciples to completely understand who Jesus is. The Isaiah text also emphasizes the idea that Jesus called the Twelve knowing that they would not be able to perfectly fulfill their mission to preach of him.

3:17 *And James the son of Zebedee, and John the brother of James:* The audience would have expected a reference to Andrew here, since he was first called immediately after Peter (1:16). Andrew is therefore conspicuous by his absence, and the reference to James[25] and John in the second and third positions in the Twelve—along with the fact that they, but not Andrew, are renamed—is significant. This reference illustrates that Jesus called to him those whom he had chosen and did not feel bound to the

---

24. Marcus, *Mark 1–8*, 263.
25. See the Notes on 1:19.

order in which the disciples had been previously called or their biological relationships to each other when determining their position in the Twelve. (Mark distinguishes Peter, James, and John from the rest of the Twelve several times [5:37; 9:2; 14:33].)

and he surnamed them Boanerges: "Surnamed" translates the same Greek phrase that was used for Peter in 3:16, so whatever the purpose was of Peter's renaming would presumably be the same here. But in this case, one new name is applied to two people, which may suggest that the renaming was not tied to a change of status but rather was a pragmatic move to distinguish them from others with the same name. Alternatively, sharing a name could imply that their status is not as great as Peter's.

Unlike in Peter's case, these brothers continue to be known as James and John for the rest of the Gospel; there is no other use of "Boanerges" in Mark.

which is, The sons of thunder: Because "boan" is not identical to "sons" and "erges" is not exactly "thunder" in Aramaic, this may be a folk etymology: it was not uncommon in the biblical world for derivations to be symbolically significant but not technically accurate. There are a few different theories as to why "sons of thunder" was chosen for their new name:

1. If "rges" was derived from the Hebrew word for thunder, then it is the same word as found in LXX Job 37:2 (KJV: "noise"). A reference to thunder would fit nicely with the motif of God's presence on a mountain in this story since thunder is an important part of theophanies. Perhaps Mark is suggesting that James and John are witnesses to God's presence through thunder; if so, this witness may explain why they, and not Andrew, hold the second and third slots in the Twelve.

2. "Sons of thunder" is a Semitic idiom suggesting that they had "a wrathful disposition,"[26] which may be suggested elsewhere in Mark's Gospel (9:38; 10:35–40).

3. Because they are called the "sons of thunder," Zebedee, not Jacob and John, is equated with the thunder. It is unclear, however, why thunder would be an appropriate epithet for Zebedee.

4. Neither for Peter nor for Jacob and John is there an explanation for the new names. This indicates that the meaning of the words was not the key issue; rather, it is the fact that a new name was granted that is emphasized.

Relationship to Israel. Because the patriarch Jacob's name was changed to Israel when Israel was established (Gen. 35:10), changing Peter, James,

---

26. Bratcher and Nida, *Translator's Handbook,* 114.

and John's names here furthers the theme of a reconstituted Israel as the background to the calling of the Twelve. The triple renaming suggests a "rebirth"[27] of Israel.

3:18 *And Andrew:* Andrew was mentioned previously (1:16, 29); he is Simon's brother. But here, he is mentioned fourth instead of second (see the Notes on 3:17).

and Philip, and Bartholomew: "Bartholomew is not a name but a patronymic, meaning son of Thalmai, so [Mark does not provide] this man's personal name."[28]

and Matthew: It is possible (if unlikely) that Matthew is another name for Levi (see the Notes on 2:14).

and Thomas, and James the son of Alphæus: See the Notes on 2:14, where Levi the son of Alphaeus is mentioned. There are several possibilities for what is happening here:

1. James is a new name for "Levi." Levi may have been renamed because "Levi" is too closely associated with the religious hierarchy. (But it is somewhat odd that the renaming is not mentioned anywhere.)

2. Jacob is Levi's brother but, if so, it is odd that Mark does not mention this.

3. The reason "son of Alphaeus" is included here is to distinguish him from Jacob the son of Zebedee.

and Thaddæus: Some manuscripts have "Lebbaeus" instead of "Thaddaeus."[29]

and Simon the Canaanite: The word translated in the KJV as "Canaanite" is more likely to mean "zealous" or "the Zealot." It is quite unlikely that "Canaanite" was intended here because:

1. If interpreted strictly, it would mean that Simon was not Jewish.

2. Matthew uses the same word here that Mark does, but in Matthew 15:22, he uses a different word for "Canaanite." This suggests that, at least for Matthew, this word was not a reference to a Canaanite.

This word is likely a transliteration of the Aramaic word meaning "zealous" instead of a reference to the land of Canaan, although the meaning of this term is debated:

1. It may point to extreme religious zeal. (See Acts 21:20; 22:3; and Gal. 1:14 for similar uses.)

---

27. Marcus, *Mark 1–8*, 268.
28. Witherington, *Gospel of Mark*, 152.
29. Metzger, *Textual Commentary*, 69.

2. Later, there would be a political group known as the Zealots who were distinguished by their Jewish nationalism. The Zealots were instrumental in the Jewish revolt that led to the destruction of the temple and Jerusalem. While this word might not have had this meaning in Jesus' time, it almost certainly did by Mark's time,[30] which means that Mark would have used it with a recognition of its political implications. The inclusion of someone vitriolically opposed to Roman rule in a group that ate with tax collectors is striking; that Jesus would call people from opposite ends of the political spectrum to work and live and travel and represent him is most telling.

3. It may refer to someone from Cana (compare John 2:1).

It is difficult to know whether this reference centers on the meaning of the word "Canaanite" or whether the point is simply to distinguish this Simon from Simon Peter.

3:19 *And Judas Iscariot:* Possible interpretations of "Iscariot" include:

1. It is the Greek rendering of the Hebrew "man from Kerioth." Kerioth was a town in Judea, although its precise location is unknown. Interestingly, this would likely make him the only disciple who was not from Galilee.

2. It derives from "bandit" or "to lie."[31]

3. It refers to a man who uses a dagger.[32]

4. It means "red haired" and is therefore another nickname, like Peter/Rocky. This would mean that the first and the last members of the Twelve had nicknames; if this is the best reading, it implies that Jesus bookended the calling of the Twelve with personal nicknames.

Judas is the only one of the Twelve about whom additional information ("Iscariot," "betrayed him") is given in this list, aside from those situations where additional information needed to be included to distinguish disciples with the same name as other disciples (Simon, Jacob [KJV: James], and John). For that reason alone, this description would have stood out to the audience. The information may have been particularly troubling to Mark's audience: "'Iscariot' is similar to the name of the revolutionary party the Sicarii at whose hands the Markan Christians may have suffered. For Mark's audience, then, the treachery of Iscariot may gain an added dimension of horror from the terror of the Sicarii."[33]

which also betrayed him: The meaning of the Greek verb translated as "betrayed" is "handed him over [to authorities]." This was, of course,

---

30. This is how Luke understands the reference (Acts 1:13).
31. France, *Gospel of Mark,* 163.
32. Marcus, *Mark 1–8,* 264,
33. Marcus, *Mark 1–8,* 269.

a betrayal, but that is not the underlying meaning of the word. It is the same verb used to describe John the Baptist's imprisonment (1:14), which emphasizes the idea that John came before Jesus and Jesus followed John. While subtle, this is the second allusion to Jesus' death in Mark.

Relationship to Genesis 29. While Judas was a common name during this period, because "Judas" is the Greek form of the Hebrew "Judah," it is possible that Judas is a type of his HB namesake because both sell their "brother" (Gen. 37:26–27), but in neither case are they able to thwart the brother's task of saving his people.

Relationship to Isaiah. The same word used here for betrayed (Greek: *paradidōmi*) is used in LXX Isaiah 53:6 (KJV: "hath laid on him") and LXX Isaiah 53:12 (KJV: "hath poured out"). This passage in Isaiah, when understood as a prophecy of the life of Jesus, implies that it was known well in advance that Jesus would be betrayed. This would have been important background material to Mark's audience because it would have shown that Jesus' betrayal was not an accident or a random event.

and they went into an house: Most modern translations place this phrase in 3:20, where it fits more felicitously, since it does not conclude the story of the call of the Twelve but rather begins the next story, which will revolve around the theme of houses and families. Moving the phrase to the next story leaves "which also betrayed him" as the last phrase in this story—a stunning, ironic ending to the story of Jesus choosing a select group of followers.

"An house" is likely an idiom meaning "at home." No particular house is specified here, but the only houses mentioned so far in Mark are Simon's and Levi's, so one of those is probably in view.

The move from the mountain to the house suggests "the family-like character of the new Israel"[34] that Jesus is creating with his disciples; the meaning of family is the theme of the next story Mark tells.

Analysis

The pattern of having a summary of Jesus' ministry followed by a scene where disciples are called was followed in 1:14–15 and again here in 3:13–19. The summaries may be designed so that an audience listening to the Gospel read aloud would be able to orient themselves to the most important parts of

---

34. Waetjen, *Reordering of Power,* 98.

the text through summary and repetition. And perhaps Mark placed the calling of the Twelve immediately after the summary statement about the large crowds and the casting out of unclean spirits in order to explain why the Twelve were needed: they will assist Jesus now that his ministry's expanding scope requires more than one person. The narrative structure positions the calling of the Twelve as a response to the increased popularity of Jesus.

In the story of the calling of the Twelve, the themes of Jesus' authority, the restoration of Israel, and the extension of Jesus' ministry take center stage. But it is also true that "the overall impression one gets is that the Twelve was a socially diverse group including both fishermen and their nemeses the tax collectors, and both a tax collector and those who opposed paying any taxes to Rome or the overlords, indeed those who had supported opposing such oppressors even by violent means."[35]

Only Peter, James, John, Andrew, and Judas are mentioned again in Mark. The fact that seven others were called but not mentioned again suggests that the symbolic nature of the number twelve was more important than the individuals who filled the ranks. It is also significant that Levi is (most likely) not included in the Twelve although his call story was recounted in chapter 2.

The first and final callings—Peter's and Judas'—stand out from the others. The renaming of Peter not only speaks to Peter's new status, but also to Jesus' authority to grant that new status to him: "We can tell from the word order . . . that emphasis falls, not on the meaning of the new name for its significance to Simon, but on the act of renaming for its signifying Jesus' authority. . . . The greater bestows a name on the lesser."[36] And with the note that Judas will betray Jesus, Mark reveals the entire plot of the Gospel—there is no suspense left now that the audience knows that Jesus will be betrayed and who will do the betraying. It is clear that Mark's emphasis is elsewhere, and so the audience knows the end of the story from the beginning. Judas' presence—with the note that he would betray Jesus—does one of two things: either (1) suggests that Jesus did not know that Judas would betray him or (2) suggests that Jesus intentionally included a betrayer among the Twelve.

Mark's arrangement links the story of the calling of the Twelve, ending with this note of betrayal, to the next story, where Jesus' family attempts to seize him. These stories contribute to the theme developed in this chapter of various reactions to Jesus.

---

35. Witherington, *Gospel of Mark,* 152–53.
36. Gundry, *Mark,* 165.

Jesus' Family and the Scribes Respond (3:20–35)

Greek Text

20 Καὶ ἔρχεται εἰς οἶκον· καὶ συνέρχεται πάλιν ὁ ὄχλος, ὥστε μὴ δύνασθαι αὐτοὺς μηδὲ ἄρτον φαγεῖν. 21 καὶ ἀκούσαντες οἱ παρ' αὐτοῦ ἐξῆλθον κρατῆσαι αὐτόν, ἔλεγον γὰρ ὅτι ἐξέστη. 22 καὶ οἱ γραμματεῖς οἱ ἀπὸ Ἱεροσολύμων καταβάντες ἔλεγον ὅτι Βεελζεβοὺλ ἔχει καὶ ὅτι ἐν τῷ ἄρχοντι τῶν δαιμονίων ἐκβάλλει τὰ δαιμόνια. 23 καὶ προσκαλεσάμενος αὐτοὺς ἐν παραβολαῖς ἔλεγεν αὐτοῖς· Πῶς δύναται Σατανᾶς Σατανᾶν ἐκβάλλειν; 24 καὶ ἐὰν βασιλεία ἐφ' ἑαυτὴν μερισθῇ, οὐ δύναται σταθῆναι ἡ βασιλεία ἐκείνη· 25 καὶ ἐὰν οἰκία ἐφ' ἑαυτὴν μερισθῇ, οὐ δυνήσεται ἡ οἰκία ἐκείνη σταθῆναι· 26 καὶ εἰ ὁ Σατανᾶς ἀνέστη ἐφ' ἑαυτὸν καὶ ἐμερίσθη, οὐ δύναται στῆναι ἀλλὰ τέλος ἔχει. 27 ἀλλ' οὐδεὶς δύναται εἰς τὴν οἰκίαν τοῦ ἰσχυροῦ εἰσελθὼν τὰ σκεύη αὐτοῦ διαρπάσαι ἐὰν μὴ πρῶτον τὸν ἰσχυρὸν δήσῃ, καὶ τότε τὴν οἰκίαν αὐτοῦ διαρπάσει.

28 Ἀμὴν λέγω ὑμῖν ὅτι πάντα ἀφεθήσεται τοῖς υἱοῖς τῶν ἀνθρώπων, τὰ ἁμαρτήματα καὶ αἱ βλασφημίαι ὅσα ἐὰν βλασφημήσωσιν· 29 ὃς δ' ἂν βλασφημήσῃ εἰς τὸ πνεῦμα τὸ ἅγιον, οὐκ ἔχει ἄφεσιν εἰς τὸν αἰῶνα, ἀλλὰ ἔνοχός ἐστιν αἰωνίου ἁμαρτήματος. 30 ὅτι ἔλεγον· Πνεῦμα ἀκάθαρτον ἔχει.

31 Καὶ ἔρχονται ἡ μήτηρ αὐτοῦ καὶ οἱ ἀδελφοὶ αὐτοῦ καὶ ἔξω στήκοντες ἀπέστειλαν πρὸς αὐτὸν καλοῦντες αὐτόν. 32 καὶ ἐκάθητο περὶ αὐτὸν ὄχλος, καὶ λέγουσιν αὐτῷ· Ἰδοὺ ἡ μήτηρ σου καὶ οἱ ἀδελφοί σου ἔξω ζητοῦσίν σε. 33 καὶ ἀποκριθεὶς αὐτοῖς λέγει· Τίς ἐστιν ἡ μήτηρ μου ἢ οἱ ἀδελφοί μου; 34 καὶ περιβλεψάμενος τοὺς περὶ αὐτὸν κύκλῳ καθημένους λέγει· Ἴδε ἡ μήτηρ μου καὶ οἱ ἀδελφοί μου· 35 ὃς γὰρ ἂν ποιήσῃ τὸ θέλημα τοῦ θεοῦ, οὗτος ἀδελφός μου καὶ ἀδελφὴ καὶ μήτηρ ἐστίν. [SBLGNT]

King James Version

20 And the multitude cometh together again, so that they could not so much as eat bread. 21 And when his friends heard of it, they went out to lay hold on him: for they said, He is beside himself.

22 And the scribes which came down from Jerusalem said, He hath Beelzebub, and by the prince of the devils casteth he out devils. 23 And he called them unto him, and said unto them in parables, How can Satan cast out Satan? 24 And if a kingdom be divided against itself, that kingdom cannot

New Rendition

20 And they went home. And again a crowd came together, so that they were not even able to eat. 21 And his family having heard about it, they went out to seize him, for they said, "He is out of his mind."

22 And the scriptorians, the ones who came down from Jerusalem, were saying, "He is possessed by Beelzebul" and "By the ruler of demons he casts out demons." 23 And having called them to him, in parables he said to them, "How can Satan cast out Satan? 24 And if

stand. 25 And if a house be divided against itself, that house cannot stand. 26 And if Satan rise up against himself, and be divided, he cannot stand, but hath an end. 27 No man can enter into a strong man's house, and spoil his goods, except he will first bind the strong man; and then he will spoil his house. 28 Verily I say unto you, All sins shall be forgiven unto the sons of men, and blasphemies wherewith soever they shall blaspheme: 29 But he that shall blaspheme against the Holy Ghost hath never forgiveness, but is in danger of eternal damnation: 30 Because they said, He hath an unclean spirit.

31 There came then his brethren and his mother, and, standing without, sent unto him, calling him. 32 And the multitude sat about him, and they said unto him, Behold, thy mother and thy brethren without seek for thee. 33 And he answered them, saying, Who is my mother, or my brethren? 34 And he looked round about on them which sat about him, and said, Behold my mother and my brethren! 35 For whosoever shall do the will of God, the same is my brother, and my sister, and mother.

a kingdom is divided against itself, that kingdom cannot endure. 25 And if a family is divided against itself, that family cannot endure. 26 And if Satan has risen up against himself and is divided, he cannot endure but has an end. 27 But no one can enter into the strong man's house to steal his possessions unless first he ties up the strong man, and then he can rob his house. 28 Amen, I say to you that all will be forgiven the people, the sins and the blasphemies, as much as they shall have blasphemed. 29 But whoever blasphemes against the Holy Spirit never has forgiveness in the eternities but will be guilty of eternal sin." 30 Because they were saying, "He has an unclean spirit."

31 And his mother and his siblings come. And standing outside, they sent to him, calling him. 32 And a crowd sat around him, and they say to him, "Look, your mother and your siblings are outside asking for you." 33 And having answered them, he says, "Who is my mother and my siblings?" 34 And having looked around at those sitting in a circle around him, he says, "Look! My mother and my siblings. 35 For whoever does the will of God is my brother and my sister and my mother."

Notes

3:20 *And the multitude cometh together again:* The "again" refers to 3:7, when the crowd was last mentioned. If this is the same house as before, this is now the second (or third; see 2:1–4) time that Mark recounts a huge crowd at the house. There is a definite escalation: first there was a huge crowd (1:33); the second time, they blocked the door (so they had to lower the lame man) (2:4); and this time, the disciples probably can't even eat. The increasing popularity of Jesus' ministry is emphasized.

so that they could not so much as eat bread: There are several possible referents for "they":

1. Jesus and the Twelve
2. the crowd
3. Jesus, the Twelve, and the crowd

There are two ways to understand the phrase "eat bread":

1. "Eat bread" is idiomatic for "eating"; there is not a focus on bread but on eating a meal.

2. Jesus wasn't even able to eat bread, let alone a complete meal; Jesus is either so busy tending to the crowd's needs that he cannot find time to eat, or the press of the crowd makes it impossible to get food into the house, or both.

One thing is clear: the double negative in the Greek text emphasizes the extent to which it was completely impossible for them to eat. The two other call stories were followed by stories of joining together for a meal (1:29–31; 2:15), so this passage features a strong contrast as the pattern of post-call meals is violated, and Jesus is unable to eat. Once again, Jesus' popularity is presented as a double-edged sword.

3:21 *And when his friends heard of it:* The Greek phrase translated as "friends" in the KJV means something like "those along with him" and could theoretically refer to friends, family, or associates. But in this context, it almost certainly means "family" since:

1. This passage is part of the first half of a Markan "sandwich" that concludes at the end of the chapter, where Jesus' family is specifically mentioned. If not read as the first half of the sandwich, then this story has no resolution—the audience is told that they want to seize him, but they never find out if they try and whether they succeed. Mark does not normally present incomplete stories, so it is better to assume that those with him are his family, whose story will be concluded at the end of the chapter.

2. The phrase is used to distinguish these people from the disciples who were mentioned in 3:20, which implies that this group is not the same as the disciples. This means that interpreting "friends" as disciples does not make sense.

3. Some later manuscripts read "the scribes and others" instead of "friends"; presumably this change was made because it was thought too embarrassing to have Jesus' own family decide that he was out of his mind.[37] The fact that Matthew and Luke omit 3:20–21 suggests that discomfort with this material began early in the tradition. So Matthew, Luke, and the later scribes apparently all understood this text as a reference to Jesus' family.

4. Other texts support the idea that Jesus' family did not always understand and/or support his mission (6:4; Luke 2:48; John 2:3–4; 7:5).

---

37. Metzger, *Textual Commentary*, 70.

It is not entirely clear what the "it" is that they had heard that motivated their intervention. It is also possible they had heard that Jesus was "at home," so they finally knew where to find him.

they went out to lay hold on him: Presumably "went out" means they went out of their own town to come to him and seize him. "Laying hold" usually implies hostility, as it is the same verb used when Jesus is seized by his enemies (12:12; 14:1 [KJV: "take him"], 44 [KJV: "take him"], 46 [KJV: "took him"]). Their goal here is to take him into custody.

for they said, He is beside himself: There are two possible referents for "they":

1. "They" refers to Jesus' family. They thought he was beside himself, so they went to seize him.

2. "They" refers to an anonymous group of other people, meaning that when Jesus' family heard that other people thought that he was beside himself, the family went to seize him. (Most scholars dismiss this reading as an attempt to exonerate Jesus' family.)

"Beside himself" means that Jesus is out of his mind. The word means literally "he has stood outside [himself]." They think he is an outsider, but when the story is completed in the other half of the sandwich at the end of the chapter, they will be the ones who are outsiders (something that the text emphasizes in several ways; see the Analysis of this section), making its use here ironic.

It was fairly common for early Christians to be accused of being insane, so this story might have been especially relevant to Mark's audience; it would have comforted them to know that Jesus faced similar accusations during his mortal life.

What is motivating Jesus' family's actions here?

1. Concerns over Jesus' safety:

   a. Jesus' inability to even eat, mentioned in 3:20, may have made his family concerned for him. They are not hostile to Jesus' mission per se, but they are not willing to permit Jesus to suffer for it. (This would be a similar concern to Peter's in 8:31–32.)

   b. If word had reached them about his Sabbath healings, they may have been worried over the authorities' reactions. (And, as the next story will indicate, they would have been right to worry.)

   Both of these readings are more sympathetic to the family: they "are portrayed as concerned for his welfare, but they fail to understand his mission."[38]

---

38. Miller, *Women in Mark's Gospel,* 37.

Perhaps Jesus' request for a boat could be read as a preempting of his family's (otherwise legitimate) concern over his fate, with the point being that he could take care of himself without their intervention. But even if Jesus' safety is their concern, the second half of the sandwich will show that it is neither innocent nor neutral: they are defining themselves as outside of Jesus' circle—even outside of his new "family"—through their efforts to control his behavior in ways that impede his ministry.

2. Concerns over shame and embarrassment. If Jesus were acting "out of his mind," he would bring shame, and perhaps legal repercussions, to his family. (This reading is undermined by the crowd's very enthusiastic response to Jesus.) This reading assumes that his family did not understand and/or accept his mission. This in turn implies that there was nothing about Jesus' physical presence or demeanor that instantly revealed his true nature (compare Isa. 53), even to family members.

There are several instances when prophets in the HB were thought to be insane (2 Kgs. 9:11; Jer. 29:26; Hosea 9:7; Zech. 13:3–6). The theme of rejection by one's own family is also prominent in Psalm 69:8. These allusions associate Jesus with the authorized messengers of the HB; they also remove some of the sting from the idea that his family thought he was insane.

3:22 *And the scribes which came down from Jerusalem said:* Because Jerusalem is in hilly country, it was common to speak of "coming down" from Jerusalem, but there might be a subtle contrast to the fact that Jesus just came down from the mountain: he had been there in order to commission followers, but the scribes come down to make false accusations. Additionally, in the HB, descent is often portrayed negatively, such as the descent of the Israelites into Egypt or Satan's descent from heaven (Isa. 30:2; 31:1; 52:4).

Because the imperfect tense is used for "saying," these scribes were repeatedly teaching that Jesus was possessed; this was not a one-time event.

The unspoken assumption here is that Jesus' ministry—which up to this point in Mark has been confined to Galilee—has been a topic of discussion in Jerusalem to the extent that the religious authorities are concerned and have come to intervene. This is an ominous development. It is likely that these scribes are on an official assignment from the religious authorities to investigate Jesus' activities.

He hath Beelzebub: Most modern translations read "Beelzebul" instead of "Beelzebub" based on a textual variant. "Beel" probably refers to Baal, the Canaanite storm god; the Hebrew root "*zebul*" means "abode," yielding a meaning for Beelzebul of something like "god of the house," which is particularly interesting in this context, where Jesus will refer to a house divided and a strong man's house in his responses to this accusation. "Beel-zebub" was a (deliberate?) mistake made in 2 Kings 1:2,[39] changing the meaning of the name from "god of the house" to "god of the flies"; this seems to have given rise to the variant text responsible for the KJV reading "Beelzebub." By Jesus' time, pagan gods such as Beelzebul were thought to be demons, so "Beelzebul" was considered a reference to Satan. Since "hath" implies possession, the idea here is that Jesus is possessed by Satan.

The wording here (literally: "saying that Beelzebub he has") is very similar to what his family said ("saying that he was insane"), emphasizing the parallel between these two responses to Jesus. At the same time, there is a departure from the family's accusation; here, they don't just think he is mad but possessed. There may be a link between the two accusations: because the family thinks that Jesus is (literally) "beside himself," it is as if he has left his body empty, which sets the stage for Beelzebul to possess that body. The family's accusation has, at least on a literary level, created the circumstances under which the scribes can make their accusation, particularly given the belief that possession and insanity were intertwined (John 10:20).

There are two ways to interpret the scribes' accusation:

1. It was not unknown for people to accuse their political enemies of being in league with evil forces as a way to discredit them; it is possible that this charge has little to do with the scribes' assessment of the real source of Jesus' power but everything to do with their concern that he will create political problems for them.

2. Determining whether a miracle worker was using God's power or Satan's power was a very real concern during Jesus' time and is addressed in a number of sources; the rule developed that miraculous ability associated with following the law of Moses was divine in origin while miracles associated with violating the law came from Satan. Given Jesus' troubled relationship with (the prevailing interpretation of) the law of Moses in 2:1–3:6, it is perhaps no surprise that these scribes have assumed that his power is satanic.

And by the prince of the devils casteth he out devils: "Prince of the devils" might be another name for Beelzebul, equating him with Satan. Jesus' response, which mentions Satan, would further this association. According to the law of Moses, a person possessed by an evil spirit must be put to death (Lev. 20:27; the context probably implies that the person has invited the possession in some way; compare Lev. 19:31).

---

39. Mann, *Mark,* 253.

There are two ways to interpret this verse:

1. The scribes from Jerusalem have been sent on a fact-finding mission to investigate Jesus, and this is their conclusion.

2. The scribes had been sent to thwart Jesus, and so they preach that Jesus gets his power from Satan.

It is difficult to determine whether this verse should be interpreted as one charge against Jesus stated in two different ways or as two different charges ("he hath Beelzebub" and "by the prince of the devils casteth he out devils"). The scribes are conceding that Jesus has the power to cast out demons. has already made clear to the audience that this accusation is not and cannot be true. The audience's insider status means that they know that this accusation is false before Jesus even responds to it.

3:23 *And he called them unto him:* The verb "called" (Greek: *proskaleomai*) is normally used for Jesus gathering the disciples to teach them, which makes its usage here unusual.

Options for the antecedent of "them" include

1. The ones close to Jesus—the family from 3:21.

2. The scribes. This statement implies that they were speaking about Jesus but not to Jesus in the previous verse; Jesus changes the dynamic by speaking directly to them. This would be a rare instance where the verb normally used to call disciples is used for those hostile to Jesus. Perhaps Jesus is treating these scribes as potential disciples.

3. The crowds.

4. The disciples.

5. Any combination of the above.

and said unto them in parables: This is the first use of the word "parable" in Mark, which is somewhat surprising since 2:19–22 contained parables, but Mark did not label them as such. Perhaps this is a bit of foreshadowing for chapter 4, which contains an entire section of parables.

In general, parables convey teachings that outsiders can't understand. This raises interesting questions about what "parable" means here because the message in this passage is unambiguous; it is just the language that is indirect. But the issue of insiders and outsiders is raised repeatedly in this chapter, and the presence of parables contributes to that theme.

How can Satan cast out Satan?: Jesus presents a logical argument here. Satan was understood to be the ruler of a hierarchy of demons, so for Satan to send Jesus to exorcise demons would make no sense—he would be fighting against himself.

Mark just told the audience that Jesus would be answering in parables, but this does not seem to be a parable. There are two ways to resolve this conundrum:

1. This statement is an introduction to the three brief parables that Jesus is about to utter.

2. There is something parabolic about this question that Jesus poses, despite appearances to the contrary. This is precisely why Mark alerted the audience that Jesus would be answering in parables (contrast 2:19–22, where Mark did not forewarn the audience when Jesus spoke in parables).

It may be significant that Jesus does not adopt their wording ("Beelzebul" or "the prince of rulers") but instead refers to "Satan"; this may be a theological correction: "by tacitly substituting 'Satan' for 'Beelzebul' Jesus brings the controversy within the perspective of his mission as a direct confrontation with Satan."[40] In other words, Jesus' mission is an affront to Satan, not merely a clash with lesser demons.

3:24 *And if a kingdom be divided against itself, that kingdom cannot stand:* Jesus' parable presents a kingdom belonging to Satan, with an organization and a leader. But perhaps Mark's note alerting the audience to the fact that Jesus would be speaking in parables was a warning that not every element of his response should be interpreted literally: if Satan does have a kingdom, then this would not be a parable.

3:25 *And if a house be divided against itself:* "House" can be understood as referring to a family or household; it connotes all of the people living under one roof, not the structure itself. It may refer to the royal family: "It may be an allusion to the rivalry over the high priesthood between the brothers Aristobulus II and Hyrcanus II, which brought an end to Jewish interdependence when Pompey led the Roman legions into Jerusalem in 63 BC."[41] If the royal family is alluded to, then Jesus has used two political examples—the first is simply on a larger scale. If the house alludes to any family, then Jesus has used one political and one familial parable. As a familial parable, it echoes the discord within Jesus' own family.

that house cannot stand: Since this text is sandwiched between references to Jesus' family's opposition to him, this verse becomes a subtle prophecy of Jesus' own death: because his family is divided against him, his household cannot stand. It is also possible, especially given the recent

40. Lane, *Gospel according to Mark,* 142.
41. Stein, *Mark,* 183.

calling of the Twelve, that one layer of meaning here is that Jesus' house (his disciples) cannot stand because of the impending betrayal by Judas. The underlying theme of 3:23–35 is that unity is a prerequisite for strength.

3:26 *And if Satan rise up against himself:* The Greek sentence assumes a situation that is contrary to fact; in other words, Jesus is implying that Satan has not risen up against himself.

and be divided, he cannot stand: "Stand" in this verse is the same verb that was used in the previous two verses.

but hath an end: The logic here assumes that Satan has no end. This is a necessary component of Jesus' argument that he is not working by Satan's power; at the same time, it could create the misunderstanding that Satan would never have an end. The next verse will clarify, showing how Satan's power will end: it will be through Jesus' actions but not, as the scribes have suggested, because Jesus is using Satan's power but rather because Jesus uses God's power to overcome Satan.

Behind Jesus' words is the belief that Satan's house/kingdom is currently standing; the reality of evil is assumed here.

3:27 *No man can enter into a strong man's house:* The KJV does not include it, but this verse begins with a strong adversative in Greek ("but"), which implies that Jesus, having demolished the theory that he exorcises using Satan's power, is now going to explain how it is that he is able to cast out demons. The opposition between this verse and the last emphasizes that the threat to Satan is not from within his realm (as it would have been if Jesus had been exorcising using Satan's power), but rather from outside, hence the need for someone from the outside to enter into the strong man's house.

"Strong man" is definite ("the strong man," not "a strong man"), which makes it more likely that this is a reference specifically to Satan, so "the parable seems to assume that, before Jesus appeared on the scene, Satan was the head of the household of this world, an identification perhaps already implied by the epithet 'Beelzebul' = 'lord of the abode.'"[42] There is a double negative here, emphasizing the impossibility of entering the strong man's house unless the man is first bound. This highlights the power that the strong man (Satan) has.

The word translated as "strong" (Greek: *ischuros*) is the same word used by John to describe the "one mightier" (1:7) than himself who was coming (in fact, these are the only two uses of this word in Mark), furthering the idea that Jesus is the "stronger man" in this passage who can bind the

---

42. Marcus, *Mark 1–8*, 274.

strong man. Perhaps John recognized that he lacked the authority that Jesus would hold—the authority to "bind the strong man," or end Satan's ability to control people.

and spoil his goods: While it can have other meanings (including "things," "possessions," or "property"), it is possible to translate "goods" as "bodies,"[43] which might best fit the context here. The New Rendition uses "possessions," which preserves the multiple possible meanings.

This parable may not point to one specific event (at least Mark doesn't make that clear here or elsewhere). If one event is in mind, it is probably Jesus' temptations (1:13), which is the only other text where Jesus' conflict with Satan is specifically mentioned.

except he will first bind the strong man: The same verb for "bind" (Greek: *deō*) is used for Jesus (15:1), so its use here hints that Jesus will have the ultimate victory. In some ancient texts, Satan binds people, so there would be an inversion here.

It is difficult to determine whether Jesus' parable describes some future day when Satan will be bound (which makes sense of the previous verses, where Satan's kingdom/house still stand) or describes the current day (given that Jesus has been performing exorcisms that, according to this parable, require Satan to be bound).

and then he will spoil his house: Jesus occupies the narrative role of a thief in this parable,[44] which means that he is violating social norms in order to accomplish his work. He is also risking his freedom and life, as all thieves do. This picture of Jesus as a robber who is stronger than the strong man is an important counterweight to the likely assumptions about a "weak" or "defeated" Jesus at the crucifixion.

It was common to portray God as the head of the household, so this parable, by picturing Satan as the head, is most unexpected. It shows that something is wrong—something that Jesus has come to fix.

Relationship to Nathan. In the HB story, Nathan employs a parable instead of making a direct accusation against King David (2 Sam. 12). (Parables were a way for lower-status people to convey truths to higher-status people

---

43. 2 Cor. 4:7 (KJV: "vessels") and 1 Thes. 4:4 (KJV: "vessel"). The only other use of "goods" (Greek: *skeuos*) in Mark is 11:16, where it refers to the vessels that Jesus would not permit people to carry through the temple.

44. Compare Matt. 24:43; 1 Thes. 5:2–4; 2 Pet. 3:10; and Rev. 3:3. Of course, on a more literal level, Jesus has a perfectly legitimate claim to enter the house and reclaim the bodies there.

without getting into trouble. Jesus may have used this approach to avoid further antagonizing the Jerusalem authorities until he had finished his mission.) If the allusion to the Nathan story was intentional, it shows Jesus in the role of a prophet and the scribes in the role of wicked leaders.

Relationship to Psalm 68. Psalm 68:18 reads, "you have taken captives captive" and thus presents the same idea as this text in Mark that captives are being transferred to a new captivity. This, too, could be understood as a prophecy of Jesus' mission.

Mark 3:27 implies that captivity (to Satan) ends, but another captivity (to Jesus) begins (compare 1 Cor. 6:19–20). A similar idea is found in the Exodus: the children of Israel are freed from slavery to Pharaoh so they can choose to become slaves to God.

Relationship to Isaiah 49 and 53. In Isaiah 49:25, the Lord explains that it is indeed possible for spoils to be taken from the one who possesses them because the Lord himself will intervene; the LXX uses very similar language as this text in Mark. This allusion is important because it identifies Jesus with the Lord in the HB, and it further suggests that Isaiah prophesied of Jesus' mission here.

Another important allusion to the present text comes from Isaiah 53:12, where the power of the strong one to claim the spoils of victory comes from his willingness to "[pour] out his soul unto death" and "bare the sin of many." Again, the saving mission of Jesus is prophesied in Isaiah and fulfilled here.

3:28 *Verily I say unto you:* This phrase "is generally agreed to be a hallmark of Jesus' distinctive style of teaching."[45] It is used many times in Mark's Gospel (6:11 [but see the Notes on that verse]; 8:12; 9:1, 41; 10:15, 29; 11:23; 12:43; 13:30; 14:9, 18, 25, 30); this is its first occurrence. The New Rendition transliterates the Greek word *amēn* (KJV: "verily"; modern English: "truly"), familiar to English speakers as the word "amen."

This phrase is akin to the "thus saith the Lord" statements of the HB. While *amēn* was commonly used to assert truthfulness and is found both within and without the HB (see, for example, 1 Chr. 16:36 [KJV: "amen"]), it was normally spoken *after* the saying to affirm its trustworthiness. Jesus uses it before the saying, which is a unique practice. This points to his authority to affirm the truthfulness of his sayings in advance; Jesus utters

---

45. France, *Gospel of Mark*, 175.

it when he wants to emphasize the seriousness of what he is about to say. Even scholars who are very skeptical of the historicity of the Gospels' portrayal of Jesus think that the "verily I say unto you" sayings go back to Jesus and were one of the main characteristics of his speaking style.

Relationship to Isaiah. Isaiah 65:16 uses "God of the Amen" (KJV: "God of truth") as a title or name for deity. This might be viewed as Isaiah's prophetic understanding that Jesus would use the phrase "truly I say unto you" in a distinct way, or perhaps Jesus deliberately modeled himself on Isaiah's usage. Either way, a link is made between Jesus and the God of the HB.

All sins shall be forgiven unto the sons of men: The phrase "sons of men" is likely an idiom meaning "people" in general. "Shall be forgiven" is probably a divine passive, implying that God is doing the forgiving.

Because of its location, the phrase "all sins" is emphasized in the Greek text. Since the context here is the sin against the Holy Ghost, it is easy to lose sight of the very significant fact that this passage announces the possibility of forgiveness for all (other) sins.

and blasphemies wherewith soever they shall blaspheme: Blasphemy merited the death penalty under the law of Moses (Lev. 24:16), so offering forgiveness for it is an immense departure from expectations and speaks to the mercy that Jesus provides.

One way of conceptualizing this verse is to understand blasphemies as offenses against God and sins as offenses against humans.

The incredible promise of forgiveness made in this verse should be read in the light of 3:27, which showed Jesus liberating Satan's captives. In this context, the implication is that liberating the captives means forgiving them of all sins, which strengthens the idea that the parable can be understood as a representation of the Atonement.

3:29 *But he that shall blaspheme:* It may seem that this verse contradicts the previous one (which promises forgiveness for all sins), but it is a common biblical idiom to first mention a general rule and then to provide an exception to it (for example, Gen. 2:16–17; Ex. 12:10).

against the Holy Ghost: The scribes from Jerusalem did not mention the Holy Ghost; they claimed that Jesus was possessed by Beelzebul. So Jesus' response here only makes sense if Jesus exorcises by the power of the Holy Ghost; that is the only way to link the Holy Ghost to this story. So the unstated assumption of this passage is that Jesus casts out demons by the power of the Holy Ghost; thus, claiming that Jesus casts out demons by Satan's power is blasphemy against the Holy Ghost because it ascribes the Holy Ghost's power to Satan. This reading furthers the idea that in this Gospel, Jesus is, in effect, possessed by the Holy Ghost.

hath never forgiveness, but is in danger of eternal damnation: There are two significant textual variants in this statement:

1. Some manuscripts have the future tense ("will be") instead of the present tense ("is") here; the future tense may have been the earlier reading; the change to the present tense was probably made so that it would agree with the previous phrase.[46] The future tense is theologically preferable, since it indicates that judgment for sin happens in the future and not at the moment of sin.

2. Earlier manuscripts have the word "sin" here instead of "damnation," rendering the phrase "guilty of eternal sin" (NIV, NRSV). It is not Mark's usual word for sin but a form that is used only here and the previous verse. Presumably the change to "damnation" (some manuscripts have the word "torment" instead; some have "sin and damnation") was made because the expression was awkward or difficult to understand.[47] Whether "sin" or "damnation" is chosen may not ultimately impact the interpretation of this verse: presumably an "eternal sin" (if taken to mean an unrepented sin) would permanently estrange one from the presence of God and therefore have the same effect as "eternal damnation." The reading "eternal sin" supports the suggestion above that the underlying problem with blasphemy against the Holy Ghost (attributing the power that Jesus gets from his "possession" by the Holy Ghost to possession by Beelzebul) is that it makes it impossible to rely on the Atonement, thus making any sins committed "eternal" in the sense that they are not forgiven because forgiveness is not sought. The awkwardness of the phrase "eternal sin" combined with the unusual term for sin likely encouraged some scribes to change it to "eternal damnation," but the original phrase makes good sense: the idea is that the sin is not forgiven and is therefore eternal.

The doubled time references in this verse also point to the idea that the sin never goes away.

Jesus has inverted their argument: they accused him of being aligned with evil, but he has made clear that they are the ones actually associated with evil and in an even greater manner than they had suggested for him. And this inversion fits the "binding the strong man" scenario perfectly—the strong man had kept others captive but then became a captive himself.

Had the scribes committed the unforgivable sin? There are a few different ways to answer this question:

---

46. Collins, *Mark,* 225 note g.
47. Metzger, *Textual Commentary,* 70.

1. The scribes had committed this sin, and

    a. they cannot repent of it, so Jesus' words are meant as a warning to others.

    b. they can repent, and Jesus' words are meant to encourage them to do so.

2. The scribes had not committed this sin, but they were engaged in behavior that was similar to it or could lead to it, and so Jesus' words are a warning to them. (In Latter-day Saint thought, an unpardonable sin requires a very high level of spiritual knowledge [D&C 76:43]; it is unlikely that the scribes would have possessed the requisite level of knowledge to be capable of committing this sin.)

3:30 *Because they said:* The verb here is imperfect ("they were saying"), which has important implications for understanding the nature of the unforgivable sin: this is not behavior that they engaged in once or accidentally but rather a deliberate and repeated pattern of behavior.

He hath an unclean spirit: "Hath" (Greek: *scheō*) is the same Greek word translated as "hath" in the previous verse. To Mark's audience, there would have been an echo from the previous verse: if Jesus *has* an unclean spirit, then one does not *have* forgiveness.[48] Further, because the same Greek word, *pneuma,* is translated as "ghost" in 3:29 but "spirit" in 3:30, the association is even tighter: Jesus is either possessed by the unclean spirit or he is possessed by the Holy Spirit.

This verse is not necessary to the flow of the narrative since the audience is already aware of this charge from 3:22. Its repetition implies that Mark wanted to be sure there was no confusion whatsoever about precisely what spurred Jesus to discuss the unforgivable sin. In this context, that sin is deliberate, repeated preaching by religious leaders that Jesus is possessed by Satan when they know that that is not the case.

3:31 *There came then his brethren:* This verse resumes the story from 3:21, which was interrupted by the scribes' accusations. "Brethren" can include brothers and sisters and would refer to Jesus' (half) siblings.[49]

and his mother: Some assume that the lack of reference to a father is because Joseph had died, but Mark is silent on this point. Mark knew the names of Jesus' family members (6:3); not naming them here focuses the audience's attention on their role as family members instead of on their personal identity.

---

48. The reverberation may have begun in 3:26, where Satan has (Greek: *scheō*) an end, continuing the theme in the passage.

49. Under influence of the (later) tradition of Mary's perpetual virginity, the case has often been made for understanding the "brethren" to be cousins, but the text itself would not encourage that reading. For a summary of the arguments, see Marcus, *Mark 1–8,* 276.

Other references to Jesus' mother in Mark include 6:3 and possibly 15:40 and 16:1 (see the Notes on these verses). There is no way to determine what else Mark's audience would have known about Jesus' mother.

and, standing without: "Standing without" is not mere stage direction; it creates a distinction between the literal "outsiders" and "insiders" to Jesus' ministry that the rest of the passage develops. Further, the word used here for "without" is similar to the word used when Jesus was accused of being "beside himself" (3:21) in the first half of this sandwich of stories. Mark cleverly manipulates narrative space throughout the Gospel. Here, the point is that it is not Jesus who is "outside of himself" but his family who is out of bounds.

sent unto him: The presumption is that it is so crowded that the family cannot even get close to Jesus. But because the word for "sent" (Greek: *apostellō*) is the same word used in 3:14 to describe the mission of the Twelve, the implication is that the family is trying to direct Jesus in the same way that he leads his disciples.

calling him: This phrase is redundant; it may have been included to imply that they are trying to call Jesus away from what he is doing in the same way that Jesus called the four fishermen and Levi away from their tasks; in fact, this is the same verb that was used in 1:20. Because of the sandwiching structure, the audience knows that this calling is not benign: they are calling him with the goal of seizing him.

3:32 *And the multitude sat about him, and they said unto him:* It is possible that this multitude includes the scribes from Jerusalem; if so, the scribes' ease in shifting from charging satanic possession to calling attention to Jesus' family is evidence that they are interested in disrupting his work by any available means.

Behold, thy mother and thy brethren without: Some manuscripts add "and your sisters" here. These words may have accidentally dropped out when a copyist's eye skipped across the text, or they may have deliberately been omitted because "sisters" are not mentioned in 3:31 or 3:34. The phrase's inclusion in the earliest text is likely, because if someone had later added "sisters" to harmonize with 3:35, the phrase would presumably also have been added to 3:31, 33, and 34 as well. On the other hand, "and your sisters" is not included in that many of the ancient texts, and it may have been unlikely that Jesus' sisters would have been involved in such a public rebuke.[50]

---

50. Metzger, *Textual Commentary,* 70.

(Of course, that may be precisely the reason why the reference was later deleted, if present originally.)

It is difficult to determine which reading is best, but it may not matter. Because plural masculine endings were used for nouns referring to groups including both genders, it is likely that—even without "and your sisters"— Jesus' sisters had been implicitly included in the word "brethren" in 3:31, 32, and 34. The fact that Jesus specifically mentions a sister in 3:35 lends weight to the idea that his sisters had been included in all of the previous references to brethren, making the phrase "and your sisters" redundant. "And your sisters" may not have been part of the earliest manuscripts of Mark, but the presence of Jesus' sisters in this scene should nonetheless be assumed.

The fact that the crowd—but not Jesus—is aware that Jesus' family is looking for him implies that the crowd has taken on the narrative role of separating Jesus from his family. The language about "sitting around him" emphasizes this motif, because they are literally closer to Jesus than his family is. It also sets the stage for Jesus' coming statement that the crowd is now his family, which is also emphasized by the fact that the family is "without" or outside and looking for him. ("Without" could mean that the family is outside, or it could mean that they want Jesus to go outside.) So in this verse alone, Mark provides three indicators of difference between the crowd and the family's position relative to Jesus.

seek for thee: The family is doing more than just seeking for Jesus: 3:21 says that they want to seize him. Either the people making this statement are unaware of the family's true plans, or they are deliberately misrepresenting the family's intentions in order to entrap Jesus. (If the latter is correct, then Jesus' answer is a very clever avoidance of that trap.) But it is also true that almost all uses of the verb "seek" in Mark have a negative connotation (for example, 8:11; 11:18 [KJV: "sought"]; 12:12; 14:11), so perhaps the statement itself indicates malicious intent.

3:33 ***And he answered them, saying, Who is my mother, or my brethren?:*** A singular form for "is" (Greek: *estin*) is used here, perhaps to emphasize his mother's role in the scene. So the New Rendition reads "who is my mother and my siblings," despite the fact that this is infelicitous in English.

The audience would find the answer to this question painfully obvious, which makes Jesus' answer all the more stunning and unexpected. He engages in an important act of redefinition here, which may have been particularly meaningful to Mark's audience, who likely experienced conflict with their own family members over their own commitment to the gospel.

3:34 *And he looked round about on them which sat about him, and said:* The KJV has "round" modify "looked," but it is better to read it as modifying "sat," meaning that the people were sitting in a circle around Jesus. There is actually triple repetition of the idea that these people are around Jesus: he looks around at those seated around him in a circle. It is likely that this circle includes the Twelve as well as other disciples; their physical location speaks to their attitude. This is another example of Mark's clever use of narrative space in this story; he shows the disciples encircling Jesus, in contrast to his family, who are literal and metaphorical outsiders.

If the scribes are part of those working with the family to seize Jesus, then this circle of disciples is something of a defensive barrier. If these are the people that Jesus called on the mountain to be with him, then part of their ministry might have been to physically protect Jesus, and the result of that service is that they now constitute his family, as 3:35 will explain.

Behold my mother and my brethren!: It is most unlikely that Jesus would have said this if women were not included in his followers.

It is perhaps surprising that Mark does not mention a father here (see also 10:30); several theories could explain this:

1. Jesus omits "father" to maintain the parallelism with the statement by the multitude, which did not mention a father; it is thus the coincidental result of the fact that no father was present.

2. Jesus did not mention a father because the role of father in the new family was limited to God alone (compare 8:38; 11:25; 13:32; 14:36).

3. No father is mentioned here (or in 10:30) because the rights and privileges that a Greco-Roman or Jewish father had were not to be exercised by the disciples.

4. In Psalm 128:3 and Job 29:5, the children sit around the patriarch of the family; perhaps this scene in Mark presents Jesus as the patriarch and all of his followers as his children. If this allusion is intentional, then the nonbiological nature of Jesus' new family is all the more remarkable by way of the contrast.

3:35 *For whosoever shall do the will of God:* The defining characteristic for being in Jesus' family is not biological relationship but rather obedience to God. The assumption is that those who are forming a circle around Jesus (and not his family outside) are those who are doing God's will, which is equated to listening to Jesus. Given that the Twelve were just called to be with Jesus, it is perhaps not surprising that being present with him is presented as the definition of doing God's will—or that a new family is constituted, much as the Twelve were presented as a restoration of Israel. There may also be a bit of foreshadowing in this section; compare 4:10–11, where the theme of insiders and outsiders will be discussed openly.

the same is my brother, and my sister, and mother: By including a specific reference to his sister, this "is an interesting example of deliberately
inclusive language."[51] Jesus makes no distinction between the roles of his
brother and his sister here; both are to do the will of God (to listen to
Jesus), which would have been most unexpected in his cultural context. It
is very significant for Jesus to include mothers and sisters in his new family and to place them on equal footing with the brothers. Given that the
disciples have several "mothers" now, "the unique relationship of mother
with child is thus undermined."[52] All of the adults in the community are
expected to provide that same kind of care to those who need it as was formerly expected only of mothers. Jesus' definition of family as duty based
instead of biologically based echoes 1:20, where James's[53] and John's duty
to follow Jesus overrode their duty to work with their father.

Relationship to Exodus 32. In Exodus 32:25–29, Moses observes chaos[54]
among the people that is causing their enemies to deride them. This is
similar to how Jesus' family's actions can be understood, at least on a literary level, to lead the scribes to accuse Jesus. Moses invites those who are on
the Lord's side to come to him, similar to how the disciples circle around
Jesus. Moses commands them to kill the wild ones, even if they are family.
This disturbing part of the story parallels Jesus' distinction between his
biological family and those who do the will of God, but Jesus' story is nonviolent; in fact, it claims that his family is implicitly welcome to join Jesus'
"new" family by simply committing to do the will of God.

Reading these stories in tandem encourages the audience to see the
dangers posed by the family's "wild" actions and the necessity of making
a choice for one side (inside, with Jesus) or the other (outside, attempting
to derail Jesus' ministry), while the contrast between the two stories highlights Jesus' mercy.

Restored Family Theme. Several HB texts indicate hope for the restoration of the family: "The picture of a new family, moreover, would probably
fit in with the Markan community's sense of eschatological advent, since
[the biblical], Jewish, and Christian traditions looked forward to the restoration of the family as a sign of the end-time (see e.g., Mal 4:6; Sir 48:10;

---

51. France, *Gospel of Mark,* 180.
52. Miller, *Women in Mark's Gospel,* 48.
53. See the Notes on 1:19.
54. The KJV translates this word as "naked," but it probably carries the metaphorical
meaning of "wild."

Lk 1:17). . . . It may not be coincidental, moreover, that Isa 49:18–21 and 60:4 express their hope for the eschatological restoration of the family in terms that are similar to the description of Jesus' glance in Mark 3:34; Zion is exhorted to *lift up her eyes, look around,* and *see* her children restored to her."[55] It is very significant in this regard that the family that Jesus constructs here is based on belief instead of biology and, due to the lack of reference to a father, is presumed to be nonhierarchical.

Analysis

There are numerous references in this story to narrative space (that is, space in a physical or geographical sense) and many indications that these are not simple "stage directions" but rather are imbued with great symbolic meaning. Significant references to narrative space in 3:31–35 include standing without, about him, without, and round about, creating an incredible concentration of references to narrative space in such a short passage.

All of these references emphasize the idea that Jesus' family is outside and the disciples are inside. Extending the use of narrative space is the family's claim that Jesus is "beside himself" (3:21). In other words, they accused him of being an outsider, but Mark shows the audience through the use of narrative space that they, the family, are actually the outsiders. The role of the disciples as insiders who are (literally) close to Jesus is emphasized. The theme of insiders and outsiders here prepares the audience for references to the same theme in the next chapter, particularly in 4:10–11.

The most poignant part of Mark's construction of narrative space is that it hints at the suffering that Jesus must have experienced during his life as his own family accused him of being an outsider.

The scribes—not local scribes, but those from Jerusalem—witness to an increasing hostility to Jesus' mission. The escalation might be related to the previous story, where Jesus called the Twelve. Now that his ministry is expanding, the opposition to it expands as well. Because this story is sandwiched between the two parts of the family's story, it is easy to lose sight of the fact that it directly follows Jesus having given the Twelve authority to cast out demons. This story raises the issue of where, precisely, that authority comes from—one of the main themes in Mark.

Jesus' parable of the strong man teaches that being possessed by an unclean spirit is like being a bound captive in Satan's household. Being

---

55. Marcus, *Mark 1–8,* 286.

exorcised is compared to having Jesus, who is stronger than even Satan, come into the house and liberate the captive. The fact that possessed humans are in the role of "goods" in this parable permits reading the exorcisms as involving people who have chosen to allow evil into their lives, since the goods are the rightful possession of the strong man.

Jesus' argument here in the strong man parable relies on the existence of unity in Satan's domain. This means that any time Jesus exorcises a demon, he is also fighting against Satan's domain, which places all of the exorcism stories into a different context because they are instances where Jesus illustrates his superiority over Satan's power. The text points to "Jesus' ability to do what no other force on earth can accomplish."[56] While Jesus will give his disciples power to expel unclean spirits, they will have difficulty exercising it (see 9:18).

Jesus teaches that it makes no sense for Satan to permit his power to be used to cast out demons who are under Satan's control. But since his opponents have already implicitly conceded that Jesus can cast out demons, the question remains: By what power is he casting them out? The only logical answer is that Jesus is casting the demons out by a power greater than Satan's, which must be God's power. There is no way that his opponents can refute this logic. Implicitly, this passage teaches that Satan's power is real, Jesus' power is real, and Jesus has a power greater than Satan's power.

It is possible to read the parable of the binding of the strong man as a depiction of the Atonement: due to sin, humans (the "goods") are bound and kept captive in Satan's house. Because of Satan's strength, there is no way for them to escape on their own. It is only through the actions of Jesus—who is stronger than Satan—that the captives can be set free. Then once the strong man is bound, Jesus is able to liberate the captives. In this reading, all of Jesus' exorcisms become symbolic preenactments of the Atonement.

Also very significant in this section is the first use of "verily I say unto you," which is a hallmark of Jesus' speaking style. In the NT uses of "verily I say unto you" that do not come from Jesus, the "amen" is always used to confirm that someone else's (that is, not the speaker's) words are true; only Jesus uses it to affirm his own words. This is important because it implies that he is claiming a special status for himself by affirming his own words. Where others would have said "thus saith the Lord," Jesus says "truly I say to you." Because Jesus' use of this phrase to affirm his own words is unique

---

56. Marcus, *Mark 1–8,* 282.

in extant writings, it is extremely important—not only as his affirmation of the statement in question but also as evidence of his unique, godlike status.

It is perhaps surprising that blasphemy against the Holy Ghost could not be forgiven when Jesus has just taught that other blasphemies—indeed, all sins—could be. The most logical way to understand this is that ascribing Jesus' power to Satan (which constitutes blasphemy against the Holy Ghost, who is the true source of Jesus' power) makes it impossible to accept Jesus' atoning mission and thus to be forgiven. It is not that Jesus refuses to forgive someone who blasphemes against the Holy Ghost, or that it would not be possible to forgive them, but rather that it is impossible for Jesus to forgive only because that person is unwilling to accept the power that would make forgiveness possible.

Jesus' statement about who is family is revolutionary. First, given the efforts that Mark has taken to suggest Jesus' exalted status and authority, to now show Jesus recognizing a large crowd as his family is quite extraordinary. Next, given the role of the biological family in this society, Jesus is presenting an absolutely revolutionary teaching.[57] The passage does leave open the door to his biological family becoming part of his new family—he has not rejected them; he just can't welcome them into the new family until they do the will of God. Jesus isn't presented as being antifamily (compare 7:9–13 and 10:1–12), but, when in conflict, doing the will of God supersedes obligation to biological family. It is important to not focus too much on the exclusion of his family (who, according to later tradition, did eventually come to believe in him [Acts 1:14]) but on the inclusiveness that Jesus is offering to all people who want to follow him. Unstated here is the cost of discipleship—all of these people have left their families, including Jesus. The rupture of family relationships is the cost of doing the will of God by being with Jesus.

The reference to Jesus' sisters is a reminder that women are often present in scenes even when they are not specifically mentioned: without the change to the singular form in Jesus' statement in this verse, the presence of women in this story would not have been obvious (see also the Notes on 15:40–41).

This story is an important counterpoint to the calling of the Twelve because it shows that not just the Twelve, but a larger group—a group that included women, a group that in effect called themselves by choosing to

---

57. This is not the only time that Jesus offers a culturally radical critique of social roles; see also 9:35–37 and 10:13–16.

encircle Jesus—constitutes his family. If the Twelve recall Israel's history, then the new family takes the audience back even farther into the HB narrative by recalling the family sagas in Genesis. The story also emphasizes that a close relationship with Jesus is not limited to the Twelve. By pointing out that anyone who chooses to can do the will of God, Jesus makes clear that his ministry is not an exclusive one but that all people—including women—can become part of his new family. The earliest audiences of Mark's Gospel would have been taught that they, too, could choose to be part of Jesus' family by doing the will of God. In this manner, Mark's audience members are not passive recipients of the story but rather invited to be a part of it. Not only that, but since Jesus is the Son of God, those who choose to follow him are his brothers and sisters and thus also sons and daughters of God.

This Gospel is well known for its use of "sandwiches"; the story about Jesus' family is divided into two parts (3:20–21 and 31–35) and surrounds the story of the scribes. On a literary level, the controversy happens at the same narrative moment when the family is traveling to meet him. This sandwich suggests that both Jesus' family and the scribes are working at cross-purposes to his ministry. Both stories ultimately concern one question: Who controls Jesus? The scribes think that it is Satan; the family wants to control Jesus themselves because they do not think that he is controlling himself (since he is "beside" himself). Mark's audience already knows that it is the Holy Spirit who controls Jesus.

There is also a contrast between the parts of the sandwich: Jesus' statement about which sins can be forgiven (particularly his teaching that all other sins and blasphemies will be forgiven) implies that his family's efforts to seize him and to find him mad will be forgiven.[58]

The sandwiching implies that Jesus' parables are also relevant to the story about his family: they are an example of the "house divided." Similarity can also be found in the fact that Jesus responds to accusations in both stories with provocative questions: "How can Satan cast out Satan?" and "Who is my mother?"

---

58. While it is possible to view Jesus' family as guilty of the unforgivable sin—since they would be blaspheming against the Holy Ghost by attributing to mental illness the power of the Holy Ghost—this reading is unlikely, largely because Mark's audience was probably aware that at least some of Jesus' family members had later joined Jesus' cause (Acts 1:14). So it is more likely that the sandwiching of the stories is implying that, while the scribes' and the family's reactions to Jesus have some similarities, there are also significant differences.

By casting his own family as outsiders and the Twelve (and others) as insiders, Jesus creates an unexpected reversal in this story. But this reversal will later be itself reversed: "The end of Mark's narrative [finds] the Twelve, demonstrating a remarkable unwillingness to understand or sympathize with Jesus's ministry and message, betray (14:10–11, 43–46), desert (14:50), and deny (14:66–72) him at the moment of his arrest, while Jesus's mother appears among the women who faithfully attend his execution and ultimately attempt to anoint his dead body (15:40; 16:1; cf. 6:3)."[59] Further, in 12:34, one of the scribes from Jerusalem will be told that he is not far from the kingdom. When read as a whole, Mark shows opportunities—in fact, multiple opportunities—for Jesus' family, friends, and enemies to accept the gospel message.

This passage concludes 3:7–35, which focuses on the various reactions that different groups of people have to Jesus. On the positive side, there is a large group of followers and the Twelve who accept calls from Jesus. But there are also the scribes from Jerusalem and Jesus' own family showing a more negative reaction to his ministry. The story of the calling of the Twelve (and others) is heightened by the contrasting reaction from Jesus' family and the scribes, and their status as outsiders is emphasized by references to those who listen to and surround Jesus.

---

59. Busch, "Questioning and Conviction," 503.

Parables
(4:1–34)

Overview

There may be a chiastic structure in this chapter:
    A Introduction (4:1–2)
        B Seed parable (4:3–9)
            C The use of parables (4:10–13)
                D Explanation of the parable (4:14–20)
            C' The use of parables (4:21–25)
        B' Seed parables (4:26–32)
    A' Conclusion (4:33–34)[1]
The very close similarity between A (4:1–2) and A' (4:33–34) suggests deliberate bookending. While the C' material (parables) is not in the same form as the C material (a dialogue), both have the same function in the text: to explain how teaching in parables works. Also, both use the same Greek word (*hina* in 4:12, 21, and 22) to indicate purpose.

This structure encourages the audience to interpret the difficult sayings found in 4:10–13 in light of 4:21–25: while the discussion of insiders and outsiders in 4:10–13 can seem exclusionary, 4:21–25 makes clear that the exclusion is only temporary, and eventually everything will be revealed to everyone.

The audience for Jesus' words in 4:21–32 is not entirely clear, but the chiasm is one of several reasons for concluding that the B and B' sections are addressed to the crowds while the C, D, and C' sections are only to the

---

1. Klyne Snodgrass, "A Hermeneutic of Hearing Informed by the Parables with Special Reference to Mark 4," *Bulletin for Biblical Research* 14, no. 1 (2004): 67.

disciples. The B and B' sections involve "public" parables (sowing), while the C section is about hidden teachings, and the C' section is a domestic parable (a lamp in a room); these observations may be an additional indication of the sections' audience and setting. Further, both of these parables have explanations, implying that they were taught to insiders. If this analysis is correct, it means that the teachings to insiders are placed literally inside while those also addressed to outsiders are structurally outside; Mark has cleverly allowed setting to echo content.

The explanation of the parable (4:14–20) occupies the central position of this structure; it emphasizes structurally Jesus' statement that understanding the parable in 4:3–9 is the key to understanding all of the parables (see 4:13).

There is another way to understand the structure of this section: it consists of parables followed by explanation:[2]

> first parable: 4:1–9
> > first explanation: 4:14–20
> second parable: 4:21
> > second explanation: 4:22
> third parable: 4:24
> > third explanation: 4:25
> fourth and fifth parables: 4:26–32
> > fourth and fifth explanations (implied): 4:34

The first parable and explanation are each much longer than the others, perhaps in order to illustrate the pattern. Located between the second and third parable in 4:23 is an exhortation to hear. The advantage of this structure is that it shows a pattern of parable followed by explanation; the disadvantage is that it does not account for the discussion between Jesus and the disciples in 4:10–13.

There are two different ways that the broader structure of 3:23–4:34 can be understood:

1. Mark 3:23–4:9 is a single block of parabolic teachings, interrupted by Jesus' family in 3:31–35. Jesus turns the interruption into a discussion of insiders and outsiders (a move that Mark emphasizes with several notes about literal insider and outsider status). Surrounding the insider/outsider discussion with parables—parables that are not understood by outsiders—emphasizes the role that the parables play in transmitting greater understanding to insiders.

---

2. Elizabeth Struthers Malbon, "Narrative Criticism: How Does the Story Mean?" in Anderson and Moore, *Mark and Method*, 43.

2. Mark 3:23–30 and 4:3–9 are blocks of parabolic teachings, each followed by discussions of insiders and outsiders (3:31–35 and 4:10–13). The repetition of this pattern stresses that teaching in parables leads to the creation of insiders and outsiders. It also emphasizes that Mark's audience must choose to become insiders by working to understand the parables.

THE PARABLE OF THE SOILS (4:1–9)

Greek Text

1 Καὶ πάλιν ἤρξατο διδάσκειν παρὰ τὴν θάλασσαν. καὶ συνάγεται πρὸς αὐτὸν ὄχλος πλεῖστος, ὥστε αὐτὸν εἰς πλοῖον ἐμβάντα καθῆσθαι ἐν τῇ θαλάσσῃ, καὶ πᾶς ὁ ὄχλος πρὸς τὴν θάλασσαν ἐπὶ τῆς γῆς ἦσαν. 2 καὶ ἐδίδασκεν αὐτοὺς ἐν παραβολαῖς πολλά, καὶ ἔλεγεν αὐτοῖς ἐν τῇ διδαχῇ αὐτοῦ· 3 Ἀκούετε. ἰδοὺ ἐξῆλθεν ὁ σπείρων σπεῖραι. 4 καὶ ἐγένετο ἐν τῷ σπείρειν ὃ μὲν ἔπεσεν παρὰ τὴν ὁδόν, καὶ ἦλθεν τὰ πετεινὰ καὶ κατέφαγεν αὐτό. 5 καὶ ἄλλο ἔπεσεν ἐπὶ τὸ πετρῶδες ὅπου οὐκ εἶχεν γῆν πολλήν, καὶ εὐθὺς ἐξανέτειλεν διὰ τὸ μὴ ἔχειν βάθος γῆς· 6 καὶ ὅτε ἀνέτειλεν ὁ ἥλιος ἐκαυματίσθη καὶ διὰ τὸ μὴ ἔχειν ῥίζαν ἐξηράνθη. 7 καὶ ἄλλο ἔπεσεν εἰς τὰς ἀκάνθας, καὶ ἀνέβησαν αἱ ἄκανθαι καὶ συνέπνιξαν αὐτό, καὶ καρπὸν οὐκ ἔδωκεν. 8 καὶ ἄλλα ἔπεσεν εἰς τὴν γῆν τὴν καλήν, καὶ ἐδίδου καρπὸν ἀναβαίνοντα καὶ αὐξανόμενα, καὶ ἔφερεν ἓν τριάκοντα καὶ ἓν ἑξήκοντα καὶ ἓν ἑκατόν. 9 καὶ ἔλεγεν· Ὃς ἔχει ὦτα ἀκούειν ἀκουέτω. [SBLGNT]

King James Version

1 And he began again to teach by the sea side: and there was gathered unto him a great multitude, so that he entered into a ship, and sat in the sea; and the whole multitude was by the sea on the land. 2 And he taught them many things by parables, and said unto them in his doctrine, 3 Hearken; Behold, there went out a sower to sow: 4 And it came to pass, as he sowed, some fell by the way side, and the fowls of the air came and devoured it up. 5 And some fell on stony ground, where it had not much earth; and immediately it sprang up, because it had no depth of earth: 6 But when the sun was up, it was scorched;

New Rendition

1 And again he began to teach beside the sea. And a large crowd was gathered to him, so having gotten into a boat, he sat in it in the sea, and all the crowd was beside the sea on the land. 2 And he taught them in parables many things and said to them in his teachings, 3 "Listen! Look! A planter went out to plant. 4 And it came to pass that as he planted, some indeed fell by the [path]way, and the birds came and ate it. 5 And other seed fell on rocky land, where it did not have much soil. And immediately it sprouted because there was no depth to the soil. 6 But after the sun rose, it was burned. And since it did not have root,

and because it had no root, it withered away. 7 And some fell among thorns, and the thorns grew up, and choked it, and it yielded no fruit. 8 And other fell on good ground, and did yield fruit that sprang up and increased; and brought forth, some thirty, and some sixty, and some an hundred. 9 And he said unto them, He that hath ears to hear, let him hear.

it withered away. 7 And other seed fell into the thorns. And the thorns came up and choked it, and it produced no crop. 8 But other seeds fell into the good soil and produced a crop, coming up and increasing, and bore thirty times and sixty times and one hundred times as much." 9 And he said, "Whoever has ears to hear, hear!"

Notes

4:1 *And he began again to teach by the sea side:* "Again" links this text to 3:7–9 (and 1:16 and 2:13), where Jesus was also at the seaside.

and there was gathered unto him a great multitude: Because a superlative is used, the phrase "a great multitude" could be translated as "the biggest crowd yet";[3] Mark emphasizes the ever-increasing crowd, which may foreshadow the enormous yield of the good soil (see 4:8).

so that he entered into a ship: Jesus had previously asked his disciples to prepare a boat, which was not needed at the time (3:9). Mark may have structured the text to show Jesus as prophetically prepared, with the boat ready before it was needed. The two boat references also bracket the text located in between, suggesting that the intervening material is unified by the theme of insiders and outsiders (see the Notes on 3:10–35), which is an appropriate theme to flank with boat references since the presence of a boat demands that everyone will be either inside or outside of it. It is also possible that the boat was physically necessary to protect Jesus from the surging crowd.

and sat in the sea: Jesus is, obviously, sitting in the boat and not in the sea itself; the awkwardness of the phrasing[4] suggests that Mark is making a theological point, the possibilities for which include:

1. Sitting was the normal posture for authority and teaching. The focus is not on the sea but on the sitting, which implies that Jesus is an authoritative teacher.

2. In 1:17, Jesus announced his plan to make his disciples into fishers of men. By sitting in the boat, Jesus himself also "fishes" for disciples from the listening crowd.

---

3. Marcus, *Mark 1–8,* 291.
4. Note that both Matthew and Luke omit the phrase (Matt. 13:1–2; Luke 8:4).

3. In the HB, the sea was a symbol for chaos; sitting in the sea implies Jesus' mastery over it. The story of the calming of the storm in 4:35–41 extends this theme. Linking Jesus' teaching in parables to his sitting in the sea associates Jesus' teaching with an end to chaos.

4. Later in this verse, Mark notes that the crowd is on the soil/land; this aligns the crowd with the parable and also alerts the audience to the relationship between the parable and its setting. So by having Jesus sitting in the sea, Mark implies that Jesus himself is not one of the soils in the parable.

Relationship to Psalm 29. In Psalm 29:10, the Lord sits on the seas (KJV: "the flood") and majestically rules. If Mark had this psalm in mind, the connection would identify Jesus with the God of the HB. Since the first five verses of the psalm emphasize the greatness of the Lord's teachings, the same theme would be suggested in Mark, and the association would also imply that Jesus rules through his teachings.

---

and the whole multitude was by the sea on the land: The Greek word translated here as "land" is the same word translated as "ground" in 4:8. Just as in 3:31–35, where the seating arrangement conveyed a theological point, Mark suggests that the crowd's location is related to the content of the parable.

In Isaiah 42:4, 10, and 12, Isaiah announces that the people along the coast (KJV: "isles") will eagerly await the decrees of the servant of the Lord, and similar ideas are expressed in Isaiah 49:1; 51:4–5; 60:9; and 66:19; perhaps Mark echoed this language to imply that Jesus is the servant of the Lord whom Isaiah had prophesied and to suggest that the crowd was eager to learn from him.

4:2 *And he taught them many things by parables:* The root meaning of the word "parable" is "to throw alongside"; a parable works by inviting the audience to compare two things that have been placed side by side and to learn from their similarities. Also, "in classical Greek literature the term designates a mode of speech distinguished by its power to convince. . . . In the LXX and Jewish apocalyptic literature, it becomes a term for a message, often encrypted in a comparison of some sort, that is difficult to comprehend and requires decipherment."[5]

and said unto them in his doctrine: The word "doctrine" is perhaps too specific for modern English readers; "teachings" better preserves the sense of the Greek.

---

5. Marcus, *Mark 1–8,* 291.

4:3 *Hearken; Behold:* These two verbs are commands from Jesus to the audience. There are several possible reasons for this dual exhortation:

1. Because "hearken" means "to listen" and "behold" means "to see," Jesus is commanding them to use more than one sense, implying that this is required to understand the parable. The command to look points to the intensely visual nature of parables; Jesus is encouraging them not only to listen to the parable but also to visualize it.

2. The command to hear links the passage to Deuteronomy 6:4–9, a text that had an important role in first-century Judaism and that also begins with a command to hear. Deuteronomy 6:4–9, known as the Shema, was regarded as the core of Judaism; linking it to this parable implies that the parable will have a similar role for Jesus' followers. It is even possible that the three unproductive soils in the parable are a commentary on the failure to observe the three parts of the Shema (to love the Lord with one's entire heart, soul, and might).

3. There is a biblical pattern of a command to hear immediately preceding symbolic teachings (Judg. 9:7; Isa. 28:23; Ezek. 20:47); Jesus follows that pattern in order to alert the audience that nonliteral teachings will follow.

4. The doubled command reflects Mark's penchant for duplication.

5. As 4:13 will indicate, this parable is very important, something that introducing it with two commands to pay attention emphasizes. At the end of the parable, Jesus also refers to hearing (4:9), thus bookending the parable with pleas to hear.

6. After the parable, Jesus will quote from Isaiah 6:9–10, a text that begins with the prophet being commissioned to tell the people to hear and see. Including those injunctions here means that Jesus is taking on the role of a prophet in this story.

7. Chapter 13 is comparable to chapter 4 as the only other extended section of Jesus' spoken teachings in Mark; the reference to looking in chapter 4 anticipates the emphasis on watching in chapter 13 and further links the two passages together.

Note: The commentary on 4:3–9 is limited to technical and factual details of the parable; interpretive comments are reserved for 4:14–20, where Jesus interprets the parable for the disciples.

there went out a sower to sow: Sowing meant walking through a field and scattering seeds along the surface; sowers generally did not dig holes in which to place the seeds. The elements of the parable would have been immediately understandable to the audience; only some modern readers need to have sowing explained to them.

Because Jesus has invited the audience to listen carefully to the parable and because the verb for "went out" translates the same Greek verb used for Jesus' mortal ministry (1:38; 2:13, 17), this may hint that Jesus is the sower.

Several HB texts picture God as a sower:

1. In Isaiah 55:10–11, God is the sower, the seed is the word, and the passage teaches that what God has promised will in fact come to pass. The Lord assures that the word "shall accomplish that which I please"; importing this idea into Mark's text implies that whatever happens to the seeds reflects God's will, which raises some interesting questions since many seeds fail to be productive.
2. Jeremiah 31:27–28 pictures God as a sower repopulating the formerly desolate Judah and Israel. As background, it implies that the sowing reflects God's action of producing a faithful people. Chapter 4 tweaks the text from Jeremiah by suggesting that only some of the seeds will produce.
3. Hosea 2:23 pictures a future day when the Lord will plant people in the land, take pity on them, and call them his people. The restoration of the covenant is emphasized. As background to chapter 4, this passage identifies Jesus with the God of the HB and shows him, as the sower, fulfilling the promises that had been made about the restoration of the covenant.

4:4 *And it came to pass, as he sowed, some fell by the way side:* The image here is of a path (KJV: "way side") through a field, with the seeds landing either by or on the path. "The way" will, by Mark's time, be one of the main designations for the Christian movement ("The Way"). If it carries that meaning here, it implies that this seed is near but not quite part of "The Way"; it would describe someone close to—but not committed to—following Jesus.

Foot traffic on a path would have caused packed soil in which a seed could not sprout. It is possible that this situation reflects the unavoidable waste inherent in hand-sowing since some seed accidentally lands on the path, but it may also reflect the practice of plowing *after* sowing, which would result in the path's hard soil being churned and the seed having a chance to sprout.

and the fowls of the air came and devoured it up: The phrase "of the air" is not in the best manuscripts.[6]

4:5 *And some fell on stony ground:* The stony ground is not rocks mixed with soil but rather a thin layer of soil over a rock layer, which means that one cannot tell simply by looking that the soil is stony.

---

6. Bratcher and Nida, *Translator's Handbook*, 129. The phrase "fowls of the air" occurs in Gen. 1:24 and may have been imported from there.

where it had not much earth; and immediately it sprang up, because it had no depth of earth: The dual references to the lack of earth point to its importance; the fact that these statements surround the seed's springing up suggests that the lack of soil is responsible for the fast sprouting. No seed could actually spring up "immediately"; rather, this implies a relatively quick sprouting compared to other seeds, reasons for which may include:

1. Because the soil was so thin, it could warm quickly, and therefore the seed would germinate more quickly.

2. The rock stopped the seed from getting pushed down more deeply into the soil where it was cooler; the warm soil helped the seed to sprout more quickly.

3. A seed could go farther down into good soil but then would require more time for the plant to be visible above the surface. So a seed in shallow soil pokes above the ground sooner, while a seed in good soil could be exactly the same size but wouldn't yet be visible because it is positioned farther below the surface.

4. In rocky soil, the seed is not devoting any of its energy to downward growth (roots). Since all growth is upward, it initially appears that there has been more growth.

4:6 *But when the sun was up, it was scorched; and because it had no root, it withered away:* "Was up" translates the same verb (minus the prefix) as "sprang up" in the previous verse; there may be wordplay indicating that the action of the plant mirrors (too closely) the action of the sun. It is as if the plant is taking its cues not from its own schedule for growth but from the sun.

4:7 *And some fell among thorns:* The rest of this verse indicates that the thorns came up only later; they were probably not visible at this point.

and the thorns grew up, and choked it: The seed does not necessarily die; it is just unable to produce fruit due to competition for resources from the thorns.

and it yielded no fruit: This is the first mention that no fruit is produced, although that would have been true for the other two soils as well.

4:8 *And other fell on good ground:* The word translated as "other" was probably first plural and then changed by copyists to the singular form in order to match 4:5 and 7.[7]

---

7. Collins, *Mark*, 238 note g.

and did yield fruit that sprang up and increased: Because the tense of the verb changes, this line "form[s] a moving picture of ongoing emergence, growth, and productivity."[8]

The phrasing here is unusual since the fruit is mentioned first with the springing up; increasing is mentioned only later. Given the final reference to the harvest, perhaps this is a deliberate chiastic structure meant to emphasize the growth of the plant by surrounding it with references to fruitfulness:

yield fruit (4:8)
>sprang up (4:8)
>increased (4:8)
brought forth (4:8)

Because there is a reference to not yielding fruit at the end of the previous verse, there could be a different chiasmus where the reference to the good soil is surrounded by references to yielding fruit, which would emphasize that the good ground triggers the fruitfulness:

did not yield fruit (4:7)
>good ground (4:8)
did yield fruit (4:8)

and brought forth, some thirty, and some sixty, and some an hundred: The reference to one hundred is unexpected; the audience would have anticipated that the third number would be ninety (if the pattern is to add thirty to the previous number) or one hundred and twenty (if the previous number is doubled). Reasons one hundred is the third yield may include:

1. If the audience was expecting it to be ninety, then one hundred is an unexpectedly bountiful harvest.

2. In Genesis 26:12, Isaac reaps one hundred times what he had sown because the Lord blessed him; perhaps the parable implies that God is blessing the activity of the sower. The successful yield is therefore not just the result of the good soil but also of divine intervention.

There is debate as to if a hundredfold yield represents divine intervention or if it would be possible under ordinary conditions. Either way, this yield more than compensates for the seed lost in the three poor soils.

For each seed, there is a three-part description of what happens to it, with the three failed seeds described in three ways each and the seed in good soil described by three different harvest levels. There are two (not mutually exclusive) reasons for this pattern:

---

8. Gundry, *Mark,* 192.

1. Because three was a number symbolic of deity, the parable hints that it is not only the condition of the soil but also divine intervention that determines the harvest.

2. Groups of three were common in oral discourse because they are easier to remember and more pleasing to the ear, so there might be a pragmatic reason for their presence here.

In Mark's setting, Jesus speaks this parable from a boat to a huge crowd on the "ground" of the shore; this massive crowd may represent Jesus' very fruitful mission.

4:9 *And he said unto them, He that hath ears to hear, let him hear:* "Let him hear" is a command ("pay attention"). This parable both begins (4:3) and ends with exhortations to listen, suggesting that it requires concerted effort to understand; pondering and thought are required for successful interpretation. The issue of the audience's (lack of) understanding of the parable gets an enormous amount of attention in this chapter.

HB Allusions in 4:9. There are several HB texts that may be echoed here:

1. This verse is a sort of parody of Jeremiah 5:21, where the audience is directly criticized for their lack of understanding. Here, the audience isn't criticized but invited to comprehend, suggesting that Jesus is different from his HB predecessors.

2. Deuteronomy 29:4 features Moses telling the people that the Lord did not give some of them understanding minds and discerning ears, implying that hearing is not possible unless the Lord equips the hearer for it. It is possible that the opening exhortation to hear the parable means, unlike the Deuteronomy passage, that all people are now invited to have understanding minds and ears.

3. Psalm 115:6 describes idols with ears that cannot hear, suggesting that those who don't hear are like idols (that is, made in the image of other gods) and not humans (who are made in God's image). If this psalm is in the background of this parable, then there is a subtle message about choosing whom one will worship.

4. In Ezekiel 12:2, Ezekiel is told that he is living among rebellious people who cannot hear; the implication is that those who cannot hear the parables are those who have chosen to rebel.

Analysis

Mark's early audiences probably wondered why Jesus' ministry created such wildly varying responses as complete devotion and plots to kill him. Mark 4:1–34, which contains several parables and a rationale for Jesus' use of parables, explains why people had such different reactions to Jesus' ministry. With these parables, Jesus gives the audience a way to think about the troubling, discouraging events of the last few chapters.

This teaching in Mark is neither the first to be labeled a parable (see 3:23) nor the first to contain parables (see 2:19–22). But unlike these previous passages, chapter 4 is self-evidently concerned with parables and their use. In what has become a famous statement on parables, C. H. Dodd wrote, "At its simplest the parable is a metaphor or simile drawn from nature or common life, arresting the hearer by its vividness or strangeness, and leaving the mind in sufficient doubt about its precise application to tease it into active thought."[9] Jesus intended for the audience to ponder the parable—the meaning would not have been obvious. Parables have a dual nature: they use very common images (seeds, birds, lamps) that were instantly familiar to Jesus' audience, but they frequently have one or more unexpected aspects; these discontinuities draw attention to themselves and therefore emphasize certain parts of the parable. Thus, Jesus' parables have a revolutionary edge to them: they "are intended to be unsettling, disturbing, sometimes even ominous and shocking. They are not told to reinforce the status quo like so many traditional proverbs are. Rather they alert people to the new and disturbing thing God is doing in their midst which involves reversal of expectations, values, social standing, roles in society."[10] Jesus' parables are "invitational rather than imperatival. Most of them are invitations to see differently rather than stories that say, 'Do this.'"[11]

In previous decades, it was generally thought that a parable had one point of comparison with reality. In recent years, scholars are more willing to find multiple points of contact between the concrete world of the parable and its abstract teachings, but this does not imply that every single element of the parable must correspond to real life. Determining which parts of the parable are significant and which are merely coincidental is one challenge for the modern reader.

Jesus' parables are filled with references to the world of poor farmers. By selecting common experiences from their lives—not from the lives of, for example, royalty or soldiers—Jesus delivered a message particularly suited to the poor and one that legitimated their experiences. It required wealthier listeners to assume the frame of reference of the peasants; Jesus

---

9. C. H. Dodd, *The Parables of the Kingdom* (New York: Charles Scribner's Sons, 1961), 5.
10. Witherington, *The Gospel of Mark*, 163.
11. Borg, *Jesus*, 155.

made it somewhat easier for the poor farmer to become an insider than for the wealthy urbanite. Because vivid parables are easier to remember than sermons, this may be one reason that Jesus used them; it is easy to imagine a farmer sowing seed years or even decades after listening to Jesus and gaining new insight into the parable. Someone initially lukewarm—or even hostile—to Jesus' message may have, over time, softened and been able to recall and then learn from a parable later.

The crucial role of 4:3–9 is emphasized in several ways. First, Mark not only includes the parable but then recounts Jesus' explanation of it (4:14–20), which means that Mark's audience hears the parable twice; this repetition gives them a second chance to understand the parable. Then, Jesus explains that understanding this parable is the key to understanding all of the parables (see 4:13). Also, Mark has very little direct instruction from Jesus; in fact, only two chapters (4 and 13) contain lengthy teachings. The parable in 4:3–9 and its explanation therefore constitute a substantial portion of Jesus' teachings in this Gospel. And perhaps most importantly, Jesus literally surrounds this parable with exhortations to hear and to listen to it (4:3, 9).

There is a clever interplay between the setting and the content of the parable: the parable is about how the soil receives the seed and whether it will be fruitful; the setting includes bookending exhortations from Jesus about how the audience receives the word and whether their understanding will be fruitful. The exhortations to listen, which bracket the text, also create an important difference between Jesus and the sower, who might be considered negligent for casting seed onto rocky and thorny soil, because Jesus does everything within his power to carefully prepare his audience to receive what he is teaching. Jesus, unlike the sower, works hard to ensure that the soil is as receptive as possible.

At the beginning of the parable, the command to listen was extended to everyone but at the end it is only for those who have ears to hear. This may be an insignificant shift for stylistic reasons, or it might imply that the parable itself has created insiders who are capable of hearing (from their very exposure to this parable and their willingness to engage it) and outsiders who are not capable of understanding the parable and therefore not even commanded to try.

Jesus Teaches about Parables (4:10–20)

Greek Text

10 Καὶ ὅτε ἐγένετο κατὰ μόνας, ἠρώτων αὐτὸν οἱ περὶ αὐτὸν σὺν τοῖς δώδεκα τὰς παραβολάς. 11 καὶ ἔλεγεν αὐτοῖς· Ὑμῖν τὸ μυστήριον δέδοται τῆς βασιλείας τοῦ θεοῦ· ἐκείνοις δὲ τοῖς ἔξω ἐν παραβολαῖς τὰ πάντα γίνεται, 12 ἵνα βλέποντες βλέπωσι καὶ μὴ ἴδωσιν, καὶ ἀκούοντες ἀκούωσι καὶ μὴ συνιῶσιν, μήποτε ἐπιστρέψωσιν καὶ ἀφεθῇ αὐτοῖς.

13 Καὶ λέγει αὐτοῖς· Οὐκ οἴδατε τὴν παραβολὴν ταύτην, καὶ πῶς πάσας τὰς παραβολὰς γνώσεσθε; 14 ὁ σπείρων τὸν λόγον σπείρει. 15 οὗτοι δέ εἰσιν οἱ παρὰ τὴν ὁδὸν ὅπου σπείρεται ὁ λόγος, καὶ ὅταν ἀκούσωσιν εὐθὺς ἔρχεται ὁ Σατανᾶς καὶ αἴρει τὸν λόγον τὸν ἐσπαρμένον εἰς αὐτούς. 16 καὶ οὗτοί εἰσιν ὁμοίως οἱ ἐπὶ τὰ πετρώδη σπειρόμενοι, οἳ ὅταν ἀκούσωσιν τὸν λόγον εὐθὺς μετὰ χαρᾶς λαμβάνουσιν αὐτόν, 17 καὶ οὐκ ἔχουσιν ῥίζαν ἐν ἑαυτοῖς ἀλλὰ πρόσκαιροί εἰσιν, εἶτα γενομένης θλίψεως ἢ διωγμοῦ διὰ τὸν λόγον εὐθὺς σκανδαλίζονται. 18 καὶ ἄλλοι εἰσὶν οἱ εἰς τὰς ἀκάνθας σπειρόμενοι· οὗτοί εἰσιν οἱ τὸν λόγον ἀκούσαντες, 19 καὶ αἱ μέριμναι τοῦ αἰῶνος καὶ ἡ ἀπάτη τοῦ πλούτου καὶ αἱ περὶ τὰ λοιπὰ ἐπιθυμίαι εἰσπορευόμεναι συμπνίγουσιν τὸν λόγον, καὶ ἄκαρπος γίνεται. 20 καὶ ἐκεῖνοί εἰσιν οἱ ἐπὶ τὴν γῆν τὴν καλὴν σπαρέντες, οἵτινες ἀκούουσιν τὸν λόγον καὶ παραδέχονται καὶ καρποφοροῦσιν ἓν τριάκοντα καὶ ἓν ἑξήκοντα καὶ ἓν ἑκατόν. [SBLGNT]

King James Version

10 And when he was alone, they that were about him with the twelve asked of him the parable. 11 And he said unto them, Unto you it is given to know the mystery of the kingdom of God: but unto them that are without, all these things are done in parables: 12 That seeing they may see, and not perceive; and hearing they may hear, and not understand; lest at any time they should be converted, and their sins should be forgiven them. 13 And he said unto them, Know ye not this parable? and how then will ye know all parables?

14 The sower soweth the word. 15 And these are they by the way side, where the word is sown; but when they have heard, Satan cometh immediately,

New Rendition

10 And when he was alone, those around him and the Twelve were asking him about the parables. 11 And he said to them, "To you the secret of the kingdom of God has been given. But to those who are outside, all things come in parables. 12 So that

> 'they might see but not perceive,
> and hear but not understand,
> to prevent them from ever
>   returning and being
>   forgiven.'"

13 And he says to them, "You don't understand this parable? Then how will you understand all of the parables? 14 The planter plants the word. 15 These are the ones along the pathway where the word is planted: and when they hear,

and taketh away the word that was sown in their hearts. 16 And these are they likewise which are sown on stony ground; who, when they have heard the word, immediately receive it with gladness; 17 And have no root in themselves, and so endure but for a time: afterward, when affliction or persecution ariseth for the word's sake, immediately they are offended. 18 And these are they which are sown among thorns; such as hear the word, 19 And the cares of this world, and the deceitfulness of riches, and the lusts of other things entering in, choke the word, and it becometh unfruitful. 20 And these are they which are sown on good ground; such as hear the word, and receive it, and bring forth fruit, some thirtyfold, some sixty, and some an hundred.

Satan immediately comes and takes away the word that has been planted in them. 16 And, similarly, these are the ones who are planted in rocky places: who, when they hear the word, immediately receive it with joy, 17 and they do not have any root in themselves but are temporary; then when trouble or persecution comes because of the word, they immediately stumble. 18 And others are the ones who are planted among the thorns: these are the ones who, having heard the word, 19 the anxieties of this life, the lure of wealth, and the desires for other things enter in, choke the word, and it becomes fruitless. 20 And these are the ones planted on the good soil: they hear the word and accept it and produce a crop, one thirty times, and one sixty times, and one a hundred times as much."

Notes

4:10 *And when he was alone:* Obviously, this phrase is not to be read literally since Jesus is with the Twelve and others; the point here is that he is no longer with the crowd.

The phrase also suggests a shift in scene. However, 4:33 assumes that Jesus had been speaking to the crowd, so there is either some imperfect editing or an unannounced shift from a private audience back to the entire crowd located somewhere between 4:10 and 4:33. It is possible that Mark structured the text with more attention to theology than to setting and thus did not particularly care about the unexplained change in audience; perhaps the point of saying "when he was alone" was to signal to the audience that Mark is departing from a chronological order of events (as if to say "later on, when he was alone") for narrative reasons, and the audience is to presume a return to the scene with the crowd at some point. In this view, 4:10 introduces a section of text (the precise ending of which is unclear) that happened *after* Jesus had related the rest of the teachings in this chapter to the larger audience. Mark may have structured the text this way so that the interpretation of 4:3–9 would be in closer proximity to the parable itself. Since Jesus says that understanding this parable is the key to understanding all of the parables, it would make sense that Mark would want the audience to understand this parable before the other parables are presented.

they that were about him with the twelve: The KJV can be interpreted so that those with him who were not part of the Twelve asked the question, but the Greek text implies that the Twelve and the others, as one group, asked about the parables.

"About him" translates the same Greek phrase found in 3:34, suggesting that this is the same group of disciples. This group is Jesus' family—not his biological family but those who are willing to do the will of God—and is composed of those who were willing to listen to Jesus (3:35). Those about him here and those about him in chapter 3 are both contrasted with another group, those who are outside. The similarities between these texts encourage a link between those who do the will of God and those who ask Jesus to explain his teachings. Thus Mark implies that seeking knowledge and asking questions are important tasks for the disciples.

It is impossible to know whether, when Jesus spoke the parable in 4:3–9, the Twelve and the other disciples were in the boat with him or if they were part of the crowd on the shore, although 4:36 may imply that they were not in the boat while Jesus taught. If they were part of the crowd on the shore, then they are enacting the role of the good soil who receive the seed (hear the word) in a different way from the rest of the soil. In this case, good hearing involves asking Jesus for clarification.

asked of him the parable: The earliest text most likely read "parables" (plural) here, although some texts have "parable" (singular).[12] The reference was presumably changed to the singular by scribes who noted that Jesus tells just one parable in this scene.

The disciples' question is ambiguous; there are several different ways to interpret it:

1. They ask for the interpretation of the parable in 4:3–9. In this reading, it is difficult to understand why they used the plural form "parables" unless one assumes that Mark has retrojected a question they asked after Jesus had taught more parables.

2. They ask about the parables Jesus taught on previous occasions (2:19–22; 3:23–27), with their question being delayed because Jesus' family interrupted the parabolic teachings in 3:31. While the explanation only interprets the parable from 4:3–9, making this reading less likely, Jesus does suggest that this

---

12. Collins, *Mark,* 247 note b.

parable is the key to understanding all other parables, so his response could still be viewed as an explanation for all of the parables that he has spoken up to this point.

3. They ask for more parables.[13] This would explain the use of the plural form. Jesus' response, which is to interpret the parable from 4:3–9, does not mesh well with this explanation unless it is assumed that Jesus did not give them what they wanted (at least right away, but compare 4:21–32).

4. They ask why Jesus taught using parables. This makes sense of the plural form. Jesus' answer, which first explains why he taught in parables, meshes well with this reading. It is even possible that the scene has already shifted so that the larger crowd is part of the audience before Jesus delivers the explanation of the parable from 4:3–9, which means that 4:14–20 was spoken to the entire crowd.

4:11 *And he said unto them, Unto you it is given:* The word "you" is plural in Greek, so it refers to the entire group of disciples. "It is given" is a divine passive, implying that God is the one doing the giving.

to know the mystery of the kingdom of God: The phrase "to know" is not in the best manuscripts;[14] it was likely added later to parallel the accounts in Matthew 13:11 and Luke 8:10. It is possible that Mark assumed that his audience would automatically fill in the phrase "to know," but it is also possible that Mark thought of the mystery as akin to a physical object that could be given to someone.

It is quite difficult to determine precisely what this mystery is. The verb "is given" in the previous phrase is in the Greek text a perfect passive ("has been given"), which means that the mystery has already been given to the disciples. So the interpretation of the parable could not be the mystery, since it has not yet been given to them. Similarly, the mystery could not be understanding Jesus' full identity, since the disciples do not yet understand that. Options for the identity of the mystery include:

1. Knowledge for insiders only: "A *mystery* in the Biblical sense is essentially knowledge which has not been known to people in general, but revealed to the initiated, i.e., to the believers."[15] While this is the usual scriptural sense, it does not mesh well with Mark's context, where there is no record of the disciples having been given insider knowledge, although it is possible that this happened when Jesus called the Twelve and others to the mountain (see 3:13–15), but Mark is silent on this point; the modern Latter-day Saint

---

13. A. M. Ambrozic, "Mark's Concept of the Parable: Mk 4, 11f. in the Context of the Second Gospel," *Catholic Biblical Quarterly* 29, no. 2 (1967): 225.

14. Bratcher and Nida, *Translator's Handbook,* 134.

15. Bratcher and Nida, *Translator's Handbook,* 135; italics in original.

practice of restricting the temple ordinances to worthy believers may be an analogous practice.

2. Knowledge that was hidden in the past but is now made known to everyone. Mark 4:22 supports this idea; the summary of Jesus' mission in 1:14–15 may be an example of it.

3. Jesus himself: "the kingdom of God has come in the person and words and works of Jesus. That is a secret because God has chosen to reveal himself indirectly and in a veiled way. The incarnate Word is not obvious. Only faith could recognize the Son of God in the lowly figure of Jesus of Nazareth."[16] The advantage of this reading is that it reconciles the paradox that the disciples already have the mystery while they still do not understand the parable: they have Jesus with them to explain the parable, and he does. This reading emphasizes the idea that truth is ultimately found not in parables but in the person of Jesus. It also coheres well with the parable in 4:21–22 on two points: first, nothing is hidden except to be revealed later, and second, that parable strongly implies that the once-hidden, now-revealed lamp is also a symbol for Jesus.

4. A veiled revelation that requires an interpreter. The same Greek word for "mystery" is used in LXX Daniel 2:18–19, 27–30, and 47, where King Nebuchadnezzar has a dream but does not know the interpretation; it is explained to him by Daniel. The disciples in Mark are a close analogue to the king, who has been given something that he does not yet understand and which requires a prophetic figure to explain. This reading emphasizes that the mystery is not decoded merely because the person is particularly clever or diligent (as the word "mystery" implies in English); rather, its meaning is first revealed in a veiled way that requires someone with prophetic authority to further explain. An important implication of this definition of mystery is that it means that the mystery will not always be secret; rather it is meant to be revealed through an authorized messenger. One strength of this reading is that it makes sense of the paradox that the disciples already possess the mystery but still do not understand the parable.

5. The knowledge that one must ask for more understanding. This reading makes sense of Jesus' statement that this parable is the key to all parables (see 4:13): if the disciples know to ask Jesus about the meaning of this parable, then they know how to understand all of the parables. This option meshes nicely with the conclusion of chapter 3, where Jesus taught that doing the will of God and becoming part of his new family meant sitting at Jesus' feet and listening to him.

6. How to apply a parable. In 2 Samuel 12, Nathan teaches a parable to David. There is a stage in that story when David understands the moral of the parable

---

16. Cranfield, *Gospel according to St Mark,* 153.

(do not take things that do not belong to you), but he does not yet understand how the parable applies to his own situation with Bathsheba. By analogy, the disciples could know the mystery (that is, the meaning of the parable) without understanding its application (to their own lives). This reading meshes well with Jesus' explanation of the parable in terms of how it should apply to the lives of the disciples as they face persecution.

7. Because Jesus will refer to the disciples' lack of knowledge in 4:13, it is possible that this verse is sarcastic or ironic. An ironic cast to these words would help make sense of the notoriously difficult-to-interpret 4:12, which would then also be read sarcastically.[17]

The mystery of the kingdom—whatever it is—is not just for the Twelve but also for the larger group of disciples with Jesus; this group would include, per 3:35, all (including women) who are willing to do the will of God by listening to Jesus and following him.

but unto them that are without: "Without" means those who are on the outside. The proximity of this passage to 3:32–35 links together these references to who is "in" and who is "out" of Jesus' circle. The precise identity of those who are without is not given here, but it probably refers to those in the crowd on the shore who did *not* seek greater understanding of the parable. The part of the crowd that is "good soil" consists of the Twelve and those with them; the rest of the crowd has chosen to take on the role of the outsiders who do not seek to become insiders. This idea of a "righteous remnant" meshes well with the quotation from Isaiah (see the Notes on 4:12). But the outsiders are not sent away empty handed: Jesus is willing to preach to them (see 4:33), and they have now heard a parable that they may decide to ponder later.

all these things are done in parables: "All these things" is a surprising phrase; it may imply that Jesus is using the word "parables" more broadly than just to describe 4:3–9; it is possible that even his miracles are considered parables since they include symbolic elements. Another hint that this is the case is found in the idea of *doing* things in parables when one might have expected Jesus to say that he was *speaking* in parables.

4:12 *That seeing they may see, and not perceive:* This verse is a quotation of Isaiah 6:9–10.

There are a few different ways that the word translated as "that" at the beginning of this verse can be understood:

---

17. Robert M. Fowler, "Reader-Response Criticism: Figuring Mark's Reader," in Anderson and Moore, *Mark and Method,* 82.

1. *Purpose.* This verse provides the purpose for what was described in the previous verse: the reason Jesus taught in parables was so some people would not repent. The presumption is that if he had taught in a different way, they would have repented, but he did not want this outcome, so he taught in parables. Many readers find this interpretation untenable since it seems contrary to Jesus' mission, but the verse does permit this reading.

2. *Result.* This verse does not address Jesus' motive in teaching in parables but presents the result of those teachings. This reading initially seems to avoid the theological difficulties of reading "that" as indicating purpose, but the issue is still murky since the audience would presume that Jesus would be able to anticipate the result of his teachings. (In other words, one might argue that there is no meaningful distinction between purpose and result for Jesus.)

3. *Fulfillment.* "That" is short for "in order that the scriptures might be fulfilled." This would be an unusual statement for Mark, who, unlike Matthew, is not much concerned with recording the fulfillment of HB prophecies. At the same time, it is a cogent explanation with less theological baggage than the above options. But it still raises the question: Why would Isaiah have been inspired to prophesy that Jesus would teach in a way that would not lead to repentance?

4. *Alternative.* "That" is translated as "otherwise." In other words, the hardness that prohibits them from hearing is precisely the same thing that makes them not want to repent.[18] There is no cause and effect here—just two outcomes stemming from the same initial situation.

5. *Restatement.* "That" is translated as "that is," meaning that the Isaiah quotation is a simple restatement of the words from the previous verse.

6. *Prerequisite.* It is possible that the Greek word translated "in order that" means "unless"—that is, it sets forth a behavior requirement so that the entire phrase would mean something like "unless they repent and are forgiven, they will not see and hear."[19] This reading fits the context; further, the idea that cognitive knowledge is not independent of morality coheres nicely with Latter-day Saint thought.

The verb for "seeing" and, in the next phrase, the verb for "hearing" are each repeated ("seeing they might not see and hearing they might not hear"), which serves to emphasize them: they look over and over, they listen again and again, but still there is no understanding.

---

18. J. R. Kirkland, "Earliest Understanding of Jesus' Use of Parables: Mark 4:10–12 in Context," *Novum Testamentum* 19, no. 1 (1977): 7.

19. Stein, *Mark,* 211.

and hearing they may hear, and not understand; lest at any time they should be converted: The word translated as "converted" implies to "turn" or "repent."

The word "lest," much like "that" in the previous phrase, can be troubling with its implication that Jesus does not want some hearers to repent. But there are other ways to understand it:

1. It could have a positive sense ("if perhaps" or "unless"): "the rabbis understood Isa 6:10 as a promise, not a threat."[20]

2. It is also possible to read the entire phrase as sarcasm ("Oh, we wouldn't want *that* to happen!").

and their sins should be forgiven them: The phrase "their sins" does not appear in the best manuscripts.[21]

In 3:29, the unpardonable sin was attributing Jesus' power to Satan, which meant that one would not seek forgiveness from Jesus and thus could not be forgiven. A parallel point is made here: if one does not seek the meaning of the parable from Jesus, one will not receive it and thus will not be forgiven. This link between seeking forgiveness and seeking the meaning of the parable implies a close relationship between Jesus' power and his teachings. In both cases, the disciples must actively seek them out in order to access them.

Relationship to 2 Samuel 12. While parables are rare in the HB, 2 Samuel 12 includes a parable spoken by the prophet Nathan to the adulterous King David. Nathan's parable provides important background to Jesus' parables. Generally in the HB, teaching in parables was a way for a lower-status person to convey truth to a higher-status person without offending them; this is certainly the case with Nathan and David. If that principle applies to Jesus' use of parables, then Jesus is implicitly presenting himself as of lower status than his audience, and his use of parables becomes evidence of his humility as he rhetorically positions himself as inferior to his audience.

Had Nathan attempted to directly approach David about his sin (in other words, had the story begun in 2 Sam. 12:7 instead of with the parable in 2 Sam. 12:1), David almost certainly would have rejected Nathan's message. By using a parable, Nathan was able to convince David of the sinfulness of

---

20. Stein, *Mark*, 211. For rabbinic discussion, see Babylonian Talmud, Seder Mo'ed IV, Rosh Hashanah 17b; and Seder Mo'ed IV, Megillah 17b. See also Craig A. Evans, "Isaiah 6:9–10 in Rabbinic and Patristic Writings," *Vigiiliae Christianae* 36 (1982): 275–81.

21. Bratcher and Nida, *Translator's Handbook*, 135.

adultery in general (by using a metaphor of theft) before asking David to apply the principle to his own circumstances. Only once David had admitted the truthfulness of the principle did Nathan apply it to David, who was not able to reject a principle to which he had already assented. One suspects that, had David's heart not been so hardened, he would have initially recognized the applicability of the parable to his own circumstances, but he does not until Nathan points it out. One level of the parable's meaning is concealed from David because of his hardness of heart (he does not realize that the parable describes his situation with Bathsheba) while another level of the parable (the general idea that it is wrong to take that which does not belong to you) is obvious to him.

Teaching in parables permits a separation of principle and application; people find it easier to accept a principle if they do not simultaneously have to condemn their own behavior. It is precisely the combination of hiddenness and revelation that allows the parable to accomplish its objective in David's case; it is because of his hardness of heart that the parable is the best method to teach him. This explains Jesus' repeated calls to hear, since there is more than one level of hearing needed to understand a parable: first, one must hear not just the image but the principle behind the image, and second, one must apply the principle to one's own behavior. For outsiders, their partial understanding of the parable makes it possible for them to learn principles without the resistance of their commitment to their sinful behavior.

Relationship to Isaiah 6:9–10. This verse quotes Isaiah 6:9–10, which is part of Isaiah's inaugural vision and prophetic commissioning. The quotation presents several interpretive challenges:[22]

1. *Omissions.* Jesus omitted the command from Isaiah to "make the mind of this people dull, and stop their ears, and shut their eyes" (NRSV Isa. 6:10). There are two different ways to explain this omission:

   a. Jesus omitted this passage because it was *not* his commission from God to deliberately blind the people. It may be that the entire point of the Isaiah quotation was to draw a distinction between Jesus' mission and Isaiah's mission.

   b. Jesus assumed that the audience would fill in the missing material, and so he intended for his audience to consider "blinding" to be a part of his mission.

---

22. It is rather ironic that a passage about understanding is so very difficult to understand.

2. *Differences.* Mark's text differs from the Isaiah text: "It [the Isaiah quotation] differs from both the [Hebrew and Greek] texts . . . in three ways: (1) it has the third person in indirect discourse rather than the second person in direct discourse; (2) it has 'forgiven' rather than 'heal'; and (3) it has the divine passive ('it shall be . . .') instead of the active ('I shall . . .')."[23] Also, the order of references to hearing and seeing is reversed.

3. *Isaiah's Meaning.* It is not entirely clear what the Isaiah quotation means in its own context.[24] Regardless, later, Isaiah notes that "eyes will no longer be blind and ears will be attentive" (NET Isa. 32:3); it is important to understand that Isaiah's mission of "blinding" was not meant to be permanent.

4. *A New Meaning?* It is not clear whether Jesus is using the quotation in its original context or whether he is changing the meaning. It is possible that Jesus is using the Isaiah text precisely to draw distinctions between his situation and Isaiah's:

   a. Isaiah is sent to preach in virtually hopeless circumstances; did Jesus see his circumstances the same way?

   b. In Isaiah, the hardening appears to be a community-wide condition: the people were, as a group, unrepentant, and hence exile was the result. But in Jesus' time, insider or outsider status is an individual decision, as 3:31–35 shows, and not a corporate one.

   c. In Isaiah, the prophet is commanded to harden, blind, and deafen the people. But in Mark, these states are entirely under the control of each individual, as Jesus' repeated commands to hear and see suggest.

   d. In Isaiah, the text implies a complete rejection, but Jesus applies it only to the outsiders. In this framing, it is actually quite merciful since room has been created for some people to hear and listen and thus avoid the fate that Isaiah describes.

   e. Isaiah asks, "how long," presumably meaning how long will the people be in a blinded state. This question—and the Lord's answer, which specifies an end date—implies that the blinding will not be permanent. Does Jesus' use of the quotation from Isaiah presume the same? Mark 4:22 would suggest that it did.

In the same chapter in Isaiah, the Lord refers to a righteous remnant who will survive and return and calls them a "holy seed" (Isa. 6:13). This reference coheres nicely with the many seed parables in chapter 4; perhaps Jesus takes the image of the holy seed from the Isaiah text and extends it to

---

23. Stein, *Mark,* 210.

24. Douglas S. McComiskey, "Exile and the Purpose of Jesus' Parables (Mark 4:10–12; Matt 13:10–17; Luke 8:9–10)," *Journal of the Evangelical Theological Society* 51 (March 2008): 59–85.

four different soils with different responses and then into two more seed parables. The hundredfold success of the seed in Jesus' parable contrasts with the one-tenth success rate in Isaiah (see Isa. 6:13).

Does 4:10–20 Stem from Jesus' Ministry or from the Early Church? This commentary does not normally engage questions concerning which portions of Mark's text stem from Jesus' life and which are later additions. In this case, the issue is raised because of its importance in the study of Mark and because there are several puzzles in this chapter that can be explained by the presence of multiple layers of tradition. Many scholars conclude that 4:10–20 does not reflect the life of Jesus but rather was composed decades later for the following reasons:

1. Allegorical interpretation is thought to be more characteristic of the early church than of Jesus' ministry.

2. There are multiple infelicities in the text that may be the result of sloppy editing when later material was added to an earlier text:

    a. Mark 4:10–20 is not clear as to whether the people or the seed are sown (see the discussion on 4:15).

    b. Mark 4:10 has Jesus alone with the disciples but 4:33–34 implies that Jesus is speaking to a larger crowd, and the text did not mention at what point between 4:10 and 4:33 the audience expanded.

    c. In 4:10, the disciples ask Jesus about the "parables" despite the fact that he has only spoken one parable.

    d. The idea that the disciples have already been given the mystery of the kingdom of God (see 4:11) does not seem to mesh well with their lack of understanding of the parable.

    e. The interpretation may not entirely fit the parable from 4:3–9.

3. Many words in this section are not used elsewhere in Mark's Gospel, possibly suggesting that they were written by a later hand.

4. The idea that Jesus tells parables in order to keep some people outside (4:12) seems to contradict 4:33–34, where the parables tell them just as much as they can learn.

Some scholars take a similar but more limited position that only 4:10–12 was not original to the text. It is true that the text would flow nicely without 4:10–12, and several of the problems mentioned above (2.c, 2.d, and 4) would be eliminated.

While it is certainly possible that some parts of Mark's Gospel were added by a later hand or were added by Mark but do not reflect Jesus' mortal ministry, the case can be made that 4:10–20 was written by Mark and originated in Jesus' ministry. Mark's Gospel is such a very careful and deliberate story that the supposed seams and sloppy editing in this section are probably better attributed to other causes, including intentional narrative design. For example, the fact that the composition of the audience silently transitions from the disciples to the crowd may simply reflect Mark's sandwiching of stories for literary and theological purposes overriding any commitment to chronological order and factual details. (See also the overview of chapter 4 above on the chiasmus in this chapter, which suggests that the entire structure is deliberate and that no group of verses is a later addition.) Additionally, Daniel 2 (which contains a dream followed by its explanation) suggests that this type of explanation is not foreign to biblical literature.

But if 4:10–12 or 4:10–20 is determined to be a later addition, this does not necessarily make it inaccurate or ahistorical. The Book of Mormon contains a fascinating account where the resurrected Christ tells his disciples to redact their sacred records, which means that the later record would have been more accurate and inspired than the earlier record (see 3 Ne. 23:7–13). By analogy, whether 4:10–20 was originally in Mark's Gospel and whether it originates in the life of Jesus are two entirely separate questions. (In other words, it could be quite historical but added to the record later.) And it is also possible that there is later embroidery on top of an earlier tradition. (In other words, perhaps the explanation of the parable originated with Jesus, but then some words were changed or added later, which would create the impression that the explanation came from the vocabulary and interests of the early church instead of from Jesus.)

Many interpreters see conflicting teachings in this chapter and resolve them by identifying several layers of tradition. But it is also possible to see Jesus teaching a nuanced or paradoxical message that, in its individual components, might seem contradictory but is instead meant to teach a message as a whole. Latter-day Saint readers would have no inherent objection to the idea that this passage reflects later strands of tradition, but at the same time, there may be benefits to grappling with the paradoxes in this chapter instead of dismissing them as evidence of multiple sources.

4:13 *And he said unto them:* The historical present tense ("he says") is used here.

Know ye not this parable?: There are several ways to understand this phrase:

1. As a question: "You don't understand this parable?"
2. As an accusation: "You don't know this parable!"

3. As a conditional statement: "If you don't know this parable, then how will you understand . . ."

One might also speculate as to Jesus' tone of voice: Is he surprised? Exasperated? Mournful? Disapproving? Encouraging self-reflection?

It is difficult to reconcile this verse with the prior statement that the disciples have been given the mystery of the kingdom, but apparently having the mystery is compatible with not understanding the parable.

and how then will ye know all parables?: This verse explains that understanding this parable is the key to understanding all the parables, but it does not explain why this is true. Options include:

1. This is a particularly easy parable, and so if they do not understand this one, they won't understand any of them.

2. If the disciples don't know that they need to ask Jesus to explain the parable, then they will never understand any parable because they will never ask Jesus for more information.

3. The content of this parable is key—perhaps because it is the first seed parable, and two more follow it—to understanding all of the parables.

4. This parable describes how the seed/word grows, so if the people do not understand this, they will not be able to get other seed/word/parables to bear fruit within them. In other words, the content of this parable describes the process of understanding parables.

It is possible that "all parables" includes Jesus' "enacted parables" (miracles that are symbolic).

4:14 *The sower soweth the word:* "Word" is likely a technical term for the gospel (see 1:45), although Mark has not developed this concept.

This verse indicates that the seed in the parable symbolizes the word. Jesus conveys this so seamlessly—"the sower soweth the word" instead of "the seed symbolizes the word"—that it is easy to miss, but the underlying premise is that the parables are to be interpreted so that one thing stands for another thing.

4:15 *And these are they by the way side, where the word is sown:* "These" (and similar words throughout the explanation) is masculine, not neuter, meaning that it probably refers to the person and not to the seed. But it is also possible that this implies that it is the seed that is sown if "these" refers to the soil by way of an abbreviated form: "these [people are represented by the seeds that are] along the pathway."

but when they have heard, Satan cometh immediately: The word "immediately" is not in the parable itself (compare 4:4) but is included in the interpretation.

Jesus' interpretation aligns Satan with the birds, an association that is also made in some ancient Jewish writings.[25] There is an intriguing inversion from the last chapter, where Jesus stole captives from Satan (3:27), to this verse, where Satan steals the word from the sower.

This part of the parable emphasizes the plight of a new follower of Jesus (unsprouted seed): before the word/seed is covered with soil and has taken root, it is in extreme danger. (A bird could not pluck out a fully grown plant with roots.)

Some interpreters fault the sower for permitting the seed to be plucked, but it is probably preferable to view this as one of the aspects of the parable that does not correspond to a symbolic meaning.

See also the section "Relationship to 4:4" after the Notes on 10:52.

and taketh away the word that was sown in their hearts: Most manuscripts read "in them" instead of "in their hearts."[26] The phrase was probably changed from the former to the latter under the influence of Luke 8:12 and Matthew 13:19.

4:16 *And these are they likewise which are sown on stony ground; who, when they have heard the word, immediately receive it with gladness:* The stony ground gets a fuller description than the other soils. With this seed, it is clear that joy is not enough and that excessive zeal may create its own problems. Since three of the four soils start out positively, the implication is that a good start is not sufficient to bear fruit.

4:17 *And have no root in themselves, and so endure but for a time: afterward, when affliction or persecution ariseth for the word's sake:* Persecution is symbolized by the sun (compare 4:6), but the sun is, of course, necessary for the growth of the seed. It is not the sun/persecution itself that is the problem; it is the lack of preparation (root system) that dooms this plant.

immediately they are offended: Notice the parallel to the phrase "immediately receive it with joy" (New Rendition) at the end of the last verse; the parallel implies that these people act too impetuously in general.

The word "offended" means "to be trapped or snared but [is] used in biblical Greek to describe apostasy or a falling away."[27] There is no adequate English translation: "the idea conveyed by the Greek verb is that of being

25. Babylonian Talmud, Seder Nezikin III, Sanhedrin 107a.
26. Collins, *Mark*, 250 note b.
27. Guelich, *Mark 1–8:26*, 222.

offended and repelled to the point of abandoning (whether temporarily or permanently, the word itself does not specify) belief in the Word or one's relation to Jesus."[28] It is the root of the English term "scandalize."

The parable suggests that the unbalanced growth of a huge top with no roots is dangerous. The big top requires more root than average to sustain it, but this is precisely what it is lacking. Further, its appearance is deceptive.

4:18 *And these are they which are sown among thorns; such as hear the word,* 19 *And the cares of this world, and the deceitfulness of riches:* "Deceitfulness" could also be translated as "seduction" or "delight."

and the lusts of other things entering in, choke the word, and it becometh unfruitful: The three poor soils are progressively more productive: the first does not sprout, the second sprouts but lacks root, and the third grows a complete plant except for fruit. This suggests that there are different points where the seed might fail, and there are different ways to fail. It is also possible to read the three unproductive soils with their varying levels of growth as analogous to the successful soil with its three levels of harvest.

Both circumstances—too difficult (persecution) and too easy (wealth)—cause trouble for the plant.

Each of the three seeds in unproductive soil comes to a violent end: they are devoured, burned, or choked. The imagery of the parable is as vivid as it is devastating.

Relationship to Jeremiah 4:3. In this text, the Lord compares removing sin to removing thorns that would otherwise compete for resources with a good seed; the symbolism of thorns as sins might carry over to this parable.

4:20 *And these are they which are sown on good ground; such as hear the word, and receive it:* In this verse, the verb "hear" is in the present tense, unlike the verbs used with the three poor soils, which were in the past tense. This implies that the kind of hearing that the good soil does is qualitatively different from what the poor soils did: there is an ongoing action of hearing on the part of the good soil that is significant given that Jesus has bounded the parable with references to the audience's "hearing" (4:3, 9). The scene is recursive and self-referential as Jesus encourages them to be the good soil.

---

28. Bratcher and Nida, *Translator's Handbook,* 139–40.

and bring forth fruit: Interestingly, Jesus does not explain what it means to bear fruit.

some thirtyfold, some sixty, and some an hundred: There is no explanation given for the growth here; contrast the three poor soils, where failure is described in detail. The emphasis is on the failures, not the successes.

Because the sower endures three losses before he enjoys a harvest, the parable suggests that while initial efforts will fail, the sower should not lose hope. In fact, the abundance of the harvest will more than make up for the seed lost in the failed attempts; this pattern may mirror Jesus' ministry where each of the three previous stories of opposition was followed by remarks about the ever-increasing crowd around Jesus (see 2:1–12 and 2:13; 3:1–6 and 7–12; and 3:20–25 and 4:1).[29] The parable thus contextualizes the previous stories by showing that Jesus was still able to engage in fruitful ministry.

In the HB, the image of fruitfulness is used to suggest God's blessings in the coming age (Jer. 31:12; Hosea 2:21–22; Joel 2:22; Amos 9:13; Zech. 8:12), and lack of fruit is a symbol for God's judgment or curse (Gen. 3:17–18; Isa. 5:10; Jer. 8:13; Joel 1:12). To the extent that Jesus is encouraging the audience to hear and to choose to be good soil, the parable implies that people choose whether to be blessed or cursed; this nuance is an important correction to the tendency to read this section of Mark in a way that denies human choice.

The Identity of the Sower. Oddly, the sower is not identified in Jesus' explanation of the parable; possibilities include:

1. The sower is God. In this reading, Jesus is the word sown by God.

2. The sower is Jesus. This reading makes sense of the dramatically varied responses to Jesus' ministry so far in Mark's Gospel. It also suggests that Jesus presents his word to all people despite their various propensities for accepting it. It also may make sense of the narrative setting, in which Jesus' audience is on the land but he alone is in the sea.

3. The sower represents all who preach the word. In this reading, the negligence of the sower (who is responsible for placing the seed in ground where it could not be expected to bear fruit) is easily attributed to the weakness of the disciples. The parable would then absolve disciples from responsibility when their preaching is unfruitful.

---

29. John Paul Heil, "Reader-Response and the Narrative Context of the Parables about Growing Seed in Mark 4:1–34," *Catholic Biblical Quarterly* 54, no. 2 (1992): 271–86.

4. The sower is not identified because the audience's attention should be elsewhere; as the narrative emphasis of the parable makes clear, it is the different soils and how they receive the word that are the focal points of the parable.

5. Jesus omitted the identity of the sower in order to leave the disciples a portion of the parable to decode on their own so they could gain personal experience in the process of understanding parables.

Characters in the Gospel and the Parable. It is possible to read this parable as describing certain people in Mark's narrative:

1. Peter as the rocky soil. The name "Peter" means "rock," and he was given that nickname without explanation only shortly before (see 3:16), so the attentive reader or hearer would have probably associated Peter with the rocky soil. The depiction of the rocky soil mirrors Peter's experience as Jesus' follower fairly closely: initial acceptance, zeal, but then an inability to stand strong in the face of persecution. This reading can be uncomfortable (but not nearly as uncomfortable as 8:33!) for audience members who think of Peter as the leader of the early church, but it does cohere with the text and, more positively, can be read as a merciful warning to Peter (and to others). This reading encourages a reconsideration of Peter's call story (see 1:16–18), where the speed of Peter's obedience now appears to be a sign of impetuousness instead of deep devotion. And yet Mark's early audiences, who perhaps would have known Peter as a leader, would have realized that the designation of soil as rocky and unfruitful was not a permanent one since Peter's repentance and restoration would have nuanced their understanding of the parable.

2. Peter as the seed planted along the pathway. In 8:31, Jesus teaches the disciples that he will suffer and die. Peter immediately rejects this seed/word/teaching (8:32), as if Satan had plucked it from hard ground. While this association is not as strong as the idea of Peter as rocky soil, it does illustrate the dynamic of the first seed.

3. In 10:17–27, a rich man rejects Jesus' teachings, making him an example of the seed choked by thorny soil. The same dynamic might be at play in 6:20, where Herod does not want to kill John the Baptist but does so under pressure.

Comparison with 1 Nephi 8–13. Mark's text presents a parable (4:3–9) and then its interpretation (4:14–20). This is similar to 1 Nephi 8–14, where Lehi's vision is recounted (1 Ne. 8) and then Nephi's vision (1 Ne. 12–14), which is similar to his father's vision but contains more interpretative material, is presented. Additionally, just as Mark's text melds setting and teaching, with its crowd on the soil hearing a parable about the soil, Lehi's vision of the fruit of the tree is prefaced by the note that his family was gathering fruit seeds (1 Ne. 8:1). In each text, one background detail is provided (the crowd on the soil will hear a parable about the soil; the family gathering fruit seeds will hear a vision about fruit); in neither text is this detail an irrelevant bit of scene setting; rather, the details serve as interpretive keys to the symbolic learning experience that follows. And while a vision is not exactly the same as a parable, both are symbolic communications and therefore require similar interpretational techniques.

The pattern in these texts served to teach their audiences through repetition and by modeling the process of determining how to gain further insight: in Mark, the audience is taught to ask Jesus for an interpretation, and in the Book of Mormon text, the reader is taught to seek one's own vision. In both cases, the symbolic material has an outsized role in the developing narrative due to its placement.

Comparison with Alma 32. Alma 32 also contains a seed parable, although it has several key differences from 4:3–9, especially the inclusion of good and bad seeds instead of good and bad soils. Yet its setting shares a focus on insiders and outsiders, and the exhortation to "give place for a portion of my words" echoes Jesus' action of teaching "as they were able to hear" (4:33).

Interestingly, the final exhortation in Alma 33 (which was part of the same chapter as Alma 32 per the original chapter divisions) is "I desire that ye shall plant this word in your hearts," which is congruent with the parable in Mark.

Analysis

The question about parables from the disciples is an instance of what will become a central theme for Mark: the incomprehension of the disciples. While fully fleshing out this theme will require the rest of the narrative, Mark crafts this story to introduce several key ideas. First, while there is some chastisement, Jesus does patiently answer their question, and thus seeking further light and knowledge is positioned as a good thing. The disciples are portrayed as learners; being a disciple of Jesus does not mean knowing all of the answers—it means seeking the answers. The disciples' lack of understanding also creates an opportunity for Mark to showcase Jesus' patience. In terms of the narrative, the disciples play a crucial role: by asking questions, they present an opportunity for Jesus to reteach (7:17; 9:28; 10:10; 13:3–4), which means that Mark's audience gets to hear the teaching again. So the disciples allow the audience to learn more. Further, the disciples' lack of understanding permits the audience to think of themselves as worthy to be disciples. If the disciples were presented as perfect characters, they would not be able to teach the audience how to grow in faith. Given the emphasis in the last chapter about Jesus' deliberate choice in calling the disciples (3:13) and their adoption as Jesus' family due to their choice to listen to him (3:35), the disciples' lack of understanding must be viewed in the context of Jesus' overt choice of them as disciples; their weaknesses did not disqualify them and may actually have been one reason that they were chosen.

Parables are a unique teaching form: they are a code that the listener can break later. This reading meshes well with the idea in 4:22 that nothing is hidden except to be later revealed. In fact, 4:22 is an interpretive limit on what Jesus' meaning could be in the present passage. The focus in that verse is not on the hiding itself but on the fact that the hiding is not meant to be permanent; it concerns not the secret but the conditions under which the secret will be revealed. This passage implies that the key to revealing the mystery is the request of the disciples: what is required to have the mystery revealed is a willingness to hear.[30]

The same language used to describe the outsiders in this passage is applied to the disciples in 8:17–18, which suggests that insider/outsider status is neither permanent nor externally imposed but rather the choice of the disciple, a point vividly made in 3:31–35. Further, the contrast between 4:11 (where the audience does not know the mystery and is an outsider) and 4:13 (where the disciples do not understand and are outsiders) points to the ease with which the role reversal from insider to outsider can happen.[31]

The Isaiah quotation is central to Jesus' explanation for teaching in parables but is, unfortunately, difficult to interpret. This Isaiah text was, more generally, important to early Christians[32] because they used it to explain why so many of the Jews rejected Jesus: God had specifically blinded them to the message. While it is uncertain whether this context reflects Mark's intent, the Isaiah quotation helps explain why some people do not respond in faith to Jesus' message. And by quoting Isaiah, Jesus positions himself as a prophet like Isaiah.

---

30. A similar sentiment is reflected in 1 Ne. 15:7–11.

31. Fowler, "Reader-Respose Criticism," 82.

32. Isa. 6:9–10 is also quoted in the NT in John 12:40; Acts 28:26–27; and Rom. 11:8–10.

The disciples' question as to why Jesus taught in parables is, despite the answer Jesus offers in this chapter, still puzzling. Reasons why Mark presents Jesus teaching in parables may include:

1. *To exclude.* Jesus taught in parables so that some people would not be able to understand his teachings. This exclusionary view seems to be the plain meaning of his words, but many interpreters find it unacceptable because they believe that Jesus wanted all people to learn from him, although it is possible that idea needs to be reconsidered in light of Jesus' explanation. If Jesus' goal was to restrict his teachings, then the next question becomes: Was this restriction permanent or temporary? It might be temporary either because everything will later be revealed to everyone or because individuals will choose to move from outsider to insider status and so teachings will be revealed to them.[33] But 4:33 argues against the idea that Jesus' goal was to exclude people from understanding because it implies that Jesus' motive was to teach them as much as they could understand.

2. *To protect Jesus.* Jesus veiled his teachings from those who would do him harm if they understood who he claimed to be and/or if the crowds around him grew even larger. Teachings hidden in parables may have kept opposition to his ministry to a minimum; one can easily imagine scouts from the Jewish leadership concluding that Jesus seemed innocent enough talking about seeds and lamps.

3. *To encourage the disciples to seek more information.* Jesus' use of parables—parables that require explanation to be understood—sets a pattern for the disciples: his teachings will require seeking further knowledge. Jesus wants to teach them a habit of seeking more knowledge. If the listener is not willing to ask Jesus about the meaning of the parable, then it remains a parable and they cannot return and repent. This reading meshes with the idea of the unpardonable sin in 3:29, where the only reason that that sin was unpardonable was because the sinner would not seek Jesus' authority to remit it. Similarly, the only reason the parables are opaque is that the listener will not seek Jesus' further teachings to explain them. It also coheres well with the idea from 3:35 that doing the will of God means sitting at Jesus' feet and learning from him. The point is that parables are not self-interpreting—they require a relationship between the listener and the teacher in which the listener seeks the teacher's further input. So people who refuse to follow Jesus are unable to understand him because his teachings do not exist as self-contained propositions of truth but rather require a community and a

---

33. While the modern Latter-day Saint practice of restricting the temple ceremony to those who are worthy might appear similar to this exclusionary reading, the analogy does not work very well since it is not the case that the temple ceremony is taught publicly and only certain people are able to understand it.

relationship to be understood. Soon, Jesus will teach that nothing is hidden except that it will be revealed—the point is the process through which a person progresses as the teaching transitions from hidden to revealed. Jesus' goal here is for the people to understand the parables, but he employs a rhetoric of indirection because the process itself of decoding parables is important. In fact, it is so important that both here and in 7:14–23 Mark will show the audience how the process works: as Jesus teaches in parables, the disciples ask questions, and Jesus further explains his teachings. By way of contrast, when Jesus later speaks "openly" about his suffering and death (8:31–32), he is rebuked; speaking in a veiled manner through parables may have avoided this problem.

4. To create space for faith. Had Jesus taught without parables, the authority of his teaching would have been such that no one could have disputed it. In other words, there would have been no space for faith: "faith is only possible where there is room for personal decision."[34] He taught in parables so that the audience would have to make an intentional choice to have enough faith in him to listen and to ask for clarification. The discussion imported from Isaiah of outsiders being prevented from repenting must be read in the light of Jesus' reiterated calls for them to hear the parable—he does not want them to be outsiders, and so he repeatedly invites them to become insiders. But he invites; he does not demand. So the difference between insiders and outsiders is whether one learns the interpretation of the parable, and that is determined by the individual choice to ask Jesus for more information. As 3:31–35 showed, anyone who wanted to could become an insider, but no one—not even Jesus' family—would be forced to become one. Read in light of 4:3–9, where the sower gives every type of soil the same seed, the implication is that Jesus gives every person the same parable, and it is the person's exercise of will (what kind of soil they choose to be) that determines their fruitfulness.

5. To create the potential for future learning. Parables are very memorable stories, which means that the audience members could choose—even years later—to reconsider a parable that they remembered and wanted to understand better. It is a merciful way of teaching because it allows a hearer with no interest today to become an insider tomorrow. Jesus' teaching in parables is a message of hope—hope that the outsiders will repent and listen in the future; this fits the context of the Isaiah quotation, which saw hope for a future remnant. It also makes sense of the fact that Jesus made his teachings available to them in parables instead of refusing to teach them. The present concealment points to the possibility of future revelation.

---

34. C. E. B. Cranfield, "Message of Hope: Mark 4:21–32," *Interpretation: A Journal of Bible and Theology* 9, no. 2 (1955): 156.

6. To teach "in riddles." The word "parable" may have more than one meaning in this chapter, and this referent means riddles, not parables per se. In other words, despite the fact that the word is the same, Jesus is not claiming that he taught in parables so that some people would not understand him; rather, he is saying that to those without the mystery of the kingdom of God his teachings are "in riddles." Mark may even have joined these sayings together from separate occasions in Jesus' ministry precisely because of the shared word, despite the fact that the meaning of "parable" is not the same in both instances.

7. To allow the hard-hearted to "hear" tough doctrine. The partial veiling of the parable permits the principle (but not yet the application) to be learned by the unrepentant and creates room for the personal application of the principle to be accepted later (see the section "Relationship to 2 Samuel 12" after the Notes on 4:12 above for a fuller discussion).

Jesus then explains the parable to the disciples. Since three out of the four scenarios are negative, it shows a concern not just with the theme of discipleship but more specifically with the circumstances under which disciples fail. The parable emphasizes the failures in a story where success (a seed bearing fruit) is the norm:[35] it is normal to be a good disciple; it is the failed disciple that requires an explanation. By contrast with the three bad soils, the good soil must accept the word immediately (so Satan can't snatch it), deeply (to protect it from the sun), and exclusively (to avoid thorns).

This parable reflects the world of farmers (which, interestingly, Jesus was not). It has a significant socioeconomic component: it implies security and prosperity for the sower as a result of the bountiful harvest from the good soil. In a world where many people were debt-plagued tenant farmers, the bumper crop described in this parable would have been enough to free them from their landlords and perhaps even transform them into landowners themselves.[36]

Some interpreters have used this parable to support predestination, which is the idea that people do not choose whether and how to respond to God's word; instead, people are like soil that has no choice whether it will host rocks or thorns. This is probably not the best reading of this parable; not every concrete element of a parable works symbolically. By introducing and concluding the parable with exhortations to hear, Jesus teaches

---

35. Tolbert, *Sowing the Gospel,* 158.
36. Myers, *Binding the Strong Man,* 177.

that the people do have a choice as to which kind of soil they will become. Mark 3:31–35, which emphasizes that the position of insider or outsider is freely chosen, coheres with this message. And Jesus' explanations of the poor soils suggest that it is how a person reacts to trials that determines what kind of soil they are; the type of soil is not predetermined.

It could even be argued that this parable advances a robust notion of human choice by presenting Jesus as "the sower broadcasting seed without prejudging the soil in terms of its potentiality."[37] The seeds all have an equal potential for growth; the parable explains the different responses to Jesus' preaching in terms of individual choices.

Neither Jesus nor Mark names this parable. One concern with naming parables is that it is impossible to do so without interpreting them; whatever name is chosen indicates a focal point for the parable. Possible names for this parable and their implications include:

1. *The Parable of the Sower.* This is the common name for this parable (and it is included in Matthew 13:18, but not in Mark) but it may focus too much on the sower, who has only a minor role in the parable and whose identity is not included in Jesus' interpretation.

2. *The Parable of the Six Seeds.* This title suggests a pleasing symmetry between the three poor soils and the three abundant harvests: just as each of the three seeds on poor soil fails at a different point in its growth, each seed in the good soil has a larger harvest than the one before it. And yet this title elides the fact that it is the nature of the soil, not of the seeds, that is the focal point of the parable.

3. *The Parable of the Soils.* Because the soils (and not the seeds or the sower) differ, it makes sense to focus attention on the soils as the key to the parable. Yet later parables in this chapter focus more on the sower and the seed, perhaps implying that those elements are important here as well.

It is no accident that a parable about how to hear the word is surrounded by exhortations to hear the word; the text is carefully structured to unify form and content. Because the audience is encouraged to do at the discourse level what the parable encourages them to do at the story level, the unity implies that the audience is supposed to be self-reflective and to link the parable to their own lives. The parable itself is about the reception of parables.

---

37. Waetjen, *Reordering of Power,* 102.

JESUS SHARES MORE PARABLES (4:21–34)

Greek Text

21 Καὶ ἔλεγεν αὐτοῖς· Μήτι ἔρχεται ὁ λύχνος ἵνα ὑπὸ τὸν μόδιον τεθῇ ἢ ὑπὸ τὴν κλίνην, οὐχ ἵνα ἐπὶ τὴν λυχνίαν τεθῇ; 22 οὐ γάρ ἐστιν κρυπτὸν ἐὰν μὴ ἵνα φανερωθῇ,
οὐδὲ ἐγένετο ἀπόκρυφον ἀλλ᾽ ἵνα ἔλθῃ εἰς φανερόν. 23 εἴ τις ἔχει ὦτα ἀκούειν
ἀκουέτω. 24 καὶ ἔλεγεν αὐτοῖς· Βλέπετε τί ἀκούετε. ἐν ᾧ μέτρῳ μετρεῖτε μετρηθή-
σεται ὑμῖν καὶ προστεθήσεται ὑμῖν. 25 ὃς γὰρ ἔχει, δοθήσεται αὐτῷ· καὶ ὃς οὐκ ἔχει,
καὶ ὃ ἔχει ἀρθήσεται ἀπ᾽ αὐτοῦ.

26 Καὶ ἔλεγεν· Οὕτως ἐστὶν ἡ βασιλεία τοῦ θεοῦ ὡς ἄνθρωπος βάλῃ τὸν σπό-
ρον ἐπὶ τῆς γῆς 27 καὶ καθεύδῃ καὶ ἐγείρηται νύκτα καὶ ἡμέραν, καὶ ὁ σπόρος βλα-
στᾷ καὶ μηκύνηται ὡς οὐκ οἶδεν αὐτός. 28 αὐτομάτη ἡ γῆ καρποφορεῖ, πρῶτον
χόρτον, εἶτα στάχυν, εἶτα πλήρης σῖτον ἐν τῷ στάχυϊ. 29 ὅταν δὲ παραδοῖ ὁ καρπός,
εὐθὺς ἀποστέλλει τὸ δρέπανον, ὅτι παρέστηκεν ὁ θερισμός.

30 Καὶ ἔλεγεν· Πῶς ὁμοιώσωμεν τὴν βασιλείαν τοῦ θεοῦ, ἢ ἐν τίνι αὐτὴν παρα-
βολῇ θῶμεν; 31 ὡς κόκκῳ σινάπεως, ὃς ὅταν σπαρῇ ἐπὶ τῆς γῆς, μικρότερον ὂν
πάντων τῶν σπερμάτων τῶν ἐπὶ τῆς γῆς— 32 καὶ ὅταν σπαρῇ, ἀναβαίνει καὶ γίνεται μεῖζον πάντων τῶν λαχάνων καὶ ποιεῖ κλάδους μεγάλους, ὥστε δύνασθαι ὑπὸ
τὴν σκιὰν αὐτοῦ τὰ πετεινὰ τοῦ οὐρανοῦ κατασκηνοῦν.

33 Καὶ τοιαύταις παραβολαῖς πολλαῖς ἐλάλει αὐτοῖς τὸν λόγον, καθὼς ἠδύναντο
ἀκούειν· 34 χωρὶς δὲ παραβολῆς οὐκ ἐλάλει αὐτοῖς, κατ᾽ ἰδίαν δὲ τοῖς ἰδίοις μαθηταῖς ἐπέλυεν πάντα. [SBLGNT]

King James Version

21 And he said unto them, Is a candle
brought to be put under a bushel, or
under a bed? and not to be set on a candlestick? 22 For there is nothing hid, which
shall not be manifested; neither was any
thing kept secret, but that it should come
abroad. 23 If any man have ears to hear, let
him hear. 24 And he said unto them, Take
heed what ye hear: with what measure
ye mete, it shall be measured to you: and
unto you that hear shall more be given.
25 For he that hath, to him shall be given:
and he that hath not, from him shall be
taken even that which he hath.

26 And he said, So is the kingdom of
God, as if a man should cast seed into

New Rendition

21 And he was saying to them, "The
lamp doesn't come so that it might be
placed under the bowl or under the
cot, does it? Doesn't it come in order
that it might be placed on a lampstand?
22 For nothing is hidden that will not
be revealed, nor is there any secret that
will not come to light. 23 Whoever has
ears to hear, hear!" 24 And he was saying to them, "Look closely at what you
hear; by what measure you measure, it
will be measured to you, and more will
be added to you. 25 Indeed, whoever
has will be given more, but whoever
does not have, even what he has will be
taken from him."

the ground; 27 And should sleep, and rise night and day, and the seed should spring and grow up, he knoweth not how. 28 For the earth bringeth forth fruit of herself; first the blade, then the ear, after that the full corn in the ear. 29 But when the fruit is brought forth, immediately he putteth in the sickle, because the harvest is come.

30 And he said, Whereunto shall we liken the kingdom of God? or with what comparison shall we compare it? 31 It is like a grain of mustard seed, which, when it is sown in the earth, is less than all the seeds that be in the earth: 32 But when it is sown, it groweth up, and becometh greater than all herbs, and shooteth out great branches; so that the fowls of the air may lodge under the shadow of it. 33 And with many such parables spake he the word unto them, as they were able to hear it. 34 But without a parable spake he not unto them: and when they were alone, he expounded all things to his disciples.

26 And he was saying, "So is the kingdom of God like a person who scatters seed upon the ground 27 and sleeps and rises, night and day, and the seed sprouts and grows, but he does not know how. 28 By itself the ground produces the crop: first a stalk, then a head, then the full grain in the head. 29 But when the crop is ready, he immediately sends in the sickle, because the harvest has come."

30 And he was saying, "To what should we compare the kingdom of God? Or, with what parable could we describe it? 31 It is like a mustard seed that, when it has been planted in the ground, is the smallest of all of the seeds that are in the ground. 32 But when it has been planted, it rises and becomes taller than all of the shrubs and produces large branches so that the birds are able to nest in its shade."

33 And with many such parables, he was speaking the word to them, as they were able to hear. 34 He was not speaking to them without a parable. But privately, alone with his own disciples, he was explaining all things.

Notes

4:21 *And he said unto them:* "Them" could refer to the disciples or to the crowd; as mentioned above, at some point the audience expands from just the disciples (see 4:10) to the crowd (see 4:33–34), but Mark does not indicate when the shift occurs.

Is a candle brought to be put under a bushel, or under a bed: This is not a candle but a lamp made of clay and filled with oil.

In Greek, there is a definite article before the word "lamp" ("the lamp," not "a lamp"), which makes it more likely that the lamp is to be interpreted symbolically, since it is a reference to one particular lamp.

The Greek verb is "coming" (not "brought"), which creates the odd picture of a lamp "coming" as if under its own volition. The combination of the definite article and the idea of the lamp coming strongly implies that the lamp is a symbol for Jesus, especially since the same verb for "coming" is used many times in Mark to characterize Jesus' ministry (1:7, 14, 24; 2:17; 8:38; 10:45; 11:9–10; 13:26, 35–36; 14:62).

The "bushel" is a bowl or basket. The word implies a container that can hold ("measure") about two gallons, which may link this parable to the counsel about measuring in 4:24. If the emphasis here is on the capacity of the bowl to measure, then the point would be that the light is not something that can or should be measured but rather something that can fill an entire room.

The phrase "does it" has been added to the New Rendition (despite the fact that it does not appear in the Greek text) to make it clear that the first question anticipates a negative answer.

The lamp may also represent the parables that Jesus was teaching by suggesting that their meaning, although initially hidden (as a lamp in a bowl), was not intended to be hidden but rather to come forth so that all could understand.

This parable can also be understood as a comment on the experience of the "rocky soil" that fears persecution. Because the purpose of the light was to come forth, Jesus teaches that the disciples should not fear the persecution that will come from sharing the light with the world; the entire reason that the light came forth was not so that it could be fearfully hidden under the bed but rather so that it would be shared with the entire house. This reading suggests that the motif of warnings to Peter extends throughout this entire chapter: he is not just the rocky soil, but he is also cautioned about the danger of hiding the light that he has been given.

It is also possible that Jesus is preempting the possibility that the disciples would misunderstand him and think that they were also supposed to teach in a method that was hidden: Jesus clarifies that that is not a way in which they should be modeling him.

Relationship to Judges 7:15–21. In Judges 7, Gideon prepared to attack the Midianites by telling his men to put their lamps under jars so they would not be seen (and perhaps so the wind would not blow them out) while they sneaked into position. At Gideon's signal, they broke their jars. Then the light (and the trumpets) terrified the enemy, who fled in confusion.

Because the idea of once-hidden lights being revealed is so obscure, it is likely that this text is behind Jesus' parable. It suggests that there would have been no purpose to hiding the light without the intention to reveal it later; the entire point of hiding the light is not so it will be hidden forever but so it can be revealed at the appropriate time—something that would not have been possible had it not been hidden first. Further, the purpose of the light is to terrify and banish the enemy; perhaps Jesus' parable has the same implication.

and not to be set on a candlestick?: This is a lampstand, not a candlestick. In Greek, this question expects an affirmative answer.

4:22 *For there is nothing hid:* The "for" at the beginning of this verse implies that Jesus is drawing a conclusion from the previous verse.

which shall not be manifested; neither was any thing kept secret, but that it should come abroad: "Abroad" means "public" in this context. Compare 9:9, where Jesus instructs the disciples not to tell anyone about the Transfiguration until after he has risen from the dead as an example of the idea that certain things might be kept private temporarily but revealed later.

Mark 4:21–25 mirrors 4:10–13, which means that 4:21–25 is an important interpretive guide to 4:10–13: the enigmatic teachings about the purpose of parables, including the teachings about insiders and outsiders and the Isaiah quotation, need to be read in light of this parable and its explanation. This verse implies that nothing that was hidden will be so permanently—it will all be made known; any exclusionary practice from the Isaiah quotation should be understood as a temporary condition.

It is possible also to read this verse with reference to the "messianic secret" in Mark: Jesus' identity must be kept (at least partially) hidden at this point, but this will not always be so.

4:23 *If any man have ears to hear, let him hear:* As with 4:9, this is not permission to hear but a command to hear.

Interpretation of this command depends in part on the composition of its audience:

1. If the audience consists only of the Twelve and those with them, then the implication is that it is possible for even the insiders to misunderstand what Jesus teaches.
2. If the audience includes the crowd, then:
   a. Jesus promises that the eventual revealing will be to everyone, including the crowd.
   b. Jesus offered explanations of his parables (see 4:22) to the crowd as well as to the disciples.

In either case, this verse, especially when combined with the next one, shows the extraordinary emphasis that Jesus placed on the need for his listeners to work hard to gain a proper understanding of his teachings.

These three references to the importance of hearing imply that what he was teaching was neither obvious nor easy to understand.

4:24 *And he said unto them, Take heed what ye hear:* Because "take heed" translates the verb "to see," there is a great play on words here: "see what you hear." The emphasis is on *what* the audience chooses to hear, not just on *how* they hear it (contrast 4:23).

with what measure ye mete: The parallelism suggests that hearing and measuring are similar; hearing should involve measuring or evaluating.

it shall be measured to you: and unto you that hear shall more be given: In Greek, the root word for "measure" is repeated three times ("with what measure you measure, it will be measured to you"). This statement appears to be a proverb, but the phrase "shall more be given" is not found in other sources; thus Jesus appears to have added that line to a preexisting proverb.

There is a divine passive here, which implies that God is the one measuring out the recompense.

The first part of this verse implies that one will be given as one has measured to others; the second part implies that one will be given more than one has measured. These ideas seem contradictory, but there are two ways they can be reconciled:

1. The phrase "take heed what ye hear" signals that the statement that follows it is spoken only in order to be refuted (compare 8:15; 12:38; 13:5, 9, 23, 33). This would mean that Jesus is quoting the proverb about measuring in order to repudiate its philosophy, which he does by teaching his audience that they will be given more than what they measure. Support for this reading comes from Ezekiel 18:1–4, where a proverb is quoted in order to be refuted (interestingly, Ezekiel 17 contains a parable with many themes similar to this chapter). Further, the parable in 4:3–9 (with its super-abundant harvests in the good soil) and the parables in 4:26–32 (with inexplicable and tremendous growth) point to the idea of receiving more than one would have expected.

2. The point of the proverb is that the measuring system used when selling is the same one that will be used when buying. So, if the seller shortchanges the buyer, she will be shortchanged when she buys. Thus, if the audience seeks more information about the parable, they will receive it; generous hearing results in a generous provision of understanding. The final line "unto you that hear shall more be given" disrupts this reciprocal relationship by introducing the element of God's abundant, merciful provision: the disciples get more than they give because God makes up the difference. In this reading, the paradox between the halves of the verse is resolved through God's excessive outpouring.

4:25 *For he that hath, to him shall be given:* The word "for" suggests that this verse explains the previous verse. There is a similar structure in 4:22

and 4:25: both are introduced by the word "for" and explain the parables that come immediately before them.

Mark 4:24 is in the second person ("you"), but this verse is in the third person ("he"). This may indicate that these sayings originated at different moments in Jesus' ministry but that Mark has linked them together since they address the same topic.[38]

and he that hath not, from him shall be taken even that which he hath: There are two options for explaining the apparent impossibility of taking something away from someone who has nothing:

1. This is hyperbole: the person does not have nothing—they have only very little.

2. In the context of the seed sown by the path, the soil does not have the ability to host the seed, and so the seed is taken away by the bird (Satan). This would explain how something (the seed) could be taken from someone who "hath not" (the resources to host the seed).

4:26 And he said, So is the kingdom of God: In 1:14–15, the introductory summary of Jesus' preaching focused on the kingdom; for Mark, this is a key concern for Jesus' ministry.

as if a man should cast seed into the ground: Comparing the kingdom of God to a peasant's daily tasks is a powerful method of validating and recognizing people who were neither important nor wealthy.

4:27 And should sleep, and rise night and day, and the seed should spring and grow up: The formula "night and day" may seem unusual, but Jews reckoned days to begin at sundown, so the phrase makes good sense in that context. No work except scattering is mentioned—no watering or weeding. The sower makes a minimal contribution, and the seed is portrayed as doing most of the work.

Several HB passages use a spring or sprout as an image for the expected Messiah:

1. In Zechariah 3:8, the Lord tells Joshua that one name for his servant is the "spring" (KJV: "branch"). The same image is used in Zechariah 6:12.

2. In Jeremiah 23:5–6, the Lord promises to send a descendant of David who will be the ideal ruler and who is called a "spring" or "branch." The same image occurs in Jeremiah 33:15.

As background to Mark, these texts identify Jesus with the seed (and not with the sower).

---

38. Note that Matthew and Luke each contain both of these sayings, but they are not contiguous in either Gospel (Matt. 13:12; 25:29; Luke 8:18; 19:26).

he knoweth not how: The sower's ignorance is further evidence that he is not a symbol for Jesus[39] or God but rather for the disciple who shares the word/seed/Jesus with other people.

Relationship to Isaiah 55. Isaiah 55:8–11 makes clear that God understands matters that humans cannot; as background to the parable, it would suggest that the sower's ignorance is meant to highlight not the futility of the situation but rather the omniscience of God. Similarly, Genesis 1:11–12 pictures the growth of plants from seeds as God's act, independent of human initiative, knowledge, or aid.

4:28 *For the earth bringeth forth fruit of herself:* The emphasis in this parable is on the idea that the earth produces "of herself"; the actions of the sower are minimized as much as possible in order to focus on the earth's own ability to bring forth. Surely all of the farmers in the audience would have known that a lot more work than is mentioned here was required to grow a crop; the surprising picture of an inactive and ignorant farmer is a deliberate effort to emphasize the self-growing nature of the seed. If Jesus is the fruit, then the point is that Jesus is sufficient in himself.

This image may also have been intended as a contrast to Hellenistic parables that compared education, which required intense effort, to a highly cultivated plant.[40] In this context, Jesus emphasizes that growth in knowledge of the good news does not require intensive intervention from anyone but God (compare 1 Cor. 4:6–7): "In both Mark and Paul the contrast with the Hellenistic emphasis on human effort is a result of the apocalyptic worldview in which God is the primary actor and humans respond to God's initiative."[41]

Relationship to Leviticus 25. In LXX Leviticus 25:11, where the laws regarding the Jubilee year are set forth, the same Greek word translated in 4:28 as "of herself" is used to describe the growth of seeds that have not been sown. Consumption of these volunteer plants is forbidden during the Jubilee year. As background to Mark, this text would suggest a departure from expectations since the parable presumes that this seed that grows by itself can be harvested and consumed. The contrast might hint at the changes that Jesus' life and death brings to the law of Moses and point to a time when observation of the Jubilee year will not be required.

---

39. But perhaps 13:32 opens the door to thinking about Jesus' mortal lack of omniscience.
40. Dowd, *Reading Mark,* 40–41.
41. Dowd, *Reading Mark,* 41.

first the blade, then the ear, after that the full corn in the ear: There are two different ways that Jesus' description of the growth process could have been perceived by early audiences:

1. This is the natural process of growth with no divine intervention. The implication is that a perfectly ordinary event can describe the kingdom of God.

2. This is a miracle, since the plant growth process was not understood anciently. The point is that God intervenes to create a fruitful plant.

4:29 *But when the fruit is brought forth:* The phrase "brought forth" translates the same Greek verb used to describe Jesus' being handed over to the authorities (3:19; 9:31; 10:33; 14:10–11, 18, 21, 41–42, 44); this is more evidence that the fruit is a symbol for Jesus.

It is unusual to think of fruit handing itself over, but "the very oddity of 'fruit' being the subject of the verb rather than its expected object should arrest the reader."[42] The odd moments in parables are deliberate moves to attract the audience's attention, in this case by implying that Jesus is the fruit and that he was willingly handed over.

immediately he putteth in the sickle, because the harvest is come: The word "immediately" seems odd coming after the description of a slow, multistage process. Its unexpectedness implies that the sickle appears at precisely the right time. In other words, there is no delay; the sower acts at exactly the time when his input is needed, and he does not otherwise act. This would have been a comforting message to Mark's audience as they grappled with the problem of God's apparent inaction in the face of the persecution and trials that they faced.

The verb translated as "putteth" (Greek: *apostellō*) is a cognate of the noun that is translated as "apostle." The underlying idea of this verb is "to send out," so the basic concept is that the sickle is sent out to harvest the crop, but the allusion to the apostles would not have been lost on Mark's audience; they would have thought of the sickle as a symbol for the apostles. The apostles (and perhaps other disciples as well) are portrayed as being sent out to harvest the fruit; this image fits in well with the motif in Jewish thought of the harvest as a metaphor for gathering people for judgment (for example, Isa. 27:12; Joel 3:13).

Harvest Metaphors in the HB. Several HB passages use harvest imagery, including:

---

42. J. Gerald Janzen, "The Verb *Paradidomi* and the Last Judgment in Mark 4:29," *Encounter* 69 (Winter 2008): 31.

1. Isaiah 17:5–8, where the harvest is a metaphor for the final days. As Isaiah 17:7–8 indicates, in that time people will worship the Lord and not false idols. In Mark's context, if the apostles are the sickles, then they will be able to reap a harvest of righteousness with Jesus as the seed/plant.

2. Isaiah 18:6–7, which pictures the sower cutting off unproductive tendrils. As background to Jesus' parable, an ignorant and minimally involved sower implies that all of the growth is permitted to remain. This reading would provide an important nuance to this chapter since it suggests that all types of growth are allowed until the time of judgment.

3. Isaiah 53:2, which is interpreted as a messianic "servant song," understood by Christians to prophesy of the coming of Jesus. The servant is described as a young plant who grows out of dry ground; the servant initially seems to be of no significance, especially given the unlikely locale of his placement. It is only as the text of Isaiah continues and the trials and successes of the servant are described that it becomes clear that the servant is a deeply significant figure. As background to Mark's text, it is further evidence that Jesus is the seed/plant. It also creates an interesting wrinkle in the interpretation of the parable from 4:3–9 by suggesting that the ground in which this seed is planted was not necessarily the best but the seed was successful anyway; this may refer to Jesus' ability to live a sinless life and die an atoning death despite the poor and obscure circumstances into which he was born.

4. Joel 3:13, which features the sickle at the harvest as a symbol for the judgment of the wicked. It is possible to find the same idea in Jesus' parable: the fruition of the seed (Jesus) means that the time has come to judge the wicked. But it is also possible that Jesus is inverting the context in order to indicate that Jesus' own coming produces a righteous harvest instead of a wicked one.

5. Micah 4:12, where the gathering of grain is a symbol for the covenant people's ability to thresh their enemies. As background to this parable, it would imply that the adversaries of Jesus' ministry will receive their retribution at the designated time.

6. Psalm 126:5, which reads, "they that sow in tears shall reap in joy." As background to the parable, this verse pictures an inversion of fortunes with the passage of time; this psalm meshes well with the view of the seed as Jesus' body laid in the tomb ("in tears") and later resurrected ("in joy").

7. Ecclesiastes 11:4–6, which shares several themes with this parable, especially the end of verse 5 and verse 6, which read:

   > you do not know the work of God who makes everything.
   > Sow your seed in the morning,
   > and do not stop working until the evening;
   > for you do not know which activity will succeed—
   > whether this one or that one, or whether both will prosper equally. (NET)

In Ecclesiastes, the ignorance of the sower is reason for him to work frantically to maximize his chances for success. In Mark, Jesus inverts the message: the sower need not work constantly. It is possible that in both texts, ignorance is a metaphor for sin, and the Ecclesiastes text describes a view centered on the law of Moses, where constant action is required to abate sin, while Jesus' parable presents a gospel-centered view, where an entirely different kind of effort is required.

Relationship to Jacob 5. This Book of Mormon text is an extended allegory featuring an olive orchard. It focuses extensively on the efforts of the sower to do everything within his power to produce a successful crop. According to the Book of Mormon, this allegory originated with an Old World prophet named Zenos, who shared it with the house of Israel.

This allegory is not recorded in any other extant sources, so there is no way to determine whether Jesus, his audience, Mark, or the Gospel's audience was familiar with it, but it is possible that they were. If so, it would nuance the interpretation of this parable, which would then be read as a virtual antitype of Zenos's allegory due to the parable's strong emphasis on the lack of action—or even knowledge—on the part of the sower. Perhaps Jesus' point was that Christian disciples, unlike the priests under the law of Moses, did not need to be so active since it was the Atonement of Christ (the seed) that would be performing all of the redemptive work.

Symbolism of the Parable. There are several different ways that this parable can be interpreted:

1. Just as the seed has a secret stage, during which its growth cannot be seen, followed by a stage when the growth is obvious, this passage pictures Jesus' mortal life with the need for secrecy and commands to silence (the sower's inaction) during his lifetime and the anticipation of the public proclamation (harvest) after his death. This reading meshes well with the previous parable, which taught that hidden things will eventually become openly known.

2. The steps of plant growth described here echo Jewish apocalyptic texts[43] by showing order and precision, progression and planning, as God's actions in history are compared to natural events such as the growth of a seed.[44] In this context, the parable contains a message about the end times and God's control of history.

3. After the initial act of sowing, the planter does nothing, implying that the fruit of the kingdom of God does not require human knowledge or effort.

---

43. *1 Enoch* 90–104.
44. Marcus, *Mark 1–8,* 328.

Most of the work happens out of sight; in fact, at first it seems as if nothing is happening at all. This may have been a corrective to those Zealots and revolutionaries who felt an urgency to bring forth the kingdom through their own efforts or even by violence.

4. Jesus is the fruit—buried in the earth, coming forth in the Resurrection—in a way the disciples do not understand, which is pictured by the ignorance of the sower. Most people—including Jesus' own disciples—did not at first comprehend his Atonement. One weakness of this reading is that it cannot explain the parable's emphasis on the stages of growth.

5. Read in light of 4:3–9, this parable fills a lacuna by providing a close-up description of the good soil, showing all of the stages of the virtually automatic growth in the good soil. Since the seed is the word, the parable points to the power of the word to bear fruit without much intervention. Additionally, this parable suggests that since the sower's duties are *only* planting and harvest, he is not culpable for the birds, rocks, or thorns that plagued the three bad soils; the good soil can produce without close attention. The structure of the text itself also serves as an example of how those who already have will be given more: those who already had the parable from 4:3–9 are taught more about the good soil. The unlikelihood of Jesus being the sower in this parable may point to a role for Jesus as the seed in 4:3–9, where interpreting Jesus as the seed would lead to the conclusion that he is also the word (see 4:14). This implies that interpreting the parables is not as simple as

   symbol (seed) → interpretation (word)

   but rather works like this:

   symbol (seed) → interpretation, which is still a symbol (word) → further interpretation (Jesus)

6. This parable, which emphasizes the sower's lack of understanding, should be read in the context of 4:10 and 13, which showcased the disciples' lack of understanding. The gaps in the disciples' knowledge will not interfere with the harvest; the parable is a message of comfort since the disciples can still be effective workers in the kingdom even if they do not understand everything. This is a key component of Mark's message about discipleship: the weaknesses of the disciples, which Mark highlights, will not stop the coming of the kingdom.

4:30 *And he said, Whereunto shall we liken the kingdom of God? or with what comparison shall we compare it?:* The word "we" is somewhat surprising in this context; it might point to the teaching role of the disciples and Jesus' inclusion of them in his ministry. It is also possible that its function is to invite the audience to ponder the question.

4:31 *It is like a grain of mustard seed:* Mustard grows wild in Palestine, into a bush that is ten to twelve feet tall when fully grown. It was known for dominating the area in which it was planted and was therefore considered undesirable, which means that there is an element of redemption in this parable as the mustard seed is shown to be useful.

which, when it is sown in the earth: Once again, the word translated as "earth" is the same Greek word translated as "ground" in the parable in 4:3–9.

Since mustard grew wild, this phrase is akin to saying, "the kingdom of God is like a person who plants a dandelion seed."[45] This is odd behavior. It suggests that the sower finds value in what others do not.

is less than all the seeds that be in the earth: This is another example of hyperbole since other seeds are smaller, although the mustard seed was proverbial as the smallest possible thing.[46]

4:32 *But when it is sown, it groweth up, and becometh greater than all herbs, and shooteth out great branches; so that the fowls of the air may lodge under the shadow of it:* The phrase "fowls of the air" is an idiom for wild (as opposed to domesticated) birds. In the HB, the image is sometimes used to represent the gentile nations.

It is unclear whether the parable pictures the birds in the branches or on the ground, but in either case, they are shaded.

HB Allusions. Several HB texts may provide background for this parable:

1. *Daniel 4.* Nebuchadnezzar has a parabolic dream that he does not understand and that his wise men are not able to interpret (which may parallel the idea in 4:11 that parables cannot be understood by outsiders; Jesus' ability to interpret parables echoes Daniel's ability to interpret dreams). Nebuchadnezzar dreams of a huge tree in which birds can nest. An angel commands that the tree be destroyed except for the roots. The purpose of this destruction is "so that those who are alive may understand that the Most High has authority over human kingdoms" (NET Dan. 4:7). Daniel explains that the tree is a symbol for the king himself and the destruction of the tree represents his (temporary) destruction, with the preservation of the roots indicating that his kingdom will be restored to him eventually. The repeated refrain is that the Most High exercises authority over human kingdoms and is capable of giving those kingdoms to whomever he wishes. As background to this parable in Mark, the Daniel text conveys a subversive message about Rome, positioning it as just another human kingdom under God's control. In Daniel, the large size of the tree is a symbol for the greatness of the gentile empire, which

---

45. Malbon, *Hearing Mark,* 33.
46. Compare Matt. 17:20 for the use of the mustard seed as the proverbial smallest thing imaginable.

means that Jesus' substitution of a shrub for the tree indicates that the appearance of the kingdom of God will be less impressive than expected (but it will still be able to fulfill its function of providing shade and shelter).

2. *Ezekiel 17.* In Ezekiel 17, an eagle symbolizes the king of Babylon and the cedar's top is the house of David. God promises to take a twig from the tree and replant it; eventually, all kinds of birds will nest in the new tree (Ezek. 17:22–24). Through the twig, the house of David will be restored. This text meshes nicely with Jesus' parable in broad terms, and perhaps Jesus tweaks the image by having the new shrub begin from a seed instead of a twig, indicating that the kingdom of God is fundamentally different from the kingdom of David. It may also "parody overblown messianic expectations. . . . Instead of a cedar they got a shrub."[47] But as with the dream in Daniel, the shrub—although it violates expectations—is able to fulfill the same purpose as the grand tree.[48] The line "I make the high tree low; I raise up the low tree" (NET Ezek. 17:24) provides a context for Jesus' use of a shrub instead of a great tree. And since in Ezekiel's text it is the Lord who performs the inversion of the high and the low tree, Jesus is identified as the God of the HB.

3. *Ezekiel 31.* This passage also contains the image of a large tree that provides refuge for birds, with a pronounced emphasis on the largeness of the tree.

Since the parable mentions that the mustard seed is the smallest seed, audiences tend to focus on the transition from small to large. But when read against similar images from the Bible, Jesus' parable suggests that the mustard shrub—even in its final form—is much smaller than what was expected. Through this important nuance to the parable, Jesus teaches that the kingdom of God is more humble than what the audience was expecting.

Interpreting this parable is an excellent example of needing ears to hear: the political message would not have been obvious to a listener who was unfamiliar with the HB images of trees as kingdoms and nesting birds as gentile nations. One reason Jesus may have taught in parables is to limit his critique of Roman authority to those who had ears to hear. These subtle references to Gentiles also set the stage for Jesus' journey to gentile lands in chapter 5.

4:33 *And with many such parables spake he the word unto them:* "Spake the word" translates what might be a technical term for "preached the

---

47. Collins, *Mark,* 256.

48. Robert W. Funk, "Looking-Glass Tree Is for the Birds: Ezekiel 17:22–24; Mark 4:30–32," *Interpretation* 27, no. 1 (1973): 3–9.

gospel." The implication is that the parables per se are not the point of the teaching—the parables are a vehicle that Jesus uses to teach the word. Mark also indicates that Jesus frequently taught in parables and only a few are included here.

Because this verse is very similar to 4:2, it bookends this section of parables, setting it off as a distinct section of the text.

as they were able to hear it: This phrase "can be translated more literally as 'just as' and mean without restriction or limitation, that is, he taught in a manner and on a level to match his hearers' ability, so that they could understand everything. Or it can mean 'to the degree that' or as far as they could understand it."[49] The interpretation chosen here will impact the understanding of Jesus' use of parables: Were they a vehicle that allowed him to teach as much as possible, or were they a way in which he limited how much he taught, or both?

This line also reinforces the message of the parable of the soils, which was that different people are able to hear the parables differently.

4:34 *But without a parable spake he not unto them:* This isn't, of course, literally true but hyperbole emphasizing how frequently Jesus taught in parables. It may also point to the fact that many of Jesus' miracles function as enacted parables due to their symbolic meaning.

and when they were alone: This phrase reveals a problem in the setting: in 4:10, Jesus was alone with the disciples, but this verse implies that Jesus had been teaching the crowd, although Mark never narrated the point at which Jesus had begun speaking to the crowd again. Mark 4:33 suggests that at least the previous two parables had been spoken to the crowd.

he expounded all things to his disciples: The word "expounded" could also be translated as "interpreted." Other examples of restricted groups receiving private teachings include 7:17–23; 8:16–21; 9:28–29; 10:10–12; 11:21–25; and 13:3–37.

This verse indicates that Jesus' teachings required further explanation and were not self-evident; the disciples had to seek the source of the teaching for more information. Further, knowledge was not conveyed outside of a relationship: the disciples needed to follow and know Jesus in order to understand the parables.

---

49. Stein, *Mark,* 237.

Analysis

In contrast with the other seed parables in this chapter, the parable of the mustard seed identifies the type of seed. Thus the three seed parables function telescopically: 4:26–29 is a close-up of the good soil from 4:8, and 4:30–32 is an even closer view of the seed from 4:26–29. This reading would serve as a good illustration of the parable of the lamp, where previously hidden material is brought into the open, as the details of the parable in 4:8 are further explained in 4:26–29, which in turn is further explained in 4:30–32.

In 4:3–9, the bird stole the seed from the path and ended the possibility for growth. In 4:30–32, the seed grows and is able to shade the birds, suggesting forgiveness and mercy. In 4:3–9, the sun threatened the seed; in 4:30–32, the grown plant is able to shade the birds from that same hot sun, implying that successfully being prepared for and meeting trials creates the ability to help others (in this case, the nations) survive the same challenges.

If the focus on the soils (and not the seeds) is extended from 4:3–9 to these other seed parables, then the transformation of the seed—especially given the sower's minimal effort and ignorance and the smallness of the seed—points to the transformative power of the soil: "Jesus, in preaching the word, does not create them or convert them; he *reveals* them."[50] The soil cannot show what it is capable of until the seed is planted in it; then, the transformation of seed into plant and fruit showcases the character of the soil.

The idea of hearing looms large in chapter 4; "hear" occurs thirteen times in the thirty-four verses of this section, creating a refrain. Further, the central parable is bracketed by references to hearing. The commands to hear mesh with the parables, since 4:3–9 concerns how the soil "hears" the seed. There may also be a link to the Shema, the key Jewish prayer, in terms of the primary religious obligation to hear. The central role of hearing in the kingdom of God, in a context where one would have expected a kingdom to involve force and power, emphasizes that "God's rule is established, not by conquest, but by speaking; and that a person participates in God's rule, not by joining an army, but by hearing the message in the right ways."[51]

---

50. Tolbert, *Sowing the Gospel,* 162; italics in original.
51. Gundry, *Mark,* 207.

Mark 4:1–34 is unusual in that Mark's Gospel is primarily a record of deeds and not words: Mark teaches about Jesus by presenting his actions, not his sermons. The two major exceptions to this tendency are found in chapters 4 and 13, which are the only times when Jesus speaks at length in the Gospel of Mark. These texts serve as twin pillars, with each one occurring about halfway through its section of the text: chapter 4 is the midpoint of the first third, which is focused on Galilee, and chapter 13 is the midpoint of the final third, which is focused on Jerusalem.[52] Both texts also follow stories of controversy, suggesting that the discourses should be interpreted in their light. The theme of persecution and how the disciples should respond to it is also a key concern in both chapters.

Mark's audience—including the modern reader—is invited to become insiders as they learn what Jesus taught solely to his disciples in this chapter. Given that a key Markan theme is discipleship, inviting the audience to join the insiders is an important narrative move that grants the Gospel's audience an insider status.

---

52. See the Notes on chapter 13 for more on its relationship to chapter 4.

Miracles
(4:35–5:43)

Overview

In 4:35–5:43, Jesus performs four miracles. Yet it is not the miracles themselves, but rather how they reveal Jesus' identity that is Mark's focal point. Jesus has power over everything that might threaten human life. It is possible to read the three healings in this section as three examples of the good soil,[1] with progressively increasing yields matching the increased level of effort required by the petitioner: the demoniac does nothing, the bleeding woman touches Jesus, and Jairus publicly debases himself. Themes of class, race, and gender permeate this section, emphasizing that Jesus' power is accessible to all people: "that a man whose home is in the Greek cities of the Decapolis (5:20), a poor woman (5:26), and a leader of a Jewish synagogue (5:22) should all prove themselves to be good earth with faith capable of producing fruit indicates the universal nature of the kingdom of God."[2] Chapter 4, with its parabolic references to the explosive growth of the kingdom, has prepared the audience for the expansion of Jesus' ministry.

The sandwiching structure that dominates 5:21–43 will be discussed at length below; there may also be a chiastic structure in this section, focused on the theme of discipleship:

> negative example: the people want Jesus to leave (5:17)
>> positive example: Jairus wants Jesus to touch his daughter (5:23)
>> positive example: the bleeding woman wants to touch Jesus (5:28)
> negative example: the people of Nazareth are offended by Jesus (6:3)

---

1. Tolbert, *Sowing the Gospel,* 166.
2. Tolbert, *Sowing the Gospel,* 170.

Jesus Stills the Sea (4:35–41)

Greek Text

35 Καὶ λέγει αὐτοῖς ἐν ἐκείνῃ τῇ ἡμέρᾳ ὀψίας γενομένης· Διέλθωμεν εἰς τὸ πέραν. 36 καὶ ἀφέντες τὸν ὄχλον παραλαμβάνουσιν αὐτὸν ὡς ἦν ἐν τῷ πλοίῳ, καὶ ἄλλα πλοῖα ἦν μετ᾽ αὐτοῦ. 37 καὶ γίνεται λαῖλαψ μεγάλη ἀνέμου, καὶ τὰ κύματα ἐπέβαλλεν εἰς τὸ πλοῖον, ὥστε ἤδη γεμίζεσθαι τὸ πλοῖον. 38 καὶ αὐτὸς ἦν ἐν τῇ πρύμνῃ ἐπὶ τὸ προσκεφάλαιον καθεύδων· καὶ ἐγείρουσιν αὐτὸν καὶ λέγουσιν αὐτῷ· Διδάσκαλε, οὐ μέλει σοι ὅτι ἀπολλύμεθα; 39 καὶ διεγερθεὶς ἐπετίμησεν τῷ ἀνέμῳ καὶ εἶπεν τῇ θαλάσσῃ· Σιώπα, πεφίμωσο. καὶ ἐκόπασεν ὁ ἄνεμος, καὶ ἐγένετο γαλήνη μεγάλη. 40 καὶ εἶπεν αὐτοῖς· Τί δειλοί ἐστε; οὔπω ἔχετε πίστιν; 41 καὶ ἐφοβήθησαν φόβον μέγαν, καὶ ἔλεγον πρὸς ἀλλήλους· Τίς ἄρα οὗτός ἐστιν ὅτι καὶ ὁ ἄνεμος καὶ ἡ θάλασσα ὑπακούει αὐτῷ; [SBLGNT]

King James Version

35 And the same day, when the even was come, he saith unto them, Let us pass over unto the other side. 36 And when they had sent away the multitude, they took him even as he was in the ship. And there were also with him other little ships. 37 And there arose a great storm of wind, and the waves beat into the ship, so that it was now full. 38 And he was in the hinder part of the ship, asleep on a pillow: and they awake him, and say unto him, Master, carest thou not that we perish? 39 And he arose, and rebuked the wind, and said unto the sea, Peace, be still. And the wind ceased, and there was a great calm. 40 And he said unto them, Why are ye so fearful? how is it that ye have no faith? 41 And they feared exceedingly, and said one to another, What manner of man is this, that even the wind and the sea obey him?

New Rendition

35 And he says to them on that day, when the evening had come, "Let's go across to the other side." 36 And leaving the crowd, they take him with them in the boat, just as he was, and other boats were with him. 37 And a great wind storm comes, and the waves beat into the boat, so that the boat is already being filled up with water. 38 And he was in the stern, sleeping on the cushion. And they wake him and say to him, "Teacher, don't you care that we are being destroyed?" 39 And awakening, he commanded the wind and said to the sea, "Be quiet! Be calm!" And the wind stopped, and there was a great calm. 40 And he said to them, "Why are you so afraid? Do you not yet have trust?" 41 And they were completely terrified and were saying to one another, "Who, then, is this? Even the wind and the sea obey him!"

Notes

4:35 *And the same day, when the even was come:* Mark emphasizes that this story occurs on the same day Jesus had been teaching in parables; this links Jesus' power to his teachings, implying that the same authority manifested in the miracles is found in the teachings.

he saith unto them, Let us pass over unto the other side: "Them" refers to the disciples (compare 4:34). The "other side" indicates the other side of the Sea of Galilee, which was gentile territory. This is Jesus' first foray into gentile lands in Mark.

4:36 *And when they had sent away the multitude:* The negative connotation of the English phrase "sent away" is not found in the Greek text, which simply indicates that the disciples left the crowd.

they took him even as he was in the ship: The phrase "took him" can sound forceful or even violent in English, but the Greek lacks this nuance. Normally Jesus would take his disciples with him (they are, after all, his followers), but this verse pictures the disciples taking Jesus with them. Since Jesus announced his intention to cross the sea in 4:35, it would probably be a mistake to picture the disciples as controlling the itinerary.

Possible meanings of the phrase "as he was" include:

1. Jesus was still in the boat, where he had been teaching in parables, and went across the sea without ever leaving the boat.

2. "As he was" means "when," so Jesus had left the boat after teaching; when he got back into the boat, they crossed to the other side.

3. The phrase functions symbolically: it links this story to Jesus' posture of sitting "in the sea" (4:1) while teaching in parables. Just as the parables illustrated his nature and teachings, this story—where he is still in the boat—will do just the same.

And there were also with him other little ships: This statement is perplexing because there is no other reference to these other boats; possible reasons for mentioning them include:

1. This is a historical remembrance, included—despite not being strictly relevant to the story—because it reflected the memory of the event.

2. These other boats, lacking Jesus' presence and power, sank in the storm.

3. Jesus' popularity is emphasized since so many boats were required to transport the people who wanted to be near him.

4. Perhaps the text is corrupt; maybe it originally indicated that there were *no* other boats with them, a situation that would have emphasized the storm's danger since they would have been without aid had their own boat sunk.

5. The presence of other boats suggests that the calming of the storm also affected other people, people who are not the focus of the story but who nonetheless were in danger and were rescued by Jesus.

6. There are many links between this story and the book of Jonah (see "Realtionship to Jonah" after the Notes on 4:41). Later Jewish traditions about Jonah included reference to other boats, which were not in danger since Jonah was not with them.[3] So perhaps Mark mentions the other boats to encourage the allusion to the story of Jonah.

4:37 *And there arose a great storm of wind:* Because the Sea of Galilee is surrounded by mountains, sudden and severe storms are frequent.[4]

Relationship to Job 38:1. The same Greek word that the KJV translates as "storm" is used in LXX Job 38:1 (KJV: "whirlwind") to name the storm out of which God spoke to Job in a text where the storm is the source for a revelation about the nature of God. There is a similar dynamic in Mark's text, where the identity of Jesus is also disclosed through a storm.

---

and the waves beat into the ship, so that it was now full: The New Rendition adds "with water" for clarity, although these words are not in the Greek text. The wind is creating waves so large that they break over the side of the boat and fill it with water. Given that several of the disciples were fishermen on this very lake, the panic they display in the next verse also indicates the ferocity of the storm. The multiple references to the strength of the storm emphasize Jesus' power when he calms it.

4:38 *And he was in the hinder part of the ship, asleep on a pillow:* In 1986, a boat dating from approximately the time of Jesus was found in the Sea of Galilee;[5] it had an elevated stern with a platform (where a sailor would sit) that would have created a protected area underneath it. Assuming this boat is similar in design to the one in Mark's story, then Jesus is asleep in this protected area under the platform in the "hinder part" of the boat. This setup explains how Jesus could have slept while waves crashed over the side of the boat.

The "pillow" is the cushion upon which the sailor would have sat; it would have accommodated Jesus' head, not his entire body.

---

3. Yalkut Shimoni to Jonah 550:2; note that this is a very late tradition.

4. It is sometimes argued that since storms on the Sea of Galilee subside just as quickly as they arise, the calming of the sea in this story may reflect natural events and not a miracle. However, the reaction of the disciples—the reaction of fishermen who worked on this very sea—strongly suggests that this calming was not typical. Eric F. F. Bishop, "Jesus and the Lake," *Catholic Biblical Quarterly* 13 (October 1951): 408.

5. Stein, *Mark*, 242.

This is the only story in the NT where Jesus sleeps.[6] Jesus' sleep may allude to the following:

1. In the HB, sleep is often associated with God (Ps. 35:23; 44:23; 59:4), which means that Jesus is identified with God in this story.

2. The still, quiet state of Jesus contrasts with the chaotic, wild state of the storm. There are some indications that this story is modeled on an exorcism; if this is the case, then Jesus personifies the opposite of the demon-possessed storm. He is possessed not by an evil spirit but by the Holy Spirit, which brings peace and (literal) rest.

3. In the HB, the faithful are able to sleep (Ps. 3:5; Prov. 3:24–25). So Jesus' undisturbed sleep implies that he is confident of divine protection.

4. Jesus was literally out of sync with his disciples who, as fishermen, were used to working at night, or alternatively, Jesus was particularly exhausted after a long day of teaching. Either or both of these images of Jesus' physical weakness would emphasize the spiritual strength that he exercised in stilling the storm in spite of his depleted physical state.

5. Jesus sleeps to test the disciples' faith: how will they respond to the situation without his intervention?

6. Jesus' sleep is mentioned to enhance the allusion to Jonah's story (Jonah 1:5).

and they awake him, and say unto him, Master, carest thou not that we perish?: This is the first use of "teacher" (KJV: "master") in Mark in reference to Jesus. Perhaps the title emphasizes Jesus' teaching role in the previous chapter. But because the audience knows that Jesus is so much more than a teacher, the title also reflects the disciples' limited knowledge of Jesus' identity, an idea also emphasized by their reaction at the end of this story (4:41).

There are two ways to understand the "we" here:

1. Inclusive. It refers to Jesus and the disciples, so the disciples think that Jesus does not care about his own safety.

2. Exclusive. It refers to the disciples only, so the disciples assume that Jesus will take care of himself but worry that he will not attend to their needs.

In Greek, the disciples' question anticipates a positive answer; they think that Jesus will say "Yes, I do care." But Jesus' answer (4:40) also guides the interpretation of the question as evidence of the disciples' current lack of faith. Further, "the rudeness of the [question] . . . is an eloquent pointer to the messianic veiledness—the Son of God subject to the rudeness of men."[7]

---

6. The reference to Jesus' sleep is included in the other synoptic accounts of this story (see Matt. 8:24–25; Luke 8:23).

7. Cranfield, *Gospel according to St Mark,* 174.

Relationship to Psalm 46. In Psalm 46, the distinguishing characteristic of the faithful is their trust in the Lord, even during storms at sea (Ps. 46:3). The fact that the disciples do not share this attitude is evidence of their immature faith.

4:39 *And he arose, and rebuked the wind:* "Rebuke" is the same word used in 1:25, where it referred to expelling demons; thus, some details in this story suggest that it is an exorcism of the sea.

and said unto the sea, Peace, be still: The word translated as "be still" is the same word that Jesus uses to command the demon to "hold thy peace" in 1:25. In both contexts, the command is joined to a rebuke. This parallel contributes to the exorcism motif.

The doubled command may reflect the fact that there are two problems to be solved: the wind is commanded to be peaceful and the waves are commanded to be still. The next line, which shows the effects of these commands, supports this reading.

And the wind ceased, and there was a great calm: Because "and there was a great calm" could be translated as "and a great calm came to pass," it is syntactically nearly identical to "there arose a great storm of wind" (4:37, which could be translated as "and a great gale came to pass"). These similar phrases bracket Jesus' commanding voice, which is shown to be the mechanism that changes a great storm to a great calm. Through this parallel, Mark emphasizes the power of Jesus' words to effect great change.

4:40 *And he said unto them, Why are ye so fearful? how is it that ye have no faith?:* There is a textual variant here: some manuscripts add the word "yet" to this verse ("how is it that ye have no faith *yet*?"). It is difficult to determine which reading is better (compare the similar variant in 8:21). Because the inclusion of "yet" is kinder to the disciples, it is easier to imagine a scribe adding "yet" than intentionally omitting it, but it is more likely—given the manuscript evidence—that the "yet" was originally present but accidentally omitted.[8] The inclusion of "yet" is probably a better reflection of Mark's view of the disciples as fallible learners since it assumes that they may have faith in the future; Jesus' question is not so much about faith as it is about timing.

Regardless of the reading, Jesus' question is perhaps surprising: isn't their question evidence of their faith? Possible explanations for this conundrum include:

---

8. J. M. Ross, "Further Unnoticed Points in the Text of the New Testament," *Novum Testamentum* 45, no. 3 (2003): 210.

1. Perhaps, given the analogy in this story between stilling the storm and exorcising a demon, Jesus expected the disciples to use the power to cast out demons that he had previously granted them (3:14–15) to calm the sea themselves. An unsolvable puzzle is why, if their request to Jesus showed a lack of faith, Jesus responded affirmatively to their implied request.

2. By analogy to the Jonah story, the expectation is that Jesus, filling the role of Jonah, will pray to God to calm the storm. (Instead, Jesus, aligned with God, calms it himself.) This leads to two possibilities:

   a. The disciples had assumed that Jesus would pray to God to end the storm. Jesus rebukes them because they themselves should have prayed to still the storm.

   b. Jesus is dismayed that the disciples thought that Jesus would need to pray to God to still the storm: not fully understanding his identity, they did not realize that he could still the storm himself.

This is the first of several rebukes of the disciples in Mark. Other rebukes of the disciples occur in 7:18; 8:17–21, 33; and 9:19.

The contrast assumed in Jesus' question is not between doubt and faith but between fear and faith. As mentioned before, in the Gospel of Mark, faith is better understood as trust than as intellectual assent to certain beliefs (9:22–24). Jesus' critique of the disciples is because they do not (yet) trust him.

4:41 *And they feared exceedingly, and said one to another:* "Feared" in this verse does not share the same root as "fearful" in the previous verse: "The fear (*phobos*) mentioned in the present verse is the proper response to a manifestation of the divine, whereas the quailing before the storm found in the previous verse (*deiloi* = 'cowardly') is reprehensible."[9] So it is not the case that they are being fearful immediately after Jesus chastises them for fearing.

It is not clear whether the disciples' fear is a response to the calming of the storm or to Jesus' words. Perhaps their question ("what manner of man is this?") indicates that their focus is on Jesus' identity.

The word translated as "exceedingly" is the same word translated as "great" when describing the storm in 4:37 and the calm in 4:39. When presented with a great storm, Jesus' actions have two similar effects: a great calm for the waters and a great fear/reverence for the disciples. The disciples' response might be considered part of the miracle, especially since these same disciples were just speaking somewhat rudely to Jesus (4:38), as if he were not worthy of reverence and awe.

---

9. Marcus, *Mark 1–8,* 334.

What manner of man is this: This line can be interpreted either as a question with an explanatory clause (as the KJV takes it) or as a question followed by an exclamation (as the New Rendition takes it). Either way, it can be understood as either:

1. A genuine question, which implies that the disciples are learning very slowly, since the HB background of God's unique ability to control the seas should have made the answer to the question obvious. But it also shows that, despite their gaps in knowledge, they were willing to follow Jesus and learn from him. Posing the question at least acknowledges that there is more to Jesus' identity than they currently know; they are aware that their knowledge is incomplete and that "teacher" is an inadequate title. A miracle, even a dramatic one such as stilling a life-threatening storm, did not reveal Jesus' identity to them.

2. A statement about Jesus' identity phrased as a question. This would imply that the disciples knew that Jesus' identity is more than they had previously imagined.

that even the wind and the sea obey him?: The answer to this question is (or, at least, should be) obvious: the HB clearly teaches that only God controls the elements.

Relationship to Psalm 107. The image in Psalm 107:23–32 is of the Lord rescuing sailors from a storm; the similarities between this psalm and the present text in Mark are significant. Interestingly, the only real point of departure is at the very end where instead of rejoicing (Ps. 107:30 KJV: "are . . . glad") at the stilling of the storm, the disciples wonder who Jesus is. Because Mark's text has followed the psalm so closely, the abrupt departure is highlighted. It emphasizes the disciples' response as unexpected and somewhat inadequate since they are still wondering who Jesus is. The weaknesses of the disciples and their identity as learners—major Markan themes—are emphasized. At the same time, both their wondering and the comparison of Jesus to the God of the HB emphasize Jesus' identity.

Relationship to Jonah. There are extensive similarities between Jonah 1 and this story in Mark:

1. The main character travels by boat to a foreign land in order to complete a mission of preaching repentance (in fact, Jonah is the only HB prophet called to preach to the Gentiles).

2. The ship is in danger of being destroyed by a storm (4:37; Jonah 1:4).

3. The main character is asleep while the others worry about their destruction (4:38; Jonah 1:5).

4. The others wake the main character and ask him questions (4:38; Jonah 1:6).

5. Questions about the main character's true identity are raised (4:41; Jonah 1:8).

6. The others fear greatly (4:41; Jonah 1:16).

7. In LXX Jonah 1, several words are identical to those found in Mark; one key word is "perish" (LXX Jonah 1:6, 14; 3:9; compare 4:38), which "expresses the leitmotiv of the entire book [of Jonah], escape from destruction at the hand of God."[10]

But the stories are not entirely similar: one theme in the book of Jonah is Jonah's unwillingness to travel to and preach in foreign lands; by contrast, Jesus initiates his journey and completes it without complaint. And, crucially, Jesus—unlike Jonah—takes responsibility for ending the storm. And, most surprisingly—since, in the Jonah story, the presumption is that Jonah would pray to God and God would calm the storm—Jesus calms the storm himself. This shifts Jesus' role in the story from prophet to God. Because the stories had been tracking each other so closely up to this point, this divergence becomes even more pronounced and important.

If Mark mentioned the other boats to encourage the allusion to the Jonah story, then when the storm arises, the audience should suspect that someone in Jesus' boat had been unrighteous. The obvious candidate for the sinner would be Jesus, since he—like Jonah—is sleeping, woken by others, and asked a question. Of course, the audience knows that it is not Jesus' unrighteousness that caused the storm. This allusion to Jonah may be part of how Mark teaches about the Atonement in this story: Mark shows Jesus accepting and mitigating the consequences for unrighteousness that he himself did not merit and was not personally troubled by. Alternatively, the Atonement imagery could be understood in a different way since Jonah will ultimately permit himself to be offered as a sacrifice to save the many on the ship; in this sense, Jonah foreshadows Jesus' self-sacrifice.

Analysis

In the HB, the sea is associated with chaos, and only God has the authority to control it (Gen. 8:1; Job 26:12; Ps. 104:3; 107:23–29; Isa. 50:2).[11] In this story, Jesus is not simply performing the miracle of stilling a storm; he is being identified with the God of the HB. This suggestion gains power through the allusions to the book of Jonah.

Jesus is able to sleep through the storm. His position in the boat means that the storm does not threaten him. On a symbolic level, this can be read

---

10. Marcus, *Mark 1–8,* 333.

11. See generally Fred E. Woods, *Water and Storm Polemics against Baalism in the Deuteronomic History* (New York: Peter Lang Publishing, 1994).

to imply that the storm of sin does not affect him. It is the disciples (symbolic of all humans threatened by sin) who ask Jesus to intervene to save them. While subtle, this story can be read as a component of Mark's Atonement theology: Jesus need not intervene for his own sake, but he does so to protect others.

The way that Mark has structured this story creates a question—who is Jesus?—that is allowed to linger, unanswered, in the audience's minds and prompt their own thinking on the subject (later, 5:7 will answer the question: Jesus is the "Son of the most high God"). The question illustrates that for Mark, this story is not primarily about the calming of the sea but rather about the question of Jesus' identity.

JESUS EXORCISES DEMONS (5:1–20)

Greek Text

1 Καὶ ἦλθον εἰς τὸ πέραν τῆς θαλάσσης εἰς τὴν χώραν τῶν Γερασηνῶν. 2 καὶ ἐξελθόντος αὐτοῦ ἐκ τοῦ πλοίου εὐθὺς ὑπήντησεν αὐτῷ ἐκ τῶν μνημείων ἄνθρωπος ἐν πνεύματι ἀκαθάρτῳ, 3 ὃς τὴν κατοίκησιν εἶχεν ἐν τοῖς μνήμασιν, καὶ οὐδὲ ἁλύσει οὐκέτι οὐδεὶς ἐδύνατο αὐτὸν δῆσαι 4 διὰ τὸ αὐτὸν πολλάκις πέδαις καὶ ἁλύσεσι δεδέσθαι καὶ διεσπάσθαι ὑπ' αὐτοῦ τὰς ἁλύσεις καὶ τὰς πέδας συντετρῖφθαι, καὶ οὐδεὶς ἴσχυεν αὐτὸν δαμάσαι· 5 καὶ διὰ παντὸς νυκτὸς καὶ ἡμέρας ἐν τοῖς μνήμασιν καὶ ἐν τοῖς ὄρεσιν ἦν κράζων καὶ κατακόπτων ἑαυτὸν λίθοις. 6 καὶ ἰδὼν τὸν Ἰησοῦν ἀπὸ μακρόθεν ἔδραμεν καὶ προσεκύνησεν αὐτόν, 7 καὶ κράξας φωνῇ μεγάλῃ λέγει· Τί ἐμοὶ καὶ σοί, Ἰησοῦ υἱὲ τοῦ θεοῦ τοῦ ὑψίστου; ὁρκίζω σε τὸν θεόν, μή με βασανίσῃς. 8 ἔλεγεν γὰρ αὐτῷ· Ἔξελθε τὸ πνεῦμα τὸ ἀκάθαρτον ἐκ τοῦ ἀνθρώπου. 9 καὶ ἐπηρώτα αὐτόν· Τί ὄνομά σοι; καὶ λέγει αὐτῷ· Λεγιὼν ὄνομά μοι, ὅτι πολλοί ἐσμεν· 10 καὶ παρεκάλει αὐτὸν πολλὰ ἵνα μὴ αὐτὰ ἀποστείλῃ ἔξω τῆς χώρας. 11 ἦν δὲ ἐκεῖ πρὸς τῷ ὄρει ἀγέλη χοίρων μεγάλη βοσκομένη· 12 καὶ παρεκάλεσαν αὐτὸν λέγοντες· Πέμψον ἡμᾶς εἰς τοὺς χοίρους, ἵνα εἰς αὐτοὺς εἰσέλθωμεν. 13 καὶ ἐπέτρεψεν αὐτοῖς. καὶ ἐξελθόντα τὰ πνεύματα τὰ ἀκάθαρτα εἰσῆλθον εἰς τοὺς χοίρους, καὶ ὥρμησεν ἡ ἀγέλη κατὰ τοῦ κρημνοῦ εἰς τὴν θάλασσαν, ὡς δισχίλιοι, καὶ ἐπνίγοντο ἐν τῇ θαλάσσῃ. 14 Καὶ οἱ βόσκοντες αὐτοὺς ἔφυγον καὶ ἀπήγγειλαν εἰς τὴν πόλιν καὶ εἰς τοὺς ἀγρούς· καὶ ἦλθον ἰδεῖν τί ἐστιν τὸ γεγονός. 15 καὶ ἔρχονται πρὸς τὸν Ἰησοῦν, καὶ θεωροῦσιν τὸν δαιμονιζόμενον καθήμενον ἱματισμένον καὶ σωφρονοῦντα, τὸν ἐσχηκότα τὸν λεγιῶνα, καὶ ἐφοβήθησαν. 16 καὶ διηγήσαντο αὐτοῖς οἱ ἰδόντες πῶς ἐγένετο τῷ δαιμονιζομένῳ καὶ περὶ τῶν χοίρων. 17 καὶ ἤρξαντο παρακαλεῖν αὐτὸν ἀπελθεῖν ἀπὸ τῶν ὁρίων αὐτῶν. 18 καὶ ἐμβαίνοντος αὐτοῦ εἰς τὸ πλοῖον παρεκάλει αὐτὸν ὁ δαιμονισθεὶς ἵνα μετ' αὐτοῦ ᾖ. 19 καὶ οὐκ ἀφῆκεν αὐτόν,

ἀλλὰ λέγει αὐτῷ· Ὕπαγε εἰς τὸν οἶκόν σου πρὸς τοὺς σούς, καὶ ἀπάγγειλον αὐτοῖς ὅσα ὁ κύριός σοι πεποίηκεν καὶ ἠλέησέν σε. 20 καὶ ἀπῆλθεν καὶ ἤρξατο κηρύσσειν ἐν τῇ Δεκαπόλει ὅσα ἐποίησεν αὐτῷ ὁ Ἰησοῦς, καὶ πάντες ἐθαύμαζον. [SBLGNT]

King James Version

1 And they came over unto the other side of the sea, into the country of the Gadarenes. 2 And when he was come out of the ship, immediately there met him out of the tombs a man with an unclean spirit, 3 Who had his dwelling among the tombs; and no man could bind him, no, not with chains: 4 Because that he had been often bound with fetters and chains, and the chains had been plucked asunder by him, and the fetters broken in pieces: neither could any man tame him. 5 And always, night and day, he was in the mountains, and in the tombs, crying, and cutting himself with stones. 6 But when he saw Jesus afar off, he ran and worshipped him, 7 And cried with a loud voice, and said, What have I to do with thee, Jesus, thou Son of the most high God? I adjure thee by God, that thou torment me not. 8 For he said unto him, Come out of the man, thou unclean spirit. 9 And he asked him, What is thy name? And he answered, saying, My name is Legion: for we are many. 10 And he besought him much that he would not send them away out of the country. 11 Now there was there nigh unto the mountains a great herd of swine feeding. 12 And all the devils besought him, saying, Send us into the swine, that we may enter into them. 13 And forthwith Jesus gave them leave. And the unclean spirits went out, and entered into the swine: and the herd ran violently down a steep place into the sea, (they were about two thousand;) and

New Rendition

1 And they came to the other side of the sea, to the region of the Gerasenes. 2 And having gone forth out of the boat, he immediately met a man from the tombs with an unclean spirit, 3 who lived in the tombs. And not even with a chain was anyone able to confine him anymore. 4 For he had often been bound with leg chains and handcuffs, but the cuffs had been wrenched apart by him, and the chains were shattered, and no one was strong enough to control him. 5 And constantly—all night and all day—in the tombs and in the mountains, he was shouting and cutting/bruising himself with rocks. 6 And having seen Jesus from a distance, he ran and knelt in front of him. 7 And having shouted with a loud voice, he says, "Mind your own business, Jesus, Son of the Most High God! I urge you by God not to torture me." 8 For he was saying to him, "Come out of the man, unclean spirit!" 9 And Jesus asked him, "What is your name?" And he says, answering, "Legion is my name, because we are many." 10 And he begged him repeatedly that he would not send them out of the region. 11 Near the mountain there was a great herd of hogs feeding. 12 And they begged him, saying, "Send us into the hogs, that we might enter into them." 13 And he permitted them. And having gone out of the man, the unclean spirits entered into the hogs and rushed the herd, numbering about two thousand, down the cliff into the sea. And they were drowned in the sea.

were choked in the sea. 14 And they that fed the swine fled, and told it in the city, and in the country. And they went out to see what it was that was done. 15 And they come to Jesus, and see him that was possessed with the devil, and had the legion, sitting, and clothed, and in his right mind: and they were afraid. 16 And they that saw it told them how it befell to him that was possessed with the devil, and also concerning the swine. 17 And they began to pray him to depart out of their coasts. 18 And when he was come into the ship, he that had been possessed with the devil prayed him that he might be with him. 19 Howbeit Jesus suffered him not, but saith unto him, Go home to thy friends, and tell them how great things the Lord hath done for thee, and hath had compassion on thee. 20 And he departed, and began to publish in Decapolis how great things Jesus had done for him: and all men did marvel.

14 And those who fed the hogs fled and told it in the city and in the countryside. And the people came to see what it is that has happened. 15 And they come to Jesus and see the demon-possessed man sitting, clothed and sane—the same one who had had the legion—and they were afraid. 16 And those who saw it related to them what happened to the demon-possessed man and about the hogs. 17 And they began to beg him to leave their region. 18 And as he was getting into the boat, the man who had been possessed by demons begged that he might go with him. 19 But he did not permit him to, but he says to him, "Go into your home, to your own people, and proclaim to them how much the Lord did for you and had mercy on you." 20 And he departed and began to proclaim in the Decapolis how much Jesus had done for him, and everyone was amazed.

Notes

5:1 *And they came over unto the other side of the sea:* Jesus' is willing to enter gentile—and therefore defiled—land to help the people there: "Christ *goes towards the other*: adversary, unbeliever, suffering human being."[12] The issue of uncleanness becomes acute in this setting, and Mark will emphasize it in several different ways as the story progresses.

into the country of the Gadarenes: The previous phrase could be literally rendered as "into the other side of the sea" and this phrase as "into the region of the Gadarenes," emphasizing that Jesus is venturing deep *into* gentile territory, a point strengthened by 4:35's note that this trip was intentionally undertaken by Jesus.

With its gentile setting, this verse signals a significant departure from what has come before. It is noteworthy that Jesus would devote some of

---

12. Jean Starobinski, "An Essay in Literary Analysis—Mark 5:1–20," *Ecumenical Review* 23, no. 4 (1971): [383]; italics in original.

his ministry to gentile lands and people. While it is clear that this is gentile territory, there are three textual variants for the name of the location:[13]

1. "Gerasenes." Gerasa was on the southeastern side of the Sea of Galilee and was part of the Decapolis (compare 5:20). Some ancient manuscripts read "Gerasenes" here. It was probably the earlier reading, but it presents problems, which may have led to the other textual variants. Gerasa was almost forty miles away from the Sea of Galilee, which makes it hard to envision the swine "immediately" running to and drowning in the sea; at the very least, there would have been no witnesses to the entire scene. But it is possible that the reference is to the region and not to the city proper, which reduces the problem. This reading has the best manuscript support and is the most difficult reading to understand; both of these factors make "Gerasenes" the most likely earliest reading. "The Hebrew root [of Gerasenes] means 'to banish' and is a common term for exorcism,"[14] so the name might be appropriate and even symbolic here as it would contribute to the exorcism motif in the story.

2. "Gadarenes." Gadara was five miles southeast of the Sea of Galilee. This variant probably reflects a change made to harmonize with Matthew 8:28,[15] but Gadara lacks any steep cliffs from which the pigs could have plunged. However, Gadara may be correct if it refers to the region of Gadara and not the city proper.

3. "Gergesenes." Gergesa has the least manuscript support and makes the most logical sense (it has a steep bank and is near the Sea of Galilee); therefore, it is the most likely to be a later scribal correction.

The place name in this verse affects the interpretation of 5:20; see the Notes on that verse.

5:2 *And when he was come out of the ship, immediately there met him out of the tombs:* The tombs are probably in caves, perhaps below ground level. The demon-possessed man is thus among the dead and, symbolically, enduring a living death. Under the law of Moses, his proximity to the dead would have made him unclean. Mark 5:3 and 5:5 also refer to the tombs; this triple repetition emphasizes the importance of the theme of death in the passage.

a man with an unclean spirit: See the discussion of unclean spirits in 1:23.

5:3 *Who had his dwelling among the tombs; and no man could bind him, no, not with chains:* In both English and Greek, there is a triple negative

---

13. Comfort, *New Testament Text and Translation Commentary,* 109.
14. Marcus, *Mark 1–8,* 342.
15. Metzger, *Textual Commentary,* 72.

repetition in this phrase, emphasizing the impossibility of binding the man and suggesting the strength of the demons that possess him.

Mark does not explain why the man was bound; possibilities include:

1. to prevent the man from hurting himself or others.
2. to keep him away from the tombs, though that was unsuccessful.
3. to keep him in the tombs, where his uncleanness would not spread to others.

5:4 *Because that he had been often bound with fetters and chains:* "Fetters" chained the feet; "chains" are handcuffs.

and the chains had been plucked asunder by him, and the fetters broken in pieces: These lines can be read as "demonic passives," an inversion of the more common "divine passives,"[16] conveying that it was the demons—not the man—who were responsible for the actions.

neither could any man tame him: The strength of the demonic possession is emphasized by yet another phrase indicating the failure of all human efforts to control the man. There may be a chiastic arrangement here:

A no one could bind him (5:3b)
  B fetters/chains (5:4a)
  B' chains/fetters (5:4a)
A' no one was strong enough to subdue him (5:4b)[17]

This structure would be an additional way of emphasizing the inability of anyone to control the man.

The word "could" (Greek: *ischuō*) is a cognate of the word "strong" (Greek: *ischuros*) in 3:27; this demon-possessed man is too strong to be bound. Jesus fills the role of the "strong man" from 3:27, but he frees instead of binds. The audience may have expected Jesus to bind the man since the story presents the inability to bind him as the problem, but that expectation will not be met. Jesus doesn't bind the man but removes the need for him to be bound: "demons themselves 'bind' people, and so our passage may contain an element of irony: the world's method for dealing with those whom Satan has enchained is to tie them up further."[18]

5:5 *And always, night and day, he was in the mountains, and in the tombs, crying:* Because the caves were probably below ground, the shift from mountains to tombs implies that the man is in frantic motion with no stable location. Combined with the phrase "night and day," it creates a picture of constant, chaotic, troubled motion.

---

16. Stein, *Mark,* 252.
17. Stein, *Mark,* 252.
18. Marcus, *Mark 1–8,* 343.

and cutting himself with stones: The verb here could refer to cutting or to bruising. It could have several possible meanings:

1. an association with worshiping demons (1 Kgs. 18:28).
2. a reflection of the demons' efforts to destroy the man.
3. a reflection of the man's efforts to release the demons or to kill himself.

According to the Talmud, the four signs of insanity are walking at night, sleeping on a grave, tearing one's clothes, and destroying things.[19] This understanding of insanity may be responsible for the elements of demonic possession described in this story, included to imply that the man is insane. Mark does not make clear if the demons had made the man insane or if an insane person had been possessed by demons.

5:6 *But when he saw Jesus afar off, he ran and worshipped him:* "Worshipped" may not have the English connotation that the man recognized Jesus as deity; the word might simply suggest the action of a servant before his master.

Once again, it is impossible to determine which actions reflect the will of the demons and which the will of the man, but it is likely that the worship reflects the man's desire to implore Jesus to free him from the demons. If this is the case, the man could exercise some control over his own body some of the time.

5:7 *And cried with a loud voice, and said, What have I to do with thee:* The question here is the same idiom used in 1:24 (see the Notes on that verse). In this context, the phrase appears to conflict with the running and bowing down and thus reflects the struggle between the man and the demons for control: 5:7 contains the words of the demons while 5:6 reflects the actions of the man.

Jesus, thou Son of the most high God?: Naming Jesus is probably an attempt to gain control over him.

The title "the most high God" fits within the gentile context quite well since the title was used for the head god in a pagan group of gods (compare Acts 16:17) and for the God of Israel in gentile settings (Gen. 14:18 [this chapter is widely believed to derive from a non-Israelite source]; Num. 24:16; Dan. 3:26). By way of contrast, the demon in 1:24 used a title more appropriate to a Jewish setting.

Mark 4:41 left unanswered the question of Jesus' identity; 5:7 supplies the answer from a supernatural (albeit demonic) source.

---

19. Babylonian Talmud, Seder Mo'ed IV, Hagigah 3b.

I adjure thee by God, that thou torment me not: This statement drips with irony:

1. "Adjure" is a technical term used by exorcists to expel a demon (compare Acts 19:13). Here it is used by the demons themselves as they take on the role of exorcist and attempt to cast out Jesus.

2. The demons adjure Jesus "by God," as if the demons are calling on God's power to command Jesus. Mark's account suggests that evil—even demons themselves—wrap themselves in the words, rituals, and appearances of righteous power.

3. Hypocritically, the demons are willing to torture the man who is possessed, but they plead that Jesus will not torture them. (Contrast how Jesus, when asked to leave the region by the people [5:17–18], goes instantly and silently.)

5:8 *For he said unto him, Come out of the man, thou unclean spirit:* "Said" is imperfect in Greek ("he was saying"), implying repeated action.

The placement of this verse is unusual because it is out of chronological order: the "for" indicates that Mark is presenting the rest of this verse as the reason for the demons' outburst in 5:7. (In other words, Jesus repeatedly told the demons to get out of the man, and this caused the demons to say what they did in 5:7.) Why might Mark have chosen to narrate the story this way? It obscures the fact that the demons were not instantly obedient to Jesus' command, a detail that is de-emphasized when the story is presented out of order. (While Matthew and Luke alter Mark's account to make it seem as if Jesus is more polished than in Mark's presentation, it is possible that this incident reflects one time when Jesus' actions were a little too rough around the edges even for Mark.)

When the story is read in chronological order, this is a "two-step" exorcism (compare 8:22–26, which is a two-step healing); Jesus does not accomplish his objective with the first effort, which is this verse's command to "come out of the man." As the previous verse indicates, the demons did not come out but rather attempted to exorcise Jesus. In this reading, there are two ways to interpret the story:

1. Jesus spoke to the demons as if there were only one demon; it is only when he learns that there are thousands of demons that he is able to successfully cast them out. (While unnarrated, it is possible that when Jesus commanded one demon to leave, it left, but that still left the man possessed by thousands of demons.)

2. The demons bargain with Jesus to neither be cast out of the region nor be left without bodies, and Jesus agrees to permit the demons to enter into the herd of swine. Only then do they leave the man.

There is no command to silence despite the fact that the demons have revealed Jesus' identity. Perhaps this is because the story is in gentile lands (where the revelation of Jesus' identity would not pose a threat to his ministry from incensed religious authorities) or, more prosaically, because Jesus cannot command the demons to silence when he still needs to hear their name(s) in order to complete the exorcism.

5:9 *And he asked him, What is thy name?:* Although the Greek text reads "he" and not "Jesus," the New Rendition includes "Jesus" for clarity, since Jesus was the last speaker and one would normally assume that the next speaker would not be the same person.

This verse would not have occurred immediately after 5:8; rather, the chronological order of events would have been 5:8, 7, 9. This means that Jesus asks the demons what their names are in response to their words in 5:7.

Mark does not indicate whether Jesus knew the answer to the question; perhaps

1. Jesus did not know the answer. This would be an example of Jesus' mortal limitations. It might also explain why the story reads as if he were unsuccessful in his first effort to expel the demons: he did not have enough information about them. Specifically, he proceeded as if there were only one demon instead of thousands. This question, along with the demons' answer ("for we are many"), informed Jesus about the correct dimensions of the problem, and only then was he able to solve it. It is interesting that the demons knew Jesus' name but he did not know their name(s).

2. Jesus knew the answer. In this case, it raises questions about why he might have asked the question: was this a learning opportunity for the audience? for the man? for the disciples?

And he answered, saying, My name is Legion: for we are many: A "legion" was a unit of the Roman military composed of five to six thousand men. Perhaps there were actually that many demons in the man; it is also possible that the name was hyperbolic. Either way, it emphasizes the demons' strength, implying that they are as strong as thousands of Roman warriors. Jesus must contend with an entire army of demons.

"Legion" could be the name of this group of demons or it could be offered instead of their name(s) ("We will not tell you our names—we will only tell you that there are thousands of us"). Because knowledge of a name was thought to give one power over the named, perhaps the demons avoid telling Jesus their name(s) so that he will not have power over them. However, Jesus' greater power is evidenced by his ability to free the man, even if he does not know the demons' name(s).

5:10 *And he besought him much:* "Besought" is imperfect, indicating that he spoke more than once. Yet again, it is not clear if it is the will of the demons or the will of the man being expressed here.

This begging emphasizes Jesus' power and strength, especially after the strength of the demons was emphasized in so many ways; if they would beg Jesus, then he must be incredibly powerful.

that he would not send them away out of the country: Both the KJV and the Greek are somewhat odd in this verse: "he [singular] besought . . . would not send them [plural] away." Reasons for this odd construction include:

1. Sometimes Mark's Greek is awkward.

2. The man's voice is singular, but it reflects the will of many demons.

3. It is deliberately awkward and confusing in order to reflect the nature of demonic possession.

5:11 *Now there was there nigh unto the mountains a great herd of swine feeding:* Swine are not herd animals; the word translated as "herd" is a military term for a group of recruits. There were about two thousand pigs (5:13); it is all but certain that a group this large would have been the food supply for the Roman army since the normal size for a group of pigs was about one hundred.

The presence of swine is another indicator of gentile territory since Jews regarded them as the paradigmatic unclean animal (Lev. 11:7–8; Isa. 65:4; 66:17) and since they were forbidden to raise pigs; in fact, "by Jesus' day the pig had become in a sense the symbol of paganism."[20]

5:12 *And all the devils besought him, saying, Send us into the swine, that we may enter into them:* Presumably the demons realize that they will not be permitted to stay in the man, but they still desire some other host. Some Latter-day Saint leaders have used this request by the demons as evidence of the desirability of possessing a physical body:[21] the demons prefer even a swine's body to having none at all.

5:13 *And forthwith Jesus gave them leave:* Jesus does not oust the demons but rather accedes to their request to enter the swine. It may be that he agreed in order to create a situation where the demons' true desire—destruction—could be illustrated through the fate of the swine. It is also possible to read this as Jesus' compassion for the demons.

---

20. Witherington, *Gospel of Mark,* 179.

21. LeGrand Richards, "What the Gospel Teaches," *Ensign* 12 (May 1982): 30; J. Reuben Clark Jr., in *The One Hundred Twenty-Seventh Semi-annual Conference of The Church of Jesus Christ of Latter-day Saints* (Salt Lake City: The Church of Jesus Christ of Latter-day Saints, 1956), 84.

And the unclean spirits went out, and entered into the swine: and the herd ran violently down a steep place into the sea: The New Rendition adds "of the man" after "went out"/"having gone out" for clarity, although this phrase is not in the Greek text.

Relationship to Leviticus 16. Leviticus 16:5–10 contains the directions for the ritual of the "scapegoat": performed on the Day of Atonement, two goats are brought forth. One is a sin offering to the Lord, and the other is sent out into the wilderness. The goat permitted to "escape" (hence "scapegoat") was understood to symbolically carry away all of the sins of the community. In this story, the pigs could be understood similarly. As pigs, they are emblematic of gentile lands. They carry the demons far away, out of the community, and the man is left clean.

they were about two thousand: It is somewhat odd that Mark mentions that there were two thousand pigs when a legion had five to six thousand men; possible explanations for this disjuncture include:

1. The exact number of soldiers in a legion was probably not common knowledge in the ancient world, so Mark may not have known it.[22]

2. In informal use, "legion" could refer to a group of 2,048 soldiers,[23] so "about two thousand" could be considered accurate.

3. Mark may be unconcerned with precise numbers; the reference to "about two thousand" is intended to make the point that the man had been inhabited by thousands of demons.

That the demons were able to control a group of two thousand swine indirectly indicates Jesus' power since he was able to remove those demons from the man.

and were choked in the sea: Under normal circumstances swine can swim, but—perhaps in a frenzy of confusion—they managed to crowd and trample each other. The death of the swine raises many questions:

1. Who caused the swine to plunge into the sea?

   a. The demons. The swine were less able to resist the demons than the human, who was able to resist the demons' impulse to destroy him.

   b. The swine. They jump to escape the demons, deciding that they are better off dead than possessed. Despite their ritual impurity, they still will not tolerate the uncleanness of demonic possession. This reading adds an interesting twist to the story regarding the demons' request to inhabit the

22. Joshua Garroway, "The Invasion of a Mustard Seed: A Reading of Mark 5.1–20," *Journal for the Study of the New Testament* 32 (September 2009): 62.

23. Gundry, *Mark*, 263.

swine: they apparently did not anticipate that the swine would choose to destroy themselves and so they would lose another host. Now Jesus appears prophetic: by granting their request, he has secured the demons' cooperation in their own destruction.

2. What would the destruction of the swine have meant to Mark's early audiences?

   a. This detail would have been perceived as a funny departure from the gravity of a story of demonic possession (and, possibly, Jesus' initial inability to stop it) and the scorn of people wanting to cast out Jesus.

   b. A Jewish audience would presumably have been pleased at the destruction of the swine; in fact, the story can be read as the purification of the land. Jesus purifies the man and then the land.

3. What happened to the demons after the swine drowned?

   a. They were destroyed.

   b. They continued to exist, without a host, in the sea. This fits ancient beliefs that the sea was associated with chaos. In this reading, Jesus is presented as limiting—but not yet ending—threats to human flourishing. Similarly, Jesus calmed the sea in the last story, but the demons in the sea suggest that the sea will not remain calm. Compare the next story: he raises Jairus's daughter, but she will die again. The temporary or partial nature of Jesus' miracles (despite the fact that they provide real relief for the afflicted) speaks to the need for an atoning act.

   c. They had to leave the region (see 5:10) in order to find new hosts, which means that Jesus did not, despite initial appearances, grant their request to remain in the region.

4. Was Jesus responsible for the destruction of property? Some readers have expressed concern that Jesus was accountable for the destruction of very valuable property. Perhaps there is an implicit assessment that the man's freedom is worth more than two thousand swine, which would make an important point about human dignity and autonomy. It is also possible that the fact that Jesus merely gave permission to the demons (instead of casting them out himself) negates his responsibility for the destruction of property. Another possibility is that, because he was a Jew of the first century, Jesus regarded the destruction of the swine as a positive good.

Political Dimensions of the Story. There are many terms in this story with strong political overtones:

1. The primary meaning of the word "legion" is a group of five to six thousand Roman soldiers, so it is as if the demons self-identify as a unit of the Roman army. Given that the number in a legion is quite different from the number of

swine in the story, perhaps the audience is supposed to realize that "legion" is not meant to be read literally but rather is a deliberate allusion to Roman power.

2. In 5:10, "send" translates a Greek word with military connotations; it suggests the way that an officer would command troops when sending them out.[24]

3. Swine would not have been kept by faithful Jews, and a group this large was almost certainly the food supply for the army. Swine were also the symbol for the Tenth Roman Legion, who served in this area a few decades after Jesus' lifetime, which may have influenced how Mark's audience understood the story.

4. In 5:11, the swine are described as a "herd," but pigs are not herd animals. The word translated as herd "is also a local term for a band of trainees."[25]

5. In 5:13, "gave them leave" seems odd because Jesus appears to be giving them permission to do what they want, but the verb is used in other ancient writings for issuing a military command.

6. In 5:13, "ran violently" is "a natural [term] for troops rushing into battle."[26]

All of these words can also be used in nonmilitary contexts, but each also has the potential to be understood as a military term. The profusion does imply a military undercurrent to the story, especially the word "legion." Other military overtones are implied by the story as well:

1. Mark notes that no one could tame the man, even with fetters and chains, which represent the unsuccessful efforts to limit Roman power.

2. The confusion over whether it is the man or the demon who is speaking/acting at any given time reflects the difficulty of knowing if the people's speech/action reflects their authentic feelings or if they act to avoid causing trouble with their Roman overlords.

3. The demons' request not to be sent out of the region mirrors the Roman desire to remain within the region. In fact, this language works better on a symbolic level than a literal one since there is no reason to believe that the demons would prefer to live in one area rather than another.

4. The depiction of the demoniac in his occupied state is a picture of the effects of Roman rule, which is shown to be akin to a living death. The Romans possess the land in the same way that demons possess the body: their occupation caused "an atmosphere of living death"[27] for the colonized people.

---

24. J. Duncan M. Derrett, "Contributions to the Study of the Gerasene Demoniac," *Journal for the Study of the New Testament* 3 (1979): 5.

25. Derrett, "Contributions to the Study of the Gerasene Demoniac," 5.

26. Derrett, "Contributions to the Study of the Gerasene Demoniac," 5.

27.Waetjen, *Reordering of Power*, 115.

5. Reading the legion as a symbol for Rome makes the analogy to Exodus 14 tighter since the drowned swine parallel the drowned army (see "HB Allusions" after the Notes on 5:20).

6. The political imagery undergirding the parable of the mustard bush, growing to shade the birds/nations (4:30–32), primed the audience to find political nuance here and thus interpret this exorcism as a clash between the kingdom of God (exemplified in Jesus' authority) and Rome (exemplified by the demons' power).

7. Just as the story of the demon in the synagogue implied that the Jewish leadership was unclean and inaugurated Jesus' ministry in Jewish lands, the demon here implies that the Roman occupation is unclean and thus begins Jesus' ministry in gentile lands.

8. Jesus does not so much destroy the symbol of Rome as permits it to self-destruct. The story suggests that though it would have been possible for Jesus to destroy Roman power, he did not choose to do so.

The setting of the story leads the audience to think that the problem is the impurity of gentile lands, but the story pivots to show that the real problem is Roman occupation. Mark has grafted the horror of impurity onto attitudes toward the Roman occupation. Those who ask Jesus to leave in 5:17 assume the role of Roman sympathizers; they do not value the man's freedom above the potential for trouble caused by his exorcism.

5:14 *And they that fed the swine fled:* Mark does not introduce these characters until the narrative requires them to act, but presumably they have been present the entire time, or they would not have witnessed the event.

and told it in the city, and in the country. And they went out to see what it was that was done: The New Rendition uses "the people" instead of "they" to make clear that it is not the swine feeders, but the people whom they had told, who went out to see. The Greek text reads "they" here.

5:15 *And they come to Jesus, and see him that was possessed with the devil, and had the legion:* The phrase "had the legion" is not strictly necessary here since there is no chance that the audience would have confused him with some other healed demoniac, so the reference emphasizes that this man had been possessed but is no longer. It sets the stage for the rest of the verse to showcase his restoration.

sitting, and clothed, and in his right mind: The reference to clothing might imply that he was previously naked, although this was not specifically mentioned. It is not unreasonable to assume that if he wouldn't stay in chains, he wouldn't stay in clothing either.

and they were afraid: The verb translated as "were afraid" is the same verb used in 4:41 for the disciples' reaction to the stilling of the storm. But the fear/awe response leads to two different secondary responses: while the disciples wondered about Jesus' identity and stayed with him (5:1), these people want Jesus to leave. Thus, one of the characteristics of Jesus' disciples is that—in spite of their incomplete understanding of Jesus and his mission—they are willing to stay with him. This concept meshes well with Jesus' teaching that those who are physically near to him are his true family (3:31–35).

5:16 *And they that saw it told them how it befell to him that was possessed with the devil, and also concerning the swine:* The reference to the swine is emphasized, suggesting that they were more concerned about the economic and political consequences of the destruction of the animals than they were about the restoration of the man. This would explain their desire to remove Jesus in the next verse: they prioritize their financial and political peace over access to Jesus' miraculous powers.

5:17 *And they began to pray him to depart out of their coasts:* "They" refers not just to the eyewitnesses but to all of the people who hear about what happened. Ironically, they are more tolerant of the presence of the demons than they are of Jesus' presence.

At this point, these people are occupying the same narrative role that the demons did: both come to Jesus, both show fear, and both request that Jesus leave them alone—except Jesus willingly, silently agrees (as 5:18 implies) to the request of the people. They are, in effect, exorcising Jesus from their midst. Significantly, Jesus does not recognize the agency of the demons, but he does recognize the choice of the people who ask him to leave. He is not like the demons who force their presence where it is not wanted. Because of the power that Jesus has shown in this story, it is clear that Jesus leaves of his own volition and not because he has no choice. The next few verses may suggest that the healed demoniac will remain as Jesus' proxy in this region.[28]

In Jewish lands, Jesus was frequently opposed by the religious leadership, but ever-larger crowds continued to gather. In this first story in gentile lands, there are no thronging crowds; rather, the crowd wants him to leave—perhaps because of the Roman legal prohibitions against magic. The gentile people are less welcoming of Jesus than the Jewish people. The

---

28. Waetjen, *Reordering of Power,* 119.

fact that Jesus receives a much better reception in Jewish lands is an important counterweight to later strands of Christian anti-Semitism.

5:18 ***And when he was come into the ship, he that had been possessed with the devil prayed him that he might be with him:*** When Jesus called the Twelve (3:14), he used similar language ("to be with him") to describe their calling. The man is thus asking to do what the Twelve do.

This request to be with Jesus is the opposite of what the rest of the people want. Mark cleverly illustrates that, despite the former demoniac's previous state of extreme uncleanness, he has been so radically transformed by Jesus' power that he now—unlike everyone else around him—wants to be one of Jesus' closest followers. By contrast, those who heard of the exorcism want to be outsiders; they want Jesus far away from them. This inversion suggests that this is not just an exorcism or a condemnation of Roman rule but also a redemption story, showcasing the effect that Jesus' power had on a desperate man. Significantly, following Jesus is not something that is ever forced on someone: "neither in this [story] nor elsewhere does Christ's mastery take the form of a dominance exercised from inside a person; it relies on an imperative *addressed to* the person. It is a call to listen and to decide."[29]

5:19 ***Howbeit Jesus suffered him not, but saith unto him:*** Interestingly, in Mark's Gospel, those who are healed do not follow Jesus: "the tradition shows that Jesus never calls those who have already been marginalized by illness or possession. Instead, he instructs these individuals to return to society but calls those who have lived an integrated life within the community to leave all behind and live a relatively marginalized life with him."[30] Like the seed that produces of itself in the good ground (4:8, 20), this man does not need to "be with" Jesus. Jesus only needed to sow the seed and leave him be. By contrast, "the disciples, the rocky ground, demand continuous cultivation, if any positive growth at all is to result."[31]

Go home to thy friends: The word that the KJV translates as "friends" can refer to friends, family, or one's own people. While these meanings may be similar, the option chosen here determines whether the man is obedient or disobedient in 5:20:

---

29. Starobinski, "Essay in Literary Analysis: Mark 5:1–20," [394]; italics in original.

30. Teresa Calpino, "The Gerasene Demoniac (Mark 5:1–20): The Pre-Markan Function of the Pericope," *Biblical Research* 53 (January 2008): 23.

31. Tolbert, *Sowing the Gospel,* 168.

1. If the man was supposed to tell his family only, then the very limited scope of his audience meshes nicely with the other commands to secrecy in Mark's Gospel, especially since family members seem to be excluded from commands to secrecy (compare 5:40–43). In this reading, preaching throughout the Decapolis (see 5:20) means that he was disobedient. There may be an analogy here to 1:40–45, where the healed leper's proclamation (probably) indicates disobedience to Jesus' command.

2. If the man was supposed to tell "his own people," then that could include those throughout the Decapolis, if "his own people" refers to the Gentiles.

In either reading, this command indicates that Jesus has made it possible for the man to go home—he will no longer be condemned to a living death isolated among the tombs.

It is also possible that Jesus isn't denying the man's request so much as suggesting that he can do an even more important work at home than he could by following Jesus: he can be a personal, living testimony of Jesus' power to those who knew him when he was demon-possessed, as the next phrase suggests ("how great things the Lord hath done for thee"); he cannot do that if he travels across the sea where he is unknown. Mark's story suggests that discipleship will not and should not look the same for everyone.

While the man is denied permission to be with Jesus, he is commanded to engage in the other portion of the Twelve's assignment—to preach. Given that the people have just asked Jesus to leave, Jesus has given the man a rather difficult task.

and tell them how great things the Lord hath done for thee: This command is an important part of the picture of the man's redemption: he had previously been limited to inarticulate shrieks, but now he can preach the gospel.

Jesus has not yet sent the Twelve on a preaching mission (6:7–13; compare 3:14). They are still with Jesus (which was part of their assignment) but not yet prepared to fulfill the second half of their commission. So one way to read the former demoniac's story is that he requests the first part of the mission of the Twelve and is denied it but is instead commanded to complete the second part. This suggests that he is, at this point, more prepared to serve than the Twelve.

The use of "Lord" here may be significant: it identifies Jesus with the Lord.

Note: See also the section "Relationship to the Gerasene Demoniac" after the Notes on 16:5.

The Messianic Secret. This command from Jesus to announce the miracle seems to conflict with the frequent commands to secrecy found in the

Gospel (see appendix H: "The 'Messianic Secret' in Mark"). Options for reconciling this paradox include:

1. Because Jesus is in gentile lands, secrecy is not important. This might be because the secrecy commands exist to

   a. protect Jesus' ministry from premature interference by Jewish religious leaders.

   b. protect Jesus' ministry from huge crowds (which is not an issue in gentile lands, where he is asked to leave).

   c. ensure that, in Jewish lands where there were (partially) incorrect expectations for the coming Messiah, people understood that Jesus was not precisely what they were expecting. (In other words, had rumors of Jesus' miracle-working spread in Jewish lands, people might have seen him only as a miracle worker and not understood the other aspects of his mission.) In gentile lands, where there were no such messianic expectations, secrecy would not be an issue.

2. The man is given permission to discuss the healing with only his family, which is compatible with the general commands to secrecy found in other stories.

---

and hath had compassion on thee: While Jesus' compassion was not mentioned in the story of the exorcism, it is here highlighted as the main point of the story. This is an interesting guide to the audience: the focus of the story, from Jesus' perspective, is that the exorcism was an act of compassion towards the man.

5:20 *And he departed, and began to publish in Decapolis:* The Decapolis was a region of gentile cities; Jesus will return to this area in 7:31. There are two ways to interpret what is happening here:

1. The man was obedient to Jesus' command and thus began preaching to the Gentiles. If "Gadara" or "Gergesa" (both of which are part of the Decapolis) is the best reading in 5:1 (see the Notes on 5:1), then the man has not left his home area and thus doesn't violate Jesus' command. It is possible to view this man as the gentile equivalent of John the Baptist, going before the Lord to prepare the way for him. Given that the disciples in 1:16–20 are called immediately before an exorcism, it is also possible to see this man as a disciple sent to the Gentiles (but contrast 7:27). The man could be viewed as a faithful disciple who was assigned a very difficult task (especially given the attitude toward Jesus in this area, even on the part of those who have seen his miracles) and nonetheless completed it. He becomes the first to do a "reverse invasion" of the gentile lands—contra the Roman occupation that was symbolically removed in this exorcism—in the name of the kingdom of God.[32] In

---

32. Garroway, "Mustard Seed," 70.

this reading, the man's actions are viewed as a good thing, and Mark suggests that Jesus' ministry is not restricted solely to the Jews, even at this early stage.

2. The man was not obedient; his preaching was contrary to Jesus' wishes. If "Gergesa" is the best reading in 5:1, then the man is leaving his home area (as the phrase "he departed" in 5:20 indicates) and thus violating Jesus' command to preach only to his close friends/family. The man is akin to the leper in 1:40–45, who is also healed by Jesus, given a specific command related to what he is and is not permitted to say about his experience, and then apparently violates that command. The fact that he was supposed to preach about "the Lord" but preaches about "Jesus" also suggests that he isn't being obedient.

how great things Jesus had done for him: "Lord" from 5:19 becomes "Jesus" here. This is either evidence of the man's disobedience or evidence of the fact that he—unlike the Twelve—understands a good bit about Jesus' identity.

and all men did marvel: "All" is likely hyperbole since some people wanted Jesus to leave (5:17). It is not clear if they are marveling at the exorcism, the fate of the swine, or the man's preaching.

HB Allusions. There are several possible allusions to the HB in this story:

1. *Isaiah 65:1–7.* Isaiah 65:1 emphasizes that the Lord is accessible to all people: "I made myself available to those who did not ask for me" (NET). This detail may make sense of the reference to Jesus' desire to go to gentile lands (4:35), as well as the fact that, at the end of this story, the people want Jesus to leave. Allusion to the Isaiah text heightens Mark's emphasis on the idea that Jesus' ministry is for all people, not just the Jews. In 65:4, Isaiah mentions sitting in tombs and eating swine flesh, which are also key themes in 5:1–20. In Isaiah 65:5, the covenant people are trying to keep unclean people away from them, which is echoed in the unclean spirit coming to Jesus, the desire of the unclean spirits to stay in the region, and the desire of the healed demoniac to be with Jesus. It is possible that the Isaiah text is a subtle prophecy of 5:1–20; it is also possible that 5:1–20 was shaped with an eye toward echoing the Isaiah text. In either case, the association between the two passages emphasizes the alignment between Jesus and the God of the HB.

2. *Exodus 14:1–15:22.* The story of the Egyptian army drowning through miraculous means is mirrored in this story when the food supply for the Roman army (which is itself described in military terms) drowns; there are also multiple verbal allusions between the two stories. And perhaps the desire for Jesus to leave gentile lands reflects the complaints of the children of Israel in the wilderness: in both cases, the complainers prefer oppressive security to the unknown freedom that they have miraculously been granted. These similarities strengthen the political undertones of 5:1–20 and symbolically

align Rome with Egypt. The alignment between the two stories also suggests that Jesus is a Moses figure, leading his people to freedom through miraculous control of natural forces. Additionally, since the climax of the Exodus narrative is not the drowning of the troops but rather the faith and praise of the Lord that it engendered (Ex. 15:1–21), it shifts attention in the demoniac's story away from the drowning of the swine and towards the man's proclamation of what the Lord had done for him: the healed demoniac is cast into the role of Moses and Miriam as joyful proclaimers of the Lord's goodness.

3. *1 Samuel 16:14–23.* In this text, Saul is tormented by an evil spirit. David plays music to comfort him, which brings him relief. As an intertext, it places Jesus into David's role, with the ability to calm one with an evil spirit. The alignment of Jesus with David emphasizes Jesus' power and authority.

Analysis

Mark 4:35–5:20 can be read to show Jesus as the lone victor against a huge demonic host. In 4:36, the separation begins as Jesus and his disciples remove themselves from the crowds. Then, because Jesus and his disciples were in the boat but only Jesus is described as leaving the boat, Jesus is (at least symbolically) separated from his disciples, and thus Jesus is presented as fighting the demons alone.[33] While the text initially presents the demon as singular, the audience later learns that there are actually thousands of demons; now the lone Jesus is terribly outnumbered. Mark's careful composition serves to emphasize Jesus' power as the one conqueror of thousands of demons. This scene may serve as a precursor to Jesus' experience in Gethsemane, where he separates first from a larger group of disciples, and then from a smaller group, to suffer alone; in both cases, Jesus vanquishes evil entirely on his own, something the structure of the text emphasizes. The motif of separation also extends to the next healing stories, where the disciples (but not Jesus) have trouble understanding the difference between a single touch and the touch of a group (5:31) and where Jesus does not permit the mourners or most of the disciples—but does permit Peter, James,[34] John, and the girl's parents (5:40)—to witness the girl's raising from the dead.

The exorcism story draws much of its power from resonances to the Exodus story, Isaiah 65, and Roman military practices. Jesus' ministry in gentile lands makes him seem very tolerant of outsiders. But what he

---

33. Starobinski, "Essay in Literary Analysis: Mark 5:1–20," [387].
34. See the Notes on 1:19.

cannot and will not tolerate is some people being denied control of their body (that is, through demonic possession). And Jesus does not tolerate the demoniac as he is—rather, he changes him into a better version of himself.[35] In terms of the parables from the last chapter, Jesus is the sower, sending forth this single seed into the good soil (soil that is good because Jesus cleansed the land from demonic forces), and the former demoniac is the mustard seed that becomes the shelter of the nations—the people might have expected a mighty cedar, but the healed demoniac is the weedy bush bringing forth the kingdom of God.

This story may have been particularly important to Mark's audience because it showed Jesus interacting with Gentiles in gentile lands. Whether gentile converts would need to be Jews (that is, conform to Jewish custom and law) as well as Christians would be an important (and heated) issue for the early church. This story may have been interpreted to imply that Gentiles did not need to become Jews in order to become Christians, since the man is given a preaching task with no hint of conforming to Jewish law first.

Mark 1:21–28 features an exorcism in a synagogue; 5:1–20 concerns one in gentile lands. Both exorcisms follow the same pattern, with narrative markers (into/out of the synagogue, sea crossing, and return crossing), symbolism (synagogue, Gentile/unclean), implied leaders (scribes, Roman legion), a demon who names Jesus, Jesus issuing commands, the demon departing, and the reaction of the crowd.[36] Each also has a title given to Jesus that includes "of God" and that is uniquely appropriate to its religious setting. The fact that Jesus performs exorcisms before beginning a new phase of his ministry implies that Jesus must actively remove evil from the area before he can begin his work and that evil forces (correctly) perceived a threat from Jesus' ministry. The first thing that Jesus encounters when he extends his ministry to a new geographical area is demonic opposition; this is true in the synagogue as well as on gentile lands.

There may be some subtle foreshadowing of the story of Jesus' Resurrection here: both texts are set among tombs, both have fear as a theme, and both feature the possessed/dead man coming forth whole again, something the language emphasizes.[37] In both stories, the idea that what has happened is to be preached is strongly emphasized. If Mark wanted his audience to

---

35. Dowd, *Reading Mark,* 55.

36. Myers, *Binding the Strong Man,* 193.

37. Christopher Burdon, "'To the Other Side': Construction of Evil and Fear of Liberation in Mark 5.1–20," *Journal for the Study of the New Testament* 27, no. 2 (2004): 163.

think of the demoniac as a forerunner of Jesus, then Jesus is identified with an unclean, possessed, outcast gentile man. This would have been a powerful commentary on Jesus' humility and solidarity with all people.

See also the section "Relationship to the Gerasene Demoniac" after the Notes on 16:5.

JESUS HEALS A WOMAN AND RAISES A GIRL (5:21–43)

Greek Text

21 Καὶ διαπεράσαντος τοῦ Ἰησοῦ ἐν τῷ πλοίῳ πάλιν εἰς τὸ πέραν συνήχθη ὄχλος πολὺς ἐπ᾽ αὐτόν, καὶ ἦν παρὰ τὴν θάλασσαν. 22 καὶ ἔρχεται εἷς τῶν ἀρχισυναγώγων, ὀνόματι Ἰάϊρος, καὶ ἰδὼν αὐτὸν πίπτει πρὸς τοὺς πόδας αὐτοῦ 23 καὶ παρακαλεῖ αὐτὸν πολλὰ λέγων ὅτι Τὸ θυγάτριόν μου ἐσχάτως ἔχει, ἵνα ἐλθὼν ἐπιθῇς τὰς χεῖρας αὐτῇ ἵνα σωθῇ καὶ ζήσῃ. 24 καὶ ἀπῆλθεν μετ᾽ αὐτοῦ.

Καὶ ἠκολούθει αὐτῷ ὄχλος πολύς, καὶ συνέθλιβον αὐτόν. 25 καὶ γυνὴ οὖσα ἐν ῥύσει αἵματος δώδεκα ἔτη 26 καὶ πολλὰ παθοῦσα ὑπὸ πολλῶν ἰατρῶν καὶ δαπανήσασα τὰ παρ᾽ αὐτῆς πάντα καὶ μηδὲν ὠφεληθεῖσα ἀλλὰ μᾶλλον εἰς τὸ χεῖρον ἐλθοῦσα, 27 ἀκούσασα περὶ τοῦ Ἰησοῦ, ἐλθοῦσα ἐν τῷ ὄχλῳ ὄπισθεν ἥψατο τοῦ ἱματίου αὐτοῦ· 28 ἔλεγεν γὰρ ὅτι Ἐὰν ἅψωμαι κἂν τῶν ἱματίων αὐτοῦ σωθήσομαι. 29 καὶ εὐθὺς ἐξηράνθη ἡ πηγὴ τοῦ αἵματος αὐτῆς, καὶ ἔγνω τῷ σώματι ὅτι ἴαται ἀπὸ τῆς μάστιγος. 30 καὶ εὐθὺς ὁ Ἰησοῦς ἐπιγνοὺς ἐν ἑαυτῷ τὴν ἐξ αὐτοῦ δύναμιν ἐξελθοῦσαν ἐπιστραφεὶς ἐν τῷ ὄχλῳ ἔλεγεν· Τίς μου ἥψατο τῶν ἱματίων; 31 καὶ ἔλεγον αὐτῷ οἱ μαθηταὶ αὐτοῦ· Βλέπεις τὸν ὄχλον συνθλίβοντά σε, καὶ λέγεις· Τίς μου ἥψατο; 32 καὶ περιεβλέπετο ἰδεῖν τὴν τοῦτο ποιήσασαν. 33 ἡ δὲ γυνὴ φοβηθεῖσα καὶ τρέμουσα, εἰδυῖα ὃ γέγονεν αὐτῇ, ἦλθεν καὶ προσέπεσεν αὐτῷ καὶ εἶπεν αὐτῷ πᾶσαν τὴν ἀλήθειαν. 34 ὁ δὲ εἶπεν αὐτῇ· Θυγάτηρ, ἡ πίστις σου σέσωκέν σε· ὕπαγε εἰς εἰρήνην, καὶ ἴσθι ὑγιὴς ἀπὸ τῆς μάστιγός σου.

35 Ἔτι αὐτοῦ λαλοῦντος ἔρχονται ἀπὸ τοῦ ἀρχισυναγώγου λέγοντες ὅτι Ἡ θυγάτηρ σου ἀπέθανεν· τί ἔτι σκύλλεις τὸν διδάσκαλον; 36 ὁ δὲ Ἰησοῦς παρακούσας τὸν λόγον λαλούμενον λέγει τῷ ἀρχισυναγώγῳ· Μὴ φοβοῦ, μόνον πίστευε. 37 καὶ οὐκ ἀφῆκεν οὐδένα μετ᾽ αὐτοῦ συνακολουθῆσαι εἰ μὴ τὸν Πέτρον καὶ Ἰάκωβον καὶ Ἰωάννην τὸν ἀδελφὸν Ἰακώβου. 38 καὶ ἔρχονται εἰς τὸν οἶκον τοῦ ἀρχισυναγώγου, καὶ θεωρεῖ θόρυβον καὶ κλαίοντας καὶ ἀλαλάζοντας πολλά, 39 καὶ εἰσελθὼν λέγει αὐτοῖς· Τί θορυβεῖσθε καὶ κλαίετε; τὸ παιδίον οὐκ ἀπέθανεν ἀλλὰ καθεύδει. 40 καὶ κατεγέλων αὐτοῦ. αὐτὸς δὲ ἐκβαλὼν πάντας παραλαμβάνει τὸν πατέρα τοῦ παιδίου καὶ τὴν μητέρα καὶ τοὺς μετ᾽ αὐτοῦ, καὶ εἰσπορεύεται ὅπου ἦν τὸ παιδίον· 41 καὶ κρατήσας τῆς χειρὸς τοῦ παιδίου λέγει αὐτῇ· Ταλιθα κουμ, ὅ ἐστιν μεθερμηνευόμενον· Τὸ κοράσιον, σοὶ λέγω, ἔγειρε. 42 καὶ εὐθὺς ἀνέστη

τὸ κοράσιον καὶ περιεπάτει, ἦν γὰρ ἐτῶν δώδεκα. καὶ ἐξέστησαν εὐθὺς ἐκστάσει μεγάλῃ. 43 καὶ διεστείλατο αὐτοῖς πολλὰ ἵνα μηδεὶς γνοῖ τοῦτο, καὶ εἶπεν δοθῆναι αὐτῇ φαγεῖν. [SBLGNT]

King James Version

21 And when Jesus was passed over again by ship unto the other side, much people gathered unto him: and he was nigh unto the sea. 22 And, behold, there cometh one of the rulers of the synagogue, Jairus by name; and when he saw him, he fell at his feet, 23 And besought him greatly, saying, My little daughter lieth at the point of death: I pray thee, come and lay thy hands on her, that she may be healed; and she shall live. 24 And Jesus went with him; and much people followed him, and thronged him. 25 And a certain woman, which had an issue of blood twelve years, 26 And had suffered many things of many physicians, and had spent all that she had, and was nothing bettered, but rather grew worse, 27 When she had heard of Jesus, came in the press behind, and touched his garment. 28 For she said, If I may touch but his clothes, I shall be whole. 29 And straightway the fountain of her blood was dried up; and she felt in her body that she was healed of that plague. 30 And Jesus, immediately knowing in himself that virtue had gone out of him, turned him about in the press, and said, Who touched my clothes? 31 And his disciples said unto him, Thou seest the multitude thronging thee, and say-est thou, Who touched me? 32 And he looked round about to see her that had done this thing. 33 But the woman fearing and trembling, knowing what was done in her, came and fell down

New Rendition

21 And Jesus having crossed over in the boat again to the other side, a great crowd was gathered to him, and he was by the sea. 22 And one of the synagogue leaders, named Jairus, comes and, hav-ing seen him, falls at his feet. 23 And he begged him urgently, saying, "My little daughter is about to die. Come, place hands on her so that she may be cured/ saved and live." 24 And he went with him.

And a large crowd followed him and clustered around him. 25 And a woman having a flow of blood for twelve years, 26 suffering many things under many doctors, spending all that she had, not improving, but getting worse, 27 hear-ing stories about Jesus, and coming after him in the crowd, touched his clothes. 28 For she said, "If I should touch even just his clothes, I shall be cured/saved." 29 And immediately her flow of blood was dried up, and she knew in her body that she had been healed of her ill-ness. 30 Jesus, having known in himself immediately that power had gone out of him, having turned to the crowd, said, "Who touched my clothes?" 31 And his disciples said to him, "You see the crowd clustered around you, and yet you say, 'Who touched me?'" 32 And he looked around to see who had done this. 33 And the woman, having been frightened and trembling, knowing what had been done to her, came and fell down in front of him and told him the whole truth. 34 And he said to her, "Daughter, your trust has cured/saved

before him, and told him all the truth. 34 And he said unto her, Daughter, thy faith hath made thee whole; go in peace, and be whole of thy plague. 35 While he yet spake, there came from the ruler of the synagogue's house certain which said, Thy daughter is dead: why troublest thou the Master any further? 36 As soon as Jesus heard the word that was spoken, he saith unto the ruler of the synagogue, Be not afraid, only believe. 37 And he suffered no man to follow him, save Peter, and James, and John the brother of James. 38 And he cometh to the house of the ruler of the synagogue, and seeth the tumult, and them that wept and wailed greatly. 39 And when he was come in, he saith unto them, Why make ye this ado, and weep? the damsel is not dead, but sleepeth. 40 And they laughed him to scorn. But when he had put them all out, he taketh the father and the mother of the damsel, and them that were with him, and entereth in where the damsel was lying. 41 And he took the damsel by the hand, and said unto her, Talitha cumi; which is, being interpreted, Damsel, I say unto thee, arise. 42 And straightway the damsel arose, and walked; for she was of the age of twelve years. And they were astonished with a great astonishment. 43 And he charged them straitly that no man should know it; and commanded that something should be given her to eat.

you. Go in peace, and be whole from your disease."

35 While he was speaking, people come from the synagogue leader's house, saying, "Your daughter is dead. Why are you still bothering the teacher?" 36 And Jesus, ignoring/overhearing what was said, says to the synagogue leader, "Don't fear—only trust." 37 And he allowed no one to follow him, except for Peter, Jacob, and John, the brother of Jacob. 38 And they come to the synagogue ruler's house, and he sees a commotion and people crying and lamenting loudly. 39 And having entered the house, he says to them, "Why are you making this commotion and crying? The child is not dead but sleeps." 40 And they were laughing at him. But he threw them all outside, keeping with him the father of the child and the mother and those with him, and he enters into where the child was. 41 And having taken the child's hand, he says to her, "Talitha koum," which is translated, "Young girl, I say to you: stand up!" 42 And immediately the girl stood up and walked, for she was twelve years old. And immediately they were amazed with great amazement. 43 And he sternly directed them that no one should know about this. And he told them to give her something to eat.

Notes

5:21 *And when Jesus was passed over again by ship unto the other side, much people gathered unto him: and he was nigh unto the sea:* Jesus has returned to Jewish lands (compare 4:35).

5:22 *And, behold, there cometh one of the rulers of the synagogue:* The word "behold" was probably not in the earliest manuscripts and may have been added later to parallel Matthew 9:18 and Luke 8:41.[38] Given that "behold" is usually reserved in Mark's Gospel for crucial events (compare 1:2; 10:33), it should probably be omitted here.

Little is known about synagogue organization at this point in history, but presumably Jairus would have had some responsibility for the facility and for the worship service. There are two options for understanding Jairus's role:

1. Each synagogue had multiple rulers; Acts 13:15 might suggest this. Thus, Jairus is one of several people who lead this synagogue.

2. Each synagogue had one ruler; Jairus is the ruler of this particular synagogue.

Either way, the construction "one of the" draws attention to the fact that this entire class of people was not opposed to Jesus. (Inversely, calling Judas "one of the Twelve" in 14:10 and 43 does similar work.)

Jairus by name: A few ancient manuscripts omit this phrase, but the majority of manuscripts include it;[39] it probably dropped out accidentally. However, it is quite unusual to have a proper name in a healing miracle. It is generally accepted that names were added to the tradition later as stories were transmitted, but it is also possible that the name was included because

1. Jairus was known to the first audience (perhaps he or his daughter became disciples of Jesus?).

2. "Jairus" can mean "he awakens/arouses" or "he will enlighten," which suggests an ironic wordplay with the events of the story, since not he but Jesus will awaken his daughter.

and when he saw him, he fell at his feet: The reference to seeing (KJV: "saw"), which is unnecessary on a literal level, may suggest that he is one of the few Jewish leaders—one of the few of all people—who perceived who Jesus really was.

5:23 *And besought him greatly, saying, My little daughter lieth at the point of death:* "Little daughter" translates the diminutive form for "daughter" and shows affection. It is noteworthy that he cares so much about the life of a child, particularly a female child. (A less sympathetic view is that Jairus is afraid that if his daughter dies, others will interpret it as God's judgment against him.)

I pray thee, come and lay thy hands on her: Laying on of hands for healing was common in the ancient world, but, except in 2 Kings 5:11, the

---

38. Collins, *Mark,* 274 note c.
39. Comfort, *New Testament Text and Translation Commentary,* 111.

practice was not used for healing—only for blessings and ordinations—in the HB.

that she may be healed: The word "healed" can mean healed or saved. In this context, it almost certainly means healed, but the New Rendition indicates both possibilities to call attention to the fact that this same verb is used in the story of the bleeding woman, where its meaning is more ambiguous.

and she shall live: "Healed" and "lived" may be two ways of expressing the same thing, or they could imply two different things ("lived" may point to how very young she is and that she has not yet really begun to live).

5:24 *And Jesus went with him; and much people followed him, and thronged him:* Jesus silently follows; this shows humility on Jesus' part.

It is, unfortunately, common for some readers to interpret the Gospels as critical of the Jews. But note the relationship here between a Jewish leader and Jesus, especially in contrast to the reception Jesus just received in gentile lands: in both stories, Jesus silently accedes to the requests (to leave, to follow) made of him, which enhances the association between the two stories, sharpens the contrast between the two receptions, and teaches that global denunciation of Jews is not an accurate reading of the text.

5:25 *And a certain woman, which had an issue of blood twelve years:* "An issue of blood" refers to unceasing menstruation (a small minority of scholars think it could be other bleeding[40]), which would have made her ritually unclean and seriously restricted her ability to interact with other people (Lev. 15:19–30).

5:26 *And had suffered many things of many physicians:* In Greek and in the KJV, the word "many" appears twice in this verse and emphasizes her suffering.

and had spent all that she had: Only the well-off would have been able to afford the services of physicians, so the woman had been wealthy but became poor due to her illness. The emphasis on money heightens, by way of contrast, the fact that she will not pay Jesus for healing her.

and was nothing bettered, but rather grew worse: The medical intervention actually made her condition worse.

5:27 *When she had heard of Jesus:* Mark's phrasing here might link to the parable of the sower in 4:3–20, where the emphasis was on hearing. It seems that this woman has never been in Jesus' presence but is reacting to what she has heard about him.

---

40. Lane, *Gospel according to Mark,* 191.

came in the press behind: The Greek word translated as "behind" is the same word as "after" from 1:17, used when Jesus invites the disciples to follow him, perhaps suggesting (at least symbolically) that the woman is acting like a disciple.

and touched his garment: This touch should have made Jesus ritually unclean; the fact that it does not (or that he is not concerned about it if it does) is a commentary about Jesus' relationship to the law of Moses.

Many readers, including most artists, imagine the woman kneeling; this is unlikely to have been the case since she would not have been able to catch up to Jesus to touch him and may have been trampled by the crowd.[41] She is probably walking and, therefore, would have touched him on the shoulder, arm, or back.[42]

"Touched" is the main verb in a sentence that extends from 5:25 through 5:27. The sentence has seven consecutive participles (*"had* an issue of blood," *"had suffered* many things," *"had spent," "was* nothing better," *"grew* worse," *"heard,"* and *"came* in the press" [italics added]). This sentence structure would be unusual in any circumstance but is particularly so in Mark, given his penchant for extremely simple sentences joined by the conjunction "and." So this description of the woman has a pronounced effect on the audience partially because it is so rare in this text. By stretching the sentence out in an almost unendurable way, it mirrors the lengthy suffering of the woman and also builds suspense for the audience. The woman's touch becomes an enormous release of pent-up feeling, serving as the perfect metaphor for her situation as all of her suffering and faith is concentrated on touching Jesus. It also invites Mark's audience to enter into the perspective of the bleeding woman and to see the touch as the culmination of everything that she has endured. For the audience, it is almost painful to read this long, drawn-out account when they are already waiting for Jesus to heal a little girl who is at the very brink of death.

5:28 *For she said, If I may touch but his clothes, I shall be whole:* Mark gives access to the woman's thoughts in this explanatory clause. Presumably, she said this to herself: because she was trying to avoid attention from the crowd, she would not have spoken out loud. Similarly, she likely adopted this secretive approach of touching his clothes without drawing

---

41. Richard W. Swanson, "Moving Bodies and Translating Scripture: Interpretation and Incarnation," *Word & World* 31 (Summer 2011): 273.

42. Readers may be interpreting Mark under the influence of Luke 8:44, where the woman touches the edge of Jesus' hem, but this is not how Mark tells the story.

any attention to herself for fear of trouble stemming from violating the norms for male-female relationships, disturbing Jesus, making him (and the crowd) unclean, or calling attention to herself, an outcast.

While unusual to most modern readers, several ideas may have contributed to her belief that touching Jesus' clothing could heal her:

1. In the HB, a holy person's body could have special powers (Ex. 17:11–12; 2 Kgs. 13:20–21), so it might be assumed that contact with the clothing of someone who was even greater than a prophet could heal. In this reading, the woman recognizes Jesus' elevated status; her recognition is quite rare at this point in the Gospel (compare 6:1–6).

2. If 1:10 is interpreted to suggest that Jesus was "clothed" by the Spirit, then she is trying to access the power of the Spirit that Jesus possesses,[43] and it was not unreasonable to think that she could access that power through his clothing.

3. The reference to "healing in his wings" in Malachi 4:2 was sometimes interpreted so that clothing stood in for the wings.[44] Further, while Mark does *not* refer to the hem of Jesus' garment here (compare 6:56 and Luke 8:44), some Jews conceptualized the fringes required by Numbers 15:38 as being like feathery edges; LXX Numbers 15:38 uses the same word for "fringes" as LXX Malachi 3:20 (KJV Malachi 4:2) uses for "wings," which would have strengthened the connection between the two concepts in the minds of Greek-speaking Jews. Thus a belief in the ability of healing to come through clothing would have been a reasonable conclusion.

4. Under the law of Moses, it was possible to become unclean as a result of touching the chair or bedding of a person who was experiencing certain types of uncleanness (Lev. 15:26–27), so it is not too far-fetched for the woman to think that touching clothing would, inversely, make her clean.

Whatever its origin, she is not alone in her belief that touching Jesus' clothes might lead to healing (see 6:56). Writing from a Latter-day Saint perspective, Mark Alan Wright argues that revelation occurs in culturally appropriate and anticipated ways.[45] So if the woman expected that touching Jesus' clothing would heal her, perhaps then it could. (See also the Notes on 5:34, which may reflect Jesus' correction of the woman's understanding.)

---

43. Miller, *Women in Mark's Gospel*, 59.

44. J. Duncan M. Derrett, "Mark's Technique: The Haemorrhaging Woman and Jairus' Daughter," *Biblica* 63, no. 4 (1982): 476.

45. Mark Alan Wright, "'According to Their Language, unto Their Understanding': The Cultural Context of Hierophanies and Theophanies in Latter-day Saint Canon," *Studies in the Bible and Antiquity* 3 (2011): 51–65.

Relationship to Zechariah 8:23. Zechariah 8:23 describes a future time when people will "take hold of the skirt of him that is a Jew, saying, We will go with you: for we have heard that God is with you." It is possible that this text pictures the actions of the bleeding woman; it would perhaps explain the nature of her faith if she thought that God was with Jesus. It also explains the curious detail that she touched Jesus' clothing.

5:29 *And straightway the fountain of her blood was dried up:* LXX Leviticus 12:7, which sets out the rules pertaining to the purification of a woman after childbirth, uses the same wording for "the fountain of her blood," which strengthens the case that this is gynecological bleeding and that it had made her ritually unclean.

and she felt in her body that she was healed of that plague: "Healed" does not translate the same Greek word as is used in either 5:28 or 5:34. It is possible that Mark varies the wording for stylistic reasons, but it is also possible that, despite the fact that her blood has stopped flowing, she has not been entirely cured/saved, something that will only come later as a result of her bold interaction with Jesus.[46] If this is the case, touching Jesus' hem was actually not enough to cure/save the woman, although it was sufficient to stop the flow of her blood; the woman had not only a flow of blood that needed healing but also a false belief in her unworthiness to merit Jesus' attention, which needed to be addressed before she could be completely cured/saved.

5:30 *And Jesus, immediately knowing in himself:* There is a parallel between the woman's body and Jesus' body: they both know immediately within themselves that something significant has happened as a result of her touch.

that virtue had gone out of him: The word "virtue" is misleading to modern English speakers; the Greek word here means "power." (The same Greek word is translated as "mighty works" in 6:2.) Mark notes that power went out of Jesus, not out of his clothes. This detail may be important to avoiding the misunderstanding that Jesus' clothing had magical powers.

Joseph Smith commented on the idea of virtue going out of Jesus in this story: "The virtue here referred to, is the spirit of life, and a man who exercises great faith in administering to the sick, blessing little children,

---

46. Frederick J. Gaiser, "In Touch with Jesus: Healing in Mark 5:21–43," *Word & World* 30 (Winter 2010): 8.

344 The Gospel according to Mark

or confirming, is liable to become weakened."[47] Joseph Smith taught this after a situation where he became "pale and [lost] strength" after performing a healing, which suggests that physical exhaustion can be the result of exercising spiritual power. Perhaps Jesus' awareness that power had gone out of him was tied to an awareness of his own physical depletion. Further, it is reasonable to think that the bleeding woman would have had anemia-like symptoms herself and would therefore have been pale and had little strength. Mark does not mention any of this, but one might speculate that the woman became physically more vigorous at precisely the same moment when Jesus became less so. This would be another instance where the woman's body and Jesus' body are paralleled; it perhaps also serves as a foreshadowing of the Atonement, where Jesus' body would experience the pains and sins of all other human bodies.[48]

turned him about in the press: Turning indicates that Jesus knew that the person who had intentionally touched him was behind him.

and said, Who touched my clothes?: A Jewish audience may have thought that Jesus wanted to know who had touched him so that she could be rebuked for transmitting impurity. The fact that the story plays out very differently would have surprised the audience.

Mark has described Jesus walking with people crowded around him; the disciples will soon wonder how Jesus can possibly ask who touched him under those circumstances. But his question shows that the bleeding woman's touch was in some way different from the touches of all the other people in the crowd. Thus it is not the case that simply touching Jesus' clothing was enough to prompt a miracle; healing also required real intent and faith. People could see without seeing, hear without hearing, and touch without touching.

Does Jesus know the answer to this question before he asks it?

1. Yes. The question was not posed to increase Jesus' knowledge but rather to invite the woman to come forward. One weakness of this reading is that asking a question to which he already knows the answer could be considered deceptive.

47. "History, 1838–1856, Volume D-1 [1 August 1842–1 July 1843]," 1497, Church History Library, available online at Church Historian's Press, *The Joseph Smith Papers,* http:// www.josephsmithpapers.org/paper-summary/history-1838-1856-volume-d-1-1-august -1842-1-july-1843/140.

48. Julie M. Smith, "A Redemptive Reading of Mark 5:25–34," *Interpreter: A Journal of Mormon Scripture* 14 (2015): 102.

2. No. Jesus asks because he does not know the answer to the question. This reading raises interesting questions about the limitations of Jesus' mortal experience: if he did not know the answer to the question, then he is not omniscient. At the same time, the fact that Jesus was able to distinguish her intentional touch from the general press of the crowd (which the disciples were not able to do) points to his miraculous powers. Latter-day Saint readers may be particularly well equipped for understanding what happens here: in modern Latter-day Saint thought, those who exercise priesthood power are viewed as conduits, not controllers, of God's power. This story illustrates that point with an extreme case: not only was Jesus a conduit, but he could be so without even being aware of it. The power here is God's, and presumably it was exercised with God's knowledge and permission, if not Jesus'.

If this were merely a healing story, then 5:30–34 is entirely unnecessary since the woman has already been healed. The inclusion of Jesus' question, the disciples' question, the woman's response, and Jesus' response indicates that there is something in addition to Jesus' ability to heal that Mark wants to explore in this story.

5:31 *And his disciples said unto him, Thou seest the multitude thronging thee, and sayest thou, Who touched me? 32 And he looked round about to see her that had done this thing:* Jesus does not respond to the disciples' question. Their question may have been a moment of humor in this intense story.

The woman's presence in the jostling crowd has, under the law of Moses, made all of them unclean. The fact that they do not realize this stands as a subtle commentary on the limits of the law.[49]

5:33 *But the woman fearing and trembling:* There are several possible explanations for her fear and trembling:

1. She fears Jesus' wrath for having used his power without his knowledge or consent.

2. She fears that the crowd will be angry with her for rendering them unclean.

3. In the HB, fearing and trembling are the classic reactions to the presence of the divine (Ex. 15:16), so her response is based on her understanding of Jesus' identity.

knowing what was done in her, came and fell down before him: "Came" carries the connotation of "came back," implying that she had already been leaving; in her mind, the encounter with Jesus was over and she was

---

49. Such accidental defilement is acknowledged in the law of Moses and is resolved by means of the trespass offering; see especially Lev. 5–6.

proceeding on her way. But like the lamp in the parable (4:21–22), the woman and the miracle that has been performed must not be hidden.

and told him all the truth: The phrase "the whole truth" often occurs in legal contexts.[50] Presumably, the truth the woman spoke includes her internal thoughts ("if I may touch but his clothes") as well as the fact that she instantly knew "in her body" that she had been healed. The whole story would have been, under then-current cultural norms, enormously embarrassing for her to relate and for the crowd to listen to. But Jesus has deemed it acceptable for her to discuss her thoughts, her medical condition, and her body in a very public setting.

In many other healing stories, the healed person engages in some form of ministry after the healing (1:31; 5:19–20). It is possible to read the woman's confession as a testimony or a proclamation following her miracle. Rather than commanding silence, Jesus has in this case solicited her story.

This verse explains the presence of some of the personal details found in this story—particularly the woman's internal thoughts and her awareness of what is happening within her body. Presumably, she shared these while telling "all the truth"; otherwise, they would have been unknown to Mark (or a source).

5:34 ***And he said unto her, Daughter:*** Mark had introduced the woman by calling her a woman with "an issue of blood." She had no name, no relationships, no geographical location; her disease is the sole marker of her identity. But in this verse, Jesus gives her a new identity marker: she is his daughter, a term implying a close relationship between the two of them. This title is not bestowed after the healing but after her act of bravery in describing her personal situation to a (potentially hostile) crowd.

The appellation "daughter" echoes 2:5 (when Jesus called the lame man his "son") and 3:31–35 (where Jesus claimed not his biological kin but rather those who listened to him as his family). Jesus here recognizes this woman as part of his new family.

thy faith hath made thee whole: The Greek verb translated as "made . . . whole" has three possible meanings here:

1. Cured, referring to physical healing. This is possible but perhaps odd for Jesus to announce at this point since she had been cured in 5:29.

2. Saved, in the sense of spiritual salvation. It is possible that the woman receives physical healing as a result of touching Jesus and spiritual salvation as a result of responding to Jesus' invitation to speak boldly of her healing before the

---

50. Miller, *Women in Mark's Gospel*, 66.

crowd. The story may be an enacted parable, showing the woman seeking salvation from Jesus and being granted it when she confesses the effect that Jesus has had on her life.

3. The word could be deliberately ambiguous with possible connotations of both physical and spiritual healing.

The recognition of the woman's faith by Jesus is particularly significant, given that the last reference to faith in the text was in the context of Jesus criticizing the disciples for their lack of faith (4:40).

In 5:28, the woman thought that if she touched Jesus, she would be saved/cured. Here, Jesus tells her that her faith has saved/cured her. This statement from Jesus affirms the woman's thought process and validates her belief in him. It may also reinterpret the woman's touch as evidence of faith so that there is no confusion on the part of the audience as to whether Jesus' clothing itself had magical properties.

Also, Jesus points to her faith—not his power—as the source of her healing. He does not castigate the woman for spreading impurity by touching him. If the crowd expected Jesus to chastise her but he instead applauds her faith, this is a substantial violation of their expectations. One element of the woman's faith that Jesus is praising here may have been her awareness that Jesus' relationship to the law of Moses was not that of the average person: her willingness to touch him signaled her faith that the touch would not make him unclean.

go in peace: This is "a Jewish mode of saying farewell."[51]

Relationship to 1 Samuel 1. There are some compelling parallels between this story and 1 Samuel 1: both feature a woman who suffers from a problem with her reproductive system (bleeding in this story and infertility in Hannah's) who approaches a male religious leader and speaks boldly of her problem and who is then told to "go in peace" (1 Sam. 1:17). At the same time, the characterization of Eli could not be worse, creating a strong contrast between his behavior and Jesus', which serves to emphasize Jesus' goodness in this story.

and be whole of thy plague: Given that the woman's healing was previously narrated, it is not obvious what work this line is doing. Options include:

1. It reinforces the healing that has already happened.
2. It indicates that there is more to "being whole" than being physically healed: it is her willingness to speak boldly in public that has led to her being made whole. Part of her illness was the resulting social marginalization; here, Jesus

---

51. Bratcher and Nida, *Translator's Handbook,* 176.

restores her to, literally, the center of society as she commands the attention of the entire group and speaks in front of them.

3. It is an assurance that the healing is permanent.

4. It makes clear that the use of Jesus' power was accompanied by his permission (if only after the fact).

5. "Go in peace" was a Jewish blessing and "be whole" a Hellenistic one, so Jesus combines the two to convey a universal approach.[52]

6. In Leviticus 15, there is a seven-day gap between the end of bleeding and the pronouncing of cleanness. By deeming the woman whole, Jesus has made the process instantaneous as well as indicated his authority over the law of Moses.

Relationship to Genesis 3. There are significant parallels between the story of the hemorrhaging woman and the Fall (Gen. 3). The stories share a dozen terms,[53] and the same theme, if not the same wording, is found in several other instances. Both passages refer to clothing, hiding, walking, becoming aware, seeing/looking, and children/daughters. But more significant than the verbal overlap are the thematic associations:

1. There are several ways in which the bleeding woman is associated with Eve. First, her condition of ceaseless menstrual bleeding is a magnification of the normal female condition. In some strains of Jewish thought, menstruation was associated with Eve's sin, and it was thought that it would not occur in the age to come. Menstruation was also associated with sin in general (Lam. 1:17; Ezek. 36:17–18). All of these associations serve to make the bleeding woman in this story the ideal narrative re-creation of Eve in her fallen state.

2. In both stories, the thought process behind the woman's decision-making is preserved; the audience knows what the woman is thinking as she takes the initiative to act in a difficult situation. This is even more significant given how rare records of women's thinking are in scripture.

3. Both stories feature a transgressive touch: Eve is not supposed to touch the fruit; the woman is not supposed to touch Jesus. Just as Eve's touch leads ultimately to death, the bleeding woman's touch leads to death by causing

---

52. Vernon K. Robbins, "The Woman Who Touched Jesus' Garment: Socio-Rhetorical Analysis of the Synoptic Accounts," *New Testament Studies* 33, no. 4 (1987): 510.

53. Shared vocabulary between chapter 5 and LXX Genesis includes the words "woman" (5:25 and LXX Gen. 3:1), "all" (5:26 and LXX Gen. 3:1), "heard" (5:27 and LXX Gen. 3:8), "know/realize" (5:29, 33 and LXX Gen. 3:5), "knowing" (5:30 and LXX Gen. 3:5), "touch" (5:28, 30, 31 and LXX Gen. 3:3), "see" (5:32 and LXX Gen. 3:6), "done" (5:32 and LXX Gen. 3:13), "fear" (5:33 and LXX Gen. 3:10), "told" (5:33 and LXX Gen. 3:13), and "said" (5:34 and LXX Gen. 3:16).

a delay that permits the girl to die. Mark's story highlights the fact that the woman's touch was unique—distinct from all of the other touches of the crowd—and thus worthy of comment from Jesus. It parallels Eve's touch, which led to unique consequences and similarly ushered in death. Because the bleeding woman is most likely standing, it is possible that she touches Jesus' side, or ribs. While speculative, this would be another point of contact with the Genesis text and suggest her role as Eve—in this case, reestablishing contact with the source of her creation. In both stories, the transgressive touch changes the nature of the women's bodies. The touching/eating in the garden passed along the contagion of sin and death to Adam. In this story, the woman should convey impurity to Jesus, but that is precisely the opposite of what happens.

4. In the garden, as recorded in the Genesis text, Adam is passive. In the bleeding woman's story, Jesus is also passive. Mark's audience assumes that Jesus will be filling the role of Adam when the stories are compared because Jesus' otherwise puzzling passivity emphasizes the association. However, when Jesus becomes the interlocutor and the pronouncer of a blessing (instead of the expected curse), it becomes clear that he is no longer filling the role of Adam but rather the role of God since in the garden it is God who asks the questions and pronounces the curses. Similar to the stilling of the storm, Mark began by encouraging the audience to think of Jesus in the role of Adam but then abruptly shifted so that Jesus was in the role of God. While modern approaches to the story of the Fall tend to interpret Adam and Eve as "every(wo)man," there are other approaches to the text, including the ancient reading that views Adam as a symbol for Christ and Eve as a symbol for the Church.[54] So it makes good sense for Jesus to take on the role of Adam as the bleeding woman reprises the role of Eve.

5. In both stories, after the transgressive touch, the woman hides from the divine presence until summoned by a question.

6. In both stories, the woman is questioned about her behavior. In the garden, God asks whether Eve has eaten; here, Jesus asks who has touched him.

7. In the Fall, when Adam is questioned, he blames Eve; when Eve is questioned, she blames the serpent. There is a pattern of avoiding responsibility by blaming others. In contrast, the bleeding woman told the whole truth when she was questioned. This difference between the two texts is very significant because it shows that this time, "Eve" (in the role of the bleeding woman) took complete responsibility for her own actions, and this is what, in terms of the narrative, results in Jesus claiming her as a daughter.

---

54. Julie M. Smith, "Paradoxes in Paradise," in *Fleeing the Garden: Reading Genesis 2–3,* ed. Adam S. Miller, Proceedings of the Mormon Theology Seminar (Provo, Utah: Neal A. Maxwell Institute for Religious Scholarship, 2017), 24–26 and n. 88.

8. The story of the Fall ends with serious consequences and curses; Mark's story ends with a blessing ("go in peace"). This shift highlights Mark's point in comparing the stories: the comparison highlights the idea of motif inversion. This time, the story is set to rights, largely through the person of Jesus. The curse was menstruation as a symbol of identification with Eve and with sin, but it is now gone. Peace is the inversion of the enmity with Satan.

9. In both stories, the focus of the passage is on the consequences of the woman's actions. But whereas Eve's choice to touch resulted in her separation from God, the bleeding woman's choice to touch resulted in her communion with Jesus and acceptance as his daughter. Because the Fall happened at the initiative of a woman, it is important in this story of redemption from the Fall that the corrective also occurs under the initiative of a woman. In other words, one of the things redeemed in this story is woman's initiative.

10. In Mark, the wording suggests that the woman came back when questioned, implying that she had already moved on. She had left Jesus' presence, analogous to leaving the garden and the presence of God. In other words, Jesus invited the now-healed woman back into his presence. This is in contrast to the story of Eve, where she is cast out from the presence of the Lord for her action.

11. Because of the association of menstruation with sin (and thus a fallen state), the bleeding woman is redeemed from her fallen state by Jesus' actions. When Jesus says that her faith has cured/saved her, this symbolizes being saved from the effects of the Fall. One of the consequences of the Fall is that Adam's body will eventually return to dust (Gen. 3:19). Jesus is the first person to whom this does not apply. In other words, Adam's curse ends with him. (This is true for Jesus in other ways as well: as the upcoming feeding miracles will show, he has ways other than by the sweat of his brow to acquire bread.) So it makes sense that in this story, Eve's curse will end with the woman. The fact that the curses end in both of them meshes well with the parallels between the woman's body and Jesus' body.

12. One of the consequences of the Fall is that Adam will have power over Eve (Gen. 3:16). In this story, that dynamic is reversed as the passive and unknowing "Adam's" power flows out of him and into "Eve" as a result of her decision to access that power. This is another way in which the story of the Fall is redeemed in Mark's text.

13. Just as the fear is that Adam and Eve will become "like the Gods," it is literally the case that this woman is like Jesus, something clearly illustrated by all of the parallels between the two of them. Because the woman's body foreshadows Jesus' suffering, the story powerfully affirms the idea that all human bodies are made in God's image.

14. The story of the Fall ends with Eve's desire for her husband; the story of the bleeding woman begins with her desire for Jesus (who is in the role of Adam). The story ends with the woman assuming the role not of wife but of daughter; this is because Jesus' role in the story has shifted from Adam to God.

(Although, interestingly, there is also a sense in which Eve is Adam's "daughter," inasmuch as she was birthed from his side.) Jesus' pronouncement of the bleeding woman's wholeness is tied not just to her physical healing but also to a broader sense of wholeness that involves her new relationship with Jesus. Just as the Fall reconfigures Eve's relationship with God, the story of the bleeding woman reconfigures the woman's relationship to Jesus; she is now his daughter. Much as Adam named his wife Eve, this story has Jesus naming the woman as his daughter. Her primary identity at the end of the story is that she is the daughter of Jesus.

15. One consequence of the Fall for Eve is that her births—and her pain—will be multiplied. Mark's story is a variation on this theme: the healing of the woman means that there is the potential for her births to be multiplied (which creates another allusion to the story of the Fall, which refers to Eve's seed), but through her encounter with Jesus, pain is removed from her—not added.

These parallels suggest that the concept of "redemptive reading," where an HB story with a less-than-perfect ending is reenacted and redeemed through the life of Jesus, is active in this text.[55] It fits comfortably with the stilling of the storm (as the reenactment and correction of the Jonah story) and the raising of Jairus's daughter (as the reenactment and correction of Jephthah's daughter). The point is to foreshadow the idea that Jesus is the means by which the effects of the Fall will be overcome. By showcasing a woman—and a woman with a uniquely female problem—the story emphasizes the fact that Jesus' ability to overcome the effects of the Fall extends to all people. By permitting this bleeding woman to take on Eve's role, Mark's text shows that the effects of the Fall have now been overcome through Jesus. Because the bleeding woman's story is sandwiched within Jairus's daughter's story, both of the main effects of the Fall—death and sin/estrangement from God—are done away with in this block of narrative. In fact, the link to the Fall story may explain why Mark chose to sandwich these stories: they highlight the themes of redemption from the Fall that permeate both texts.

One objection to reading Mark's story here as an intertext to the story of the Fall may be that "there is no mention or allusion to the first woman/Eve in the Hebrew Scriptures beyond Genesis 5."[56] But it is also true that, during Jesus' time, there was a renewed interest in this text: "Jewish

---

55. Smith, "Redemptive Reading of Mark 5:25–34," 95–105.
56. Kristen E. Kvam, Linda S. Schearing, and Valarie H. Ziegler, *Eve and Adam: Jewish, Christian, and Muslim Readings on Genesis and Gender* (Bloomington: Indiana University Press, 1999), 19.

literature from 200 BCE to 200 CE reflects an interest in Eve and Adam far beyond that found in the Hebrew Scriptures. [These works] retell, expand, and comment on Genesis 1–5."[57] So this reading would have fit well in its historical context. While it is unknown which reflections on and expansions of the Fall story were current in Jesus' time and/or known to Mark and the audience, it is nonetheless true that some themes from the extant sources are reflected in Mark's text. For example, the *Apocalypse of Moses* relates the story of the Fall from the perspective of Eve and includes the Lord telling Eve that the time will come when she will say, "Lord, Lord, save me."[58] Clearly, there is some thematic overlap with Mark's story. So while Mark's text is a correction and a redemptive reading, it also fits into its cultural context of interest in the Fall.

Relationship to Jeremiah 8. There may be subtle allusions to Jeremiah 8, which contains the Lord's statement that neglect of God will lead to destruction and the people's response of lament. The passage includes a picture of ineffectual help (Jer. 8:10–11), paralleling the doctors who failed the bleeding woman; a lament (Jer. 8:19) similar to Jairus's; public mourning (Jer. 8:21) similar to that at Jairus's home; and a reference to the true physician (Jer. 8:22).

Menstruation. As one scholar described it, "ancient man reacted to the phenomenon of menstruation with a horror that seems to us grotesque and hysterical."[59] In addition to that general disdain, Jewish tradition included several negative symbolic referents for menstruation:

1. One tradition held that being near a menstruating woman could be fatal.[60] In the context of Mark's story, this tradition is particularly interesting because it is inverted: not only does the woman's touch not cause Jesus' death, but it also enhances her life. And, as the sandwich story suggests, it might permit the girl's death by delaying Jesus but ultimately does not impede Jesus' ability to overcome her death.

2. Another tradition maintained that even minimal contact with a menstruating woman might counteract a healer's ability.[61] Again, in Mark's context, this

57. Kvam, Schearing, and Ziegler, *Eve and Adam,* 41.

58. Kvam, Schearing, and Ziegler, *Eve and Adam,* 62.

59. Bernard J. Bamberger, "Defilement by Discharge from the Sex Organs," in *The Torah: A Modern Commentary,* ed. W. Gunther Plaut (New York: Union of American Hebrew Congregations, 1981), 849.

60. Babylonian Talmud, Seder Mo'ed II, Pesahim 111a.

61. Hekhalot Rabbati 18, §226 in *Synopse zur Hekhalot-Literatur,* ed. Peter Schäfer, Margarete Schlüter, and Hans Georg von Mutius (Tübingen: Mohr-Siebeck, 1981).

tradition is invalidated since Jesus' powers are not negated by the woman's touch. Rather, the tradition is upended since the touch of a menstruating woman initiates her healing.

3. In another traditional belief, menstruation was thought to be a curse for Eve's sin.[62] In light of Mark's story, this would picture Jesus removing the curse; in the sandwich story, Jesus would be removing the other curse associated with the Fall—death. The sandwich structure would then emphasize Jesus' role in removing the effects of the Fall.

It is unknowable whether any of these traditions were on the minds of Mark or the audience, but there is no doubt that this story would have been an uncomfortable one for the audience—particularly the male portion of the audience—to hear: discussing vaginal bleeding in mixed company was certainly not the norm in the ancient world. The fact that Mark included this story in the record challenges the then-current (and still-extant) discomfort with the functions of the female body. This story requires male audience members to relate to and sympathize with uniquely female concerns, and it suggests that Jesus shared these concerns: "Jesus' healing of this woman expresses an attitude of outreach to the 'unclean' rather than one of judgment and exclusion."[63]

Parallels between the Woman and Jesus. Many similarities lead to the conclusion that Mark intended for the audience to parallel the woman and Jesus, with a particular focus on their bodies:

1. The same adverb (Greek: *polus*) translated as "many" is used for both of them to describe their suffering (5:26; 8:31).

2. The same verb for "suffer" (Greek: *penthō*) is used for both of them (and for no one else) in Mark (5:26; 8:31; 9:12).

3. The same root word describes their suffering (5:29 [KJV: "plague"]; 10:34 [KJV: "scourge"]).

4. The word "body" is used for both of them (5:29; 14:22).

5. Due to purity law and social taboo, her condition was considered shameful and embarrassing; similarly, Jesus' torture and crucifixion as a criminal would have been an embarrassment.

6. Blood pours out from both the woman and Jesus (14:24). Associating Jesus' blood with menstrual blood would have emphasized the theme of embarrassment.

---

62. Genesis Rabbah 17:8.

63. Marie Sabin, "Women Transformed: The Ending of Mark Is the Beginning of Wisdom," *Cross Currents* 48 (Summer 1998): 152.

7. In this story, both the woman and Jesus instantly know in their bodies that something has happened; the same verb is used in 5:29 and 5:30 for their "knowing." This association creates a strong parallel between their two bodies.

These robust similarities imply that Mark wants the audience to think of the woman—and particularly the woman's body—as a foreshadowing of Jesus and his body. She is a type of Christ, and her suffering is a type of his suffering. The fact that she is female makes this comparison very significant since women were regarded as inferior, and the fact that the suffering of her body involves a uniquely female problem amplifies the unexpectedness of the comparison. Mark's story redeems the female body, allowing it to stand proxy for Jesus' body.

In the view of the HB, the blood contained the life (Lev. 17:10–14), leading to the ritual prohibitions related to blood. The story of the bleeding woman requires the audience to rethink the symbolism of blood since it impedes the woman's life (and her life-giving ability). At the same time, this rethinking of blood sets the stage for the shedding of Jesus' blood, where life and death will be interwoven. The story of the bleeding woman is thus an important prelude to understanding the symbolism of Jesus' blood.

5:35 *While he yet spake:* This line emphasizes that the stories are intertwined and that the girl dies at the moment when the woman is healed. From the perspective of the crowd, the bleeding woman has delayed Jesus and led to the girl's death. This is another reason, in addition to the impurity, for the crowd to be hostile to the bleeding woman; it makes Jesus' kindness and praise all the more surprising.

there came from the ruler of the synagogue's house certain which said, Thy daughter is dead: why troublest thou the Master any further?: The cruel abruptness of this line and the one before it may represent Mark's telescoping of the story, or it might represent their attitude toward the death of a female child, who would have been an economic liability to the household.

These messengers presume that there is nothing that Jesus can do; they may have believed in his ability to heal the sick but not to raise the dead. As with the other miracle stories in this section, the difficulty of the situation is emphasized: the boat was already swamped, the demoniac couldn't be bound, the woman had been to many doctors, and, now, the little girl is dead. These references not only heighten the drama of the story but also emphasize Jesus' power.

5:36 *As soon as Jesus heard the word that was spoken, he saith unto the ruler of the synagogue:* There is some uncertainty over the verb that the KJV translates as "heard": most ancient manuscripts have the word *parakousas,* which can mean "overheard" or "ignored."[64] Others have *akousas,* which means "heard." Given how similar the verbs are, it is possible that the variant reflects a scribal mistake. It is also possible that, given the ambiguity of *parakousas,* a scribe changed it to make clear that Jesus heard (not ignored) what was said and was responding to it. Given the context, it seems that Jesus is responding to the message that was spoken.

Be not afraid, only believe: The verb translated as "believe" recalls the word used to describe the woman's faith in 5:34. So Jesus is asking Jairus to model himself on the bleeding woman; given their disparate social locations, this is most remarkable.[65] It is not specified precisely what it is that Jairus should believe, but this is probably because belief was not assent to theological propositions but rather trust. In other words, Jesus is commanding Jairus to trust him. Unlike in modern thought, fear—not doubt—is the opposite of belief.

Jesus teaches how the faithful should respond to challenges, even to those that seem insurmountable. He tells Jairus to do precisely what his own disciples should do (but do not do) when confronted with the knowledge of Jesus' own death. There are several ways in which the girl's experience foreshadows Jesus' death and Resurrection; the girl is a type of Christ in that her death is not permanent and therefore not sufficient cause for a lack of faith.

At this point in the narrative, Jesus has, from Jairus's perspective, failed by not arriving in time to heal his daughter. Knowing how the story will end, it can be difficult for the audience to sympathize with Jairus. But in this moment, Jairus has reason to be not only personally shattered but also disappointed in Jesus' (apparently) failed offer to heal his daughter. Further, Jesus' statement to the woman—calling her a daughter and saying that her faith had healed her—would have been very difficult for Jairus to hear given the desperate state of his own daughter. From Jairus's perspective at this moment, this situation is not just bleak but punishingly ironic. But Jesus will come through for Jairus in a way that Jairus simply could not have anticipated. What is required of Jairus is to continue following Jesus and to trust him. This story can be read as an enacted parable where initial disappointment is transformed into rejoicing for those willing to trust and follow Jesus.

---

64. Bratcher and Nida, *Translator's Handbook,* 177.

65. James R. Edwards, "Markan Sandwiches: The Significance of Interpolations in Markan Narratives," *Novum Testamentum* 31, no. 3 (1989): 204–5.

Relationship to Habakkuk 2:4. LXX Habakkuk 2:4 (NRSV: "the righteous live by their faith") uses the same words for "live" as in 5:23 and "believe" as in 5:36 and teaches that "the just shall live by his faith," which parallels the bleeding woman's situation. Habakkuk 2:3 exhorts: "even if the message is not fulfilled right away, wait patiently; for it will certainly come to pass" (NET), which has an obvious parallel to Jesus' implied message to Jairus in 5:36. (This verse in Habakkuk played an important role in the thinking of other NT authors on the subject of faith and works [see Rom. 1:17; Gal. 3:11; and Heb. 10:38], but its meaning is disputed.)

5:37 *And he suffered no man to follow him:* This is another example of an absolute statement followed by exceptions: as the next line will show, the prohibition on following Jesus was not absolute.

save Peter, and James, and John the brother of James: No explanation is given as to why the other disciples are excluded; one possibility is that, like the other occasions when a core group of disciples is singled out (9:2; 14:33), this, too, will be an event of key importance. As the only raising from the dead in Mark (except, of course, of Jesus), this is a very significant event. It is intriguing that Mark uses the composition of the audience to signal the importance of the event.

While Mark never explicitly explains that Peter, James,[66] and John occupy a leadership role within the Twelve, the Greek text indicates that they form an inner circle: only one article is used for all three of their names, implying that they are a distinct group.

5:38 *And he cometh to the house of the ruler of the synagogue, and seeth the tumult, and them that wept and wailed greatly:* A commotion is made by professional mourners who, according to custom, would have been hired to weep and wail over the death of the girl.

5:39 *And when he was come in, he saith unto them, Why make ye this ado, and weep? the damsel is not dead, but sleepeth:* Jesus has not yet seen the child; it seems that his knowledge of her state is miraculous.

It is difficult to explain Jesus' statement that the girl is sleeping. Options include:

1. It is factually true: the girl is not dead—she is in a coma or a similar state. Jesus' knowledge of her condition, especially when the family thinks otherwise, would point to his miraculous ability. This reading explains why Jesus told Jairus to believe and not to fear: the reports of his daughter's death were inaccurate and thus not to be believed. In this reading, the messengers from

---

66. See the Notes on 1:19.

Jairus's house and the mourners are akin to the bleeding woman's many doctors who have misdiagnosed the patient; Jesus is, in both stories, the true physician who understands what is actually wrong and how to fix it. To the extent that the girl is a symbol for Israel, the fact that she is presumed dead when she is not suggests that Israel is not truly dead but merely awaiting restoration. One weakness of this reading is that, as will be shown below, the numerous parallels between the girl's story and Jesus' own raising from the dead suggest that the girl, like Jesus, was literally dead. (In fact, one could argue that Mark would not have highlighted the association between the girl and Jesus had the girl not died because it might have aided opponents of the early Christian movement who argued that Jesus himself had not really died.)

2. It is not factually true because the girl is literally dead. There are two different ways to understand this statement if it is not factually true:

   a. Jesus did not tell the truth. For whatever reason, he deliberately wanted to create a false impression in the minds of the crowd about the girl's state. Many readers would find this kind of duplicity on Jesus' part difficult to accept.

   b. "Sleep" is used sometimes in the NT to describe death (Matt. 27:52; John 11:12; Acts 7:60; 13:36; 1 Cor. 7:39; the same verb can also be used for literal sleep [4:27] or figurative sleep [1 Thes. 5:6]), particularly in contexts where the speaker believes in the resurrection from the dead. So Jesus would be recognizing her death but also claiming that it is temporary. She isn't dead in the commonly understood sense of death as a permanent state; her death is akin to sleep because it is about to end. This reading makes good sense of the ridicule in 5:40, since the onlookers would not have understood or accepted the idea of a temporary death. It is even possible that, as with the parables of the last chapter, there is one meaning for outsiders (who take the sleep literally) and another for insiders (who understand that Jesus can raise the dead). This story continues the motif of insiders and outsiders established in chapter 3 and expanded upon in chapter 4, as Jesus literally creates outsiders and insiders by inviting some people but prohibiting others from witnessing the miracle. If this is the best reading, then, as suggested in the last chapter, the insider/outsider status is temporary: presumably these people will see the girl alive and realize that they had misunderstood. And yet one weakness of this reading is that, for the insiders who interpret the reference to sleep as a sort of temporary death, Jesus is saying, in effect, "she isn't dead, she's dead"; this phrasing is difficult to explain.

3. Jesus was deliberately ambiguous in order to give different messages to insiders and outsiders, as if this speech were a parable. Perhaps this statement relates to Jesus' command at the end of the story that no one be told that the girl has been raised: if Jesus' intention was that the story not become general knowledge (as that verse suggests), then he has laid the groundwork for a

plausible alternative explanation for the girl's reappearance. Nonetheless, it is difficult to determine how Jesus expected the raising to be kept private when hired mourners were already on the scene.

5:40 *And they laughed him to scorn:* "They" could theoretically include the girl's family as well as Jesus' disciples, but it is more likely to include only the hired mourners since the girl's parents and Peter, James, and John are invited to witness the girl's raising. Given that the hired mourners were just described as weeping and wailing, the sudden shift to scornful laughter speaks to their lack of genuine emotion.

The idea of Jesus' announcement being greeted with derision may have been particularly meaningful to Mark's audience, who were probably used to a similar response to their proclamations that Jesus was no longer dead. This is one way in which this girl's story foreshadows Jesus' own story.

But when he had put them all out: The Greek verb translated as "put ... out" is the same word used when Jesus performs exorcisms (1:34; 3:22 [KJV: "cast out"]). The immediate result of their lack of faith, manifested as scornful laughter, is that they are denied the opportunity to witness a miracle.

The insider/outsider motif may be on display here: if Jesus' words about the girl's "sleep" were interpreted one way by outsiders (those who misunderstand him and mock) but differently by insiders (those who understand him—the girl's parents, Peter, James, and John), then Mark is presenting an enacted parable where the outsiders lack understanding and the insiders are given an even greater opportunity to understand.

he taketh the father and the mother of the damsel: Mark does not explain why Jesus permitted the girl's parents to witness the miracle, but perhaps he intended for them—along with Peter, James, and John—to serve as witnesses.

As suggested above, Mark signals the importance of this event via the composition of the audience. The inclusion of the mother is noteworthy, especially by way of contrast with the two HB stories that are most similar to this one (see the sections "Relationship to Judges 11" and "Relationship to 1 Kings 17:17–23 and 2 Kings 4:18–37" after the Notes on 5:43 below). The girl's mother also prefigures the role of the women at the tomb (16:1–8) as a witness to the conquering of death.

and them that were with him: The word "them" refers to Peter, James, and John (compare 5:37).

and entereth in where the damsel was lying: This line indicates that there was more than one room in their house and thus attests to their wealth. According to Numbers 19:14, anyone who enters into a room with a corpse becomes unclean.

5:41 ***And he took the damsel by the hand, and said unto her, Talitha cumi:*** Mark preserves the Aramaic words and then translates them for the audience. Presumably, Jesus spoke Aramaic, his native language, which Mark has translated into Greek without comment since the beginning of the text. Reasons for the inclusion of the Aramaic in this case may include:

1. There is something ritualistic about this command; perhaps the words constitute some sort of ritual formula. Hence the precise wording was preserved. Of the other instances where Mark preserves Aramaic wording, some support—but others do not support—this reading (compare 7:34; contrast 3:17; 7:11).

2. Mark uses Aramaic (only?) in the instances when he has the actual words that Jesus used (which means that all other words attributed to Jesus are paraphrases).

3. Inclusion of the Aramaic words and their translation slows the pace of the narrative and thus builds suspense at this crucial moment when the girl is about to rise from the dead.

which is, being interpreted, Damsel, I say unto thee, arise: The word "interpreted" does not carry its normal English connotation but rather means "translated"; Mark gives the Greek translation of the Aramaic words. "I say unto thee" is not part of the Aramaic words quoted. Mark may have provided this translation so that his non-Aramaic-speaking audience would not think that Jesus had just pronounced a magical healing formula on the girl but rather would realize that Jesus' words were a simple command. This may be another instance of Mark's penchant for creating and then dashing the audience's expectations: they may have initially assumed that Jesus was uttering some sort of magical incantation (which was the practice of other healers), but then they discover that he was simply commanding the girl to rise in his usual language.

Once again, as has been the pattern in Mark, the words Jesus speaks at a healing are a command to the person that requires the person to have been healed in order to execute.

5:42 ***And straightway the damsel arose, and walked:*** The word "straightway" emphasizes Jesus' power. It occurs twice in this verse: to describe the girl rising and to describe the response to it.

for she was of the age of twelve years: Note the odd placement of the girl's age; it would have made much more sense to note it at the beginning of the story. But its very awkwardness highlights its importance: here it cannot be dismissed as simple scene-setting, as it might have been when the girl was first introduced.

The number twelve had symbolic value and referred to Israel and its leadership (Gen. 17:20; 35:22; 49:28; Ex. 24:4; 39:14; Lev. 24:5; Num. 7:84–87; Josh. 4:3; 1 Kgs. 7:25). See the sections "Relationship to 1 Kings 17:17–23 and 2 Kings 4:18–37" and "The Relationship between the Bleeding Woman and Jairus's Daughter" after the Notes on 5:43 below for discussions of the girl as a symbol for Israel and the contrast with the bleeding woman (who had her condition for, as Mark notes, twelve years).

And they were astonished with a great astonishment: The word "they" refers to Peter, James, John, the parents, and, possibly, the girl. The KJV and the New Rendition reflect the repetition of the root word for "astonish," which functions to emphasize the reaction. The KJV does not translate the second instance of "immediately" (Greek: *euthys*) in this verse; including it would yield "they were immediately astonished."

Relationship to the Resurrection. Many similarities tie the story of the raising of Jairus's daughter to the story of Jesus' Resurrection:

1. These are the only two times in Mark's Gospel when someone is raised from the dead.
2. The same Greek word translated as "rise" in 5:41 is used in 16:6 to describe Jesus' rising.
3. In both stories, Jesus is mocked (14:65).
4. The Greek word for astonishment (*ekstasis*) is used in Mark only for the reaction to the girl's raising and the reaction to Jesus' raising (16:8).
5. In Aramaic, "talitha" can refer to a lamb, which further encourages the association between the girl and Jesus. (Although Mark does not use the symbolism of the lamb to directly refer to Jesus [compare John 1:29], it is probably implicit in the links between the Last Supper and the Passover.)

Thus, the girl's story foreshadows Jesus' Resurrection.

5:43 *And he charged them straitly that no man should know it:* Why does Jesus command them not to tell anyone about the raising? Possibilities include:

1. Jesus had specifically invited the girl's father and mother to witness the raising, so they obviously are part of the group that should know about the miracle. This accords with the story of the Gerasene demoniac, in which Jesus commands the man to tell what has happened to him to those close to him. The pattern suggests that Jesus sees a privileged role for family members (and, perhaps, families in general), which makes for an interesting contrast to the lack of privilege that he grants to his own family at the end of chapter 3.

2. The word "it" has several possible referents here: the raising of the girl, the method of the raising, or the identity of the person who raised her. So perhaps what is to be kept secret is Jesus' role in the miracle: people would know that the girl was raised, but they need not know who had done it.

3. Perhaps Jesus' hope was that the raising could be kept private long enough for Jesus and his disciples to move on to the next town without being mobbed or arrested.

4. Perhaps the commands to secrecy in Mark exist because, at the time that they are given, the characters in the story do not know enough about Jesus' nature and mission to accurately preach about who he is. In other words, telling people who do not understand Jesus' role about his ability to raise people from the dead would result in misunderstanding. (Interestingly, this theory suggests that the parents and the three disciples do understand who Jesus is.)

5. Perhaps the girl's raising is an enactment of the same principle articulated in the parable: nothing is hidden except to be made clear later (4:22). Eventually, all will know about the girl's raising (it is included in the Gospel of Mark, after all), but in the short-term, only those who are prepared will know about it. (The presence of the girl's mother affirms that women can be insiders.)

The command here is in contrast with the earlier story in this chapter, where the healed demoniac is specifically told to tell others about his healing. Efforts to explain the secrecy command in this story must, therefore, grapple with the previous command to proclaim. One way to reconcile these is to note that Jesus is now in Jewish territory; perhaps the secrecy commands are designed to limit awareness of Jesus' ministry in areas where there could be repercussions from the religious authorities.

Of all of the secrecy commands in Mark (1:34, 44; 7:36; 9:9), this is the only one that was not violated (or, at least, whose violation was not narrated).

and commanded that something should be given her to eat: Reasons why Jesus might have issued this command include:

1. It is a characteristic of healing miracles to show the healed person engaged in some activity that illustrates that they have truly been healed; eating would show that the girl was truly alive again.

2. The command shows Jesus' concern with the details of common life. It was not enough for him to use his spectacular power to raise her from the dead; he also used his authority to ensure that her more mundane needs were met.

3. Some scriptures, including Isaiah 25:6–8, picture what would later be called "the messianic feast," where the time of the Messiah is characterized by lavish banquets. Jesus' concern with food here might echo that theme, especially since the girl has just been raised from the dead.

4. In the story of the Gerasene demoniac, it is the swine feeders who served as eyewitnesses of the miracle. The fact that the girl's mother and father and

Peter, James, and John take the same role in this story might have been something that Mark wanted to highlight, emphasizing that they had the same narrative role as providers of food for the person whom Jesus had helped.

5. There are extensive similarities between the story of the raising of Jairus's daughter and the raising of Jesus (see 16:1–8). In both stories, women are given a specific task to do after the raising, and so the command to the mother to feed her daughter would parallel the command to the women at the tomb to tell the disciples that Jesus is going to Galilee.

Relationship to Judges 11. Judges 11 relates the sad tale of Jephthah and his daughter. Similar to Jairus, Jephthah, as a judge, is also a prominent religious leader. Both Jephthah and Jairus are distraught at the thought of the death of their daughters, and both fathers are met with noise and chaos when they return home. But Jairus (who, perhaps not coincidentally, shares the name of the judge who served immediately before Jephthah; this may explain the inclusion of his name in this story when that was not common for healing miracles) intercedes to avoid the death of his daughter, while it was Jephthah's own foolishness that led to his daughter's death.

Just as the story of the calming of the sea mirrored Jonah's story only long enough to develop certain expectations in the minds of the audience and then proceeded to violate those expectations, the story of Jairus follows the story of Jephthah just long enough to suggest the similarity but then pivots to illustrate that Jairus is very different from Jephthah. Mark shows that the activities of Jesus' life (literally) redeem the mistakes and errors of history: Jonah is now Jesus; Jephthah is now Jairus.[67]

Relationship to 1 Kings 17:17–23 and 2 Kings 4:18–37. In 1 Kings 17, the prophet Elijah raises a child from the dead; in 2 Kings 4, Elisha does the same. Both of these stories involve a woman and her son, who would have most likely been her sole source of financial support. In Mark's story, the death of the daughter of a prominent man lacks that dynamic: the girl is financially useless to Jairus. Nonetheless, she is just as valued in the story. Mark has thus woven into the account a commentary on the value of women. Additionally, in the HB stories, the mother is not permitted to witness the raising, but Jairus's wife is; this implies a more inclusive role for women, even as eyewitnesses, in Jesus' ministry and anticipates the role of the women at the tomb as witnesses to Jesus' own Resurrection.

---

67. Mary Ann Beavis, "The Resurrection of Jephthah's Daughter: Judges 11:34–40 and Mark 5:21–24, 35–43," *Catholic Biblical Quarterly* 72, no. 1 (2010): 60–61.

The similarities between the stories imply Jesus' identification with the HB prophets and demonstrate his superiority to them: Jesus need only speak to raise the dead, while Elijah and Elisha had to engage in ritual actions (1 Kgs. 17:21; 2 Kgs. 4:34–35). Also, both HB raisings are of non-Israelites, which heightens the significance of the fact that this girl is not just an Israelite but also literally a daughter of the synagogue. The point is that even the house of Israel is in need of Jesus' ministry—even the ruler of the synagogue is just as dependent on Jesus' power as a gentile woman. These gentile women may have pleaded for their sons because of their financial dependence on them, but the picture of a father appealing for his daughter is rather different and suggests her inherent value.

Relationship to Chapter 1. Mark 1:23–31 features the same pattern of an exorcism followed by the healing of a woman. In both healings, the woman, who is identified by her relationship to a prominent male, is "raised" in a private venue and then returns to typical behavior. The difference is that chapter 1 inaugurates Jesus' ministry in Jewish territory while chapter 5 begins his ministry in gentile lands. The pattern suggests that the inaugural exorcism was necessary for ridding the land of the demonic presence that infested it before Jesus began his ministry. The healings—particularly since both are of women—suggest the scope and extent of Jesus' ministry, which includes all people.

The Relationship between the Bleeding Woman and Jairus's Daughter. The story of the bleeding woman is sandwiched in between the two halves of the story of Jairus's daughter. Mark frequently employs this sandwiching technique to encourage the audience to compare the bracketed stories. Indeed, the bleeding woman and Jairus's daughter have many similarities:

1. *Women.* In both stories, the key characters are female. This, in itself, is unusual in the ancient world. Not only does this convey how central women were in Jesus' ministry and Mark's telling of it, but in the story of the bleeding woman, Jesus also extends a specific invitation for the woman to literally and specifically assume central space and become the focal point of the story, despite the fact that she would clearly prefer to remain in the background. And not only is a young girl a main character in her own story, but her mother is also mentioned as a witness to a miracle and thus grouped in the elite company of the inner circle of disciples.

2. *Bodies.* The similar language describing the bleeding woman's knowledge of what happens in her body and Jesus' knowledge of what happens in his body encourages the comparison between their bodies. Similarly, corresponding language and themes invite the audience to read the death and raising of the

girl's body as a template for Jesus' body. And because these two stories are sandwiched, Mark conveys the idea that females prefigure Jesus' suffering as well as his death and rising.

3. *Life, Death, and Blood.* While one story involves illness and the other death, they may be more similar than they initially seem since the HB teaches that life is in the blood (Gen. 9:4; Lev. 17:11); thus, the loss of blood from the bleeding woman serves, at least symbolically, to indicate the loss of life. This similarity between the stories may help explain Jesus' counsel to Jairus to have faith: Jairus should expect that if Jesus can stop the metaphorical death of the bleeding woman, then he should be able to stop the death of the girl. The stories link to death in another way: the girl is dead before (in fact, right on the cusp of when) she could have children, and the bleeding woman is unable to have children due to her condition. The fact that the woman's blood is, in this story, not a symbol for life but rather indicates that she cannot create new life points to the limitations of the law of Moses.

4. *Twelve.* The bleeding woman has had her condition for twelve years, and the little girl is, as Mark awkwardly relates, twelve years old. Not only do these references serve to link the two stories together, but they also associate both stories with the symbolic meaning of the number twelve. Based on its HB usage, twelve became a symbol for Israel, its leadership, and its hopes for restoration. The unrelieved suffering of both females would symbolically correspond to the idea that the house of Israel was suffering (under sin and under Roman oppression), and no human could solve these problems. Much as Jesus restores both females to wholeness, Jesus' ministry and death will restore Israel. The Twelve function as a symbol for Israel, and these two females do so as well; the fact that women are associated with the number twelve in Mark's story is remarkable and would have surprised the audience. As a literal "daughter of the synagogue," Jairus's daughter functions as a symbol for Israel, dead (which, in a sense, it was, given that ten of the tribes had been "lost") without Jesus' touch. But she is redeemable and not beyond hope.

5. *Faith.* Both stories contain references to faith. Jesus references (but does not solicit) the faith of the bleeding woman, but, by contrast, he exhorts Jairus to have faith. Given that the bleeding woman and Jairus occupy functionally opposite social locations, the fact that the poor, marginalized woman serves as a model of faith for the wealthy male religious leader is remarkable.

6. *Fear.* Fear is mentioned in both stories: the woman fears to tell Jesus what she has done, and Jesus tells Jairus not to fear.

7. *Violation of Expectations.* Both the bleeding woman and Jairus have to violate social expectations: the woman by touching Jesus and Jairus by being humble enough to seek Jesus' help when Jairus, as a ruler of the synagogue, is the religious authority.

8. *Ritual Purity.* Both stories should involve the transmission of ritual impurity to Jesus, through the bleeding woman's touch and contact with a corpse. But

Jesus does not become impure; rather, he transmits healing and life through touch. This suggests something very important about his relationship to the law of Moses, which means that there is an important message here about Jesus' nature and identity.

9. *Touch.* The woman touches Jesus (at least, his clothing), and Jesus touches the girl.

10. *Falling at Jesus' Feet.* Both Jairus and the bleeding woman are described as falling at Jesus' feet. Despite the fact that different verbs are used, the action is similar, and the fact that both respond to Jesus in the same way heightens the similarity.

11. *Daughter.* Both stories use the word "daughter": in Jairus's story, with reference to his biological daughter and, in the story of the bleeding woman, through Jesus' honorary title for the woman. To be Jesus' daughter means to seek one's own healing, to act on one's own faith, to claim Jesus' power, to come forward even when afraid, to speak in front of a crowd, and not to worry about violating social convention. Being a daughter of the synagogue means being silent and passive and having one's father intercede. This reality is reflected in the fact that "the bleeding woman plays the two roles in her story that are divided between Jairus and his daughter in their story; she is both the one who needs healing and the one who believes in Jesus' power and seeks his help."[68] The message is that being a daughter of Jesus is a much more active role than being a daughter of the synagogue.

12. *Relationships.* Both females are introduced in the text in terms of how they relate to the power structure of Judaism: the girl in terms of her father (who personifies power as a ruler of the synagogue) and the woman in terms of her violation of the purity laws. But by the end of the story, they are identified differently: "In both her impending death (v. 23) and death (v. 35) the child is referred to as 'daughter', but in her sleep (v. 39) and her recovery (v. 41) she is a 'girl'. The transition from death to life transforms the 'daughter' into a 'girl' in much the same way as the hemorrhaging woman experiences a transition from 'woman' to 'daughter' through her interaction with Jesus. Both experience life-affirming changes in their identities."[69] In both cases, Jesus speaks to them in a way that reorients their relationships and identifies them in new terms. Jesus takes the unaffiliated bleeding woman and gives her a relationship (as his daughter), and he takes the affiliated daughter and makes her independent of the synagogue by calling her a little girl. The idea is not that familial affiliation is negative in itself but rather that Jesus heals and redeems the affiliation: Jesus removes the girl from the relationship with the

---

68. Dowd, *Reading Mark,* 56.

69. Susan Haber, "A Woman's Touch: Feminist Encounters with the Hemorrhaging Woman in Mark 5.24–34," *Journal for the Study of the New Testament* 26 (December 1, 2003): 188.

synagogue (that has resulted in her death) and makes her independent. Jesus takes the bleeding woman, whose independence has not been a blessing to her, and embeds her in a relationship with him.

13. *Fertility.* The woman has not been fertile because of her bleeding (and her uncleanness) and so is restored to fertility. The little girl's age means that she is on the cusp of fertility and marriageability. Not only is this significant on a literal level, but it may also have had a metaphorical resonance since some HB texts (for example, Isa. 54:1–3) use fertility images to describe the new age.

14. *The Failed Physician.* References to the motif of a failed physician are explicit in the story of the bleeding woman (see 5:26) and implicit in the story of Jairus's daughter, when the crowd mocks Jesus' misdiagnosis of the girl as being asleep. In both cases, Jesus is—most unexpectedly—the great physician who, unlike all others, can restore both the woman and the girl.

While these similarities are significant and imply that Mark wants the audience to compare the two stories, there are also substantial differences that are instructive:

1. Jairus thought a grand gesture (namely, having Jesus come to his home and lay hands on the girl) was required; the bleeding woman thought that a very small gesture (quietly touching the edge of his clothes) would suffice. They were both right; Jesus' power can be accessed in a variety of ways.

2. Jairus and the bleeding woman are both supplicants but in very different ways: he has no problem boldly and publicly approaching Jesus and asking for something very specific, as if it is reasonable to expect Jesus to stop what he is doing to tend to Jairus's needs. The woman, on the other hand, does not approach Jesus this way; she does not speak, make her action publicly known, or intend to draw attention to herself in any way. She thinks she might be healed without interrupting him. But Jesus will not let her do this; Jesus implies that, like Jairus, she has a right to his attention, to distract him from his appointed course, and to command center stage. She has a right to have her "whole story" heard by the crowd, and they should listen to her. The fact that the girl dies while this happens means that the woman has, in a sense, done a terrible thing by delaying Jesus. (Surely it was better for her to bleed than for the girl to die.) But the story implies that her conversation with Jesus and her appearance as the center of attention is so significant that it outweighs saving the girl's life. The bleeding woman wants to be the narrative equivalent of Jairus's daughter (who is silent and passive), but Jesus requires her to be the equivalent of Jairus (who speaks from center stage). Jesus did not need to break his stride to heal her; that happened without him stopping. What Jesus considers worth stopping for is teaching her about her value.

3. Clearly, the wealthy male synagogue leader enjoys many positive status markers while the poor, unprotected, unclean woman has none. The fact

that Jesus not only treats them as equals but also delays helping the high-class supplicant to aid the lower-class one is extremely significant. Because he is named, Jairus is presented as if he were a main character in the story, but by the end of the story, it is clear that he is not as significant as the unnamed bleeding woman (for whom Jesus makes him wait) or his own daughter (who becomes the focal point of the story). There is a status reversal as Jesus makes Jairus wait while he speaks to the bleeding woman, as if she were more important; the fact that she is already healed by that point heightens the message. Jairus must renounce his high status by kneeling before Jesus; the bleeding woman must claim a higher status by speaking boldly with Jesus from center stage. (The woman's new, higher status is also manifest in the fact that she is Jesus' daughter by the end of the story.) Interestingly, Jairus is asked to keep the girl's raising quiet, but the bleeding woman is invited to share her experience with the crowd.[70]

4. The woman wants only a quiet, private encounter with Jesus, but Jesus turns it into a very public situation. Jairus is comfortable with a very public request, but Jesus raises his daughter in a very private setting (and with a command to keep it circumspect).

Later, the audience will learn that many people touched Jesus' clothing in order to be healed (6:56). Perhaps Mark chose to include the full story of this particular touch because it not only illustrated the principle that Jesus could heal but also contained additional teachings communicated by sandwiching this particular healing story within the story of the raising of Jairus's daughter.

Analysis

The intertwined stories of the bleeding woman and Jairus's daughter may be Mark's most intricately plotted and symbolically rich text.

Mark highlights several key themes through the inclusion of the disciples' question about why Jesus is asking who touched him. First, the disciples' question provides an opportunity for the audience to reassess Jesus' question and recognize that Jesus realizes that the woman's touch is categorically different from the random touches of the rest of the crowd. Next, a perennial Markan theme, the incomprehension of the disciples, is on display: the audience already knows that Jesus has been purposefully touched by a woman, so the disciples' question shows a lacuna not shared by the audience. While the disciples are unaware of this exchange, the

---

70. Credit for this insight belongs to Lauree Strong.

fact that they continue to follow Jesus means that they will continue to learn about him; the disciples' lack of knowledge does not disqualify them from discipleship. Third, since every person in this crowd who had had any physical contact with the bleeding woman is unclean until the evening, the disciples' question is an implicit critique of the purity laws since it would have been impossible for the crowd to determine whether they were ritually clean. This is an important commentary on the limits of the purity requirements and the sanctity of temple worship.

The bleeding woman, linked by the number twelve as a symbol for the house of Israel, was—like Israel specifically and humanity generally—unable to escape the suffering of a fallen world through her own efforts. Jesus invites the woman to enter into a new covenant with him, one symbolized by his use of the word "daughter," which implies a new relationship between himself and the woman. Because Jesus calls her daughter, the type of woman who is a part of Jesus' new family is the kind who is willing to violate social conventions and to respond to Jesus' invitation to take center stage and become the audience's focus of attention. At his baptism, Jesus was declared the Son of God; this woman is now God's "granddaughter." Just as Jesus' faithful decision to be baptized led to the declaration of sonship, her faith led to this declaration. The fact that Jesus is willing to delay helping Jairus indicates the value that he placed on the bleeding woman—not just on her healing (which has already occurred), but on the conversation that he has with her.

The effect (if not the purpose) of the purity regulations related to menstruation was to severely restrict female activity and public presence. The woman should not be in a crowd and should not be touching Jesus, but Jesus not only permits but celebrates these things and requires her to take a more public position than she herself is willing to inhabit. To then go a step further and compare the woman's body to Jesus' body is a departure from social norms and a radical affirmation of the goodness of women's bodies.

Much as the stilling of the storm "redeemed" the Jonah story, the story of the bleeding woman redeems the story of Eve's fall. The principle of motif inversion[71]—where a theme from an HB story is partially reenacted and then inverted—is a key literary strategy for Mark in this section of the Gospel. This method is not only a clever literary device that rewards close attention from the audience, but it also allows form to follow function: the form of the story is to "redeem" the reading of an HB text while simultaneously introducing the idea of Jesus as the redeemer.

---

71. Beavis, "Jephthah's Daughter," 61.

A compelling inversion occurs here as the end of the woman's uncontrollable flow of blood happens in the same moment when Jesus experiences an uncontrollable flow of power. There is a sense in which she exerts some control over Jesus (by drawing on the power he holds) at the same time that Jesus exerts control over her (by healing her). Once again, the woman's body and Jesus' body are paralleled. And since under the law of Moses, any sort of bodily discharge rendered the person unclean, Jesus' discharge of power as evidence of strength suggests a novel reordering and points to his unique relationship to the law of Moses. Inasmuch as this story suggests a similarity between blood and power, it establishes the groundwork for the shedding of Jesus' own blood to be viewed as an example of his power.

The story of the raising of Jairus's daughter shows Jesus' power over death, but it also shows his concern for children (who were not highly regarded in antiquity), including young girls. There is no canonized story of a raising from the dead that does not have a female witness to the event,[72] so the presence of the mother is not an extraneous detail but rather a key part of that pattern. The raising of the girl foreshadows Jesus' Resurrection. It is significant that it is the body of a young girl that is the proxy for the body of Jesus (whose body is the proxy for everyone else's bodies). The fact that she is not a mother (motherhood was seen as the primary value of female bodies) extends the countercultural nature of this message. One important aspect of this story is the work that it does in requiring the audience to reimagine the function and worth of female bodies. Given the disdain in which women's bodies (and women in general) were held in the ancient world, the idea that Mark would present women and their bodies as a worthy comparison to Jesus and his body serves to, in a metaphorical sense, redeem women's bodies.

Given the similar treatment that Jesus shows to Jairus and the bleeding woman despite their disparate statuses, it is very clear that Mark wants

---

72. There may be a few exceptions to this general rule, but each is debatable: (1) 2 Kings 13:20–21 depicts a dead man who revives when buried with Elisha's corpse; this story seems more mythical than historical. (2) Acts 20:9–12 may depict Paul raising Eutychus from the dead, but it is possible that Eutychus had not actually died. (3) 3 Nephi 7:19 and 19:4 are not the accounts of a raising from the dead but merely a statement in passing. Given the paucity of female characters in the Book of Mormon, the presence of women in Alma 19 is a notable example of the pattern of including female witnesses whenever there is a raising from the dead or anything symbolically similar. Stories of raisings from the dead that include a female character include 16:1–8; 1 Kings 17:17–24; 2 Kings 4:16–37; Luke 7:12–15; John 11; Acts 9:36–41; and Hebrews 11:35.

the audience to understand that Jesus' ministry was to bless and help all people regardless of their social or cultural status. At the same time, Jairus loses nothing—his daughter is, ultimately, returned to health. It is the way of the fallen world to think of resources (such as Jesus' time) as limited and thus to allocate them on the basis of status, but this story shows that Jesus' ministry is not restricted in that way.

Purity laws (and their violation) undergird the story of the Gerasene demoniac, the bleeding woman, and the raising of Jairus's daughter. The presence of impurity in all three of these stories conveys that it is not only in gentile lands where impurity is a problem. Further, Jesus' relationship to the law of Moses is unique. The priests had no mechanism by which they could make the bleeding woman or Jairus's daughter clean; they could merely pronounce them ritually clean after they had become clean through other means. Jesus could actually cleanse them, which indicates his greater power and authority. Numbers 5:1–4 lists the people who must be excluded from the camp of Israel due to impurity: lepers, those with a bodily discharge, and corpses. Jesus has now healed people in all three categories, symbolically welcoming them back into the camp of Israel and inviting them not only back into the community of the covenant but also into the presence of the Lord.

The miracles in 4:35–5:43 show Jesus' control over all of the ways in which a person could be threatened—by nature, demons, disease, and death—and thus work together to illustrate the totality of Jesus' authority and power. Mark's text teaches that Jesus will protect those who welcome him from anything that threatens them. Much as the five controversy stories in 2:1–3:6 feature an ever-increasing level of hostility directed toward Jesus, these miracles feature a pattern of increasing levels of miraculousness—from the disciples' fear that they will die, to a living death among the tombs, to sickness, and finally to literal death. In each case, Jesus' power is sufficient to meet the challenge. The varied cast of characters—the chosen disciples, unnamed Gentiles, men, women, the wealthy, the poor—also highlights the scope of Jesus' authority and power.

Mission and Rejection
(6:1–31)

The previous section, 4:35–5:43, highlighted miracles and emphasized the role of faith. In contrast, chapter 6 begins with Jesus' experience in Nazareth, where the people's lack of faith made it all but impossible for him to perform miracles. The bulk of this section concerns the story of the death of John the Baptist. One theme weaving through these stories is that people stumble when they do not understand Jesus' true identity. Mark uses the story of John's death to teach about Jesus' ministry since John is the forerunner who shows the path that Jesus will follow.

John's imprisonment (which was already mentioned in 1:14) and death are narrated as a flashback and bracketed by references to the sending out of the Twelve; this structure is a classic Markan sandwich. Because the text flows very smoothly when omitting 6:14–29, it appears that Mark has very deliberately placed the account of John's death in the middle of another narrative, most likely in order to emphasize the theme of discipleship. First, Jesus' mission was rejected in his hometown; now Mark wants the audience to think about the mission of the Twelve in terms of the mission of John the Baptist.

Jesus Is Rejected
(6:1–6)

Greek Text

1 Καὶ ἐξῆλθεν ἐκεῖθεν, καὶ ἔρχεται εἰς τὴν πατρίδα αὐτοῦ, καὶ ἀκολουθοῦσιν αὐτῷ οἱ μαθηταὶ αὐτοῦ. 2 καὶ γενομένου σαββάτου ἤρξατο διδάσκειν ἐν τῇ συναγωγῇ· καὶ οἱ πολλοὶ ἀκούοντες ἐξεπλήσσοντο λέγοντες· Πόθεν τούτῳ ταῦτα, καὶ τίς ἡ σοφία ἡ δοθεῖσα τούτῳ, καὶ αἱ δυνάμεις τοιαῦται διὰ τῶν χειρῶν αὐτοῦ γινόμεναι; 3 οὐχ οὗτός ἐστιν ὁ τέκτων, ὁ υἱὸς τῆς Μαρίας καὶ ἀδελφὸς Ἰακώβου καὶ Ἰωσῆτος καὶ Ἰούδα καὶ Σίμωνος; καὶ οὐκ εἰσὶν αἱ ἀδελφαὶ αὐτοῦ ὧδε πρὸς ἡμᾶς; καὶ ἐσκανδαλίζοντο ἐν αὐτῷ. 4 καὶ ἔλεγεν αὐτοῖς ὁ Ἰησοῦς ὅτι Οὐκ ἔστιν προφήτης ἄτιμος εἰ μὴ ἐν τῇ πατρίδι αὐτοῦ καὶ ἐν τοῖς συγγενεῦσιν αὐτοῦ καὶ ἐν τῇ οἰκίᾳ αὐτοῦ. 5 καὶ οὐκ ἐδύνατο ἐκεῖ ποιῆσαι οὐδεμίαν δύναμιν, εἰ μὴ ὀλίγοις ἀρρώστοις ἐπιθεὶς τὰς χεῖρας ἐθεράπευσεν· 6 καὶ ἐθαύμαζεν διὰ τὴν ἀπιστίαν αὐτῶν.

Καὶ περιῆγεν τὰς κώμας κύκλῳ διδάσκων. [SBLGNT]

King James Version

1 And he went out from thence, and came into his own country; and his disciples follow him. 2 And when the sabbath day was come, he began to teach in the synagogue: and many hearing him were astonished, saying, From whence hath this man these things? and what wisdom is this which is given unto him, that even such mighty works are wrought by his hands? 3 Is not this the carpenter, the son of Mary, the brother of James, and Joses, and of Juda, and Simon? and are not his sisters here with us? And they were offended at him. 4 But Jesus said unto them, A prophet is not without honour, but in his own country, and among his own kin, and in his own house. 5 And he could there do no mighty work, save that he laid his hands upon a few sick folk, and healed them. 6 And he marvelled because of their unbelief. And he went round about the villages, teaching.

New Rendition

1 And he went out from there and came to his hometown. And his disciples follow him. 2 And the Sabbath having come, he began to teach in the synagogue. And many hearing him were astonished, saying, "Where did this one get these things? And what is this wisdom that has been given to him? What miracles are done by his hands? 3 Isn't this the builder? Mary's son, and the brother of Jacob, Joses, Judas, and Simon? And aren't his sisters here with us?" And they did not respect him. 4 And Jesus said to them, "A prophet is not without honor except in his hometown and among his relatives and in his own household." 5 And he wasn't able to perform any miracle there, except on a few sick people: having laid on hands, he healed them. 6 And he was amazed at their lack of belief.

Notes

6:1 *and he went out from thence:* "Thence" probably refers to Jairus's house (5:38).

and came into his own country: Jesus' "own country" is Nazareth (1:9, 24). (There is no reference to Bethlehem in Mark's Gospel.)

and his disciples follow him: The disciples have no role in this story. Mark probably mentions them because it is important that they witness Jesus' rejection as the prelude to their own missions, for which Jesus specifically prepares them for the possibility of rejection (6:11).

6:2 *And when the sabbath day was come, he began to teach in the synagogue: and many hearing him were astonished, saying:* Some manuscripts read "most" instead of "many" here.[1] The textual history is disputed, and it is difficult to determine which reading is better.

From whence hath this man these things: The phrase "this man" "expresses contempt."[2] Both this line and the next can be read as questions ("From whence hath this man these things? What wisdom is this that is given unto him?") or as exclamations ("From whence hath this man these things! What wisdom is this that is given unto him!"). These are both incomplete sentences; lacking finite verbs, they reflect the people's astonishment. It is as if they are so amazed that they cannot even form complete sentences.

Of course, Mark's audience already knows the answers to these questions: Jesus has power from God through the Holy Spirit at his baptism. The questions permit the audience to examine their own thinking about Jesus and to realize that they are now "insiders" to Jesus' ministry—even more so than the people who lived in his hometown.

The people of Nazareth are not in doubt about the reality of Jesus' power. Throughout Mark's text (see 3:20–30), no one denies that Jesus has special powers; rather, they debate the source of those powers. In this case, "more than just a matter of familiarity breeding contempt, this comes from the ancient mentality that geographical and [hereditary] origins determine who a person is and what his capacities will always be. They see Jesus as someone who is not merely exceeding expectations but rather is overreaching. This will in fact be the last time in Mark that we find Jesus in

---

1. Collins, *Mark,* 287 note a.
2. Bratcher and Nida, *Translator's Handbook,* 183.

a synagogue and is the last mention that Jesus taught."[3] Much as Jesus silently and willingly left after exorcising the man when the people asked him to, he stops teaching and visiting the synagogue when he is rejected.

and what wisdom is this which is given unto him: The emphasis here is on the phrase "unto him," as if to say, "and how did he *of all people* end up with this wisdom?" The phrasing suggests a divine passive ("which is given"), which ironically means that they are answering their own question: Jesus' wisdom comes from God. But they are not willing to accept the implications of that fact.

that even such mighty works are wrought by his hands: Some manuscripts change the end of the verse to a declaration instead of a question—"'and such powerful works occur through his hands!'"[4] The sentiment might be understood a little differently depending on whether they are asking questions and then making a proclamation that recognized Jesus' abilities or voicing a string of questions. If the variant reading is adopted, there is a parallel between 6:2 and 6:3: both involve a list of questions followed by a statement; however, in 6:2, the statement is a recognition of Jesus' abilities, but in 6:3, it is an offended response.

The mention of Jesus' hands emphasizes the idea that he is the last person they would have expected to be a conduit for miracles because his hands are the hands of a laborer, not a miracle worker.

It is difficult to know how closely this story is linked to the previous section, but it is possible that word of Jesus calming the storm, healing the demoniac and the bleeding woman, and raising the girl (but compare 5:43) has reached Nazareth, and these are the miracles to which they refer.

Given that the phrasing of this verse implies hostility, it is unlikely that these would be genuine questions but are instead probably criticism hiding behind questions. At the same time, these questions encourage the audience to think about the questions and their true answers. The crowd serves an important narrative role by creating an opening for the audience to ponder sincerely, even if the questions have been asked derisively.

Allusion to Isaiah. According to Isaiah 11:2, the combination of wisdom and might belongs to the Davidic ruler who will come in the future. This allusion may be strengthened by the word "branch," which is very similar to the word for "Nazareth" in the previous verse. Once again, the people

---

3. Witherington, *Gospel of Mark,* 192.
4. Collins, *Mark,* 287 note c.

seem to be unwittingly answering their own question: Jesus is the promised ruler from the line of David.

6:3 *Is not this the carpenter:* Some manuscripts read "the son of the carpenter," although the KJV reading is more likely to have been the earlier one.[5] Perhaps the wording was changed because:

1. It was considered insulting to call Jesus a carpenter, since this would have situated him within the lower classes.

2. The change to "the son of the carpenter" was made to harmonize with Matthew.

3. It would have been considered offensive to refer to Jesus as only his mother's son and not also as the son of his (legal) father.

Reading "the son of a carpenter" changes the nuance of the verse, not only because of what it might imply about Jesus' socioeconomic position but also because it would mean every description of him in this verse is relational (son, son, brother). In other words, Jesus' family makes his power and authority difficult to believe. For Mark, recognizing who Jesus is requires the audience to not be limited by the assumption that one's background has any relation to one's spiritual power.

The word that the KJV translates as "carpenter" can refer to a builder working with any material (wood, stone, metal, etc.); because Nazareth was so small, Jesus may have worked with a variety of materials. (It is also possible that Jesus worked in Sepphoris, which was only a few miles from Nazareth; it was undergoing something of a building boom during Jesus' life, and there would have been ample—and more specialized—work opportunities there.) The New Rendition uses the word "builder," which covers all of the options.

In Jesus' world, manual labor was considered degrading, so this question is insulting. The presumption is that Jesus' occupation implies that he has no extraordinary powers. The complaint is that he is not trained as a religious authority but rather worked as a common laborer. Interestingly, "the problem with hometown folks is that they know both too much and too little about a person."[6] Mark wants the audience to realize that a person is not limited by his family of origin; in its historical context, this is a radical notion.

---

5. Metzger, *Textual Commentary,* 75–76.
6. Witherington, *Gospel of Mark,* 200.

Two absences are significant here:

1. Mark has not mentioned before that Jesus is a carpenter. His occupation is only important to the critical townspeople and not to Mark's presentation of Jesus.

2. Most of Jesus' parables and teachings refer to farming, not to construction. Jesus taught in a manner that would be relevant to his audience—not in a way that was necessarily familiar and comfortable to him personally.

the son of Mary: There are a variety of opinions as to how the words "the son of Mary" should be interpreted:

1. There is general (but not universal) agreement that to refer to a man as the son of his mother is an insult implying illegitimacy. (But the alternative phrasing—"the son of Joseph"—may have been problematic for Mark.[7]) The reference to Jesus as a carpenter in the previous phrase increases the likelihood that calling him Mary's son is an insult given the context of derogatory speech. If Mark and the audience were aware of the circumstances of Jesus' birth, then the audience might be expected to interpret this insult ironically: the people thought they were questioning Jesus' legitimacy, but they had no idea that they were being precisely accurate since Joseph was not really his biological father.

2. The phrase "son of Mary" is meant to indicate a difference between Jesus and his brothers, who were more properly the sons of Joseph.

3. Both the heavens and the demons have recognized Jesus as the Son of God; the reference to Jesus as the son of Mary highlights the gulf between the true identity of Jesus and the incorrect assumptions that people make about him.

4. "Son of Mary" indicates that Joseph is deceased. It may even be informal ("you know, the son of Mary, who lives over there").

5. In 6:1, the word for "hometown" (KJV: "country") can be translated as "fatherland"; it contains the same root word as "father." Mark heightens the irony that within his fatherland, Jesus' father is not recognized—neither his supposed father, Joseph, nor his eternal father, God.

6. There are some ancient instances of a son referred to as his mother's son without implied insult.[8] This usage seems to occur when the mother had a higher, even royal, status, but it may not fit the context here, where the point of the townspeople's complaint is that Jesus' background is entirely ordinary.

---

7. Note, however, that Mark does not mention the idea of a virgin birth. Mark may have omitted this as irrelevant to a focus on discipleship; it is also possible that the author is unaware of the circumstances of Jesus' birth.

8. Tal Ilan, "'Man Born of Woman . . .' (Job 14:1): The Phenomenon of Men Bearing Metronymes at the Time of Jesus," *Novum Testamentum* 34, no. 1 (1992): 23–45.

7. The reference "places [Jesus] outside the kingly line and emphasizes his very ordinariness ... [and] it indicates ... that the Markan Jesus represents all humanity, female as well as male."[9]

the brother of James, and Joses, and of Juda, and Simon?: Some ancient Christian traditions, in an effort to defend the idea of the perpetual virginity of Mary, postulated that these were not siblings but cousins, or perhaps half-siblings from a (hypothetical) previous marriage of Joseph's. But absent a desire to defend that doctrine, there is no reason to think that the people named here are anything other than Mary's biological children.

It may be significant that all four of these brothers share their names with HB patriarchs: "James" is the KJV translation of "Jacob"[10] and "Joses" is short for "Joseph."

and are not his sisters here with us?: The phrase "here with us" may indicate that the brothers, by contrast, were not with them in Nazareth; perhaps they were following Jesus in Capernaum, or they had moved away for other reasons. The sisters, who might be literally present in the synagogue as this scene unfolds, may be young enough to still live at home with Mary, or they may have married local men. They are mentioned as evidence of Jesus' unexceptional background.

The lack of reference to Joseph (who is never mentioned in Mark's Gospel) may suggest that he was deceased by this point, but this is speculative.

And they were offended at him: "Offended" is imperfect, implying an ongoing (not a one-time) action. Because the same word is used in 4:17, the people of Nazareth are associated with the stony ground. This link may explain an odd dynamic in this text: the people go from amazement and questions to offense within the space of a few verses because, like the plant on stony ground, they immediately received the word but then became offended.

These offended people are aware of Jesus' miracles, so Mark makes the point that witnessing miracles is not sufficient for developing faith. But there is no record of Jesus performing miracles in Nazareth; perhaps these folks are offended that they were not the beneficiaries of the miraculous powers of which they have heard so much. The references to his family would then imply something like "you'd think he would perform miracles here, where his family would benefit from them." This reading makes sense

---

9. Mary Noonan Sabin, *Reopening the Word: Reading Mark as Theology in the Context of Early Judaism* (Oxford: Oxford University Press, 2011), 147.

10. See the Notes on 1:19.

of their offense, which can otherwise be difficult to understand given how quickly it follows their astonishment. This reaction by the people becomes ironic proof that Jesus is a prophet, given his proverb (see the Notes on 6:4) that prophets are not honored in their own lands.

Allusion to Isaiah. In Isaiah 8:14, the Lord of Hosts is described as "a stone of stumbling" and a "rock of offence" to some people. Mark's text may be a deliberate allusion to that prophecy or even a fulfillment of it.

6:4 *But Jesus said unto them, A prophet is not without honour:* It is not clear whether "them" refers to Jesus' disciples, to the people of Nazareth, or to both.

Is Jesus claiming to be a prophet here?

1. Yes. He describes himself as a prophet through the use of this proverb and thus aligns himself with the prophets of the HB.

2. No. Other texts in Mark make clear that "prophet" is an inadequate title for Jesus because it minimizes his mission (6:15; 8:28). He is no more claiming to be a prophet than he was claiming to be a physician when he used a proverb about physicians (2:17). Jesus is a physician and a prophet only in a metaphorical sense.

Regardless, this proverb about prophets fits the context well, since so many HB prophets were rejected. In an ironic twist, rejection becomes an indicator of the veracity of the prophetic calling.

but in his own country, and among his own kin, and in his own house: This verse is a proverb with Hellenistic and Jewish parallels that convey the idea that proximity makes it difficult to recognize superiority ("familiarity breeds contempt"). As is normally the case with proverbs, this one is generally applicable but not absolute: after all, Jesus was just rejected in gentile lands (5:17). The proverb also supplies a thematic link to the story of John's death later in this chapter. The rejection of Jesus by those closest to him is a theme that Mark has explored before (3:20–21, 31–35).

The word that the KJV translates as "country" is the same word used in 6:1. Additionally, the Greek word translated as "his own kin" (Greek: *sungenēs*) sounds similar to the word for "synagogue" (Greek: *sunagōgē*) in 6:2; these echoes highlight that Jesus was in his native land.

6:5 *And he could there do no mighty work:* It may be that it was not possible for Jesus to perform miracles, or perhaps he chose not to in the absence of faith. Jesus has healed before in the presence of a hostile audience (3:1–6), and a healing has occurred apparently without his foreknowledge (5:25–34). Jesus generally heals only in response to requests for healing (but contrast 3:1–6); if there were no faith, no one would ask him to heal, and therefore there would be no healings.

There is quite a bit of irony here: it was witnessing Jesus' mighty works that led the people of Nazareth to be offended by him, which led to Jesus no longer performing mighty works. Their attitude is a self-fulfilling prophecy: they did not believe that Jesus could do mighty works, and so he did not.

save that he laid his hands upon a few sick folk, and healed them: While unusual to modern ears, this verse uses a common speech pattern in which a general rule ("no mighty works") is followed by an exception to the rule ("a few sick folk [were] healed"). Mark does not clarify whether these people had faith and so were able to be healed or whether they were healed in the absence of faith. The previous story made it clear that the woman's faith made her healing possible (5:34). It is also possible that he performed some miracles "based on his mercy and not on faith."[11] Another possibility is that healing a few people did not, in Mark's mind, qualify as "mighty works."

This verse provides a good example of the role of the Gospel writer in shaping the account. It would have been possible for Mark to omit that Jesus could do no mighty works in Nazareth and instead to emphasize the healings that he did perform; this would have created a radically different impression of the situation in the minds of the audience. By framing it this way, the text stresses the lack of miracles in Nazareth.

6:6 *And he marvelled because of their unbelief:* While "marvelled" in this verse does not translate the same Greek verb as "astonished" in 6:2, the sentiment is similar. This incident is therefore bounded by references to the amazed state of the people of Nazareth and of Jesus.

It seems that for Jesus to marvel, he must be surprised by events, which would indicate a lack of foreknowledge. Elsewhere, Mark's text suggests that Jesus is, during mortality, not omniscient (5:30; 13:32), so it is possible that Jesus is genuinely surprised by their reaction to him. Note the irony: when the people expect that Jesus has no special ability, he acts in accordance with that expectation and shows no special ability, marveling in surprise just as any ordinary person would.

The word "unbelief" is interesting here, given that the people previously confessed a knowledge of Jesus' mighty works. The fact that unbelief can coexist with belief in mighty works is very telling; it points to the inability of miracles to create belief. As mentioned previously, "faith" in Mark's

---

11. Stein, *Mark,* 284.

Gospel generally does not mean assent to statements of fact but rather trust in Jesus. These people clearly do not trust Jesus, despite their belief that he could perform mighty works.

Parallels with 1:21–28. This text in Mark shares extensive similarities with the inaugural exorcism in 1:21–28, which also has reference to the Sabbath, the synagogue, Jesus' teachings, the amazement of the people, and questions about Jesus' actions and powers. The fact that this story ends on a much more negative note than chapter 1 may imply something about increasing hostility to Jesus. Or, it may point to the fact that, surprisingly, demons are easier to exorcise than false beliefs: Jesus will command the one but not the other. That is, he does not recognize the agency of the demons to dwell in humans, but he acknowledges the right of humans to willingly host false beliefs if they choose to.

And he went round about the villages, teaching: "Round about" implies that Jesus is traveling to the villages surrounding Nazareth.

The New Rendition takes this sentence as the beginning of the next story, not the end of the scene in Nazareth. It seems to fit better in that context. While it is possible to view this teaching as a response to the lack of faith in Nazareth, it also sets the stage for Jesus to call the Twelve to do what he has been doing: traveling and teaching.

In the next story, Jesus will tell the Twelve to shake the dust off of their feet in the villages that do not accept them. It may be significant that Jesus himself does not do this in Nazareth.

Analysis

The people of Nazareth are engaging in the normal, expected behavior of assuming that Jesus was a product of his familial background. (Interestingly, their attitude suggests that there was nothing exceptional about Jesus' childhood.) Clearly, Mark rejects that assumption. Jesus has already set the stage to abandon this belief in 3:31–35, where he proclaimed his true family to be not his biological family but rather those who are willing to follow him.

Note the paradox: the combination of aspects of Jesus that seem divine (mighty works, wisdom) alongside aspects that seem normal (family relations, occupation) make it impossible for them to believe in him. As the story of Jesus' anointing will show (see the Notes on 14:3–9), it is the combination of Jesus' identities (sufferer, priest, and king) that make it difficult for most people—but not the woman who anoints him—to understand who he is. There is a preview of that motif here as the people from his hometown struggle to understand how his hands can do manual labor as well as miracles.

Some commenters find evidence of a poorly edited text in the note of Jesus' marveling here: after all, he just recited a proverb that explains that people normally reject prophets in their own land, so there is no reason to marvel at this behavior as if it were unexpected. But rather than seeing this incident as the result of sloppy editing, it probably makes more sense to read the marveling in the context of the normal pattern of a healing miracle. (Also, just because a coherent explanation for an event can be articulated does not mean that the event is not surprising.) Usually, the pattern of a miracle story is for the onlookers to react with amazement to the miracle; here, Jesus reacts with amazement at what is, in effect, an anti-miracle story. There is a sense in which Jesus has traded places with the people because he is marveling when they should be; this might be a subtle allusion to the theology of the Atonement that Mark develops throughout this text.

In a typical healing story, someone presents Jesus with a physical ailment and he corrects it, making the person whole again. In this story, which is an inversion of the typical healing narrative, the people present Jesus with their objections to him. But this is a disease of the will, not of the body, and Jesus is thus powerless to fix it because that would require overriding their will. He cannot heal their moral agency because it belongs to them. Their malady, which only they can heal for themselves, is their false assumptions about Jesus' identity.

Much as the story of John's death later in this chapter foreshadows Jesus' own death, Jesus' rejection in Nazareth sets the stage for his ultimate rejection later on. Because the string of miracle stories in chapter 5 presented such a positive vision of Jesus' ministry, Mark may have chosen to include this story to emphasize the theme of opposition to Jesus, particularly with the terribly dark story of John's death looming over this chapter.

The people in Nazareth are asking good questions about Jesus, but they are not reaching the right answers. This story indicates that merely posing proper questions is not enough to ensure successful discipleship. These people are not willing to ask Jesus for his help (which would show faith and give him an opportunity to perform miracles) nor are they willing to follow him; they thus lack the characteristics of true disciples.

JESUS SENDS OUT THE TWELVE (6:7–13)

Greek Text

7 καὶ προσκαλεῖται τοὺς δώδεκα, καὶ ἤρξατο αὐτοὺς ἀποστέλλειν δύο δύο, καὶ ἐδίδου αὐτοῖς ἐξουσίαν τῶν πνευμάτων τῶν ἀκαθάρτων, 8 καὶ παρήγγειλεν αὐτοῖς ἵνα μηδὲν αἴρωσιν εἰς ὁδὸν εἰ μὴ ῥάβδον μόνον, μὴ ἄρτον, μὴ πήραν, μὴ εἰς τὴν ζώνην χαλκόν, 9 ἀλλὰ ὑποδεδεμένους σανδάλια, καὶ μὴ ἐνδύσησθε δύο χιτῶνας. 10 καὶ ἔλεγεν αὐτοῖς· Ὅπου ἐὰν εἰσέλθητε εἰς οἰκίαν, ἐκεῖ μένετε ἕως ἂν ἐξέλθητε ἐκεῖθεν. 11 καὶ ὃς ἂν τόπος μὴ δέξηται ὑμᾶς μηδὲ ἀκούσωσιν ὑμῶν, ἐκπορευόμενοι ἐκεῖθεν ἐκτινάξατε τὸν χοῦν τὸν ὑποκάτω τῶν ποδῶν ὑμῶν εἰς μαρτύριον αὐτοῖς. 12 Καὶ ἐξελθόντες ἐκήρυξαν ἵνα μετανοῶσιν, 13 καὶ δαιμόνια πολλὰ ἐξέβαλλον, καὶ ἤλειφον ἐλαίῳ πολλοὺς ἀρρώστους καὶ ἐθεράπευον. [SBLGNT]

King James Version

7 And he called unto him the twelve, and began to send them forth by two and two; and gave them power over unclean spirits; 8 And commanded them that they should take nothing for their journey, save a staff only; no scrip, no bread, no money in their purse: 9 But be shod with sandals; and not put on two coats. 10 And he said unto them, In what place soever ye enter into an house, there abide till ye depart from that place. 11 And whosoever shall not receive you, nor hear you, when ye depart thence, shake off the dust under your feet for a testimony against them. Verily I say unto you, It shall be more tolerable for Sodom and Gomorrha in the day of judgment, than for that city. 12 And they went out, and preached that men should repent. 13 And they cast out many devils, and anointed with oil many that were sick, and healed them.

New Rendition

And he went around among the villages teaching. 7 And he calls the Twelve to him and began to send them out two by two and gave them power/authority over unclean spirits. 8 He instructed them that they should take nothing for the way except for a staff only—no bread, no satchel, no money in their belts— 9 "but wear sandals and don't wear two tunics." 10 And he said to them, "Wherever you enter a house, stay there until you leave that area. 11 And if any place will not accept you or hear you, depart from there and shake the dirt off of your feet as a testimony to/against them." 12 And having gone out, they proclaimed that people should change their minds. 13 And they drove out many demons and anointed many sick people with oil and healed them.

Notes

6:7 *And he called unto him the twelve, and began to send them forth by two and two:* The verb translated as "send" is a cognate of the word for "apostle." Further, "the verb used for sending is a technical term for a delegation. It carries the notion of a special commission and the delegation of authority to accomplish that commission."[12]

In Mark's story, "there is in the context no thought of the creation at this time of a permanent office, but rather the fulfillment of a specific commission. This is an important consideration; it signifies that the instructions which Jesus gave to the disciples do not have a general and permanent validity. They are relevant to this particular commission."[13] While Latter-day Saints believe that these disciples were later called to apostleship as a permanent office, it does not appear to be the case that that calling came at this point. If this distinction is not maintained, it can (and has) led to confusion regarding whether the restrictions that Jesus articulates here are expected to be followed by the Twelve at all times. To put the case in modern Latter-day Saint terms, it is preferable to think of this text as a missionary call and not an apostolic call.

This section creates the expectation in the audience that the Twelve will organize a similar mission after Jesus dies, particularly if the negative response to Jesus' ministry in Nazareth is a foreshadowing of Jesus' death. The fact that they don't, but scatter in lack of faith and fear,[14] emphasizes their failure at the cross and the tomb and advances Mark's theme of discipleship.

and gave them power over unclean spirits: Mark 3:15 also gave the Twelve power over unclean spirits. No specific mention is made of teaching or healing; perhaps these are to be presumed.

6:8 *And commanded them that they should take nothing for their journey:* The New Rendition translates "way" instead of "journey" here; while both are adequate, "way" was chosen since "The Way" was a common designation for the early Christian movement (for example, Acts 9:2), and that meaning may have resonated with Mark's audience.

---

12. Collins, *Mark,* 297.

13. Lane, *Gospel according to Mark,* 207.

14. See 16:1–8 and the Notes on those verses (16:9–20 was not originally part of Mark's Gospel).

The command to take nothing must be read in light of the exceptions that follow it.

save a staff only: Staffs were a protection against human and animal predators as well as an aid to walking. If they are to take a staff, the presumption is that they will not be enjoying divine protection from threats. Rather, the reference to the staff—especially as the first item on the list—indicates that they will need to protect themselves.

Relationship to 2 Kings 4:29. In 2 Kings 4:29, Elisha's commissioning of Gehazi includes the command to take Elisha's staff. Interestingly, Gehazi does not successfully complete the task for which he has been sent out: Gehazi was supposed to use the staff to raise a dead child but was unsuccessful, so the raising had to wait for the appearance of Elisha. If the reference to the staff is supposed to encourage an allusion in the minds of the audience, then there is a hint that the Twelve will not be successful in their mission—only the one who sent them will succeed.

---

no scrip, no bread, no money in their purse: Various theories are offered to explain the items that Jesus allows (a staff) and forbids (money, bread, purse):

1. The forbidden items would be needed on longer journeys, but the towns in Galilee are close enough to each other that there would be no need for bread to eat en route, money to buy food between towns, or a second tunic for warmth at night while sleeping in the open. The Twelve will sleep and eat in towns, relying on the hospitality of the people. The fact that Jesus permits a staff suggests that they are to rely on others for everything that other people could be expected to provide, but it is unreasonable to think that someone else would protect them while traveling, so they will need their own staffs. They are not supposed to be self-sufficient: they are to have faith that God, through the people they teach, will provide for them. However, if this command is read in light of the warnings about being rejected, then perhaps they should expect to do without.

2. When the children of Israel prepare for the Exodus from Egypt, there is reference to a staff (Ex. 12:11), bread (from heaven [Ex. 16]), sandals (Ex. 12:11), and a single item of clothing (which does not wear out, even after forty years, due to divine intervention [Deut. 8:4; 29:5–6]). If Mark's text mirrors the Exodus, these allusions would imply that the mission of the Twelve is akin to leaving slavery and entering the wilderness. One theme of the Exodus narrative is that God will care for the people in the wilderness; the allusion might suggest that God will similarly care for the Twelve. Given Israel's experience in the wilderness, this parallel suggests that the disciples will have trials and will not always act in accord with the Lord's expectations.

6:9 *But be shod with sandals:* The New Rendition is somewhat awkward as it reflects how Mark's text shifts from the narrator's words to Jesus' words without the standard introductory phrase "Jesus said" as preface.

Why does Jesus tell them to wear sandals?

1. The reference to (money) belts and sandals alludes to John the Baptist (1:6), which sets the stage for the coming story of the death of John.

2. Jesus does not permit them to wear more expensive shoes, which would have covered the top of the foot. The simple footwear would signify their commitment to avoiding luxury.

and not put on two coats: There is no adequate English translation for "coats"; the text refers to an inner garment (not a coat) that is not precisely a shirt (because it is longer) but not underwear (because it is the shape of a long shirt). Options for understanding the prohibition on two coats include:

1. Wealthier people wore inner and outer tunics, so the disciples should distinguish themselves from the wealthy. The point is that they should dress like poorer people.

2. Cynic philosophers traveled around and were known to carry these cloaks; "cynics were despised by the public and . . . their cloak, begging bag, and staff were objects of contempt."[15] Jesus wants to ensure that his disciples are not confused with Cynics.

While the reasons behind these particular commands and prohibitions can be difficult to discern at this historical distance, one thing is clear: "These strict instructions indicate both the extreme urgency of their mission and the greatness of the power they have been given."[16]

6:10 *And he said unto them, In what place soever ye enter into an house, there abide till ye depart from that place:* The disciples are not to move from home to home within one village if they are offered superior accommodations; they are to stay in one place to avoid offending their hosts. Once again, the Twelve are encouraged to identify themselves with the poorer classes of people.

6:11 *And whosoever shall not receive you, nor hear you:* Many manuscripts read "when a place" instead of "whosoever" here, with the former likely to be the earlier reading and the latter reflecting a change made either to harmonize with Luke 9:5 or so the verse will flow more smoothly.[17] The

---

15. Collins, *Mark*, 299.
16. Heil, *Gospel of Mark as a Model for Action*, 135.
17. Collins, *Mark*, 293 note d.

ritual of dusting off the feet seems to better fit rejection by a place than rejection by a person.

when ye depart thence, shake off the dust under your feet for a testimony against them: The phrase "when ye depart" can be read as a command to depart.

Shaking off the dust can have several different meanings:

1. The disciples are not required to be tainted by their failures—they are to move forward without past setbacks clinging to them.

2. The transition from stranger to guest was made as the host either provided water or actually washed the feet of the guest.[18] So shaking dust off of the feet is evidence that they were not offered hospitality. This reading coheres well with the reference to Sodom and Gomorrah, since lack of hospitality was understood to be a major reason why those cities were destroyed (Ezek. 16:49). This reading has the advantage of making every item in the list of instructions connected to hospitality (since the point of prohibiting certain items would have made it necessary for them to rely on hospitality).

3. Jewish tradition called for those who had ventured outside of Israel to cleanse all dust from foreign lands from their clothing and body,[19] as if the very ground were ritually impure. If this understanding is behind the prohibition, then Jesus has portrayed the nonreceptive people as foreigners and their land as unclean.

4. In the early Christian tradition, shaking dust off of the feet was a protest and sign of judgment when the disciples were rejected (Acts 13:51; 18:6). While that practice might be the natural result of this text, it is also possible that that sentiment predated Mark's Gospel and is thus reflected here.

5. In some Jewish traditions, entering the temple area with a staff, sandals, money belt, or dusty feet was prohibited.[20] The similarities may imply that Jesus conceived of their mission experience as sacred ground, although the overlap in items is not perfect.

The "testimony against them" can be understood as positive (a witness, which offers a chance to repent) or negative (a judgment against them [compare D&C 24:15; 60:15]).

Verily I say unto you, It shall be more tolerable for Sodom and Gomorrha in the day of judgment, than for that city: This sentence is omitted in

---

18. T. J. Rogers, "Shaking the Dust off the Markan Mission Discourse," *Journal for the Study of the New Testament* 27 (December 2004): 171.

19. Tosefta Kelim Bava Kamma 1:5.

20. Mishna Berakhot 9:5.

many of the earliest manuscripts; it was probably added to parallel Matthew 10:15.[21] The line implies that the sin of the people who reject the Twelve is a lack of hospitality, as was the case with Sodom and Gomorrha.

6:12 *And they went out, and preached that men should repent:* The Twelve were called to two seemingly contradictory tasks: to be with Jesus and to go out. They have been with Jesus since chapter 3, and now it is time for them to go out.

6:13 *And they cast out many devils, and anointed with oil many that were sick:* Jesus never anoints with oil in this Gospel (although he himself is anointed; see chapter 14). In the HB, oil was used medicinally (Isa. 1:6; Jer. 8:22; 51:8) and had a ritual function (Lev. 14:15–18). The only other NT reference to healing with oil is in James 5:14.

Jesus normally heals by touching people. Is it significant, then, that the disciples are using oil instead of touch? It may reflect their adoption of a "medical" approach—perhaps even aping secular physicians—to healing, or it might suggest that, since Jesus is the source of the disciples' power and authority, the oil functions as an intermediary.

and healed them: Given the previous story about Jesus' inability to perform many miracles in Nazareth, the disciples' ability to heal stands in sharp relief. This may be an example of Markan irony. Or perhaps the disciples are successful because they are not locals, and so the people are willing to believe that they have healing powers.[22] This would ironically highlight the foolishness of the people of Nazareth.

Analysis

Jesus' response to rejection is not to scale down but to expand his ministry. At the same time, given that Jesus himself was just rejected (and has already been the target of an effort to plot his demise), there is an ominous note here in calling the Twelve to do what he does—the audience can only expect that they will have the same experience of rejection that he has had.

Sending out the disciples two by two may reflect a pragmatic concern for their safety. It may also fulfill the law of witnesses (Deut. 19:15), which has two functions: it benefits the audience by providing more than one

---

21. Comfort, *New Testament Text and Translation Commentary,* 113–14.

22. Stephen A. Knapp, "He Could Do No Mighty Deed There . . . Mark 6:1–6," *Proceedings* (Grand Rapids, Mich.) 12 (January 1992): 163.

testimony, and it also mitigates the human weaknesses of each testator. The Twelve were first called (as a group, not as individual disciples; contrast 1:16–20) in chapter 3. At that time, they were given two tasks: to be with Jesus and to be sent out. They have been with Jesus to hear the parables and see the miracles and witness his rejection in Nazareth. The previously promised moment for them to be sent out has now arrived. The intervening time was a period of learning so that they would be prepared for this ministry.

The concepts of receiving the Twelve and hearing the Twelve are linked, so accepting the message of the Twelve and providing them with hospitality were united. One cannot accept the message without accepting the messengers. A large part of Jesus' counsel concerns what to do when they are rejected. Jesus is warning his disciples to expect the same treatment that he received in Nazareth. (Significantly, he does not discuss the possibility of success: there are no directions on how to baptize, organize a community, etc.) While this counsel is tempered by the assumption that some homes will extend hospitality to them, it is nonetheless true that there is a focus on rejection.

The description of their activities aligns closely with John's actions in chapter 1, so Jesus' disciples are now doing what John did. But when they come back with a positive report of their mission, the audience will perhaps wonder if something is amiss since neither John nor Jesus has had uniformly successful experiences. Either the disciples have erred in some way, or their initial success should not be expected to last.

The rest of Mark's Gospel will reveal that the disciples continue to face challenges and obstacles in their efforts to follow Jesus. The fact that Jesus is willing to send them out as emissaries, as well as their apparent successes in that endeavor, are therefore somewhat surprising. What is clear is that Mark does not advance a standard that requires perfection for a worthy disciple.

At the same time, there are hints that something is amiss in this mission. Jesus prepares them for rejection, but they come back with reports of success. Further, as the rest of this chapter will show, the story of their success is juxtaposed against the death of John the Baptist, which makes the disciples' apparent success appear to be opposed to John's mission. This perhaps implies that the disciples have done something wrong and that this is why they have a very different experience than either Jesus in Nazareth or John the Baptist in Herod's court.

John the Baptist Is Killed (6:14–31)

Greek Text

14 Καὶ ἤκουσεν ὁ βασιλεὺς Ἡρῴδης, φανερὸν γὰρ ἐγένετο τὸ ὄνομα αὐτοῦ, καὶ ἔλεγον ὅτι Ἰωάννης ὁ βαπτίζων ἐγήγερται ἐκ νεκρῶν, καὶ διὰ τοῦτο ἐνεργοῦσιν αἱ δυνάμεις ἐν αὐτῷ· 15 ἄλλοι δὲ ἔλεγον ὅτι Ἡλίας ἐστίν· ἄλλοι δὲ ἔλεγον ὅτι προφήτης ὡς εἷς τῶν προφητῶν. 16 ἀκούσας δὲ ὁ Ἡρῴδης ἔλεγεν· Ὃν ἐγὼ ἀπεκεφάλισα Ἰωάννην, οὗτος ἠγέρθη.

17 Αὐτὸς γὰρ ὁ Ἡρῴδης ἀποστείλας ἐκράτησεν τὸν Ἰωάννην καὶ ἔδησεν αὐτὸν ἐν φυλακῇ διὰ Ἡρῳδιάδα τὴν γυναῖκα Φιλίππου τοῦ ἀδελφοῦ αὐτοῦ, ὅτι αὐτὴν ἐγάμησεν· 18 ἔλεγεν γὰρ ὁ Ἰωάννης τῷ Ἡρῴδῃ ὅτι Οὐκ ἔξεστίν σοι ἔχειν τὴν γυναῖκα τοῦ ἀδελφοῦ σου. 19 ἡ δὲ Ἡρῳδιὰς ἐνεῖχεν αὐτῷ καὶ ἤθελεν αὐτὸν ἀποκτεῖναι, καὶ οὐκ ἠδύνατο· 20 ὁ γὰρ Ἡρῴδης ἐφοβεῖτο τὸν Ἰωάννην, εἰδὼς αὐτὸν ἄνδρα δίκαιον καὶ ἅγιον, καὶ συνετήρει αὐτόν, καὶ ἀκούσας αὐτοῦ πολλὰ ἠπόρει, καὶ ἡδέως αὐτοῦ ἤκουεν. 21 Καὶ γενομένης ἡμέρας εὐκαίρου ὅτε Ἡρῴδης τοῖς γενεσίοις αὐτοῦ δεῖπνον ἐποίησεν τοῖς μεγιστᾶσιν αὐτοῦ καὶ τοῖς χιλιάρχοις καὶ τοῖς πρώτοις τῆς Γαλιλαίας, 22 καὶ εἰσελθούσης τῆς θυγατρὸς αὐτῆς τῆς Ἡρῳδιάδος καὶ ὀρχησαμένης καὶ ἀρεσάσης τῷ Ἡρῴδῃ καὶ τοῖς συνανακειμένοις, εἶπεν ὁ βασιλεὺς τῷ κορασίῳ· Αἴτησόν με ὃ ἐὰν θέλῃς, καὶ δώσω σοι· 23 καὶ ὤμοσεν αὐτῇ· Ὅ τι ἐάν με αἰτήσῃς δώσω σοι ἕως ἡμίσους τῆς βασιλείας μου. 24 καὶ ἐξελθοῦσα εἶπεν τῇ μητρὶ αὐτῆς· Τί αἰτήσωμαι; ἡ δὲ εἶπεν· Τὴν κεφαλὴν Ἰωάννου τοῦ βαπτίζοντος. 25 καὶ εἰσελθοῦσα εὐθὺς μετὰ σπουδῆς πρὸς τὸν βασιλέα ᾐτήσατο λέγουσα· Θέλω ἵνα ἐξαυτῆς δῷς μοι ἐπὶ πίνακι τὴν κεφαλὴν Ἰωάννου τοῦ βαπτιστοῦ. 26 καὶ περίλυπος γενόμενος ὁ βασιλεὺς διὰ τοὺς ὅρκους καὶ τοὺς ἀνακειμένους οὐκ ἠθέλησεν ἀθετῆσαι αὐτήν· 27 καὶ εὐθὺς ἀποστείλας ὁ βασιλεὺς σπεκουλάτορα ἐπέταξεν ἐνέγκαι τὴν κεφαλὴν αὐτοῦ. καὶ ἀπελθὼν ἀπεκεφάλισεν αὐτὸν ἐν τῇ φυλακῇ 28 καὶ ἤνεγκεν τὴν κεφαλὴν αὐτοῦ ἐπὶ πίνακι καὶ ἔδωκεν αὐτὴν τῷ κορασίῳ, καὶ τὸ κοράσιον ἔδωκεν αὐτὴν τῇ μητρὶ αὐτῆς. 29 καὶ ἀκούσαντες οἱ μαθηταὶ αὐτοῦ ἦλθον καὶ ἦραν τὸ πτῶμα αὐτοῦ καὶ ἔθηκαν αὐτὸ ἐν μνημείῳ.

30 Καὶ συνάγονται οἱ ἀπόστολοι πρὸς τὸν Ἰησοῦν, καὶ ἀπήγγειλαν αὐτῷ πάντα ὅσα ἐποίησαν καὶ ὅσα ἐδίδαξαν. 31 καὶ λέγει αὐτοῖς· Δεῦτε ὑμεῖς αὐτοὶ κατ᾽ ἰδίαν εἰς ἔρημον τόπον καὶ ἀναπαύσασθε ὀλίγον. ἦσαν γὰρ οἱ ἐρχόμενοι καὶ οἱ ὑπάγοντες πολλοί, καὶ οὐδὲ φαγεῖν εὐκαίρουν. [SBLGNT]

King James Version

14 And king Herod heard of him; (for his name was spread abroad:) and he said, That John the Baptist was risen from the dead, and therefore mighty

New Rendition

14 And King Herod heard of him, for indeed his name became known. And some said, "John the Baptizer has been raised from the dead—because of this,

works do shew forth themselves in him. 15 Others said, That it is Elias. And others said, That it is a prophet, or as one of the prophets. 16 But when Herod heard thereof, he said, It is John, whom I beheaded: he is risen from the dead. 17 For Herod himself had sent forth and laid hold upon John, and bound him in prison for Herodias' sake, his brother Philip's wife: for he had married her. 18 For John had said unto Herod, It is not lawful for thee to have thy brother's wife. 19 Therefore Herodias had a quarrel against him, and would have killed him; but she could not: 20 For Herod feared John, knowing that he was a just man and an holy, and observed him; and when he heard him, he did many things, and heard him gladly. 21 And when a convenient day was come, that Herod on his birthday made a supper to his lords, high captains, and chief estates of Galilee; 22 And when the daughter of the said Herodias came in, and danced, and pleased Herod and them that sat with him, the king said unto the damsel, Ask of me whatsoever thou wilt, and I will give it thee. 23 And he sware unto her, Whatsoever thou shalt ask of me, I will give it thee, unto the half of my kingdom. 24 And she went forth, and said unto her mother, What shall I ask? And she said, The head of John the Baptist. 25 And she came in straightway with haste unto the king, and asked, saying, I will that thou give me by and by in a charger the head of John the Baptist. 26 And the king was exceeding sorry; yet for his oath's sake, and for their sakes which sat with him, he would not reject her. 27 And immediately the king sent an executioner, and commanded his head to be

miraculous powers are at work in him." 15 But others said, "He is Elijah." And others said, "He is a prophet like one of the prophets of old." 16 But Herod having heard, said, "John—whom I beheaded—has been raised!" 17 For Herod himself had John arrested and bound in prison because of Herodias, his brother Philip's wife, because Herod had married her. 18 For John had been telling Herod, "It is not lawful for you to have your brother's wife." 19 And Herodias had a grudge against him and wanted to kill him, but she could not 20 because Herod revered John, knowing him to be a righteous and holy man, and so protected him. And having heard him, he, Herod, was greatly perplexed but heard him gladly. 21 And an opportunity came when Herod on his birthday hosted a banquet for the court officials, the military officers, and the prominent people of Galilee. 22 And his daughter Herodias, having come in and danced, delighted Herod and those dining with him. And the king said to the girl, "Ask me for whatever you want, and I will give it to you." 23 And he swore to her, "Whatever you ask me, I will give it to you, up to half of my kingdom." 24 And having gone out, she asked her mother, "What should I ask?" She said, "the head of John the Baptizer." 25 And having entered immediately—with haste—to the king, she asked, saying, "I want you to give me at once upon a plate the head of John the Baptizer." 26 And the king was very sorrowful, but because of his oath and because of those dining with him, he would not refuse her. 27 And immediately having sent for an executioner, he commanded that John's head be brought. And having gone, he cut

brought: and he went and beheaded him in the prison, 28 And brought his head in a charger, and gave it to the damsel: and the damsel gave it to her mother. 29 And when his disciples heard of it, they came and took up his corpse, and laid it in a tomb. 30 And the apostles gathered themselves together unto Jesus, and told him all things, both what they had done, and what they had taught. 31 And he said unto them, Come ye yourselves apart into a desert place, and rest a while: for there were many coming and going, and they had no leisure so much as to eat.

off his head in the cell, 28 and brought the head upon a plate and gave it to the girl, and the girl gave it to her mother. 29 And having heard about it, his disciples came and took his body and placed it in a grave. 30 And the apostles are gathered to Jesus. And they told him everything—what they had done and what they had taught. 31 And he says to them, "Come by yourselves into a deserted place and rest a little." For there were so many people coming and going that they did not even have enough time to eat.

Notes

6:14 *And king Herod heard of him:* Herod Antipas, son of Herod the Great, was the tetrarch of Galilee and Perea. He ruled until 39 CE, when he was deposed.

Herod is not a king, as Mark calls him, but a tetrarch, meaning that he ruled one-fourth of the kingdom, under the authority of the Roman emperor. The title "king" is technically inaccurate but was probably used because:

1. It reflected popular usage.
2. Herod was later removed from power because he sought the title of king;[23] if Mark and the audience know about this, then calling him a king is a pointed barb at his failed aspirations.
3. The title of king strengthens the allusion between Herod and the king in the story of Esther (see the section "Relationship to Esther" after the Notes on 6:31).
4. In this story, Herod will be trapped and limited by the actions of other people. Perhaps calling him a king is meant to highlight the weaknesses and failings of human kings and, by way of contrast, the difference with the kingdom of God.

(for his name was spread abroad:) and he said, That John the Baptist was risen from the dead: There are two textual variants in this verse:

1. Some manuscripts have "and they said" (instead of "and he said"), which is probably the earlier reading, since what follows contains what was said by more than one person. The text was probably changed by copyists who

---

23. Miller, *Women in Mark's Gospel,* 76.

presumed that Herod (mentioned at the beginning of the verse) was the one speaking and since Herod will once again be the subject in 6:16.[24] Given that the difference between "he said" and "they said" in Greek is only one letter, it is also possible that the change arose by accident. If "he said" is preferred, then Herod initiates the idea that John the Baptist is raised from the dead and is willing to argue for that position (see 6:16). If "they said" is preferred, then Herod parrots the thinking of others.

2. Many manuscripts read "the baptizer" instead of "the Baptist" here.[25] It may nuance the audience's understanding of John to think of him as someone who was known as one who did baptisms instead of by a title (and one that can be confused today with a denominational affiliation). The same variant exists in 6:24.

Given that John and Jesus are contemporaries, it is unlikely that the idea of Jesus being John raised from the dead was meant in a literal sense, as if John had been reincarnated. It is more likely that the thinking was that Jesus was granted a portion of John's spirit when John died, similar to what had happened with Elijah and Elisha (2 Kgs. 2:1–15; see the section "Relationship to 2 Kings 2" below). It is also possible that Herod does not believe that Jesus is John raised from the dead in any sense, but rather he is expressing a sentiment to the effect of "I thought I solved the problem by beheading John, but Jesus is just as much of a problem as if John were back from the dead!"[26] If this is the best reading, it is somewhat ironic since Mark's audience knows from the story of Jairus's daughter that it is literally possible for someone to be raised from the dead. And much as the account of Jesus' death will be laced with irony (see the Notes on chapter 15), John's death is as well.

Either way, Herod's statement unintentionally acknowledges Jesus' power. A theme throughout Mark's text is that even those opposed to Jesus (and John) recognize that they have power and authority.

Relationship to 2 Kings 2. In 2 Kings 2, Elijah asks Elisha what he wants from him before he (Elijah) is taken away. Elisha asks for a double portion of Elijah's prophetic spirit to rest upon him. Later, it is recognized that Elijah's spirit rests on Elisha. It is possible that this story lies in the background of Mark's text and that Herod's words are meant to indicate that John's prophetic spirit rested upon Jesus after John died.

---

24. Comfort, *New Testament Text and Translation Commentary,* 114.
25. Collins, *Mark,* 295 note q.
26. Stein, *Mark,* 301.

and therefore mighty works do shew forth themselves in him: Both Herod and the people of Nazareth recognize that Jesus is able to do miracles. But in both cases, they draw the wrong conclusions from this information.

It is possible, but not certain, that Herod believed that John had performed miracles, which is interesting because there is no evidence in Mark that John had done so.

6:15 *Others said, That it is Elias:* Most first-century Jews anticipated that Elijah (the KJV transliterates his name as "Elias") would come before the Messiah (9:11–13); this idea was based on Malachi 4:5–6.

And others said, That it is a prophet, or as one of the prophets: Most modern translations use the phrase "prophets of old" here to capture the sense that this line compares Jesus with the known prophets of the past. The idea is that he is a great prophet or a true prophet, not merely as one of the many contemporary people who claimed to be prophets. Some HB texts reflect the belief that God would again raise up a prophet (Deut. 18:18).

Ironically, no one speculates that Jesus is the Messiah. At the same time, no one thinks that Jesus is merely a regular person. There is clear recognition, even on the part of those opposed to him and those who do not understand him, that there is something special about him.

6:16 *But when Herod heard thereof, he said, It is John, whom I beheaded:* The word "I" is emphasized, not to suggest that Herod himself killed John, but rather that it was done on his personal order. Mark's editorial hand is obvious here: the story of John's death reads very differently given that Herod claims responsibility for it before the story is told to the audience. Without this note, the audience likely would have concluded that Herodias deserved most of the blame. Comparisons of this story with several HB texts to which it probably alludes (see the "Relationship" sections after the Notes on 6:31) strongly suggest that Herod is not as responsible for the death as Herodias. His claim to responsibility can then be read either as the result of Herodias duping him into taking the blame or his false sense of his own self-importance. Perhaps it should not be assumed that Mark agrees with Herod's assessment of who deserves the blame.

Mark may be highlighting the limits of Herod's (or of any earthly ruler's) power: the worst punishment that Herod can deliver is death, but here Herod has to reckon with the possibility that death may not have neutralized the threat that he perceived from John.

he is risen from the dead: This is the same word for "risen" that the young man uses at Jesus' tomb. This detail is important, since the story of John's death will serve as a template for the audience's thinking about Jesus' death.

6:17 ***For Herod himself had sent forth and laid hold upon John:*** What happens here is unusual: Mark begins a flashback of the story of John's death. The results of the story (namely, John's death and Herod's responsibility for it) have already been narrated, so the story is not told in order to create suspense or to provide new information to the audience. Oddly, the story unfolds in reverse order: Herod's worry about Jesus, the beheading, the imprisoning, Herod's marriage, and then John's preaching against it. Mark is telling the story backwards.

The word translated as "sent" is a cognate for the word "apostle," so it may reflect the idea that Herod's sending for John is a perversion of Jesus' sending out the Twelve. Jesus' act of sending out leads to healing of sick folk, but Herod's act of sending out leads to death.

and bound him in prison for Herodias' sake: Herodias is not called a "queen" in this story; Mark may be indicating that that title is not legitimate since her marriage was not legitimate.

The imprisonment of John was mentioned in 1:14. It is possible that John has been languishing in prison since that point in the narrative; it is also possible that John was not imprisoned until later but that Mark chose to mention it in chapter 1 for literary reasons.

Generally, imprisonment was not used as punishment and only applied until the charge was adjudicated. It is possible that Herod has imprisoned John to protect him from Herodias.

his brother Philip's wife: Josephus records that Herodias's first husband was (also) named Herod. It is possible that Mark is mistaken in calling her first husband Philip, or he may have been known by more than one name.

for he had married her: The New Rendition uses "Herod" instead of "he" here (despite the fact that the Greek has the pronoun) to make clear the referent.

6:18 ***For John had said unto Herod, It is not lawful for thee to have thy brother's wife:*** John refers to the HB law that prohibits a woman from marrying her husband's brother[27] (see also 10:2–12). Herod had divorced his previous wife in order to marry Herodias.

John's words show commitment to the law of Moses. John did not believe that royal status or political power meant that the law need not apply. In a sense, this is the other side of the coin of Jesus' ministry, where the blessings of the gospel apply to all people.

---

27. See Lev. 18:16; 20:21. There is an exception to this rule if the first husband dies without progeny (see Deut. 25:5), but that is not the case here.

There are multiple occasions in the HB where a prophet criticizes a king (1 Sam. 15:16–31; 2 Sam. 12:1–12; 2 Kgs. 20:16–18; Jer. 38:14–23); this background means that John is akin to the HB prophets.

Relationship to Josephus. Josephus was a first-century historian and one of the few Jewish writers contemporary with Jesus. He likely wrote in the 80s in Rome but had lived previously in Palestine. He wrote that Herod had John arrested because he feared that John would provide leadership for a revolt;[28] he does not mention John's critique of Herod's marriage. This has led scholars to two different schools of thought:

1. Josephus and Mark cannot be reconciled. Perhaps Mark has embroidered the historical situation in order to make theological sense of John's death. It is difficult to determine how Mark would have learned about the events of Herod's birthday banquet—not to mention the private conversation between mother and daughter that happened outside of it—in the first place, which might further suggest that parts of this story do not reflect history. It is also possible that Josephus' account is wrong; Josephus himself is not consistent in what he has to say about Herod and his family.[29]

2. Josephus and Mark can be reconciled. The subtext of John's preaching was that Herod was not a legitimate leader for Jews, which could have led to Herod's concern that John might lead a revolt. (This would also explain why Herod kept John in prison: it prevented him from leading a revolt but did not create a martyr.) Further, since Herod's first marriage (which he ended to marry Herodias) was a political alliance, there was obviously a political underpinning to the situation. So while Mark's and Josephus's emphases are different, there is no inherent conflict between their accounts. This is especially true if, despite the religious formulation of John's words, his "criticism challenges the status of Herod as king because the true ruler was expected to uphold the law"[30] and "to claim rule over the Jewish people is legitimate only if Jewish law is recognized."[31]

6:19 *Therefore Herodias had a quarrel against him, and would have killed him; but she could not:* Despite the fact that John addressed Herod, Herodias is the one incensed by his words. This is probably because, were Herod to repent of his decision to marry Herodias and renounce her, she would be bereft of power.

---

28. Josephus, *Antiquities* 18.5.2.

29. Ross S. Kraemer, "Implicating Herodias and Her Daughter in the Death of John the Baptizer: A (Christian) Theological Strategy?" *Journal of Biblical Literature* 125, no. 2 (2006): 321–349.

30. Miller, *Women in Mark's Gospel,* 75.

31. Myers, *Binding the Strong Man,* 216.

6:20 *For Herod feared John, knowing that he was a just man and an holy, and observed him:* These two verses create an interesting picture of marital tension.

Much as the demon-possessed seem to be simultaneously attracted to and hateful toward Jesus, Herod has roughly the same attitude toward John. Mark may have deliberately painted Herod in these tones.

and when he heard him, he did many things: The New Rendition adds "he, Herod" to make the referent clear, but the noun does not occur here.

Many manuscripts have "he was greatly perplexed" instead of "he did many things."[32] It is possible that the text was changed to "perplexed" based on Luke 9:7, or since both words look very similar (*ēporei* and *epoiei*), it is possible that the variant was accidental. "He did many things" is difficult to understand because it is vague (why bother mentioning it if the audience does not learn what he did?), although it may be a Semitic idiom for listening to him often. At the same time, "he was perplexed" may be hard to mesh with the idea of Herod's gladly hearing John. So both variants can make the case for being the more difficult, and therefore the earlier, reading. "Perplexed" does have better support from the extant manuscripts. In addition to meaning "perplexed," it can mean that Herod was undecided about John's preaching or that John's words raised questions for him (the verb's root meaning is "without a way").

"Many" can be taken as an adverb instead of an adjective, so that it would describe either how perplexed Herod was or how often he heard John.

and heard him gladly: It is possible that the imprisonment (which may have been to protect John from Herodias) actually made it possible for Herod to hear from John more often. (If so, there might be some interesting comparisons between John and Joseph in Egypt.)

6:21 *And when a convenient day was come:* The word translated as "convenient" (Greek: *eukairos*) will echo the word "conveniently" (Greek: *eukairōs*) in 14:11, where it is used to describe the plot to kill Jesus; this creates another link between these two stories.

that Herod on his birthday made a supper: The celebration of birthdays is a pagan custom that was denounced in ancient Jewish sources;[33] what seems like an innocent line to modern readers would have been an indicator to many listeners of debauchery and lawlessness.

---

32. Collins, *Mark,* 294–95 note k.
33. Mishnah Avodah Zarah 1:3.

In the Greco-Roman tradition, a ruler's birthday was usually a celebration of life and frequently featured a release of prisoners,[34] so there is a cruel irony here.

to his lords, high captains, and chief estates of Galilee: The term "high captains" has "distinctly Roman overtones"[35] and implies that Herod patterns his court after a Roman court. The third group is literally "first ones" and perhaps applies to prominent businessmen.

6:22 ***And when the daughter of the said Herodias came in:*** Some manuscripts read "his daughter Herodias" here; this reading makes two important changes:

1. The girl is the daughter of Herod (not, as the KJV has it, Herodias' daughter from her previous marriage and thus Herod's stepdaughter). It is possible that Mark could have had in mind that the girl was Herod's stepdaughter but nonetheless described her as Herod's daughter in order to highlight the debauchery of the dancing scene. It is also possible that, given how very complicated Herod's family tree is, Mark was simply confused about the girl's parentage. If this girl is the biological daughter of Herod and Herodias, then she is the fruit of the union that John has condemned as illegal, and her seductive dance before her father is even more depraved.

2. The daughter is named Herodias. This would not agree with Josephus, who calls the girl Salome.[36] (Mark never names her, save in this verse if this variant is correct.) Of course, it is possible that Josephus was wrong.

It is hard to determine which variant is more likely to have been original.[37]

The same word for "daughter" was used in the previous chapter to describe Jairus's daughter, and the girls are probably close in age.

That the girl "came in" (see also 6:24 and 25) probably indicates that she was not herself attending the banquet.

and danced, and pleased Herod and them that sat with him: The word "pleased" can have a sexual connotation.[38] Some have doubted that the dance had a seductive quality, but if it did not, it is difficult to determine what would have prompted Herod's offer of compensation, an offer that Herod makes against his better instincts.

---

34. Miller, *Women in Mark's Gospel*, 84.
35. Lane, *Gospel according to Mark*, 220.
36. Josephus, *Wars of the Jews* 1.8.9; see also Collins, *Mark*, 295 note l.
37. Metzger, *Textual Commentary*, 77.
38. LXX Gen. 19:8 (KJV: "do . . . as is good in your eyes"); LXX Judg. 14:1 (the phrase "and she was pleasing" is not in the KJV text); LXX Esth. 2:4 (KJV: "pleased"); LXX Job 31:10 (KJV: "grind").

Many scholars have questioned the historicity of this account because it is all but inconceivable that a royal daughter would attend, let alone dance in a seductive way, at a banquet.[39] (Mark's numerous references to her comings and goings do make it clear that she and her mother were not guests at the banquet.) It is possible that Mark has fabricated this detail, but perhaps it is more likely that her dancing points to the utter depravity of Herod's court, which is a constant theme in this passage: "A man who has already married a woman who is both his niece and his sister-in-law may well ogle that woman's daughter."[40]

The picture of Herod's pleasure at the dance of a girl who was his step-daughter and his niece—or, if the other variant is preferred, his own biological daughter—is perverse. (It is possible that, much as Herod replaced his first wife, he may be considering replacing Herodias with her daughter.) At the same time, if Herod is this depraved and can still recognize both John's and Jesus' power and authority, Mark has recorded a substantive (if most unlikely, not to mention unsavory) testimony of them both.

The audience just learned that listening to John pleased Herod; now, they see that the dancing girl pleases him as well. Herod is shown to be poorly rooted.

Mark does not explain whose idea it was for the girl to dance. Either Herodias takes advantage of a fortuitous situation, or she creates the situation with the goal of causing John's death.

the king said unto the damsel, Ask of me whatsoever thou wilt, and I will give it thee: There is great irony in this scene: all the powers of Galilee are gathered together, but it is a young girl who controls the situation.

6:23 ***And he sware unto her, Whatsoever thou shalt ask of me, I will give it thee, unto the half of my kingdom:*** "Half the kingdom" may be proverbial for a great amount of money (compare Alma 20:23).

Herod repeats his offer from the previous verse. This might be for emphasis or because he is drunken (or drunk with lust), a theory suggested by his later remorse. He does modify somewhat his offer from "whatsoever" to "unto the half of my kingdom," perhaps indicating that he is already having second thoughts about his rashness. Regardless, as a client king, he has no authority to make this offer in the first place. And given his dispute with his wife over the fate of John, it was a foolish offer to make to her daughter in any case.

---

39. Miller, *Women in Mark's Gospel*, 77–78.

40. Jennifer A. Glancy, "Unveiling Masculinity: The Construction of Gender in Mark 6:17–29," *Biblical Interpretation* 2, no. 1 (1994): 40.

6:24 *And she went forth, and said unto her mother, What shall I ask?:* The girl must "go forth" because her mother was not attending the banquet. (Although she did permit, or even arrange, for her daughter to be present.)

And she said, The head of John the Baptist: See the note on 6:14 regarding the textual variant "baptizer."

By asking for John's head instead of for half the kingdom, the girl will not be in competition with her mother for power and status. Ironically, Herodias's request implies that the life of John the Baptist is worth more than half of Herod's kingdom.

6:25 *And she came in straightway with haste unto the king, and asked, saying:* Note the repetition: "straightway" and "with haste" each convey the idea that the girl moved quickly.

I will that thou give me by and by in a charger the head of John the Baptist: "By and by" means "immediately." The girl adds the detail "in a charger" (on a plate) to her mother's request. This detail, combined with the mention of her haste, suggests that she is a willing participant in these events.

The girl asks that, metaphorically, John's head be served at the banquet; this may be a gross parody of the Last Supper.

6:26 *And the king was exceeding sorry:* "Sorry" is the same word used in 14:34 (KJV: "sorrowful") to describe Jesus' sorrow (the only other time this word is used in Mark). Jesus is willing to endure untold suffering despite his sorrow, but Herod is completely unwilling to change his mind due to his own sorrow. The issue of personal volition is key in both stories.

It is ironic that John will not bow to social pressure to soften his message while Herod completely capitulates to social pressure by refusing to rescind his foolish offer.

yet for his oath's sake, and for their sakes which sat with him, he would not reject her: Mark paints Herod as the seed among thorns, which hears the word but is unfruitful because of the "cares of this world" (4:18–19).

6:27 *And immediately the king sent an executioner, and commanded his head to be brought: and he went and beheaded him in the prison:* The New Rendition has "John's" instead of "his" for clarity, but in Greek, the pronoun is used.

The word translated as "sent" is the verb form of the noun for "apostle" (which means "one who is sent out"). Much as Jesus sends out the apostles in the story that sandwiches the sad tale of John's death, Herod also sends out a personal emissary, but his deputy brings death instead of life.

6:28 *And brought his head in a charger, and gave it to the damsel: and the damsel gave it to her mother. 29 And when his disciples heard of it,*

they came and took up his corpse, and laid it in a tomb: The undercurrent of cannibalism stemming from the presentation of John's head on a plate at a banquet suggests the debauchery of Herod's court. Because of the parallels between Jesus' fate and John's, this story has been described as a "demonic eucharist."[41]

6:30 ***And the apostles gathered themselves together unto Jesus:*** With one possible exception,[42] Mark does not usually use the word "apostles," preferring the terms "the disciples" and "the Twelve." Why was the word "apostle" used here?

1. It echoes the verb from 6:7 (KJV: "send"), and these two texts form a sandwich around the story of the death of John the Baptist, where Herod also sends out (6:17, 27) emissaries.

2. Mark is showing a progression in discipleship: first called to follow Jesus (1:16–20), then called to the Twelve (3:13–14), only now—after their successful missions—are they considered apostles. (The fact that this term is not used later in the text is a weakness of this reading.)

3. Because the root meaning of the word "apostle" is "one who is sent out," the term emphasizes that they derive their authority from Jesus.

4. Because the previous verse mentioned John's disciples, Mark calls Jesus' followers "apostles" in order to distinguish between the two groups.

5. Mark understands the title "apostle" to refer to a specific task (being sent out to preach and to exercise Jesus' authority) and so only refers to them as apostles in that capacity: "When they return from their mission they return as apostles (6:30). . . . Henceforth he will continue to call them disciples. It was the nature of the missionary journey to initiate them into the nature of apostleship. While they are disciples in the presence of Jesus, they will become apostles apart from and in the absence of Jesus. The missionary journey has thus prepared the disciples for the future, when they will have to function as apostles in Jesus' absence."[43] (But by the time Mark writes the Gospel, "apostle" was regarded as a title for an office.)

and told him all things, both what they had done, and what they had taught: Because Jesus was rejected in Nazareth and John was killed by Herod, the Twelve's report—lacking any detail of persecution or suffering—is somewhat suspect: either they have done something wrong (perhaps by not teaching that Jesus will suffer and die; compare 8:31–32), or they are experiencing an initial success that will not last (compare 4:16–17). Also,

41. Marcus, *Mark 1–8*, 403.
42. See the Notes on the textual variant in 3:14.
43. Kelber, *Mark's Story of Jesus*, 34.

the Twelve are implicitly contrasted with John's disciples, who care for their teacher's corpse.

6:31 *And he said unto them, Come ye yourselves apart into a desert place, and rest a while:* The word "yourselves" is emphatic.

"Desert" means lonely or uninhabited, not barren (it has green grass; see 6:39). They will go to an area without inhabitants so that they can rest from the crowds.

In several HB scriptures, God provides rest for the faithful in the wilderness (Deut. 12:9; 25:19; Josh. 1:13; 21:44; Ps. 95:7–11; Isa. 63:14). So Jesus is not just suggesting a break from the crowds but is also positioning himself as the God of the scriptures. This allusion implies that the Twelve were faithful in their mission: they have fulfilled it to the best of their abilities and so are now worthy of rest. Since this rest can be understood as a type of the final rest that God grants to the righteous, this verse may foreshadow Jesus' role in saving his people.

Narrative Structure. While 6:30–31 introduces the feeding miracle, it also concludes the previous section of text:

    A the Twelve are sent out (6:7–13)
        B the death of John the Baptist (6:14–29)
    A' the Twelve return (6:30–31)

Mark interrupts the mission of the Twelve with the story of the death of John, thus encouraging the audience to interpret each text in light of the other.

---

for there were many coming and going, and they had no leisure so much as to eat: The word translated as "leisure" (Greek: *eukaireō*) is very similar to the word translated as "convenient" (Greek: *eukairos*) in 6:21, which heightens the parallels between the two stories and sets the stage to view this wilderness feeding as an inversion of Herod's lavish and debauched banquet. What was convenient for Herodias is not convenient for the disciples.

Relationship to Genesis 3. In a climactic moment, Adam endures serious consequences for obeying the voice of his wife (Gen. 3:17), as does Herod. In both stories, death enters the world because of the desires of the woman. The stories are further linked by John acting in the role of God by issuing a commandment. Herodias is similar to Eve or can be understood as the serpent whispering into her daughter's ear and prompting her behavior to convince a man to go against his better judgment in agreeing with her plan.

If the bleeding woman's story is understood as a redemptive rereading of Eve, then this story shows a retrogression. The Christ-focused reenactment of the Fall results in healing for the bleeding woman, but the worldly-oriented version of Herod results in death yet again. John's death still needs to be overcome; that will happen with Jesus' Resurrection.

Mark's structure in this section looks something like this:

A the bleeding woman
> B rejection in Nazareth
> B' sending out of the Twelve

A' Herod

It is possible to view this structure to suggest that sandwiched between the two retellings of the Fall (A and A') is a reenactment of the effects of the Fall, as Jesus is the God cast out (of Nazareth) by his people—an ironic reworking of the people cast out of the garden by their God—and as the Twelve (like Adam and Eve) are sent out into the world.

Relationship to Judges 11. In Judges 11, Jephthah makes a foolish vow: in exchange for success in battle, he will offer as a burnt offering the first person who comes through his door when he returns home. Tragically, the first person is his daughter, who comes out dancing to celebrate his victory. Themes of foolish oaths, death, daughters, and dancing unite these passages. What is interesting is that the role of Jephthah's daughter is played, at least in part, by John the Baptist, who is the one—not Herodias's daughter—who dies as a result of the foolish vow. The fact that a recent story, the raising of Jairus's daughter, also had some compelling echoes with Judges 11 increases the likelihood that Mark intended for the audience to think about Jephthah's story here.

Relationship to 1 Kings 19. Jezebel, like Herodias, was married to a man who was the ruler of the northern portion of Israel; both men were waverers under the sway of their wives (1 Kgs. 19:1–14). In both stories, there is a conflict spear-headed by the woman against a messenger from God who asks them to change their ways. Jezebel plots against Elijah; Mark makes clear that John is an Elijah figure. Ahab and Elijah have several interactions, as do John and Herod, but the women never meet the prophet in either story, presumably because "such a meeting would have been too volatile."[44] However, Jezebel's plot against Elijah does not succeed.

---

44. David M. Hoffeditz and Gary E. Yates, "Femme Fatale *Redux*: Intertextual Connection to the Elijah/Jezebel Narratives in Mark 6:14–29," *Bulletin for Biblical Research* 15, no. 2 (2005): 203.

Because Jezebel's husband is described as Israel's worst king (1 Kgs. 16:29–33; 21:25–26), the allusions between Herodias's and Jezebel's stories function as Mark's commentary on Herod's dreadful rule. Further, 1 Kings implies that the death of the prophets was Jezebel's—not Ahab's—fault. Perhaps the allusion is Mark's way of getting the audience to question Herod's claim of responsibility for the death of John. After all, it is somewhat odd that the audience would be expected to take Herod at his word, given the way that Mark portrays his character. It is even possible that Herodias has somehow convinced Herod that he is responsible for John's death as a way of deflecting blame from herself.

Mark may be using the allusion to make another point: "In her execution of the plot against Naboth, Jezebel appears to be the human embodiment of the Canaanite goddess Anat, the sister/consort of Baal known for her bloodshed and violence. Jezebel's actions in the Naboth incident seem especially to parallel the actions of Anat in the Canaanite legend of Aqhat."[45] This is important because Mark has already suggested that the real battle is not between human actors but rather between divine and satanic ones, so positioning Herodias as a pagan goddess suggests that she is the embodiment of demonic power. Because Herodias's story is sandwiched between reports of the mission of the Twelve, where their power to cast out demonic forces is emphasized, the allusion is strengthened. It is possible to read Mark's text as implying that John lacked the power to bind the demonic Herodias; rather, John was bound and killed. This notion meshes well with Jesus' parable of the binding of the strong man and John's preaching that one stronger than he was coming. John's powerlessness in the face of his own death points to Jesus' unique saving power.

Because Elijah is taken straight to heaven without experiencing death, John's death comes as a shock—especially after the lengths that Mark has gone to in order to portray John as Elijah. Perhaps Mark's goal was to prepare the audience for the suffering and death of Jesus, something that was similarly not expected to be part of the experience of the Messiah.

Relationship to Esther. There are some verbal similarities between LXX Esther and Herodias' story in Mark, namely the same words for "daughter" and "pleasure" are used. Further, in later Jewish tradition (which may have been familiar to Mark and his audience), the head of Vashti is brought to the king on a platter. When Esther is offered half of a kingdom, she instead asks for the liberation of her people from death (Esth. 7:2–4). When Herodias's

---

45. Hoffeditz and Yates, "Femme Fatale *Redux*," 206.

daughter is given the same offer, she asks for the death of John the Baptist. Esther's story is saved from being a tragedy by the presence of a woman who is willing to risk her own life for her people and who could guide an easily duped king to make the right choice, a plot with several similarities to Mark 6. Herodias's story becomes a tragedy because a woman protects her own power by demanding the life of someone else; she is the one who dupes the king. Herodias is thus an anti-Esther. In this reading, the death of John stands in for the death of all of the Jewish people in Esther's story.

Relationship to Judith. The book of Judith, while not canonical in the Protestant or Latter-day Saint traditions, was part of the LXX. In this story, Judith attends a banquet hosted by the evil Holofernes. She brings her own food to ensure that it meets the requirements of the law of Moses. Once Holofernes is passed out from drunkenness, she cuts off his head and puts it in her food bag. She is a hero since the enemy of Israel is destroyed by her hand.

The almost perfect inversion of this story in the tale of Herodias should be obvious. Mark spotlights Herodias' treachery by contrasting it with Judith's courage and emphasizes John's important role by inverting it against the enemy of Israel. Once again, the active involvement of the woman is emphasized, casting further doubt on Herod's claim to responsibility for the beheading.

Both Judith and Herodias use sexual appeal as a source of power. The fact that Judith used her power to achieve such a noble end stresses that Herodias is making a deliberate choice to advance evil: "The positive counterparts of Herodias in the biblical tradition include Jael, Esther, and Judith, all of whom use cunning and/or deceit to secure the death of a powerful enemy. Jael and Judith each inflicts a mortal head wound to the enemy of God's people."[46]

Relationship to Ether 8. In the Book of Mormon, there is a story with many similarities to this one: in Ether 8:7–15, a woman identified as the daughter of Jared dances for a man named Akish with the goal of causing him to desire her for a wife. She tells her father that when Akish asks for her in marriage, her father should agree only if Akish will give him the head of the king. So the story has potent similarities—but also some significant differences—from John's story in Mark. It is possible that both Mark and the

---

46. Dowd, *Reading Mark*, 67.

writer of the story in the Book of Mormon are relying on an ancient (and otherwise unknown) tale that shapes their stories of power and murder (the reference to "the record" in Ether 8:9 may support this idea). It is also possible that there is not an earlier tradition upon which they both rely and that the similarities are, rather, due to the fact that sexual seduction (which would, logically, be manifested in a dance) was one of the few routes to power available to women anciently.

Daughters in the Gospel of Mark. Two stories about daughters in the Gospel of Mark provide compelling comparisons with the story of Herodias's daughter:

1. *Jairus's Daughter.* Not only are these stories located close together in the narrative, but both feature

   a. daughters responding to similar physical commands (rise, dance [implied]).

   b. themes of eating (as Jesus commands in chapter 5, the banquet and the head on a platter).

   c. daughters in important roles.

   d. a highly placed male leader who is shown to be dependent upon the actions of others and not quite so powerful as the audience might initially assume.

   e. an interruption by a woman seeking power (Jairus's story by the bleeding woman who grabs for Jesus' power, and Herod's by Herodias, who grabs for the power to kill John).

   But while Jairus is willing to sacrifice his honor to beg Jesus to come to his home, Herod is not willing to sacrifice his honor by reneging on his promise to his stepdaughter. In a world with Jesus and the kingdom of heaven at its center, power is used to promote life and healing. In the world centered around a royal court, power is used to end life.

2. *The Syrophenician Woman's Daughter.* In this story, a woman speaks to Jesus to request that a demon be cast out of her daughter. This story features another woman with another request, but this time, it is a positive story, unlike the death of John. (See also the Notes on 7:24–30.)

These two other stories about parent-daughter pairs can be read as a triptych (a picture in three panels), with the story of Herodias's daughter in the center serving as the evil example of the relationship and its ramifications, located between two positive stories. The inversions concern life and death and the wholeness that Jesus brings. While Herodias typifies the "trickster" style popular in ancient literature that features powerless women tricking male authorities into granting them what they want, the women who follow Jesus display a different style: they ask outright.

Relationship between John and Jesus. Because 6:14–29 is the only story in Mark's Gospel that does not involve Jesus, it has long puzzled readers: Why did Mark devote so much space to a text that seems not entirely relevant to the Gospel's purposes and themes?

It seems that Mark intends the audience to view 6:14–29 as being very much about Jesus and his mission; the purpose of relating the story of John's death in such detail is that it provides the template for Jesus' own death. The parallels are extensive:

1. Both are arrested because of their teachings; both realize that persisting in preaching will result in their deaths.

2. The fact that Herod—of all people—thinks that Jesus is John raised from the dead emphasizes the links between Jesus' and John's ministries in an ironic way. In fact, Herod's comment is the interpretive key to the entire scene, given the structure of the story, which hinges on explaining Herod's comment since the story is told as a flashback.

3. Herodias wants to kill John, and the Sanhedrin wants to kill Jesus, but neither has the power to do so themselves.

4. A second entity is manipulated in order to make the death possible: in John's case, it is Herodias's daughter, and in Jesus' case, it is the crowds.[47]

5. A third person, a civic authority (Herod and Pilate), who does have the authority to order the death, does not want to do so but is reluctantly convinced: "Both Herod and Pilate are depicted as weak rulers, who knowingly hand over innocent men to death in order to preserve their own status."[48]

6. The death in both cases is caused not by one person but by three separate entities inadvertently working together despite their different motives and desires.

7. The presentation of John's head on a platter at the banquet may be a debased foreshadowing of Jesus offering his body and blood at the Last Supper.

8. The story of John's death creates a space in the narrative to allow for the mission of the Twelve to be completed. So there is a sense in which the death of John creates space in which the Twelve can spread the good news and exercise Jesus' power. John's death foreshadows Jesus' death by making it literally possible for the good news to be preached.

9. Mark cleverly introduces the theme of being raised from the dead into this story by including Herod's belief that Jesus is John raised from the dead.

---

47. Jean Delorme, "John the Baptist's Head—the Word Perverted: A Reading of a Narrative (Mark 6:14–29)," *Semeia* 81 (1998): 127.

48. Miller, *Women in Mark's Gospel,* 83.

This foreshadows the theme of resurrection in Jesus' own story. It is literally *through Jesus* that John is thought to be resurrected, so there is an ironic sense in which Herod has gotten the topic of resurrection and how it works exactly right, despite the fact that he is so obviously wrong.

10. In 9:12–13, Jesus declares the link between John's death and his own.

11. The one significant difference in the stories is the reaction of the teachers' disciples after the death.

Mark has already noted that Herod's people were plotting Jesus' death (3:6), so the audience has every reason to think that John's fate will one day be Jesus' fate.

Interestingly, the disciples are absent, and so they miss the connection between John and Jesus that the audience learns. At no point in the Gospel will the Twelve understand that Jesus must suffer the same fate as John.

As mentioned above, John's death is shocking for an audience who has been groomed to see him in the role of Elijah, since Elijah was taken to heaven without experiencing death. The idea of the suffering innocent sets the stage for understanding Jesus' own suffering and death.

Tyrant Type Scene. Mark's story here follows the "tyrant type scene,"[49] which has four distinct parts:

1. The tyrant is paranoid about being overthrown (while Mark doesn't dwell on this theme, Josephus mentions it).

2. The tyrant has a bodyguard (typified by Herod's men in 6:17 and 6:27).

3. The tyrant displays excess (as the banquet scene implies).

4. The tyrant interacts with a wise man (John the Baptist).

If Mark intended to follow the conventions of this type scene, then it stresses that Herod is a tyrant. Further, Mark shows Jesus as the opposite of a tyrant by inverting each of the items on the list in the framing story of the mission of the Twelve:

1. Far from being paranoid about being overthrown, Jesus shares his power with his disciples and commissions them to do what he does.

2. Jesus not only does not have a bodyguard but, by sending the Twelve out, is also left unprotected.

3. Not only does Jesus not display excess but also sends out his disciples without bread or an extra cloak.

---

49. Abraham Smith, "Tyranny Exposed: Mark's Typological Characterization of Herod Antipas (Mark 6:14–29)," *Biblical Interpretation* 14 (January 2006): 271.

4. Jesus does not interact with a wise man but rather asks his disciples to present themselves in such a way that they are less likely to be confused with Cynic philosophers.

Thus, Mark defines what Jesus' kingship means by presenting it as the opposite of tyranny.

Analysis

Because the last story related the success of the mission of the Twelve, it is likely that this is what Herod has heard about. The irony here is that the success of the Twelve leads, ultimately, to the death of John the Baptist. This odd situation primes the audience for the idea that missionary success often has a high cost in terms of subsequent persecution.

The story of Herodias and her daughter might not seem like a victory for feminist interpreters of Mark, but it is. Without including a story showing a woman acting from evil intentions and misusing her power, Mark's Gospel would present women only in positive roles and thus run the risk of reaffirming the notion that women lack full moral capacity. In other words, if women can freely choose the right, they must also have the ability to make wrong choices, and Herodias does that abundantly. Given Mark's emphasis on discipleship, the portrayal of women in this story is an important component of the idea that women can choose (but must choose) to be disciples.

Further, this story has an important message about men's perceptions and choices. Herod lusts after his stepdaughter but he "does not anticipate that his (step)daughter will express a desire separate from and even counter to his own desires; her expression of a will independent of Herod's allows the female characters to emerge not as objects but as subjects."[50] When men view females as objects with which to fill their own desires, they lose control of the narrative. The opposite phenomenon is presented in chapter 5, where Jesus claims the healed woman as daughter, not, obviously, because he desires her, but rather because he approves of her show of courage and faith. Jesus invites women to center stage—not to dance but to testify. In the worldy setting of Herod's court, women have power only through their sexual appeal and their trickery. In Jesus' world, women exercise power through their faith (5:34), their persuasive appeal (7:29), their charity (12:43–44), and their prophetic knowledge (14:8).

---

50. Glancy, "Unveiling Masculinity," 40.

One of the key features of Mark's Gospel is the insertion of one story into the middle of another in order to encourage the audience to compare them. In chapter 6, the death of John the Baptist is intercalated within the story of the mission of the Twelve. Had the text moved directly from 6:13 to 6:30, the audience would not have felt that anything was missing; rather, the story actually flows more smoothly without the intervening material. The odds of this being a deliberate literary technique increase since there is only one verse describing the return of the Twelve after the sandwich,[51] which is somewhat unusual.

The mission of the Twelve is described in positive terms. The audience may have already been a little suspicious of this pleasant outcome since Jesus had devoted most of his counsel regarding their service to the topic of what to do when they were rejected—a plausible outcome since Jesus himself has just been rejected in Nazareth. And yet no such rejection is narrated. Interrupting the story of that mission with a report of the death of John—a story that teaches that preaching repentance results in imprisonment and death—raises further concerns about the experience of the Twelve. It is also possible that if Mark is the John Mark who had his own experience of a failed mission,[52] he prefers to talk about Herod than about the successes of the Twelve.

In both stories, the verb "to send" is used: Jesus sends out the Twelve, and Herod sends out men to seize John and, later, to kill him (6:17, 27). The noun form reappears in 6:30 when the Twelve return, in what is probably Mark's only use[53] of the word "apostle" (that is, "one sent out"). Mark encourages a comparison between Jesus and Herod. A further contrast exists between Herod's lavish banquet and Jesus' directions to his disciples to live simply.

In addition to the sandwiching structure, there is a second important narrative technique in this section: it is told in reverse chronological order. Mark begins with Herod's conclusion and then works backwards in order to show how he reached that conclusion. The story of John's death also appears to be out of chronological order; compare 1:14. This placement increases the probability that Mark has very purposefully inserted the story of John's death at this juncture in order to make a theological point—or, rather, several theological points.

---

51. Edwards, "Markan Sandwiches," 206.
52. See appendix A: "Authorship and Date."
53. See the Notes on the textual variant in 3:14.

The final—and, thus, emphasized—line in the story of John's death is that his disciples claimed and buried his body. (Had Mark told the story in order, it would have ended with Herod wondering if Jesus was John raised from the dead. Instead, the tale is punctuated by the actions of John's disciples.) Given that the frame story about the mission of the Twelve encourages the audience to read John's death in light of that mission, it is very significant that John's disciples claim and bury him. While Mark does not narrate it, they must have stayed nearby during John's imprisonment in order to be able to perform this service. Of course, the Twelve will not do this for Jesus: they have fled and are not at the cross to claim his body and bury it. As a result of the similarities between John's and Jesus' deaths, the audience probably expected Jesus' disciples to do as John's had done, so the fact that they do not is all the more stark.

The sandwiching structure also moderates the positive elements of the mission of the Twelve by reminding the audience that discipleship is not always a successful endeavor. The juxtaposition with John's story emphasizes that the earthly fate of those who preach the word of God is fraught.

The theme of the incomprehension of the disciples pulses throughout Mark's text. The main matter that they do not understand is that Jesus will suffer and die. This is because they literally missed the story—the tale of John's death is one of the stronger narrative clues in the Gospel (before the eighth chapter) that Jesus will suffer and die, but the apostles are away when it happens.

The word "for" at the beginning of 6:17 and 18 indicates that the story of John's death is being told in order to explain why Herod thought that Jesus was John raised from the dead which, in turn, is part of the story of Jesus' identity. In other words, the point in telling this story is it is background to the discussion of Jesus' identity. The audience should therefore consider John's death to understand Jesus' identity. One answer to the question "who is Jesus?" is he is someone who will die as John did.

Food and Gentiles
(6:32–8:21)

OVERVIEW

Mark 6:32–8:21 functions as one integrated section, unified by references to loaves and eating in virtually every story; these stories build on each other in ways both explicit and implicit.

Mark 6:32–44 introduces this section of the text. It is the first reference to loaves, as well as one of the two feeding miracles that bracket 6:32–8:21. Jesus walks on water in 6:45–52; while the story is formally a nature miracle, it is also profoundly concerned with revealing Jesus' identity. It links to the feeding miracle through the concluding note that the disciples "considered not the miracle of the loaves" (6:52). And it echoes the previous sea miracle (4:35–41) but also anticipates a future scene in a boat, one that will also immediately follow a feeding miracle and will show the disciples' incomprehension despite that miracle (8:14–21). Chapter 6 ends with a summary of Jesus' activities.

Chapter 7 is located in the middle of a section of text that consists of two parallel blocks of stories: both 6:32–56 and 8:1–21 contain feeding miracles and stories about misunderstandings that occur in a boat. The theme of bread and eating is at the forefront of the material in chapter 7, which is also distinguished by its focus on Gentiles; the chapter begins as Jesus is confronted about his disciples' (lack of) observance of the customs of the Pharisees—customs that created a boundary between Jew and Gentile. In the middle of the chapter, Jesus initially refuses a gentile woman's request for a miracle but then exorcises her daughter. Finally, Jesus heals a gentile man. Jesus' conversation with the gentile woman is the turning point for this section of the text; it shows his ministry expanding to include Gentiles. One major theme in these three stories is the (in)ability of people to recognize Jesus. In the first and third stories, the crowds instantly recognize Jesus; in fact, their recognition is the event that initiates the plot. But in the middle story, the disciples—those who are closest to Jesus—are unable to recognize him when he approaches them. Mark arranges the stories in order to highlight the continuing inability of the disciples to recognize Jesus.

JESUS FEEDS FIVE THOUSAND MEN (6:32–44)

Greek Text

32 καὶ ἀπῆλθον ἐν τῷ πλοίῳ εἰς ἔρημον τόπον κατ᾽ ἰδίαν. 33 καὶ εἶδον αὐτοὺς ὑπάγοντας καὶ ἐπέγνωσαν πολλοί, καὶ πεζῇ ἀπὸ πασῶν τῶν πόλεων συνέδραμον ἐκεῖ καὶ προῆλθον αὐτούς. 34 καὶ ἐξελθὼν εἶδεν πολὺν ὄχλον, καὶ ἐσπλαγχνίσθη ἐπ᾽ αὐτοὺς ὅτι ἦσαν ὡς πρόβατα μὴ ἔχοντα ποιμένα, καὶ ἤρξατο διδάσκειν αὐτοὺς πολλά. 35 Καὶ ἤδη ὥρας πολλῆς γενομένης προσελθόντες αὐτῷ οἱ μαθηταὶ αὐτοῦ ἔλεγον ὅτι "Ερημός ἐστιν ὁ τόπος, καὶ ἤδη ὥρα πολλή· 36 ἀπόλυσον αὐτούς, ἵνα ἀπελθόντες εἰς τοὺς κύκλῳ ἀγροὺς καὶ κώμας ἀγοράσωσιν ἑαυτοῖς τί φάγωσιν. 37 ὁ δὲ ἀποκριθεὶς εἶπεν αὐτοῖς· Δότε αὐτοῖς ὑμεῖς φαγεῖν. καὶ λέγουσιν αὐτῷ· Ἀπελθόντες ἀγοράσωμεν δηναρίων διακοσίων ἄρτους καὶ δώσομεν αὐτοῖς φαγεῖν; 38 ὁ δὲ λέγει αὐτοῖς· Πόσους ἔχετε ἄρτους; ὑπάγετε ἴδετε. καὶ γνόντες λέγουσιν· Πέντε, καὶ δύο ἰχθύας. 39 καὶ ἐπέταξεν αὐτοῖς ἀνακλῖναι πάντας συμπόσια συμπόσια ἐπὶ τῷ χλωρῷ χόρτῳ. 40 καὶ ἀνέπεσαν πρασιαὶ πρασιαὶ κατὰ ἑκατὸν καὶ κατὰ πεντήκοντα. 41 καὶ λαβὼν τοὺς πέντε ἄρτους καὶ τοὺς δύο ἰχθύας ἀναβλέψας εἰς τὸν οὐρανὸν εὐλόγησεν καὶ κατέκλασεν τοὺς ἄρτους καὶ ἐδίδου τοῖς μαθηταῖς αὐτοῦ ἵνα παρατιθῶσιν αὐτοῖς, καὶ τοὺς δύο ἰχθύας ἐμέρισεν πᾶσιν. 42 καὶ ἔφαγον πάντες καὶ ἐχορτάσθησαν· 43 καὶ ἦραν κλάσματα δώδεκα κοφίνων πληρώματα καὶ ἀπὸ τῶν ἰχθύων. 44 καὶ ἦσαν οἱ φαγόντες τοὺς ἄρτους πεντακισχίλιοι ἄνδρες. [SBLGNT]

King James Version

32 And they departed into a desert place by ship privately. 33 And the people saw them departing, and many knew him, and ran afoot thither out of all cities, and outwent them, and came together unto him. 34 And Jesus, when he came out, saw much people, and was moved with

New Rendition

32 And they went in the boat into a deserted place by themselves. 33 And many saw them going and recognized them, and they ran together there by land from all the towns and arrived before them. 34 And having gone out [of the boat], he saw a large crowd and

compassion toward them, because they were as sheep not having a shepherd: and he began to teach them many things. 35 And when the day was now far spent, his disciples came unto him, and said, This is a desert place, and now the time is far passed: 36 Send them away, that they may go into the country round about, and into the villages, and buy themselves bread: for they have nothing to eat. 37 He answered and said unto them, Give ye them to eat. And they say unto him, Shall we go and buy two hundred pennyworth of bread, and give them to eat? 38 He saith unto them, How many loaves have ye? go and see. And when they knew, they say, Five, and two fishes. 39 And he commanded them to make all sit down by companies upon the green grass. 40 And they sat down in ranks, by hundreds, and by fifties. 41 And when he had taken the five loaves and the two fishes, he looked up to heaven, and blessed, and brake the loaves, and gave them to his disciples to set before them; and the two fishes divided he among them all. 42 And they did all eat, and were filled. 43 And they took up twelve baskets full of the fragments, and of the fishes. 44 And they that did eat of the loaves were about five thousand men.

was filled with compassion toward them because they were like sheep not having a shepherd. And he began to teach them many things. 35 And already the hour was late, having come to him, his disciples were saying to him, "This is a deserted place, and already the hour is late. 36 Send them away, so that having gone into the surrounding countryside and towns, they might buy themselves something to eat." 37 But answering, he said to them, "You give them something to eat." And they say to him, "Having gone out, should we buy two hundred days' wages worth of bread and give it to them to eat?" 38 And he says to them, "How many loaves of bread do you have? Go and see." And having found out, they say, "Five, and two fish." 39 And he commanded them to make everyone in groups on the green grass. 40 And they sat down in rows, by hundreds and by fifties. 41 And having taken the five loaves and the two fish, having looked up into/to heaven, he blessed and broke the loaves and gave them to his disciples so that they might present them to the people. And the two fish he divided among them all. 42 And they all ate and were filled. 43 And they picked up twelve basketfuls of scraps [of bread] and of the fish. 44 And those having eaten of the loaves were five thousand males.

Notes

6:32 *And they departed into a desert place by ship privately.* 33 *And the people saw them departing, and many knew him, and ran afoot thither out of all cities:* "Afoot" indicates that the crowd travels on land, while Jesus and the disciples are in the boat.

The phrase "all cities," while hyperbolic, draws attention to the fact that the crowd is very large.

and outwent them: The crowd arrives before Jesus; apparently, it was faster to travel by foot than by boat in this case.

It is incredibly ironic that the crowd arrives first, given that Jesus' intent was to take his disciples to an uninhabited place. Mark is comfortable with Jesus' lack of omniscience in this context.

It is difficult to imagine how a large crowd could arrive before Jesus (how would they even have known where he was going?). While it is possible that Jesus was sailing along the shore and the crowd paralleled his journey by land, it is also possible that Mark has adjusted some of the details in order to point to larger truths. What is clear from Mark's story is that the crowd is highly motivated to be in Jesus' presence.

and came together unto him: This line is not in the oldest manuscripts and probably does not reflect the earliest text of Mark.[1] But even with it excluded, the sentiment is the same: the people gather at Jesus' destination.

6:34 *And Jesus, when he came out, saw much people, and was moved with compassion toward them:* Jesus' reaction is noteworthy for several reasons:

1. The audience might have expected Jesus to be angry since his intention was for his disciples to have some time away from the crowds, yet this crowd has foiled his plan by arriving even before he did. But instead of anger, Jesus responds with compassion; he prioritizes the needs of the crowd above the needs of his own disciples.

2. His compassion is a result of the crowd being like sheep without a shepherd, which means that they are leaderless. Jesus' response is not anger towards those who should have been their leaders but rather compassion for the people who were left leaderless.

3. Normally in the Gospels, Jesus' compassion leads to miracles. While there will eventually be a miracle in this story, Jesus first teaches the people. It is significant that his compassion leads to teaching. This is a powerful commentary on the role and importance of teaching; it also suggests that Jesus' teaching is akin to a miracle.

because they were as sheep not having a shepherd: Figurative language is used to explain Jesus' compassionate response. Several HB texts use the imagery of sheep without a shepherd to bemoan a lack of leadership (1 Kgs. 22:17; Zech. 11:15–17). Particularly interesting is Numbers 27:15–18, where Moses' absence creates a leadership vacuum that Joshua will fill ("Jesus" is the Greek iteration of the Hebrew name "Joshua"); similarly, Ezekiel 34:23

---

1. Metzger, *Textual Commentary*, 78.

promises a future shepherd—a messianic king, like David—who will lead and feed the people, as Jesus does here in Mark's text. The image is a biting commentary on Herod, who should have been a shepherd to his people but instead offered failed leadership through his debauched court and his murder of John.

and he began to teach them many things: "Many" can be adverbial ("began to do a lot of teaching") or adjectival ("began to teach them many things").

The problem is a lack of leadership, but the solution is teaching: "in Jewish literature the 'feeding' of Israel is often associated with their being taught the Torah."[2] The content of Jesus' teachings is not given; the emphasis is on the fact of the teaching itself. Once again, Mark's portrayal of Jesus emphasizes deeds and not words.

6:35 *And when the day was now far spent his disciples came unto him, and said, This is a desert place, and now the time is far passed:* It is likely late afternoon, since the disciples believe that there is still time to travel to a market and purchase food for the evening meal.

6:36 *Send them away:* There are two different ways to understand the disciples' motivation:

1. They are upset that their promised rest has been interrupted by the crowd, so they use the lack of food as an excuse to banish them.

2. They are concerned that the crowd will go hungry and are trying to prevent that outcome. While this is a more positive reading of the disciples' motivation, it means that they prioritize physical food over Jesus' teachings. Jesus' response will show that this is a false dilemma. And they are once again (compare 4:38) attempting to counsel Jesus as to how to run his ministry.

Ironically, the disciples' request to send the people away would accomplish Jesus' original goal of being in an uninhabited place to rest. But the disciples are not sensitive to the fact that changed circumstances require that the plan change; instead, they show inappropriate rigidity, which is the opposite of Jesus' compassion.

Had Jesus sent them away, he would have been the shepherd who scatters the sheep (compare 6:34). Jesus cannot turn them away because he is the good shepherd who will care for them.

that they may go into the country round about, and into the villages, and buy themselves bread: for they have nothing to eat: The best ancient

---

2. Stein, *Mark,* 313.

manuscripts read "buy themselves something to eat" instead of "buy themselves bread: for they have nothing to eat."[3]

The disciples do not consider the possibility of a miraculous solution here—the only solution that they can envision is for Jesus to stop teaching and send the people away.

Of course, at any time, anyone in the crowd could have left to buy food; Jesus does not need to send the crowd away for this to be an option, which means that:

1. The fact that they haven't left implies that the crowd, unlike the disciples, prioritizes Jesus' teachings above their physical needs. Jesus' miraculous powers mean that they will not have to choose between the two.

2. The disciples' request is somewhat puzzling. Why do the disciples make their request when nothing was preventing the crowd from leaving? Perhaps they want Jesus to command the crowd to leave so that they will not feel pressured to share their meager provisions with them. If this is the case, the fact that Jesus' miraculous power makes the scant provisions sufficient for the crowd becomes an ironic aspect of the story.

6:37 *He answered and said unto them, Give ye them to eat:* The word "ye" is emphatic in Greek—Jesus underscores that the disciples themselves should provide food for the crowd.

Perhaps Jesus expects that the disciples will use the power that he has already given them in order to multiply the loaves and fishes themselves. This would parallel 4:35–41, where the implication behind Jesus' chastisement for their lack of faith is that they should have acted themselves instead of asking Jesus to act for them (see the Notes on 4:35–41).

Neither Jesus nor the disciples treat the need for food as unimportant. The issue at hand is whether the crowd should buy their own food or whether the disciples should provide it; neither assumes that meeting spiritual needs will meet physical needs.

And they say unto him, Shall we go and buy two hundred pennyworth of bread, and give them to eat?: "Pennyworth" is the translation for the Greek word *dēnarion,* which was the average daily wage for an unskilled laborer. It would require a very large amount of money (hence the New Rendition's "two hundred days' wages") to purchase enough bread for a crowd so large.

There are several ways to interpret this question:

---

3. Comfort, *New Testament Text and Translation Commentary,* 116.

1. Sarcastic, as if it should be obvious that such a thing would not be possible because they do not have that much money.

2. Incredulous, as if the disciples cannot imagine that this is what Jesus truly wants to happen.

3. Genuine, so they are requesting permission to spend this much of the group's funds.

4. Rhetorical, meant to show that Jesus' plan is unworkable because they do not have enough money to do this.

The disciples still do not consider a miraculous solution, even though Jesus' command to them to provide the food hints in that direction.

6:38 *He saith unto them, How many loaves have ye? go and see:* Jesus does not answer their question but rather poses his own. His query requires them to focus on what they do have instead of on what they are lacking.

And when they knew, they say, Five, and two fishes: This verse may picture the disciples going back to the boat to see what was in it.

This is probably barley bread. A loaf was about eight inches in diameter and one inch thick and would have been sufficient for one person for one day. Salted and dried fish was commonly taken on journeys. While Mark does not mention exactly how many disciples are traveling with Jesus, this is a small amount of food for a group that is planning on spending time in an uninhabited place.

There may be a link between the five loaves of bread and the five books of the Torah. If this allusion is intentional, then the disciples have the Torah, but it is not enough to feed the people. However, through Jesus' power, it will become enough to meet their needs.

6:39 *And he commanded them to make all sit down:* The Greek text uses the verb for "recline," not "sit." Reclining would have, at this time and in a Jewish context, been the customary posture at formal meals such as Passover[4] but not at everyday meals. So the command to recline may indicate that Jesus is preparing them for a special meal, not merely a casual picnic in the wilderness. It may even point to the idea of a messianic banquet (see "Allusion to the Messianic Banquet" after the Notes on 6:42).

by companies upon the green grass: The word translated as "companies" often refers to social groups at drinking parties, so the people are treated as friends gathering together for a social occasion and not just a random gathering who happened to be in the same place at the same time.

---

4. Mishnah Pesahim 10:1.

While Mark's Gospel is known for its vivid detail, the reference to the green grass is unusually specific even by Mark's standards.

6:40 *And they sat down in ranks, by hundreds, and by fifties:* "Ranks" here and "companies" (in the previous verse) translate two different Greek words. "In ranks" means "a garden plot or flower bed and is not elsewhere used to describe people, so that [it] offers a remarkably visual impression of the scene, with men lined up in groups like plots of vegetables on the green grass."[5] This image suggests that the hungry people are the seeds that Jesus plants in good soil (4:20).

It is possible that the crowd is seated in fifty rows of one hundred, which would explain how the headcount in 6:44 was determined; it is also possible that the details are not precisely historical but rather meant to be allusive.

It is not unreasonable to think that a crowd this large with such meager provisions might riot when food became available; perhaps the orderly rows are the first miracle of the story, showing Jesus' control over the crowd.

Relationship to the Exodus. During the Exodus, Moses commanded the people to form groups of hundreds and fifties (Ex. 18:25; Deut. 1:15). If Mark is alluding to this, it positions Jesus as the new Moses, leading these people as if in a new exodus. Interestingly, this time the exodus is into the wilderness instead of out of it.

Relationship to 1 Kings 18. In this text, Obadiah takes one hundred prophets, divided into two groups of fifty, and hides them from Jezebel. He brings them food and water to sustain them (1 Kgs. 18:4). If Mark intends for there to be an allusion, it identifies Jesus as a prophet in the biblical tradition and suggests that the crowd and the disciples may be at risk from evil leaders, particularly if the story of Herod's court alludes to the story of Jezebel; see the section "Relationship to 1 Kings 19" after the Notes on 6:31.

6:41 *And when he had taken the five loaves and the two fishes, he looked up to heaven, and blessed, and brake the loaves:* "Blessed" can refer to the bread or to God. In other words, Jesus may be asking God to bless the bread, or he may be blessing God for providing the bread.

Jewish tradition prescribed prayer before eating, but the normal prayer posture was downward-looking. Thus, looking up to heaven would have

---

5. France, *Gospel of Mark,* 267.

been a departure from common practice that the audience would have noticed. It probably suggests Jesus' intimate communion with heaven.

and gave them to his disciples to set before them: It is significant that the disciples, not Jesus, provide the food to the crowd. Jesus had given the disciples a command ("give ye them to eat") that seemed impossible to fulfill, but then, through his own miraculous power, he made it possible.

and the two fishes divided he among them all: It is possible that Jesus personally distributed the fish to each member of the crowd; while this is uncertain, the syntax of the sentence does permit it.

6:42 *And they did all eat, and were filled:* The actual miracle—the multiplication of the loaves and fishes—is not narrated. The audience discovers it through the description of its results (they "were filled"). This story fits the pattern of a "gift miracle," where a need is filled without the beneficiary requesting it and without describing the miracle itself.[6]

An ancient audience was far more likely to know hunger than a modern Western one; eating to fullness would have been, for many people, a rare event. The green grass indicates that it was springtime, when the supply of grain would be at its lowest for the year, which means that a full meal would have been even more appreciated.

Allusion to the Messianic Banquet. Isaiah 25:6–9 symbolizes the coming of the Messiah with a lavish banquet. It may be that Mark narrates this feeding miracle in a way that foreshadows the messianic banquet and thus subtly teaches that Jesus is the long-awaited Messiah.

Allusion to Abundant Food. Deuteronomy 8:10 describes the promised land as a good land where the people will be able to eat until they are filled. If Mark is alluding to that text, the text is suggesting that Jesus' presence— even in an uninhabited place—makes that place the promised land. (This allusion may work in tandem with the Exodus imagery.) Similarly, NET Psalm 78:29 reads, "they ate until they were stuffed; he gave them what they desired." Mark's story can be read as a fulfillment of that promise.

6:43 *And they took up twelve baskets full of the fragments, and of the fishes:* The word translated as "basket" is an unusual one; it was specifically associated with Jews in the ancient world.[7]

---

6. 1 Kgs. 17; 2 Kgs. 4; Luke 5. This type of miracle is also found in some rabbinic sources.

7. "The term for 'basket,' *kophinos,* is a different one from *kanoun,* the usual word for a basket in Attic Greek and the LXX; it also differs from *spyris,* the word used in the parallel

The twelve baskets might result from the Twelve having one basket each, or it might symbolize sufficient food for the entire restored house of Israel (see also the Notes on 8:19–21 regarding the symbolic meaning of the numbers in this story; a significant part of the impact of this feeding miracle stems from its relationship to the second feeding miracle).

No purpose is given for collecting the leftovers; possibilities include:

1. It is primarily a symbolic detail instead of a pragmatic one; consider 6:52 and 7:2, 28.

2. It may be evidence of Jesus' lack of omniscience (since he did not provide the precise amount of food that would be needed), showing him erring on the side of overabundance.

3. Mark may have wanted to convey that, even when it was not needed and was miraculously supplied, Jesus did not permit food to be wasted; this would contrast with the lavishness of Herod's banquet.

By serving the food and collecting the leftovers, the Twelve are functioning as waiters. Given that the word "minister" morphed under Christian usage from meaning "to serve at table" (compare Acts 6:2) to "to lead," it is most appropriate that Jesus is teaching the Twelve how to serve/minister in this story.

There is more food after everyone has eaten than there was before anyone ate. This superabundance teaches that God, through Jesus, is excessively gracious. It also attests to Jesus' powers.

6:44 *And they that did eat of the loaves:* Some manuscripts omit "the loaves."[8] It may have accidentally been excluded, or it might have been added later to highlight the link to the Last Supper. Or perhaps it was deliberately omitted because it seemed odd to mention the loaves and not the fish.

were about five thousand men: Once again, Mark mentions a detail at an unusual time in order to draw attention to it (compare 5:42). There are two reasons why Mark may have noted the size of the crowd:

1. It is a historical detail, evidence of an eyewitness. If the crowd sat by rows, then observers would have known precisely how many people were present. The fact that five thousand were filled by five loaves attests to the incredible nature of this miracle, particularly since Mark's audience probably would have assumed that the crowd was much smaller.

---

story in 8:8. *Kophinos* seems to designate a kind of basket particularly associated with Jews; Juvenal twice satirizes Jewish travelers with their *kophinoi* (*Satires* 3.14; 6.542), and a related word, *qûpāh/qūpā'*, is present in Rabbinic Hebrew and Aramaic (see Jastrow, 1337)." Marcus, *Mark 1–8*, 411.

8. Comfort, *New Testament Text and Translation Commentary*, 116.

2. There were normally about five thousand men in a Roman legion, so Mark may be suggesting a military overtone. There may also be a contrast with 5:1–20: a legion of Satan's followers takes a man to the brink of death, but a legion of Jesus' followers enjoys a peaceful banquet.

While there are many references to "men" in Mark's Gospel, these are translations of a Greek term that refers to a generic man ("human being"; for example, 8:24; 11:32; 12:14). But in this case, a different word is used (Greek: *anēr*), one that refers specifically to males. Perhaps women and children were present in addition to the five thousand men, but this is probably not the best reading of this passage; it seems that Mark envisions this as a male-only crowd (see the Notes on 8:19–21).

Relationship to Numbers 11. In Numbers 11, Moses despairs of feeding the people in the wilderness without sufficient resources; his complaint mirrors that of the disciples in Mark's text. The Lord intervenes by showing Moses how he will be able to feed all of the people. This allusion honors the disciples by showing them in the role of Moses (if at a moment when Moses is complaining). Similarly, it aligns Jesus with the God of the Bible as the miraculous provider of food to those in need.

There are significant contrasts between this feeding miracle and the story of the manna:

1. In the Exodus, much emphasis is placed on the fact that the people were forbidden to gather the leftovers (Ex. 16:19–20). But in Mark's account, the collection of leftovers is highlighted. Perhaps the point is to suggest that the new age that Jesus inaugurates is not one of limits but rather of abundance. Since it was permitted to gather extra manna to eat on the Sabbath (Ex. 16:22–23), Mark's story might imply that Jesus' presence heralded the time of Sabbath rest.

2. In the wilderness, the children of Israel ate manna and quail; in this feeding story, they eat bread and fish. And Mark's story is not in the desert but in a place with green grass.

3. The manna came from heaven, but the bread and fish come from the disciples' personal provisions.

Relationship to 2 Kings 4. In 2 Kings 4:42–44, Elisha's servant asks how there can possibly be enough food for such a large crowd (in a question that sounds much like the one that Jesus' disciples raise), but Elisha turns twenty loaves of bread into a meal for one hundred people. And as in Mark's text, there is reference to the leftovers.

This close parallel strongly suggests a relationship between the two texts. And not only is Jesus aligned with the prophet Elisha but he is also shown to be superior to him: instead of feeding one hundred people with twenty loaves, he feeds five thousand with five loaves. Given that Mark has suggested that John the Baptist fills the role of Elijah (see the Notes on 1:6), it makes sense that Jesus would fill the role of Elisha.

Relationship to Psalm 23. Many concepts from this psalm overlap with Mark's story, including references to green grass, shepherds, being commanded to sit, having needs met, and resting. While the wording is often different from the LXX, the ideas in Mark are the same: Jesus is shown to be the shepherd who attends to all of the needs of his flock.

Comparison with Herod's Banquet. Jesus' feeding of the five thousand is a nearly perfect inversion of Herod's banquet earlier in this chapter (6:14–31). The people Jesus feeds are not a small group of the elites; they are a large group of common people who run to be with Jesus, who are taught by Jesus, and who cannot meet their own needs. Instead of agreeing to provide "food" (in the form of John's head) because he doesn't have the courage to go back on a foolish oath, Jesus instead uses his power to provide food for all of the people. And far from the general atmosphere of licentiousness and excess of the banquet, this situation is controlled in both the provision (to orderly groups sitting row by row who are given simple food) and in the collection of the food.

Military Motifs. This feeding miracle can be read as "a purposeful gathering of men determined to persuade (or if necessary force) Jesus, now recognised as a man of undoubted charisma and leadership, to take up the role of military leadership in a popular movement of insurrection."[9] There are many indicators of a military motif in this story:

1. The odd fact that the crowd outruns Jesus' boat makes more sense if they are a would-be army.

2. It was customary for military movements to start in the wilderness.

3. As mentioned above, the reference to an all-male audience is unique in Mark's Gospel; in a military setting, this audience makes sense.

4. The reference to five thousand diners might imply a legion, meaning a unit of the Roman military.

5. Companies of fifties and hundreds further the military imagery.

---

9. France, *Gospel of Mark*, 261.

6. Jesus has compassion on the crowd because they are like sheep without a shepherd—an image that implies leaderlessness, especially in a military context.

7. The crowd's desire for a revolt may have been spurred by Herod's murder of John the Baptist (particularly if Herod believed that John was going to incite insurrection against him, as Josephus reports; this crowd may be turning to Jesus to lead a revolt against Roman rule).

8. Immediately after this story, Jesus and the disciples leave the scene quickly, which may be the result of Jesus' desire to avoid giving the crowd and/or the authorities the impression that he will provide military leadership.

9. Immediately after the feeding miracle in John's Gospel, the crowd desires to make Jesus their king (John 6:15). (Of course, it is not certain that the different Gospel writers had identical understandings of the same story.)

What is most important about this military motif is how Jesus subverts it: instead of providing military leadership, he provides compassion and dinner. And while it may have been customary for military movements to begin in the wilderness, Jesus articulated his reason for going into the deserted place—and it was not to begin a revolt. Also, he leaves quickly at the end, making it clear that his purpose was not to lead a revolt. If this is Jesus' legion, they are shown not to be fierce warriors but more like plants completely dependent upon Jesus for their care and survival. Taken together, this is a good example of Mark's tendency to establish an expectation in the minds of the audience and then subvert it. It also sharpens the contrast with Herod, who used his power not out of compassion but out of pride, not to benefit life but to end it.

See also the Notes on 6:52 and 8:19–21, where this story will again be referenced; these are important texts for understanding what meaning Mark wants the audience to find in 6:30–44.

Analysis

It is typical for miracle stories to end with a note of amazement by the witnesses. The fact that this does not happen in this story is a very loud silence: it suggests that the crowd was not aware that a miracle had taken place. The story implies that the miracle is "for" the disciples more than the crowd, since Jesus teaches his followers how to use his power and authority to bless the lives of others. Soon, Mark will chastise them for not thinking about the implications of this miracle (6:52), which is further evidence that the miracle is primarily for the disciples' benefit.

The theme of discipleship is easy to overlook in this story due to the impressiveness of the miracle. But the focus is clearly on the experience of the disciples, especially if the crowd is not even aware that a miracle has happened and if it were possible for the crowd and/or the disciples to purchase food in nearby towns.

Jesus teaches the disciples how to use their (insufficient) personal resources combined with his (infinite) powers in order to achieve a seemingly impossible outcome. Further, contrary to Jesus' usual practice, the disciples have a role in the miracle itself: they are the ones who provide the initial material, who distribute the food to the crowd whom they have seated and organized, and who collect the leftovers. Later, two passages will assume that the disciples should have learned something from this experience. So while this story reveals Jesus' power, it is also a teaching moment for the disciples: they are involved in this miracle and expected to learn from their participation in it. The story begins with the disciples assuming that they cannot feed the crowd, but as it unfolds, Jesus shows them how they are able to do so if they rely on his power. While the Markan motif of the incomprehension of the disciples is present, Jesus uses it as a teaching opportunity.

JESUS WALKS ON WATER (6:45–52)

Greek Text

45 Καὶ εὐθὺς ἠνάγκασεν τοὺς μαθητὰς αὐτοῦ ἐμβῆναι εἰς τὸ πλοῖον καὶ προάγειν εἰς τὸ πέραν πρὸς Βηθσαϊδάν, ἕως αὐτὸς ἀπολύει τὸν ὄχλον. 46 καὶ ἀποταξάμενος αὐτοῖς ἀπῆλθεν εἰς τὸ ὄρος προσεύξασθαι.

47 Καὶ ὀψίας γενομένης ἦν τὸ πλοῖον ἐν μέσῳ τῆς θαλάσσης, καὶ αὐτὸς μόνος ἐπὶ τῆς γῆς. 48 καὶ ἰδὼν αὐτοὺς βασανιζομένους ἐν τῷ ἐλαύνειν, ἦν γὰρ ὁ ἄνεμος ἐναντίος αὐτοῖς, περὶ τετάρτην φυλακὴν τῆς νυκτὸς ἔρχεται πρὸς αὐτοὺς περιπατῶν ἐπὶ τῆς θαλάσσης· καὶ ἤθελεν παρελθεῖν αὐτούς. 49 οἱ δὲ ἰδόντες αὐτὸν ἐπὶ τῆς θαλάσσης περιπατοῦντα ἔδοξαν ὅτι φάντασμά ἐστιν καὶ ἀνέκραξαν, 50 πάντες γὰρ αὐτὸν εἶδον καὶ ἐταράχθησαν. ὁ δὲ εὐθὺς ἐλάλησεν μετ' αὐτῶν, καὶ λέγει αὐτοῖς· Θαρσεῖτε, ἐγώ εἰμι, μὴ φοβεῖσθε. 51 καὶ ἀνέβη πρὸς αὐτοὺς εἰς τὸ πλοῖον, καὶ ἐκόπασεν ὁ ἄνεμος. καὶ λίαν ἐκ περισσοῦ ἐν ἑαυτοῖς ἐξίσταντο, 52 οὐ γὰρ συνῆκαν ἐπὶ τοῖς ἄρτοις, ἀλλ' ἦν αὐτῶν ἡ καρδία πεπωρωμένη. [SBLGNT]

King James Version

45 And straightway he constrained his disciples to get into the ship, and to go to the other side before unto Bethsaida, while he sent away the people. 46 And when he had sent them away, he departed into a mountain to pray. 47 And when even was come, the ship was in the midst of the sea, and he alone on the land. 48 And he saw them toiling in rowing; for the wind was contrary unto them: and about the fourth watch of the night he cometh unto them, walking upon the sea, and would have passed by them. 49 But when they saw him walking upon the sea, they supposed it had been a spirit, and cried out: 50 For they all saw him, and were troubled. And immediately he talked with them, and saith unto them, Be of good cheer: it is I; be not afraid. 51 And he went up unto them into the ship; and the wind ceased: and they were sore amazed in themselves beyond measure, and wondered. 52 For they considered not the miracle of the loaves: for their heart was hardened.

New Rendition

45 And immediately he required his disciples to enter into the boat and to go on ahead to the other side, to Bethsaida, while he dismisses the crowd. 46 And having left them, he went to the mountain to pray. 47 And evening having come, the boat was in the middle of the sea, and he was alone on the land. 48 And having seen them straining at rowing, for the wind was against them, as the night was ending, he comes to them walking on the sea and intending to pass by them. 49 And having seen him walking on the sea, they thought that it is a ghost and screamed. 50 For all saw him and were terrified. And immediately he spoke with them and says to them, "Have courage. I am [here]. Do not fear." 51 And he went up into the boat to them, and the wind stopped. And they were extremely, utterly amazed. 52 For they did not understand about the loaves, but their heart was hardened.

Notes

6:45 *And straightway he constrained his disciples to get into the ship:* The word "straightway" indicates rushing, perhaps to escape the crowd's attempt to recruit Jesus to lead a revolt.

"Constrained" is a strong word; it is possible that Jesus strongly encouraged the disciples to enter the boat when they would have preferred not to. Perhaps they did not want to be separated from Jesus—especially after what happened during the last sea crossing (4:35–41)—and so they resisted his efforts.

and to go to the other side before unto Bethsaida, while he sent away the people: They will not end up in Bethsaida (see 6:53 and the Notes there; compare 8:22 and its Notes). Some ancient manuscripts omit the phrase "to go to the other side";[10] this phrase was probably present originally but omitted since it did not match the outcome of the story.

6:46 *And when he had sent them away:* The word "them" is ambiguous; it could refer to the crowd, the disciples, or both.

he departed into a mountain to pray: Because there is a definite article before "mountain" ("the mountain," not "a mountain"), the mountain is more likely to have symbolic meaning. Because Moses goes up into a mountain to be with God (Ex. 24:15), mountains are symbolically understood as the place where God is revealed to humans (Deut. 33:2; Hab. 3:3). It is possible that this reference is meant to prime Mark's audience for the idea that Jesus will be revealed to the disciples in the story of the walking on water.

6:47 *And when even was come, the ship was in the midst of the sea, and he alone on the land. 48 And he saw them toiling in rowing; for the wind was contrary unto them:* Jesus may still be on the mountain in these verses; he may be able to see their struggle either because of his vantage point or as a result of divine perception. The latter option may be more likely since it is nighttime.

The word "toiling" can connote torment, so the disciples are pictured as struggling mightily.

and about the fourth watch of the night he cometh unto them, walking upon the sea: Jews divided the night into three watches (shifts for watchmen) while the Romans had four watches, so Mark is using the Roman system here.

The fourth watch was approximately three to six in the morning. The New Rendition uses the phrase "as the night was ending" to convey that it was almost morning and that the disciples had been struggling for the entire night. There must have been a small amount of early morning light already: the disciples think that they see a ghost, but in the ancient world, ghosts did not glow and therefore could be seen only if there were another light source.

Allusion: God Controls the Seas. Only God controlled the seas, and therefore only God could have walked on water in the biblical view of the world. In Job 9:8, the LXX reads that God "walks upon the sea as upon dry ground." An allusion to that text would thus align Jesus with God (see also Job 38:16; Ps. 77:19–20).

---

10. Metzger, *Textual Commentary*, 79.

and would have passed by them: This line has puzzled interpreters of Mark. Some have understood it to reflect the perspective of the disciples: they thought that Jesus was going to pass them by (and while Jesus' own intentions are not stated in the text, one can presume that he was not going to pass them by). However, this reading does not cohere well with the disciples' fear: Would they have screamed in terror at a ghost that appeared to be passing them by, or would they have been silently watchful? So a more likely reading is that "pass by them" indicates Jesus' intention to parade by as a divine being. Several biblical texts make reference to a divine "parade," in which God "passes by" a person as a way of revealing the divine presence. In the LXX, "to pass by" is "almost a technical term for a divine epiphany."[11] For example, Job 9:11 reads, "he goeth by me, and I see him not: he passeth on also, but I perceive him not." Not only is the divine presence "passing by" Job, but Job is unaware of it, which is also the case for the disciples in Mark's story. This text from Job may have particular resonance for Mark's story since just a few verses before (Job 9:8), Job described God as walking upon the sea: "thus, in Job 9 the image of God's walking on the sea is linked with a confession of God's mysterious transcendence of human comprehension: God's 'passing by' is a metaphor for our inability to grasp his power."[12] This theme fits well into Mark's message about the disciples' lack of understanding.

Other instances of God "passing by" humans include Exodus 33:19–34:8 and 1 Kings 19:11. In both of these texts, there is a water barrier that must be overcome; the fact that Moses and Elijah part the waters but Jesus walks on them indicates Jesus' similarity to, but also his superiority to, these prophets. If these texts are the background to Mark's story, it shifts the emphasis from Jesus walking on water to the manifestation of the divine. It appears that Jesus' intention was to reveal himself as a divine being by "passing them by" as he walked on the water.

6:49 ***But when they saw him walking upon the sea:*** Note the contrast: the disciples use all of their physical strength but make little progress, while Jesus—without boat or oars—walks past them.

they supposed it had been a spirit, and cried out: The KJV's "spirit" is problematic because this is not the same word used for holy and unclean

---

11. Marcus, *Mark 1–8*, 426.

12. Richard B. Hays, "Can the Gospels Teach Us How to Read the Old Testament?" *Pro Ecclesia* 11, no. 4 (2002): 410.

spirits in Mark. Rather, this word is best translated as "ghost." The crying out of the disciples is screaming in terror.

Mark is telling a ghost story that fits the conventions of Roman ghost stories, including a night setting and a fearful response. However, the one defining characteristic of ancient ghost stories is that ghosts could not walk on water: "Mark suggests that the disciples thought that Jesus was a ghost when they witnessed him doing one thing that ghosts absolutely cannot do: walk on water. The Jewish and Greco-Roman audience . . . would have been particularly dumbfounded by the disciples' misunderstanding."[13] The idea that someone walking on water was a ghost was a comically illogical mistake.

6:50 *For they all saw him, and were troubled. And immediately he talked with them, and saith unto them, Be of good cheer: it is I; be not afraid:* "Be of good cheer" means that they should have courage (not that they should be cheerful).

"I am" (KJV: "it is I") is one of the names of God in the HB. When God appears to Moses through the burning bush, Moses asks by what name he should refer to God. God replies, "I AM" (Ex. 3:14). Jesus uses the same words as the LXX for this passage, which means that he is claiming the distinct name of God for himself. This is incredibly significant in terms of Mark's presentation of the nature and identity of Jesus. If Jesus is deliberately using this title for himself, then the scene drips with irony: on one level, he is assuaging the fears of his disciples who think that he is a ghost by telling them that he is Jesus. But on another level, he is not saying, "It's me—Jesus"; rather, he is saying, "I am God."

Relationship to Exodus 20:18–20. In this story, the people are aware of God's presence on the mountain, and they are afraid. They want to keep their distance, and they want Moses (and only Moses) to speak with God. Moses tells them to have courage and that God has come to them to test them.

The parallels to Mark's story are instructive: Jesus too was in the mountain as the story begins, and the disciples are also afraid of him. In both cases the message to have courage is conveyed. An allusion to the Exodus text implies that the purpose of God's presence was to test the people. So Jesus' divine "passing by" and walking on the water is a test that, as Mark explains in 6:52, the disciples did not pass. But their continued presence with Jesus signals their ongoing willingness to learn and Jesus' continued willingness to teach them.

---

13. Jason Robert Combs, "A Ghost on the Water? Understanding an Absurdity in Mark 6:49–50," *Journal of Biblical Literature* 127, no. 2 (2008): 358.

6:51 *And he went up unto them into the ship; and the wind ceased:* Unlike the other sea crossing story, Jesus does not command calm. Here, it just happens when he enters the boat; it is possible that his mere presence stills the wind.

and they were sore amazed in themselves beyond measure, and wondered: There are two textual variants here:[14]

1. Some ancient manuscripts omit "beyond measure." In either case, the meaning is clear, and the only issue is the degree of amazement: with "beyond measure" included in the text, there are three references to their state ("amazed," "sore," and "beyond measure"), but without it, there are two references ("amazed" and "sore").

2. Some ancient manuscripts omit "and wondered." The phrase appears to have been added later by scribes who were perhaps thinking of Acts 2:7, where the same two verbs are used.[15] It makes better sense in context to omit "and wondered" because the next verse indicates that their problem was that they were *not* wondering (or considering) what they had seen.

6:52 *For they considered not the miracle of the loaves:* This line is an aside from the author to the audience. It implies that the point of the feeding miracle was not just the provision of food, but rather the story contained some deeper message that the disciples should have considered. While Mark does not mention it, it is possible that the baskets of leftovers are in the boat with the disciples. If so, their failure to think about what is literally in front of their faces is all the more ironic. But what precisely should they have considered?

1. Jesus' passing by, walking on water, and "I am" statement were supposed to be interpreted by the disciples as evidence that he is the God of the HB. But the disciples were not able to understand this message because they did not consider how the feeding miracle also showed Jesus to be like God, who provided manna to the people in the wilderness.

2. Mark refers to "the loaves," not "the loaves and fishes" or "the feeding miracle" or to any other miracle or event in Jesus' ministry. Mark thus focuses attention on the loaves. Perhaps the point is that the disciples were the ones who distributed the loaves to the crowd, and so they should have learned about the exercise of Jesus' power and authority from their own participation in it.

3. If the ancient belief that demons controlled the seas is behind this story, then the point would be that the disciples should have used the power that Jesus had delegated to them to control demons (a power that they had just used to distribute miraculously produced bread) in order to cross the sea. And as in

---

14. Comfort, *New Testament Text and Translation Commentary,* 116–17.
15. Metzger, *Textual Commentary* 79–80.

the feeding miracle, where they wanted to buy bread with money, here they use human resources (rowing) instead of relying on spiritual power to solve their problems.

4. If the multiplication of the loaves was a reiteration of the miracle of the manna, then it should be no surprise that Jesus could walk on water, a miracle that is very similar to the parting of the Red Sea. Had the disciples understood the first miracle (that the multiplication of the loaves meant that Jesus was the new Moses), then they should have had no trouble understanding the second (that Jesus was able to cross the hostile waters, as Moses did).

Relationship to Joshua 1. In Joshua 1:10–18, the children of Israel stop receiving manna and have to prepare rations. They eat manna and fish on the banks of the Jordan River. A few items link to the previous story of the feeding miracle:[16] they are to pass over in groups of fifty, the twelve men make a memorial, and Numbers 27:17 uses sheep/shepherd imagery to describe Joshua taking over for Moses. Jesus' compassion could be understood as his desire for them to have a leader who could lead them to the promised land. This reading explains the military imagery: they are the force that will invade the promised land under the direction of Joshua/Jesus. Perhaps the baskets of leftovers were taken up in analogy to some manna being kept "as a testimony." (That idea fits nicely with the idea that Jesus will later ask them what they took up [8:19–21]; they were supposed to remember it as a memorial). Moses told his people to leave, just as Jesus dismisses the Twelve, and then both Jesus and Moses go up the mountain to be with God.

This intertext might explain why considering the loaves would have made it possible for the disciples to have understood this miracle better: the feeding miracle—with its groups of fifty, divine provision of food, and memorial related to the number twelve (the twelve baskets of leftovers)— began the reiteration of the story of Joshua 1, which continued as Jesus asked the disciples to cross over in the boat without him, as a reenactment of entering the promised land. Because chapter 7 shows Jesus in gentile territory, there is even the hint that the "new promised land" is not traditionally Jewish territory. The importance of the allusion to Joshua 1 is that it links the feeding miracle with the sea crossing and then explains why the disciples should have considered them together.

for their heart was hardened: There are two different ways to understand the logic of this verse:

---

16. J. Duncan M. Derrett, "Why and How Jesus Walked on the Sea," *Novum Testamentum* 23, no. 4 (1981): 330–48.

1. Because the disciples' hearts were hardened, they did not consider the miracle of the loaves.
2. Because they did not consider the miracle of the loaves, their hearts were hardened.

In 3:15, Jesus' opponents are described as having hard hearts, so this is quite an indictment. The implication is that the disciples are acting like outsiders. (The fact that they used to be insiders—and will be treated as insiders again later—implies that this is not a permanent status.)

Relationship to the Exodus. A key theme in the story of the Exodus is the progressive hardening of Pharaoh's heart as he rejects the implications of the plagues. Here, the disciples are acting as Pharaoh did by refusing to consider the meaning of the miracles that they have witnessed. Of course, Jesus' miracles are not plagues but rather displays of power that bless those impacted by them. Much as the point of the plagues was so that Pharaoh would know the Lord, the disciples should have learned more about the identity of Jesus. Jesus is a new Moses, leading a new exodus, bringing his people out from slavery and into freedom. The motif of freedom bridges nicely into the next chapter, with its focus on Jesus' interpretation of the purity laws.

Analysis

This story is not primarily about Jesus walking on water but rather about Jesus' attempt to reveal his true nature to his disciples and their (comical) failure to understand him. Jesus presents himself in this story in a manner by which it should have been clear to his disciples that he is doing what only God can do (by walking on water and by passing them by), but they don't understand; rather, they assume that he is the one thing that he cannot possibly be. They not only do not recognize Jesus as God, but they also do not recognize him as Jesus. Mark's irony is as overwhelming as it is sad.

The story is also an excellent example of Mark's unique mixture of high and low Christology: Jesus intends to reveal himself as God but is thwarted by his disciples' screaming, yet he ultimately accomplishes the revelation to the audience, if not to the disciples.[17] Jesus appears to abandon his plans in order to help his ignorant and screaming disciples, but he is still able to accomplish those plans. In the first sea miracle in Mark, the story ended

---

17. Marcus, *Mark 1–8*, 432.

with the question "what manner of man is this, that even the wind and the sea obey him?" This sea miracle answers that question via Jesus' announcement that he is the great "I am."

Mark's note that the disciples didn't consider the loaves is telling: it points out that that was not just a feeding miracle but also a teaching moment. Mark's aside makes it less likely that the audience will also miss the point; the incomprehension of the disciples has an important role in teaching the audience. The aside should teach the audience that Mark's stories are not independent; one is expected to read them in light of each other. The audience should compare them and learn from them as they build one upon another. (And this will not be the last reference to the loaves: the theme will continue through chapter 7 and into chapter 8.)

Mark does not say what exactly it was about the loaves that the disciples should have considered, so the text is wonderfully elliptical; Mark has left some of the task of consideration to the audience so they can learn for themselves.

JESUS' MINISTRY SUMMARIZED (6:53–56)

Greek Text

53 Καὶ διαπεράσαντες ἐπὶ τὴν γῆν ἦλθον εἰς Γεννησαρὲτ καὶ προσωρμίσθησαν. 54 καὶ ἐξελθόντων αὐτῶν ἐκ τοῦ πλοίου εὐθὺς ἐπιγνόντες αὐτὸν 55 περιέδραμον ὅλην τὴν χώραν ἐκείνην καὶ ἤρξαντο ἐπὶ τοῖς κραβάττοις τοὺς κακῶς ἔχοντας περιφέρειν ὅπου ἤκουον ὅτι ἐστίν. 56 καὶ ὅπου ἂν εἰσεπορεύετο εἰς κώμας ἢ εἰς πόλεις ἢ εἰς ἀγροὺς ἐν ταῖς ἀγοραῖς ἐτίθεσαν τοὺς ἀσθενοῦντας, καὶ παρεκάλουν αὐτὸν ἵνα κἂν τοῦ κρασπέδου τοῦ ἱματίου αὐτοῦ ἅψωνται· καὶ ὅσοι ἂν ἥψαντο αὐτοῦ ἐσῴζοντο. [SBLGNT]

King James Version

53 And when they had passed over, they came into the land of Gennesaret, and drew to the shore. 54 And when they were come out of the ship, straightway they knew him, 55 And ran through that whole region round about, and began to carry about in beds those that were sick, where they heard he was. 56 And whithersoever he entered, into

New Rendition

53 And having crossed over to the land, they came to Gennesaret and anchored there. 54 And having come out of the boat, Jesus was immediately recognized. 55 They were running through all of that region, and they began to carry on mats those who were sick to wherever they were hearing that he is. 56 And wherever he entered—into villages or into towns

villages, or cities, or country, they laid the sick in the streets, and besought him that they might touch if it were but the border of his garment: and as many as touched him were made whole.

or into the countryside—they laid down those who were sick in the marketplaces, and they were begging him that they might touch just the fringe of his clothing. And as many as touched him were cured/saved.

Notes

6:53 *And when they had passed over, they came into the land of Gennesaret, and drew to the shore:* The disciples were headed for Bethsaida (compare 6:45) but end up in Gennesaret, which is to the southwest of Bethsaida. Several theories could explain the discrepancy:

1. Mark is not telling the stories in order and/or has omitted some intervening material.
2. Mark is alluding to Jonah 1:2–3, where Jonah travels by sea in the opposite direction from which he was called; the point may be that the disciples, with their lack of understanding and their hardened hearts, are acting like Jonah.
3. Mark is not clear on the geography and makes a mistake here.
4. The strong winds had pushed them off course.

Gennesaret is a plain roughly 3.5 miles in length between Tiberias and Capernaum.

6:54 *And when they were come out of the ship, straightway they knew him:* The New Rendition substitutes "Jesus" for "him" for clarity, but the Greek text has the pronoun.

6:55 *And ran through that whole region round about, and began to carry about in beds those that were sick, where they heard he was. 56 And whithersoever he entered, into villages, or cities, or country, they laid the sick in the streets, and besought him that they might touch if it were but the border of his garment:* The "border of his garment" is probably the fringe that Jewish men wore to comply with the law of Moses (Num. 15:38–39). If so, this picture of Jesus as a law-abiding Jew is an important counterweight to chapter 7, where Jesus will challenge prevailing interpretations of the law of Moses.

While this summary shows some similarities to the story of the bleeding woman in 5:25–34, there are also some significant differences: here, they ask for permission before touching him and are content with touching just the border of his clothing.

and as many as touched him were made whole: This section is a summary of Jesus' activities (compare 1:14–15, 39; 2:13; 4:1–2, 33). This time, Mark does not mention teaching or exorcism.

Analysis

Given that a focal point of the previous story was the disciples' inability to recognize Jesus (in fact, they think that he is a ghost), it is most ironic that the crowd is immediately able to recognize Jesus. Since the feeding of the five thousand also mentioned the crowd's instant ability to recognize Jesus, the disciples' lack of recognition is literally surrounded by stories where Jesus is recognized; this emphasizes the incomprehension of the disciples.

JESUS TEACHES ABOUT FOOD TRADITIONS (7:1–23)

Greek Text

7:1 Καὶ συνάγονται πρὸς αὐτὸν οἱ Φαρισαῖοι καί τινες τῶν γραμματέων ἐλθόντες ἀπὸ Ἱεροσολύμων 2 καὶ ἰδόντες τινὰς τῶν μαθητῶν αὐτοῦ ὅτι κοιναῖς χερσίν, τοῦτ' ἔστιν ἀνίπτοις, ἐσθίουσιν τοὺς ἄρτους — 3 οἱ γὰρ Φαρισαῖοι καὶ πάντες οἱ Ἰου-δαῖοι ἐὰν μὴ πυγμῇ νίψωνται τὰς χεῖρας οὐκ ἐσθίουσιν, κρατοῦντες τὴν παράδοσιν τῶν πρεσβυτέρων, 4 καὶ ἀπ' ἀγορᾶς ἐὰν μὴ βαπτίσωνται οὐκ ἐσθίουσιν, καὶ ἄλλα πολλά ἐστιν ἃ παρέλαβον κρατεῖν, βαπτισμοὺς ποτηρίων καὶ ξεστῶν καὶ χαλκίων καὶ κλινῶν— 5 καὶ ἐπερωτῶσιν αὐτὸν οἱ Φαρισαῖοι καὶ οἱ γραμματεῖς· Διὰ τί ᾽οὐ περιπατοῦσιν οἱ μαθηταί σου κατὰ τὴν παράδοσιν τῶν πρεσβυτέρων, ἀλλὰ κοιναῖς χερσὶν ἐσθίουσιν τὸν ἄρτον; 6 ὁ δὲ εἶπεν αὐτοῖς· Καλῶς ἐπροφήτευσεν Ἡσαΐας περὶ ὑμῶν τῶν ὑποκριτῶν, ὡς γέγραπται ὅτι Οὗτος ὁ λαὸς τοῖς χείλεσίν με τιμᾷ, ἡ δὲ καρδία αὐτῶν πόρρω ἀπέχει ἀπ' ἐμοῦ· 7 μάτην δὲ σέβονταί με, διδάσκοντες διδασκαλίας ἐντάλματα ἀνθρώπων· 8 ἀφέντες τὴν ἐντολὴν τοῦ θεοῦ κρατεῖτε τὴν παράδοσιν τῶν ἀνθρώπων.

9 Καὶ ἔλεγεν αὐτοῖς· Καλῶς ἀθετεῖτε τὴν ἐντολὴν τοῦ θεοῦ, ἵνα τὴν παράδοσιν ὑμῶν τηρήσητε· 10 Μωϋσῆς γὰρ εἶπεν· Τίμα τὸν πατέρα σου καὶ τὴν μητέρα σου, καί· Ὁ κακολογῶν πατέρα ἢ μητέρα θανάτῳ τελευτάτω· 11 ὑμεῖς δὲ λέγετε· Ἐὰν εἴπῃ ἄνθρωπος τῷ πατρὶ ἢ τῇ μητρί· Κορβᾶν, ὅ ἐστιν Δῶρον, ὃ ἐὰν ἐξ ἐμοῦ ὠφελη-θῇς, 12 οὐκέτι ἀφίετε αὐτὸν οὐδὲν ποιῆσαι τῷ πατρὶ ἢ τῇ μητρί, 13 ἀκυροῦντες τὸν λόγον τοῦ θεοῦ τῇ παραδόσει ὑμῶν ᾗ παρεδώκατε· καὶ παρόμοια τοιαῦτα πολλὰ ποιεῖτε.

14 Καὶ προσκαλεσάμενος πάλιν τὸν ὄχλον ἔλεγεν αὐτοῖς· Ἀκούσατέ μου πάντες καὶ σύνετε. 15 οὐδέν ἐστιν ἔξωθεν τοῦ ἀνθρώπου εἰσπορευόμενον εἰς αὐτὸν ὃ δύναται κοινῶσαι αὐτόν· ἀλλὰ τὰ ἐκ τοῦ ἀνθρώπου ἐκπορευόμενά ἐστιν τὰ κοι-νοῦντα τὸν ἄνθρωπον.

17 Καὶ ὅτε εἰσῆλθεν εἰς οἶκον ἀπὸ τοῦ ὄχλου, ἐπηρώτων αὐτὸν οἱ μαθηταὶ αὐτοῦ τὴν παραβολήν. 18 καὶ λέγει αὐτοῖς· Οὕτως καὶ ὑμεῖς ἀσύνετοί ἐστε; οὐ νοεῖτε ὅτι

πᾶν τὸ ἔξωθεν εἰσπορευόμενον εἰς τὸν ἄνθρωπον οὐ δύναται αὐτὸν κοινῶσαι, 19 ὅτι οὐκ εἰσπορεύεται αὐτοῦ εἰς τὴν καρδίαν ἀλλ᾽ εἰς τὴν κοιλίαν, καὶ εἰς τὸν ἀφεδρῶνα ἐκπορεύεται; —καθαρίζων πάντα τὰ βρώματα. 20 ἔλεγεν δὲ ὅτι Τὸ ἐκ τοῦ ἀνθρώπου ἐκπορευόμενον ἐκεῖνο κοινοῖ τὸν ἄνθρωπον· 21 ἔσωθεν γὰρ ἐκ τῆς καρδίας τῶν ἀνθρώπων οἱ διαλογισμοὶ οἱ κακοὶ ἐκπορεύονται, πορνεῖαι, κλοπαί, φόνοι, 22 μοιχεῖαι, πλεονεξίαι, πονηρίαι, δόλος, ἀσέλγεια, ὀφθαλμὸς πονηρός, βλασφημία, ὑπερηφανία, ἀφροσύνη· 23 πάντα ταῦτα τὰ πονηρὰ ἔσωθεν ἐκπορεύεται καὶ κοινοῖ τὸν ἄνθρωπον. [SBLGNT]

King James Version

1 Then came together unto him the Pharisees, and certain of the scribes, which came from Jerusalem. 2 And when they saw some of his disciples eat bread with defiled, that is to say, with unwashen, hands, they found fault. 3 For the Pharisees, and all the Jews, except they wash their hands oft, eat not, holding the tradition of the elders. 4 And when they come from the market, except they wash, they eat not. And many other things there be, which they have received to hold, as the washing of cups, and pots, brasen vessels, and of tables. 5 Then the Pharisees and scribes asked him, Why walk not thy disciples according to the tradition of the elders, but eat bread with unwashen hands? 6 He answered and said unto them, Well hath Esaias prophesied of you hypocrites, as it is written, This people honoureth me with their lips, but their heart is far from me. 7 Howbeit in vain do they worship me, teaching for doctrines the commandments of men. 8 For laying aside the commandment of God, ye hold the tradition of men, as the washing of pots and cups: and many other such like things ye do. 9 And he said unto them, Full well ye reject the commandment of God, that ye may keep your own tradition. 10 For Moses

New Rendition

1 And the Pharisees and some of the scriptorians, having come from Jerusalem, gather to him. 2 And having seen some of his disciples who with impure hands (that is, unwashed [hands]) are eating the loaves— 3 (For the Pharisees, and all the Jews, if they do not ritually wash the hands, they do not eat, keeping to the tradition of the ancestors. 4 And coming from the market, if they do not ritually immerse, they do not eat. And there are many other things that they received to keep, the ritual immersion of cups and pots and kettles.) 5 And the Pharisees and the scriptorians asked him, "Why don't your disciples live according to the tradition of the ancestors, but with impure hands they eat the loaf?" 6 But he said to them, "Isaiah correctly prophesied about you pretenders. It stands written,

'This people honors me with
                their lips,
    but their heart is very far away
                from me.
7 They worship me uselessly,
    teaching human rules as doctrines.'
8 "Abandoning the commandment of God, you keep the human tradition."
9 And he was saying to them, "'Correctly' you set aside the commandment of God so that you can observe your

said, Honour thy father and thy mother; and, Whoso curseth father or mother, let him die the death: 11 But ye say, If a man shall say to his father or mother, It is Corban, that is to say, a gift, by whatsoever thou mightest be profited by me; he shall be free. 12 And ye suffer him no more to do ought for his father or his mother; 13 Making the word of God of none effect through your tradition, which ye have delivered: and many such like things do ye.

14 And when he had called all the people unto him, he said unto them, Hearken unto me every one of you, and understand: 15 There is nothing from without a man, that entering into him can defile him: but the things which come out of him, those are they that defile the man. 16 If any man have ears to hear, let him hear. 17 And when he was entered into the house from the people, his disciples asked him concerning the parable. 18 And he saith unto them, Are ye so without understanding also? Do ye not perceive, that whatsoever thing from without entereth into the man, it cannot defile him; 19 Because it entereth not into his heart, but into the belly, and goeth out into the draught, purging all meats? 20 And he said, That which cometh out of the man, that defileth the man. 21 For from within, out of the heart of men, proceed evil thoughts, adulteries, fornications, murders, 22 Thefts, covetousness, wickedness, deceit, lasciviousness, an evil eye, blasphemy, pride, foolishness: 23 All these evil things come from within, and defile the man.

tradition. 10 For Moses said, 'Honor your father and your mother' and 'The one who speaks evil of father or mother must be put to death.' 11 But you say, 'If a person says to the father or the mother, "It is korban (that is, a gift [for God]), whatever you might otherwise have gotten from me,"' 12 so you don't permit him or her to do anything for the father or the mother, 13 canceling the word of God for your tradition that you have handed down. And you do many similar things."

14 And having called the crowd to him again, he was saying to them, "All of you hear me and understand. 15 There is nothing outside of a person that has the power to defile him or her by entering in. But the things coming out of the person are the things defiling the person." [16]

17 And when he went into a house away from the crowd, his disciples asked him about the parable. 18 And he says to them, "So you also lack understanding? You don't realize that everything from the outside entering into a person cannot defile him or her 19 because it does not enter into his or her heart but into the stomach and goes out into the latrine?" (He was declaring clean all food.) 20 And he was saying, "What comes out of a person—that defiles the person. 21 For from within, out of the human heart, evil ideas go out: sexual immoralities, thefts, murders, adulteries, 22 covetings, wickedness, deceit, indecency, envy/malice, slander, pride, and foolishness. 23 All of these evils from within go out and defile the person."

Notes

7:1 ***Then came together unto him the Pharisees, and certain of the scribes:***
The verb translated as "came together" (Greek: *sunagō*) has the implication of "ganging up against";[18] it is also a cognate of the word "synagogue" (Greek: *sunagōgē*), which may have sounded ironic to Mark's audience. Mark may be alluding to Psalm 2:2 (which in the LXX uses the same verb; the KJV translates it is "take counsel together"), where the leaders gather against the Lord and his anointed.

   which came from Jerusalem: In Greek, the phrasing implies that the Pharisees were local but that the scribes had come from Jerusalem. It is likely that these scribes are also Pharisees, given their concern with the purity laws, and that they had been sent to investigate reports of Jesus' actions and/or to stir up animosity against him (compare 3:22).

   7:2 ***And when they saw some of his disciples:*** It is possible that only "some" of Jesus' disciples are of concern here because other disciples kept the traditions; this would reflect the diversity of practice in the early Christian church. But it is also possible that none of Jesus' disciples kept to the tradition: the word translated as "some" is the same word translated in 7:1 as "certain," so perhaps Mark wanted to draw a contrast between some of the scribes and some of the disciples.

   Once again (2:18, 23–24), the focus is on the behavior of Jesus' disciples and not Jesus himself, with the assumption that the teacher is responsible for the behavior of his followers.

   eat bread with defiled: "Bread" is plural here, which is unusual. It may reflect Mark's desire to link this story to the feeding miracle, which noted at the beginning that the disciples did not have time to eat (6:31) and may suggest that they never did eat (they may not have had time to, since they were distributing the food, gathering the leftovers, and then crossing the sea). So it is possible that this is their first chance to eat, and they are eating the leftovers of the miraculously supplied food. It would be most ironic if the scribes and Pharisees are focusing on the violation of custom instead of the visible evidence before their eyes of a miracle.

   The concern here is not hygiene but ritual purity. The law of Moses prescribed washing to mitigate impurity (Lev. 15:11–12) but did not apply the practice to handwashing before eating; the Pharisees extended the rule. (The Pharisees most likely believed that these traditions were given

---

18. Stein, *Mark,* 338.

to Moses orally on Mt. Sinai.) During Jesus' time, many Jews did not observe these ritual washings, but purity laws related to food consumption still had an outsized role in first-century Judaism: they made it impossible for the observant to dine with others and thus were a boundary marker for the community.

that is to say, with unwashen, hands: Mark felt the need to explain the custom to the audience: apparently, at least part of his intended audience was not familiar with these practices.

they found fault: This phrase is not included in the best ancient manuscripts.[19] Without it, 7:2 is an incomplete sentence: there is a digression composing 7:3–4, and then 7:5 begins a new sentence.

7:3 *For the Pharisees, and all the Jews:* This verse begins a fuller explanation of the handwashing practice.

It was not actually the case that "all the Jews" observed the practices described in these verses. Why then did Mark use this phrase?

1. Mark employs it to anticipate the quotation from Isaiah in 7:6–7, which refers to all the people.
2. Mark was simplifying the explanation by speaking generally.
3. It is yet another instance of hyperbole.
4. Mark was unaware of the details of Jewish customs.
5. While not all Jews kept the practice, it was regarded as an ideal.

except they wash their hands oft: The word translated as "oft" in the KJV presents quite a puzzle. The Greek word most likely to have been original here, *pugmē,* probably means something like "with the fist"[20] or "up to the elbow."[21] The difficulty of making sense of that word in this context apparently led some scribes to omit it and others to replace it with the word *pukna,* which means "carefully" or "oft(en)" (hence the KJV reading). Because the word *pugmē* is not used elsewhere in the NT, it is difficult to determine its meaning. Suggestions for the meaning of "with the fist" include: rubbing the fist into the other hand while washing, using a fist full of water, using "elbow grease," having water poured over the fist, or having water poured into a cupped hand.[22] The New Rendition translates the

---

19. Comfort, *New Testament Text and Translation Commentary,* 118.

20. Metzger, *Textual Commentary,* 80.

21. Collins, *Mark,* 339 note c.

22. Stephen M. Reynolds, "Πυγμῇ (Mark 7 3) as 'Cupped Hand,'" *Journal of Biblical Literature* 85, no. 1 (1966): 87–88.

word as "ritually" to reflect what appears to be a ritual element of it, but any greater level of specificity is not possible.

eat not, holding the tradition of the elders: The word translated as "tradition" means "things handed down" and is very similar to the word used when Jesus is "handed over." So traditions are handed down from person to person, usually orally.

The "tradition of the elders" refers to those rules that were believed to have been delivered orally to Moses on Mt. Sinai (the "oral Torah"). These rules were later written down in the Mishnah (around 200 CE). Since many practices in the Mishnah date from a much earlier time, they could have been current during Jesus' life.

The implication here is that the antiquity of a tradition is not evidence of its validity.

7:4 *And when they come from the market, except they wash, they eat not:* There are two different ways that this phrase can be interpreted:

1. When they return from the market, they wash themselves. (But there is not much evidence for the idea that a person would become defiled from visiting a market.)

2. When they return from the market, they wash whatever they have purchased.

and many other things there be, which they have received to hold, as the washing of cups, and pots, brasen vessels, and of tables: These washings were required by the law, unlike the hand washing.

Some manuscripts omit the reference to "tables,"[23] perhaps because it seems unusual, but it is also possible that Mark mentioned tables as a sarcastic commentary on the Pharisees' overzealous interpretation of the law (see also the Notes on 7:30). The term translated as "tables" (Greek: *klinē*) should probably be translated as "dining couches"; these were used to eat in a reclined position. Washing dining chairs seems odd and cumbersome, although there is some evidence that this was done.[24]

Mark 7:2 provided a brief explanation of the practice of handwashing, while 7:3–4 comprise a fuller account. It is possible that 7:3–4 is a later addition to the story, from a time when more explanation was needed for an audience who was even less familiar with the Pharisees' practice.

---

23. Comfort, *New Testament Text and Translation Commentary*, 119.

24. James G. Crossley, "Halakah and Mark 7.4: '. . . and Beds,'" *Journal for the Study of the New Testament* 25, no. 4 (2003): 433–47.

7:5 *Then the Pharisees and scribes asked him:* This verse resumes the train of thought from 7:2 (which was not a complete sentence; this verse begins a new sentence).

As is usually the case with Mark, Jesus' teachings are a response to challenges that he faced and are not initiated by him (compare 2:16, 23–24; and 3:1–2).

Why walk not thy disciples according to the tradition of the elders, but eat bread with unwashen hands: Here, "walk" refers to the manner of life one lives. It may be relevant that a word deriving from "walk" is the word used for a legal decision in the rabbinic tradition.

Handwashing here is not an end in itself, but rather it is framed as a litmus test for valuing and following the tradition of the elders.

7:6 *He answered and said unto them, Well hath Esaias prophesied of you hypocrites:* "Esaias" refers to Isaiah. "Well hath" may be somewhat sarcastic in tone.

The Greek word "hypocrite" originally referred to an actor playing a role—that is, someone pretending to be something that he is not; "it does not carry the moral overtone of fraud that our English word does today."[25] The implication of the word "hypocrites" is that Jesus sees the Pharisees as playing a role, perhaps by viewing the law as a tool that they can manipulate for their own ends.

as it is written, This people honoureth me with their lip, but their heart is far from me: This verse quotes Isaiah 29:13. But in that passage, Isaiah appears to be speaking of his own day. What, then, did Jesus mean by calling this a prophecy of Isaiah's?

1. What was true in Isaiah's day is still true in Jesus' own time.

2. Given that Jesus' phrase "well hath" was sarcastic, perhaps the reference to prophesying is sarcastic as well: this is not a genuine prophecy but rather a way to call out the Pharisees for their hypocrisy.

3. While it might appear that Isaiah was speaking only to his own time, his words also had a future fulfillment (which he may or may not have been aware of). If this reading is best, it becomes an important data point for understanding how Isaiah, and HB prophecy in general, should be interpreted.

The quotation from Isaiah suggests an overemphasis on the lips, to the detriment of the heart (mind). This sentiment is particularly fitting for a discussion of ritual purity and the Pharisees' focus on what touches the lips.

---

25. Guelich, *Mark 1–8:26*, 366.

7:7 ***Howbeit in vain do they worship me, teaching for doctrines the commandments of men:*** Some manuscripts place the word "and" in between "doctrines" and "commandments" ("teaching doctrines and commandments").[26] This change makes the passage more similar to LXX Isaiah 29:13.

The words translated "teachings" and "doctrines" are very similar ("teaching teachings"). The Pharisees describe these as traditions "of the elders," but Jesus says that they are "of men." He thus downgrades the tradition, denying its claims to any special authority via antique status.

7:8 ***For laying aside the commandment of God:*** "Commandment" is singular—if this is significant, it might allude to the "great commandment" of Deuteronomy 6:4–5, a link that might be further suggested by the recent reference to hearts.

ye hold the tradition of men: Jesus establishes three points of opposition in this verse—lay aside/hold, command/tradition, and God/man. Each one emphasizes the difference between the Pharisees' teachings and his own.

as the washing of pots and cups: and many other such like things ye do: This line is absent from most of the oldest manuscripts and is likely a later addition,[27] probably accidentally copied from 7:4. It may be better to omit it as Jesus' critique is not limited to ritually washing cooking equipment but includes greater moral issues (see 7:10).

7:9 ***And he said unto them:*** This phrase is often used by Mark to signal the introduction of a new scene, so it is possible that what follows was taught on a separate occasion, and Mark placed it here because the theme was the same.

Full well ye reject the commandment of God: "Full well" translates the same Greek word as "well" in 7:6, which implies that the Pharisaical practice is viewed as a mockery of Isaiah's prophetic act.

that ye may keep your own tradition: Some ancient manuscripts have "establish" instead of "keep" here.[28] There may be a distinction between keeping (where the commandments are rejected because they conflict with already-extant tradition) and establishing (where the commandments are rejected so that a new tradition can begin) in this context.

---

26. Collins, *Mark,* 340 note k.
27. Metzger, *Textual Commentary,* 80–81.
28. Collins, *Mark,* 340 note n.

Jesus' statement suggests that "the problem for Jesus is not the traditions per se, but rather in the use of that tradition to turn aside the specific commandment of God."[29]

7:10 *For Moses said, Honour thy father and thy mother:* Jesus quotes Exodus 20:12 here. It was common to interpret the honor owed to parents to include financial support.

Because this verse uses the same word for "honor" as 7:6, it suggests that they were guilty of honoring their parents just with their lips (by announcing that their wealth is corban) instead of with their hearts (by actually supporting their parents).

Note the reference to the mother as well as the father, "which may be especially significant since some early Jewish teachers said the father was to be honored more than the mother."[30] Jesus rejects that tradition.

and, Whoso curseth father or mother, let him die the death: Jesus quotes Exodus 21:17 here. Cursing would be an extreme example of not honoring.

7:11 *But ye say, If a man shall say to his father or mother:* The word "ye" is emphatic, emphasizing the role of the Pharisees in interpreting the law, as well as the contrast between what Moses said (see the previous verse) and what the Pharisees say. This is an important rhetorical move because the Pharisees are claiming that Jesus is the one opposed to Moses for not requiring his disciples to follow the tradition; here, Jesus positions the Pharisees as the ones truly opposed to Moses.

The language "if a man shall say" presumes that an oath has been entered; oaths were not revocable.

It is Corban: While it is not completely clear how the "corban" oath worked, it probably meant that resources that should have been used for the financial support of parents are declared to be "a gift to God" and therefore off-limits to the parents but still available for the child's use. It is thus "a legal fiction."[31]

that is to say, a gift, by whatsoever thou mightest be profited by me; he shall be free: Mark apparently felt that at least some of the audience would not be familiar with this practice and so added this explanation by way of translation.

---

29. Avram R. Shannon, "Torah in the Mouth: An Introduction to Jewish Oral Law," *Religious Educator* 19, no. 1 (2018): 143.

30. Witherington, *Gospel of Mark*, 226.

31. Marcus, *Mark 1–8*, 452.

The New Rendition adds "for God" to the text here; these words are not in the Greek text but have been added to explain what kind of gift is envisioned.

7:12 *And ye suffer him no more to do ought for his father or his mother:* Jesus is describing a case where someone vowed his wealth as corban (and, therefore, inaccessible to parents) but later changed his mind (perhaps in the face of future parental need or a recognition that the vow was rashly undertaken) and so went to the authorities for permission to have the vow rescinded. But, as Jesus explains, the authorities would not allow it. While the scribes or Pharisees probably would not have encouraged such vows in the first place, they required people to honor them once they had been made since the law of Moses does not permit vows to be revoked (Num. 30:2). In this case, then, there is a conflict between the commandment to honor parents and the commandment that vows be permanent. The Pharisees' support for the vows made it possible for people to violate the commandment to honor father and mother. (Later rabbis would rule that corban vows could not override the obligation to support parents.)

7:13 *Making the word of God of none effect through your tradition:* "None effect" is a formal legal term meaning to annul or repeal.

which ye have delivered: Jesus does not picture them as passive observers whose hands are tied by the law that vows are not to be undone. Instead, "which ye have delivered" positions these scribes and Pharisees as interpreters who are guilty of promulgating a particular viewpoint.

and many such like things do ye: This line implies that the corban practice is a representative example of many other practices that permit the violation of the law.

Mark 7:6–8 and 9–13 have the same structure: they each begin with "he . . . said unto them," feature an HB quotation (Isa. 29:13; Ex. 20:12), and then contrast what the Pharisees do with what the HB commands. This pattern illustrates that, while Jesus is rejecting a particular interpretation of the HB, he is not rejecting the HB itself but rather using it as normative (but contrast 7:19).

7:14 *And when he had called all the people unto him:* Some older manuscripts included the word "again" at the beginning of this verse,[32] which may imply that 7:14 records an event occurring at a different time than 7:13.

Note the implication that the previous conversation was a private one between Jesus and the religious leaders, while this verse introduces teachings for the entire crowd.

---

32. Collins, *Mark,* 340 note o.

he said unto them, Hearken unto me every one of you, and understand:
This line strongly emphasizes the importance of the coming teachings[33] and
shows that Jesus wanted the audience—composed of all of the people—to
pay close attention to what he was about to say, which will include a strong
departure from the Pharisees' tradition. This statement is similar to what
Jesus said before teaching in parables (compare 4:3) and may imply that
the meaning will not be obvious but will require close attention in order to
be comprehended.

   **7:15 *There is nothing from without a man, that entering into him can
defile him:*** Because the law of Moses very clearly states that some foods are
defiling (Lev. 11), the interpretation of this verse is not obvious. Options
include:

1. Jesus is ending the food purity laws. While this is possible, it is not a perfect
   fit for this context, since Jesus just made two arguments (see 7:6 and 10)
   based on the assumption that the requirements of the law were inviolable.
   Further, it was not the case that Jesus' earliest disciples thought that the food
   laws had been rescinded; rather, the topic was intensely disputed (even for
   gentile converts to Christianity; Acts 10–11, 15; contrast Rom. 14:14, 20). It is
   possible that Jesus' intent here was to end the food purity laws but that his
   disciples did not understand this. If Jesus did intend to end the food laws, this
   is an enormously important text, especially given the central role that the
   dietary laws played as a boundary marker between Jews and Gentiles.

2. This is hyperbole or dialectical negation, meant to de-emphasize the food
   laws without intending to revoke them entirely. Some HB texts (Isa. 1:11–
   17; Hosea 6:6; Amos 5:21–27) are similar to Jesus' words here; these texts
   emphasize the requirement of moral purity and de-emphasize ritual purity
   without intending to overturn the law. Hence, Jesus' teachings are not quite
   as radical as they might seem. While Mark elsewhere features hyperbole and
   dialectical negation, these readings may not mesh well with Mark's declaration that Jesus declared all foods clean (but see the Notes on 7:19).

3. This verse refers only to food eaten with defiled hands—which is the immediate context—and not to all defiled foods. This position is consistent with the
   law of Moses (which did not require ritually clean hands for eating). This
   reading requires the word "nothing" at the beginning of the verse be read as
   hyperbole.

4. This passage has many indicators that 7:15 should be interpreted as a parable,
   including (1) the call to hearken in 7:14, (2) the call to hear in 7:16 (if 7:16
   is accepted as original; see the Notes on 7:16), (3) the identification of the
   parable in 7:17, and (4) the repetition of the pattern from chapter 4 (where

---

33. Compare Deut. 6:4.

a public teaching results in a private request from the disciples for more clarification). If read parabolically, this verse would not be a renunciation of food laws but something else entirely. What that might be, however, is not entirely clear (but see "Symbolism of the Loaves" after the Notes on 8:9).

but the things which come out of him, those are they that defile the man: The law of Moses considered many bodily emissions to result in ritual defilement, but Jesus will soon explain that he is not envisioning physical discharges but moral sins. A similar sentiment can be found in Jeremiah 4:3–4 and 9:23–26, so this is not a radical departure from the HB tradition.

7:16 *If any man have ears to hear, let him hear:* This verse is missing from some of the ancient manuscripts;[34] it appears to be a note made by a later scribe that was accidentally incorporated from the margin into the text.[35] It is omitted in the New Rendition.

7:17 *And when he was entered into the house from the people, his disciples asked him concerning the parable:* As mentioned above, it is not entirely obvious in what sense 7:15 constitutes a parable, but this section of text does follow the structure of chapter 4 (which was composed of parables) rather closely. It is possible that the teaching in 7:15 struck the disciples as a "riddle" (which is a possible translation of the word "parable").

7:18 *And he saith unto them, Are ye so without understanding also?:* Jesus expresses something akin to surprise; he did not anticipate that his teaching would be opaque to his disciples.

Do ye not perceive, that whatsoever thing from without entereth into the man, it cannot defile him: This line is basically a restatement of 7:15, while the next verse will begin to explain this teaching. This question expects a positive answer.

7:19 *Because it entereth not into his heart, but into the belly, and goeth out into the draught:* Food cannot result in impurity because it travels through the digestive system without coming into contact with the heart. This question, like the previous verse, anticipates a positive answer.

purging all meats: This phrase is a dangling participle that could be rendered "cleansing all the foods." While the KJV takes it to refer to the draught's ability to purge all meats (that is, from the human being), the phrase probably refers instead to Jesus' ability to declare all foods clean because the participle is in the masculine form (if it meant that the body was cleansing

---

34. Metzger, *Textual Commentary,* 81.

35. Lincoln H. Blumell, "A Text-Critical Comparison of the King James New Testament with Certain Modern Translations," *Studies in the Bible and Antiquity* 3 (2011): 85.

all foods, it would need to be neuter, which it is not, save in a very poorly attested variant reading). The fact that the next verse beings with "and he said," a phrase that reintroduces Jesus as the speaker, increases the odds that these are the narrator's words used to clarify what Jesus has just taught.

It is possible that Mark's interpretation of Jesus' statement as declaring all foods clean does not reflect Jesus' meaning: perhaps Jesus intended dialectical negation or hyperbole, but the narrator overinterpreted it as an announcement that all foods were clean. Or perhaps Jesus' teaching was ambiguous (hence the later debate in the Church over the role of the food laws), and this narrator's comment, written later, reflects a later state of surety over the matter. Given that Mark was probably written for a gentile audience, it is also possible that the teaching that all foods are clean was only meant to apply to Gentiles.

7:20 *And he said, That which cometh out of the man, that defileth the man:* See the Notes on 7:15.

7:21 *For from within, out of the heart of men, proceed evil thoughts, adulteries, fornications, murders:* Defecation is not defiling under the law of Moses,[36] so the description of these sins as defiling shows that Jesus is, in a sense, extending the definition of defilement.

"Evil thoughts" suggests making plans with an intention to act on them. Because it comes before the verb and the other items on the list come after it, it serves as an umbrella term that gives an overview of what will follow. It is followed by a list of six plural actions and then six singular vices; this type of list was common in both Jewish and Greek writings.

"Adulteries" can refer to sexual immorality generally.

7:22 *Thefts, covetousness, wickedness, deceit, lasciviousness:* "Covetousness" refers to the desire for power as well as for wealth. "Lasciviousness" means lacking in self-control.

an evil eye, blasphemy, pride, foolishness: "An evil eye" can refer to envy (compare 15:10; KJV: "envy"), malice, or jealousy.

"Blasphemy" is probably, in this context, directed not at God but at humans (that is, slander or evil-speaking). It may refer to abusive speech in general.

"Foolishness" refers to moral foolishness, not ignorance. It may be a summary of all that has been listed, much as "evil thoughts" served the same function at the beginning of the list.

---

36. Dowd, *Reading Mark*, 74.

There is a mixture of thoughts and actions in this list; there is no distinction made between the two as moral sins. Many of these sins are condemned in Leviticus 18, but the focus is on ritual impurity; here, Jesus emphasizes the moral component to these sins.

7:23 *all these evil things come from within, and defile the man:* Jesus is not claiming that defilement is not a concern but rather that moral sin (which begins within the person) defiles—not ritual sin (which begins in the outer environment). Jesus' call to a greater concern about what is coming out of a person than what is going in to her fundamentally reorients the sinner's relationship to the world.

Analysis

Underlying this discussion of purity laws is an implicit discussion of authority: the real issue is not whether one can eat with defiled hands but rather who has the authority to interpret the law and whether the "tradition of the elders" has the same binding status as the law itself. Jesus' pronouncements speak to his authority in this matter. If he declared all foods clean (or if Mark understood him to be doing such), then his authority is even greater: he has the authority to announce that even parts of the written law itself are no longer binding.

Jesus and the Greek Woman (7:24–30)

Greek Text

24 Ἐκεῖθεν δὲ ἀναστὰς ἀπῆλθεν εἰς τὰ ὅρια Τύρου. καὶ εἰσελθὼν εἰς οἰκίαν οὐδένα ἤθελεν γνῶναι, καὶ οὐκ ἠδυνήθη λαθεῖν· 25 ἀλλ᾽ εὐθὺς ἀκούσασα γυνὴ περὶ αὐτοῦ, ἧς εἶχεν τὸ θυγάτριον αὐτῆς πνεῦμα ἀκάθαρτον, ἐλθοῦσα προσέπεσεν πρὸς τοὺς πόδας αὐτοῦ· 26 ἡ δὲ γυνὴ ἦν Ἑλληνίς, Συροφοινίκισσα τῷ γένει· καὶ ἠρώτα αὐτὸν ἵνα τὸ δαιμόνιον ἐκβάλῃ ἐκ τῆς θυγατρὸς αὐτῆς. 27 καὶ ἔλεγεν αὐτῇ· Ἄφες πρῶτον χορτασθῆναι τὰ τέκνα, οὐ γὰρ καλόν ἐστιν λαβεῖν τὸν ἄρτον τῶν τέκνων καὶ τοῖς κυναρίοις βαλεῖν. 28 ἡ δὲ ἀπεκρίθη καὶ λέγει αὐτῷ· Κύριε, καὶ τὰ κυνάρια ὑποκάτω τῆς τραπέζης ἐσθίουσιν ἀπὸ τῶν ψιχίων τῶν παιδίων. 29 καὶ εἶπεν αὐτῇ· Διὰ τοῦτον τὸν λόγον ὕπαγε, ἐξελήλυθεν ἐκ τῆς θυγατρός σου τὸ δαιμόνιον. 30 καὶ ἀπελθοῦσα εἰς τὸν οἶκον αὐτῆς εὗρεν τὸ παιδίον βεβλημένον ἐπὶ τὴν κλίνην καὶ τὸ δαιμόνιον ἐξεληλυθός. [SBLGNT]

King James Version

24 And from thence he arose, and went into the borders of Tyre and Sidon, and entered into an house, and would have no man know it: but he could not be hid. 25 For a certain woman, whose young daughter had an unclean spirit, heard of him, and came and fell at his feet: 26 The woman was a Greek, a Syrophenician by nation; and she besought him that he would cast forth the devil out of her daughter. 27 But Jesus said unto her, Let the children first be filled: for it is not meet to take the children's bread, and to cast it unto the dogs. 28 And she answered and said unto him, Yes, Lord: yet the dogs under the table eat of the children's crumbs. 29 And he said unto her, For this saying go thy way; the devil is gone out of thy daughter. 30 And when she was come to her house, she found the devil gone out, and her daughter laid upon the bed.

New Rendition

24 From there, having risen up, he went away into the region of Tyre. And having entered into a house, he wanted no one to know, but he was not able to be hidden. 25 But immediately, a woman, having heard about him and having a little daughter with an unclean spirit, having come, fell at his feet. 26 But the woman was a Greek, a Syrophenician by origin, and she was asking him to cast the demon out of her daughter. 27 And he was saying to her, "First let the children be filled. For it is not right to take the children's loaf and throw it to the dogs." 28 And she answered and says to him, "Sir/Lord, but the dogs under the table eat the children's crumbs." 29 And he said to her, "For this answer, go. The demon has gone out of your daughter." 30 And having gone away to her home, she found the child lying on the bed and the demon having gone out.

Notes

7:24 *And from thence he arose:* "Thence" probably refers to the house that Jesus just left.

   and went into the borders of Tyre and Sidon: Some manuscripts omit the words "and Sidon," which were probably added later to harmonize with 7:31 and Matthew 15:21.[37]

   This verse probably refers not to the city of Tyre but to its borders, or the edges of the district, since Jesus generally doesn't go into cities but into the surrounding countryside; this is a gentile area. In the HB, Tyre and Sidon are portrayed negatively (Isa. 23:1–12; Jer. 47:4; Ezek. 26–28; Joel 3:4–8; Amos 1:9–10; Zech. 9:2–4). Josephus describes the people of Tyre as the bitterest enemy of Galilee.

---

37. Metzger, *Textual Commentary*, 82.

and entered into an house, and would have no man know it: Jesus' motive for privacy is not stated: perhaps he wanted to rest, to escape Herod, or to consider the next step for his ministry.

but he could not be hid: It is curious that Mark included the detail that Jesus' intention to hide was foiled (by, as the audience will soon discover, a gentile woman). Reasons for mentioning this might include:

1. Mark wants to show that Jesus is not omnipotent or omniscient.

2. One interpretation of this story is that the woman changes Jesus' mind with her words. Showing her stymieing his intention to be hidden introduces the theme of Jesus' willingness to be flexible: just as the woman will redirect Jesus' plan not to heal the girl, she first redirected his plan to be alone.

3. Mark illustrates Jesus' popularity by showing that he could not be alone even when he wanted to, even in gentile lands.

4. This story reenacts the first feeding miracle (6:31–44) by repeating the pattern of Jesus wanting to be alone but then compassionately meeting a real human need for "food." It shows that Jesus' miraculous ability extends not just to Jewish men (as in the first feeding miracle) or a large crowd (as in the second; see 8:1–9) but also to a sole Greek woman.

7:25 *For a certain woman, whose young daughter had an unclean spirit, heard of him, and came and fell at his feet:* Note the similarities to Jairus's approach to Jesus, but also note the differences, since Jairus was of a very high status (as a male Jewish synagogue leader). Like the bleeding woman (5:27), she acts as good soil (4:20) by hearing and then responding in faith.

7:26 *The woman was a Greek:* "Greek" indicates her cultural background and also that she is not Jewish. The "but" (Greek: *de*) at the beginning of this verse (which is left untranslated in the KJV) may be a clue to Jesus' initial refusal of her request—the woman fell at his feet (like Jairus), but she was a Greek, so Jesus did not intend to exorcise her daughter. Mark highlights her gentile status as central to the plot.

a Syrophenician by nation: This line refers to the region of her birth. References to Syrophenicia are rare, but when they do occur, they imply something unsavory. Every identity marker (female, Greek, Syrophenician, an unclean daughter) works against a positive impression of this person. But she will soon show an incredible understanding of Jesus and his mission, particularly when contrasted with the disciples.

and she besought him: "Besought" is imperfect, implying that she asks repeatedly.

that he would cast forth the devil out of her daughter: Compare the Gerasene demoniac (see 5:3–4) who was bound and shunned; this Greek woman instead pleads for her daughter—and keeps her at home. Like Jairus, she shows an unexpectedly high level of concern for a female child.

7:27 ***But Jesus said unto her, Let the children first be filled: for it is not meet to take the children's bread, and to cast it unto the dogs:*** "Take" is *labein* in Greek and "cast" is *balein,* so this wordplay highlights the opposing nature of "taking" and "casting."

The word for "dogs" is diminutive, but the diminutive can lack force so it may not signify anything particular. Regardless, in Jesus' world, dogs—even small ones—were not regarded affectionately but rather were considered unclean. They were not kept as pets but lived outside the city as wild scavengers (thus the use of "cast" to describe feeding them). In the HB, references to dogs are never positive (Deut. 23:18 [where "dog" is a euphemism for a male prostitute]; 1 Sam. 17:43; 2 Kgs. 8:13), and Jews insulted Gentiles by referring to them as dogs. Further, "in rabbinic literature, 'dog' is used metaphorically for a person who is unlearned in the scripture, Mishnah, and Talmud."[38] (This meaning may be ironic in the story, where the woman will show herself capable of understanding Jesus' words rather well.)

Jesus places himself in the role of the mother—one who is responsible for serving food to the family.

Is Jesus insulting this woman by calling her a dog? This verse should be read in the context of his recent declaration that what enters a person (which was the main dividing line between Jews and Gentiles) does not defile a person, as well as 5:1–20 (where he cast a legion of demons out of a Gentile); these passages imply acceptance of Gentiles. At the same time, Jesus' statement remains a challenge to interpreters (see the Notes on 7:29).

Jesus compares his ability to exorcise the girl to eating bread, which makes this passage a hinge between the two feeding miracles (see the Notes after 8:9 on the symbolism of the loaves).

7:28 *And she answered and said unto him, Yes, Lord: yet the dogs under the table eat of the children's crumbs:* Some manuscripts omit the word "yes." It is likely that this word was added to harmonize with Matthew 15:27.[39]

"Lord" can be translated as "sir," "master," "lord," or "Lord," so it is difficult to determine what this woman knows about Jesus' identity, but she

---

38. Collins, *Mark,* 367; see also Babylonian Talmud, Seder Mo'ed IV, Megillah 7b.
39. Metzger, *Textual Commentary,* 82.

recognizes his authority, and she begins her response respectfully. For Mark's audience, "Lord" was an important title for Jesus.

It may be significant that Jesus uses the word *teknon* to refer to children in the previous verse, but the Greek woman uses *paidion*. If so, then Jesus is envisioning the children he feeds as biological children, while the woman's words picture them as more akin to slaves and not necessarily biologically related.

Like Jesus' statement in the last verse, the woman's words here challenge interpreters. The crux of the difficulty is that her statement results in a shift from Jesus refusing her request (in the previous verse) to granting it (in the next verse). Why, precisely, does her statement—which includes but tweaks Jesus' metaphor—have this effect?

1. She employs her own saying, which "does not contradict but extends"[40] Jesus' saying.

2. She corrects his metaphor and thus changes his understanding of the limits of his ministry. There are two ways in which this might occur:

    a. Jesus said that the dogs needed to wait to be fed to ensure that the children would receive adequate food. The woman presents a scenario where both could be fed at the same time that still prioritized the children's access to the food.

    b. Jesus' metaphor imagined the dogs as scavengers who lived outside of the house. The woman's response pictures the dogs as pets who live in the house and hence are under the table. The woman encourages Jesus to reimagine the dogs, not as dangerous outsiders but as part of the household.

3. The woman shows prophetic understanding of Jesus' ministry. Unlike the disciples, she has "considered the loaves" (see 6:52) and so realizes the children have already been fed and there is food left over from the feeding miracle. Unlike the disciples who have to seek clarification of Jesus' enigmatic teachings, the woman not only understands his metaphorical reference to bread but is able to employ it to support her own ends. As a result of this prophetic understanding, Jesus grants her request. Perhaps Jesus' statement was, as a parable, something of a test to determine if she was an outsider (who would not understand it) or an insider (who would, and could therefore have access to his power).

4. Jesus' reference to dogs can be interpreted as an insult, even an ethnic slur. The woman responds by ignoring the slur and reframing the metaphor in a

---

40. David M. Rhoads, *Reading Mark: Engaging the Gospel* (Minneapolis, Minn.: Fortress Press, 2004), 80.

way that will meet her needs (exorcism) as well as Jesus' (feeding the children first). Thus, she is a model of responding to troubling statements, and it is for this reason that Jesus says that her saying has cleansed her daughter. She cleansed his metaphor; he cleanses her daughter.

5. She shows humility by accepting that she is a "dog" and not a child. In both her initial approach to Jesus (which was begging at his feet, doglike) and with the metaphor, she is willing to make herself into "the least in the kingdom" for the sake of her daught er. Jesus changes his mind to reward the woman for her humility.

These options are not mutually exclusive.

While the woman's statement does not specify why the children are dropping crumbs, the possibilities include:

1. The children are messy eaters due to immaturity. In this case, the woman has recognized that (some of) the Jews will neglect the gift of being fed first, which will create an opportunity for the bread to be fed to the dogs.

2. The children are deliberately sharing their crumbs with the dogs—an obligation that accompanies the privilege of being fed first.

7:29 *And he said unto her, For this saying go thy way:* At this point, the audience may suspect that Jesus is casting the woman out of his presence ("for this saying go thy way") for her impudence. But Mark will soon show that what has been cast out is not the woman but the demon.

The importance of the woman's saying is emphasized in two ways in the text: by Jesus' words and also in the structure of the text itself, where it is literally the turning point of the narrative:

    A. Jesus goes to Tyre
        B. the woman comes to Jesus
            C. the woman asks Jesus
                D. Jesus responds
                    E. the woman's saying
                D'. Jesus responds again
            C'. the woman's request is granted
        B'. the woman returns home
    A'. Jesus leaves Tyre[41]

In this structure, the woman's saying is the centerpiece of the story.

the devil is gone out of thy daughter: Because "gone out" is in the past tense, it indicates that the exorcism has already happened; this is a further

---

41. Adapted from Christopher E. Alt, "The Dynamic of Humility and Wisdom: The Syrophoenician Woman and Jesus in Mark 7:24–31a," *Lumen et Vita* 2 (2012): 3.

indication that the woman's saying—not Jesus' words—caused the exorcism. If this is the best reading, there is a compelling parallel between the woman's saying in 7:28 (which shows an understanding of Jesus' ministry) and Jesus' prophetic saying here (which shows an understanding of the woman's daughter).

Both Jesus' initial refusal to aid the woman as well as his apparent change of mind are difficult to interpret. The difficulty is compounded because:

1. Jesus, ironically, uses a figure of speech about the importance of tending to the needs of children as part of his explanation for declining to help a child.

2. Jesus has previously exorcised demons from a Gentile (5:1–20).

3. While the reference to "dogs" can be understood as an ethnic slur, the previous story showed that people—presumably including Gentiles—were not in fact polluted by what they ate, making it less likely that Jesus would speak disparagingly of Gentiles.

4. There has been nothing in Mark's text that would lead the audience to anticipate that Jesus would refuse this request and insult the woman in the process.

7:30 *And when she was come to her house:* Her willingness to leave Jesus' presence and go home illustrates her faith in his word: she believed that her daughter had been healed and so does not refuse to leave his presence.

In most healing stories, people do not follow Jesus' directions after the healing, but this woman does. It is perhaps ironic—given her willingness to dispute Jesus' initial refusal to help her daughter—that she now follows his counsel.

she found the devil gone out: Mark's note that the exorcism had in fact happened emphasizes Jesus' authority; this theme is particularly important in a story where Jesus appears to change his mind.

Because the woman came to Jesus seeking an exorcism for her daughter but ended up extending the scope of Jesus' mission to include the Gentiles, the daughter's exorcism becomes a symbol for the gentile mission. Given that Jesus' first ministerial forays into both Jewish and gentile lands involved exorcisms (1:21–27; 5:1–20), it is most appropriate that an exorcism occurs here; it emphasizes that a fundamental aspect of Jesus' ministry is casting out evil and releasing humans from bondage.

and her daughter laid upon the bed: The same word for "bed" was used in 7:4; Mark may be suggesting a contrast between the Pharisees' ritual cleansing of beds and Jesus' far more profound cleansing of demons. (This contrast may in fact explain the odd reference to beds in 7:4.)

Note: The story of the Syrophenician woman functions as the hinge between the two feeding miracles (6:32–44; 8:1–9); see the Notes after 8:9.

HB Allusions to the Trickster. Recurring in the HB is the portrayal of a female who is a "trickster." This is a woman who, denied access to power, instead resorts to trickery to accomplish her goals (Gen. 27:1–29; 31:34; 38:14; Judg. 16:4–30; 1 Kgs. 21:1–16). This pattern suggests that women denied power seek it through subversive means. But the Greek woman asks Jesus outright for what she needs. And then, when she is denied, she does not use trickery but rather continues to ask openly.

Relationship to 1 Samuel 1–2. There are extensive parallels between the Greek woman's story and Hannah's story[42] (1 Sam. 1–2). Both feature a desperate woman from the geographic periphery of their respective narratives who struggles under the weight of a problem that threatens her progeny. In both cases, the women approach the location of divine comfort (Hannah's story refers to the "house of the Lord"; Mark's text uses the same two words for "house" and "Lord" as the LXX), each with an unorthodox approach (Hannah by praying silently and the Greek woman by boldly making her request). The women are initially rebuffed by a religious leader, but both meet his rejection with kind but firm words that result in a changed approach from the male leader. They both go home with a promise of healing (but without any evidence of it yet). Each woman is granted what she wanted.

Interestingly, both texts refer to food in similar ways: Hannah does not eat for her grief, and Jesus compares the Greek woman's situation to begging for bread that she cannot have. There may also be a parallel in that Hannah's silent prayer cannot be heard by Eli much as the Greek woman's initial request isn't "heard" by Jesus until she clarifies her position by responding to his initial refusal. Similarly, when the women respond to the initial rebuff, both stories use the same verb (Greek: *apekrithē*), both have a doubled verb to introduce her response, and both responses have the woman call her conversation partner "Lord" (Greek: *kyrie*). And while the same words are not used in the Greek, there is a high degree of similarity in the sentiment after the women's second statements, with both Eli and Jesus telling the women to "go"; but where Eli says, "may the God of Israel grant your petition," Jesus announces that the devil has gone out of the daughter. In other words, at this moment in the story when an audience alert to the allusion would expect Jesus to refer to the God of Israel, he announces on his own authority

---

42. Julie M. Smith, "A Double Portion: An Intertextual Reading of Hannah (1 Samuel 1–2) and Mark's Greek Woman (Mark 7:24–30)," *Dialogue* 50 (Summer 2017): 125–38.

that the woman's request has been granted and therefore aligns himself with the God of Israel. Both women then return to their own homes and find that their request has been granted and their posterity is secure.

One result of comparing these two stories is that it aligns Hannah's child, the prophet Samuel who will anoint Israel's first king, with an anonymous gentile daughter; the fact that the Greek woman's daughter is paralleled to Hannah's son emphasizes the equal value of female children—a principle that would not have been widely acknowledged. And the granting of Hannah's request ushers in the era of peak biblical nationalism, but the story of the Greek woman is an important marker of precisely the opposite phenomenon: the spread of Jesus' ministry to the Gentiles.

Relationship to 1 Kings 17. Facing a famine, the widow of Zarephath (which is located to the south of Sidon and to the North of Tyre), who is also a Gentile, begins to prepare one final meal for herself and her son when she is approached by the prophet Elijah, who asks to be fed first. The issue of who is permitted to eat first creates a resonance with the Greek woman's story in Mark. In both stories, however, there is enough food so that all who are in need can be fed. And in both stories, the prophet heals the woman's child.[43]

Daughters in the Gospel of Mark. This story is the third text in Mark that features a daughter as a key character: "In the overall Markan context it forms an inclusion with the narrative of the woman with the hemorrhage in 5:21–34. The latter is, like the heroine of our story, an anonymous, plucky, ritually unclean woman who 'hears about Jesus' and received healing from him, and is coupled with a younger girl (Jairus's daughter, the Syrophenician's daughter) who is healed. These two female combinations surround a more sinister mother/daughter combination, Herodias and her daughter (6:14–29). It is hard to believe that this arrangement is accidental."[44]

Analysis

Immediately before this story, Jesus taught that what came out of—not what entered—a person defiled her. Here, this principle is put into action as the woman is not deemed defiled because of the foods that, as a Gentile,

---

43. J. Duncan M. Derrett, "Law in the New Testament: The Syro-Phoenician Woman and the Centurion of Capernaum," *Novum Testamentum* 15, no. 3 (1973): 167–86.
44. Marcus, *Mark 1–8*, 466.

she eats; rather, it is what comes out of her—a saying—which results not in defilement but in purification. In other words, what comes out of this Greek woman makes her daughter clean.

It is sometimes suggested that Jesus always intended to exorcise the girl but first refuses in order to test the mother, but this is unlikely because:

1. Jesus does not similarly test anyone else who approaches him for a miracle, so it is difficult to explain why he would in this case.

2. The audience would conclude that sometimes a negative answer from Jesus (or another leader) is an invitation to press for a different answer.

3. If Jesus needed to test her faith, then he apparently was not aware of it without the test. Hence, he is not omniscient. One of the reasons for advocating the idea that he was testing her faith is to preserve Jesus' omniscience (that is, he did not change his mind in this story), but this reading itself undermines his omniscience.

How, then, might his refusal and subsequent agreement be understood? The following are (not mutually exclusive) possibilities:

1. Jesus begins by stating that the children should be fed first, so he is not claiming that the "dogs" (Gentiles) will not be fed but rather that the "children" (Jews) must be fed first. The woman's statement is a recognition that the children have already been fed (symbolically, through the first feeding miracle); hence, it is now appropriate to begin feeding the dogs.

2. There was a very high level of animosity between Jews and Tyrians: "The Tyrian region was one that was badly hit by the Jewish/gentile tension that led up to and accompanied [the Jewish] war. Josephus reports that the Tyrians were among the Jews' bitterest enemies and cites pogroms going back to the first century B.C.E. During the Jewish War, Tyrian Gentiles killed a considerable number of their Jewish neighbors and imprisoned the rest in chains, and a Tyrian army burned the Jewish fortress of Gischala. This poisonous atmosphere may well have infected the fledgling Christian church in Tyre, the majority of whose members were probably Gentiles. . . . [Mark] may feel that Christian communities in this region . . . need to be sharply reminded of God's continuing favor for his ancient people."[45] In this light, Jesus' initial statement about the priority of the Jews can be read as an appropriate corrective. It would reflect, in a limited sense, the dislike for the people of Tyre, and when Jesus agrees to accede to the woman's request, he would be displaying an unexpected kindness toward them. The fact that he was willing to listen to and change his mind based on the woman's words would have been an important moment for the audience since it models reconciliation between

---

45. Marcus, *Mark 1–8*, 471.

the warring factions. This would have been a powerful way for Mark to show Jesus demonstrating love for an enemy.

3. Jesus has a sense of his own mission as requiring a focus on the "children" (Jews), so he cannot envision a way to meet the woman's request. As a mortal, he is limited in his experience and therefore needs to learn from others "line upon line." The woman is able to show him how to accommodate her request while, at the same time, being true to his sense of mission. Jesus thus learns from the woman and, in the process, models how to learn from others in a humble and gracious manner. A situation like this would be the only way for him to model careful listening, reasoning, and the humility necessary to change one's mind in the face of new information. (This may be analogous to his baptism: while not necessary for the remission of sin, it was performed as a model for his followers.) The fact that the other party in this dialogue is female and Gentile emphasizes Jesus' respectful listening to all people and willingness to change based on their perspectives, opinions, and needs. Mark has already suggested that Jesus is not, as a mortal, omniscient or omnipotent; in the conflict between humility and omniscience, Mark chooses to downplay Jesus' knowledge in favor of his humility. Not only does he model humility, but the story shows a dual humility: the woman is willing to humbly approach Jesus and to accept his categorization of her as a "dog," which was probably interpreted by her as an ethnic slur, much as Jesus is willing to learn from her. Thus the story models mutual submission and humility.

4. The last time Jesus cast out demons from a Gentile, he was asked to leave the area (5:17). Perhaps this led to his conclusion that the time was not right to perform miracles for Gentiles, but the woman's words—which display a sophisticated understanding of his ministry—illustrated that this was no longer the case. In the face of this new evidence, Jesus is able to extend his mission and exorcise the daughter.

5. Galilee was the bread basket for Tyre, which was wealthy from trade but could not sustain robust agriculture. This meant that "the Galileans went hungry in times of food shortage in order to supply the people of Tyre."[46] If the backdrop to this story is that Jesus' people were literally going hungry because the "dogs" of Tyre had first access to their food, then the woman is the one in a position of (economic) power, now demanding more power (this time, spiritual) from Galilee, in the person of Jesus. Jesus' refusal to accommodate an entitled woman who is asking for even more is then understandable. The woman's answer suggests that both groups might eat at the same time and have enough, but with the Galileans/children having first right to the food and the Tyrians now being in second position. This role reversal required the audience to see the Tyrians and the Galileans in a new light: their spiritual reality is the opposite of their economic reality. The woman shows how the

---

46. Miller, *Women in Mark's Gospel*, 91–92.

last will be first and the first will be last and makes clear that she is willing to undergo economic loss (that is, to have only secondary access to the bread as crumbs under the table) in exchange for access to Jesus' power. She contrasts sharply with the Gentiles of Gerasa (5:1–20), who preferred Jesus' departure over enduring the economic loss that accompanied his presence. Her similarity to Jairus is highlighted: not only does she approach Jesus on bended knee pleading for a daughter's healing as he does, but she also is willing to withdraw claims to social prestige and power, as he does.

6. The backdrop of this story is the Greek philosophical school known as Cynicism: "the term Cynic itself is derived from the Greek *kynicos,* an adjectival form of the noun for dog; referring to the Cynics' dog-like appearance and behavior . . . [including] scavenging for scraps of food. Where others used it as a term of derision, the Cynics embraced their doggish behavior as a positive choice of lifestyle."[47] They were also known for their "impudent, argumentative style:"[48] a common Cynic technique was "a cutting remark following a question or brief statement."[49] And "it is only among Cynics that we find examples of women philosophizing in public."[50] Thus, there are several points of contact between Cynicism and Mark's story, including the word "dog," the apparent argument between the woman and Jesus, and particularly the fact that the dispute involves a woman. In the context of Cynic practice, Jesus' statement is not a refusal but rather an engagement, and the woman is not a "dog" (in the derogatory sense) but rather a legitimate debate partner.

7. Jesus' desire to be alone means that he is seeking further direction for his mission (compare 1:35–38). It is possible that he initially refuses the woman because he sees her request as an obstacle to his quest, but then her response reveals that she is actually providing the answer to his request for further direction: his mission is now to be extended to the Gentiles (as the next story—where he heals a gentile man—indicates, and as the next feeding miracle—which is very similar to the previous one save it is for a gentile audience— also indicates). There is a compelling mutuality in Jesus' response to the woman's request for exorcism and the woman's response to Jesus' (implicit) request for new guidance for his mission. Interestingly, in this reading, the divine insight Jesus sought about his mission came through an anonymous gentile woman.

8. If Jesus did not perform the exorcism but rather the woman's saying made the demon flee, then it is possible that Jesus' initial refusal to perform the exorcism never changes. If the woman's saying is what causes the exorcism, it is

---

47. Ian Cutler, "A Tale of Two Cynics: The Philosophic Duel between Jesus and the Woman from Syrophoenicia," *Philosophical Forum* 41 (Winter 2010): 381.

48. Tolbert, *Sowing the Gospel,* 185 n. 15.

49. Cutler, "Tale of Two Cynics," 369.

50. Cutler, "Tale of Two Cynics," 382.

not the case that Jesus changes his mind: he refuses to perform the exorcism, the woman's saying causes the exorcism, and Jesus simply announces what has happened.

9. While controversial to many readers, it could be argued that the woman bests Jesus in a debate: "the clear outcome of the contest is that the woman wins the argument."[51] Mark has laid the groundwork for this reading by beginning the story with the note that she has already bested Jesus by ruining his plan for solitude. Mark then uses this incident to point to Jesus' humility: he is comfortable being bested (by a gentile woman, nonetheless); he doesn't attempt to hide behind any rationalizations. Modern readers may not be at ease with the woman's aggressive approach to Jesus, but it is not unprecedented: near the end of the book of Job, God praises Job's willingness to speak honestly, in contrast with his friends: "Job's God seems to make it clear that He would rather we challenge Him vigorously than affirm Him uncritically."[52] And while the idea of someone changing Jesus' mind seems unusual, it actually aligns Jesus with the God of the HB, who is depicted as experiencing a change of heart (Gen. 18:20–33; Ex. 32:11–14; Num. 14:11–20; 27:1–17). It is not necessary to abandon the idea of Jesus' perfection in order to adopt this reading, but it might be necessary to reframe what it means to be perfect: Jesus is shown as perfectly willing to learn, grow, and be humble.[53] This kind of perfection may also be on display in the two-step healing in 8:22–26: Jesus' perfection is not found in an initially perfect healing of the man but rather in his willingness to ask, listen, learn, and continue to serve the man until he can see properly.

Regardless, one thing stands out: the woman's response to Jesus' initial refusal is not regarded as inappropriate or out of bounds; he does not rebuke her for it. Jesus attributes the exorcism not to his own power or to the woman's faith, but to her saying. Her word—which reshaped Jesus' saying so that it could accommodate her request—caused an exorcism. The woman is powerful: evil flees at her word. It is even possible to read Jesus' words to indicate that he did not perform the exorcism: the woman did through the power of her own word. (This is the only case in Mark where Jesus does not speak a command to cause a miracle or does not see the person who is healed.) The ability to cast out demons is one that disciples are given—but will have trouble using. As is often the case in Mark, an otherwise-unknown woman is shown to be a more mature disciple than

---

51. Cutler, "Tale of Two Cynics," 380.

52. Michael Austin, *Re-reading Job: Understanding the Ancient World's Greatest Poem* (Salt Lake City: Greg Kofford Books, 2014), 130.

53. Credit for this observation belongs to Ben Peters.

the male disciples whom Jesus has chosen. This woman is able to exercise this power on the basis of her insight into Jesus' mission.

The Greek woman can be viewed as a type of Christ because she is willing to be humble and to put herself in a position where she suffers in order to effect the healing of another person. Just as the Greek woman turns the dog metaphor into something positive, Jesus will turn his suffering into something salvific.

Once again, there is an interesting mix of high and low Christology as, in the very same story, Jesus is bested in an argument by a gentile woman but performs (or, at the very least, is aware of) an exorcism that happens at a distance.

As is clear in this story (and even clearer when it is compared with the story of the bleeding woman), Jesus expects and desires women to act in ways that were unthinkably aggressive in their cultural context, particularly when advocating for themselves and their children. One function of this story is to show that Jesus supports women who are strong advocates for their children's needs and are not submissive, even when their actions constitute a gross breach of social convention. Further, this story teaches that women are capable not only of holding their own in conversation but also of changing the minds of religious leaders.

Jesus Heals a Disabled Man (7:31–37)

Greek Text

31 Καὶ πάλιν ἐξελθὼν ἐκ τῶν ὁρίων Τύρου ἦλθεν διὰ Σιδῶνος εἰς τὴν θάλασσαν τῆς Γαλιλαίας ἀνὰ μέσον τῶν ὁρίων Δεκαπόλεως. 32 καὶ φέρουσιν αὐτῷ κωφὸν καὶ μογιλάλον, καὶ παρακαλοῦσιν αὐτὸν ἵνα ἐπιθῇ αὐτῷ τὴν χεῖρα. 33 καὶ ἀπολαβόμενος αὐτὸν ἀπὸ τοῦ ὄχλου κατ' ἰδίαν ἔβαλεν τοὺς δακτύλους αὐτοῦ εἰς τὰ ὦτα αὐτοῦ καὶ πτύσας ἥψατο τῆς γλώσσης αὐτοῦ, 34 καὶ ἀναβλέψας εἰς τὸν οὐρανὸν ἐστέναξεν, καὶ λέγει αὐτῷ· Εφφαθα, ὅ ἐστιν Διανοίχθητι· 35 καὶ ἠνοίγησαν αὐτοῦ αἱ ἀκοαί, καὶ ἐλύθη ὁ δεσμὸς τῆς γλώσσης αὐτοῦ, καὶ ἐλάλει ὀρθῶς· 36 καὶ διεστείλατο αὐτοῖς ἵνα μηδενὶ λέγωσιν· ὅσον δὲ αὐτοῖς διεστέλλετο, αὐτοὶ μᾶλλον περισσότερον ἐκήρυσσον. 37 καὶ ὑπερπερισσῶς ἐξεπλήσσοντο λέγοντες· Καλῶς πάντα πεποίηκεν, καὶ τοὺς κωφοὺς ποιεῖ ἀκούειν καὶ ἀλάλους λαλεῖν. [SBLGNT]

King James Version

31 And again, departing from the coasts of Tyre and Sidon, he came unto the sea of Galilee, through the midst of the coasts of Decapolis. 32 And they bring unto him one that was deaf, and had an impediment in his speech; and they beseech him to put his hand upon him. 33 And he took him aside from the multitude, and put his fingers into his ears, and he spit, and touched his tongue; 34 And looking up to heaven, he sighed, and saith unto him, Ephphatha, that is, Be opened. 35 And straightway his ears were opened, and the string of his tongue was loosed, and he spake plain. 36 And he charged them that they should tell no man: but the more he charged them, so much the more a great deal they published it; 37 And were beyond measure astonished, saying, He hath done all things well: he maketh both the deaf to hear, and the dumb to speak.

New Rendition

31 And again having departed from the region of Tyre, he came through Sidon, to the sea of Galilee through the middle of the region of the Decapolis. 32 And they bring him a man who was deaf and who couldn't speak well, and they begged him that he would place a hand on him. 33 And having taken him aside from the crowd privately, he put his fingers into the man's ears. And having spit, he touched his tongue. 34 And having looked up to heaven, he groaned and says to him, "Ephphatha" (that is, be opened). 35 And his ears were opened, the bond of his tongue was loosened, and he spoke clearly. 36 And he instructed them that they should tell no one. But as much as he instructed them, they proclaimed it even more zealously. 37 And they were completely astonished, saying, "He has done all things well—he makes the deaf to hear and the mute to speak."

Notes

7:31 *And again, departing from the coasts of Tyre and Sidon:* "Again" could modify either "departing" or "came."

The Greek text has the following word order: "having departed from the region of Tyre he came through Sidon." Many later manuscripts omit the phrase "he came through Sidon" because this would have been a circuitous route, but the difficulty of this reading suggests that it is earlier.[54]

he came unto the sea of Galilee, through the midst of the coasts of Decapolis: It is significant that the first thing that Jesus does after his encounter with the gentile woman is to go into the heart of gentile territory; it suggests that she has shifted the course of his ministry by making it more inclusive of Gentiles.

---

54. Metzger, *Textual Commentary,* 82.

The route is difficult to understand: "The difficulty of Jesus's itinerary described here is obvious when one traces the journey on a map. Jesus leaves Tyre to go to the Sea of Galilee (which is southeast of Tyre) by way of Sidon (which is about 22 miles north of Tyre) and through the middle of the Decapolis (which is east of Sidon and north of the Sea of Galilee)."[55] Explanations for this route include:

1. Mark was confused about the geography (a likely possibility in a world without accurate maps).

2. Efficiency was not Jesus' goal; rather, his route is the result of some purpose not explained in the text. Perhaps he was avoiding Herod or the religious authorities or had a particular reason to visit Sidon that Mark does not mention.

3. Mark is using the geography to make a theological point: one impact of Jesus' conversation with the Syrophenician woman is that a visit to the gentile-identified Decapolis is appropriate for this moment of his ministry.

But it is clear that the Decapolis is gentile territory.

7:32 *And they bring unto him one that was deaf:* This man is likely a Gentile. In the HB, the deaf are associated with Gentiles since they don't "hear" God (Isa. 42:17–19; 43:8–9; Micah 7:16).

and had an impediment in his speech: This man is not mute but has a speech problem; perhaps he never learned to speak properly because of his deafness.

The word for the speech defect is incredibly rare (this is the only NT use) and was probably chosen to allude to Isaiah 35:6, which is its only LXX use.

and they beseech him to put his hand upon him: It is atypical that the word "hand" is singular. (They will not get "a hand" but something far more involved and intimate.)

7:33 *And he took him aside from the multitude:* Mark does not explain why Jesus removed the man from the crowd (contrast 3:3; 5:31–32), but this setting implies that the purpose of this miracle was not to teach the crowd. Given that a symbolic reading of this miracle is that it showcases Jesus' ability to open minds to greater understanding, then it is possible that the private setting suggests that these teachings occur in private, which has in fact been the case previously when Jesus has taught his disciples more about his parables (4:10; 7:17).

and put his fingers into his ears, and he spit: Where Jesus spits (on his fingers? on the man? on the ground?) is not explained (but compare 8:23).

---

55. Stein, *Mark,* 357.

There are records of other ancient healers using saliva, which was thought to have healing properties, so this is not as odd as it seems to the modern reader (although Matthew and Luke do omit this story). This practice may have reflected a belief that saliva from Jesus' tongue could make the man's tongue work as well.

According to one reading of the Talmud, Leviticus 15:8 deems saliva unclean. This background would tie this practice to the themes of Gentiles and ritual impurity that have persisted throughout this chapter, continuing the inversion of expectations about uncleanness.

and touched his tongue: Symbolically, it may be that Jesus is opening the man's ears to the gospel and loosening his tongue so he can preach.

7:34 And looking up to heaven, he sighed: Various theories can explain Jesus' sighing:

1. It is an expression of compassion in response to the man's suffering.
2. It is an element of prayer, linked to looking up to heaven.
3. It is part of the emotional engagement that was expected of a healer.

and saith unto him, Ephphatha: "Ephphatha" is an Aramaic word, but its use does not necessarily imply a Jewish setting, since some Gentiles in this area spoke Aramaic. Of course, if this command is addressed to the man, he should not have been able to hear it; if he does, then this miracle is similar to others in Mark where Jesus' command requires miraculous healing in order to be fulfilled (for example, 3:5; 5:41).

that is, Be opened: Mark translates the Aramaic for the benefit of the audience. The passive construction may indicate that Jesus envisions God as the one who is doing the opening.

Most interpreters assume that it is the man's ears that are to be opened, but given that Jesus was just looking into heaven, it is possible that he is (also) asking for the heavens to be opened. If a metaphorical approach to this miracle is taken (where the healing is symbolic of Jesus' ability to open up new means of perception in his disciples), then asking that the heavens be opened is most appropriate (compare 1:10).

7:35 And straightway his ears were opened, and the string of his tongue was loosed, and he spake plain: Some ancient manuscripts lack the word "straightway" in this verse. While that word is characteristic of Mark's Gospel, it may not have been in this context originally,[56] especially since it is in a form (*eutheos* instead of *euthys*) that is never otherwise used by Mark.

---

56. Metzger, *Textual Commentary,* 82–83.

The context also suggests against it, since his ears were not in fact opened immediately but only after both action and speech on Jesus' part.

7:36 *And he charged them that they should tell no man:* Mark does not explain who the "they" are.

but the more he charged them, so much the more a great deal they published it: Note the inverse relationship here: "The goal is to impress on the audience that the mighty deeds of Jesus are so extraordinary that they cannot be hidden. His glory shines forth in spite of his attempt to conceal it."[57]

7:37 *And were beyond measure astonished, saying:* This is a very different reaction from the last time Jesus healed on gentile lands; compare 5:17.

He hath done all things well: Although the speakers may not realize it, they are comparing Jesus to the God of the HB (Gen. 1:31 [the wording in the LXX is very similar]; Eccl. 3:11), especially since God is the one who makes it possible for humans to speak (Ex. 4:11).

he maketh both the deaf to hear, and the dumb to speak: Given that Jesus had specifically requested that no one publicize this miracle, there is a bit of irony here: Jesus will control human bodies (by making them able to hear and speak) but not human wills.

There is likely a symbolic level, heightened by this response from the observers, showing Jesus' ability to make new avenues of understanding possible. The disciples will continue to struggle with truly seeing and hearing what Jesus wants to teach them.

Analysis

As mentioned above, the only other biblical usage of "an impediment in his speech" (Greek: *mogilalos*) is found in Isaiah 35:6, so it is likely that Mark wanted to draw attention to this text. This suggests that Jesus' ministry is a fulfillment of Isaiah's prophecy and that this healing has a symbolic meaning as well as a literal one. It is significant that Isaiah is describing a future day when Israel comes back to Zion, which makes the gentile setting of this healing miracle all the more intriguing: in Isaiah 35, God takes vengeance against Israel's enemies, but in this story, Jesus heals a Gentile, inverting expectations. Through this link to the Isaiah passage, Mark shows that Jesus' ministry extends to all people the ability to truly hear his message and to speak it to the world.

---

57. Collins, *Mark,* 374.

Jesus Feeds Four Thousand People (8:1–10)

Greek Text

1 Ἐν ἐκείναις ταῖς ἡμέραις πάλιν πολλοῦ ὄχλου ὄντος καὶ μὴ ἐχόντων τί φάγωσιν, προσκαλεσάμενος τοὺς μαθητὰς λέγει αὐτοῖς· 2 Σπλαγχνίζομαι ἐπὶ τὸν ὄχλον ὅτι ἤδη ἡμέραι τρεῖς προσμένουσίν μοι καὶ οὐκ ἔχουσιν τί φάγωσιν· 3 καὶ ἐὰν ἀπολύσω αὐτοὺς νήστεις εἰς οἶκον αὐτῶν, ἐκλυθήσονται ἐν τῇ ὁδῷ· καί τινες αὐτῶν ἀπὸ μακρόθεν ἥκασιν. 4 καὶ ἀπεκρίθησαν αὐτῷ οἱ μαθηταὶ αὐτοῦ ὅτι Πόθεν τούτους δυνήσεταί τις ὧδε χορτάσαι ἄρτων ἐπ᾽ ἐρημίας; 5 καὶ ἠρώτα αὐτούς· Πόσους ἔχετε ἄρτους; οἱ δὲ εἶπαν· Ἑπτά. 6 καὶ παραγγέλλει τῷ ὄχλῳ ἀναπεσεῖν ἐπὶ τῆς γῆς· καὶ λαβὼν τοὺς ἑπτὰ ἄρτους εὐχαριστήσας ἔκλασεν καὶ ἐδίδου τοῖς μαθηταῖς αὐτοῦ ἵνα παρατιθῶσιν καὶ παρέθηκαν τῷ ὄχλῳ. 7 καὶ εἶχον ἰχθύδια ὀλίγα· καὶ εὐλογήσας αὐτὰ εἶπεν καὶ ταῦτα παρατιθέναι. 8 καὶ ἔφαγον καὶ ἐχορτάσθησαν, καὶ ἦραν περισσεύματα κλασμάτων ἑπτὰ σπυρίδας. 9 ἦσαν δὲ ὡς τετρακισχίλιοι. καὶ ἀπέλυσεν αὐτούς. 10 καὶ εὐθὺς ἐμβὰς εἰς τὸ πλοῖον μετὰ τῶν μαθητῶν αὐτοῦ ἦλθεν εἰς τὰ μέρη Δαλμανουθά. [SBLGNT]

King James Version

1 In those days the multitude being very great, and having nothing to eat, Jesus called his disciples unto him, and saith unto them, 2 I have compassion on the multitude, because they have now been with me three days, and have nothing to eat: 3 And if I send them away fasting to their own houses, they will faint by the way: for divers of them came from far. 4 And his disciples answered him, From whence can a man satisfy these men with bread here in the wilderness? 5 And he asked them, How many loaves have ye? And they said, Seven. 6 And he commanded the people to sit down on the ground: and he took the seven loaves, and gave thanks, and brake, and gave to his disciples to set before them; and they did set them before the people. 7 And they had a few small fishes: and he blessed, and commanded to set them also before them. 8 So they did

New Rendition

1 In those days, again, the crowd being large and not having anything they might eat, having called to him the disciples, Jesus says to them, 2 "I have empathy for the crowd because they have continued with me for three days and have had nothing that they might eat. 3 And if I send them away hungry to their homes, they will collapse on the way. For some of them are come from far away." 4 And his disciples answered him, "From where could anyone satisfy these people with loaves of bread in this desert?" 5 And he was asking them, "How many loaves do you have?" And they said, "Seven." 6 And he commands the crowd to sit on the ground. And having taken the seven loaves and having given thanks, he broke them and gave them to his disciples so that they might set it before them. And they set it before the crowd. 7 And they had

eat, and were filled: and they took up of the broken meat that was left seven baskets. 9 And they that had eaten were about four thousand: and he sent them away.

10 And straightway he entered into a ship with his disciples, and came into the parts of Dalmanutha.

a few small fish. And having blessed them, he also wanted these to be set before them. 8 And they ate and were satisfied. And they picked up the left-over pieces, seven baskets. 9 And there were about four thousand people. And he sent them away. 10 And immediately having entered into the boat with his disciples, he came into the district of Dalmanutha.

Notes

8:1 *In those days the multitude being very great:* Although not in the KJV (because it was not in the manuscripts available to the KJV translators), the word "again" (Greek: *palin*) occurs in this verse.[58] Since the last reference to a great multitude was in the previous feeding miracle (6:34), the word "again" brings that story to the audience's attention here; Mark intends for the two feeding miracles to be closely compared (see "Symbolism of the Loaves" after the Notes on 8:10).

This story is set in gentile territory since Jesus is still in the Decapolis (compare 7:31).

and having nothing to eat, Jesus called his disciples unto him, and saith unto them: The Greek text has a pronoun ("he") instead of the proper name "Jesus," but both the KJV and the New Rendition translate it as "Jesus" for clarity.

8:2 *I have compassion on the multitude:* It is interesting that Jesus felt the need to inform his disciples of his emotions here.

because they have now been with me three days, and have nothing to eat: The crowd "chose to be nourished by Jesus' word rather than bread,"[59] but opting to stay with Jesus meant that they eventually—after an initial period of suffering—enjoyed both.

HB Allusions. In Psalm 107:4–8, travelers are depicted as wandering and hungry until the Lord delivers them from their suffering; references to the desert, hunger, and fainting occur in the text. If Mark intended an allusion, then Jesus is pictured as the Lord who feeds and guides the people.

---

58. Comfort, *New Testament Text and Translation Commentary*, 123.
59. Lane, *Gospel according to Mark*, 273.

In several HB texts—including Genesis 40:13; Joshua 1:11; and Hosea 6:2—God's aid arrives after three days. If Mark continues this motif, then Jesus is aligned with the God of the HB. Particularly interesting is Joshua 1:11, where the Canaanites are enslaved after three days; in Mark, the (Gentile) people are liberated from want after three days, so there is a compelling inversion prompted by Jesus' care for them.

8:3 *And if I send them away fasting to their own houses:* This is not purposeful fasting but mere hunger.

Obviously, the crowd was free to leave whenever they wanted, but the reference to sending them away hints at Jesus' authority over the crowd: if he dismisses them, they will go. Otherwise, they prefer to stay with him—even if it means being hungry.

they will faint by the way: The situation is more dire than the first feeding miracle, where purchasing food was an option (6:37).

"The way" may be a mundane reference to the road home, but in later usage it designated the Christian movement ("The Way"), and so it probably carried that meaning for Mark's audience here. This would encourage a symbolic reading of other elements of the passage, so that Jesus' miraculous provision makes the Christian disciples' journey possible for those who are willing to sacrifice physical comforts to be with him and learn from him.

for divers of them came from far: These words could be Mark's note to the audience or Jesus' words to his disciples.

"From far" suggests that this crowd consists of Gentiles, since several HB texts[60] associate long travel with Gentiles and since "from the Jewish point of view Gentiles were people who were 'far away' from God, and some early Christian texts reflect this image."[61] At the same time, the lack of a specific description of the crowd[62] may indicate that it is mixed, consisting of Jews and Gentiles. Given that the last chapter saw Jesus de-emphasizing (or ending) the food purity laws (see the Notes on 7:19), a mixed gathering would be most appropriate here.

8:4 *And his disciples answered him, From whence can a man satisfy these men with bread here in the wilderness:* Because the disciples not only witnessed but participated in the first feeding miracle, the answer

60. See Josh. 9:6–9; Isa. 60:4; Jer. 46:27, all of which use the same wording in the LXX for "came from far" as Mark does here.

61. Marcus, *Mark 1–8*, 492.

62. Contrast 7:26, which provides a very specific ethnic description.

to this question should be obvious, but it is not because they "considered not the miracle of the loaves" (6:52). Once again, the major motif of the incomprehension of the disciples is emphasized through what appears to be "truly monumental stupidity,"[63] but three things nuance the situation:

1. The disciples' ignorance must be viewed in the context of Jesus' response to it: he does not reject them but rather invites them to continue to participate in his mission by distributing the food to the crowd. So their incomprehension is not a barrier to their continued discipleship or evidence of their perpetual ignorance. Further, their lack of understanding creates an opportunity for Jesus to model patience and kindness towards them.

2. In between the two feeding miracles, the audience learns that the disciples were not able to understand what Jesus was doing because they did not consider the miracle of the loaves (6:52). So the second feeding miracle is another opportunity for the disciples to consider the miracle of the loaves. Thus, it illustrates Jesus' pattern of giving them repeated opportunities to learn.

3. The story in the boat at the end of this chapter (8:19–21) will illustrate that the disciples had not forgotten about the previous feeding; rather, they can even recall its details. So it is not that they have literally forgotten what has happened; rather, they have failed to learn what they needed to from it.

Another function of this question is to show that—despite the fact that the disciples will later help Jesus by distributing the food—it is solely Jesus' power that makes the miracle possible and not any merit or effort of the disciples. Further, the question emphasizes the magnificence of the miracle by indicating how difficult it is to feed such a large group in the wilderness.

HB Allusions. This question echoes three HB texts:

1. Elijah fears Jezebel even after seeing God's power (compare 1 Kings 17:1–18:46 with 1 Kings 19:1–4). In this story, Elijah's previous experience is such that he should know better than to fear Jezebel, and yet he still does. If Mark intended for an allusion to that story, then it places the disciples into the role of Elijah. It can be difficult for modern readers to respond sympathetically to the disciples' lack of comprehension in Mark, but this allusion would help the audience understand that even prophets can struggle to trust in divine power in the face of overwhelming physical odds.

2. In Psalm 78:19–20, the people "tempt" God by wondering if God really could feed them in the wilderness. If Mark intended this allusion, it puts the disciples into the role of the faithless children of Israel, who tempted God during the Exodus, and puts Jesus into the role of the God of Israel, who is challenged regarding the ability to provide food. Picturing the gentile crowd at

---

63. Marcus, *Mark 1–8*, 497.

the feeding miracle as experiencing their own exodus is a powerful way to show the integration of Gentiles into Jesus' ministry.

3. In Numbers 11:13–14, Moses asks the Lord, "Whence should I have flesh to give unto all this people? for they weep unto me, saying, Give us flesh, that we may eat. I am not able to bear all this people alone, because it is too heavy for me." The similar sentiment makes for an intriguing contrast with Mark's feeding miracle: Jesus is a prophet greater than Moses because he does not doubt his ability to provide food for a large crowd in the wilderness. Additionally, the fact that the question about providing food is not on Jesus' lips but on the disciples', combined with the fact that it is the Lord (Num. 11:18) who provides food during the Exodus and Jesus who provides food in Mark's text, aligns Jesus with the God of the HB.

8:5 *And he asked them, How many loaves have ye:* Jesus ignores their question, neither answering it nor rebuking them for asking. Jesus announces his compassion for the hungry crowd, but he also enacts his compassion for his slowly learning disciples.

And they said, Seven: The number seven symbolized completeness and perfection and, thus, the entire world. This meaning stems from several HB references,[64] including:

1. Genesis 9:4–7, which was interpreted to present the seven commandments that were obligatory for the entire world
2. Genesis 10:2–31, which divides humanity into seventy nations
3. Deuteronomy 7:1, which describes the seven nations of Canaan

This symbolism is appropriate to the gentile setting of this miracle.

8:6 *And he commanded the people to sit down on the ground:* Jesus' command once again signals his authority. The Greek verb translated as "to sit" indicates reclining, which was the customary posture for eating meals.

It is curious that Mark includes the phrase "on the ground," since it is obvious that they would sit on the ground. It is possible that he is linking these Gentiles (who have chosen, at great personal sacrifice, to follow Jesus) to the good soil from 4:8; the same word translated "soil" there is "ground" here.

and he took the seven loaves, and gave thanks, and brake and gave to his disciples to set before them and they did set them before the people: The disciples' uncomprehending question does not preclude their participation in the miracle.

---

64. This usage is also reflected in Acts 6:3 and 13:19.

8:7 *And they had a few small fishes: and he blessed, and commanded to set them also before them:* Most manuscripts have "blessed these" instead of "blessed" here. If "blessed these" was the earlier reading, "these" was probably later omitted to reflect the Jewish practice of blessing God instead of blessing the food.[65] But in keeping with the gentile context of this miracle, it is also possible that Jesus was observing Greek practice by blessing the food.

8:8 *So they did eat, and were filled:* All of the diners were filled: they weren't given just enough food to stave off hunger for the journey home but an abundance that would even result in leftovers.

and they took up of the broken meat that was left seven baskets: As mentioned above, the number seven symbolizes completeness, which suggests an infinite number of leftovers—more than anyone could ever want or need.

These baskets could be quite large; the same word is used for a basket into which the apostle Paul could fit (Acts 9:25). This is not the same word for basket used in the first feeding story but rather a more generic term (without specifically Jewish connotations), a detail that contributes to the gentile setting of this miracle.

8:9 *And they that had eaten were about four thousand:* If the reference to four has symbolic meaning, it would suggest universality or the entire earth (13:27 [four winds]; Rev. 7:1 [four corners]).

and he sent them away: Once again, Jesus' authority is emphasized via his control over the entire crowd.

As with the other feeding miracle (6:42–44), there is no expression of amazement, so it is possible that the crowd was not aware that a miracle had happened.

8:10 *And straightway he entered into a ship with his disciples, and came into the parts of Dalmanutha:* Dalmanutha is not referenced in any other ancient text, so its location cannot be determined; the ancient tradition that Dalmanutha is Magdala is possible but unverifiable. The first event that happens to Jesus after coming into Dalmanutha is that Pharisees argue with him, which strongly implies that he is in Galilee.[66]

It is difficult to determine whether verse 10 should be read as the end of the feeding miracle or as the beginning of the next story. Mark normally mentions a shift in location at the beginning of a story, which would argue for grouping this verse with 8:11–13.

---

65. Comfort, *New Testament Text and Translation Commentary*, 124.
66. Malbon, "Narrative Criticism," 52.

Symbolism of the Loaves. As 8:19–21 will show, Jesus expected the disciples to think about the two feeding miracles, with particular attention paid to the numbers involved. These two stories contain a compelling mixture of similarities and differences:

1. The first feeding (6:30–44) takes place in Jewish lands and the second in gentile lands (see the Notes on 8:1).

2. The first feeding is initiated by the disciples' concern (6:35–36) and the second by Jesus' concern (8:1–2). If the first feeding is read as a miracle "for the Jews" and the second "for the Gentiles," this difference may indicate that the disciples' concern did not extend to the Gentiles, but Jesus' did (and, further, that Jesus' concern for the Gentiles was developed through his experience with the Syrophenician woman [see the Notes on 7:24–30]).

3. Jesus has compassion for the crowd in both stories; in the first feeding, it is because they are as sheep without a shepherd (6:34) and in the second, it is because they have not eaten for three days (8:2). In the HB, the image of sheep without a shepherd is used to describe a failure of leadership, while hunger is "a universal human problem,"[67] so the different reasons for compassion contribute to the Jewish setting of the first story and the gentile setting of the second.

4. Both stories feature Jesus teaching the crowd: this is explicit in the first story (6:34) and implicit in the second story (since the crowd has been with Jesus for three days).

5. Only in the first feeding does Jesus command the crowd to sit by companies (6:39–40), which probably reflects the similar practice in military contexts in the HB. So the first story follows the pattern for Israel while the second does not.

6. The blessing that Jesus offers over the food differs slightly in each story, with the second feeding miracle reflecting Greek practice more than Jewish practice.

7. In the second feeding, there are seven loaves, in contrast to the first feeding miracle, which began with five loaves. The seven loaves might symbolize the seven commandments obligatory for the entire world, while the five loaves could symbolize the five books of Moses (and thus Jewish law in general; some Jewish interpretations of Proverbs 9:5 and 25:21 "suggest nourishment from the bread of the Torah"[68]). This symbolism would show that in neither

---

67. Malbon, "Narrative Criticism," 52.

68. Camille Focant, *The Gospel according to Mark: A Commentary*, trans. Leslie Robert Keylock (Eugene, Ore.: Pickwick Publications, 2012), 260, although he ultimately rejects this reading.

case were the commandments sufficient to "fill" the people, but they did serve as the raw material that Jesus transmuted through his own power.

8. A different word for baskets is used in each story. In the first miracle, the word is one specifically associated with the Jews; this is not true for the second story. The fact that both words for "basket" are used in 8:19–21 suggests that the difference between the two is significant and not coincidental.

9. The first miracle ends with twelve (a symbol for Israel) baskets of leftovers but the second ends with seven (a symbol of completeness). This is one of the strongest indications that the first feeding is for the Jews and the second is for the Gentiles.

10. The number of diners is given, oddly enough, at the end of each story: there are five thousand in the first but (and the Greek text uses the word "but" [Greek: *de*] here, indicating a deliberate contrast to the first feeding miracle) four thousand in the second. The five thousand is an exact number (which would have been possible to determine, given that the people ate in rows) while the "about" four thousand in the second may refer to the four corners of the world, creating a further link to the gentile setting. At the same time, five thousand and "about" four thousand are close enough numerically to imply parity between the miracles.

11. The second miracle is set "in those days"—an odd phrase given its lack of specificity, but a phrase that is used in the HB to indicate the time when the covenant will be extended to the Gentiles.[69] Thus its use in Mark suggests that the second miracle relates to the inclusion of the Gentiles.

12. The first story refers to five thousand men (males) while the second story does not, implying that there were women present. In 1 Samuel 21, which was referred to specifically by Jesus only a few chapters ago (2:25–26), David is traveling with a group and has asked the priest for some bread (that story refers to five loaves). The priest says that if David and his men have not had intercourse for three days,[70] they are pure enough to eat the consecrated bread that is normally restricted to the priests. In the first feeding miracle, the audience consisted only of Jewish males—symbolically pure in that they have not associated with women. Hence they are worthy to partake of the miraculous bread. In the second story, the diners are of both genders. But they, too, are worthy to partake of the miraculous bread because they have been doing something else purifying for the last three days: abstaining from food or, symbolically, fasting. The suggestion is that when the kingdom of God spreads throughout the world, it will be gender inclusive and purity will not be measured by the absence of women but rather by adherence to personal devotional practices.

---

69. Joel 3:1; see also Deppe, *Theological Intentions,* 379.

70. Sexual intercourse—even for married people—renders the male unclean; see Lev. 15:16.

13. Shortly after each story, the disciples are in a boat where they cannot comprehend what happens, and it is made very clear to the audience that the reason they do not understand what has happened is because they did not carefully consider the feeding miracle(s) (6:45–52; 8:13–21).

Analysis

In 8:19–21, Jesus will make specific reference to the two feeding miracles and the numbers involved. The disciples—and the audience—are expected to compare the miracles and learn from them. Thus, a close examination of these stories is warranted, with particular attention paid to the number symbolism, which reveals that the second feeding miracle is for the Gentiles just as the first feeding miracle was for the Jews. So Jesus tends to the needs of Gentiles as well as Jews, and his miraculous power is for all people.

The two feeding miracles are also linked by the story of the Syrophenician woman (7:24–31), which serves as a hinge between them. In that story, Jesus' initial refusal to extend his ministry to Gentiles is couched in a metaphor about bread and uses the same word for "filled."[71] The woman recasts his metaphor so that the Gentiles might partake also, and Jesus grants her request; the key issue in her story is whether the Gentiles will be able to eat bread. She is aware (at least on the narrative level, if not historically) that the "children" have already been filled with bread: there are leftovers from the first feeding miracle. This is something the disciples—to their detriment—did not consider, as Mark makes the point of telling the audience (6:52). Thus, this story serves as a bridge from a ministry limited to Jews to one that re-creates that same ministry in the gentile realm. Mark has thus laid the groundwork for a gentile feeding miracle; the discussion with the Pharisees about defilement (7:1–23) also contributes to this theme. And since in the Greek woman's story, eating bread serves as a metaphor for access to Jesus' power, the feeding miracles can also be read not just as miracles but also as metaphors for access to Jesus' healing power. This reading, in turn, may encourage a rereading of Simon's mother-in-law serving (1:31) after her miracle or Jairus's daughter being offered food by Jesus after her raising (5:43). And this is not the last time in the story that the audience will be aware of the symbolic meaning of eating, a theme that will reach fruition at the Last Supper (14:17–25).

---

71. The only uses of the term in Mark are 6:42; 8:4, 8.

Jesus Reviews the Feeding Miracles (8:11–21)

Greek Text

11 Καὶ ἐξῆλθον οἱ Φαρισαῖοι καὶ ἤρξαντο συζητεῖν αὐτῷ, ζητοῦντες παρ' αὐτοῦ σημεῖον ἀπὸ τοῦ οὐρανοῦ, πειράζοντες αὐτόν. 12 καὶ ἀναστενάξας τῷ πνεύματι αὐτοῦ λέγει· Τί ἡ γενεὰ αὕτη ζητεῖ σημεῖον; ἀμὴν λέγω ὑμῖν, εἰ δοθήσεται τῇ γενεᾷ ταύτῃ σημεῖον. 13 καὶ ἀφεὶς αὐτοὺς πάλιν ἐμβὰς ἀπῆλθεν εἰς τὸ πέραν.

14 Καὶ ἐπελάθοντο λαβεῖν ἄρτους, καὶ εἰ μὴ ἕνα ἄρτον οὐκ εἶχον μεθ' ἑαυτῶν ἐν τῷ πλοίῳ. 15 καὶ διεστέλλετο αὐτοῖς λέγων· Ὁρᾶτε, βλέπετε ἀπὸ τῆς ζύμης τῶν Φαρισαίων καὶ τῆς ζύμης Ἡρῴδου. 16 καὶ διελογίζοντο πρὸς ἀλλήλους ὅτι ἄρτους οὐκ ἔχουσιν. 17 καὶ γνοὺς λέγει αὐτοῖς· Τί διαλογίζεσθε ὅτι ἄρτους οὐκ ἔχετε; οὔπω νοεῖτε οὐδὲ συνίετε; πεπωρωμένην ἔχετε τὴν καρδίαν ὑμῶν; 18 ὀφθαλμοὺς ἔχοντες οὐ βλέπετε καὶ ὦτα ἔχοντες οὐκ ἀκούετε; καὶ οὐ μνημονεύετε 19 ὅτε τοὺς πέντε ἄρτους ἔκλασα εἰς τοὺς πεντακισχιλίους, πόσους κοφίνους κλασμάτων πλήρεις ἤρατε; λέγουσιν αὐτῷ· Δώδεκα. 20 ὅτε καὶ τοὺς ἑπτὰ εἰς τοὺς τετρακισχιλίους, πόσων σπυρίδων πληρώματα κλασμάτων ἤρατε; καὶ λέγουσιν αὐτῷ· Ἑπτά. 21 καὶ ἔλεγεν αὐτοῖς· Οὔπω συνίετε; [SBLGNT]

King James Version

11 And the Pharisees came forth, and began to question with him, seeking of him a sign from heaven, tempting him. 12 And he sighed deeply in his spirit, and saith, Why doth this generation seek after a sign? verily I say unto you, There shall no sign be given unto this generation. 13 And he left them, and entering into the ship again departed to the other side.

14 Now the disciples had forgotten to take bread, neither had they in the ship with them more than one loaf. 15 And he charged them, saying, Take heed, beware of the leaven of the Pharisees, and of the leaven of Herod. 16 And they reasoned among themselves, saying, It is because we have no bread. 17 And when Jesus knew it, he saith unto them, Why reason ye, because ye have no bread? perceive ye not yet, neither understand? have ye your heart yet

New Rendition

11 And the Pharisees went out and began to argue with him, seeking a sign from heaven from him, testing him. 12 And having sighed deeply in his spirit, he says, "Why does this generation seek a sign? Amen, I say to you, [may God's judgment come upon me] if a sign will be given to this generation." 13 And having left them, again having entered the boat, he went away to the other side. 14 And they forgot to take loaves, except they did have one loaf with them in the boat. 15 And he ordered them, saying, "Watch out! Beware of the leaven of the Pharisees and of the leaven of Herod." 16 And they were discussing with one another, because they did not have loaves. 17 And having known it, he says to them, "Why are you discussing that you do not have loaves? Do you not yet perceive or understand? Have your hearts been hardened? 18 Having eyes,

hardened? 18 Having eyes, see ye not? and having ears, hear ye not? and do ye not remember? 19 When I brake the five loaves among five thousand, how many baskets full of fragments took ye up? They say unto him, Twelve. 20 And when the seven among four thousand, how many baskets full of fragments took ye up? And they said, Seven. 21 And he said unto them, How is it that ye do not understand?	do you not see? And having ears, do you not hear? And do you not remember? 19 When I broke the five loaves for the five thousand, how many baskets full of pieces did you collect?" They say to him, "Twelve." 20 "And when I broke the seven to the four thousand, how many baskets full of pieces did you collect?" And they say, "Seven." 21 And he said to them, "Do you still not understand?"

Notes

8:11 *And the Pharisees came forth, and began to question with him, seeking of him a sign from heaven:* "Question" and "seeking" share the same root word, so there might be a bit of wordplay here.

While the modern reader might assume that desire for a sign reflects a lack of faith, this is not the case in the HB, where prophets frequently produce signs to authenticate their ministry.[72] (In Isa. 7:10–12, a king is actually rebuked for refusing to seek a sign.) It is possible to read 2:1–12, particularly 2:10, as Jesus providing a sign (the man's ability to walk) to authenticate his ability to forgive sins. Similarly, in 13:4, the disciples ask for a sign and Jesus obliges.

The phrase "from heaven" has two possible meanings:

1. It may be a circumlocution for "from God." Implicit in their request is the judgment that previous "signs" in Jesus' ministry have not actually come from God (3:22). Or perhaps they want God to do something to authenticate Jesus' ministry: they reject anything that Jesus might do to validate his own ministry, which would be considered signs "on earth."

2. It could mean "from the sky," indicating that the Pharisees want an astronomical sign to validate Jesus' ministry.

The word "sign" is never used by Mark to describe any of Jesus' miracles, so the Pharisees are probably not seeking a miracle here. But at the same time, the story immediately preceding this one can be interpreted as a sign due to its symbolic elements, which makes this request ironically inappropriate. Precisely because the word "sign" isn't used for "miracles" in Mark,

---

72. Judg. 6:36–40; 1 Sam. 14:10; 1 Kgs. 18:37–38; 2 Kgs. 20:8–11; Isa. 38:1–20. Ex. 4 and 7 contain signs intended to show that Moses is a prophet. See also Deut. 13:1–6; 18:18–22; D&C 129.

the audience has to grapple with the fact that the Pharisees want a sign when they have just witnessed many miracles, which implicitly dismisses all of Jesus' miracles, exorcisms, and teaching with authority as not having any signifying function. So the Pharisees do not believe what Jesus has done up to this point in his ministry is adequate.

tempting him: Mark reveals the Pharisees' motives: they have no genuine interest in evaluating Jesus' ministry but are simply testing him. How precisely would this test work? If Jesus had requested a sign from God and that sign had not come, then he would have appeared to be a fraud. But if the sign had come, he would have been implying that previous displays of God's power through him (the healings, exorcisms, teaching with authority, etc.) were inadequate.

That Mark specified that they were tempting him is further evidence that there is nothing inherently wrong with seeking a sign to authenticate a prophet. The fact that Jesus will ask *why* they seek a sign is a further indication that the issue at hand is their motive for sign seeking. It is theoretically possible that, had their motives been pure, they would have been given the sign that they were seeking.

Jesus was tempted by Satan (1:13),[73] which means that, in this story, the Pharisees are taking on the role of Satan. For Jesus to provide a sign here would be giving in to temptation just as if he had conceded to Satan in the wilderness.

In Exodus 17:1–7, the children of Israel are portrayed as testing God through Moses. If Mark intended an allusion to that story, then Jesus is the God who is being tested.

8:12 *And he sighed deeply in his spirit:* "Sighed" translates the same verb as in 7:34, but here it has a prefix indicating intensification (hence "sighed deeply").

The emotion reflected in the sighing is not explained but may be:

1. a deep emotional reaction to their lack of faith, as if it is personally painful to Jesus. This would be an especially poignant display, since these are Jesus' enemies who have sought and will seek his life, but he is still emotionally affected by their lack of faith.

2. a reflection of his anger or grief.

3. an indication that Jesus is marshaling his emotions to make the coming pronouncement. Because that statement may not strike the audience as particularly important, the reference to Jesus' emotion was included to indicate how very seriously Jesus took this situation.

---

73. Note that the same Greek word is used in 1:13 for temptation.

Neither does Mark explain what it means to sigh in the spirit as opposed to in the body.

and saith, Why doth this generation seek after a sign: The reference to "this generation" is curious; it may be that:

1. The Pharisees represent the entire generation of people (and hence they are the ones who voice the question).

2. There is an allusion to Genesis 7:1 (where the people in Noah's day are described as "this generation," using the same term in the LXX as is used here) or to Psalm 95:10–11.

3. There is an allusion to the generation that wandered in the wilderness.

verily I say unto you: See the Notes on 3:28.

There shall no sign be given unto this generation: The Greek phrasing suggests that Jesus is making an oath, of which only half is presented ("if there shall be a sign given to this generation . . ." with the implied notion that Jesus would be cursed if this were the case). So it is an oath formula without the penalty for breaking the oath articulated;[74] the New Rendition reflects this by including the unstated part of the oath in brackets.

This curse formula could function as a sort of negative sign: if a sign is given, then Jesus will be cursed, which would be, in effect, a sign. The fact that Jesus is not cursed then serves as evidence that a sign will not be given to this generation. This response suggests a certain cleverness and playfulness on Jesus' part.

This statement is somewhat difficult to parse: Does it mean that Jesus has never given signs? (What then of 2:10?) That he has before, but will no longer? (What then of the miracles he will yet perform?) Or, that no signs will be given to "this generation" (which consists of whom?), perhaps indicating that signs may be performed in their very presence, but they will not be able to recognize them (4:25; 6:52)?

8:13 ***And he left them, and entering into the ship again departed to the other side:*** "Them" refers to the Pharisees. It is likely that Jesus' leave-taking has symbolic connotations and represents a profound rupture with the Pharisees. There may be an allusion to Deuteronomy 32:20, where the Lord announces that he will reject a faithless generation. The contrast with the disciples continues: they, like the Pharisees, misunderstand Jesus' ministry, but Jesus does not leave them because they are trying to learn. The dividing line between insiders and outsiders is not ignorance but teachability.

---

74. Compare, for example, 2 Kgs. 6:31. Such constructions are fairly common in the HB.

While Mark will often use a change in location to signal the beginning of a new story, it is perhaps better in this instance to read this verse as the end of the preceding story instead of the beginning of the next one in order to make clear that Jesus' leave-taking is related to the Pharisees' request for a sign. The Pharisees and Galilee will no longer be the focus of the Gospel, which will shift to the disciples and Jerusalem.

Relationship to Psalm 95. Verses 8–11 of Psalm 95 contain references to hardened hearts, testing in the wilderness, and a generation. And the idea of the Lord being grieved in Psalm 95:10 might link to Jesus' sighing in Mark, providing the motivation for the sighing. If Mark intended this allusion, then it aligns Jesus with the God of the HB and the Pharisees with the faithless children of Israel who want to test God.

8:14 *Now the disciples had forgotten to take bread:* While Mark does not specify, it is possible that the disciples were still supposed to be carrying the leftover baskets from the feeding miracles. That they did not is a physical indication of the fact that they have forgotten to consider the miracle of the loaves (6:52).

neither had they in the ship with them more than one loaf: The phrasing here is somewhat awkward, but the point is that they have (only) one loaf with them ("they forgot to take loaves, but they had one loaf"). The "one loaf" may be an allusion to Jesus (compare 14:22); in this case, it would reflect the truth that they are ignoring Jesus' presence. Regardless, it is not clear whether the disciples recognize that they have one loaf or whether this statement reflects the narrator's perspective. (Soon, Jesus will chastise them for their lack of understanding; the presence of one loaf may be part of what they do not understand.)

8:15 *And he charged them, saying, Take heed, beware of the leaven of the Pharisees:* Jesus' voice of warning—emphasized by the use of "charge," "take heed," and "beware"—is vigorous.

What constitutes the leaven of the Pharisees is not made clear,[75] but the last reference to the Pharisees was their desire for a sign (8:11); Jesus may be warning his disciples against sign seeking.

and of the leaven of Herod: The last reference to Herod was in the context of the death of John the Baptist (6:14–30); Mark has also mentioned Herod and the Pharisees together in the context of their plan to kill Jesus (3:6). The reference was unusual because the Pharisees and Herod(ians)

---

75. Interestingly, Matthew resolves the ambiguity by interpreting the leaven as false teachings (Matt. 16:12), but Luke resolves it by interpreting it as hypocrisy (Luke 12:1).

were normally opposed to each other (see the Notes on 3:6). If the request for a sign was a trap that might have cost Jesus his life, then perhaps the leaven of the Pharisees and Herod involves plotting against Jesus; specifically, it might be a warning for Judas. So what initially appears to be a stern admonition may also be a merciful expression designed to protect Judas from himself. This interpretation also clarifies the apparent disconnect between the reference to having bread in the boat and the reference to leaven: if Jesus is the one loaf and the leaven reflects the plot to kill Jesus, then the warning against leaven speaks to the fear that it will corrupt the bread, or kill Jesus. They should remove all of the leaven, as if they were preparing for Passover. This reading is particularly appropriate if the warning about leaven is read parabolically, a reading that may be encouraged by the reference to Isaiah 6:9, which was a centerpiece of the parable chapter (4:12) and is repeated here, along with the theme of lack of understanding.

8:16 *And they reasoned among themselves, saying:* Because "reasoned" is imperfect, it implies that the disciples ignore Jesus' warning in the previous verse and instead continue to fret about the situation from 8:14 as if Jesus had not said anything.

It is because we have no bread: In some manuscripts, a variant makes it possible to translate this as indirect speech ("that they did not have bread").[76] Perhaps a change was made to parallel Matthew 16:7, where direct speech is used.

The disciples take Jesus' symbolic referent to leaven to be a literal reference to their lack of bread. Since "leaven" can be a shorter way to refer to "leavened bread," they may have thought that Jesus did not want them to remedy their lack by purchasing bread from supporters of the Pharisees or Herod. Or, they may have assumed that Jesus was speaking generally to their immediate physical need. Either way, the disciples interpret on a literal level a saying meant to communicate symbolically; Mark, instead, teaches that sometimes Jesus' words need to be interpreted nonliterally.

8:17 *And when Jesus knew it, he saith unto them:* Given that they are in a boat, Jesus' "knowing" is most likely simple overhearing and not miraculous, but this raises the question of why Mark would bother mentioning that Jesus "knew it." Perhaps Mark wanted to contrast Jesus' knowledge of what was happening around him with the incomprehension of the disciples.

Why reason ye, because ye have no bread?: Jesus indicates that their lack of bread should not have bothered them because, after two feeding miracles, they should be well aware of Jesus' ability to provide food to

---

76. Collins, *Mark,* 382 note g.

those in need. They should not be thinking about their bread shortage but rather about what Jesus has just warned them about: the leaven of the Pharisees and Herod.

perceive ye not yet, neither understand?: The word "yet" probably points to the second feeding miracle, indicating that the pattern should be clear to them by now that Jesus can rectify their lack of bread; "yet" also has a positive force, suggesting that Jesus has hope that they will at some future point be able to understand.

have ye your heart yet hardened?: In 3:5, it is the Pharisees (who are beginning to plot to kill Jesus) who have hard hearts, so here Jesus' question puts his disciples into unpleasant company. But by framing it as a question instead of a statement, Jesus introduces the possibility without demanding it. He is encouraging his disciples to be reflective.

8:18 *Having eyes, see ye not? and having ears, hear ye not?:* This language is similar to that found in several HB sources (Deut. 29:2–4; Ps. 115:5–6; Jer. 5:21; Ezek. 12:2), especially Isaiah 6:9–10, which was quoted in 4:12. This question is definitely not flattering to the disciples, and the previous reference to it in Mark intimates that the disciples are acting as if they are outsiders to Jesus' ministry.

Previously, a deaf man was healed (7:31–37) and soon a blind man will be (8:22–26). It is possible that these healings have symbolic reference to the blindness and deafness of the disciples, and, in turn, the disciples' state is mirrored in the unseeing and unhearing state of those who need Jesus to heal them.

and do ye not remember?: This question expects a positive answer. Interestingly, the dialogue will show that the disciples do in fact remember the stories, but they do not comprehend their symbolism or implications.

8:19 *When I brake the five loaves among five thousand, how many baskets full of fragments took ye up? They say unto him, Twelve:* Jesus is encouraging them to be reflective about past events in his ministry.

8:20 *And when the seven among four thousand, how many baskets full of fragments took ye up? And they said, Seven:* The Greek text reflects the two different words for baskets used in the two feeding miracles, suggesting that they are significant.

8:21 *And he said unto them, How is it that ye do not understand?:* Some manuscripts add the word "yet" to the question ("Do you not yet understand?"),[77] which is likely to be the earlier reading; it is also more

---

77. Collins, *Mark,* 383 note i.

congruent with the idea that the disciples would be able to understand Jesus in the future. On the other hand, it is difficult to understand why scribes would have changed the text to a reading that was harder on the disciples when the general tendency seems to be the opposite (compare the similar variant in 4:40).

A similar line can be found in 4:40, where Jesus was discussing their fear. The reprise of the line here suggests a similar dynamic, but this time, it is a miracle instead of a parable that they do not understand. This may be significant, implying that Jesus' miracles are, like the parables, to be understood as symbolic teaching.[78]

Analysis

Jesus focuses on the leftovers and the numbers involved in each miracle. The focal points of Jesus' questioning are the answers twelve and seven. These numbers have crucial symbolic value, with twelve pointing to the house of Israel and seven to the entire world. This suggests that the Jewish and gentile settings of the feeding miracles were a key constituent of their meaning. If this is specifically linked to the leaven of the Pharisees and Herod, then one implication would be that Jesus' work—unlike that of the Pharisees and Herod—is not nationalistic but rather focused on the extension of the blessings of the gospel to all people. Jesus, the one loaf in the boat, can be understood as the leaven[79]—this makes sense of his warning about the (alternative) leaven of the Pharisees and Herod as well as metaphorically explaining Jesus' ability to multiply the loaves in the feeding miracle, much as leaven appears to multiply dough.

Because Jesus' questioning focuses on the issue of leftovers, it may also speak directly to the disciples' concern that they do not have (enough) bread in the boat: Has he not already shown them twice that he is capable of producing enough food not just to meet human needs but with ample amounts left over? And, given this ability, shouldn't they focus on what he is trying to teach them about the dangerous leaven instead of focusing on their immediate physical needs? Jesus teaches that there is cause for concern—it is not their lack of bread but the leaven of their enemies.

Not only does Jesus want them to remember the factual details of what has happened, but he wants them to understand the greater significance

---

78. Frank Kermode, *The Genesis of Secrecy: On the Interpretation of Narrative* (Cambridge: Harvard University Press, 1979), 46.

79. Credit for this insight belongs to Chris Mierzejewski.

of these facts and their symbolism. Instead, the disciples display a gap between their factual knowledge (which is faultless) and their understanding (which is lacking). The fact that they can answer the questions correctly suggests that working eyes and ears and a soft heart require more than simple recollection. Jesus is asking them to do something else: to think about miracles in a symbolic way.

This story relates structurally to two others in Mark. First, in a previous scene on a boat, the disciples suffered from a lack of understanding, which was specifically tied to their lack of consideration of the miracle of the loaves (4:36–41). That story also ended with an unanswered question. Mark emphasizes through repetition the idea that the disciples are supposed to remember something more than the mere facts about the feeding miracles, but they still are not getting that message. This becomes guidance to the audience, who is shown what they should think about: the deeper meaning of the feeding miracles. The next story in Mark is a two-stage healing; previously, a man who was deaf and could not speak well was healed. These healings sandwich the experience of the disciples, suggesting the gradual process of coming to knowledge and also showing that Jesus' intervention is a necessary precondition to gaining insight.

This scene in general and the way in which it ends with an unanswered question in particular (compare 4:41) would have had a significant effect on the audience. The narrator has already warned them that the disciples were guilty of not considering the miracle of the loaves (6:52), and so they already know to pay close attention to the symbolic nature of Jesus' miracles. When listening to this dialogue, then, the audience realizes that they know more than the disciples do.

Mark 8:21 is the end of the first third of the Gospel. The numerous references to Galilee and travel by boat will recede, and a focus on "the way" and Jerusalem will emerge after 8:21. The sea crossings are symbolic of Jesus' ability to unify Jews and Gentiles, who live on opposite sides but who are united by Jesus' ability to cross over. The disciples are unable to cross the sea without him—they are thus unable to unify Jews and Gentiles without him. Plus, they show a lack of understanding every time they get in a boat—they simply don't understand the crossings.[80]

The first portion of the Gospel is also roughly bracketed by references to Jesus being tempted (first by Satan and then by the Pharisees), which highlight the theme of temptation throughout the Galilean ministry.

---

80. Kelber, *Mark's Story of Jesus*, 41–42.

PART 2: ON THE WAY (8:22–10:52)

As the second act of the Gospel, this section is rather different from the previous portion of Mark. Journeys are taken by foot, not by boat, and most of Jesus' teachings are directed at the disciples, not the crowds. This section is bookended by stories of Jesus healing the blind (8:22–26; 10:46–52), healings that stand out in a text that does not include many other healing miracles. Since every story between these two healings focuses, at least in part, on the (spiritual) blindness of the disciples, these miracles operate on a symbolic level as well as a literal one: they show that the disciples lack sight (8:18) and thus require healing. They also teach that Jesus is capable of providing this healing. The first restoration of sight requires two steps, which implies that healing the disciples' blindness will also require more than one intervention.

The most significant difference in the three sections is geographical: the first section is in Galilee and the final one in (and around) Jerusalem, but the middle section is "on the way," which is the controlling metaphor in this section. Because "The Way" was one of the first terms used to describe early Christianity (for example, Acts 9:2), this is not just a literal journey but also "the way" of discipleship, as the stories in this section will indicate. The symbolic journey involves the disciples following Jesus and increasing in understanding.

The structural backbone of this section consists of three prophecies that Jesus makes of his death and Resurrection. They each have the same format:

	First	Second	Third
Prediction	8:31	9:30–32	10:32–34
Error by Disciples	8:32–33	9:33–34	10:35–37
Jesus Teaches about Discipleship	8:34–9:1	9:35–10:31	10:38–45

Each prediction that Jesus makes of his suffering and death is immediately followed by a mistake made by the disciples that, in turn, is immediately followed by Jesus' teachings about discipleship. Each of these discipleship teachings includes a paradoxical saying (8:35; 9:35; 10:43–44). This tight pattern suggests that the Passion predictions not only are important in their own right but also develop their meaning through this structure (see the Analysis of 10:32–45).

On the Way
(8:22–10:52)

Jesus Heals a Blind Man
(8:22–26)

Greek Text

22 Καὶ ἔρχονται εἰς Βηθσαϊδάν. καὶ φέρουσιν αὐτῷ τυφλὸν καὶ παρακαλοῦσιν αὐτὸν ἵνα αὐτοῦ ἅψηται. 23 καὶ ἐπιλαβόμενος τῆς χειρὸς τοῦ τυφλοῦ ἐξήνεγκεν αὐτὸν ἔξω τῆς κώμης, καὶ πτύσας εἰς τὰ ὄμματα αὐτοῦ, ἐπιθεὶς τὰς χεῖρας αὐτῷ, ἐπηρώτα αὐτόν· Εἴ τι βλέπεις; 24 καὶ ἀναβλέψας ἔλεγεν· Βλέπω τοὺς ἀνθρώπους ὅτι ὡς δένδρα ὁρῶ περιπατοῦντας. 25 εἶτα πάλιν ἐπέθηκεν τὰς χεῖρας ἐπὶ τοὺς ὀφθαλμοὺς αὐτοῦ, καὶ διέβλεψεν καὶ ἀπεκατέστη καὶ ἐνέβλεπεν τηλαυγῶς ἅπαντα. 26 καὶ ἀπέστειλεν αὐτὸν εἰς οἶκον αὐτοῦ λέγων· Μηδὲ εἰς τὴν κώμην εἰσέλθῃς. [SBLGNT]

King James Version

22 And he cometh to Bethsaida; and they bring a blind man unto him, and besought him to touch him. 23 And he took the blind man by the hand, and led him out of the town; and when he had spit on his eyes, and put his hands upon him, he asked him if he saw ought. 24 And he looked up, and said, I see men as trees, walking. 25 After that he put his hands again upon his eyes, and made him look up: and he was restored, and saw every man clearly. 26 And he sent him away to his house, saying, Neither go into the town, nor tell it to any in the town.

New Rendition

22 And they come to Bethsaida, and they bring him a blind man and begged him to touch him. 23 And having taken hold of the blind man's hand, he led him out of the village. And having spit upon his eyes, having laid hands on him, he asked him, "Do you see anything?" 24 And having looked up [or gaining his sight], he said, "I see people; as trees I see them walking." 25 Then again he laid hands upon his eyes, and he opened his eyes, and he was restored, and he saw everything clearly. 26 And he sent him to his home saying, "Do not even go into the village."

Notes

8:22 *And he cometh to Bethsaida; and they bring a blind man unto him, and besought him to touch him. 23 And he took the blind man by the hand, and led him out of the town:* In other healing miracles, Jesus has positioned the person in the center of the crowd (3:3; 5:30), but here he takes the man aside. It is not clear why he does this, but it may be related to the later command not to go into the village.

and when he had spit on his eyes: It was believed that saliva had healing properties (see the commentary on 7:33).

Here, the typical word for "eyes" (Greek: *ophthalmos,* which is used in 8:25) is not used but a different word (Greek: *omma*), "a more poetic term . . . [that is] frequently employed in philosophical contexts in which physical sight becomes an image for spiritual insight."[1] This unusual term encourages the symbolic reading of this miracle, pointing to the blindness of the disciples that Jesus must overcome.

and put his hands upon him: This verse does not specify precisely where Jesus put his hands, but since 8:25 will say that Jesus placed his hands on the man's eyes *again,* he presumably did so here.

he asked him if he saw ought: In some manuscripts, a textual variant[2] makes it possible to read this as direct speech ("Do you see anything?").

This is the only instance where Jesus asks whether a miracle has been completed. It is somewhat surprising, especially since the normal pattern is for Jesus to issue a command that requires that the miracle has already taken place in order for the command to be fulfilled.

Interpreting this question leads to a paradox: on the one hand, Jesus' words introduce the possibility that the healing has not been (completely) successful and therefore implies his own lack of omniscience. On the other hand, the fact that Jesus knew to ask whether the healing had been completely successful points to his miraculous powers.

8:24 *And he looked up, and said, I see men as trees, walking:* The man's statement is virtually impossible to translate precisely due to the strange syntax.[3] Options for understanding it include:

1. It is meant to be opaque and confusing in order to convey the man's confusion.

---

1. Joel Marcus, *Mark 8–16: A New Translation with Introduction and Commentary,* vol. 27A of the Anchor Yale Bible (New Haven, Conn.: Yale University Press, 2009), 593.

2. Collins, *Mark,* 388–89 note b.

3. Waetjen, *Reordering of Power,* 142.

2. It is a factual representation of what he sees, with no symbolic level.

3. The statement has symbolic meaning, which should be expected since the miracle itself functions as an enacted parable to describe the process by which disciples learn to "see" Jesus.[4] Options for the symbolism include:

   a. Jesus' cross. The image of men walking like trees symbolically describes a man carrying a cross (or cross beam) of wood. If the man is seeing Jesus' cross being carried, there are two different ways to interpret the scene:

      i. His vision—while unusual in the Gospel of Mark, which does not have other visions—is appropriate to a story that symbolically conveys what it means to gain (in)sight into Jesus' mission, especially since, as the next story will show, the vision of Jesus that the disciples were most lacking was understanding that Jesus must suffer and die. This healed man is then a foil for Peter's lack of knowledge since he is able to clearly see who Jesus really is. The man's vision is true and appropriate.

      ii. This story is, at least on a symbolic level, akin to an exorcism. The man's blindness is the result of demon possession. The first attempt at healing essentially fails (as was the case with the first attempt at exorcism in 5:8). The statement about seeing men walking as trees is similar to the statements that the demon-possessed make: it reveals Jesus' true identity (that is, that he will carry a cross) but is not an appropriate revelation and so Jesus will silence it—in this case, by attempting the healing again.[5] The man's vision is true but not appropriate.

   b. HB allusions:

      i. In Jeremiah 1:11–13, Jeremiah has a vision. The Lord asks him what he sees—this has significant resonance with Mark's text, where Jesus asks the man what he sees. Jeremiah replies that he sees part of a tree, and the Lord responds that he has seen correctly and that the branch is a symbol for the curses to come. If Mark intended an allusion to this text, it is significant because:

         A. Jesus is associated with the Lord of the HB. His questioning whether the man sees is not evidence of a lack of omniscience but rather that he is taking on the role of the Lord in guiding the visionary. But, in an interesting bit of Atonement theology, he extends the role of guide by presenting himself as the one who removes the curses.

         B. The blind man is associated with the prophet—a significant theme in itself, since physical deformity, including blindness, prohibited one from participating as a priest in the temple rituals (Lev. 21:18).

---

4. Eric D. Huntsman, *The Miracles of Jesus* (Salt Lake City: Deseret Book, 2014), 95–96, 103.

5. J. Duncan M. Derrett, "Trees Walking, Prophecy, and Christology," *Studia Theologica* 35 (1981): 33–54.

    C. Seeing men as trees walking is not evidence of imperfect sight but rather of a vision. This would encourage a symbolic reading of this passage regarding the disciples' enhanced sight.

  ii. In Zechariah 4:1–6, Zechariah has a vision. The angelic messenger asks him what he sees (again, echoing this passage). He sees a menorah and olive trees. He says he does not understand what he sees and asks for clarification; the messenger tells him that the items symbolize "the word of the Lord to Zerubbabel: 'Not by strength and not by power, but by my Spirit,' says the Lord who rules over all" (NET). If an allusion is intended, it suggests that

    A. once again, Jesus is associated with the divine—in this case, a messenger for the Lord—and the blind man is associated with a prophet.

    B. the trees in the blind man's vision are not evidence of lack of sight but of visionary sight.

    C. the trees symbolize precisely what it is that Peter and the other disciples will need to learn about Jesus' ministry: that it will happen not by strength and power (which is what Peter and many others had expected of the coming Messiah) but rather by the Spirit. Thus, the two-step healing of the blind man becomes the perfect expression of the increased (in)sight that the disciples need.

  iii. Judges 9:7–15 consists of "a fable about walking (and talking) trees [that] is used to criticize kingship."[6] This text might link to Peter's coming confession that Jesus is the Christ (8:29): the state of half-sight represented by Peter's rebuke of Jesus in that scene (8:32) aligns very nicely with the idea of criticizing kingship and glory. This allusion might have reminded Mark's audience of 4:30–32, which associated kingdoms and trees.

  iv. In Isaiah 6:9—a text that has already been referenced twice by Mark—people look but don't see. In Mark's text, the man looks (Greek: *anablepō*) and sees (Greek: *horaō*) men as trees. Perhaps Mark chose these verbs to allude to the Isaiah text and to suggest that the man was looking but not seeing. This would point to the need for another way of seeing; the second stage of the healing would teach that Jesus is the one who provides the much-needed new way of seeing.

8:25 *After that he put his hands again upon his eyes, and made him look up: and he was restored, and saw every man clearly:* The word translated as "clearly" means "in a far-shining way." This term probably reflects the ancient belief that sight involved an internal beam of light coming out

---

6. Marcus, *Mark 8–16*, 595, although he calls this reading "overstated."

of the person and resting upon an object;[7] one would be blind if the light were trapped inside.

This two-step restoration is somewhat puzzling. Why did it require two attempts for Jesus to heal this man?

1. The two stages reflect the way this text echoes HB texts (see the Notes on 8:24).

2. That his sight returns in stages instead of instantaneously might reflect the idea of a symbolic "restoration:" the idea is that restoring insight is not instantaneous. This aligns nicely with the symbolic use of this miracle in Mark, where the gradual gaining of sight mirrors the disciples' continuous quest for greater insight into Jesus' identity and mission.

3. While modern readers might interpret Jesus' initially imperfect effort at healing as evidence of his lack of omniscience, it instead reflects the humility that is indicative of his mission. A healing that presents Jesus as humble is the ideal context for the miracle, since it is precisely Jesus' humility and willingness to suffer that his disciples seem unable to understand and that would be suggested by a symbolic reading of this miracle.

4. The miracle is meant to emphasize Jesus' lack of omniscience. Mark presents Jesus as a miracle worker and inspired teacher, even the Son of God, but not omniscient during his mortal ministry (13:32).

5. As a mortal, Jesus is not capable of seeing what another person sees. (In other words, he cannot know what they can see through their eyes; Jesus is limited to his own perspective.) Even today, eye doctors have to ask a lengthy series of questions in order to determine what their patients can see. That Jesus was able to heal after only two tries when he cannot see through the man's eyes is actually a testament to his powers.

6. This story requires Mark's audience to reimagine what it means to be perfect. Jesus is presented as perfect in this story, but it is not the anticipated form of perfection, where he would automatically perform the healing flawlessly on the first attempt. Rather, Jesus is perfect in the sense of being perfectly willing to ask questions, to listen to the answers, to continue trying to solve the problem, and to serve the man until his vision is flawless (see also the Notes on 7:29).

7. That this miracle required multiple stages does not imply a lack on Jesus' part any more than the Creation account reflects divine deficiency because it required six days. Not all miracles are instantaneous.

---

7. Modern readers may be troubled by the idea that the scriptures could reflect incorrect scientific notions, but this is to be expected. As John A. Widtsoe wrote, "The Bible is not a treatise on science. Naturally, the knowledge of the day is reflected in the telling of the story." John A. Widtsoe, *In Search of Truth: Comments on the Gospel and Modern Thought* (Salt Lake City: Deseret Book, 1930), 86.

8. Modern science suggests that patients with newly restored sight require time for their brains to learn to process images before they can see correctly.[8] Therefore, the two-stage healing reflects the expected progression of events, with the second part of the healing concerning not his eyes but rather his brain's ability to process the image. One weakness of this reading is that this processing problem normally corrects itself with time, making it difficult to understand why Jesus would intervene here.

Relationship to Isaiah 42. In Isaiah 42:6–7, God appoints a spokesman who will open the eyes of the blind as a token of the ability to mediate the covenant. If Mark is alluding to this text, it is an important indication of Jesus' special role and commission, as well as a fulfillment of prophecy.

8:26 *And he sent him away to his house, saying:* There may be an ironic wordplay here since "sent" stems from the same root word as "apostle," but the sending is with a commission of silence, not proclamation. "Sent him away" does not have the negative connotation in Greek that it does in English.

Unlike most miracles, there appears to be nothing in this one that illustrates to the audience that the man has in fact been healed. But the command to return home can be read as evidence of the man's healing if it is assumed that he returns on his own (not with those who brought him; contrast 8:22), which he would not have been able to do if he were still blind.

Neither go into the town: The town here is Bethsaida. The command to avoid the town might have been given because

1. as with some other miracles, Jesus does not want the story of this healing to spread. It is difficult to determine precisely why this counsel was given and how it could have been followed when it would have been obvious that the man was healed as a result of his encounter with Jesus.

2. often, the blind were beggars. Perhaps now that the man has no need to beg, he can avoid going into town.

nor tell it to any in the town: Some manuscripts omit this phrase so that Jesus does not prohibit the man specifically from speaking about his healing but only prohibits him from entering the town.[9] Perhaps this is a distinction without a difference since he can't tell anyone in the town if he doesn't enter the town.

---

8. John W. Welch, "Evidence for a New Testament Miracle," *BYU Studies* 37, no. 4 (1997–98): 173–75.

9. Collins, *Mark,* 389 note d.

Analysis

Jesus' intention to travel to Bethsaida was announced in 6:45, but he and his disciples did not arrive there until this point in the narrative. It is likely that Mark has deliberately structured the text so that they do not arrive in Bethsaida until the appropriate moment, having accomplished certain things first. Perhaps the disciples cannot arrive in the place where eyes are opened until they have first had several teaching experiences, including the second feeding miracle, the discussion about defilement, and the exorcism of the Greek woman's daughter. In other words, the reason that Jesus wanted to be in Bethsaida was to open their eyes to his identity and mission, but this was not possible (as the repeated instances of the incomprehension of the disciples indicated) until this point in the story.

The two-step healing is likely not meant to reflect Jesus' inability to heal the man in one step but rather his choice to heal him gradually for symbolic reasons. The analogy between literal and spiritual vision was common in ancient writings. Thus the healing is a metaphor for the partial sight of the disciples who can, for example, recite the numbers involved in the feeding miracles but cannot see the deeper meaning (8:19–21), as happens in the story immediately before this one. Jesus' role is to ask questions, ascertain the problem, and further heal. The metaphor of seeing also overlaps the metaphor of being "on the way," since someone who is blind cannot follow Jesus on the road of discipleship. Mark is preparing the careful listener for Peter's (half-correct) confession in the next story. Much as Jesus uncharacteristically asks in this story if the man can see, Jesus will ask in the next story who people think that he is. (The common expectation that the Messiah would be able to give sight to the blind [Ps. 146:8; Isa. 29:18; 32:3; 35:5] also links the two stories.) So this scene exonerates Peter in advance for not being able to understand what it means to say that Jesus is the Christ. Because the full sight of Peter and the other disciples is never narrated in this Gospel, the symbolic reading of this healing becomes a prophecy of future action, providing a hint as to how to read Mark's curious ending (see the Notes on 16:8). In sum, this story is an enacted parable describing how the disciples come to see who Jesus really is. There might also be some irony in terms of how the audience understands the story: they may initially think it is solely a physical healing, but later events in Mark will make clear that that reading is only half-correct, as the audience's own sight expands to include the symbolic elements of the story. The audience would thus have the same experience as the blind man.

While there are many miracles in the HB, including raisings from the dead, there is no record of sight being restored to the blind. Perhaps precisely because there were no instances of healing the blind in the HB, the tradition developed that only the Messiah or the Lord would be able to do this. Thus, when Jesus heals a blind man, he is doing something that many people believed only the Messiah could do. For many audience members, this story would reveal Jesus as the Messiah.

This story has extensive similarities with 7:31–37. In both stories, a man is brought to Jesus, a healing is requested, Jesus takes the man away from the crowd, Jesus uses spit, the person is healed from a sensory-related disability, and there is a command to secrecy.

Mark has probably structured the text so that these two very similar miracles bookend the material in between, all of which concerns the incomprehension of the disciples focused on the questions Jesus poses to his followers in 8:18: "Having eyes, see ye not? and having ears, hear ye not?" The miracles that bracket this discussion show that Jesus is capable of opening eyes that can't see and ears that can't hear; the implication is that the incomprehension of the disciples is something that Jesus will eventually be able to overcome. The symbolism also suggests that the disciples currently have closed ears and eyes. The fact that the second healing occurs in two steps implies that Jesus' ability to make his disciples hear and see will not be instantaneous; the good news is that Jesus is patient. There may also be a bit of irony in the idea that Jesus will not override their agency to instantly open their spiritual ears or eyes and cause a quick (if two-step) healing in the same way that he will heal physical disabilities.

A First Prediction of Death (8:27–9:1)

Greek Text

27 Καὶ ἐξῆλθεν ὁ Ἰησοῦς καὶ οἱ μαθηταὶ αὐτοῦ εἰς τὰς κώμας Καισαρείας τῆς Φιλίππου· καὶ ἐν τῇ ὁδῷ ἐπηρώτα τοὺς μαθητὰς αὐτοῦ λέγων αὐτοῖς· Τίνα με λέγουσιν οἱ ἄνθρωποι εἶναι; 28 οἱ δὲ εἶπαν αὐτῷ λέγοντες ὅτι Ἰωάννην τὸν βαπτιστήν, καὶ ἄλλοι Ἠλίαν, ἄλλοι δὲ ὅτι εἷς τῶν προφητῶν. 29 καὶ αὐτὸς ἐπηρώτα αὐτούς· Ὑμεῖς δὲ τίνα με λέγετε εἶναι; ἀποκριθεὶς ὁ Πέτρος λέγει αὐτῷ· Σὺ εἶ ὁ χριστός. 30 καὶ ἐπετίμησεν αὐτοῖς ἵνα μηδενὶ λέγωσιν περὶ αὐτοῦ.

31 Καὶ ἤρξατο διδάσκειν αὐτοὺς ὅτι δεῖ τὸν υἱὸν τοῦ ἀνθρώπου πολλὰ παθεῖν καὶ ἀποδοκιμασθῆναι ὑπὸ τῶν πρεσβυτέρων καὶ τῶν ἀρχιερέων καὶ τῶν γραμματέων καὶ ἀποκτανθῆναι καὶ μετὰ τρεῖς ἡμέρας ἀναστῆναι· 32 καὶ παρρησίᾳ τὸν λόγον ἐλάλει. καὶ προσλαβόμενος ὁ Πέτρος αὐτὸν ἤρξατο ἐπιτιμᾶν αὐτῷ. 33 ὁ δὲ ἐπιστραφεὶς καὶ ἰδὼν τοὺς μαθητὰς αὐτοῦ ἐπετίμησεν Πέτρῳ καὶ λέγει· Ὕπαγε ὀπίσω μου, Σατανᾶ, ὅτι οὐ φρονεῖς τὰ τοῦ θεοῦ ἀλλὰ τὰ τῶν ἀνθρώπων.

34 Καὶ προσκαλεσάμενος τὸν ὄχλον σὺν τοῖς μαθηταῖς αὐτοῦ εἶπεν αὐτοῖς· Εἴ τις θέλει ὀπίσω μου ἐλθεῖν, ἀπαρνησάσθω ἑαυτὸν καὶ ἀράτω τὸν σταυρὸν αὐτοῦ καὶ ἀκολουθείτω μοι. 35 ὃς γὰρ ἐὰν θέλῃ τὴν ψυχὴν αὐτοῦ σῶσαι ἀπολέσει αὐτήν· ὃς δ' ἂν ἀπολέσει τὴν ψυχὴν αὐτοῦ ἕνεκεν ἐμοῦ καὶ τοῦ εὐαγγελίου σώσει αὐτήν. 36 τί γὰρ ὠφελεῖ ἄνθρωπον κερδῆσαι τὸν κόσμον ὅλον καὶ ζημιωθῆναι τὴν ψυχὴν αὐτοῦ; 37 τί γὰρ δοῖ ἄνθρωπος ἀντάλλαγμα τῆς ψυχῆς αὐτοῦ; 38 ὃς γὰρ ἐὰν ἐπαισχυνθῇ με καὶ τοὺς ἐμοὺς λόγους ἐν τῇ γενεᾷ ταύτῃ τῇ μοιχαλίδι καὶ ἁμαρτωλῷ, καὶ ὁ υἱὸς τοῦ ἀνθρώπου ἐπαισχυνθήσεται αὐτὸν ὅταν ἔλθῃ ἐν τῇ δόξῃ τοῦ πατρὸς αὐτοῦ μετὰ τῶν ἀγγέλων τῶν ἁγίων. 9:1 καὶ ἔλεγεν αὐτοῖς· Ἀμὴν λέγω ὑμῖν ὅτι εἰσίν τινες τῶν ὧδε ἑστηκότων οἵτινες οὐ μὴ γεύσωνται θανάτου ἕως ἂν ἴδωσιν τὴν βασιλείαν τοῦ θεοῦ ἐληλυθυῖαν ἐν δυνάμει. [SBLGNT]

King James Version

27 And Jesus went out, and his disciples, into the towns of Cæsarea Philippi: and by the way he asked his disciples, saying unto them, Whom do men say that I am? 28 And they answered, John the Baptist: but some say, Elias; and others, One of the prophets. 29 And he saith unto them, But whom say ye that I am? And Peter answereth and saith unto him, Thou art the Christ. 30 And he charged them that they should tell no man of him. 31 And he began to teach them, that the Son of man must suffer many things, and be rejected of the elders, and of the chief priests, and scribes, and be killed, and after three days rise again. 32 And he spake that saying openly. And Peter took him, and began to rebuke him. 33 But when he had turned about and looked on his disciples, he rebuked Peter, saying, Get thee behind me, Satan: for thou

New Rendition

27 And Jesus and his disciples went out into the villages of Caesarea Philippi. And on the way, he was questioning his disciples, saying to them, "Who do people say I am?" 28 And they told him, saying, "John the Baptizer, and others [say] Elijah, but others [say] one of the prophets." 29 And he questioned them, "But [all of] you—who do you say I am?" Answering, Peter says to him, "You are the anointed one." 30 And he rebuked them that they should tell no one about him.

31 And he began to teach them that it is necessary for the son of man to suffer many things and to be rejected by the elders and the chief priests and the scriptorians and to be killed and after three days to rise again. 32 And he spoke the word openly. And Peter, having taken him aside, began to rebuke him. 33 And [Jesus] having turned and having

savourest not the things that be of God, but the things that be of men.

34 And when he had called the people unto him with his disciples also, he said unto them, Whosoever will come after me, let him deny himself, and take up his cross, and follow me. 35 For whosoever will save his life shall lose it; but whosoever shall lose his life for my sake and the gospel's, the same shall save it. 36 For what shall it profit a man, if he shall gain the whole world, and lose his own soul? 37 Or what shall a man give in exchange for his soul? 38 Whosoever therefore shall be ashamed of me and of my words in this adulterous and sinful generation; of him also shall the Son of man be ashamed, when he cometh in the glory of his Father with the holy angels. 9:1 And he said unto them, Verily I say unto you, That there be some of them that stand here, which shall not taste of death, till they have seen the kingdom of God come with power.

seen his disciples, he rebuked Peter and says, "Follow me, Satan! For you are not on God's side, but the side of people."

34 And having called the crowd to him, along with his disciples, he said to them, "If anyone wants to come follow me, they must deny themselves and take up their crosses and follow me. 35 For whoever wants to save their souls/lives will destroy them. But whoever destroys their souls/lives for me and for the good news will save them. 36 For what good does it do them to gain the entire world and to lose their souls/lives? 37 For what should they give in exchange for their souls/lives? 38 For if anyone is ashamed of me and my words in this adulterous and sinful generation, the son of man will be ashamed of him or her, when he shall come in the glory of his father, with the holy angels." 9:1 And he was saying to them, "Amen, I say to you: there are some standing here who will not die before they see the kingdom of God having come in power."

Notes

8:27 *And Jesus went out, and his disciples, into the towns of Cæsarea Philippi:* Caesarea Philippi is a region with a main city and smaller settlements; here, as is usually the case, Jesus is going in to the smaller towns and not the main city. This area was associated with the idea of Caesar as lord and with the emperor cult, so the setting is ironically appropriate for the confession of Jesus as the anointed one. The area is also associated with Herod, a link furthered by the fact that the same three answers about Jesus' identity will be given here (8:28) as were given in Herod's story (6:14–16).

This is the extreme northern point of Jesus' ministry, at about twenty-five miles north of the Sea of Galilee, beginning "the way" south to Jerusalem. It is thus an appropriate place to begin this section of his ministry where Jesus is "on the way."

and by the way he asked his disciples, saying unto them: Because "the way" was a technical term for the Christian movement, the setting is not incidental but rather essential: Jesus is asking them this question as part of their discipleship on "the way." The point of being "on the way" is that they learn about Jesus' identity as they proceed.

Normally, students would have asked their rabbi questions, so this question is unexpected, much as when Jesus chose his own disciples (see the Notes on 1:17).

Whom do men say that I am?: While it is possible that Jesus knew the answer to this question before he asked, it is also possible that he is aware that people might not be entirely forthright with him, and he therefore relies on his disciples for access to information: "It is quite possible that the disciples would have had chances of gathering information of this sort, which he would not have himself—for they could mingle with the crowds unnoticed."[10] Regardless, by posing the question, Jesus begins a conversation about his identity. Mark's audience is also invited to ponder the question.

8:28 *And they answered, John the Baptist:* Belief that Jesus was John the Baptist may have been literal (in which case it would reflect ignorance of their overlapping lifespans) or may reflect the sentiment that Jesus' ministry was similar to John's.

but some say, Elias: It was expected that Elijah would return at the end of time (Mal. 4:5–6).

and others, One of the prophets: Ironically, the disciples reveal in this scene that they've done a better job of absorbing what other people say about Jesus than what Jesus says about himself.

No one thinks of Jesus as an ordinary person; all of these options speak to a special status. All three answers include the idea of Jesus being a prophet. That Jesus was considered one of the prophets may reflect the promise of Deuteronomy 18:15–19 that the Lord would someday raise up a prophet.

8:29 *And he saith unto them, But whom say ye that I am?:* "Say" and "ye" are plural here, so the question is directed at all of the disciples—not just Peter. (The New Rendition adds "all of" in brackets to make this point.) The "ye" is emphatic; the New Rendition reflects this by moving it forward and repeating it. The word "but" also suggests a distinction between the

---

10. Cranfield, *Gospel according to St Mark,* 268.

disciples and the others. This question invites the disciples to distinguish themselves from other people.

And Peter answereth and saith unto him, Thou art the Christ: Since 8:30–31 was addressed to all of the disciples and since 8:32 will be as well, Peter is speaking not just for himself but for all of the disciples here. Peter is a leader of the disciples in the sense of speaking for them to Jesus (not, at this point, in the sense of speaking for Jesus to them).

"Christ" could also be translated as "Messiah" or "anointed one" (see the Notes on 1:1). For Mark's audience, "Christ" is a title for Jesus, but when Peter spoke it, he may have simply meant "the anointed one" in a more limited sense. (As the rest of this passage will show, Peter does not yet have a full understanding of what it means to say that Jesus is the Christ.) While there was quite a bit of messianic expectation at this time, there was "little or no expectation in early Judaism that Messiah would come and suffer."[11] Rather, the expectation was for a victorious military and political figure who would throw off the shackles of Roman rule.

The audience has known since 1:1 that Jesus is the anointed one. Part of the experience that the audience has in listening to Mark's Gospel is to witness the disciples coming to the same knowledge.

See also the Notes on 8:32.

8:30 *And he charged them that they should tell no man of him:* "Charged" is the same word translated as "rebuked" when Jesus exorcises demons (1:25; 3:12; 9:25). Peter has just announced Jesus' identity; to rebuke Peter using the same language used to rebuke demons suggests some parallels between this incident and the exorcisms, with Peter in the role of the demon—a shocking association to be sure, which will be further enhanced when Jesus calls Peter "Satan." These overtones of exorcism point to the idea that, like the demonic proclamations of Jesus' identity, Peter's statement may be technically true but nonetheless inappropriate.

Why does Jesus command secrecy about his identity?

1. Because "Rome would not have tolerated an open proclamation of messiahship by so popular and influential a leader."[12] This means that, ironically, Peter's proclamation that Jesus is the Christ puts Jesus' life in danger.

2. It will not be until Jesus' trial in 14:61–62 when he publicly claims the title Messiah: "Only when Jesus was a helpless prisoner in the hands of his enemies and his messianic claims must seem ridiculous was his messiahship to

---

11. Witherington, *Gospel of Mark*, 240.
12. Stein, *Mark*, 400.

be openly proclaimed."[13] This is a crucial data point in understanding Jesus' identity and the importance of intertwining the suffering and glorious aspects of his messiahship. It is immediately after Peter's confession that Jesus begins to teach that he will suffer and die.

3. The anointing of Jesus will explain what it means for Jesus to be the anointed/Messiah/Christ (see the Analysis of 14:3–9). Until that point, the title "Christ" would be misunderstood and therefore should not be used.

8:31 *And he began to teach them:* The use of "began" signals that Jesus is initiating a new teaching here. It appears that his teachings about his suffering and death are prompted by Peter's declaration that Jesus is the Christ.

that the Son of man must suffer many things: Jesus refers to himself as "the Son of Man," not as the Christ. He may have regarded the former title as more appropriate since it did not have the political connotations that "Christ" had.

"Must" translates a Greek word (*dei*) that points to the necessity for something to happen. Some interpret it as reflecting God's will, although in this case that would suggest that those who caused Jesus to suffer were doing God's will—a questionable position. Thus, it probably implies inevitability: given how Jesus chose to minister and teach, his death was inevitable.[14]

"Many things" could also be translated as "much suffering" or "great suffering."

The concept that the Messiah would die was unprecedented in first-century Judaism since the title was linked to kingship, which explains why this teaching was a difficult one for the disciples to accept.

and be rejected of the elders: The elders, combined with the chief priests and the scribes, formed the Sanhedrin, which was the leading Jewish council.

Mark's only other use of the word "rejected" is in 12:10, quoting Psalm 118:22, where the rejected cornerstone becomes the chief cornerstone.

The phrasing of this verse implies that the rejection by religious leaders is just as much a component of Jesus' prophesied Passion as the suffering, dying, and rising, although the element of rejection garners much less attention than the other three items in nearly all Christian traditions.

and of the chief priests, and scribes: "Chief priests" refers to the high priests, former and current, and possibly their family members as well.

---

13. Cranfield, *Gospel according to St Mark,* 271.

14. Raquel A. St. Clair, *Call and Consequence: A Womanist Reading of Mark* (Minneapolis: Fortress Press, 2008), 113–14.

and be killed: Nothing specific about the method of Jesus' death is mentioned here, which is especially intriguing in light of the coming reference to taking up the cross (8:34). It is interesting to speculate as to what level of knowledge Jesus had about his death—this verse indicates that he may not have been aware of its precise circumstances (compare 13:32). It is also possible that he was aware but chose not to share details with his disciples at this point.

Because "killed" is mentioned separately from "be rejected," it distances responsibility for Jesus' death from the Jewish leaders. While Roman leaders are immediately responsible for Jesus' death, they are not named specifically in this verse. This may reflect Jesus' (and/or Mark's) need to be circumspect to avoid trouble with the authorities. Nonetheless, the text suggests that the Jewish leaders are responsible for rejecting Jesus but the Roman leaders are responsible for killing him.

and after three days rise again: The phrase "after three days" implies "on the fourth day." Mark will later describe Jesus' rising as happening on the third day (16:1); there are three ways to interpret this apparent discrepancy:

1. It is possible that Mark's writing is sloppy here and thus creates a chronological problem.

2. In the HB, "three days" sometimes means a short, indeterminate amount of time,[15] so it is possible that Jesus is speaking generally here and not specifically. This general language regarding timing would match the reference to Jesus' dying, which also lacks specifics. So Jesus prophesies his coming death and Resurrection but does not do so with specificity. There would then be some irony in the fact that Mark's audience was likely aware that Jesus' language was very close to being literally true. The HB idiom may particularly relate to Hosea 6:2, which has been interpreted to picture the Lord raising up the dead after three days.

3. The Resurrection is in fact *after* three days when timed from the rejection or the suffering (not from Jesus' death, as it is usually calculated). This approach may be of particular interest to Latter-day Saint readers, who emphasize Jesus' suffering in Gethsemane as much as—if not more than—his suffering on the cross.

8:32 *And he spake that saying openly:* "That saying" refers to the Passion prediction; it can be translated as "the word" and may be a technical term for preaching the gospel, which is how the New Rendition takes it. It is possible to translate this as "he spoke this saying openly," and perhaps Mark is

15. Mark Proctor, "'After Three Days' in Mark 8:31; 9:31; 10:34: Subordinating Jesus' Resurrection in the Second Gospel," *Perspectives in Religious Studies* 30, no. 4 (2003): 399–424.

playing with the ambiguity (which is then doubly ironic because then this phrase itself is not open but rather has a veiled meaning). The technical reading of "the word" emphasizes the idea that this passage reveals a new stage of Jesus' teachings to the disciples.

Mark makes several grammatical moves to emphasize the idea that Jesus taught about his death in advance: "The addition of ['openly'], its placement in first position after the conjunction, and the advance of ['the saying'] to second position, ahead of the verb, put great weight on the point that Jesus really did teach the disciples beforehand about his passion and resurrection."[16]

There may also be a layer of irony in the contrast between this "open" teaching and the command not to tell anyone that Jesus was the Christ: suffering can be spoken of openly, but the glorious identity of Jesus as the Christ must be kept hidden. In fact, Jesus will speak of the necessity of suffering openly beginning in 8:34. Speaking openly also contrasts with how Jesus previously spoke in parables. Contra the parables, this time the meaning should be plain and should not require any special effort at hearing on the part of the audience. When Jesus speaks clearly, he is rebuked, as happens in this verse ("And Peter . . . began to rebuke him"). By contrast, when he spoke in a veiled manner through parables, the disciples sought clarification; this dynamic might explain why Jesus spoke in parables.

As mentioned previously, Jesus' two-step healing of the blind man serves as an enacted parable for his teaching of the disciples. The use of the word "openly" in this verse may point to the process of opening their eyes.[17]

And Peter took him, and began to rebuke him: Peter's action of "taking" Jesus indicates that Peter took Jesus aside from the other disciples. It "may portray a gesture of superiority or patronization."[18] Peter apparently thought Jesus' prophecy was embarrassing, and so he wants to correct Jesus privately. Just as Jesus has taught his disciples privately concerning matters that he did not teach to the crowd, here Peter assumes the role of Jesus' teacher. The wrongheadedness of taking Jesus aside is highlighted by Jesus' response in the next verse, where he answers Peter in front of the entire group. Further, given that Jesus is "on the way," Peter's action of taking him aside symbolically suggests that he is trying to divert Jesus

---

16. Gundry, *Mark,* 431.

17. Kevin W. Larsen, "A Focused Christological Reading of Mark 8:22–9:13," *Trinity Journal,* n.s., 26 (Spring 2005): 41.

18. Stein, *Mark,* 402.

from "the way"; Peter literally attempts to remove Jesus from the path of discipleship. But as the next verse will indicate, Jesus immediately returns.

The word "began" translates the same word used to describe Jesus beginning to teach about his Passion (8:31), so there is a verbal echo: as Jesus began to teach, Peter began to rebuke. This is another indication that Peter is usurping Jesus' role. And much as Jesus had been performing miracles but then shifted to teaching about his Passion, the disciples had previously been merely confused but have now shifted to rebuking Jesus.

The Passion prediction ended on a positive note: Jesus would rise from the dead. But presumably, this is not what Peter is rebuking Jesus for saying; rather, Peter has focused on the less pleasant aspects of the prediction.

In 1:11, immediately after the announcement that Jesus was God's son, Jesus was tempted. Here, immediately after the announcement that Jesus is the Christ, Jesus is tempted by Peter's effort to get him to renounce his mission.

See also the Notes on 9:11, where the scribes' teachings about Elijah's role is implicated in the disciples' inability to understand that the Son of Man will need to suffer and die.

8:33 *But when he had turned about and looked on his disciples:* Mark cleverly uses indicators of narrative space here: Jesus turns and thus includes the other disciples in a conversation that Peter had tried to have privately. Thus Jesus rejects Peter's effort to treat Jesus as a disciple who needs to be privately corrected; instead, Jesus assumes the role of teacher addressing the entire group of disciples.

It is possible that the phrase "his disciples" is meant to suggest that, at this moment, Peter is not counted as one of the disciples (compare 16:7, where Peter is also mentioned separately from the disciples; in both texts there is the implied promise that Peter may choose to rejoin the disciples).

he rebuked Peter, saying: This is the same word for rebuke as in 8:32, so Peter and Jesus are rebuking each other. The language evokes an exorcism since those stories also use the same word for rebuke, show concern for how Jesus should be named, and include references to Satan. Much as the demons were able to correctly identify Jesus but their proclamation was not appropriate and therefore needed to be silenced, Peter was able to identify Jesus as the Christ but was commanded not to do so.

Get thee behind me, Satan: While it is possible to read "get thee behind me" to mean that Jesus wants Peter to get out of his sight, it is preferable to read it as a command for Peter to resume being Jesus' disciple. The words translated as "behind me" (Greek: *opisō mou*) are precisely the same words used when Jesus called Peter to follow him initially (1:17; KJV: "after me"). In other words, Jesus is ordering Peter to resume being a disciple and to stop treating Jesus as his disciple. This language also acknowledges that Jesus is "on the way" of discipleship and that Peter's taking him aside interferes with that path; Peter is thus asked to fall in line behind Jesus so Jesus can resume leading the journey of discipleship. Peter had attempted to get Jesus off the path literally (by taking Jesus aside) and symbolically (by rebuking Jesus' prophecy of his suffering); Jesus responds by returning to the path of discipleship literally (by turning back to the disciples) and symbolically (by inviting Peter to follow him). Interestingly, it is not only the suffering and death themselves that will be a trial for Jesus, but even teaching his own closest disciples about it will result in difficulties.

"Satan" is the appropriate and necessary label for someone who rebukes Jesus, the Christ, for announcing God's will. In other words, Jesus has just taught that his suffering and death reflects God's will; for Peter to rebuke Jesus for this teaching is to rebuke God's plan. It is Satan who rebukes God's plan; hence, it is appropriate for Jesus to call Peter "Satan" since that is the role that Peter assumes in this exchange. Ultimately, this dialogue between Jesus and Peter boils down to an issue of authority: is it Jesus or is it Peter who has the authority to determine God's will for Jesus' life? Calling Peter "Satan" is harsh, but it needs to be read in the context of the invitation to Peter to resume the path of discipleship. Thus, identifying Peter with Satan does not disqualify him from discipleship; rather, he is specifically invited to return to acting as a disciple. Jesus' further teachings on what it means to be a disciple (8:34) also make the point that Jesus' response to Peter is not rejection but correction and invitation.

The use of the term "Satan" extends the exorcism motif of the passage by clarifying that Peter is on Satan's side. Since names are frequently used in exorcisms as an effort to gain control over the other party, it is possible that Peter thinks that his "naming" of Jesus as the Christ gave him some measure of control over Jesus, which he then exercises by removing Jesus from his path and attempting to correct him via rebuke. Jesus' calling Peter "Satan" thus makes clear that it is Jesus who is in control in this encounter and Jesus who will succeed in this (symbolic) exorcism. This is not the first time that Jesus has renamed Peter, who was first called Simon, and thus shows his authority over Peter.

The reference to Satan also forges a link to the story of Jesus' temptation: the initial proclamation of Jesus as the Son of God at his baptism was immediately followed by temptation from Satan; the proclamation of

Jesus as the Christ is immediately followed by the temptation to avoid the path of suffering, from one who takes on the role of Satan. At the inauguration of both halves of his ministry, Jesus is tested by the satanic temptation to depart from the mission that has been set for him. Calling Peter "Satan" may also have suggested a link to Jesus' efforts to silence the demons when they inappropriately tried to name Jesus (1:25, 34).

In chapter 4, the stony soil (Greek: *petrōdēs*; compare "Peter," Greek: *petros*) initially experiences explosive growth, which might be compared to Peter's confession that Jesus is the Christ, but as soon as the sun rises, the plant is scorched, which might be compared to Jesus' teachings about his suffering and death.

for thou savourest not the things that be of God, but the things that be of men: This line is an explanation of what has come before it, justifying Jesus' calling Peter "Satan."

Most translations take this line to refer to Peter thinking the way people think and not the way God thinks, but the New Rendition takes it instead to refer to being on God's side or the side of people, based on the idea that the Greek reflects an idiom that refers to taking sides.[19]

The structure is somewhat surprising: it would perhaps have been more logical to conclude with a reference to the things of Satan instead of the things of men. But Jesus' words implicitly teach that "the natural man is an enemy to God" (Mosiah 3:19). In this case, avoidance of suffering and death are the "things of men" upon which Peter is focused; these are not the things of God—an idea that should have been clear when Jesus explained the necessity for his suffering and death in 8:31. The next section of text contains Jesus' teachings on the need for disciples to be willing to suffer and so continues the teachings in this section. It is thus still part of the response to Peter's rebuke.

8:34 And when he had called the people unto him with his disciples also, he said unto them: A crowd is summoned, but the topic of the last section continues as Jesus explains more about what Peter did not understand: the need for Jesus and his disciples to be willing to suffer. In that sense, there is a strong continuity between 8:33 and 8:34.

Mark calls attention to the fact that Jesus gathers the crowd here, indicating that suffering as a part of discipleship is not limited just to Jesus or to his inner circle of disciples but rather extends to all who choose to

---

19. Gerald Wheaton, "Thinking the Things of God? The Translation and Meaning of Mark 8:33c," *Novum Testamentum* 56 (2015): 42–56.

follow him. Because Jesus is in gentile lands, the broadest possible crowd is invited to follow the path of discipleship and warned that suffering is to be expected.

In LXX Exodus 3:18 and 5:3, the same Greek word is used as is here translated as "called," so there might be an allusion to the Lord calling the children of Israel to follow Moses.

Whosoever will come after me, let him deny himself: "Whosoever" suggests that discipleship is open to all who would follow Jesus' conditions. "After me" translates the same phrase as was found in 8:33 (KJV: "behind me") and in the original calls of the disciples (1:17, 18, 20; 2:14). Here, a new level of commitment is required as Jesus explains that coming after him requires self-denial. This is a response to Peter's rebuke on two levels: first, as the leader and teacher, Jesus' own suffering implies that his disciples will need to suffer as well. Second, Peter's desires to direct Jesus' ministry and to follow a Messiah who does not suffer are impulses that must be denied.

"Let him deny himself" is a singular third-person command ("he or she should deny himself or herself"). The New Rendition renders it as a plural in order to make it gender inclusive while avoiding the awkward multiple pronouns.

In the last verse, Jesus commanded Peter to resume being a disciple. In this verse, he describes precisely what it means to be a disciple. So Jesus' response to Peter's mistake includes an invitation to return and the teachings that make that return possible.

The idea of denying oneself will be shown to be limited to those spheres where one's will conflicts with God's; it is not a blanket denial of the self. For example, in 5:26–29, Jesus ends human suffering, suggesting limits to self-denial. As the line below indicates, self-denial is linked to the persecution that comes from following Jesus.

and take up his cross, and follow me: The idea of taking up a cross refers to the practice of the condemned having to carry his own cross (technically, just the beam) to the crucifixion site. Jesus has not spoken specifically of his own crucifixion in Mark, so it is possible but unlikely that Jesus' audience would have heard a specific allusion to Jesus' own death here. Mark's audience knows better, of course.

In modern usage, taking up one's cross serves as a figurative description of enduring even minor hardship, but in Jesus' and in Mark's contexts, it would have been heard as a literal invitation not just to suffering but also to martyrdom. The cross was used for the torture and execution of political prisoners; one generally had to have challenged Roman authority in some manner to merit death on the cross. To take up one's cross means to die in an extremely painful, public, and humiliating manner; thus "Jesus' statement must have sounded repugnant to the crowd and the disciples alike."[20] So Jesus' words here "would not be seen as an appealing call to discipleship."[21]

8:35 *For whosoever will save his life shall lose it:* There is a fourfold repetition of the word "for" (Greek: *gar*) in 8:35, 36, 37, and 38. Each instance serves as an explanation for why one would want to follow Jesus given the terrible cost that discipleship will demand.

Once again, the New Rendition translates singular pronouns as plural in order to avoid specifying a gender. Given that Jesus is addressing a crowd, the plural is not inappropriate although the invitation is issued to each individual and not to the crowd collectively.

The word "life" can also be translated as "soul" or "oneself." The word also appears in 8:36 and 8:37, and the passage seems to play with the multiple possible meanings of the word: in 8:35, it refers to the physical body, but 8:36 and 8:37 probably refer to the soul. Thus there are different nuances of meaning in the same word in its various occurrences.

but whosoever shall lose his life for my sake and the gospel's, the same shall save it: This statement directly responds to Peter's desire to "save" Jesus' life (by discouraging him from a mission of suffering and death), which, as Jesus explains here, would result in Jesus eventually losing his life. Jesus' self-abnegation serves as a model for his disciples.

The reference to taking up one's cross was shocking. Here, in explaining why anyone would still want to follow Jesus in the face of that warning/promise, Jesus explains that anyone willing to give up her life/soul for him will actually save her life/soul. Jesus relativizes Rome's power by showing that Rome only has control over the physical body, but following Jesus means saving one's soul.

8:36 *For what shall it profit a man, if he shall gain the whole world, and lose his own soul?:* Again, the New Rendition translates singulars as plurals in order to avoid gendered pronouns.

The phrase "gain the whole world" probably means to possess all of the wealth in the world. Jesus' message is that economic gain—even extreme economic gain—is not worth as much as one's soul.

---

20. Lane, *Gospel according to Mark*, 307.
21. Witherington, *Gospel of Mark*, 245.

8:37 *Or what shall a man give in exchange for his soul?:* This rhetorical question points out that there is nothing worth exchanging one's soul for—not even, as the last verse indicated, all of the wealth in the world. Therefore, denying oneself in order to follow Jesus is a reasonable course of action.

Relationship to Psalm 49. Psalm 49 has important resonances with this passage in Mark and may have inspired Jesus' statements here. The psalm begins by announcing that the speaker will speak important truths (verse 3). Then Psalm 49:6–7 argues that no amount of money is enough to ransom a human being from her final destiny. Psalm 49:10–13 points to death as the end for those who cared about wealth. But Psalm 49:15 indicates that God will rescue the speaker's life. The psalm highlights the theme of God's intervention as making the saving of souls possible and thus points to a theology of Atonement behind Jesus' words here in Mark.

8:38 *Whosoever therefore shall be ashamed of me and of my words:* Some manuscripts omit the word "words,"[22] which gives the text the meaning of "my followers" (the noun for "followers" is not present, but the "my" is read as "mine," implying "my people," or more specifically "my followers"). It is possible that the word for "words" was there originally and accidentally dropped out, making the KJV reading the earlier one, but it is also possible that "my words" is a later addition, perhaps added to parallel Luke 9:26. If "my followers" is the better reading, it creates a nice parallel to the reference to the angels at the end of the verse. In either case, Jesus presents being ashamed of him and his words/followers as the opposite of following him.

In chapter 14, Peter will reveal himself to be ashamed of Jesus, but 16:7 holds out hope for Peter's return to discipleship. So by analogy, this verse probably assumes that repentance is possible as well, although it is not specifically mentioned here.

In Isaiah 52–53, many people are ashamed of the suffering servant, who was interpreted by early Christians as a symbol for Jesus. It is possible that the language here in Mark is meant to evoke that text.

in this adulterous and sinful generation: While it is possible that literal adultery is meant here, it is perhaps more likely that adultery is functioning as a symbol for idolatry, which would extend the metaphor of denying

---

22. Metzger, *Textual Commentary*, 84.

oneself—in this case, denying one's desire to follow another god, one whose path did not involve suffering.

of him also shall the Son of man be ashamed: There is a strong note of reciprocity between the person ashamed of Jesus and Jesus' shame at that person.

when he cometh in the glory of his Father with the holy angels: "Father" is an unusual term for Mark but also a logical counterpart to the reference to the son in the previous verse.

Many interpreters assume that Jesus is describing the Second Coming here, but it is also possible that Jesus is describing the Transfiguration (see 9:2–9; "angels" can be translated as "messengers" and thus could describe Elijah and Moses). It might also describe Jesus' ascension after his death (in this reading, he would be coming into the presence of God) and subsequent enthronement. Regardless of which particular moment is envisioned here, the picture is a profound contrast with Jesus' recent teachings about his suffering. It is clear that suffering is not a permanent state but rather has an end.

In Daniel 7:13–14, one like the Son of Man is given great glory in the presence of God. If this allusion is intentional, it supports the reading of this text as describing the time when Jesus is enthroned in the presence of God. (See the discussion of the title "Son of Man" in appendix F: "Titles for Jesus in Mark.")

9:1 ***And he said unto them, Verily I say unto you:*** This verse is probably better understood as the conclusion to chapter 8 rather than the first words of chapter 9 for the following reasons:

1. When it is placed at the beginning of chapter 9, it is orphaned without a setting or an audience.

2. Mark generally begins scenes by making reference to a new location, which means that 9:2 reads more naturally as the beginning of the story.

3. Reading 9:1 as the beginning of the story of the Transfiguration strongly encourages the audience to view it as the introduction to the Transfiguration, which is not the only possible interpretation.

4. The link between 9:1's reference to the kingdom of God coming and 8:38's reference to the Son of Man coming (in glory) is obscured by the chapter division.

5. To the extent that 8:38 is a warning, 9:1 is a corresponding promise, and thus they should be read together.

Of course, in the context of an oral performance, the placement of the chapter division is not an issue since the audience perceives the story as a unified whole.

See the Notes on 3:28 regarding the importance of the phrase "verily I say unto you," which serves as Jesus' attestation of the authenticity of what he is about to say.

That there be some of them that stand here, which shall not taste of death: The word "not" is emphatic.

till they have seen the kingdom of God come with power: The word "see" may echo the two-step healing of the blind man. The word translated as "power" is the same term used to describe Jesus' miracles, although it is possible that a broader view of power is intended here.

This verse is rather difficult to understand because it is not entirely clear what is meant by the kingdom of God coming with power. Interpretation of this verse depends on the interpretation of 1:15, which also mentioned the coming of the kingdom:

1. If 1:15 implies that the kingdom had already come, then the emphasis in this verse is on its coming "in power." This reading is supported by the fact that the word "coming" is perfect in this verse (this is why the New Rendition uses "having come," even though it is somewhat awkward in English), which implies that the kingdom has already come (although people may not yet be aware of it). Thus, the change is not in the coming of the kingdom; the change is in people's awareness of what has happened. There may be a link to the parable in 4:30–32, where the seed was always present, but its growth was not initially obvious. If this is the better reading, then Jesus' message is that the kingdom has already come, but it will take time for some people to realize it and some may die without realizing it.

2. If 1:15 implies that the kingdom has not yet come and this verse thus describes the coming of the kingdom, there are several options for the event to which it refers:

    a. The Transfiguration. This reading makes sense of the fact that this verse comes immediately before Mark's account of the Transfiguration. If this is the best reading, it is an important interpretive clue to an otherwise enigmatic story since it indicates that the point of the Transfiguration is to show the kingdom of God coming in power. In this reading, there are two options for the identity of those who do not experience death before they see the coming of the kingdom:

        i. This group consists of Peter, James,[23] and John, who witness the Transfiguration. The problem with this reading is that it is odd to describe them as not dying before an event that happens barely a week later.

        ii. Those who would not die refers to Moses and Elijah. (It was believed that Moses had not died; see the Notes on 9:4.) This interpretation,

---

23. See the Notes on 1:19.

however, seems to require that Moses and Elijah are present when Jesus speaks these words—something that the text otherwise doesn't suggest.

b. Jesus' death on the cross.

c. The Resurrection.

d. The bestowal of the Spirit at Pentecost (see Acts 2).

e. The growth of the early Christian church, understood as a "kingdom" of saints.

f. The Second Coming of Jesus, which means that this prophecy was not fulfilled. (Latter-day Saints would probably not ascribe a false prophecy to Jesus but might consider this verse a later tradition incorrectly attributed to Jesus. Latter-day Saint readers might, under the influence of 3 Nephi 28 and D&C 7, read this passage as a reference to a disciple who will not die, but this interpretation probably would not have occurred to Mark's early audiences.)

g. Jesus' appearance in the Book of Mormon. Heather Hardy makes the case that "an Israelite remnant . . . recognized the resurrected Jesus as the promised Messiah, and he established God's kingdom among them within the lifetime of the generation that had rejected him a hemisphere away,"[24] thus fulfilling the prophesy in 9:1. One weakness of this reading is that it would imply that there were some in Jesus' presence who would witness the kingdom established in the Book of Mormon; the only possible contender for this seems to be Jesus, and that would require a rather elliptical way of speaking.

While this verse presents difficult interpretive issues, it is also, ironically enough, perhaps a testament to the fidelity of the biblical record: given the potential for this passage to be understood as a false prophecy by Jesus, one could understand the desire of scribes to delete it from the record. So its inclusion in the text speaks to the scribes' faithfulness to the tradition, even under difficult circumstances.

Analysis

When Peter calls Jesus the Christ, there is a sense in which he uses the correct term to describe Jesus but almost certainly attaches the wrong meaning to it, as 8:32 will suggest. This usage of a correct term with an incorrect meaning is an example of Mark's irony. It will remain for Jesus to redefine

---

24. Heather Hardy, "'Saving Christianity': The Nephite Fulfillment of Jesus' Eschatological Prophecies," *Journal of Book of Mormon Studies* 23 (2014): 28.

the term (see the Analysis of 14:3–9); until that point, Jesus asks his disciples not to use this confusing term (8:30), and he refers to himself as the Son of Man (8:31). As Jesus' rebuke in 8:30 will indicate, Peter's announcement is akin to the demons' ability to correctly identify Jesus: the correct words are used, but the proclamation is still not appropriate. The fact that Peter rebukes Jesus also indicates that Peter does not fully understand what it means to say that Jesus is the Christ.

Because this passage began with the disciples relaying to Jesus some misconceptions about his identity (that is, that Jesus is John the Baptist, Elijah, or one of the prophets) and ends with Jesus' command to silence, the necessary result is that people will continue to operate under false beliefs about Jesus' true identity. It is interesting that, at this point in the narrative, correcting those false beliefs is not Jesus' first priority.

Jesus' description of his suffering and death nuances Peter's confession by explaining what it means for Jesus to be the anointed one: it will involve suffering, rejection, death, and then being raised from the dead. Jesus calls himself the Son of Man and not Christ, and he focuses on suffering and death, not on glory, royal power, or victory. And yet the note of victory is still present, not in the expected political terms but rather when Jesus is raised from the dead.

Jesus' prophecy of his suffering and death begins a new stage of his teaching, signaled by the phrase "began to teach." (There were only the most subtle of allusions to Jesus' death previously, in 2:20; 3:6; and 6:17–29.) This is the first of three Passion predictions in Mark (9:31; 10:33–34), each of which involve direct teaching on the subject of Jesus' death and Resurrection. It seems that the "Christ" proclamation by Peter prompted this new stage of teaching because the disciples were now ready for it: now that Peter and the disciples have the half-sight that Jesus is the Christ, Jesus begins teaching them about the second component of his mission, which involves suffering and death.

Peter's rebuke shows how a high level of understanding ("thou art the Christ") can co-exist with a very low level of understanding (that it was appropriate for Peter to rebuke Jesus). This rebuke is crucial to understanding Peter's frame of mind when he said that Jesus was the Christ: at this point, Peter cannot accept the idea that the Christ will suffer and die. He also does not recognize Jesus' supreme authority but instead considers it his role to correct Jesus. If the two-step healing of the blind is an enacted parable to explain Jesus' granting spiritual insight to his disciples, then Peter is half-blind at this point.

Mark's penchant for irony shines here as the first thing that happens after Jesus prophesies that he will be rejected is that Jesus' teachings are rejected—and by one of his own disciples. This event also foreshadows Peter's later rejection of Jesus (14:68).

Jesus teaches that the disciples must deny themselves. To deny does not mean merely to deny oneself certain pleasures but more fundamentally to deny one's own will—in this case, by choosing a path that involves suffering. It does not imply that the disciple does not have a will but rather that she chooses to follow God's will when it conflicts with her own (see also 14:36 and the Notes on that verse). This should not be interpreted as a general command to deny all aspects of human will; it only applies in instances where human will conflicts with divine will (as the incident above with Peter demonstrated). The point here is that when Jesus' ministry leads to persecution, Jesus and his disciples must deny themselves in order to endure that persecution.

In a sense, Jesus' invitation to self-denial constitutes a second calling of his disciples: they are now asked not only to follow him (which, in the early chapters of Mark, involved abandoning one's occupation), but they are also being asked to be prepared to die an excruciating death. Just as Jesus' presentation of himself shifts from an authoritative, miracle-working teacher in the first portion of the Gospel to someone on his way to suffering and death here, the duties of discipleship shift as well. Significantly, the invitation to discipleship is accompanied not by promises of blessings but rather by promises of suffering.[25]

There appears to be a paradoxical relationship between Jesus' distancing himself from the political connotations of the title "Christ" and his exhortation to take up the cross—the instrument of death for political enemies of Rome—here. But this is the essence of Jesus' message to his disciples: be prepared to be treated as a political enemy even though you are not one.

The interpretation of Jesus' words about the kingdom coming in power generally focuses on the coming of the kingdom, but it may be that Jesus is emphasizing instead the impending deaths of some of his audience: many of them will not have the opportunity to see the kingdom come in power before they die. Thus, this is a warning that the path of discipleship, full of persecution, does not necessarily include dramatic spiritual manifestations.

---

25. Dewey, "Women in the Gospel of Mark," 25.

JESUS IS TRANSFIGURED (9:2–13)

Greek Text

2 Καὶ μετὰ ἡμέρας ἓξ παραλαμβάνει ὁ Ἰησοῦς τὸν Πέτρον καὶ τὸν Ἰάκωβον καὶ Ἰωάννην, καὶ ἀναφέρει αὐτοὺς εἰς ὄρος ὑψηλὸν κατ' ἰδίαν μόνους. καὶ μετεμορφώθη ἔμπροσθεν αὐτῶν, 3 καὶ τὰ ἱμάτια αὐτοῦ ἐγένετο στίλβοντα λευκὰ λίαν οἷα γναφεὺς ἐπὶ τῆς γῆς οὐ δύναται οὕτως λευκᾶναι. 4 καὶ ὤφθη αὐτοῖς Ἠλίας σὺν Μωϋσεῖ, καὶ ἦσαν συλλαλοῦντες τῷ Ἰησοῦ. 5 καὶ ἀποκριθεὶς ὁ Πέτρος λέγει τῷ Ἰησοῦ· Ῥαββί, καλόν ἐστιν ἡμᾶς ὧδε εἶναι, καὶ ποιήσωμεν τρεῖς σκηνάς, σοὶ μίαν καὶ Μωϋσεῖ μίαν καὶ Ἠλίᾳμίαν. 6 οὐ γὰρ ᾔδει τί ἀποκριθῇ, ἔκφοβοι γὰρ ἐγένοντο. 7 καὶ ἐγένετο νεφέλη ἐπισκιάζουσα αὐτοῖς, καὶ ἐγένετο φωνὴ ἐκ τῆς νεφέλης· Οὗτός ἐστιν ὁ υἱός μου ὁ ἀγαπητός, ἀκούετε αὐτοῦ. 8 καὶ ἐξάπινα περιβλεψάμενοι οὐκέτι οὐδένα εἶδον ἀλλὰ τὸν Ἰησοῦν μόνον μεθ' ἑαυτῶν.

9 Καὶ καταβαινόντων αὐτῶν ἐκ τοῦ ὄρους διεστείλατο αὐτοῖς ἵνα μηδενὶ ἃ εἶδον διηγήσωνται, εἰ μὴ ὅταν ὁ υἱὸς τοῦ ἀνθρώπου ἐκ νεκρῶν ἀναστῇ. 10 καὶ τὸν λόγον ἐκράτησαν πρὸς ἑαυτοὺς συζητοῦντες τί ἐστιν τὸ ἐκ νεκρῶν ἀναστῆναι. 11 καὶ ἐπηρώτων αὐτὸν λέγοντες· Ὅτι λέγουσιν οἱ γραμματεῖς ὅτι Ἠλίαν δεῖ ἐλθεῖν πρῶτον; 12 ὁ δὲ ἔφη αὐτοῖς· Ἠλίας μὲν ἐλθὼν πρῶτον ἀποκαθιστάνει πάντα, καὶ πῶς γέγραπται ἐπὶ τὸν υἱὸν τοῦ ἀνθρώπου ἵνα πολλὰ πάθῃ καὶ ἐξουδενηθῇ; 13 ἀλλὰ λέγω ὑμῖν ὅτι καὶ Ἠλίας ἐλήλυθεν, καὶ ἐποίησαν αὐτῷ ὅσα ἤθελον, καθὼς γέγραπται ἐπ' αὐτόν. [SBLGNT]

King James Version

2 And after six days Jesus taketh with him Peter, and James, and John, and leadeth them up into an high mountain apart by themselves: and he was transfigured before them. 3 And his raiment became shining, exceeding white as snow; so as no fuller on earth can white them. 4 And there appeared unto them Elias with Moses: and they were talking with Jesus. 5 And Peter answered and said to Jesus, Master, it is good for us to be here: and let us make three tabernacles; one for thee, and one for Moses, and one for Elias. 6 For he wist not what to say; for they were sore afraid. 7 And there was a cloud that overshadowed them: and a voice came out of

New Rendition

2 And after six days, Jesus takes with him Peter and Jacob and John and leads them up apart into a high mountain themselves alone. And he was changed in appearance in their presence. 3 And his clothing became intensely, brilliantly white, as no launderer on the earth is able to whiten it. 4 And Elijah with Moses appeared to them, and they were talking with Jesus. 5 And interjecting, Peter says to Jesus, "Rabbi, it is good for us to be here. And let us make three shelters—one for you and one for Moses and one for Elijah." 6 For he did not know what he should say, for they were terrified. 7 And a cloud came, covering them, and a voice came out of the

the cloud, saying, This is my beloved Son: hear him. 8 And suddenly, when they had looked round about, they saw no man any more, save Jesus only with themselves. 9 And as they came down from the mountain, he charged them that they should tell no man what things they had seen, till the Son of man were risen from the dead. 10 And they kept that saying with themselves, questioning one with another what the rising from the dead should mean.

11 And they asked him, saying, Why say the scribes that Elias must first come? 12 And he answered and told them, Elias verily cometh first, and restoreth all things; and how it is written of the Son of man, that he must suffer many things, and be set at nought. 13 But I say unto you, That Elias is indeed come, and they have done unto him whatsoever they listed, as it is written of him.

cloud: "This is my son, the beloved one. Listen to him." 8 And suddenly, having looked around, they no longer saw anyone except Jesus alone with them.

9 And as they were descending from the mountain, he instructed them that they should tell no one what they had seen, not until after the son of man had risen from the dead. 10 And they kept that matter to themselves, questioning what it is to rise from the dead. 11 And they were asking him, saying, "Why do the scriptorians say that it is necessary for Elijah to come first?" 12 And he was saying to them, "Does Elijah indeed, having come first, restore everything? And why is it written of the son of man that he should suffer many things and be scorned? 13 But I say to you that Elijah has come, and they did to him whatever they wanted, as it has been written of him."

Notes

9:2 *And after six days:* "After six days" is one of the only time references in the first two-thirds of Mark's story. Why does Mark employ a concrete time marker here?

1. If it has been six days since Jesus' words in the previous verse, then the phrase "after six days" links the Transfiguration to 9:1, which verse can then be read as a prophecy of the Transfiguration. While this reading fits the context, it is not without difficulty: in 9:1, Jesus said that there were some present who would not die until they saw the kingdom come, but that is unusual language for an event that happens barely a week later (unless the point is that the kingdom came even more quickly than Jesus himself had anticipated). At the same time, it would serve as a powerful reminder to Mark's audience that Jesus' prophecies would actually come to pass—and quickly.

2. If 9:1 is read as the conclusion to chapter 8 (see the Notes on 9:1), then Mark does not reveal what event the Transfiguration is six days after. This would suggest a symbolic meaning for the time referent:

   a. The Transfiguration has much in common with Exodus 24 (see "Relationship to Exodus 24" after the Notes on 9:8), which also includes a reference to six days, so the time marker heightens the association between the two stories.

b. "After six days" means "on the seventh day" and thus alludes to the Sabbath, perhaps even the Sabbath of the Creation week. This reading would position the Transfiguration as, symbolically, a time of rest for Jesus after his "week" of ministry. (The phrasing "after six days" instead of "on the seventh day" would still require explanation, however.) But if an allusion to the Creation account was deliberate here, it would imply that Jesus is the "new creation," an idea that meshes well with the image of Jesus as the new Adam that Mark developed in chapter 1 (see the Notes on 1:13).

Jesus taketh with him Peter, and James, and John, and leadeth them up into an high mountain apart by themselves: The Transfiguration is traditionally thought to have occurred on Mount Tabor, but with a fortress on its two-thousand-foot summit, this site does not appear to be likely. Efforts to identify the mountain are inconclusive since there are no particularly high mountains in Galilee. But this may miss the point: "high" is relative and most likely symbolic here, especially since in the HB, mountains were a frequent location for contact between humans and God.

There is a repeated emphasis ("taketh," "leadeth," "apart," "by themselves") on the idea that Jesus took only these three disciples with him. There will be further indicators that this experience is for and about these disciples.

and he was transfigured before them: While "transfigured" would later be a technical term in the Christian tradition, here it simply means "change," with the implication of a visual change. The word (Greek: *metamorphoō*) is a cognate of the English "metamorphosize." Mark does not specify precisely what it was about Jesus that was changed (but see 9:3). This verb is probably a divine passive, meaning that God caused the change.

There are two different ways to understand what happens here: "One is that Jesus walked the earth as a divine being, whose true nature is momentarily revealed in the Transfiguration. The other is that the Transfiguration is a temporary change that Jesus undergoes here as an anticipation of his glorification after death."[26] In either case, the manifestation was probably intended to help these three disciples better understand who Jesus is. This experience may also have better fortified Jesus to face the challenges that his ministry would soon bring.

9:3 *And his raiment became shining, exceeding white as snow:* The phrase "as snow" is not in the best ancient manuscripts and appears to be a later addition.[27]

---

26. Collins, *Mark*, 421.
27. Bratcher and Nida, *Translator's Handbook*, 273.

There are two different ways to understand the role that this verse plays in Mark's account:

1. It is an explanation of the word "changed" (KJV: "transfigured") from 9:2. That is, what it means to be transfigured is that one's clothing shines and is very white.

2. It is something that happens in addition to, perhaps as a result of, the change in the previous verse, but that original change is left unspecified. Thus the shiny white clothing is the result of the Transfiguration, not the Transfiguration itself.

The reference to the shining white clothing may have evoked one or more of the following ideas for Mark's early audiences:

1. Some Jewish texts suggest that Adam had radiant garments that were taken away at the time of the Fall but that would be returned to the Messiah.[28] Thus one function of this story is to reveal Jesus as the anticipated Messiah.

2. In many Greek myths, when a god is revealed, a key characteristic is the blinding brightness of his or her clothing.[29] So the shiny clothing would reveal Jesus' divine identity to a Greek audience.

3. White garments are associated with martyrs in some ancient texts including the book of Revelation (Rev. 6:11). In Mark's context, an allusion to martyrdom is particularly appropriate since Jesus has been teaching about his coming suffering and death. This scene intertwines concepts of glorification and suffering, which is precisely the admixture that Peter does not yet understand.

so as no fuller on earth can white them: In the HB, the process of bleaching clothing can symbolize becoming spiritually pure (Ps. 51:7; Jer. 2:22; Mal. 3:2–3), so the exceptionally white clothing would indicate Jesus' own purity.

If taken literally, this description would imply that Jesus' clothing was not earthly but rather had a divine origin.

9:4 *And there appeared unto them Elias with Moses:* The KJV "Elias" refers to Elijah. The phrasing "Elijah with Moses" is unusual since Moses lived before Elijah and was regarded as the more prominent figure. Why did Moses and Elijah, as opposed to any other figures from the HB, appear? Possibilities include:

1. Moses appeared as a representation of the law and Elijah as a representation of the prophets. And since the law and the prophets can symbolize all of scripture, it is as if all scripture is attesting to Jesus. This adds an element of irony

---

28. Genesis Rabbah 20:12.

29. Candida R. Moss, "The Transfiguration: An Exercise in Markan Accommodation," *Biblical Interpretation* 12, no. 1 (2004): 79.

to the discussion about the proper interpretation of scripture that occurs between Jesus and Peter, James,[30] and John as they descend the mountain.

2. It was believed that neither Moses nor Elijah had died a mortal death, so they would have been able to appear to Jesus. (While Deuteronomy 34:5–6 describes the death of Moses, Josephus argued that Moses did not die but was taken up to heaven and included the note of his death in Deuteronomy out of modesty.[31]) If Moses and Elijah were able to avoid death, then their presence here is a powerful reminder of the possibility that Jesus, too, might transcend death (compare 9:10).

3. Moses and Elijah are "the only OT figures to have seen a theophany on a mountain."[32]

4. Moses and Elijah have epiphanies where the Lord passes them by (Ex. 33:17–23; 1 Kgs. 19:11–13), making their presence in this scene—where God's voice issues from a cloud—most appropriate.

As with the reference to Jesus' clothing, there are two ways to understand the presence of Elijah and Moses:

1. The Transfiguration itself happened in 9:2, and the appearance of Elijah and Moses happens after the Transfiguration but is not formally part of it.

2. The appearance of Elijah and Moses—and their subsequent conversation with Jesus—is part of the Transfiguration.

Relationship to 1 Kings 18:41–46. This text from 1 Kings has several interesting similarities to Mark's text, including a reference to Elijah, an encounter with God on a mountain, and a symbolically significant cloud. At the end of the story, "the Lord energized Elijah with power" (NET 1 Kgs. 18:46). If the allusion is intentional, it would encourage Mark's audience to read the Transfiguration as Jesus being endowed with power from on high.

Relationship to Malachi 4:4–5. The unusual phrasing "Elijah with Moses" almost certainly alludes to Malachi 4:4–5, where the two prophets are mentioned together. In the LXX, the order of the verses differs so that Elijah is mentioned before Moses (the LXX has verse 5, then 6, then verse 4[33]), which may explain Mark's unusual phrasing. Other points of contact with the text from Malachi include:

1. The LXX uses the word *apostello* for the sending of Elijah, which might allude to the apostles, who are given a special role in Mark's account of the

---

30. See the Notes on 1:19.

31. Josephus, *Antiquities* 4.8.48.

32. Gundry, *Mark,* 459.

33. The chapter and verse numbers in the LXX differ from the KJV; the KJV references have been used; in the LXX, this passage is Mal. 3:22–24.

Transfiguration. This would imply that Elijah should be a role model for the disciples, who are similarly sent out by the Lord.

2. In Malachi 4:5, the Lord states that he will send Elijah before the day of the Lord. This suggests that Elijah has a preparatory role: as the next verse indicates, he will reunite the hearts of the children and the fathers. This role may include the events that transpired on the mount. The conversation that the disciples initiate as they descend from the mountain supports this focus on Elijah's role.

3. In LXX Malachi 3:26 (KJV Mal. 4:6), the reference to the child and the father is in the singular ("the heart of the father to the son"). Since the voice from heaven in Mark's text proclaims that Jesus is the beloved son, this line from Malachi may well have been interpreted by Mark's early audiences with reference to Jesus and God, so that God's heart had been linked to Jesus' heart. In context, the point would not be that there had been any conflict between the two but rather that God accepted and approved of Jesus' teachings about his coming suffering and death; in other words, their hearts were united on this matter.

4. In both the KJV and the LXX, there is reference to Mount Horeb as the site where the law was given to Moses. This may explain the mountain setting of the Transfiguration and suggest that the Transfiguration positions Jesus himself as the new law.

---

and they were talking with Jesus: Mark's wording suggests that Peter, James, and John do not hear what Elijah and Moses say to Jesus.

9:5 *And Peter answered and said to Jesus, Master, it is good for us to be here:* What the KJV translates as "master" could also be transliterated as "rabbi."

Peter is enjoying this moment of being present for Jesus' glorification; this will be in stark contrast to Jesus' experience in Gethsemane (when Peter sleeps), in his interrogations (when Peter remains outside, denying Jesus), and in his crucifixion (when Peter is not present).

and let us make three tabernacles; one for thee, and one for Moses, and one for Elias: "Tabernacles" refers to a tent, booth, or other dwelling place. It might suggest the tent of meeting, which was the precursor to the temple (Ex. 27) or the booths used at the Feast of Tabernacles (Lev. 23:33–43). While Peter's reaction might initially seem appropriate, 9:6 makes clear that it was not. What was wrong with Peter's proposal here?

1. The only other person who calls Jesus "master" is Judas at the betrayal (14:45),[34] suggesting that the title is insincere or otherwise problematic. Even if the title were neutral, it might reflect a retrogression on Peter's part since he last

---

34. A different form of the word is used in 10:51 (see the Notes on that verse).

called Jesus "the Christ." It is even possible that, as a result of comparison with the heavenly messengers, Peter has in effect downgraded his opinion of Jesus from "Christ" to "master."

2. Peter may interpret this scene of glorification of Jesus and conversation with heavenly beings as appropriate because it suggests that Jesus is honored. This would fit with Peter's previous objection to Jesus teaching about his suffering and dying and imply that he still cannot accept Jesus' fate. That the voice from heaven will say to Peter "hear him" suggests the correction to this attitude: he cannot merely enjoy the pleasant parts of Jesus' ministry without simultaneously accepting what Jesus teaches about his future when he "hear[s] him."

3. If Peter wants the booths to protect Jesus but God instead uses the cloud to protect Jesus, then Peter has offered an inferior solution to the problem. Perhaps Peter wants to protect Jesus (as he did with his rebuke [8:32]), but once again the point is made that Jesus does not need Peter's protection since he has God's protection.

4. Peter is attempting to offer the traditional and expected response to the revelation of a god, a shrine.[35] This would show Peter once again trying to be in charge of Jesus' ministry.[36] But the voice from heaven explains that what is needed is not a physical shrine but rather obedience to Jesus' words.

5. If the time marker "after six days" was meant to be interpreted as "on the seventh day" and thus allude to the week of Creation, it is Peter who is assuming the role of God by announcing what is "good," using the same Greek word for "good" as is found in LXX Genesis 1. Thus Peter attempts to usurp God's role, just as he usurped Jesus' role in directing his ministry in the last chapter. The voice of God from the cloud thus serves as a corrective, explaining that what is genuinely good is not Peter's assessment but hearing Jesus.

6. If Peter's desire to build "booths" means that he wants to build something akin to the tabernacle used in the HB, then it suggests that he probably thought that Jesus' glorified condition was (or, at least, should be) a permanent condition and that he should have a "house," much as the HB tabernacle was a house for the Lord. Once again, this would reflect Peter's thinking that Jesus need not suffer and die to achieve glory. But the Transfiguration is not intended to be permanent. It thus shows Peter's fundamental misunderstanding of the experience. (This line of thinking might explain why Jesus will soon tell Peter and the others not to discuss the Transfiguration until after his Resurrection: they are incapable of understanding the former until they have experienced the latter.)

7. The desire to build *three* booths suggests that Peter views Jesus, Moses, and Elijah as worthy of equal treatment and honor. But one point of the

---

35. Collins, *Mark,* 418–19.
36. Contrast 14:9, where Jesus suggests a memorial; see also the Notes on 14:3–9.

Transfiguration is that this is not the case: the voice from heaven tells them to hear "him" and not "them" and thus corrects Peter's mistaken belief that Jesus is merely the equal of the HB prophets.

8. The point of the shelters was to provide a more "dignified"[37] place for the visitors.

9. The text implies that Peter (and James and John) do not hear the conversation between Jesus and Moses and Elijah. Perhaps Peter's desire to build booths reflects an attempt to be an active participant and not merely a witness of the Transfiguration.

10. The booths might suggest a permanent residence, which would be incompatible with the idea of being "on the way" in this section of Mark—something that is necessary for Jesus to fulfill his mission. These booths might seem innocent, but in this light, they are an effort to divert Jesus from fulfilling God's plan for him.

11. Perhaps there is no logical reason for Peter's reaction; as the next line indicates, he speaks unknowingly and out of fear.

9:6 *For he wist not what to say:* Mark clearly signals that Peter's response in the previous verse was not appropriate.

for they were sore afraid: There is a disconnect between Peter's statement that it is good for the disciples to be on the mount and Mark's note that they were afraid. It is possible that Peter's statement was an attempt to cover up his fear.

9:7 *And there was a cloud that overshadowed them:* In the HB, a cloud is a symbol for God's presence (Ex. 16:10; 19:9; 40:34–38).

It is not entirely clear at this point who is overshadowed by the cloud: grammatically, it is more than one person, but it could be any combination of the six people on the mountain. However, when the cloud leaves, the disciples see Jesus alone; this strongly implies that Jesus, Elijah, and Moses—but not the disciples—were covered by the cloud.

While it serves other roles in the narrative, the overshadowing cloud is also a response to Peter's desire to make tabernacles. But rather than a human-made structure, the cover is a divine cloud, much as how during the Exodus the cloud is the Lord's "tent."

In Psalm 91:4, the promise is made that God will provide shelter; the same word for "overshadow" is used in the LXX (Ps. 90:4) as is found in Mark. The point is that the Lord provides shelter and protection, and Peter doesn't need to do that with the booths.

---

37. France, *Gospel of Mark*, 354.

and a voice came out of the cloud, saying, This is my beloved Son: This language is virtually identical to that used by the voice from heaven immediately after Jesus' baptism (see the Notes on 1:11), except here it is directed to the disciples ("this is") and not to Jesus ("thou art"). Knowledge that only Jesus used to have (that is, that he was God's son) is now extended to the disciples.

hear him: At the baptism, the statement after "you are my beloved Son" was "in you I am well pleased"; here, it is "hear him." So instead of approval directed to Jesus, there is a command directed to the disciples. This fits with the idea of the Transfiguration being an experience primarily for the benefit of the disciples.

9:8 *And suddenly, when they had looked round about, they saw no man any more, save Jesus only with themselves:* "Suddenly" is a very unusual word and not Mark's typical term for "immediately."

"Round about" implies that they had been hiding their faces.

Relationship to Genesis 22. There are extensive verbal and thematic similarities between the story of the near-sacrifice of Isaac and Jesus' Transfiguration.[38] The point of the intertext is to emphasize "Jesus' status as God's beloved son. The intertextual parallels between 9:2–9 and Gen 22:1–19 reinforce the portrayal of Jesus as an Isaac figure whose identity as a beloved son involves a journey toward possible death. Perhaps not coincidentally, Mark explicitly refers to Jesus' death at the conclusion of the Transfiguration episode."[39]

Relationship to Exodus 24. Exodus 24 contains many motifs similar to the Transfiguration account:

1. *Six Days.* In Exodus, this is the time period during which the glory of the Lord is covered by a cloud while Moses is on the mountain and before the Lord speaks to Moses from the cloud. It thus suggests a period of preparation.

2. *Mountain.* In both stories, contact with the divine is made on a mountain, a traditional symbol for proximity to God.

3. *Disciples.* Moses ascends the mountain with Joshua (the name "Joshua" in Hebrew is "Jesus" in Greek). Other disciples are not invited on the ascent but remain below.

---

38. Matthew S. Rindge, "Reconfiguring the Akedah and Recasting God: Lament and Divine Abandonment in Mark," *Journal of Biblical Literature* 131, no. 4 (2012): 766–67.

39. Rindge, "Reconfiguring the Akedah and Recasting God," 767.

4. *The Cloud.* In both texts, the divine voice comes from the cloud, and the cloud protects mortals from the divine presence.

5. Moses is given the stone tablets at the climax of the encounter. There is no analogy to this in the Transfiguration unless the divine voice's command to "hear him" indicates that Jesus himself is the new law.

The Transfiguration in Restoration Thought. The story of the Transfiguration is one of the few instances where the Latter-day Saint tradition offers a unique reading of Mark's Gospel. Yet while the Transfiguration has been a rich site for Restoration thought (see Moses 1:14), the evidence is partial and, in some cases, not entirely clear. This is perhaps not surprising given that a revelation through Joseph Smith stated that a complete account of the Transfiguration did not yet exist.[40]

Based on a statement made by Joseph Smith,[41] Latter-day Saints have believed that Jesus conferred priesthood keys on Peter, James, and John on the Mount of Transfiguration. While this conferral is not mentioned in Mark's text, there is some evidence that could support it:

1. The only previous instance where Peter, James, and John were singled out from the other disciples was at the raising of Jairus's daughter. If that story were patterned after Elijah's raising of the widow's son (see the Notes on 5:43), there might be a pattern of selecting only Peter, James, and John to accompany Jesus when—to use terminology that Mark does not use—higher priesthood is in view, since Elijah's raising of the widow's son could be taken as the key instance of his use of the sealing power.

2. The last time Jesus invited disciples to join him on a mountain was at the calling of the Twelve (3:13–14), so perhaps the mountain setting implies the bestowal of special authority.

3. Because the voice from heaven spoke in the second person at the baptism but speaks in the third person at the Transfiguration, it is implied that the Transfiguration is for the benefit of the disciples, as the baptism was for Jesus himself. If that is the case, and if the baptism is read as a bestowal of power on Jesus (via the descent of the Spirit), then it would follow that the Transfiguration involved a similar bestowal of power on the disciples.

---

40. D&C 63:21. It is not entirely certain that D&C 63 is referring to the same event recounted in chapter 9.

41. "History, 1838–1856, Volume C-1 [2 November 1838–31 July 1842]," 11 [addenda], The Joseph Smith Papers, http://www.josephsmithpapers.org/paper-summary/history -1838-1856-volume-c-1-2-november-1838-31-july-1842/546; see also "Discourse, between circa 26 June and circa 4 August 1839–A, as Reported by Unknown Scribe," p. [3], The Joseph Smith Papers, http://www.joseph smith papers.org/paper-summary/discourse -between-circa-26-june-and-circa-4-august-1839-a-as-reported-by-unknown-scribe/2.

However, there may also be room to reconsider the traditional Latter-day Saint viewpoint. The original statement from Joseph Smith reads, "The Savior, Moses, and, Elias gave the Keys to Peter, James and John on the Mount when they were transfigured before him."[42] But Joseph Smith did not specify that this was the same event described in 9:2–9; in fact, Joseph Smith says that "they" were transfigured—presumably referring to Peter, James, and John—but only Jesus is transfigured in 9:2–9. So it is possible that Joseph Smith was referring to a different occasion, one not included in Mark. Given Mark's portrayal of the disciples, it could easily be argued that the disciples are not yet mature enough in their discipleship to be given the responsibility of priesthood keys.

Some Latter-day Saint thinkers have speculated that Peter, James, and John were endowed[43] (or something akin to it) on the Mount of Transfiguration.[44] It may also be worth exploring whether Jesus' own experience in 9:2–9 constituted something akin to the modern Latter-day Saint practice of receiving a temple endowment:

1. As mentioned above, some Jewish traditions held that Adam's garments lost in the Fall would be restored to the Messiah, which may be what is happening in the Transfiguration.

2. The reference to divinely pure clothing echoes the ritual role of clothing in the endowment, as does the presence of heavenly messengers and a voice from heaven.

3. Peter, James, and John's inability to hear the conversation between Jesus, Moses, and Elijah may imply that they are not allowed to know what was discussed on the mount, perhaps suggesting a ritual that they were not participating in.

4. The larger purpose of the Transfiguration in Mark's telling is opaque; if Mark intended to veil the endowment, that opaqueness would make sense. It is also possible that Mark was personally unaware of all that had happened.

5. If 9:1 applies to the Transfiguration, then that event is conceived as the kingdom of God coming in power. It would then make sense to read Jesus' experience on the mount as a bestowal of power.

---

42. "History, 1838–1856, Volume C-1," 11 [addenda].

43. Alma P. Burton, "Endowment," in Ludlow, *Encyclopedia of Mormonism*, 2:454–56.

44. Joseph Fielding Smith, *Doctrines of Salvation,* comp. Bruce R. McConkie, 3 vols. (Salt Lake City: Bookcraft, 1954–56), 2:165.

9:9 *And as they came down from the mountain, he charged them that they should tell no man what things they had seen, till the Son of man were risen from the dead:* This verse, by linking the story of the Transfiguration to the Resurrection, suggests that these two events should be understood in light of each other. This is emphasized by the fact that the final words spoken in the Transfiguration account consisted of the voice from heaven commanding the disciples to hear Jesus; this verse contains the first thing that Jesus says to his disciples after that important commandment. A prophecy of the Resurrection is in effect hidden in Jesus' statement here.

9:10 *And they kept that saying with themselves, questioning one with another what the rising from the dead should mean:* The phrase "kept that saying with themselves" signals obedience to the previous command not to tell anyone about the Transfiguration.

Because the concept of resurrection was not foreign to first-century Judaism, it is unlikely that the disciples are questioning the idea of resurrection per se but rather the idea that the Son of Man would be resurrected—which would have required him to have died. The need for the Son of Man to die is what they do not (yet) understand.

9:11 *And they asked him, saying, Why say the scribes that Elias must first come?:* The word "must" translates the same Greek word (*dei*) that Jesus used in his prediction of his suffering and death to indicate the necessity of the event.

The link between the disciples' question here and their questioning what the rising from the dead meant in the previous verse seems to be this: Malachi 4:5 teaches that Elijah would be sent before the day of the Lord, and thus the scribes intuited that Elijah would restore all things,[45] an idea not actually found in Malachi. If Elijah were to restore all things, nothing would be amiss, and thus there would be no need for the Son of Man to suffer and die. So the (false) teaching of the scribes that Elijah would restore all things is the underpinning of the disciples' belief that the Son of Man would not need to suffer and die, hence their question. The underlying cause of the misunderstanding is the disciples' reliance on the scribes' interpretation of Malachi 4:5. As Jesus' response in the next verse will indicate, the flaw in the logic is the presumption that Elijah will restore all things.

---

45. Ben Sira 48:1–11. It is true that LXX Malachi 3:23 (KJV Malachi 4:5) indicates that when Elijah comes, he will "restore" (using the same word for "restore" as in 9:12) the heart of the father to the son, but then (according to the disciples) the scribes equate that with restoring "all things," which is not what the text says.

9:12 *And he answered and told them, Elias verily cometh first, and restoreth all things:* Jesus' statement here can be read as a question, which makes better sense in context (see the Notes on 9:11). Malachi 4:5 states that Elijah would come before the day of the Lord, but it does not state that he would restore all things. Jesus' next words, a question about the need for the Son of Man to suffer, confirm this line of thought. So Jesus debunks the scribes' interpretation of Malachi 4:5.

and how it is written of the Son of man, that he must suffer many things, and be set at nought: There is no HB passage that refers to the suffering of the Son of Man, so

1. Jesus may be referring to a lost text.

2. Jesus may be referring to texts that refer to suffering (for example, Ps. 22; 41; 69; Isa. 50:4–9; 52:13–53:12) but not to the Son of Man specifically.

3. the phrase "it is written" can be used when drawing a conclusion, so there is no scripture that refers to the Son of Man suffering in view; rather, this is the conclusion Jesus reaches from combining references to suffering and the Son of Man from separate passages.

4. "Son of Man" is a modest way for Jesus to refer to himself, not a reference to HB passages that use the title. So Jesus is applying passages from the HB about the suffering servant of God to himself.

9:13 *But I say unto you, that Elias is indeed come:* At this point, it is likely that the audience would assume that Jesus was speaking of the presence of Elijah in 9:4. But as the rest of this verse will indicate, this is not who Jesus is talking about—he is instead referring to John the Baptist fulfilling the role of Elijah, as was suggested in 1:2 and 1:6.

and they have done unto him whatsoever they listed, as it is written of him: There are no extant texts indicating that Elijah would suffer after his return (although he did suffer during his mortal life [1 Kgs. 19:2–10]). It is possible that this statement refers to now-lost prophecies that John the Baptist would suffer.[46]

This line makes clear that when Jesus speaks about "Elijah," he is referring not to the literal Elijah who just appeared but rather to John the Baptist in the role of Elijah.

46. Daniel H. Ludlow, *A Companion to Your Study of the New Testament* (Salt Lake City: Deseret Book, 1982), 234.

Analysis

The Transfiguration is unlike any other scene in Mark. How would early audiences have understood this event?

1. *Royal Investiture.* Particularly if the Transfiguration is linked to 9:1's promise that the kingdom will come in power, it can be viewed as a royal investiture scene where Jesus is clothed in divine vestments to signal his status as a king.

2. *Glorification.* The Transfiguration shows Jesus' glory, either the glory that he always possessed—but that is normally hidden in his mortal state—or a foretaste of the glory that he will enjoy after his Resurrection. (By contrast, a cloud covers God's glory during the Transfiguration so that the disciples do not witness it.) This glimpse of Jesus' glorification occurs immediately after he begins to prophesy of his death, thereby tying his suffering to his glory: "the two realities are in constant tension."[47] The representation of Jesus' glorification would have provided the audience with a vision of Jesus' true identity to have in mind as they proceed through Mark's portrayal of Jesus' suffering and death.

3. *Divine Approval.* In context, the Transfiguration is the divine response to Peter's rejection of Jesus' teachings about his suffering and death. The purpose of the voice from the cloud is to show that Jesus still enjoys the same approval of his ministry that he had at his baptism, even now that he is prophesying about his coming suffering and death.

4. *A Symbol of the Resurrection.* There are several similarities between the Transfiguration and Resurrection appearances; the fact that Mark's text does not have a Resurrection appearance (see the Notes on 16:8) may imply that the Transfiguration should be read as a pattern for the Resurrection.

These readings are not mutually exclusive.

Once again, the disciples are not clear about what to do, as Peter's proposal suggests. In this context, it is important to remember that Jesus chose his disciples and then specifically chose these three to accompany him up the mountain. Their ignorance does not disqualify them from the work: Jesus has chosen them so he can teach them. Once again, the lack of understanding on the part of the disciples provides an opportunity to showcase Jesus' patience with them and provides an opportunity for them to be taught by him.

It is ironic that Peter, who seems to understand the glorious aspect of Jesus' identity but struggles with the idea that Jesus will suffer and die, would have an experience where he sees Jesus glorified; this would seem

---

47. Focant, *Gospel according to Mark,* 354.

to exacerbate his misunderstanding. However, the command by the divine voice for Peter to hear signals divine approval for Jesus' teachings, including those about his coming suffering and death. Thus the glorification of Jesus must be understood in the context of the climax of the story, which is not the Transfiguration itself but rather the divine voice commanding the disciples to listen to what Jesus is teaching them. Repeat auditors of Mark's Gospel would likely note that Peter's experience here did not prevent him from denying Jesus later; they would likely conclude that this type of experience does not guarantee faith and commitment, especially in the face of persecution.

The voice makes no reference to Elijah or to Moses; that Jesus has a unique role and an authority above even that of beings who come from the heavenly sphere and did not experience death is emphasized.

While there have been previous commands to secrecy in Mark, this is the first case where there is a time limit attached (but see the Notes on 1:45). It may be that the timing of the Resurrection is the key to understanding all of Mark's secrecy commands: either Jesus did not want the authorities to end his ministry before the proper time, and/or some events are simply not understandable without knowledge of the Resurrection and therefore must be kept private until that time. Interestingly, the other nine members of the Twelve will not know about the Transfiguration until after the Resurrection.

This command to secrecy would have had a profound impact on Mark's audience. While they might initially suspect that the disciples did not follow Jesus' counsel to keep quiet, the next verse makes clear that they did. So if the story of the Transfiguration is being discussed, as it is here in Mark's text, it demonstrates that the Son of Man has in fact risen from the dead. So for Mark's audience to hear about the Transfiguration shows that the Resurrection really happened; it is thus a witness to the audience of the truthfulness of the Resurrection.

While it initially appears that Jesus' reference to Elijah refers to the very literal appearance of Elijah in the preceding story, this is not actually the case. Instead, he is referring to John the Baptist in the role of Elijah. This is a crucial data point in understanding how Jesus interpreted scripture: in this case, the obvious and literal interpretation is not correct. Rather, a subtle, allusive interpretation is what Jesus intended.

The Disciples Fail to Heal (9:14–29)

Greek Text

14 Καὶ ἐλθόντες πρὸς τοὺς μαθητὰς εἶδον ὄχλον πολὺν περὶ αὐτοὺς καὶ γραμματεῖς συζητοῦντας πρὸς αὐτούς. 15 καὶ εὐθὺς πᾶς ὁ ὄχλος ἰδόντες αὐτὸν ἐξεθαμβήθησαν, καὶ προστρέχοντες ἠσπάζοντο αὐτόν. 16 καὶ ἐπηρώτησεν αὐτούς· Τί συζητεῖτε πρὸς αὐτούς; 17 καὶ ἀπεκρίθη αὐτῷ εἷς ἐκ τοῦ ὄχλου· Διδάσκαλε, ἤνεγκα τὸν υἱόν μου πρὸς σέ, ἔχοντα πνεῦμα ἄλαλον· 18 καὶ ὅπου ἐὰν αὐτὸν καταλάβῃ ῥήσσει αὐτόν, καὶ ἀφρίζει καὶ τρίζει τοὺς ὀδόντας καὶ ξηραίνεται· καὶ εἶπα τοῖς μαθηταῖς σου ἵνα αὐτὸ ἐκβάλωσιν, καὶ οὐκ ἴσχυσαν. 19 ὁ δὲ ἀποκριθεὶς αὐτοῖς λέγει· Ὦ γενεὰ ἄπιστος, ἕως πότε πρὸς ὑμᾶς ἔσομαι; ἕως πότε ἀνέξομαι ὑμῶν; φέρετε αὐτὸνπρός με. 20 καὶ ἤνεγκαν αὐτὸν πρὸς αὐτόν. καὶ ἰδὼν αὐτὸν τὸ πνεῦμα εὐθὺς συνεσπάραξεν αὐτόν, καὶ πεσὼν ἐπὶ τῆς γῆς ἐκυλίετο ἀφρίζων. 21 καὶ ἐπηρώτησεν τὸν πατέρα αὐτοῦ· Πόσος χρόνος ἐστὶν ὡς τοῦτο γέγονεν αὐτῷ; ὁ δὲ εἶπεν· Ἐκ παιδιόθεν· 22 καὶ πολλάκις καὶ εἰς πῦρ αὐτὸν ἔβαλεν καὶ εἰς ὕδατα ἵνα ἀπολέσῃ αὐτόν· ἀλλ᾽ εἴ τι δύνῃ, βοήθησον ἡμῖν σπλαγχνισθεὶς ἐφ᾽ ἡμᾶς. 23 ὁ δὲ Ἰησοῦς εἶπεν αὐτῷ· Τὸ Εἰ δύνῃ, πάντα δυνατὰ τῷ πιστεύοντι.

24 εὐθὺς κράξας ὁ πατὴρ τοῦ παιδίου ἔλεγεν· Πιστεύω· βοήθει μου τῇ ἀπιστίᾳ. 25 ἰδὼν δὲ ὁ Ἰησοῦς ὅτι ἐπισυντρέχει ὄχλος ἐπετίμησεν τῷ πνεύματι τῷ ἀκαθάρτῳ λέγων αὐτῷ· Τὸ ἄλαλον καὶ κωφὸν πνεῦμα, ἐγὼ ἐπιτάσσω σοι, ἔξελθε ἐξ αὐτοῦ καὶ μηκέτι εἰσέλθῃς εἰς αὐτόν. 26 καὶ κράξας καὶ πολλὰ σπαράξας ἐξῆλθεν· καὶ ἐγένετο ὡσεὶ νεκρὸς ὥστε τοὺς πολλοὺς λέγειν ὅτι ἀπέθανεν. 27 ὁ δὲ Ἰησοῦς κρατήσας τῆς χειρὸς αὐτοῦ ἤγειρεν αὐτόν, καὶ ἀνέστη. 28 καὶ εἰσελθόντος αὐτοῦ εἰς οἶκον οἱ μαθηταὶ αὐτοῦ κατ᾽ ἰδίαν ἐπηρώτων αὐτόν· Ὅτι ἡμεῖς οὐκ ἠδυνήθημεν ἐκβαλεῖν αὐτό; 29 καὶ εἶπεν αὐτοῖς· Τοῦτο τὸ γένος ἐν οὐδενὶ δύναται ἐξελθεῖν εἰ μὴ ἐν προσευχῇ. [SBLGNT]

King James Version

14 And when he came to his disciples, he saw a great multitude about them, and the scribes questioning with them. 15 And straightway all the people, when they beheld him, were greatly amazed, and running to him saluted him. 16 And he asked the scribes, What question ye with them? 17 And one of the multitude answered and said, Master, I have brought unto thee my son, which hath a dumb spirit; 18 And wheresoever

New Rendition

14 And having come to the disciples, they saw a large crowd around them and scriptorians arguing with them. 15 And immediately all the crowd, having seen him, were stunned and, running to him, greeted him. 16 And he asked them, "What are you arguing about with them?" 17 And one out of the crowd answered him, "Teacher, I brought you my son, who is possessed by a spirit that makes him mute. 18 And when it seizes

he taketh him, he teareth him: and he foameth, and gnasheth with his teeth, and pineth away: and I spake to thy disciples that they should cast him out; and they could not. 19 He answereth him, and saith, O faithless generation, how long shall I be with you? how long shall I suffer you? bring him unto me. 20 And they brought him unto him: and when he saw him, straightway the spirit tare him; and he fell on the ground, and wallowed foaming. 21 And he asked his father, How long is it ago since this came unto him? And he said, Of a child. 22 And ofttimes it hath cast him into the fire, and into the waters, to destroy him: but if thou canst do any thing, have compassion on us, and help us. 23 Jesus said unto him, If thou canst believe, all things are possible to him that believeth. 24 And straightway the father of the child cried out, and said with tears, Lord, I believe; help thou mine unbelief. 25 When Jesus saw that the people came running together, he rebuked the foul spirit, saying unto him, Thou dumb and deaf spirit, I charge thee, come out of him, and enter no more into him. 26 And the spirit cried, and rent him sore, and came out of him: and he was as one dead; insomuch that many said, He is dead. 27 But Jesus took him by the hand, and lifted him up; and he arose. 28 And when he was come into the house, his disciples asked him privately, Why could not we cast him out? 29 And he said unto them, This kind can come forth by nothing, but by prayer and fasting.

him, it throws him down, and he foams [at the mouth] and grinds his teeth and becomes rigid. And I spoke to your disciples, if they might cast it out, and they did not have the power to do it." 19 And answering them, he says, "You faithless generation! How long must I be with you? How much longer do I have to put up with you? Bring him to me." 20 And they brought him to him. And having seen him, the spirit immediately caused the boy to go into spasms. And having fallen upon the ground, he rolled around, foaming at the mouth. 21 And he asked his father, "How long has he been like this?" And he said, "From childhood, 22 and it often throws him into the fire and into the water, so that it might destroy him. But if you can do anything, help us and have compassion on us!" 23 And Jesus said to him, "'If you can do anything'? All things can be done for one who trusts." 24 Immediately having cried out, the father of the child was saying, "I trust you! Help my lack of trust!" 25 Jesus, having seen that a crowd was gathering, rebuked the unclean spirit, saying to it, "Mute and deaf spirit, I command you: come out of him and never enter him again." 26 And having cried out and having caused many spasms, it came out, and he became as if dead, so that most were saying, "He is dead." 27 And Jesus, having taken him by the hand, raised him, and he arose. 28 And having entered into a house, his disciples asked him privately, "Why were we not able to cast it out?" 29 And he said to them, "This kind cannot be cast out except by prayer."

Notes

9:14 *And when he came to his disciples, he saw a great multitude about them, and the scribes questioning with them:* There is a textual variant here: instead of "he came" and "he saw," some manuscripts read "they came" and "they saw."[48]

The audience will soon learn that this questioning stemmed from the scribes' conclusion that the disciples do not have access to God's power since they were unable to exorcise the demon. This is ironic since the scribes had previously criticized Jesus precisely because he had cast out demons (3:22). The implication is that the scribes will oppose the work of Jesus and his disciples no matter what they do or do not do. And there is another layer of irony: this dispute is happening at the same moment in narrative time as the voice from heaven confirms Jesus' authority by commanding the disciples to "hear him."

The same word translated as "questioning" here was used to describe what the disciples were doing in 9:10; since the scribes are opposed to Jesus, it implies that the disciples were as well.

9:15 *And straightway all the people, when they beheld him, were greatly amazed, and running to him saluted him:* This verse seems to interrupt the narrative, which would flow nicely from 9:14 to 9:16 without this verse.

Their amazement is strongly emphasized—they were not just amazed but greatly amazed. It is not clear why the people were amazed since that is the typical reaction to Jesus performing a miracle. Perhaps Jesus' clothing continued to shine after the Transfiguration (compare Ex. 34:30), and this caused the amazement, but this is speculative. And yet if this is the case, the questioning of the disciples and of the scribes becomes all the more inappropriate in the presence of Jesus' shining robes. They either cannot see that Jesus' clothing is changed (because their eyes are only half-opened) or they are so focused on other matters that they simply do not notice.

9:16 *And he asked the scribes, What question ye with them:* "The scribes" translates a pronoun ("asked them"), so it is not clear whom Jesus is asking—it might have been the scribes, the disciples, the crowd, or some combination. But it seems most likely that he would ask his own disciples for clarification. But it will be one of the crowd who answers him; perhaps an uncomfortable pause followed his question (compare 9:34) since the disciples may not have wanted to admit their failure to exorcise.

---

48. Collins, *Mark,* 433 note d.

9:17 *And one of the multitude answered and said, Master, I have brought unto thee my son, which hath a dumb spirit:* It is unlikely that the spirit is dumb (that is, mute) but more likely that the spirit makes the son mute. This muteness may explain why this story does not follow the regular pattern of an exorcism where the spirit speaks to Jesus.

9:18 *And wheresoever he taketh him, he teareth him:* The translation "throws him down" instead of "tears him" is preferable here; it seems to fit better the descriptions in 9:20 ("fell on the ground") and 9:22 ("cast him into the fire and into the waters").

and he foameth, and gnasheth with his teeth, and pineth away: and I spake to thy disciples that they should cast him out; and they could not: The inability of the disciples to cast out this spirit is striking given that they were specifically empowered by Jesus to cast out demons (3:15; 6:7, 13).

9:19 *He answereth him, and saith, O faithless generation, how long shall I be with you?:* "Them" instead of "him" is a variant and a better reading since the word "you" is plural. Thus Jesus is responding not just to the father but to a larger group that may consist of the crowd, the scribes, and the disciples.

The word "faithless" shares a root with the command to "believe" in 1:15, so they have not followed Jesus' call to believe.

While interpretations of this statement usually focus on Jesus' criticism of their lack of faith, there is also a covert prophecy here: Jesus' words assume that he will not be with them much longer. Whether his question should be taken rhetorically as a lament for the difficulty of being with faithless people or rather reflects Jesus' actual lack of knowledge about the timing of his death is difficult to determine (compare 13:32).

Relationship to Deuteronomy 32:5. Containing references to people unfaithful to the Lord as a deceitful generation, Deuteronomy 32:5 has several points of contact with Jesus' lament here in Mark. Interestingly, the line "they have not acted like his children" (NET) may be compared to the relationship between the father and the son in Mark's story: the son is damaged, in pain, and in danger but has no way to save himself. The father is willing and able to intercede for him. An allusion would suggest that the faithless generation is like a possessed child—in dire straits with no way to change the situation for themselves. By contrast, the father is like Jesus, intervening through humility to save his son. And because it is the voice of the Lord lamenting in the Deuteronomy text, the allusion would reveal Jesus as the Lord of the HB. (Similar laments occur in Num. 14:27 and Isa. 6:11.)

how long shall I suffer you? bring him unto me: The words "bring" and "you" are plural, so Jesus is not (just) addressing the father here. Jesus immediately gives them something to do to show a little faith.

9:20 *And they brought him unto him: and when he saw him, straightway the spirit tare him; and he fell on the ground, and wallowed foaming:* It is unclear whether the phrase "when he saw him" refers to Jesus seeing the son or to the son seeing Jesus.

9:21 *And he asked his father, How long is it ago since this came unto him?:* While the wording is not identical in Greek, the question is similar to 9:19: Jesus asked how long he would need to remain with the faithless generation, and he asks how long the unclean spirit has remained with the boy.

and he said, Of a child: If the son had been having seizures since he was a child, that implies that he is no longer a youth.

9:22 *And ofttimes it hath cast him into the fire, and into the waters, to destroy him: but if thou canst do any thing, have compassion on us, and help us:* The word "us" pairs the father and the son in an effort to decouple the unclean spirit and the son: the father speaks for and seeks healing for the child while the spirit silences and seeks to hurt the child.[49]

The father's doubt should be viewed sympathetically in light of the failure of the disciples to exorcise the spirit.

9:23 *Jesus said unto him, If thou canst believe, all things are possible to him that believeth:* The word translated as "believe" seems to have been added by copyists who were flummoxed by the brevity of Jesus' statement and overlooked that he was repeating the father's words.[50] Modern English translations show how the phrase might be handled: ""'If you can'?' said Jesus. 'Everything is possible for him who believes'" (NIV) or "Jesus said to him, 'If you are able!—All things can be done for the one who believes'" (NRSV). These readings change Jesus' words from a call for more belief to a call to better understand Jesus' powers, while simultaneously expressing incredulity that the father would question Jesus' ability to help.

9:24 *And straightway the father of the child cried out, and said with tears:* The phrase "with tears" appears to have been added by copyists to increase the drama in the story; it does not appear in the earliest manuscripts.[51]

49. Focant, *Gospel according to Mark,* 370.
50. Metzger, *Textual Commentary,* 85.
51. Metzger, *Textual Commentary,* 85.

Lord, I believe; help thou mine unbelief: "Lord" is not in the best manuscripts.[52]

Much as Jesus echoed the father's words in 9:23, here the father echoes Jesus' words.

9:25 *When Jesus saw that the people came running together:* It is difficult to determine why Mark included this note since a crowd was already present; perhaps Jesus ceased the conversation and began the exorcism before the crowd could get any larger.

he rebuked the foul spirit, saying unto him, Thou dumb and deaf spirit, I charge thee, come out of him, and enter no more into him: This is the first indication that the spirit is deaf. Jesus' power is emphasized by the fact that this deaf spirit can hear his command to depart from the son.

9:26 *And the spirit cried, and rent him sore, and came out of him: and he was as one dead; insomuch that many said, He is dead:* The phrase "as one dead" implies that he was not actually dead.

One of the father's fears was that the demon would destroy the child; here it appears that this fear has been realized. In this moment, there is ample reason for the father (and the audience) to have their faith crushed, particularly in light of the disciples' failure to exorcise the demon.

9:27 *But Jesus took him by the hand, and lifted him up; and he arose:* While not a literal raising from the dead, the story alludes to death and resurrection.

Relationship to the Raising of Jairus's Daughter. While this exorcism is not a literal raising from the dead, it contains extensive similarities to the story of the raising of Jairus's daughter: in both cases, a father intercedes on behalf of his child, there is a delay in the miracle that leads to a discussion about the need for faith, the child seems (or is) dead, Jesus takes the child by the hand, and Jesus raises the child.

What the stories do not have in common is the identity of the child; the fact that Jesus' power is accessible to both a girl and a boy, to a (literal) child of the synagogue and to an unclean child, is significant. Further, the delay in each story and the discussion of faith that ensues is a significant pattern: Mark's audience is taught to expect delays in desired healings and to look to those delays as a time for developing faith through dialogue with Jesus.

---

52. Bratcher and Nida, *Translator's Handbook,* 288.

9:28 *And when he was come into the house, his disciples asked him privately, Why could not we cast him out? 29 And he said unto them, This kind can come forth by nothing, but by prayer and fasting:* "This kind" may refer to demons in general or to this specific kind of demon (unlike in the other cases of possession in Mark, this story has a deaf and dumb spirit that does not speak to Jesus).

The phrase "and fasting" was probably not in this verse originally.[53] It may have been added as a result of the increased emphasis on fasting in later centuries. Mark 2:18–20 makes two points that are relevant here: first, that Jesus' disciples are not supposed to fast when they are with him and, second, that the disciples will fast in the future.

There appears to be something of a disconnect in this passage since there is no reference to prayer in this story, but there is ample discussion of (lack of) faith. Options for resolving this disparity include:

1. If one has faith, one is prayerful, so there is no conflict.

2. The father's statement "help my unbelief" functions as a prayer, so there is no conflict. This would imply that the disciples failed because they did not seek help for their lack of faith. Thus the father is a model for the disciples to follow.

3. The requirements for the disciples to perform an exorcism are different from those for Jesus; had the disciples prayed, they would have been able to perform it. They needed to pray, but Jesus need not pray because he has the power of God within him in a unique way.

4. Jesus' reference to prayer does not refer to offering a prayer in the middle of an exorcism but rather to an ongoing prayerful relationship with God. So while there is no specific reference to prayer in this text, Jesus had the power to perform this exorcism because he prayed regularly.

Relationship to Exodus 32. In Exodus 32, when Moses came down the mountain, he found that the people had built a golden calf to worship. This might parallel Jesus finding a dispute over his disciples' inability to exorcise when he came down the mountain after the Transfiguration. Aaron took charge of the false worship in Exodus 32, much as nine of the Twelve are implicated in the failure to exorcise the demon. If Mark intended for there to be an allusion here, it would align idol worship with the failure to exorcise, and it would suggest that just as the people of Israel floundered without Moses' direction, the disciples did the same without Jesus.

---

53. Metzger, *Textual Commentary*, 85.

Analysis

Bracketing the exorcism with references to the disciples suggests that, unlike with the previous exorcisms in Mark's Gospel, this one is primarily focused on the disciples' lack of understanding, a theme that is emphasized throughout this section.

There are several indicators that demonic possession symbolizes faithlessness in this story:

1. When Jesus asks (presumably his disciples) what the dispute with the scribes is about, they do not reply. This meshes with the idea of a dumb (mute) spirit possession.

2. Jesus asks how long he must remain with the faithless generation and then asks how long the spirit has been in the son. The similarity between these questions encourages a comparison between them and explains the otherwise-puzzling fact that Jesus delays the exorcism to ask how long the demoniac has been possessed at a time when the demoniac is in dire physical distress.

3. The same Greek word is used for the cry of the father in 9:24 as for the cry of the spirit in 9:26, suggesting a similarity between the two.

4. The father's statement of belief combined with a plea for Jesus to help his lack of belief shows precisely the kind of half-sight that plagues the disciples and frames this section of Mark's Gospel; it also suggests that Jesus' task in this story is not just to exorcise the demon but to aid the father's lack of belief, which heightens the association between the possession and the lack of belief. Lack of belief is presented as something that the man cannot fix for himself any more than he could exorcise the demon.

In the past, the disciples had been able to cast out demons (6:13). Perhaps the problem here is that they had become prideful in their own ability and had forgotten to recognize the source of their power.

A SECOND PREDICTION OF DEATH (9:30–37)

Greek Text

30 Κἀκεῖθεν ἐξελθόντες παρεπορεύοντο διὰ τῆς Γαλιλαίας, καὶ οὐκ ἤθελεν ἵνα τις γνοῖ· 31 ἐδίδασκεν γὰρ τοὺς μαθητὰς αὐτοῦ καὶ ἔλεγεν αὐτοῖς ὅτι Ὁ υἱὸς τοῦ ἀνθρώπου παραδίδοται εἰς χεῖρας ἀνθρώπων, καὶ ἀποκτενοῦσιν αὐτόν, καὶ ἀποκτανθεὶς μετὰ τρεῖς ἡμέρας ἀναστήσεται. 32 οἱ δὲ ἠγνόουν τὸ ῥῆμα, καὶ ἐφοβοῦντο αὐτὸν ἐπερωτῆσαι.

33 Καὶ ἦλθον εἰς Καφαρναούμ. καὶ ἐν τῇ οἰκίᾳ γενόμενος ἐπηρώτα αὐτούς· Τί ἐν τῇ ὁδῷ διελογίζεσθε; 34 οἱ δὲ ἐσιώπων, πρὸς ἀλλήλους γὰρ διελέχθησαν ἐν τῇ ὁδῷ τίς μείζων. 35 καὶ καθίσας ἐφώνησεν τοὺς δώδεκα καὶ λέγει αὐτοῖς· Εἴ τις θέλει πρῶτος εἶναι ἔσται πάντων ἔσχατος καὶ πάντων διάκονος. 36 καὶ λαβὼν παιδίον ἔστησεν αὐτὸ ἐν μέσῳ αὐτῶν καὶ ἐναγκαλισάμενος αὐτὸ εἶπεν αὐτοῖς· 37 Ὃς ἂν ἓν τῶν τοιούτων παιδίων δέξηται ἐπὶ τῷ ὀνόματί μου, ἐμὲ δέχεται· καὶ ὃς ἂν ἐμὲ δέχηται, οὐκ ἐμὲ δέχεται ἀλλὰ τὸν ἀποστείλαντά με. [SBLGNT]

King James Version

30 And they departed thence, and passed through Galilee; and he would not that any man should know it. 31 For he taught his disciples, and said unto them, The Son of man is delivered into the hands of men, and they shall kill him; and after that he is killed, he shall rise the third day. 32 But they understood not that saying, and were afraid to ask him.

33 And he came to Capernaum: and being in the house he asked them, What was it that ye disputed among yourselves by the way? 34 But they held their peace: for by the way they had disputed among themselves, who should be the greatest. 35 And he sat down, and called the twelve, and saith unto them, If any man desire to be first, the same shall be last of all, and servant of all. 36 And he took a child, and set him in the midst of them: and when he had taken him in his arms, he said unto them, 37 Whosoever shall receive one of such children in my name, receiveth me: and whosoever shall receive me, receiveth not me, but him that sent me.

New Rendition

30 Having gone out from there, they passed through Galilee, and he did not want anyone to know it. 31 For he was teaching his disciples and was saying to them, "The son of man is delivered into the hands of humans, and they will kill him. And having been killed, after three days, he will arise." 32 But they did not understand the statement, and they were afraid to ask him.

33 And they came to Capernaum. And when he was in the house, he asked them, "What were you discussing on the way?" 34 But they were silent, for on the way they had been discussing with one another who was the greatest. 35 And having sat down, he called the Twelve, and he says to them, "If anyone wants to be first, he or she must be last of all and servant of all." 36 And having taken a child, he put him/her in the middle of them, and hugging him/her, he said to them, 37 "Whoever welcomes one of these children in my name welcomes me. And whoever will welcome me does not welcome me, but the one having sent me."

Notes

9:30 *And they departed thence, and passed through Galilee; and he would not that any man should know it:* Perhaps Jesus did not want his presence known either because this was not a teaching and healing ministry but rather "the way" to Jerusalem or because his intention was to teach his disciples privately.

9:31 *For he taught his disciples, and said unto them, The Son of man is delivered into the hands of men, and they shall kill him:* "Taught" is imperfect, indicating that Jesus taught this on more than one occasion.

In Greek and in English, there is a play on words as "the Son of man" is delivered to "men," highlighting the tragedy and irrationality of people harming their own (figurative) son: "It is consonant with this pessimistic interpretation of 'to the hands of human beings' that in 2 Sam 24:14/ 1 Chron 21:13 falling into human hands is considered a terrible fate because of the ruthlessness of humankind."[54]

There is a lack of specificity in this prophecy: the identity of the killers and the method of execution is not revealed.

and after that he is killed, he shall rise the third day: The reference to killing is repeated in this verse for emphasis.

Some ancient manuscripts have "after three days" instead of "the third day," with the latter likely a change made to bring the passage into harmony with the way that the Resurrection is normally described in the NT.[55] See also the Notes on 8:31.

9:32 *But they understood not that saying, and were afraid to ask him:* For the disciples to fear, they must have had some inkling of what the answer would be. (If they had absolutely no clue as to what Jesus had meant, they would not have been afraid to ask—Jesus has previously shown himself receptive to questions such as this.) In other words, the fear is not about the process of asking a question; the fear is about the content of the answer. Their fear likely stems from their budding understanding that Jesus must suffer and die and, if they are to follow him, that this is likely to be their fate as well.

9:33 *And he came to Capernaum: and being in the house he asked them:* Some manuscripts read "they came" instead of "he came" here. It is possible that "he came" was a correction made by scribes who thought that the subject of this sentence should be "he" in anticipation of the next sentence.[56]

It may be significant that it was in a house in Capernaum that the inaugural healing of Jesus' ministry took place when Simon's mother-in-law was

---

54. Marcus, *Mark 8–16,* 669.
55. Collins, *Mark,* 440 note a.
56. Collins, *Mark,* 441 note a.

restored and served. There may be some irony here as her service is shown, per Jesus' statements later in this story, to be evidence that she is the greatest among them.

What was it that ye disputed among yourselves by the way?: The phrase "among yourselves" is not in the best ancient manuscripts,[57] although the sense is the same with or without it.

"The way" describes the symbolic journey that Jesus and the disciples are taking to Jerusalem and to his suffering and death. Jesus' use of the phrase here, when it is not necessary for his question to make sense, points to the symbolic meaning and heightens attention to the error of the disciples in disputing about greatness when they should have been learning about Jesus' ministry.

9:34 *But they held their peace:* Their silence probably indicates that they knew that Jesus would not approve of their discussion. It may parallel their (implied) silence in the previous story, when they did not answer Jesus' question about the dispute over the failed exorcism (see the Notes on 9:16).

for by the way they had disputed among themselves, who should be the greatest: The repetition of "by the way," which already occurred in 9:33, suggests its symbolic function. They were supposed to be on "the way" of discipleship, but instead they had been bickering about hierarchy. They have not yet applied to themselves Jesus' counsel to deny themselves and their desire for greatness.

A chiasmus has been identified in this text:

    A what (*ti*)
       B in the way
          C were you discussing?
            D they were silent
          C' for . . . they had been discussing
       B' in the way
    A' who (*tis*) was the greatest[58]

This structure focuses attention on a rather unexpected place: the silence of the disciples; perhaps Mark's goal was to highlight the wrongness of that silence. Particularly when read in light of the previous story—where the father's willingness to speak up contrasts with the muteness of the demon—Mark may be emphasizing the need to speak out. This would be an important lesson for the disciples to learn "on the way" of discipleship.

---

57. Bratcher and Nida, *Translator's Handbook,* 293.
58. Marcus, *Mark 8–16,* 680.

9:35 *And he sat down, and called the twelve, and saith unto them:* Sitting down implies assuming the posture of a teacher. This is significant because it indicates that Jesus is the greatest among them.

Because the Twelve were already present, there is technically no need for Jesus to call them to him; the fact that Mark mentions it suggests that it is a bit of stage-setting to present Jesus as the teacher of the Twelve, the one who gives orders that are followed.

If any man desire to be first, the same shall be last of all, and servant of all: "First" means to have a prominent position; to be the last or to be a servant means to have no prominence. Jesus' words are not only paradoxical but radically countercultural in a setting where no esteem was granted to servants. Jesus is, in effect, redefining the terms and teaching that humility is greatness.

While Mark informed the audience of the topic of dispute, no one in the story informed Jesus. His knowledge suggests either that he has used miraculous powers of discernment or that he knew what they were discussing before he asked but had given them a chance to confess.

9:36 *And he took a child, and set him in the midst of them:* Contrary to modern notions of children as innocent and pure, "in the ancient world, a child was mainly symbolic of powerlessness."[59]

All of the words used to refer to the child are gender-neutral, so it is not clear whether this is a boy or a girl.

In Aramaic, the same word can be translated as "servant" or "child," so there might have been a play on words in the original statement.

Jesus is, through his treatment of the child, enacting his own teachings by welcoming and receiving the child. This is a parabolic act.

and when he had taken him in his arms, he said unto them: Jesus' hugging of the child would have been perceived as a rather maternal act. It is possible to imagine the storyteller of Mark's Gospel taking a child from the audience into his or her arms when delivering this line.

9:37 *Whosoever shall receive one of such children in my name, receiveth me:* "Receive" connotes offering hospitality. In the ancient world, children required hospitality when they were orphaned or abandoned. Caring for such a child would have been seen as precisely the opposite of an act of greatness. Further, serving a child "reverses the ancient protocol where slaves and children, indeed all the subordinate members of the household, were to serve the male head of the household."[60]

---

59. Malbon, *Hearing Mark*, 64.
60. Witherington, *Gospel of Mark*, 270.

and whosoever shall receive me, receiveth not me, but him that sent me: The idea that by receiving a child one would actually be receiving Jesus means that Jesus is equating himself with children, the least powerful people. Jesus is taking on the role of greatest in this story by sitting and teaching, but he then aligns himself with a child, taking the role of the least. Thus his own actions in this story mirror his teachings precisely.

The phrase "receiveth not me" may be dialectical negation: it would not mean that Jesus was not received, but that, more significantly, God was received more so. Much as Jesus identifies himself with a child, he also identifies himself with God here. Jesus has presented a blueprint for receiving God: it involves receiving those with the least power. Further, "the logical corollary is that the community in which the non-persons of society find no welcome is a community without the presence of God."[61]

A greater honor than receiving (in the sense of providing hospitality for) God cannot be imagined; Jesus shows that one can receive God by receiving a child. Thus, Jesus has answered their question about who is the greatest by teaching them how to be the greatest. It is a counterintuitive process.

Analysis

The dispute over who is greatest probably has its origin in the previous two stories—the Transfiguration and failed exorcism—that featured Peter, James,[62] and John in a special role and the remaining nine flummoxed by their inability to perform a miracle. The singling out of Peter, James, and John followed by the failure of the other nine may have led Peter, James, and/or John to conclude that they were better than the others.

Because 9:32 indicated that the disciples did not understand Jesus' prophecy and were afraid to ask about it, the natural conclusion for the audience to reach is that the disciples were disputing about that prophecy. So Mark's explanation that they were disputing over who was the greatest would have come as a surprise. The complete inappropriateness of debating who is greatest is magnified by the audience's expectation that what they were actually doing was trying to better understand Jesus' suffering and death. They were fixated on their own prominence even at the expense of better understanding Jesus' ministry. It may even be the case that their growing understanding that Jesus would die had led them to dispute who would take his place as leader and teacher after his death.

---

61. Dowd, *Reading Mark,* 97.
62. See the Notes on 1:19.

All three predictions of Jesus' suffering and death in Mark are followed by an error made by the disciples, each of which involves assuming a role that is not theirs (see the Notes after 10:45).

By positioning the stereotypically female actions of holding and caring for children as paradigmatic of true greatness, Jesus is presenting a countercultural message:

> None of the Twelve could nominate himself for the position of "greatest" after seeing Jesus demonstrate greatness by taking a little child in his arms. Rather, Jesus implies, they should nominate the women they saw attending to the children in the household in Capernaum where Jesus and the Twelve had come: the mothers, grandmothers, aunts, and sisters who took care of children as part of their daily duties. The women were the greatest among them. . . . The women's practice of receiving little children made them able to receive Jesus in his role as the suffering Son of Man, for in his passion Jesus is like the little child who is rejected and killed [as children often were via infanticide].[63]

THE DISCIPLES FAIL TO WELCOME (9:38–50)

Greek Text

38 Ἔφη αὐτῷ ὁ Ἰωάννης· Διδάσκαλε, εἴδομέν τινα ἐν τῷ ὀνόματί σου ἐκβάλλοντα δαιμόνια, καὶ ἐκωλύομεν αὐτόν, ὅτι οὐκ ἠκολούθει ἡμῖν. 39 ὁ δὲ Ἰησοῦς εἶπεν· Μὴ κωλύετε αὐτόν, οὐδεὶς γάρ ἐστιν ὃς ποιήσει δύναμιν ἐπὶ τῷ ὀνόματί μου καὶ δυνήσεται ταχὺ κακολογῆσαί με· 40 ὃς γὰρ οὐκ ἔστιν καθ᾽ ἡμῶν, ὑπὲρ ἡμῶν ἐστιν. 41 Ὃς γὰρ ἂν ποτίσῃ ὑμᾶς ποτήριον ὕδατος ἐν ὀνόματι ὅτι χριστοῦ ἐστε, ἀμὴν λέγω ὑμῖν ὅτι οὐ μὴ ἀπολέσῃ τὸν μισθὸν αὐτοῦ.

42 Καὶ ὃς ἂν σκανδαλίσῃ ἕνα τῶν μικρῶν τούτων τῶν πιστευόντων εἰς ἐμέ, καλόν ἐστιν αὐτῷ μᾶλλον εἰ περίκειται μύλος ὀνικὸς περὶ τὸν τράχηλον αὐτοῦ καὶ βέβληται εἰς τὴν θάλασσαν. 43 Καὶ ἐὰν σκανδαλίζῃ σε ἡ χείρ σου, ἀπόκοψον αὐτήν· καλόν ἐστίν σε κυλλὸν εἰσελθεῖν εἰς τὴν ζωὴν ἢ τὰς δύο χεῖρας ἔχοντα ἀπελθεῖν εἰς τὴν γέενναν, εἰς τὸ πῦρ τὸ ἄσβεστον. 45 καὶ ἐὰν ὁ πούς σου σκανδαλίζῃ σε, ἀπόκοψον αὐτόν· καλόν ἐστίν σε εἰσελθεῖν εἰς τὴν ζωὴν χωλὸν ἢ τοὺς δύο πόδας ἔχοντα βληθῆναι εἰς τὴν γέενναν. 47 καὶ ἐὰν ὁ ὀφθαλμός σου σκανδαλίζῃ σε, ἔκβαλε αὐτόν· καλόν σέ ἐστιν μονόφθαλμον εἰσελθεῖν εἰς τὴν βασιλείαν τοῦ θεοῦ ἢ δύο

---

63. Judith M. Gundry-Volf, "Between the Text and Sermon: Mark 9:33–37," *Interpretation* 53, no. 1 (1999): 59, 60.

ὀφθαλμοὺς ἔχοντα βληθῆναι εἰς τὴν γέενναν, 48 ὅπου ὁ σκώληξ αὐτῶν οὐ τελευτᾷ καὶ τὸ πῦρ οὐ σβέννυται.

49 Πᾶς γὰρ πυρὶ ἁλισθήσεται. 50 καλὸν τὸ ἅλας· ἐὰν δὲ τὸ ἅλας ἄναλον γένηται, ἐν τίνι αὐτὸ ἀρτύσετε; ἔχετε ἐν ἑαυτοῖς ἅλα, καὶ εἰρηνεύετε ἐν ἀλλήλοις. [SBLGNT]

King James Version

38 And John answered him, saying, Master, we saw one casting out devils in thy name, and he followeth not us: and we forbad him, because he followeth not us. 39 But Jesus said, Forbid him not: for there is no man which shall do a miracle in my name, that can lightly speak evil of me. 40 For he that is not against us is on our part. 41 For whosoever shall give you a cup of water to drink in my name, because ye belong to Christ, verily I say unto you, he shall not lose his reward. 42 And whosoever shall offend one of these little ones that believe in me, it is better for him that a millstone were hanged about his neck, and he were cast into the sea. 43 And if thy hand offend thee, cut it off: it is better for thee to enter into life maimed, than having two hands to go into hell, into the fire that never shall be quenched: 44 Where their worm dieth not, and the fire is not quenched. 45 And if thy foot offend thee, cut it off: it is better for thee to enter halt into life, than having two feet to be cast into hell, into the fire that never shall be quenched: 46 Where their worm dieth not, and the fire is not quenched. 47 And if thine eye offend thee, pluck it out: it is better for thee to enter into the kingdom of God with one eye, than having two eyes to be cast into hell fire: 48 Where their worm dieth not, and the fire is not quenched. 49 For every one shall be salted with fire, and every sacrifice shall be salted with salt. 50 Salt is good: but if the salt have

New Rendition

38 John was saying to him, "Teacher, we saw someone casting out demons in your name. And we tried to stop him because he was not following us." 39 And Jesus said, "Do not stop him. For there is no one who will do a miracle in my name who will be able soon after to revile me. 40 For whoever is not against us is for us. 41 For whoever should give you a cup of water because you are the anointed one's—amen, I say to you—that person will not destroy his/her reward. 42 And whoever causes one of these little ones who trusts me to stumble, it would be better for them if a large millstone were put around their neck and they were cast into the sea. 43 And if your hand should cause you to stumble, cut it off. It is better for you to enter into life maimed instead of going away into hell with two hands, into the unquenchable fire. [44] 45 And if your foot should cause you to stumble, cut it off. It is better for you to enter into life maimed instead of having two feet [and] being cast into hell. [46] 47 And if your eye causes you to stumble, cast it out. It is better for you to enter into the kingdom of God with one eye, rather than having two eyes and having to be cast into hell, 48 where their worm does not die and the fire is not quenched. 49 For everyone will be salted with fire. 50 Salt is good, but if the salt becomes unsalty, how could you season it? Have

lost his saltness, wherewith will ye season it? Have salt in yourselves, and have peace one with another.

salt in yourselves, and be at peace with one another."

Notes

9:38 *And John answered him, saying, Master, we saw one casting out devils in thy name, and he followeth not us:* The phrase "and he followeth not us" is not in the best manuscripts,[64] so it is not included in the New Rendition (it is, however, at the end of the verse).

In other instances, Peter has been the spokesperson for the disciples. It is not clear why John assumes that role (via his use of "we") here; perhaps it points to a fluidity in leadership roles during Jesus' ministry, which would be consonant with the previous conversation about who was the greatest.

and we forbad him, because he followeth not us: This response is ironic since the disciples were recently unable to exorcise a demon themselves.

John's use of the word "us" is also suspect—Jesus has not taught that anyone should be following the disciples; rather, people are to follow Jesus. It is even possible that this unknown exorcist was actually following Jesus but did not follow the disciples.

9:39 *But Jesus said, Forbid him not:* "Forbid" is plural, so while John may have asked the question, he appears, based on Jesus' response, to be speaking for all of the disciples.

for there is no man which shall do a miracle in my name, that can lightly speak evil of me: Because "miracle" (Greek: *dunamis*) and "can" (Greek: *dunamai*) are very similar, there is a play on words here.

Jesus' words imply that he did not intend for the performance of miracles to be limited to his disciples. The subtext of his statement is that all people have the power to perform miracles in his name. There may also be a layer of irony in Jesus' reply if it is assumed that John is "speaking evil" of the unknown exorcist.

Relationship to Numbers 11. In Numbers 11:27–29, Joshua and others ask Moses to stop Eldad and Medad from prophesying. (The LXX uses the same verb as Mark does for "forbid.") Moses refuses and expresses his wish that all people were prophets. There are similarities between the two texts: Moses and Jesus have an expansionist view, but some of their followers want to restrict spiritual manifestations. Comparing these texts encourages

---

64. Metzger, *Textual Commentary*, 86.

a link between prophesying and exorcising. And since Moses asks if they are jealous, comparing the two stories may hint at John's motivation.

9:40 *For he that is not against us is on our part:* This line is a common proverb, but it can also be read as "a prophecy of the future":[65] someone who is not actively opposed to Jesus and who performs exorcisms in Jesus' name will, in the future, desire to be on Jesus' side.

9:41 *For whosoever shall give you a cup of water to drink in my name:* This verse pictures someone who is not a disciple but who makes life easier for the disciples in the smallest possible way.

There are two ways in which this verse might relate to the situation with the unknown exorcist: both picture nondisciples contributing to Jesus' cause, and both make reference to doing things in the name of Jesus.

because ye belong to Christ: While the ancient manuscripts firmly support the text, some scholars still wonder if the reference to Christ is a later addition because it is so out of character[66] to use the title "Christ" in Mark's Gospel and also because the syntax is awkward.

It is not the provisioning of the water per se but rather providing it to advance the ministry of Christ that is in view here.

verily I say unto you, he shall not lose his reward: The duty to provide food and water as part of basic hospitality was well established, so the idea of a reward being attached to it is surprising. Jesus rewards even the simplest acts of kindness; this speaks to his own generosity. Further, the language posits eternal rewards even for those not fully committed to following Jesus (compare D&C 76:74–76).

See also the Notes on 3:28 regarding the phrase "verily I say unto you."

9:42 *And whosoever shall offend one of these little ones that believe in me:* The word "offend" means "to stumble" and thus integrates well with the imagery of being "on the way" of discipleship. Metaphorically, it means "to sin" or "to go astray."

By "little one," Jesus may mean a literal child, which would make sense given the previous story's reference to an actual child. But it could also refer to the unknown exorcist as one exercising a small amount of belief, which makes sense given the immediate context of this saying. In the latter case, John is the one who is at risk of offending the one who believes, the exorcist.

The phrase "in me" is missing from some of the ancient manuscripts;[67] perhaps it was added to harmonize with Matthew 18:6. Omitting this

---

65. Marcus, *Mark 8–16*, 686.

66. Waetjen, *Reordering of Power*, 160–61.

67. Metzger, *Textual Commentary*, 86.

phrase makes Jesus' admonition applicable to all children and not just children who believe in him; given the context, this is probably the preferable reading.

The relationship of this verse to the previous verse may rely on antithetical parallelism: 9:41 describes the blessings of helping those who believe, and this verse describes the curse accruing to those who harm believers.

Jesus' primary concern here is not with restricting authority but rather with not causing offense.

it is better for him that a millstone were hanged about his neck, and he were cast into the sea: While the Greek text uses singular forms for "him," "his," and "he," the New Rendition uses plural forms in order to avoid gender-specific pronouns.

Unlike small millstones that could be operated by hand, the Greek word here describes a large millstone that would have been pulled by a draft animal.

The image in this verse is based on an actual practice: "The graphic reference to the millstone around the neck and being cast into the sea would not have been lost upon the disciples, who undoubtedly had heard of the punishment inflicted by the Romans in Galilee on some of the leaders of the insurrection under the early Zealot leader, Judas the Galilean."[68] The vivid picture uses a real-world example to emphasize the strict importance of not offending the little ones.

9:43 *And if thy hand offend thee, cut it off:* There is a shift from the previous verse, which was concerned with offending other people, to this verse's concern with offending oneself.

The hand could symbolize accomplishing one's intentions in the physical world; it could also symbolize sexual sin. While Judaism prohibited self-mutilation (Deut. 14:1), amputation was used as punishment under the law of Moses (Ex. 21:23–25; Deut. 25:11–12) and in the Greco-Roman world.

it is better for thee to enter into life maimed, than having two hands to go into hell, into the fire that never shall be quenched: "Hell" translates the name of a valley south of Jerusalem, the Valley of Hinnom. It was thought to be the site of infant sacrifice (Jer. 7:31).[69] It became a garbage dump under the Josian reforms and refuse was burned there so that it was normally smoldering. Because of the association with pagan ritual, garbage, and perpetual fire, the valley became a metaphor for eternal punishment and thus for hell.

---

68. Lane, *Gospel according to Mark,* 346.

69. The idea that this was the site of infant sacrifices might be propaganda, but it was nonetheless a common belief, if inaccurate.

9:44 ***Where their worm dieth not, and the fire is not quenched:*** Neither 9:44 nor 9:46 appear in the earliest manuscripts;[70] these verses seem to have been copied—either accidentally or intentionally to improve the style—from 9:48. The New Rendition omits both verses.

9:45 ***And if thy foot offend thee, cut it off: it is better for thee to enter halt into life, than having two feet to be cast into hell:*** Foot can be a euphemism for penis in the HB[71] but also a metaphor for walking, and thus perhaps another reference to the way of discipleship.

into the fire that never shall be quenched: This phrase is not in many of the ancient manuscripts and was probably added later—either accidentally based on the parallel in 9:43 or deliberately to improve the style by creating a parallel to that verse.[72]

9:46 ***Where their worm dieth not, and the fire is not quenched:*** See the Notes on 9:44.

9:47 ***And if thine eye offend thee, pluck it out:*** The eye can symbolize sins of attitude and intention or could "be understood in the context of the erotic gaze."[73]

it is better for thee to enter into the kingdom of God with one eye, than having two eyes to be cast into hell fire: The word "fire" is not in the best manuscripts.[74]

9:48 ***Where their worm dieth not, and the fire is not quenched:*** "Their worm" refers to the maggots in the dead bodies of those who go to hell.

This verse is a paraphrase of Isaiah 66:24. In this, the final verse of Isaiah, the people who worship the Lord see the corpses of those who rebelled against God attacked by maggots and consuming fire.

9:49 ***For every one shall be salted with fire:*** This verse is quite a puzzle to interpret, partially because there are no ancient parallels to being "salted with fire" and it is not precisely clear what this phrase might mean. (This confusion may be reflected in Matthew's and Luke's decision to omit it.) Possible interpretations include:

1. Under the law of Moses, sacrifices were salted (Lev. 2:13). Here, instead of the sacrifice being salted, the person is salted, as if she were the sacrifice. Perhaps this imagery relates to the idea of self-mutilation described above, moderating it by suggesting that every disciple will eventually sacrifice herself anyway and thus the sacrifice of an offending body part is minimized.

---

70. Metzger, *Textual Commentary*, 86–87.
71. See perhaps Ex. 4:25; Judg. 3:24; Ruth 3:7; 1 Sam. 24:3; and Isa. 6:2.
72. Collins, *Mark*, 443 note g.
73. Collins, *Mark*, 454.
74. Bratcher and Nida, *Translator's Handbook*, 303.

2. Salting with fire points to the need for purification and thus the idea that everyone will be salted with fire teaches that everyone must be purified. The depiction of maimings points to the importance of this purification process.

3. "Salted with fire" represents an Aramaic or Hebrew idiom that was translated literally but that meant "destroyed with fire."[75] (The idiom stems from the practice of destroying fields by salting them.) In this reading, "everyone" refers to everyone who enters hell and who is thus destroyed with fire.

and every sacrifice shall be salted with salt: This phrase does not seem to have been in the earliest texts but rather appears to be an explanatory marginal note—perhaps made by a scribe who thought that Leviticus 2:13 would help explain Jesus' teachings—that was accidentally incorporated into the text.[76]

9:50 *Salt is good: but if the salt have lost his saltness, wherewith will ye season it?:* Salt does not lose its saltiness, so options for interpreting this phrase include:

1. Salt that was mixed with impurities could lose its saltiness. The idea of a mixture of impurities and genuine salt fits well in the context of the discussion of impure desires.

2. Because genuine salt cannot lose its saltiness, the saying presupposes fake salt as a metaphor for fake discipleship. In other words, there is no way to make a fake disciple into a genuine disciple. That would be an interesting statement in the context of the discussion of the unknown exorcist: it would seem based on context that, ironically, Jesus is suggesting that John—not the unknown exorcist—is the fake disciple.

3. The idea of salt losing its saltiness is a metaphor for losing the very purpose of one's being.

4. Because salt could kill worms, there may be a link between this saying and the previous one based on the idea that salt would be the one thing that could stop the undying worms. In this view, the worms on the corpse in hell could be eradicated by salt—assuming it is genuine salt—that then becomes a metaphor for Jesus' saving power.

5. In rabbinic tradition[77] and in other ancient texts, salt is associated with wisdom. In context, this would mean that wisdom is necessary to living peacefully together, including specifically the wisdom needed to recognize that the unknown exorcist should be applauded, not shut down.

75. Weston W. Fields, "'Everyone Will Be Salted with Fire' (Mark 9:49)," *Grace Theological Journal* 6, no. 2 (1985): 299–304.

76. Metzger, *Textual Commentary,* 87.

77. See Evans, *Mark 8:27–16:20,* 73.

6. There are several HB references (Num. 18:19; 2 Chr. 13:5) that link the covenant to salt since salt was one of the few known substances that would not be changed or destroyed by fire or by the passage of time.

7. As a result of the link of salt to the covenant described above, salt was also a symbol for purity (Ex. 30:34–36). (Perhaps this symbolism arose since salt could prevent food from spoiling.)

8. Salt was a preservative, so the disciples' job is to preserve Jesus' teachings from corruption.

Several of these readings, particularly numbers 6 and 8, mesh well with modern Latter-day Saint thought about the role of covenants and apostasy: if salt is a symbol for the covenant, then the disciples' job is to preserve that covenant. If they do not, it will be lost and cannot be instantly restored, hence the risk of apostasy. Interestingly, in this reading this danger of apostasy is tied to the disciples' desire to stop the unknown exorcist.

Have salt in yourselves, and have peace one with another: If both of the imperatives ("have salt" and "have peace") are synonymous, this counsel suggests that the result of having salt is being at peace. Assuming that Jesus' teachings here are still a response to John's desire to stop the unknown exorcist, then this is the final exhortation: it is important to be at peace with him. It may also link to the previous dispute regarding which disciple was the greatest.

Analysis

Jesus' sayings found in 9:38–50 are some of the most difficult to interpret in the entire text. There are two different options for understanding the arrangement of these sayings:

1. The sayings were likely delivered by Jesus at various times and on various occasions during his ministry; they were grouped together by keywords, which would have aided memorization. The keywords are: in my name (9:37, 38, 39, 41), offend (9:42, 43, 45, 47), child (9:36, 37, 42), hell (9:43, 45, 47), salt (9:49, 50), and fire (9:43, 48, 49). Thus, there is no internal logic to the section, and the sayings do not relate to each other.

2. The sayings do relate to each other and form one integrated discourse, composing Jesus' response to John's desire to stop the unknown exorcist. The entire section concerns this desire, which Jesus compares unfavorably to self-mutilation; he then exhorts peace among those who use his name.

It is difficult to determine which approach is preferable.

The general thrust of Mark's message concerning discipleship is that the disciples are learners who follow Jesus and learn from him. This story adds a nuance to that presentation through an unknown exorcist who does not follow Jesus and his disciples but who is able to exorcise in Jesus' name and is not condemned by him for so doing. Particularly when compared with the disciples' recent inability to perform an exorcism, this exorcist stands as a model disciple.

Jesus' refusal to forbid this unknown exorcist is particularly noteworthy since authority to cast out demons was specifically given to the disciples (3:15). Further, performing an exorcism was the first formal act of Jesus' ministry (1:21–28) and one of the key tasks of the ministry of the Twelve (6:7, 13). All the same, this power is not meant to be restricted just to this inner circle, as Jesus' approval of this exorcist illustrates. Apparently John thought that this power and authority should have been restricted to the Twelve only, but Jesus' perspective is different. Further, Jesus' words indicate that it is not the role of the Twelve to mediate Jesus' authority at this point.

Jesus' counsel to get rid of hand, foot, and eye rather than sin has different interpretations, including the following:

1. As euphemisms for sexual sins. The reference to little ones refers to pederasty, the hand to masturbation, the foot (as a symbol for genitals) to adultery, and the eye to lust. The oblique language stems from a desire not to speak openly about sexual sin. The point is that it would be better to drown or maim the body than to give in to its unrighteous desires. While this reading has the advantage of including the millstone reference along with the three instances of maiming, it does not fit well in the larger context, which does not involve sexual sins.

2. As a response to John's request to forbid the unknown exorcist. The point is that the disciples would be better off drowning or maiming themselves than causing offense to another. The graphic language suggests that it is better to cut off part of one's own body than to cut off one who performs miracles in Jesus' name; the disciples should be more concerned about the fate of "little ones" than they are about their own bodies.

3. As a metaphor for the path of discipleship. If the hand (symbolizing action), the foot (motion), or eye (planning) distracts from that path, it is better to remove the offending part than to be removed from the path.

It is often suggested that Jesus did not intend for these verses to be taken literally. That reading misses the point: it is literally true that it would be preferable to be physically maimed than to sin. Physical defects do not isolate one from God, but sin does, therefore the sin is worse. However, Jesus is not teaching that maiming is a solution to sin. His statement, even when read literally, in no way encourages physical maiming because that would not remit the sin.

Under the law of Moses, those who were physically imperfect could not serve as priests (Lev. 21:17) and thus could not serve the Lord in the temple or symbolically enter the Lord's presence. Jesus' teachings here suggest that not only is it possible to enter the presence of the Lord when maimed, it is preferable to sinning. This is an important commentary on the law of Moses; it is also significant in the context of Jesus' healing ministry: his miracles do not support the notion that physical perfection is required in order to enter the presence of the Lord.

Jesus Teaches about Divorce (10:1–12)

Greek Text

1 Καὶ ἐκεῖθεν ἀναστὰς ἔρχεται εἰς τὰ ὅρια τῆς Ἰουδαίας καὶ πέραν τοῦ Ἰορδάνου, καὶ συμπορεύονται πάλιν ὄχλοι πρὸς αὐτόν, καὶ ὡς εἰώθει πάλιν ἐδίδασκεν αὐτούς.

2 Καὶ ἐπηρώτων αὐτὸν εἰ ἔξεστιν ἀνδρὶ γυναῖκα ἀπολῦσαι, πειράζοντες αὐτόν. 3 ὁ δὲ ἀποκριθεὶς εἶπεν αὐτοῖς· Τί ὑμῖν ἐνετείλατο Μωϋσῆς; 4 οἱ δὲ εἶπαν· Ἐπέτρεψεν Μωϋσῆς βιβλίον ἀποστασίου γράψαι καὶ ἀπολῦσαι. 5 ὁ δὲ Ἰησοῦς εἶπεν αὐτοῖς· Πρὸς τὴν σκληροκαρδίαν ὑμῶν ἔγραψεν ὑμῖν τὴν ἐντολὴν ταύτην· 6 ἀπὸ δὲ ἀρχῆς κτίσεως ἄρσεν καὶ θῆλυ ἐποίησεν αὐτούς· 7 ἕνεκεν τούτου καταλείψει ἄνθρωπος τὸν πατέρα αὐτοῦ καὶ τὴν μητέρα καὶ προσκολληθήσεται πρὸς τὴν γυναῖκα αὐτοῦ, 8 καὶ ἔσονται οἱ δύο εἰς σάρκα μίαν· ὥστε οὐκέτι εἰσὶν δύο ἀλλὰ μία σάρξ. 9 ὃ οὖν ὁ θεὸς συνέζευξεν ἄνθρωπος μὴ χωριζέτω.

10 Καὶ εἰς τὴν οἰκίαν πάλιν οἱ μαθηταὶ περὶ τούτου ἐπηρώτων αὐτόν. 11 καὶ λέγει αὐτοῖς· Ὃς ἂν ἀπολύσῃ τὴν γυναῖκα αὐτοῦ καὶ γαμήσῃ ἄλλην μοιχᾶται ἐπ᾽ αὐτήν, 12 καὶ ἐὰν αὐτὴ ἀπολύσασα τὸν ἄνδρα αὐτῆς γαμήσῃ ἄλλον μοιχᾶται. [SBLGNT]

King James Version

1 And he arose from thence, and cometh into the coasts of Judæa by the farther side of Jordan: and the people resort unto him again; and, as he was wont, he taught them again.

2 And the Pharisees came to him, and asked him, Is it lawful for a man to put away his wife? tempting him. 3 And he answered and said unto them, What did Moses command you? 4 And they said, Moses suffered to write a bill of

New Rendition

1 And having risen up from there, he comes through the region of Judea and beyond the Jordan. And the crowds again come together to him, and as again, as was his habit, he was teaching them. 2 And having come to him, they demanded of him, "Is it lawful for a husband to divorce his wife?" testing him. 3 But answering he said to them, "What did Moses command you?" 4 And they said, "Moses permitted [a man] to write a divorce decree and to

divorcement, and to put her away. 5 And Jesus answered and said unto them, For the hardness of your heart he wrote you this precept. 6 But from the beginning of the creation God made them male and female. 7 For this cause shall a man leave his father and mother, and cleave to his wife; 8 And they twain shall be one flesh: so then they are no more twain, but one flesh. 9 What therefore God hath joined together, let not man put asunder. 10 And in the house his disciples asked him again of the same matter. 11 And he saith unto them, Whosoever shall put away his wife, and marry another, committeth adultery against her. 12 And if a woman shall put away her husband, and be married to another, she committeth adultery.

send her away." 5 But Jesus said to them, "Because of the hardness of your heart, he wrote this commandment for you. 6 But from the beginning of creation he 'made them male and female.' 7 'Because of this, a man will leave his father and mother, 8 and the two will be one flesh,' so that they are no longer two but one flesh. 9 Therefore, what God has united together, let no one separate." 10 And in the house the disciples were asking him, once again, about this. 11 And he says to them, "Whoever divorces his wife and marries another commits adultery against her. 12 And if a woman divorces her husband and marries another, she commits adultery."

Notes

10:1 *And he arose from thence, and cometh into the coasts of Judæa:* "Thence" refers to Capernaum, which was the last place mentioned (9:33).

by the farther side of Jordan: and the people resort unto him again; and, as he was wont, he taught them again: The word "people" translates "crowds," which is a common enough word in Mark, although this is the only time where the plural form is used, perhaps because two different locations have been mentioned.

10:2 *And the Pharisees came to him, and asked him:* It is likely that the earliest texts of Mark did not here include reference to the Pharisees (so instead of "the Pharisees came" the text would have read "they came"), with the identity of Jesus' interlocutors omitted; the reference to the Pharisees may have been added later by scribes in order to parallel Matthew 19:3.[78]

Is it lawful for a man to put away his wife?: The Greek permits this line to be read as direct speech ("asked him, 'Is it lawful'") or indirect speech ("asked him whether it was lawful").

Deuteronomy 24:1 permits divorce in cases of "uncleanness." First-century Judaism therefore authorized divorce, although the conditions that justified it

---

78. Metzger, *Textual Commentary*, 88.

were debated[79] based on varying interpretations of what constituted "unclean-ness." The minority view was that divorce was only permitted in cases of adul-tery, but most authorities allowed it for much broader reasons, including very minor ones. In context, then, the question posed to Jesus would most likely have struck Mark's audience as insincere (even without Mark's note that they were trying to tempt Jesus) since there was general agreement that divorce was permitted. There are two ways in which their question might have entrapped Jesus:

1. John the Baptist lost his head largely because of his criticism of Herod's mari-tal situation (6:18). So the questioners might hope that Jesus will teach as John did and thus create political trouble for himself; the issue is particularly salient at this moment in the narrative since 10:1 made it clear that Jesus had entered territory controlled by Herod.

2. Deuteronomy 24:1–4 assumes that divorces will occur and regulates it, but in Malachi 2:16, God proclaims hatred for divorce. So Jesus' interlocutors may have intended to show Jesus in violation of sacred writ regardless of which position he took.

The inquirers do not ask whether a woman might divorce her husband; neither the law of Moses nor then-contemporary Jewish practice permit-ted women to initiate divorce proceedings.[80]

tempting him: Mark clearly signals to the audience that this is not a genuine question.

10:3 *And he answered and said unto them, What did Moses command you?:* Jesus does not ask what Moses commanded "us" but rather what he commanded "you," which may indicate his unique position in relation to the law of Moses. It could also anticipate the fact that the law was given because of their hardheartedness, a condition that would not apply to him.

Some interpreters have used this passage to argue that Moses wrote Deuteronomy, but that line of reasoning is suspect: Jesus may either be speaking traditionally, or he may be using "Moses" to refer to a certain sec-tion of scripture without commenting on authorship at all.

10:4 *And they said, Moses suffered to write a bill of divorcement, and to put her away:* Jesus' questioners refer to Deuteronomy 24:1–4, which regulated divorce. But the answer here only mentions the man: "the

---

79. France, *Gospel,* 387–88. One exception appears to be among the community at Qumran, where divorce was banned; interestingly, they also appealed to Gen. 1:27, as Jesus will, to bar divorce. See Evans, *Mark 8:27–16:20,* 81.

80. While Jewish women in the Elephantine could initiate divorce (Collins, *Mark,* 459), this practice is probably too distant from Mark's text to be relevant (Gundry, *Mark,* 543).

questioners are portrayed as construing divorce entirely from the male point of view. They speak only of writing the certificate; they omit the formal step of putting it into the woman's hand, thus guaranteeing that she can show the specific reason for her ex-husband's rejection of her, leaving nothing to rumor and speculation."[81] In this passage, Jesus will treat both genders with parity at every turn, but this response to his question ironically ignores women when the very purpose of the legislation in Deuteronomy was to protect women who were divorced by their husbands.

While Jesus asks what Moses "commanded," they answer concerning what Moses "permitted." This difference is significant because Moses did not command divorce; rather, Deuteronomy regulates divorce without necessarily condoning it.[82]

10:5 *And Jesus answered and said unto them, For the hardness of your heart he wrote you this precept:* The word "your" probably refers to all of fallen humanity, since it is unlikely that Jesus meant that the people listening to him were uniquely the cause of what was written in the law of Moses.

Possibilities for how hardness of heart motivated the divorce regulations in Deuteronomy include:

1. In the absence of a legal mechanism for divorce, some hardhearted men might have killed their wives to be free of them.
2. Adultery (as the motive for divorce) would suggest hardness of heart.
3. The regulations in Deuteronomy specifically prohibit the remarriage of divorced spouses if the wife had remarried and divorced (or been widowed) in the interim. Hence, temporary marriages, a practice that would have indicated hardness of heart, were prohibited.

Jesus does not indicate whether God had inspired this regulation. While it is possible that Deuteronomy 24:1–4 was inspired, it is also possible that Jesus indicates that it was written without divine guidance. Either way, "first principles must take primacy over subsequent remedial provisions."[83]

10:6 *But from the beginning of the creation God made them male and female:* Jesus quotes from Genesis 1:27. Mark's original text probably read "he" instead of "God," with later scribes changing the text so that the audience would not think that Moses (the closest referent for "he") had created men and women.[84]

---

81. Dowd, *Reading Mark,* 101.
82. Collins, *Mark,* 459.
83. France, *Gospel,* 392.
84. Metzger, *Textual Commentary,* 88.

10:7 *For this cause shall a man leave his father and mother:* This line is a quotation from Genesis 2:24. In that context, it introduces the conclusion drawn from Adam's statement that the woman is bone of his bone and flesh of his flesh. However, Jesus uses it differently here: in this context, it is the conclusion drawn not from Adam's statement, but rather from the narrator's statement that God created humans as male and female (Gen. 1:27, quoted in 10:6). Jesus combines the two statements from Genesis to suggest that a man leaves his parents in order to join with his wife because they were created for each other. Jesus' questioners would, of course, have been familiar with these passages. However, they probably had not combined them in this way and may not have applied them to the issue of divorce.

Genesis 2:24 describes a matrilocal system, where a man left his parents' home to live with his wife's family. While there is no evidence that this was the practice either in ancient Israel or in Jesus' time, the text nonetheless reflects this custom.

and cleave to his wife: Some ancient manuscripts omit this phrase. There are two possibilities for what has happened here:

1. The phrase was originally in the text but was accidentally omitted when a scribe's eye skipped from the "and" at the beginning of this phrase to the "and" at the beginning of 10:8.

2. It was not originally included but was added by a later scribe to complete the quotation from Genesis 2:24.[85]

If the phrase is not included, the closest antecedent for the word "they" in 10:8 would be the man's mother and father—clearly not what the text intended. This could argue either for the original inclusion of the phrase "and cleave unto his wife" (since it makes better sense of the text) or for its exclusion (since it may have been later scribes who improved the text precisely so that it would make better sense).

If the phrase is omitted, Jesus' entire quotation from Genesis is gender-neutral. In this reading, the "man" who in 10:9 is not to separate what man had joined could be either the male or the female, which sets the stage for Jesus' later reference to women as initiators of divorce in 10:12.

10:8 *And they twain shall be one flesh:* This line is also a quotation from Genesis 2:24. While most interpreters take "one flesh" to refer to sexual union or to marital unity in general, in some strands of Jewish thought it was believed to refer to the couple's children. All three of these readings would support Jesus' argument concerning the undesirability of divorce.

---

85. Metzger, *Textual Commentary*, 88–89.

Jesus' quotations from Genesis raise the issue of the authorship of Genesis. Traditionally, it was thought that Moses wrote the first five books of the HB, but virtually all modern scholars reject this idea.[86] On the one hand, it is possible to take the disjunction between how Jesus introduces the Deuteronomy text and the Genesis texts ("[Moses] wrote this precept" in 10:5 regarding Deuteronomy 24:1–4, versus no author named for the Genesis quotations—despite the fact that Jesus actually quotes from Genesis) as evidence that Jesus was not attributing the authorship of Genesis to Moses. But on the other hand, the fact that Jesus' line of inquiry began with "What did Moses command you?" suggests that he views Genesis as containing Moses' commands. It is possible that Jesus is speaking conventionally here, meaning that he is attributing the authorship of Genesis to Moses as was commonly done, and yet to use his words as an argument for Mosaic authorship is to overread his meaning here.

so then they are no more twain, but one flesh: To conclude that a married couple is one flesh, it would have been logical to refer to the story of Eve's creation from Adam's rib. (In fact, the idea that God created humans as male and female would seem to imply the opposite: that humans are, originally and through the perfect order of creation, two fleshes and not one.) That Jesus does not refer to the rib story—despite quoting from both before and from after it in the Genesis text—is intriguing.

10:9 *What therefore God hath joined together:* Some interpreters have suggested that Jesus' prohibition on divorce did *not* apply to couples whom God had not joined together (including, perhaps, nonbelievers or those who married contrary to the law).[87] This would seem to be the case in 6:18, where John the Baptist preaches that Herod's marriage is not legitimate; presumably John would not have thought that God had joined them together nor thought that God prohibited their separation. Jesus' contemporaries debated the acceptable motives for divorce, but Jesus focuses on something else entirely: whether God was involved in the original decision to marry.

let not man put asunder: "Let" is an imperative, so Jesus is forbidding anyone from separating a married couple, including, perhaps, someone who would woo a married person.

The parallelism of the verse makes a strong distinction between God's role as the creator of men, women, and their union, and human inability to end that union.

---

86. David E. Bokovoy, *Authoring the Old Testament: Genesis–Deuteronomy* (Salt Lake City: Greg Kofford Books, 2014).

87. Witherington, *Gospel of Mark,* 277.

It might be noted that there is no "scriptural justification to assume and teach that death should annul the marriage covenant."[88] Here, the union is presented as existing before the Fall, with no mechanism for its ending.

Modern readers might assume that the man who would put a marriage asunder would be a judge in a court of law, but this was not the case under the law of Moses, where the husband would simply give his wife a written statement ending the marriage (Deut. 24:1–4). Hence, the "man" here is the husband. (It is also possible that the man is Moses, the giver of the law that permitted divorce.)

10:10 *And in the house his disciples asked him again of the same matter:* Which house is not mentioned, and, in fact, the location is surprising since Jesus has not been in this geographical area before. This suggests a symbolic function for the location and/or Mark's omission of details not relevant to the story. Given the private location, Mark's audience likely would have assumed that the following teachings were for insiders only.

The word "again" modifies "in the house," not "asked," so Mark is not suggesting that the disciples had previously asked about this matter; rather, Mark emphasizes that the disciples often ask Jesus to clarify his teachings in private. As with all of the material in this section of Mark, the disciples fail to understand what Jesus is teaching, but their need for repetition provides the audience with another chance to hear Jesus' words.

Mark does not specify exactly what they asked, but it will be clear from Jesus' answer that it concerned the divorce teachings.

10:11 *And he saith unto them, Whosoever shall put away his wife, and marry another, committeth adultery against her:* Jesus teaches that the man is guilty of adultery against the first wife. In the HB, adultery is always a crime against a male (Deut. 22:22–24; Lev. 20:10) and never against a female. Rather, if a man and a woman had an affair, the man would have committed adultery against the woman's husband (given his property right in his wife) and not against his own wife (who had no right to her husband's fidelity).

10:12 *And if a woman shall put away her husband, and be married to another, she committeth adultery:* There are four theories as to why Jesus would mention women divorcing given that Jewish law did not permit women to initiate divorce:

---

88. LeGrand Richards, "One Lord, One Faith," in *Official Report of the One Hundred Thirty-ninth Annual General Conference of The Church of Jesus Christ of Latter-day Saints* (Salt Lake City: The Church of Jesus Christ of Latter-day Saints, 1969), 90.

1. He was anticipating the spread of the gospel to areas under Roman law, where women could initiate divorce. (Some scholars even suggest this verse is a later addition to the text intended to apply Jesus' teachings to the expanding early church.)

2. While not legally permitted, some women, including Herodias, did divorce. Also, there was something of a loophole: while women could not initiate a divorce, they may have been able to maneuver their husbands into initiating a divorce. So Jesus' statement addresses these extralegal divorces and makes clear that they are not acceptable.

3. Because Jesus' teachings in this passage have been scrupulously gender-neutral to this point, this teaching is presented in a way that fits that pattern: "among the Gospel writers only the author of Mark sees women not as victims but as responsible moral agents."[89] From start to finish, Jesus treats men and women as equals in this section of the text.

4. If the best interpretation of the passage is that Jesus is prohibiting remarriage but not divorce, then he would be extending the right to divorce to women.

In 6:11 and 12, Jesus clearly prohibits remarriage. What is not clear is whether divorce itself is also prohibited; this would have allowed marriage partners a degree of autonomy without permitting subsequent remarriage for economic or political gain (which seems to have been the case with Herod and Herodias in chapter 6). Complicating the situation is the fact that remarriage was the norm so that to prohibit remarriage was, in effect, likely to prohibit divorce. And while Jesus' teachings make clear that initiating a divorce and then remarrying is sinful, it is not clear whether a spouse who is rejected when his or her spouse initiates a divorce is similarly banned from remarrying.

Comparison to 7:1–23. Mark 10:1–12 bears the following similarities to 7:1–23:

1. Jesus is publicly questioned in a hostile manner.

2. There is a legal debate.

3. Jesus offers a statement that is considered radical relative to the common positions in his day.

4. Jesus' response includes a citation from the HB.

5. Jesus further explains his teachings to his disciples in a private setting.

While Jesus is more strict than his interlocutors in chapter 10 but more permissive in chapter 7, in both stories the same dynamic is at work: the

---

89. Dowd, *Reading Mark,* 102.

questioners think themselves to be more righteous than Jesus. Jesus disabuses them of that notion by outlining a position that relies not on common interpretive traditions but rather on the text of the HB applied in an unconventional manner.

Analysis

The tenth chapter of Mark, which ends with the healing of a blind man, concludes a section that began—also with the healing of a blind man—in 8:22. All of the material bookended by these stories concerns the symbolic blindness of the disciples. In this story, that dynamic plays out as the disciples privately receive clarification about Jesus' teachings about divorce.

Further uniting this section of text is its geographical progression: it begins in Caesarea Philippi (8:27), which is the extreme northern point of Jesus' ministry, and proceeds southward to Jerusalem. Mark presents this as not just a physical journey but also as an enacted parable of the symbolic journey of discipleship, an idea emphasized through the repeated use of the phrase "the way" (8:27; 9:34; 10:17, 32, 46, 52), which was one of the first designations for the early Christian movement.

Jesus' short statement about divorce being permitted because of hardness of heart is extremely significant: he teaches that not everything included in scripture perfectly reflects the will of God; rather, some of it represents an accommodation to human weakness.[90] The implication is that some laws function to reduce the consequences of sin without entirely eliminating them. This is a radical view regarding the law of Moses: "For the Jewish people, at least for those who were Torah observant, appeal to the commandments of Moses was an appeal to the highest authority on any question."[91] But here Jesus suggests that the law of Moses is neither a uniform authority nor the highest authority.

Interestingly, Jesus departs from his usual practice of being more lenient in his interpretation of the law than his contemporaries (compare 2:16–20 and 7:15) when he adopts a stricter position regarding divorce; perhaps this is a response to the unique harms that divorce presented to women and children in the ancient world. In this light, his position is not so much a divergence from his usual lenience as it is consonant with his concern for the most vulnerable members of society.

---

90. A similar concept is found in Ezek. 20:25.
91. Evans, *Mark 8:27–16:20*, 83.

The most common interpretation of this passage is that Jesus is replacing an old law that permitted divorce with a new law that does not. However, this reading may be the result of (inappropriately) assuming that the antithesis language ("ye have heard that it was said by them of old time . . . but I say unto you") from the Sermon on the Mount is implied here. Rather, it is possible that Jesus still permits divorce (per Deut. 24:1–4) as a concession to hardheartedness while simultaneously teaching that divorce does not reflect God's design for marriage and would not be necessary in ideal circumstances. (The clarifying teachings that Jesus delivers privately to his disciples do not prohibit divorce but remarriage.)

Jesus' quotation of Genesis 1:17 suggests that sexual differentiation ("male and female"), which was part of the Creation, declares God's purposes for marriage, which did not include divorce. As will be the case with all of Jesus' statements in this story, he is gender-neutral, with his use of the Genesis text "present[ing] an interesting contrast with Jubilees 3:4–7 (second century BCE), in which the creation of the *female* is for the purpose of marriage. For the author of Mark, God created both female *and* male in sexual differentiation from each other so that they might be joined in marriage and become one."[92] While it could be argued that Jesus is merely quoting the Genesis text and thus not uniquely responsible for the radical gender neutrality of the message, the fact that he does not quote the Creation account in Genesis 2 (where the woman is created "for" the man) is indicative of his emphasis here. So Jesus' teaching suggests a level of independence for the female and interdependence for the male that was unusual in his cultural context. Thus, part of Jesus' teaching is that the order of creation speaks to the equality of the male and female: they were *both* created for the purpose of being married to each other. A system that permitted only the male to initiate divorce would destroy this equality.

Jesus explains the undesirability of divorce based on the idea that the married couple is "one" and thus cannot be separated. In Genesis 2:24, the man was to leave his parents and stay with his wife; Jesus teaches that that pattern forbids divorce. The argument relies on the idea that the order of creation is a higher law than the law of Moses: before the Fall, the created order represents God's ideal pattern for human life. Hence, some scholars speak of these "creation ordinances" as laws,[93] despite the fact that

---

92. Dowd, *Reading Mark,* 102; italics in original.

93. C. John Collins, *Genesis 1–4: A Linguistic, Literary, and Theological Commentary* (Phillipsburg, N.J.: P and R Publishing, 2006), 129–32.

the Creation account does not present laws per se. Jesus' use of these texts from Genesis imply two significant teachings: that Adam and Eve were married before the Fall and that they are meant to be models for all humans. Both of these ideas are important in Latter-day Saint thought.

Jesus' statement that a man can commit adultery against his own wife is revolutionary. It indicates that married women had rights and were, in this matter, equal to men in terms of their expectation of fidelity. Adultery is no longer a property crime against the "owner" of the woman's fidelity but rather a sin against a spouse of either gender.[94]

A modern reader, faced with the gender inequity of the HB's view of adultery, might expect Jesus to have liberated women from this slanted regime by declaring a woman no longer the property of her husband. But this is not what Jesus does; instead, he subjugated husbands so that they are now the property of their wives. Jesus presents a vision for spouses not of independence but of interdependence. He thus reimagines the marriage relationship and, indeed, male and female bodies. In the past, the female body (but only the female body) belonged to the spouse, hence if someone else had sex with her, it was a crime against him because of his property right. But Jesus puts male bodies under precisely the same restrictions: women now have a right to their husband's fidelity. Men do not own their own bodies anymore: "the sharp intensification of the concept of adultery had the effect of elevating the status of the wife to the same dignity as her husband and placed the husband under an obligation of fidelity."[95] Both the Deuteronomy text and then-current Pharisaic disputes aimed to protect women's rights in the context of the unequal standing of men and women under the law. By contrast, Jesus levels the playing field for men and women by placing equal responsibilities on husbands and wives.

Because Jesus sees the relationship with the second wife as adultery, it is as if the divorce had not occurred. (Had the divorce occurred but the second marriage was invalid, then the sin would be fornication, not adultery.) Thus Jesus' point is not so much that divorce is wrong as that it is impossible: humans are not physically capable of separating what God has joined, and thus a second marriage is adulterous. Jesus is not specifically prohibiting divorce here; he is prohibiting remarriage. What Jesus describes here does not mesh well with modern Latter-day Saint practice, which permits divorce

---

94. Compare 1 Cor. 11:11–12, which makes the radical argument that a man's body belongs to his wife.

95. Lane, *Gospel according to Mark*, 357.

and remarriage, even for those who have been sealed eternally in Latter-day Saint temples. It may be that the cancelation of temple sealings reflects a necessary accommodation for modern hardness of heart. It is also possible that Jesus' teachings were meant to be applicable only in certain social situations: in his world, divorce was almost always a disaster for women; perhaps this justified a ban that would not be necessary in other cultural settings.

Under the law of Moses, a priest was not permitted to be married to a divorced woman (Lev. 21:7). If this practice is behind Jesus' restrictions on remarriage, then he is extending a rule that had previously applied only to priests to all people. Interestingly, many of the Pharisees' innovations involved extending rules that had applied only to priests to the general population; Jesus frequently disapproves of these practices (7:3–13). In fact, this would be the one case where Jesus was stricter than the Pharisees in the application of the law of Moses' priestly requirements to non-priests. In this light, Jesus' inclusion of women is particularly significant.

JESUS TEACHES ABOUT CHILDREN (10:13–16)

Greek Text

13 Καὶ προσέφερον αὐτῷ παιδία ἵνα αὐτῶν ἅψηται· οἱ δὲ μαθηταὶ ἐπετίμησαν αὐτοῖς. 14 ἰδὼν δὲ ὁ Ἰησοῦς ἠγανάκτησεν καὶ εἶπεν αὐτοῖς· Ἄφετε τὰ παιδία ἔρχεσθαι πρός με, μὴ κωλύετε αὐτά, τῶν γὰρ τοιούτων ἐστὶν ἡ βασιλεία τοῦ θεοῦ. 15 ἀμὴν λέγω ὑμῖν, ὃς ἂν μὴ δέξηται τὴν βασιλείαν τοῦ θεοῦ ὡς παιδίον, οὐ μὴ εἰσέλθῃ εἰς αὐτήν. 16 καὶ ἐναγκαλισάμενος αὐτὰ κατευλόγει τιθεὶς τὰς χεῖρας ἐπ' αὐτά. [SBLGNT]

King James Version

13 And they brought young children to him, that he should touch them: and his disciples rebuked those that brought them. 14 But when Jesus saw it, he was much displeased, and said unto them, Suffer the little children to come unto me, and forbid them not: for of such is the kingdom of God. 15 Verily I say unto you, Whosoever shall not receive the kingdom of God as a little

New Rendition

13 And they were bringing little children to him, so that he might touch them. But the disciples rebuked them. 14 But having seen this, Jesus was angry and said to them, "Let the little children come to me—don't stop them. The kingdom of God belongs to such as these. 15 Amen, I say to you, whoever will not receive the kingdom of God like a little child will never enter into

child, he shall not enter therein. 16 And he took them up in his arms, put his hands upon them, and blessed them.

it." 16 And having hugged them, he was blessing them, having laid hands on them.

Notes

10:13 *And they brought young children to him, that he should touch them:* The identity of those who bring the children is unspecified. The term "children" could refer to infants through age twelve. If Jesus is still in the house (compare 10:17), then perhaps the residents of the home are bringing their own children to Jesus. Regardless, it is likely that the children's parents bring them to Jesus: "Their very anonymity helps to make the point about status: they, and their children, and not anybody special."[96]

Mark does not indicate the purpose of the touching. In all other cases in Mark, touching is used for healing, not for blessing, so it is possible that these children were ill, but 10:16 says that Jesus did bless the children. Those bringing the children may have hoped that Jesus would perform the kind of blessing that the HB patriarchs did (Gen. 9:26–27; 27; 48). If that is the case, it is interesting that they want Jesus to assume the role of father and patriarch to these children.

and his disciples rebuked those that brought them: Some manuscripts read "rebuked them" instead of "rebuked those that brought them." It is likely that the former is the earlier reading, with the latter attempting to make clear that the disciples did not rebuke the children.[97] However, the earlier text was ambiguous regarding who was being rebuked, so it may have been the children or those who brought them.

The word "rebuke" is the same Greek word used when demons are rebuked, which emphasizes the disciples' hostility to the children. Because Jesus has just taught that welcoming a child meant welcoming him (9:36–37), Mark's audience would have been most surprised by this rebuke. Much as with the two feeding miracles, the two stories about welcoming children work together to show the disciples' lack of comprehension, but they also provide repetition in order to help the audience learn. And as with each of the stories bookended by the two accounts of Jesus giving sight to the blind, the theme of the incomprehension of the disciples is a key concern of this story.

---

96. France, *Gospel of Mark,* 395.
97. Metzger, *Textual Commentary,* 89.

10:14 *But when Jesus saw it, he was much displeased, and said unto them:* The word "displeased" signals irritation, anger, and even repugnance at their attitude.

Left unresolved is this question: Does Jesus disapprove in general of the disciples' role as gatekeeper, or would he have approved of the disciples' limiting access to him if they had done so in ways consistent with Jesus' understanding of his mission?

Suffer the little children to come unto me, and forbid them not: There is a doubled command (suffer/allow and forbid not), employed here for emphasis.

for of such is the kingdom of God: This line implies that children are entitled to a place in the kingdom of God. A logical conclusion from this sentiment is that there is no original sin or need for infant baptism. Jesus' words are also a defense of the children's right to his attention: just as children have a share of the kingdom of God, they merit a share of Jesus' power.

Relationship to Deuteronomy 1. In Deuteronomy 1:35–39, the Lord vows that only the children—who are not tainted by the wrong choices made by their parents' generation—will be allowed to enter the promised land. It is possible that Jesus' words here in Mark suggest a similar sentiment, with a contrast made between the children who are admitted to the kingdom and the adult disciples who attempt to stop them and thus show their own lack of readiness for the kingdom.

10:15 *Verily I say unto you:* See the Notes on 3:28.

Whosoever shall not receive the kingdom of God as a little child, he shall not enter therein: In the Greek, the negative is doubled in this line for emphasis.

10:16 *And he took them up in his arms, put his hands upon them, and blessed them:* Jesus here models what it looks like when one receives a child (and, thus, receives the kingdom).

Relationship to Genesis 48. Jesus' action in blessing these children is akin to the blessings that Jacob gives to his children in Genesis 48. Those blessings ignore age/seniority as well. Because the timing of those blessings was determined by the fact that the patriarch's death was approaching (Gen. 48:1), the fact that Jesus gives blessings in a parallel text becomes, in effect, another prediction of the nearness of his own death.

Relationship to 2 Kings 4. In 2 Kings 4:27, a gatekeeper attempts to stop someone from approaching but is, like the disciples in Mark's story, in the wrong. If Mark intended an allusion here, it would reemphasize that Jesus is a prophet. It would also place the disciples in the role of servants to the prophet.

Analysis

The disciples rebuke those who bring children to Jesus. In the disciples' defense, they may have thought that since Jesus was "on the way," interrupting him with the needs of children was not an appropriate use of his time. This passage thus makes the point that caring for the needs of children is precisely the kind of action one engages in when one is "on the way" of discipleship.

Jesus uses the same language here as he did when telling the disciples not to stop the unknown exorcist (see 9:39). In both stories, the disciples were attempting to limit access to Jesus' power, but Jesus responds by instead limiting the disciples.

Jesus teaches that his disciples must receive the kingdom as a little child. There are two ways in which "as a little child" could be understood:

1. As a subject ("as a little child receives the kingdom of God"). This reading raises the question: How does a little child receive the kingdom of God? Interpretations focus on the characteristics of children, but modern notions of children (as innocent, precious, close to heaven, etc.), which were entirely foreign to the ancient world, must not be imported into the text. Rather, in Jesus' time, children occupied a very low status: they were vulnerable and easily exploited, they were humbled by necessity, and they had no rights. To receive the kingdom as a child thus means to receive it as one expecting only the lowliest of positions within it (compare Mosiah 3:16–19). The child, emblematic of "the least," becomes the paradigm for discipleship. Jesus' followers only receive the kingdom inasmuch as they are willing to inhabit a role without any social, economic, or political power, placing themselves at the mercy of others for even the most basic of their needs. By inviting the disciples to assume the role of the most exploitable, Jesus is inviting them to establish a system that does not tolerate exploitation.

2. As a direct object ("the kingdom must be received as one receives a child"). This reading fits the context particularly well since the disciples are literally rejecting children in this passage while Jesus literally receives them and demonstrates how to receive them: by hugging them, blessing them, and placing his hands on them. By rejecting the children, the disciples are rejecting the kingdom; by welcoming the children, Jesus welcomes the kingdom. And not only does Jesus welcome the kingdom/child, but he does so despite opposition from his closest followers. Further, in this passage, the children do

not themselves receive something but rather are received. So the physical actions of Jesus become an enacted parable of the teaching about welcoming the kingdom. Since children would be the last people one would receive (because of their low status), the idea of receiving the kingdom as a child is rather surprising. This reading meshes well with Jesus' parable of the mustard seed (4:30–32), where the smallest seed is a metaphor for the kingdom; it would also have important implications for female audience members since it would traditionally be the role of women to care for children; here, Jesus presents that task as the metaphor for welcoming the kingdom of God. He is thus asking his disciples to act more like women, particularly mothers.

Those who brought the children to Jesus had asked him to touch them, but Jesus hugs them, lays hands on them, and blesses them. In other words, he does far more than they had asked him to.

If the blessings Jesus gives are modeled on the HB blessings of patriarchs, then there is a certain logic that pervades this entire section of the text based on the idea of inheritance: the previous discussion on divorce concerns keeping the lines of inheritance legitimate while the subsequent discussion about "inheriting" the kingdom and the use of wealth concerns precisely what one should and should not do with that inheritance.

Mark 9:33–10:16 can be read as having the following structure:

> 9:33–37: in a house, the disciples' (inappropriate) conversation; Jesus' response about welcoming children, followed by hugging a child
>
>> 9:38–41: disciples try to get rid of unknown exorcist—to stop his access to Jesus' power
>>
>>> 9:42–50: Jesus teaches: separate one flesh to avoid sin
>>>
>>> 10:1–12: Jesus teaches: refuse to separate flesh to avoid sin
>>
>> 10:13: disciples try to get rid of unwelcome children—to stop their access to Jesus' power
>
> 10:14–16: in a house, the disciples' (inappropriate) action; Jesus' response about welcoming children, followed by hugging a child

What is perhaps most interesting about this structure is the inversion between 9:42–50, where Jesus advocates the separation of body parts to avoid sin and 10:1–12, where Jesus teaches that husband and wife are one flesh and thus cannot be separated. The paradox of these two teachings serves to emphasize Jesus' words about marriage and divorce by implying that the wife's relationship to her husband is more integral than that of his own hand.

Jesus Teaches about Wealth (10:17–31)

Greek Text

17 Καὶ ἐκπορευομένου αὐτοῦ εἰς ὁδὸν προσδραμὼν εἷς καὶ γονυπετήσας αὐτὸν ἐπηρώτα αὐτόν· Διδάσκαλε ἀγαθέ, τί ποιήσω ἵνα ζωὴν αἰώνιον κληρονομήσω; 18 ὁ δὲ Ἰησοῦς εἶπεν αὐτῷ· Τί με λέγεις ἀγαθόν; οὐδεὶς ἀγαθὸς εἰ μὴ εἷς ὁ θεός. 19 τὰς ἐντολὰς οἶδας· Μὴ φονεύσῃς, Μὴ μοιχεύσῃς, Μὴ κλέψῃς, Μὴ ψευδομαρτυρήσῃς, Μὴ ἀποστερήσῃς, Τίμα τὸν πατέρα σου καὶ τὴν μητέρα. 20 ὁ δὲ ἔφη αὐτῷ· Διδάσκαλε, ταῦτα πάντα ἐφυλαξάμην ἐκ νεότητός μου. 21 ὁ δὲ Ἰησοῦς ἐμβλέψας αὐτῷ ἠγάπησεν αὐτὸν καὶ εἶπεν αὐτῷ· Ἕν σε ὑστερεῖ· ὕπαγε ὅσα ἔχεις πώλησον καὶ δὸς τοῖς πτωχοῖς, καὶ ἕξεις θησαυρὸν ἐν οὐρανῷ, καὶ δεῦρο ἀκολούθει μοι. 22 ὁ δὲ στυγνάσας ἐπὶ τῷ λόγῳ ἀπῆλθεν λυπούμενος, ἦν γὰρ ἔχων κτήματα πολλά.

23 Καὶ περιβλεψάμενος ὁ Ἰησοῦς λέγει τοῖς μαθηταῖς αὐτοῦ· Πῶς δυσκόλως οἱ τὰ χρήματα ἔχοντες εἰς τὴν βασιλείαν τοῦ θεοῦ εἰσελεύσονται. 24 οἱ δὲ μαθηταὶ ἐθαμβοῦντο ἐπὶ τοῖς λόγοις αὐτοῦ. ὁ δὲ Ἰησοῦς πάλιν ἀποκριθεὶς λέγει αὐτοῖς· Τέκνα, πῶς δύσκολόν ἐστιν εἰς τὴν βασιλείαν τοῦ θεοῦ εἰσελθεῖν· 25 εὐκοπώτερόν ἐστιν κάμηλον διὰ τῆς τρυμαλιᾶς τῆς ῥαφίδος διελθεῖν ἢ πλούσιον εἰς τὴν βασιλείαν τοῦ θεοῦ εἰσελθεῖν. 26 οἱ δὲ περισσῶς ἐξεπλήσσοντο λέγοντες πρὸς ἑαυτούς· Καὶ τίς δύναται σωθῆναι; 27 ἐμβλέψας αὐτοῖς ὁ Ἰησοῦς λέγει· Παρὰ ἀνθρώποις ἀδύνατον ἀλλ᾽ οὐ παρὰ θεῷ, πάντα γὰρ δυνατὰ παρὰ τῷ θεῷ.

28 Ἤρξατο λέγειν ὁ Πέτρος αὐτῷ· Ἰδοὺ ἡμεῖς ἀφήκαμεν πάντα καὶ ἠκολουθήκαμέν σοι. 29 ἔφη ὁ Ἰησοῦς· Ἀμὴν λέγω ὑμῖν, οὐδείς ἐστιν ὃς ἀφῆκεν οἰκίαν ἢ ἀδελφοὺς ἢ ἀδελφὰς ἢ μητέρα ἢ πατέρα ἢ τέκνα ἢ ἀγροὺς ἕνεκεν ἐμοῦ καὶ ἕνεκεν τοῦ εὐαγγελίου, 30 ἐὰν μὴ λάβῃ ἑκατονταπλασίονα νῦν ἐν τῷ καιρῷ τούτῳ οἰκίας καὶ ἀδελφοὺς καὶ ἀδελφὰς καὶ μητέρας καὶ τέκνα καὶ ἀγροὺς μετὰ διωγμῶν, καὶ ἐν τῷ αἰῶνι τῷ ἐρχομένῳ ζωὴν αἰώνιον. 31 πολλοὶ δὲ ἔσονται πρῶτοι ἔσχατοι καὶ οἱ ἔσχατοι πρῶτοι. [SBLGNT]

King James Version

17 And when he was gone forth into the way, there came one running, and kneeled to him, and asked him, Good Master, what shall I do that I may inherit eternal life? 18 And Jesus said unto him, Why callest thou me good? there is none good but one, that is, God. 19 Thou knowest the commandments, Do not commit adultery, Do not kill, Do not steal, Do not bear false witness, Defraud not, Honour thy father

New Rendition

17 Now as he went forth on the way, a man having run up to him and having knelt down, asked him, "Good teacher, what should I do so that I might inherit eternal life?" 18 But Jesus said to him, "Why do you call me good? No one is good except God alone. 19 You know the commandments: 'Do not commit adultery. Do not murder. Do not steal. Do not give false testimony. Do not defraud. Respect your father

and mother. 20 And he answered and said unto him, Master, all these have I observed from my youth. 21 Then Jesus beholding him loved him, and said unto him, One thing thou lackest: go thy way, sell whatsoever thou hast, and give to the poor, and thou shalt have treasure in heaven: and come, take up the cross, and follow me. 22 And he was sad at that saying, and went away grieved: for he had great possessions.

23 And Jesus looked round about, and saith unto his disciples, How hardly shall they that have riches enter into the kingdom of God! 24 And the disciples were astonished at his words. But Jesus answereth again, and saith unto them, Children, how hard is it for them that trust in riches to enter into the kingdom of God! 25 It is easier for a camel to go through the eye of a needle, than for a rich man to enter into the kingdom of God. 26 And they were astonished out of measure, saying among themselves, Who then can be saved? 27 And Jesus looking upon them saith, With men it is impossible, but not with God: for with God all things are possible.

28 Then Peter began to say unto him, Lo, we have left all, and have followed thee. 29 And Jesus answered and said, Verily I say unto you, There is no man that hath left house, or brethren, or sisters, or father, or mother, or wife, or children, or lands, for my sake, and the gospel's, 30 But he shall receive an hundredfold now in this time, houses, and brethren, and sisters, and mothers, and children, and lands, with persecutions; and in the world to come eternal life. 31 But many that are first shall be last; and the last first.

and mother.'" 20 But he said to him, "Teacher, all of these I have strictly obeyed from my youth." 21 But Jesus, having looked at him, loved him, and said to him, "One thing of yours is lacking: go, as much as you have—sell, and give [the money] to the poor, and you will have treasure in heaven. And come, follow me." 22 But he, his face falling at this saying, went away grieving, for he was one who had many possessions.

23 And having looked around, Jesus says to his disciples, "How hard it is for those having riches to enter into the kingdom of God!" 24 But the disciples were astonished at his words. But Jesus again answering says to them, "Children, how hard it is to enter the kingdom of God. 25 It is easier for a camel to go through the eye of a needle than for a rich person to enter into the kingdom of heaven." 26 But they were extremely astonished, saying to him, "Then who can be saved?" 27 Jesus, having looked at them, says, "With mortals it is impossible, but not with God. Indeed, all things are possible with God."

28 Peter began to say to him, "Look, we have left all things and are following you." 29 Jesus said, "Amen, I say to you, there is no one who has left home or brothers or sisters or mother or father or children or land for my sake and for the good news 30 who will not take a hundred times as much now in this time—homes and brothers and sisters and mothers and children and land, with persecution—and in the age which is coming, eternal life. 31 But many who are first will be last, and the last first."

Notes

10:17 *And when he was gone forth into the way, there came one running, and kneeled to him, and asked him, Good Master, what shall I do that I may inherit eternal life?:* The man's question relies on some problematic assumptions:

1. Whether it is appropriate to call Jesus "good" (see the next verse).
2. Whether eternal life requires certain actions in order to "inherit" it. This idea does not mesh well with Jesus' teachings about receiving the kingdom as a child. The question is also somewhat self-contradictory since one normally does not need to do anything in order to receive an inheritance.

Neither the man's wealth (which Mark's audience will not learn about until the very end of the story) nor his commandment-keeping has left him feeling secure about his prospects for eternal life; this is especially significant if the man's statement that he has kept all of the commandments (see 10:20) is accepted as accurate.

10:18 *And Jesus said unto him, Why callest thou me good?:* The word "me" is emphatic here.

Jesus' refusal to accept being called "good" can be difficult to understand; possible interpretations include:

1. The man may have called Jesus "good" in order to obligate Jesus to address him with a similarly flattering title. Jesus' refusal to accept being called "good" thus signals his unwillingness to engage in mutual flattery, despite social convention.
2. Many HB texts praise God as good (1 Chr. 16:34; 2 Chr. 5:13; Ps. 100:5; 106:1; 107:1; 136:1). Perhaps Jesus was not willing to permit this man to lavish praise on him that properly belongs only to God. Jesus may be, in a hyperbolic way, shifting the glory from himself to God as a way to highlight God's glory. If this is the best reading, it is a departure from the frequent tendency in Mark to place Jesus in narrative roles where he is identified with the God of the HB; perhaps it is the case that the narrative can reveal Jesus' role as God but the discourse cannot.
3. Jesus' refusal to be called "good" may indicate his refusal to identify with the privileged members of the household; the point would be that God alone is good while all others are equal.

there is none good but one, that is, God: Jesus' statement opens up some distance between himself and God and thus could be weighed in later debates regarding the nature of the relationship between Jesus and God, although this is not Mark's concern here.

10:19 *Thou knowest the commandments:* Focusing on the Ten Commandments is interesting in light of 10:1–12, where Jesus downplayed the law of Moses in favor of the creation ordinances.

Do not commit adultery, Do not kill, Do not steal, Do not bear false witness: Jesus recites the sixth, seventh, eighth, and ninth commandments, following the Hebrew order.

Defraud not: This phrase appears to have been in the earliest manuscripts but was omitted by some later scribes, probably because they realized that "defraud not" did not belong to a listing of the Ten Commandments.[98] And surely the audience would have expected a reference to the tenth commandment, which prohibited coveting, here. But instead Jesus violates their expectations with the command not to defraud. Why does Jesus mention defrauding in a manner designed for maximum audience impact? Perhaps because "the command, 'You shall not defraud,' would have immediately elicited in the minds of Jesus' listeners the whole constellation of images which associated elite wealth with greed, land acquisition, and the abuse of day laborers."[99] While Mark's audience has not yet been informed of it, this man is wealthy. So the reference to defrauding is most appropriate to his personal situation and speaks to Jesus' prophetic gifts. (It may also reflect the commandments in Lev. 19:13 and/or Deut. 24:14–15.) In the economic reality of Jesus' time, there was no path to wealth except to defraud others: "In the localized zero-sum economy of agrarian Palestine, there was little chance one could become rich without having defrauded people along the way."[100] Also, through the act of altering the list of the Ten Commandments in order to reflect the personal situation of his interlocutor, Jesus makes clear his own relationship to the law.[101]

Honour thy father and mother: Jesus returns to the Ten Commandments but presents the fifth commandment out of order. It is not clear why Jesus mentions this commandment last; it may be because it is the

---

98. Metzger, *Textual Commentary*, 89.

99. Joseph H. Hellerman, "Wealth and Sacrifice in Early Christianity: Revisiting Mark's Presentation of Jesus' Encounter with the Rich Young Ruler," *Trinity Journal*, n.s., 21 (Fall 2000): 155.

100. Michael Peppard, "Torah for the Man Who Has Everything: 'Do Not Defraud' in Mark 10:19," *Journal of Biblical Literature* 134, no. 3 (2015): 604.

101. Richard Hicks, "Markan Discipleship according to Malachi: The Significance of *Me Aposterēsēs* in the Story of the Rich Man (Mark 10:17–22)," *Journal of Biblical Literature* 132, no. 1 (2013): 182.

only commandment with a promise attached, and that promise is long life (Ex. 20:12), which is related—at least tangentially—to the man's question about eternal life. It is also possible that the man's wealth may have provided special temptations for not honoring parents, perhaps through a vow of corban (see the Notes on 7:11).

10:20 *And he answered and said unto him, Master, all these have I observed from my youth:* There are two different approaches to the man's answer:

1. He is sincere. Otherwise, it would be hard to explain why Jesus loved him in the next verse. Also, he now addresses Jesus as "teacher" (KJV: "master") instead of "good teacher," so he is teachable and willing to accommodate his behavior to Jesus' request.

2. He had not kept all of the commandments, although perhaps he didn't realize it.

While this character is often called "the rich young man," Mark does not present him as young, as the phrase "from my youth" indicates.

10:21 *Then Jesus beholding him loved him, and said unto him:* There is a good chance, based on context and language, that "loved" includes a physical gesture such as hugging or putting his arm around him.

One thing thou lackest: There is an interesting irony here: despite all of his riches, he lacks something.

go thy way, sell whatsoever thou hast, and give to the poor: Because the word "go" is common in healing stories, it hints that the man's possessions are like a disease from which he must be liberated.

In some strains of Jewish thought, selling everything was forbidden because it would make the giver dependent upon others.

and thou shalt have treasure in heaven: The language here is not coincidental: the man has to give up his treasures on earth in order to get treasures in heaven.

It would have been nearly impossible to become wealthy without collaborating with Rome, so Jesus is inviting this man to focus on a different kingdom.

and come, take up the cross, and follow me: The phrase "take up the cross" is not in the best ancient manuscripts.[102]

The invitation to follow Jesus is the same invitation extended to the other disciples, supporting the reading that this is also a call story, distinctive as the only call that is refused.

---

102. Metzger, *Textual Commentary*, 89.

10:22 *And he was sad at that saying, and went away grieved:* Without saying a word, the man's face falls and he walks away. His reaction contrasts to Jesus, who looked at him and loved him; he shows his lack of love for Jesus by being unwilling to follow him. He is, as a wealthy man who attempts to engage in mutual flattery, the opposite of the child who welcomes the kingdom.

for he had great possessions: Possessions would include land and property.

Relationship to Malachi 3. In Malachi 3, the Lord is on the way to the temple to examine its corruption, as Jesus is "on the way" to the temple in Mark's text. Malachi asks who will be able to stand when the Lord comes, which means that the rich man's kneeling in this text could be read as a narrative signal that the man cannot "stand" in the Lord's presence,[103] as his unwillingness to divest of his possessions indicates. An allusion to Malachi might help explain Jesus' puzzling objection to calling him good, since in Malachi, apparently innocuous questions weary the Lord (see Mal. 2:17).[104] A close link between the two texts comes with Malachi 3:5, which in the LXX uses the same Greek word for "defraud" (KJV: "oppress") as is found in 10:19. If Mark's audience caught an allusion to Malachi 3:5 in Jesus' mention of not defrauding, they likely would have presumed that this man was guilty of oppressing his employees by withholding wages or by paying unfair wages. Another verbal link exists with the word "observed" (10:20), which is also found in LXX Malachi 3:7 (KJV: "kept"): in Mark, the rich man insists that he has observed the commandments, but the link to the Malachi texts suggests that the Lord's complaint is that he has not, in fact, done so. Further, Jesus' reference to "treasures in heaven" (10:21) echoes Malachi 3:10's use of "treasure" (KJV: "storehouse" or treasury) and "heaven." But the rich man rejects Jesus' offer, just as the audience rejects the Lord's offer in Malachi. The reference to Jesus' love for the man echoes the "theme of God's covenantal love for unfaithful Israel [that] underlies the entire book of Malachi."[105] These allusions to the Malachi text would place Jesus in the narrative role of the God of the HB.

---

103. Hicks, "Markan Discipleship," 189.
104. Hicks, "Markan Discipleship," 190.
105. Hicks, "Markan Discipleship," 194.

10:23 *And Jesus looked round about, and saith unto his disciples, How hardly shall they that have riches enter into the kingdom of God!*: The Greek text permits the possibility that the wealthy can enter the kingdom.

The discussion of entering the kingdom relates this scene to the previous one, which couched receiving the kingdom in terms of receiving a child.

Interpretation of this teaching hinges on whether the man's statement that he had kept all of the commandments is accepted as accurate. If he had kept them, then the point is clear: keeping the commandments while refusing to follow Jesus does not permit eternal life.

10:24 *And the disciples were astonished at his words*: The disciples' astonishment is explained by the idea in the HB that wealth is a blessing from God (Gen. 24:35; 26:12–14; 33:11; Lev. 26:3–10; Ps. 112:3). Their assumption would likely have been that only the righteous were blessed with wealth, so the wealthy would be the ones most likely to enter the kingdom. Thus, for Jesus to say that it was extremely difficult for the wealthy to enter the kingdom would be difficult to comprehend.

But Jesus answereth again, and saith unto them, Children, how hard is it for them that trust in riches to enter into the kingdom of God!: The oldest manuscripts omit the phrase "for them that trust in riches," so that Jesus is saying that it is hard for everyone to enter the kingdom of God. The modifying phrase appears to have been added to soften Jesus' statement or to make it more specifically relevant to the immediate situation.[106] But 10:26 requires a blanket statement before it in order to make sense; otherwise, the answer to 10:26 would have been obvious: anyone who was not wealthy could enter the kingdom. On the other hand, it is possible that the phrase might have been present initially; the disciples' astonishment in the next phrase would be understandable in terms of their belief that the wealthy were blessed. So, if the wealthy, the most blessed of people, could not enter the kingdom of God, that would indeed be surprising.

10:25 *It is easier for a camel to go through the eye of a needle*: Some of the later manuscripts have the word *kamilon* ("rope") instead of *kamelon* ("camel").[107] The change to rope was probably made because the image of a camel going through a needle's eye seemed bizarre or impossible.[108] Given

---

106. Metzger, *Textual Commentary*, 90.

107. Metzger, *Textual Commentary*, 40.

108. John A. Tvedtnes debunked the explanation that the "eye of the needle" was a gate to Jerusalem through which a camel could enter, but only on its knees, by explaining that a camel's anatomy would not permit this. He suggested one of two possibilities for understanding this verse: either that the word originally used was "rope" or that this

how similar the two words are in Greek, it is also possible that the change happened accidentally.[109]

A camel was the largest animal in Palestine at the time and the eye of a needle was the smallest opening with which they would have been familiar. Thus, the image plays on the reputation of camels and needles as the most extreme members of their respective classes in order to emphasize the impossibility of the situation. Further, camels were beasts of burden, weighed down by many "possessions," and thus the ideal symbol for the wealthy man who refuses to put down his own possessions.

than for a rich man to enter into the kingdom of God: Both 10:23 and 24 make the point that it was extremely difficult for a rich person to enter the kingdom; this verse suggests that it is impossible. Embedded within Jesus' teaching is the assumption that human effort—even keeping all of the commandments, as the rich man had done—is insufficient to enter the kingdom of God. This explains why the man needed to follow Jesus; it also hints at the need for Jesus' ministry.

10:26 *And they were astonished out of measure, saying among themselves, Who then can be saved?:* The disciples, operating under the influence of HB teachings that equated riches with God's blessings, cannot understand how anyone can be saved if the wealthy cannot be.

10:27 *And Jesus looking upon them saith:* The reference to Jesus looking is the third and final reference to his gaze in this passage (see also 10:21 and 23). Symbolically, Mark may be suggesting that Jesus' viewpoint should be an object of focus and that it is, as the previous verse made clear, significantly different from the viewpoint of others in this story.

With men it is impossible, but not with God, for with God all things are possible: Once again, the idea that humans—wealthy or otherwise—can enter the kingdom on their own merit is debunked. A subtle indication of the need for an atonement is suggested here.

---

was "deliberate hyperbole," which, he notes, was a characteristic of Jesus' speaking style specifically and of his environment in general. He concludes that "all three possible explanations of Matthew 19:24—the gate, the rope, and the Jewish figure of speech—have been mentioned by prominent Latter-day Saint leaders. (See James E. Talmage, *Jesus the Christ*, Salt Lake City: Deseret Book, 1973, pp. 485–6; Bruce R. McConkie, *Doctrinal New Testament Commentary*, 3 vols., Salt Lake City: Bookcraft, 1965–73, 1:556.) In any event, the idea is clear—riches can become a serious stumbling block to a person seeking eternal life." John A. Tvedtnes, "I Have a Question," *Ensign* 15 (March 1985): 29.

109. Collins, *Mark,* 474 note f.

Relationship to Genesis 18. In Genesis 18:14, the Lord rhetorically asks Abraham if anything is impossible for the Lord in reference to the idea of Sarah having a child at an advanced age. Jesus' use of similar language in Mark would indicate that he is fulfilling the same narrative role as the Lord. Further, the passage compares God's ability to welcome someone into the kingdom of heaven with Sarah's ability to bear a child. This feminized metaphor for God's welcoming meshes well with Mark's frequent concern with showing women as full participants in Jesus' ministry.

10:28 *Then Peter began to say unto him, Lo, we have left all, and have followed thee:* "All" in this verse translates the same Greek word that Jesus used for "all things" in the last verse, suggesting that Peter is making a link between his own actions and God's.

Peter seems to be reenacting the approach of the wealthy man (who called Jesus "good") by making a statement designed to elicit praise from Jesus—praise that Jesus does not offer.

10:29 *And Jesus answered and said, Verily I say unto you, there is no man that hath left house:* Jesus' reference to leaving one's "house" has the following possible referents:

1. Leaving home in order to preach the gospel.

2. Losing one's home because of persecution.

3. Selling one's possessions to follow Jesus, as the rich man was invited to do. One weakness of this reading is that, as previous instances in Mark have shown (1:29; 3:9), the disciples still had access to their property even after leaving to follow Jesus.

4. The inhabitants of one's household who are left behind when one leaves to preach. In this reading, the remainder of the verse would describe those left behind. (This structure would parallel the structure of the tenth commandment, which commands not coveting a neighbor's house[hold] and then lists the occupants of it.[110]) In this case, Jesus is not only requiring that they do not covet what belongs to other people but also that they freely give up what belongs to them.

or brethren, or sisters, or father, or mother, or wife, or children, or lands, for my sake, and the gospel's: The earliest manuscripts do not include the word "wife" in this verse;[111] indeed, it would be surprising for Jesus to suggest that people leave their spouses in light of his teachings on divorce at the beginning of this chapter.

---

110. Robert H. Gundry, "Mark 10:29: Order in the List," *Catholic Biblical Quarterly* 59, no. 3 (1997): 467.

111. Bratcher and Nida, *Translator's Handbook,* 326.

There may be some tension between the idea of leaving father and mother and of honoring them, a commandment that Jesus has recently mentioned. Perhaps the very reason that he referred to the fifth commandment—out of order, nonetheless—in 10:19 was to prepare for the statement here by indicating that the need to leave father and mother for the sake of the gospel did not negate the commandment to honor them. See also 7:10–13.

10:30 *But he shall receive an hundredfold now in this time, houses, and brethren, and sisters, and mothers, and children, and lands:* The terms in 10:29 were joined by the word "or" while those in this verse are joined by the word "and," implying that if a disciple leaves behind but one item mentioned in 10:29, she or he will receive everything listed in this verse.

with persecutions: This phrase is quite a startling conclusion to the previous list of blessings. While 10:29 and 30 contain parallel (if not identical) lists, 10:29 ends with "for my sake, and the gospel's" while 10:30 ends with "with persecution." Thus Jesus clearly links following him to enduring persecution. Interestingly, this verse could be interpreted to say that persecution is a blessing and, in light of the obstacle which wealth was to the man asking about eternal life, this reading fits the context particularly well.

Relationship to Job. Job gives up all of his possessions and family relations and is persecuted but, at the end of his story, has everything returned to him doubled (Job 42:10). If Jesus was alluding to Job's story, then the point would be that the follower of Jesus has even more restored to him or her as persecutions are righteously endured.

---

and in the world to come eternal life: Here Jesus returns the conversation to the impetus for the scene—the question regarding eternal life. Jesus' message is that the way to eternal life is through sacrifice. The wealthy man's refusal to follow Jesus now appears all the more short-sighted in light of this teaching.

Jesus' response to Peter, when taken in its entirety, emphasizes not eternal life but rather the blessings of gospel living during mortal life (namely, fellowship and hospitality).

10:31 *But many that are first shall be last; and the last first:* The word translated as "but" (Greek: *de*) could be an explanatory "for," which would mean that this verse explains why the last verse is true.

This line links to the plight of the wealthy man, who in refusing to make himself last will have no chance to be first. But those, as Jesus has taught, who are willing to take last place will in fact end up being first.

This teaching serves as a warning to Peter who, as a leading disciple, is in spiritual danger, as his bragging about leaving everything to follow Jesus has indicated.

Analysis

This passage contains the only reference to Jesus' love for another in Mark's Gospel; "While Jesus may be *reciting* the Decalogue, he is in fact *practicing* the 'great commandment.'"[112] On the one hand, Jesus loves this man despite his errors. On the other hand, this love does not stop Jesus from correcting him and encouraging him to change his behavior.

While the impulse to minimize Jesus' teachings should generally be avoided, there is good reason to believe that the command to sell all was not meant to be a universal command but rather was unique to this man's situation:

1. Even after their call to follow Jesus, Peter still had a house and (presumably) James[113] and John still had a boat—evidence that they, even as apostles, were not under a similar command.

2. In chapter 6, the apostles were sent out as missionaries without provisions with the understanding that other people would provide for their needs—something that would have been impossible had everyone given away all of their goods. Similarly, 10:29 pictures a situation where followers of Jesus pool their goods and share them, which would be impossible if everyone had sold everything.

3. In 14:3–9, a woman spends a year's wages on anointing oil for Jesus. Observers object that the woman should have sold the ointment and given the proceeds to the poor, echoing the commandment here. And yet Jesus defends the woman's actions, strongly suggesting that the counsel to sell all is not universal.

4. The man approached Jesus with a personal question ("What must I do to inherit eternal life?"), not a general one ("What must one do?"), suggesting that Jesus' answer would likewise be personal and not general.

Why was it necessary for this man to sell everything? Most likely because his wealth was not acquired legitimately; in fact, such a thing was generally not possible: "The only way someone became wealthy in Israelite society (as in any traditional agrarian society) was to take advantage of someone else who was vulnerable, to defraud others by charging interest on loans, which was forbidden in covenant law, and eventually gaining

---

112. Myers, *Binding the Strong Man*, 273.
113. See the Notes on 1:19.

control of others' possessions (labor, fields, households)."[114] (Thus there are numerous protections built into the law of Moses to limit the concentration of wealth [Lev. 19:9–10; 25:8–55; Deut. 14:28–29; 15:1–11; 24:14–15; 24:19–22].)

This command to sell all is similar to the call stories in 1:16–20 and 3:14 because the man is being asked to leave his worldly goods. This is, in effect, a failed call story; contrast the next story, the healing of Bartimaeus, which has elements of a successful call story. It is painfully ironic that the only person who Jesus is said to love rejects Jesus' call to follow him.

Mark withholds the detail that the man was rich until the end of the story; it is a common technique for Mark to delay crucial information in order to emphasize it and to heighten the suspense in the story (compare 5:42; 6:44; 15:41). The late placement of this detail also emphasizes Jesus' prophetic ability since he presumably already knew about the man's wealth.

The great wealth explains the man's refusal to follow Jesus; implicit is that the man's love for his possessions contrasts with Jesus' love for the man. But Jesus loved him even in his prideful ignorance. Leaving the detail about the man's wealth out of the story permits the audience to share Jesus' love for the man; had they known earlier that he was wealthy, it likely would have been impossible for them to love him. Oddly, a lack of information makes it easier for the audience to adopt Jesus' perspective—a perspective that comes from an abundance of information (as Jesus' command to the man to "defraud not" indicated).

In the HB, riches were usually regarded as a blessing from God or as evidence that one was blessed by God.[115] Here, the riches are an obstacle to blessings; the man's wealth keeps him from eternal life despite his explicit desire for it. Perhaps Mark has withheld the information about the man's riches from the audience until the end of the story to suggest that one may not realize what an impediment wealth is to eternal life until it is, in effect, too late.

It is significant that this man is genuinely interested in eternal life and willing to be corrected by Jesus (in the matter of calling him "good"). That is, his questions are not like those in the controversy stories that are posed only in order to trick Jesus. The point is that even a fundamentally good person can be misled by an attachment to wealth. This story could have

---

114. Richard A. Horsley, *Hearing the Whole Story: The Politics of Plot in Mark's Gospel* (Louisville, Ky.: Westminster John Knox Press, 2001), 191.

115. Although note the countertradition: Jer. 9:22–23; Micah 2:1–2; and especially Amos 2:6–8.

provided solace to the poor, who knew that this was not a temptation that they faced.

When Mark's audience finds out about the man's great wealth at the end of the story, they might wonder if he viewed eternal life as just another possession that he wanted to add to his collection; this would explain why he wasn't willing to give up his other possessions in order to qualify for eternal life.

The reference to "hundredfold" links this teaching to the harvest from the good soil in the seed parable in chapter 4, particularly in light of the recent picture of the man whose attachment to riches choked the seed. It also suggests that this is not a promise of private, literal possession—a reading contradicted not only by common sense but also lived experience. Rather, the promise here is that the disciple will enjoy the fellowship and hospitality of the Christian community, which will include access to hundreds of houses to stay in and fellow followers of Jesus who will be, in effect, a new family (compare 3:31–35). This may also explain the lack of reference to spouses here, since a disciple would not treat all other Christians as a spouse. Given that family relationships in antiquity signified economic security as much as—if not more so—than they signified sentimentality, this is an important promise. Additionally, this passage is an important component of Jesus' teachings on renunciation of property: "Jesus' intention was not to call people into poverty but into community."[116] There are rewards—even immediate rewards—for following Jesus. At the same time, as the next phrase will indicate, those rewards will be accompanied by persecution.

The lack of reference to fathers in 10:30 is significant, particularly since fathers were mentioned in the previous verse (compare 3:31–35, which does not include fathers in the "new family" either). The omission may be due to the fact that the new community has but one father, the Father in Heaven. It may also stem from the reality that the outsized power that fathers had in the ancient world could not be appropriately exercised among Jesus' followers (compare 10:43). Or, Jesus may be the unmentioned father, especially since he has taken on the role of father as the one who blesses children and since he has just referred to his audience as "children" (10:24; see also 2:5; 5:34). Jesus' statement refutes Peter's claim to have given up everything by showing that Peter has actually gained more than he forfeited.

---

116. Steve Barr, "The Eye of the Needle—Power and Money in the New Community: A Look at Mark 10:17–31," *Andover Newton Review* 3, no. 1 (1992): 42.

A Third Prediction of Death (10:32–45)

Greek Text

32 Ἦσαν δὲ ἐν τῇ ὁδῷ ἀναβαίνοντες εἰς Ἱεροσόλυμα, καὶ ἦν προάγων αὐτοὺς ὁ Ἰησοῦς, καὶ ἐθαμβοῦντο, οἱ δὲ ἀκολουθοῦντες ἐφοβοῦντο. καὶ παραλαβὼν πάλιν τοὺς δώδεκα ἤρξατο αὐτοῖς λέγειν τὰ μέλλοντα αὐτῷ συμβαίνειν 33 ὅτι Ἰδοὺ ἀναβαίνομεν εἰς Ἱεροσόλυμα, καὶ ὁ υἱὸς τοῦ ἀνθρώπου παραδοθήσεται τοῖς ἀρχιερεῦσιν καὶ τοῖς γραμματεῦσιν, καὶ κατακρινοῦσιν αὐτὸν θανάτῳ καὶ παραδώσουσιν αὐτὸν τοῖς ἔθνεσιν 34 καὶ ἐμπαίξουσιν αὐτῷ καὶ ἐμπτύσουσιν αὐτῷ καὶ μαστιγώσουσιν αὐτὸν καὶ ἀποκτενοῦσιν, καὶ μετὰ τρεῖς ἡμέρας ἀναστήσεται.

35 Καὶ προσπορεύονται αὐτῷ Ἰάκωβος καὶ Ἰωάννης οἱ υἱοὶ Ζεβεδαίου λέγοντες αὐτῷ· Διδάσκαλε, θέλομεν ἵνα ὃ ἐὰν αἰτήσωμέν σε ποιήσῃς ἡμῖν. 36 ὁ δὲ εἶπεν αὐτοῖς· Τί θέλετε ποιήσω ὑμῖν; 37 οἱ δὲ εἶπαν αὐτῷ· Δὸς ἡμῖν ἵνα εἷς σου ἐκ δεξιῶν καὶ εἷς ἐξ ἀριστερῶν καθίσωμεν ἐν τῇ δόξῃ σου. 38 ὁ δὲ Ἰησοῦς εἶπεν αὐτοῖς· Οὐκ οἴδατε τί αἰτεῖσθε· δύνασθε πιεῖν τὸ ποτήριον ὃ ἐγὼ πίνω, ἢ τὸ βάπτισμα ὃ ἐγὼ βαπτίζομαι βαπτισθῆναι; 39 οἱ δὲ εἶπαν αὐτῷ· Δυνάμεθα. ὁ δὲ Ἰησοῦς εἶπεν αὐτοῖς· Τὸ ποτήριον ὃ ἐγὼ πίνω πίεσθε καὶ τὸ βάπτισμα ὃ ἐγὼ βαπτίζομαι βαπτισθήσεσθε, 40 τὸ δὲ καθίσαι ἐκ δεξιῶν μου ἢ ἐξ εὐωνύμων οὐκ ἔστιν ἐμὸν δοῦναι, ἀλλ᾽ οἷς ἡτοίμασται.

41 Καὶ ἀκούσαντες οἱ δέκα ἤρξαντο ἀγανακτεῖν περὶ Ἰακώβου καὶ Ἰωάννου. 42 καὶ προσκαλεσάμενος αὐτοὺς ὁ Ἰησοῦς λέγει αὐτοῖς· Οἴδατε ὅτι οἱ δοκοῦντες ἄρχειν τῶν ἐθνῶν κατακυριεύουσιν αὐτῶν καὶ οἱ μεγάλοι αὐτῶν κατεξουσιάζουσιν αὐτῶν. 43 οὐχ οὕτως δέ ἐστιν ἐν ὑμῖν· ἀλλ᾽ ὃς ἂν θέλῃ μέγας γενέσθαι ἐν ὑμῖν, ἔσται ὑμῶν διάκονος, 44 καὶ ὃς ἂν θέλῃ ἐν ὑμῖν εἶναι πρῶτος, ἔσται πάντων δοῦλος· 45 καὶ γὰρ ὁ υἱὸς τοῦ ἀνθρώπου οὐκ ἦλθεν διακονηθῆναι ἀλλὰ διακονῆσαι καὶ δοῦναι τὴν ψυχὴν αὐτοῦ λύτρον ἀντὶ πολλῶν. [SBLGNT]

King James Version

32 And they were in the way going up to Jerusalem; and Jesus went before them: and they were amazed; and as they followed, they were afraid. And he took again the twelve, and began to tell them what things should happen unto him, 33 Saying, Behold, we go up to Jerusalem; and the Son of man shall be delivered unto the chief priests, and unto the scribes; and they shall condemn him to death, and shall deliver him to the Gentiles: 34 And they shall mock him, and shall scourge him, and shall spit upon

New Rendition

32 They were on the way, going up to Jerusalem. And Jesus was going before them, and they were astonished. And those following were afraid. And having taken to him the Twelve again, he began to tell about the things that were going to happen to him. 33 "Look, we are going up to Jerusalem, and the son of man will be handed over to the chief priests and the scriptorians. And they will condemn him to death, and they will hand him over to the Gentiles. 34 And they will mock him and spit on him and whip him

him, and shall kill him: and the third day he shall rise again.

35 And James and John, the sons of Zebedee, come unto him, saying, Master, we would that thou shouldest do for us whatsoever we shall desire. 36 And he said unto them, What would ye that I should do for you? 37 They said unto him, Grant unto us that we may sit, one on thy right hand, and the other on thy left hand, in thy glory. 38 But Jesus said unto them, Ye know not what ye ask: can ye drink of the cup that I drink of? and be baptized with the baptism that I am baptized with? 39 And they said unto him, We can. And Jesus said unto them, Ye shall indeed drink of the cup that I drink of; and with the baptism that I am baptized withal shall ye be baptized: 40 But to sit on my right hand and on my left hand is not mine to give; but it shall be given to them for whom it is prepared. 41 And when the ten heard it, they began to be much displeased with James and John. 42 But Jesus called them to him, and saith unto them, Ye know that they which are accounted to rule over the Gentiles exercise lordship over them; and their great ones exercise authority upon them. 43 But so shall it not be among you: but whosoever will be great among you, shall be your minister: 44 And whosoever of you will be the chiefest, shall be servant of all. 45 For even the Son of man came not to be ministered unto, but to minister, and to give his life a ransom for many.

and kill him, and after three days he will rise again."

35 And Jacob and John, the sons of Zebedee, come up to him, saying to him, "Teacher, we want you to do for us whatever we ask you." 36 But he said to them, "What do you want me to do for you?" 37 And they said to him, "Grant us that one of us will sit at your right hand and one at your left hand, in your glory." 38 But Jesus said to them, "You do not know what you are asking for. Can you drink the cup that I drink and be baptized with the baptism that I am baptized with?" 39 But they said to him, "We can!" But Jesus said to them, "The cup that I drink, you will drink. And the baptism that I am baptized with, you will be baptized with. 40 But to sit at my right hand or at my left hand is not mine to give but [is] for those for whom it has been prepared." 41 And having heard this, the ten began to be angry with Jacob and John. 42 And having called them to him, Jesus says to them, "You know that those recognized to rule over the Gentiles exercise lordship over them, and their great ones exercise authority/power over them. 43 But it is not this way among you. Whoever wants to become great among you will be your servant, 44 and whoever wants to be first among you will be the slave of all. 45 For even the son of man did not come to be served but to serve and to give his life for the release of many."

Notes

10:32 *And they were in the way going up to Jerusalem:* "Going up" was a common way of describing travel to Jerusalem since it was literally higher than the surrounding area. But it may also echo language describing a pilgrim's ascent to the holy city (compare Ps. 24:3; 122:4; Isa. 2:2–3), which would be most fitting since this is the time when pilgrims ascended to Jerusalem to celebrate the Passover. This is the first time that Jerusalem is named as Jesus' destination.

and Jesus went before them: While this statement may be literally true, it is likely that Mark mentions it for its symbolic value, suggesting that Jesus is traveling the road of discipleship as a model for his followers (compare 14:28; 16:7).

and they were amazed: While not specified, it is likely that they are amazed that Jesus would willingly go to Jerusalem where he would presumably be killed (compare 3:6). Lurking behind this amazement is a lack of understanding of Jesus' mission.

and as they followed, they were afraid: There are two ways to interpret this verse:

1. There are two groups: the disciples who are amazed and the followers who are afraid.
2. There is one group; they are first amazed as they realize Jesus' destination, and then they are afraid as they continue to follow him.

Normally, fear and amazement result from witnessing miracles. But this story is different. Inasmuch as this journey is symbolic of the journey of discipleship, Mark suggests that the normal response to following is astonishment and fear since these emotions are tied to following Jesus to Jerusalem. Significantly, Jesus' response to these emotions is to teach his followers more about his ministry.

And he took again the twelve, and began to tell them what things should happen unto him: "Again" signals to the audience that these are not new teachings. (In fact, this is the third Passion prediction.)

The fact that Jesus takes "the Twelve" implies that a larger group is traveling with him; later, it will be made clear that this group included women (compare 15:41 and 16:7).

10:33 *Saying, Behold, we go up to Jerusalem:* "Behold" translates the same Greek word (*idou*) that Peter used in 10:28. The proximity of the references suggests a contrast between Peter's self-focused statement about his material sacrifices and Jesus' prophecy of his own suffering and death.

and the Son of man shall be delivered unto the chief priests, and unto the scribes: It is the Jewish leaders—not the Jewish masses—who will condemn Jesus. (The crowds are actually an obstacle to their plans [11:32; 14:1–2, 10–11].)

and they shall condemn him to death, and shall deliver him to the Gentiles: In this, the most specific of the prophecies of Jesus' suffering and death, the blame for his death is spread between the Jewish leaders who condemn him and the Gentiles who execute him. While only the Jewish leaders are implicated (via the reference to the chief priests and the scribes), "the Gentiles" more generally are responsible for his death. Unfortunately, the history of interpretation has been precisely the opposite, with only a few Gentiles held responsible but the Jewish people generally blamed, to horrific effect historically. But this is the inverse of Jesus' statement here.

10:34 *And they shall mock him, and shall scourge him, and shall spit upon him, and shall kill him: and the third day he shall rise again:* Some manuscripts have "on the third day"; others have "after the third day." "After three days" is more likely to be the earlier reading as it is the harder reading; "on the third day" may have been chosen to harmonize with Matthew 20:19 and Luke 18:33.[117] (Compare 8:31 and 9:31 and especially the Notes on 8:31. See also the Analysis for this section.)

The Secret Gospel of Mark. A letter purporting to be written by Clement of Alexandria near the end of the second century contains two excerpts claiming to be from the "secret Gospel of Mark." The excerpts consist of

1. a story where Jesus raises a man from the dead, resides in his home for nearly a week, and then teaches him the mysteries of the kingdom. This passage is inserted between 10:34 and 10:35. Because the teaching of the mysteries has some resonances with modern Latter-day Saint temple ritual, this text has been of interest to some Latter-day Saint scholars.[118]

2. a brief report of Jesus' refusal to meet with two female disciples. This incident is placed in the middle of 10:46. This text can be viewed as

   a. likely to be original and capable of explaining the odd situation of Mark recounting that Jesus went to Jericho but then not recording what he did there (see the Notes on 10:46).

   b. likely to be unoriginal but rather a later attempt to fill what was perceived to be a gap in the text. Had Secret Mark been the original version of the text, a redactor would likely have excised all reference to Jericho instead of leaving behind a confusing reference to the city.

---

117. Metzger, *Textual Commentary*, 91.

118. William J. Hamblin, "Aspects of an Early Christian Initiation Ritual," in *By Study and Also By Faith: Essays in Honor of Hugh W. Nibley on the Occasion of his Eightieth Birthday, 27 March 1990*, ed. John M. Lundquist and Stephen D. Ricks, 2 vols. (Provo, Utah: FARMS; Salt Lake City: Deseret Book, 1990), 1:202–21.

There are solid reasons to question the legitimacy of Secret Mark, including:

1. Morton Smith, a biblical scholar, claimed in 1958 to have discovered the letter. It is possible that he forged the letter.

2. What Smith found was a copy of the letter made in the eighteenth century, so it is possible that the letter was forged before Morton Smith found it.

3. If the letter does derive from Clement, his belief that Mark wrote one Gospel for the public (now known as the canonical Gospel of Mark) and another, secret Gospel for "insiders" may not be accurate.

4. It is unclear whether Secret Mark was written by the same person who wrote canonical Mark and which text was written first.

5. The themes in Secret Mark do not fit well with canonical Mark:

   a. Because Jesus does not elsewhere refuse female disciples in Mark, this material does not mesh well with Mark's portrayal of Jesus and may instead stem from divisions in the early church regarding the legitimacy of female discipleship.

   b. The three Passion predictions in Mark follow a very precise pattern (see the Analysis for this section), but the inclusion of Secret Mark disrupts that pattern.[119]

   c. Generally, Secret Mark reads like "a confused pastiche of phrases gathered from elsewhere in Mark and the other canonical gospels."[120]

   d. In Secret Mark, the "mysteries" are transmitted via ritual, but in canonical Mark, they come through the parables.

While certainty is not possible on this subject, the weight of the evidence currently available suggests that the Secret Gospel of Mark was written after canonical Mark and by a different author; whether that author lived in the second century, the twentieth century, or at some point in between may never be known.[121] Secret Mark may have some value in determining Christian concerns and beliefs in the time in which it was composed, but it is unlikely to be helpful in understanding either canonical Mark or the life of Jesus.

10:35 *And James and John, the sons of Zebedee, come unto him, saying, Master, we would that thou shouldest do for us whatsoever we shall desire:* This request is similar to Herod's poorly considered offer to give

---

119. Collins, *Mark,* 485.
120. Gundry, *Mark,* 621.
121. See Collins, *Mark,* 491–93, for a summary of recent arguments.

his stepdaughter whatever she asks for (6:23). But Jesus will show greater wisdom than Herod.

James[122] and John are asking for a "blank check"; Jesus refuses to give it (contrast Hel. 10:5 and especially 3 Ne. 28:1).

10:36 *And he said unto them, What would ye that I should do for you?* 37 *They said unto him, Grant unto us that we may sit, one on thy right hand, and the other on thy left hand:* Their request envisions Jesus seated on a throne (compare Ps. 110:1); they want the seats on either side of him, which would be the seats of highest honor. They leave no place for Peter; in fact, their request comes immediately after Peter's self-aggrandizing statement about his selflessness and may have been timed to capitalize on Peter's mistake. They sense a weakness in Peter's leadership and attempt to ingratiate themselves with Jesus.

Ironically, the disciples' immediate response to Jesus' teaching that leaders will attempt to kill him is to ask if they might themselves become leaders.

in thy glory: Jesus does not speak of his own glory but rather his Father's glory (8:38). But it is as if the disciples have not understood Jesus' teachings about his coming death at all and think that they are entering Jerusalem so that Jesus might be glorified in the normal way; their main concern is sharing in his glory. Their incomprehension (in which they will soon be joined by the rest of the Twelve) also speaks to "the cruel loneliness with which Jesus faced the journey to Jerusalem."[123]

10:38 *But Jesus said unto them, Ye know not what ye ask:* Jesus explains that they do not know what they are asking for because they do not yet understand that glorification cannot happen without suffering first.

can ye drink of the cup that I drink of?: The cup has several possible (overlapping) symbolic meanings:

1. *Suffering* (see especially 14:36).

2. *The King's Fate.* In this context where they have requested seats next to the king, they will drink of whatever the king does, which means that if the king is poisoned, they will be as well (Gen. 40:1–13; Neh. 1:11–2:1).

3. *Blessings* (Ps. 16:5; 23:5; 116:13). While perhaps surprising in this context, it is nonetheless true that James and John are asking for blessings that Jesus will enjoy.

---

122. See the Notes on 1:19.
123. Lane, *Gospel according to Mark*, 382.

4. *Judgment* (Ps. 75:8; Ezek. 23:31–34). This would hint at an Atonement theology since any judgment that Jesus suffers will not reflect his own sins.

5. *Suffering Transferred to Another* (Lam. 4:21; Jer. 25:15). In some HB passages, the cup describes how the covenant people will suffer but also how God will then transfer that suffering to those who have oppressed them (Isa. 51:17–23). This, too, might hint of an Atonement theology inasmuch as it pictures transferred suffering, but it would do so ironically since the suffering would be transferred from the guilty to the innocent through Jesus' Atonement.

Regardless of which combination of referents Jesus intended here, the larger point is clear: glory is tied to suffering. This is one teaching that the disciples will struggle to comprehend throughout Mark's narrative.

and be baptized with the baptism that I am baptized with?: This is Jesus' only reference to his own baptism; here, it is a metaphor for his suffering and death. (As the ancient writer Chrysostom suggested, "he called his death a baptism because by it he cleansed the world."[124]) Because one possible meaning of "baptism" is "to destroy" (by drowning), this statement may be a play on words.

Jesus' questions involve two verbs: drink and baptize. Both involve liquid, but the former involves ingesting liquid and the latter being immersed in it. Perhaps Jesus wanted to indicate the complete nature of his suffering, both internal and external.

See also the Analysis on 15:38–41 for more on the meaning of Jesus' death.

Relationship to Isaiah 53. Jesus' intimations of his own suffering suggest a link to the suffering servant in Isaiah 53. Yet to read Isaiah 53 as just a description of Jesus seems counter to the text itself and to its earlier interpreters (as well as its modern Jewish interpreters), since Isaiah 53 can also be understood with reference to the suffering of the covenant people in the role of the suffering servant. This leads nicely to Jesus' point here in Mark as he explains that James and John (and, indeed, all who follow him) will share his fate of suffering for the benefit of others.

10:39 *And they said unto him, We can:* The easy agreement of James and John contrasts radically with Jesus' pleas in Gethsemane that the cup be taken away from him (14:36). (Both texts refer to the cup.) Significantly, their exuberant embrace of suffering does not follow Jesus' example. Once again, the theme of the incomprehension of the disciples takes center stage.

---

124. Oden and Hall, *Mark,* 150–51.

At the same time, it is fair to say that "they may lack understanding, but not loyalty or courage."[125]

James and John contrast with the wealthy man who refused to follow Jesus: in both stories, something is asked of Jesus and Jesus responds by asking for something difficult. The rich man went away sorrowful while James and John readily agree to the hard task, but neither of these responses is appropriate.

And Jesus said unto them, Ye shall indeed drink of the cup that I drink of; and with the baptism that I am baptized withal shall ye be baptized: It is paradoxical that Jesus' words here reveal a knowledge of James and John's fates while the very next verse shows Jesus' limitations since the honored seats next to him are not his to give. Mark once again presents a compelling portrait of Jesus' mixture of human and divine nature.

10:40 *But to sit on my right hand and on my left hand is not mine to give; but it shall be given to them for whom it is prepared:* The full irony of these words will not be apparent until the crucifixion, when very similar language is used to describe those crucified on Jesus' left and right hand (15:27). Sitting on Jesus' left and right hand involves dying with him, despite the disciples' belief that it involves being honored with him. Suffering is inexorably tied to glory throughout this Gospel.

It is curious that Jesus asked them about their willingness to drink the cup and to be baptized, when the places of honor were not his to give in the first place. Perhaps he was offering them a way to step away from their question. Or perhaps "the cup and the baptism thus prove not to be qualifying conditions at all, but rather a way of indicating that their whole conception of [glory] and of the way it is to be achieved is misguided."[126]

Once again, Mark is comfortable showing the limitations of Jesus' powers.

10:41 *And when the ten heard it, they began to be much displeased with James and John:* "The ten" would include Peter. The displeasure seems to be tied to their concern that James and John will be given honors that the others will miss out on. Of course, this is ironic since Jesus has just denied them these honors. Once again, the disciples seem to only selectively hear what Jesus says.

10:42 *But Jesus called them to him, and saith unto them, Ye know that they which are accounted to rule over the Gentiles exercise lordship over them:* The phrase "are accounted to rule" means that they do not in fact

---

125. France, *Gospel,* 417.
126. France, *Gospel,* 417.

rule; Jesus is calling worldly systems of power a sham. There is perhaps some irony in that Jesus just told his disciples that they did not know what they were asking for, but here he points out that they do know how authority works for the Gentiles (both 10:38 and this verse use the same verb for "know").

"Exercise lordship" translates the same verb as is found in LXX Psalm 109:2 (KJV Ps. 110:2), where the Lord gives the Davidic ruler the right to rule his enemies. Jesus' point is that his followers do not exercise this kind of leadership (compare D&C 121:36–46).

and their great ones exercise authority upon them: While this was generally true in practice, it is worth noting that within the Hellenistic tradition there were exhortations for leaders to act as servants.[127] So Jesus is not presenting a new ideal; he is calling them to live up to an existing ideal.

10:43 *But so shall it not be among you:* Some ancient manuscripts have the future tense ("shall . . . be"); others have the present tense ("it is"). The present tense seems more likely to have been original; perhaps scribes softened the saying[128] in order to justify Christian leaders enjoying a higher status than others in mortality by suggesting that Jesus' words here only applied to the future or, alternatively, to explain early Christianity's failure to live up to this ideal.

but whosoever will be great among you, shall be your minister: The word "minister" is better translated as "servant"; it is the same word used to describe the actions of Simon's mother-in-law after she was healed (1:31). This verse thus encourages a reexamination of that healing story now that Jesus teaches that her actions epitomize true greatness. Once again, Jesus suggests that behavior associated with women is a model for all of his disciples (compare 10:15).

10:44 *And whosoever of you will be the chiefest, shall be servant of all:* The word translated as "servant" can be translated as "slave"; it is not the same Greek word as minister/servant in the previous verse. While different terms are used, the effect is to restate for emphasis the teaching of the previous line.

It is intriguing that Jesus does not encourage them to squelch their desire for greatness; rather, he channels it into a motive to serve.

---

127. David Seeley, "Rulership and Service in Mark 10:41–45," *Novum Testamentum* 35, no. 3 (1993): 234–50.

128. Metzger, *Textual Commentary,* 91.

10:45 For even the Son of man came not to be ministered unto, but to minister: The "for" introducing this verse serves to make the verse an example of the principle articulated in the previous verse. In other words, Jesus' life is a model of greatness through service.

The tense of the verb "came" suggests that it refers to Jesus' entire life, not just to his suffering and death, which suggests that Jesus' entire mortal experience involved ministering to others. This statement thus serves as Jesus' summary of his life and its purpose. Ironically, it shifts James and John's image of Jesus being on a throne to an image of Jesus as a servant.

Relationship to Daniel 7. In Daniel 7:13–14, the one like the Son of Man is given power and authority, and all people are to serve him. Thus, Jesus' statement here that the Son of Man has come to serve, not to be served, recites but then rebuts the expectation of Daniel 7.

and to give his life a ransom for many: The HB mentions several reasons for which a ransom might be paid, including to free a slave, a prisoner, or a hostage. In other contexts, God is the one who (figuratively) redeems people (Isa. 41:14; 43:1; 44:22). In Mark's context of a discussion of serving and slaves, the most likely meaning would be to liberate a slave (Lev. 25:47–55).

Jesus' statement does not make clear from whom the people are ransomed; options include:

1. Earthly masters (literal or figurative), so that people are free to serve God instead of humans. This reading makes good sense in the context of a discussion of gentile rulers.
2. God, who as the universal administrator of justice requires a ransom in order to free those enslaved by sin.
3. Satan, who has claim on those who sin.
4. Justice anthropomorphized, to whom a ransom is due in order to free sinners.

It is also possible that more than one meaning is intended here. Regardless, Jesus' focus is on the one offering the ransom, not the one to whom the ransom is given.

The use of "many" instead of "all" is unexpected; options for its meaning include the following:

1. "All": "In Semitic usage 'many' tends to be used inclusively as a synonym for 'all.'"[129]

---

129. Stein, *Mark,* 489.

2. "The elect": "In rabbinic literature, and even more strikingly at Qumran, 'the many' is a technical term for the elect community, the eschatological people of God."[130] This concept would need to be nuanced by the idea that Jesus inverts the very idea of the elect by lauding children, criticizing his disciples for trying to assume honors, and presenting servants and slaves as models.

3. The word "many" may not be in opposition to "all" but rather may contrast with the quest for glory that focuses on the individual. In other words, Jesus' ministry did not focus on himself as one glorified individual but rather on the needs of the many.

4. "Many" may have been chosen to echo the language of Isaiah 53:11 ("my righteous servant [shall] justify many") and Isaiah 53:12 ("he bare the sin of many") and thus connect Jesus' mission to that text.

Relationship to Isaiah 53. Isaiah 53 describes one who will suffer for the benefit of the many, so Mark 10:45 might be read as a summary of the entire chapter of Isaiah.

Analysis

Interpreters generally read 10:45 to describe Jesus' death, but, in Mark's context, the idea of Jesus as a "ransom" seems to apply more to his life than to his death. In that light, it is very significant that Jesus' topic here is not his own death but rather discipleship. Jesus' life and death are presented as a pattern for his disciples to follow. Jesus asks his disciples to choose to be slaves but then promises that he will ransom them from that slavery.

While Mark occasionally hints that Jesus will suffer and die (2:20), there are three developed passages where Jesus specifically prophesies concerning his suffering and death; these are known as the Passion predictions. All three occur in 8:31–10:45, as Jesus is "on the way" to Jerusalem. They share many similar features:

1. Jesus prophesies of his suffering and death (8:31; 9:30–32; 10:32–34).
2. Each prediction is followed by the disciples' misunderstanding (8:32–33; 9:33–34; 10:35–37).
3. Jesus responds to the misunderstanding with teachings that are paradoxical in nature (8:34–9:1; 9:35–10:31; 10:38–45).[131]

---

130. Lane, *Gospel according to Mark,* 384.
131. Stein, *Mark,* 386.

Each prediction refers to Jesus rising from the dead after three days. And while the same format is followed for all three prophecies, each one becomes more specific. So as the disciples are willing to continue following Jesus "on the way," they become privy to more information about his life and death. In each case, a lack of understanding is the first response to prophecy. Learning more about Jesus reveals more about the disciples; in each case, they seek self-aggrandizement. The pattern of showing evidence of the disciples' misunderstanding immediately after each Passion prediction is extremely significant, since it intertwines Jesus' mission with the theme of discipleship. In other words, understanding who he is is closely tied to behaving appropriately as disciples. The link between discipleship and prophecies also suggests that Jesus' suffering and death is the automatic outgrowth of living a certain way; thus, discipleship and suffering are linked. These predictions are not then just about Jesus' identity but also about the identity of his disciples. The two are inseparably linked.

After each prophecy, after the disciples have misunderstood, Jesus teaches them; these teachings always contain a paradox. Jesus makes clear in each case that the teaching applies to everyone, not just to the disciples who are present. The pattern implies that discipleship necessarily involves paradoxical elements. It is precisely these paradoxes Jesus' disciples struggle to understand—they always favor one element of the paradox but cannot accept the other element.

While some scholars dispute the historicity of the Passion predictions, the fact that (1) the three statements show increased specificity, (2) none specifically mention the cross, and (3) even the final and most specific prophecy does not use the same vocabulary as the crucifixion account (including no reference to "the elders" in the Passion, different words for scourging [compare 10:34 and 15:15], and a different order of the events), combine to make it at least plausible that the Passion predictions stemmed from Jesus' teachings.

JESUS HEALS ANOTHER BLIND MAN (10:46–52)

Greek Text

46 Καὶ ἔρχονται εἰς Ἰεριχώ. καὶ ἐκπορευομένου αὐτοῦ ἀπὸ Ἰεριχὼ καὶ τῶν μαθητῶν αὐτοῦ καὶ ὄχλου ἱκανοῦ ὁ υἱὸς Τιμαίου Βαρτιμαῖος τυφλὸς προσαίτης ἐκάθητο παρὰ τὴν ὁδόν. 47 καὶ ἀκούσας ὅτι Ἰησοῦς ὁ Ναζαρηνός ἐστιν ἤρξατο κράζειν καὶ

λέγειν· Υἱὲ Δαυὶδ Ἰησοῦ, ἐλέησόν με. 48 καὶ ἐπετίμων αὐτῷ πολλοὶ ἵνα σιωπήσῃ· ὁ δὲ πολλῷ μᾶλλον ἔκραζεν· Υἱὲ Δαυίδ, ἐλέησόν με. 49 καὶ στὰς ὁ Ἰησοῦς εἶπεν· Φωνήσατε αὐτόν. καὶ φωνοῦσι τὸν τυφλὸν λέγοντες αὐτῷ· Θάρσει, ἔγειρε, φωνεῖ σε. 50 ὁ δὲ ἀποβαλὼν τὸ ἱμάτιον αὐτοῦ ἀναπηδήσας ἦλθεν πρὸς τὸν Ἰησοῦν. 51 καὶ ἀποκριθεὶς αὐτῷ ὁ Ἰησοῦς εἶπεν· Τί σοι θέλεις ποιήσω; ὁ δὲ τυφλὸς εἶπεν αὐτῷ· Ῥαββουνι, ἵνα ἀναβλέψω. 52 καὶ ὁ Ἰησοῦς εἶπεν αὐτῷ· Ὕπαγε, ἡ πίστις σου σέσωκέν σε. καὶ εὐθὺς ἀνέβλεψεν, καὶ ἠκολούθει αὐτῷ ἐν τῇ ὁδῷ. [SBLGNT]

King James Version

46 And they came to Jericho: and as he went out of Jericho with his disciples and a great number of people, blind Bartimaeus, the son of Timaeus, sat by the highway side begging. 47 And when he heard that it was Jesus of Nazareth, he began to cry out, and say, Jesus, thou Son of David, have mercy on me. 48 And many charged him that he should hold his peace: but he cried the more a great deal, Thou Son of David, have mercy on me. 49 And Jesus stood still, and commanded him to be called. And they call the blind man, saying unto him, Be of good comfort, rise; he calleth thee. 50 And he, casting away his garment, rose, and came to Jesus. 51 And Jesus answered and said unto him, What wilt thou that I should do unto thee? The blind man said unto him, Lord, that I might receive my sight. 52 And Jesus said unto him, Go thy way; thy faith hath made thee whole. And immediately he received his sight, and followed Jesus in the way.

New Rendition

46 And they come to Jericho. And as he was going out of Jericho with his disciples and a large crowd, the son of Timaeus, Bartimaeus, a blind beggar, was sitting beside the way. 47 And having heard that it is Jesus of Nazareth, he began to shout and to say, "Son of David, Jesus, have mercy on me!" 48 And many were rebuking him that he should be silent, but he shouted all the more, "Son of David, have mercy on me!" 49 And having stopped, Jesus commanded, "Call him." And they call the blind man, saying to him, "Have courage—rise up! He is calling you." 50 And having thrown off his cloak, having jumped up, he came to Jesus. 51 And answering him, Jesus says, "What do you want me to do for you?" And the blind man said to him, "Rabbi, that I may see." 52 And Jesus said to him, "Go. Your trust has healed/saved you. And immediately he could see and followed him on the way."

Notes

10:46 *And they came to Jericho: and as he went out of Jericho with his disciples and a great number of people:* The reference to Jesus entering Jericho only to leave without doing anything there is surprising. Possible reasons for Mark to mention it include:

1. Mark references Jericho symbolically: "[Jericho's] great importance flows from the fact that it was the first city captured by the invading Israelites and

the staging ground for the conquest of the rest of Canaan under Joshua."[132] Thus, Jesus is the new Joshua, staging a new invasion of Jerusalem. The reference to Jesus as a son of David in this story would emphasize this theme. But this time the son of David does not conquer; he heals.

2. The text could be understood to say that they passed through Jericho, which makes the reference to Jericho less obscure. The point would be that Jesus is progressing on his journey to Jerusalem.

blind Bartimaeus, the son of Timæus: Because "Bartimaeus" means "son of Timaeus," it is difficult to understand why Mark provided the translation here; it seems redundant. While there are other occasions where Mark includes Aramaic and then translates it, this is the only instance where the Greek translation appears before the Aramaic word. These two unusual details may imply that Mark's purpose here is more than simple translation. Additionally, including names in healing miracles is most unusual; this is the only time in Mark's Gospel that the name of a healed person is given.[133] Reasons for Mark's unprecedented phrasing might include:

1. Bartimaeus or, more likely, his father was known to Mark's audience.

2. The word "Timaeus" can mean "honored" in Greek; given that his son is a blind beggar—one of the least honored members of society—the name would be ironic. But it would also be most appropriate—even prophetic— given how Jesus treats Bartimaeus and publicly recognizes his faith.

3. While this story is obviously a healing, it also shares several features with the calls to discipleship (see the Notes on 10:49); it is typical for call stories to include the name of the person called. Hence, the inclusion of the name is not inappropriate.

sat by the highway side begging: "The way" (KJV: "highway") likely has symbolic meaning here: Bartimaeus is next to—but not on—the way of discipleship, but this will change by the end of the story.

10:47 *And when he heard that it was Jesus of Nazareth:* "Of Nazareth" distinguishes Jesus from others with the same first name.

he began to cry out, and say, Jesus, thou Son of David: This and the next verse are the only use of the title "Son of David" in Mark; it is debated whether it is an accurate title for Jesus:

---

132. Marcus, *Mark 8–16*, 758; see also Josh. 2.

133. In 1:30, the name of the son-in-law of the woman with the fever is given and in 5:22, the name of the father of the girl raised from the dead is given, but the given name of the recipient of the miracle herself is not provided. Interestingly, in all three of these stories, the person is named in relation to other people (mother-in-law, daughter, son).

1. *Inaccurate.* This is not a title that Mark uses for Jesus or that Jesus uses for himself; the fact that the speaker is blind and in need of healing suggests the symbolic blindness of the title. Support for this reading may come from 12:35–37, depending on how that text is interpreted (see the Notes on those verses). While it is true that Bartimaeus will soon be praised for his faith, this does not necessarily imply that his understanding of Jesus is complete (especially since the incomprehension of the disciples is a major theme in Mark's Gospel). There may also be echoes here of the story of the hemorrhaging woman, who was also praised for her faith, but who may have misunderstood the nature of Jesus' power when she thought she could be healed by touching his clothes. Or perhaps this title is, if not entirely inaccurate, short-sighted or incomplete, which would symbolically echo the man's blindness. In either case, after Bartimaeus is healed, he simply follows Jesus without titling him, which seems to fit Mark's privileging of deeds over words as evidence of discipleship. So in a story where blindness refers symbolically to the spiritual blindness of the disciples, perhaps the blind man's utterance should not be accepted at face value.

2. *Accurate.* There would be typical Markan irony in the fact that the blind man is capable of identifying Jesus while Jesus' disciples continually struggle to understand who Jesus is. The irony is amplified by Jesus' frequent suggestion that his disciples are blind. This reading prompts the question: What would Bartimaeus have meant—and what would Mark's audience have understood—by a reference to Jesus as a son of David? First Kings 4:29–34 portrays Solomon (a son of David) as a miracle worker, leading to the idea current in the first century that the title "son of David" referred to a miracle worker; thus it would make sense for Bartimaeus to address Jesus as a healer since he was requesting a healing. Further, Jesus does not correct Bartimaeus (contrast 10:18). Bartimaeus' knowledge is highlighted since the crowd called Jesus "Jesus of Nazareth" and Bartimaeus does not simply echo that title but replaces it with "son of David."

Regardless of the aptness of the title, there may be a link between "son of Timaeus" and "son of David" in terms of equating Jesus and Bartimaeus in this story: Bartimaeus is the son of the honored one, as is Jesus.

Relationship to 2 Samuel 5. In 2 Samuel 5:6, David is approaching Jerusalem to occupy it. He is taunted with the idea that even the blind and lame will turn him back. David then specifically identifies the lame and the blind as his enemies (see 2 Sam. 5:8). Connections to Mark's story include the reference to David, the idea of approaching Jerusalem, and the presence of the blind man. Significantly, blind Bartimaeus is seen by the crowd as an obstacle to Jesus' journey much as the blind were to David. Thus Jesus ironically meets the same condition that David did regarding entry to Jerusalem: they both must overcome the obstacle of the blind. And yet "Jesus . . . has removed the blindness rather than the blind as he goes up to the Holy City."[134] Jesus, as the son of David, does the bidding of the blind man (as his question asking Bartimaeus what he wants makes clear), exemplifying his recent teachings about serving instead of being served.

have mercy on me: Because a plea for mercy directed to God was common in the HB (Ps. 4:1; 6:2), Bartimaeus here associates Jesus with the God of the Bible.

10:48 *And many charged him that he should hold his peace:* The crowd's motivation is not made clear: Do they assume that Bartimaeus is begging for money? That his plight is not worth Jesus' attention? That Jesus will be unable to heal him? Are they concerned about the political repercussions of the title "Son of David"? Regardless, their interference violates HB strictures to treat the blind well (Lev. 19:14; Deut. 27:18; Job 29:15).

It is possible that the word "many" in this verse is meant to evoke Jesus' recent announcement that he would be a ransom for many (10:45). In this context, the many are, ironically, trying to keep Bartimaeus away from him, and yet Jesus is still willing to ransom them.

but he cried the more a great deal, Thou Son of David, have mercy on me: The only other use of the Greek word translated here as "have mercy" is when Jesus commands the healed demoniac to tell of the mercy (KJV: "compassion") that the Lord has had for him (5:19). In this context, it is likely that the blind man sees mercy as displayed through acts of healing.

10:49 *And Jesus stood still:* The idea of Jesus stopping for a beggar, especially in the face of his determination to go to Jerusalem, is extremely significant; it is likely that Mark is pointing out the contrast between standing still and being on the way. Significantly, for Jesus, being on the way sometimes involves standing still in order to meet the needs of others.

and commanded him to be called: Jesus' command shows that he—not the crowd—exercises authority in this interaction. Interestingly, Jesus' words suggest that he can hear but not see Bartimaeus, and so he wants Bartimaeus brought closer to him; there is a sense in which Jesus is also "blind" at the beginning of their interaction. The language suggests that this might even be a call story, in the sense that Jesus is calling Bartimaeus as a disciple.

---

134. Witherington, *Gospel of Mark*, 292.

And they call the blind man, saying unto him, Be of good comfort, rise; he calleth thee: Notice the triple repetition of the word "call" in this verse, which may suggest that this is the story of Bartimaeus' call by Jesus (although a different word is used here than in the other call accounts).

10:50 *And he, casting away his garment, rose, and came to Jesus:* The reference to the garment seems an odd detail; Mark may have mentioned it because

1. it reflects a historical reminiscence from Mark's source for the story but has no particular symbolic role.

2. it shows the blind man's excitement at Jesus' invitation.

3. it is meant to contrast with the rich man who would not sacrifice any of his possessions.

4. beggars would often spread their garments out in front of them to collect alms, so abandoning them signifies his faith that, after his interaction with Jesus, he will no longer need to beg because he will not be blind.

5. if this story is read as a call to discipleship and the garment is the tool of his trade as a beggar,[135] then his abandonment of it is similar to when Peter and Andrew left their nets and Levi left his customs booth.

10:51 *And Jesus answered and said unto him, What wilt thou that I should do unto thee?:* While the answer to this question might seem obvious, the query introduces the possibility that Bartimaeus may have simply been asking for money. After all, he is a beggar. But the fact that he asks for a healing highlights that Bartimaeus understands Jesus' extraordinary powers.

The blind man said unto him, Lord, that I might receive my sight: The KJV translates an unusual Greek word (Greek: *rhabbouni*) as "Lord" here. (Its only other NT usage is John 20:16.)

10:52 *And Jesus said unto him, Go thy way; thy faith hath made thee whole:* The word "go" is frequently used by Jesus after miracles are performed. It is difficult to determine whether Jesus is telling Bartimaeus to go away or to walk to demonstrate his sight.

The theme of vision intensifies as Jesus' words show "that he can see what others cannot: Bartimaeus' faith."[136] Jesus' vision is superior to the

---

135. The law of Moses provided special protections to a beggar's cloak for this reason (Deut. 24:12–13).

136. Juan Carlos Ossandón, "Bartimaeus' Faith: Plot and Point of View in Mark 10,46–52," *Biblica* 93, no. 3 (2012): 395.

crowd's, who saw in Bartimaeus only an unwarranted interruption. Even before his healing, Bartimaeus could see who Jesus was better than the crowd could.

How did Jesus see Bartimaeus' faith? Through Bartimaeus' calling out to Jesus, his continuing to do so even when the crowd chastised him, and his willingness to cast aside his garment and come when Jesus called him.

The same verb here translated as "whole" was translated as "saved" in the disciples' question concerning who could be saved in 10:26. Thus, Mark's audience likely would have heard Jesus' statement to Bartimaeus as an answer to that question: Bartimaeus can be saved because of his faith.

And immediately he received his sight, and followed Jesus in the way: As is usually the case in this section of Mark, the language of "following" and being on "the way" is symbolic of the path of discipleship. This is particularly the case given the shift from 10:46, where Bartimaeus was "by" (Greek: *para*) the way to this verse, where he is "in" (Greek: *en*) the way as a result of his healing by Jesus.

Relationship to 4:4. The references to being next to the way and the idea of hearing (see 10:47) would remind the audience of the seed that the bird devoured from Jesus' parable (see 4:4). In other words, Bartimaeus is in a vulnerable position. The crowd is in the role of the bird/Satan in attempting to keep Bartimaeus from Jesus. But they are ultimately unsuccessful because of Jesus' intervention; this story thus becomes an important commentary on the parable and on Jesus' power to overcome Satan.

Relationship to 5:25–34. Using very similar wording, Jesus tells both Bartimaeus and the woman with a hemorrhage of blood that their faith has made them whole (or saved them). Both stories also involve a healed person on the margins of society (an unclean woman and a disabled man) who acts in socially inappropriate ways (by calling out, even after the crowd discourages him, and by touching Jesus in a crowd) in order to access Jesus' power. Further, both the bleeding woman and Bartimaeus interrupt Jesus as he is "on the way" to another location, and, while the audience might expect them to be chastised for this, they are instead two of the very limited cohort of characters in Mark's Gospel who receive a positive word from Jesus. Further, each story has an impact far beyond its own characters since the bleeding woman represents the house of Israel (see the Notes on chapter 5) and Bartimaeus represents all disciples who have their (spiritual) blindness healed by Jesus.

Relationship to 10:35–40. In both the Bartimaeus story and the story of the request of James[137] and John, characters approach Jesus with a plea. And Jesus responds with virtually identical language to both requests (10:36: "What would ye that I should do for you?" and 10:51: "What wilt thou that I should do unto thee?" The Greek for both questions is also very similar). But Bartimaeus asked for mercy while James and John asked for honors (after first asking for anything they wanted). James and John request honors as if that were their due, while Bartimaeus asks for mercy, which is framed as something he does not deserve. Mark places both stories in proximity to heighten the contrast.

Analysis

The note that Bartimaeus followed Jesus strongly suggests that this account is a call story, similar to the calls of Peter, Andrew, James, John, and Levi (1:16–20; 2:14). The normal pattern of a call story involves Jesus walking by, Jesus seeing the person, the person being named and his occupation given, and the person abandoning the tasks of daily life at Jesus' call to follow Jesus. The major tweak to that pattern in this story is the healing miracle, but there is a minor tweak as well: instead of Jesus seeing Bartimaeus, it is implied that Jesus cannot see him and thus he calls for him to come to him (10:49). This inversion may suggest Jesus' identification with the blind Bartimaeus. Or perhaps it represents his presenting the crowd with a chance to "repent" for their actions: they had previously attempted to keep Bartimaeus away from Jesus, but they are now given a chance to help Bartimaeus come to Jesus.

If this text is read as a call story, then 1:16–10:52 is framed by callings. This would be an appropriate move for Mark, who consistently emphasizes discipleship. And given the metaphorical framing of 8:22–10:52 as Jesus being "on the way" to Jerusalem and concerned with the issue of discipleship, it makes sense that the final story in this section would be a call to discipleship. While this is a healing miracle, it is also a story that downplays the healing elements in order to emphasize Bartimaeus' call to discipleship.

It is likely that Mark intended for the audience to compare Bartimaeus with the wealthy man who refused Jesus' call. The two men exist at opposite

---

137. See the Notes on 1:19.

ends of the economic spectrum, with Bartimaeus as a beggar in contrast to the wealthy man. Both stories start with the men making a request of Jesus. The comparison may explain the unusual detail that Bartimaeus left behind his garment: this was his only possession, but he was willing to jettison it at Jesus' call in contrast to the wealthy man who was unwilling to abandon his own vast possessions. And while the wealthy man is specifically invited to follow Jesus—and refuses—Bartimaeus is not invited (in fact, the command to "go" may be read as precisely the opposite of an invitation to discipleship), and yet Mark narrates that he followed Jesus. In this light, Bartimaeus' poverty is a blessing: it makes it easier to follow Jesus because he has much less to leave behind; his material goods exert a much smaller call on him.

The symbolic lesson is clear: the rich man chose to be blind (or revealed his blindness) by selecting wealth over eternal life. Further, Bartimaeus is shown to be more blessed than the rich man; this would have been a radical idea.

Hellenistic household codes were written to instruct people in their ethical obligations: "Ancient household codes customarily treat, along with the subject of acquiring wealth, three relationships: husband-wife, father-children, and master-slave."[138] (There are household codes within the NT itself; see Col. 3:18–4:1; Eph. 5:20–6:9; Titus 2:1–10; 1 Pet. 2:18–3:7.) It is possible that chapter 10 should be read as a household code, but in the usual fashion, Mark violates expectations by inverting the typical household code:

1. Mark 10:1–12 concerns divorce but very deliberately positions women as equal to their husbands, thus subverting the expected code that rendered fewer rights to the wife than to the husband.

2. Mark 10:13–16 concerns children and places Jesus into the role of the father (through his action of blessing the children), inverting the typical household code that subjugated children to their fathers.

3. Mark 10:17–31 concerns wealth, but instead of presenting the owner as superior to the slave, it positions the rich man who refuses to divest from his wealth as a slave to his passions.

While subtle, this pattern fits well into Mark's tendency to present instances where Jesus rejects social conventions when they contradict the gospel that he preaches in favor of a radical equality among all people. The divorce section teaches that men do not have more rights than women, the

---

138. Marcus, *Mark 8–16*, 715.

next section teaches that adults are not more valuable than children, and the final section teaches that the wealthy are not more blessed than the poor, including servants and slaves.

With the healing of Bartimaeus, a large block of Mark's Gospel (8:22–10:52) comes to a close. This section features Jesus "on the way" to Jerusalem and is bounded by stories involving the healing of the blind. But the blindness is not just literal but also a metaphor for the state of spiritual blindness that afflicts the disciples. Further, each incident occurring in between the two sight restorations involves in some way the theme of the spiritual blindness of the disciples. (Also emphasizing the message are Jesus' frequent explicit references to the blindness of the disciples [4:11–13; 7:18; 8:17–18].) Bartimaeus' ability to identify Jesus as a healer and a son of David despite his blindness further emphasizes Mark's theme that physical sight and spiritual insight do not necessarily overlap. Ironically, Bartimaeus seems capable of seeing who Jesus really is, even when he is blind. As discussed above, it is possible that Bartimaeus misuses the title he applies to Jesus, but this is not an impediment to Mark's portrayal of Bartimaeus as an ideal disciple. Rather, it is part of his message: proper discipleship involves following Jesus; the ability to correctly name Jesus is incidental. (And, as Peter's confession of Jesus as the Christ indicated, sometimes the correct title is more of an obstacle than an aid to understanding.)

The elements of Bartimaeus' story that overlap with the standard call story emphasize the theme of Bartimaeus as the ideal disciple. The fact that Bartimaeus—and not Peter, James, or John—is presented as the ideal, faithful disciple is significant because it means that Mark is encouraging his audience to aspire to be like faithful followers of Jesus, not like leaders. This is an important element to Mark's picture of discipleship: had the Twelve been presented as ideal followers, then the audience would have aspired to be like them. But Mark does not want the audience to aspire to be leaders but rather to be servants. This requires positioning people like Simon's mother-in-law and Bartimaeus as ideal followers of Jesus. Bartimaeus may also be a living testimony to Jesus' teaching that the last shall be first and the first shall be last: he is the last person healed in Mark's Gospel but "first" in terms of being an ideal disciple.

PART 3: JERUSALEM (11:1–16:8)

Mark 1:1–8:21 features Jesus in Galilee, 8:22–10:52 shows Jesus "on the way" to Jerusalem, and 11–16 locates Jesus in and around Jerusalem. This third and final division is focused particularly around the temple, which was not a significant presence in the first two sections of Mark.

These chapters comprise about one-third of Mark's narrative and yet cover only one week of Jesus' life. This section of Mark is organized and demarcated chronologically:

Sunday: 11:1–11
Monday: 11:12–19 ("on the next day")
Tuesday: 11:20–13:37 ("in the morning")
Wednesday: 14:1–11 ("two days before Passover")
Thursday: 14:12–72 ("first day of unleavened bread")
Friday: 15:1–47 ("immediately, early in the morning")
Saturday: no events narrated
Sunday: 16:1–8 ("when the Sabbath had passed")

This pattern may reflect the actual chronology of events; however, since the other three Gospels arrange the material differently, it is possible that this structure is a literary creation of Mark's designed to reflect theological truths and perhaps to mirror a new week of creation (compare Gen. 1).

In this section, Jerusalem is presented as the site of Jesus' betrayal, abandonment, denial, condemnation, suffering, mocking, and death—in stark contrast to both the usual depiction of Jerusalem as a sacred center and to Jesus' successful ministry in Galilee. This is one more way in which Jesus' ministry inverts expectations. The invitation to return to Galilee at the end of the text is another way in which the centrality of Jerusalem is diminished.

The Temple
(11:1–13:37)

OVERVIEW OF CHAPTERS 11–12

It is possible to identify five controversy stories in this section of Mark's text:

1. 11:27–12:12: Jesus Questioned about His Authority
2. 12:13–17: Jesus Questioned about Paying Taxes
3. 12:18–27: Jesus Questioned about Resurrection
4. 12:28–34: Jesus Questioned about the Commandments
5. 12:35–37: Jesus Questions the Scribes

Of course, the structure is not perfect since the final story (12:35–37) does not consist of Jesus being questioned but rather features Jesus asking a question. Nonetheless, the structure is similar enough to the five controversy stories in 2:1–3:6 to warrant comparison, since each set of stories is followed fairly closely by the only instances in Mark where Jesus speaks at length (see chapters 4 and 13).

It may be that 12:35–37 departs from the standard form of a controversy story for rhetorical effect: 12:34 notes that after Jesus' response to the scribe, the fact that no one dared to ask him any more questions may signal to the audience that Jesus has triumphed over those who would attempt to entrap him in his words.

JESUS ENTERS JERUSALEM (11:1–11)

Greek Text

1 Καὶ ὅτε ἐγγίζουσιν εἰς Ἰεροσόλυμα εἰς Βηθφαγὴ καὶ Βηθανίαν πρὸς τὸ Ὄρος τῶν Ἐλαιῶν, ἀποστέλλει δύο τῶν μαθητῶν αὐτοῦ 2 καὶ λέγει αὐτοῖς· Ὑπάγετε εἰς τὴν κώμην τὴν κατέναντι ὑμῶν, καὶ εὐθὺς εἰσπορευόμενοι εἰς αὐτὴν εὑρήσετε πῶλον δεδεμένον ἐφ᾽ ὃν οὐδεὶς οὔπω ἀνθρώπων ἐκάθισεν· λύσατε αὐτὸν καὶ φέρετε. 3 καὶ ἐάν τις ὑμῖν εἴπῃ· Τί ποιεῖτε τοῦτο; εἴπατε ὅτι Ὁ κύριος αὐτοῦ χρείαν ἔχει· καὶ εὐθὺς αὐτὸν ἀποστέλλει πάλιν ὧδε. 4 καὶ ἀπῆλθον καὶ εὗρον πῶλον δεδεμένον πρὸς θύραν ἔξω ἐπὶ τοῦ ἀμφόδου, καὶ λύουσιν αὐτόν. 5 καί τινες τῶν ἐκεῖ ἑστηκότων ἔλεγον αὐτοῖς· Τί ποιεῖτε λύοντες τὸν πῶλον; 6 οἱ δὲ εἶπαν αὐτοῖς καθὼς εἶπεν ὁ Ἰησοῦς· καὶ ἀφῆκαν αὐτούς. 7 καὶ φέρουσιν τὸν πῶλον πρὸς τὸν Ἰησοῦν, καὶ ἐπιβάλλουσιν αὐτῷ τὰ ἱμάτια αὐτῶν, καὶ ἐκάθισεν ἐπ᾽ αὐτόν. 8 καὶ πολλοὶ τὰ ἱμάτια αὐτῶν ἔστρωσαν εἰς τὴν ὁδόν, ἄλλοι δὲ στιβάδας κόψαντες ἐκ τῶν ἀγρῶν. 9 καὶ οἱ προάγοντες καὶ οἱ ἀκολουθοῦντες ἔκραζον· Ὡσαννά· Εὐλογημένος ὁ ἐρχόμενος ἐν ὀνόματι κυρίου· 10 Εὐλογημένη ἡ ἐρχομένη βασιλεία τοῦ πατρὸς ἡμῶν Δαυίδ· Ὡσαννὰ ἐν τοῖς ὑψίστοις.

11 Καὶ εἰσῆλθεν εἰς Ἰεροσόλυμα εἰς τὸ ἱερόν· καὶ περιβλεψάμενος πάντα ὀψὲ ἤδη οὔσης τῆς ὥρας ἐξῆλθεν εἰς Βηθανίαν μετὰ τῶν δώδεκα. [SBLGNT]

The Kings James Version

1 And when they came nigh to Jerusalem, unto Bethphage and Bethany, at the mount of Olives, he sendeth forth two of his disciples, 2 And saith unto them, Go your way into the village over against you: and as soon as ye be entered into it, ye shall find a colt tied, whereon never man sat; loose him, and bring him. 3 And if any man say unto you, Why do ye this? say ye that the Lord hath need of him; and straightway he will send him hither. 4 And they went their way, and found the colt tied by the door without in a place where two ways met; and they loose him. 5 And certain of them that stood there said unto them, What do ye, loosing the colt? 6 And they said unto them even as Jesus had commanded: and they let them go. 7 And they brought the

New Rendition

1 And when they are coming near to Jerusalem, to Bethphage and Bethany, near the Mount of Olives, he sends two of his disciples. 2 And he says to them, "Go into the village ahead of you and immediately entering into it, you will find a colt having been tied up, upon which no one has ever sat. Untie it and bring it. 3 And if anyone says to you, 'Why are you doing this?' say, 'The master has need of it, and he will send it back here immediately.'" 4 And they left and found a colt having been tied at the door, out in the road, and they untied it. 5 And some of those who were standing there were saying to them, "What are you doing untying the colt?" 6 But they spoke to them as Jesus had commanded, and they allowed them [to go]. 7 And they

colt to Jesus, and cast their garments on him; and he sat upon him. 8 And many spread their garments in the way: and others cut down branches off the trees, and strawed them in the way. 9 And they that went before, and they that followed, cried, saying, Hosanna; Blessed is he that cometh in the name of the Lord: 10 Blessed be the kingdom of our father David, that cometh in the name of the Lord: Hosanna in the highest. 11 And Jesus entered into Jerusalem, and into the temple: and when he had looked round about upon all things, and now the eventide was come, he went out unto Bethany with the twelve.

lead the colt to Jesus. And they threw their cloaks on it, and he sat on it. 8 And many spread their cloaks on the way, but others cut leafy branches from the fields. 9 And those going in front and those going behind were shouting, "Hosanna! Blessed is the one coming in the name of the Lord! 10 Blessed [is] the coming kingdom of our father David! Hosanna in the highest!" 11 And he entered into Jerusalem, into the temple. And having looked around at everything, the hour already being late, he went to Bethany with the Twelve.

Notes

11:1 *And when they came nigh to Jerusalem:* This verse indicates a significant turning point in Mark's account: Jesus is no longer "on the way," as he was in the middle section of Mark, but is now arriving in Jerusalem. The third and final major division of the text begins here as Jesus approaches Jerusalem. Since Jesus has prophesied that he will die in Jerusalem (10:33), an ominous undercurrent runs through this verse.

Jesus and his disciples would have approached Bethphage, Bethany, and the Mount of Olives before they reached Jerusalem, but Mark mentions the locations out of order, most likely to emphasize Jerusalem as their intended destination.

unto Bethphage and Bethany: The name "Bethphage" probably derives from the Aramaic meaning "house of unripe [or: early] figs" and thus might set the stage for the withering of the fig tree (11:12–14). Bethphage is less than a mile away from Jerusalem, and Bethany is about two miles away.

Mark is again narrating out of order: the group would have first come to Bethany and then to Bethphage. Mark may have listed Bethphage first because it was better known or perhaps because it was closer to Jerusalem, which was named immediately before it.

at the mount of Olives: In modern English, this is a hill and not a mountain, but the New Rendition maintains the customary usage.

Given that the Mount of Olives is the fourth geographic reference in this verse, it is puzzling as to why it was mentioned. Perhaps Mark wanted to allude to Zechariah 14:4, a passage that links to events in the last days, emphasizing the kingship of the chosen ruler, who comes from the Mount of Olives. There will be many other allusions to Zechariah in chapter 11. The only other HB reference to the Mount of Olives is in 2 Samuel 15:30, where David weeps over the people's rejection of him, so perhaps this reference hints at Jesus' coming rejection. The combination of these two HB references to the Mount of Olives, in light of Jesus' coming messianic actions and his coming rejection, is very powerful. The Mount of Olives is also mentioned at the end of chapter 13, which may imply that chapters 11–13 should be understood as a literary unit focused on Jesus and the temple.

he sendeth forth two of his disciples: The word translated as "send" (Greek: *apostellō*) is a cognate of "apostle," although these disciples are not necessarily apostles. The disciples are not named in this instance; sending them out in a pair follows the pattern established in 6:6–7.

11:2 *And saith unto them, Go your way into the village over against you:* "Over against" could mean "in front of" or "on the opposing side." It is unclear whether Jesus is referring to Bethphage, Bethany, or a third, unnamed village.

and as soon as ye be entered into it, ye shall find a colt tied: "Colt" refers to a young animal; the species is not specified. It might be a horse or a donkey, but the latter is more likely since they were less valuable and therefore more likely to be found in a small village.

whereon never man sat; loose him, and bring him: In the HB, unused animals are considered preferable for special tasks (Num. 19:2; Deut. 21:3; 1 Sam. 6:7). This language probably alludes to Zechariah 9:9, where Jerusalem is promised that her future king will come to her riding on a new colt. Significantly, the allusion to Zechariah uses the language of kingship that Christians would come to associate with Jesus: "This king, riding on a donkey, will banish war from the land—no more chariots, war-horses, or bows. Commanding peace to the nations, he will be a king of peace."[1]

11:3 *And if any man say unto you, Why do ye this? say ye that the Lord hath need of him:* The line "the Lord hath need of him" permits several interpretations:

---

1. Marcus J. Borg and John Dominic Crossan, *The Last Week: The Day-by-Day Account of Jesus's Final Week in Jerusalem* (San Francisco: HarperSanFrancisco, 2006), 4. It is worth noting that, within its context, the full portait of kingship in Zechariah does not completely fit Jesus: Zechariah's king achieves peace through victorious conquest.

1. "The Lord" refers to Jesus. A custom of forced service permitted animal and human labor to be claimed by rulers (compare 15:21; see also Matt. 5:41), and the phrase "the Lord hath need of him" may have been almost a technical term for this practice.[2] Unsurprisingly, this custom was a detested part of Roman rule.[3] If this is the correct background to this passage, Jesus is positioning himself—not the Romans—as the legitimate ruler when he claims the right to impress the animal.

2. "The Lord" refers to God. The point is that God wants Jesus to enter Jerusalem on the colt. This reading recognizes God as the true creator and thus controller of all creation, including animals.

3. "The Lord" means simply "the master" and refers to the literal owner of the animal. This reading leads to two possibilities:

   a. Jesus has already arranged with the owner to borrow the animal. (But see below for why this is unlikely.)

   b. Jesus is instructing his disciples to convey an untruth, as there was no arrangement with the animal's owner. Modern readers would likely find this incongruent with their picture of Jesus. At the same time, sometimes readings that don't work well on the literal level (see the Notes on 11:13: "the time of figs was not yet") are an indication on Mark's part that the text should be approached on a symbolic level, and that may be the case here. Thus the unlikely picture of Jesus encouraging his disciples to convey a falsehood is an indicator that the story should be interpreted symbolically.

It is possible that Mark is exploiting the ambiguity in this verse to make a point: God, as the creator of the animal, is its Lord; Jesus is the Lord to whom that title would be primarily applied by Mark's audience (even though no one in Mark's narrative would likely have recognized that the title applied to him), and the earthly owner of the colt functions as its master.

and straightway he will send him hither: This line can be read as the conclusion to what Jesus wants the disciples to say ("The Lord has need of him and will immediately return him") or Jesus' announcement of what the response will be to the disciples' words ("'The Lord has need of him.' [Then] he will immediately send him.")

It is possible that this passage implies that Jesus had made a previous arrangement with the owner of the animal, but this is unlikely, mostly because it is difficult (1) to imagine Mark leaving out that fact in this rather

2. Hans Leander, "With Homi Bhabha at the Jerusalem City Gates: A Postcolonial Reading of the 'Triumphant' Entry (Mark 11.1–11)," *Journal for the Study of the New Testament* 32, no. 3 (2010): 325.

3. Leander, "With Homi Bhabha at the Jerusalem City Gates," 324–25.

detailed account and (2) to determine why Mark would have spent so much time relating these details to the audience. It is much more likely that this passage is pregnant with symbolic meaning, similar to 1 Samuel 10:1–9, where Samuel also announces a quickly filled prophecy as a sign of his authenticity (compare 14:13–16, a passage that is very similar, and the Notes on those verses).

Relationship to 1 Kings 1. In 1 Kings 1:33–40, David, nearing death, announces plans to enthrone his son Solomon, including seating Solomon on his mule for a procession. Since this is the first time kingship passes from David, it becomes a template and is thus probably responsible for the portrait in Zechariah 9.[4]

11:4 *And they went their way, and found the colt tied by the door without in a place where two ways met; and they loose him. 5 And certain of them that stood there said unto them, What do ye, loosing the colt? 6 And they said unto them even as Jesus had commanded: and they let them go:* These bystanders apparently assume that the disciples are the agents of the animal's owner (the "Lord").

In this incident, the disciples are literally preparing the way of the Lord and thus partially fulfilling 1:2.

11:7 *And they brought the colt to Jesus, and cast their garments on him:* The disciples bring—they don't ride—the animal, thus preserving it for Jesus. The two disciples place their clothing on the animal, presumably because, having never been ridden, it lacks a saddle.

In the previous story, Bartimaeus cast away his garment to follow Jesus (10:50); here, Jesus' two unnamed disciples engage in a similar action. Thus, there might be an element of symbolism here as these two disciples show themselves willing to sacrifice their possessions in order to follow Jesus and prepare the way for him.

and he sat upon him: A typical pilgrim to Jerusalem at the time of the festivals would have entered on foot, so Jesus' entry is distinctive, especially since he was riding an unused animal. The scene likely alludes to Zechariah 9:9: "Rejoice greatly, O daughter of Zion; shout, O daughter of Jerusalem: behold, thy King cometh unto thee: he is just, and having salvation; lowly, and riding upon an ass, and upon a colt the foal of an ass." Jesus

---

4. Brent Kinman, "Jesus' Royal Entry into Jerusalem," *Bulletin for Biblical Research* 15, no. 2 (2005): 240.

is thus portrayed (by his own very deliberate actions) as the long-awaited king. This is a very significant moment in Mark's narrative.

11:8 *And many spread their garments in the way:* It is likely that "many" refers to many (i.e., not all) of the disciples who were traveling with Jesus: he is not yet in Jerusalem, so these are not the people of Jerusalem but rather those who have been traveling with Jesus.

"In the way" may be symbolic as well as literal. Being "in the way" involves recognizing Jesus as the coming king (but a king who, by his own prophecies, is on the way to his death).

This scene may allude to 2 Kings 9:13, where the people place their garments on the stairs and announce that Jehu is king. Placing clothing on the ground was also a ritual used to show honor in Roman culture.[5]

and others cut down branches off the trees, and strawed them in the way: The phrase "and strawed them in the way" seems to be a later addition, probably added to harmonize with Matthew 21:8[6] or because the passage seems incomplete without it since it doesn't explain what they did with the branches. Perhaps they are cutting the branches to clear a path for Jesus (which would be similar to 2:23; see the Notes on that verse).

The picture here is the ancient equivalent of rolling out the red carpet; the combination of the road, the animal, the garments, and the branches (whether just cut or cut and spread) implies a welcome fit for royalty.

11:9 *And they that went before, and they that followed, cried, saying, Hosanna:* Some people go in front of Jesus (presumably to put straw down), and some follow after. All cry "hosanna," a Hebrew and Aramaic expression meaning "O Lord, save" that had morphed into a generic expression of jubilation by Jesus' time. There may be some irony in the word: those who considered the word's meaning would recognize that the crowd was proclaiming an important truth about Jesus' identity, but many saying it would not have attributed any special significance to it.

The people are quoting Psalm 118:25–26. This psalm was part of the Passover liturgy and thus functioned to help people remember the Exodus. There may be in its use an undercurrent of an expectation that Jesus would help liberate the people from Roman rule, much as Moses liberated the people from Egyptian rule. Jesus himself will quote from this psalm (118:22–23) in 12:10–11.

---

5. Collins, *Mark,* 519.
6. Collins, *Mark,* 512 note c.

Blessed is he that cometh in the name of the Lord: "In the name of the Lord" might modify "blessed" ("blessed in the name of the Lord") or "cometh" ("cometh in the name of the Lord"). To do something "in the name of" someone means to do it with their authority; thus, the people are either blessing Jesus with the Lord's authority or claiming that he comes with the Lord's authority.

11:10 ***Blessed be the kingdom of our father David, that cometh in the name of the Lord:*** The phrase "in the name of the Lord" is not found in the best ancient manuscripts.[7]

Hosanna in the highest: "In the highest" might refer to the angels (those who live on high) who should praise God, or it might refer to God (who is the highest), or it could refer to the highest places (that is, the highest heavens).

11:11 ***And Jesus entered into Jerusalem, and into the temple: and when he had looked round about upon all things, and now the eventide was come, he went out unto Bethany with the twelve:*** This verse seems anticlimactic, but that is precisely the point. Certain expectations would have accompanied a kingly procession into the city: Josephus recounts that Alexander the Great's entry into Jerusalem involved him being greeted by all of the people, welcomed by the high priest, and offering sacrifices in the temple. While it is unlikely that that account is historically accurate, "it reflects Greco-Roman entrance processions of his time."[8] The fact that failure to properly welcome a king to a city could lead to punishments, including the destruction of the city, may have resonated with the audiences of Mark who heard the gospel after the destruction of Jerusalem.

Jesus' looking around may be significant here: he may be assessing the situation inside the temple in preparation for his action in the temple the next day. Similarly, the reference to it being late in the day (KJV: "eventide") may have symbolic resonance: as the rest of the chapter will suggest, it is too late for an appropriate response to Jesus on the part of some of the city's elites.

The departure shows that Jesus' base of operations this week will be in Bethany, not Jerusalem. This may reflect the simple historical reality that he was granted hospitality in Bethany but not Jerusalem, or it may also

---

7. Bratcher and Nida, *Translator's Handbook,* 347.

8. Paul Brooks Duff, "The March of the Divine Warrior and the Advent of the Greco-Roman King: Mark's Account of Jesus' Entry into Jerusalem," *Journal of Biblical Literature* 111, no. 1 (1992): 59.

have a theological meaning: he is more closely aligned with the small town of Bethany than with the large city that rejects him.

Relationship to 10:46–52. The chapter break obscures the relationship between the healing of blind Bartimaeus and Jesus' entry into Jerusalem, but the stories are linked by multiple verbal echoes including references to "the way," removing clothing (perhaps for ritual use), the theme of salvation, following Jesus, and the son of David (which is implicit in the procession into Jerusalem). These similarities position Bartimaeus as the model for the behavior of the disciples.

While Bartimaeus went out of his way to emphatically welcome Jesus, the religious leaders in Jerusalem who should have welcomed Jesus after the procession do not do so. The contrast between the literally blind Bartimaeus and the spiritually blind leaders is stark.

Analysis

Even though this story is formally placed in the third section of Mark (Jerusalem) and not the second section (on the way), it is something of a transitional story since it shows Jesus' entry into the city.

Mark devotes a considerable portion of this account not to the entry into Jerusalem itself but rather to the planning for that event, which is related twice (once in Jesus' words and again as it actually happens). Mark's purpose seems to be to emphasize that Jesus' entry into the city was neither haphazard nor random but rather was carefully and deliberately planned: his precisely orchestrated entry "is a nonverbal way of making a messianic claim."[9] The note "even as Jesus had commanded" is key to this passage since it shows Jesus' prophetic ability and narrates the fulfillment of his words. The portrait of Jesus that emerges is one in which he is in control, has planned for every detail, and where what he says will happen actually happens. (Mark will introduce the Last Supper in a similar way in 14:12–16.) This is an important beginning to this third section of the Gospel, where Mark's early audiences would have had to cope with the embarrassment of Jesus' arrest and crucifixion. This portrait serves as a counterpoint to the idea of Jesus dying as a condemned criminal. In Mark's telling, this incident is not primarily about Jesus' manner of entry in Jerusalem but rather attests to his prophetic ability and control.

---

9. Collins, *Mark,* 518.

The portrait that Mark paints of Jesus' entry implies that it is a kingly procession into the city. Jesus is entering as any king would enter. It is possible that Jesus' disciples did not recognize the full import of the scene, but—at least as it is presented to Mark's audience—Jesus is very intentionally presenting himself as a Davidic king entering the city in a royal procession.

Mark's audience would perhaps have known of another processional entrance into Jerusalem: "The meaning of Jesus's mode of entry is amplified by the realization that two processions entered Jerusalem that Passover. The other procession was an imperial one. On or about the same day, the Roman governor Pontius Pilate rode into the city from the opposite side, the west, at the head of a very different kind of procession: imperial cavalry and foot soldiers arriving to reinforce the garrison on the Temple Mount."[10] The similarities would have suggested Jesus' kingly status, but the differences (namely, Jesus' lack of an army) would have implied the nonviolent nature of his kingship.

The Romans would have instantly quashed any event appearing to them as an insurrection, and a kingly procession entering Jerusalem at the time of Passover certainly would have qualified. Therefore it is likely that Jesus' entry into Jerusalem was a very small event, perhaps involving only the disciples who had been traveling with him, which did not draw the attention of the authorities. Given that Passover involved hundreds if not thousands of people entering Jerusalem each day,[11] they likely did not even notice Jesus and his small band of followers.

Mark's audience would have assumed that Jesus was entering Jerusalem triumphantly, an assumption encouraged by Mark's detailed account of Jesus' careful preparations for the event. But in 11:11, their anticipation is dashed by the lack of welcome afforded to Jesus. The city's elites should have been present to welcome Jesus into the city and to invite him to participate in a ritual of some sort.[12] Jesus and his disciples have carefully orchestrated his arrival in Jerusalem, but the city's leaders are absent. While this story is traditionally called "the triumphal entry," that is a misnomer since the climax of the story is anything but a triumph—rather, it is an embarrassment. (Modern audiences are used to thinking of this event as a triumphal and grandiose entry based on John's version of the story.) It

---

10. Borg, *Jesus*, 232.

11. Kinman, "Royal Entry," 252.

12. Leander, "With Homi Bhabha at the Jerusalem City Gates," 319.

thus becomes another instance of Mark's irony: Jesus presents himself as a messianic king, in a way that is deliberately provocative, and no one reacts. No one pays any attention at all.

There may be another layer of irony here as well. The understanding of the various groups in this story likely differs (with Jesus displaying messianic intent, the disciples perhaps showing less understanding of Jesus' true identity but still welcoming a great teacher whom they chose to follow, and the authorities not even noticing anything unusual). Mark's audience would be aware of these various levels of understanding and realize that Jesus' ministry was not uniformly understood.

THE FIG TREE AND THE TEMPLE (11:12–26)

Greek Text

12 Καὶ τῇ ἐπαύριον ἐξελθόντων αὐτῶν ἀπὸ Βηθανίας ἐπείνασεν. 13 καὶ ἰδὼν συκῆν ἀπὸ μακρόθεν ἔχουσαν φύλλα ἦλθεν εἰ ἄρα τι εὑρήσει ἐν αὐτῇ, καὶ ἐλθὼν ἐπ’ αὐτὴν οὐδὲν εὗρεν εἰ μὴ φύλλα, ὁ γὰρ καιρὸς οὐκ ἦν σύκων. 14 καὶ ἀποκριθεὶς εἶπεν αὐτῇ· Μηκέτι εἰς τὸν αἰῶνα ἐκ σοῦ μηδεὶς καρπὸν φάγοι. καὶ ἤκουον οἱ μαθηταὶ αὐτοῦ.

15 Καὶ ἔρχονται εἰς Ἱεροσόλυμα. καὶ εἰσελθὼν εἰς τὸ ἱερὸν ἤρξατο ἐκβάλλειν τοὺς πωλοῦντας καὶ τοὺς ἀγοράζοντας ἐν τῷ ἱερῷ, καὶ τὰς τραπέζας τῶν κολλυβιστῶν καὶ τὰς καθέδρας τῶν πωλούντων τὰς περιστερὰς κατέστρεψεν 16 καὶ οὐκ ἤφιεν ἵνα τις διενέγκῃ σκεῦος διὰ τοῦ ἱεροῦ, 17 καὶ ἐδίδασκεν καὶ ἔλεγεν αὐτοῖς· Οὐ γέγραπται ὅτι Ὁ οἶκός μου οἶκος προσευχῆς κληθήσεται πᾶσιν τοῖς ἔθνεσιν; ὑμεῖς δὲ πεποιήκατε αὐτὸν σπήλαιον λῃστῶν. 18 καὶ ἤκουσαν οἱ ἀρχιερεῖς καὶ οἱ γραμματεῖς, καὶ ἐζήτουν πῶς αὐτὸν ἀπολέσωσιν· ἐφοβοῦντο γὰρ αὐτόν, πᾶς γὰρ ὁ ὄχλος ἐξεπλήσσετο ἐπὶ τῇ διδαχῇ αὐτοῦ. 19 Καὶ ὅταν ὀψὲ ἐγένετο, ἐξεπορεύοντο ἔξω τῆς πόλεως.

20 Καὶ παραπορευόμενοι πρωῒ εἶδον τὴν συκῆν ἐξηραμμένην ἐκ ῥιζῶν. 21 καὶ ἀναμνησθεὶς ὁ Πέτρος λέγει αὐτῷ· Ῥαββί, ἴδε ἡ συκῆ ἣν κατηράσω ἐξήρανται. 22 καὶ ἀποκριθεὶς ὁ Ἰησοῦς λέγει αὐτοῖς· Ἔχετε πίστιν θεοῦ· 23 ἀμὴν λέγω ὑμῖν ὅτι ὃς ἂν εἴπῃ τῷ ὄρει τούτῳ· Ἄρθητι καὶ βλήθητι εἰς τὴν θάλασσαν, καὶ μὴ διακριθῇ ἐν τῇ καρδίᾳ αὐτοῦ ἀλλὰ πιστεύῃ ὅτι ὃ λαλεῖ γίνεται, ἔσται αὐτῷ. 24 διὰ τοῦτο λέγω ὑμῖν, πάντα ὅσα προσεύχεσθε καὶ αἰτεῖσθε, πιστεύετε ὅτι ἐλάβετε, καὶ ἔσται ὑμῖν.

25 καὶ ὅταν στήκετε προσευχόμενοι, ἀφίετε εἴ τι ἔχετε κατά τινος, ἵνα καὶ ὁ πατὴρ ὑμῶν ὁ ἐν τοῖς οὐρανοῖς ἀφῇ ὑμῖν τὰ παραπτώματα ὑμῶν. [SBLGNT]

King James Version

12 And on the morrow, when they were come from Bethany, he was hungry: 13 And seeing a fig tree afar off having leaves, he came, if haply he might find any thing thereon: and when he came to it, he found nothing but leaves; for the time of figs was not yet. 14 And Jesus answered and said unto it, No man eat fruit of thee hereafter for ever. And his disciples heard it.

15 And they come to Jerusalem: and Jesus went into the temple, and began to cast out them that sold and bought in the temple, and overthrew the tables of the moneychangers, and the seats of them that sold doves; 16 And would not suffer that any man should carry any vessel through the temple. 17 And he taught, saying unto them, Is it not written, My house shall be called of all nations the house of prayer? but ye have made it a den of thieves. 18 And the scribes and chief priests heard it, and sought how they might destroy him: for they feared him, because all the people was astonished at his doctrine. 19 And when even was come, he went out of the city.

20 And in the morning, as they passed by, they saw the fig tree dried up from the roots. 21 And Peter calling to remembrance saith unto him, Master, behold, the fig tree which thou cursedst is withered away. 22 And Jesus answering saith unto them, Have faith in God. 23 For verily I say unto you, That whosoever shall say unto this mountain, Be thou removed, and be thou cast into the sea; and shall not doubt in his heart, but shall believe that those things which he saith shall come to pass; he shall have

New Rendition

12 And on the next day, as they went out from Bethany, he was hungry. 13 And having seen in the distance a fig tree having leaves, he went [to see] if perhaps he would find any [figs] on it. And having come to it, he found nothing but leaves, for it was not fig season. 14 And answering, he said to it, "May no one ever again eat your fruit." And his disciples heard.

15 And they come to Jerusalem. And having entered into the temple, he began to cast out those selling and those buying in the temple. And he toppled the moneychangers' tables and the chairs of those selling the doves. 16 And he didn't permit anyone to carry any goods through the temple. 17 And he was teaching and was saying to them, "Has it not been written 'My house will be called a house of prayer for all the nations'? But you have made it 'a hideout for robbers.'" 18 And the chief priests and the scriptorians heard [it], and they sought how they could destroy him because they feared him because all of the crowd was astonished at his teaching. 19 And when evening came, they went out of the city.

20 And passing by in the morning, they saw the fig tree, withered from the roots. 21 And having remembered, Peter says to him, "Rabbi, look, the fig tree that you cursed has withered." 22 And answering, Jesus says to them, "Have trust in God. 23 Amen, I say to you, if you say to this mountain, 'Be lifted and thrown into the sea,' and you do not waver in your heart, but trust that what you say will happen, it will happen for you. 24 Therefore I say to you, all things you pray and ask for, trust

whatsoever he saith. 24 Therefore I say unto you, What things soever ye desire, when ye pray, believe that ye receive them, and ye shall have them. 25 And when ye stand praying, forgive, if ye have ought against any: that your Father also which is in heaven may forgive you your trespasses. 26 But if ye do not forgive, neither will your Father which is in heaven forgive your trespasses.

that you have received it, and it will be yours. 25 And whenever you stand praying, forgive anything you have against anyone, so that your father who is in the heavens will forgive your sins." [26]

Notes

11:12 *And on the morrow, when they were come from Bethany, he was hungry:* The note that Jesus was hungry fits into Mark's portrait of Jesus as genuinely human. At the same time, Jesus' hunger is likely more symbolic than literal. This becomes more obvious as the story develops.

11:13 *And seeing a fig tree afar off having leaves, he came, if haply he might find any thing thereon:* It would have been typical for a fig tree to be in leaf the week before Passover (compare 13:28); it would not have been expected, however, for it to bear fruit at this time (figs ripen between May and October). According to Pliny the Elder, the fig tree was unique because it produced leaves before fruit. (Some commentators suggest that Jesus expected to find early buds or leftover figs from the previous season, but these possibilities are contradicted by Mark's note that it was not the season for figs.)

and when he came to it, he found nothing but leaves; for the time of figs was not yet: Mark mentions that it was not the right time of year for figs. This is an indication that Jesus' expectation of figs simply does not make sense on a logical level and therefore must be considered on another level. It is a strong hint that this scene should be interpreted as an enacted parable, meaning that Jesus' actions themselves are like a parable: the literal meaning is not nearly as important as the symbolic meaning:[13] "The best interpretation views Jesus' behavior as deliberately incongruous in order to alert his disciples to a metaphorical meaning."[14] Further, the Greek word

---

13. Examples of enacted prophecies in the HB include Isa. 20:1–6; Jer. 13:1–11; 19:1–15; and Ezek. 4:1–17.

14. Craig L. Blomberg, "New Testament Miracles and Higher Criticism: Climbing Up the Slippery Slope," *Journal of the Evangelical Theological Society* 27 (December 1984): 428.

translated as "time" is *kairos,* which can refer to a specifically appointed time, as opposed to chronological time (Greek: *chronos*); *kairos* is the same word used in 1:15 ("the time is fulfilled") when Jesus announces that the time for his ministry has come. Thus this word choice also points to a symbolic meaning for the curse on the fig tree; had it been simply literal, it is likely that *chronos,* not *kairos,* would have been used.

11:14 *And Jesus answered and said unto it, No man eat fruit of thee hereafter for ever:* The word "answered" is sometimes used without its full meaning by Mark, but in this context may imply that the tree has "spoken" to Jesus by presenting leaves but no fruit.

This story vexes interpreters, who sometimes dismiss Jesus' reaction as illogical, capricious, or petty. But Mark notes carefully that it was not the time for figs, thus suggesting a symbolic interpretation. And while Jesus' statement is often considered a curse (based on Peter's words in 11:21), in Mark's Gospel, Peter is not always a reliable source of information. Additionally, the word "fruit" instead of "fig" may point less to the tree than to the general concept of fruitfulness (Ps. 92:12–15; Hosea 10:1, 13): it "invokes the biblical motif of fruitfulness or fruitlessness as a symbol of spiritual health or disease."[15] So it makes sense to view Jesus' words as a prophetic statement and the scene with the fig tree as an enacted parable.

And his disciples heard it: This is an odd thing to note. Presumably the disciples heard everything that Jesus said in Mark's Gospel (otherwise, how would Mark have found out about it?), so this comment strikes the audience as unusual and suggests some significance beyond the obvious. Because this is the first half of a sandwich story, the hearing of the disciples is significant: when Mark returns to the story, the fact that the disciples had heard and remembered what Jesus said here is crucial to the development of the plot. Further, it might point to the symbolic nature of the event, especially since an emphasis on hearing is a key element of both the parable of the sower and the discussion surrounding the parable (see the Notes on chapter 4).

Note: The story of the fig tree resumes in 11:20; see the Notes there.

11:15 *And they come to Jerusalem: and Jesus went into the temple, and began to cast out them that sold and bought in the temple:* At Passover, pilgrims would have come to the temple from long distances; because it was impractical for them to bring sacrificial animals with them, they purchased what they needed once they arrived in Jerusalem.

and overthrew the tables of the moneychangers, and the seats of them that sold doves: In Jesus' time, the half-shekel temple tax had to be paid in

---

15. Marcus, *Mark 8–16,* 782.

Tyrian coins.[16] Moneychangers would have exchanged the coins brought by pilgrims for these Tyrian coins (and, of course, made some money for themselves in the process).

11:16 *And would not suffer that any man should carry any vessel through the temple:* "Vessel" can mean "thing" and so is a very generic word. Jesus' actions here might be interpreted several different ways:

1. The temple was sometimes used as a shortcut; Jesus objects to this practice as disrespectful to the temple and thus stops people who are just crossing through it carrying common things.

2. It would have been necessary to carry things through the temple in order for the temple to fulfill its functions; by stopping this practice, Jesus is, in effect, prohibiting the temple from functioning. (This would then be a parabolic action, perhaps a prophecy of the coming destruction of the temple; compare 13:2.)

3. This action relates to Zechariah 14:21, which envisions a future day when everything will be so holy that a common vessel will be as holy as what is used in the temple. Perhaps Jesus envisions what is happening in his day to be an inversion of that practice, where these common vessels are treated as if they were holy by carrying them through the temple. Interestingly, the Zechariah passage pictures a time when there will be no Gentiles in the temple, which also suggests an inversion of Jesus' actions.

4. This scene almost certainly happens in the outer court of the temple, or the court of the Gentiles. This space was regarded as much less sacred than the inner areas of the temple. But Jesus' actions imply that the portion of the temple where Gentiles were permitted (who, presumably, would come there to pray) should be treated as if it were holy and not as a thoroughfare or market. Interestingly, in this reading, Jesus is arguing for the extension of holiness, which is counter to the normal pattern in Mark where the Pharisees want to extend the realm of holiness, but Jesus objects.

11:17 *And he taught, saying unto them, Is it not written, My house shall be called of all nations the house of prayer? but ye have made it a den of thieves:* The language "my house shall be called of all nations the house of prayer" quotes Isaiah 56:47, which envisions eunuchs and foreigners welcome in the temple, in contrast with Deuteronomy 23:1–4, which prohibited their presence. Both the Isaiah quotation and Jesus' use of it emphasize the role of prayer in the temple; this will become an important theme in this section of Mark (see the Notes on 11:23). The reference to the "den of thieves" quotes Jeremiah 7:11 (the LXX uses the same Greek word). In context, Jeremiah is fulfilling the command that he has been given to prophesy of the destruction of the temple. By framing the justification for his action

---

16. Mishah Berakhot 9:5.

with two quotations from the HB, Jesus is positioning himself as a prophet. Interestingly, Jeremiah 7:11 speaks against the entry of foreigners into the temple, but Isaiah 56:7 supports it.[17]

"Den" refers to a cave, but the implication of the word is not neutral; rather, a hideout for robbers is pictured here. Many readers take the reference to thieves as an indictment of the moneychangers and merchants, but a robber's hideout is not the place where a crime is committed but rather the place where robbers hide afterward.[18] So the implication is that the crime was committed elsewhere and the temple is the hideout, a presumed safe place. This perhaps reflects the common belief that the temple would not be destroyed, and so those inside of it would be safe, no matter what they had done. Perhaps one reason why Jesus quotes from Jeremiah 7 is to emphasize the idea that the temple could in fact be destroyed (Jer. 7:4).

The word "thieves" presents some interpretive difficulties. To Mark's audience, the word is the same as that used to describe the Zealots, who sought to end Roman occupation, especially if Mark is writing after 67 CE, when the Zealots were operating from within the temple. In this context, it sounds as if Jesus is decrying the presence of Zealots (as members of a revolutionary movement) within the temple and perhaps suggesting that their presence would lead to the destruction of the temple.[19] But the word stems from the quotation of Jeremiah 7:11, when it did not have that connotation, although it did suggest thievery involving violence.

Relationship to Nehemiah 2:11–18. There are some intriguing similarities and differences between Mark's account and Nehemiah 2:11–18. In both, the entry into Jerusalem on an animal is pictured as well as the examination of the temple area. However, Nehemiah, after looking around, announces plans to rebuild the temple—precisely the opposite of what Jesus is doing if he is prophesying of the temple's coming destruction. If this is a deliberate allusion, Mark has followed a pattern used elsewhere in this Gospel where an HB text is followed to a point but then inverted.

11:18 *And the scribes and chief priests heard it:* Mark's careful note here parallels 11:14 where Jesus' disciples heard what he said to the fig tree. The

---

17. Sabin, *Reopening the Word,* 80.

18. J. R. Daniel Kirk, "Time for Figs, Temple Destruction, and Houses of Prayer in Mark 11:12–25," *Catholic Biblical Quarterly* 74, no. 3 (2012): 518.

19. J. Bradley Chance, "The Cursing of the Temple and the Tearing of the Veil in the Gospel of Mark," *Biblical Interpretation* 15, no. 3 (2007): 276.

parallel does two things: it aligns the disciples with the religious leaders (which is not flattering to the disciples) and aligns the fig tree incident with the action in the temple.

and sought how they might destroy him: Because everything that happened in the temple was controlled by the chief priests, "in attacking the vendors and money-changers, Jesus had attacked the priesthood."[20] This explains why they want to destroy Jesus. But it is also a fulfillment of 8:31, when Jesus prophesied to his disciples that these leaders would seek to destroy him.

for they feared him, because all the people was astonished at his doctrine: Mark distinguishes between the religious leadership and the common people: the leaders are opposed to Jesus, but the people would be opposed to any action against Jesus. This speaks to Jesus' popularity. Not only is this an important nuance to Mark's story, but it is also a significant hedge against anti-Semitic readings of scripture: it is not "the Jews" who are seeking to destroy Jesus. Rather, the common people support him; it is the leadership class that feels threatened by his popularity and wants to destroy him. If it is the case that the presence of moneychangers and merchants in the temple is a fairly new development, then a disconnect between the wishes of the religious leadership (who probably profited from the new arrangement) and the people (who may have perceived it as an unfortunate development) fits well historically and may make sense of why the leaders were reluctant to stop Jesus in the moment but would explain "how Jesus could have done something that led to his eventual, but not immediate, arrest."[21]

11:19 *And when even was come, he went out of the city:* Most manuscripts read "they went" instead of "he went" here.[22] Presumably, the reference is to Jesus and his disciples, not to the scribes and chief priests in the previous verse.

11:20 *And in the morning, as they passed by, they saw the fig tree dried up from the roots:* Of course, it would not have been possible for the disciples to see the roots of the tree to determine whether they were withered; the phrasing points to a meaning more symbolic than literal, which

---

20. Evans, *Mark 8:27–16:20*, 180.
21. Craig A. Evans, "Jesus' Action in the Temple: Cleansing or Portent of Destruction?" *Catholic Biblical Quarterly* 51, no. 2 (1989):266.
22. Metzger, *Textual Commentary*, 92.

supports the conclusion that the incident with the fig tree is best understood not as a simple literal action but rather as an enacted parable.

11:21 *And Peter calling to remembrance saith unto him:* Because the phrase "calling to remembrance" is not strictly necessary to the progression of the narrative, it stands out as Mark's hint to the audience. It may suggest that Peter (and, by extension, the other disciples) will not understand certain aspects of Jesus' ministry at first (compare 11:14, with its note that the disciples heard what Jesus had said) but will only come to a fuller understanding later on.

Master, behold, the fig tree which thou cursedst is withered away: Much as with the quickly fulfilled prophecies surrounding the arrangements for the entry into Jerusalem, Jesus' words about the future fruitlessness of the fig tree (11:14) are almost instantly fulfilled. This pattern encourages Mark's audience to trust in Jesus' promises. This is an important aspect of Mark's narrative art since some of Jesus' promises are not fulfilled during the course of the narrative (see especially chapter 13) but await fulfillment after the story ends.

A "curse" is Peter's characterization—not the narrator's and not Jesus'[23]—but Mark's audience knows that Peter does not always fully understand Jesus.

11:22 *And Jesus answering saith unto them, Have faith in God:* The command to have faith is plural, as are the commands in 11:24–25. So while Jesus may be answering Peter, he is addressing the other disciples as well; these teachings are not exclusively for Peter.

11:23 *For verily I say unto you, That whosoever shall say unto this mountain, Be thou removed:* The word "this" implies that Jesus is speaking about a specific mountain; given their location, this would likely be the Mount of Olives or the temple mount. In context, a reference to the temple mount makes more sense since the removal of the temple mount would cause the destruction of the temple (already alluded to via Jesus' temple action in the central story that the withered fig tree surrounds).

One major function of the temple was as a place of prayer, with the concomitant belief that prayer offered from the temple was easily heard[24]—an idea emphasized by Jesus' reference to prayer during his temple action (see 11:17). Thus the ability of prayer to be efficacious when the temple has been destroyed would have been a pressing concern.

---

23. Sharyn Echols Dowd, *Prayer, Power, and the Problem of Suffering: Mark 11:22–25 in the Context of Markan Theology* (Atlanta, Ga.: Scholars Press, 1988), 58.

24. 1 Sam. 1:10–11; 1 Kgs. 8:12–30; 2 Kgs. 19:14–37; Jonah 3:2. See also Dowd, *Problem of Suffering*, 45.

Job 9:5 explains the gulf between God and humans via the fact that God is able to move mountains, something humans cannot do; in that context, Jesus' statement here means that through prayer, humans can become like God and share in God's power. Additional meaning may come from the fact that, in the rabbinic writings, the phrase "he who uproots mountains" referred to someone with such excellent skills that he could solve extremely difficult legal problems.[25] This positions Jesus and his faithful followers as those with the ability to solve difficult problems; this sets the scene for the following stories in Mark's Gospel, which show Jesus successfully responding to the efforts of various leaders to entrap him in his words.

If Jesus' words in 11:14 were a prayer, then Jesus is teaching Peter that he prayed, and his prayer had been answered. Similarly, the disciples can pray and have their prayers answered. In both cases, the content of the prayer is the same: the (symbolic) destruction of the temple (via Jesus' prayer about the fruitlessness of the tree and the disciples' hypothetical prayer about moving mountains). The inability of the average Christian to move a mountain is best explained by 14:36: answers to prayers depend not solely on the will of the person but also on God's will.

Zechariah 14:4 teaches that on the day of the Lord, the Mount of Olives will be split in half. (See also Zech. 4:7, where the temple mount becomes a plain.) It "speaks of an eschatological fissure of this mountain [the Mount of Olives] running from east to west, a term that literally means 'to the sea.'"[26] If that is the background to Mark's text, then what is really being prayed for is not the destruction of a mountain but rather that the Lord will come (see also Isa. 40:4; 49:11). And Jesus assures them that the Lord really will come.

Apparently there was a belief that mountains had roots (see Job 28:9), which makes the link between the mountain and the fig tree even tighter (especially since the roots of the fig tree are specifically mentioned; in fact, it might be precisely to encourage the audience to think about roots that Mark mentioned the fig tree's roots when the disciples cannot see them). This supports the reading that what Jesus did to the fig tree is possible for anyone to do in prayer. It also suggests that moving a mountain would have seemed even harder to them than it does today: not only does the mountain itself need to be moved, but the roots as well!

---

25. Babylonian Talmud, Seder Nezikin IV, Horayoth 14a.

26. Marcus, *Mark 8–16*, 785, although he ultimately rejects this reading.

and be thou cast into the sea: The only other reference to being cast into the sea in Mark's Gospel is the swine possessed by demons (5:1–20). If there is an echo of that story here, it would emphasize the uncleanness of the mountain as a symbol for the uncleanness of the temple.

and shall not doubt in his heart, but shall believe that those things which he saith shall come to pass; he shall have whatsoever he saith: The New Rendition uses plural forms—despite the fact that the Greek text uses singular forms—in order to keep this verse gender neutral since the material before and after this verse is in the plural and since women are presumably being addressed.

Once again, the absolutist language here needs to be balanced against other references to prayer in Mark's Gospel, such as when Jesus prays in Gethsemane. His words there make clear that God is all powerful, and humans must subordinate their desires to God's will. Jesus' prophecies of the coming persecution of his disciples (13:9) suggest that the disciples will not be given what they want.

11:24 ***Therefore I say unto you, What things soever ye desire, when ye pray, believe that ye receive them, and ye shall have them:*** Because the aorist form is used for "receive" ("have received"), Jesus tells them that they should believe that they have already received what they are asking for in prayer.

While Jesus' statement here might be hyperbolic, it is significant because it shows that their prayers can be answered—even without access to the temple. This is an important teaching in light of the theme of temple destruction in this chapter.

11:25 ***And when ye stand praying, forgive, if ye have ought against any:*** Standing as the typical position for prayer is reflected in the language of this verse. Once again, it might seem as if the discussion of forgiveness is misplaced as part of Jesus' response to Peter's reaction to the withered fig tree, but it is not: along with prayer, forgiveness was a primary purpose of the temple (via the sacrificial system). Hence, Jesus is explaining to his disciples how they might find forgiveness in a world without a functioning temple—by forgiving each other.

Additionally, sin (in the form of not forgiving others) makes it difficult for one's prayers to be heard. Since the verbs in this verse are in the plural form, community prayer might be envisioned here; the lesson is that a lack of forgiveness for anyone who is joined in prayer in the community might impede the prayer. At the same time, the teaching is even broader than that: Jesus does not limit the need to forgive to those in the community but extends it to any who stand in need of it. This is an important idea to introduce at the moment in the narrative when the plot against Jesus' life is gaining momentum (compare 11:18).

This reference to forgiveness also functions as a control against reading Jesus' prayer regarding a fig tree as a curse and thinking that one might similarly pray for the destruction of those whom one is unwilling to forgive.[27]

that your Father also which is in heaven may forgive you your trespasses: Jesus teaches that God will forgive them if they forgive others. In other words, they are invited to act as God does in extending forgiveness to others.

It is possible that "which is in heaven" is meant to emphasize that God is not (solely) in the temple, and so prayers will still be efficacious in a world where the temple has been destroyed.

11:26 *But if ye do not forgive, neither will your Father which is in heaven forgive your trespasses:* Because such a variety of early manuscripts omit this verse, it is likely that it was not there originally but was added later in order to harmonize with Matthew 6:15.[28] It is possible that the verse was originally present and was accidentally omitted since 11:25 and 26 both end with the same three words,[29] but this is less likely. This verse is not included in the New Rendition. The presence or absence of 11:26 does not change the thrust of the message because the idea that the Father will not forgive unless one forgives others is presumed in the previous verse.

See also the discussion of the fate of the temple under "Narrative Space: Temple and Leper's House" after 14:9.

Analysis

Given that the fig tree was known as the only tree known to have fruit before it had leaves,[30] and given that the fig tree was a symbol for Israel (Jer. 24:1–10; Amos 8:1–3), this scene suggests that Israel (and, in particular, its religious institutions) gives the appearance of fruitfulness since, for any other kind of tree, the presence of leaves indicates the presence of fruit. But in this case, the leaves are akin to false advertising: they suggest the presence of fruit but do not deliver. In fact, they hide barrenness.

The symbolism of the fig tree would have been well-known to Mark's early audiences since the HB uses the fig tree as a symbol for Israel on many occasions (Isa. 28:3–4; Jer. 8:13; Hosea 9:10, 16; Joel 1:7, 12; Micah

---

27. Dowd, *Prayer, Power, and the Problem of Suffering,* 124.
28. Blumell, "Text Critical Comparison," 87.
29. Ross, "Further Unnoticed Points," 213.
30. France, *Gospel of Mark,* 440.

7:1). In particular, Micah 7:1–2 describes the wickedness of the times in terms of a lack of figs. And in 13:28, a fig tree will be used again as a symbol of judgment, on the temple in particular. When read in this light, Jesus is approaching the fig tree as a symbolic representation of the house of Israel. He is hungry for their righteousness. They have leaves, meaning that they appear to promise fruitfulness. But on further inspection, it becomes obvious that they are actually barren. The figless tree is thus a symbol for the failures of the house of Israel.

His pronouncement on the tree is likely less a curse than a prophetic announcement of the fruitlessness of Israel. The note that it was not the season for figs in a sense absolves the leadership: figs were simply not something that they could have been expected to provide at this time. There might be a wisp of Atonement theology here, as the fruitfulness that Jesus desires to see is something that no human can be expected to provide.

Jesus' experience with the fig tree is intimately linked to its larger setting in Mark. The scene points backwards to the entry into Jerusalem: "The 'leaves' on the fig tree correspond to the acclamations of the crowd, and the lack of fruit corresponds to the missing welcome by the leaders."[31] But it also points forward: in the beginning of the next chapter, Jesus will tell a parable about a vineyard, where the religious leadership is represented by those who should have been tending the vineyard but who were negligent. The parable will bring the image to fruition with the idea that those who should have been tending the vineyard will kill the one who came to set things aright. Most significantly, the story of the fig tree surrounds Jesus' actions in the temple, and both stories interpret each other.

One important lesson for the disciples (and for Mark's audience) from the fig tree is that not all of Jesus' actions are meant to be understood on a strictly literal level (compare 8:14–21).

Jesus' action in the temple is traditionally interpreted as a cleansing of the temple, that is, the removing of impure elements so that the temple might return to its proper function. This interpretation meshes well with Malachi 3:1–5, which envisions the Lord coming suddenly to the temple to purify it so that offerings can be offered properly. The Lord comes in judgment against those who oppress the poor. However, this interpretation does not otherwise fit well into Mark's context and relies overmuch on John's account of Jesus' temple action (John 2:12–22). In Mark's context, the temple action is literally surrounded by the story of the withered fig

---

31. Collins, *Mark*, 526.

tree and "a tree withered from the roots up makes for a poor illustration of a purified temple."[32] It is sometimes suggested that Jesus objected to the moneychangers and merchants taking advantage of the pilgrims through unfair rates of exchange. However, this reading seems unlikely since Jesus casts out the buyers as well when they would have been the victims of unfair trade.[33] Perhaps the most that can be said for the "cleansing" interpretation is that Jesus anticipates that the temple will be destroyed if it does not remain cleansed.[34]

While moneychangers and animal sellers were necessary in order for pilgrims to worship in the temple, their presence in the temple courts—as opposed to in other areas of the city—appears to have been a very recent innovation during Jesus' lifetime,[35] with a portion of the money collected going to the temple authorities. Jesus may be objecting to their presence within the temple itself, particularly if they made it difficult for Gentiles to pray in the temple. Also, since the Tyrian coins used to pay the temple tax "bore the head of the town god Melqart (identified with Heracles) on the front,"[36] another objection would be that permitting the merchants and moneychangers within the temple effectively permitted idolatry within the temple itself. This reading links to Isaiah 56:11, where the leaders are criticized for profiting from their roles. It also fits well in Mark's context: this scene begins Jesus' interactions with the temple, which end with his directing attention to the widow who supports the temple (when the temple is supposed to be supporting her). There may also be a link to Jesus' quotation of Jeremiah 7 here since Jeremiah 7:5–6 condemns the people for not taking care of widows.

Jesus' actions in the temple are an enacted parable, a prophetic preenactment of the coming destruction of the temple (compare 13:2). In this reading, the temple is not cleansed—it is too late for that. Rather, Jesus looked around the temple on his first visit, noticed its corruption, and has returned to announce—for those with ears to hear, those who observe the symbolic meaning of his action—that the temple will be destroyed because it is not fulfilling its purpose, particularly by not welcoming him after his procession into the city. This temple action is framed by the story of the

---

32. Kirk, "Time for Figs," 520.
33. Malbon, *Hearing Mark*, 79.
34. David Seeley, "Jesus' Temple Act," *Catholic Biblical Quarterly* 55, no. 2 (1993): 279.
35. Evans, "Jesus' Action in the Temple," 267.
36. Collins, *Mark*, 528.

withered fig tree, which is also an enacted parable of the coming destruction of Israel; both the fig tree and the temple action have not only the same message but also the same medium (an enacted parable) for conveying that message. Further, the similarities between 11:21 and 13:1 (both feature the disciples' surprised reactions) hint at other similarities between the stories, which reinforce the idea that Jesus' action in the temple parallels his teachings about its coming destruction in chapter 13. Additionally, at his trial, Jesus will be accused of promising to destroy and rebuild the temple (see 14:58); while Mark dismisses the accuracy of the testimony, the grain of truth behind it is that people had (correctly) interpreted Jesus' action here in the temple as a promise that the temple would be destroyed. In this reading, the coming destruction of the temple might have reference to:

1. Jesus' atoning act, which would negate the need for the sacrificial system of the temple.

2. The rending of the temple veil at Jesus' death, which symbolically ended the temple's role in dividing the sacred from the common.

3. The destruction of the temple in 70 CE by the Romans. It is believed that Mark's Gospel was written around this time (see appendix A: "Authorship and Date"); if this is the case, then Mark's audience would have interpreted Jesus' temple action not as a random historical event but rather as a prophesied part of God's plan, as articulated by Jesus. The HB records the idea of using foreign nations to accomplish God's will in the chastisement of Israel (Deut. 28:25–37), so the concept that Rome, as the destroyer of the temple, could be God's agent in fulfilling the very thing that Jesus had prophesied is not unlikely.

The temple tax paid for the daily sacrifice, which was offered for the remission of the sins for all of the people.[37] By (at least symbolically) making it impossible for that to happen, Jesus is in effect ending the sacrificial system and implicitly indicating that something will replace it. Thus his actions subtly hint at Atonement theology.

It is likely that Jesus' action in the temple was primarily symbolic since the temple was a huge complex—about 450 meters by 300 meters—so "most people . . . that day would not have even noticed him."[38] (Nothing indicates that his disciples or any others joined in the action, which means that Jesus would have disrupted just a few people.)

---

37. Barry D. Smith, "Objections to the Authenticity of Mark 11:17 Reconsidered," *Westminster Theological Journal* 54, no. 2 (1992): 262.

38. Evans, *Mark 8:27–16:20*, 167.

Part of prevailing messianic expectations during Jesus' time was that the Messiah would cleanse the temple by purging it of foreign influences. For Jesus to approach the temple and act in a way to encourage foreign influences—by clearing (part of) the court of the Gentiles so that the temple could be a house of prayer for all people—would have been a reversal of expectations and therefore ironic. Mark hints in 11:18 that it is the temple action that ultimately (although not immediately) leads to Jesus' arrest. This means that the temple action is extremely important as the proximate cause of Jesus' death.

The response of the leaders is fear; this is an important component of Mark's portrayal of Jesus because it indicates his power: "He will be crucified, then, not because of any weakness in him. Quite the oppositely, because of his power!"[39]

The people are described as being "astonished at his doctrine." In other words, in Mark's narrative the temple action was regarded as "doctrine," and it was astonishing to the people. This supports reading the temple action as an enacted parable since the people realize that there is doctrinal teaching embedded within it. Further, that the people find it astonishing supports reading it as an enacted prophecy and not as a cleansing: many people in Jesus' time might have thought that the temple was in need of cleansing so it is difficult to see how that would have been regarded as astonishing. More astonishing was the idea that this enormous temple could be destroyed.

By returning to the story of the fig tree after the temple action, Mark creates a sandwich that suggests that the story of the fig tree and the story of Jesus' actions in the temple should be used to interpret each other. Because the barren, fruitless tree is an HB symbol of destruction and judgment for evil (see Hosea 9:16), it suggests that the temple action should also be viewed as an enacted prophecy of destruction, not of cleansing. Further, Jesus quoted from Jeremiah 7:11 during the temple action; Jeremiah 8:13 refers to barren fig trees and thus links these passages together, especially since the Jeremiah text shows the Lord wanting to gather figs when there are none to be found.

Readers have puzzled over the relationship between Jesus' reaction and Peter's statement—how is it that faith and prayer relate to the withered fig tree? The association between the withered fig tree and the promised destruction of the temple (which is implicit in Jesus' action at the temple)

---

39. Gundry, *Mark,* 641.

makes sense of Jesus' statement: in the ancient world, gods are linked to temples, which meant that the destruction of the temple came perilously close to suggesting the destruction of God. With this response, Jesus severs the link between the temple and God by showing how it is possible for them to have faith in God even without a temple.[40]

More generally, the intertwined destruction of the temple and fig tree suggests that the special role of the temple in mediating prayer and forgiveness will no longer exist and that it will belong to the prayer and actions of the individual. Mark paints a portrait of Jesus' mercy as he prepares his disciples for a world where the temple has been destroyed.

JESUS QUESTIONED ABOUT HIS AUTHORITY (11:27–12:12)

Greek Text

27 Καὶ ἔρχονται πάλιν εἰς Ἱεροσόλυμα. καὶ ἐν τῷ ἱερῷ περιπατοῦντος αὐτοῦ ἔρχονται πρὸς αὐτὸν οἱ ἀρχιερεῖς καὶ οἱ γραμματεῖς καὶ οἱ πρεσβύτεροι 28 καὶ ἔλεγον αὐτῷ· Ἐν ποίᾳ ἐξουσίᾳ ταῦτα ποιεῖς; ἢ τίς σοι ἔδωκεν τὴν ἐξουσίαν ταύτην ἵνα ταῦτα ποιῇς; 29 ὁ δὲ Ἰησοῦς εἶπεν αὐτοῖς· Ἐπερωτήσω ὑμᾶς ἕνα λόγον, καὶ ἀποκρίθητέ μοι, καὶ ἐρῶ ὑμῖν ἐν ποίᾳ ἐξουσίᾳ ταῦτα ποιῶ· 30 τὸ βάπτισμα τὸ Ἰωάννου ἐξ οὐρανοῦ ἦν ἢ ἐξ ἀνθρώπων; ἀποκρίθητέ μοι. 31 καὶ διελογίζοντο πρὸς ἑαυτοὺς λέγοντες· Τί εἴπωμεν; ἐὰν εἴπωμεν· Ἐξ οὐρανοῦ, ἐρεῖ· Διὰ τί οὖν οὐκ ἐπιστεύσατε αὐτῷ; 32 ἀλλὰ εἴπωμεν· Ἐξ ἀνθρώπων;— ἐφοβοῦντο τὸν ὄχλον, ἅπαντες γὰρ εἶχον τὸν Ἰωάννην ὄντως ὅτι προφήτης ἦν. 33 καὶ ἀποκριθέντες τῷ Ἰησοῦ λέγουσιν· Οὐκ οἴδαμεν. καὶ ὁ Ἰησοῦς λέγει αὐτοῖς· Οὐδὲ ἐγὼ λέγω ὑμῖν ἐν ποίᾳ ἐξουσίᾳ ταῦτα ποιῶ.

12:1 Καὶ ἤρξατο αὐτοῖς ἐν παραβολαῖς λαλεῖν· Ἀμπελῶνα ἄνθρωπος ἐφύτευσεν, καὶ περιέθηκεν φραγμὸν καὶ ὤρυξεν ὑπολήνιον καὶ ᾠκοδόμησεν πύργον, καὶ ἐξέδετο αὐτὸν γεωργοῖς, καὶ ἀπεδήμησεν. 2 καὶ ἀπέστειλεν πρὸς τοὺς γεωργοὺς τῷ καιρῷ δοῦλον, ἵνα παρὰ τῶν γεωργῶν λάβῃ ἀπὸ τῶν καρπῶν τοῦ ἀμπελῶνος· 3 καὶ λαβόντες αὐτὸν ἔδειραν καὶ ἀπέστειλαν κενόν. 4 καὶ πάλιν ἀπέστειλεν πρὸς αὐτοὺς ἄλλον δοῦλον· κἀκεῖνον ἐκεφαλίωσαν καὶ ἠτίμασαν. 5 καὶ ἄλλον ἀπέστειλεν· κἀκεῖνον ἀπέκτειναν, καὶ πολλοὺς ἄλλους, οὓς μὲν δέροντες οὓς δὲ ἀποκτέννοντες. 6 ἔτι ἕνα εἶχεν, υἱὸν ἀγαπητόν· ἀπέστειλεν αὐτὸν ἔσχατον πρὸς αὐτοὺς λέγων ὅτι Ἐντραπήσονται τὸν υἱόν μου. 7 ἐκεῖνοι δὲ οἱ γεωργοὶ πρὸς ἑαυτοὺς εἶπαν ὅτι Οὗτός ἐστιν ὁ κληρονόμος· δεῦτε ἀποκτείνωμεν αὐτόν, καὶ ἡμῶν

---

40. Myers, *Binding the Strong Man*, 304–5.

ἔσται ἡ κληρονομία. 8 καὶ λαβόντες ἀπέκτειναν αὐτόν, καὶ ἐξέβαλον αὐτὸν ἔξω τοῦ ἀμπελῶνος. 9 τί ποιήσει ὁ κύριος τοῦ ἀμπελῶνος; ἐλεύσεται καὶ ἀπολέσει τοὺς γεωργούς, καὶ δώσει τὸν ἀμπελῶνα ἄλλοις. 10 οὐδὲ τὴν γραφὴν ταύτην ἀνέγνωτε· Λίθον ὃν ἀπεδοκίμασαν οἱ οἰκοδομοῦντες, οὗτος ἐγενήθη εἰς κεφαλὴν γωνίας· 11 παρὰ κυρίου ἐγένετο αὕτη, καὶ ἔστιν θαυμαστὴ ἐν ὀφθαλμοῖς ἡμῶν;

12 Καὶ ἐζήτουν αὐτὸν κρατῆσαι, καὶ ἐφοβήθησαν τὸν ὄχλον, ἔγνωσαν γὰρ ὅτι πρὸς αὐτοὺς τὴν παραβολὴν εἶπεν. καὶ ἀφέντες αὐτὸν ἀπῆλθον. [SBLGNT]

King James Version	New Rendition
27 And they come again to Jerusalem: and as he was walking in the temple, there come to him the chief priests, and the scribes, and the elders, 28 And say unto him, By what authority doest thou these things? and who gave thee this authority to do these things? 29 And Jesus answered and said unto them, I will also ask of you one question, and answer me, and I will tell you by what authority I do these things. 30 The baptism of John, was it from heaven, or of men? answer me. 31 And they reasoned with themselves, saying, If we shall say, From heaven; he will say, Why then did ye not believe him? 32 But if we shall say, Of men; they feared the people: for all men counted John, that he was a prophet indeed. 33 And they answered and said unto Jesus, We cannot tell. And Jesus answering saith unto them, Neither do I tell you by what authority I do these things.	27 And they come again to Jerusalem. And as he is walking in the temple, the chief priests and the scriptorians and the elders come to him. 28 And they were saying to him, "By what authority are you doing these things? Or, who gave you this authority, that you should do these things?" 29 But Jesus was saying to them, "I will ask you one thing, and if you answer me, then I will tell you by what authority I do these things. 30 The baptism of John: was it from heaven, or from humans? Answer me." 31 And they were reasoning with each other, saying, "If we say from heaven, he will say, 'Then why did you not trust him?' 32 But if we should say from humans . . ."—they feared the crowd, for all held that John indeed was a prophet. 33 And answering Jesus, they say, "We do not know." And Jesus says to them, "Neither will I tell you by what authority I do these things."
12:1 And he began to speak unto them by parables. A certain man planted a vineyard, and set an hedge about it, and digged a place for the winefat, and built a tower, and let it out to husbandmen, and went into a far country. 2 And at the season he sent to the husbandmen a servant, that he might receive from the husbandmen of the fruit of the vineyard. 3 And they caught him, and beat	12:1 And he began to say to them in parables, "A man planted a vineyard and placed around it a wall and dug a pit for the winepress and built a watchtower and rented it to tenant farmers and went on a journey. 2 And he sent a slave to the tenant farmers at the right time, so that he might receive the fruits of the vineyard from the tenant farmers. 3 But seizing him, they beat him

him, and sent him away empty. 4 And again he sent unto them another servant; and at him they cast stones, and wounded him in the head, and sent him away shamefully handled. 5 And again he sent another; and him they killed, and many others; beating some, and killing some. 6 Having yet therefore one son, his wellbeloved, he sent him also last unto them, saying, They will reverence my son. 7 But those husbandmen said among themselves, This is the heir; come, let us kill him, and the inheritance shall be ours. 8 And they took him, and killed him, and cast him out of the vineyard. 9 What shall therefore the lord of the vineyard do? he will come and destroy the husbandmen, and will give the vineyard unto others. 10 And have ye not read this scripture; The stone which the builders rejected is become the head of the corner: 11 This was the Lord's doing, and it is marvellous in our eyes? 12 And they sought to lay hold on him, but feared the people: for they knew that he had spoken the parable against them: and they left him, and went their way.

and sent him away with nothing. 4 And again he sent another slave to them; this one they beat on the head and treated shamefully. 5 And he sent another, and this one they killed. And many others, beating some and killing others. 6 Yet having one beloved son, he sent him to them last, saying, 'They will have respect for my son.' 7 But those tenant farmers said to one another, 'This is the heir. Come, let's kill him, and the inheritance will be ours.' 8 And seizing him, they killed him and cast him out of the vineyard. 9 So what will the owner of the vineyard do? He will come and will destroy the tenants and will give the vineyard to others. 10 Have you not even read this scripture:

'The stone the builders rejected
has become the cornerstone.
11 This was from the Lord,
and it is wonderful in our eyes'?"

12 And they wanted to arrest him—but they feared the crowd—for they knew that he had spoken the parable against them. And having left him, they went away.

Notes

11:27 *And they come again to Jerusalem: and as he was walking in the temple:* Mark's use of "again" takes the audience back to 11:15 and reminds them of Jesus' previous actions in the temple, including the note that the religious authorities wanted to kill him. Jesus has every reason to believe that he could be arrested and killed after his previous activity in the temple and the leaders' response to it, so he shows great courage and commitment to his mission by returning.

   there come to him the chief priests, and the scribes, and the elders: While these three groups compromised the Sanhedrin, this does not appear to be a formal meeting.

   In 8:31, Jesus prophesied that these three groups would be involved in his death, so there is an ominous note to Mark's text.

11:28 *And say unto him, By what authority doest thou these things?:* "These things" may refer generally to Jesus' ministry, but more likely it refers to Jesus' action of removing the moneychangers and merchants from the temple. Jesus' entry into Jerusalem, with its messianic overtones, may also be in view here. The chief priests had responsibility for what happened in the temple, so implicit in this question is the idea that Jesus has usurped their authority by setting his own standard for what is permissible there.[41] While it is not likely that these religious authorities were aware of Jesus' recent teachings about prayer and forgiveness (unless the audience is to imagine that one of Jesus' disciples told them about it), in the context of Mark's narrative it may also be the case that they object to Jesus' idea that prayer and forgiveness can happen without the mediation of the temple—which would profoundly undercut the power and control of these leaders. This is particularly likely given the reference that Jesus will soon make to John the Baptist since John also promised forgiveness independent of the temple (1:4).

and who gave thee this authority to do these things?: The repetition of their question in slightly different terms emphasizes that the real issue is Jesus' authority. This is a major theme in this chapter (and in the entire Gospel of Mark).

Narratively, the repeated question serves as an invitation to Mark's audience to think about the question for themselves. By this point, Mark has given them the tools to reach the correct answer. Ironically, their line of inquiry makes clear that (1) Jesus does have authority and that (2) the religious leadership did not give it to him. Hence, an obvious conclusion is that it came from God. This is the conclusion that Mark's audience has been led to.

According to the law of Moses, those who acted in God's name without proper authority were to be executed (Deut. 13:1–5), so the subtext of these questions is a threat of death.

11:29 *And Jesus answered and said unto them, I will also ask of you one question, and answer me:* The word "one" may be significant here: they had asked two questions—neither of which flummoxed Jesus—but he is able to demonstrate their lack of authority with just one question.

and I will tell you by what authority I do these things: Mark's penchant for irony shines through in this passage. Jesus sets the terms of the exchange by stating that he will answer their questions only under certain conditions. This means that he has more authority than the religious

---

41. Hans Dieter Betz, "Jesus and the Purity of the Temple (Mark 11:15–18): A Comparative Religion Approach," *Journal of Biblical Literature* 116, no. 3 (1997): 459.

leaders. (The religious leaders will further undercut their own authority in 11:33.) So Jesus demonstrates his superior authority in this passage, and the leaders accept it when they accept his terms for the conversation.

11:30 *The baptism of John, was it from heaven, or of men? answer me:* "Heaven" is a common euphemism used in place of "God" in Jewish texts, and that is probably its use here. There are two ways to understand the rhetorical move that Jesus is making with his question here:

1. The leaders have approached Jesus with questions about his authority. But their unwillingness to answer Jesus' question about John's authority will show that they are not ultimately concerned with whether authority is derived from God but rather with whether they can maintain their own authority in the face of the will of the crowd.

2. If the leaders acknowledged John's authority, then they would have the answer to their questions about Jesus' authority, since Jesus' authority (symbolized by the voice from heaven at his baptism and the descent of the dove) is directly related to John's authority to baptize him.

The positioning of "from heaven" and "from man" in opposition is consistent with several other passages including 7:20–23; 8:33; and 10:5–6. The mention of John—who was killed for his preaching—adds another ominous note to the story. The phrase "Answer me" "borders on disrespect,"[42] which is significant in terms of the authority dynamic in the narrative.

11:31 *And they reasoned with themselves, saying, If we shall say, From heaven:* This might be understood either as their internal thought processes or as a group discussion between them before answering Jesus.

he will say, Why then did ye not believe him?: Their focus is on how the debate will proceed, not on what is true.

11:32 *But if we shall say, Of men; they feared the people: for all men counted John, that he was a prophet indeed:* Mark's audience likely would have picked up on the close similarity between the sentiment here and that in 11:18, where the desired actions of the religious leadership are shaped by their fear of the people, especially in contrast to Jesus, who has reentered the temple despite the very real possibility (which he does not fear) that he might be arrested.

Their line of thought is cut off in the middle and replaced with Mark's conclusion. This creates a dramatic moment as their unstated supposition is allowed to linger. The audience, of course, fills in the blank themselves with the cowardly conclusion.

---

42. Evans, *Mark 8:27–16:20*, 205.

11:33 *And they answered and said unto Jesus, We cannot tell:* They refuse to answer after considering the implications (not the facts) of their possible answers. Their refusal undermines their own claims to authority if they are unwilling to exercise that authority to determine whether John is a legitimate prophet.

And Jesus answering saith unto them, Neither do I tell you by what authority I do these things: The irony is that Jesus' actions in this story (namely, setting the conditions under which he would answer their question) revealed his authority. So he does not explain his authority on the discourse level but does so on the narrative level.

12:1 *And he began to speak unto them by parables:* The chapter division obscures that Jesus is still in the temple and still speaking to the chief priests, scribes, and elders who asked him about his authority (11:27–28). In fact, this parable continues the conversation regarding Jesus' authority.

The word translated as "parables" is plural here, although Jesus will only deliver one parable. It may be that Jesus told several parables but Mark chose to only include one, or "by parables" may refer generically to Jesus' mode of teaching.

A certain man planted a vineyard: Frequently in the HB, the vineyard (or vine) is a symbol for Israel (Ps. 80:8–13; Isa. 1:8; 3:14; 27:2–6; Jer. 2:21; 12:10; Ezek. 19:10; Hosea 10:1; Micah 7:1).

and set an hedge about it, and digged a place for the winefat, and built a tower: The "hedge" is a fence, necessary to protect a very valuable crop. The "place for the winefat" is a trough dug underneath the wine press to collect the wine. The tower provided security and perhaps also sleeping quarters and storage for tools. As this verse suggests, an enormous financial outlay was required in order to establish a vineyard—which would not produce a crop for three to five years—so the man in the parable must have been quite wealthy. He offers everything that his tenants would need to be successful, in advance and at his own expense.

There are two explanations for mentioning the hedge, winefat, and tower:

1. The parable follows Isaiah 5:1–7 closely, as that text also mentions the hedge, winefat, and tower. It is likely that these elements are included in order to suggest the connection to Isaiah and not because they have any allegorical value.

2. Some Jewish writings took the tower and winepress mentioned in Isaiah 5:1–2 as symbols for the temple and the altar,[43] so it is possible that that meaning is intended here. Read in this vein, the fence might symbolize the law and the tower would be the location for the watchmen (prophets).

---

43. Tosefta Sukkot 3:15.

and let it out to husbandmen: "Husbandmen" are tenant farmers: they would farm the land (or, more likely, hire laborers to do it for them) and then provide a share of the crop (or money from its sale) to the owner. The tenants were normally paid wages during the first four or five years when there was not yet a crop; once the vineyard was productive, they would keep one third of the crop.[44] There is some evidence of wealthy tenant farmers although most were poor.

There are two schools of thought regarding the identity of the tenants in the parable:

1. Scholars generally agree that the tenant farmers represent the religious leadership of Jesus' day. The parable suggests that the tenants enter into something akin to a covenant with the vineyard owner: in exchange for the vineyard owner providing them with everything needed to produce a productive crop, they promise to give the owner a portion of the crop. Thus, the religious leaders at one point had had legitimate authority, but the parable suggests that they did not uphold their end of the agreement.

2. A minority position suggests that the tenants represent the Romans and their willing helpers who occupied Israel.[45] Reading the tenants as Romans fits well with the fact that the tenants' sole interest in the vineyard is financial gain. If the tenants are Romans, then the destruction at the end of the parable (12:9) refers to the end of Roman rule in Israel.

and went into a far country: In Jesus' day, there were many absentee landlords. Partly due to foreign oppression, small landholders lost their land (often as a result of unpaid taxes), and landowning was thus consolidated in the hands of the wealthy. Particularly with vineyards—which required a large up-front investment and were not productive for half a decade—owners tended to be wealthy outsiders. These owners were generally disliked; it is therefore somewhat odd that Jesus' parable places God into this role. However, Jesus is telling this parable not to the peasant farmers of Galilee but to the elite in Jerusalem—and placing that elite into the role of the tenant farmers. The audience is reminded that while they might enjoy the privileges of the elite in relation to displaced tenant farmers, they themselves are in the role of humble tenants in relation to God.

12:2 *And at the season he sent to the husbandmen a servant:* The Greek word translated as "season" is *kairos,* which implies an appointed time (it is used in 13:33 to refer to the time of the coming of the Son of Man). It indicates the time of harvest in this parable.

---

44. Ernest Van Eck, "The Tenants in the Vineyard (GThom 65/Mark 12:1–12): A Realistic and Social-Scientific Reading," *Hervormde Teologiese Studies* 63, no. 3 (2007): 914, 925.

45. Sabin, *Reopening the Word,* 87.

Referring to the prophets as servants is common in the HB (Josh. 14:7; 2 Sam. 3:18; Ps. 105:26; Amos 3:7).

It is possible that there was little or no contact between the owner and the tenant farmers during the years before the vineyard became productive. Read symbolically, the point is that the owner did not forget about his tenants despite the years when he had no direct involvement with them.

that he might receive from the husbandmen of the fruit of the vineyard: This fruit (or, technically, the money from the sale of the fruit) was what the tenants owed the owner for use of the vineyard and its fence, wine trough, and tower.

12:3 ***And they caught him, and beat him, and sent him away empty:*** The tenants owed the owner, but not only did they not pay, they wounded the servant who came to collect. Ancient sources describe tenants behaving precisely in this way: once the tenants had enjoyed the use of the land and its improvements, the temptation to keep the harvest for themselves was great. "In not only refusing the rent but also assaulting and insulting the collectors the tenants are in the plainest terms repudiating the owner's claim to the vineyard and challenging him to enforce payment if he can."[46]

12:4 ***And again he sent unto them another servant; and at him they cast stones, and wounded him in the head, and sent him away shamefully handled:*** The phrase "and at him they cast stones" is missing from the best ancient manuscripts.[47] The translation of "wounded him in the head" is uncertain. It is remotely possible that the reference to wounding the head could refer to decapitation and thus the fate of John the Baptist.

12:5 ***And again he sent another; and him they killed, and many others; beating some, and killing some:*** The HB contains many references to prophets who were killed (1 Kgs. 18:13; 19:10; Neh. 9:25–26; Jer. 26:23). To continue to send servants is extravagant, illogical behavior on the part of the vineyard owner, but that is precisely the point: the owner was merciful and patient and willing to risk his slaves (KJV: "servants") beyond what anyone would reasonably expect in order to give the tenants a chance to fulfill their obligations.

12:6 ***Having yet therefore one son, his wellbeloved:*** The same Greek word for "wellbeloved" is used to describe Jesus by the voice from heaven at his baptism (1:11) and at the Transfiguration (9:7). Because these are the only three uses of this term in Mark, it would be clear to the audience that the vineyard owner represents God, and the son represents Jesus in this

---

46. France, *Gospel of Mark*, 459.
47. Bratcher and Nida, *Translator's Handbook*, 365.

parable. And because the owner was originally called "a man," the well-beloved is therefore "the Son of Man."[48]

he sent him also last unto them, saying, They will reverence my son: It seems that the owner thought that, due to his son's higher status, the tenants would have more respect for him than they did for the slaves. (Ironically, Jesus' socioeconomic status in mortality was rather low.) Read symbolically, it seems that God was wrong about the response to Jesus' ministry. There are two options for interpretation here:

1. Not every facet of a parable can (or should) correspond with reality. Thus, the error in judgment here is not a commentary on God's (lack of) judgment.

2. Taking a longer view, the tenants will eventually respect the son—when the tenants are destroyed and the vineyard given to others (see 12:9) and the son becomes the cornerstone. Because the son eventually triumphs, the audience is required to confront their initial assumption that the owner erred when the son was killed; one can easily imagine the same dynamic playing out in early Christianity.

12:7 ***But those husbandmen said among themselves, This is the heir; come, let us kill him, and the inheritance shall be ours:*** Immediately after hearing the word "come," the audience would likely assume that the tenants are going to fulfill their obligations because they have recognized the status of the heir. So the words "let us kill him" come as a shock. "Their recognition of the son, then, turns out to be analogous to that of the demons, who realize that Jesus is God's son, but for that very reason oppose him . . . and thereby seal their own destruction."[49]

There are two ways to think about the tenant farmers' thought process here:

1. Their thoughts are simply illogical. It makes no sense to think that they would inherit the land by killing the son, as they had no actual claim to it. The irrational thought process is read parabolically as reflecting the irrationally of rejecting Jesus.

2. Because they use the terms "heir" and "inheritance," they probably believe that the father is dead, ill, or preoccupied. At the very least, eliminating the son buys them some more time living on the land. If they kill the son, there might not be another claimant, and they may, by adverse possession (acquiring possession of another's land by occupying it, a principle that was probably

---

48. Johannes C. de Moor, "The Targumic Background of Mark 12:1–12: The Parable of the Wicked Tenants," *Journal for the Study of Judaism in the Persian, Hellenistic, and Roman Periods* 29, no. 1 (1998): 66–67.

49. Marcus, *Mark 8–16*, 313.

operative in Jesus' time), end up with claim to the vineyard. What is interesting about this view, especially when read parabolically, is how it

a. Constitutes a breach of covenant on the part of the tenants: they had agreed to provide a share of the crop in exchange for use of the land and the improvements on it, but now they refuse to do so.

b. Constitutes an acknowledgment of the legitimate authority of the son. Ironically, their actions only make sense if they acknowledge the right of the son—otherwise, there would be no purpose in killing him. Further, the language used very specifically identifies the son as the owner's heir. So it is very clear that the parable is suggesting that the religious leaders recognize Jesus' legitimate authority from God.

The sentiment of the tenants mirrors Isaiah 55:8's "my thoughts are not your thoughts"; the owner believes that the tenants will honor the son, but the tenants scheme to kill him.

Relationship to Genesis 37. In Genesis 37:20, when Joseph's brothers plan to kill him, the same three words (Greek: *deute apokteinōmen auton*) are used in the LXX to articulate their plan as are used in this parable (KJV: "come, let us kill him"). If the allusion is intentional, then Jesus (or Mark) positions Jesus as akin to Joseph in Egypt, perhaps hinting that he would be in a unique position to save his people but only after undergoing a great deal of suffering. The parallel would emphasize the idea that the religious leaders of Jesus' day are akin to Joseph's scheming brothers.

Relationship to 1 Kings 21. In this passage, King Ahab wants Naboth's vineyard, but Naboth refuses to sell or trade it. Ahab's wife Jezebel arranges to have two men falsely accuse Naboth of blaspheming God and the king, resulting in his stoning. The same word for "inheritance" is used in the LXX. His plan to acquire the vineyard is most clearly not a legal one, which suggests that in Jesus' parable, the tenants are not hoping to claim the vineyard under a law of adverse possession but rather under a clearly illegal scheme.[50] When Ahab hears that Naboth is dead, he goes to possess the vineyard. In 1 Kings 21, the response of God is the same as what Jesus says will be the vineyard owner's: the destruction of the tenants (1 Kgs. 21:19, 21). It is possible that Jesus modeled his parable on this story.

---

50. Klyne Snodgrass, "Recent Research on the Parable of the Wicked Tenants: An Assessment," *Bulletin for Biblical Research* 8 (1998): 196.

12:8 *And they took him, and killed him, and cast him out of the vineyard:* Casting the corpse out of the vineyard is an additional insult since it denies a proper burial. It is parallel to Jesus' own death, which was also perceived as shameful.

12:9 *What shall therefore the lord of the vineyard do?:* Notice the shift: Jesus introduced the owner as simply "a man" but here calls him "the lord of the vineyard." The word "lord" (Greek: *kyrios*) can be translated as master, lord, or Lord, but to Mark's audience, it was, by that time, used as a title for Jesus. There is a sense in which the parable is falling away and the true identity of the owner is revealed—but only at the point when it is too late for the tenants to choose wisely.

he will come and destroy the husbandmen, and will give the vineyard unto others: This line, the climax of the story, would have been surprising to the audience. First, the idea of destroying the tenants himself and not making an appeal to the courts would probably have been historically unusual[51] and therefore have stood out to the audience. Second, the actions depicted here depart from the pattern of the parallel text in Isaiah (Isa. 5:1–7), where the vineyard is destroyed. One conclusion that might be drawn is that the people in general will not be punished for the death of Jesus—just the leaders. "Destroy" translates the same word used to describe what the religious leaders want to do to Jesus (3:6; 11:18) and thus probably implies that he will kill the tenants. It may also point to the destruction of Jerusalem, although perhaps that is pushing the parable too far.

The identity of the "others" is not specified here; it is most likely the Gentiles, but it can also be read as other (but still Jewish) leaders. Perhaps it refers to the Sanhedrin, who would lose their role when the temple was destroyed. The others might also be "the disenfranchised lower classes to whom and for whom Jesus has directed his ministry."[52]

There are two ways to interpret the role of the "others" to whom the vineyard is given:

1. The language suggests that the others are actually the new owners of the vineyard. If this is the case, the shift from tenants to owners carries significant implications. First, it would reflect a new arrangement, parabolically akin to a new covenant. Second, the new owners are in a sense elevated to the status that only God had previously enjoyed.

51. John S. Kloppenborg, "Self-Help or *Deus ex Machina* in Mark 12.9?" *New Testament Studies* 50, no. 4 (2004): 516.

52. Waetjen, *Reordering of Power*, 188.

2. The vineyard is given to new tenants—a reading that the Greek does permit. This reading subtly lays the foundation for the idea of an apostasy since one would presume that if the new tenants refuse to provide fruit to the owner by keeping the terms of the agreement, then they, too, would be removed.

Relationship to Genesis 22. In LXX Genesis 22:2, the same Greek word for "wellbeloved" is used to describe Isaac in the story of his near-sacrifice. If Mark's audience caught an allusion to that text, they may have assumed that the owner's intent was to sacrifice his son—but then the reference to the owner's thought that the tenants would reverence his son destroys that expectation. And just as the planned sacrifice of Isaac seemed as if it would have negated the promises that God made to Abraham, the death of the son in this parable seems as if it would be the end of the owner and his son's claim on the vineyard, but the parallel shows that neither was actually the case. The sacrifice of the son of the vineyard seems like it will end the inheritance but actually ensures it. The reference to Psalm 118 (see Notes on 12:10, 11) extends this paradoxical theme.

Relationship to Isaiah 5. Multiple shared themes link this parable to the parable in Isaiah 5 (see especially 12:1 and Isa. 5:2). Significantly, both the parable in Isaiah and the parable in Mark pose questions to the audience regarding what the owner will do in response to the failure to produce fruit. But there are some differences:

1. There is no figure analogous to the son of the owner in Isaiah 5. And yet the same Greek word translated as "beloved" makes an appearance in both stories, since in chapter 12 the son is described as "beloved" while in Isaiah 5 the parable is introduced by the narrator saying that he will "sing to my well-beloved a song of my beloved touching his vineyard." So while the beloved is the audience for the parable in Isaiah 5, the beloved has become a character in the parable in chapter 12.

2. In Isaiah, the vineyard is not productive; the grapes it produces are sour. In Mark, the vineyard has produced good fruit, but the tenants refuse to relinquish what they owe to the owner of the vineyard. The flaw is not with the fruit but rather with the tenants. The goodness of the fruit in Mark is an important hedge against anti-Semitic readings of the scripture.

12:10 *And have ye not read this scripture; The stone which the builders rejected is become the head of the corner:* It is possible to translate "head of the corner" as either "cornerstone" or "keystone." But because the word "head" is used, it is more likely to refer to the keystone (or perhaps the stone on the top of a column), since a cornerstone would probably not have been thought of as a "head" stone. The irregular shape of a keystone means that it would not have made a very good cornerstone, which is why they rejected it in the first place, but the shape makes it ideal for its intended purpose.

Here, Jesus quotes Psalm 118:22. There is a bit of sarcasm in the question "have ye not read," since of course they had read it; the question assumes an affirmative answer. Jesus is criticizing their ability to truly understand the scriptures.

The larger context of chapters 11–13 concerns the end of the temple in Jerusalem; perhaps this metaphor positions Jesus as the cornerstone of the new temple. In other words, it is his body—through his Atonement—which is the new temple, the new site of the sacrifice, that makes it possible for sins to be remitted and the petitioner to return to the presence of God.

12:11 *This was the Lord's doing, and it is marvellous in our eyes?*: This line completes the quotation of Psalm 118:22–23. It makes explicit the divine role in the elevation of the rejected stone to a place of prominence.

12:12 *And they sought to lay hold on him, but feared the people*: "They" refers to the chief priests, scribes, and elders; compare 11:27.

Mark's irony is trenchant here: the desire of the chief priests, scribes, and elders to arrest Jesus (presumably for the purpose of killing him) shows them enacting the role of the tenants in the parable who want to kill the son. The second level of irony is highlighted by the inheritance in the parable representing religious power. But if they don't arrest Jesus solely from fear of the crowd, then they clearly do not possess any power—the people wield it and thus determine the outcome. The religious leadership is shown to have sacrificed all (since they will be destroyed) in order to claim the inheritance of power, but they do not in fact possess that power.

They are portrayed as succumbing to popular pressure here. They fully desire to arrest Jesus; they hesitate not from uncertainty about the propriety of this action but out of fear. In 12:13, "they" (presumably these same leaders) will send others to challenge Jesus. While other readings are possible, it seems quite likely that they have left Jesus' presence out of fear and then send others to argue with Jesus.

"The people" are the Jewish crowd in Jerusalem. Recognition of this fact is an important check against anti-Semitic readings of the parable: it would be absolutely incorrect to say that "the Jews" were the tenants, because "the people" were clearly opposed to the arrest of Jesus. The tenants are the religious leadership only, not the masses of people (compare 15:9, 12, 14).

***for they knew that he had spoken the parable against them*:** The word "for" (Greek: *gar*) indicates that this line explains why they feared the people. Most interpreters take "they" to refer to the chief priests, scribes, and elders who are the audience for the parable, but it is perhaps more likely that it refers to "the people" because:

1. "People" is the immediate antecedent.
2. Usually, the religious leaders display a lack of understanding of what Jesus is teaching.
3. It would explain why the leaders feared the people: the people knew that Jesus had spoken the parable against the leaders, and the people support Jesus, not the leaders, in this dispute over authority.

In this reading, the sense of this verse is that the leaders feared the people because the people knew that the parable had implicated the religious leaders. Regardless, *someone* understood the parable, in sharp contrast to 4:11–13, where even the disciples do not understand the parable. It is perhaps another instance of Mark's irony that these outsiders can understand Jesus when his own disciples cannot.

The phrase "against them" could also be translated as "for them." In that reading, the parable was perceived by the religious leaders not as hostile to them but rather as an opportunity to help them repent (although they reject this opportunity).

and they left him, and went their way: The phrasing here is redundant ("left him" and "went their way"), which is probably deliberate in order to emphasize that they are symbolically turning away from Jesus.

Analysis

In the discussion with the religious leaders, Mark shows Jesus as clever and in control as he asserts his authority, and the leaders implicitly show their lack of concern with true authority as they are more concerned with the implications of their response than its truthfulness.

Despite the chapter break, the parable of the vineyard is a continuation of the discussion with the religious leaders regarding Jesus' authority. The parable makes clear that Jesus not only has authority from God but that his authority supersedes that of the prophets since he is not servant but son, even a beloved son. The parable contains Jesus' answer to the question regarding his authority, and the answer is simple: it is God's authority, given to Jesus as the Son of God.

The owner of the vineyard does not meet the tenants' violence with violence but rather with yet another opportunity to set things right. Nonetheless, it is illogical behavior to risk the well-being and life of one's beloved son. The picture is not rational; rather, it highlights the mercy and care of the owner toward the tenants. "For modern readers, centuries of familiarity with this image may have dulled the absurd charity of endangering a loved relative in order to give murderers a final chance to turn around. . . . This act defies common sense and surpasses human compassion."[53] It also pictures repentance: even after all that they have done, the owner is providing them another chance to make things right.[54]

While the actions of the owner—destroying the tenants and giving the vineyard to others—may appear harsh, it is also the case that the owner showed unexpected and undeserved mercy and patience: he has given the tenants multiple opportunities to live up to their end of the agreement. In other words, the parable shows that the destruction of the tenants was more than justified. Positioning the leaders as tenants shows the elite (who would have naturally identified with the owners) that they have actually been treated far more mercifully by God than they would have treated scheming tenants.

Linked by the words "time" (Greek: *kairos*) and "fruit" (Greek: *karpos*), the story of the cursing of the fig tree in chapter 11 parallels the parable of the vineyard. Just as Jesus inspected the actual fig tree and found it lacked the expected fruit, in the parable, the owner of the vineyard inspects (through the intermediary of his servants and son) the vineyard and finds it similarly lacking in fruit. In both cases, the lack of productivity results in a curse. This parable suggests that, as the son, Jesus was clearly entitled to the fruit that the tree (in chapter 11) and the tenants (in chapter 12) refused to give him.

In chapter 11, the two halves of the story of the cursing of the fig tree surround and thus interpret Jesus' action in the temple, where Jesus calls his audience a den of robbers. Similarly, in this parable, the tenants act as robbers as they hold back what they owe from the owner.

This parable suggests that the vineyard will not be destroyed but handed over to others—a point that is especially emphasized in contrast with the parallel parable in Isaiah. This is important because it then implies to Mark's audience that what was envisioned in chapter 11 was not so much the ultimate and final destruction of the temple but rather the handing over of its functions to others. This idea gains further support from 13:28–29, which will return to the image of the fig tree. Further, under the presumption

---

53. Tolbert, *Sowing the Gospel*, 236.
54. Focant, *Gospel according to Mark*, 474.

that the "others" who will be given the vineyard are Gentiles, this connects to the statement (from Jesus' action in the temple) that the temple was intended to be a house of prayer for all nations. Thus, the theme of the incorporation of the Gentiles into the covenant is present in both stories, if subtly.

The rejection pictured in 12:10 has just happened in Mark's Gospel: Jesus very deliberately presented himself in the beginning of chapter 11 as the triumphant ruler, but the religious leadership rejected him by ignoring him. This link between the stories is strengthened by the fact that both quote from Psalm 118. Interestingly, Psalm 118 concerns the removal of the Gentiles (Ps. 118:10), so there is a surprising inversion here as the "others" (presumably Gentiles) are given the vineyard. One function of Jesus' use of Psalm 118 is to justify the judgment rendered on the tenants/builders. Clearly, they are not being unfairly punished but rather are receiving the natural consequences of their actions. It also makes the point that rejection is not a proxy for usefulness. But the main function of the use of this psalm is to vindicate the son: in the world of the parable, the son is killed and conquered. But the quotation from the psalm has the important function of clarifying that the death of the son was not his end; it is an implicit hint of the Resurrection of Jesus. It is also possible that the rejected stone refers not to the son but rather to the rejected people, those "others" who are given the vineyard when the original tenants are destroyed.[55]

From a later vantage point—after Jesus has been killed—the parable might appear to be prophetic and condemnatory (and certainly it is), but at the time it was delivered, when the "tenants" still had another chance to permit the son to claim what was his, the focus was more on warning and mercy. In fact, the beginning of 12:12—with its reference to the idea that while they wanted to arrest Jesus, they did not—may hint at the possibility that the tenants will not kill the son, even if for craven motives. To the extent that this is a judgment parable, it is also about how to escape judgment: do not kill the son and produce the fruits of righteousness that you owe to God. The parable also contains a word of comfort to the people: they have indeed been fruitful; the fault lies solely with the leaders who have kept those fruits for themselves. The parable enacts that reality on the narrative level when it shows the crowd wanting to protect Jesus from the leaders who would kill him. The fact that the son is not yet dead means that they are still, in the terms of the parable, being offered a

---

55. Waetjen, *Reordering of Power,* 188.

chance to provide the owner what they owe. The entire point of the parable is that the owner gives multiple chances for the tenants to do right, even after they have done wrong. The idea that Jesus' invitation to repent was correctly interpreted as such by leaders who nonetheless decided to have him arrested (and thus likely killed) for it is as ironic as it is tragic.

Most of Jesus' parables show his knowledge of and identification with the poor. This parable is different since the tenant farmers are the antagonists and the wealthy land owner is the protagonist. Jesus lived in a world of "great landed estates and the inevitable tension between the absentee-owners and the dispossessed, land-hungry peasantry who cultivated the land as tenant-farmers."[56] The audience for this parable is the religious elite, who are either themselves wealthy or who would have identified with and associated with the wealthy. Interestingly, this parable puts Jesus' privileged audience in the position not of the wealthy protagonist of the parable but of the tenant farmers. Thus one thing this parable does is to insist that those who enjoy privileges identify themselves with the poor. Interestingly, Mark takes pains to relate that the audience did in fact understand this parable (contrast chapter 4, which indicates several times that the parables are not understood). This parable may be an invitation for the religious leadership to follow Jesus, but it is embedded in a requirement that they identify with the poor in order to do so. Any poor peasants who later heard this story would have delighted in hearing the leadership class positioned as tenants instead of owners, especially since at the end of the parable, the vineyard is given to others.

JESUS QUESTIONED ABOUT PAYING TAXES (12:13–17)

Greek Text

13 Καὶ ἀποστέλλουσιν πρὸς αὐτόν τινας τῶν Φαρισαίων καὶ τῶν Ἡρῳδιανῶν ἵνα αὐτὸν ἀγρεύσωσιν λόγῳ. 14 καὶ ἐλθόντες λέγουσιν αὐτῷ· Διδάσκαλε, οἴδαμεν ὅτι ἀληθὴς εἶ καὶ οὐ μέλει σοι περὶ οὐδενός, οὐ γὰρ βλέπεις εἰς πρόσωπον ἀνθρώπων, ἀλλ' ἐπ' ἀληθείας τὴν ὁδὸν τοῦ θεοῦ διδάσκεις· ἔξεστιν δοῦναι κῆνσον Καίσαρι ἢ οὔ; δῶμεν ἢ μὴ δῶμεν; 15 ὁ δὲ εἰδὼς αὐτῶν τὴν ὑπόκρισιν εἶπεν αὐτοῖς· Τί με

---

56. Lane, *Gospel according to Mark*, 416.

πειράζετε; φέρετέ μοι δηνάριον ἵνα ἴδω. 16 οἱ δὲ ἤνεγκαν. καὶ λέγει αὐτοῖς· Τίνος ἡ εἰκὼν αὕτη καὶ ἡ ἐπιγραφή; οἱ δὲ εἶπαν αὐτῷ· Καίσαρος. 17 ὁ δὲ Ἰησοῦς εἶπεν αὐτοῖς· Τὰ Καίσαρος ἀπόδοτε Καίσαρι καὶ τὰ τοῦ θεοῦ τῷ θεῷ. καὶ ἐξεθαύμαζον ἐπ᾽ αὐτῷ. [SBLGNT]

King James Version

13 And they send unto him certain of the Pharisees and of the Herodians, to catch him in his words. 14 And when they were come, they say unto him, Master, we know that thou art true, and carest for no man: for thou regardest not the person of men, but teachest the way of God in truth: Is it lawful to give tribute to Caesar, or not? 15 Shall we give, or shall we not give? But he, knowing their hypocrisy, said unto them, Why tempt ye me? bring me a penny, that I may see it. 16 And they brought it. And he saith unto them, Whose is this image and superscription? And they said unto him, Caesar's. 17 And Jesus answering said unto them, Render to Caesar the things that are Caesar's, and to God the things that are God's. And they marvelled at him.

New Rendition

13 And they send to him some of the Pharisees and the Herodians, so that they might trap him in his words. 14 And having come, they say to him, "Teacher, we know that you are truthful and do not cater to anyone, for you are impartial, but with truth you teach the way of God. Is it right to pay taxes to Caesar or not? Should we pay or not pay?" 15 And knowing of their pretending, he said to them, "Why do you test me? Bring me a coin, so that I might see it." 16 And they brought it. And he says to them, "Whose image is this? And the inscription?" And they said to him, "Caesar's." 17 And Jesus said to them, "The things of Caesar you give to Caesar, and the things of God [you give] to God." And they were amazed at him.

Notes

12:13 ***And they send unto him certain of the Pharisees and of the Herodians:*** "They" likely refers to the chief priests, scribes, and elders who have just questioned Jesus' authority and then left him (compare 11:27 and 12:12).

The precise identity of the Herodians is unknown (see the Notes on 3:6), although they were clearly supportive of Roman rule—a detail that will be crucial to their role in this encounter with Jesus. Herod ruled in Galilee, which was not under direct Roman rule. This means that the Galileans do not have to pay the tax that will be the topic of this encounter with Jesus. Their interest in this question is thus not genuine but rather focused on causing trouble for Jesus.

Historically, it seems unlikely that the Pharisees (who supported stricter interpretation of the law of Moses, especially separation of the clean and unclean) and the Herodians (who collaborated with Roman rulers) would join forces. It may be that their antipathy for Jesus outweighed their nor-mal disdain for each other, but it is more likely that their presence in this story is designed to represent the two opposing sides in the controversy over paying tribute to Caesar.

to catch him in his words: The verb "catch" is "borrowed from the lan-guage of hunting and fishing."[57] It implies that they want to trap Jesus like an animal. Because the Pharisees and Herodians take opposite sides on this issue, they presume that any response Jesus makes will offend at least some of them. In 11:30–33, Jesus caught them in their own words; here they will attempt to turn the tables on him. They were forced to claim they didn't know the source of John's authority, and they probably expected Jesus to do the same thing here.

12:14 *And when they were come, they say unto him, Master, we know that thou art true, and carest for no man:* This line creates a stark contrast to 11:33, where the religious leaders claimed that they did not know if John the Baptist's authority came from God or from man, using the same verb for "know." The audience appreciates the irony that these leaders are not "true" themselves because they are seeking to cause trouble for Jesus.

The gist of "caring for no man" is that Jesus does not care about anyone's opinion of him, not that he is uncaring in general. This flattery appears to be an effort to goad him into saying that paying taxes is wrong, since he must maintain his reputation of not caring for the opinion of those who would arrest him for opposing Roman rule.

for thou regardest not the person of men, but teachest the way of God in truth: The idea of "regarding not the person" is that Jesus does not teach differently based on the social location of his audience but, by contrast, teaches God's truth to everyone. The literal rendering would be "you do not look on the face of people." While different wording is used in 12:16 when Jesus asks whose picture is on the coin, the conceptual similarities still resonate: his interlocutors have stated that Jesus doesn't care about the "face" of people, but Jesus will avoid their trap through reference to whose face is on the coin. Also, the idea of not respecting "the face" could be taken to mean that Jesus won't care that Caesar's image appears on the coin. This reading would be an effort to convince Jesus to adopt the Hero-dian position (which will upset the Pharisees). Further, Mark notes that Jesus knows of their hypocrisy (12:15); the word translated as "hypocrisy"

---

57. Focant, *Gospel according to Mark,* 488.

stems from the practice of wearing masks in a theatrical performance, and so the implication is that Jesus can see right through their masks.

Because "the way" was one of the most common designations for the early church, Mark's audience would have heard a deeper level of meaning in these words than their speakers intended. Of course, everything that has been said by the religious leaders about Jesus is completely true—despite the fact that the speakers did not believe it. Mark's audience would have recognized this irony.

There is redundancy in this verse: they thickly apply flattery to Jesus. Their language echoes Isaiah 11:3, which was interpreted to mean that the Messiah would not judge by appearances; thus, Jesus is required to be impartial or to lose his claim to being the Messiah. So this is not merely another challenge regarding the proper interpretation of the scriptures or the proper level of accommodation to an occupying power but more fundamentally a challenge to his claim to be the Messiah.

In 1 Samuel 16:7, the Lord tells Samuel that humans look on the face, but God looks on the heart. The concept is very similar to what the Herodians and Pharisees say to Jesus. Mark's audience recognizes the truth in these words even though the speakers do not, and thus the audience aligns Jesus with the God of the HB.

Is it lawful to give tribute to Caesar, or not?: "Lawful" means permissible according to the law of Moses. Payment of the tax was mandated by Roman law. "Caesar" might be translated as "emperor" and is the title applied to whomever the current ruler was; at this point, Tiberius was Caesar.

Judea had been paying tribute to Roman rulers since 63 BCE. When Judea came under direct Roman rule in 6 CE, a poll tax (a per capita tax) was first imposed,[58] and it led to a revolt because people detested it so much. (Interestingly, "As a Galilean [Jesus] was not liable to pay the [poll tax], which applied only to provinces such as Judaea which were under direct Roman rule."[59]) "Although [the revolt] was quickly crushed by the Romans, the issue of paying taxes to Caesar (i.e., to Rome) was a continual irritant to the Jews of Palestine. It was a continual reminder of their captivity to the Romans, and along with other grievances led to the Zealot

---

58. Collins, *Mark,* 552.
59. France, *Gospel,* 465.

revolt of AD 66 and its disastrous consequences."[60] The tax was regarded as particularly egregious because "failure to meet the tribute demand often resulted in expropriation of the land of small holders."[61]

12:15 *Shall we give, or shall we not give?:* And now the trap is sprung: if Jesus says yes, he looks like a Roman collaborator. (The previous parable, which made Jesus appear sympathetic to landowners instead of tenants, would encourage that viewpoint.) But if he says no, he looks like a revolutionary, and the Romans will be after him. It is important for modern audiences to realize that this is not a dispute about the morality of taxation itself but rather about the morality of paying taxes to an occupying power. The impending Passover celebration, with its focus on remembering the signal act of liberation in the nation's history, would have heightened the point of the question regarding the legitimacy of cooperating with an oppressive foreign power.

The doubled question (compare 12:14) is not just redundant: first they asked if the payment was lawful under the law of Moses, and here they ask if they should pay it. These are two different questions. There was a general consensus that Jewish law did not permit them to be a subjugated people paying taxes using coins to a foreign power. Despite these issues, most Jews paid the tax anyway, either because they were benefiting from Roman rule (like the Herodians) or because they feared the consequences of noncompliance.

But he, knowing their hypocrisy, said unto them: A textual variant replaces "knowing" with "seeing" here,[62] although this would not substantially change the meaning of the verse.

Why tempt ye me? bring me a penny, that I may see it: The "penny" is a denarius, which had the image of Caesar on it. It was the typical day's wage for an average laborer.

The most logical reading of this verse is that Jesus does not have a denarius with him—but the Pharisees and the Herodians do.

12:16 *And they brought it. And he saith unto them, Whose is this image and superscription?:* The image on the coin was that of Caesar; the Ten Commandments prohibited such images (Ex. 20:4–6). The superscription proclaimed that Caesar was the son of the divine Augustus and was the high priest. "For everyday commerce the Jews were able to avoid 'idolatry'

60. Stein, *Mark,* 544.
61. Myers, *Binding the Strong Man,* 313.
62. Marcus, *Mark 8–16,* 817.

by using copper coins, locally minted, which bore no image,"[63] but they had to pay the tax with the denarius, which would have offended Jewish sensibilities. Further, to use the coin was to accept and to legitimate the rule of Rome.[64] It is these offensive aspects of the coin to which Jesus draws attention, and it is perhaps not coincidental that his critical interlocutors have this coin with them (in the temple, of all places) and Jesus apparently does not.

And they said unto him, Caesar's: Their laconic answer is not a full answer:[65] the coin contained Caesar's image, but they do not answer Jesus' question about the superscription ("Caesar Augustus Tiberius, son of the Divine Augustus"). Their nonresponse would have been noted by Mark's audience and would have impugned their credibility, particularly in contrast with Jesus as "true" (see the Notes on 12:14).

12:17 *And Jesus answering said unto them, Render to Caesar the things that are Caesar's, and to God the things that are God's. And they marvelled at him:* The word "render" has the implication not just of "to give" but "to give back," implying that one is divesting oneself of the coin and thus avoiding contamination and complicity with Roman rule.

The verb form here implies that they were extremely amazed, with their amazement emphasized by the intensified form. This line has to control interpretation of the story: their intention was to trap him, but they ended up marveling instead.

Analysis

In later times, there would be stories of rabbis so virtuous that they refused to even look at the images on coins.[66] Here, Jesus asks them to look, and they look. In the very acts of the narrative, Jesus is shown to be the good and "true" teacher they had posited him to be—a faithful follower of the law. His adversaries are willing to obey his authority by bringing the coin and looking at the coin, even though "gazing at a Roman denarius would

---

63. France, *Gospel of Mark,* 466.

64. Justin S. Ukpong, "Tribute to Caesar, Mark 12:13–17 (Mt 22:15–22; Lk 20:20–26)," *Neotestamentica* 33, no. 2 (1999): 440.

65. William R. Herzog II, "Dissembling, a Weapon of the Weak: The Case of Christ and Caesar in Mark 12:13–17 and Romans 13:1–7," *Perspectives in Religious Studies* 21, no. 4 (1994): 347.

66. Paul Corby Finney, "The Rabbi and the Coin Portrait (Mark 12:15B, 16): Rigorism Manqué," *Journal of Biblical Literature* 112, no. 4 (1993): 636.

have raised certain problems for all Jews."[67] So they implicate themselves for having (or having easy access to) the coin, for obeying Jesus' authority, and for looking at the coin. By contrast, Jesus does not implicate himself: he does not have the coin, does not look at the coin, and will offer an answer that causes all to marvel.

Jesus' response is usually interpreted to mean that the tax should simply be paid. However, it could not have been interpreted this way by his entire audience: the goal was to entrap Jesus in his words since the Herodians were protax while the Pharisees were antitax. So if Jesus is just counseling them to pay the tax, that does not account for the reaction of amazement at the end of the story since it is one of the two answers that they had anticipated that he would give and believed would trap him.

Rather, Jesus' answer would have been interpreted differently by different parts of his audience. The Romans would have heard an admonition to pay the tax in the phrase "render to Caesar." This would have satisfied them. On the other hand, the Jews would have heard an admonition not to pay the tax because they believed everything belonged to God (Ps. 24:1). Support for the idea of everything belonging to God comes from Jesus' previous question that asked about the "image" on the coin: this is the same Greek word (*eikon*) used in LXX Genesis 1:26, suggesting that what is in the "image" of God is humans. Thus, the mere coin belongs to Caesar ("During that reign it was the common understanding that the coins actually belonged to Caesar, since he minted them."[68]), but the human is given to God. The comparison is an insult to Caesar: the only thing he made is an insignificant piece of metal, which he is welcome to claim; by contrast, God made humans and can claim them. To give the coin back to Caesar is no loss but rather a gain since the coin is polluting the temple.[69] To get rid of the problematic coin is a good deed that would equal or even outweigh the idea of paying the tax.

Further, the inscription on the coin combined religious and political status. But here, Jesus separates them. Thus there are limits on what Caesar can demand—he can demand a coin but not what belongs to God. Jesus' point is that, contra the Zealots, there is no conflict because one owes different things to God than to Caesar. His stance isn't pro-Roman (because

---

67. Finney, "Rabbi and the Coin Portrait," 634.

68. Witherington, *Gospel of Mark,* 325.

69. Herzog, "Dissembling, a Weapon of the Weak," 350.

it shows that one owes something to God), but neither is it pro-Zealot (because it permits giving to Caesar). This statement makes a clear line of demarcation between Caesar and God—which is the opposite of what the coin does. Given the parallelism of Jesus' response, he is implicitly claiming that Caesar is not divine by comparing him to God, who is divine. Jesus cleverly teaches that Caesar is not divine while avoiding the wrath of the Romans.

Additionally, Jesus avoids the trap by not specifying what is owed to God and what is owed to Caesar; he leaves this implicit. Jesus' answer forces them to decide what they owe to Caesar and what they owe to God and thus gets Jesus out of the trap because he doesn't make the decision for them.

Jesus' counsel to give to God what belongs to God describes the opposite of the behavior of the tenants who withheld the fruit that rightfully belonged to God. The stories are also linked by the fact that the hated poll tax often resulted in farmers losing title to their land and being forced to become tenant farmers. Further linking the two stories is the fact that the "marvelling" in 12:17 uses the same root word as the marveling in 12:11, suggesting that, despite their rejection of Jesus (represented by their asking a question designed to trap him), they end up marveling at him. This is another instance in Mark where the narrative is saying something rather different from the discourse, and a perceptive audience would learn a great deal from the story itself.

Offering an answer that each group will interpret differently is the way in which Jesus escapes their trap and causes them to marvel at his response. Jesus' response may seem vaguely unsatisfying to the modern reader who wants guidance on how to balance the duties owed to God and government, but this is not what Jesus is offering here; he's responding to antagonists who are attempting to force him to say something that will cause him political problems. One should not expect him to cast pearls before swine but rather to cleverly escape the trap with an answer that conceals as much as it reveals, and this is precisely what he does, which is similar to (if more subtle than) his refusal to answer the question about his authority (see 11:33). Approaching this story as a definitive doctrinal statement would not then be appropriate. Jesus responds in a manner appropriate to the venue and the intent of the questioner.

JESUS QUESTIONED ABOUT RESURRECTION (12:18–27)

Greek Text

18 Καὶ ἔρχονται Σαδδουκαῖοι πρὸς αὐτόν, οἵτινες λέγουσιν ἀνάστασιν μὴ εἶναι, καὶ ἐπηρώτων αὐτὸν λέγοντες· 19 Διδάσκαλε, Μωϋσῆς ἔγραψεν ἡμῖν ὅτι ἐάν τινος ἀδελφὸς ἀποθάνῃ καὶ καταλίπῃ γυναῖκα καὶ μὴ ἀφῇ τέκνον, ἵνα λάβῃ ὁ ἀδελφὸς αὐτοῦ τὴν γυναῖκα καὶ ἐξαναστήσῃ σπέρμα τῷ ἀδελφῷ αὐτοῦ. 20 ἑπτὰ ἀδελφοὶ ἦσαν· καὶ ὁ πρῶτος ἔλαβεν γυναῖκα, καὶ ἀποθνῄσκων οὐκ ἀφῆκεν σπέρμα· 21 καὶ ὁ δεύτερος ἔλαβεν αὐτήν, καὶ ἀπέθανεν μὴ καταλιπὼν σπέρμα, καὶ ὁ τρίτος ὡσαύτως· 22 καὶ οἱ ἑπτὰ᾽ οὐκ ἀφῆκαν σπέρμα· ἔσχατον πάντων καὶ ἡ γυνὴ ἀπέθανεν. 23 ἐν τῇ ἀναστάσει ὅταν ἀναστῶσιν τίνος αὐτῶν ἔσται γυνή; οἱ γὰρ ἑπτὰ ἔσχον αὐτὴν γυναῖκα.

24 ἔφη αὐτοῖς ὁ Ἰησοῦς· Οὐ διὰ τοῦτο πλανᾶσθε μὴ εἰδότες τὰς γραφὰς μηδὲ τὴν δύναμιν τοῦ θεοῦ; 25 ὅταν γὰρ ἐκ νεκρῶν ἀναστῶσιν, οὔτε γαμοῦσιν οὔτε γαμίζονται, ἀλλ᾽ εἰσὶν ὡς ἄγγελοι ἐν τοῖς οὐρανοῖς· 26 περὶ δὲ τῶν νεκρῶν ὅτι ἐγείρονται οὐκ ἀνέγνωτε ἐν τῇ βίβλῳ Μωϋσέως ἐπὶ τοῦ βάτου πῶς εἶπεν αὐτῷ ὁ θεὸς λέγων· Ἐγὼ ὁ θεὸς Ἀβραὰμ καὶ ὁ θεὸς Ἰσαὰκ καὶ ὁ θεὸς Ἰακώβ; 27 οὐκ ἔστιν θεὸς νεκρῶν ἀλλὰ ζώντων· πολὺ πλανᾶσθε. [SBLGNT]

King James Version

18 Then come unto him the Sadducees, which say there is no resurrection; and they asked him, saying, 19 Master, Moses wrote unto us, If a man's brother die, and leave his wife behind him, and leave no children, that his brother should take his wife, and raise up seed unto his brother. 20 Now there were seven brethren: and the first took a wife, and dying left no seed. 21 And the second took her, and died, neither left he any seed: and the third likewise. 22 And the seven had her, and left no seed: last of all the woman died also. 23 In the resurrection therefore, when they shall rise, whose wife shall she be of them? for the seven had her to wife. 24 And Jesus answering said unto them, Do ye not therefore err, because ye know not the scriptures, neither the power of God? 25 For when they shall

New Rendition

18 And Sadducees—who say there is no resurrection—come to him. And they were questioning him, saying, 19 "Teacher, Moses wrote for us, 'If a man's brother should die and leave behind a wife and not leave children, he should marry his brother's wife, and he should raise children for his brother.' 20 There were seven brothers, and the first took a wife and, dying, left no children. 21 And the second took her and died, not having left children, and the third, the same. 22 And none of the seven had children. And last of all, the woman died. 23 In the resurrection whose wife will she be? For the seven had her as a wife." 24 Jesus said to them, "Aren't you mistaken because you do not know the scriptures or the power of God? 25 For when they rise from the dead, they do

rise from the dead, they neither marry, nor are given in marriage; but are as the angels which are in heaven. 26 And as touching the dead, that they rise: have ye not read in the book of Moses, how in the bush God spake unto him, saying, I am the God of Abraham, and the God of Isaac, and the God of Jacob? 27 He is not the God of the dead, but the God of the living: ye therefore do greatly err.

not marry nor are they given in marriage but are like angels in heaven. 26 Now as for the dead—that they are raised—have you not read in the book of Moses, in the passage about the [burning] bush, how God spoke to him, saying, 'I am the God of Abraham and the God of Isaac and the God of Jacob?' 27 He is not the God of the dead but of the living. [So] you are very mistaken."

Notes

12:18 ***Then come unto him the Sadducees, which say there is no resurrection; and they asked him, saying:*** This is the only reference to Sadducees in Mark's Gospel. "They were not so much a religious party (as the Pharisees), but more of a social class, or elite, composed mostly of the priests. The traditionalists of their day, they rejected all 'innovations,' including the idea of the resurrection, angels, etc."[70] In addition to the priests themselves, the term "the Sadducees" probably includes their family members and followers.

Interestingly, in the HB, the only generally accepted references to life after death are in Isaiah 26:19 and Daniel 2:2 (although many other texts are interpreted to refer to postmortal life by some). The Pharisees and other Jews did believe in resurrection, so, interestingly, Jesus will side with the Pharisees here.

12:19 ***Master, Moses wrote unto us, If a man's brother die, and leave his wife behind him, and leave no children, that his brother should take his wife, and raise up seed unto his brother:*** This verse quotes Deuteronomy 25:5, which describes levirate marriage, the practice of a childless widow marrying her deceased husband's brother so that she might have children. Those children were regarded as belonging to the deceased brother and thus continuing his line and memory.

It is perhaps no coincidence that the term for "raise up" (Greek: *exanistēmi*) is similar to the term for "resurrection" (Greek: *anastasis*). The implication for the Sadducees is that an actual resurrection is not necessary since the children produced by the levirate marriage serve whatever purpose would be filled by resurrection: people would, in effect, live forever

---

70. Bratcher and Nida, *Translator's Handbook,* 374.

through their children. Of course, in this case, even six levirate marriages did not "raise up" anything, so their own example undermines the idea that levirate marriage negates the need for resurrection.

12:20 *Now there were seven brethren: and the first took a wife, and dying left no seed. 21 And the second took her, and died, neither left he any seed: and the third likewise. 22 And the seven had her, and left no seed: last of all the woman died also. 23 In the resurrection therefore, when they shall rise, whose wife shall she be of them? for the seven had her to wife. 24 And Jesus answering said unto them, Do ye not therefore err, because ye know not the scriptures, neither the power of God:* It may seem a little odd that Jesus says that they "err" when they have only asked a question, but their question contained erroneous assumptions. These assumptions would include that (1) levirate marriages would be eternal or that (2) polyandry in the next life is so unthinkable that it could be used to deny the Resurrection. (One way to avoid polyandry in this situation would be for the woman to be given a choice of husbands, but apparently the Sadducees find that notion equally impossible.) The possibility of polyandry may seem excessively speculative, but in the last instance when Jesus was challenged about marriage relationships, he took the argument in a decidedly nonandrocentric direction that was almost certainly unanticipated by his audience (10:12), so perhaps the same thing happens here. That said, the first option is more likely: Jesus is teaching here that contra the assumption of the Sadducees, not all marriages are eternal. (This is likely to strike Latter-day Saint readers as ironic.) The Sadducees have asked whose wife she would be, but Jesus does not say "the first man's" or "all of theirs." Jesus' answer in 12:25 suggests that none of these marriages will be eternally valid—even the first one, which was not a levirate marriage, apparently wasn't eternally permanent either. But particularly for the levirate marriages, there is a good case to be made that they would not be expected to be eternal. In chapter 10, Jesus explains that marriages stem from the original order of creation, but only the Fall—by bringing death into the world—would provide a scenario where levirate marriage was required. Thus, many Jews (and, apparently, Jesus here as well) separated regular marriage from levirate marriage.

What does it mean to say that the Sadducees do not know the power of God? At its most basic, this phrase means that resurrected life is different from earth life. First, concerns about dying without seed would not be applicable, so levirate marriage would not be necessary. Second, God's power permits some (but not all) marriages to be eternal. And life in the resurrection is different from earthly life—to the point where the potential for polyandry is not a reason to discount the Resurrection.

12:25 ***For when they shall rise from the dead, they neither marry, nor are given in marriage; but are as the angels which are in heaven:*** At its most basic level, this statement goads the Sadducees, who apparently did not believe in angels.[71] It is easy to imagine Mark's early audiences laughing at this line. While most interpreters assume that the reference to angels means that angels will be unmarried,[72] this is not necessarily the case. The HB does not describe angels as asexual (Gen. 6:1–4). Rather, being like the angels means not being subject to death and therefore not requiring levirate marriage.

12:26 ***And as touching the dead, that they rise: have ye not read in the book of Moses, how in the bush God spake unto him, saying:*** This question indicates that Jesus was well aware that the Sadducees' question was not really about marriage but rather about resurrection.

The phrase "in the bush" probably functioned much as chapter and verse divisions do today: it was a short-hand way of saying "in the story of the burning bush" and calling the audience's attention to the story to which he was referring. At the same time, the fact that the bush was on fire but was not consumed serves as an example of the power of God, specifically (if subtly) of the power of God to preserve life from death.

I am the God of Abraham, and the God of Isaac, and the God of Jacob?: This is a quote from Exodus 3:6. In context, God is self-identifying to Moses to prepare Moses to return to the people. If Abraham, Isaac, and Jacob no longer existed at the time this was spoken, then it would have made no sense for God to mention their names. The fact that God does use them leads to the conclusion that Abraham, Isaac, and Jacob must have existed after death (as Jesus explains in the next verse). Further, "God had made promises to these patriarchs, and since they had not all yet been fulfilled, it must be assumed that they are still alive."[73] So the continued existence of the patriarchs negates the Sadducees' beliefs.

While some have emphasized the tense of the verb "am" (as opposed to "was"), Mark does not actually have that verb in the text (it is assumed but not included), and so that does not appear to be the point of the statement.

---

71. Acts 23:8. However, there are several references to angels in the first five books of the HB (for example, Gen. 22:15), which the Sadducees did accept as scripture, so it is difficult to know what to make of this evidence.

72. This is contra the position of D&C 132:16, which takes the angelic state as an unmarried one, but in terms of determining how Mark's audience would have interpreted the reference to angels, it does not seem likely that they would have assumed that the angelic state was an unmarried one.

73. Witherington, *Gospel of Mark*, 329.

12:27 *He is not the God of the dead, but the God of the living: ye therefore do greatly err:* Jesus explains that, in a sense, there are no dead people: God can self-define in terms of Abraham, Isaac, and Jacob because they are still living.

"Ye . . . do . . . err" translates the same Greek verb (*planaō*) as "ye . . . err" in 12:24, framing Jesus' remarks and emphasizing the idea that the Sadducees' question relies on erroneous assumptions.

Analysis

The point of the Sadducees' (highly unlikely) scenario is to suggest that resurrection cannot be possible because if it were, a woman might end up with seven husbands in the next life. The Sadducees would rather deny the Resurrection than countenance the possibility of polyandry. Given that they presumably had no problem with polygyny (which is mentioned in their scriptures), this serves as a startling example of sexist thought. Further, this scenario is only a problem for them if they assume that all marriages are eternal. If there was any possibility in their minds that marriages were not eternal, then the solution to their question is simple: most or all of her marriages would not be eternal. (Even for Latter-day Saints, who believe in the possibility of eternal marriages, there is doubt as to whether levirate marriages would be eternal since the purpose of the marriage was to provide children to the deceased brother, not to be a permanent match.)

This story is not solely a dispute about this one unusual case. To the extent that the Sadducees (or Mark's audience) understood that Jesus would die and be resurrected, it is important for Jesus to be able to defend the idea of resurrection; otherwise, his entire ministry is undermined.

Jesus' teachings here also imply that it is not the mere fact of a marriage that makes it eternal, but rather a marriage requires something else (what Latter-day Saints would now call the sealing authority) to render it a post-mortally valid marriage. Apparently, the Sadducees did not realize this, hence Jesus' comment that they do not understand the scriptures (which reference covenants and ordinances and sealing power, if not with the clarity that Latter-day Saint readers sometimes superimpose on them) or the power of God (which makes it possible for some, if not all, marriages to be eternal).

The obvious way out of the Sadducees' trap is for Jesus to say that there are no marriages in heaven; the fact that the Sadducees do not consider this a possibility (and thus think that their question proves that there can be no resurrection) suggests that the Sadducees assumed that Jesus would believe in marriage after death so strongly that he would be more likely to concede the Resurrection than postmortal marriage. In other words, this trap question is a testament to the strength of Jesus' (and the Sadducees') belief in marriage after death.

Jesus' warning about not knowing the scriptures fits into a pattern in Mark's Gospel where knowledge of the scriptures is shown to be different from understanding of the scriptures; this would have been a powerful warning for Mark's audience. The Sadducees assumed that the law of Moses was a template for the eternal order, but this is not correct: Jesus' answer implies that the law of Moses was, in at least some respects, an accommodation to the problems of a fallen world. It may have been a particularly relevant statement for the Sadducees, since they rejected most of the scriptural record. (While the evidence is scant, it is likely that the Sadducees only accepted the first five books of the HB as scripture.)

Jesus' teachings about marrying in heaven may appear to be contrary to Latter-day Saint ideas about the eternal potential of marriages. But given that the Sadducees are not actually interested in learning from Jesus but rather just trying to trip him up, one should not be surprised that Jesus chose not to teach them anything else about marriage at this point (compare 11:33). Of course, there may be a hint of a higher teaching in the note that God has powers that they do not understand. In other instances in Mark, Jesus hints at the eternal nature of marriage (see 10:8–9, where it is difficult to imagine that God would "tear asunder" the "one flesh" after death). Further, the wording used in this passage refers to the contracting of new marriages ("marry" and "given in marriage"; not "continue to be married"). This idea is wholly congruent with Latter-day Saint thought: it is precisely because new marriages are not believed to be contracted in the next life (D&C 132:16)[74] that proxy marriages are performed in this life and that eternal marriages are regarded as so very important. Even some non–Latter-day Saint interpreters take this view (although, admittedly, the sentiment is rare): "Notice what Jesus does not say. He does not say that there will be no marriage in the age to come. The use of the terms [marry] and [are given in marriage] is important, for these terms refer to the gender-specific roles played in early Jewish society by the man and the woman in the process of getting married. . . . Thus Mark has Jesus saying that no new marriages will be initiated . . . this is surely not the same as claiming that all existing marriages will disappear."[75]

---

74. Note that the language appears to echo this very passage in Mark with its references to marrying, being given in marriage, and being as angels.

75. Witherington, *Gospel of Mark*, 328; compare Collins, *Mark*, 561–62.

JESUS QUESTIONED ABOUT THE COMMANDMENTS (12:28–34)

Greek Text

28 Καὶ προσελθὼν εἷς τῶν γραμματέων ἀκούσας αὐτῶν συζητούντων, ἰδὼν ὅτι καλῶς ἀπεκρίθη αὐτοῖς, ἐπηρώτησεν αὐτόν· Ποία ἐστὶν ἐντολὴ πρώτη πάντων; 29 ἀπεκρίθη ὁ Ἰησοῦς ὅτι Πρώτη ἐστίν· Ἄκουε, Ἰσραήλ, κύριος ὁ θεὸς ἡμῶν κύριος εἷς ἐστιν, 30 καὶ ἀγαπήσεις κύριον τὸν θεόν σου ἐξ ὅλης τῆς καρδίας σου καὶ ἐξ ὅλης τῆς ψυχῆς σου καὶ ἐξ ὅλης τῆς διανοίας σου καὶ ἐξ ὅλης τῆς ἰσχύος σου. 31 δευτέρα αὕτη· Ἀγαπήσεις τὸν πλησίον σου ὡς σεαυτόν. μείζων τούτων ἄλλη ἐντολὴ οὐκ ἔστιν. 32 καὶ εἶπεν αὐτῷ ὁ γραμματεύς· Καλῶς, διδάσκαλε, ἐπ' ἀληθείας εἶπες ὅτι εἷς ἐστιν καὶ οὐκ ἔστιν ἄλλος πλὴν αὐτοῦ· 33 καὶ τὸ ἀγαπᾶν αὐτὸν ἐξ ὅλης τῆς καρδίας καὶ ἐξ ὅλης τῆς συνέσεως καὶ ἐξ ὅλης τῆς ἰσχύος καὶ τὸ ἀγαπᾶν τὸν πλησίον ὡς ἑαυτὸν περισσότερόν ἐστιν πάντων τῶν ὁλοκαυτωμάτων καὶ θυσιῶν. 34 καὶ ὁ Ἰησοῦς ἰδὼν αὐτὸν ὅτι νουνεχῶς ἀπεκρίθη εἶπεν αὐτῷ· Οὐ μακρὰν εἶ ἀπὸ τῆς βασιλείας τοῦ θεοῦ. καὶ οὐδεὶς οὐκέτι ἐτόλμα αὐτὸν ἐπερωτῆσαι. [SBLGNT]

King James Version

28 And one of the scribes came, and having heard them reasoning together, and perceiving that he had answered them well, asked him, Which is the first commandment of all? 29 And Jesus answered him, The first of all the commandments is, Hear, O Israel; The Lord our God is one Lord: 30 And thou shalt love the Lord thy God with all thy heart, and with all thy soul, and with all thy mind, and with all thy strength: this is the first commandment. 31 And the second is like, namely this, Thou shalt love thy neighbour as thyself. There is none other commandment greater than these. 32 And the scribe said unto him, Well, Master, thou hast said the truth: for there is one God; and there is none other but he: 33 And to love him with all the heart, and with all the understanding, and with all the soul, and with all the strength, and to love his neighbour as himself, is more than all whole burnt offerings and sacrifices.

New Rendition

28 And having come up, one of the scriptorians having heard them reasoning together, having known that he answered them well, he asked him, "Which is the first commandment of all?" 29 Jesus answered, "The first is, 'Listen, Israel: The Lord our God, the Lord is one. 30 And love the Lord your God, with all your heart and with all your soul and with all your mind and with all your strength.' 31 The second is this: 'Love your neighbor as yourself.' There is no other commandment greater than these." 32 And the scriptorian said to him, "Right, teacher, you have spoken truthfully that 'he is one and there is no one else besides him.' 33 And to love him with all the heart and with all the understanding and with all the strength and to love a neighbor as oneself is more important than all the burnt offerings and sacrifices." 34 And Jesus, having seen that he answered wisely,

34 And when Jesus saw that he answered discreetly, he said unto him, Thou art not far from the kingdom of God. And no man after that durst ask him any question. said to him, "You are not far from the kingdom of God." And no one dared any longer to question him.

Notes

12:28 *And one of the scribes came, and having heard them reasoning together, and perceiving that he had answered them well, asked him, Which is the first commandment of all?*: This question asks which commandment is most important (not which one was given first). It is an interesting contrast to the previous question—which was about as obscure and pedantic as imaginable—by virtue of its importance and practicality.

12:29 *And Jesus answered him, The first of all the commandments is, Hear, O Israel; The Lord our God is one Lord:* Jesus quotes Deuteronomy 6:4–5, which was known as the Shema and was recited twice per day by adult male Jews. Thus, this would have been a very familiar text to his audience.

12:30 *And thou shalt love the Lord thy God with all thy heart, and with all thy soul, and with all thy mind, and with all thy strength: this is the first commandment:* The quotation from Deuteronomy 6:4–5 continues, but that text does not include a reference to "mind" (Greek: *dianoia*). Perhaps "mind" is added to apply to the situation of a scribe, particularly given the larger context of Jesus being asked hard questions to trip him up—clearly not an instance of them using their minds to love God. The fourfold repetition of "all" (Greek: *holos*) serves to emphasize the totality of devotion that is expected.

12:31 *And the second is like, namely this, Thou shalt love thy neighbour as thyself:* Here, Jesus quotes Leviticus 19:18. Leviticus 19 contains many commandments that prohibit the exploitation of the poor and defenseless. The scribe didn't ask for a second commandment, but Jesus offers it anyway: "Evidently the commandment that is first of all cannot stand alone."[76] Perhaps there is a necessary balance and corollary to loving God in loving neighbor, especially for a scribe who may be overly zealous. Jesus' answer places God before all other humans, but it also places all humans on equal footing with each other, especially since—given Jesus' treatment of Gentiles—the word "neighbor" should be read broadly.

---

76. Waetjen, *Reordering of Power*, 193.

There is none other commandment greater than these: The word "com-mandment" is singular: in a sense, Jesus regards love of God and love of neighbor as composing one commandment. At the same time, the identi-fication between the two is not total since Jesus does label them "first" and "second."

12:32 *And the scribe said unto him, Well, Master, thou hast said the truth: for there is one God; and there is none other but he:* The scribe quotes Deuteronomy 4:35.

12:33 *And to love him with all the heart, and with all the understand-ing, and with all the soul, and with all the strength, and to love his neigh-bour as himself, is more than all whole burnt offerings and sacrifices:* The scribe quotes Hosea 6:6 (a similar sentiment is expressed in 1 Sam. 15:22); nonetheless, this is a pretty stunning statement for a scribe since it sug-gests a secondary status for sacrifices and offerings. In a classic example of Mark's irony, the statement is offered while Jesus and the scribe are actu-ally in the temple. And much as with the fig tree story, it simultaneously deprioritizes the temple while offering an alternative to temple worship. In this case, love of God and neighbor substitute for temple rituals.

For Mark's audience, this statement is also significant on another level: "By quoting this principle [that there is no other besides God, which was often used against Christians] in a context that suggests a Jewish scribe's *approval* of Jesus, the Markan narrative implies that the Shema's affirma-tion of divine oneness is compatible with reverence for Jesus."[77]

Combining 12:30 and 33 gives a sevenfold repetition of the word "all" (Greek: *holos*). The number seven symbolizes totality; perhaps Mark's audience would have picked up on this nuance that once again emphasizes the need for complete devotion to God.

12:34 *And when Jesus saw that he answered discreetly, he said unto him, Thou art not far from the kingdom of God:* Much of the scribe's answer was a basic restatement of what Jesus had said and thus unlikely to result in Jesus' response. But the scribe added the idea that love was worth more than sacrifice, and it seems to be this analysis that Jesus praises because it shows the scribe's ability to extend Jesus' teachings and to realize their implications.

Jesus' statement that the scribe is not far from the kingdom of God may be an example of litotes (a literary device in which the speaker negates the opposite of what they want to affirm as a way of understating their case); if

---

77. Marcus, *Mark 8–16*, 844.

this is the case, then being "not far from the kingdom of God" would actually imply being part of the kingdom.

And no man after that durst ask him any question: Chapters 11–12 have featured a series of questions aimed at Jesus; it is somewhat curious that the questions would stop now. After all, it isn't as if Jesus had condemned the scribe; certainly he was more stern with the Sadducees when he told them more than once that they had erred and didn't understand the power of God. Perhaps the questions stop because the others are afraid that they, like the scribes, will come to see the wisdom in Jesus' teachings. Or perhaps Jesus' verdict that this scribe was not far from the kingdom has left no one else willing to be judged by Jesus. The lack of questions also provides the setup to the next story, which begins with Jesus—not one of his adversaries—asking a question.

Analysis

Most interpreters take the scribe's question as a genuine, respectful question (based on the scribe's statement in 12:32–33 and Jesus' response to the scribe in 13:34), but it is possible that his initial approach is hostile. Because the scribe thought that Jesus had provided good answers to the difficult questions posed to him so far, he may have been motivated to present Jesus with a question that he could not answer well in order to undermine Jesus. Under that reading, the fact that Jesus' answer is acceptable to the scribe leads to the scribe undergoing a change of heart in this passage. The result of this change of heart is Jesus' statement that the scribe is not far from the kingdom. This reading makes better sense of the final line of the passage: no one else dared to ask Jesus any questions because they saw that it led the scribe to improve his opinion of Jesus' teachings.

Jesus' praise of the scribe stands out in a text where the scribes are often positioned as the enemies of Jesus. This is an important counterweight to the potential for anti-Semitic interpretations of the text: it is of signal importance to note that neither the Jews in general, nor even the Jewish leadership in particular, is uniformly opposed to Jesus in this Gospel. Further, Jesus' praise of the scribe may be even more positive than it seems if it is read as litotes. It is perhaps no accident that the command to love neighbors is a focal point in a story featuring two stereotypical antagonists (Jesus and the scribe) who both have positive things to say about each other. The story models at the discourse level what is preached at the narrative level.

Jesus' statement puts him in the position of judging the scribe and thus showcases his authority. This is especially significant since the scribe has just judged Jesus' answer, but "the scribe may have the power to evaluate Jesus' mastery of the law, but Jesus possesses the greater power, the power to determine that the scribe is 'not far from the kingdom of God.'"[78]

JESUS QUESTIONS THE SCRIBES (12:35–37)

Greek Text

35 Καὶ ἀποκριθεὶς ὁ Ἰησοῦς ἔλεγεν διδάσκων ἐν τῷ ἱερῷ· Πῶς λέγουσιν οἱ γραμ-ματεῖς ὅτι ὁ χριστὸς υἱὸς Δαυίδ ἐστιν; 36 αὐτὸς Δαυὶδ εἶπεν ἐν τῷ πνεύματι τῷ ἁγίῳ· Εἶπεν κύριος τῷ κυρίῳ μου· Κάθου ἐκ δεξιῶν μου ἕως ἂν θῶ τοὺς ἐχθρούς σου ὑποκάτω τῶν ποδῶν σου. 37 αὐτὸς Δαυὶδ λέγει αὐτὸν κύριον, καὶ πόθεν αὐτοῦ ἐστιν υἱός; καὶ ὁ πολὺς ὄχλος ἤκουεν αὐτοῦ ἡδέως. [SBLGNT]

King James Version

35 And Jesus answered and said, while he taught in the temple, How say the scribes that Christ is the Son of David? 36 For David himself said by the Holy Ghost, The Lord said to my Lord, Sit thou on my right hand, till I make thine enemies thy footstool. 37 David therefore himself calleth him Lord; and whence is he then his son? And the common people heard him gladly.

New Rendition

35 While teaching in the temple, answering, Jesus said, "Why do the scriptorians say that the anointed one is a son of David? 36 David himself said by the Holy Spirit,

'The Lord said to my Lord,
"Sit at my right hand
until I place your enemies under
your feet."'

37 "David himself calls him Lord. So how is he his son?" And the large crowd happily heard him.

Notes

12:35 *And Jesus answered and said, while he taught in the temple, How say the scribes that Christ is the Son of David?*: Since no one was willing to ask Jesus any more questions (12:34), Jesus asks a question of his own. Because it was already clear that Jesus was in the temple, this additional reference to being in the temple emphasizes the setting.

Mark's audience may have assumed that this teaching is incorrect since Jesus presents it as what the scribes teach, but that instinct must be

---

78. Tolbert, *Sowing the Gospel*, 255.

balanced against the fact that a scribe has just shown himself to be close to the kingdom of God. So it would not have been clear to Mark's audience whether the teaching should be presumed correct or incorrect.

Many HB passages were interpreted to mean that the Christ (or Messiah; "Christ" transliterates a Greek word meaning "the anointed one" while "Messiah" is a Hebrew word meaning the same thing) would be a son of David (Isa. 9:5–6; 11:1; Jer. 23:5; 33:15–17; Ezek. 34:23–24; Zech. 3:8), so this does not seem like an unreasonable thing for the scribes to teach.

12:36 *For David himself said by the Holy Ghost:* This reference to the Spirit is atypical for Mark; this is the only time in Mark in which the Spirit is said specifically to speak. It suggests authority, much as the descent of the Spirit at Jesus' baptism implied his authority.[79] It may relate to the sentiment in 2 Samuel 23:1–2, where David's inspiration is also referenced. It claims a special authority for David's words. Perhaps Jesus emphasizes the inspired nature of David's utterance in order to emphasize that David himself actually spoke these words (today, Davidic authorship of the psalms is not generally accepted) and that they had the meaning that Jesus will ascribe to them. (Contrast 12:10, where no issue is raised regarding the authorship or inspiration of the psalm there quoted.) Because the Holy Ghost is sometimes associated with anointing (1 Sam. 16:13; 2 Sam. 23:1–2; Acts 10:38; 1 Cor. 1:21–22), Jesus might also be emphasizing David's own messiahship.

The Lord said to my Lord, Sit thou on my right hand, till I make thine enemies thy footstool: Some manuscripts contain the variant "underneath your feet" instead of a reference to a "footstool."[80] The sense is the same in either case.

Mark's text uses the same word for "Lord" (Greek: *kyrios*) twice in this verse. This mirrors LXX Psalm 109:1 (KJV Ps. 110:1), where the same Greek word is also used twice. But the Hebrew text uses two different words, so there is a distinction in the Hebrew text that is missing from the LXX.

12:37 *David therefore himself calleth him Lord; and whence is he then his son? And the common people heard him gladly:* Because Herod also gladly heard John the Baptist shortly before ordering John's execution (6:20), this line may have carried an ominous tone for Mark's audience.

---

79. Emerson B. Powery, "The Spirit, the Scripture(s), and the Gospel of Mark: Pneumatology and Hermeneutics in Narrative Perspective," *Journal of Pentecostal Theology* 11, no. 2 (2003): 184–98.

80. Collins, *Mark,* 577 note a.

Even without that association, one presumes that Jesus' goal was "the stirring up of reflection and not pleasure,"[81] which suggests that the crowd is reacting inappropriately to Jesus, perhaps by focusing on the glee of seeing the scribes chastised instead of focusing on the point of Jesus' message.

Analysis

Jesus quotes Psalm 110:1 here. This verse is very difficult to understand because of the two uses of the title "Lord," but it is probably best understood as God speaking to the Messiah, with God offering the Messiah a seat of honor.[82] The point of Jesus' reference is that David refers to the Messiah as "my Lord," and one would not speak to one's descendant with such language.

While not the point of the quotation, it is nonetheless true that in Jesus' usage, God is promising to put the Messiah's enemies under his feet. This provides an explanation for Jesus' nonmilitaristic ministry here: it is God who will subdue the enemies, not the Messiah. It suggests the same kind of vindication as was pictured by the psalm quote following the parable at the beginning of the chapter (12:10).

While other NT texts conceptualize Jesus as a son of David (Matt. 1:1), it seems that Mark did not share this viewpoint: 12:37 suggests that Jesus, contrary to the scribes, did not consider it appropriate to view the Messiah as a son of David. (While Jesus is called "son of David" in 10:47–48, Mark may be implying that Bartimaeus's use of this title reflects his blindness.) It could also be argued that Mark is not rejecting the idea of the Messiah as the son of David entirely but rather arguing that "son of David" is an accurate but inadequate description of the Messiah, perhaps because of the militaristic and nationalistic aspects of that title.

Jesus' argument, using the beliefs common to a first-century Jew, relies on the assumption that (1) David authored this psalm, (2) that David himself was the speaker in the psalm (even had David authored the psalm, he might not be its narrator), and (3) that the "lord" in the psalm can be unquestionably equated with the Messiah. Most interpreters would not

---

81. Focant, *Gospel according to Mark,* 507.

82. Modern Latter-day Saint thought makes a clean distinction between Elohim (the Father) and Jehovah (Jesus Christ), but this has not been the case throughout all of Latter-day Saint Church history, let alone the scriptures. See Ryan Conrad Davis and Paul Y. Hoskisson, "Usage of the Title Elohim," *Religious Educator* 14, no. 1 (2013): 109–27; and Boyd Kirkland, "Elohim and Jehovah in Mormonism and the Bible," *Dialogue* 19 (Spring 1986): 79–93.

accept all three of these assumptions today and therefore would not find Jesus' use of this psalm persuasive. Of course, Jesus was speaking to an ancient audience, not a modern one; presumably he would use different evidence if making the argument today. But "given the way Jesus and his contemporaries read Psalm 110, the argument is convincing enough."[83]

JESUS PRAISES THE WIDOW (12:38–44)

Greek Text

38 Καὶ ἐν τῇ διδαχῇ αὐτοῦ ἔλεγεν· Βλέπετε ἀπὸ τῶν γραμματέων τῶν θελόντων ἐν στολαῖς περιπατεῖν καὶ ἀσπασμοὺς ἐν ταῖς ἀγοραῖς 39 καὶ πρωτοκαθεδρίας ἐν ταῖς συναγωγαῖς καὶ πρωτοκλισίας ἐν τοῖς δείπνοις, 40 οἱ κατεσθίοντες τὰς οἰκίας τῶν χηρῶν καὶ προφάσει μακρὰ προσευχόμενοι· οὗτοι λήμψονται περισσότερον κρίμα.

41 Καὶ καθίσας κατέναντι τοῦ γαζοφυλακίου ἐθεώρει πῶς ὁ ὄχλος βάλλει χαλκὸν εἰς τὸ γαζοφυλάκιον· καὶ πολλοὶ πλούσιοι ἔβαλλον πολλά· 42 καὶ ἐλθοῦσα μία χήρα πτωχὴ ἔβαλεν λεπτὰ δύο, ὅ ἐστιν κοδράντης. 43 καὶ προσκαλεσάμενος τοὺς μαθητὰς αὐτοῦ εἶπεν αὐτοῖς· Ἀμὴν λέγω ὑμῖν ὅτι ἡ χήρα αὕτη ἡ πτωχὴ πλεῖον πάντων ἔβαλεν τῶν βαλλόντων εἰς τὸ γαζοφυλάκιον· 44 πάντες γὰρ ἐκ τοῦ περισσεύοντος αὐτοῖς ἔβαλον, αὕτη δὲ ἐκ τῆς ὑστερήσεως αὐτῆς πάντα ὅσα εἶχεν ἔβαλεν, ὅλον τὸν βίον αὐτῆς. [SBLGNT]

King James Version

38 And he said unto them in his doctrine, Beware of the scribes, which love to go in long clothing, and love salutations in the marketplaces, 39 And the chief seats in the synagogues, and the uppermost rooms at feasts: 40 Which devour widows' houses, and for a pretence make long prayers: these shall receive greater damnation.

41 And Jesus sat over against the treasury, and beheld how the people cast money into the treasury: and many that were rich cast in much. 42 And there came a certain poor widow, and

New Rendition

38 And in his teaching, he said, "Watch out for the scriptorians who like walking around in long robes and greetings in the markets, 39 the first seats in the synagogues and the first places at banquets, 40 the ones consuming the property of widows and, on a pretext, [making] long prayers. These will be more harshly punished." 41 And having sat down opposite the temple treasury, he watched the crowd put money into the treasury, and many rich people were putting in much. 42 And having come, one poor widow put in two coins, which equals less than

83. France, *Gospel*, 487.

she threw in two mites, which make a farthing. 43 And he called unto him his disciples, and saith unto them, Verily I say unto you, That this poor widow hath cast more in, than all they which have cast into the treasury: 44 For all they did cast in of their abundance; but she of her want did cast in all that she had, even all her living.

a penny. 43 And having called his disciples to him, he says to them, "Amen, I say to you that this poor widow has put in more than all of those [who are] putting in to the treasury, 44 for they put in out of their abundance. However, she put in out of her poverty as much as she had—her whole life."

Notes

12:38 *And he said unto them in his doctrine, Beware of the scribes, which love to go in long clothing, and love salutations in the marketplaces:* Given that Jesus has recently had a positive interaction with a scribe, it is important to read this warning as applying not to all scribes but rather to those who exhibit these behaviors.

The word "beware" (Greek: *blepō*) will be a refrain throughout chapter 13, where the disciples will be repeatedly warned to watch/beware (see the Notes on 13:2).

The long clothing may refer to clothing worn by scribes that was intended to imitate priestly robes, or it may have simply been expensive clothing that would have signaled the wearer's wealth, or even just special occasion clothing worn to signal that the wearer was engaged in special activities. It was intended to cause others to recognize their elevated status, which would result in special greetings as people recognized and honored them. Jesus is telling them to be suspicious of those who seek social status for their religious learning.

12:39 *And the chief seats in the synagogues, and the uppermost rooms at feasts:* The "chief seats" faced the people and were next to the scrolls of scripture; they were considered places of honor. The reference to feasts implies that these scribes seek not only religious honors but social ones as well.

12:40 *Which devour widows' houses, and for a pretence make long prayers: these shall receive greater damnation:* The only other Markan use of the word "devour" (Greek: *katesthiō*) describes a bird (a figure for Satan) eating the seed in a parable (4:4), so it has very negative associations.

Devouring widows' houses refers to unfairly profiting from the estates of widows, but precisely how this was done is open to a variety of interpretations:

1. The scribes accepted money for making long prayers on behalf of the widows, thus depleting their savings. This reading has the advantage of explaining

the context: the long prayers are the mechanism by which the estates are destroyed. An interesting implication of this reading is that it implies that the women should be making their own prayers and not relying on male authority figures to mediate their relationship to God.

2. "Devouring" may refer to accepting too much in hospitality and leaving the widow without enough resources to meet her own needs.

3. Perhaps the scribes are the legal guardians of the widows' estates and are managing them to their own benefit, at the widows' expense.

Regardless, the passage shows these scribes violating both of the great commandments by not loving God or neighbor. Because the HB evinces a special concern for widows (Ex. 22:22–24; Isa. 1:23; Jer. 7:6; 22:3; Zech. 7:10), this behavior is particularly egregious. It is precisely the opposite of the self-sacrificial care that followers of Jesus are to show to others.

The Greek word translated as "pretence" means "things put in front." So it could suggest that these are false prayers or that the prayers are meant to be a "front" for the abuse of widows. Or perhaps scribes faked long prayers so that they would seem righteous and be chosen to become estate agents.[84]

12:41 *And Jesus sat over against the treasury, and beheld how the people cast money into the treasury: and many that were rich cast in much:* Some manuscripts read "he" instead of "Jesus," and that is probably the earlier reading. The subject of the sentence is not in doubt, but scribes probably replaced the pronoun with the noun for clarity[85] since Jesus has not been mentioned by name since 12:35. Sitting was the position of an authoritative teacher. "Over against" may signal Jesus' opposition to the treasury; compare 13:3.

In the temple courtyard, there were thirteen receptacles for offerings. With narrow bases and wide tops, they looked like trumpets. People would have paid the half-shekel temple tax here and also made additional offerings; "the offerings to the temple treasury were meant for redistribution among the poor."[86] Hence, the widow's offering is ironic since she is poor.

12:42 *And there came a certain poor widow, and she threw in two mites, which make a farthing:* "In patriarchal societies the worst and most tragic thing for a woman is to become a widow."[87] The mere presence of a poor

---

84. J. Duncan M. Derrett, "Eating Up the Houses of Widows: Jesus' Comment on Lawyers?" *Novum Testamentum* 14, no. 1 (1972): 1–9.

85. Metzger, *Textual Commentary,* 94.

86. Hisako Kinukawa, *Women and Jesus in Mark: A Japanese Feminist Perspective* (Maryknoll, N.Y.: Orbis Books, 1994), 72.

87. Kinukawa, *Women and Jesus in Mark,* 68.

widow—even absent scribes attempting to steal her money—is an indictment against the religious authorities for not following the law of Moses (Deut. 14:29 mandates the care of widows). The verse division obscures the very close but inverted parallel between the "many rich people [who] were throwing many things" and the "one poor widow [who] threw two *lepta.*"[88] There is a difference in verb tense: the rich "are throwing" (an imperfect form, indicating repeated action) while the widow "threw" (a singular event). And in contrast to the "many" rich is "one" widow. This is not Mark's usual word for "certain" (Greek: *tis*) but another term indicating "one" (Greek: *mia*), which emphasizes her singular contrast to the crowd of the wealthy.

"Mites" translates the Greek word *lepton,* which "does not seem to have been a recognized monetary unit"[89] but rather a generic term for the smallest coin in circulation. Hence Mark's explanation, which provides the Roman equivalent of a "farthing" or quadrant (the smallest Roman coin in circulation), which was one-sixtieth of a denarius and thus about one-sixtieth of a day's wage for an average laborer—a very small amount indeed. The fact that she throws in two mites may seem to negate this point, but rather it suggests that it would have been possible for her to donate while still holding back something for herself. And yet she chose not to do this. This is a freewill offering (not something required by the law of Moses) and thus emphasizes her generosity.

12:43 *And he called unto him his disciples, and saith unto them, Verily I say unto you:* The "verily" saying emphasizes the truthfulness and importance of what Jesus is about to say (see the Notes on 3:28). Interestingly, this is the only one of Jesus' "verily" sayings that points to a past action instead of a future action.[90]

The widow's story is surrounded by Jesus' admonition of his disciples to "watch/beware" (Greek: *blepō*; see the Notes on 12:38 and 13:2); while the same Greek word is not used in this verse, Jesus is calling his disciples to watch this woman and to learn from her.

That this poor widow hath cast more in, than all they which have cast into the treasury: Clearly, Jesus is using a metric other than the market value of the coins in order to determine the worth of her offering, especially

88. Marcus, *Mark 8–16,* 860.
89. Focant, *Gospel according to Mark,* 518.
90. Kinukawa, *Women and Jesus in Mark,* 76.

since "the strict, literal meaning of the Greek is that she put in more than all others *together* put in."[91]

12:44 *For all they did cast in of their abundance; but she of her want did cast in all that she had, even all her living:* It is possible to read this verse as the conclusion to Jesus' remarks or as Mark's explanation of Jesus' enigmatic remark.

Note the repetition in Jesus' answer: "all that she had" and "all her living" serve to emphasize the point that she has truly given everything. The premise of the HB's concern for widows (and orphans) is that they are incapable of meeting their own needs; interestingly, in this story, the widow is, in effect, caring for the temple. Jesus calls attention to this role reversal.

The reference to her whole life (KJV: "all her living") may foreshadow Jesus' coming gift of his whole life.

See also the section "Relationship to the Widow's Offering" after the Notes on 14:3–9, since the anointer's story parallels the widow's story in significant ways.

Analysis

The widow contrasts sharply with Jesus' recent criticism of the scribes. They sought attention in the temple through their displays of wealth (and perhaps the rich did with their huge offerings did as well), but the point is that Jesus calls attention to the offering of this poor widow. She does not seek attention for herself. Jesus has to call the disciples' attention to her because she is not doing anything to draw attention to herself. And yet her small gift becomes great when Jesus consecrates it with his attention. Part of the significance of this story lies in the fact that the woman does nothing to seek out attention (unlike Bartimaeus or the criticized scribes who sought attention).

This story has something of a surprise ending. One would presume that, even for a poor widow, two mites was a small portion of her money. But only after the fact does the audience discover that it is all the money that she had. This forces the audience to reevaluate the meaning and import of her gift and Jesus' statement. The experience of listening to this story causes the audience to undergo a reassessment of the value of her contribution; listening to it is a transformative experience. Her story makes a subtle contrast with the good scribe: she is praised fully whereas his praise

---

91. Bratcher and Nida, *Translator's Handbook,* 394; italics in original.

is more limited because he is all talk and no action, whereas she is all action and no talk.

Jesus' statement can be interpreted several ways:

1. *Lament.* It is clear in Mark that the temple is corrupt and will soon be destroyed. In that context, the widow's gift is wasted, and thus Jesus laments it.[92] This reading is adopted by only a minority of scholars,[93] but it is supported by the idea that human needs trump traditions and even commandments (3:1–5; 12:28–34).

2. *Praise.* Jesus' words are, on their face, positive. He calls his disciples' attention to her in order to praise her action. This widow is not giving her money to the scribes who would devour her house but to the temple. And she's not doing it under duress—no one is even paying attention to her. The fact that the temple is soon to be destroyed does not mean that it is wrong to donate to it (a useful parallel from a Latter-day Saint perspective can be found in how the Nephites in the Book of Mormon continue to keep the law of Moses even as they anticipate a higher law that will supersede it). This widow exemplifies what Jesus has taught about true discipleship (8:35). She is clearly following the admonition of the Shema to give her "all" to God, something that would be particularly resonant if Mark's audience agreed with the Dead Sea Scrolls' understanding that the "whole strength" of the Shema referred to all of one's wealth. Further, the widow's story closely parallels 14:3–9 (see the section "Relationship to Other Stories in Mark" after the Notes on 14:8), which means that, just as Jesus praises the anointing woman, he is praising the widow.

3. *Multivalence.* It is possible to read Jesus' statement as deliberately ambiguous or even ambivalent.

4. *Typological Reading.* Much as Jesus gives his whole life to save a fallen and corrupt humanity, the woman gives her whole life to a fallen temple: "His death . . . will also be mysteriously intertwined with the destruction of the present Temple."[94] Her sacrifice for the temple is not logical, but then neither is Jesus' sacrifice of his life. Because the widow's story is aligned with the anointer's story (see the section "Relationship to Other Stories in Mark" after the Notes on 14:8), both women are giving gifts to the doomed: the widow to the temple and the anointer to Jesus. But, as Jesus explains in the anointing story, the gift is not wasted but rather attains a higher purpose. In the case of the widow, the higher purpose is that Jesus is able to use her experience as a teaching moment for his disciples about what it looks like to give one's "all." And much as Jesus' anointed body will return to life, perhaps this story implicitly hints that the temple, though corrupt during Jesus' time, will return as well (this idea is supported by 13:28).

92. Addison G. Wright, "The Widow's Mites: Praise or Lament—a Matter of Context," *Catholic Biblical Quarterly* 44, no. 2 (1982): 256–65.

93. Evans, *Mark 8:27–16:20*, 282.

94. Marcus, *Mark 8–16*, 863.

Regardless of which reading is preferable, one notable fact about this story stands out: Jesus knows that the woman is poor, a widow, and that this donation represents all of her wealth. It seems likely that he is relying on suprahuman knowledge in this instance. Normally, Mark is in the role of the omniscient narrator, but Jesus steps in to that role in this story. Many HB stories speak of God's special concern for widows. In this story, Jesus is placed into the narrative role of God as he is the one evincing the special concern for the widow, who is ignored by all those around her.

In 13:2, Jesus will prophesy the destruction of the temple. Because that scene immediately follows the widow's experience in the temple, she is its immediate catalyst, and it is likely that her experience of supporting the temple (when, according to the law of Moses, the temple and surrounding religious infrastructure should have been supporting her) is, in terms of the narrative, the proximate cause of the temple's destruction.

OVERVIEW OF CHAPTER 13

Chapter 13 is sometimes referred to as the Olivet Discourse since Jesus speaks from the Mount of Olives. The interpretation of chapter 13 presents several complications:

1. The genre of the chapter is difficult to determine:

   a. It has some characteristics of apocalyptic writings (similar to Daniel, the book of Revelation, and many texts from Jesus' lifetime), particularly a concern with future events. And one of the hallmarks of apocalyptic writing is a veiledness so that outsiders (who might constitute a political threat) are unable to understand the material. So perhaps some of the difficulty in interpreting this chapter may be deliberate (or, at least, an unavoidable side effect of the genre). However, chapter 13 is missing many of the usual elements of apocalyptic writing, including a vision of the heavens, a review of history, an angelic mediator, numbers related to time calculations (contrast 13:32), warnings of judgment, a final battle, a description of the afterlife, and bizarre symbols.[95] It also contains elements not usually found in apocalyptic texts, such as the repeated admonition to watch and a high number of commands. And the apocalyptic elements that it does contain (such as references to wars and earthquakes) are not mentioned for their own sake but rather in the context of Jesus' other teachings (see 13:7–9). In fact, some interpreters describe the text as anti-apocalyptic: it introduces apocalyptic themes only in order to minimize them.

---

95. Focant, *Gospel according to Mark*, 521; see also Gundry, *Mark*, 751–52.

b. Chapter 13 contains some characteristics of a farewell discourse (compare Gen. 49:2–27; Deut. 32; 1 Chr. 28–29; John 13–17) since it contains Jesus' final teachings to his disciples before his death. But it omits other common elements of that genre, including moral teachings and a review of the past.

So while Mark contains aspects reminiscent of apocalyptic and farewell discourses, it also departs significantly from what would have been expected from both of those genres. Much as Mark appears to have invented the genre of "gospel," chapter 13 seems to be a genre unto itself.

2. The chapter contains many ambiguous terms: "these things" in 13:4, 29, and 30; the "abomination of desolation" in 13:14; "those days" in 13:17, 19, 20, and 24; "this generation" in 13:30; and "that day" in 13:32. Because the interpreter cannot always be sure of the correct referent, it is difficult to interpret the text. The chapter contains numerous indicators of time sequence ("when" in 13:7, 11, 14, and 29; "and then" in 13:21, 26, and 27), which might help elucidate these ambiguous terms. However, one characteristic of apocalyptic writing is a disregard for chronological order; this problematizes the use of these time markers.

3. There is no consensus on the structure of the text, with a variety of proposed structures stemming from the interpreter's understanding of the meaning of the chapter which, of course, is debated. The following proposal for the structure reflects this commentary's position that virtually the entire discourse refers to the events of the Jewish War (other interpreters see all or part of 13:24–31 or even 13:5–31 as referring to the return of the Son of Man):

> disciples' questions, 13:1–4
> A "these things" (the end of the temple/Jerusalem), 13:5–27
> B parable: end of the temple/Jerusalem, 13:28–31
> A' "that day" (the return of the son), 13:32–33
> B' parable: the return of the son, 13:34–36
> conclusion, 13:37

But this structure and the interpretation that gives rise to it should be regarded as tentative in light of the interpretive challenges mentioned above. And yet despite these compounding complexities, chapter 13 fascinates as a result of its distinctive nature: it is the single longest discourse by Jesus in the Gospel, and it "has a larger number of imperatives than any other single chapter in Mark. . . . The ratios indicate that the frequency of imperatives in 13:5–37 is more than twice that of any other chapter in the Gospel."[96] This is clearly an important part of Mark's story of Jesus' life and his message about discipleship.

---

96. Stanley E. Porter, *Linguistic Analysis of the Greek New Testament: Studies in Tools, Methods, and Practice* (Grand Rapids, Mich.: Baker Academic, 2015), 228–29.

JESUS PROPHESIES ABOUT THE TEMPLE (13:1–4)

Greek Text

1 Καὶ ἐκπορευομένου αὐτοῦ ἐκ τοῦ ἱεροῦ λέγει αὐτῷ εἷς τῶν μαθητῶν αὐτοῦ· Διδά-σκαλε, ἴδε ποταποὶ λίθοι καὶ ποταπαὶ οἰκοδομαί. 2 καὶ ὁ Ἰησοῦς εἶπεν αὐτῷ· Βλέ-πεις ταύτας τὰς μεγάλας οἰκοδομάς; οὐ μὴ ἀφεθῇ ὧδε λίθος ἐπὶ λίθον ὃς οὐ μὴ καταλυθῇ.

3 Καὶ καθημένου αὐτοῦ εἰς τὸ Ὄρος τῶν Ἐλαιῶν κατέναντι τοῦ ἱεροῦ ἐπηρώτα αὐτὸν κατ᾿ ἰδίαν Πέτρος καὶ Ἰάκωβος καὶ Ἰωάννης καὶ Ἀνδρέας· 4 Εἰπὸν ἡμῖν πότε ταῦτα ἔσται, καὶ τί τὸ σημεῖον ὅταν μέλλῃ ταῦτα συντελεῖσθαι πάντα. [SBLGNT]

King James Version

1 And as he went out of the temple, one of his disciples saith unto him, Master, see what manner of stones and what buildings are here! 2 And Jesus answering said unto him, Seest thou these great buildings? there shall not be left one stone upon another, that shall not be thrown down. 3 And as he sat upon the mount of Olives over against the temple, Peter and James and John and Andrew asked him privately, 4 Tell us, when shall these things be? and what shall be the sign when all these things shall be fulfilled?

New Rendition

1 And as he is leaving the temple, one of his disciples says to him, "Teacher, look! What [impressive] stones and what [impressive] buildings!" 2 And Jesus said to him, "You are watching these great buildings? There will not be left one stone upon [another] stone here that shall not be thrown down." 3 And while he is sitting upon the Mount of Olives—opposite the temple—Peter, Jacob, John, and Andrew asked him privately, 4 "Tell us when these things will be. And what will be the sign when these things are all going to happen?"

Notes

13:1 *And as he went out of the temple, one of his disciples saith unto him:* The Greek indicates that the disciple asking this question is male, but that is all the text reveals about the speaker; he may or may not be one of the disciples named in 13:3.

Master, see what manner of stones and what buildings are here!: The New Rendition adds "impressive" in brackets to convey the gist of the disciple's observation. Other modern translations add words such as "magnificent," "large," or "massive" to describe the stones and buildings; while none of these words are in the Greek text, they help communicate the disciple's point. "Buildings" refers to the many structures that made up the temple complex.

The temple was undoubtedly a wondrous sight to behold. "The magnificence of the city and temple complex cannot be exaggerated. The majesty and grandeur of the temple complex would have made even some of the seven wonders of the world pale in comparison."[97] Stones measuring an incredible 42 by 14 by 11 feet have been identified.

13:2 *And Jesus answering said unto him, Seest thou these great buildings? there shall not be left one stone upon another, that shall not be thrown down:* The words "seest thou these great buildings" can be read as a question (as the KJV takes it) or as a statement ("You see these great buildings"). While either reading is possible, the latter calls the audience's attention to the fact that the disciple is looking at the wrong thing. The word "seest" translates the same Greek verb (*blepō*) as "take heed," which is used so often in this chapter that it forms a refrain (13:5, 9, 23, 33). (Hence the use of "watching" in the New Rendition to echo the other uses, despite its awkwardness in English.) So in the context of the entire chapter, the word "seest" almost certainly has symbolic connotations as well: this disciple is focused on the physical grandeur of what he is seeing instead of what he should really be watching out for (compare 13:9, 14, 23, 35, 37).

In the phrase "there shall not be left," the negative is doubled in Greek, making Jesus' words particularly emphatic. Many manuscripts add the word "here" ("one stone here upon another"); it is probably the earlier reading, with the omission reflecting Luke 21:6.[98]

13:3 *And as he sat upon the mount of Olives over against the temple:* Sitting is the position of the authoritative teacher, a role Jesus assumes in this chapter. Once again, symbolically significant "stage directions" make it clear that Jesus is "against" the temple. As is common in Mark, narrative markers foreshadow and reinforce discourse. Because this is the position from which Jesus will deliver the discourse that composes the rest of this chapter—his longest discourse in the entire text—the overarching setting for chapter 13 is "against the temple." The language also echoes Jesus being "against the treasury" (12:41) and thus implies a causal link between the widow's experience and Jesus' words against the temple.

The reference to the Mount of Olives may echo the text of Ezekiel (Ezek. 9–11), where God's glory departs the temple and goes to the Mount of Olives. In Zechariah 14, it is prophesied that redemption will come from

---

97. Stein, *Mark*, 588.
98. Metzger, *Textual Commentary*, 94.

the Mount of Olives, which, in Mark's context, implies that Jesus—not the temple sacrifices—will be the source of that redemption.

Peter and James and John and Andrew asked him privately: Their question follows a well-established pattern in Mark (4:10; 7:17; 10:10) where the disciples privately ask Jesus for more clarification when they do not understand what he has taught publicly.

13:4 *Tell us, when shall these things be? and what shall be the sign when all these things shall be fulfilled?:* It is likely the word "us" connotes that the disciples want Jesus to tell them (that is, the inner circle of disciples) about the coming signs but that they do not want Jesus to teach everybody these things; this makes Jesus' statement at the end of this discourse "and what I say unto you I say unto all" (13:37) a rebuke.

As mentioned in the "Overview of Chapter 13" above, ambiguous language such as "these things" makes this chapter tricky to interpret. Jesus has referred to the destruction of the temple, but the disciples ask when "these things"—in the plural—will be. It is most unlikely that "these things" could refer to the destruction of the temple itself (as the plural form would make no sense) or only to the end times (because nothing would have prompted that question—they do not know what Jesus will say in the rest of this chapter). These disciples apparently think that the destruction of the temple will occur at the same time as the end of the world (an idea that Jesus will correct later; see the Notes on 13:4), and thus they ask two questions about that end: when it will be and what signs will precede it. Thus one major function of Jesus' speech in this chapter is to separate these two events so that the disciples will understand that the end of the temple is not the end of the world.

Sign seeking does not appear to be a problem for Mark (see the Notes on 8:11); Jesus does not rebuke them for asking for a sign.

This chapter contains many allusions to Daniel; the first question asked in this verse may echo Daniel 12:6–7, which asks how long certain events will take.

Analysis

It is likely that leaving the temple is an enacted parable of Jesus' rejection of the temple (perhaps also echoing Ezekiel 10, where God's spirit leaves the temple before it is destroyed), prompted by the corruption evident in the widow's support of the institution when the law of Moses mandated that the temple support her.

The disciples would not have been new to the sight of the temple, so interpreters who read their comment about the stones as the reflection of awestruck tourists are missing the mark. Rather, it is likely that Mark's early audiences would have laughed at how preposterous this praise of the temple is in light of Jesus' recent experiences in the temple and, in particular, his enacted parable of its coming destruction (see the Notes on 11:12–14). And there is an ironic contrast between this disciple's awe at the buildings and the fact that even a scribe was able to recognize that the commandments were of more worth than the temple's sacrificial system (12:33). Finally, Jesus' proclamation that the widow's meager offering was worth more than all the other gifts—gifts that would have constituted the wealth of the temple and funded its operation—implies that the great buildings are not quite as great as the widow's two small coins.[99] So in context, the awe for the temple expressed here suggests that this disciple does not understand what Jesus has been teaching in the last few chapters; rather, he is focusing on outward appearances while ignoring inward corruption. The most charitable reading is that the disciple's comment reflects that he is beginning to understand Jesus' critique of the temple but is unable to reconcile it with some HB passages that imply that the temple will stand forever (Ps. 48:8–9, 12–14); implicit in that belief is the notion that the sacrificial system at the core of temple worship would also stand forever, thus eliding the need for Jesus' atoning act.

The prophecy of the destruction of the temple is the immediate result of Jesus' experience in the temple, specifically of the treatment of the poor widow; the chapter division may mislead the audience if they ignore the link between the widow's story and Jesus' exit from the temple. It may have better reflected Mark's intention to begin this chapter with 13:3, since that would have emphasized that Jesus' pronouncement concerning the destruction of the temple is the last thing that he says in the temple before he leaves and thus the last words he says publicly in the text. This placement lends added weight to his words. For an ancient audience, a prophecy of the temple's destruction would have immediately raised the question of how sins could be forgiven if the temple's sacrificial system ceases to function. So to place Jesus' prophecy of destruction as the final words of his public ministry is to raise the question to which his suffering and death are the answer.

---

99. John Paul Heil, "The Narrative Strategy and Pragmatics of the Temple Theme in Mark," *Catholic Biblical Quarterly* 59, no. 1 (1997): 89.

There are competing strands of thought in the HB regarding the temple, with some texts intimating that the temple will stand forever and others prophesying of its destruction (1 Kgs. 9:8; Micah 3:12; Jer. 26:18). Jesus' words place him within the latter tradition, but with a distinction: prophecies of the temple's destruction are normally conditional ("if you do not repent") but Jesus does not mention any way to avoid the coming calamity. He is speaking at a moment when the opportunity for repentance has passed; his experience within the temple—particularly with the widow— has led to this point.

In the ancient world, it was believed that in order for a temple to be destroyed, the god whom it honored would have had to have abandoned it.[100] Thus, this prophecy of the destruction of the temple strengthens the case that Jesus' leaving the temple in 13:1 was symbolic: he is the God leaving the temple—and leaving it to its destruction. And because Jesus' words are spoken publicly, his statement about the coming destruction of the temple is likely one of the proximate causes of his death.

Many sources contemporaneous with Mark predicted the destruction of the temple, so in this respect Jesus' statement was not unusual. However, his prophecy that not one stone would be left upon another is startling given that some of these stones weighed over five hundred tons. Whether Jesus' words were literally fulfilled—and whether they were intended to be read literally in the first place—is a matter of some debate. On the one hand, the destruction of the temple by the Romans in 70 CE was so extensive that virtually all of these enormous stones were, in fact, displaced. On the other hand, some stones are still one upon another to this very day, forming what is now commonly called the Western Wall.[101] But these stones were originally part of a retaining wall and not the temple proper, so to some interpreters they do not count as temple stones. Yet others claim that the use of the word "buildings" instead of "temple" means that Jesus was referring to the entire temple complex, and thus his words were not literally fulfilled. If one concludes, as appears to be more likely, that Jesus' words were not literally fulfilled, then they might be:

1. *Hyperbolic.* This would fit the pattern of hyperbole in Mark and suggest the immense devastation that did indeed occur.[102]

---

100. John S. Kloppenborg, "*Evocatio Deorum* and the Date of Mark," *Journal of Biblical Literature* 124, no. 3 (2005): 441.

101. Collins, "Apocalyptic Rhetoric," 22.

102. Collins, "Apocalyptic Rhetoric," 22.

2. *Referential.* Options include:

  a. See the section "Relationship to Other Stories in Mark" after the Notes on 14:9 concerning the idea that 11–14:9 replicates the procedure for the treatment of a leprous house as outlined in Leviticus 14, but with the temple as the leprous house. In that reading, the reference here to "one stone upon another" echoes the language from Leviticus 14:45 used for disassembling a hopelessly leprous house stone by stone. The point is to suggest that the temple is as corrupt as a leprous house.

  b. 2 Samuel 17:13 describes Israel destroying its enemy's city so that not even one "small stone" will be left. Perhaps this language was a common way to express the threat of complete destruction.

  c. Haggai 2:15 describes the construction of the temple, when one stone was laid upon another, using very similar language in the LXX to what is here in Mark. Jesus' language might then suggest the inverse: the destruction of the temple will be precisely the opposite of its construction.

Regardless, Mark has structured the narrative to encourage the audience to believe this prophecy of the temple's destruction, despite the grandeur of the temple and despite the fact that the prophecy is not fulfilled within the narrative itself: this prophecy (as well as the others in chapter 13) is sandwiched between 11:1–7 and 14:12–16, both of which contain prophecies made by Jesus that are quickly fulfilled within the narrative. This structure encourages the audience to believe in Jesus' prophetic ability. In this context, Jesus' point is that despite the temple's physical grandeur, it is still subject to complete destruction. Given the probable date of Mark's Gospel, it is likely that most of the audience heard the Gospel after the destruction of the temple, when they knew that Jesus' prediction was accurate (even if hyperbolic or echoing HB texts) despite its incredible claims.

With the reference to stones, this passage picks up the theme of the Psalm 118 quotation that Jesus spoke after the parable of the wicked tenants (12:10–11; compare Ps. 118:22–23). The fact that there will not be left one stone upon another indicates a need to rebuild, and now it can commence with Jesus, the previously rejected stone who is the new cornerstone. Given the central role of the temple in the remission of sins, profound Atonement theology lies beneath this prophecy of the destruction of the temple when it is read in light of the parable of the wicked tenants. The physical stones of the temple, enabling the sacrificial system for forgiveness of sins, will be replaced with the cornerstone of Jesus' body, sacrificed for sins.

JESUS TEACHES ABOUT THE DESTRUCTION OF THE TEMPLE (13:5–31)

Greek Text

5 ὁ δὲ Ἰησοῦς ἤρξατο λέγειν αὐτοῖς· Βλέπετε μή τις ὑμᾶς πλανήσῃ· 6 πολλοὶ ἐλεύσονται ἐπὶ τῷ ὀνόματί μου λέγοντες ὅτι Ἐγώ εἰμι, καὶ πολλοὺς πλανήσουσιν. 7 ὅταν δὲ ἀκούσητε πολέμους καὶ ἀκοὰς πολέμων, μὴ θροεῖσθε· δεῖ γενέσθαι, ἀλλ᾽ οὔπω τὸ τέλος. 8 ἐγερθήσεται γὰρ ἔθνος ἐπ᾽ ἔθνος καὶ βασιλεία ἐπὶ βασιλείαν, ἔσονται σεισμοὶ κατὰ τόπους, ἔσονται λιμοί· ἀρχὴ ὠδίνων ταῦτα.

9 βλέπετε δὲ ὑμεῖς ἑαυτούς· παραδώσουσιν ὑμᾶς εἰς συνέδρια καὶ εἰς συναγωγὰς δαρήσεσθε καὶ ἐπὶ ἡγεμόνων καὶ βασιλέων σταθήσεσθε ἕνεκεν ἐμοῦ εἰς μαρτύριον αὐτοῖς. 10 καὶ εἰς πάντα τὰ ἔθνη πρῶτον δεῖ κηρυχθῆναι τὸ εὐαγγέλιον. 11 καὶ ὅταν ἄγωσιν ὑμᾶς παραδιδόντες, μὴ προμεριμνᾶτε τί λαλήσητε, ἀλλ᾽ ὃ ἐὰν δοθῇ ὑμῖν ἐν ἐκείνῃ τῇ ὥρᾳ τοῦτο λαλεῖτε, οὐ γάρ ἐστε ὑμεῖς οἱ λαλοῦντες ἀλλὰ τὸ πνεῦμα τὸ ἅγιον. 12 καὶ παραδώσει ἀδελφὸς ἀδελφὸν εἰς θάνατον καὶ πατὴρ τέκνον, καὶ ἐπαναστήσονται τέκνα ἐπὶ γονεῖς καὶ θανατώσουσιν αὐτούς· 13 καὶ ἔσεσθε μισούμενοι ὑπὸ πάντων διὰ τὸ ὄνομά μου. ὁ δὲ ὑπομείνας εἰς τέλος οὗτος σωθήσεται.

14 Ὅταν δὲ ἴδητε τὸ βδέλυγμα τῆς ἐρημώσεως ἑστηκότα ὅπου οὐ δεῖ, ὁ ἀναγινώσκων νοείτω, τότε οἱ ἐν τῇ Ἰουδαίᾳ φευγέτωσαν εἰς τὰ ὄρη, 15 ὁ ἐπὶ τοῦ δώματος μὴ καταβάτω μηδὲ εἰσελθάτω τι ἆραι ἐκ τῆς οἰκίας αὐτοῦ, 16 καὶ ὁ εἰς τὸν ἀγρὸν μὴ ἐπιστρεψάτω εἰς τὰ ὀπίσω ἆραι τὸ ἱμάτιον αὐτοῦ. 17 οὐαὶ δὲ ταῖς ἐν γαστρὶ ἐχούσαις καὶ ταῖς θηλαζούσαις ἐν ἐκείναις ταῖς ἡμέραις. 18 προσεύχεσθε δὲ ἵνα μὴ γένηται χειμῶνος· 19 ἔσονται γὰρ αἱ ἡμέραι ἐκεῖναι θλῖψις οἵα οὐ γέγονεν τοιαύτη ἀπ᾽ ἀρχῆς κτίσεως ἣν ἔκτισεν ὁ θεὸς ἕως τοῦ νῦν καὶ οὐ μὴ γένηται. 20 καὶ εἰ μὴ ἐκολόβωσεν κύριος τὰς ἡμέρας, οὐκ ἂν ἐσώθη πᾶσα σάρξ. ἀλλὰ διὰ τοὺς ἐκλεκτοὺς οὓς ἐξελέξατο ἐκολόβωσεν τὰς ἡμέρας. 21 καὶ τότε ἐάν τις ὑμῖν εἴπῃ· Ἴδε ὧδε ὁ χριστός, Ἴδε ἐκεῖ, μὴ πιστεύετε· 22 ἐγερθήσονται γὰρ ψευδόχριστοι καὶ ψευδοπροφῆται καὶ δώσουσιν σημεῖα καὶ τέρατα πρὸς τὸ ἀποπλανᾶν εἰ δυνατὸν τοὺς ἐκλεκτούς· 23 ὑμεῖς δὲ βλέπετε· προείρηκα ὑμῖν πάντα.

24 Ἀλλὰ ἐν ἐκείναις ταῖς ἡμέραις μετὰ τὴν θλῖψιν ἐκείνην ὁ ἥλιος σκοτισθήσεται, καὶ ἡ σελήνη οὐ δώσει τὸ φέγγος αὐτῆς, 25 καὶ οἱ ἀστέρες ἔσονται ἐκ τοῦ οὐρανοῦ πίπτοντες, καὶ αἱ δυνάμεις αἱ ἐν τοῖς οὐρανοῖς σαλευθήσονται. 26 καὶ τότε ὄψονται τὸν υἱὸν τοῦ ἀνθρώπου ἐρχόμενον ἐν νεφέλαις μετὰ δυνάμεως πολλῆς καὶ δόξης· 27 καὶ τότε ἀποστελεῖ τοὺς ἀγγέλους καὶ ἐπισυνάξει τοὺς ἐκλεκτοὺς ἐκ τῶν τεσσάρων ἀνέμων ἀπ᾽ ἄκρου γῆς ἕως ἄκρου οὐρανοῦ.

28 Ἀπὸ δὲ τῆς συκῆς μάθετε τὴν παραβολήν· ὅταν ἤδη ὁ κλάδος αὐτῆς ἁπαλὸς γένηται καὶ ἐκφύῃ τὰ φύλλα, γινώσκετε ὅτι ἐγγὺς τὸ θέρος ἐστίν· 29 οὕτως καὶ ὑμεῖς, ὅταν ἴδητε ταῦτα γινόμενα, γινώσκετε ὅτι ἐγγύς ἐστιν ἐπὶ θύραις. 30 ἀμὴν λέγω ὑμῖν ὅτι οὐ μὴ παρέλθῃ ἡ γενεὰ αὕτη μέχρις οὗ ταῦτα πάντα γένηται. 31 ὁ οὐρανὸς καὶ ἡ γῆ παρελεύσονται, οἱ δὲ λόγοι μου οὐ μὴ παρελεύσονται. [SBLGNT]

King James Version

5 And Jesus answering them began to say, Take heed lest any man deceive you: 6 For many shall come in my name, saying, I am Christ; and shall deceive many. 7 And when ye shall hear of wars and rumours of wars, be ye not troubled: for such things must needs be; but the end shall not be yet. 8 For nation shall rise against nation, and kingdom against kingdom: and there shall be earthquakes in divers places, and there shall be famines and troubles: these are the beginnings of sorrows.

9 But take heed to yourselves: for they shall deliver you up to councils; and in the synagogues ye shall be beaten: and ye shall be brought before rulers and kings for my sake, for a testimony against them. 10 And the gospel must first be published among all nations. 11 But when they shall lead you, and deliver you up, take no thought beforehand what ye shall speak, neither do ye premeditate: but whatsoever shall be given you in that hour, that speak ye: for it is not ye that speak, but the Holy Ghost. 12 Now the brother shall betray the brother to death, and the father the son; and children shall rise up against their parents, and shall cause them to be put to death. 13 And ye shall be hated of all men for my name's sake: but he that shall endure unto the end, the same shall be saved.

14 But when ye shall see the abomination of desolation, spoken of by Daniel the prophet, standing where it ought not, (let him that readeth understand,) then let them that be in Judaea flee to the mountains: 15 And let him that is on the housetop not go down into the

New Rendition

5 But Jesus began to say to them, "Watch, so that no one misleads you. 6 Many will come in my name, saying, 'I am [he],' and they will mislead many people. 7 And when you hear of wars and reports of wars, do not be alarmed—it must be. But the end is not yet. 8 For nation will rise up against nation, and kingdom against kingdom. There will be earthquakes in [various] places. There will be famines. These are the beginning of labor pains.

9 "But watch yourselves: they will hand you over to courts and in synagogue councils. You will be beaten. And you will be brought before governors and kings because of me, for a witness to them. 10 And first, the good news must be proclaimed to all nations. 11 And when they lead you away, handing you over, do not worry ahead of time about what you should say, but say what is given you at that time—for you are not speaking, but the Holy Spirit. 12 And sibling will hand over sibling to death, and a father his child. And children will rise up against parents and will put them to death. 13 And you will be hated by all because of my name. But the one having persevered to the end will be saved.

14 "But when you observe 'the detestable [thing] causing desolation' standing where he should not (let the one reading understand), then those people in Judea should flee into the mountains. 15 But the one on the roof must not come down to go inside to take anything out of the house. 16 And the one in the field should not return to the things left behind to take clothing.

house, neither enter therein, to take any thing out of his house: 16 And let him that is in the field not turn back again for to take up his garment. 17 But woe to them that are with child, and to them that give suck in those days! 18 And pray ye that your flight be not in the winter. 19 For in those days shall be affliction, such as was not from the beginning of the creation which God created unto this time, neither shall be. 20 And except that the Lord had shortened those days, no flesh should be saved: but for the elect's sake, whom he hath chosen, he hath shortened the days. 21 And then if any man shall say to you, Lo, here is Christ; or, lo, he is there; believe him not: 22 For false Christs and false prophets shall rise, and shall shew signs and wonders, to seduce, if it were possible, even the elect. 23 But take ye heed: behold, I have foretold you all things.

24 But in those days, after that tribulation, the sun shall be darkened, and the moon shall not give her light, 25 And the stars of heaven shall fall, and the powers that are in heaven shall be shaken. 26 And then shall they see the Son of man coming in the clouds with great power and glory. 27 And then shall he send his angels, and shall gather together his elect from the four winds, from the uttermost part of the earth to the uttermost part of heaven. 28 Now learn a parable of the fig tree; When her branch is yet tender, and putteth forth leaves, ye know that summer is near: 29 So ye in like manner, when ye shall see these things come to pass, know that it is nigh, even at the doors. 30 Verily I say unto you, that this generation shall not pass, till all these things be

17 But alas to those who are pregnant and to those who are breastfeeding in those days! 18 And pray that it may not be during the winter. 19 For there will be suffering in those days such as there has never been from the beginning of creation, which God created, until now and never shall be [again]. 20 And if the Lord had not limited the days, no one would have been saved. But on account of the elect whom he chose, he has limited the days. 21 And if anyone says to you, 'Look! Here is the anointed one!' or 'Look! There!' you should not trust it. 22 For there will arise fake anointed ones and fake prophets, and they will give signs and wonders to deceive, if possible, the elect. 23 But you—watch! I have told you all things ahead of time.

24 "But in those days, after that suffering, the sun will be darkened, and the moon will not give its light. 25 And the stars will be falling out of the sky/heaven, and the powers that are in the skies/heavens will be shaken. 26 And then they will see 'the son of man coming in clouds,' with great power and glory. 27 And then he will send the angels/messengers, and he will gather together his elect from the four winds—from the end of earth to the end of the sky/heaven.

28 "But you know the parable of the fig tree: when the branch is already tender and has put out its leaves, you know that summer is near. 29 So when you see these things happen, know that it/he is near, at the door. 30 Amen, I say to you, this generation will not pass away until these things all have taken place. 31 The sky/heaven and the earth will pass away, but my words will not pass away.

done. 31 Heaven and earth shall pass
away: but my words shall not pass away.

Notes

13:5 *And Jesus answering them began to say, Take heed lest any man deceive you:* The fact that this verse—despite the KJV translation—uses "but" (Greek: *de*) and not "and" (Greek: *kai*) suggests that Mark wanted to be clear that Jesus is not (at least, initially) going to answer their question. It is extremely significant that Jesus instead begins by warning the disciples how easy it is to be deceived on this topic. Jesus, in speaking to his inner circle of four disciples, warns them about the potential for even them to be misled.

"Take heed" translates a Greek verb (*blepō*) that means to watch or to be careful. It is a keyword in this text, repeated in 13:5, 9, 23, and 33.

13:6 *For many shall come in my name, saying, I am Christ; and shall deceive many:* "In my name" can be understood two different ways:

1. It refers to those who come with legitimate authority (hence "in my name") but are nonetheless misled and misleading.

2. It refers to pretenders who claim the name of the Messiah for themselves (thus "I am Christ"). Not only do they claim to be Christ, but the Greek title for the self-identification of God (*ego eimi*; see the Notes on 6:50) is used here, indicating that they are not just claiming to be the Messiah but also claiming to be God. There were in fact several self-proclaimed Messiahs in the years leading up to the Jewish War.

The key point here, as 13:7 ("but the end shall not be yet") will make clear, is that the false claimants are *not* a sign. Rather, their activities explain why the disciples are to be alert—hence the word "for" at the beginning of 13:6.

13:7 *And when ye shall hear of wars and rumours of wars, be ye not troubled:* Prophetic statements not to fear reports of current events are also found in the HB (Jer. 51:46; Dan. 11:44–12:1). The point is that reports of war do not require action on the part of the disciples; in the context of the Jewish War, this is significant counsel since there was a sense of patriotic duty to fight.

It is likely that this verse is closely linked to the previous verse because the messianic pretenders are also revolutionaries who view the Messiah as one who will throw off Roman rule. There were in fact several such figures during the 60s.

for such things must needs be; but the end shall not be yet: Jesus explains that the false teachers and reports of war are not to be interpreted as signs. Rather, these are things that simply happen.

13:8 *For nation shall rise against nation, and kingdom against king-dom:* Similar language is found in Isaiah 19:2.

and there shall be earthquakes in divers places, and there shall be fam-ines and troubles: The phrase "and troubles" is not in many of the ancient manuscripts; perhaps it was accidentally omitted as a scribe's eye skipped from one word to the next, but it is more likely that it was added to make the teaching more generally applicable.[103] Several HB texts suggest that God's judgment is made manifest in earthquakes (Micah 1:3–4; Hab. 3:6) and famines (Jer. 11:22).

these are the beginnings of sorrows: Many manuscripts have the singu-lar form of "beginning,"[104] which is probably original and may have been changed since a plural form seemed a better fit for the list in this verse, which includes multiple items.

The word translated as "sorrows" means labor pains, implying a birth metaphor here. Labor pains are used frequently as an image of God's judg-ment in the HB (Isa. 13:8; 26:17; Micah 4:9; Jer. 4:31; Hosea 13:13). Impor-tantly, "with this metaphor, Mark prepares the reader for a discourse not of revolutionary triumphalism, but of suffering and tribulation."[105] Jesus asks his audience to think about a quintessentially female experience and to see the world through female eyes as they work to comprehend the events surrounding the destruction of the temple and their own experience of persecution.

13:9 *But take heed to yourselves: for they shall deliver you up to coun-cils; and in the synagogues ye shall be beaten:* Notice the adversative ("but") beginning the verse. The point is that the disciples should not be obsessed with current events but rather are to watch themselves. They don't need to be concerned with earthquakes and wars but with their own ministries. Jesus does not teach them how to avoid persecution; he pre-pares them for its inevitability.

Because the predictions of Jesus' suffering and death include the idea that he would be delivered up (9:31; 10:33), the implication is that the dis-ciples will have the same experience as Jesus; this is part of what it means to follow him.

"Councils" refers to local Jewish councils.[106]

---

103. Metzger, *Textual Commentary,* 95.
104. Collins, *Mark,* 591 note d.
105. Myers, *Binding the Strong Man,* 333.
106. The precedent for these councils stems from Deut. 25:1–3.

and ye shall be brought before rulers and kings for my sake, for a testimony against them: These are Gentile, not Jewish, rulers. It is significant that Jesus is predicting that his disciples, common fishermen, would speak before kings.

"Against them" could be translated as "for them" (see 1:44 and the Notes there; the only other use of this phrase in Mark is in 6:11, where "against them" is the only possible meaning). The next verse, with its reference to proclaiming the gospel, encourages reading this phrase as "for them," although either reading is possible.

Note the emphasis here: Jesus responds to their request for signs with, instead, a prophecy of their ministry and persecution. Instead of thinking about signs, they are supposed to be testifying, even under difficult circumstances.

13:10 *And the gospel must first be published among all nations:* In this context, "all nations" would have referred to the then-known world. Thus, Mark's audience would have interpreted this as a fulfilled prophecy (Rom. 16:26; Col. 1:6) and regarded it as a signal that Jesus' words are trustworthy.

Note how closely the idea of preaching the gospel is linked to persecution: it is literally surrounded by references to persecution (13:9, 11) resulting from discipleship.

13:11 *But when they shall lead you, and deliver you up, take no thought beforehand what ye shall speak, neither do ye premeditate:* It would have been terrifying for average folks such as Jesus' disciples to contemplate speaking in front of religious and civic leaders. And yet Jesus tells them not to worry about it. Interestingly, his advice "is contrary to the method of the rhetorical tradition, which stressed careful preparation that would present the appearance of spontaneity."[107] It also places the disciples into the role of prophets, since in the HB, prophets were given similar advice not to be concerned with their speaking ability (Ex. 4:10; Jer. 1:6).

but whatsoever shall be given you in that hour, that speak ye: for it is not ye that speak, but the Holy Ghost: "Shall be given you" is a divine passive, indicating that it is God who is giving them what they will speak. The idea that the Spirit inspired speakers is well-attested in the HB (Num. 24:2–3; 1 Kgs. 22:24; 2 Sam. 23:2) and is also mentioned elsewhere in Mark (12:35–37).

It is possible that this verse is the fulfillment of the promise John the Baptist made (see 1:8) that Jesus would baptize with the Holy Spirit. It is

---

107. Whitney Shiner, *Proclaiming the Gospel: First-Century Performance of Mark* (Harrisburg, Pa.: Trinity Press International, 2003), 109.

also another data point suggesting that in Mark, one is either possessed by a demonic spirit or by the Holy Spirit. Here, it is not the speaker herself who will be speaking but rather the Holy Spirit who will be speaking through her body, analogous to the case of demonic possession, where the unclean spirit speaks through the body (1:24; 5:7).

In context, the relationship between this verse and 13:10 implies that God takes the terrible circumstance of persecution and, through the Holy Spirit acting through the disciple, is able to transform the occasion into one where the gospel is preached.

13:12 *Now the brother shall betray the brother to death, and the father the son; and children shall rise up against their parents, and shall cause them to be put to death:* This verse extends opposition to the disciples from the religious and the political realms into the familial realm, and because "brother [was] a common early Christian term for 'fellow Christian,'"[108] this verse could also picture conflict within the community of disciples.

This verse also places the disciples into a role that Jesus has occupied since his own family opposed his ministry (see Notes on 3:21, 32). It reflects a sentiment similar to that found in Micah 7:6 and Isaiah 19:2. It also represents an inversion of Malachi 4:5–6: instead of the hearts of parents and children turning to one another, they will instead betray each other.

13:13 *And ye shall be hated of all men for my name's sake:* While "all" might be hyperbolic, it is also fitting, given that Jesus has just explained how they will be persecuted in the religious, civil, and familial spheres.

but *he that shall endure unto the end, the same shall be saved:* The "but" at the beginning of this line makes a contrast between the hatred the disciples will experience and the salvation that will come later.

This line is difficult to interpret because "end" could refer to the end of the disciple's life or the end of times, and "saved" can refer to saving one's life or to spiritual salvation, thus yielding four possible interpretations for this saying.

13:14 *But when ye shall see the abomination of desolation, spoken of by Daniel the prophet, standing where it ought not:* The phrase "spoken of by Daniel the prophet" is not in the best ancient manuscripts and was likely added later to explain the preceding phrase, which is in fact a quotation from Daniel 11:31. Note that "it is generally held that the phrase in Daniel referred to the heathen altar erected in the Temple in Jerusalem by

---

108. Marcus, *Mark 8–16*, 888.

Antiochus Epiphanes in 168 BCE."[109] The precise nature of the abomination of desolation is disputed, but "it came to symbolize an unspeakable affront to the sanctity of God's house and to God himself."[110]

The word "standing" is masculine, but it refers to "the abomination of desolation," which is neuter. This may be a grammatical error, but it is more likely that the abomination is personified as male. It may refer to the fact that in Daniel, the abomination was probably a statue of Zeus (and hence male) and/or that in Mark, the abomination is a male. Hence the New Rendition's translation of "standing where he should not."

The basic idea of "the abomination of desolation" is something so offensive (abominable) that it causes the temple to be abandoned and thus left desolate. There are several possibilities for its specific identity:

1. Pontius Pilate attempted to have Roman soldiers enter Jerusalem with their standards. This reading is rather unlikely since it probably happened in the late 20s and was ultimately unsuccessful.

2. In 40 CE, Caligula attempted to put a statue of himself in the temple; he failed because he was assassinated. This reading is somewhat unlikely since it is a full thirty years before the destruction of the temple.

3. In 67/8 CE, the Zealots entered the temple and took control of it, including investing a "mock high priest to carry out a travesty of temple ritual."[111] While certainty is impossible, this event is the most likely candidate for the fulfillment of this prophecy in Mark. The timing is right since the event is shortly before the destruction of the temple but early enough that there was still time to flee the city. Further, the Zealots prohibited Gentiles from entering the temple complex, which could have been viewed as an abomination (especially in light of 11:17).

4. In 70 CE, Titus entered the temple and the Holy of Holies. His soldiers put their standards (which would have had images of gods on them) in the temple courtyard and offered sacrifices to them. However, the counsel to flee at the end of this verse makes little sense as a response to Titus's actions, since it would have been too late to flee at that point.[112] Further, this event is not a sign of the coming destruction of the temple but rather the beginning of the destruction itself.

5. There are many resonances between the book of Jeremiah and this section of Mark's Gospel:

   a. LXX Jeremiah 7:10 and 30 use the word "abomination" (Greek *bdelugma*) and LXX Jeremiah 7:34 contains the word "desolate" (Greek *erēmōsis*).

---

109. Bratcher and Nida, *Translator's Handbook*, 405.

110. Evans, *Mark 8:27–16:20*, 318.

111. France, *Gospel of Mark*, 525.

112. Kloppenborg, "*Evocatio Deorum* and the Date of Mark," 424.

b. Jesus condemned the temple as a "den of thieves" (11:17), borrowing the phrase "den of robbers" from Jeremiah 7:11.

c. The parable of the wicked tenants (12:2–5) echoes Jeremiah 7:25–26.

d. The commands regarding sacrifice in 12:28–34 may allude to Jeremiah 7:21–22.

e. The prediction of the destruction of the temple (13:2) echoes Jeremiah 7:34, especially since the verb translated as "destroy" in 13:2 is only used three times in Mark (13:2; 14:58; 15:29–30) and always with reference to the temple. It is the same verb as is found in LXX Jeremiah 7:34, where it refers to destruction stemming from the violation of the covenant.

These parallels are significant because in Jeremiah 7:30, the people are warned that housing their abominations in the temple will lead to their land becoming desolate. In this case, there is not one specific referent for the abomination; rather, it refers to all manner of covenant violations.[113] If Mark intended to echo Jeremiah's usage, it suggests that the "abomination" is not one particular historical event but rather a pattern of covenant betrayal. (Of course, it could also be both.) However, one weakness of this reading is that covenant violation in general would be a difficult sign to discern.

This line signals a major turning point in Jesus' speech, as the following pattern suggests:

13:7: when you hear . . . do not be afraid
13:11: when you are . . . do not worry
13:14: when you see . . . let them flee

Jesus has previously addressed two situations that might cause alarm, but he told the disciples not to worry or take action. But 13:14 is different: when they see the abomination, they are to take action by fleeing. The similarity in the structure between the three verses highlights the difference in content of the final verse.

(let him that readeth understand): This unusual line clearly breaks "the fourth wall" by addressing the audience directly (compare 13:37). It is unclear whether this line should be understood as (1) something Jesus said to Peter, James,[114] John, and Andrew, (2) something Mark said to the audience, or (3) a later marginal note that was accidentally incorporated into the text. This is a command (not the granting of permission): the one who is reading must understand.

This command is addressed to the audience, in the third person singular (he or she who reads is commanded to understand). While it perhaps

---

113. Robert S. Snow, "Let the Reader Understand: Mark's Use of Jeremiah 7 in Mark 13:14," *Bulletin for Biblical Research* 21, no. 4 (2011): 476.

114. See the Notes on 1:19.

sounds unusual to modern ears, it is possible that this refers to the audience who "hears" Mark, despite the fact that they are not technically "readers"[115] (compare 2:25; 12:10; 12:26), especially if they are thought of as "readers" of the HB. Similarly, the singular (as opposed to plural) form might have been used to refer to the entire audience: "Mark uses the singular 'addressee' in order to include each reader or listener individually."[116]

It is difficult to determine precisely what it was that the audience is commanded to understand:

1. The audience needs to catch the allusion to the text of Daniel. However, Mark contains many HB references, and it is difficult to determine why this one would merit special signaling.

2. The audience should be aware that the grammatical mismatch in the preceding line was deliberate—to emphasize that the abomination is a person—and not a simple grammatical error that should be corrected. It is even possible that the line was not supposed to be read out loud to Mark's audience but rather was a note to the audience of the Gospel not to correct the grammatical mismatch when performing or copying the text.

3. The abomination is not a reference to Caligula, which might have been a logical assumption for the audience to make, knowing that Jesus taught roughly a decade before that time.

4. Much as 4:9 and 23 contain admonitions to hear, this line serves to emphasize the importance of Jesus' message and the need to understand it properly. This interpretation fits well with the other similarities between chapters 4 and 13 (see the section "Relationship to Chapter 4" after the Notes on 13:37). In this reading, this line is a general reminder to think about what Jesus is teaching: "the primary verb that the author uses here occurs in two other Markan settings . . . In both cases Jesus is addressing his disciples and upbraiding them for their failure to grasp his teaching and the significance of his miracles."

then let them that be in Judæa flee to the mountains: "Let them . . . flee" is imperative, so this is a command. Fleeing to the mountains as a refuge is a common image in the HB (Gen. 19:17; Judg. 6:2; Jer. 16:16; Zech. 14:5). However, the city of Jerusalem is also regarded as a refuge, so the idea of fleeing from Jerusalem would have been shocking, especially in light of the ancient idea that safety could be found in a walled city. This verse may have reminded Mark's audiences of the situation of Sodom and Gomorrah, where the corruption of a city necessitated flight, yet picturing the holy city Jerusalem in the role of Sodom and Gomorrah would surely

---

115. Shiner, *Proclaiming the Gospel,* 177.
116. Shiner, *Proclaiming the Gospel,* 177.

have shocked contemporary sensibilities.[117] Additionally, in the context of Jewish patriotism and the resulting belief in the importance of defending Jerusalem and the temple, the idea that Jesus' disciples would flee would have been surprising.

Because an action is commanded here, it makes clear that the sign that the disciples had asked for has been given: it is the abomination of desolation that is the sign that the destruction of the temple will soon happen.

It is possible to view this verse less literally and more symbolically—a reading that perhaps better fits the other symbols in the chapter. In a symbolic reading, Jesus would not be commanding literal flight but rather commanding his disciples to seek the mountains—the paradigmatic meeting place between humans and God—at the moment when the temple ceases to function as that meeting place. This reading would be symbolic of the break between Jesus' followers and other Jews.

13:15 *And let him that is on the housetop not go down into the house, neither enter therein, to take any thing out of his house:* Roofs were flat and were used as extra living space, so being on a roof was not unusual. The KJV is confusing here: obviously, the person was permitted to go down from the roof; what was prohibited was taking time to enter the house to gather possessions.

13:16 *And let him that is in the field not turn back again for to take up his garment:* The cloak (KJV: "garment") served as a blanket at night, so counsel to leave without it emphasizes the need to flee instantly.

The admonition not to turn back is very similar to the language used for Lot's wife (Gen. 19) and may have furthered the surprising connection between Sodom and Jerusalem.

13:17 *But woe to them that are with child, and to them that give suck in those days!:* Jesus' concern here is for the unique experiences of vulnerable women and their children, especially when read in the context of "the ancient wartime practice of disemboweling pregnant women and murdering their infant or unborn children."[118] The dangers that war posed to women and children is a common HB theme (Amos 1:13; 2 Kgs. 8:12; Ps. 137:9; Isa. 13:16; Hosea 10:14; Nahum 3:10. Hosea 9:11–16 is particularly relevant).

---

117. Such shock tactics were also used by prophets like Isaiah (Isa. 1:9–11) and Jeremiah (Jer. 23:14).

118. Brant James Pitre, "Blessing the Barren and Warning the Fecund: Jesus' Message for Women Concerning Pregnancy and Childbirth," *Journal for the Study of the New Testament* 81 (March 2001): 69.

13:18 *And pray ye that your flight be not in the winter:* The word translated as "winter" could also be understood as "storms." Either way, the idea is the same: winter rains could lead to floods that would make flight difficult if not impossible.

Interestingly, this verse seems to suggest that while it is not possible to stop this catastrophic event, it might be possible through prayer to alter the timing to make enduring it as easy as possible.

13:19 *For in those days shall be affliction, such as was not from the beginning of the creation which God created unto this time, neither shall be:* This verse is probably hyperbole: while the suffering of the Jewish War was immense, it is difficult to believe that it was worse than Jesus' own suffering or all subsequent historical events. The use of similar language in the HB (Ex. 9:18; Dan. 12:1) suggests that perhaps Jesus was echoing those texts. Thus, these are likely "stock expressions for unparalleled suffering, and are not to be pressed literally."[119]

13:20 *And except that the Lord had shortened those days, no flesh should be saved:* Once again, the word "saved" can refer to saving human life or to salvation, although the former is more likely in this case. The language here is likely hyperbolic or metaphorical, since obviously humans in other parts of the world—even in other parts of the Roman empire—would have survived the Jewish War without divine intervention. Similar language in the LXX (LXX Jer. 12:12; LXX Ezek. 21:4) suggests that the reference to all flesh being destroyed is intended to echo those texts and not to be taken literally. One implication of this verse is that God is indeed acting to preserve some people, despite the devastation.

but for the elect's sake, whom he hath chosen, he hath shortened the days: In the first century, "elect" referred to the chosen community during an end-times event.

13:21 *And then if any man shall say to you, Lo, here is Christ; or, lo, he is there; believe him not:* This is not a false Christ but rather a false disciple.

13:22 *For false Christs and false prophets shall rise:* Jesus fits within the tradition that warned of false prophets (Deut. 13:1–5).

and shall shew signs and wonders: Mark 13:21–22 returns to the theme of false preachers that was mentioned previously in 13:5–6. Thus, Jesus' teachings in this section about the coming destruction of the temple are literally surrounded by warnings about false teachers. This is particularly significant given that what the disciples had asked for was a sign, but what

---

119. France, *Gospel of Mark,* 527.

Jesus emphasizes is that most of the signs that they will see will come from people who would (inadvertently or deliberately) deceive them. In a move typical of Markan irony, the disciples have asked for signs and Jesus warns them about false signs.

to seduce, if it were possible, even the elect: Commentators debate over whether "if it were possible" implies that Jesus does not know if they will be seduced; compare the Notes on 13:32.

The possibility that the elect might be seduced is significant: it implies that the elect are not beyond being tempted and falling into temptation.

13:23 *But take ye heed: behold, I have foretold you all things:* The word "ye" is not necessary and is therefore emphatic. This verse continues the refrain (compare 13:5, 9, and 33) of admonitions to watch (KJV: "take ye heed") that undergird the chapter.

Obviously, Jesus has not told them "all" things; this hyperbolic language signals that he has told them all that they need to know about the sign of the destruction of the temple.

13:24 *But in those days, after that tribulation, the sun shall be darkened, and the moon shall not give her light:* Jesus does not give the referent for "in those days," and thus scholars debate whether 13:24–27 describes the time of the destruction of Jerusalem and the temple or the end times.

13:25 *And the stars of heaven shall fall, and the powers that are in heaven shall be shaken:* It is debatable whether Mark's audience would have understood this as a prediction of a physical event. Rather, their interpretation would have been shaped by the perspective of many HB passages where celestial bodies served as symbols for the nations: "such cosmic terminology is frequently used to describe divine interventions via 'normal' historical events and means [as] is evident from such passages as Isa. 13:9–11 [the destruction of Babylon by the Medes], Jer. 4:23–28; 15:9 [the destruction of Jerusalem by Babylon]; Ezek. 32:7–8 [the destruction of Pharaoh's army]."[120] Other NT passages show that this type of language was not taken literally.[121]

Again, it is difficult to determine whether this language refers to the time of the destruction of the temple/Jerusalem, or to the last days, or to both, or even as a more general depiction of God's intervention into and control of human affairs. Because this kind of language is used in the HB

---

120. Stein, *Mark*, 612.

121. See Acts 2:19–20, where Peter states that a prophecy from Joel involving celestial signs was fulfilled on the Day of Pentecost.

for the destruction of gentile powers, if it is here applied to the destruction of Jerusalem and the temple, that would be a significant inversion of the tradition.

13:26 *And then shall they see the Son of man coming in the clouds with great power and glory:* In the HB, clouds often accompany God's visits to the people (Ex. 34:5; Lev. 16:2; Num. 11:25; Dan. 7:13). So Jesus is aligned here with the God of the HB. The entire phrase "Son of man coming in the clouds" quotes Daniel 7:13. However, in the Danielic context, it is a picture of the Son coming to heaven—not to earth—and being enthroned in the heavens. This leaves Mark's audience with two options:

1. The Markan context of the phrase is the same, which means that this verse refers to Jesus being enthroned in the heavens, not the Second Coming. This reading meshes well with the recent reference to the end of earthly kingdoms (symbolized by stars falling and powers being shaken in 13:25), because their loss would happen as the Son of Man was given full authority over the kingdom after his ascent into heaven. It also makes good sense of 13:30, which states that "this generation" would know of these events and thus points to Jesus' enthronement and not his return to earth (but see the Notes on 13:30). But one challenge to this reading is that it ties the coming of the Son of Man in power to the destruction of the temple—not to his death, Resurrection, or Ascension, which are surely more likely candidates for his coming in power. On the other hand, Jesus prophesies the destruction of the temple in this chapter. Thus, the destruction validates him. In that sense, the destruction of the temple could be interpreted as *seeing* the coming of the Son of Man in power. That is, Jesus has previously (at his death, Resurrection, or Ascension) come in power, but people do not see that power until the temple is destroyed.

2. The Markan context is different, despite the use of the quote. In Mark's context, the image is inverted so that the Son is coming to earth, and thus the verse pictures the Second Coming. One difficulty with this reading is reconciling it with 13:30's intimation that this would happen during the lifetime of the current generation (but see the Notes on 13:30).

This is an important interpretive decision since it determines whether the previous verses refer to the end of the temple or to the Second Coming. However, each option presents difficulties. Further complicating the situation here is the word "they" at the beginning of the verse: To whom does this pronoun refer? In Daniel, it is the visionary who sees the Son coming. But in the immediate Markan context, the antecedent for "they" would be the celestial bodies—symbolizing political powers—who see the Son coming. So perhaps there is a sense in which the failing political powers "see" the coming of the Son—if not literally, then they "see" it through their own defeats.

See also the Notes on 14:62.

13:27 *And then shall he send his angels, and shall gather together his elect from the four winds, from the uttermost part of the earth to the uttermost part of heaven:* The word "his" means that the angels are the possession of the Son of Man—an idea that is truly "astounding"[122] because it means that Jesus, not God, is in control of the angels.

"Gather" is singular, so it is the Son of Man who is gathering together, not the angels. Deuteronomy 30:4 speaks of a future time of gathering.

The event to which the interpreter ascribes the coming of the Son of Man in 13:26 (see the Notes on that verse) will determine the referent for the gathering in 13:27:

1. If the coming of the Son of Man is linked to the destruction of the temple, then the gathering in this verse would refer to missionary efforts after that time. Given that "angels" could be translated as "messengers," this would make sense and would prophetically describe missionary work. Since the idea of gathering was often linked to gathering to the temple in the HB, the idea that gathering would continue after the destruction of the temple would have been an important solace to early Christians.

2. If the coming of the Son of Man is interpreted to refer to the Second Coming, then the gathering would refer to the gathering of the faithful after that event.

13:28 *Now learn a parable of the fig tree; When her branch is yet tender, and putteth forth leaves, ye know that summer is near:* The "tender" branch results from the sap, which rises in the spring, making the branch more pliable than it would have been in the winter. There were fig trees on the Mount of Olives that would have been in leaf during Passover time, so Jesus is speaking about something that his disciples can see in their immediate vicinity. It echoes the beginning of the chapter, which included references to the temple stones that they could see.

The verb translated as "know" can be imperative ("I command you to know") or indicative ("you [already] know"), but the latter is more likely in this case. (In the next verse, the opposite is the case.)[123]

13:29 *So ye in like manner, when ye shall see these things come to pass, know that it is nigh, even at the doors:* Although it is plural, "these things" appears to refer to the abomination in the temple. Jesus emphasizes that, just as the presence of leaves on a fig tree signals summer, the abomination signals that the temple is about to be destroyed.

---

122. Evans, *Mark 8:27–16:20*, 329.

123. J. Lyle Story, "The Parable of the Budding Fig Tree (Mark 13:28–31)," *American Theological Inquiry* 4, no. 1 (2011): 91.

The word "door" (*thyra*) is very similar in Greek to the word "harvest" (*therismos*),[124] so the image of a door—while seemingly out of place in an agricultural metaphor—probably would have made a pleasant play on words for Mark's audience.

13:30 *Verily I say unto you:* See the Notes on 3:28.

that this generation shall not pass, till all these things be done: This verse is, as is much of chapter 13, difficult to interpret. The referent for "this generation" has several possibilities; options include:

1. The logical reading is that it refers to people alive when Jesus is speaking, meaning that this generation would pass by forty years later (which is the biblical reckoning of a generation). The similarities between this verses and 9:1 suggest this reading. Approximately forty years after Jesus' life ended, the temple was destroyed. This literal interpretation of "this generation" leads to two options:

   a. "These things" refers to the destruction of the temple, which did in fact occur about forty years after the events recorded in the Gospel of Mark.

   b. "These things" refers to the return of the Son of Man, and so this is an inaccurate prediction. Latter-day Saint theology does not have room for a false prophecy by the mortal Jesus (especially in light of the fact that 13:30 is bounded by reference to its trustworthiness; see the Notes on 13:31), but it could accommodate an incorrect record of his words. There are other problems with this reading: it does not make good sense of 13:32, since if the Son of Man does not know when he will return, then he cannot know that it will be while this generation is still alive. It is also difficult to determine why early Christians would have performed the Gospel of Mark if it contained a failed prophecy. To sum, it is unlikely, based on the context, that "these things" refers to the return of the Son of Man.[125]

2. "This generation" refers to those who oppose Jesus.[126] In this reading, Jesus' point is that these opponents will exist until the Son of Man comes. This reading fits well with the idea of the false messengers mentioned repeatedly in this chapter. The larger point of this passage would be that only Jesus is a

---

124. Story, "Parable of the Budding Fig Tree," 92.

125. Many Latter-day Saint readers have seen in this verse an allusion to the Apostle John, who is described in Restoration scripture as being granted immortality until Jesus' Second Coming (3 Ne. 28:6; D&C 7). While such a reading would make it possible to interpret "these things" in this verse as referring to the coming of the Son of Man, this option never would have occurred to Mark's original audience (who, to our knowledge, had no such tradition about John), and the other contextual concerns mentioned here still make it unlikely that "these things" refers to Jesus' return in Mark.

126. Compare 8:12, 38; 9:19; 13:30; see also Tolbert, *Sowing the Gospel*, 268.

trustworthy messenger—something that the next verse and the "verily, I say unto you" that begins this verse would emphasize.

3. As with some other moments in this chapter (compare 13:2, 13, 20, 23), this is a hyperbolic reference to the closeness of the event with no intention of chronological precision.

13:31 *Heaven and earth shall pass away: but my words shall not pass away:* This verse is probably an example of dialectical negation, which means that Jesus is not suggesting that heaven and earth will pass away but rather that it is more likely that heaven and earth would pass away than it is that his words will pass away.

This verse and the "verily" statement in the previous verse literally surround Jesus' statement that "these things" will be done. This structure emphasizes the truthfulness of Jesus' saying. There is also a contrast between "this generation"—which will pass away—and Jesus' words, which will not pass away. The point, again, is that his words are reliable.

Several HB texts emphasize the reliability and permanence of God's words (compare Ps. 102:25–27 and Isa. 40:7–8). Thus, this statement aligns Jesus with the God of the Bible.

Analysis

When the disciples ask Jesus for signs, the first thing Jesus does is warn them about their propensity to be misled. This is extremely significant. The refrain "take heed" shows that Jesus' main message is that the disciples' response to the end of the temple and the end of the world should be, primarily, watchfulness. The disciples ask about signs and timing, but Jesus instead emphasizes that watchfulness—not knowledge of times and signs—should be their key concern. Jesus refers to false prophets—not that they are a sign of the times but rather that his disciples need to watch out for them. Further, while many interpreters have assumed that much of this chapter applies to the last days, it is far more likely that the bulk of it refers to the time of the destruction of the temple.[127]

The reference to the fig tree in leaf would have called to mind the enacted parable of the withered fig tree in 11:12–14 and 20–21. Much as Jesus cursed the tree because its leaves without fruit signaled corruption, in this chapter, the leaves signal that the time for the destruction of the temple has

---

127. Latter-day Saint readers often interpret this material in light of Joseph Smith—Matthew, which does seem to be more oriented toward a discussion of the last days. However, this is not how Mark presents the material and not how early audiences would have interpreted it.

come. At the same time, the reference to a blooming fig tree hints at the potential for the return of the temple. These two stories of the fig trees effectively bookend Jesus' experience in the temple and serve as narrative markers of this section of the text. This is one more reason to believe that 13:5–29 concerns the destruction of the temple and not the return of the Son of Man at the last days.

Jesus Teaches about the Future (13:32–37)

Greek Text

32 Περὶ δὲ τῆς ἡμέρας ἐκείνης ἢ τῆς ὥρας οὐδεὶς οἶδεν, οὐδὲ οἱ ἄγγελοι ἐν οὐρανῷ οὐδὲ ὁ υἱός, εἰ μὴ ὁ πατήρ. 33 βλέπετε ἀγρυπνεῖτε, οὐκ οἴδατε γὰρ πότε ὁ καιρός ἐστιν· 34 ὡς ἄνθρωπος ἀπόδημος ἀφεὶς τὴν οἰκίαν αὐτοῦ καὶ δοὺς τοῖς δούλοις αὐτοῦ τὴν ἐξουσίαν, ἑκάστῳ τὸ ἔργον αὐτοῦ, καὶ τῷ θυρωρῷ ἐνετείλατο ἵνα γρηγορῇ. 35 γρηγορεῖτε οὖν, οὐκ οἴδατε γὰρ πότε ὁ κύριος τῆς οἰκίας ἔρχεται, ἢ ὀψὲ ἢ μεσονύκτιον ἢ ἀλεκτοροφωνίας ἢ πρωΐ, 36 μὴ ἐλθὼν ἐξαίφνης εὕρῃ ὑμᾶς καθεύδοντας· 37 ὃ δὲ ὑμῖν λέγω πᾶσιν λέγω· γρηγορεῖτε. [SBLGNT]

King James Version

32 But of that day and that hour knoweth no man, no, not the angels which are in heaven, neither the Son, but the Father. 33 Take ye heed, watch and pray: for ye know not when the time is. 34 For the Son of man is as a man taking a far journey, who left his house, and gave authority to his servants, and to every man his work, and commanded the porter to watch. 35 Watch ye therefore: for ye know not when the master of the house cometh, at even, or at midnight, or at the cockcrowing, or in the morning: 36 Lest coming suddenly he find you sleeping. 37 And what I say unto you I say unto all, Watch.

New Rendition

32 "But of the day or the hour no one knows—not even the angels in the sky/heaven, nor the Son—except the Father. 33 Watch; keep alert, for you do not know when the appointed time is. 34 It is like a person going on a journey, having left his house, having given his slaves authority, [assigning] to each his work. And he commanded the doorkeeper to be on guard. 35 Therefore be on guard, for you do not know when the master of the house will come—in the evening or at midnight or when the rooster crows or in the morning—36 or else, having come suddenly, he should find you sleeping. 37 And what I say to you, I say to all: be on guard!"

Notes

13:32 *But of that day and that hour knoweth no man, no, not the angels which are in heaven, neither the Son, but the Father:* The adversative ("but") that begins this sentence suggests a contrast. The reference to the (singular) day and hour (as opposed to the "these things" in 13:31) also implies a contrast. The third way in which a contrast is implied is in the content: 13:31 gave a time frame for "these things," but this verse indicates that no one knows the day and hour. These sharp contrasts lead to the conclusion that Jesus changes topic here; 13:5–31 concerns the destruction of the temple while this verse and the rest of the chapter discuss the return of the Son of Man. Enmeshed with the reference to the abomination of desolation in Daniel 12:11–13 is extensive emphasis on the precise timing of the event. Obviously, this disavowal of knowledge of the timing of the return of the Son stands in stark contrast to that passage, further suggesting that this verse refers not to the destruction of the temple but to a different event. Now, and unlike with the destruction of the temple, "vigilance, not calculation, is required."[128]

There is an interesting juxtaposition of this verse—which points to a gap in Jesus' knowledge—and the last, which posited that Jesus' words were more stable than heaven and earth. Often overlooked is the implication that the Father does know the time and that the return of the Son will in fact happen.

13:33 *Take ye heed, watch and pray: for ye know not when the time is:* Jesus again emphasizes that the disciples will not know the time of his return because there is no need for them to know (despite the disciples' question that launched this chapter). Rather, what is needed is that they pay attention and pray, neither of which require them to know the timing of events.

13:34 *For the Son of man is as a man taking a far journey, who left his house, and gave authority to his servants, and to every man his work, and commanded the porter to watch:* The porter's role is to guard the door. A string of participles ("taking," "leaving" [KJV: "left"], "giving" [KJV: "gave"]) followed by the main verb "commanded" emphasizes this point. This is, in the world of the parable, the role of Jesus' disciples: to watch the door. (This is not the same verb that forms the refrain of "watching" throughout this chapter, but the sentiment is the same.) The disciples' role is to protect the owner's property while he is away; 13:37 extends this role to the entire community.

---

128. Lane, *Gospel according to Mark,* 482.

13:35 *Watch ye therefore: for ye know not when the master of the house cometh, at even, or at midnight, or at the cockcrowing, or in the morning:* These four time references demarcate the four watches of the night (as calculated by the Romans; the Jews had a system with three watches, although there might be some mixing of the systems here as the Romans numbered the watches while the Jews named them[129]). The idea of returning from a journey at midnight would have been most unusual: ancient people did not travel in the middle of the night for obvious safety reasons. The mismatch between the timing of the return in the parable and the customary expectation would have caused this element of the story to stand out to Mark's audience; it strongly emphasized the idea that the Son of Man might very well return at the least expected time possible.

Relationship to Chapters 14–15. The account of Jesus' Passion makes reference to the same four watches of the night mentioned here: the last supper happens during the evening (14:17), Peter's denial is linked to midnight (14:30, 72) and cock crow (14:72), and Jesus is given to the Romans at dawn (15:1). The repeated admonitions from Jesus to the disciples to watch also link chapter 13 to the story of the Passion. It is possible that the similarities are merely coincidental, but it is also possible that Jesus' Passion is the first test of discipleship in difficult circumstances for which the counsel in chapter 13 was meant to prepare the disciples.

13:36 *Lest coming suddenly he find you sleeping:* Watching is not understood as watching for signs but rather as watching in preparation to complete one's assignment—something that can't be done while sleeping. It is possible that this verse should be understood in relation to the disciples' inability to stay awake in Gethsemane (see the Notes on 14:34–41).

13:37 *And what I say unto you I say unto all, Watch:* This verse extends the audience of this chapter: these teachings are not merely for Peter, James,[130] John, and Andrew, but for all who would listen to Jesus and to Mark. Similar to 13:14, this line appears to breach the "fourth wall" by speaking directly to the audience and inviting them to act as disciples act. The same verb translated as "watch" here was used to describe the porter's role in 13:34.

---

129. Troy W. Martin, "Watch During the Watches (Mark 13:35)," *Journal of Biblical Literature* 120, no. 4 (2001): 694.

130. See the Notes on 1:19.

This moment constitutes Jesus' final preaching at the end of his longest discourse in Mark: "It is probably not insignificant that the last word before the narrative of the passion is, 'Watch!'"[131]

Allusions to Zechariah 14. The Olivet Discourse has the following echoes of Zechariah 14:

1. The Lord stands on the Mount of Olives.

2. Reference to earthquakes and wars.

3. Command to flee to the mountains when a specified event occurs.

4. Reference to the coming of the Lord God.

5. Reference to the ceasing of celestial lights.

6. Zechariah 14:7 reads: "It will happen in one day (a day known to the Lord); not in the day or the night, but in the evening there will be light" (NET). This intersects with chapter 13 in two interesting ways:

   a. The idea that Jesus does not know when this day will be appears to distance him from the role of the Lord, which is counter to the usual impulse in Mark.

   b. The timing of this event at evening differs from the unknown timing mentioned in 13:35.

7. Reference to the season when these events will happen.

The promise in Zechariah that "the Lord shall be king over all the earth" (Zech. 14:9) is the key point of connection between the two passages. Mark's echoes of the language from Zechariah point to Jesus' reign.

Relationship to Chapter 4. In general, Mark emphasizes Jesus' actions and not his teachings. The two great exceptions to this pattern occur in chapter 4 and chapter 13. Both of these chapters pause the action by presenting relatively lengthy teachings. Both chapters also share the following points of contact:

1. The use of parables and symbolic speech to teach about the nature of the kingdom. In particular, "the use of the growth of a plant as a metaphor for the manifestation of the dominion of God is one of several links between 13:28–29 and the parabolic discourse in 4:1–34."[132]

2. Both chapters are directed (at least in part) to the inner circle of disciples.

3. Both chapters involve teachings in special locations: a boat in chapter 4 and the mountain in chapter 13.

---

131. Focant, *Gospel according to Mark*, 555.
132. Marcus, *Mark 8–16*, 910.

4. Both chapters are deeply concerned with the concept of discipleship.

5. Chapter 4 contains admonitions to hear and chapter 13 contains admonitions to watch. Both function to signal the key characteristic of discipleship as active engagement by paying attention.

Note: See the section "Relationship to Other Stories in Mark" after the Notes on 14:9 for a discussion of how chapter 13 fits into the larger structure of the text.

Analysis

While certainty is unobtainable, it seems most likely that 13:32 signals a shift: before it, Jesus was speaking about the destruction of the temple but then pivots to the time of the return of the Son of Man. It should be clear from Jesus' statement that he does not know the timing of his own return, so this chapter would not and could not give signs of that return.

There is a tension between the two parables in this chapter: on the one hand, the parable of the fig tree indicates that there will be distinct signs that one should look toward in order to anticipate events. On the other hand, the parable of the servants suggests constant vigilance because there is no sign of the coming event. The tension between these two parables is best dissolved by seeing the parable of the fig tree as the conclusion to Jesus' teachings about the destruction of the temple/Jerusalem but the parable of the doorkeeper as concerning the return of the Son of Man.

As mentioned in the overview of chapter 13, it is by far the most difficult chapter to interpret due to ambiguous words and phrases. While it seems fairly clear that 13:2 refers to the destruction of the temple and 13:32 refers to the return of the Son of Man, it is debated precisely where in between 13:2 and 13:32 the topic changes from the destruction of the temple to the return of the Son. This commentary takes the position that virtually the entire chapter concerns the destruction of the temple, with the return of the Son not mentioned until 13:32. Jesus provides a sign (the abomination of desolation, which refers to the Zealot presence in the temple; see the Notes on 13:14) for the former but none for the latter. In this chapter, Jesus corrects the disciples' assumption that the end of the temple was the end of the world by separating the two events. Obviously, other interpretations of this chapter are plausible, but this one seems to best take the various data points into account. While modern readers often view this chapter as presenting "the signs of the times," in its Markan context, Jesus' words serve to tamp down a focus on these signs and substitute instead an attitude of watchfulness and an emphasis on discipleship, even under persecution. They are counseled not to believe most of what they hear from those who teach and prophesy about the future. It is an excellent example of Markan irony that when Jesus is asked for signs, the bulk of his response is that those who announce signs are false teachers and that things they might interpret as signs (such as wars) are not signs.

The theme of discipleship has frequently been overlooked in this chapter, despite a general recognition that discipleship is the signal theme of Mark's Gospel. It is significant that what might initially appear to be typical apocalyptic material (such as reference to wars and earthquakes) instead becomes warnings to the disciples not to focus on these things. Jesus warns that they can expect to be persecuted as they preach the gospel. In some senses, this chapter is "the passion of the community"[133] because it teaches about the suffering that disciples will undergo.

The theme of discipleship is emphasized by the stories that surround this chapter: the story of the widow who gives all that she has (12:41–44) and the story of the woman who does all she can for Jesus (14:3–9). These stories show what the self-sacrificial discipleship of which Jesus speaks in this chapter looks like in practice.

This emphasis on discipleship, although rarely appreciated, is a key part of this chapter—more important than the supposed apocalyptic elements that are more frequently noted: "Instead of giving signs, which only false christs and false prophets do, the Jesus of Mark teaches his disciples to live in incertitude as to times and seasons."[134]

Many interpreters view chapter 13 as showing Jesus' eschatological focus, but when closely read, it is more accurate to say that chapter 13 is anti-eschatological: it discourages the desire for signs, announces that things normally regarded as signs (false prophets, wars, etc.) are in fact not signs, and instead counsels calm watching. They are not to watch for signs; rather, they are to watch their own behavior.

---

133. Focant, *Gospel according to Mark,* 520.
134. Focant, *Gospel according to Mark,* 522.

Approaching Death
(Chapter 14)

Overview

The term "Passion narrative" describes the accounts of Jesus' suffering and death. (The word "Passion" derives from the Latin for "suffering," *passio*.) It has become a cliché to describe the Gospel of Mark as a Passion narrative with a lengthy introduction,[1] but it is true that Mark grants disproportionate attention to the final days of Jesus' life: about one-third of the text is devoted to Jesus' final week and about one-sixth to his final day.

It is possible that the stories of the Passion narrative were told together before the Gospel of Mark existed, so the audience of Mark may have been familiar with this portion of the text (or, at least, a similar version of it).

Chapter 14, a lengthy chapter, contains some of the most significant events of Jesus' story: his anointing, his observance of Passover, his prayer in Gethsemane, his abandonment and betrayal by his disciples, his arrest, his examination by the Jewish leaders, and Peter's denial of him. While other options are possible, this is one proposal for the structure of this chapter:

---

1. Martin Kahler, *The So-called Historical Jesus and the Historic, Biblical Christ* (Philadelphia: Fortress Press, 1964), 80 n. 11.

1. Death Plot (14:1–2)

2.   Anointing of Jesus (14:3–9)

3. Death Plot (14:10–11)

4. Preparation for the Passover (14:12–16)

5. Prediction of Judas' Betrayal (14:17–21)

6.   Last Supper (14:22–25)

7. Prediction of Peter's Betrayal (14:26–31)

8. Preparation for the Passion (Gethsemane Prayer and Arrest) (14:32–52)

9. Peter Positioned to Deny Jesus (14:53–54)

10.   Jesus Is Examined by the Sanhedrin (14:55–65)

11. Peter Denies Jesus (14:66–72)

The chapter has three main scenes (14:3–9, 22–25, and 55–65); each one focuses on the topic of Jesus' identity (see the Notes on those verses). Each is bracketed by reference to the betrayal of Jesus (14:1–2, 10–11, 17–21, 26–31, 53–54, 66–72). In between the three main scenes are scenes focused on the idea of preparation: first, the preparation for the Passover (14:12–16) and then preparation for the Passion (including Jesus' arrest; 14:32–52). The framing of the Gethsemane scene in Mark's story of Jesus is noteworthy: it prepares Jesus to face his suffering and death, and it should have prepared the disciples as well.

In this structure, the main theme of chapter 14 concerns Jesus' identity. Significantly, each foray into that identity (14:3–9, 22–25, 55–65) is literally surrounded by the idea of betraying Jesus. The fact that he is betrayed, abandoned, and denied by those closest to him is crucial to the way Mark presents Jesus and a significant component of Mark's message about discipleship.

The anointing of Jesus (14:3–9) is the centerpiece of Mark's Gospel, thus it is given extensive analysis in the commentary. For Mark, this is where Jesus literally becomes the Christ, since "Christ" means the Anointed One. It is not coincidental that Jesus says that wherever the gospel is preached, the story of his anointing must be told.

Jesus Is Anointed (14:1–11)

Greek Text

1 Ἦν δὲ τὸ πάσχα καὶ τὰ ἄζυμα μετὰ δύο ἡμέρας. καὶ ἐζήτουν οἱ ἀρχιερεῖς καὶ οἱ γραμματεῖς πῶς αὐτὸν ἐν δόλῳ κρατήσαντες ἀποκτείνωσιν, 2 ἔλεγον γάρ· Μὴ ἐν τῇ ἑορτῇ, μήποτε ἔσται θόρυβος τοῦ λαοῦ.

3 Καὶ ὄντος αὐτοῦ ἐν Βηθανίᾳ ἐν τῇ οἰκίᾳ Σίμωνος τοῦ λεπροῦ κατακειμένου αὐτοῦ ἦλθεν γυνὴ ἔχουσα ἀλάβαστρον μύρου νάρδου πιστικῆς πολυτελοῦς· συντρίψασα τὴν ἀλάβαστρον κατέχεεν αὐτοῦ τῆς κεφαλῆς. 4 ἦσαν δέ τινες ἀγανακτοῦντες πρὸς ἑαυτούς· Εἰς τί ἡ ἀπώλεια αὕτη τοῦ μύρου γέγονεν; 5 ἠδύνατο γὰρ τοῦτο τὸ μύρον πραθῆναι ἐπάνω δηναρίων τριακοσίων καὶ δοθῆναι τοῖς πτωχοῖς· καὶ ἐνεβριμῶντο αὐτῇ. 6 ὁ δὲ Ἰησοῦς εἶπεν· Ἄφετε αὐτήν· τί αὐτῇ κόπους παρέχετε; καλὸν ἔργον ἠργάσατο ἐν ἐμοί· 7 πάντοτε γὰρ τοὺς πτωχοὺς ἔχετε μεθ᾽ ἑαυτῶν, καὶ ὅταν θέλητε δύνασθε αὐτοῖς εὖ ποιῆσαι, ἐμὲ δὲ οὐ πάντοτε ἔχετε· 8 ὃ ἔσχεν ἐποίησεν, προέλαβεν μυρίσαι τὸ σῶμά μου εἰς τὸν ἐνταφιασμόν. 9 ἀμὴν δὲ λέγω ὑμῖν, ὅπου ἐὰν κηρυχθῇ τὸ εὐαγγέλιον εἰς ὅλον τὸν κόσμον, καὶ ὃ ἐποίησεν αὕτη λαληθήσεται εἰς μνημόσυνον αὐτῆς.

10 Καὶ Ἰούδας Ἰσκαριὼθ ὁ εἷς τῶν δώδεκα ἀπῆλθεν πρὸς τοὺς ἀρχιερεῖς ἵνα αὐτὸν παραδοῖ αὐτοῖς. 11 οἱ δὲ ἀκούσαντες ἐχάρησαν καὶ ἐπηγγείλαντο αὐτῷ ἀργύριον δοῦναι. καὶ ἐζήτει πῶς αὐτὸν εὐκαίρως παραδοῖ. [SBLGNT]

King James Version

1 After two days was the feast of the passover, and of unleavened bread: and the chief priests and the scribes sought how they might take him by craft, and put him to death. 2 But they said, Not on the feast day, lest there be an uproar of the people.

3 And being in Bethany in the house of Simon the leper, as he sat at meat, there came a woman having an alabaster box of ointment of spikenard very precious; and she brake the box, and poured it on his head. 4 And there were some that had indignation within themselves, and said, Why was this waste of the ointment made? 5 For it might have been sold for more than three hundred pence, and have been given to the poor.

New Rendition

1 It would be the Passover, and the feast of unleavened bread, after two days. And the chief priests and the scriptorians were looking for a way that they might kill him [after] having taken him by stealth. 2 For they were saying, "Not during the feast, or there will be a riot by the people."

3 And being in Bethany, in the house of Simon the leper, being reclined [at the table], there came a woman having an alabaster flask of expensive ointment of pure nard; having broken the alabaster flask, she poured it on his head. 4 But some were angry among themselves: "Why was this ointment wasted? 5 For this ointment could have been sold for more than a year's wages

And they murmured against her. 6 And Jesus said, Let her alone; why trouble ye her? she hath wrought a good work on me. 7 For ye have the poor with you always, and whensoever ye will ye may do them good: but me ye have not always. 8 She hath done what she could: she is come aforehand to anoint my body to the burying. 9 Verily I say unto you, Wheresoever this gospel shall be preached throughout the whole world, this also that she hath done shall be spoken of for a memorial of her.

10 And Judas Iscariot, one of the twelve, went unto the chief priests, to betray him unto them. 11 And when they heard it, they were glad, and promised to give him money. And he sought how he might conveniently betray him.

and [the money] have been given to the poor." And they were scolding her. 6 But Jesus said, "Leave her alone. Why do you bother her? She did a good work in me. 7 For 'you always have the poor with you,' and whenever you want to, you are able to do them good. But me you do not always have. 8 She did what she could: she came before the fact to anoint my body for burial. 9 Amen, I say to you: wherever the good news is proclaimed in the whole world, what she has done will also be told in memory of her."

10 And Judas Iscariot, the one of the Twelve, went away to the chief priests that he might betray Jesus to them. 11 And having heard, they rejoiced and promised to give him money. And he was looking for a good opportunity to betray him.

Notes

14:1 *After two days was the feast of the passover, and of unleavened bread:* In first-century Jewish time keeping, "after two days" meant what modern readers would consider to be the next day, so Mark is describing the day before Passover (Ex. 12), or the Wednesday of the final week of Jesus' life.

The word "Passover" in Mark is the transliteration of the Aramaic term for Passover. The Passover lamb was ritually sacrificed in the afternoon of the 14th day of the month of Nisan (which corresponds to March or April) and then eaten after sunset, which was the 15th of Nisan (since the new day began at sunset). The dates for the feast of unleavened bread were the 15th to the 21st of Nisan (Ex. 12:15–20). Originally, the Passover and the feast of unleavened bread were two separate celebrations, but they had merged into one before Jesus' time as a result of the proximity of their dates.

This verse is the first instance in Mark when a time reference can be linked to a specific date on the calendar; it contrasts with Mark's frequent use of the term "immediately." The specificity of this date would have signaled to the audience that something different—something extremely important—was about to happen. It is thus an ideal introduction to the Passion narrative in general and the anointing of Jesus in particular.

There is great irony in the celebration of Passover in Roman-occupied Jerusalem. The volatility of celebrating the liberation from a foreign power in a city controlled by a foreign power was not lost on the Romans, who recognized that rebellion was more likely during Passover.[2]

and the chief priests and the scribes sought how they might take him by craft, and put him to death: The audience has already learned of the plot to arrest Jesus (11:18; 12:12), so this is not new information. The only novel element is the idea of taking Jesus by stealth. It underlines Jesus' innocence.[3]

Because Jesus' prophecies of his death mentioned the role of these religious leaders (8:31; 10:33), the audience understands that Jesus is not losing control of events; rather, this is an illustration of his prophetic ability.

14:2 *But they said, Not on the feast day, lest there be an uproar of the people:* The concern is that the people assembled for Passover would riot (KJV: "uproar") if they knew that Jesus was arrested. This fear was not unreasonable: the Passover celebration swelled the population of Jerusalem to perhaps half a million people, and they were primed by the celebration itself to react to the oppressive behavior of a foreign power.

The concern with rioting implies that Jesus was popular with the crowd. There is a substantial difference between the leadership (who want Jesus arrested) and the people (who would riot if that happened). This distinction is important: it is not the case that "the Jews" were hostile to Jesus in Mark's Gospel; the opposition is limited to (some of) the Jewish leadership. The Jewish people supported Jesus to the point of making his arrest difficult.

Jesus will eventually be arrested during the Passover (14:43–53) but only because of Judas' betrayal.

14:3 *And being in Bethany in the house of Simon the leper, as he sat at meat:* During Jesus' time in Jerusalem, he retires to Bethany overnight and then returns to the city each day.

The reference to Simon "the leper" is surprising. Lepers were considered ritually unclean (Lev. 13), and as a result they were not permitted to mingle freely with others and certainly not to host meals in their homes. There are several possible explanations for why the meal is set in a leper's home:

1. Most interpreters assume that Simon had previously been healed, perhaps even by Jesus. Jesus has previously healed a leper (1:40–45), but since that

---

2. Josephus, *Antiquities* 14.2.1; 17.9.3; 20.5.3.
3. Heil, *Gospel of Mark as a Model for Action*, 274.

leper was not named it is rather unlikely that Mark's audience would have associated Simon the leper with that story.

2. Jesus has in the past eaten with people who were ritually unclean (2:16), so perhaps he was willing to eat in the home of a leper. If so, Jesus' willingness to take on uncleanness on the eve of Passover is a significant departure from Mosaic law (Num. 9:6–12).

3. Mark states that the meal was in Simon's home, which does not necessarily mean that Simon was present: he may have been away or even deceased.

4. Simon was a fairly common name, so Mark may not have intended to call attention to his leprosy but rather to distinguish him from Simon Peter. There may even be a contrast to Simon Peter, who might have been expected to arrange hospitality for Jesus.

5. Perhaps Simon the leper was known to Mark's early audiences and this is why Mark mentions his name (see the Notes on 15:21).

6. In 14:9, Jesus says that the anointing woman's story will be told worldwide, but her name is not included in the text. This is a classic example of Markan irony, heightened by way of contrast with the host of the meal, who plays no real role in the story but is nonetheless named.

Deciding between these options is difficult. Regardless, the reference to leprosy would have surprised—if not shocked—the audience with its implication of uncleanness. Further, lepers were regarded as the equivalent of the dead,[4] and so the reference primes the audience for the themes explored in this story: Jesus' later statement about his burial (14:8) garners new meaning if understood to have figuratively taken place in the realm of the dead. And if the leper had been healed, it is as if he had returned from the dead. Mark might be intentionally playing on the audience's inability to determine whether Simon is recovered in order to emphasize how life and death intertwine: the infected leper casts the pall of death while the audience's likely conclusion that the leper is healed suggests a return from the dead.

The word translated as "sat" implies that they were reclining on their sides. By Jesus' time, Greek custom had prevailed among Jews—at least among those who could afford reclining couches—so that festive meals (and perhaps other meals as well) were usually eaten while reclining.

there came a woman having an alabaster box of ointment of spikenard very precious: The word "came" implies that this woman is not a guest at the dinner; rather, she enters the home during the meal—which is unusual behavior.

---

4. Josephus, *Antiquities* 3.11.3.

The woman is not identified, which is ironic given that Jesus will later say that her story should be told wherever the gospel is preached. Her name-lessness makes her paradigmatic of a woman completely devoted to Jesus. She will receive more praise from Jesus than anyone else in this Gospel; her anonymity may be a necessary counterpart to this high praise.

The phrase "alabaster box" translates a Greek word that refers to a vial made of alabaster. It would have had a long, narrow neck. "Ointment" refers to a liquid oil while "spikenard" is the oil from the root of nard, a plant from India. Left untranslated in the KJV is the Greek word *pistikos*, whose meaning is uncertain (this is its only use in Mark), but possibilities include:

1. The oil is pure or unadulterated, which would suggest its value.
2. The word *pistikos* sounds similar to the word "pistachio" in Aramaic, so it is possible that it is describing the kind of oil used, although this seems to conflict with the idea that it is nard.
3. Perhaps Mark has transliterated the name of the plant into Greek, but this suffers from the same problem as option two above.

While certainty is not possible, it is clear that Mark's ample description of the ointment indicates its significance.

and she brake the box, and poured it on his head: Contra the KJV, this is not a box but a vial. She has snapped (KJV: "brake") the neck of the vial. Breaking the vial was not necessary. After all, there must have been an opening to put the oil into the vial in the first place; it would have had a stopper of some sort, perhaps wax or cloth. The breaking of the vial indicates that the woman is not preserving either the container or any oil for future use. And because broken vials were sometimes left in the tombs after corpses were anointed, the broken vial itself became a symbol for death (Eccl. 12:6; Jer. 13:12–14) and thus might have suggested that association for Mark's audience.

Four different verbs describe the woman's actions ("came," "having," "brake," and "poured") in this verse, while Jesus is passive.

There are many reasons for anointing in the biblical world: it could be a simple act of hospitality, the coronation of a king, the ordination of a priest, or the preparation of a body for burial (see the Analysis of 14:1–11).

14:4 *And there were some that had indignation within themselves, and said:* The "some" are not identified; they are presumably other diners at the meal and may or may not be disciples.

Why was this waste of the ointment made: The word "waste" (Greek: *apōleia*) could be translated as "destruction"; it is a cognate of the word for "destroy" (Greek: *apollumi*) used in the plot against Jesus' life (3:6; 11:18). The objectors believe the ointment to have been wasted, but Jesus' response will show that they are sorely mistaken: they only recognize the financial value of the ointment and not the symbolic value of the anointing. Their objection and Jesus' response to it point to a crucial symbolic meaning for the anointing; otherwise, its use would indeed have been a waste.

And yet, in an ironic sense, the woman has "destroyed" the oil—through an enacted parable of the destruction of Jesus' body, which she prophetically anticipates.

14:5 *For it might have been sold for more than three hundred pence, and have been given to the poor:* "Pence" translates the Greek word *dēnarion,* which was roughly one day's wage for a common worker,[5] so the ointment cost more than a year's wages. This is an incredibly large sum of money to spend on anointing oil. Further, the word translated as "more than" makes the oil of limitless value.

And they murmured against her: It is unclear whether this murmuring is internal to the group of objectors or whether they are speaking directly to the woman, but Jesus' command to leave her alone (see the next verse) probably implies the latter. In either case, this line emphasizes their complaint against her.

14:6 *And Jesus said, Let her alone; why trouble ye her? she hath wrought a good work on me:* Jesus does not permit their criticism of the anointing to stand unchallenged. The word "good" intimates moral goodness and is an important element in the story: a surprisingly large number of interpreters assume that the woman's anointing had no particular purpose to her, but Jesus would not have labeled her action as good if it had no motive or intent.

It is probably preferable to translate "in me" instead of "on me" since the Greek preposition *en* is used here. "In me" connotes the anointing affects Jesus in a profound and deeper sense than "on me" might suggest and is therefore more appropriate given the significant symbolism of the anointing (see the Notes on 14:8 on the symbolism of the anointing).

The story of Jesus' anointing shares vocabulary with the story of the Creation. The word "work" (Greek: *ergon*) is closely associated with God's work[6] in creation, suggesting that the anointing woman was doing the work of

---

5. Compare Matt. 20:2. Two hundred denarii would have been enough to feed five thousand people (see 6:37).

6. Sabin, *Reopening the Word,* 194.

God. God's work in the Creation is repeatedly described as "good" (Greek: *kalos*) (LXX Gen. 1:4, 10, 12, 18, 21, 25, 31), using the same Greek word that Jesus uses to describe the anointing woman's action and thus further suggesting a link between God and the anointing woman.

14:7 *For ye have the poor with you always:* Jesus' words allude to Deuteronomy 15:11, where the statement that the poor would always be with them is immediately followed by a command to help them. That text describes the practice of releasing debts every seventh year, which was designed to minimize economic inequality (Deut. 15:4). Deuteronomy focuses on the motivation for lending money—which should not be to gain wealth by accumulating interest but rather to assist someone in need— in light of the knowledge that the year of debt release is approaching; it asserts that one who refuses to lend money under these circumstances is sinful (Deut. 15:9–10). By referencing this text, Jesus intimates that the woman, although aware that his death is near and that she will not have her generosity repaid, still chose to give to him freely and thus honored the law. By contrast, those who object to the anointing are like those who do not lend money for fear of the impending debt release. The allusion to the Deuteronomy text might also contain an implicit criticism of the objectors' plan: selling the oil and giving the proceeds to the poor is not enough; what is required is a regular release of debts and a willingness to loan money even when the year of release is approaching.

and whensoever ye will ye may do them good: but me ye have not always: The word "me" is emphasized in this line.

The contrast is not between Jesus and the poor but rather between "whensoever" and "not always." In other words, the obligation to care for the poor is ongoing; one can always help the poor. But the opportunity to do a good work for Jesus in his mortal life is almost over. The objectors do not realize that this is a special time—the last few days of Jesus' mortal life—but the woman does recognize this, and she acts according to her prophetic foreknowledge. This line constitutes another prediction of Jesus' death.

14:8 *She hath done what she could:* This line is a classic example of Markan irony: it suggests that she did (only) what she was capable of doing. And yet, as the story suggests, what she was capable of doing was performing an anointing that explained Jesus' identity—not a minor feat by any measure.

Note: See also the discussion of the JST for 14:8 in appendix I: "The Joseph Smith Translation."

she is come aforehand to anoint my body to the burying: The use of "aforehand" affirms that the woman understood that Jesus was going to die soon. This is especially significant given the reaction to Jesus' prophecies of his coming death: the disciples have been told three times that Jesus will suffer and die, but they still struggle to understand what this means and sometimes actively reject his teachings. By contrast, the anointing woman understands that his death is near, and she responds appropriately.

The fact that this oil was extremely costly—which is emphasized in this story—suggests that something in addition to a standard burial anointing was intended.

14:9 ***Verily I say unto you:*** This phrase is used by Jesus to emphasize the truthfulness and importance of whatever follows it; see also the Notes on 3:28. It is significant that "Jesus' comment on the woman's prophetic anointing is his lengthiest and most positive pronouncement on the words or deeds of any person preserved by the evangelist Mark."[7]

Wheresoever this gospel shall be preached throughout the whole world: This verse points to the Resurrection: Jesus just mentioned his own death, and the preaching of the gospel presumes that his death is not the end of his relevance. It also prophesies the spread of the gospel to the entire world.

One can only imagine how Mark's audience would have reacted to hearing this line since they were, in the moment of hearing it, witnessing that this statement had come true: the gospel was being preached and the story of the anointing was being told to them.[8]

this also that she hath done shall be spoken of for a memorial of her: Both "preached" (in the previous line) and "spoken of" envision the oral presentation of the gospel (not the spread of a written text).

The word translated as "shall be spoken of" is in the future tense, so Jesus is indicating—either prophetically or as a commandment—that the anointing story will be told.

The term "memorial" is used in LXX Exodus for the way in which God remembers the people of Israel and the way in which the people are to remember God (Ex. 3:15; 12:14; 13:9; 28:12). If Mark's audience caught this allusion, it would have strongly emphasized the importance of the anointing by associating it with the biblical rituals of remembrance. It

7. Mary Ann Beavis, "Women as Models of Faith in Mark," *Biblical Theology Bulletin* 18, no. 1 (1988): 7.

8. John R. Donahue, *Are You the Christ? The Trial Narrative in the Gospel of Mark* (Missoula, Mont.: Society of Biblical Literature, 1973), 231.

would have suggested a dimension of covenant enactment or renewal to the woman's actions. The anointing would be taken as evidence of God's involvement with the people; the woman's act manifests this involvement by demonstrating the accessibility of God's power to all people who would use it to honor Jesus.

The phrase "for a memorial" is often found in funerary inscriptions. Its use here would then be ironic since the death in view is Jesus'—not the woman's. There might be a bit of Atonement theology at play, since she is the one garnering a memorial for an action related to his death. And to the extent that "for a memorial" evokes the thought of the woman's death in the minds of Mark's audience, Jesus is suggesting that his death is profoundly related to her death, an idea that also points to the Atonement.

Relationship to HB Texts. The story of Jesus' anointing in Mark gains nuance from its relationship to several different HB texts:

1. *Hannah* (1 Sam. 2). Hannah shares an important trait with the anointing woman. In Hannah's song of praise, she is the first regular Israelite to refer to the coming anointed one (1 Sam. 2:10).[9] It is significant that the first person in the HB to recognize the coming Messiah, as well as the first person in Mark's story of Jesus to recognize him, are both female.

2. *Samuel* (1 Sam. 10). The story of the anointing of Saul as king by the prophet Samuel forms a significant backdrop to Jesus' anointing in Mark. An allusion to Samuel's act of pouring oil on Saul's head would have signified to Mark's audience that Jesus was being anointed as a king. And given that 1 Samuel 9:15–16 shows the Lord telling Samuel whom to anoint (see also 1 Sam. 16:12), a comparison of these texts suggests that the anointing woman had a similar revelation regarding whom she should anoint. Although not in the KJV, the LXX (and most modern English translations) includes the following text at the end of 1 Samuel 10:1: "And you shall reign over the people of the Lord and you will save them from the hand of their enemies round about. And this shall be the sign to you that the Lord has anointed you to be prince over his heritage." Next, a very specific prophecy of instruction is given and immediately fulfilled (1 Sam. 10:2–9). A similar story follows Jesus' anointing: Jesus tells some of his disciples about arrangements for the Last Supper, and they find everything to be as he predicted (14:13–16). In both cases, the quickly filled prophecy verifies the authenticity of the anointing.

---

9. In Hannah's case, the coming anointed one was the Israelite king. See also Julie M. Smith, "'I Will Sing to the Lord': Women's Songs in the Scriptures," *Dialogue: A Journal of Mormon Thought* 45 (Fall 2012): 56–69.

3. *Psalm 23.* Psalm 23 has several interesting resonances with the anointing story, particularly in its LXX iteration (LXX Ps. 22). Both texts involve the anointing of the head at a meal in the presence of enemies. Psalm 23:5 mentions preparing a table for a meal, which resonates with the next story in Mark, where two disciples prepare the Passover meal for Jesus. In the context of the entire psalm, Psalm 23:5 implies that the anointing is a comfort to the speaker and may therefore suggest that the anointing would be a comfort to Jesus as he faces his suffering and death.

4. *Song of Solomon.* A passage from the Song of Solomon—a book that was read as part of the Passover observance—reads: "your anointing oils are fragrant; your name is oil poured out" (ESV Song 1:3). The references in Song 1:12 to a king and to nard are also echoed in the anointing story. Note that "the word *shem*, which means name or reputation, resembled the word *shemen*, which means oil or ointment, and the two words are associated with Ecclesiastes vii. 1: 'A good *name* is better than precious *oil.*'"[10] These echoes would have primed Mark's audience to link Jesus' anointing with naming (see the Analysis of 14:1–11 on the symbolism of the anointing).

5. *The Messianic Feast.* The messianic feast is the idea that the coming of the Messiah can be symbolized by a lavish banquet. Isaiah 25 develops this imagery. LXX Isaiah 25:6 departs from the Hebrew text in a significant way: it describes the messianic banquet as including anointing with ointment. The significance of this allusion is that it implies that the woman turned an otherwise-ordinary meal into a messianic feast, reflecting her knowledge that the Messiah was indeed present.

Relationship to Other Stories in Mark. The anointing takes pride of place in Mark's Gospel and it has significant resonances with many other stories in Mark:

1. *John the Baptist.* John the Baptist and the anointing woman effectively bookend Jesus' public ministry. In both cases, a ritual action (baptism and anointing) is performed by a faithful disciple. Both John and the anointer prepare the way of the Lord (1:3). Substantial parallels link Jesus' baptism and his anointing.[11] At the baptism, the Spirit descends on (or "into"; see the Notes on 1:10) him. Because Isaiah 61:1 links having the Spirit with being anointed,[12] a close auditor of Mark's text might have found a link between Jesus' baptism (which inaugurates his public ministry) and his anointing (which concludes it). Much as the Spirit equipped Jesus for his life's work, the anointing

---

10. Philip Carrington, *According to Mark: A Running Commentary on the Oldest Gospel* (Cambridge Eng.: University Press, 1960), 306; italics in original.

11. Miller, *Women in Mark's Gospel*, 142–43.

12. This link is also found in other texts where the Spirit is "poured out" like oil, including Isa. 44:3 and Joel 2:28–29.

prepares Jesus for his suffering and death. Both stories include the idea of descent, with the Spirit descending at baptism and the oil descending at the anointing. Both stories teach Mark's audience about Jesus' identity: much as the voice from heaven proclaims that Jesus is the beloved Son, the anointing enacts Jesus' identity as a royal but suffering Messiah. Each of these events is followed by temptations: the baptism by the temptations in the wilderness and the anointing by the temptation to avoid suffering (14:36), and both events would have prepared Jesus to be successful in the face of these temptations. Part of this preparation stemmed from the fact that both actions reinforced his identity.

2. *The Healings of Simon's Mother-in-Law and the Leper* (1:29–31, 40–45). In Mark, Jesus' ministry was inaugurated with the healing of a woman and of a leper, so it is appropriate that a woman and a leper have key roles in the final story of that ministry. His ministry began and ended in the house of a Simon (1:29; 14:3). But now, the woman and the leper are serving Jesus instead of being served by him; this inversion suggests that one result of Jesus' life is that those who once needed his care will now be able to serve others.[13] While extremely speculative, it is worth considering whether the woman and leper of chapter 1 could be the same people as in 14:3–9. There are some significant resonances between the stories: Simon's mother-in-law ministers (Greek: *diakoneō*) to Jesus and his disciples (1:31), and the anointing woman's act could be described as ministering. In chapter 1, the woman is named and the leper is not, while the reverse is the case in chapter 14. Jesus commanded the leper to "say nothing to any [one]" (1:44), but in chapter 14, Jesus states that the story of the anointing will be told wherever the gospel is preached. This inversion suggests that the anointing is crucial to understanding Jesus' identity, but the healing of the leper might, on the other hand, sow confusion. The leper violates Jesus' command by proclaiming (KJV: "publishing"; Greek: *kēryssō*); the same verb is used when Jesus refers to the proclamation of the woman's deed (KJV: "preached"). Similarly, the same Greek verb (*embrimaomai*) is used to describe Jesus' "straitly charg[ing]" (1:43) the leper and for the objectors' "murmur[ing]" (14:5) against the woman. The purpose of this echo might be to emphasize the emotional content of each incident. And much as the proclamation of the leper's healing made it difficult for Jesus to freely enter a town (1:45), the anointing apparently made it impossible for Jesus to openly enter Jerusalem (the preparations for the Last Supper suggest this) and led to Judas' betrayal.

3. *The Bleeding Woman* (5:25–34). The story of the bleeding woman shares many similarities with the story of the anointing woman. First, both are structured to emphasize the theme of death: the bleeding woman's story is surrounded by the story of the death of Jairus's daughter, and the anointing is

---

13. Sabin, *Reopening the Word,* 192.

surrounded by the story of the plot to kill Jesus. Since Jairus's daughter's death foreshadows Jesus' death (see the section "Relationship to the Resurrection" after the Notes on 5:42), the link between the two texts is strengthened. Both the bleeding woman and the anointing woman approach Jesus in socially unacceptable ways, but this does not concern Jesus in either story. In both cases an objection (the disciples wonder how Jesus can isolate one touch from the crowd; some complain about the waste of ointment) comes from those who do not understand what is happening. While the anointing woman prepares Jesus for his suffering and burial, the bleeding woman suffered many things—a word (Greek: *penthō*) used only for her and for Jesus in this Gospel (5:26; 8:31; 9:12). Additionally, the bleeding woman's story indicates that she had spent all of her money (5:26); like the anointer, she is willing to give everything. The sandwiching of the bleeding woman's story with that of Jairus's daughter emphasizes each woman's link to the tribes of Israel since the number twelve is associated with both (5:25, 42), while the anointing woman fills the role of Israel's prophet by anointing Israel's new king. Most importantly, like the other pivotal, truthful occurrences in Mark, these events are tactile instead of being primarily verbal. A chain of touching and reaction stretches through Mark, always involving women and Jesus: "The touch of the woman with the flow of blood preceded the raising of Jairus's daughter. The touch of this [anointing] woman precedes the flow of Jesus' own blood which in turn will precede his resurrection. She is in touch with him, present to him in a way that no one else is, in one act both preparing his body for death and acknowledging him as the anointed one, the Messiah."[14]

4. *Peter's Confession* (8:27–30). While both stories are concerned with Jesus' identity, there are profound differences between Peter's announcement that Jesus is the Christ and the woman's anointing act. The fact that Peter rebukes Jesus for teaching about his coming suffering suggests that Peter does not understand what it means to say that Jesus is the Christ (8:31–33). But the woman's anointing act—which is both a royal and a burial anointing—shows that she does indeed understand that suffering is an integral part of Jesus' messiahship. More significantly, Peter, upon learning that Jesus will suffer and die, attempts to change Jesus' mind about his fate (8:32). But the woman, who has knowledge of Jesus' coming suffering and death, does not try to dissuade him from his mission but rather honors that death through the act of anointing. Further, the woman uses actions (but no words) to convey this knowledge—a stark contrast to Peter, who struggles with the correct actions to correlate with his often-impetuous words. This explains why the anointing woman's act proclaiming that Jesus is the Anointed One is a story that must be told, while Peter was cautioned not to tell anyone that Jesus was the Anointed One.

---

14. Susan Lochrie Graham, "Silent Voices: Women in the Gospel of Mark," *Semeia* 54 (1991): 153.

5. *Jesus' Temple Action* (11:15–19). Mark has patterned Jesus' relationship to the temple after the procedure outlined in Leviticus for dealing with a leprous house.[15] Leviticus prescribes, first, an examination of a leprous home where the priest empties it for inspection (Lev. 14:36–37), which is mirrored in Jesus' examination of the temple (11:15–19). Later, the priest will return to inspect the house, and if it is still corrupt, "he shall break down the house, the stones of it, and the timber thereof, and all the mortar of the house; and he shall carry them forth out of the city into an unclean place" (Lev. 14:45). This line is echoed in Jesus' prophecy that "there shall not be left one stone upon another, that shall not be thrown down" (13:2). Given that it was not literally true that one stone was not left upon another, an allusion to Leviticus is all the more likely here. The leper's possessions would be scattered since it was probably the leper's greed (that is, the leper's own unwillingness to charitably "scatter" his/her possessions) that was believed to have caused the disease in the first place. Jesus predicts the destruction of the temple shortly after noting the corruption and greed of the Jerusalem religious establishment. It is significant that most of the material between Jesus' action in the temple and the prediction of its demise concerns Jesus' encounters with the religious authorities; Jesus is, through these encounters, gathering evidence that the temple, as paradigmatic of the religious establishment, is as unclean as a leper's house. Mark has condemned the temple as hopelessly leprous and incapable of fulfilling its functions. At the same time, it is in the actual house of a real leper that the anointing of the king occurs. Mark has made the leper's house into a temple and the temple into a leper's house. This is a classic example of Markan irony. Further, since burial anointings would normally take place in a tomb and lepers were often associated with the dead, the leper's home is an entirely (ironically) appropriate place for a burial anointing.

6. *The Widow's Offering* (12:41–44). While the anointing story is linked to many other episodes in Mark's Gospel, some of its closest ties are to the story of the widow in chapter 12:

   a. Both stories involve unnamed women.

   b. Both have a double mention of the poor, and both contrast the offerings of the rich and the poor.

   c. Jesus proclaims that each woman has given all that she has in a statement that defends the activities of each woman from a presumed or actual objection.

   d. A solemn saying (KJV: "verily") concludes each story.

   e. Each of the widow's coins total $\frac{1}{128}$ of a denarius; thus the value of the widow's gift contrasts sharply with the anointer's gift, which was almost

---

15. J. Duncan M. Derrett, "No Stone upon Another: Leprosy and the Temple," *Journal for the Study of the New Testament* 30 (1987): 3–20.

twenty thousand times more valuable. Mark suggests that the actual value of the gift is irrelevant; what really matters is giving all that one has. The widow's gift of her whole life parallels Jesus' gift, and the anointing woman's gift defines what it means for Jesus to give his life, as well as predicting that event. Since both the temple and Jesus' body are, in Mark's Gospel, expected to be destroyed, in both cases the woman is making a gift to something doomed.

f. Both the anointer and the widow are silent, yet both teach important truths through their actions.

g. The gift, in a way, causes the destruction: the widow's gift to the temple seems to be the catalyst for Jesus leaving the temple and prophesying its destruction, while the anointing motivates Judas to betray Jesus.

h. Much as the idea of the blooming fig tree in chapter 13 points to the eventual return of the temple, a royal anointing of Jesus implies that his death is not permanent.

These numerous parallels suggest that the two stories are intended to frame the teachings of chapter 13:

> evil scribes denounced (12:38–40)
>> the widow's offering (12:41–44)
>>> teachings about discipleship (13:1–37)
>> the anointing (14:1–9)
> plot to kill Jesus (14:10–11)

Jesus' teachings in chapter 13 are framed and illustrated first by righteous women and then by evil men.[16] The evilness and the righteousness of each deed is emphasized via stark contrast. And much as the particular crime of "devour[ing] widows' houses" (12:40) is contrasted with the widow's offering, the plot to kill Jesus emphasizes the death motifs of the anointing.

Note: See also the discussions of the anointing story after 14:11, 16, 21; and 16:8.

***

14:10 *And Judas Iscariot, one of the twelve:* The odd triple naming here (Judas, Iscariot, one of the Twelve) is especially unusual since Judas has already been introduced (3:19). The point is to emphasize his nefariousness: it is one of Jesus' closest disciples who betrays him. The article before the word "one" ("the one of the Twelve") is as awkward in Greek as it is in English; this further emphasizes Judas' position in the Twelve.

---

16. Joanna Dewey, *The Oral Ethos of the Early Church: Speaking, Writing, and the Gospel of Mark* (Eugene, Ore.: Cascade Books, 2013), 75.

went unto the chief priests, to betray him unto them: The New Rendition changes "him" to "Jesus" (despite the fact that the Greek text has the pronoun) for clarity.

The most likely scenario is that the act of betrayal was for Judas to tell the authorities when Jesus is in Gethsemane; by providing them with information about a time and a place to arrest Jesus away from the crowd, Judas makes it possible for them to capture Jesus without causing a riot (compare 14:1–2).

In Mark's Gospel, the immediate cause of Judas' desire to betray Jesus is the anointing, perhaps due to its symbolic connotations. But it is also possible that there is an undercurrent of sexism, since "Men can get very angry when other men elevate women over them."[17]

Relationship to the Suffering Servant (Isaiah 53). Several HB texts refer to the "suffering servant," who was interpreted by early Christians to be Jesus. In LXX Isaiah 53:6 and 12, language very similar to what is here translated as "betray him unto them" is used. Mark's audience might have caught the allusion and understood Jesus to be the suffering servant who was handed over.

14:11 *And when they heard it, they were glad, and promised to give him money:* Mark's Gospel never suggests that Judas' motive is money; his motive is not stated in the text, although the anointing seems to be the precipitating event. Rather, money is only mentioned after Judas approaches the authorities.

The chief priests are glad because their problem (a desire to arrest Jesus without causing a riot) has been solved via Judas' willingness to betray Jesus. They do not give Judas money here; presumably, that would only happen after Jesus was arrested.

And he sought how he might conveniently betray him: The words translated as "sought" and "how" are the same two words used in 14:1; this verbal similarity emphasizes Judas' affinity with the chief priests and suggests that these verses bracket the anointing.

---

17. Thomas E. Boomershine, *The Messiah of Peace: A Performance-Criticism Commentary on Mark's Passion-Resurrection Narrative* (Eugene, Ore.: Cascade Books, 2015), 66.

Analysis

As Jesus' statement that the anointing story should be told wherever the gospel is preached should suggest, the anointing is an extremely important story. "Christ" is the Greek equivalent of the Hebrew "Messiah," which means "the Anointed One," and this is the story of his anointing—of what it means to say that Jesus is the Messiah or the Christ. It is likely that Jesus' different reactions to being called "Christ" in 8:30–33 (where he limits the title) and 14:61–62 (where he accepts it) are attributable to the fact that one takes place before the anointing and the other after.

Anointing was a common practice in antiquity and was done for many different reasons: to begin a feast (Amos 6:6), to hallow objects (Gen. 31:13; Lev. 8:10), to adorn the body (Ruth 3:3), or to consecrate priests (Ex. 28:41) and kings (1 Sam. 15:1). Several themes developed around the concept of anointing, but particularly it served as an acknowledgment of divine election, implied an endowment of power from God, and conferred a spirit of wisdom. In general, anointing suggests "status transformation" that leads to a "new social role."[18] And while anointing was a common practice in the ancient world, Mark's story—particularly Jesus' statement that it should be told whenever the gospel is preached—suggests that this is not an ordinary anointing. It has several symbolic meanings in Mark:

1. *A Burial Anointing.* Jesus states that the woman has anointed his body for burying. Some interpreters think that the only reason the anointing is in the text is because Mark's audience would have been distressed that Jesus' corpse was not properly anointed after burial (16:1–8). However, it is more likely that early Christians would have denied the need for a proper burial since Jesus was resurrected, especially since the anointing story raises the question of whether this anointing would even constitute a proper burial anointing since it was performed before death. Nonetheless, this is a burial anointing and abounds in death symbolism. The same item of furniture (Greek: *klinē*) is used to recline at a dinner and to lay out a corpse. The broken vial of oil, which was often left in the tomb with the dead, is itself a symbol of death and destruction (Eccl. 12:6; Jer. 13:12–14). And there is the suggestion that the house is a tomb since it is the home of a leper.

2. *A Royal Anointing.* The anointing is in a context of profuse royal imagery, which began with Jesus' entry into Jerusalem. The anointing continues the messianic imagery that reaches its ironic climax in the mockery of the crucifixion (see the Analysis of 15:16–32). The fact that Jesus' head is anointed

---

18. Santiago Guijarro and Ana Rodríguez, "The 'Messianic' Anointing of Jesus," *Biblical Theology Bulletin* 41, no. 3 (2011): 137.

supports the idea of it being a royal anointing; there is ample HB precedent for the anointing of the king's head as part of the coronation ritual (1 Sam. 10:1; 1 Kgs. 1:39; 2 Kgs. 9:1–6; 2 Kgs. 11:12). Particularly relevant is Samuel's anointing of Saul as king since both are followed by a quickly filled prophecy as a sign of authenticity. Although not every king in Israel was anointed, a king whose right to reign was disputed would have been anointed, and the kingship of Jesus is certainly disputed. Of course, the woman's anointing inverts expectations at least as much as it fulfills them since she is not a prophet in Israel. But when Jesus says that she has anointed his body ahead of time for burial, he suggests that the woman has in fact acted prophetically. The royal anointing would normally take place in the most sacred of locations (a temple), but Jesus' occurs in one of its most polluted (a leper's home). While the audience would have understood that this was a royal anointing, they also would have seen it as reimagined in significant ways.

It is not the case that one or the other meaning for the anointing must be chosen. Rather, the symbolism of the anointing is multifaceted: Mark intends for the audience to view this as both a burial anointing *and* a royal anointing. The combination of meanings is essential to understanding the nature of Jesus' mission: he is the Messiah, but he suffers and dies. An anointing that is at once a royal anointing and a burial anointing is the ideal vehicle by which to teach this truth: "It is no diminution of its royal significance when Jesus declares the anointing to be for his burial, for it is precisely the paradox of Christ's royalty that he is enthroned through being entombed."[19]

Taking both meanings simultaneously allows the interpreter to view the anointing as consistent with Mark's major theological focus: the paradox of the victorious death. To see the royal, glorious Jesus without understanding the reality of his suffering and death is to make Peter's mistake (8:31–33); to see Jesus as one who suffers without any royal underpinning is to make the mistake of those who mock him in chapter 15.

The objection regarding the use of money in this story fits the pattern established in Mark: concern with money in Mark's Gospel is always presented as negative. Two other references in Mark mention a *denarius*: the feeding miracle (6:37) and the controversy over paying taxes to Caesar (12:13–17). In these stories, money is the concern of those who do not understand Jesus. And yet the objection to the anointing is by far the most understandable of all of the criticisms lobbed at Jesus in the Gospel of Mark. Jesus had, after all, told the rich man to sell what he had and give to the poor (10:21), and the

---

19. Austin Marsden Farrer, *A Study in St. Mark* (London: Dacre Press, 1951), 129–30.

objectors are merely echoing that counsel here. And because the poor were given special gifts at Passover, their needs would have specifically been on the minds of those present. Jesus' response will show that this objection is nonetheless mistaken and that a wooden, literalist approach to Jesus' teachings is not appropriate: what he counseled in one setting is not necessarily appropriate in a different context. The fact that Jesus has taught that helping the poor is important implies that this act of anointing is even more important than aiding the poor; this is another factor pointing to the extreme significance of this anointing.

What the objectors had interpreted to be a waste, Jesus interprets as a good work. He is not focused on the monetary cost of the anointing (which, out of context, makes the act seem wasteful) but rather on its symbolic meaning, which renders it a good work. Obviously, caring for the poor is a good thing; Jesus' words in 14:6 affirm as much. The point of Jesus' response is not to downplay the need to care for the poor but rather to build on it: one of the clues for the audience to the importance of the anointing is precisely that it is even more important than care for the poor. Jesus has already taught this principle in the controversy concerning fasting (2:19), where he explained that his presence alleviated the obligation to fast. The anointing is another case where the presence of Jesus triggers unusual circumstances and requires a disciple to act in ways in which she or he might not otherwise act.

In Jewish tradition, there was a hierarchy where an unclean male was less unclean than an unclean woman, who was less unclean than a leper, who was less unclean than a corpse.[20] The anointing story involves a man, a woman, a leper, and a (future) corpse, and thus it makes Jesus' verdict that her deed is "good" all the more significant: it is a strong commentary on Jesus' relationship to the law of Moses.

The only other use of the word "work" (Greek: *ergon*) in Mark is to describe the assignments given to the servants in the parable at the end of the previous chapter (13:34). The proximity of that parable to the anointing makes it very likely that Mark's early audiences would have interpreted the anointing woman's work in its light. They would likely have concluded that she had been given her task by her master, that she had not undertaken it by her own initiative, and that she was faithfully completing her assigned task and thus observing the commandment to "watch." This relationship is especially significant in light of the scene in Gethsemane, where Jesus'

---

20. Mishah Kelim 1:4.

inner circle of disciples will fail to watch despite repeated reminders from Jesus to do so.

Jesus' quotation of Deuteronomy 15:11 evoked a text that criticized those who gave to the poor anticipating recompense. His praise of the woman implied that she, on the contrary, had acted without expectation of reward. And yet, in a classic instance of Markan irony, the woman is recompensed—richly—not only by Jesus' praise but by his statement that turns her deed into a memorial to her wherever the gospel is preached. His words invite the audience to participate in the woman's memorial by retelling her story. Jesus' statement is unique in Mark: the woman's action is permanently connected to Jesus' story, a privilege given to no one else. Some interpreters suggest that the memorial is of Jesus, not of the woman, or that her memorial will be that her good deed is remembered by God on the day of judgment, but neither of these readings seem likely given the actual wording of Jesus' statement.

Significantly, Mark's Gospel contains no command to memorialize the Last Supper. The only event in Mark that Jesus asks to be remembered is his anointing. Mark's Gospel envisions a continued role in the life of the early church, not for the ritual reenactment of the Last Supper but rather for storytelling and, particularly, telling the story of the anointing. This story can be read as the centerpiece of Mark's Gospel. It is thus ironic that the woman's name is not included in the account by which she will be memorialized. And yet the lack of a name is, in a sense, appropriate: "throughout the Gospel, naming has often been associated with the human desire for fame, glory, status, and authority, all longings that harden the heart and encourage fear rather than faith."[21] And there might be yet another layer of irony in that the unnamed woman "names" Jesus through an act that explains what it means to say that Jesus is the Christ.

Latter-day Saint readers will find a parallel between Jesus' command that the woman's deed be memorialized and the scene in the Book of Mormon where Jesus reviews the Nephite record and requests that the prophecies of Samuel the Lamanite be included (3 Ne. 23:7–13). In both cases, Jesus commands that certain material be included in the record; it is likely that, given cultural biases (against Lamanites and women) these particular stories might have otherwise been lost to history without Jesus' intervention. Most significantly, both Samuel and the anointing woman testify of Jesus in profound ways.

---

21. Tolbert, *Sowing the Gospel*, 293.

It is likely that one reason why the anointing story has received less attention than it should is that the woman does not say anything. But Mark's Gospel prefers deeds to words: Jesus does not speak nearly as often in Mark as in the other Gospels; he is more active and less verbal. The preference for action is particularly notable in the women in the text: although often silent, they are generally the true followers.

As discussed above, the allusion to the Song of Solomon primed the audience to think of the anointing as bestowing a name despite the silence of the woman. This type of naming is most appropriate to the Gospel of Mark where more traditional methods of naming often fail. It is particularly in the outbursts from the demons that the audience realizes that merely confessing the identity of Jesus verbally is not sufficient by Mark's standards, especially in light of the ancient belief that to name someone is to gain power over him or her. The perverse proliferation of abused and abusive titles in the next chapter further shows their unreliability for Mark.

The only fact known about the anointer is that she is female—not that she is a Gentile, not that she is from Galilee, not that she is someone's wife. (One can assume that she was a woman of means because she had expensive ointment at her disposal, but her only positive identifying marker is her gender.) The lack of other identifiers forces the audience to focus on her gender while making her femaleness the most relevant requirement for her task. It is possible that Mark leaves out her name in order to spare her dishonor. But other stories in Mark show a disregard for this type of social norm, so it is perhaps ironic that he leaves out her name (which is usually done to protect a woman's modesty) in a situation where she is acting boldly and where Jesus proclaims that the entire world will know of her act. Names are suspect in Mark: Judas, with his triple naming (14:10), stands in sharp relief to the anonymous woman. Unnamed, the woman is more of a type (of the ideal disciple) than she is a distinct character, which is significant since she is taking on the role usually restricted to the one identified as a prophet in Israel.

The anointing story has much to contribute to the idea of discipleship in Mark's Gospel. First, within the story itself, participants are given the opportunity to act as disciples—or not. "The anointing of Jesus by the woman may be interpreted as a prophetic sign which has the effect of a parable, dividing those present into two groups."[22] Much as the parables in chapter 4, the anointing can be considered an enacted parable, revealing something about those who observe it. Describing the objectors as "some" implies the

---

22. Miller, *Women in Mark's Gospel*, 134.

presence of others who do not disapprove of the anointing, and thus the woman's action would have served the purpose of creating two groups: those who did and those who did not understand. This division exemplifies a pattern found throughout the Passion narrative: Jesus' attackers speak out, but his defenders are silent.

But the key way in which discipleship operates in this story is to show the anointing woman as a model disciple. In Mark's Gospel, it is not the Twelve but the anointing woman (among others) who is presented as an ideal. The disciples deny and avoid Jesus' death, but the woman acknowledges it, honors it, and responds appropriately to it. Mark's Gospel is focused on the theme of discipleship, and the anointing woman is presented as a model disciple.[23]

She also fits the pattern of other female characters who are exemplary minor characters, but the command to commemorate her act means that her link to Jesus is not as short-lived as most of the other stories in Mark. The anointer is the only person in Mark's Gospel who understands Jesus' identity during his mortal life. It is precisely because she presents a model for discipleship that makes it necessary for the story to be remembered. The broken vial and the complete use of the ointment serve as symbols of the completeness of her sacrifice and thus suggest that she foreshadows Jesus and his own sacrifice.

The anointing is the chief Christological material in the Gospel; this would explain why Jesus states that the story will be told wherever the gospel is preached. Because the anointing is a ritual action and not a simple spoken title (such as "Christ" or "Son of Man"), it is best able to reflect Mark's Christological vision: "it is only in the relationship of the two facts—his identity as Messiah and his appearance as the crucified King of the Jews—that the truth of the story can be expressed."[24] Jesus is named, not with a title, but through the silent action of a faithful follower. This type of naming is most appropriate to the Gospel of Mark where more traditional methods of naming fail. And the layered truth that Jesus must be simultaneously understood as a dying and a royal Messiah simply cannot be expressed in one small word. Mark's Christology encapsulates a nuanced understanding, so one title cannot capture the full meaning. Even the title "Christ" is

---

23. Julie M. Smith, "'She Hath Wrought a Good Work': The Anointing of Jesus in Mark's Gospel," *Studies in the Bible and Antiquity* 5 (2013): 31–46.

24. Donald Juel, *A Master of Surprise: Mark Interpreted* (Minneapolis: Fortress Press, 1994), 41.

insufficient since, through the anointing, Mark redefines its meaning. The very fact that Mark is a narrative should suggest that Mark believes that truth is best conveyed by telling a story—not by one title or phrase.

Jesus links the woman's deed to the proclamation of the gospel—the good news—of Jesus Christ. What is that good news and what are the implications of this Christological vision? The good news is that traditional expectations are inverted in the face of the inbreaking kingdom of God. Life and death are mysteriously intertwined, purity and impurity play, outsiders become insiders and insiders become outsiders, power comes from silence, words speak only betrayal, and gender barriers are shattered. But the most important and most curious paradox in Mark is the concept of the victorious death and the suffering Messiah.

Far removed from Jesus' commands to silence (1:44; 5:43) is his statement that the anointing will be told wherever the gospel is preached. What accounts for the difference? The anointing story holds the key to the messianic secret in Mark: because the anointing encapsulates all of the significant dimensions of Jesus' identity, it can be—it must be—told. By contrast, the healing of a leper or the exorcism of a demon or the Transfiguration would only reveal one aspect of Jesus' identity and therefore lead to more confusion than clarity.

Oddly, many interpreters downplay the significance of the anointing. One suspects an androcentric perspective is the problem; this suspicion is sometimes confirmed outright, as when one interpreter writes that "in 14.8–9, Jesus speaks of his death and of the future of the gospel. The aura of this event is reduced, however, when the woman implicitly shares this knowledge."[25] Equally disappointing is the way that the anointing story has been (mis)treated by feminist interpreters. Perhaps they, too, have been hemmed in by their own preconceptions, particularly the idea that an anonymous, silent woman cannot be a key character. But in Mark's presentation, this woman foreshadows Jesus: he "cast[s] the anonymous woman as a Christ-figure. Her extravagant love, expressed in an act of self-giving which provokes conflict, is an anticipation in the narrative of what will happen to Jesus himself."[26] Much as Jesus will be vindicated by the empty tomb, the woman is vindicated by his words.

---

25. Edwin K. Broadhead, *Teaching with Authority: Miracles and Christology in the Gospel of Mark*, vol. 74 of Journal for the Study of the New Testament Supplement Series (Sheffield, Eng.: JSOT Press, 1992): 180.

26. Stephen C. Barton, "Mark As Narrative: The Story of the Anointing Woman (Mk 14:3–9)," *Expository Times* 102, no. 8 (1990–91), 232.

Many interpreters argue that the woman anointed him for no particular reason or simply as a kind gesture. But it is highly implausible that the woman had no symbolic intention. The fact that she is not given a motivation in the text is not a sufficient reason to assume that she has none: "for each person who acts with purpose a commission or task can be assumed."[27] In cases where a person commits a deed with a duplicitous motive, Mark makes that motive clear so that the audience will not perceive the act as virtuous (9:5–6; 10:2; 11:28–32; 12:13). Since the woman's act is specifically praised and no nefarious motivation is given, it is logical to assume that she intended the full symbolic meaning of the anointing. It is difficult to explain the lavish praise that Jesus gives to her act if she had no particular reason for anointing him.

With the key teaching that disciples are supposed to watch (13:33–37) fresh in their ears, Mark's audience would have "watched" the anointing and realized its importance. Further, the only two concrete time references in the Gospel (14:1, 12) bracket the story of the anointing, which means that it is the only precisely timed act in the text and therefore forms a break in the narrative, reminiscent of a slow-motion scene in an action movie. So the narrative structure itself emphasizes the importance of the anointing.

Mark 14:1–11 is one of the clearest examples of Mark's sandwiching technique:

> A plot to kill Jesus (14:1–2)
>> B the anointing (14:3–9)
> A plot to kill Jesus (14:10–11)

The shared language in 14:1 and 14:11 emphasizes that both passages concern the plot to kill. The framing of the anointing by the treacherous murder plans emphasizes the goodness of the woman's deed. The terseness of 14:1–2 and 10–11 contrasts sharply with the details of the anointing, and, while the anointing is primarily concerned with actions instead of words, the murder plot is merely talk at this point. The furtiveness of the plotters is contrasted with the openness of the woman's actions. Jesus' prophecy that the woman's act will be remembered throughout the whole world sharply contrasts with the desire that Jesus' death plot be kept from the people. Finding out about the anointing is a part of the "good news"; finding out about the death plot would cause a riot. Further, there are strong contrasts between Judas and the anointing woman; Judas functions as a foil

---

27. Robert C. Tannehill, *The Shape of the Gospels: New Testament Essays* (Eugene, Ore.: Cascade Books, 2007), 165.

for the nameless, laudable woman. In the only two instances in the Gospel where money is spent on Jesus, the woman sacrifices her own great sum in order to show her love for Jesus while Judas receives compensation for betraying him. And while Judas is triply, redundantly named, the anointing woman is unnamed. Judas, the insider, betrays Jesus while the anointing woman, a literal outsider, enters the house to honor him. Additionally, the religious leaders (who should be insiders) show themselves to be outsiders—by plotting against Jesus and by their narrative position outside the meal scene—while a leper, the consummate outsider, becomes an insider since the anointing happens in his home.

The sandwiching structure also implies that it is the anointing that causes Judas to desire to betray Jesus. Similar to how the healing of the bleeding woman changes the trajectory of the story of Jairus's daughter (in that case, from a healing to a raising), the anointing changes the frustration of the plotters, who cannot figure out how to arrest Jesus without causing a riot, to gladness because Judas has stepped forward to betray Jesus. It was probably the very act of the anointing—with its messianic connotations, flouting of social norms, and intimation of Jesus' coming death—that pushed Judas to betray Jesus. One function of the sandwiching structure is to emphasize the relationship between the anointing and the plot to kill Jesus.

The anointing story is also the narrative bridge between Jesus' life and death; it is both the last story relating events from his daily life and the first part of the story of his death. It is the hinge between the accounts of his life and his death; its location in the text mirrors its theological function since the anointing story explores the link between Jesus' life and death.

JESUS OBSERVES PASSOVER (14:12–25)

Greek Text

12 Καὶ τῇ πρώτῃ ἡμέρᾳ τῶν ἀζύμων, ὅτε τὸ πάσχα ἔθυον, λέγουσιν αὐτῷ οἱ μαθηταὶ αὐτοῦ· Ποῦ θέλεις ἀπελθόντες ἑτοιμάσωμεν ἵνα φάγῃς τὸ πάσχα; 13 καὶ ἀποστέλλει δύο τῶν μαθητῶν αὐτοῦ καὶ λέγει αὐτοῖς· Ὑπάγετε εἰς τὴν πόλιν, καὶ ἀπαντήσει ὑμῖν ἄνθρωπος κεράμιον ὕδατος βαστάζων· ἀκολουθήσατε αὐτῷ, 14 καὶ ὅπου ἐὰν εἰσέλθῃ εἴπατε τῷ οἰκοδεσπότῃ ὅτι Ὁ διδάσκαλος λέγει· Ποῦ ἐστιν τὸ κατάλυμά μου ὅπου τὸ πάσχα μετὰ τῶν μαθητῶν μου φάγω; 15 καὶ αὐτὸς ὑμῖν δείξει ἀνάγαιον μέγα ἐστρωμένον ἕτοιμον· καὶ ἐκεῖ ἑτοιμάσατε ἡμῖν. 16 καὶ ἐξῆλθον οἱ μαθηταὶ καὶ ἦλθον εἰς τὴν πόλιν καὶ εὗρον καθὼς εἶπεν αὐτοῖς, καὶ ἡτοίμασαν τὸ πάσχα.

17 Καὶ ὀψίας γενομένης ἔρχεται μετὰ τῶν δώδεκα. 18 καὶ ἀνακειμένων αὐτῶν καὶ ἐσθιόντων ὁ Ἰησοῦς εἶπεν· Ἀμὴν λέγω ὑμῖν ὅτι εἷς ἐξ ὑμῶν παραδώσει με ὁ ἐσθίων μετ’ ἐμοῦ. 19 ἤρξαντο λυπεῖσθαι καὶ λέγειν αὐτῷ εἷς κατὰ εἷς· Μήτι ἐγώ; 20 ὁ δὲ εἶπεν αὐτοῖς· Εἷς τῶν δώδεκα, ὁ ἐμβαπτόμενος μετ’ ἐμοῦ εἰς τὸ τρύβλιον· 21 ὅτι ὁ μὲν υἱὸς τοῦ ἀνθρώπου ὑπάγει καθὼς γέγραπται περὶ αὐτοῦ, οὐαὶ δὲ τῷ ἀνθρώπῳ ἐκείνῳ δι’ οὗ ὁ υἱὸς τοῦ ἀνθρώπου παραδίδοται· καλὸν αὐτῷ εἰ οὐκ ἐγεννήθη ὁ ἄνθρωπος ἐκεῖνος.

22 Καὶ ἐσθιόντων αὐτῶν λαβὼν ἄρτον εὐλογήσας ἔκλασεν καὶ ἔδωκεν αὐτοῖς καὶ εἶπεν· Λάβετε, τοῦτό ἐστιν τὸ σῶμά μου. 23 καὶ λαβὼν ποτήριον εὐχαριστήσας ἔδωκεν αὐτοῖς, καὶ ἔπιον ἐξ αὐτοῦ πάντες. 24 καὶ εἶπεν αὐτοῖς· Τοῦτό ἐστιν τὸ αἷμά μου τῆς διαθήκης τὸ ἐκχυννόμενον ὑπὲρ πολλῶν. 25 ἀμὴν λέγω ὑμῖν ὅτι οὐκέτι οὐ μὴ πίω ἐκ τοῦ γενήματος τῆς ἀμπέλου ἕως τῆς ἡμέρας ἐκείνης ὅταν αὐτὸ πίνω καινὸν ἐν τῇ βασιλείᾳ τοῦ θεοῦ. [SBLGNT]

King James Version

12 And the first day of unleavened bread, when they killed the passover, his disciples said unto him, Where wilt thou that we go and prepare that thou mayest eat the passover? 13 And he sendeth forth two of his disciples, and saith unto them, Go ye into the city, and there shall meet you a man bearing a pitcher of water: follow him. 14 And wheresoever he shall go in, say ye to the goodman of the house, The Master saith, Where is the guestchamber, where I shall eat the passover with my disciples? 15 And he will shew you a large upper room furnished and prepared: there make ready for us. 16 And his disciples went forth, and came into the city, and found as he had said unto them: and they made ready the passover. 17 And in the evening he cometh with the twelve. 18 And as they sat and did eat, Jesus said, Verily I say unto you, One of you which eateth with me shall betray me. 19 And they began to be sorrowful, and to say unto him one by one, Is it I? and another said, Is it I? 20 And he answered and said unto them, It is one of the twelve, that dippeth with me in the dish. 21 The

New Rendition

12 And on the first day of [the feast of] unleavened bread, when the Passover lamb was being sacrificed, his disciples say to him, "Where do you want us to go to prepare for you to eat the Passover meal?" 13 And he sends out two of his disciples and says to them, "Go into the city and a man carrying a jar of water will meet you. Follow him. 14 And wherever he enters, say to the owner of the house, 'The teacher says, "Where is my guest room, where I might eat the Passover with my disciples?"' 15 And he will show you a big room upstairs, furnished and ready. Prepare for us there." 16 And the disciples left and came into the city. And they found things just as he had said to them. And they prepared the Passover.

17 And when it was evening, he comes with the Twelve. 18 And as they were reclining and as they were eating, Jesus said, "Amen, I say to you: one of you will betray me, the one who is eating with me." 19 They began to be distressed and to say to him, one by one, "Not me, right?" 20 But he said to them, "[It is] one

Son of man indeed goeth, as it is written of him: but woe to that man by whom the Son of man is betrayed! good were it for that man if he had never been born.

22 And as they did eat, Jesus took bread, and blessed, and brake it, and gave to them, and said, Take, eat: this is my body. 23 And he took the cup, and when he had given thanks, he gave it to them: and they all drank of it. 24 And he said unto them, This is my blood of the new testament, which is shed for many. 25 Verily I say unto you, I will drink no more of the fruit of the vine, until that day that I drink it new in the kingdom of God.

of the Twelve, who is dipping [his hand] in the bowl with me. 21 For the son of man goes, as it has been written about him, but woe to the man who betrays the son of man! It would have been better for that man had he never been born."

22 And while they were eating, having taken bread, [and] having blessed, he broke [it] and gave [it] to them and said, "Take [it]. This is my body." 23 And having taken a cup, having given thanks, he gave [it] to them, and they all drank of it. 24 And he said to them, "This is my blood of the covenant being poured out for many. 25 Amen, I say to you that I will never drink of the fruit of the vine until the day when I drink it new in the kingdom of God."

Notes

14:12 *And the first day of unleavened bread, when they killed the passover:* See 14:1 for a discussion of the festival of unleavened bread; this time reference places this story on Thursday.

"Killed the passover" means to kill the Passover lamb (Ex. 12).

"They" could refer generically to everyone who will observe Passover, or it might refer specifically to Jesus and his disciples. It is possible that the latter is the better reading since it explains why Mark would bother mentioning this seemingly mundane detail. On the other hand, Jesus' command to go into the city in the next verse makes more sense if they are outside of the city than if they are in the temple. But if this verse does refer to Jesus and the disciples, then Mark's audience would have visualized a poignant scene because "according to Jewish convention, Jesus would have slit the animal's throat, its blood would have been drained into a silver or gold basin held by a priest, and the priest would have taken the basin to the altar where he would have sprinkled the blood at the base of the altar."[28] It would be easy for Mark's audience to imagine Jesus' emotional reaction to performing this ritual when he knew that he himself would soon suffer and die.

---

28. Evans, *Mark 8:27–16:20*, 373.

his disciples said unto him, Where wilt thou that we go and prepare that thou mayest eat the passover?: Jesus and his disciples have been retiring to Bethany from Jerusalem each night, but they must make new arrangements since they were required to eat the Passover meal in the city (Deut. 16:5–7).

The Passover was normally celebrated as a family, so this question extends the idea in Mark that Jesus and his disciples have formed a new family (compare 3:31–35).

14:13 *And he sendeth forth two of his disciples, and saith unto them:* The sending of two disciples may be so that the law of witnesses will be honored, and thus Jesus' prophetic foreknowledge can be attested. The disciples are not identified, although 14:17 implies that they are not members of the Twelve. The Greek wording permits the possibility that one of the disciples was female. Traditionally, women prepared the Passover, so it is not unlikely that Mark's audience would have assumed the presence of a female disciple here.

Go ye into the city, and there shall meet you a man bearing a pitcher of water: follow him: Carrying water, especially in jars (KJV: "pitcher"), was considered women's work.

While some interpreters have suggested that this passage implies that Jesus has made prior arrangements for the Passover, this reading is unlikely because it does not explain why Mark would bother including this story. Rather, it seems to have been included to show Jesus' prophetic foreknowledge: Jesus made no previous arrangement; rather, he demonstrates prophetic insight into the circumstances. Another factor making the idea of prearrangement unlikely is that Jesus would surely have given more specific directions than simply to "go into the city," which was brimming with Passover visitors. And the Greek text implies that the man meets the disciples—not the other way around. So this scene shows Jesus (but not the disciples) as having a prophetic understanding of coming events, a theme frequently developed in Mark's Gospel.

14:14 *And wheresoever he shall go in, say ye to the goodman of the house:* This line pictures the man entering one particular house and the disciples following; if the KJV's "wheresoever" suggests to the modern reader that they entered many different houses, it misleads.

The Master saith, Where is the guestchamber, where I shall eat the passover with my disciples: Jesus' reference to the "teacher" (KJV: "Master") would have primed Mark's audience to think of Jesus assuming a teaching role during the Passover meal, which is precisely what he will do when he reinterprets the symbols of the Passover. The Greek text refers to "the teacher," not "a teacher," perhaps suggesting that Jesus was known to the homeowner. The master (or teacher) refers to his own ("my," contra the KJV's "the") guestroom here, so the implication is that the homeowner is a humble figure who welcomes Jesus, even when Jesus claims the guestroom as his own. There may be some similarity to the anointing woman—another anonymous, wealthy person whose generosity to Jesus makes it possible for the plot to advance.

14:15 *And he will shew you a large upper room furnished and prepared: there make ready for us:* It is surprising that a large room would be available at the last minute during Passover; it probably suggests divine intervention.

"Prepared" probably means that the furniture was arranged for the meal; the next verse suggests that the disciples prepared the food.

14:16 *And his disciples went forth, and came into the city, and found as he had said unto them: and they made ready the passover:* "The disciples" (as opposed to "his disciples") is probably the better reading here. "Made ready" implies that they are preparing the food for the meal.

14:17 *And in the evening he cometh with the twelve:* This line suggests that the two disciples sent to make arrangements for the Passover were not part of the Twelve (see also the Notes on 14:20). Mark's Gospel implies that women were present at the Last Supper:

1. Mark 14:17 suggests that Jesus arrived with the Twelve after two other disciples had made preparations. The grammar permits one of these other disciples to be female, and given that their task included meal preparation, it is even more likely that this person was female.

2. Mark describes the room where the meal was held as "large" (14:15), suggesting that a large group was expected.

3. The Passover ritual required the participation of children (Ex. 12:26–27) and was celebrated in family groups, so the presence of children and women was the norm historically. It seems likely that if Jesus' observance of Passover departed from these norms, Mark would have mentioned it. However, nowhere in Mark are women more limited in their sphere than they are in the larger culture.

4. Jesus will tell those who celebrated the Passover with him that, after he is raised, he will go before them to Galilee (14:28). At the tomb, the young man tells the women that Jesus has gone before them to Galilee "as he said unto you" (16:7). The most likely explanation is that women were at the Last Supper and so had heard Jesus' prophetic words. If women had not been at the Last Supper, the young man's statement would require the audience to

hypothesize another (unnarrated) occasion when Jesus told the women that he would go before them to Galilee.

5. Mark 15:41 notes that some women "came up with [Jesus] unto Jerusalem," and the reason that Jesus went to Jerusalem was to celebrate the Passover. The logical conclusion is that women celebrated the Passover with him.

14:18 *And as they sat and did eat, Jesus said, Verily I say unto you, One of you which eateth with me shall betray me:* The Greek verb implies reclining, not sitting. (Ex. 12:11 required standing while eating the Passover, but that was not generally practiced in the first century.)

On the phrase "verily I say unto you," see the Notes on 3:28.

Because others beside the Twelve are present with Jesus (see the Notes on 14:17), it is not clear at this point whether one of the Twelve or another disciple will betray Jesus; later, Jesus will clarify that it is one of the Twelve (14:20).

The word "betray" is in the future tense, which is interesting since 14:10–11 could be interpreted to mean that Judas has already betrayed Jesus. However, the future tense here may be intentionally used to imply that Judas has not yet completed the betrayal and may still choose not to go through with it. Perhaps this passage is intended to be a merciful warning to Judas that there is still time to change his mind.

Because of the role meals played in ancient hospitality and relationships, Jesus is describing a particularly heinous betrayal here: "the idea that one who shares another's food will then become a betrayer was viewed with loathing and outrage."[29]

Mark's audience has known about Judas's betrayal since Judas was introduced at the beginning of the Gospel (3:19). Thus, this verse is not news to the audience; rather, Mark included it to show the audience how the disciples reacted to Jesus' announcement.

Relationship to Psalm 41. Psalm 41 describes the betrayal of the psalmist; its ninth verse reads, "Yea, mine own familiar friend, in whom I trusted, which did eat of my bread, hath lifted up his heel against me." In Mark, the phrase "one of you which eateth with me" is awkward in Greek but may be a deliberate echo of this verse from Psalm 41 (LXX Ps. 40:10), which would explain its clumsiness. Later verses of the psalm speak of how, despite the betrayal of friends, the psalmist still enjoys the approval of God and thus suggests Jesus' innocence and ultimate victory despite betrayal.

---

29. Evans, *Mark 8:27–16:20*, 375.

14:19 *And they began to be sorrowful, and to say unto him one by one, Is it I? and another said, Is it I?:* It is unlikely that "and another said, is it I?" was in the earliest texts of Mark,[30] but the sense is the same either way.

"One by one" emphasizes that everyone at the meal (which is almost certainly more than the Twelve) asked this question. In the Greek text, the question presumes a negative answer (hence the New Rendition's "Not me, right?"), so it is unlikely that any disciple thought that he or she would be the one to betray Jesus. In fact, it is possible to read the question as an attempt to elicit a statement from Jesus exonerating the speaker.

It is significant that no disciple responds by identifying Judas. None of them thought Judas had behaved in such a way as to make him the obvious culprit; nothing about Judas's persona or behavior indicated his treachery. While Mark's audience has known since 3:18 that Judas would betray Jesus, the disciples are still unaware.

14:20 *And he answered and said unto them, It is one of the twelve, that dippeth with me in the dish:* Part of the Passover ritual involves dipping bitter herbs into salty water or vinegar.

Jesus' words add more specificity to his previous statement: it is one of the Twelve who will betray him. This verse, when contrasted with 14:18, implies that people besides the Twelve are present at the Last Supper. Jesus' answer provides those present who are not part of the Twelve the reassurance they were seeking that they would not betray him, but Jesus provides no similar comfort to the Twelve.

14:21 *The Son of man indeed goeth, as it is written of him:* The concept of going (KJV: "goeth") is probably a metaphor for dying.

"As it is written" refers to something written in the scriptures, but Jesus does not specify what scripture he has in mind. Possibilities include Psalm 41 (see the section "Relationship to Psalm 41" after the Notes on 14:18), Daniel 7 (since verses 21–25 refer to the idea that evil will prevail for a short time), and Daniel 9 (which teaches that the anointed one will be cut off). The idea of fulfillment of scripture is also mentioned in 14:27 and 49; these references are not typical of Mark, and so their rarity has two significant effects: they emphasize that this portion of Jesus' life is different from what has come before, and they show that the events surrounding Jesus' arrest are not accidental but rather are part of God's plan.

but woe to that man by whom the Son of man is betrayed! good were it for that man if he had never been born: It has puzzled some interpreters

---

30. Comfort, *New Testament Text and Translation Commentary*, 148.

that Jesus' death was apparently both a necessity as well as a cause for woe for Judas. But Jesus' death did not require Judas's involvement: presumably the leaders could have continued with their original plan to arrest Jesus after Passover.

Judas is never named as the betrayer in this passage. There are two possible reasons for this:

1. Jesus himself did not know that Judas would betray him. Mark's audience has known since 3:18 that Judas will betray Jesus, but it is possible Jesus does not share this knowledge; there are other instances in Mark where Jesus' knowledge is incomplete.[31]

2. Judas was excessively named in the previous part of this chapter (see 14:10–11 and the Notes there); perhaps there is an ironic contrast here.

The word "woe" indicates that this is "pronounced in grief."[32]

14:22 *And as they did eat, Jesus took bread, and blessed, and brake it, and gave to them, and said, Take, eat: this is my body:* Some manuscripts omit the command "eat" here; "eat" may have been added to conform with Matthew 26:26.[33] The absence of a command to eat may be significant if the disciples are invited—not commanded—to participate in this ritual with Jesus.

Because the same word for "body" is used to refer to Jesus' corpse (15:43), it would be possible to translate this line as "this is my corpse."[34] Given that Jesus' body has already been anointed for burial (14:8), this reading is not implausible.

14:23 *And he took the cup, and when he had given thanks, he gave it to them: and they all drank of it:* The cup would have contained wine; while not part of the HB account, wine was included in the Passover ritual by Jesus' time. No definite article precedes the word "cup," so "a cup" (not a specific cup) is meant here. It is not known whether first-century Jewish custom involved one cup shared by the entire group or individual cups. In later times, the Passover ritual would involve four cups of wine, but it is not clear if that tradition was observed here.

In two other instances in Mark, the word "cup" has symbolic value. When James[35] and John asked for seats of honor, Jesus referred to his suffering as

---

31. See appendix G: "Mark's Christology."
32. Boomershine, *Messiah of Peace,* 87.
33. Collins, *Mark,* 653 note d.
34. Gundry, *Mark,* 831.
35. See the Notes on 1:19.

drinking from the cup he drinks from (10:38). And Jesus will, in his prayer in Gethsemane, describe his suffering as a cup that he wants his Father to remove from him (14:36). So it is likely that part of the symbolism of the Passover cup is that Jesus is inviting his disciples to share in his suffering, a concept that chapter 13 also suggests. There would have been a gap in time between the bread and the cup when the main part of the meal was served, but Mark elides that.

14:24 *And he said unto them, This is my blood of the new testament, which is shed for many:* The word "new" was probably a later addition, intended to harmonize the text with Luke 22:20 and 1 Corinthians 11:25,[36] although it is also possible that it was accidentally omitted. Including the word "new" emphasizes a break with the past (and perhaps echoes Jer. 31:31–34); omitting it suggests that Jesus is not presenting a new covenant but rather renewing the original covenant with new symbols that speak specifically to his role in the covenant.

The word "testament" (especially when prefaced by the word "new") can be confusing for modern English speakers, but here "testament" carries the sense of "covenant." This is not a reference to the collection of documents that would later be known as the New Testament.

The phrase "which is shed" translates a present participle but can apply to the future and thus to the shedding of Jesus' blood.[37] The phrase also suggests a link to the passages that describe the shedding of blood of the sacrificed animals in Leviticus, where similar language is used in the LXX (LXX Lev. 4:7, 18, 25, 30, 34). This shared usage would imply a link between Jesus' death and that of the animals sacrificed, and thus it hints at a theology of the Atonement.

The word "many" has led some interpreters to conclude that Jesus' blood was shed for many—but not all—people. But this reading is unlikely since "many" was sometimes used to connote "all" (Rom. 5:15). The word "many" may have been meant to echo LXX Isaiah 53:11, where the death of the suffering servant will "justify many."

Relationship to Exodus. Exodus 24:8 is the only HB verse that contains both the words "blood" and "covenant" as does this verse in Mark. Jesus is in a sense reenacting the scene from Exodus, which was the ratification of the covenant, except now it is Jesus' blood (symbolized by wine) instead

---

36. Metzger, *Textual Commentary,* 95.
37. Lynne C. Boughton, "'Being Shed for You/Many': Time-Sense and Consequences in the Synoptic Cup Citations," *Tyndale Bulletin* 48, no. 2 (1997): 250.

of animal blood as the token of the covenant. In Exodus, the people verbalize their assent to the covenant; this makes a strong contrast to the Markan context, where the story of the Last Supper is literally surrounded by references to the failure of the disciples.

Relationship to the Anointing (14:3–9). There are substantial similarities between the anointing and the Last Supper:

1. Both the anointing and the Passover are meals with substantial ritual content, with Jesus articulating the interpretation of both rituals.

2. While the same verb isn't used, the anointing involves breaking (of the flask) and the Last Supper (of the bread).

3. Just as the anointing retains but nuances the symbolism of anointing, Jesus does the same with the tradition of the Passover symbols.

4. The woman pours out the contents of her broken flask much as Jesus pours out his blood from his broken body. Jesus explains that the woman has anointed his body for burial, and he then shares his body with the disciples; both incidents are made possible by the complete pouring out of the valuable liquids, nard and blood.

5. Both stories are explicitly focused on Jesus' body and predictions about its future, with reference to his coming death. The phrase "my body" appears only in these two contexts in Mark, with the touch of the anointing and the shared bread of the supper emphasizing the physicality of Jesus' work.

6. Both incidents are followed in close proximity by a "verily" saying (14:9, 25), the former concerning the future of the gospel and the latter concerning Jesus' own future.

7. Both the anointing and the Last Supper are literally surrounded by references to the failure of the disciples. Through this pattern, Mark suggests that the response to the rituals that teach about Jesus is that he is betrayed by those closest to him.

These similarities suggest that the anointer and Jesus should be paralleled. Additionally, the anointing should be regarded as an event of at least equal importance to the Last Supper given the links between them. Perhaps, in Mark, the anointing is more important since it has a statement from Jesus that it should be told wherever the gospel is preached while the text of the Last Supper contains no similar comment about memorializing it; this seems to indicate that, in Mark, the anointing is the key text.

14:25 *Verily I say unto you, I will drink no more of the fruit of the vine, until that day that I drink it new in the kingdom of God:* See the Notes on 3:28 for the significance of "verily I say unto you." Because Jesus uses a "verily" saying here, he emphasizes his prophecy of the future—not the explanation of the symbolism of the bread or the wine—as the key material for the Last Supper. The Greek text contains a triple negation in this verse, which serves to highlight the emphatic nature of Jesus' statement. This verse links Jesus' death to the coming of the kingdom.

The word "new" can refer to Jesus, to imply that he will be new (or renewed) the next time he drinks. It is thus a prophecy of his coming Resurrection.

Jesus' language is literal, pointing to the nearness of his death. But it also has a symbolic aspect, probably relying on Isaiah 25:6–8, which describes the day of the Lord as a banquet including "a feast of wine." This echo points to the fact that Jesus' statement is not only about his imminent fast but also about the coming feast: "There is here a clear anticipation of the messianic banquet when the Passover fellowship with his followers will be renewed in the Kingdom of God."[38] Generally, in the HB, new wine is "a mark of prosperity and good living."[39]

Jesus' statement suggests that this meal is truly a "last" supper—the end of the old order of things—so that "the celebration of the Lord's Supper should not be simply a sorrowful, backward recollection of Jesus' suffering and death but should also conclude with a hopeful looking forward to and joyous anticipation of that glorious day when believers will share with Jesus the 'new' wine/food of the messianic banquet."[40] His statement may also recall his aphorism about not putting new wine into old wine skins (2:22).

See also the Notes on 15:23.

Analysis

In 1 Samuel 10, Samuel anoints Saul to be the king of Israel. Then, as a sign of the authenticity of the kingship, Samuel issues a prophecy that is fulfilled very quickly. Similarly, Jesus was just anointed in 14:3–9. Now, Jesus delivers a prophecy regarding Passover preparation that is quickly fulfilled. Interestingly, both Samuel's and Jesus' prophecies contain references to men carrying liquids (see 1 Sam. 10:3). Thus, this story serves to authenticate Jesus' anointing. This allusion explains why Mark would have included this story about the seemingly mundane details concerning their preparation for the Passover: this is not really a story about preparing for the meal but rather a story showing that Jesus' kingship is legitimate.

---

38. Lane, *Gospel according to Mark*, 508.
39. France, *Gospel of Mark*, 572; see also Gen. 27:28; Deut. 33:28; and Joel 3:18.
40. Stein, *Mark*, 653.

Two characters in this story have intriguing parallels to the anointing woman:

1. The man carrying the water. Because carrying water was considered women's work, this man may echo the previous scene, where a woman—who was also described only as carrying a container of liquid—anointed Jesus. Each one advances the plot in a crucial way, and each acts contrary to expectations of their gender role.

2. The owner of the house. This is obviously a person of some wealth, who is willing to give lavishly to Jesus as the anointing woman did. The generosity of both of these anonymous characters is essential to teaching about who Jesus is in a ritualized setting.

Many similarities also link Jesus' preparations to enter Jerusalem and his preparations for the Passover. Both stories seem somewhat out of place in the text as they describe incidents that could have been omitted without disrupting the flow of the story. The stories share eleven consecutive words (Greek: *apostellei duo tōn mathētōn autou kai legei autois hypagete eis tēn* in 11:1–2 [KJV: "he sendeth forth two of his disciples, and saith unto them, go your way into the . . ."] and 14:13 [KJV: "he sendeth forth two of his disciples, and saith unto them, go ye into the . . ."]), an echo that Mark's listening audience was likely to catch. Both involve Jesus' prophetic knowledge of events, and both show clearly and quickly that his prophecy is correct. Thus one function of these two stories might be to affirm Jesus' prophetic ability and thus to increase the audience's level of trust in Jesus regarding the prophetic statements whose fulfillment is not narrated within the text (such as the prophecies in chapter 13).

Another function of the similarities between these stories is to bracket the material that occurs between them (11:12–14:11), much as the two similar healings bracketed the middle section of Mark's Gospel. And much as those healings inform the interpretation of the stories that they surround, showing the need for and Jesus' ability to open the eyes of his disciples, this bracketing suggests that Jesus' prophetic ability surrounds and therefore must guide the interpretation of his controversies in the temple and his teachings in chapter 13. Intriguingly, this structure groups the anointing story with this bracketed material as well; this is not normally done by interpreters, but it does make good sense given that the anointing story has elements of controversy and shows Jesus teaching the objectors. And inasmuch as all of 11:12–13:37 either occurs in or is focused on the temple, it suggests that the anointing story would also contain temple themes (see "Jesus' Temple Action" within the section "Relationship to Other Stories in Mark" after the Notes on 14:9).

At the Last Supper, Jesus aligns a broken piece of bread with his own body. This scene shows Jesus "symbolically enacting"[41] his death. Much as the withering of the fig tree was an enacted parable for the destruction of the temple,[42] the Last Supper is an enacted parable for the destruction of Jesus' body. But the implication is that the destruction of the bread is not its final end because it will nourish the disciples, just as Jesus' life will continue to animate the lives of his disciples. So "when [Jesus] wanted fully to explain what his forthcoming death was all about, he didn't give them a theory. He didn't even give them a set of scriptural texts. He gave them a meal."[43]

The Passover ritual included a meal where the head of the household presented a symbolic interpretation of the foods consumed; in this sense the Last Supper is a typical Passover meal. The bread of the Passover meal represented the suffering of Israel's ancestors in Egypt; Jesus shifts that so that the bread suggests his own suffering. Because the suffering in Egypt led to liberation, the hint is that Jesus' suffering body will lead to liberation as well. The bread was eaten unleavened, which symbolized the fact that the children of Israel had to be ready to leave Egypt at a moment's notice when the opportunity for freedom came. The implication is that Jesus' body symbolizes quickly coming deliverance from evil. This reinterpretation of the symbolism makes Jesus' body (represented by the bread) into the site for God's act of liberation. Jesus shifts the symbolism in another way: the elements of the meal no longer point to a past event but rather one in the future.

It may be significant that the lamb is not mentioned in the account of the Last Supper despite the fact that it was central to the Passover observance and was already mentioned in 14:12. It would have been logical for Jesus to compare his body to the sacrificial lamb; other early Christian writings develop this idea (1 Cor. 5:7). And yet Mark's account does not mention it. It is possible that if Mark's account were written after the destruction of the temple, when it was no longer possible to have a ritually sacrificed Passover lamb, anything Jesus had said about the lamb at the Last Supper would have had less immediate relevance to early Christians, and so they may not have included them in the record.

---

41. France, *Gospel of Mark*, 568.

42. See the Notes on 11:12–14 and 20–26.

43. N. T. Wright, *Simply Jesus: A New Vision of Who He Was, What He Did, and Why He Matters* (New York: HarperOne, 2011), 180.

With both the bread and the wine, there is a strong element of community participation in the meal: "The essential action which accompanied this word was not the breaking of the bread, but its distribution."[44] Jesus is inviting the disciples to join in his body and blood as they join in a communal meal. The idea of drinking blood would have been anathema to Jews: the covenant God made with Noah prohibited human consumption of blood on the grounds that it contained the life force (Gen. 9:4–6). (In fact, the radicalness of associating the wine with his blood may explain why, unlike with the bread, Jesus has them consume the wine before the interpretation of the symbol is given.) Because of the equation of blood with life, the disciples are in a sense taking Jesus' life when they drink the wine. Once again, there is Atonement theology here.

The Passover wine recalls an event where blood on the doorposts prevented the angel of death from harming the inhabitants of the home. Here, the blood is taken internally, from the cup that symbolizes suffering. The symbolism suggests that the wine, as the lamb's blood, will protect them from death. Much as the blood of the Passover lamb made escape from Egypt possible, Jesus' blood makes escape from spiritual slavery possible (compare 3:27).

Mark includes no command to repeat the ritual of the Passover in the future. Mark's approach emphasizes the symbolism of the meal instead of its repetition.

JESUS PROPHESIES BETRAYAL (14:26–31)

Greek Text

26 Καὶ ὑμνήσαντες ἐξῆλθον εἰς τὸ Ὄρος τῶν Ἐλαιῶν. 27 Καὶ λέγει αὐτοῖς ὁ Ἰησοῦς ὅτι Πάντες σκανδαλισθήσεσθε, ὅτι γέγραπται· Πατάξω τὸν ποιμένα, καὶ τὰ πρόβατα διασκορπισθήσονται. 28 ἀλλὰ μετὰ τὸ ἐγερθῆναί με προάξω ὑμᾶς εἰς τὴν Γαλιλαίαν. 29 ὁ δὲ Πέτρος ἔφη αὐτῷ· Εἰ καὶ πάντες σκανδαλισθήσονται, ἀλλ᾽ οὐκ ἐγώ. 30 καὶ λέγει αὐτῷ ὁ Ἰησοῦς· Ἀμὴν λέγω σοι ὅτι σὺ σήμερον ταύτῃ τῇ νυκτὶ πρὶν ἢ δὶς ἀλέκτορα φωνῆσαι τρίς με ἀπαρνήσῃ. 31 ὁ δὲ ἐκπερισσῶς ἐλάλει· Ἐὰν δέῃ με συναποθανεῖν σοι, οὐ μή σε ἀπαρνήσομαι. ὡσαύτως δὲ καὶ πάντες ἔλεγον. [SBLGNT]

---

44. Lane, *Gospel according to Mark*, 506.

King James Version

26 And when they had sung an hymn, they went out into the mount of Olives. 27 And Jesus saith unto them, All ye shall be offended because of me this night: for it is written, I will smite the shepherd, and the sheep shall be scattered. 28 But after that I am risen, I will go before you into Galilee. 29 But Peter said unto him, Although all shall be offended, yet will not I. 30 And Jesus saith unto him, Verily I say unto thee, That this day, even in this night, before the cock crow twice, thou shalt deny me thrice. 31 But he spake the more vehemently, If I should die with thee, I will not deny thee in any wise. Likewise also said they all.

New Rendition

26 And having sung a hymn, they went out to the Mount of Olives. 27 And Jesus says to them, "All of you will desert me, for it has been written, 'I will strike down the shepherd, and the sheep will be scattered.' 28 But after I am raised, I will go ahead of you into Galilee." 29 But Peter said to him, "Even if everyone deserts you, I will not!" 30 And Jesus says to him, "Amen, I say to you: today—this very night—before the rooster crows twice, you will deny me three times." 31 But he was insisting, "Even if I have to die with you, I will never deny you!" And they all said the same thing.

Notes

14:26 *And when they had sung an hymn, they went out into the mount of Olives:* It was customary to sing Psalms 115–18 after the Passover meal. The line "I shall not die, but live" in Psalm 118:17 would have several layers of irony on this occasion.

The Mount of Olives is the same location as Jesus' teachings in chapter 13.

14:27 *And Jesus saith unto them, All ye shall be offended because of me this night:* Many manuscripts omit the phrase "because of me this night"; it was probably added to harmonize with Matthew 26:31, but it is possible that the phrase was accidentally omitted.[45]

The word "offended" implies being ensnared, turning against Jesus, or being scandalized.

At the meal, the disciples learned that one of them would betray Jesus. Here, they find out that none of them will be successful disciples in the short term.

for it is written, I will smite the shepherd, and the sheep shall be scattered: It is not clear whether this line should be read as a continuation of Jesus' statement or as Mark's commentary on Jesus' statement. Because the word "strike" implies causing death, this is another prediction of Jesus' death.

---

45. Collins, *Mark,* 657–58 note a.

This line is a quotation of Zechariah 13:7. (This portion of Zechariah is frequently quoted in the Passion narrative.) In Zechariah, the Lord commands that the shepherds (unfaithful kings) are smitten with the result that the sheep (the people of Israel) are scattered. Many HB texts use the imagery of gathering sheep to describe the role of a leader (Num. 27:17; 1 Kgs. 22:17; Ezek. 34:8–15; Zech. 10:2). This means that the shepherd in Zechariah is portrayed negatively as an unfaithful king, making this an odd scripture to be applied to Jesus. However, it is possible that the intended association is simply that when a shepherd is struck, the sheep are scattered and no other parallels should be drawn. Zechariah 10:6–12 pictures the regathering of the scattered because of the compassion of the Lord, so the imagery from Zechariah might lead to the idea of Jesus' return, mentioned in the next verse in Mark.

14:28 But after that I am risen, I will go before you into Galilee: It is possible that this verse is a later addition to Mark: it is missing from one third-century copy of Mark,[46] and the next verse seems to answer the previous verse and ignore this verse. It is also easy to imagine a later scribe adding this verse so that 16:7 would make better sense. And yet most of the ancient manuscripts do contain this verse, and the fact that in the next verse, Peter responds to 14:27 (not 14:28) does seem to be in character with Peter's myopic focus.

This is a prophecy of the resurrection from the dead; the passive verb form suggests that God is the one who will do the raising. The verse could be interpreted to mean that Jesus will be in Galilee and the disciples are to meet him there, or that Jesus will lead them to Galilee.

See also 16:7, which makes reference to this verse.

14:29 But Peter said unto him, Although all shall be offended, yet will not I: What is most striking about Peter's response is that he is responding to 14:27, not to 14:28. He demonstrates his inability to hear—in a very literal sense—Jesus' prophecy of the Resurrection and the way that the disciples are invited to continue their ministry, even after their failure. Peter responds to none of this; rather, he disputes Jesus' contention that he (Peter) will be offended. Of course, this is rather ironic since Peter is, in this moment, showing himself to be offended by what Jesus said. Further, Peter thrusts himself into the role of a prophet as he attempts to predict the future better than Jesus can. As if this weren't bad enough, he is also boasting that he is stronger than all of the other disciples. (There will be a special irony in that he will fail Jesus more than they will—not just abandoning

---

46. Lane, *Gospel according to Mark,* 510 n. 63.

Jesus but also denying him.) There is a warning about self-aggrandizing discipleship woven into Peter's story.

A case can be made that Jesus' suffering begins here: in this scene, Jesus is experiencing the distress that comes from being misunderstood and from having those close to him not accept his leadership.

14:30 *And Jesus saith unto him, verily I say unto thee, That this day, even in this night, before the cock crow twice, thou shalt deny me thrice:* See the Notes on 3:28 on "verily I say unto thee." The phrase "this day, even in this night" makes sense in a Jewish context where the day was considered to begin at sunset.

The verb tense used here makes it unlikely that Jesus commanded Peter to betray him[47] and more likely that this is a prophetic statement.

14:31 *But he spake the more vehemently, If I should die with thee, I will not deny thee in any wise. Likewise also said they all:* It is extremely ironic that Peter's claim that he will not deny Jesus is in fact a denial of what Jesus has said. Once again, Peter is acting as if he has a greater prophetic gift than Jesus. And because Peter is in the very act of denying Jesus, Jesus' words are coming true in this moment, showing the audience that Jesus' prophetic ability is superior to Peter's. The message to the audience would have been clear: the disciples are not as trustworthy as Jesus is. It is even possible that Mark's audience might have laughed at this line because Peter is so obviously wrong. This exchange could be viewed as a moment of comic relief in between the heavy scenes of Passover and Gethsemane.

Because 14:32 suggests that they are walking while this conversation is occurring, the "journey" motif from the middle section of Mark's Gospel is reenacted here. Once again, a literal journey is tied to the journey of discipleship.

Jesus does not respond to this statement. Mark's audience would have been struck by a conversation that seems to end in the middle, with no final word from Jesus.

Analysis

Jesus' quotation from Zechariah removes some of the culpability from the disciples (the "sheep") for their scattering (abandoning Jesus) by framing the scattering of the sheep as the natural result of the death of the shepherd. Thus, one important aspect of the discipleship theme in Mark

---

47. Eric D. Huntsman, "The Accounts of Peter's Denial," in Judd, Huntsman, and Hopkin, *Ministry of Peter*, 134–36.

is the inability of the disciples to function properly without Jesus' guidance. This reflects the importance of Jesus more than the weakness of the disciples.

Mark's Gospel has a strong sense of symbolic narrative space. The first third of the Gospel is centered in Galilee and the final third in Jerusalem. Mark 14:28 and 16:7 (which refers to 14:28) are the only references to Galilee in the final third of the Gospel, but they have an outsized effect. While first-century conventional wisdom in the Jewish world held Jerusalem to be the central focal point, Jesus' ministry inverts this logic by showing Jerusalem to be the place of his death but Galilee to be the central location of both his mortal and postmortal ministry. The statement that Jesus will go before them to Galilee implies that Jesus' return will be a continuation of his Galilean ministry (not a continuation of the middle section of the Gospel, which was his journey to Jerusalem, or a continuation of the final third, which focused mostly on his suffering and death). The kinds of things Jesus did in Galilee—healing miracles, exorcisms, and teaching with authority—will continue to be the focus. There is also a sense, particularly with 16:7, of the story starting all over again via the return to Galilee.

Jesus' words about going before them to Galilee imply that he will continue to lead the disciples after he is raised up. He has posited a time when his death would mean that his sheep would be scattered, but then he shows that that is a temporary condition. This strongly suggests that the disciples' failures in the remainder of the text are not permanent. Jesus prophesies his return as the shepherd who gathers and leads the sheep. The journey from Galilee to Jerusalem that constituted the middle section of the Gospel text will be reversed via the return journey. Since the middle section of Mark was focused on discipleship, the implication is that this return journey will also teach them how to be better disciples.

Their return to discipleship is prophesied here and is tied to the Resurrection: it is the Resurrection that makes renewed discipleship possible after failure.

Peter boasts that he would not desert Jesus, but Jesus responds that Peter will not only desert but also deny Jesus. There is irony here: Peter had claimed that he was different from the other disciples; Jesus responds that Peter is indeed distinct—but in a negative sense. The only use of the word "deny" outside of the story of Peter's denial is when Jesus taught that following him required self-denial (8:34). Ironically, Peter will not deny himself but rather deny Jesus.

Because roosters crow before first light, Jesus is prophesying that Peter's denial will happen very soon. When Jesus' prediction is fulfilled (14:72), Mark's audience would once again have evidence that Jesus is a prophet indeed. (See also the discussion of the symbolism of cocks in the Notes on 14:72.)

It is significant that Jesus was described as specifically and deliberately selecting Peter as a disciple (1:16–17; 3:14–16). Jesus did not choose his disciples based on their perfection or devotion; in Mark's Gospel, the disciples are primarily learners who in turn teach the audience to be better disciples through the story of their experiences with Jesus, including their missteps.

In Mark's Gospel, the story of the Last Supper is bracketed by references to the failure of the disciples. In fact, very little attention is paid to the Last Supper per se in Mark's narrative. Rather, the Last Supper is primarily a story about discipleship: "The theme of failed discipleship continues to be central; more than half of Mark's narration of Thursday evening and night is devoted to it (thirty-three of sixty-one verses: 14:18–21, 27–45, 50–52, 66–72)."[48]

The emphasis on betrayal and failure would have been heightened by the audience's expectation that the Passover would be a celebration and remembrance of liberation; instead, it is shot through with references to Jesus' capture and his disciples' role in exacerbating the situation. The implication is that something about the Last Supper makes it possible for the disciples to rebound from failure. The reimagining of the Passover symbolism as Jesus' body and blood and his invitation to the disciples to participate in the ritual suggest a continual invitation to discipleship. Because the Last Supper is literally surrounded by references to the betrayal of Jesus by the disciples, the focal point of the meal is that Jesus is willing to give his body and blood to people that he knows are not going to live up to their obligations to him and will instead cause his suffering.

JESUS PRAYS
(14:32–42)

Greek Text

32 Καὶ ἔρχονται εἰς χωρίον οὗ τὸ ὄνομα Γεθσημανί, καὶ λέγει τοῖς μαθηταῖς αὐτοῦ· Καθίσατε ὧδε ἕως προσεύξωμαι. 33 καὶ παραλαμβάνει τὸν Πέτρον καὶ Ἰάκωβον καὶ Ἰωάννην μετ' αὐτοῦ, καὶ ἤρξατο ἐκθαμβεῖσθαι καὶ ἀδημονεῖν, 34 καὶ λέγει αὐτοῖς· Περίλυπός ἐστιν ἡ ψυχή μου ἕως θανάτου· μείνατε ὧδε καὶ γρηγορεῖτε.

---

48. Borg and Crossan, *Last Week*, 113.

35 καὶ προελθὼν μικρὸν ἔπιπτεν ἐπὶ τῆς γῆς, καὶ προσηύχετο ἵνα εἰ δυνατόν ἐστιν παρέλθῃ ἀπ᾽ αὐτοῦ ἡ ὥρα, 36 καὶ ἔλεγεν· Αββα ὁ πατήρ, πάντα δυνατά σοι· παρένεγκε τὸ ποτήριον τοῦτο ἀπ᾽ ἐμοῦ· ἀλλ᾽ οὐ τί ἐγὼ θέλω ἀλλὰ τί σύ. 37 καὶ ἔρχεται καὶ εὑρίσκει αὐτοὺς καθεύδοντας, καὶ λέγει τῷ Πέτρῳ· Σίμων, καθεύδεις; οὐκ ἴσχυσας μίαν ὥραν γρηγορῆσαι; 38 γρηγορεῖτε καὶ προσεύχεσθε, ἵνα μὴ ἔλθητε εἰς πειρασμόν· τὸ μὲν πνεῦμα πρόθυμον ἡ δὲ σὰρξ ἀσθενής. 39 καὶ πάλιν ἀπελθὼν προσηύξατο τὸν αὐτὸν λόγον εἰπών. 40 καὶ πάλιν ἐλθὼν εὗρεν αὐτοὺς καθεύδοντας, ἦσαν γὰρ αὐτῶν οἱ ὀφθαλμοὶ καταβαρυνόμενοι, καὶ οὐκ ᾔδεισαν τί ἀποκριθῶσιν αὐτῷ. 41 καὶ ἔρχεται τὸ τρίτον καὶ λέγει αὐτοῖς· Καθεύδετε τὸ λοιπὸν καὶ ἀναπαύεσθε· ἀπέχει· ἦλθεν ἡ ὥρα, ἰδοὺ παραδίδοται ὁ υἱὸς τοῦ ἀνθρώπου εἰς τὰς χεῖρας τῶν ἁμαρτωλῶν. 42 ἐγείρεσθε ἄγωμεν· ἰδοὺ ὁ παραδιδούς με ἤγγικεν.
[SBLGNT]

King James Version

32 And they came to a place which was named Gethsemane: and he saith to his disciples, Sit ye here, while I shall pray. 33 And he taketh with him Peter and James and John, and began to be sore amazed, and to be very heavy; 34 And saith unto them, My soul is exceeding sorrowful unto death: tarry ye here, and watch. 35 And he went forward a little, and fell on the ground, and prayed that, if it were possible, the hour might pass from him. 36 And he said, Abba, Father, all things are possible unto thee; take away this cup from me: nevertheless not what I will, but what thou wilt. 37 And he cometh, and findeth them sleeping, and saith unto Peter, Simon, sleepest thou? couldest not thou watch one hour? 38 Watch ye and pray, lest ye enter into temptation. The spirit truly is ready, but the flesh is weak. 39 And again he went away, and prayed, and spake the same words. 40 And when he returned, he found them asleep again, (for their eyes were heavy,) neither wist they what to answer him. 41 And he cometh the third time, and saith unto them, Sleep on now, and take your rest: it is enough,

New Rendition

32 And they come to a place that is called Gethsemane. And he says to his disciples, "Sit here while I pray." 33 And he takes Peter, Jacob, and John with him. And he began to be stunned and deeply distressed. 34 And he says to them, "My soul is greatly grieved—even to death. Stay here and watch." 35 And having moved forward a little, he threw himself on the ground and prayed that, if it is possible, the hour might pass from him. 36 And he was saying, "Abba, Father, all things are possible for you. Take away this cup from me. But not what I want, but what you want." 37 And he comes and finds them sleeping. And he says to Peter, "Simon, are you asleep? Were you not strong enough to watch for one hour? 38 Watch and pray so that you don't enter into temptation. The spirit is willing, but the flesh is weak." 39 And having gone away again, he prayed, having said the same words. 40 And having returned again, he found them sleeping—because they could not keep their eyes open. And they didn't know what to tell him. 41 And he comes the third time, and he says to them, "Are you still

the hour is come; behold, the Son of man is betrayed into the hands of sinners. 42 Rise up, let us go; lo, he that betrayeth me is at hand.

sleeping and resting? Enough. The hour has come. Look: the son of man is delivered into the hands of sinners. 42 Rise up, let's go. Look: the one who is betraying me is approaching."

Notes

14:32 *And they came to a place which was named Gethsemane:* Gethsemane is described as a "place" (Greek: *chōrion*), which probably implies an estate; Mark does not use the word "garden" to describe it. It is possible that it is a cave.[49] "Gethsemane" means "oil press" in Hebrew and Aramaic. Because they are still on the Mount of Olives, it is likely that Gethsemane was an olive grove (if it refers to the cave, there is evidence that the cave was used for the preparation of oil).[50] Given that Mark emphasizes the name (not "they came to Gethsemane" but "they came to a place which was named Gethsemane"), the location likely has symbolic meaning. In the HB, olive oil had a consecrating function (Ex. 30:22–38).

and he saith to his disciples, Sit ye here, while I shall pray: Presumably "disciples" refers to the same group that observed the Passover with Jesus—so the Twelve plus other disciples, including women.

14:33 *And he taketh with him Peter and James and John:* Jesus first has a larger group of disciples in Gethsemane, but then singles out Peter, James,[51] and John to be closer to where he will pray. It is not clear whether future references to the disciples in this scene—including 14:37–38, 40, and 41–42—refer just to Peter, James, and John or to the larger group. There are two reasons why Jesus might have isolated a smaller group of disciples here:

1. This fits a pattern evident at the raising of Jairus's daughter (which also included her parents), the Transfiguration, and chapter 13 (which also included Andrew) of Jesus selecting a smaller group of disciples to witness events of key importance.

2. These three are the only disciples who have boasted of their ability to endure without fail (10:38–39; 14:29). Jesus has thus allowed them to watch him prepare for suffering so that they will be able to endure as he does. Of course, this

---

49. Joan E. Taylor, "The Garden of Gethsemane: Not the Place of Jesus' Arrest," *Biblical Archaeology Review* 21 (July/August 1995): 26–30.

50. Taylor, "Garden of Gethsemane," 26–30.

51. See the Notes on 1:19.

does not work since they fall asleep. But the point is that Jesus has provided them with an opportunity to learn to endure suffering.

and began to be sore amazed, and to be very heavy: The language used here to describe Jesus' mental distress is strong: "The two verbs together describe an extremely acute emotion, a compound of bewilderment, fear, uncertainty and anxiety."[52] Jesus' attitude is not "contemplative detachment, but . . . genuine human terror."[53]

14:34 ***And saith unto them, My soul is exceeding sorrowful unto death:*** Jesus' sentiment is that his grief is so great that it feels as if it might kill him. There is a certain tragic irony in the idea that his coming death grieves him to the point of death.

The audience gets a picture of Jesus' emotions not only from the narrator but also from Jesus himself, which highlights his emotional state by noting it twice.

Jesus' language describing his sorrow echoes Psalm 42:4–11, which speaks of the suffering of the psalmist but then pivots to an affirmation that, after a time, God will intervene.

tarry ye here, and watch: "Tarry" means to remain: Jesus has invited Peter, James, and John to move away from the other disciples, but he does not want them to follow him when he moves on.

Why does Jesus tell them to watch? Possibilities include:

1. The Passover observance was to be a night of watching for the Lord (Ex. 12:42), which suggests that Jesus' actions in Gethsemane are similar to the Lord "passing over" the people in the Exodus account. This is a significant part of Mark's presentation of the Atonement.

2. Watching "is the proper response to suffering,"[54] so Jesus is teaching the disciples how to respond to the suffering of others.

3. The disciples are to watch so that they can be witnesses to Jesus' suffering. One problem with this reading is that they repeatedly fail to watch, suggesting that it was not actually necessary for them to witness Jesus' suffering.

4. The disciples are to watch so that they can prevent the disciple who will betray Jesus from leaving and/or protect Jesus from those who would arrest him. Once again, a problem with these interpretations is that the disciples fail at this task. But it is possible that the failure is precisely the point: had the disciples been more vigilant, Jesus would not have been arrested. Their sleeping

---

52. Bratcher and Nida, *Translator's Handbook,* 446.
53. Myers, *Binding the Strong Man,* 366.
54. Dowd, *Reading Mark,* 152.

becomes a symbol of their weakness and thus functions theologically: it is human weakness that causes Jesus' death.

5. Jesus has singled out the three disciples who have boasted of their ability to suffer with him (10:38–39; 14:29–31). They are now to watch him to learn how to prevail against suffering. But they don't watch, so they aren't able to prevail when the time comes. This reading is significant because it casts Jesus' prayer in Gethsemane as the model of the preparation necessary to endure suffering; as his prayer will show, submission of one's will to the Father is the key to successfully enduring suffering. But the disciples sleep instead of watching (despite the fact that they were taught in chapter 13 to watch), and so they are left unready for their own challenges. Significantly, Mark's audience stays awake throughout the story, and so they are prepared to be successful disciples and follow Jesus' model.

6. They are to stay awake in order to support Jesus.[55] In this reading, Jesus' suffering is worse than it otherwise would have been because his disciples are not providing him the support that he requested.

14:35 *And he went forward a little, and fell on the ground:* The idea that Jesus "fell" may mean that he intentionally prostrated himself, it might be a physical manifestation of his grief, or it might be a sign of his exhaustion. This is not a normal prayer posture, although falling on one's face before prayer is not unknown in the HB (Gen. 17:3).

First Samuel chapter 28 contains a similar story: "King Saul hear[s] a prophecy of his violent death and collaps[es] on the ground (*epesen . . . epi tēn gēn*) in great fear (1 Sam 28:20 LXX). The parallel is especially striking because Saul is the Lord's anointed (1 Sam 10:1, etc.), but God has now rejected him and refuses to hear his prayer (1 Sam 28:6) and he will subsequently be 'turned over to the hands' of his enemies (1 Sam 28:19) to be killed."[56]

and prayed that, if it were possible, the hour might pass from him: The "hour" refers to the time when Jesus is handed over (14:41).

Jesus has previously made many predictions of his suffering and death; if it were to not happen, he would be shown to be a false prophet. Nonetheless, Jesus prays to avoid his fate.

14:36 *And he said, Abba, Father, all things are possible unto thee:* Because "he said" is imperfect ("he was saying"), it probably anticipates the threefold repetition of the prayer.

55. Collins, *Mark*, 677.
56. Marcus, *Mark 8–16*, 977.

"Abba" is Aramaic for "father." Mark also provides the Greek word for "father." (It may be the case that Mark records the Aramaic word and its Greek translation when the actual words of Jesus are included.) While this word could be used by a small child for its father, it is used in other situations as well. It is a "somewhat unconventional"[57] term for God, but it is probably not unique. The idea of God as a father has strong HB precedent (Deut. 32:6; Isa. 63:16; Jer. 31:19; Mal. 1:6).

The narrator described Jesus' prayer in the previous verse; this verse is the prayer in Jesus' own words. The narrator used the phrase "if it were possible," but Jesus says, "all things are possible." There appears to be a distinction between the perspective of the narrator and Jesus' perspective.

take away this cup from me: Jesus uses a cup as a metaphor for his suffering and death. Additional resonances of this metaphor include:

1. *The Cup of Wrath.* Several HB texts use a cup as a metaphor for the wrath of God (Isa. 51:17; Lam. 4:21; Ezek. 23:32–34), and Jesus has already used the cup metaphor with this meaning (10:38). Its use in Isaiah 51:22 is particularly significant because it presents God as removing the cup of wrath; Jesus' words indicate that he hopes the same thing will happen in his case. Jesus' language may also echo Jeremiah 49:12, where the Lord says that even the one who did not deserve it must drink of his wrath. If Mark's audience recognized that allusion, they would have found in Jesus' words an acknowledgment of his innocence. Further, in some HB texts, the cup is linked to the "theme of the judgment of the nations."[58] This would suggest that Jesus will take on himself the judgment that all nations deserve; this would point to a theology of Atonement.

2. *The Passover Cup.* The most recent reference to a cup in Mark's text has been at the Passover meal (14:23). However, it is difficult to make a connection between these two texts because Jesus promised his disciples he would not drink again, but here he asks God to take the cup away. Despite their proximity and shared vocabulary, these texts are probably not otherwise linked.

3. *The Cup of Salvation.* The disciples would have just sung Psalm 116, so Psalm 116:13, "I will take the cup of salvation," may have been in mind, suggesting a link between the cup that Jesus will drink and the idea of salvation. The fourth verse of the psalm also contains a plea to God to spare the psalmist's life, which also fits the context here well.

nevertheless not what I will, but what thou wilt: It is significant that Mark presents Jesus' will as being different from his Father's. Nonetheless,

---

57. Evans, *Mark 8:27–16:20,* 412.
58. Collins, *Mark,* 680.

Jesus is willing to choose his Father's will instead of his own will, even when it will cause him intense suffering; he enacts the principle he taught in 8:33–34. Jesus does not view the point of prayer as solely to change God's will; nonetheless, he does make the request.

Mark's account gives no indication that Jesus suffers physically in Gethsemane (except possibly for physical suffering resulting from emotional distress). One cause—perhaps the cause—of his emotional distress is his recognition that his will and his Father's will do not align and he must choose his Father's will.

14:37 *And he cometh, and findeth them sleeping:* It is not clear whether "they" refers solely to Peter, James, and John or to all of the disciples.

and saith unto Peter, Simon, sleepest thou?: "Sleepest thou" could be read as a question ("Are you asleep?"). Jesus calls Peter "Simon" here; this seems particularly significant since the narrator has just referred to him as Peter. The odd naming might imply that Peter has (temporarily; compare 16:7) lost the right to the new name Jesus had given him (3:16). Peter's sleeping is a failing; he is not acting like the "rock" he was called to be. The next line, which questions Peter's lack of strength, supports this idea.

This is not the first time Jesus has renamed Peter but the third. The first renaming was at Peter's calling to the Twelve. The second was another instance when Peter's weakness was apparent, and Jesus thus referred to him as "Satan" (8:33).

couldest not thou watch one hour?: The verb translated as "couldest" means to have the strength or power to do something, so the implication of this question is that Peter lacked the strength that he was supposed to have.

This question should be read in light of Peter's recent boast that he would be able to stand with Jesus even to death (14:31). The fact that he lacked the strength to stay awake illustrates his weakness by sharp contrast to his bluster.

14:38 *Watch ye and pray, lest ye enter into temptation:* Unlike the previous verse, the verbs here are plural, indicating that Jesus is no longer speaking just to Peter.

"Temptation" could refer to temptation or to testing. In either case, given the context, it would most likely refer to the temptation to abandon Jesus. There are two ways to understand the logic of this verse:

1. The disciples are to pray. What they are to pray for is that they will not enter into temptation.
2. The disciples are to pray, but the content of the prayer is not specified. The result of praying is that they will not be tempted.

It is difficult to decide between these two options. In either case, it is clear that avoiding temptation is linked to prayer.

Jesus had not initially told them to pray, although he does tell them now. It may be significant that he provides a model of prayer before commanding them to pray.

The spirit truly is ready, but the flesh is weak: Most interpreters find a contrast between the human spirit and human flesh here, but it is also possible that Jesus is referring to the Holy Spirit in contrast to human flesh. The prayers in Gethsemane show how to follow the Spirit instead of the flesh; the disciples' task is to watch this model of prayer. Had they done so, they would have known how to subjugate the flesh to the spirit.

Soon, the narrator will explain that the disciples' sleep was the result of their eyes being "heavy" (14:40). In other words, the problem is a weakness of the flesh. Read in that context, this verse implies that the disciples' spirits are willing to follow Jesus but that their flesh is too weak.

14:39 ***And again he went away, and prayed, and spake the same words:*** Jesus repeats his prayer from 14:36, but Mark does not repeat his words in the text. It may be that Mark does not include the words of the prayer to downplay the fact that it had not been answered (compare 5:8, where Mark reorders the narrative to obscure the fact that an exorcism is not successful on the first try; see the Notes on that verse). The lack of repetition of the prayer is particularly striking given that not only does Mark repeat that the disciples were sleeping but also adds an explanation to it (see the next verse). In addition to wanting to elide the fact that Jesus' prayer was not immediately answered, Mark's focus in this story—as in all stories—is on the experience of discipleship.

14:40 ***And when he returned, he found them asleep again, (for their eyes were heavy,):*** This verse repeats 14:37 but adds the explanation that their eyes were heavy. But this is a nonexplanation; it is as if Mark had said "they were sleepy because they were tired." Perhaps the reference is symbolic: the disciples cannot see and therefore are acting like outsiders (compare 4:12 and 8:18). The heavy eyes may also exemplify the weak flesh from 14:38.

neither wist they what to answer him: This line implies that Jesus has asked them a question (compare 14:37), although Mark does not narrate the question.

14:41 ***And he cometh the third time, and saith unto them, Sleep on now, and take your rest:*** "Sleep" can be read as

1. a question ("Are you sleeping?").

2. a command, which could be

   a. sarcastic ("Fine then—sleep!").

   b. genuine. This would suggest that the disciples had stayed awake this time and were now given permission to sleep. There is an element of irony that they had previously slept when they were supposed to be awake but now need to be commanded to sleep.

it is enough, the hour is come: The meaning of "it is enough" is extremely difficult to determine. Options include:

1. "It is enough sleeping." This would add irony to the passage: the disciples were supposed to be watching Jesus, but Jesus ends up watching them.

2. "It is distant." This meaning comports with the only other Markan usage (7:6) and its usual meaning in other literature. It may mean that Judas is distant, so that they may sleep for awhile longer. When Judas approaches, Jesus will tell them to rise up.

3. "Is it distant?" Perhaps it is a question where the answer is "no." The point would be that Jesus' hour is not far distant. This meaning fits the context well: Jesus has asked them if they were still sleeping and if they think the end is far away. They shouldn't be asleep because his hour is near.

4. "It is enough of a rebuke." In this case, the point would be that Jesus is finished rebuking the disciples for sleeping instead of watching.

5. "It is enough praying." Jesus has finished his prayer. Perhaps this indicates that his prayer has been answered. This interpretation would link nicely to the next line: the betrayal of the Son of Man is part of the hour that has come.

6. "It is paid."[59] This would refer to the money given to Judas. It would suggest Jesus' prophetic awareness of what had transpired.

This is the hour that Jesus had prayed to have pass from him.

In this story, Mark's audience is allowed to be insiders in a way that even Peter, James, and John are not. Presumably, Mark's audience stays awake throughout the story.

See also the section "Relationship to Gethsemane" after the Notes on 14:72.

Relationship to the Transfiguration. There are several similarities between the Transfiguration and Gethsemane: both scenes single out Peter, James, and John, and both note that the disciples did not know what to say (9:6). But there is also an interesting inversion: at the Transfiguration, they did not understand Jesus' glorification; in Gethsemane, they do not understand his suffering. Both stories showcase the lack of understanding of the disciples.

---

59. Bratcher and Nida, *Translator's Handbook,* 452. "The money has been paid."

Relationship to Chapter 13. The prayer in Gethsemane and chapter 13 both take place on the Mount of Olives. In both scenes, Jesus tells the disciples to watch three times—a link made more significant by the fact that these are the only uses of the word "watch" (Greek *grēgoreuō*) in Mark (13:34, 35, 37; 14:34, 37, 38). This strong echo would have encouraged Mark's audience to compare these scenes. Jesus has warned them in chapter 13 that the key duty for disciples in perilous times is to watch; the reminders to watch in Gethsemane indicate that the time has come. This makes the failure of the disciples to watch (which is symbolized by their sleeping) all the more stark.

behold, the Son of man is betrayed into the hands of sinners: Mark's audience knows that Jesus has repeatedly predicted this moment (8:31; 9:31; 10:33–34). So despite appearances, events are not spinning out of Jesus' control; rather, his prophecies are being fulfilled.

Jesus' words here echo some HB texts: being turned over into others' hands (KJV: "betrayed into the hands") is the language used to describe what God does to Israel as a result of Israel's wickedness (Jer. 21:10; 22:25; Ezek. 7:21; 11:9). Thus, Jesus is being treated the way that Israel is treated when it violates the covenant. Because Mark's audience knows that Jesus has been faithful, this language suggests that Jesus is taking on himself a punishment that others deserved. Similarly, in Daniel 7:13–14, the Son of Man is given dominion and authority—the opposite of being given into the hands of sinners. This inversion is ironic: Jesus deserves to be rewarded by God but is instead taking on punishment.

14:42 *Rise up, let us go:* In the previous verse, Jesus told the disciples to sleep, so the command to rise up seems jarring. Perhaps time has passed; one might imagine a performer pausing at the end of the last verse to suggest the passage of time.

"Let us go" implies that they are going to meet Judas, not going to escape. Mark presents Jesus as accepting his fate.

lo, he that betrayeth me is at hand: Judas is not named here; this is perhaps ironic given the abundant naming of Judas earlier in the chapter and in the next verse. (And, again, it is possible in Mark's narrative that Jesus did not know—or at least did not announce to his disciples—the name of the disciple who would betray him.)

It is possible that the command to watch meant that the disciples were supposed to protect Jesus from Judas. Under that reading, this line is ironic because it is Jesus who announces Judas's arrival.

Analysis

Being "sore amazed" implies alarm and distress or astonishment from a surprise; the implication is that the actual experience of suffering was a surprise to Jesus. Given that Jesus has predicted his suffering and death three times, Mark's audience likely would have been astonished at Jesus' astonishment. But the idea is not foreign to Latter-day Saint thought; as Elder Neal A. Maxwell explained, "Jesus knew cognitively what He must do, but not experientially. He had never personally known the exquisite and exacting process of an atonement before. Thus, when the agony came in its fulness, it was so much, much worse than even He with his unique intellect had ever imagined!"[60] Jesus' prophecies about his suffering and death (8:31–32; 9:30–32; 10:32–34) have an unemotional, detached quality; they are delivered in the third person. But when Jesus begins to actually experience suffering, he begs his Father to avoid it. Mark's Gospel contains a strong message about the difference between prophecy and experience.

Jesus' reaction is not culturally appropriate and would have been embarrassing to the audience. Martyrs were expected to approach their death with equanimity, so the picture of Jesus' emotions here "is a striking contrast between Jesus' frame of mind in the face of death and the joyful courage of Jewish and Christian martyrs or the [happy] serenity of a Socrates."[61] Praying that the hour would pass was not considered worthy of martyrs, who were expected to face death stoically. Jesus' prayer in Gethsemane was actually used by anti-Christians to discredit him: "The late-second-century pagan critic Celsus, for example, regarded Jesus' lamentation and prayer as proof that he was not divine."[62] Jesus' attitude toward death would have likely struck Mark's early audiences as cowardly. This is significant: it suggests that Jesus is, in his cultural context, rejecting suffering as much as possible—not glorifying it. This is an important corrective to the mistaken notion that suffering should be sought out or glorified. Mark's story does not permit the audience to conclude that suffering is desirable; to the extent that Mark's audience models Jesus, they will seek to avoid suffering unless there is no other way to accomplish God's will.

Mark describes Jesus' suffering as if it were entirely emotional; nothing in Mark suggests a physical component of Jesus' suffering in Gethsemane

---

60. Neal A. Maxwell, "Willing to Submit," *Ensign* 15 (May 1985): 72–73.
61. Cranfield, *Gospel according to St Mark,* 431.
62. Marcus, *Mark 8–16,* 986.

except inasmuch as the emotional distress causes him physical suffering.[63] One advantage of reading Jesus' physical distress in Gethsemane as stemming from his emotional distress is that otherwise the source of the physical distress is unclear, leaving many interpreters to posit a situation where God inflicts physical pain on Jesus, which is not an idea that resonates with the concept of God developed in Mark's Gospel.

Jesus' response to extreme distress is to pray. The other recorded prayers of Jesus in Mark are at the beginning and middle of his ministry (1:35; 6:46), so prayer bookends and centers Jesus' ministry. In the other cases, Jesus sought solitude; here, he does not. This is also the only instance where the content of the prayer is recorded. It would not have been lost on Mark's audience that the Messiah prayed but his request was not granted. At this point, they would need to reassess Jesus' words from 11:24 ("What things soever ye desire, when ye pray, believe that ye receive them, and ye shall have them"); see the Notes on 11:23–24. This prayer does make clear that suffering is not the result of a lack of faith.[64]

The sleeping of the disciples has a symbolic element in Mark's text. Perhaps stemming from HB passages that suggest that the troubled cannot sleep (Dan. 2:1), the contrast between Jesus' severe emotional distress and the disciples' sleep is profound: "The emotional abandonment of Jesus by his disciples during his time of prayer in Gethsemane portends the literal abandonment that will take place soon."[65]

Jesus expected the disciples to stay awake, to watch, and to pray. But they do not. Mark's scene in Gethsemane suggests an Atonement theology because Jesus does what the disciples are unable or unwilling to do.

While less is said about each of the three prayers, the structure of the passage conveys that Jesus repeated his prayer three times. This implies that the prayer was not answered the first or second time; the idea that God would not immediately answer the prayer of the Messiah is striking. Perhaps some of Jesus' suffering in Gethsemane was tied to the fact that his prayer was going unanswered. It is possible that this experience nuances some of Jesus' previous sayings about prayer (9:23; 11:23). The triple-repetition of the prayer also serves as a model of persistent prayer.[66]

---

63. This does not mean that there was not a physical component, only that Mark's text does not mention it.

64. Dowd, *Reading Mark,* 151.

65. Evans, *Mark 8:27–16:20,* 414.

66. Curtis C. Mitchell, "The Case for Persistence in Prayer," *Journal of the Evangelical Theological Society* 27 (June 1984): 161–68.

The perspective of the narrator differs from that of Jesus three times in this scene: when Jesus' emotions are described (compare 14:33 with 34), in the description of God's power ("if it were possible" in 14:35 and "all things are possible" in 14:36), and in the naming of Simon Peter ("Peter" by the narrator but "Simon" by Jesus in 14:37). These instances, happening in quick succession, are particularly noteworthy since the story contains no other examples of this type of distance between the narrator and Jesus. It may be part of Mark's narrative art to suggest that in Jesus' time in Gethsemane, his aloneness is so profound that he is even distanced from the narrator of the story.

JESUS IS ARRESTED (14:43–52)

Greek Text

43 Καὶ εὐθὺς ἔτι αὐτοῦ λαλοῦντος παραγίνεται Ἰούδας εἷς τῶν δώδεκα καὶ μετ' αὐτοῦ ὄχλος μετὰ μαχαιρῶν καὶ ξύλων παρὰ τῶν ἀρχιερέων καὶ τῶν γραμματέων καὶ τῶν πρεσβυτέρων. 44 δεδώκει δὲ ὁ παραδιδοὺς αὐτὸν σύσσημον αὐτοῖς λέγων· Ὃν ἂν φιλήσω αὐτός ἐστιν· κρατήσατε αὐτὸν καὶ ἀπάγετε ἀσφαλῶς. 45 καὶ ἐλθὼν εὐθὺς προσελθὼν αὐτῷ λέγει· Ῥαββί, καὶ κατεφίλησεν αὐτόν. 46 οἱ δὲ ἐπέβαλαν τὰς χεῖρας αὐτῷ καὶ ἐκράτησαν αὐτόν. 47 εἷς δέ τις τῶν παρεστηκότων σπασάμενος τὴν μάχαιραν ἔπαισεν τὸν δοῦλον τοῦ ἀρχιερέως καὶ ἀφεῖλεν αὐτοῦ τὸ ὠτάριον. 48 καὶ ἀποκριθεὶς ὁ Ἰησοῦς εἶπεν αὐτοῖς· Ὡς ἐπὶ λῃστὴν ἐξήλθατε μετὰ μαχαιρῶν καὶ ξύλων συλλαβεῖν με; 49 καθ' ἡμέραν ἤμην πρὸς ὑμᾶς ἐν τῷ ἱερῷ διδάσκων καὶ οὐκ ἐκρατήσατέ με· ἀλλ' ἵνα πληρωθῶσιν αἱ γραφαί. 50 καὶ ἀφέντες αὐτὸν ἔφυγον πάντες.

51 Καὶ νεανίσκος τις συνηκολούθει αὐτῷ περιβεβλημένος σινδόνα ἐπὶ γυμνοῦ, καὶ κρατοῦσιν αὐτόν, 52 ὁ δὲ καταλιπὼν τὴν σινδόνα γυμνὸς ἔφυγεν. [SBLGNT]

King James Version	New Rendition
43 And immediately, while he yet spake, cometh Judas, one of the twelve, and with him a great multitude with swords and staves, from the chief priests and the scribes and the elders. 44 And he that betrayed him had given them a token, saying, Whomsoever I shall kiss, that same is he; take him, and lead him	43 And immediately—while Jesus was still speaking—Judas, one of the Twelve, arrives. And a crowd [was] with him, with swords and clubs, [sent] from the chief priests and the scriptorians and the elders. 44 The one who was betraying him had given a signal to them, saying, "Whomever I kiss is he. Arrest him

away safely. 45 And as soon as he was come, he goeth straightway to him, and saith, Master, master; and kissed him.

46 And they laid their hands on him, and took him. 47 And one of them that stood by drew a sword, and smote a servant of the high priest, and cut off his ear. 48 And Jesus answered and said unto them, Are ye come out, as against a thief, with swords and with staves to take me? 49 I was daily with you in the temple teaching, and ye took me not: but the scriptures must be fulfilled. 50 And they all forsook him, and fled. 51 And there followed him a certain young man, having a linen cloth cast about his naked body; and the young men laid hold on him: 52 And he left the linen cloth, and fled from them naked.

and securely lead him away." 45 And having arrived, immediately having come up to him, he says, "Rabbi." And he kissed him. 46 And they took hold of him and arrested him. 47 But one who was standing there, having drawn his sword, struck the high priest's slave and cut off his ear. 48 And answering, Jesus said to them, "Are you come out, as [if] against a bandit, with swords and clubs to capture me? 49 Every day I was with you in the temple teaching—and you did not arrest me. But the scriptures must be fulfilled." 50 And having deserted him, they all fled.

51 And a certain young man was following him, wearing a linen cloth on his naked body. And they seize him. 52 But having left behind the linen cloth, he fled naked.

Notes

14:43 *And immediately, while he yet spake, cometh Judas, one of the twelve, and with him a great multitude with swords and staves, from the chief priests and the scribes and the elders:* The word "immediately" shows the fast fulfillment of Jesus' words (see 14:42); "while he yet spake" emphasizes this idea even more. Once again, Mark has carefully structured the narrative to suggest not that Jesus is losing control of events but rather that his prophetic ability is verified.

The phrase "one of the Twelve" is not providing the audience with any new information; rather, it emphasizes that Jesus' prophecy that one of the Twelve would betray him is in fact fulfilled.

The word "great" is likely a later addition.[67]

The word "from" has the connotation of "sent by." The leading council, the Sanhedrin, was composed of the chief priests, the scribes, and the elders; this is not a mob but rather a delegation sent by the Sanhedrin to arrest Jesus.

---

67. Bratcher and Nida, *Translator's Handbook,* 454.

Mark does not specify how Judas knew where to find Jesus, but the most likely explanation is that Judas was with the disciples when they arrived in Gethsemane and then left to inform the authorities of Jesus' location.

14:44 *And he that betrayed him had given them a token, saying, Whomsoever I shall kiss, that same is he; take him, and lead him away safely:* The implication is that the arresting party would not have been able to identify Jesus unless Judas pointed him out to them. This highlights Judas's treachery; it made the arrest of Jesus possible. Since they apparently would not have been able to identify Jesus without Judas, this implies that Jesus was not very well known.

In the HB, kisses were sometimes used in greetings (Gen. 33:4; Ex. 4:27), but it is debated whether this was still common Jewish practice in Jesus' time. Mark's audience, like other early Christian groups, may have customarily greeted one another with a kiss (Rom. 16:16; 1 Cor. 13:12; 1 Thes. 5:26). The idea of using a kiss to betray is as ironic as it is deceitful (2 Sam. 20:9–10; Prov. 27:6).

Jesus had taught the disciples to expect that people would betray those who were close to them (13:12). Once again, while to the casual observer it might appear that Jesus has lost control, the careful audience of Mark realizes that events are transpiring precisely as Jesus said that they would.

"Safely" does not suggest that Judas is concerned about Jesus' safety; rather, it means that they should keep Jesus safely guarded so that he cannot escape, which would endanger Judas' reward. Because Jesus' recent words made clear that he knew the arresting party was coming but chose not to escape when he had the chance, the point is made that Judas does not understand Jesus. The idea of being arrested under heavy guard is part of the betrayal and humiliation of Jesus and therefore a part of his suffering.

14:45 *And as soon as he was come, he goeth straightway to him, and saith, Master, master; and kissed him:* The second instance of "master" was probably not in the earliest texts of Mark.

This is the only time in Mark's Gospel where one of the Twelve touches Jesus; on the other hand, Jesus has had frequent physical contact with children and those he has healed.

14:46 *And they laid their hands on him, and took him. 47 And one of them that stood by drew a sword, and smote a servant of the high priest, and cut off his ear:* Because a definite article comes before "servant" ("the servant," not "a servant"), the implication is that this is an important functionary of the high priest; perhaps he is the one in charge of the arrest.

Because a diminutive form is used, it may be better to translate the word as "earlobe" instead of "ear."

Under the influence of John's Gospel, the sword-wielder has frequently been understood to be Peter (John 18:10), but in Mark, this person is described as "one of them," which means a member of the arresting party. It is unlikely to have been Peter since his visit to the high priest's courtyard, which included his mingling with the servants, would almost certainly have ended in his arrest. Further, Jesus' statement in the next verse (which notes that he is "answering" what has just happened) criticizes his arresting party for having swords; this comment would be nonsensical if a sword had just been used by one of Jesus' disciples, but it makes perfect sense if a sword has been wielded by one of the arresting party. And if the swordsman were Peter, then the incident passes without commentary, consequence, or any discernible reason for its inclusion in the Gospel. Thus, this verse describes "friendly fire," as one of the arresting party harms one of their own number. Interestingly, this injury makes this servant unfit to officiate in the temple and thus symbolically points to the illegitimacy of the current high priest. Because robbers in antiquity had an ear cut off, the implication is that the arresting party harbors a robber—one who is trying to "steal" Jesus. Ironically, Jesus will ask in the next verse why they are treating him as a robber, but the audience knows that the arresting party has unwittingly revealed themselves as the real robbers.

14:48 *And Jesus answered and said unto them, Are ye come out, as against a thief, with swords and with staves to take me:* Because this verse begins with Jesus "answering," it implies that this is a response to the sword incident in the previous verse. The most logical reading is that the swordsman is one of the arresting party who injures another member of that party; this verse is Jesus' response to their violence.

The word "thief" would, at least by Mark's time, have had a political connotation, and so Mark's audience would have heard Jesus asking if they thought he was a political revolutionary.

14:49 *I was daily with you in the temple teaching, and ye took me not:* "Daily" probably means every day, but it could also mean "in the day time" (as opposed to this middle-of-the-night arrest). The point is to show their cowardice: they chose not to arrest Jesus during the day because they knew the people would have supported him.

It is significant that Jesus highlights teaching as his main activity in the temple.

Jesus knows that these words will have no effect on the arresting party; his message is for the disciples and the audience.

but the scriptures must be fulfilled: No specific scripture is named, and "scripture" is plural here, suggesting a combination of passages or scripture in a general sense. Texts that might be in mind could include

1. Isaiah 53:12, which refers to one who was counted a rebel and willingly went to his death—a death that would benefit others.

2. Zechariah 13:7, which states that if the shepherd is struck, the flock will scatter. This passage is particularly relevant given that Jesus recently quoted it (14:27) and that the next event recorded is the scattering of the disciples.

3. Amos 2:16, where the stout of heart flee naked, which would speak to the gravity of the situation and explain the unusual incident with the naked young man (14:51–52).

14:50 *And they all forsook him, and fled:* The word "all" is not strictly accurate: the audience will soon learn that Peter and another disciple have not fled. "All" might be hyperbolic, or it could echo the promise by "all" of the disciples at the Last Supper that they would never flee (14:31).

The disciples did not flee at the first sign of the arresting party but after Jesus' words. It is likely that Mark has structured the scene to emphasize that their flight is in fulfillment of scripture.

14:51 *And there followed him a certain young man, having a linen cloth cast about his naked body; and the young men laid hold on him:* The word "following" is imperfect, so that suggests that this young man has been a disciple for awhile. Additionally, the word "following" has a prefix that intensifies it (Greek: *sunakoloutheō*). Its only other Markan usage is in reference to the inner circle of disciples (5:37).

"Young men" was probably "they" in earlier iterations of Mark's Gospel.[68]

If the young man has a cloth over his body, he is not naked. The reference to his nakedness is thus somewhat forced and suggests a symbolic meaning (see the Notes on 14:52).

14:52 *And he left the linen cloth, and fled from them naked:* "From them" should probably be omitted.[69]

Mark 14:51–52 may be the most enigmatic passage in the entire text. Theories for the meaning of the story of the naked young man include:

1. This is a historical reminiscence with no particular theological meaning. The major problem with this reading is that it is unlikely that storytellers would

---

68. Bratcher and Nida, *Translator's Handbook,* 459.
69. Comfort, *New Testament Text and Translation Commentary,* 151.

have continued to include it in the text if it did not contribute to the story of Jesus.

2. This is a "cameo appearance" by the author of the Gospel. While this theory was popular in older scholarship, it has little to recommend it. It doesn't fit well with the idea of the Gospel as an oral text (since the story would not have first been told by the author), and it is difficult to imagine how audiences were supposed to figure out that it was a reference to the author.

3. Some interpreters have found baptism imagery here, based on the idea that early Christian baptism involved the removal and replacement of clothing, but this reading is disputed:[70] it is unclear in any case how baptismal imagery would function at Jesus' arrest.

4. This scene is the fulfillment of Amos 2:16, which speaks of a time of such threat that even the brave will flee naked.

5. Normally in the HB, nakedness symbolizes shame (Gen. 3:7; 2 Chr. 28:15; Hosea 2:3; Amos 2:16). Here, the young man's nakedness might indicate the shame he should feel at fleeing instead of following Jesus.

6. These verses are probably best understood with reference to 16:1–8, the story of the women approaching the sepulchre, which has the following similarities to this text:

    a. These are the only two passages in Mark that use the word "young man" (Greek: *neaniskos*).

    b. Both passages use the same word for "clothed" (Greek: *periballō*), a term not used elsewhere in Mark, to refer to the young man and hence draw significant attention to his clothing.

Given the similarities, it seems that 14:51–52 and 16:1–8 are intended to work together. Thus, the role of the young man is not clear in this chapter; it only becomes clear after Jesus is resurrected. This is an important message for the audience: some things are inexplicable, except in the light of the Resurrection (see the section "Relationship to the Naked Young Man" after the Notes on 16:1).

Analysis

If the swordsman is part of the arresting party, the moral is clear: attempting to harm Jesus results in harm to oneself. There may be some irony in that these religious leaders had expressed a desire to avoid a riot when arresting Jesus (14:2) and then nearly start their own skirmish through their own bumbling. It is possible that the incident with the sword functioned

---

70. Collins, *Mark*, 690.

for Mark's audience as a moment of comic relief in the middle of an otherwise somber narrative. Its portrayal of the arresting party would have been a bit of "grim humor."[71]

With the flight of the disciples, Jesus' prophecy about the failure of the disciples is fulfilled (14:27). Once again, emphasizing a strong theme throughout the Passion narrative, it is not the case that events are out of Jesus' control, despite all appearances; rather, Jesus' prophecies are being affirmed. And since the disciples assured Jesus that they would not deny him, the contrast between their predictive ability and his is highlighted. The irony is overwhelming: just as everything that Jesus had prophesied is happening, his disciples flee from him.

JESUS IS QUESTIONED BY JEWISH LEADERS (14:53–65)

Greek Text

53 Καὶ ἀπήγαγον τὸν Ἰησοῦν πρὸς τὸν ἀρχιερέα, καὶ συνέρχονται πάντες οἱ ἀρχιερεῖς καὶ οἱ πρεσβύτεροι καὶ οἱ γραμματεῖς. 54 καὶ ὁ Πέτρος ἀπὸ μακρόθεν ἠκολούθησεν αὐτῷ ἕως ἔσω εἰς τὴν αὐλὴν τοῦ ἀρχιερέως καὶ ἦν συγκαθήμενος μετὰ τῶν ὑπηρετῶν καὶ θερμαινόμενος πρὸς τὸ φῶς. 55 οἱ δὲ ἀρχιερεῖς καὶ ὅλον τὸ συνέδριον ἐζήτουν κατὰ τοῦ Ἰησοῦ μαρτυρίαν εἰς τὸ θανατῶσαι αὐτόν, καὶ οὐχ ηὕρισκον· 56 πολλοὶ γὰρ ἐψευδομαρτύρουν κατ' αὐτοῦ, καὶ ἴσαι αἱ μαρτυρίαι οὐκ ἦσαν. 57 καί τινες ἀναστάντες ἐψευδομαρτύρουν κατ' αὐτοῦ λέγοντες 58 ὅτι Ἡμεῖς ἠκούσαμεν αὐτοῦ λέγοντος ὅτι Ἐγὼ καταλύσω τὸν ναὸν τοῦτον τὸν χειροποίητον καὶ διὰ τριῶν ἡμερῶν ἄλλον ἀχειροποίητον οἰκοδομήσω· 59 καὶ οὐδὲ οὕτως ἴση ἦν ἡ μαρτυρία αὐτῶν. 60 καὶ ἀναστὰς ὁ ἀρχιερεὺς εἰς μέσον ἐπηρώτησεν τὸν Ἰησοῦν λέγων· Οὐκ ἀποκρίνῃ οὐδέν; τί οὗτοί σου καταμαρτυροῦσιν; 61 ὁ δὲ ἐσιώπα καὶ οὐκ ἀπεκρίνατο οὐδέν. πάλιν ὁ ἀρχιερεὺς ἐπηρώτα αὐτὸν καὶ λέγει αὐτῷ· Σὺ εἶ ὁ χριστὸς ὁ υἱὸς τοῦ εὐλογητοῦ; 62 ὁ δὲ Ἰησοῦς εἶπεν· Ἐγώ εἰμι, καὶ ὄψεσθε τὸν υἱὸν τοῦ ἀνθρώπου ἐκ δεξιῶν καθήμενον τῆς δυνάμεως καὶ ἐρχόμενον μετὰ τῶν νεφελῶν τοῦ οὐρανοῦ. 63 ὁ δὲ ἀρχιερεὺς διαρρήξας τοὺς χιτῶνας αὐτοῦ λέγει· Τί ἔτι χρείαν ἔχομεν μαρτύρων; 64 ἠκούσατε τῆς βλασφημίας· τί ὑμῖν φαίνεται; οἱ δὲ πάντες κατέκριναν αὐτὸν ἔνοχον εἶναι θανάτου. 65 καὶ ἤρξαντό τινες ἐμπτύειν αὐτῷ καὶ περικαλύπτειν αὐτοῦ τὸ πρόσωπον καὶ κολαφίζειν αὐτὸν καὶ λέγειν αὐτῷ· Προφήτευσον, καὶ οἱ ὑπηρέται ῥαπίσμασιν αὐτὸν ἔλαβον. [SBLGNT]

---

71. Gundry, *Mark*, 860.

King James Version

53 And they led Jesus away to the high priest: and with him were assembled all the chief priests and the elders and the scribes. 54 And Peter followed him afar off, even into the palace of the high priest: and he sat with the servants, and warmed himself at the fire. 55 And the chief priests and all the council sought for witness against Jesus to put him to death; and found none. 56 For many bare false witness against him, but their witness agreed not together. 57 And there arose certain, and bare false witness against him, saying, 58 We heard him say, I will destroy this temple that is made with hands, and within three days I will build another made without hands. 59 But neither so did their witness agree together. 60 And the high priest stood up in the midst, and asked Jesus, saying, Answerest thou nothing? what is it which these witness against thee? 61 But he held his peace, and answered nothing. Again the high priest asked him, and said unto him, Art thou the Christ, the Son of the Blessed? 62 And Jesus said, I am: and ye shall see the Son of man sitting on the right hand of power, and coming in the clouds of heaven. 63 Then the high priest rent his clothes, and saith, What need we any further witnesses? 64 Ye have heard the blasphemy: what think ye? And they all condemned him to be guilty of death. 65 And some began to spit on him, and to cover his face, and to buffet him, and to say unto him, Prophesy: and the servants did strike him with the palms of their hands.

New Rendition

53 And they led Jesus to the high priest. And all of the chief priests, elders, and scriptorians assembled. 54 And Peter followed him from a distance, up to the high priest's courtyard. And he was sitting with the guards and warming himself at the fire. 55 But the chief priests and the whole Sanhedrin were seeking testimony against Jesus, to put him to death, but they were not finding any. 56 For many were falsely testifying against him, but their testimonies were not consistent. 57 And some, having risen up, falsely testified against him, saying, 58 "We heard him saying, 'I will destroy this temple, the one made with hands, and in three days another one—not made with hands—I will build.'" 59 And thus their testimony did not agree. 60 And having stood up in the middle, the high priest questioned Jesus, saying, "Do you have no answer? What is it that these people testify against you?" 61 But he was being silent and did not answer at all. Again the high priest was questioning him and says to him, "Are you the anointed one, the son of the Blessed One?" 62 And Jesus said, "I am. And you will see the son of man 'sitting at the right hand' of the Power and 'coming with the clouds of heaven.'" 63 But the high priest, having torn his clothing, says, "Why do we still need witnesses? 64 You heard the blasphemy. What do you decide?" And all judged him to be deserving of death. 65 And some began to spit on him and to cover his face and hit him and to say to him, "Prophesy!" And the guards slapped him.

Notes

14:53 *And they led Jesus away to the high priest: and with him were assembled all the chief priests and the elders and the scribes:* Although Mark doesn't identify him by name, the high priest would have been Caiaphas, who served from 18 to 36 CE (compare Matt. 26:3 and John 11:49).

The phrase "with him" is not in the best manuscripts.[72] "All" is probably hyperbole.

14:54 *And Peter followed him afar off, even into the palace of the high priest: and he sat with the servants, and warmed himself at the fire:* Contra the KJV, Peter is with not servants but guards, probably including members of the arresting party. The image of Peter sharing a fire with them comes close to implying that he has joined with them; he is "afar off" from Jesus but nestled close to the guards.

Here, the common word for "fire" (Greek: *pur*) is not used but rather the word that is normally translated as "light" (Greek: *phōs*). It thus likely has a symbolic connotation.

14:55 *And the chief priests and all the council sought for witness against Jesus to put him to death; and found none:* "Council" refers to the Sanhedrin, or leading council.

Mark is clear that they are not seeking the truth about Jesus but rather are seeking evidence to justify his death.

14:56 *For many bare false witness against him, but their witness agreed not together:* The Mosaic law required two witnesses (Num. 35:30; Deut. 17:6).

It is perhaps surprising that Judas is not one of the witnesses; this supports the idea that Judas's role was to reveal Jesus' location, not his teachings.

This verse echoes the sentiment of Psalm 27:12, where false witnesses attempt to destroy the psalmist.

14:57 *And there arose certain, and bare false witness against him, saying:* Mark very clearly signals that the testimony is false; this framing is crucial to the interpretation of the next verse.

14:58 *We heard him say, I will destroy this temple that is made with hands, and within three days I will build another made without hands:* In this line, "we heard" is emphatic, so those who testify emphasize that

---

72. Collins, *Mark*, 696 note a.

they themselves have heard Jesus say this, which highlights the falseness of their testimony. Then, they emphasize the first occurrence of "I," so that the stress is not on the destruction of the temple but rather on the fact that Jesus himself will destroy it.

Jesus spoke of the destruction of the temple in chapter 13, but he did not say that he himself would destroy it. Further, a different word for temple was used: chapter 13 referred to the *hieron* (a broader term for the entire temple complex, used in 11:11, 15, 27; 12:35; 13:1, 3; 14:49) while this verse uses *naos* (which narrowly refers to the sanctuary; this term is also found in 15:29 and 15:38). Jesus had referred to "three days" in the context of his prophecies about his suffering and death (8:31; 9:31; 10:34), but he had not described the rebuilding of the temple this way or specifically referred to his body as a temple. Jesus had not used the "made with(out) hands" language either. Calling the current temple "made with hands" would have offended the council because it denies divine involvement in its creation; worse, the idea of something being made by (human) hands suggests idolatry (Lev. 26:1; Ps. 115:4).

In sum, this accusation reads like a confused scramble of Jesus' teachings. One point of this scene is that people's inability to understand Jesus' teachings led, in a very literal sense, to his death. Because this statement is partially true, Mark has carefully framed the statement with three attestations of its falsity (see 14:56, 57, 59) so that the audience will not be confused.

Relationship to Jeremiah 26. The prophet Jeremiah was tried for claiming that the temple would be destroyed—and he did not even claim to be the one who would destroy it. The portion of Mark's audience who was familiar with this story would have recognized that this accusation aligns Jesus with this HB prophet.

14:59 *But neither so did their witness agree together:* It is difficult to determine precisely what did not agree, unless some of the witnesses said, "I will destroy this temple" and others said, "I will build another" and this was thought to contradict.[73]

Deuteronomy 19:15–19 relates penalties for those who give false testimony.

---

73. James A. Kleist, "The Two False Witnesses (Mk. 14:55 ff)," *Catholic Biblical Quarterly* 9, no. 3 (1947): 321–23.

14:60 And the high priest stood up in the midst, and asked Jesus, saying, Answerest thou nothing? what is it which these witness against thee? 61 but he held his peace, and answered nothing: Jesus' lack of response is described by an emphatic double negative.

Many HB texts emphasize the idea of the quiet suffering of a just person (Ps. 38:12–15; Isa. 53:7; Lam. 3:28–30).

Again the high priest asked him, and said unto him, Art thou the Christ, the Son of the Blessed: The word "thou" is emphatic, scornfully emphasizing that Jesus is an unlikely Messiah.

"Christ" is the Greek word used to translate the Hebrew "Messiah," with the underlying meaning of "the anointed one"; the New Rendition uses "anointed one" to emphasize the link to the anointing story (14:3–9).

"Blessed" is a common Jewish circumlocution to avoid saying the name of God, so the high priest is asking if Jesus is the Son of God. The use of "blessed" here is ironic: the high priest is willing to blaspheme through his treatment of Jesus but won't risk blaspheming by speaking the name of God.

14:62 And Jesus said, I am: Some ancient manuscripts read "you say that I am" instead of "I am." The phrase "you say that" is probably the result of scribes wanting to harmonize the text with Matthew 26:64 and Luke 22:70; it is unlikely to be original.[74]

"I am" uses the same Greek words that the Lord used to self-identify to Moses (Ex. 3:14). As 14:63–64 will make clear, for Jesus to use this name was regarded as blasphemy. Jesus' previous refusal to respond adds even more weight to his words here.

and ye shall see the Son of man sitting on the right hand of power: The idea of "seeing" suggests that the high priest will know that Jesus has been vindicated. Jesus' words prophesy that God's justice will override the decision of the Sanhedrin.

The reference to the Son of Man quotes Daniel 7:13 which, in the LXX, aligns the Son of Man with God (see the Notes on 2:10).

Jesus' language about sitting on the right hand quotes Psalm 110:1. In this psalm, God invites the Messiah to sit on the right hand, which symbolizes being given a place of authority. Jesus adds "of power" to the quotation; this is a euphemism to avoid speaking the name of God. It is surprising that Jesus would use a euphemism for the name of God here when he has not done so elsewhere. Mark is strongly making the point that there are no grounds to accuse Jesus of blasphemy in this case.

---

74. Comfort, *New Testament Text and Translation Commentary,* 151.

and coming in the clouds of heaven: This concept also comes from Daniel 7:13. But in Daniel, the Son of Man is coming into heaven—not to earth. This is significant. While is it possible that Jesus is using the image in a context other than its original one, it is more likely that Jesus' words are describing the Son of Man's entrance into heaven. (While the high priest would not literally see this, the idea of seeing should probably not be pressed too literally; see also the Notes on 13:26.)

In the HB, only God travels on the clouds (Num. 10:34; Ps. 104:3; Isa. 19:1), so by claiming that the Son of Man will, Jesus opens himself again to blasphemy charges. Further, in Daniel 7:27, the Son of Man is worshiped, and so Jesus is suggesting that he will be an object of worship. Not only that, but the people on this very council will worship him.

There appears to be some tension between the last phrase, where Jesus was seated, and this phrase, where he is in motion. There are two possible solutions to this:

1. neither image should be read overly literally; both are metaphorical pictures of enthronement.

2. the image is of a chariot throne (Ezek. 1:10).

In either reading, the key issue is that Jesus is providing an image of ultimate vindication. This would have been important for Mark's audience to understand, at the moment when Jesus appears—by earthly standards—to be powerless before the Sanhedrin. But Jesus is not on trial in front of anyone who has the power to exercise control over his destiny.

Jesus has taught previously that when the righteous are brought before councils, the Spirit will tell them what to say (13:11). So Mark's audience would therefore assume that the Spirit is here speaking through Jesus as he addresses the council. This would add weight to his words.

14:63 *Then the high priest rent his clothes, and saith, What need we any further witnesses?:* Tearing clothing was a way of expressing horror and was probably a ritual response to blasphemy. (High priests are forbidden [Lev. 21:10] to rend their priestly robes, but he would not have been wearing those in his home in the middle of the night.)

The thrust of this statement is that Jesus' words constituted blasphemy, so there is no reason to seek any more witnesses.

14:64 *Ye have heard the blasphemy: what think ye?:* Blasphemy is, most commonly, misuse of the divine name, but Mark is clear that Jesus has not used God's name here. The claim to be the Messiah was probably not considered blasphemy; others made this claim and were not deemed blasphemous. Jesus' "I am" saying could have easily been regarded as blasphemous, since this is the language the Lord uses to self-identify to Moses. Blasphemy might also have been found in the idea of sitting at the right hand of God and thus sharing power or in claiming to be the Son of Man.

The question here could have been presented by the storyteller to Mark's early audiences in such a way that would have encouraged them to contemplate for themselves what they thought of Jesus. If they were to do that, then the next line, condemning Jesus to death, would be all the more devastating.

And they all condemned him to be guilty of death: The "all" may be hyperbole (contrast 15:43).

According to the law of Moses, death by stoning is the penalty for blasphemy (Lev. 24:13–14). Obviously, that is not what happens here. This suggests that the religious leaders lacked the authority to execute Jesus; instead, they hand him over to the Romans.

This verdict violates many trial rules under Jewish law, but it is not clear whether this is a formal trial or merely a hearing[75] and whether those rules, which are only known from later documents, were operative in the first century.

14:65 And some began to spit on him, and to cover his face, and to buffet him, and to say unto him, Prophesy: and the servants did strike him with the palms of their hands: Some manuscripts omit the phrase "and to cover his face";[76] it seems to have been added to conform to Luke's account.

The "some" who torment Jesus are members of the Sanhedrin. Mark later records that they turned Jesus over to the Romans because they "envied" him (15:10). Spitting conveyed contempt (Num. 12:14; Job 30:9–10). The demand to prophesy probably means that they mockingly want Jesus to identify who has hit him. Of course, Mark's audience is aware that many of Jesus' prophecies have in fact come true in this scene, including his prediction that the religious leaders would mock him and spit on him (10:34). So the irony is overwhelming.

Analysis

The idea of a messianic secret in Mark is complicated, but to the extent that there was one, it ends with Jesus' "I am" statement to the high priest. In this context of persecution and suffering, Jesus can now reveal to all that he is the Anointed One (contrast 8:30). In these circumstances—unlike after

---

75. Darrell Bock, "Blasphemy and the Jewish Examination of Jesus," *Bulletin for Biblical Research* 17, no. 1 (2007): 65–66.

76. Collins, *Mark,* 696 note e.

healing miracles—when it requires faith to believe it, Jesus can proclaim that he is the Christ. The next line, with its focus on what they will see in the future in contrast to how things now appear, emphasizes this idea by showing Jesus' future vindication.

With the condemnation to death, Jesus' prophecy is fulfilled (10:33). The constant refrain of fulfilled prophecies in the Passion narrative make clear that, despite appearances, Jesus is in control.

Peter Denies Jesus (14:66–72)

Greek Text

66 Καὶ ὄντος τοῦ Πέτρου κάτω ἐν τῇ αὐλῇ ἔρχεται μία τῶν παιδισκῶν τοῦ ἀρχιερέως, 67 καὶ ἰδοῦσα τὸν Πέτρον θερμαινόμενον ἐμβλέψασα αὐτῷ λέγει· Καὶ σὺ μετὰ τοῦ Ναζαρηνοῦ ἦσθα τοῦ Ἰησοῦ· 68 ὁ δὲ ἠρνήσατο λέγων· Οὔτε οἶδα οὔτε ἐπίσταμαι σὺ τί λέγεις, καὶ ἐξῆλθεν ἔξω εἰς τὸ προαύλιον καὶ ἀλέκτωρ ἐφώνησεν. 69 καὶ ἡ παιδίσκη ἰδοῦσα αὐτὸν ἤρξατο πάλιν λέγειν τοῖς παρεστῶσιν ὅτι Οὗτος ἐξ αὐτῶν ἐστιν. 70 ὁ δὲ πάλιν ἠρνεῖτο. καὶ μετὰ μικρὸν πάλιν οἱ παρεστῶτες ἔλεγον τῷ Πέτρῳ· Ἀληθῶς ἐξ αὐτῶν εἶ, καὶ γὰρ Γαλιλαῖος εἶ καὶ ἡ λαλιά σου ὁμοιάζει· 71 ὁ δὲ ἤρξατο ἀναθεματίζειν καὶ ὀμνύναι ὅτι Οὐκ οἶδα τὸν ἄνθρωπον τοῦτον ὃν λέγετε. 72 καὶ εὐθὺς ἐκ δευτέρου ἀλέκτωρ ἐφώνησεν· καὶ ἀνεμνήσθη ὁ Πέτρος τὸ ῥῆμα ὡς εἶπεν αὐτῷ ὁ Ἰησοῦς ὅτι Πρὶν ἀλέκτορα φωνῆσαι δὶς τρίς με ἀπαρνήσῃ, καὶ ἐπιβαλὼν ἔκλαιεν. [SBLGNT]

King James Version

66 And as Peter was beneath in the palace, there cometh one of the maids of the high priest: 67 And when she saw Peter warming himself, she looked upon him, and said, And thou also wast with Jesus of Nazareth. 68 But he denied, saying, I know not, neither understand I what thou sayest. And he went out into the porch; and the cock crew. 69 And a maid saw him again, and began to say to them that stood by, This is one of them. 70 And he denied it again. And a little after, they that stood by said again to Peter, Surely thou art

New Rendition

66 And while Peter was below, in the courtyard, one of the female servants of the high priest comes. 67 And having seen Peter warming himself, having looked at him, she says, "And you were with the Nazarene, Jesus." 68 But he denied it, saying, "I don't know, or even understand, what you say." And he went out onto the entryway. 69 And the servant, having seen him, began again to say to those nearby, "This is one of them!" 70 But again he was denying it. And after a little while, again those nearby were saying to Peter, "Surely you are

one of them: for thou art a Galilaean, and thy speech agreeth thereto. 71 But he began to curse and to swear, saying, I know not this man of whom ye speak. 72 And the second time the cock crew. And Peter called to mind the word that Jesus said unto him, Before the cock crow twice, thou shalt deny me thrice. And when he thought thereon, he wept.

with them. For you are definitely a Galilean." 71 But he began to curse and to swear [an oath]: "I don't know this man you are talking about!" 72 And immediately, a rooster crowed the second time. And Peter remembered what Jesus had said to him: "Before the rooster crows twice, you will deny me three times." And having broken down, he cried.

Notes

14:66 *And as Peter was beneath in the palace, there cometh one of the maids of the high priest:* Peter is not in a "palace" but rather in a courtyard.

14:67 *And when she saw Peter warming himself, she looked upon him, and said, And thou also wast with Jesus of Nazareth:* "Looked upon" implies that the woman did a double take. It seems that she has seen Peter with Jesus on some other occasion and thus recognizes him. It is possible that her statement is an observation and not an accusation, which makes Peter's denial of Jesus even less understandable.

14:68 *But he denied, saying, I know not, neither understand I what thou sayest. And he went out into the porch; and the cock crew:* The evidence is mixed regarding whether the words "and the cock crew" were in the early manuscripts of Mark.[77] Without this line, it is as if neither Peter nor Mark's audience "hears" the first crow—they only hear the second, when it is too late and Jesus' prophecy (14:30) is fulfilled. Of course, the reference to the second crowing makes clear that there was a first, but Mark's story makes more sense if the first crowing is left unnarrated.

Peter's words can be taken as a statement followed by a question ("I don't know or understand. What are you saying?") or as one statement ("I don't know or understand what you are saying"). The former is less likely because Peter would not want to encourage further conversation. It is possible that Peter's claim not to understand refers to her accent, but it is clear that he does indeed understand her. There is "exquisite irony"[78] in that what Peter says is, in a sense, true: he actually does not know who Jesus is.

---

77. Metzger, *Textual Commentary,* 97.
78. Dowd, *Reading Mark,* 155.

Peter's move onto the porch is probably an effort to get away from the woman and to get out of the light by which she can see him.

14:69 *And a maid saw him again, and began to say to them that stood by, This is one of them:* This verse refers to the same maid mentioned previously (the word "again" makes that point).

This group probably included some of those who arrested Jesus; they would have been able to confirm the identification of Peter as "one of them" and perhaps arrest him as well.

14:70 *And he denied it again. And a little after, they that stood by said again to Peter, Surely thou art one of them: for thou art a Galilaean, and thy speech agreeth thereto:* The phrase "and thy speech agreeth thereto" is missing from many manuscripts. It appears to have been added to later copies of Mark either to clarify how Peter was recognized as a Galilean or to harmonize with Matthew's account (Matt. 26:73).[79]

14:71 *But he began to curse and to swear, saying, I know not this man of whom ye speak:* To "curse" means to call down a curse upon someone if what is said is not true (compare 2 Sam. 3:9 and Acts 23:12). Normally, there would have been a direct object following it (that is, "to curse [name of person]"), but there is not in this case; it is possible that Peter cursed Jesus, but Mark chose to elide this fact. Because "cursing Jesus served as proof of innocence before a Roman tribunal when a person was accused of unlawfully being a Christian"[80] (not during Jesus' time, but later and thus relevant for Mark's audience), it would have been reassuring for Mark's audience to know that even the lead disciple failed when faced with a similar test. Because they know of Peter's later position, they would realize that even a setback as grave as this need not be permanent.

To "swear" means to swear an oath—a promise that what is being said is true.

Notice that Peter expends a lot of effort to avoid saying Jesus' name: he instead says, "this man of whom ye speak."

14:72 *And the second time the cock crew. And Peter called to mind the word that Jesus said unto him, Before the cock crow twice, thou shalt deny me thrice:* Although not included in the KJV, this verse begins with the Greek word for "immediately," which emphasizes that Jesus' prophecy came true with precision.

---

79. See also Collins, *Mark,* 697–98 note i.
80. Deppe, *Theological Intentions,* 82.

Some ancient manuscripts omit the words "the second time," probably to harmonize with versions of Mark that omitted the crowing in 14:68.[81] But the best reading probably includes "the second time," assuming that the first crowing happened but was left unnarrated.

In the ancient world, cocks "primarily epitomized virile aggression"[82] due to their association with cockfighting. Their crow was "not a cry of submission or an empty vaunt of superiority, rather it is affirmation of the cock's readiness to fight on to its death,"[83] so when Jesus' prophecy links Peter's denial to the cock crow, Jesus has suggested that Peter will behave spinelessly at precisely the moment when courage to the death is expected. Because "value was also placed upon cocks which might lose but fight to the death anyway,"[84] Peter's unwillingness to stand up for Jesus is emphasized by way of contrast. It would have been considered honorable for Peter to die while defending Jesus, but this is not what happens. Jesus' linking of Peter's denial to the crowing of the cock is a profound example of Markan irony. Cocks that lost their fights were "thought to lose free status and are referred to as slaves,"[85] so there is another layer of irony in the fact that it is a female slave who bests Peter here. It is also ironic that cocks were thought to be "vigilantly wakeful,"[86] which the disciples were supposed to be but were not. It is as if with the crowing of the cock, Peter finally wakes up to what is happening, as the next line suggests.

And when he thought thereon, he wept: The precise meaning of the verb translated as "thought thereon" is unknown. It may mean that Peter rushed outside. The New Rendition uses "breaking down," but this is uncertain.

Relationship to the Death of John the Baptist (6:14–29). Peter's denial of Jesus and the story of the death of John the Baptist are the only stories in Mark that do not feature Jesus. However, they are very much about Jesus: both showcase the response of disciples under persecution. John, too, could have denied his testimony and been spared as Peter was. They further Mark's theme of discipleship by showing how disciples respond to threats to their lives.

---

81. Metzger, *Textual Commentary,* 97.

82. Michael Pope, "The Cockcrow in Greco-Roman Context," unpublished, copy in possession of the author.

83. Pope, "Cockcrow in Greco-Roman Context."

84. Pope, "Cockcrow in Greco-Roman Context."

85. Pope, "Cockcrow in Greco-Roman Context."

86. Pope, "Cockcrow in Greco-Roman Context."

Analysis

Peter denies Jesus three times; the denials escalate from a simple denial to one accompanied by a curse and an oath. This obviously reflects poorly on Peter, but it reflects even more on Jesus' mercy: the end of the Gospel will make clear that Peter will be offered an opportunity to return to discipleship (16:7).

In chapter 13, Jesus taught the disciples that they would need to watch to be prepared to face the challenges of persecution. In the Gethsemane scene, Jesus repeated the command to watch. But the disciples did not; instead, they slept. Because they slept, they did not witness Jesus' prayer. If they had, they would have known how to remain true in the face of suffering by placing God's will above their own. The triple repetition of watching in chapter 13 and in Gethsemane and the triple repetition of Peter's denial suggest this link. In this scene, Peter fails as a disciple by denying Jesus because he did not place God's will first. In Mark's Gospel, the prayer in Gethsemane is the key to strong discipleship, serving as a model for the disciples.

At the same time that Peter is outside and denying Jesus to the high priest's maid, Jesus is inside and identifying himself to the high priest; this juxtaposing encourages the hearer to compare Peter's denial with Jesus' confession. In the narrative, Peter's denial happens at precisely the same moment that Jesus confesses himself, which shows in the starkest terms the difference between the two, especially since Jesus is being interrogated by the high priest while Peter is only being questioned by the high priest's servant. (In fact, the irregularity of Jesus' "trial" before the high priest may be shown by the fact that the high priest is doing no more than his serving woman, who also presents "evidence" and "witnesses" of Peter's identity.) As some mock Jesus by ordering him to prophesy, his prophecy concerning Peter is simultaneously coming true in the courtyard. Indeed, both the act of testifying before rulers and his betrayal by his disciples have been prophesied by Jesus.

The crowing of the cock is clearly linked to Peter's denials, but it is also, through the juxtaposing structure, linked to Jesus' victory: the cock crow was associated with the proclamation of victory. Since Peter's denial and Jesus' confession happen at the same time, the cock crow also announces Jesus' victory in submitting his will to the will of God. To an outside observer, it would appear that Jesus loses (since he is handed over to the Romans) and Peter wins (since he goes free), but the crowing of the cock shows that, ironically, it is Jesus who gains the victory by losing his life to save it. The audience is led to see victory in Jesus' scene, despite all evidence to the contrary, through the crowing of the cock.

There are also several similarities between this juxtaposition and the previous one in chapter 14, where the anointing was sandwiched by references to the plot to kill Jesus. In both, someone who should be an insider (Judas, Peter) is outside betraying Jesus while Jesus is inside in a scene where his identity is confirmed. Perhaps most significantly, this reading draws a parallel between the woman and Jesus since both proclaim his identity. By repeating the sandwiching pattern, Mark emphasizes to the audience that even Jesus' closest disciples failed him; further, the ironic link between the establishment of Jesus' identity and the failure of the disciples is highlighted. Both sandwiched stories convey the idea that Jesus' true identity as the Christ can only be understood in the context of his betrayal and subsequent suffering and death. He is clearly not the Messiah that they were expecting.

Death and Resurrection (15:1–16:8)

Overview

This chapter includes precise time markers:

    Mark 15:1: morning
    Mark 15:25: the third hour (9 a.m.)
    Mark 15:33: the sixth hour (noon)
    Mark 15:34: the ninth hour (3 p.m.)
    Mark 15:42: evening

No other story in Mark has references to the time of day. Rather, Mark's Gospel began with a profusion of the word "immediately" but no specific time references. During the Passion narrative, there are references to the days of the week. And now, on the final day of Jesus' life, there are even more specific time references. The overall effect is one of time slowing down as the story progresses which, like a slow motion sequence in a movie, emphasizes the events of this chapter. Further, the time references in chapter 15, "like the series of sevens in the book of Revelation, impl[y] that this dark epoch is nevertheless under the firm control of an all-powerful God."[1]

---

1. Marcus, *Mark 8–16*, 1050.

Jesus before Pilate (15:1–15)

Greek Text

1 Καὶ εὐθὺς πρωῒ συμβούλιον ποιήσαντες οἱ ἀρχιερεῖς μετὰ τῶν πρεσβυτέρων καὶ γραμματέων καὶ ὅλον τὸ συνέδριον δήσαντες τὸν Ἰησοῦν ἀπήνεγκαν καὶ παρέδωκαν Πιλάτῳ. 2 καὶ ἐπηρώτησεν αὐτὸν ὁ Πιλᾶτος· Σὺ εἶ ὁ βασιλεὺς τῶν Ἰουδαίων; ὁ δὲ ἀποκριθεὶς αὐτῷ λέγει· Σὺ λέγεις. 3 καὶ κατηγόρουν αὐτοῦ οἱ ἀρχιερεῖς πολλά. 4 ὁ δὲ Πιλᾶτος πάλιν ἐπηρώτα αὐτὸν λέγων· Οὐκ ἀποκρίνῃ οὐδέν; ἴδε πόσα σου κατηγοροῦσιν. 5 ὁ δὲ Ἰησοῦς οὐκέτι οὐδὲν ἀπεκρίθη, ὥστε θαυμάζειν τὸν Πιλᾶτον.

6 Κατὰ δὲ ἑορτὴν ἀπέλυεν αὐτοῖς ἕνα δέσμιον ὃν παρῃτοῦντο. 7 ἦν δὲ ὁ λεγόμενος Βαραββᾶς μετὰ τῶν στασιαστῶν δεδεμένος οἵτινες ἐν τῇ στάσει φόνον πεποιήκεισαν. 8 καὶ ἀναβὰς ὁ ὄχλος ἤρξατο αἰτεῖσθαι καθὼς ἐποίει αὐτοῖς. 9 ὁ δὲ Πιλᾶτος ἀπεκρίθη αὐτοῖς λέγων· Θέλετε ἀπολύσω ὑμῖν τὸν βασιλέα τῶν Ἰουδαίων; 10 ἐγίνωσκεν γὰρ ὅτι διὰ φθόνον παραδεδώκεισαν αὐτὸν οἱ ἀρχιερεῖς. 11 οἱ δὲ ἀρχιερεῖς ἀνέσεισαν τὸν ὄχλον ἵνα μᾶλλον τὸν Βαραββᾶν ἀπολύσῃ αὐτοῖς. 12 ὁ δὲ Πιλᾶτος πάλιν ἀποκριθεὶς ἔλεγεν αὐτοῖς· Τί οὖν θέλετε ποιήσω ὃν λέγετε τὸν βασιλέα τῶν Ἰουδαίων; 13 οἱ δὲ πάλιν ἔκραξαν· Σταύρωσον αὐτόν. 14 ὁ δὲ Πιλᾶτος ἔλεγεν αὐτοῖς· Τί γὰρ ἐποίησεν κακόν; οἱ δὲ περισσῶς ἔκραξαν· Σταύρωσον αὐτόν. 15 ὁ δὲ Πιλᾶτος βουλόμενος τῷ ὄχλῳ τὸ ἱκανὸν ποιῆσαι ἀπέλυσεν αὐτοῖς τὸν Βαραββᾶν, καὶ παρέδωκεν τὸν Ἰησοῦν φραγελλώσας ἵνα σταυρωθῇ. [SBLGNT]

King James Version

1 And straightway in the morning the chief priests held a consultation with the elders and scribes and the whole council, and bound Jesus, and carried him away, and delivered him to Pilate. 2 And Pilate asked him, Art thou the King of the Jews? And he answering said unto him, Thou sayest it. 3 And the chief priests accused him of many things: but he answered nothing. 4 And Pilate asked him again, saying, Answerest thou nothing? behold how many things they witness against thee. 5 But Jesus yet answered nothing; so that Pilate marvelled. 6 Now at that feast he released unto them one prisoner, whomsoever they desired. 7 And there

New Rendition

1 And immediately, in the morning, having held a hearing, the chief priests, with the elders and scriptorians and all the Sanhedrin, having bound Jesus, led him away and handed him over to Pilate. 2 And Pilate questioned him: "Are you the king of the Jews?" And answering him, he says: "You say so." 3 And the chief priests were repeatedly accusing him. 4 And again Pilate questioned him, saying, "You do not answer? Look, they accuse you of many things!" 5 But Jesus answered nothing, so that Pilate was amazed.

6 And at the feast, he used to release to them one prisoner whom they were requesting. 7 And there was one called

was one named Barabbas, which lay bound with them that had made insurrection with him, who had committed murder in the insurrection. 8 And the multitude crying aloud began to desire him to do as he had ever done unto them. 9 But Pilate answered them, saying, Will ye that I release unto you the King of the Jews? 10 For he knew that the chief priests had delivered him for envy. 11 But the chief priests moved the people, that he should rather release Barabbas unto them. 12 And Pilate answered and said again unto them, What will ye then that I shall do unto him whom ye call the King of the Jews? 13 And they cried out again, Crucify him. 14 Then Pilate said unto them, Why, what evil hath he done? And they cried out the more exceedingly, Crucify him.

15 And so Pilate, willing to content the people, released Barabbas unto them, and delivered Jesus, when he had scourged him, to be crucified.

Barabbas having been bound with the rebels who in the uprising had committed murder. 8 And having come up, the crowd began to ask him to do as he usually did for them. 9 But Pilate answered them, saying, "Do you want me to release the king of the Jews to you?" 10 (For he knew that it was because of envy that the chief priests had handed him over.) 11 And the chief priests incited the crowd, so that he might release Barabbas to them instead. 12 Again answering, Pilate was saying to them, "Then what do you want me to do to him that you call the King of the Jews?" 13 And again they shouted, "Crucify him!" 14 And Pilate was saying to them, "Why? What has he done wrong?" But they shouted all the more: "Crucify him!" 15 But Pilate, desiring to do what the crowd wanted, released Barabbas to them and handed over Jesus, having whipped him, that he might be crucified.

Notes

15:1 *And straightway in the morning the chief priests held a consultation with the elders and scribes and the whole council:* The word "straightway" points to the quick fulfillment of what Jesus had prophesied about his fate.

"In the morning" could simply mean "early," or it could refer more specifically to the fourth watch of the night, which was from three to six in the morning.

The "consultation" can be understood several ways:

1. It refers to the meeting of Jewish leaders that was described in 14:55–65. Mark mentions it again in order to reorient the audience to this thread of the narrative after telling the story of Peter's denial.

2. It refers to another meeting of Jewish leaders, held after the one described in 14:55–65.

3. The Greek text could be translated as "made a plan." The plan probably concerned how they would present Jesus' situation to Pilate, given that he would not be terribly interested in a charge of blasphemy (see the Notes on 15:2).

The text emphasizes that the chief priests played the leading role in this event. But the phrasing is unusual because the Sanhedrin (KJV: "council") was composed of the chief priests, elders, and scribes, which means that the reference to "the whole council" is redundant. Perhaps Mark wanted to emphasize that the entire council was complicit (which would include Joseph of Arimathea; compare 15:43).

and bound Jesus, and carried him away, and delivered him to Pilate: "Delivered" (Greek: *paradidōmi*) translates the same verb used in Jesus' predictions of his fate (9:31; 10:33). Once again, a surface reading of the story might suggest that Jesus is losing control of his fate, but Mark's audience knows that Jesus' prophetic ability is being confirmed. This is also the same verb used to describe John the Baptist's imprisonment (1:14 [KJV: "was put"]), which emphasizes that Jesus is likely to experience the same fate as John. This is also the same verb found in LXX Isaiah 53:6 (KJV: "hath laid on"), where it is the sins of "all" that is "laid on."

Jesus has been deemed guilty of blasphemy by the Jewish authorities; blasphemy carried the penalty of stoning (Lev. 24:16). It is debated whether the Jewish leadership had the authority to inflict a death sentence at this time. It may be that Rome did not permit conquered people to enact death sentences (at least, without Roman permission) for fear that they would deploy them against those who aided Rome. But it is also possible that the Jewish leadership could have stoned Jesus but chose not to in order to avoid permitting him the same (honorable) fate of stoning as many prophets in the HB;[2] crucifixion, by contrast, was regarded as a dishonorable death (Deut. 21:23). It has also been suggested that the Sanhedrin could have stoned Jesus in an extrajudicial killing, but they preferred for his death to be state-sanctioned in order to underscore Jesus' guilt.

This portion of the text may have been particularly poignant for Mark's audience, who may have similarly worried about being handed over to gentile courts—something that Jesus had prophesied would be one of the consequences of following him (13:11).

Pilate was the Roman governor of Judea from 26–36 CE. His usual residence was Caesarea Maritima, but he came to Jerusalem for Passover. Mark's Gospel contains no overt indications of Jesus' age or the length of his ministry; only the dating of Pilate's rule places Jesus' death within 26–36 CE.

---

2. While the HB itself contains no accounts of prophets being stoned to death, compare Matt. 23:37; Luke 13:34.

15:2 ***And Pilate asked him, Art thou the King of the Jews?:*** The word
"thou" is emphatic—Pilate cannot fathom how Jesus could be the king of
the Jews. The image of a tortured and bound peasant claiming to be a king
must have struck Pilate as absurd, and so his question is sarcastic or perhaps incredulous.

This question "can only have been based on the information supplied
by the Sanhedrin,"[3] but Pilate does not mention blasphemy—the charge
made by the Jewish leadership—rather, he accuses Jesus of being the king
of the Jews. How best to explain this difference is debated:

1. This is an entirely separate charge. The Jewish leadership realized that Pilate
   would have no interest in punishing a blasphemer, so they presented Jesus
   as a political threat instead. The implication is that the Jewish leadership has
   lied about Jesus to Pilate.

2. This is functionally the same charge as blasphemy, reworded to be understandable to a gentile audience. The blasphemy stemmed from Jesus' claim
   to be the Anointed One (see the Notes on 14:61–64), which is essentially a
   claim to kingship.

Either way, claiming to be the king of the Jews would have been understood as a threat to Roman rule since it implied the desire to establish Jewish lands as a kingdom independent of Rome.

And he answering said unto him, Thou sayest it: Jesus' response is
somewhat ambiguous. It must contain a denial ("*You* say that—I don't say
that") in order to make sense of Pilate's continued investigation: had this
been an unambiguous claim to be king, it is unlikely that the chief priests
would have continued to accuse him, that Pilate would have asked the
question again, or that Pilate would later conclude that Jesus had been
brought to him out of envy. At the same time, it is not a complete renunciation of the title.

This ambiguity is most appropriate given that Jesus is the king of the
Jews, but only in a most unexpected sense and with a completely unexpected mission: to die instead of to throw off Roman rule. The ambiguity
guides the audience to think about the senses in which "king" both is and
is not an appropriate title for Jesus.

Because he repeats Pilate's use of the word "thou" at the beginning of his
response, Jesus' statement has an impudent tone. It is a bit cheeky, especially when voiced by a peasant to a governor. This is ironic: on the level
of the words, the response is ambiguous as to whether Jesus is claiming to

---

3. France, *Gospel of Mark,* 628.

be the king of the Jews, but this audacious tone implies that Jesus considers himself to be superior to the governor and thus in that sense affirms his kingship.

15:3 *And the chief priests accused him of many things:* "Many things" could mean either:

1. They level many charges against Jesus. This could reflect desperation: as it becomes apparent that their charge of being the king of the Jews may not stick, they try to make the case for Jesus' death on other grounds. Or it might have reflected the standard procedure of adding charges to malign the character of the accused.

2. They accuse him with vigor (harshly or repeatedly). This reading may be preferable since only one accusation is mentioned in the story.

Regardless, this line makes clear that the chief priests are occupying the same narrative role in this story as those who falsely accused Jesus to the Sanhedrin.

but he answered nothing: These words are not in the best ancient manuscripts.[4] They were likely added so that Pilate's question in the next verse would seem less abrupt.

15:4 *And Pilate asked him again, saying, Answerest thou nothing? behold how many things they witness against thee:* Pilate's question echoes that posed to Jesus by the Sanhedrin (14:60–61), suggesting an affinity between Pilate and the Jewish leaders.

Once again, "many" could refer to quantity or intensity (see the Notes on 15:3).

15:5 *But Jesus yet answered nothing:* This line may echo Isaiah 53:7, where the afflicted one kept silent, especially since there are other allusions to Isaiah in this chapter.

so that Pilate marvelled: Pilate's reaction may stem from the fact that "Roman law apparently presumed the guilt of those who refused to defend themselves."[5] Pilate may wonder why Jesus is in effect confessing to this most unlikely of charges. Because the verb translated as "marvelled" "often carries a note of admiration,"[6] it may also suggest that Pilate was impressed by Jesus' silence in contrast to the accusations made by the chief priests.

The word "marvelled" may also echo LXX Isaiah 52:15, where the same Greek verb is used to describe how the nations will be surprised by the

---

4. See SBLGNT above.

5. Evans, *Mark 8:27–16:20*, 479.

6. N. T. France, *Gospel of Mark*, 629.

Lord's servant. Interestingly, in that passage, it is the kings who shut their mouths in his presence, so Jesus is placed into the role of king by this intertext. The larger context of the Isaiah passage is the glorification of the servant, despite the fact that his glory will not be evident; it is thus an evocative passage to apply to Jesus' current situation.

15:6 *Now at that feast he released unto them one prisoner, whomsoever they desired:* There is no external evidence of a custom of releasing a prisoner at Passover (in fact, Acts 25:16 suggests the opposite), although there is evidence of occasional prisoner releases as a gesture of good will. It is possible that the Jews had a custom of asking for a prisoner at Passover—a request that was not regularly fulfilled. It is also possible that this was a personal custom of Pilate's, and thus no record of it exists.

15:7 *And there was one named Barabbas:* The phrasing "one named Barabbas" (as opposed to simply "Barabbas") signals that Mark is calling attention to the name Barabbas, which transliterates the Aramaic for "son of the father." It seems that Mark's purpose for including this story is to suggest that Barabbas is an alternative to Jesus—another "son of the father"—but that his brand of liberation, attempting to cast off Roman rule, was the one which the people chose instead of Jesus'.

which lay bound with them that had made insurrection with him: "Lay bound" means that Barabbas was imprisoned. Due to his involvement with the insurrection, there is a political component to Barabbas's crime.

who had committed murder in the insurrection: The word "who" is plural, so the implication is that not just Barabbas but all of these rebels were murderers. It is also possible that Barabbas wasn't accused of murder but that he was arrested with others who had committed murder; this is perhaps the more likely reading since it is hard to imagine Pilate releasing someone accused of murdering Romans, the presumed victims of murder committed in the context of an insurrection.

The article before the word "insurrection" ("the insurrection") implies that Mark's audience was familiar with this event.

It is possible that these other insurrectionists are the ones crucified alongside Jesus.

15:8 *And the multitude crying aloud began to desire him to do as he had ever done unto them:* Many manuscripts read "went up" instead of "crying aloud" here;[7] the former is probably the earlier reading.[8] The variant may

---

7. Collins, *Mark,* 711 note b.
8. Collins, *Mark,* 719.

have occurred either because the idea of going up didn't make sense to a copyist (although it is appropriate if the crowd is going up to Jerusalem or to Pilate's residence) or because it was simply a mistake since the words appear similar (*anabas* ["went up"] and *anaboēsas* ["called out"]). The idea of this being a "new" crowd recently come into Jerusalem might explain the fact that previously the chief priests had feared the crowd's excessive devotion to Jesus (14:2), which clearly is not the case with this crowd.

It is possible that, at this point, the crowd is not concerned with which prisoner is released but merely wants any of them released as a token of goodwill.

15:9 But Pilate answered them, saying, Will ye that I release unto you the King of the Jews?: Pilate does not refer to Jesus by name but by his purported title. It is possible that Pilate does not even know Jesus' proper name, which would be an ironic reflection of how little Pilate "knows" of Jesus' true identity. Nonetheless, it seems that Pilate is here encouraging the crowd to ask for Jesus' release.

It is also possible that the crowd does not know that it is Jesus who is being offered here; perhaps they would have requested Jesus' release had they known. The idea that Jesus would die as a result of mistaken identity (either on Pilate's part or the crowds') is a profound instance of Markan irony. It is also possible that the audience is pressed into a corner here (and the chief priests may be manipulating them on this basis): if they ask for the king of the Jews, they may in turn be accused of supporting a threat to Rome by expressing their desire for the Jews to have their own king.

15:10 For he knew that the chief priests had delivered him for envy: This aside is very revealing: it not only condemns the chief priests for being motivated not by justice but by envy, but it condemns Pilate for acquiescing to the crowd when he knew Jesus was not guilty. It also suggests to Mark's audience that, despite Jesus' treatment at the hands of both Jewish and Roman leadership, he was innocent. The fact that Pilate found Jesus blameless—even after the accusations against him, and even in the face of Jesus' silence—is a strong condemnation of the charges against Jesus.

Envy implies that they recognized something of value in Jesus, but envy seeks to punish the possessor of good qualities;[9] by contrast, discipleship seeks to reproduce those qualities.

---

9. Anselm C. Hagedorn and Jerome H. Neyrey, "'It Was Out of Envy That They Handed Jesus Over' (Mark 15:10): The Anatomy of Envy and the Gospel of Mark," *Journal for the Study of the New Testament* 69 (1998): 52–53.

How did Pilate know the chief priests' motivation?[10] Perhaps he heard an edge of envy in their voices as they made their accusations against Jesus. In any case, the text implies that Pilate was skilled at discernment, which is ironic given his inability to determine Jesus' identity.

15:11 *But the chief priests moved the people, that he should rather release Barabbas unto them:* This verse suggests that it was not the natural inclination of the crowd to prefer Barabbas to Jesus but that this position was only reached after the chief priests manipulated the crowd. One implication of this is that, contrary to the ugly trend of some Christian history, "the Jews" are not guilty for the death of Jesus—rather, some of the Jewish religious establishment were culpable.

This verse and 14:1–2 suggest that the leadership regarded the crowd as a force to be manipulated, which further suggests Jesus' innocence: Jesus is not killed because the Roman judicial system brought about a fair verdict.

Mark does not record what, precisely, the leaders said to sway the crowd. This enhances the nefariousness of their deed.

15:12 *And Pilate answered and said again unto them, What will ye then that I shall do unto him whom ye call the King of the Jews?:* Some manuscripts omit the phrase "him whom ye call."[11] It probably was added by a scribe to clarify that Pilate did not think that Jesus was the king of the Jews (compare 15:9 and the variant on 14:62).

The crowd decided to release Barabbas, but it is left unclear what fate they wanted for Jesus; hence Pilate's question here. The crowd could have asked for Jesus' release (they may have thought Pilate unlikely to grant freedom to a second prisoner, but they still could have asked; Pilate's unwillingness to condemn Jesus suggests that he might well have released him) or for his imprisonment. But instead, they demand his death.

15:13 *And they cried out again, Crucify him:* Save Jesus' reference to taking up one's cross (8:34), this is the first mention of crucifixion in Mark's Gospel. Crucifixion was an incredibly cruel punishment, applied only to the gravest crimes and even then not to Roman citizens—some of whom spoke out against the practice as being too barbaric.

15:14 *Then Pilate said unto them, Why, what evil hath he done?:* The imperfect form of "said" ("was saying") implies that Pilate made more than

---

10. John W. Welch, "The Factor of Fear in the Trial of Jesus," in *Jesus Christ: Son of God, Savior,* ed. Paul H. Peterson, Gary L. Hatch, and Laura D. Card (Provo, Utah: Religious Studies Center, 2002), 288.

11. Collins, *Mark,* 711 note d.

one effort to reason with the crowd. This question suggests "the need to make the point that Jesus was indeed innocent; he was not a criminal justly convicted by a Roman official."[12]

And they cried out the more exceedingly, Crucify him: The crowd does not answer Pilate's question, leaving Mark's audience with the realization that Jesus has done no evil.

15:15 ***And so Pilate, willing to content the people, released Barabbas unto them:*** Mark provides Pilate's motive: Pilate did not find Jesus guilty (compare 15:13), but he releases Barabbas to appease the crowd. Throughout Christian history, Pilate has usually been viewed as wishy-washy, but it might be more accurate to think of him as shrewd and calculating.

Pilate and the crowd have, in a sense, switched roles: now the crowd is ruling Pilate. To show a leader turning over decision-making to a crowd inverts the very concept of a just trial. This scene is a parody of a trial, which Mark's audience would have interpreted as indicting Pilate—not, as the modern reader might suppose, the Jews.

It is significant that Pilate quickly determines Jesus' innocence; that portion of this hearing is brief. Then, Pilate devotes a fairly long time to trying to sway the crowd. This is another way in which Mark emphasizes Jesus' innocence.

and delivered Jesus, when he had scourged him, to be crucified: Because "scourged" is a participle and not the main verb, it is de-emphasized; the downplaying of Jesus' physical torture will be consistent in this chapter. Scourging, which was standard practice before crucifixion, involved flogging with a multipiece whip with sharp items embedded in it. Sometimes it was fatal.

This torture fulfills Jesus' prophecy from 10:34, although, interestingly, that verse uses a different Greek term to describe the scourging.

Relationship to the Death of John the Baptist. Both Herod and Pilate are willing to accede their authority to others: Herod to his wife's daughter and Pilate to the crowd. The result in both cases is that a righteous man is killed.

Comparison between the Two Hearings. In chapter 14, Jesus is interrogated by the Sanhedrin; in chapter 15, he undergoes a very similar questioning by Pilate, a Roman leader. Parallels between the two scenes include:[13]

---

12. Collins, *Mark*, 721.
13. Deppe, *Theological Intentions*, 92–93.

1. question about Jesus' identity (14:61 and 15:2)
2. Jesus' answer (14:62 and 15:2)
3. question about Jesus' silence (14:64 and 15:2)
4. false witnesses (14:56–59 and 15:3)
5. Jesus remains silent (14:61 and 15:5)
6. agreement to kill Jesus (14:64 and 15:13–14)
7. Jesus tortured (14:65 and 15:15)
8. Jesus is mocked (14:65 and 15:16–20)

Some differences may also be significant: when Jesus was asked by the Sanhedrin if he was the Messiah, his response was "I am" (14:62)—a response with no trace of ambiguity. But his response of "thou sayest" to Pilate is ambiguous. Nonetheless, these are "amazingly similar"[14] accounts. One result of the parallel is to suggest an equivalence between the Jewish leadership and the Roman leadership—an idea that would have offended most Jews. The parallel also implies that responsibility for Jesus' death is diffuse: contra the historical impulse to blame the Jews (an impulse aided, no doubt, by the extensive presence of Romans—but not Jews—in the Christian church and in positions of political authority), in Mark's story, they carry no more blame than the Romans—and probably a good bit less.

Paralleling the two hearings of Jesus is not the first time that Mark has paralleled a Jewish and a gentile scene: it happened with the inaugurating exorcisms and the feeding miracles (compare 1:21–28 with 5:1–20 and 6:30–44 with 8:1–10). Just as both groups shared responsibility for Jesus' death, both groups were beneficiaries of his miracles.

Analysis

Up to this point in Mark's Gospel, references to kings and kingdoms have referred to God, not to Jesus. But in this chapter, a plethora of references to kingship refers to Jesus. Jesus was proclaimed the Son of God at his baptism, but Mark suggests (primarily through the use of irony) that Jesus is king through his death.

It is, of course, ironic that the crowd chooses Barabbas, the other "son of the father," as his name suggests. In Mark's story, Jesus, although innocent, takes the place of another "son of the father," a son who merited death but was spared from it only because Jesus died for him.

---

14. Marcus, *Mark 8–16,* 1031.

Both Jesus and Barabbas present a challenge to Roman rule as they advocate respectively for a kingdom of the Jews and a kingdom of God. Part of the point of this story is that the crowd chose physical salvation (from Rome) over spiritual salvation. The people are coerced by their leaders into choosing Barabbas over Jesus; they chose the killer over the savior.

JESUS IS CRUCIFIED (15:16–32)

Greek Text

16 Οἱ δὲ στρατιῶται ἀπήγαγον αὐτὸν ἔσω τῆς αὐλῆς, ὅ ἐστιν πραιτώριον, καὶ συγκαλοῦσιν ὅλην τὴν σπεῖραν. 17 καὶ ἐνδιδύσκουσιν αὐτὸν πορφύραν καὶ περιτιθέασιν αὐτῷ πλέξαντες ἀκάνθινον στέφανον· 18 καὶ ἤρξαντο ἀσπάζεσθαι αὐτόν· Χαῖρε, βασιλεῦ τῶν Ἰουδαίων· 19 καὶ ἔτυπτον αὐτοῦ τὴν κεφαλὴν καλάμῳ καὶ ἐνέπτυον αὐτῷ, καὶ τιθέντες τὰ γόνατα προσεκύνουν αὐτῷ. 20 καὶ ὅτε ἐνέπαιξαν αὐτῷ, ἐξέδυσαν αὐτὸν τὴν πορφύραν καὶ ἐνέδυσαν αὐτὸν τὰ ἱμάτια τὰ ἴδια. καὶ ἐξάγουσιν αὐτὸν ἵνα σταυρώσωσιν αὐτόν.

21 Καὶ ἀγγαρεύουσιν παράγοντά τινα Σίμωνα Κυρηναῖον ἐρχόμενον ἀπ' ἀγροῦ, τὸν πατέρα Ἀλεξάνδρου καὶ Ῥούφου, ἵνα ἄρῃ τὸν σταυρὸν αὐτοῦ. 22 καὶ φέρουσιν αὐτὸν ἐπὶ τὸν Γολγοθᾶν τόπον, ὅ ἐστιν μεθερμηνευόμενον Κρανίου Τόπος. 23 καὶ ἐδίδουν αὐτῷ ἐσμυρνισμένον οἶνον, ὃς δὲ οὐκ ἔλαβεν. 24 καὶ σταυροῦσιν αὐτὸν καὶ διαμερίζονται τὰ ἱμάτια αὐτοῦ, βάλλοντες κλῆρον ἐπ' αὐτὰ τίς τί ἄρῃ.

25 Ἦν δὲ ὥρα τρίτη καὶ ἐσταύρωσαν αὐτόν. 26 καὶ ἦν ἡ ἐπιγραφὴ τῆς αἰτίας αὐτοῦ ἐπιγεγραμμένη· Ὁ βασιλεὺς τῶν Ἰουδαίων. 27 καὶ σὺν αὐτῷ σταυροῦσιν δύο λῃστάς, ἕνα ἐκ δεξιῶν καὶ ἕνα ἐξ εὐωνύμων αὐτοῦ. 29 Καὶ οἱ παραπορευόμενοι ἐβλασφήμουν αὐτὸν κινοῦντες τὰς κεφαλὰς αὐτῶν καὶ λέγοντες· Οὐὰ ὁ καταλύων τὸν ναὸν καὶ οἰκοδομῶν ἐν τρισὶν ἡμέραις, 30 σῶσον σεαυτὸν καταβὰς ἀπὸ τοῦ σταυροῦ. 31 ὁμοίως καὶ οἱ ἀρχιερεῖς ἐμπαίζοντες πρὸς ἀλλήλους μετὰ τῶν γραμματέων ἔλεγον· Ἄλλους ἔσωσεν, ἑαυτὸν οὐ δύναται σῶσαι· 32 ὁ χριστὸς ὁ βασιλεὺς Ἰσραὴλ καταβάτω νῦν ἀπὸ τοῦ σταυροῦ, ἵνα ἴδωμεν καὶ πιστεύσωμεν. καὶ οἱ συνεσταυρωμένοι σὺν αὐτῷ ὠνείδιζον αὐτόν. [SBLGNT]

King James Version

16 And the soldiers led him away into the hall, called Praetorium; and they call together the whole band. 17 And they clothed him with purple, and platted a crown of thorns, and put it about

New Rendition

16 And the soldiers led him away into the courtyard of the governor's house, and they called the entire band of soldiers together. 17 And they put a purple cloak on him and placed on him a thorn

his head, 18 And began to salute him, Hail, King of the Jews! 19 And they smote him on the head with a reed, and did spit upon him, and bowing their knees worshipped him. 20 And when they had mocked him, they took off the purple from him, and put his own clothes on him, and led him out to crucify him. 21 And they compel one Simon a Cyrenian, who passed by, coming out of the country, the father of Alexander and Rufus, to bear his cross. 22 And they bring him unto the place Golgotha, which is, being interpreted, The place of a skull. 23 And they gave him to drink wine mingled with myrrh: but he received it not. 24 And when they had crucified him, they parted his garments, casting lots upon them, what every man should take. 25 And it was the third hour, and they crucified him. 26 And the superscription of his accusation was written over, THE KING OF THE JEWS. 27 And with him they crucify two thieves; the one on his right hand, and the other on his left. 28 And the scripture was fulfilled, which saith, And he was numbered with the transgressors. 29 And they that passed by railed on him, wagging their heads, and saying, Ah, thou that destroyest the temple, and buildest it in three days, 30 Save thyself, and come down from the cross. 31 Likewise also the chief priests mocking said among themselves with the scribes, He saved others; himself he cannot save. 32 Let Christ the King of Israel descend now from the cross, that we may see and believe. And they that were crucified with him reviled him.

crown, having woven it. 18 And they began to salute him: "Hail, King of the Jews!" 19 And they hit his head with a staff, and they spit on him. And, kneeling down, they paid homage to him. 20 And when they had ridiculed him, they took the purple cloak off of him and put his own clothes on him and led him out to crucify him.

21 And they forced a passerby, Simon of Cyrene—the father of Alexander and Rufus—who was coming from the fields, to carry his cross. 22 And they bring him to a place called Golgotha (which means "the place of a skull"). 23 And they gave him wine mixed with myrrh, but he did not take it. 24 And having crucified him, "they divided his clothes, throwing dice for them" [to see] who should take what.

25 And it was about nine in the morning when they crucified him. 26 And the inscription of the charge against him read, "The King of the Jews." 27 And they crucified two outlaws with him, one on the right side and one on his left. [28] 29 And those passing by blasphemed him, shaking their heads and saying, "Ha! The one destroying the temple and building it in three days, 30 save yourself by coming down from the cross!" 31 In the same way, the chief priests were mocking, together with the scriptorians, [and] saying among themselves, "He saved/healed others, but he does not have the power to save/heal himself. 32 Let the anointed one, the King of Israel, come down now from the cross so that we might see and trust!" And those being crucified with him insulted him.

Notes

15:16 *And the soldiers led him away into the hall, called Prætorium:* "Hall" may connote a courtyard and thus an exterior space.[15] "Praetorium" is a loanword from Latin that refers to the governor's official residence. It is possible that "hall" and "praetorium" mean the same thing, with the latter term used to make the sense intelligible to Mark's audience.

and they call together the whole band: A "band" is a military term referring to several hundred men. It may begin a series of allusions to the Roman triumphal procession (see the Analysis of this section).

15:17 *And they clothed him with purple:* This is not the standard verb for "clothe" but rather a vaunted one, perhaps used to suggest the ritual mocking.

Due to the cost of producing purple dye, purple clothing was associated with kings. It is debated whether those outside the nobility were even permitted to wear purple.

The mockery inherent in this scene would have been exacerbated by Jesus' appearance as a victim of torture, weakened and bloody.

and platted a crown of thorns, and put it about his head: The emperor would have worn a laurel wreath during processions, so this is another mocking action. In contrast to the purple clothing, Mark never says that the crown is removed, so it is likely that Jesus was crucified wearing it.

15:18 *And began to salute him, Hail, King of the Jews!:* Their words mockingly mimic how one would address a king or emperor.

15:19 *And they smote him on the head with a reed, and did spit upon him, and bowing their knees worshipped him:* An unusual word for "reed" is used, perhaps to echo LXX Isaiah 42:3.

The reed mockingly represents the king's scepter, but instead of giving it to Jesus as a sign of his rule, they use it to hurt him. The pain of these blows to the head would have been amplified by the crown of thorns.

Previously, demons have bowed down to Jesus (5:6); these are the only two uses of this Greek verb in Mark, so audience members who noticed the connection would have concluded that these soldiers—the personification of Roman power—were acting demonically.

15:20 *And when they had mocked him, they took off the purple from him, and put his own clothes on him, and led him out to crucify him:* Normally, victims were transported and crucified naked, so the reference

---

15. Collins, *Mark,* 725.

to returning Jesus' clothes to him may have surprised Mark's audience. Permitting the victim to wear clothing may have been a concession to Jewish sensibilities (but see 15:24).

15:21 *And they compel one Simon a Cyrenian, who passed by, coming out of the country, the father of Alexander and Rufus, to bear his cross:* "Compel" refers to the practice of soldiers requiring a person in an occupied territory to assist them (Matt. 5:41). Normally, a victim was required to carry his own cross (technically, just the cross beam since the upright beam was permanently mounted in the ground); the compelling of Simon probably indicates that Jesus was not physically capable—as a result of the previous torture—to carry his own cross. Once again, Mark minimizes the attention devoted to Jesus' physical suffering by not directly mentioning Jesus' physical state.

Simon is described as being from Cyrene, which was in present-day Libya. Simon is thus an African, and it is "quite plausible"[16] that he was black. The reference to his children implies that they were known to Mark's audience; otherwise, it is difficult to imagine why they would have been mentioned. There is no way to determine whether Mark is referring to the same Alexander and Rufus who are mentioned elsewhere in the NT (Acts 19:33; 1 Tim. 1:20; and 2 Tim. 4:14 mention Alexander; see Rom. 16:13 for a reference to Rufus).

"Out of the country" can also mean "from the fields." Some have objected to the latter reading if it implies that Simon was working on the Passover, but a long journey from "the country" on the Passover would also have violated the law. Either way, the implication is that Simon is a peasant; Mark may intend a contrast to Joseph of Arimathea, who also aids Jesus but is of much higher status.

Jesus explained that following him required taking up one's cross (8:34). Simon of Cyrene fulfills this mandate in a concrete manner, although that picture is complicated by the fact that Simon did not choose to carry Jesus' cross but rather was compelled to do so. So perhaps Simon's story is not an example of taking up the cross, although it is possible that Mark intended—in spite of Simon's lack of choice—that he be interpreted as an ideal disciple. The fact that his children are known to Mark's audience does suggest that his family was associated with the early Christians. The fact that he shares a name with Simon Peter may imply a contrast between Peter's stalled discipleship (which is especially surprising in light of Peter's promise to stay

---

16. Witherington, *Gospel of Mark,* 392.

with Jesus even if it costs him his life; see 14:31) and Simon of Cyrene's aid during Jesus' most trying hours.

15:22 *And they bring him unto the place Golgotha, which is, being interpreted, The place of a skull:* The word translated as "bring" often means "carry" (2:3; 6:27–28; 12:15), so it is possible that Jesus, being too weak to walk, was carried.

Golgotha was outside of Jerusalem on a hill. "Golgotha" is an Aramaic word meaning "skull." ("Calvary" is derived from the Latin word for "skull.") This hill may have been so named (1) because of a traditional (but historically unlikely) belief that it was the burial place of Adam's skull, (2) for the presence of bones since it was an execution site, or (3) because the hill itself was shaped like a skull. By presenting the Aramaic name and then the translation, Mark calls attention to the symbolic resonances of the name.

Jesus' experience in this chapter follows the pattern of a triumphal procession (see the Analysis of this section) that ended on a hill that was also associated with a skull, which may explain why Mark emphasizes the name.

15:23 *And they gave him to drink wine mingled with myrrh: but he received it not:* It is not clear to whom "they" refers:

1. *The women* (who will not be introduced until 15:40–41). Later Jewish writings refer to honorable women who gave numbing drinks to those being crucified, so perhaps they were offering to reduce Jesus' pain (Prov. 31:6–7). (It is debated whether myrrh actually deadens pain, but they may have believed that it did.) There may be a link to Jesus' prayer in Gethsemane requesting that the "cup" pass from him: Jesus is here refusing an alternative cup—one which would have diminished his suffering. Mark is showing that Jesus is still capable of making choices, and his choice is to drink the cup his Father has asked him to drink and not escape from it by drinking from another cup. The scene shows his commitment—even during this moment of torture and impending death—to following his Father's will.

2. *The soldiers.* They are the immediate antecedent of the word "they." This leads to three possibilities:

   a. It seems unlikely that they would have wanted to diminish Jesus' pain, but it is possible—albeit speculative—that they were acting at the request of Pilate, who is sympathetic to Jesus. If so, his refusal to drink would be for the same reasons outlined above.

   b. Because wine with myrrh was something only kings could afford to drink, its offer may have continued the mocking of Jesus with symbols of kingship. Jesus' refusal signals his refusal to participate in his own mockery.

   c. While a small amount of myrrh would have pleasantly spiced the wine, myrrh itself was bitter, so a large amount would have been unpleasant. The soldiers may be tormenting Jesus by offering him what appears to be a thirst-quencher but that would actually have been undrinkable. Jesus' refusal of the cup shows his ability to discern the true nature of what they are offering him.

Regardless of which of these readings is preferred, Jesus' refusal to drink may relate to his promise at the Last Supper that he would not drink wine again until he drinks it in the kingdom of God (14:25). His refusal to drink here shows his ability to keep his promises, even under extreme physical duress.

This scene may echo the portion of the Roman triumphal procession where "at the moment of sacrifice at the end of a triumph, a cup of wine was handed to the one performing the sacrifice; he did not drink it, but poured it out as a libation to the gods."[17] This, then, would explain his refusal to drink.

15:24 *And when they had crucified him, they parted his garments, casting lots upon them, what every man should take:* Crucifixion involved either tying or nailing[18] the arms and legs to a cross. As is typical of Mark's account, the torturous aspects of the crucifixion are minimized, and the focus is on other elements of the experience: it is telling that Jesus' pain is not mentioned but the dispersal of his clothing is.

Clothing was relatively expensive in antiquity; one of the perks of performing an execution was the right to the victim's clothing. This verse probably indicates that Jesus was crucified naked, which was standard practice in order to humiliate the victim.

"Casting lots" refers to a method of determination by chance, perhaps using pebbles with markings on them, pottery shards, or dice.

When the soldiers cast lots to divide Jesus' garments, it echoes Psalm 22:18, where the division of clothing by lots signals impending death. In the context of the psalm, the sufferer is innocent, which is important background to Mark's story.

15:25 *And it was the third hour, and they crucified him:* The third hour is 9 a.m.

Continuing with the theme of mocking Jesus as a pretend king, crucifixion itself was understood as a "burlesque kingship [ritual]."[19]

---

17. Dowd, *Reading Mark,* 159.

18. In 1968, the ossuary of a crucifixion victim from the late 20s CE was discovered. There was an iron spike of 11.5 cm found through the right ankle bone; apparently the spike could not be removed, so the victim was buried with it and a fragment of the olive wood to which the spike was attached. Evans, *Mark 8:27–16:20,* 501.

19. Marcus, *Mark 8–16,* 1050.

15:26 *And the superscription of his accusation was written over, THE KING OF THE JEWS:* It is more likely that this placard was placed around Jesus' neck than attached to the cross above his head.

In the Roman triumphal procession, "Signs proclaiming the triumphator's achievements are carried in procession with him"[20] and then raised up at the end.

15:27 *And with him they crucify two thieves; the one on his right hand, and the other on his left:* "Thieves" has a political connotation, so these are not common thieves but rebels. Simple theft was not a capital offense. These two are most likely those with whom Barabbas was arrested; they were part of an insurrection.

This verse echoes Isaiah 53:12; see the Notes on 15:28.

15:28 *And the scripture was fulfilled, which saith, And he was numbered with the transgressors:* No early NT manuscript includes this verse;[21] it appears to be a marginal note (quoting Isa. 53:12) that was accidentally incorporated into the text by a later copyist or was added to harmonize with Luke 22:37.[22] It is therefore omitted from the New Rendition. But 15:27 does allude to Isaiah 53:12, so the sentiment is not inappropriate.

15:29 *And they that passed by railed on him, wagging their heads, and saying, Ah, thou that destroyest the temple, and buildest it in three days:* Crucifixions were intentionally located along roads to maximize the presence of passersby and contribute to a deterrent effect. Here, those who pass by taunt Jesus.

"Railed on" translates the Greek word *blasphēmeō,* which means "blasphemes" in its three other Markan occurrences (2:7; 3:28, 29). It is possible that it carries the generic sense of abusive speech, but it is more likely that, ironically, people are blaspheming Jesus while Jesus is being killed on charges of blasphemy.

Wagging the head is a sign of scorn (Ps. 109:25; Isa. 37:22). It also alludes to Psalm 22:7, where the suffering one is mocked by those who wag their heads. In Mark, these scorners call on Jesus to save himself, but in the psalm, God is called on to save the innocent sufferer. Mockingly, and thus ironically, they align Jesus with the God of the Bible. A similar mocking is described in Lamentations 2:15; with that intertext, interestingly, Jesus would be aligned with the "daughter of Jerusalem."

---

20. Dowd, *Reading Mark,* 159.

21. Blumell, "Text Critical Comparison," 88.

22. Metzger, *Textual Commentary,* 99.

This accusation repeats the one made at Jesus' appearance before the Sanhedrin (compare 14:58). There is some irony in that Jesus' body will be restored after three days.

15:30 *Save thyself, and come down from the cross:* They assume that because Jesus does not save himself, he cannot save himself and, therefore, could not save others. They do not realize that, according to the logic of the narrative as established in the Gethsemane prayer, Jesus is choosing to lose his life. This fulfills Jesus' teaching that the only way to truly save one's life is to lose it (8:35).

This taunt is probably why Mark referred to their words as blasphemy: "The final blasphemy is to say that God would send a Messiah who would rather save himself than others."[23]

15:31 *Likewise also the chief priests mocking said among themselves with the scribes, He saved others; himself he cannot save:* Introducing this verse with "likewise" signals that it constitutes blasphemy as well. The verb translated as "saved" can mean "saved" or "healed," so the chief priests are implicitly admitting that Jesus healed others, and Mark's audience would probably have understood this as an unintentional confession of Jesus' ability to save others.

15:32 *Let Christ the King of Israel descend now from the cross, that we may see and believe:* The title "king of Israel" is used only here in Mark, but it appears to be the Jewish equivalent to "king of the Jews."[24]

And they that were crucified with him reviled him: "Reviled" is imperfect, implying that they repeatedly insulted him. In a sense, this is the ultimate insult: even those who are suffering the same fate as Jesus are not sympathetic to him. But it also suggests that Jesus is not dying as one of them. This incident suggests that the experience of crucifixion is not necessarily sufficient to create empathy.

Analysis

This scene appears to be patterned after the Roman triumphal procession.[25] It would have begun with the gathering of the troops (hence the reference to "the whole band" in 15:16) and involved a crowned emperor wearing purple who is hailed by the gathered crowd. So these are not isolated

---

23. Joel F. Williams, "Foreshadowing, Echoes, and the Blasphemy at the Cross (Mark 15:29)," *Journal of Biblical Literature* 132, no. 4 (2013): 916.

24. France, *Gospel of Mark*, 648.

25. Dowd, *Reading Mark*, 158.

incidents of mockery but rather a developed allusion to the concept of Jesus as king. Of course, it is ironically true that Jesus is a king and should be treated as such. His kingly nature is highlighted through the mockery, as is the idea that people do not realize his true identity. Perhaps most significantly, the kingly procession would normally "end with the sacrifice of a bull and the epiphany of the king as god to the accompaniment of a ritual shout from the people."[26] Of course, it is Jesus who is sacrificed in Mark's story and the centurion who recognizes Jesus' real identity after his death.

"The one on his right hand, and the other on his left" (15:27) is not only an odd detail to include but also a very long alternative to having Jesus "between" two thieves. This language is almost surely used to echo the intemperate request of James[27] and John to be given the seats of honor on Jesus' left and right hand (10:37–40). The alert audience member would thus realize that the crucifixion is, shockingly, the "glory" of Jesus. This connection is strengthened by the fact that, in the exchange with James and John, Jesus referred to his suffering and death as his "baptism" and "cup" and asked if they were capable of participating in those with him. Despite James and John's affirmations, it is not them but rather two strangers who are at Jesus' right and left here. Thus, the reference to the thieves is a commentary on the disciples' abandonment of Jesus (but see 15:40–41).

The taunt to "save thyself" implies that power should always be used to one's own benefit; Jesus' behavior suggests otherwise. Similarly, they are challenging his truthfulness (via his [supposed] prophecy that the temple will be destroyed), but Jesus' three prophecies about his suffering and death are currently being fulfilled. The passersby are positioned as those who have eyes but do not see; Mark's audience, however, sees what is really going on here.

The requirement to see before one believes is framed negatively here, especially since the audience will remember that previously, the religious leaders saw Jesus' ability to exorcise but chose to attribute his power to Satan instead of to God (3:22). To Mark's audience, the demand for a sign is ironic since Jesus' suffering and death fulfill his multiple prophecies of these events and thus constitute a sign of his reliability. These religious authorities are examples of those with eyes who do not see (4:11–12).

---

26. Dowd, *Reading Mark,* 158.
27. See the Notes on 1:19.

Mark's telling of this story minimizes Jesus' physical suffering, which is omitted along with details of the torture and crucifixion. One can imagine the story told in a much different manner so that the audience would focus on the physical agony of the cross. But instead, Mark's emphasis is on the emotional torture of mockery, insult, and misunderstanding.

JESUS DIES (15:33–41)

Greek Text

33 Καὶ γενομένης ὥρας ἕκτης σκότος ἐγένετο ἐφ᾽ ὅλην τὴν γῆν ἕως ὥρας ἐνάτης. 34 καὶ τῇ ἐνάτῃ ὥρᾳ ἐβόησεν ὁ Ἰησοῦς φωνῇ μεγάλῃ· Ἐλωῒ ἐλωῒ λεμὰ σαβαχθάνι; ὅ ἐστιν μεθερμηνευόμενον Ὁ θεός μου ὁ θεός μου, εἰς τί ἐγκατέλιπές με; 35 καί τινες τῶν παρεστηκότων ἀκούσαντες ἔλεγον· Ἴδε Ἠλίαν φωνεῖ. 36 δραμὼν δέ τις καὶ γεμίσας σπόγγον ὄξους περιθεὶς καλάμῳ ἐπότιζεν αὐτόν, λέγων· Ἄφετε ἴδωμεν εἰ ἔρχεται Ἠλίας καθελεῖν αὐτόν. 37 ὁ δὲ Ἰησοῦς ἀφεὶς φωνὴν μεγάλην ἐξέπνευσεν. 38 καὶ τὸ καταπέτασμα τοῦ ναοῦ ἐσχίσθη εἰς δύο ἀπ᾽ ἄνωθεν ἕως κάτω. 39 ἰδὼν δὲ ὁ κεντυρίων ὁ παρεστηκὼς ἐξ ἐναντίας αὐτοῦ ὅτι οὕτως ἐξέπνευσεν εἶπεν· Ἀληθῶς οὗτος ὁ ἄνθρωπος υἱὸς θεοῦ ἦν.

40 Ἦσαν δὲ καὶ γυναῖκες ἀπὸ μακρόθεν θεωροῦσαι, ἐν αἷς καὶ Μαρία ἡ Μαγδαληνὴ καὶ Μαρία ἡ Ἰακώβου τοῦ μικροῦ καὶ Ἰωσῆτος μήτηρ καὶ Σαλώμη, 41 αἳ ὅτε ἦν ἐν τῇ Γαλιλαίᾳ ἠκολούθουν αὐτῷ καὶ διηκόνουν αὐτῷ, καὶ ἄλλαι πολλαὶ αἱ συναναβᾶσαι αὐτῷ εἰς Ἱεροσόλυμα. [SBLGNT]

King James Version

33 And when the sixth hour was come, there was darkness over the whole land until the ninth hour. 34 And at the ninth hour Jesus cried with a loud voice, saying, Eloi, Eloi, lama sabachthani? which is, being interpreted, My God, my God, why hast thou forsaken me? 35 And some of them that stood by, when they heard it, said, Behold, he calleth Elias. 36 And one ran and filled a spunge full of vinegar, and put it on a reed, and gave him to drink, saying, Let alone; let us see whether Elias will come to take him down. 37 And Jesus

New Rendition

33 And at about noon, darkness came over all the land until about three o'clock. 34 And at around three o'clock, Jesus screamed with a loud voice, "Eloi, Eloi, lema sabachthani?"—which means, "'My God, my God, why have you abandoned me?'" 35 And some of those standing by, having heard, were saying, "Look, he calls Elijah." 36 But someone, having run, and having filled a sponge with wine, having put it on a stick, was giving him a drink, saying, "Leave him be! Let's see if Elijah comes to take him down." 37 And Jesus, having

cried with a loud voice, and gave up the ghost. 38 And the veil of the temple was rent in twain from the top to the bottom.

39 And when the centurion, which stood over against him, saw that he so cried out, and gave up the ghost, he said, Truly this man was the Son of God. 40 There were also women looking on afar off: among whom was Mary Magdalene, and Mary the mother of James the less and of Joses, and Salome; 41 (Who also, when he was in Galilee, followed him, and ministered unto him;) and many other women which came up with him unto Jerusalem.

uttered a loud cry, breathed his last breath. 38 And the temple veil was torn in two—from top to bottom. 39 But the centurion, standing against him, having seen that he breathed his last breath, said, "Truly this man was God's son!"

40 There were also women looking on from a distance, including Mary of Magdala and Mary the mother of Jacob the Younger and the mother of Joses and Salome, 41 who, when he was in Galilee, followed him and ministered to him. And many other women, those having come up with him to Jerusalem, [were there].

Notes

15:33 ***And when the sixth hour was come, there was darkness over the whole land until the ninth hour:*** The sixth hour is noon, and the ninth hour is 3 p.m. "The whole land" could refer to the entire earth or to a localized area. In the HB, darkness is generally a symbol of God's judgment but presumed only to cover the land of Israel (Joel 2:2; Zeph. 1:15; Jer. 15:9); if it here covers the entire earth, it suggests that Jesus' death has a universal impact.

It is not clear whether the darkness dissipates immediately before Jesus dies or continues after his death. In either case, the darkness occurs at noon, which should be the time of greatest light. An eclipse has been suggested as the cause of the darkness, but this would not have been physically possible at the time of Passover and it would not have lasted long enough. Sometimes direct divine intervention is posited as a cause of complete darkness, but this is most unlikely: the religious leaders have just demanded a sign so that they might "see and believe" (15:32), and an indisputable sign would have been, in effect, a capitulation to their demands. So the darkness was probably something such as a dust storm or dark cloud cover that would have been significant to those with eyes to see but unrecognized by everyone else. (The lack of reaction to the darkness on the part of the soldiers and bystanders implies that they are not aware of it.) To those who perceived it, the darkness would have had symbolic resonances including:

1. An inversion of creation. The darkness inverts God's command that there be light on the first day of the Creation, which implies that Jesus' death suggests a new creation is approaching. The reference in 16:2 to the sun rising may enhance this motif.

2. The plague of darkness from the Exodus. LXX Exodus 10:21–22 has very strong verbal similarities to 15:33; the darkness lasts for three days in Exodus and three hours in Mark. This would suggest divine judgment on the actions of the leadership, with the Jewish and Roman leaders who have condemned Jesus in the role of Pharaoh. Additionally, the idea of freeing the people from slavery is linked to the idea of Jesus' death.

3. A symbol of God's abandonment. God's presence is associated with light in the HB (Num. 6:25–26; Ps. 89:15), and so the darkness implies that God is not present. This might make sense of Jesus' cry of abandonment.

4. A reference to Jesus' teachings in chapter 13, where he explained that during times of suffering, the sun would refuse to give its light (13:24), which was an allusion to Isaiah 13:10 and 34:4.

5. The closest HB allusion is Amos 8:9–10, which refers to God making the earth dark at noon, turning a festival (Passover) into a time of mourning as if for an only son. The reference to mourning for an only son is probably picked up in the centurion's coming reference to Jesus as God's son (even if the centurion himself would have been unaware of the Amos text).

15:34 *And at the ninth hour Jesus cried with a loud voice, saying, Eloi, Eloi, lama sabachthani?:* By the ninth hour (3 p.m.), Jesus had been on the cross for six hours.

"Eloi, Eloi, lama sabachthani" is Aramaic; Mark will soon provide the translation. Reasons why Mark would have included the Aramaic words may include:

1. Perhaps some members of Mark's audience understood Aramaic.[28]

2. The Aramaic rendering is required in order for Mark's Greek-speaking audience to understand why some people thought Jesus was calling Elijah: in Aramaic, the similarity between the words "Elijah" and "God" is apparent.

3. In this and in the two other cases where Mark provides and then translates the Aramaic of Jesus' words (5:41; 14:36), Mark may have done so because in these (and only these?) cases, Jesus' actual words are preserved. All three are signal moments in the story: a raising from the dead, Jesus' address to his father in Gethsemane, and his plea on the cross.

which is, being interpreted, My God, my God, why hast thou forsaken me?: Here, Mark provides the Greek translation of Jesus' words.

---

28. Collins, *Mark,* 755.

Jesus' question quotes Psalm 22:1. The thrust of Jesus' quotation from this psalm is debated:

1. It reflects a genuine sense of temporary abandonment, but it also anticipates future vindication. While Psalm 22 begins with a sentiment of abandonment, it ends with reconciliation. (Given the density of allusions to Psalm 22 in chapter 15, it is likely that Mark has the entire psalm—not just the first line—in mind.) By quoting from the beginning, Jesus' words presume the entire psalm, which means that while the sense of abandonment is real, it also anticipates a future reconciliation.

2. It reflects a genuine sense of complete abandonment. While the rest of the psalm envisions a restoration of the relationship, that is not the part that is quoted; Jesus could have substituted or added material from Psalm 22:22–31 had he wanted to indicate a future hope for vindication; the fact that he did not must be taken seriously. Further, the allusions from Psalm 22 are in inverse order in Mark, which means that in its Markan context, the psalm is not pointing toward a future vindication.

Either way, the text suggests that "the presence of God does not depend on the knowledge or emotional experience of the Markan Jesus."[29] Despite his sense of abandonment, Jesus is still calling on God.

15:35 *And some of them that stood by, when they heard it, said, Behold, he calleth Elias:* In Aramaic, Jesus' plea to God could have been misunderstood as a call to Elijah, especially given the common belief that Elijah would rescue the righteous (but contrast 9:11–13: Elijah has, according to Jesus, already come in the form of John the Baptist, and instead of saving the innocent he prepared the way for the innocent to die). This scene would then reflect a consistent theme in Mark: people frequently misunderstand Jesus; Jesus' experience of suffering on the cross included the anguish of being misunderstood. But it is also possible that these bystanders understood Jesus perfectly well and that this is "a malicious twisting"[30] of his words.

15:36 *And one ran and filled a sponge full of vinegar, and put it on a reed, and gave him to drink, saying:* This person is more likely to be a Jewish passerby than a Roman soldier, because he understood the reference to Elijah and, apparently, the expectation that Elijah would rescue the righteous.

While many crosses were quite low to the ground, the use of a reed suggests that Jesus' cross was higher.

---

29. Elizabeth S. Malbon, *Mark's Jesus: Characterization As Narrative Christology* (Waco, Tex.: Baylor University Press, 2009), 189.

30. France, *Gospel of Mark*, 654.

This verse probably alludes to Psalm 69:21–23; in the psalm, the speaker's enemies give him vinegar to drink. Psalm 69:23's reference to their darkened eyes prohibiting sight also relates to this scene in Mark, where there is darkness and where the mockers do not really "see" what they are doing.

Let alone; let us see whether Elias will come to take him down: It is possible that this is an act of mercy, but it is more likely mockery and torture: the drink would prolong Jesus' life and, hence, his suffering. Part of Jesus' distress was this deliberate effort to prolong his agony, apparently for sport.

It is, presumably, still dark, which makes the desire to "see" if Elijah will come ironic.

Mark's audience knows that these mockers are in the wrong since Elijah has already returned (9:13).

15:37 *And Jesus cried with a loud voice, and gave up the ghost:* This is Jesus' second cry from the cross; it seems to reflect either "the intensity of his suffering or . . . a cry of triumph or defiance."[31]

The Greek word translated as "gave up the ghost" could be rendered as "the spirit went out of him," an idiomatic way to describe dying. It is possible that the cry with a loud voice is Jesus' last breath and thus is the spirit going out of him. Because the same words for "loud cry" are used in Mark elsewhere only to describe the expelling of unclean spirits (1:26; 5:7; the phrase is also used in 15:34), it is possible that this phrasing points to the idea that Jesus is having his own (holy) spirit expelled here.

Mark's audience may have been surprised by the reference to a loud voice since crucifixion victims on the verge of death were normally too weak to be loud.

15:38 *And the veil of the temple was rent in twain from the top to the bottom:* The immediate response to Jesus' death is the ripping of the veil of the temple.

The text is unclear on whether the outer veil (which separated the temple proper from the courtyard) or the inner veil (which separated the main worship space of the temple from the Holy of Holies) is indicated since the same word could be used for both, but it is more likely to be the inner veil.[32] However, to the extent that the curtains are symbolically similar (since both restrict access to the worthy only, and both suggest the heavens/creation), choosing between the two may not matter.

---

31. Witherington, *Gospel of Mark,* 399.

32. Daniel M. Gurtner, "LXX Syntax and the Identity of the NT Veil," *Novum Testamentum* 47, no. 4 (2005): 344–53.

The outer veil had embroidery depicting the cosmos, but the inner veil had similar symbolism: Josephus described the Holy of Holies imitating heaven, so "the tearing of the inner veil could also symbolize the rending of the heavens."[33]

The symbolic nature of the rending of the veil is apparent not only because of the symbolism of the veil itself but also as a result of how Mark weaves the ripping into the story: telling the audience about the veil requires Mark to abruptly shift the narrative to a different geographical location and then to bring the audience back to the foot of the cross. No one in the story is aware of the rending of the veil as it would not have been visible from Golgotha—this is information for Mark's audience only. Mark implies that God has ripped the veil because the rip starts at the top of the curtain (which was about twenty-five meters or eighty-five feet tall) and because it is described with a passive verb form, used to connote divine action.[34]

It is possible that the ripping connotes judgment (on the Jewish leadership, enacted on the symbol of their leadership, the temple): Jesus' death results, ironically, not in the end of his own power but in the end of their power. However, it is more likely that Mark's audience would have interpreted the rending as a symbol of increased access. This is not the destruction of the temple: "far from destroying the sanctuary, Jesus opens it up."[35] Jesus has been twice accused of prophesying the destruction of the temple (14:58; 15:29), but what he actually does is extend the power of the temple by making it possible for more people to be in the presence of God.

The ripping of the veil may symbolize the destruction of the temple, since the temple sacrifices (which mediated access to God) are no longer necessary after Jesus' death. In this sense, the enacted parable of Jesus' temple action in chapter 11 is here fulfilled, and the temple is "destroyed." Now, everyone can access God without the mediation of the physical temple or its ritual.

Isaiah 64:1 is a prayer that God would open the heavens and come to earth. If that text is alluded to here, the implication is that the tearing of the veil makes it possible for God's presence to be available outside of the Holy of Holies.

---

33. Collins, *Mark*, 762.

34. Matthew L. Bowen, "'Thy Will Be Done': The Savior's Use of the Divine Passive," in *The Sermon on the Mount in Latter-day Scripture: The 39th Annual BYU Sydney B. Sperry Symposium*, ed. Gaye Strathearn, Thomas A. Wayment, and Daniel L. Belnap (Salt Lake City: Deseret Book, 2010), 230–48.

35. Sabin, *Reopening the Word*, 108.

15:39 ***And when the centurion, which stood over against him:*** A centurion was an officer who commanded about eighty soldiers; it is likely that this centurion was in charge of Jesus' crucifixion. Mark's early audiences would have seen that Jesus' death had an impact even on those who were responsible for executing him.

The phrase "over against" permits more than one meaning:

1. It is often used in the LXX for spatial position in the context of battle, so it might suggest that the centurion is positioned as Jesus' enemy.

2. It is one of the expressions used "for standing 'in the presence' of God" in the LXX.[36] This would suggest, as the centurion's words do, that the centurion recognizes that he is in the presence of the divine.

It is likely that both meanings are intended here: Jesus' death transforms the centurion's relationship to Jesus, and this transformation is reflected in the ambiguous phrasing.

saw that he so cried out, and gave up the ghost, he said, Truly this man was the Son of God: The phrase "so cried out, and" is missing from the best manuscripts. It may have been accidentally omitted as a scribe's eye skipped, or it may have been added to harmonize with Matthew 27:50.[37]

The centurion's description of Jesus presents two interpretive challenges:

1. Although the KJV includes "the" before "Son of God," the Greek text lacks the article. This leads some interpreters to translate the phrase as "a son of God," which implies a less important role than "the Son of God." However, it is probably better to translate "the Son of God," despite the absent article, because (1) Greek probably does not require the article here and (2) Mark's audience would have heard this statement in light of other references to Jesus as the unique Son of God in Mark and understood it accordingly.

2. An imperfect form is used so that the phrase might be translated "this man *was* the Son of God," as if Jesus' death ended his special status. However, this reading is unlikely for two reasons: had the present tense been used ("is the Son of God") it may have (1) inadvertently conveyed that Jesus was adopted by God at his death and (2) elided the important point that Jesus was God's son during his suffering and death. Further, because the Resurrection has not yet happened (and would be unimaginable from the centurion's viewpoint), the "was" may be appropriate to describe Jesus at this point.

Despite these interpretive difficulties, it is almost certain that Mark's audience would have thought that this confession was very meaningful: the

---

36. Harry L. Chronis, "The Torn Veil: Cultus and Christology in Mark 15:37–39," *Journal of Biblical Literature* 101, no. 1 (1982): 110.

37. Comfort, *Translator's Handbook,* 494.

centurion was recognizing that Jesus was and is the (unique) Son of God. All of the previous uses of "Son of God" (1:1, 11; 3:11; 5:7; 9:7; 13:32; 14:61–62) predispose Mark's audience to put full weight on this title. A Roman centurion normally subscribed to the view that the emperor was the son of God, so there is rich irony in the idea that Jesus is killed as a rebel against Rome, but his death turns the centurion into a rebel. It is likely that this centurion had experience with other crucifixions, so his response to Jesus reflects the uniqueness of Jesus' death, not his naiveté.

15:40 ***There were also women looking on afar off:*** Some interpreters take the women being "afar off" as indicating a deliberate choice to distance themselves from Jesus (compare Peter's similar stance outside of Jesus' interrogation [14:54]), especially in light of Psalm 38:11, where part of the suffering of the innocent is that his friends stay far away from him. (It is even possible that Jesus is not aware of their presence. These women could be like God: present at the cross but not recognized by Jesus.) However, "afar off" does not necessarily imply deliberate distance: the same Greek words are used when the demons observe Jesus before worshiping him (5:6) and for Jesus seeing the fig tree from a distance (11:13). Given the other indications of a positive portrayal of the women, it is not likely that "afar off" is meant to imply something negative. It is also possible that the phrase should be translated as "women from afar" (compare the similar usage to describe the Gentiles at the feeding miracle [8:3]), which would emphasize that they have traveled a great distance to be with Jesus. It is also possible that "afar off" signals that they are at a (symbolic) distance from the mockery of Jesus.

among whom was Mary Magdalene, and Mary the mother of James the less and of Joses, and Salome: Some manuscripts add an article ("the"),[38] which means that this list would refer to four women and not three since the phrase "the mother of James and Joses" would not apply to Mary but to another (unnamed) woman. In this reading, the four women would be Mary Magdalene; Mary; the mother of James[39] and Joses; and Salome. However, the KJV rendering is probably preferable.

It is difficult to determine the precise identity of these women, especially since half the Jewish women at this time were named Mary or Salome![40] But the following can be deduced about each woman:

---

38. Collins, *Mark,* 772 note a.

39. See the Notes on 1:19.

40. Marcus, *Mark 8–16,* 1060.

1. This is the first reference to Mary Magdalene in Mark's Gospel. Her name probably means that Mary is from Magdala and would imply that she had relocated from Magdala to somewhere else.[41] It is possible that "her name is thus an indication of her role as a disciple who has left her home and family to follow Jesus during his mission."[42] (This may also be the case for the other two characters named by their hometowns in the Passion narrative: Simon of Cyrene and Joseph of Arimathea.)

2. Mary is described as the mother of two sons, James the less (the small one or younger one) and Joses. Because James and Joses are named in 6:3 as the sons of Jesus' mother Mary, it is sometimes suggested that this Mary is Jesus' mother. However, this is unlikely because (1) she probably would have been mentioned before Mary Magdalene since she has already been introduced to Mark's audience, (2) she is not described as Jesus' mother, and (3) Jesus' brother James was known in the early church as "James the Just," not "James the less."[43] So it is more likely that this is a different Mary; it is probable that the reference to "James the less" is used to distinguish this Mary from Jesus' mother. It is possible that, as is the case with Simon of Cyrene, Mary's children are mentioned because they were known to Mark's audience.

3. Salome is the third (or possibly fourth) woman named; unfortunately, Mark provides no more information about her.

A similar (but not identical) list of named women will appear at Jesus' burial and Resurrection (15:47; 16:1).

15:41 *(who also, when he was in Galilee, followed him, and ministered unto him):* The word "followed" indicates that these women have been Jesus' disciples—they have answered the call to follow him. The word "ministered" is used to describe the actions of Jesus, of angels, and of women in Mark's Gospel, but never of other mortal males. While this word can refer to simple table service, it connotes a greater service in Mark—especially since all of the meals are laden with symbolic meaning. Additionally, this is the term used by Jesus to describe his own ministry: he came not to be ministered to but to minister to others (10:45). By noting that the women ministered to Jesus, Mark is describing them as successful disciples. The fact that "ministered" is imperfect ("was ministering") emphasizes this point.

Mark employs a flashback here to show that women were part of Jesus' Galilean ministry and followed him as disciples. Mark has not previously mentioned female disciples specifically; it is likely that they are mentioned here because Jesus' death makes it possible for their ministry to be

---

41. Miller, *Women in Mark's Gospel,* 154.

42. Miller, *Women in Mark's Gospel,* 154.

43. Marcus, *Mark 8–16,* 1060.

acknowledged. One of the significant effects of Jesus' death in Mark is to inaugurate the ministry of women—a ministry that had been occurring but was not publicly acknowledged. In a sense, women's ministry is parallel to the messianic secret in Mark.

and many other women which came up with him unto Jerusalem: While only three (possibly four) women are named, Mark notes that there were additional women (but apparently not any male disciples) present at Jesus' death.

Jesus as Ishmael. Profound similarities link Jesus' death and Genesis 21:

1. Both Jesus and Ishmael are positioned as the rejected son, especially in light of the scene where the crowd chooses Barabbas, the counterfeit "son of the father."

2. The same word for the women watching from "afar off" (Greek: *makrothen*) is used for Hagar watching Ishmael from far off (LXX Gen. 21:16).

3. Jesus describes himself as feeling abandoned on the cross; Ishmael is similarly abandoned by his mother because she cannot bear to see the death of her child. This is an important resonance because it provides a motive for the abandonment, which is otherwise missing in Mark. But in light of the intertext, it is clear that God's abandonment of Jesus is not an actual abandonment (inasmuch as Hagar is still there), but rather that God has, like Hagar, withdrawn from the scene out of anguish (Gen. 21:16). Further, the idea of Mark representing God as not only a woman but as a slave is a powerful commentary.

4. Both Jesus and Ishmael cry out when facing death.

5. In Genesis 21:18, Hagar is promised that Ishmael will be made into a great nation. By analogy, this is a subtle promise of Jesus' ultimate victory.

While the similarities between Jesus' death and the sacrifice of Isaac are frequently noted, the similarities between Jesus' death and the story of Ishmael are also important, and that story may actually provide a stronger parallel than Isaac's. In Abraham's story, he is being obedient to a higher authority when he chooses to sacrifice Isaac, but one would not describe God's role in Jesus' death in those terms. On the contrary, the analogy with Hagar seems more apt and certainly more theologically intriguing: she neither chooses Ishmael's death nor consents to it. This parallel would then nuance the view of God's role in Jesus' death.

Relationship to Jesus' Baptism. There are significant links between Mark's accounts of Jesus' baptism and Jesus' death:[44]

---

44. Julie M. Smith, "Narrative Atonement Theology in the Gospel of Mark," *BYU Studies Quarterly* 54, no. 1 (2015): 29–41.

1. Mark uses the Greek verb *schizō* to describe what happens to the veil. It is a rare verb,[45] vivid and violent, used only one other time in Mark—to characterize the opening of the heavens immediately after Jesus was baptized. One can imagine a storyteller using the same ripping motion in both stories to emphasize the link.[46] The temple veil restricted access to the Holy of Holies (which was understood as God's abode), so the symbolism of the ripping of the temple veil echoes the ripping of the heavens at the baptism: in both cases, the ripping action removes the barrier between heaven and earth.[47] The two occurrences of this verb invite comparison of the baptism and the death.[48] Mark encourages the audience to interpret the rending of the temple veil in light of the rending of the heavens, and thus the death in light of the baptism. By presenting masses of people ("all") coming from the south for baptism (1:5), while Jesus comes for baptism as a lone figure from the north (1:9), Mark presents Jesus as the embodiment of all of Israel. In Mark's Gospel, the postbaptismal vision appears to be experienced by Jesus alone, so the fact that the death of Jesus opens up access to the divine presence for all people, and not just Jesus, conveys Mark's understanding of the Atonement. Both the baptism and the death also have the same narrative pattern, with the main event narrated only briefly and greater attention given to the results; the several reactions to the baptism parallel the several reactions to the death. Echoing backwards through Mark, the rent veil echoes Jesus' torn flesh, echoes the heavens ripped after Jesus' baptism—all instances where old wineskins ripped under the pressure of new wine.[49] Jesus' death ends the need for a high priest, now that everyone has access to the Holy of Holies (Heb. 4:14–16). Similarly, at Jesus' baptism, the rent heavens dethrone the old order of things under John, who had recognized that a stronger one was coming (1:7). Both rendings are divine actions: after the baptism, the Spirit tears through the heavens to descend into Jesus (1:10); after the death, God's action rends the veil, implying that neither the baptism nor the death were random events but divinely orchestrated ones, a point further emphasized by how the death follows the pattern set by the baptism.

2. Both stories reference Elijah: at the baptism, John the Baptist is dressed as Elijah, and at Jesus' death, bystanders think that he is calling Elijah. But

---

45. *Schizō* is used only nine times in the NT; by way of comparison, *anoigo,* the common word for "open," occurs seventy-five times in the NT.

46. Kelly R. Iverson, "A Centurion's 'Confession': A Performance-Critical Analysis of Mark 15:39," *Journal of Biblical Literature* 130, no. 2 (2011): 342.

47. Marcus, *Mark 8–16,* 1057.

48. Daniel M. Gurtner, "The Rending of the Veil and Markan Christology: 'Unveiling' the HUIOS THEOU (Mark 15:38–39)," *Biblical Interpretation* 15, no. 3 (2007): 292–306; see also David Ulansey, "The Heavenly Veil Torn: Mark's Cosmic *Inclusio,*" *Journal of Biblical Literature* 110, no. 1 (1991): 123–25.

49. Mark 2:21 uses the noun form of *schizō* (Greek: *schisma*; KJV: "rent") in the context of the inability to mix the new with the old.

Jesus is calling God, not Elijah; Elijah is not actually present at the cross. Because Elijah's return was associated with turning "the heart of the fathers to the children, and the heart of the children to their fathers" (Mal. 4:6), his absence at the cross highlights the lacuna in the relationship between Jesus and God at this moment.

3. Both stories make reference to the Spirit's relationship to Jesus: at the baptism, the Spirit descends on (or "into") Jesus, while the word used to describe Jesus' death is literally "out-spirited" (which carries the idiomatic meaning of "died").[50] Additionally, Jesus' death scene is full of references to descent, the most significant being the rend in the veil that runs from top to bottom, but with no fewer than six other references to downward motion at Jesus' death scene.[51] In the baptism scene, it is clear that the descent of the Spirit represents a new bestowal of God's power, and at the death, the rip in the veil makes possible increased access to God's power. But this time, the new power is not restricted to Jesus: it extends to all people. His death broadens access to God's Spirit that he alone enjoyed previously. In both stories, Isaiah's plea "Oh that thou wouldest rend the heavens, that thou wouldest come down, that the mountains might flow down [or quake] at thy presence" (Isa. 64:1) is fulfilled as the presence and power of God are accessible on earth in new ways. The manner in which Mark narrates Jesus' temptation in the wilderness implies that it is a direct result of his baptism; the Spirit that descended into Jesus immediately casts him into the wilderness (1:12), using the same verb found in the LXX when Adam and Eve were cast out of the garden after the Fall (LXX Gen. 3:24). So the result of Jesus being baptized is that he suffers the same consequence that Adam and Eve suffered, despite the fact that he did not sin as they had. Similarly, he dies on the cross because of charges that do not apply to him (14:56)—charges that stem from his effort to restore to other people the wholeness that he already enjoys. Jesus' willingness to experience suffering that he has not merited is emphasized in both stories. And because his death restores access to God's presence, his death overcomes the effects of the Fall that buffeted him after his baptism.

4. Both scenes use the same Greek word for "voice" (*phōnē*): at the baptism, the voice from heaven quotes a psalm when speaking to Jesus (1:11; Ps. 2:7), and at the cross, Jesus quotes a psalm when speaking to God (15:34; Ps. 22:1). In both instances, psalms are the medium of communication between God and Jesus, but there is a stark inversion of sentiment, with the first psalm announcing, "Thou art my beloved Son," and the second psalm asking, "My God, my God, why hast thou forsaken me?" The similarity of the form heightens the clash in content and thus the rupture in the relationship.

---

50. Gundry, *Mark*, 948.
51. Tolbert, *Sowing the Gospel*, 282.

Analysis

It is significant that in his moment of feeling abandoned by God, Jesus' response is to speak to God. In other words, Jesus does not abandon God just because he feels that God has abandoned him. The address as "my God" (especially since the "my" is doubled relative to the source text) emphasizes that Jesus still recognizes his relationship with God. Jesus does not curse God when he feels abandoned (compare Job 1:11; 2:5, 9) but prays to God instead. Part of Jesus' suffering is a sense of feeling abandoned by God. His statement also enhances the motif of ironic kingship since kings were supposed to enjoy God's approval and support.

Jesus' question raises two difficult interpretative issues:

1. Was Jesus actually abandoned or did he just feel abandoned? In other words, had God actually abandoned Jesus, or was Jesus unable to perceive God's presence? Mark's text does not answer this question.

2. What precisely constituted the abandonment: Does it mean being abandoned to death, or does it mean that Jesus could not perceive God's presence? Mark does not answer this question either.

Most later Christians would believe that Jesus' feeling of abandonment was the result of sin that Jesus took on himself, but this is not made explicit in Mark; rather, Mark "wants us to feel Jesus' agony, not to explain it."[52] Although a voice speaks from heaven elsewhere in Mark's Gospel, Mark records no response to this plea (1:11; 9:7). These are the last words Jesus speaks in this story. In contemporary accounts of the deaths of martyrs (Dan. 3:15–28), they are perfectly brave and stoic as they approach death. Jesus is not. His prayer in Gethsemane to avoid suffering and his cry on the cross would have been perceived as out of line with expectations and thus embarrassing to Mark's early audiences.

While Jesus prays elsewhere in Mark's Gospel, in Gethsemane and on the cross are the only times when the wording of Jesus' prayer to God is recorded. In both instances, Jesus gives God a title: "abba" in Gethsemane and "my God" on the cross. It is possible that the relative familiarity of "abba" implies that Jesus feels a greater distance from God when he is on the cross; his words suggest as much. Interestingly, in both prayer accounts, Mark includes the Aramaic words.

There is no answer to Jesus' prayer in Gethsemane recorded in the text; there is no answer to Jesus' question from the cross. This is stunning: in the only two instances in Mark where Jesus' words to God are recorded,

---

52. France, *Gospel of Mark,* 653.

God gives no direct answer, and the implied answer (that Jesus will have to suffer; that God has apparently abandoned Jesus) is the last response one would expect to be the answer to the Messiah's prayers.

Jesus dies at (or perhaps just after) the ninth hour, or about three in the afternoon. This is the time when a lamb would have been sacrificed in the temple (as part of the daily sacrifice). While Mark does not directly develop the lamb imagery (despite an opportunity to do so at the Last Supper) or the idea of Jesus as a sacrifice, both of those motifs may be subtly present due to the time reference.

The audience would likely have been surprised at how quick Jesus' death was: by Mark's reckoning, Jesus was on the cross for six hours, but sometimes victims of crucifixion lingered for days. Again, the focus of Jesus' death in Mark is not the physical aspects of his suffering. The emphasis is on the symbolic details of the story and the emotional insults.

What precisely is the centurion reacting to when he concludes that Jesus is the Son of God? Mark does not make the answer entirely clear. It could be Jesus' death in general, it could be the speed of his death (which was unusually quick for a crucifixion), or it could be the darkness. He would not have been able to see the rending of the temple veil and, even if he had, he probably would not have understood its significance. At the same time, it is the rending of the veil—which allows knowledge of God to extend beyond the Holy of Holies—that makes the centurion's confession possible. He, in a clever inversion of the demand of the chief priests above, does not see, but he does believe.

While it is possible that the centurion's statement is mocking (which would fit the other instances of mockery in chapter 15), it is more likely to be genuine, since he is impacted by the death of Jesus and, implicitly, the rending of the temple veil. The word "truly" would have helped Mark's audience break out of the habit of hearing mockery and move to hearing a genuine statement. While it is possible that the written word can be ambiguous, it is much harder to imagine an oral performer delivering these words ambiguously: spoken aloud, they would be either reverent or mocking.

It is sometimes argued that a centurion could not be expected to give a genuine confession of Jesus, but Mark has a penchant for characterizing a group and then presenting one individual who violates expectations of that group: an honorable synagogue ruler, a wicked woman, a decent scribe, a good member of the Sanhedrin. Significantly, each of these out-of-type characters appear after Jesus has had several typical interactions with group members,[53] so it is likely that Mark's audience would have been predisposed to accept him as a "good" centurion and thus view his confession as genuine. Further, it was common in martyrdom accounts for the executioner to be converted,[54] so a genuine confession would not have been unexpected by Mark's audience. And yet given the context of mockery, it is easy to imagine that Mark's audience, when hearing this confession, would need to pause for a moment of mental recalibration before realizing that the centurion's words are genuine. It is a powerful experience for the audience because they have to profoundly shift how they interpret what they hear; it is theologically significant because it means that Jesus' death has an immediate impact on them and instantly changes how they view the world.

And yet this confession would have been unexpected in some ways: not only is he not a follower of Jesus, but he is not even Jewish, and he probably was in charge of the crucifixion and a participant in the mockery of Jesus. He is perhaps the last person who should have been able to understand Jesus' identity. And yet Mark presents him as reaching this realization only after Jesus dies. In terms of the narrative, it is a substantive theological statement: it is only through his death that Jesus' identity is recognizable by humans.[55] It is possible that this would have been a moment when Mark's early audiences would have applauded while listening to the Gospel.[56]

The centurion's reference to Jesus as "this man" echoes how Peter used similar language to deny knowing "this man" (14:71). Once again, Mark's audience would be struck by the irony that the lead disciple denied knowing Jesus while the centurion who helped ensure Jesus' death is able to identify Jesus as the Son of God.

The women function as the witnesses to Jesus' death; the same verb for "looking" is used two more times (15:47; 16:4) to describe the women's actions. They see Jesus die on the cross, they see where he is buried, and they see the empty tomb. These women are the witnesses to his death and Resurrection; their witness is essential to the story and is unparalleled in Mark. Further, they are fulfilling the command from chapter 13 to "watch," something the other disciples failed to do in Gethsemane. The primary function of these women is to witness to Jesus' death, burial, and

---

53. Iverson, "Centurion's 'Confession,'" 339–40.
54. Iverson, "Centurion's 'Confession,'" 344.
55. But the anointing woman seems to have anticipated this; see the Notes on 14:3–9.
56. Iverson, "Centurion's 'Confession,'" 343–4.

Resurrection, which probably explains why their names are included when Mark does not typically provide the names of model disciples. Much as Peter, James, and John had a role in witnessing to key events in Jesus' ministry—the raising of Jairus's daughter, the Transfiguration, and Jesus' prayer in Gethsemane—the women witness to the key events of his Passion. They also take the place of the male disciples, who—despite repeated admonitions to "watch"—chose to flee and to deny Jesus instead.[57] The Twelve, as male Jews, symbolized the restoration of the house of Israel, but after their failure, the women's key witnessing role signifies the expansion of discipleship to all people, something made possible through the death of Jesus.

The parallels between the baptism and the death encourage the audience to read these stories as the bookends around Jesus' life. Bracketing Jesus' life by his baptism and death emphasizes the theme of breaking barriers and implies that the granting of access to God's power and presence is a key element in the Gospel story. This narrative structure can then guide the interpretation of the text. For example, some scholars argue that the rending of the temple veil is an expression of either God's displeasure with the temple system or of mourning at Jesus' death. In isolation, these readings are possible, but when read in light of the baptism, the audience would note that the rending of the heavens at the baptism did not express God's displeasure or mourning, so reading the baptism and death stories together guides the interpretation of the death scene. This bookending of the baptism and the death scenes might also explain why Mark includes neither nativity nor Resurrection appearances.

It is significant that the only time Jesus refers to baptism in Mark's Gospel is as a metaphor for death (10:38–39). This would have further encouraged Mark's audience to think about Jesus' baptism in light of his death and vice versa. In Mark, the symbolic linkage of baptism to death is stronger than the link between baptism and rebirth, which is developed in other sources but not in Mark. The links between the baptism and the death lead to a somber conclusion: in Mark, baptism is intertwined with death. Jesus' baptism sets the pattern—quite literally—for his death.

As Mark tells the story, Jesus' death has three immediate—and symbolically significant—repercussions:[58]

---

57. Sabin, *Reopening the Word*, 195.

58. See Julie M. Smith, "Narrative Atonement Theology in the Gospel of Mark," *BYU Studies Quarterly* 54, no. 1 (2015): 29–41.

1. *The Veil.* Immediately after Jesus dies, the veil of the temple is torn in two from top to bottom. This veil was the barrier between the main area of the temple and the Holy of Holies (Ex. 26:33), which was the sacred space that could only be entered once per year and only by the High Priest. It was the appointed site where the Lord would visit his people, sitting on the mercy seat (Ex. 25:22). Its rending signifies that this most sacred of spaces is now accessible to all people because of Jesus' death. The barrier between God and humans has been torn asunder. Access to the divine is no longer limited to one person and to one day of the year but is now available to all as a direct result of the death of Jesus. The fact that the rending of the veil is the very first thing that Mark mentions after Jesus' death highlights its importance. The one day when the high priest was permitted to enter the Holy of Holies was on the Day of Atonement (Lev. 16). Via the ripping of the veil, Mark implies that Jesus' death is the Day of Atonement[59] and that his death has an atoning effect. Because there were cherubim woven onto the temple curtain (Ex. 36:35) and because the Holy of Holies was the place where the Lord could be present, it is possible to think of those worked cherubim as the embroidered equivalent of the fiery cherubim who guarded the Garden of Eden after the Fall (Gen. 3:24). The rending of the veil thus suggests that the cherubim are no longer performing that function and because of the death of Jesus, humans can once again enter the presence of God. To be sure, this development is something of a double-edged sword: entering the Holy of Holies was regarded as dangerous (Ex. 19:12, 21; 20:18–19; 28:43; Lev. 16:2, 13; Isa. 6:5); surely the unworthy would be in grave danger if they attempted to approach the Lord, so it is unlikely that the average person would have desired to enter the Holy of Holies. Following Jesus can be terrifying in Mark's Gospel (5:17, 30; 6:49; 13:9), but the implicit promise is that Jesus will support his disciples and that his death will make it possible for them to enter into the divine presence without fatal effect (Isa. 6:5–7). The invitation for all to enter the Holy of Holies—which, presumably, is not an invitation that will endanger their lives—itself implies an atoning aspect to Jesus' death. The idea that Jesus' death permits access to God's presence is a key component of Mark's theology of the Atonement.

2. *The Centurion.* Immediately after the temple veil is ripped, Mark returns to the scene of the crucifixion and relates a response of incredible narrative importance: the first human reaction to Jesus' death. Here is where one would expect a significant statement from Mark about what difference Jesus' death makes to human beings. Mark has a centurion announce, "Truly this

---

59. In 2:19–20, Jesus taught that his disciples did not fast, but they would fast on the day when he was taken from them. Given that the only mandated fast in the law of Moses was on the Day of Atonement, this would have been Mark's audience's first hint that Jesus' death would be a figurative Day of Atonement.

man was the Son of God." This statement is a remarkable reaction to Jesus' death for several reasons, not the least of which is that the man was a Gentile, so for the centurion to understand that Jesus was the Son of God would be extraordinary in any case but even more so in this context because he did not reach this conclusion after watching Jesus walk on water or raise the dead but rather after seeing him die as a condemned criminal. For that event to result in a recognition of Jesus' true identity speaks volumes about the impact of Jesus' death on a bystander: it makes it possible for the least likely person to gain vital knowledge that has previously been unattainable. In fact, up to this point in Mark's narrative, no human being has been able to articulate that Jesus was the Son of God. After Jesus' baptism, the voice from heaven said, "You are my Son, the Beloved," and the demons recognized Jesus as the Son of God (3:11; 5:7; 9:7; 13:32), but even Jesus' closest disciples struggled, and largely failed, to understand who he was. So the idea that a centurion could recognize the Son of God extends the theme established in the rending of the veil that access to and knowledge about God was being extended. The ripped veil symbolized the ability of people to "see" God; the announcement of the centurion is an example of that insight. Two thousand years of Christian tradition have probably made it impossible to appreciate how odd it was for a soldier to look at the corpse of a criminal and announce that the dead man was God's Son. The parallel with the baptism, where the voice from heaven pronounces Jesus to be God's Son, makes the centurion's exclamation all the more profound because he is occupying the narrative role of God when he is the voice that attests to Jesus' identity. Just as the rending of the heavens comes immediately before the divine announcement that Jesus is God's son at the baptism, the rending of the temple veil comes immediately before the centurion's announcement that Jesus is God's son. In other words, Mark's narrative teaches that the death of Jesus makes it possible for a centurion to do what God does. Even a hated pagan soldier can be elevated to a godlike status and possess a godlike knowledge because of the death of Jesus. It required the severing of the heavens and the temple veil, but the removal of these barriers has made possible the transmission of God's knowledge to humans in a new way.

3. *The Women.* After the centurion's statement, Mark narrates the presence and ministry of Jesus' female followers. The primary role of the women here is watching; they are witnesses to Jesus' death. Because most strains of Jewish thought interpreted the Torah to forbid female witnesses, the implication in Mark is that Jesus' death has opened new roles and responsibilities for women. And not only does this affect the women but the entire community: one literally cannot be a Christian without accepting their witness because their testimony is crucial to the story of Jesus' death; it is how the story was preserved since all of the male disciples had fled. The fact that the women's ministry is presented out of chronological order suggests that Mark wants to emphasize that the death of Jesus extends ministry opportunities to women or, at least,

makes possible their public recognition. What happens here underscores the importance of the narrative art of Mark: it is through manipulating the time sequence that Mark is able to make the point about the women's ministry. The text rewards the audience's careful attention to narrative. It is only now, after Jesus' death, that the audience finds out that there were women present all along, being disciples and engaging in ministry,[60] a reality that Mark had largely hidden from the audience's view. And so the audience, like the centurion, gains new knowledge—this time, knowledge about the effect that Jesus' death has on women's opportunities to minister and witness. While Mark's Gospel hints that Jesus has female disciples (3:31–35), the idea is not developed. Just as his baptism led directly to the angels' ministry, his death leads directly to the women's ministry. Mark also notes that, in addition to the women that are named, many other unnamed women also came up to Jerusalem with Jesus and were present at the crucifixion. This large group of women creates a compelling contrast to the single centurion and suggests that the effects of Jesus' ministry are not limited to select individuals or even to people whose names are known but extend to all who are willing to follow Jesus.

These three reactions show that Mark is outcome-oriented, not process-oriented, as the story constructs the meaning of Jesus' death. In not one of the three cases does Mark describe precisely how it is that Jesus' death was able to rend the veil, enlighten the centurion, or empower the women; rather, the text simply states that it was so. The focus is on the outcome, not the process; the result, not the method. Mark's approach contrasts with most Christian thought about the Atonement, which examines the way the Atonement worked instead of its results. Mark's example suggests that analogies are more productive when focused on the end and not the means of the Atonement.

The three results of Jesus' death can all be unified under the banner of increased access to God. The rent veil, the centurion, and the women all show that what was previously restricted is no longer—the divine presence, knowledge, and ministry are now available to all. Mark cleverly manipulates narrative space in order to show how this is so. Because the temple veil was not visible from the cross, Mark must transport the audience and therefore grants a heavenly perspective on events. Similarly, the centurion is described as being "over against" Jesus, probably suggesting opposition. But his proclamation shows that his position has changed—he may have begun "over against" Jesus, but after Jesus' death, the centurion knows who Jesus is—he is, in other words, now with him. Along the same lines,

---

60. Miller, *Women in Mark's Gospel.*

the women are described as being "afar off," a distance that they overcome as their contribution to Jesus' ministry can now be observed and described in the narrative at close hand. Mark has carefully constructed narrative space in each of the three reactions to Jesus' death in order to suggest that distance is overcome by Jesus' death—the distance between the audience and the temple, the distance between the centurion and Jesus, and the distance between the women and the audience.

In addition to narrative space, Mark employs careful characterization to show that access to God is extended through Jesus' death. By featuring a Gentile and women, Mark makes clear that the previously restricted access to God has now been expanded. In Jesus' time, the temple complex included a "court of the Gentiles" and a "court of women." So it is perhaps no surprise that Mark has chosen a Gentile and women to showcase the human responses to Jesus' death as these were the people who had been formally excluded from the symbolic presence of the Lord. Now, as a result of Jesus' death, they can be invited into the presence of the Lord, where they can share God's knowledge and have a role in Jesus' ministry.

JESUS IS BURIED (15:42–47)

Greek Text

42 Καὶ ἤδη ὀψίας γενομένης, ἐπεὶ ἦν παρασκευή, ὅ ἐστιν προσάββατον, 43 ἐλθὼν Ἰωσὴφ ὁ ἀπὸ Ἁριμαθαίας εὐσχήμων βουλευτής, ὃς καὶ αὐτὸς ἦν προσδεχόμενος τὴν βασιλείαν τοῦ θεοῦ, τολμήσας εἰσῆλθεν πρὸς τὸν Πιλᾶτον καὶ ᾐτήσατο τὸ σῶμα τοῦ Ἰησοῦ. 44 ὁ δὲ Πιλᾶτος ἐθαύμασεν εἰ ἤδη τέθνηκεν, καὶ προσκαλεσάμενος τὸν κεντυρίωνα ἐπηρώτησεν αὐτὸν εἰ πάλαι ἀπέθανεν· 45 καὶ γνοὺς ἀπὸ τοῦ κεντυρίωνος ἐδωρήσατο τὸ πτῶμα τῷ Ἰωσήφ. 46 καὶ ἀγοράσας σινδόνα καθελὼν αὐτὸν ἐνείλησεν τῇ σινδόνι καὶ ἔθηκεν αὐτὸν ἐν μνημείῳ ὃ ἦν λελατομημένον ἐκ πέτρας, καὶ προσεκύλισεν λίθον ἐπὶ τὴν θύραν τοῦ μνημείου. 47 ἡ δὲ Μαρία ἡ Μαγδαληνὴ καὶ Μαρία ἡ Ἰωσῆτος ἐθεώρουν ποῦ τέθειται. [SBLGNT]

King James Version

42 And now when the even was come, because it was the preparation, that is, the day before the sabbath, 43 Joseph of Arimathæa, an honourable counsellor, which also waited for the kingdom

New Rendition

42 And already evening had arrived. Since it was the day for preparation (that is, the day before the Sabbath), 43 Joseph of Arimathea, a prominent member of the council who also himself

of God, came, and went in boldly unto Pilate, and craved the body of Jesus. 44 And Pilate marvelled if he were already dead: and calling unto him the centurion, he asked him whether he had been any while dead. 45 And when he knew it of the centurion, he gave the body to Joseph. 46 And he bought fine linen, and took him down, and wrapped him in the linen, and laid him in a sepulchre which was hewn out of a rock, and rolled a stone unto the door of the sepulchre. 47 And Mary Magdalene and Mary the mother of Joses beheld where he was laid.

was looking forward to the kingdom of God, having come with boldness, went to Pilate and asked for Jesus' body. 44 And Pilate wondered if Jesus was already dead. And having summoned the centurion, he asked him if Jesus was now dead. 45 And learning [that Jesus was dead] from the centurion, he gave the body to Joseph. 46 And having bought a linen cloth, having taken him down, he wrapped him in the linen cloth and placed him in a tomb, which was cut out of a rock. And he rolled a stone across the entrance to the tomb. 47 And Mary Magdalene and Mary the mother of Joses saw where he was placed.

Notes

15:42 *And now when the even was come, because it was the preparation, that is, the day before the sabbath:* Jesus dies at or just after 3 p.m.; the syntax here indicates that it is almost nightfall, so it is perhaps 4 or 5 p.m., and the Sabbath will begin at 6 p.m.

"The preparation" refers to the time for those tasks that should not be performed on the Sabbath, including burials.

15:43 *Joseph of Arimathæa, an honourable counsellor, which also waited for the kingdom of God:* Arimathea is about twenty miles northwest of Jerusalem. It is possible that Joseph was a member of the local council in Arimathea, but it is more likely that he was a member of the council in Jerusalem, the Sanhedrin, because his access to a tomb in Jerusalem implies his residence there.

Mark specified that all of the council found Jesus worthy of death and that all of the council condemned Jesus (14:55, 64); unless Mark was speaking hyperbolically, this would have included Joseph. This leads to two possibilities for understanding Joseph's motive and characterization here:

1. Joseph has had a change of heart about Jesus. Like the centurion—who was also involved in Jesus' death—Joseph was deeply impacted by Jesus' death. One of the points of Mark's story would then be that even those implicated in Jesus' death can change their minds. Joseph should then be contrasted with Simon of Cyrene: despite their inverted social locations, both of them serve Jesus in his hour of need. (They are also similar to the widow and the

anointing woman, who both engage in charitable acts from opposite ends of the social spectrum.)

2. Joseph still does not approve of Jesus, but he wants him to be properly buried nonetheless. It is not likely that Joseph is a disciple because (1) Pilate would have been rather unlikely to grant a disciple's request and (2) the reference to "wait[ing] for the kingdom of God" implies that he does not think it has yet arrived.[61] Joseph may have been motivated by a desire to fulfill Jewish law by ensuring that Jesus was not left unburied (Deut. 21:22–23), especially with the Sabbath approaching. (It is sometimes argued that the fact that Joseph does not make arrangements for the burial of the other two victims argues against this reading, but it is quite likely that neither was dead yet.) One reason to include this story if Joseph was not a disciple is to emphasize that even someone who did not believe in Jesus' Resurrection would have been able to attest to the reality of his death (see also the Notes on 15:47). It is even possible that Joseph wants Jesus' body in a secure tomb precisely in order to ward off stories of his Resurrection.

came, and went in boldly unto Pilate, and craved the body of Jesus: Boldness was required because Joseph was putting himself at risk by appearing to be sympathetic to Jesus; his boldness contrasts with Jesus' faint-of-heart disciples.

15:44 *And Pilate marvelled if he were already dead:* The New Rendition replaces the pronoun "he" with the noun "Jesus" for clarity in two instances in this verse. Pilate has previously "marvelled" at Jesus' silence (15:5); these two emotional reactions from Pilate frame the story of Jesus' death. Significantly, this verb is used elsewhere in Mark to describe the reactions to Jesus' miracles and authoritative teachings (5:20; 12:17), so its use here suggests that Jesus' death is not—as would have been expected—an embarrassing failure but rather another way in which Jesus taught those around him.

Jesus was on the cross for six hours; this was rather quick for a crucifixion, which sometimes took days. This speed explains Pilate's reaction; he is surprised that Jesus has already died. While later Christian tradition would emphasize Jesus' suffering on the cross, to contemporary observers the most noteworthy aspect of Jesus' time on the cross was its brevity. (This may hint to the severity of his torture before the crucifixion.)

and calling unto him the centurion, he asked him whether he had been any while dead: This is presumably the same centurion (at least on a literary level, if not a literal level) who was in charge of the crucifixion and who recognized Jesus' identity as the Son of God.

---

61. Dowd, *Reading Mark,* 164.

15:45 *And when he knew it of the centurion, he gave the body to Joseph:* One reason for including this scene may have been to make clear to Mark's early audiences (as well as adversaries of early Christianity) that Jesus really had died.

Typically, the body of a crucifixion victim would have been either left hanging on a cross until animals destroyed it or placed into a mass grave.

15:46 *And he bought fine linen, and took him down, and wrapped him in the linen:* The presumption is that Joseph's servants or slaves do the actual work here. Joseph's ability to quickly purchase linen (as well as his access to a tomb) speak to his wealth. As a result, there may be a subtle allusion to the idea found in Isaiah 53:9 of one making his grave with the rich.

It is curious that Joseph was able to purchase linen on Passover, which would have probably been prohibited (Lev. 23:7–8), but there may have been exceptions made if payment was delayed.

Wrapping a corpse in linen was standard practice.

Because the definite article is included, Joseph was purchasing "the linen cloth," not "a linen cloth." It is likely that Mark's audience would have therefore associated this cloth with the one left by the young man when he fled from Gethsemane. On a symbolic level (if not a literal one), Jesus' body is wrapped in the young man's linen garment.

and laid him in a sepulchre which was hewn out of a rock, and rolled a stone unto the door of the sepulchre: Burial was a two-stage process: the body would be placed on a shelf in a tomb for about a year, and then the bones would be moved to a box called an ossuary. Tombs would normally hold multiple bodies due to the difficulty of carving them out of the rock. Mark does not specify, but the audience would have assumed that this tomb belonged to Joseph of Arimathea's family. Because "the shame of a criminal's execution extended into the postmortem period[,] ... [the] tomb of Jesus was therefore regarded as a place of shame (which probably explains why no tomb was venerated in Christian circles until well into the fourth century)"[62] and explains why the precise location of the tomb is still debated today.

The purpose of the stone was to prevent grave robbers; it was probably flat and circular and capable of being rolled along an indentation in the ground so that it could cover the entrance to the tomb.

15:47 *And Mary Magdalene and Mary the mother of Joses beheld where he was laid:* Once again, the witnessing function of the women is emphasized. Mark shows the women as knowing where Jesus is buried so that

---

62. Evans, *Mark 8:27–16:20*, 520.

they are in a position to verify later that his body is no longer there. While Mark does not narrate it, it seems that the women stayed at the cross with Jesus' body until Joseph arrived to remove the body—otherwise it is difficult to explain how they would have known where and when to be present to witness the burial. Once again, the contrast between Jesus' male and female disciples is stark: "The women have done the two things that the males in the community found impossible: they have been servants, and they continued to follow Jesus even *after* he was arrested and executed."[63]

In contrast to the scene at the cross, Salome is not mentioned, and Mary is described only as the mother of Joses (James the less is not mentioned). The shortening of the description of Mary could be a simple shorthand, but it is more difficult to account for the absence of Salome. It may reflect the historical situation that she, for whatever reason, was not present at Jesus' interment.

While the women are witnesses, it appears that they do not interact with Joseph. This supports the reading that Joseph was probably not a disciple.

Relationship to Psalm 22. There are several echoes of Psalm 22 in Mark's story of Jesus' death. They include

1. the division of clothing preparatory to death (15:24 and Ps. 22:18)
2. head-wagging (15:29 and Ps. 22:7)
3. the call to save oneself (15:30 and Ps. 22:8)
4. mockery and insults (15:31 and Ps. 22:8)
5. a loud cry (15:43 and Ps. 22:2)
6. question about abandonment (15:34 and Ps. 22:1)

Because Psalm 22:1 is quoted in 15:34, it appears Mark intends for the story of Jesus' death to echo Psalm 22. The references to the psalm appear in roughly reverse order in Mark's account, which means that while the psalm moves from lament and despair to praise and hope, Mark's text moves in the opposite direction, with vindication absent from this chapter. All of the allusions to Psalm 22 in chapter 15 focus on suffering; none of the praise material has been included.

Also significant is the adaption of Psalm 22:8: in the psalm, the antagonists cry for the Lord to save the psalmist, but in 15:30, the call is to "save yourself." This is another instance where Jesus is placed in the role of the God of the HB.

---

63. Myers, *Binding the Strong Man*, 396; italics in original.

Analysis

It is significant that none of Jesus' family, friends, or disciples make arrangements for his body. While this might have been in part due to the need for someone of significant social standing to speak to Pilate, it is Joseph alone who sees to the burial, without assistance. This contrasts with the death of John the Baptist (6:29) and highlights the failure of Jesus' disciples.

Obviously, the meaning of Jesus' death is a crucial part of Mark's story. Significant elements include:

1. While later Christian thinking would see Jesus' death as a ransom given to God (expanding on one possible reading of 10:45), this is not how Mark presents Jesus' death; rather, "Jesus' life is given as a ransom to the murderous authorities of this generation, the price required to sow the word abroad, to awaken the good earth into abundant fruitfulness."[64]

2. While Mark does present Jesus as the Messiah, it is not the Messiah most people were expecting: "One of the major aims of the Markan narrative as a whole seems to be the reinterpretation of messiahship to include the degrading suffering and death experienced by Jesus."[65]

3. Because of the miracles that Jesus has performed, the audience presumes that Jesus was capable of stopping his own death if he had chosen to. In Gethsemane, it was made clear to the audience that Jesus would have preferred not to suffer and die. And yet despite his ability to stop his death and his preference not to die, he nonetheless does die. The implication is that he chose to submit his will to his Father's; he did not have to, and he did not want to, but he did. This leads to the conclusion that "Mark presents God as one who willed and participated in Jesus' suffering and death and did not—even when asked—deliver him."[66] The portrait of Pilate shows that "no human power, not even that of a sympathetic governor, can stand in the way of the accomplishment of [God's] will."[67]

4. While later Christian tradition would emphasize that Jesus' death made forgiveness possible, "The Gospel of Mark makes no explicit connection between the death of Jesus and the forgiveness of sins."[68] In Mark, forgiveness of sins was tied to John's baptism; Jesus was able to forgive sins well before his death (1:4; 2:1–12).

5. According to then-contemporary cultural standards, Jesus is completely and utterly dishonored when he suffers a humiliating death. But Mark's audience knows that that isn't really the case, which means that cultural standards have

---

64. Tolbert, *Sowing the Gospel,* 262–63.
65. Collins, *Mark,* 750.
66. Rindge, "Reconfiguring the Akedah," 772.
67. Marcus, *Mark 8–16,* 1035.
68. Dowd and Malbon, "Significance of Jesus' Death," 271.

to be reconsidered. Thus, one impact of Jesus' death on Mark's audience is that they are called to look beyond the standards of their own culture.

6. In Mark, the blame for Jesus' death is shared by multiple parties: the disciples for betraying and deserting him, the religious leaders for handing him over to the Romans, the crowd for choosing Barabbas, and the Roman government (in the person of Pilate). While later history foisted most of the blame onto the Jewish people (with horrific results), Mark's "Gentile audience would likely have read [the story of Jesus' death] with acute embarrassment, for many Roman Christians were likely proud of their Roman heritage."[69]

The scene at the cross is replete with irony: virtually everything said by everyone other than Jesus in chapter 15 is insulting mockery, but the audience knows these statements to actually be true even though the speaker does not. The irony extends beyond the verbal to the situational as well: James and John wanted to and/or should have been on the crosses around Jesus, but they weren't. Similarly, Barabbas should have been on the cross instead of Jesus, but he wasn't. And Jesus has primed the audience to think about crucifixion as glorification (10:35–39). Mark does use irony elsewhere in the story but not in such a profusion or concentration; it is the main storytelling technique in this section. This is a rather unusual way to tell a story. It permits Jesus' identity (as king) to be conveyed to the audience, despite the fact that those in the story do not actually believe it to be true.

Jesus' Resurrection Is Announced (16:1–8)

Greek Text

1 Καὶ διαγενομένου τοῦ σαββάτου Μαρία ἡ Μαγδαληνὴ καὶ Μαρία ἡ τοῦ Ἰακώβου καὶ Σαλώμη ἠγόρασαν ἀρώματα ἵνα ἐλθοῦσαι ἀλείψωσιν αὐτόν. 2 καὶ λίαν πρωῒ τῇ μιᾷ τῶν σαββάτων ἔρχονται ἐπὶ τὸ μνημεῖον ἀνατείλαντος τοῦ ἡλίου. 3 καὶ ἔλεγον πρὸς ἑαυτάς· Τίς ἀποκυλίσει ἡμῖν τὸν λίθον ἐκ τῆς θύρας τοῦ μνημείου; 4 καὶ ἀναβλέψασαι θεωροῦσιν ὅτι ἀποκεκύλισται ὁ λίθος, ἦν γὰρ μέγας σφόδρα. 5 καὶ εἰσελθοῦσαι εἰς τὸ μνημεῖον εἶδον νεανίσκον καθήμενον ἐν τοῖς δεξιοῖς περιβεβλημένον στολὴν λευκήν, καὶ ἐξεθαμβήθησαν. 6 ὁ δὲ λέγει αὐταῖς· Μὴ ἐκθαμβεῖσθε· Ἰησοῦν ζητεῖτε τὸν Ναζαρηνὸν τὸν ἐσταυρωμένον· ἠγέρθη, οὐκ ἔστιν ὧδε· ἴδε ὁ τόπος ὅπου ἔθηκαν αὐτόν· 7 ἀλλὰ ὑπάγετε εἴπατε τοῖς μαθηταῖς αὐτοῦ καὶ τῷ

---

69. Witherington, *Gospel of Mark*, 393.

Πέτρῳ ὅτι Προάγει ὑμᾶς εἰς τὴν Γαλιλαίαν· ἐκεῖ αὐτὸν ὄψεσθε, καθὼς εἶπεν ὑμῖν. 8 καὶ ἐξελθοῦσαι ἔφυγον ἀπὸ τοῦ μνημείου, εἶχεν γὰρ αὐτὰς τρόμος καὶ ἔκστασις· καὶ οὐδενὶ οὐδὲν εἶπαν, ἐφοβοῦντο γάρ. [SBLGNT]

King James Version	New Rendition
1 And when the sabbath was past, Mary Magdalene, and Mary the mother of James, and Salome, had bought sweet spices, that they might come and anoint him. 2 And very early in the morning the first day of the week, they came unto the sepulchre at the rising of the sun. 3 And they said among themselves, Who shall roll us away the stone from the door of the sepulchre? 4 And when they looked, they saw that the stone was rolled away: for it was very great. 5 And entering into the sepulchre, they saw a young man sitting on the right side, clothed in a long white garment; and they were affrighted. 6 And he saith unto them, Be not affrighted: Ye seek Jesus of Nazareth, which was crucified: he is risen; he is not here: behold the place where they laid him. 7 But go your way, tell his disciples and Peter that he goeth before you into Galilee: there shall ye see him, as he said unto you. 8 And they went out quickly, and fled from the sepulchre; for they trembled and were amazed: neither said they any thing to any man; for they were afraid.	1 And the Sabbath having passed, Mary of Magdala, and Mary [the mother] of Jacob, and Salome bought spices so that they might go and anoint him. 2 And very early on the first day of the week, the sun having risen, they come to the tomb. 3 And they were saying to each other, "Who will roll away for us the stone from the entrance to the tomb?" 4 And having looked up, they see that the stone had been rolled away—it was extremely large indeed! 5 And having entered into the tomb, they saw a young man sitting on the right, wearing a white robe, and they were really stunned. 6 But he says to them, "Don't be stunned. You seek Jesus the Nazarene—the one who was crucified. He has been raised. He is not here. Look! [This is] the place where they laid him. 7 But go. Say to his disciples and to Peter that he goes before you into Galilee. There you will see him, as he said to you." 8 And having gone out, they fled from the tomb, trembling and amazement having taken hold of them, and they said nothing to anyone because they were awestruck.

Notes

16:1 *And when the sabbath was past:* This time notation could indicate any time after about 6 p.m. on Saturday.

   Mary Magdalene, and Mary the mother of James, and Salome: "Mary the mother of James" is probably the same woman who was called "Mary the mother of James the younger and of Joses" in 15:40 and "Mary the mother of James" in 15:47. It is sometimes suggested that this woman is Jesus' mother since 6:3 names James and Joses as Jesus' brothers, but if this is indeed the case, it is puzzling that Mark does not refer to her as Jesus' mother—unless the intention was to emphasize that she is present as a disciple, not in her role as a biological relative of Jesus (compare 3:31–35).

Note that these women were named in the previous verse, so it is rather odd to immediately name them again. The repetition probably points to their role as the primary eyewitnesses of Jesus' burial and Resurrection.

had bought sweet spices, that they might come and anoint him: Most interpreters assume that the women intended to perform a burial anointing and thus conclude that they did not expect Jesus to be resurrected. (It is also possible that they were coming to anoint the risen Jesus as the Messiah-King,[70] but this seems less likely.) The purpose of burial anointing, which was a common practice, was to mask the smell of decomposition, although many interpreters find the idea of anointing after three days in the tomb to be unusual.[71] If they are attempting a burial anointing, it shows that they did not anticipate Jesus' Resurrection (8:31; 9:31; 10:34). It is surprising that these women, who apparently have no inkling that Jesus will be resurrected, are the first ones to receive the news of it.[72]

Since "ordinarily, nobody would think to give a victim of crucifixion the dignity of an anointing,"[73] their attempt signals devotion to Jesus; they may have wanted to remedy Joseph of Arimathea's lack of anointing.

This text has an interesting impact on the audience: they know that Jesus has already been anointed for burying (14:3–9) and that Jesus will be resurrected, so they know that the women's goal will not be achieved.

16:2 ***And very early in the morning the first day of the week, they came unto the sepulchre at the rising of the sun:*** Mark 16:1–2 contains four time references. This is quite a bit of redundancy: it is, by necessity, very early in the morning if the sun is rising, and it is obviously the first day of the week if the Sabbath has just ended. This is rather significant repetition, especially in a Gospel that is short on specific time references. But all of these references point to the idea of newness, which is an appropriate note to strike in preparation for the news of the Resurrection.

---

70. Tolbert, *Sowing the Gospel,* 294.
71. Collins, *Mark,* 794.
72. Kinukawa, *Women and Jesus in Mark,* 109.
73. Gundry, *Mark,* 989.

Mark's audience is not given any information as to the actual time of Jesus' Resurrection—only that it was before first light on Sunday morning. Jesus has been in the tomb three days—according to ancient Jewish reckoning, if not modern timekeeping. Jesus is buried just before sunset on Friday night, and he is raised by Sunday morning, so he is in the tomb for Friday afternoon, Saturday, and Sunday morning.

16:3 *And they said among themselves, Who shall roll us away the stone from the door of the sepulchre?:* This question increases the suspense of the story; it may also be a subtle reminder that all of Jesus' male disciples have fled and are not there to assist. It is unclear whether the lack of preparation to move the stone reflects poor planning or reflects faith that the problem would somehow be resolved. It is also possible that the women are asking each other which one of them will move the stone away, and thus the verse should be interpreted as evidence of their intention to solve the problem themselves.

16:4 *And when they looked, they saw that the stone was rolled away: for it was very great:* "Saw" is in the present tense in Greek ("see"), which draws the audience in to the scene as if it were happening in that moment.

Mark does not specify who rolled the stone away, which creates a bit of suspense. (It is possible that God, Jesus, or the young man has moved the stone.) The focus on the stone—especially in a laconically narrated story—is rather surprising and might suggest a symbolic element. Perhaps the stone is a symbol of the Resurrection: the women have not anticipated that it would move, and yet it has. Mark's silence regarding who moves the stone is a good analogue to his silence about the Resurrection itself, which is also not narrated. It is also possible that the stone is a symbol "of the opening of the gates of the kingdom of death represented by the tomb. . . . The opening of the tomb is not the work of a human force, but instead of a divine force."[74]

The detail about the stone being large (KJV: "great") seems as if it would fit better at the end of verse 3 than in its current position. However, it is a characteristic of Mark's style to provide details later in the narrative than might be expected (compare 5:42).

16:5 *And entering into the sepulchre, they saw a young man sitting on the right side, clothed in a long white garment; and they were affrighted:* The young man is described as "sitting on the right side," which is somewhat

---

74. Focant, *Gospel according to Mark,* 656.

awkward when taken literally (on the right side of what?), but both the sitting position and being on the right side connote authority;[75] thus, this detail is probably included for symbolic reasons.

Interpreters often claim that this young man is actually an angel since that is how Matthew tells the story (Matt. 28:5) and since in some contemporary texts, the Greek word used in Mark for "young man" is used for angels.[76] However, it is unlikely that Mark wanted his audience to think of this young man as an angel: in other instances (1:2, 13; 8:38; 12:25; 13:27; 13:32), Mark uses the term angel (Greek: *angelos*) but not here, and in Luke's account, there are men—not angels—at the tomb (Luke 24:4).

However, Mark's young man is filling the role of an angel: he comes with a message from God, he inspires fear, and he commands his audience not to be afraid; these are the stereotypical actions of angels in the biblical tradition. But it is important for Mark's purposes that this character is understood to be a young man taking on the role of an angel and not an angel per se. (See the discussion in the Analysis.)

In previous uses in Mark's Gospel, sitting on the right side has been associated with Jesus in his glorified state (10:36–40; 14:62). But here, it is the young man who is on the right side, which means that, symbolically, the young man is allowed to share in Jesus' glory.

The women respond by being "affrighted"; the same Greek verb is used to describe Jesus' emotional state in Gethsemane (14:33). It is not clear to what they are responding with fear: they do not yet realize that Jesus' body is gone, so they might be reacting either to the presence of a living human being in the tomb or to the profound change in the young man since they last saw him in Gethsemane (see the Analysis below).

This might have been a moment of humor for Mark's audience: normally, one would be stunned to find a corpse where a living person was expected, but there is something delightfully ironic about finding a living person where a corpse was expected to be.

Relationship to the Gerasene Demoniac (5:1–20). The demon-possessed man in 5:1–20 begins his story by being poorly dressed and out of control, but then, under the care of Jesus, becomes appropriately dressed, returns to his right mind, and desires to spread the gospel; both stories also occur

---

75. Compare 10:37; 12:35–37; and 14:62; see also France, *Gospel of Mark,* 678.

76. Abraham Kuruvilla, "The Naked Runaway and the Enrobed Reporter of Mark 14 and 16: What Is the Author Doing with What He Is Saying?" *Journal of the Evangelical Theological Society* 54 (September 2011): 541.

in tombs. Thus his story follows the same basic pattern as the story of the young man. These echoes were likely more apparent to Mark's listening audience than they are to the modern reader. If Mark's early audiences had picked up on this echo, they would have concluded that the exorcism story functioned as an enacted parable for the effect that Jesus' Resurrection could have on a disciple. Additionally, this intertext may help explain the women's fear: it is parallel to the fear experienced by those who saw Jesus heal the demoniac.

16:6 *And he saith unto them, Be not affrighted:* Discouraging fear is a typical statement for an angel to make (Judg. 6:23; Dan. 10:12) and thus suggests that the young man is filling the role of an angel.

Ye seek Jesus of Nazareth, which was crucified: It is possible to read this as a question ("Are you looking for Jesus?"), but that is perhaps less likely.

It is fascinating that the young man refers to Jesus as "Jesus of Nazareth" and not by one of the many titles he might have chosen, such as Son of God or Messiah.

he is risen; he is not here: behold the place where they laid him: "Is risen" is a divine passive, suggesting that God raised him. "Behold" is singular, which is probably a grammatical error, since the young man is speaking to more than one person.

This verse features "the staccato style of five short utterances without conjunction of any sort,"[77] which lends a certain urgency and artlessness to the young man's announcement.

16:7 *But go your way, tell his disciples and Peter that he goeth before you into Galilee:* With this line, the women are commissioned by one in the role of an angel to announce the Resurrection to Jesus' other disciples. The women are given a special task as agents who extend Jesus' forgiveness and an invitation to follow him. Generally, women were not permitted to be witnesses under Jewish law,[78] which means that in order for the disciples, Peter, and Mark's audience to accept the invitation to follow Jesus, they need to discard the cultural norm of distrusting women's words.

Peter is mentioned separately from the disciples, perhaps suggesting that he is distanced from the other disciples by his denial of Jesus. However, the implication of the young man's words is that Peter is invited to return to the way by following Jesus to Galilee. While Peter's current state is dire,

---

77. France, *Gospel of Mark,* 680.
78. Mishah Niddah 6:4.

the clear message is that he will be given the opportunity to return to full fellowship; Peter and the disciples who fled in fear are being given another chance to follow Jesus "on the way"—literally on the way to Galilee. It was evidence of mercy to specifically mention Peter and to make clear that the invitation applied to him as well, despite his denial of Jesus. The promise of restoration to discipleship requires that they act in faith by choosing to follow Jesus to Galilee. They are all expected to act on the announcement of Jesus' Resurrection.

"Goeth" could mean that Jesus will lead them to Galilee or that he is going to Galilee before they do. "Goeth" is in the present tense, suggesting that Jesus is going to Galilee as the young man is speaking.

there shall ye see him, as he said unto you: "As he said unto you" refers to Jesus' words in 14:28, the only time when he spoke specifically on this topic. This reference reveals that women were present at the Last Supper.

The final words spoken by any character in this text are "as he told you," which is an appropriate summation of the prophetic nature of Jesus' ministry.

16:8 *And they went out quickly, and fled from the sepulcher:* It is unclear whether the women's fleeing stems from fear of their commission or whether it indicates that they are hurrying to complete their assignment.

for they trembled and were amazed: neither said they any thing to any man; for they were afraid: The Greek text contains a double negative that serves to emphasize their silence.

Relationship to Genesis 18. In LXX Genesis 18:15, where Sarah overhears the messenger tell Abraham that she will have a child, the first sentence ends with "for she was afraid," with the same verb for "afraid" and the same Greek word for "for" (Greek: *gar*). There are also several thematic connections between Sarah's story and that of the women at the tomb, including the promise of a return, fear, a female character, and the suggestion of new life where it seems impossible.[79] If Mark's audience realized that Mark's text was alluding to Genesis 18, the audience would have been reminded that the seemingly impossible can in fact happen, as the rhetorical question "Is any thing too hard for the Lord?" (Gen. 18:14) suggests.

Note: Mark 16:9–20 was almost certainly not originally part of the Gospel of Mark and is therefore treated in appendix D: "Mark 16:9–20."

---

79. Marcus, *Mark 8–16,* 1082.

Analysis

In 14:3–9, a woman anoints Jesus for his burial. In 16:1–8, women attempt to anoint Jesus for his burial, but they are unsuccessful because he has already been raised. The two stories are linked in other ways: both involve rare time references (14:1–2; 16:1–2) and both focus heavily on the theme of Jesus' death and burial.

Mark's audience would almost certainly have associated this young man at the tomb with the young man who fled arrest in Gethsemane (14:51–52) since the same Greek word (*neaniskos*) is used for both (and nowhere else in Mark), in both cases their clothing is described, and they both appear to the audience without introduction. The association would have been stronger had the definite article been used ("the young man"), but Mark calls him "a young man," which has led some interpreters to think that this young man has nothing to do with the young man in Gethsemane. However, this interpretation is less persuasive because the enigmatic young man in the Gethsemane story would have left Mark's audience wondering about his identity and role, while the reference here to a young man and his clothing encourages the connection.

The young man in Gethsemane was dressed in a linen cloth (using the same Greek word as is used to describe Jesus' burial shroud—where it is described as "the linen cloth," not "a linen cloth" [15:46]), and he runs away—sans clothing—when the authorities attempt to arrest him. He was initially described as following Jesus, using an unusual prefix on the verb for "following"; the only other use of that combination is in 5:37, where the idea of being a close disciple (and, incidentally, raising of the dead) is mentioned. So the young man is presented as a close follower—at least before he flees. That is a picture of shame: the cloth suggests that he showed up with the intent of dying with Jesus but, under pressure, preferred the humiliation of running away naked to the pain of death.[80] Jesus is crucified without clothing, just as the young man runs away without clothing, implying that Jesus is symbolically taking the young man's shame upon himself. When the young man reappears at the tomb, he is now wearing clothing associated with honor and glory—clothing described as being like Jesus' clothing at the Transfiguration (these are the only two instances in Mark where clothing is described as being "white") and assuming a position of authority. In other words, he has not only been restored from shame

---

80. Kuruvilla, "Naked Runaway," 541.

but is now assuming an even more honorable position. In effect, Jesus has swapped roles with this young man and thus made the young man's restoration and glorification possible.

The subtle but clear implication is that Jesus' death and Resurrection have made this change possible for the young man. It is then most fitting that the young man announces that not only the scattered disciples but also Peter will be given an opportunity to follow Jesus again, the same opportunity that the young man has been given and is reflected by his position and clothing. The young man has also been given the angel-like task of announcing the Resurrection. Now that Jesus is raised, a simple young man—even the kind who would flee instead of standing by Jesus—can fulfill the function of an angel, just as a centurion can fill the function of God. The two scenes with the young man show the effect of the Resurrection on the life of the disciple: Jesus' suffering, death, and Resurrection make it possible for this young man to escape the shame of failed discipleship and to take on the role of authoritative messenger. He is the idealized picture of failed discipleship restored under the influence of Jesus' life and death. He personally encapsulates the main themes of the Gospel of Mark. He is, through the transformation that has happened to him, the primary Resurrection witness in Mark's Gospel. In Gethsemane, he literally ran away from the idea of Jesus' death; in the tomb—transformed by Jesus' suffering, death, and Resurrection—he is able to sit and proclaim that death. And now the young man's role is to ask the women to join in and to be the authoritative messengers who tell the other disciples about the Resurrection.

Part of the puzzle of Mark's ending is solved when the young man at the tomb is understood as a picture of the ideal disciple—failed, restored, glorified, and providing a template for the rehabilitation of the disciples.

The reference to Galilee invites the audience to return to the beginning of Mark's Gospel, which recounted Jesus' ministry in Galilee. The middle of the story focused on the journey to Jerusalem, and the final portion takes place in and around Jerusalem, but Jesus will be reuniting with his disciples in Galilee. This is significant precisely because Galilee was thought to be insignificant and marginal, while Jerusalem was the center of religious leadership and the location of the temple.[81] The return of Jesus' ministry to Galilee is one more way in which Jesus inverts expectations. Further, it means that the geographical movement in Mark's Gospel is not

---

81. Kinukawa, *Women and Jesus in Mark*, 111.

linear (from Galilee to Jerusalem) but circular (from Galilee to Jerusalem to Galilee).

The KJV includes 16:9–20, but Mark's Gospel, in its earliest manuscripts, ended with 16:8. It is almost an understatement to say that "Mark's ending is a surprise grammatically, literarily, thematically, theologically, and stylistically."[82] This enigmatic ending has spawned numerous possibilities for interpreting the text.

One theory is that Mark's Gospel originally extended beyond 16:8, but that this ending was somehow lost. Support for this idea comes from the fact that 16:8 ends with the word translated as "for," which is a very unorthodox manner to end a work. In general, 16:8 seems to be an overly abrupt ending. This leads some scholars to conclude that, while KJV 16:9–20 is not the original ending of Mark, neither is 16:8; rather, a now-lost ending was the earliest ending to the text. Another possibility is that the original manuscript ended at 16:8, not by Mark's design but only because some outside factor (illness, persecution, death, etc.) prohibited Mark from finishing the text.

Nonetheless, it is not likely that there was an original, now missing, ending to Mark. On a practical level, the first copies of Mark were probably scrolls, not codices, which makes it more difficult to imagine an ending becoming lost since the ending of the scroll would have been rolled into the center.[83] Also, Matthew and Luke (who are otherwise following Mark fairly closely in this section of the text) are radically different after 16:8, which means that a lost ending would have to have been lost quite early (before Matthew and Luke wrote) and lost from the copies from which both Matthew and Luke were working.[84] Thus it is likely that Mark intended to end with 16:8. What is one to make of this enigmatic ending?

First, while ending with the word "for" might seem unusual to modern ears, it is not unprecedented in ancient literature.[85] It may even be characteristic of oral speech. Mark sometimes uses these "for" clauses to provide needed background explanations for the audience,[86] so perhaps 16:8 is not

---

82. Deppe, *Theological Intentions,* 2.

83. Daniel B. Wallace, "Mark 16:8 as the Conclusion to the Second Gospel," in *Perspectives on the Ending of Mark: 4 Views,* ed. David Alan Black (Nashville: B&H Academic, 2008), 35–36.

84. Wallace, "Mark 16:8 as the Conclusion," 31.

85. Deppe, *Theological Intentions,* 274.

86. Thomas E. Boomershine and Gilbert L. Bartholomew, "The Narrative Technique of Mark 16:8," *Journal of Biblical Literature* 100, no. 2 (1981): 215.

as abrupt as it seems: rather, the climax is 16:7 (which has the feel of an appropriate ending) and 16:8 is merely an explanation, perhaps somewhat akin to the modern footnote.

One similar incident from another ancient text is revealing. Plato writes of an instance where Socrates is listening to a speech by Protagoras that ends with the word "for" (Greek: *gar*). Socrates describes how this ending affected him: "I stayed gazing at him, quite spellbound, for a long time, thinking that he was going to say something more, and anxious to hear it; but when I saw that he had really finished, I collected myself with an effort . . ."[87] This example shows that a work could end with "for" and it hints at the effect that it would have on an audience: they would anticipate more to come and only slowly realize that the speaker had ended. It is easy to imagine Mark's audience having a similar response as anticipation of continued speech morphs into the realization that the story has already ended. So the argument that Mark could not have ended at 16:8 because it would be too awkward should be discarded; perhaps awkwardness was his very intention. Further, other ancient texts—even scriptural texts—feature open and provocative endings (Jonah 4:11).

Another argument against accepting 16:8 as the original ending is that it means that Mark's Gospel does not contain a Resurrection appearance. But this might be intentional: it is possible that Hellenistic members of Mark's audience would not have expected a Resurrection appearance but rather would have thought that the empty tomb scene adequately conveyed the reality of Jesus' Resurrection, as this was common in Hellenistic literature: "Indeed, it would have been the body's absence, not its presence, that would have signaled the provocative moment for the ancient reader."[88] Additionally, it is only by comparison with the other canonized Gospels that the lack of Resurrection appearance seems to be a problem: on its own, Mark's Gospel has no inherent lack. (None of the canonized Gospels relate the actual Resurrection but only tell of later appearances of the resurrected Jesus, and yet readers generally do not think the Gospels are defective due to this lack.) In fact, it is possible that the later endings of Mark were written precisely because the compilation of Mark and the other Gospels made Mark's ending begin to seem inadequate. Another factor that makes 16:8 less abrupt than it might initially seem involves the promise of 1:1: if Mark

---

87. Plato, *Protagoras* 328d, trans. C. C. W. Taylor (Oxford: Clarendon Press, 1991), 20.

88. Richard C. Miller, "Mark's Empty Tomb and Other Translation Fables in Classical Antiquity," *Journal of Biblical Literature* 129, no. 4 (2010): 767.

truly is the beginning of the gospel, then it makes sense that the text would end without telling the complete story or "the end" of the gospel.

Accepting 16:8 as the original and intentional ending of Mark raises the question of what, precisely, this ending means. This can be difficult to determine in part because the actions of the women at the tomb are difficult to parse. It seems that they fail in the task that the young man gives them: they leave in fear and say nothing to anyone. It is difficult to read their flight as positive when the same verb is used to describe the flight of the disciples at Jesus' arrest (14:50). (Alternatively, there may be an ironic inversion here, with the male disciples' flight resulting from cowardice while the female disciples' flight reflects quick observance of the young man's commission, which requires them to flee from the tomb.)

If the women are thought to fail at their task, this would have a profound effect on the audience. In this reading, there are no successful disciples within the text, which creates pressure on the audience to become the ideal disciple and to spread the message of the Resurrection. Interestingly, it means that the male disciples failed under suffering and the women failed under glory—suggesting a tweak to conventional gender stereotypes that must be overcome in order to be successful disciples. The audience focuses on the young man as the ideal disciple and models themselves on his pattern of success after failure. One point of this reading would be to suggest that the end of the text is obviously not the end of the story: the disciples— including Mark's audience—have an important role to play in preaching the good news that extends well beyond the confines of the text. If the reaction of the audience is akin to "how on earth could they not say anything to anyone?" then Mark has successfully ensnared the audience in an enacted parable—just as Nathan did to David[89]—where they are made to realize how critical it is that they take corrective action.

But given the context—especially regarding the presence of the young man as the failed-but-redeemed disciple and his message of an opportunity for the reinstatement of Peter and the other disciples—to the extent that these women are viewed as failing by fleeing in fear and saying nothing to anyone, Mark has already built into the narrative the opportunity for their future redemption. The failure of the present moment does not negate the possibility of future success. Ultimately, however, the weight of the evidence suggests that the women are successful at their task. It is also possible—if less

---

89. Compare 2 Sam.12:7; see also Timothy J. Geddert, "Beginning Again (Mark 16:1–8)," *Direction* 33 (Fall 2004): 156.

likely—that Mark intended the ending to be ambiguous. That is, the audience is deliberately unable to determine if the women succeeded or failed at their commission. This ending would leave Mark's audience with the promise of Jesus' return but without evidence of it—which is precisely the situation of the audience in regard to Jesus' return to earth. An ambiguous ending might have spurred audience engagement with the story, which was perhaps a more important goal for Mark than supplying a crisp ending. One can easily imagine the audience highly motivated to discuss the story and its ambiguity and to act to share the news of the Resurrection: "the real ending of Mark's Gospel is in the response of its hearers."[90] All of the endings later added—in 16:9–20, in Matthew, and in Luke—witness to the success of Mark's strategy of spurring others to, in effect, continue the story themselves. Given that the entire point of the scene at the tomb is that death is not the end, it makes sense that the text does not really end. An ambiguous ending is a powerful way in which to convey the hope of return to discipleship.

Another way to interpret the ending is to focus not on the women but rather on the young man. He is the idealized disciple, moved from fear and shame to glory by the power of Jesus' death and Resurrection. He is the one who announces the Resurrection. His proclamation of the Resurrection is the high point of the Gospel, and the women are something of an afterthought. Both the male and female disciples are left at loose ends in the text: they have the option of returning to discipleship if they choose. But in the young man is a model of what that return looks like.

While it is possible that the women fail, that the ending is ambiguous, or that the focal point should be the young man, the best-supported interpretation is that, despite the surface reading, the women are successful in their task. First, that they fear may not quite represent their state, which may have more in common with reverent awe—an entirely appropriate response to the absence of Jesus' corpse, the announcement of the Resurrection, and their commission. Further, in previous instances, fear has not been incompatible with following Jesus (10:32), so their fear may not indicate failure. The women experience the same emotion that Jesus does in Gethsemane, but that did not prevent him from completing the assignment that he had been given.

It is possible that "saying nothing to anyone" only applies to the time when they were afraid—a time that certainly would not last forever; there

---

90. Joan L. Mitchell, *Beyond Fear and Silence: A Feminist-Literary Approach to the Gospel of Mark* (New York: Continuum, 2001), 23.

may be a parallel with Mark's bleeding woman, who also fears before she testifies to her experience. And it is quite likely that the audience would presume that the women succeeded in their mission—if they had not, no one (not the disciples, not Peter) would have known to go to Galilee, and there would have been no Resurrection appearances and thus no continuation of the Christian story beyond Jesus' death. In fact, if they really said nothing to anyone, the story of what happened at the tomb would itself never have become public knowledge! Thus the presumption must be that the women succeeded in their assignment. Additionally, the fact that the Passion narrative is framed by stories of women (attempting to) anoint Jesus suggests that the women at the tomb should be regarded as being successful disciples, parallel to the anointing woman of chapter 14. It is possible that flight is precisely the correct, obedient response to have in this situation—after all, they were initially seeking Jesus' body, they realized it was not in the tomb, and they were given a message to relay to the disciples. The obedient choice at that moment is to flee the tomb; that flight was the wrong response to Jesus' arrest does not mandate that it is the wrong response at the tomb. The women's silence may also be appropriate: Mark's language does not require that it be interpreted as complete and total silence; Jesus told the leper to say nothing to anyone but to go to the priest (1:40–45) using very similar language. In that case, the command to silence did not mean total silence; rather, it meant that the news must only be shared with specific parties and no one else. In this reading, the women are obedient because they share the news of the Resurrection only with the disciples and Peter. Had they not been, Jesus' prophecy of going before the disciples to Galilee (to which the young man specifically refers; compare 14:27–28) would have been left unfulfilled, and that is not a likely scenario in Mark's Gospel.

While extremely speculative, it is interesting to contemplate how the ending of the Gospel would be interpreted by Mark's audience if the storytellers from whom they were hearing the Gospel were the women who were at the tomb. Given that the text has emphasized their role of witnessing to the death, burial, and empty tomb, it is not implausible that this witnessing task would have continued in the early Christian community. But even if the women are not the storytellers for Mark's Gospel, it is still almost certain that they are ultimately successful in the assignment that the young man had given them.

So there are many indicators that, despite its abrupt rendering, the ending of Mark shows the women as successful, obedient disciples. If this is how Mark's audience interpreted the ending, then this picture of female disciples announcing the Resurrection is the final image that the story leaves with them. This is an extremely pro-female message, particularly in a cultural context in which women were not given equal rights and where women's testimonies were not permitted in court. The final note of the Gospel, by contrast, is that one cannot be a follower of Jesus—indeed, one will not be given the opportunity to follow Jesus—if one is not willing to listen to women and believe their words.

Interestingly, the Gospel ends with Mark's audience still in the tomb,[91] left to contemplate, facing the reality that Jesus is no longer there. They are left with the invitation to leave the tomb and proceed to Galilee to continue following Jesus, so that "the ending of the Gospel of Mark is not a conclusion but rather an invitation."[92] Mark's audience members are invited to seek their own resurrection appearance by choosing to follow Jesus.

The Gospel of Mark is neatly bookended by messengers who go ahead to prepare the way: "John, clothed in animal skins and sent 'ahead' to 'proclaim' the one stronger than him, and the young man dressed in white, who at the conclusion will say that Jesus 'goes before' the disciples into Galilee (16:7) with the aim of launching the mission of 'proclaiming' the gospel."[93] This bracketing suggests that 16:8 is the original intended ending of the Gospel; it also implies that discipleship and following are key themes in the text.

The commissioning of women as authorized agents to spread the most important message of human history is a fitting capstone to the portrait of women in Mark's Gospel. Beginning with the serving/ministering role of Peter's mother-in-law, women occupy understated roles throughout the text until a crucial moment at the foot of the cross when their ministering can be recognized. At that point, women take over as Jesus' closest disciples—since the male disciples have fled—and are the only witnesses to Jesus' death, burial, and Resurrection. They will be the only primary eyewitnesses to these events in Mark's Gospel and, thus, to the early Christian movement. By the end of the text, "women are the only figures who faithfully follow and serve and the only witnesses to the crucifixion and empty

---

91. William F. McInerny, "An Unresolved Question in the Gospel Called Mark: 'Who Is This Whom Even Wind and Sea Obey?' (4:41)." *Perspectives In Religious Studies* 23, no. 3 (1996): 266.

92. Raymond Pickett, "Following Jesus in Galilee: Resurrection as Empowerment in the Gospel of Mark," *Currents in Theology and Mission* 32 (December 2005): 435.

93. Focant, *Gospel according to Mark*, 35.

tomb—and the only links to the implied continuation of the movement in Galilee and outwards."[94]

Given this signal role, it is probable that women were involved in the transmission of the Gospel of Mark. It is difficult to imagine a group of men telling and hearing the menstruation-focused story of 5:25–34, for example, so it is likely that women were among the early storytellers of the Gospel.[95] But the implication that the male disciples, even Peter, will be given another chance to follow Jesus points to the involvement of men and women together in the early Christian movement. Interestingly, there were only male witnesses to the Transfiguration and only female witnesses to the empty tomb, so in order for the complete story of Jesus to be told, both groups will have to rely on each other.

Throughout Mark's Gospel, the disciples have frequently stumbled in their attempts to follow Jesus. The nadir occurs with Peter's denial of Jesus. But the message of the young man at the tomb is not just that Jesus has been raised but that an invitation is to be extended to Jesus' fallen disciples— even to Peter—to resume following Jesus. This, ultimately, is Mark's main message: disciples will fail, and Jesus will invite them to try again.

---

94. Horsley, *Hearing the Whole Story*, xv.

95. Antoinette Clark Wire, *The Case for Mark Composed in Performance* (Eugene, Ore.: Cascade Books, 2011), 168.

Appendix A:
Authorship and Date

What Does the Gospel Indicate about Its Author?

The Gospel of Mark is formally anonymous, meaning that the name of the author does not occur within the text (contrast Rev. 1:1). The writer may not have felt any need to include his or her name, being well known to the community or may have omitted a name for rhetorical reasons, perhaps to focus the text on Jesus Christ instead.[1] The author does not claim to be a follower of Jesus, an eyewitness to his ministry, or to have any specific personal connection to the people in the Gospel.[2] Nothing indicates how the author learned the stories that are in the Gospel. Apparently, the author did not think that the reader needed to know his or her name or connection to Jesus' life. This has not stopped scholars from trying to figure out as much as possible about who wrote the Gospel.

The first clue is the title. The Gospel was likely originally without title since "in ancient book production and publication, the title belonged more to the stage of reception than to that of production."[3] Perhaps the Gospels were initially without titles because the titles would have been obvious to all readers, because the authors hoped to avoid persecution from having

---

1. It is theoretically possible that the author of Mark was female, but given the extremely low rates of female literacy in the ancient world, this is unlikely.

2. Older scholarship often associated the author of the Gospel with the young man who flees when Jesus is arrested in 14:51, but this is unlikely. The association probably stemmed from a desire to explain the function of the young man in the narrative, but there are now better readings of this enigmatic character. See the Notes on that verse for more information.

3. Collins, *Mark,* 129.

their names associated with Christian writings, or because they did not consider the text their unique creation but rather a communal project. It may have been that a title was only added after other Gospels were written and it became necessary to distinguish them. Or a title may not have been necessary until the Gospel circulated beyond its original location.[4]

The title of Mark's Gospel is very old, but it is not attached to all ancient manuscripts. It was most likely added in the late first century or early second century, although there were some copies even in the fourth century that did not have a title.[5] The oldest manuscript of the second Gospel does not have a title, although many other manuscripts from that era do contain titles.[6] The title is likely to date from before the mid-second century because by then Gospels were normally attributed to apostles to increase their authority and prestige. Presumably, had a title-less Gospel of Mark been circulating and someone had decided to give it a title at that point, it would have been given the name of an apostle.

Because the title appears at the beginning, the end, the side, or both the beginning and the end, depending on the manuscript, it seems that the title was not there originally but was added later and thus placed in a variety of locations. The fact that the only author associated with this text is Mark is an indication of the accuracy of the attribution; by contrast, Galen, a second-century physician, had an untitled work that was later given more than one title, which is precisely what one would expect to happen if many different hands were generating a title for a book.

There is a curious situation regarding the title of this Gospel in the Joseph Smith Translation: while Latter-day Saint Bibles indicate in the footnotes that the JST titles the book "The Testimony of St. Mark," this is apparently an error; the JST does change the titles of Matthew and John from "The Gospel of" to "The Testimony of," but apparently the titles of Mark and Luke were not changed. Some Latter-day Saint scholars conclude that the title change, limited to Matthew and John, reflects their apostolic status.[7]

---

4. For a general discussion of Gospel authorship from a Latter-day Saint perspective, see Frank F. Judd Jr., "Who Really Wrote the Gospels? A Study of Traditional Authorship," in *How the New Testament Came To Be: The Thirty-fifth Annual Sidney B. Sperry Symposium*, ed. Kent P. Jackson and Frank F. Judd Jr. (Provo, Utah: Religious Studies Center; Salt Lake City: Deseret Book, 2006), 129–30.

5. Marcus, *Mark 1–8*, 17.

6. Collins, *Mark*, 3.

7. Barney, "Joseph Smith Translation," 88.

So there is very good—but not airtight—evidence that the author of this Gospel was named Mark. Unfortunately, "Mark" was one of the most common male names in the Roman Empire.[8] (It was, however, rare for Jews.[9]) What else can be known about him? Some characteristics of the author can be deduced from the text, although most of these conclusions are not without counterpoint:

1. *Latinisms.* Mark's use of Latin terms[10] suggests that (some of) the audience was more familiar with Latin than Greek, especially since there are two occasions when Greek words are explained in Latin terms.[11]

2. *Aramaic Words and Phrases.* Mark's Gospel contains a surprisingly high number of Aramaic terms[12] for a text of its length. In all cases, these are translated into Greek, leading to the conclusion that the author, but not (all of) the audience, knew Aramaic.

3. *Geographical Descriptions.* Some scholars find errors in Mark's descriptions of geography,[13] which might indicate a lack of familiarity with Palestine. (Other scholars point out that ancient people would not have known their own geography nearly as well as those who have access to maps.[14]) On the other hand, it is likely that Mark is more concerned with theology than geography and therefore adapts the physical setting to fit the rhetorical needs.

4. *Understanding of Judaism.* Mark explains some Jewish customs. Traditionally, it was assumed that this was because Mark (but not the audience) was

---

8. Marcus, *Mark 1–8,* 17.

9. David E. Garland, *A Theology of Mark's Gospel: Good News about Jesus the Messiah, the Son of God,* ed. Andreas J. Köstenberger (Grand Rapids, Mich.: Zondervan, 2015), 50.

10. Latinisms in Mark's Gospel include *legion* (5:9, 15), *speculator* (KJV: "executioner"; 6:27), *denarius* (KJV: "penny"; 6:37; 12:15; 14:5), *quadrans* (KJV: "mite"; 12:42), *flagellare* (KJV: "scourge"; 15:15), *praetorium* (15:16), and *centurion* (15:39, 44, 45). See also Stein, *Mark,* 11–12.

11. "Two mites, which make a farthing" (12:42); "the hall, called Praetorium" (15:16).

12. "Boanerges, which is, The sons of thunder" (3:17), "Talitha cumi; which is, being interpreted, Damsel, I say unto thee, arise" (5:41), "Corban, that is to say, a gift" (7:11), "Ephphatha, that is, Be opened" (7:34), "hell, into the fire that never shall be quenched" (9:43), "Bartimaeus, the son of Timaeus" (10:46), "Abba, Father" (14:36), "Golgotha, which is, being interpreted, The place of a skull" (15:22), "Eloi, Eloi, lama sabachthani? which is, being interpreted, My God, my God, why hast thou forsaken me?" (15:34).

13. In 5:1, the earliest texts of the Gospel have the pigs running 35 miles (!) to "Gerasa." Later texts read "Gadara," but that area has no cliffs (Stein, *Mark,* 250). In 7:31, the journey from Tyre to the Sea of Galilee by way of Sidon is an unnecessary detour (Stein, *Mark,* 357). In 11:1, a similar "detour" is described (Stein, *Mark,* 503).

14. Collins, *Mark,* 8.

familiar with them.[15] Alternatively, some scholars feel that these descriptions show a limited understanding of Judaism,[16] perhaps implying that Mark was not Jewish, but this is disputed,[17] especially since Mark contains many biblical allusions. It is also possible that these descriptions are provided for dramatic effect and not because they provide new information to the audience.[18]

5. *System of Timekeeping.* In 6:48 and 13:35, Mark uses the Roman system of four watches per night, instead of the Jewish reckoning of three watches per night, to delineate time, perhaps serving as further evidence for a Roman setting of the Gospel. But it is also possible that Mark used Roman time either in order to make the text understandable to gentile audience members, or because he or she was not being precise, or perhaps because Jews used the Roman system as well.

6. *Writing Style.* Mark's Gospel is written in very poor Greek.[19] For example, in 16:6, the word "behold" is in the singular form despite the fact that more than one person is being addressed.

It can be difficult to evaluate what some of this evidence implies about Mark, and scholars draw opposite conclusions from it. Perhaps it is safe to say that the data suggests that the author knew (at least some) Aramaic, knew Greek (but wrote it poorly), was likely to have been a Jew, and is associated with Rome.

---

15. For example, washing customs of Pharisees (7:3), explanation of the Passover (14:12), and preparation for the Sabbath (15:42).

16. Mark 15:42 can be read to suggest that Mark did not understand that the Sabbath began at sundown, therefore preparation for the Sabbath would not have occurred during the evening as that would have already been considered the Sabbath; Luke 23:56 may be a commentary on this (see Marcus, *Mark 1–8*, 20). Mark 1:2 (which ascribes quotations from Isaiah and Malachi to Isaiah only) and 2:26 (which names Abiathar as the high priest when the high priest was Ahimelech [see 1 Sam. 21]) may show a lack of familiarity with Jewish scripture (although there are other explanations for these "mistakes"; see the Notes on each verse).

17. For example, 7:3–4 (washing customs of the Pharisees) is widely regarded to be erroneous, but some disagree with this assessment. Marcus, *Mark 1–8*, 20.

18. For example, the description of Judas as one of the Twelve in 14:10 does not provide the audience with new information but rather serves to emphasize Judas' treachery. Similarly, the description of Jewish custom in 7:3–4 may not be new information to the audience but rather serve to emphasize the reliance on the tradition on the elders and the absurdity of washing dining couches.

19. To the extent that the KJV translation sounds refined and elegant to modern ears, it does not represent Mark's writing style.

What Other Information Is There about the Author?

The oldest statement about the authorship of Mark's Gospel comes from Papias, who was the bishop of Hieropolis (in what is now Turkey) and lived from about 60 CE to 130 CE. Most scholars date Papias's statement about Mark's Gospel to close to 130 CE,[20] but a few think his statement might have been made closer to 100 CE[21] and that he was referencing information that he learned at an earlier time, perhaps 80 CE.[22] Unfortunately, Papias's original works are lost and survive only through quotations contained in Eusebius, who was a bishop in Palestine and lived c. 260–340 CE. The statement from Papias (preserved by Eusebius) concerning Mark's Gospel reads as follows:

> And the Presbyter [or: elder] used to say this, "Mark became Peter's inter-preter and wrote accurately all that he remembered, not, indeed, in order, of the things said or done by the Lord. For he had not heard the Lord, nor had he followed him, but later on, as I said, followed Peter, who used to give teaching as necessity demanded but not making, as it were, an arrangement of the Lord's oracles, so that Mark did nothing wrong in thus writing down single points as he remembered them. For to one thing he gave attention, to leave out nothing of what he had heard and to make no false statements in them."[23]

The information in this statement is a treasure trove of background infor-mation about Mark's Gospel, but it raises as many questions as it answers:

1. *Is Eusebius likely to have accurately conveyed Papias's words?* Eusebius had a low opinion of Papias; at one point he calls him "a man of very little intel-ligence, as is clear from his books."[24] This may imply that Eusebius would have been comfortable editing Papias's work as he thought necessary, mak-ing the tradition less trustworthy. On the other hand, if Eusebius were going to concoct a story about the origins of Mark's Gospel, he presumably would not have placed that origin story in the mouth of someone whom he tells his

---

20. Witherington, *Gospel of Mark,* 22.

21. Gundry, *Mark,* 1027–28; see also Richard Bauckham, *Jesus and the Eyewitnesses: The Gospels as Eyewitness Testimony* (Grand Rapids, Mich.: William B. Eerdmans Publish-ing, 2006), 14.

22. Bauckham, *Jesus and the Eyewitnesses,* 14.

23. Eusebius, *The Ecclesiastical History,* translated by Kirsopp Lake (New York: G. P. Putnam's Sons, 1926), 297.

24. Eusebius, *History,* 297.

readers is stupid; the fact that he does this probably indicates that the tradition is trustworthy.

2. *Is Papias likely to have accurately conveyed the Presbyter's words?* There is nothing in Papias's statement that will answer this question, but it is worth remembering that one cannot assess this link in the chain.

3. *Who was "the Presbyter"?* Earlier in his text, Eusebius identifies the person called "the Presbyter" (Greek: "the elder") as "John." But who is this John? Historians disagree here: some understand this to be the apostle John and others to be a different John, a second-generation church leader.[25]

4. *Did John the Presbyter have accurate information about the Gospel?* Nothing in Papias's statement can confirm this.

5. *Who said what?* In the text from Eusebius, it is difficult to determine if the entire statement consists of Papias's quotation of the Presbyter, or if some of the text is Papias's commentary on what the Presbyter said, or even Eusebius's commentary on what the Elder (or Papias) said. A tradition dating from the time of Eusebius would be less trustworthy than one dating from Papias's time.

6. *What does it mean to say that Mark was Peter's "interpreter"?* There are several different theories about what "interpreter" might have meant here. Perhaps Peter only spoke Aramaic (although other scholars find this unlikely[26]), so he needed Mark to translate into Latin or Greek when he preached in areas where the audience did not know Aramaic. Had Mark translated frequently, he would have become very familiar with Peter's stories of Jesus and therefore would have been capable of writing a Gospel. Another possibility is that Mark's "translating" occurred when recording Peter's (Aramaic) memories in the form of a (Greek) written gospel.[27] Or perhaps Mark was Peter's "transmitter,"[28] with responsibility for conveying Peter's teachings to others. In this view, writing the Gospel would have been a part—perhaps the main part—of the interpreting role. Another possibility is that Mark is providing his own interpretation of Peter's teachings, perhaps similar to the tradition of Jewish midrash.[29]

7. *What does it mean to say that Mark's Gospel is "not in order"?* The obvious interpretation of this statement is that the events in Mark's Gospel are not in chronological order: Peter would not necessarily have told stories about

---

25. The situation is complicated by the fact that, while Eusebius seems to distinguish between the Apostle John and the Presbyter John, some interpreters think that Eusebius has created a distinction between the two Johns where none existed because of his hostility to the Apostle! Oden and Hall, *Mark*, xxi n. 1; Gundry, *Mark*, 1029–30.

26. Terence Y. Mullins, "Papias on Mark's Gospel," *Vigiliae Christianae* 14, no. 4 (1960): 220–21; see also Gundry, *Mark*, 1035.

27. Bauckham, *Jesus and the Eyewitnesses*, 205–6.

28. Guelich, *Mark 1–8:26*, xxvii.

29. Sabin, *Reopening the Word*, 12.

Jesus in chronological order (especially if he were telling them "as necessity demanded"), and therefore Mark, not an eyewitness to Jesus' ministry, would have had no idea how to order the events in the Gospel. However, other scholars take Papias's comment as referring not to chronological order but to topical order.[30] But most scholars feel that there is quite a bit of order to Mark's work; perhaps Papias did not appreciate the order and just noticed the lack of chronology? And how can one explain the similarity in Mark's and Matthew's orders if one is chronological but the other is not? Other scholars read the idea of the Gospel not being in order as implying "gaps"[31] in the record.

8. *What does it mean to say that Peter taught "as necessity demanded"?* While this phrase has normally been understood to mean that Peter recounted stories of Jesus' ministry that were appropriate to the situation of his audience, there is another view. It keeps untranslated the term *chreia* as "a technical rhetorical term to describe the form in which Peter delivered his teachings."[32] An appropriate English synonym might be "anecdotes." In other words, the Gospel is not a systematic or sequential presentation of Jesus' life but rather a collection of anecdotes.

9. *How likely is it that Mark "left out nothing of what he had heard"?* Of all of the components of Papias's statement, this one is perhaps most disputed. Particularly if the Mark who wrote the Gospel is the Mark who is Peter's associate, then for it to be true that Mark left nothing out would mean that Mark was only familiar with about an hour and a half of spoken stories about Jesus; it is unlikely that Mark could have spent any amount of time with Peter and not have learned more. Further, given that some stories about Peter appear in Matthew and Luke but not in Mark, if it is true that Mark left nothing out, it must mean that those stories were never recounted in Mark's hearing and yet were told to others, which also seems unlikely. One scholar reads this statement as referring not to Mark leaving anything out but rather to Peter not leaving out anything that he remembered about Jesus.[33] Again, however, it is difficult to imagine that Peter would only have had an hour and a half of stories to tell about Jesus and that the material about Peter that is in Matthew and Luke but not in Mark was known to someone other than Peter but not Peter himself. It seems safest to conclude that Mark (or Peter) did leave some stories of Jesus out of this account and that perhaps the Presbyter (or Papias or Eusebius) is engaged in a bit of hyperbole here.

10. *What was the purpose of Papias's statement?* Papias's statement seems like a defense of Mark's Gospel ("Mark did nothing wrong" and left nothing out and made no false statements); the precise nature of what Papias was

---

30. Witherington, *Gospel of Mark*, 22–23.
31. Gundry, *Mark*, 1036–37.
32. Bauckham, *Jesus and the Eyewitnesses*, 215.
33. Gundry, *Mark*, 1036.

defending Mark against is not clear, although it seems to be either the criticism that his Gospel is not in the proper order, that he merely had written down what he had remembered (as opposed to providing a complete account or as opposed to writing things down from a written source), or that he had added to Peter's words his own ideas (something that Rev. 22:18–19 suggests was not considered acceptable in the ancient world).[34] Papias seems open to acknowledging some weaknesses in the Gospel, but ultimately finds it reliable and trustworthy.

11. *What other evidence is there that Peter is associated with Mark's Gospel?* The evidence for an association between Mark and Peter is as follows:

   a. Both 1:16 and 16:7 call unusual levels of attention to Peter's name, thus bookending the Gospel with references to Peter, indicating that he was an eyewitness source to the events included in the Gospel.[35]

   b. Simon Peter's name is mentioned far more frequently (relative to overall length) in the Gospel of Mark than in the other Gospels, indicating that Peter is given special prominence in the Gospel.[36]

   c. In addition to Papias's statement associating Peter with Mark's Gospel, Clement in Alexandria and Irenaeus in Gaul also attest to an association between Mark and Peter.[37]

   d. There is also an independent witness to the idea that Mark was the interpreter of Peter, found in the Anti-Marcionite Prologue (c. 160–180 CE). This prologue to the Gospel adds the detail that Mark was stump-fingered, as his fingers were disproportionately short compared to the rest of his body. This tradition is likely to be historically accurate, because no one would have fabricated a story about the author of the Gospel being "stump-fingered" to bolster its credibility!

   e. Despite the fact that more than 90 percent of Mark's text is in Matthew, the second Gospel stayed in the canon. Why keep a copy? One possible reason is that the work was tied to the authority of Peter. (Of course, belief in the link to Peter's authority may be an entirely separate issues from the Gospel actually having had Peter's authority.)

   f. The Gospel contains many passages that are quite critical of Peter,[38] and it may be easier to imagine these stories coming from Peter himself than from any other source.

---

34. Mullins, "Papias on Mark's Gospel," 216–24.

35. Bauckham, *Jesus and the Eyewitnesses,* 124–27.

36. Bauckham, *Jesus and the Eyewitnesses,* 124–26.

37. Oden and Hall, *Mark,* xxv.

38. The disciples do not understand Jesus (8:14–18); Jesus says to Peter, "get thee behind me Satan" (8:33); and after proclaiming his loyalty in 14:29, Peter denies that he knows Jesus (14:66–72).

g. The fact that the other Gospels follow Mark's chronology—when Mark is unlikely to accurately reflect the chronology of Jesus' life—may speak to the authority of Peter behind Mark's text: "Particularly in the case of Matthew, the fact that a gospel either written by or held to be so closely associated with one of the Twelve would follow Mark even when his chronology is not likely to have been accurate is striking."[39]

On the other hand, many scholars doubt any association between Peter and Mark's Gospel. They find the above evidence unsatisfactory: "The truth is that, were it not for Papias, one would never suspect that the Second Gospel was particularly Petrine."[40] They point to the follow evidence:

a. It is hard to understand the absence of the many stories about Peter[41] from Mark's Gospel if Peter were the main information source.

b. What would have been Mark's source for the stories where Peter would not have been an eyewitness?[42] (At the very least, one needs to question the idea that Peter is the sole source for this Gospel.)

c. Had the Gospel of Mark been regarded as the record of the lead apostle, it is difficult to understand why it was neglected throughout Christian history[43] in favor of Matthew's Gospel, which does not claim a special tie to the lead apostles.

d. Mark 7:19 has the narrator summarize Jesus' statement by saying that he has just declared all foods to be clean. It is extremely difficult to explain why Peter needed a visionary experience to teach him that all foods were clean (see Acts 10:9–16[44]) if he were the source for the story in chapter 7.

---

39. See Eric D. Huntsman, "The Petrine *Kērygma* and the Gospel according to Mark," in Judd, Huntsman, and Hopkin, *Ministry of Peter,* 184.

40. Marcus, *Mark 1–8,* 24.

41. Matt. 14:28–31; 16:17–19; 17:24–27; Luke 8:45; 12:41; 22:8, 31; and 24:12–35, as well as the Aramaic form of Peter's name ("Cephas"). One has to wonder how Matthew and Luke knew about these stories but Mark did not, especially if Mark wrote down, as Eusebius indicates, everything that Peter said. Similarly, one might have expected a little more elaboration on the stories that do involve Peter: if this were Peter's recollections, then wouldn't 1:16–18, for example, be a little more developed, perhaps explaining why Peter would have wanted to follow Jesus?

42. Mark 1:1–15 and 14:53–16:8. See also Marcus, *Mark 1–8,* 23.

43. Wire, *Case for Mark Composed in Performance,* 33. The Gospel of Mark was widely thought to be an abbreviated version of Matthew's Gospel and therefore virtually ignored until the nineteenth century, when a closer examination of the Gospels suggested that Mark was written first and that Matthew and Luke used it as a main source. Since that time, attention to Mark's Gospel has expanded exponentially. Francis J. Moloney, *The Gospel of Mark: A Commentary* (Peabody, Mass.: Hendrickson, 2002), 1–2.

44. There are questions about the historical veracity of all details in Acts that should be considered here. Additionally, there is a real possibility that Acts was not well known in the early church.

So the evidence is contradictory and difficult to evaluate. From a Latter-day Saint perspective, the fact that the JST leaves the title as "gospel" and does not change it to "testimony" (as the JST does for Matthew and John) may be evidence for a lack of association with Peter, or at least enough of a lack of association that Mark isn't just a mechanical scribe or translator.

12. *In general, how reliable is Papias's statement about the origins of the Gospel of Mark?* The modern scholarly consensus is that Papias's statement should not be given much weight at all. Representative of this sentiment is Mary Ann Tolbert, who writes that "an anonymous author writing in *koine* Greek to a Greek-speaking, predominantly Gentile audience during the second half of the first century C.E. is about as specific as our knowledge can be concerning the history of the Gospel's production."[45] Joel Marcus adds: "the very vehemence of Papias's insistence upon the connection with Peter creates suspicion."[46] There are also concerns about Eusebius's general level of accuracy: he writes that Papias claimed that Matthew wrote his Gospel in Hebrew, but this is extremely unlikely;[47] this error might call Eusebius's other statements into question. It is worth noting that Papias is in error in other statements that he makes.[48] And it is certainly true that third-hand information (from John the Presbyter—if it was John—to Papias to Eusebius) should receive exceptionally close scrutiny. But there are also solid reasons for trusting the tradition associating Peter with Mark's Gospel, not the least of which is the somewhat defensive tone of the statement: Papias appears to be defending the Gospel of Mark and concluding that it is trustworthy despite its shortcomings. While Papias was familiar with 1 Peter and could therefore have built a theory of a relationship between Peter and Mark from that letter, if someone were going to embellish or even fabricate a history of a Gospel, this is not the story that he would generate. He would have attributed the book to an apostle, not the "interpreter" of an apostle. There is no important early church leader named Mark and therefore no incentive to attribute a Gospel to him. If this Mark is the same person described in the New Testament (more on this below), then he does not have a flawless reputation (Acts 15:38). If the goal were to concoct a pedigree for an anonymous Gospel, Papias would presumably not have criticized the author for writing in the wrong order[49] or have emphasized the fact that he was not an eyewitness. Ironically, the unflattering elements of Markan authorship are an indication of its truthfulness: when people tell tales, they usually tell much prettier ones.

---

45. For example, Tolbert, *Sowing the Gospel*, 36.

46. Marcus, *Mark 1–8*, 22.

47. Some interpreters excuse this by claiming that Papias meant that Matthew wrote not in Hebrew, but in the Semitic style.

48. Ehrman, *Jesus, Interrupted*, 109–10.

49. For a different perspective on Papias's statement—that he was exonerating and not accusing Mark—see Witherington, *Gospel of Mark*, 23.

At this point, it might be helpful to revisit the list above concerning the information from internal evidence about the author of the Gospel while thinking about a possible role for Peter as the source for (some of) Mark's information. The numerous Latinisms and the use of Aramaic are easy to understand as Mark's (Latin) and Peter's (Aramaic) contribution to the Gospel. The apparent errors in geographical descriptions and the depiction of Jewish customs are perhaps more difficult to understand if Peter is Mark's source. Neither the system of timekeeping nor the style of the Greek is likely to be affected by thinking of Peter as Mark's source.

Since the association of Peter with Mark's Gospel is only as strong as one's assessment of Papias's statement, an examination of the evidence from the New Testament about Mark and his relationship to Peter is in order. As mentioned above, "Mark" was one of the most common male names in the Roman empire, so one cannot be sure that every reference to Mark in the NT is a reference to the same person. (Although some scholars think it is likely—but still not certain—that all of the references are to one person.[50]) With those caveats, here is what the NT references to Mark might suggest about the author of the Gospel:

1. Acts 12:12 records that Peter "came to the house of Mary the mother of John, whose surname was Mark; where many were gathered together praying," and Acts 12:25 describes John Mark serving as a missionary with Barnabas and Paul. This Mark was called "John Mark"; it was fairly common at this time for Jews to have a Hebrew name (John, as it comes into English, or Yohanan in Hebrew) and a Roman name (Mark). It is possible that the reference to his surname served to distinguish him from other Marks who were known to the audience. He lived in Jerusalem and his mother was named Mary. A home used for church gatherings would have been large, indicating their wealth, which makes it more likely that John Mark would have been literate, a characteristic he would have shared with only a tiny fraction of the population.[51] This evidence links Peter and John Mark. Since few Romans would have known Aramaic, the presence of Aramaic in Mark lends support to the idea of the author being John Mark, since he had a home in Jerusalem. On the other hand, John Mark is a Jew, but several passages in the Gospel of Mark suggest a lack of familiarity with Jewish customs, so that might indicate that this is not a reference to the author of the second Gospel.[52] Overall, the evidence

---

50. Marcus, *Mark 1–8*, 18.

51. Literacy rates were probably between 2 percent and 10 percent. Horsley, *Hearing the Whole*, 53–55.

52. Pierson Parker, "The Authorship of the Second Gospel," *Perspectives in Religious Studies* 5, no. 1 (1978): 6.

from this passage is mixed, but much of it is congruent with the picture of the author of Mark's Gospel.

2. 2 Timothy 4:11 reads: "Only Luke is with me. Take Mark, and bring him with thee: for he is profitable to me for the ministry." The author of the letter (traditionally presumed to be Paul, but most modern interpreters dispute this) felt that Mark would be "profitable." This passage does not call Mark "John Mark," which may imply that this is not the same Mark who is mentioned in Acts.

3. Acts 15:36–39 describes a falling out between Paul and Barnabas over John Mark. Paul did not want to take John Mark on the missionary tour that he was proposing because John Mark had abandoned him in the middle of a previous tour (see Acts 13:13). While this is certainly not a flattering portrait of John Mark, its inclusion in the record actually serves as support for Mark's authorship of the Gospel since it is unlikely that an early Christian writer would have forged a connection between an absconding missionary and a Gospel.[53] On the other hand, if Mark's personal history included the abandonment of missionary service, then the theme of discipleship (especially failures of discipleship), a theme generally recognized as one of the key concerns in Mark's Gospel, becomes particularly personal and poignant.

4. In 1 Peter 5:13, Peter[54] refers to "Marcus my son." Most scholars take the reference to "son" as an honorific, but it certainly suggests the kind of close association that would have made Mark an excellent recorder of Peter's memories. "Marcus" is not called "John" here.

5. While it does not mention Mark, Romans 16:13 may be informative. If the "Rufus" of Romans 16:13 is the same Rufus mentioned in Mark 15:21— where the verse makes it sound as if he were known to the first audience of the Gospel—then it strengthens the connection that most scholars find between the Gospel and a Roman setting.

Again, there is no way to know if these references are to the author of the second Gospel and/or if they all refer to the same person. Some scholars do not think that "Mark" and "John Mark" are the same person; rather, the entire point of calling one of them "John Mark" would have been to distinguish him from the other Mark(s).[55] The evidence concerning (John) Mark from Acts and the epistles suggests an association between Mark and Peter.

---

53. Depending on how the materials are dated and whether they refer to the same person, it is possible that Philem. 24 and Col. 4:10 indicate that the rift between Mark and Paul was later mended.

54. This reference is complicated by the fact that it is unlikely that Peter himself wrote 1 Peter. See Collins, *Mark,* 4.

55. Guelich, *Mark 1–8:26,* xxviii. He reviews the evidence but ultimately rejects this theory.

It implies that Mark had a besmirched reputation in the Church and did not hold any sort of high office and therefore would not have been anyone's first choice when developing a story about Gospel authorship. So while these passages do not prove that Peter was Mark's source, they do not contradict that theory either, and to some extent they support the association of the Gospel with Mark and with Peter.

To What Extent Did Mark Shape the Gospel?

One might wonder to what extent the writer simply transmitted the traditions about Jesus that were received (from Peter or from others) or, on the other hand, actively reshaped them. As Joel Marcus phrased the question, was Mark a "conservative redactor [editor] or creative theologian?"[56] There is no definitive answer to this question, but given the highly literary quality of the Gospel, it seems likely that Mark (or someone before Mark) carefully shaped the source material in order to carefully convey the good news of Jesus Christ. This is not to suggest that Mark invented material but rather that Mark shaped the materials to emphasize what was important. Two examples will suffice, one that shows a shaping hand and another that shows restraint. Mark 6:56 relates that, wherever Jesus went, people "besought him that they might touch if it were but the border of his garment: and as many as touched him were made whole." But that is all the audience learns about these countless people. Contrast 5:25–34, which provides, in great detail, the story of one such person who touched Jesus and was made whole. Mark told this story in detail, despite apparently knowing of many similar ones, because this particular healing allowed Mark to explore several other themes as well (including the house of Israel, gender roles, and discipleship), particularly as Mark "sandwiches" this story with the raising of Jairus's daughter. So there is a creative hand in the structure of the Gospel.

But Mark also exhibits some restraint: in 1:24, a demon calls Jesus "the Holy One of God," a title that is not otherwise used in the Gospel. Had Mark been concocting this story, the temptation would have been to substitute one of the usual titles for Jesus, such as "Son of God."[57] Had Mark felt

---

56. Marcus, *Mark 1–8*, 59.
57. Marcus, *Mark 1–8*, 60.

free to tinker with the source material, Mark may have changed "the Holy One of God" to a more familiar title. The fact that Mark does not becomes evidence of respect for the source material. Similarly, in Mark's chronology, Jesus is not raised "on the third day," but slightly before; the fact that Mark records Jesus' prophecies that he would be raised on the third day suggests Mark's unwillingness to alter the sources used (see the Notes on 8:31).

These examples are open to other interpretations, but they can be read to suggest that Mark exercised some control in the selection and arrangement of stories in the Gospel but did not entirely fabricate them.

Was the Gospel of Mark Originally a Written Text or an Oral Performance?

In recent years, many scholars have advanced the idea that Mark is closely tied to oral traditions about Jesus and that the Gospel may have existed as an oral performance before it was written down. It does contain many characteristics of oral performances.[58] If this Gospel began as an oral composition, then Mark may have written it down but had only a minimal hand in its creation. Mark's role would be akin to that of a modern court reporter. As one scholar described it, "Mark was building on, refining, and developing an oral tradition that had already created a continuous, more-or-less coherent narrative."[59] Perhaps the greatest challenge to the idea of Markan authorship is not the traditional doubts about whether the author was actually named Mark or whether Mark worked with Peter, but the growing consensus that Mark's Gospel was primarily an oral story, one refined, shaped, and delivered by a variety of anonymous performers, and Mark was simply the one who committed the story to written form.

Using traditional theories of authorship, it has been difficult to explain why Mark was included in the canon. After all, if Mark was (as it was thought previously) simply an abbreviation of Matthew, what is the point of including it in the NT? But if Mark existed primarily as an oral performance, then its inclusion in the canon is easy to understand: Mark was simply too popular to ignore; a collection of Gospels without Mark would not have been seen as legitimate any more than a modern collection of great plays that did not include *Hamlet* could be taken as definitive. Further evidence for the primarily oral nature of Mark stems from the fact that

---

58. Wire, *Case for Mark Composed in Performance.*

59. Joanna Dewey, "The Survival of Mark's Gospel: A Good Story?" *Journal of Biblical Literature* 123, no. 3 (2004): 503.

it has more textual variants than the other Gospels and has fewer ancient manuscripts.[60]

It is likely the case that Mark's (written) Gospel is much like one of Shakespeare's plays: the intention was for the audience to experience the story in a live, oral performance, and the written text is a tool intended to help the performer. It was not the intention of the writer that the audience would use the written text; the primary state of the story is the oral performance. It is useful for the modern reader of Mark to be aware of this dynamic as it can impact interpretation. (It is beneficial to experience Mark's Gospel as an oral performance; many are available online.)

One important implication of thinking about the Gospel of Mark as primarily an oral performance is that it opens up the possibility that women were some of the early tellers of Mark's story. In a world with near-total female illiteracy, it is highly unlikely that women would have had a role in the promulgation of written texts. But it is likely that women were storytellers. In the case of the Gospel of Mark, it is highly likely that women were involved in telling and listening to the stories; it is difficult to imagine, for example, that an all-male storyteller and audience would have found much personal resonance in the story of the woman with the menstrual hemorrhage (see 5:25–34).

WHEN WAS THE GOSPEL WRITTEN?

The Gospel does not contain any specific dates for its contents or writing (contrast Ezek. 1:2). It is possible that Mark was written in stages (either because Mark wrote the Gospel over a number of years or because Mark incorporated passages that were written by someone else at an earlier time, or both). Most scholars concur that the Gospel of Mark was written in the late 60s. Generally, efforts to date Mark rely heavily on the interpretation of chapter 13 (which contains predictions of travails that will come in the future) in light of then-current events in order to date the entire text. Most scholars think that one of two events might have been the special focus of the Gospel and therefore help date Mark:

1. In 64 CE, Christians were persecuted by Nero when he attempted to blame them for a fire that leveled Rome. In this context, the Gospel of Mark is seen

---

60. Dewey, "Survival of Mark's Gospel," 505.

as an aid to understanding the role of suffering and martyrdom in Christian life, with not only chapter 13 but also passages such as 8:34 (where the disciples' suffering is prophesied) and 4:17–19 (where the betrayal of close friends is prophesied) taking on deeper meaning. If the author is John Mark, then according to 1 Peter 5:13, he would have been in Rome at the time Christians were being blamed for the fire and, presumably, would have personally known some of those who were tortured and killed. But other scholars note that persecution was present at many times in early Christianity, including, obviously, in the life of Jesus himself, which means that Mark may not have been specifically written as a response to the persecution in Rome. Note that "Christians would have been even more vulnerable in Rome in the late 60s because Nero appears to have been the first Roman ruler to actually distinguish Jews from Christians when he singled them out and blamed them for the fire.[61] Christians were no longer associated with a religion of long standing which at least officially was not prohibited or banned by Roman law."[62]

2. The second event to which chapter 13 is linked is the Jewish War of 66–73 CE, which included the destruction of the temple. Scholars point to several ties between the Gospel and the setting of the Jewish War; for example, the reference to "thieves" in 11:17 uses a Greek word that is also used by Josephus to describe the would-be Jewish revolutionaries who encouraged conflict with Rome, so "if Mark understands the term similarly, then the Markan Jesus' reproach exactly fits what happened early in the Jewish revolt: in the winter of 67–68 C.E. a group of revolutionary 'brigands' or Zealots moved into Jerusalem under the leadership of Eleazar son of Simon and set up their headquarters in the inner Temple itself, remaining there until the fall of the city in 70 C.E."[63] In this reading, the leaders of the attempted revolution are the "abomination of desolation" (13:14) in the temple. So perhaps Mark was composed at the time of the Jewish War near Palestine, perhaps in Syria, then a Roman province and a mostly gentile area. As one scholar describes the situation: "Most scholars have concluded that [chapter 13] reflects some knowledge or even experience of the first Jewish war with Rome."[64]

The dating of Mark may relate to the location of its writing and first audience: if the Gospel was written in response to the fire in Rome in the mid-60s, then it probably has a Roman setting; if it was written in response to the Jewish War in the later 60s, then it may have a Syrian setting. Unfortunately, neither date is without problems.

---

61. Tacitus, *Annales* 15.44.2–8.
62. Witherington, *Gospel of Mark,* 34.
63. Marcus, *Mark 1–8,* 35.
64. Collins, *Mark,* 11.

One issue for Latter-day Saint readers is that both scenarios tend to assume that chapter 13 contains not Jesus' prophecies but rather ex post facto prophecies (written by Mark and attributed to Jesus) that are applicable to then-current events. But even bracketing this concern, dating Mark on the basis of the content of chapter 13 requires certain interpretive moves that may not be warranted; chapter 13 is notoriously difficult to interpret with any precision. At the least, if the data can be said to fit both the context of the mid-60s and the late-60s, then it must be admitted that the data cannot determine the date. The prophecies in chapter 13 are general enough that they can be applied to a wide variety of situations, making their use in dating the Gospel tenuous at best. Also, one would think that if this were a description of the destruction of Jerusalem, the author would have mentioned the fire in Jerusalem as well. As one scholar described it, "the use of Mark 13 to date Mark is highly questionable."[65]

On the other hand, one specific item in chapter 13 may point to a date for the Gospel. In 13:2, Jesus prophesies that there will not be one stone of the temple left upon another after the temple is destroyed. The temple *was* destroyed in 70 CE, but some of the stones remain stacked to this day.[66] Given that the prophecy was not literally fulfilled, it is likely that the Gospel would have been written before the temple was destroyed, or the author would not have portrayed Jesus as making what could appear to be a false prophecy. While this viewpoint is widespread, it assumes that a very literal interpretation of Jesus' words was intended, which may not have been the case.

One other data point sometimes used to date Mark's Gospel is the death of Peter, which was probably related to Nero's persecution in 64 CE. Unfortunately, the ancient sources vary as to whether Mark was written before or after Peter died; most ancient sources have Mark write the Gospel after the death of Peter, although others disagree. If Mark wrote near or after the end of Peter's life, then the Gospel was not written before the mid 60s.

One can also attempt to date Mark based on its textual history. If Mark was a written source used by Matthew and Luke, which is almost certainly the case, then it must also predate those Gospels. There are not indisputable dates for Matthew or Luke either, but their Gospels are normally dated to the late 70s or 80s. Additionally, Mark was included in a harmony of the

---

65. Stein, *Mark*, 15.

66. Josephus, *Wars of the Jews* 7.1.1. These "stacked stones" are now called the Western Wall.

four Gospels that dates to about 175 CE, and the oldest fragments of the Gospel of Mark are dated to the first half of the third century. On the basis of these dates, Mark must date before, say, 75 CE, but we cannot get more specific than that.

One significant factor on the issue of the date of Mark is that the date in question is more about *compilation* than *creation,* as it is highly unlikely that Mark was written without reference to previously extant sources that, obviously, would predate it. These sources likely included oral stories as well as written sources. One of the more likely candidates for a source that would predate Mark would be the material behind chapters 14–16, the story of Jesus' death and Resurrection.

Unfortunately, this leaves very little to go on when trying to establish when the Gospel was written. Fortunately, the answer to this question is not crucial to the interpretation of the text.

WHO WAS MARK'S AUDIENCE?

In the twentieth century, it was generally assumed that each Gospel was written for a geographically distinct audience. But this idea has less favor than it once did.[67] The oral nature, particularly of Mark, suggests that the Gospels would have circulated widely as their storytellers traveled. If the Gospel had been meant for one specific geographical area only, it is less likely that it would have been written down, given the very high rates of illiteracy. In an oral context, it is likely that the audience is not homogenous: it probably contained many poor people, but also a few wealthy ones, and it likely contained Jews and Gentiles. In short, very little can be said with certainty about the composition of Mark's audience.

CONCLUSIONS

Because the Gospel does not reveal its author, date, or location, one has to assess indirect and external evidence—all of which is illuminating, none of which is conclusive. There is some evidence, certainly not irrefutable, that

---

67. Collins, *Mark,* 96–100.

"Mark" was the author. It may be the case that Peter was a major source of information, but this seems to be unlikely. Papias's statement raises as many questions as it settles: there is no way to determine with certainty whether this tradition is accurate, in whole or in part. Perhaps the best evidence for the traditional reading of the second Gospel as being written by Mark and relying on Peter's memories is the absence of any counter-tradition—no other contenders for authorship or source as there presumably would have been had later writers fabricated a background for an originally anonymous Gospel.[68]

James Talmage, then a member of the Quorum of the Twelve, approvingly quotes from Austin Farrer's *Life of Christ* the idea that Jesus was born in a cave as being "one of the few [traditions], though unrecorded in the Gospel history, [to which] we may attach a reasonable probability."[69] While it is difficult to know how much weight Elder Talmage gave to Farrer's position, the claim itself is nonetheless helpful to the extent that it emphasizes the difference between the data in the scriptures themselves and the data from other sources. In the case of the authorship of Mark, if limited to the canonical data, one would not conclude that the author of this Gospel was John Mark or that Peter was a major source of information. If one is willing to accept data from outside of the canon, then it is possible—but definitely not certain—that Mark was a close associate of Peter. Taken at face value, this might imply that one should give very little weight to Papias's statement. On the other hand, Latter-day Saints have generally been comfortable with the traditional attributions of authorship. (No Restoration scripture specifically mentions the Gospel of Mark as a text [contrast 1 Ne. 14:19–30; 2 Ne. 25:1; D&C 113].) And, as discussed above, if Papias had been fabricating a story, it is very unlikely that this is the one he would have told.

If the standard is "beyond all reasonable doubt," then one would not feel comfortable concluding that John Mark is the author of the Gospel and that Peter was his main source. However, if the standard is "a preponderance of the evidence," then John Mark is likely to have been the author (at

---

68. The contrast with the Letter to the Hebrews may be instructive here: since antiquity, it has been recognized that there are enormous problems with attributing the letter to Paul, and thus no fewer than a half dozen possible authors have been postulated. See Luke Timothy Johnson, *Hebrews: A Commentary* (Louisville, Ky.: Westminster John Knox Press, 2006), 41.

69. James E. Talmage, *Jesus the Christ* (Salt Lake City: The Church of Jesus Christ of Latter-day Saints, 1981), 100.

least in the sense of writing down the storytellers' stories), and it is possible that Peter was his source.

Fortunately, the stakes here are not enormous:[70] for Latter-day Saints, "Who wrote this text?" and "Was this text inspired?" are two independent questions. As President J. Reuben Clark explained:

> I am not really concerned, and no man of faith should be, about the exact authorship of the books of the Bible. More than one Prophet may well have written parts of books now collected under one heading. I do not know. There may have been 'ghost writers' in those days, as now. The Lord gave Aaron to Moses in an equivalent capacity, and spoke to Israel through Moses by the mouth of Aaron. He may have done the same in other cases. If so, what of it?[71]

Given that the author does not claim to be an eyewitness, his or her identity is perhaps less important than it would otherwise be since one is not relying on the author's personal witness in any case. (Further, passages like 9:6—which show the benefits of later thought and knowledge—raise question about the benefits of eyewitness testimony as the benchmark for accuracy in the first place.) When it comes to authorship and date, perhaps the real reason to be concerned with these issues is their link to the reliability and accuracy of the Gospel text. That Mark includes "embarrassing" details speaks to the text's reliability; the fact that Matthew and Luke often tone down or eliminate these details[72] is telling.[73] The presence of these unflattering elements becomes a kind of testimony to the trustworthiness of the text and can therefore compensate to some extent for the unanswerable questions concerning authorship and date. The identity of the author (and the sources) has a minimal impact on the far more important question of how one interprets the text itself. In the thicket of these concerns about the origin of the Gospel, it is easy to lose sight of what one can know, beyond a doubt, about this author: Mark is a Christian who believes in Jesus Christ and wants to persuade the audience to do the same.[74]

---

70. Huntsman, "Petrine Kērygma," 174–75.

71. J. Reuben Clark, *On the Way to Immortality and Eternal Life* (Salt Lake City: Deseret Book, 1950), 210.

72. Compare 10:35–37 with Matt. 20:20–23; 14:33 is omitted by Luke and tamed in Matt. 26:37.

73. Cranfield, *Gospel according to St Mark,* 15.

74. Witherington, *Gospel of Mark,* 20.

Appendix B: Style

Although not always apparent in the English translation or to the casual reader, many features of Mark's writing style are not as common in (or are completely absent from) the other Gospels. Many of these features show more affinity to the spoken word than the written word, perhaps indicating that Mark's Gospel was primarily an oral composition. The distinctive aspects of Mark's writing style include:

1. Mark uses Aramaic words and phrases[1] with disproportionate frequency relative to the length of the Gospel.[2] Scholars debate why Mark included the Aramaic words in the Gospel; since Jesus spoke in Aramaic, everything

---

1. Mark 3:17 ("Boanerges, which is, The sons of thunder"; omitted in Matt. 10:2 and Luke 6:14); 5:41 ("Talitha cumi; which is, being interpreted, Damsel, I say unto thee, arise"; omitted in Matt. 9:25 and Luke 8:54); 7:11 ("Corban, that is to say, a gift"; omitted in Matt. 15:5 and no similar story in Luke); 7:34 ("Ephphatha, that is, Be opened"; omitted in Matt. 15:29–31 and no similar story in Luke); 9:5 ("rabbi," KJV: "master"; Matt. 17:4 uses "Lord" instead, and Luke 9:33 uses "master" [Greek: *epistatēs*] instead); 9:43 ("hell, into the fire that never shall be quenched"; omitted in Matt. 18:9 and Luke 17:2); 10:46 ("Bartimaeus, the son of Timaeus"; omitted in Matt. 20:30 and Luke 18:35); 10:51 ("rabbouni," KJV: "Lord"; Matt. 20:33 and Luke 18:41 use "Lord" [Greek: *kurios*] instead); 11:9–10 ("hosanna"; Matt. 21:9 keeps the usage, but it is omitted in Luke 19:38); 11:21 ("rabbi," KJV: "Master"; Matt. 21:20 omits it and no similar story in Luke); 14:36 ("Abba, Father"; Matt. 26:39, 42; and Luke 22:42 omit it); 14:45 ("rabbi," KJV: "master"; Matt. 26:49 uses it, and Luke 22:47 omits it); 15:22 ("Golgotha, which is, being interpreted, The place of a skull"; Matt. 27:33 uses it, and Luke 23:33 omits it); 15:34 ("Eloi, Eloi, lama sabachthani? which is, being interpreted, My God, my God, why hast thou forsaken me?"; Matt. 27:46 uses it while Luke 23:45–46 omits it). The overall pattern is clear: Mark is far more likely to use Aramaic; only rarely will Matthew retain the Aramaic and Luke will almost always omit it.

2. Also as discussed in appendix A: "Authorship and Date," there are many Latinisms in Mark's Gospel, including a few that are unique to Mark. These do not appear to be a

he said could have been presented in this Gospel in Aramaic. So why were these particular words and phrases included untranslated? Notice that some of the Aramaic words are in the context of healing (for example, 5:41; 7:34), perhaps Mark felt it was important to include the actual wording because these had ritual or historical significance. It has also been suggested that the Aramaic phrases represent the (only) times where Jesus' actual words (as opposed to a paraphrase) are preserved in the account, but there is no way to verify this.

2. While the Gospel of Mark is substantially shorter than the other three Gospels,[3] the tendency in Mark is for an individual story to be longer than Matthew, Luke, or John's account of the same event. For example, Matthew and Mark both contain stories of a woman who comes to anoint Jesus at a dinner, but Mark's account has significantly more detail.[4] Similarly, Mark tells the story of the hemorrhaging woman in 153 Greek words while Matthew uses only 48 words and Luke 110 words (5:25–34; Matt. 9:20–22; Luke 8:43–48). The story of a man healed from a demon takes 20 verses for Mark to relate; Matthew tells the story in a mere 7 verses, and the details that Matthew omits scrub the story of its political implications, which are front and center in Mark (5:1–20; Matt. 8:28–34).[5] The details in Mark's stories would have added vividness and drama and perhaps accounted for some of its popularity as an oral narrative. Since Mark not only includes more detail but also has a shorter text length, this means that Mark tells substantially fewer stories than the other Gospels.

---

significant literary part of Mark's writing style, however, but more related to the fact that the audience was likely to be Latin-speaking.

3. Mark has sixteen chapters to Matthew's twenty-eight, Luke's twenty-four, and John's twenty-one.

4. Matthew omits the following details when compared with Mark's account: the ointment was spikenard (14:3; contrast Matt. 26:7), the woman broke the box (14:3; contrast Matt. 26:7), the cost for which the anointing oil could have been sold (14:5; contrast Matt. 26:9), the murmuring against the woman (14:5; contrast Matt. 26:8), Jesus' statement to leave the woman alone (14:6; contrast Matt. 26:10), Jesus' statement that they can help the poor at any time (14:7; contrast Matt. 26:11), and Jesus' statement that the woman did what she could (14:8; contrast Matt. 26:12). Matthew adds this phrase: "For in that she hath poured this ointment on my body" (Matt. 26:12), presumably so the sense of Jesus' comment won't be lost. Luke also has a story of a woman who anoints Jesus, although it is debatable whether it is based on the same historical incident that gave rise to Matt. 26 and Mark 14. In this case, Luke's account of the anointing is longer because Jesus tells a parable in the story, but this expansion is an exception to the general rule that Matthew and Luke will normally tell the same story as Mark in a shorter form.

5. Interestingly, in this case, Luke's account is roughly the same length as Mark's (see Luke 8:26–39).

3. Mark's Gospel consists of episodes connected only loosely. (The technical term for this is parataxis.) About two-thirds of the verses[6] in Mark begin with the word "and." This is not a writing style that wins kudos from those who appreciate sophisticated literary creations, but it is a characteristic of oral narratives. The simple presentation may also be an appropriate manner in which to tell the story of a Son of God who chose to live an unadorned human life.

4. One of the most distinctive characteristics of Mark's Gospel is the frequent use of the word *euthys* ("immediately").[7] This word is used 41 times in the Gospel, or, on average, more than twice per chapter (although it is concentrated at the beginning of the gospel, with ten occurrences in the first chapter). It creates a sense of a rapidly rushing narrative.

5. Mark features many instances of triple repetition, sometimes in an intensifying sequence.[8] This may serve a theological purpose, especially since the number three was a symbol for God. It may also be a sign of an oral composition: groups of three are common to oral materials because they are easier to memorize and are pleasing to the ear.

---

6. Verse numbers were added in the sixteenth century and so are not original to the Gospel; they are used here for convenience.

7. *Eutheos* or *euthys* ("immediately") in Mark's Gospel: 1:10 (KJV: "straightway"), 12, 18 (KJV: "straightway"), 20 (KJV: "straightway"), 21 (KJV: "straightway"), 23 (not translated in the KJV), 28, 29 (KJV: "forthwith"), 30 (KJV: "anon"), 42, 43 (KJV: "forthwith"); 2:8, 12; 3:6 (KJV: "straightway"); 4:5, 15, 16, 17, 29; 5:2, 29 (KJV: "straightway"), 30, 42 (KJV: "straightway"); 6:25 (KJV: "straightway"), 27, 45 (KJV: "straightway"), 50, 54 ("straightway"); 7:25 (not translated in the KJV), 35 (KJV: "straightway"; note that there is a textual variant that omits the word here); 8:10 (KJV: "straightway"); 9:15 (KJV: "straightway"), 20 (KJV: "straightway"), 24 (KJV: "straightway"); 10:52; 11:2 (KJV: "as soon as"), 3 (KJV: "straightway"); 14:43, 45 (KJV: "as soon as"), 72 (not translated in the KJV); and 15:1.

8. The threefold pattern is found in the responses to Jesus' baptism (opening heavens, descending Spirit, hearing a voice; 1:10–11), the calling of the disciples (fishermen, Levi, the Twelve; 1:16–20; 2:14; 3:13–19), Jesus' prophecies of his suffering and death (which contains three elements that are repeated three times; 8:31; 9:31; 10:33–34), Jesus' warnings ("if your hand/foot/eye offend thee . . ."; 9:43, 45, 47), Jesus' return to the disciples in Gethsemane (14:32–41), Peter denies Jesus (14:66–72), time mentioned during the crucifixion (15:25, 33- 34), groups mocking Jesus on the cross (passersby, chief priests and scribes, and the others being crucified; 15:29–32), reactions to Jesus' death (the veil of the temple, the centurion, and the women; 15:38–40). The pattern is also found in the grouping of disciples (Peter, James, and John; 5:37; 9:2; 14:33), the adversaries to Jesus (chief priests, scribes, and elders; 8:31; 11:27; 14:43, 53; 15:1), the women at the cross and tomb (Mary Magdalene and other women; 15:40; 16:1), and the references to three days (8:2, 31, 14:58; 15:29).

6. Mark has a tendency to organize the Gospel by the type of material (miracles, controversies, parables),[9] not by theme (faith, patience, repentance) or chronologically. It is important for the reader to realize that the material is thus organized (see the outline in the introduction).

7. Mark frequently uses foreshadowing, mentioning to the audience something that will not be more fully revealed until later in the narrative.[10] Mark also foreshadows events that will not happen in the Gospel text but at a future point in history.[11] The fact that foreshadowed events are fulfilled within the text cultivates the trust of the audience, who then assumes that the events foreshadowed beyond the text will actually come to pass.

8. Mark frequently "sandwiches" a story in between two other sections of text with the goal of encouraging the audience to understand the center story in light of its surrounding material.[12] Recognition of this pattern is very important to understanding the purpose and point of the stories that Mark tells. The reader who is aware of this pattern will gain far more from her study of Mark's Gospel, as the "meat" of the sandwich is typically explained in more

---

9. Mark places together miracles (1:21–45; 4:35–5:43), controversies (2:1–3:6; 11:27–12:44), parables (4:1–34), prophecies of Jesus' suffering and death (three within a narrow section of text: 8:31–10:34), and teachings about the last days/persecution (13:1–37).

10. Examples of foreshadowing in Mark's Gospel include the coming of someone mightier than John the Baptist (mentioned in 1:7; fulfilled in 1:21–28), the arrest of John the Baptist (mentioned in 1:14; fulfilled in 6:14–27), taking away of the "bridegroom" (mentioned in 2:20; fulfilled in 14:43–46), the plot to destroy Jesus (mentioned in 3:6; fulfilled in 15:37), Jesus prophesies of his suffering and death (8:31, 9:31, and 10:32–33; fulfilled in 14:43–46), Jesus tells the disciples to find a man with a pitcher of water (14:13; fulfilled in 14:16), Jesus prophesies that he will be betrayed by a close associate (14:18; fulfilled in 14:43), Jesus prophesies Peter's denial (14:30; fulfilled in 14:66–72).

11. Prophecies that will be fulfilled after the end of the text include: Jesus baptizing with the Holy Spirit (1:8), the deaths of James and John (10:38–39), the destruction of the Temple (13:2), the story of the anointing told all over the world (14:9), Jesus will drink of the fruit of the vine in the kingdom (14:25), and Jesus will meet the disciples after the Resurrection (16:7).

12. Examples of "sandwiched" stories in Mark's Gospel include the discussion of Jesus' authority to forgive sins (2:6–10) surrounded by the story of a lame man whose sins he forgives (2:1–5, 11–12), a controversy about Satan (3:22–30) surrounded by references to Jesus' family (3:20–21, 31–35), a question about why Jesus taught in parables (4:10–12) surrounded by the parable of the sower (4:3–9, 13–20), the healing of the hemorrhaging woman (5:25–34) surrounded by the story of Jairus's daughter (5:21–24, 35–43), the death of John the Baptist (6:14–29) surrounded by the mission of the Twelve (6:7–13, 30–31), the Transfiguration (9:2–8) surrounded by references to who/what is coming (9:1, 9–13), casting the moneychangers out of the temple (11:15–19) surrounded by references to the fig tree (11:12–14, 20–26), Jesus' anointing (14:3–9) surrounded by references to the plot to kill him (14:1–2, 10–11), and Jesus' trial (14:55–65) surrounded by references to Peter (14:54, 66–72).

detail by way of comparison with the "bread." This pattern may also have made it easier to remember the story as it was being transmitted orally.

9. Mark's Gospel includes a lot of questions.[13] These are rarely straightforward requests for information but usually an indication of controversy; Jesus and his opponents frequently ask questions that spark debate and discussion.[14] The questions engage the audience of the Gospel as they ponder the questions themselves. The questions also provide teaching opportunities for Jesus. Many of these questions, intended to entrap Jesus, end up "showcas[ing] the wisdom and cleverness of Jesus."[15] It is easy to imagine how these questions would have captured the attention of an audience listening to the Gospel orally.

10. Mark frequently uses the historical present tense, which means recounting events that happened in the past using the present tense. As one scholar writes, Mark "is especially fond of using the present tense to relay past happenings. Mark employs this 'historical present' over 150 times when other writers would have used the simple past tense."[16] This might have been particularly appropriate in oral story telling; it certainly creates a sense for the reader of being right in the middle of the action. Matthew and Luke will frequently change these verbs to the past tense.

11. The quality of Mark's Greek is very poor: "Mark [writes] in an extremely plain, abrupt, often unidiomatic and dogged Koine [Greek] which has generally been made to seem falsely natural, even eloquent, in English translations."[17] To create the appropriate effect in an English translation, it would need to include actual grammatical errors. Other interpreters have understood Mark's poor Greek as intentionally simple in a way that "serve[s] to make Jesus the contemporary of those who hear or read the account."[18] In either case, it is good for the reader to remember that she is not reading a polished literary text (compare Luke's Gospel, where that description does fit).

12. Mark is also known for the use of irony, which often exists on multiple levels. For example, Jesus heals a leper and tells the leper not to tell anyone (1:44–45). In the first bit of irony, the leper disobeys the one who has healed him. In the next layer, Jesus himself has to act like a leper and live in the wilderness in order to escape the crowds. In the final layer of irony, Jesus' efforts to

---

13. Jerome H. Neyrey, "Questions, *Chreiai,* and Challenges to Honor: The Interface of Rhetoric and Culture in Mark's Gospel," *Catholic Biblical Quarterly* 60, no. 4 (1998): 657–81.

14. Mark 2:7–9, 16, 18–19, 24–26; 3:4, 23, 33; 4:38, 40–41; 5:39; 6:2–3, 38; 7:5, 18–19; 8:4–5, 12, 17–21, 27–29, 36–37; 9:11, 19, 33; 10:2, 17, 26, 38, 51; 11:3, 17, 28, 31; 12:9, 14–16, 23–24, 26, 28, 35; 13:2, 4; 14:4, 6, 14, 19, 37, 48, 60, 63–64; 15:2, 9, 12, 34; 16:3.

15. Neyrey, "Questions," 657-681.

16. Lane, *Gospel according to Mark,* 26.

17. Reynolds Price, *Three Gospels* (New York: Touchstone, 1997), 17.

18. Lane, *Gospel according to Mark,* 26.

escape the crowds fail, and they come to him in the desert. Irony plays into other themes that Mark develops, such as discipleship: while the Twelve repeatedly struggle to understand Jesus' identity and teachings, despite his repeated efforts to teach them, the literally blind Bartimaeus is able to identify Jesus (10:47). In another example, the same Pharisees who watch Jesus closely so they can accuse him of Sabbath-breaking for healing someone on the Sabbath will then, ironically, begin on the Sabbath to plot Jesus' death (3:6). The touch of the hemorrhaging woman, which, under the law of Moses, should have rendered Jesus ritually unclean, instead renders the woman healed (5:34). In 6:29, the disciples of John the Baptist come forward to claim his corpse and bury him; later, it is Joseph of Arimathea (15:43)—not one of Jesus' chosen inner circle of disciples—who will request and bury his body; Jesus' closest male disciples have fled (although the women will look on from afar). The irony in Mark's Gospel reaches its climax with the death of Jesus, where Jesus is mocked with symbols of kingship (15:1–39); the reader understands that Jesus is the true king, making the mockery ironic. Irony is an appropriate literary device for a Gospel that teaches that you save your life by losing it (8:35) and that the Christ must suffer and die. It also would have created an affinity between writer and audience, because the audience, by recognizing the irony, attains the "insider" status that allows them to see themselves as part of Jesus' inner circle of disciples and followers.

13. This Gospel is very much focused on deeds; Jesus does not say much. There is no Sermon on the Mount (see Matt. 5–7) or Farewell Discourse (see John 14–17). This may also be an indicator of an oral narrative. It creates a picture of Jesus as active and dynamic.

As the above evidence suggests, it seems likely that Mark's Gospel was originally more closely tied to oral presentation rather than written composition. Perhaps this is because it was originally Peter's memoirs, perhaps because Mark designed it to meet the needs of an almost entirely illiterate group of Christians, or perhaps for some other reason. Regardless, it seems to bear the marks of a text that was transmitted orally. The normal method for the audience to experience this Gospel would have been for them to have listened to it being read out loud, most likely in one sitting.[19] Awareness of Mark's likely history as an oral composition can nuance how some parts of the text are interpreted. For example, references to "to hear" (4:9, 12, 23) would have been understood the way references to "to see" are in a literate, visually focused culture; in both cases, they are metaphors for "to

---

19. It takes between an hour and a half and two hours to listen to Mark's Gospel read aloud.

understand."[20] In an oral text, keywords and repetition are generally appreciated more than they are in written texts, which are generally not read in one sitting or with the same awareness of this sort of detail.

Mark's history as an oral composition may explain why it was included in the NT. Joanna Dewey argues that the reason Mark survived is that it worked so well for oral performance and was popular and therefore spread. In fact, it is likely that even after a written copy of the Gospel of Mark existed, oral performances independent of the written text persisted: "Even after it was committed to writing around 70 C.E., it continued to be performed orally, with minimal dependence on or even connection to manuscripts. In the process of being told and retold orally during the first century or two of Christianity, it became widely known orally to Christians in diverse parts of the empire."[21]

---

20. Tolbert, *Sowing the Gospel,* 44–45.
21. Dewey, "Survival of Mark's Gospel," 496.

Appendix C:
Distinctive Material in
the Gospel of Mark[1]

The influential Christian scholar Augustine (354–430 CE) championed the position that the Gospel of Mark was an abbreviated version of the Gospel of Matthew.[2] Thus, Mark was thought to have nothing unique to offer the reader, and so it was neglected for centuries. In fact, the first full-length commentary on Mark didn't appear until the seventh century, and Mark was only sparsely commented on until the nineteenth century. At that time, scholars theorized that Mark was actually the first Gospel written and one of the main sources for Matthew and Luke; this belief that Mark was the oldest Gospel—and therefore the record closest to the life of Jesus Christ—created a frenzy of interest in the text that has not abated to this day. Scholars have closely analyzed it and have discovered many aspects that differ greatly from the other three Gospels.

It might seem that analysis of the material unique to Mark's Gospel would provide good insight into Mark as a writer, but there is one caution: since Mark wrote first, the material that is unique to Mark is only unique because Matthew and Luke chose to omit it, not because Mark made the choice to include it. So looking at the material unique to Mark says more about Matthew and Luke than it does about Mark. That said, an examination of this material, when carefully considered, can hint at Mark's unique preferences.

---

1. Originally published as Julie M. Smith, "Mark's Unique Contribution," *Religious Educator* 17, no. 2 (2016): 56–85.

2. Augustine, *Harmony of the Gospels* 1.2.4.

Surprisingly little material occurs in only Mark's Gospel; one estimate is that fewer than two dozen out of over 650 verses are unparalleled.[3] The following material is unique to this Gospel:

1. "Mark is the only one of the canonical Gospels to use the term [gospel] at the beginning as a summary of its own contents."[4] It is curious that Matthew and Luke did not continue with this usage.

2. In 1:13, when Jesus is tempted in the wilderness, wild beasts are present; this detail is not included in the other Gospel accounts. If Mark's Gospel is, at least in part, meant to help Christians survive the terrible persecution that resulted from blame heaped upon them after a fire destroyed most of Rome in 64 CE, then this detail would have been of great comfort to its audience, who might literally be thrown to the lions in the arena.

3. The teaching that "for every one shall be salted with fire, and every sacrifice shall be salted with salt" (9:49) is unique to Mark. (The second half of that verse is unlikely to be original to the Gospel of Mark because it does not appear in many of the oldest manuscripts.[5]) Perhaps Matthew and Luke chose not to include this saying because its meaning was unclear, or perhaps it was particularly important to Mark because it spoke to the persecuted status of his audience: "Jesus' enigmatic statement had found fulfillment in the trial and persecution of Roman Christians under Nero."[6]

4. The teaching that "the sabbath was made for man, and not man for the sabbath" (2:27) is not found in any of the other Gospels. Perhaps Matthew and Luke were uncomfortable with a teaching that might be (mis)interpreted to condone lawlessness.

5. While both Matthew and Luke tell the story of the healing of blind Bartimaeus, only Mark includes the man's name (compare 10:46–52 with Matt. 20:29–34 and Luke 18:35–43). Usually, names were added to the tradition as time goes on, which makes the absence of Bartimaeus's name in Matthew's and Luke's accounts all the more surprising. However, it is possible that in this case Mark included the name because Bartimaeus was known to the audience and Matthew and Luke omitted it because he was not known to theirs. Similarly, Mark names the sons of Simon of Cyrene, but Matthew and Luke, while they include this story in their accounts, omit their names (compare 15:21 with Matt. 27:32 and Luke 23:26).[7]

---

3. According to Robert H. Stein, 23 out of 666 verses are unique. See Stein, *Mark,* 16.

4. Collins, *Mark,* 3.

5. Metzger, *Textual Commentary,* 87.

6. Lane, *Gospel according to Mark,* 24.

7. Interestingly, the JST will change "Alexander" to "Alexandria."

6. In 3:20–21, Mark records that Jesus' own family thought that he had lost his mind.[8] Matthew omits the reference (compare Matt. 12:25–29), as does Luke. In general, Mark seems to have a much higher tolerance for material that might be perceived as embarrassing; Matthew and Luke tend to omit this material.

7. Mark places the teachings in 4:24 ("with what measure ye mete, it shall be measured to you: and unto you that hear shall more be given") and 4:25 ("For he that hath, to him shall be given: and he that hath not, from him shall be taken even that which he hath") sequentially. In Matthew, this material is divided between Matthew 7:2 and Matthew 13:12, and in Luke it is divided between Luke 8:18 and Luke 19:26.

8. Mark's Gospel is the only account to contain the parable of the seed growing secretly (4:26–29). Perhaps Matthew and Luke omitted this story because it was so similar to the parable in 4:3–9.

9. Only Mark includes a reference to Jesus as "the son of Mary" (6:3). Matthew recasts it into a question: "is not his mother called Mary?" (Matt. 13:55). There may have been discomfort associated with thinking of Jesus as "Mary's son" because, for those who did not understand or believe in the virgin birth, it would have carried the taint of scandal to identify him by his mother and not his father. Once again, Mark's Gospel appears more comfortable with potentially embarrassing material about Jesus. Similarly, Mark is the only Gospel where Jesus is called a carpenter (6:3); in Matthew 13:55, he is the son of a carpenter. Also, Mark mentions Jesus' sisters (6:3); the other Gospel writers do not.

10. Mark 6:8–10 permits the Twelve to take a staff (Greek: *rhabdos*) and directs them to take sandals (Greek: *sandalion*) when they go out to preach. Matthew 10:10 forbids the taking of a staff (Greek *rhabdos,* KJV: "staves"). Matthew 10:10 also prohibits the taking of "shoes" (Greek: *hypodēma*; this is a different Greek word than the one used in Mark, so it is hard to make a direct comparison). In Luke 9:3, no footwear is mentioned, but the prohibition on staffs (Greek: *rhabdos,* KJV: "staves") is present. This is one of the few outright contradictions between the synoptic Gospels; most of the variation has to do with omissions or matters of emphasis. It is difficult to determine why Mark's text is different from Matthew's and Luke's here. Perhaps the various sources for the Gospels remembered Jesus' counsel differently; perhaps the writers were willing to shape Jesus' words to fit the current expectations for missionaries even at the cost of altering how Jesus had originally presented his teachings.

11. Mark explains Jewish customs that neither Matthew nor Luke explains to their audiences (see 7:3–4; compare Matt. 15:2–3). It is likely that this

---

8. The KJV for 3:21 reads, "and when his friends heard of it, they went out to lay hold on him: for they said, He is beside himself." This verse more likely refers to family, not friends; the end of the verse implies that Jesus is "out of his mind."

information was necessary for Mark's audience, which likely was at least in part Gentile, but not for Matthew's, which is more likely to have been Jewish.

12. Mark's Gospel is the only one to contain the declaration by the narrator "thus he declared all foods clean" (7:19 [KJV: "purging all meats"]; contrast Matt. 15:17–20). As Acts and Paul's letters make clear (Acts 10:9–19; Gal. 2:11–18), dietary rules were a difficult issue for early Christians to navigate, and it is easy to imagine Mark including this note for the (likely) gentile audience and Matthew omitting it, given his emphasis on Jesus as the fulfillment of the Mosaic law. It is possible to view the statement as an editorial comment by Mark that offered an interpretation of Jesus' words with which Matthew did not agree.

13. Unlike Matthew, Luke, and John, Mark contains no reference to Samaritans. Perhaps the conflicts between Jews and Samaritans held less relevance to Mark's audience. But given the paucity of references to Samaritans in the other Gospels, this may just be a coincidence.

14. Mark's Gospel is the only one to contain a "two-step" miracle: Jesus heals a blind man in stages (8:23–25). Matthew and Luke omit this story, perhaps over discomfort at the idea that Jesus was not completely successful in his first attempt to heal the man.

15. In 9:38–41, the disciples complain that someone who was not following them was casting out demons in Jesus' name. Part of Jesus' response ("For he that is not against us is on our part. For whosoever shall give you a cup of water to drink in my name, because ye belong to Christ, verily I say unto you, he shall not lose his reward") is not included in the other Gospels.

16. In 12:32–34, after the scribe responds to Jesus' explanation of the greatest commandment, Jesus says that he is "not far from the kingdom of God" (12:34), which is not found in any other Gospel. Matthew and Luke may have been uncomfortable with Jesus' praise of the scribe.

17. In what is probably the most enigmatic episode in the entire Gospel, a young man flees naked when Jesus is arrested (14:51–52). Nothing clarifies who this young man is[9] or anything else about him, although he may reappear to announce Jesus' Resurrection. This story is not included in any of the other Gospels, perhaps because their authors didn't know what to make of it.

18. While other Gospels contain a reference to the person cutting the ear of the servant of the high priest with a sword when Jesus is arrested, only in Mark's Gospel is the sword wielded by one of the arresting party (14:47; contrast Matt. 26:51; Luke 22:50; John 18:10).

19. In Mark's Gospel, the centurion proclaims, "truly this man was the Son of God" (15:39) when Jesus dies. In Matthew's Gospel, the centurion makes a

---

9. A few interpreters have suggested that this is an oblique reference to the author of the Gospel, but that seems excessively speculative.

similar proclamation when he witnesses an earthquake at the time of Jesus' death (Matt. 27:54); Mark does not mention an earthquake. In Luke's Gospel, the centurion praises God and announces that Jesus was innocent (Luke 23:47): "Only Mark retains a truly creative tension in the confession of the centurion."[10] Matthew eliminates the tension by having the centurion witness something spectacular (an earthquake) and Luke does so by focusing on Jesus' innocence instead of his identity; only Mark contains the paradoxical image of a Gentile, a Roman soldier, realizing that the humiliating death of a political prisoner could be the death of the Son of God.[11]

20. Only Mark includes the detail that Pilate asked a centurion whether Jesus was already dead (see 15:44–45; compare Matt. 27:58; Luke 23:52–53; John 19:38). While the text is not specific, it may be that this is the same centurion from 15:39 (and, if not actually the same centurion, then filling the same literary role as a gentile witness to Jesus' death) and so Mark's inclusion of this brief exchange may further cement the centurion's testimony from 15:39. But it is also possible that Matthew, Luke, and John omit this detail because it wasn't required to move the story forward.

21. All four Gospels feature women visiting the tomb, but only in Mark's Gospel do they wonder about how they will move the stone from the tomb's entrance (16:3; compare Matt. 28:2; Luke 24:2; John 20:1). This is the sort of detail that would have heightened the drama in an oral presentation of Mark's Gospel but perhaps seemed unnecessary in the accounts of the other evangelists.

22. In Mark's Gospel, a "young man" (16:5) is in the tomb, Matthew's Gospel has the angel of the Lord (Matt. 28:2), Luke's Gospel has two men in shining clothing (Luke 24:4), and John's Gospel has no messenger—divine or otherwise—in the tomb (John 20:1–10). While multiple theories attempt to explain the differences between the four accounts, one way to understand Mark's presentation is to see it as part of the emphasis on discipleship.

It is difficult to analyze the unique material in Mark's Gospel because it may tell more about Matthew's and Luke's editorial choices than Mark's particular interests. But there does appear to be some patterns in the material unique to Mark: Mark seems to be more comfortable with stories that show the "human" side of Jesus than the other writers are. From a Latter-day Saint perspective, it is theologically important to maintain that Jesus had both divine and human aspects during mortality, and thus Mark's unique material can be an important counterweight to the other Gospels, particularly John, where Jesus is presented as more perfect and therefore less human.

---

10. Marvin Meyer, "Taking Up the Cross and Following Jesus: Discipleship in the Gospel of Mark," *Calvin Theological Journal* 37, no. 2 (2002): 230–38.

11. It is possible to interpret the centurion's statement ironically, although this is less likely. See the Notes on 15:39.

Appendix D:
Mark 16:9–20

Without a doubt, the ending of Mark's text is the most significant textual variant in the Gospel of Mark. Virtually all scholars believe that 16:9–20[1] was *not* originally part of the Gospel for the following reasons:

1. The two oldest Greek manuscripts omit the longer ending. Other ancient manuscripts that include it append a note indicating that the text is uncertain.

2. It is difficult to imagine why a copyist would omit it; it is much easier to imagine a copyist adding it.

3. Several early Christian writers appear to know copies of the Gospel of Mark that do not include 16:9–20.[2]

4. The style differs substantially from the rest of the Gospel. (These problems not only suggest that 16:9–20 was not original to Mark but also that it was not written afresh to end the text but rather was a preexisting text.[3]) Stylistic infelicities include the following:

   a. The transition between 16:8 and 16:9 is awkward: the implied antecedent of "he" is Jesus, but 16:8 was about the women, not Jesus.

   b. The time reference is unnecessarily repeated in 16:9. Also, it is inconsistent to have Jesus rise very early in the morning when that was the time the women went to the tomb and found it empty.

---

1. Within 16:9–20, there are a few textual variants. In 16:18, some manuscripts add "with their hands" to the beginning of the verse. In 16:19, some manuscripts add "Jesus" before "Lord"; this is perhaps more likely to have been the earlier reading. In 16:20, the word "amen" is not in the earlier texts but was probably added later to reflect how the Gospel was used in the church. Metzger, *Textual Commentary,* 107.

2. Robert H. Stein, "The Ending of Mark," *Bulletin for Biblical Research* 18, no. 1 (2008): 79–98.

3. Metzger, *Textual Commentary,* 105.

    c. Mary Magdalene is introduced to the audience in 16:9 as if they were unfamiliar with her despite the fact that she was mentioned just a few verses before. The other Mary and Salome drop out of the text without explanation.

    d. Mark has no story of demons having been cast out of Mary Magdalene, making 16:9 difficult to understand.

    e. The fear of the women was underscored in 16:8, but it disappears without explanation in 16:9.[4]

    f. In 16:10, the identity of the "them" is unexplained. Presumably it would be the disciples, but no antecedent is given. Further, their mourning is difficult to understand when their last action was to abandon Jesus.

    g. Mark 16:12 refers to Jesus appearing in different forms but nowhere explains what these forms were.

    h. The summary nature of 16:9–20 would not have been consistent with an oral performance and therefore does not fit well with the rest of Mark's Gospel. It is very different from Mark's storytelling style: Jesus appears to Mary Magdalene, but no details whatsoever of the incident are given.

    i. Over a dozen words included in 16:9–20 are not found elsewhere in Mark.[5] For example, the title "Lord Jesus" is not used elsewhere in Mark.

    j. The setting of 16:9–20 appears to be Jerusalem, but the young man at the tomb told the women that Jesus would meet them in Galilee.

    k. In 16:1–8, the women are given a task, but that task has disappeared from 16:9–20.

    l. There is no evidence of the fulfillment of Jesus' prophecy that he will meet his disciples in Galilee (14:28).

5. Substantive theological differences distinguish 16:9–20 from the rest of Mark's Gospel:

    a. The theology of belief and baptism in 16:16 is foreign to Mark's Gospel.

    b. The idea of signs following believers is foreign to Mark. Nowhere else in the NT are believers promised immunity from threats such as poison and snakes. (In fact, Jesus' instructions to the Twelve in 6:8 to take a staff imply the need to fend off dangers.) The desire for signs is criticized explicitly in 8:11–13 and, implicitly, in 15:32.

---

4. Thomas A. Wayment, "The Endings of Mark and Revelation," in *The King James Bible and the Restoration,* ed. Kent P. Jackson (Provo, Utah: Religious Studies Center, Brigham Young University, 2011), 80.

5. Bratcher and Nida, *Translator's Handbook,* 519–20.

6. Many elements of 16:9–20 seem borrowed from other NT texts and do not relate to Mark's concerns, including the scene with two disciples on the road (Luke 24:13–35), the reproach for unbelief (John 20:19, 26), the great commission (Matt. 28:19), salvation (John 3:18, 36), speaking in tongues (Acts 2:4; 10:46), and the ascension (Luke 24:51).[6]

7. Matthew and Luke follow Mark quite closely until 16:8, and then their texts diverge substantially; this suggests that they had copies of Mark that ended at 16:8.

8. The existence of other endings (see the end of this appendix) strongly suggests that 16:9–20 was not present originally. It implies that some found 16:8 to be inadequate and decided to add to the ending.

For these reasons, 16:9–20 was almost certainly not originally part of the Gospel of Mark. Based on its theological concerns and when it is attested, it was probably written in the second century. Because the focus of this commentary is how the first audiences of Mark would have understood the Gospel, exegetical notes and commentary are not provided for 16:9–20.

As mentioned above, in addition to 16:9–20, a few ancient manuscripts contain other material or combinations of material, but none of these has a good claim for being the earliest ending. What is known as the Shorter Ending of Mark reads: "'But they reported briefly to Peter and those with him all that they had been told. And after these things Jesus himself sent out through them, from east to west, the sacred and imperishable proclamation of eternal salvation.'"[7] It uses many words that Mark normally does not: it is only thirty-four words long but uses nine words not used elsewhere in Mark.[8] Also, it has a much different "rhetorical tone,"[9] as the phrase "the sacred and imperishable proclamation of eternal salvation" should indicate. And it is found alone in only one manuscript (although some other manuscripts have this ending plus 16:9–20, and another manuscript, now defective, may have contained it).[10] The manuscripts that include it date from the seventh century or later.[11]

Another ending, called the Freer Logion, adds the following text after 16:14:

6. Evans, *Mark 8:27–16*, 546.
7. Metzger, *Textual Commentary*, 103.
8. Stein, "Ending of Mark," 81.
9. Metzger, *Textual Commentary*, 105.
10. Collins, *Mark*, 802.
11. Metzger and Ehrman, *Text of the New*, 323.

"And they excused themselves, saying, 'This age of lawlessness and unbelief is under Satan, who does not allow the truth and power of God to prevail over the unclean things of the spirits. ... Therefore reveal your righteousness now'—thus they spoke to Christ. And Christ replied to them, 'The term of years of Satan's power has been fulfilled, but other terrible things draw near. And for those who have sinned I was handed over to death, that they may return to the truth and sin no more, in order that they may inherit the spiritual and incorruptible glory of righteousness that is in heaven.'"[12]

Attestation for the Freer Logion is very poor.[13]

While there are very few certainties when it comes to the study of ancient texts, the overwhelming weight of the evidence suggests that the earliest manuscripts of Mark did not include what is now 16:9–20, the Shorter Ending, or the Freer Logion.

Latter-day Saint readers might wonder what to make of the fact that material similar to 16:9–20 appears in the Book of Mormon (compare 16:15–18 with Morm. 9:22–24). There are several ways to explain this shared material:

1. Despite the evidence to the contrary, 16:9–20 is original to the Gospel. (In light of the available evidence, this option is unlikely.)

2. Mark 16:9–20 is not original to the Gospel but nonetheless contain some of Jesus' words; these words are also included in the Book of Mormon.

3. The similarities between the two texts are the result of Joseph Smith employing language and concepts already familiar to him from the KJV in his translation of the Book of Mormon.

4. It is also possible that in the Book of Mormon story, Jesus used language that he knew would be familiar and meaningful to the Book of Mormon's modern audience because it was in KJV Mark.

---

12. Metzger, *Textual Commentary,* 104.
13. Metzger, *Textual Commentary,* 104.

Appendix E:
Demonology in Mark's Gospel

The concept of unclean spirits or demons[1] is largely foreign to modern audiences, and there are several possibilities as to what it meant for someone to have an unclean spirit:

1. *Mental Illness.* This theory makes sense of some of the symptoms of possessions, but it does not explain why, in Mark's Gospel, people with unclean spirits have a special ability to identify Jesus (for example, 1:24).

2. *Epilepsy or Seizure Disorders.* As with #1, it explains some symptoms but does not explain why the sufferers would have been able to identify Jesus.

3. *Literal Possession of a Human Body by a Demon.* This viewpoint might be a challenge to notions of moral agency and individual choice. But in Mark's Gospel, the existence of demons does not absolve humans from responsibility for their deeds, especially since a major theme in this text is discipleship, which involves how people choose to respond to Jesus. And as one scholar noted, "to suggest that there may be more truth here in the N.T. picture than has sometimes been allowed is not to wish to turn the clock back on scientific progress. . . . The question whether the spread of a confident certainty of the demons' non-existence has not been their greatest triumph gets tragic urgency from such twentieth-century features as Nazism."[2] It is possible that the modern commitment to a scientific approach to the world makes it difficult for people today to recognize the reality of demonic possession.

4. *A Distress Response.* An extreme psychological response to debilitating social conditions may explain the phenomenon: "some data from anthropology and social psychology suggest that conditions of political oppression, social deprivation, and rapid social change (all of which characterized the Jewish

---

1. Mark seems to use these two terms interchangeably. See Stein, *Mark,* 87.
2. Cranfield, *Gospel according to St Mark,* 75.

homeland in the first century) are correlated with increased frequency of possession."[3]

It is difficult to determine which option is best here.[4] (See the Analysis of 3:20–35 for a discussion of Jesus' parabolic explanation of exorcisms.) Mark does not explain precisely which phenomenon is in mind, either because it was common knowledge to the audience or because it was not the focal point of the story. But the message is clear: however it is that evil gains a foothold, whatever metaphorical or actual evil is present, Jesus has the power and authority to uproot it. While rare, exorcisms were sometimes performed; the practice was not unique to Jesus. But Jesus' practice differed in two significant ways from exorcisms recorded outside of the NT:

1. Exorcists in the ancient world normally did something physical—offered an incantation, performed a ritual, or used some physical object—but Jesus does none of this. His power and authority are highlighted by the fact that he need not rely on magical devices or intermediaries but simply uses the power of his word.

2. If the demon's naming of Jesus is an attempt to gain control over him, then it is very significant that Jesus does not name the demon: he simply commands silence without engaging the demon according to the standard procedure. This would show his superior power.

Mark's Gospel can be read to suggest that Jesus was "possessed" by the Holy Spirit at his baptism (see the Notes on 1:10). Immediately after Jesus' baptism, a dove descends from heaven. It is likely that earlier iterations of Mark's text had the dove descend "into" Jesus,[5] which serves as the first hint that the Spirit possesses Jesus. The second hint comes when the Spirit immediately thrusts Jesus into the wilderness (1:12). The next hint is in the fact that the language used to describe unclean spirits in Mark is often quite similar to the language used to the describe the Holy Spirit.[6] The Greek word translated as "gave up the ghost" could be rendered as "the Spirit

3. Borg, *Jesus,* 150.

4. Note that while there are many stories of unclean spirits in Jesus' ministry, demons are largely absent from other volumes of scripture (but see Mosiah 3:5–6; Hel. 13:37; and D&C 35:9 for a few exceptions).

5. Collins, *Mark,* 133–34 note h.

6. Compare 1:8 ("with the Holy Ghost"; presumably this is the same as in Jesus' baptism, although the word "holy" is not repeated) with 1:23 ("with an unclean spirit"). This aural similarity would have been notable to Mark's original, oral audience.

went out of him." It is an idiomatic way to describe dying.[7] It is possible that the cry with a loud voice is Jesus' last breath and is thus the Spirit going out of him.[8] Because the same words for "loud cry" are used elsewhere in Mark only to describe the expelling of demons (1:26; 5:7), it is possible that this phrasing points to the idea that Jesus is having his own (holy) Spirit expelled here.

It seems that in Mark, one is possessed either by the Holy Spirit or by an unclean spirit, so that these are, in effect, two sides of the same coin. This theory gains traction in chapter 3, where Jesus has been accused by the scribes of using demonic power in order to cast out demons (3:22). He addresses this charge and then states that people will be forgiven all blasphemies, save those against the Holy Spirit (3:28–29). The relationship between the Holy Spirit and the rest of the conversation seems tenuous, unrelated to the discussion about casting out demons using demonic power. Perhaps aware that the audience might miss the connection, Mark quickly explains that Jesus' reference to the Holy Spirit was a direct response to the accusation that Jesus had an unclean spirit (3:30). Mark's careful guidance here makes clear to the audience that suggesting that Jesus had an unclean spirit risks blasphemy against the Holy Spirit. But why is this so? A close reading of Mark's story of Jesus implies that it is because possession by the Holy Spirit and possession by an unclean spirit are the same phenomenon, which means that to accuse Jesus of having an unclean spirit is functionally the same thing as denying that the Holy Spirit was influencing him; this is what would constitute blasphemy against the Holy Spirit.

While the idea of demonic possession and "possession" by the Holy Spirit being essentially the same phenomenon is unusual, it does seem to be supported by Mark's Gospel. And it is a useful framework for Latter-day Saint readers because it can explain how it is that demonic possession does *not* override human agency: just as one would invite the Holy Spirit into her life and become more and more attuned to and responsive to it, one might invite an unclean spirit through sinful behavior and, as time passes, become more attuned and responsive to it.

---

7. France, *Gospel of Mark,* 655-56.
8. Gundry, *Mark,* 948.

Appendix F:
Titles for Jesus in Mark

Traditionally, most efforts to understand Christology were moored in the effort to understand the names and titles applied to Jesus. In Mark, key names for Jesus may include:

1. *"Son of Man."* While most NT writers prefer to call Jesus "Christ" or "Lord," Jesus usually referred to himself as the Son of Man, making it an important title in Mark's Gospel. But it is enigmatic; there are several possible meanings for this phrase:

    a. It is a humble way to refer to oneself (although some scholars dispute the idea that "Son of Man" was ever a circumlocution for "I"[1]). The phrase is an ideal encapsulation of Mark's view of Jesus as one who is exalted but simultaneously meek. Jesus used this term as "as a form of deliberately oblique or ambiguous self-reference."[2] Jesus never says that he is the Son of Man. He always speaks of the Son of Man in the third person, but the audience is invited to make the connection (see 2:5, 10).[3]

    b. It alludes to Daniel 7:13–14, linking Jesus and the person Daniel saw in a vision who was given "dominion, and glory, and a kingdom, that all people, nations, and languages, should serve him: his dominion is an everlasting dominion, which shall not pass away, and his kingdom that which shall not be destroyed" (Dan. 7:14), although other scholars dispute the connection to Daniel 7.[4] While other iterations of the text have the Son of Man approaching the Ancient of Days, some manuscripts of LXX Daniel 7:13 state that the one like the Son of Man is the Ancient of Days.[5] It is not

---

1. Collins, *Mark,* 187–89.
2. Richard Bauckham, "The Son of Man: 'A Man in My Position' or 'Someone'?" *Journal for the Study of the New Testament* 23 (1985): 29.
3. Malbon, "Narrative Christology," 373–85.
4. Bauckham, "Son of Man," 27.
5. Michael B. Shepherd, "Daniel 7:13 and the New Testament Son of Man," *Westminster Theological Journal* 68, no. 1 (2006): 102; see also Benjamin E. Reynolds, "The 'One Like

clear whether this reading is the cascading result of a scribal error or a deliberate theological move,[6] but in either case, this may be the text Mark is working from and thus how Mark would have understood the text. The idea that the Son of Man is the Ancient of Days is extremely significant for the NT use of Daniel 7:13, because Jesus would then be claiming to be not just the Son of Man but also the Ancient of Days, who was understood to be God. Jesus would then be aligning himself with the God of the HB when he uses this title. Interestingly, the text in Daniel contains the idea that all the people will serve the Son of Man, but in Mark, Jesus states that the Son of Man will serve (KJV: "minister unto") the people (10:45); this inversion is a key part of the concept of Jesus as the Son of Man in Mark's Gospel.

Because first-century Judaism did not associate the title "Son of Man" with the Messiah, Jesus could use it without any of the nationalistic or political overtones that "Son of David" would have had. Different audience members may have had divergent understandings of what "Son of Man" meant: a Greek speaker would not have recognized "Son of Man" as a title but would have simply taken the words at face value. Therefore, this title could have had the paradoxical function of both revealing and concealing Jesus' identity. Only Jesus uses the title "Son of Man" to describe himself in the Gospel;[7] other people do not use it.

2. *"Master."* The title most commonly used by other people to address Jesus in Mark's Gospel is "Master"; modern translations usually translate this word (Greek: *didaskalos*) as "teacher."[8] This title does not mean that Jesus was divine but rather suggests that most of the people around Jesus do not really understand his identity. Perhaps as part of Mark's thinking on discipleship or as part of the extensive irony in this Gospel, it seems that the people who call Jesus "Master" do not usually accept him as such (12:14, 19) or in their very statement show that they do not understand what he is teaching/doing (4:38; 5:35; 9:17, 38; 10:35; 13:1). The incident in 10:17–22 particularly exemplifies this situation since the rich man does not grasp what Jesus has to teach. This is also true of Peter's and Judas's identification of Jesus as "Master" (11:21;

---

a Son of Man' According to the Old Greek of Daniel 7,13–14," *Biblica* 89, no. 1 (2008): 71–72.

6. H. Daniel Zacharias, "Old Greek Daniel 7:13–14 and Matthew's Son of Man," *Bulletin for Biblical Research* 21, no. 4 (2011): 454–55.

7. Occurrences of the "Son of Man" in Mark's Gospel: 2:10, 28; 8:31, 38; 9:9, 12, 31; 10:33, 45; 13:26; 14:21, 41, 62. (As the italics in 13:34 indicate, the phrase "Son of Man" is not present in the Greek text; it simply reads "man.")

8. Occurrences of *didaskalos* in Mark's Gospel include 4:38; 5:35; 9:17, 38; 10:17, 20, 35; 12:14, 19, 32; 13:1; and 14:14. (The KJV for 9:5; 11:21; and 14:45 read "master," but the Greek word here is *rabbi*, not *didaskalos*. KJV 13:35 has "master," but the Greek word is *kyrios*, usually translated in the KJV as "Lord.")

14:45). There is one exception to this pattern: 12:32 seems genuine since Jesus' interlocutor repeats his words in agreement. But 12:34 makes it problematic: while the scribe is close to the kingdom of God, nothing indicates that he either asks more questions or follows Jesus.

3. *"Son of God."* "Son (of God)" is another title applied to Jesus.[9] It is used by nonhuman beings (God and the demons), by the narrator, by Jesus as a direct reference to himself, and by the centurion. Because it is used in the confession at the cross (15:39), some have argued that it is the most important title for Jesus in Mark's Gospel.[10] Some scholars believe that Mark's original audience would have understood that the phrase "Son of God" implied "preexistence and deity."[11] (Other scholars reject this association, pointing out that the HB uses it for mortal kings; see 2 Sam. 7:14 and Ps. 2:7. There may be a distinction here based on the audience, with Jews thinking that a mere mortal could be God's son but Gentiles thinking that "Son of God" implied a divine status.) Additionally, some have understood "Christ" and "Son of God" to be synonymous because they seem to be used that way in 2 Samuel 7:14 and Psalm 2:7; some Jews in the first century understood that the Messiah was "God's son" based on these verses. The theme of Jesus as God's son is an important one to Mark, and the Gospel will have a lot to say about it (1:11, 24; 3:11; 5:7; 9:7; 12:6–8, 25–26; 13:32; 14:61–62; 15:39).

4. *"Christ."* Another title is "Christ."[12] Some scholars argue that this title is the most important one in Mark's Gospel because it is key to Peter's confession (8:29) and it is unambiguously claimed by Jesus during his trial (14:62). The fact that Peter can be rebuked by Jesus right after proclaiming that Jesus is the Christ (8:33) suggests that Mark has something complicated to say about this title. As soon as Peter makes that confession and Jesus begins to teach that he must suffer and die, Peter rebukes Jesus: clearly, suffering and death were not a part of Peter's conception of who the Christ was and what he did. At this point, the Gospel text pivots, and the remaining narrative will be largely concerned with presenting the suffering and death of Jesus, hence redefining what it means to be "the Christ." The story of the anointing in chapter 14 functions as a narrative hinge between the life and death of Jesus and explains what it means to be the Christ by showing his anointing as a burial anointing

---

9. Instances of "Son of God" (or similar titles, as indicated) in Mark's Gospel include 1:1 (although the text here is disputed; see the Notes on 1:1); 1:11 ("Thou art my beloved Son"); 3:11; 5:7 ("Son of the Most high God"); 9:7 ("This is my beloved Son"); 12:6 ("one son, his wellbeloved"); 13:32 ("the Son [of the Father]"); 14:61–62 ("Art thou . . . the Son of the Blessed? . . . I am"); and 15:39.

10. Norman Perrin, "The Creative Use of the Son of Man Traditions by Mark," *Union Seminary Quarterly Review* 23 (Summer 1968): 358.

11. Stein, *Mark,* 41.

12. Instances of "Christ" in Mark's Gospel include 1:1; 8:29; 9:41; 12:35; 13:21, 22; 14:61; and 15:32. While the KJV for 13:6 contains the word "Christ," the Greek text does not.

and a royal anointing. Since "Christ" is the Greek word for "anointed," the anointing story defines what it means to say that Jesus is "the Christ."

5. *"Lord."* Another title for Jesus is "Lord."[13] Because it can also be translated as "sir" and since it sometimes refers to God the Father, many scholars dismiss "Lord" as an important title because it is so difficult to interpret its use. But a minority suggest that that very ambiguity, which serves to affiliate Jesus with God, might be important to fleshing out Mark's understanding of who Jesus was.[14]

6. *"Son of David."* The title "Son of David" does not seem to be a key title in this Gospel. Bartimaeus twice calls Jesus "Son of David" (10:47, 48). While Jesus does not rebuke Bartimaeus, Jesus will later specifically eschew identification of the Christ as the Son of David (12:35–37). The title "Son of David" is perhaps insufficient because it presumes a purely Davidic kingship, which would not have the connotations of suffering and death that are a crucial part of Jesus' messiahship.

7. *"King of the Jews."* Another title is "King of the Jews."[15] It is certainly no accident that references to Jesus as the "King of the Jews" cluster around his trial and that the title is frequently used in ironic mockery of Jesus.

8. *"Rabbi," "Prophet."* Other titles for Jesus in this Gospel include "rabbi"[16] and "prophet,"[17] although these do not seem to be key titles for Jesus.

9. *"Jesus of Nazareth."* There are also multiple times when Jesus is referred to as simply Jesus of Nazareth.[18] Because "Jesus" (from the Hebrew "Joshua") was a very common male name for this time and place, it would have been necessary to identify him by a town name or in some other way. To call him "Jesus of Nazareth" is sort of an "antititle," suggesting that he did not have any special status. Of the five uses of "Jesus of Nazareth" in Mark's Gospel, one is

---

13. Occurrences of "Lord" include 1:3; 2:28; 5:19; 7:28 (it may mean "sir" here); 9:24; 11:3, 9, 10; 12:9, 11, 29, 30, 36, 37; 13:20, and 35 (KJV: "master"). The KJV for 6:21 contains "lords," but this is a different Greek word; similarly, 10:51 contains "Lord" in the KJV, but the Greek word is different.

14. Daniel Johansson, "Kyrios in the Gospel of Mark," *Journal for the Study of the New Testament* 33, no. 1 (2010): 101–24.

15. The title "King of the Jews" is found in 15:2, 9, 12, 18, 26, and 32 ("king of Israel").

16. Occurrences of "rabbi" include 9:5 (KJV: "Master"); 10:51 (KJV: "Lord," the Greek here is *rhabbouni*); 11:21 (KJV: "Master"); and 14:45 (KJV: "Master"). It is worth noting that the Gospel of Mark is the earliest text containing the title "rabbi," although later rabbinic texts indicate that the term may have been in use before the time of Jesus.

17. Instances of "prophet" include 1:2 (where "the [HB] prophets" are mentioned); 6:4 (where Jesus alludes to the idea of being a prophet); 6:15; and 8:28 (in both verses, unnamed people think he might be a prophet). In 11:32, John the Baptist is considered a prophet by Jesus' adversaries. In 13:14, Daniel is called a prophet.

18. Occurrences of "Jesus of Nazareth" include 1:24; 10:47; 14:67; and 16:6.

from a demon (1:24); despite their evil character, the demons in this Gospel have accurate information. Bartimaeus, who is presented as a model follower, also uses this title (10:47), further suggesting that it is an appropriate one. The narrator uses it in the beginning of the Gospel (1:19) and the woman who speaks with Peter after Jesus is arrested uses it (14:67); these two uses are perhaps expected. What is very surprising is that the young man at the tomb, when speaking to the women who have come to anoint Jesus' body for burial, calls Jesus simply "Jesus of Nazareth" (16:6), when the audience would have likely expected one of the dramatic titles (Christ, Son of God, etc.) to be used at this crucial moment. The fact that this most modest of titles suggests that Mark doesn't think very highly of titles for Jesus in general.

While the titles applied to Jesus are certainly important and would have impacted how the audience understood Mark's story, it is also important to consider the narrative elements of Mark's Christology.

Appendix G:
Mark's Christology

"Christology" is the term used to describe an author's depiction of Jesus Christ's nature. A Christology is considered low if it focuses on Jesus' human aspects or high if it stresses his divine attributes. Traditionally, Mark's Gospel has been thought to have the lowest Christology—and John's the highest—of the Gospels, with Matthew's and Luke's in between. Yet Mark exhibits elements of high Christology as well, stemming from how Jesus' story echoes HB texts. Clearly, Mark contains elements of a low Christology but also contains elements of a very high Christology, so that if Mark's portrait of Jesus must be reduced to one word, the best choice is neither "low" nor "high" but rather "full."

Jesus Exercises God's Powers

Jesus acts in a way that only the God of the HB was expected to act. This happens over two dozen times in Mark:

1. Mark 1:8: John the Baptist teaches that the one coming after him would bestow the Holy Spirit upon them. But in the HB, only God gives the Spirit to people, so one effect of John's statement is to equate Jesus with the God of the Bible. John's statement may echo Ezekiel 39:29, where the Lord God promises to pour out the Spirit on the house of Israel. This allusion would further strengthen the case for identifying Jesus with the biblical God.

2. Mark 1:17: Standard practice was for students to choose which teacher to follow, so Jesus upsets expectations here by calling disciples: Jesus acts, not like a rabbi or a philosopher, but like the God of the HB, who calls Abraham (Gen. 12:1, 4).

3. Mark 1:41: Because only God could heal lepers, Jesus does not merely heal a leper; he also identifies himself with the God of the HB.

4. Mark 2:8: In the HB, God (and only God) can know what is in people's hearts, so this phrase identifies Jesus with the God of the HB.

5. Mark 2:12: In Isaiah 64:4, the speaker expresses amazement at acts that have never been seen before, perhaps making a link to the similar exclamation in the present text in Mark. In Isaiah, it is God who is performing the new acts, suggesting a link between Jesus and the God of the HB.

6. Mark 2:17: In Exodus 15:26, the Lord announces, "I am the Lord that healeth thee." If that text is alluded to here, then it is an important piece of self-revelation as Jesus identifies with the God of the HB.

7. Mark 2:28: In the HB, God—who organizes the Sabbath—is thus the Lord of the Sabbath. Jesus is subtly identifying himself with the God of the HB.

8. Mark 3:6: In Deuteronomy 29:18-20, the text warns those who imagine that they can keep their evil plans secret that they will be met with the Lord's anger. The parallel to the Mark story (where Jesus is aware—even beforehand—of the secret plot to kill him) provides a context for Jesus' anger here and aligns him with the God of the HB.

9. Mark 3:28: When others in the NT use "verily I say unto you," the statement is always used to confirm that someone else's (that is, not the speaker's) words are true; only Jesus uses it to affirm his own words. This is important because it implies that he is claiming a special status for himself by affirming his own words. Where others would have said, "thus saith the Lord," Jesus says, "truly I say to you." Because Jesus' use of this phrase to affirm his own words is unique in extant writings, it is extremely important—not only as his affirmation of the statement in question but as evidence of his unique, godlike status.

10. Mark 4:1: In Psalm 29:10, the Lord sits on the seas (KJV: "the flood") and majestically rules. If Mark had this psalm in mind, the connection would identify Jesus with the God of the HB.

11. Mark 6:31: In several HB scriptures, God provides rest for the faithful in the wilderness. So Jesus is not just suggesting a break from the crowds but is also positioning himself as the God of the scriptures.

12. Mark 6:48: Only God controlled the seas and therefore only God could have walked on water in the biblical view of the world. In Job 9:8, the LXX reads that God "walks upon the sea as upon dry ground." An allusion to that text would thus align Jesus with God (see also Job 38:16 and Ps. 77:19-20).

13. Mark 7:27-29: Modern readers are generally not at ease with the woman's aggressive approach to Jesus, but it is not unprecedented: near the end of the book of Job, God praises Job's willingness to speak honestly, in contrast with his friends. And while the idea of someone changing Jesus' mind seems unusual, it actually aligns Jesus with the God of the HB, who is depicted as experiencing a change of heart.

14. Mark 7:37: Although the speakers may not realize it, they are comparing Jesus to the God of the HB, especially since God is the one who makes it possible for humans to speak.

15. Mark 8:1–10: In Psalm 107:4–8, travelers are depicted as wandering and hungry until the Lord delivers them from their suffering; references to the desert, hunger, and fainting occur in the text. If Mark intended an allusion, then Jesus is pictured as the Lord who feeds and guides the people.

16. Mark 8:2: In several HB texts—including Genesis 40:13, Joshua 1:11, and Hosea 6:2—God's aid arrives after three days. If Mark continues this motif, then Jesus is aligned with the God of the HB. Particularly interesting is Joshua 1:11, where the Canaanites are enslaved after three days; in Mark, the (Gentile) people are liberated from want after three days, so there is a compelling inversion prompted by Jesus' care for them.

17. Mark 8:4: In Psalm 78:19–20, the people "tempt" God by wondering if God really could feed them in the wilderness. If Mark intended for this allusion, then it puts the disciples into the role of the faithless children of Israel who tempted God during the Exodus and puts Jesus into the role of God.

18. Mark 8:6: In Numbers 11:13–14, Moses asks the Lord, "Whence should I have flesh to give unto all this people? for they weep unto me, saying, Give us flesh, that we may eat. I am not able to bear all this people alone, because it is too heavy for me." The similar sentiment makes for an intriguing contrast with Mark's feeding miracle: Jesus is a prophet greater than Moses because he does not doubt his ability to provide food for a large crowd in the wilderness. Additionally, Jesus is aligned with the God of the HB by the fact that the question about providing food is on the lips not of Jesus but of the disciples, combined with the fact that it is the Lord who provides food during the Exodus (Num. 11:18) and Jesus who provides food in Mark's text.

19. Mark 8:11: In Exodus 17:1–7, the children of Israel are portrayed as testing God through Moses. If Mark intended an allusion to that story, then Jesus is the God who is being tested.

20. Mark 8:13: Psalm 95:8–10 contains references to hardened hearts, testing in the wilderness, and a generation. And the idea of the Lord being grieved might link to Jesus' sighing in Mark, which would provide the motivation for the sighing. If Mark intended this allusion, then it aligns Jesus with the God of the HB and the Pharisees with the faithless children of Israel who want to test God.

21. Mark 10:47: Because a plea for mercy directed to God, such as the one in Psalm 4:1, was common in the HB, Bartimaeus here associates Jesus with the God of the Bible.

22. Mark 12:14: In 1 Samuel 16:7, the Lord tells Samuel that humans look on the face, but God looks on the heart. The concept is very similar to what the Herodians and Pharisees say to Jesus. Mark's audience recognizes the truth

in these words even though the speakers do not, and thus they align Jesus with the God of the HB.

23. Mark 12:41–44: Many HB stories speak of God's special concern for widows. In this story, Jesus is placed into the narrative role of God as he is the one evincing the special concern for the widow, who is ignored by all those around her.

24. Mark 13:26: Usually in the HB, it is God who is associated with clouds, so this image suggests the divinization of the Son.

25. Mark 13:27: The Son of Man is sending "his" angels. This is significant because it means that he has authority over the angels.

26. Mark 13:31: Compare the attestation of Jesus' words to Isaiah 40:7–8. This is significant because it parallels Jesus' word with God's word in terms of being reliable and permanent.

Taken together, all of these instances of Jesus exercising powers believed to be restricted to God alone would probably have suggested to Mark's early audiences a very high Christology, if not an outright identification—in some sense—between Jesus and the God of the scriptures. But this reading raises an important question: Is it safe to conclude that Jesus is identified with God, or is it better to think that powers previously restricted to God alone are now being shared with Jesus? Jesus' exercise of God's power may signal the extension of God's power instead of an identification of Jesus with God. So while ample evidence in Mark suggests that Jesus exercises powers previously restricted to God, this is suggestive, but not definitive proof, that Jesus occupies God's role.

JESUS IN GOD'S NARRATIVE ROLE

There is another manner in which Mark's Christology is clearly very high: Mark frequently presents Jesus occupying the narrative role of the God of the HB. In about a half dozen major instances—and an even larger number of minor ones—Mark's text echoes one or more stories from the HB and places Jesus unequivocally into the role of God.

Jesus Forgives Sins

In 2:5, Jesus announces that a man's sins are forgiven. While some interpreters have suggested that, since the verse uses a passive construction, Jesus is merely announcing that God had forgiven the man's sins and not forgiving the sins himself, that interpretation flounders on the objection of the scribes: they would not have objected in the same way to Jesus announcing God's forgiveness since there is precedent for a prophet or priest proclaiming that God had forgiven sins (2 Sam. 12:13).[1] Any remaining ambiguity regarding who is doing the forgiving is eliminated by 2:10 because, unlike the reference to forgiving sins in 2:5, this reference is not passive. So it is clear that the story portrays Jesus' own ability to forgive sins. Thus Jesus is clearly exercising God's unique prerogative here, as the question of his adversaries suggests: "Who can forgive sins but God only?" The phrasing here implies an allusion to Deuteronomy 6:4, with its reference to God being "one." The idea that God—and only God—could forgive sins is well established in the HB (Ex. 34:6–7; 1 Kgs. 8:39; Isa. 43:25; 44:22). The power and authority to forgive sins is quite a claim, as the question of the scribes make clear, because it means that Jesus is exercising a right that only God has. Prophecies about the Messiah do not state that the Messiah will forgive sins, so Jesus is something more than just the anticipated Messiah here.

This question from the scribes about who may forgive sins fits a pattern in Mark's Gospel of presenting provocative questions that the audience should be able to answer if they will but ponder them. The question creates an opportunity for the idea that Jesus is acting in the role of God to sink into their minds, despite the rush of the narrative.

The suggestion that Jesus is in God's role is strengthened by a possible echo of Psalm 103:3 in 2:9. In that psalm, the very structure of the verse parallels forgiving sins with healing. Because the psalmist was speaking about the Lord, an allusion between that text and Mark would further associate Jesus with the God of the Bible.

In sum, this story places Jesus in the role of the God of the HB in a unique and distinct way. Unlike the examples discussed previously, it really is not possible to argue that God is granting powers to Jesus that were previously restricted to God alone because Mark's text goes out of its way to make clear that powers uniquely associated with God are being exercised by Jesus. Thus, a very high Christology emerges from this narrative as Jesus is identified with the God of the Bible.

---

1. If they had thought Jesus was announcing forgiveness that God had granted, they might have accused him of presuming to be a prophet, but not of blasphemy.

Jesus Calms the Sea

In 4:39, Jesus calms a storm. This incident echoes HB texts in multiple ways and places Jesus into God's role. First, the same Greek word that the KJV translates as "storm" is used in LXX Job 38:1 to name the storm out of which God spoke to Job in a text where the storm is the source for a revelation about the nature of God. A similar dynamic exists in Mark's text, where the identity of Jesus is also disclosed through the storm (see under the heading "Jesus Passes By" in this appendix). Additionally, in the Bible, sleep is often associated with God (Ps. 35:23; 44:23; 59:4), which means that when Jesus is asleep in the boat, he is identified with God. Plus, the sea is related to chaos and only God has the ability to control it (Gen. 8:1; Job 26:12; Ps.104:3; Isa. 50:2; Ps. 107). Texts such as Psalm 107:23–32, where the Lord rescues sailors from a storm, suggest this unique power. And finally, over a half dozen distinct echoes, including much shared vocabulary, link Mark's text to the book of Jonah.

Echoes include:

1. The main character travels by boat to a foreign land in order to complete a mission of preaching repentance (in fact, Jonah is the only HB prophet called to preach to the Gentiles).
2. The ship is in danger of being destroyed by a storm.
3. The main character is asleep while the others worry about their destruction.
4. The other sailors wake the main character and ask him questions.
5. Questions about the main character's true identity are raised.
6. The other sailors fear greatly.
7. In LXX Jonah 1, several words are identical to those found in Mark; one key word is "perish," which "expresses the leitmotiv of the entire book [of Jonah], escape from destruction at the hand of God."[2]

These connections would have suggested to Mark's audience that Jesus was filling the role of Jonah but, of course, they would have expected Jesus, unlike Jonah, to do the right thing and pray to God for the storm to cease. But this is where Mark departs from the expected track of the story of Jonah: Jesus does not, in fact, pray for the storm to cease but rather himself commands the storm to stop. In other words, Jesus pivots from occupying the narrative role of Jonah to occupying the narrative role of God. This would have made a powerful impression on Mark's audience:

---

2. Marcus, *Mark 1–8*, 333.

the sudden and unexpected placing of Jesus into God's role would surely have impacted their understanding of Jesus' nature and identity. And, once again, Mark allows a significant question posed in the story to work on the audience: when the disciples ask, "What manner of man is this, that even the wind and the sea obey him?" the audience has been given enough information to figure out the answer to that question, which is that Jesus is doing what only God can do.

Jesus as God in the Garden of Eden

In 5:29, a woman's unceasing menstruation ends when she touches Jesus' clothing. There are significant parallels between this text and Eve's Fall as recorded in Genesis 3. The stories share a dozen terms,[3] and the same concepts, if not the same wording, are found in several other instances—both passages refer to clothing, hiding, walking, becoming aware, seeing/looking, and children/daughters. But more significant than the verbal overlap are the extensive thematic associations. The bleeding woman is associated with Eve; in some strains of Jewish thought, menstruation was associated with Eve's sin[4] or with sin in general (Lam. 1:17; Ezek. 36:17–18). In both stories, the thought process behind the woman's decision-making is preserved; the audience knows what the woman is thinking as she takes the initiative to act in a difficult situation. Both stories feature a transgressive touch: Eve is not supposed to touch the fruit; the woman is not supposed to touch Jesus. Just as Eve's touch leads ultimately to death, the bleeding woman's touch leads to death by causing a delay that permits Jairus's daughter to die since Jesus' journey to her is interrupted by the bleeding woman's story. Mark's story highlights the fact that the woman's touch was unique—distinct from all of the other touches of the crowd and thus worthy of comment from Jesus. It parallels Eve's touch, which led to unique consequences and similarly ushered in death. In both stories, the transgressive touch changes the nature of their bodies. The touch/eating in the garden passed along the contagion of sin and death to Adam. In this story, the woman should convey impurity to Jesus, but that is precisely

---

3. Shared vocabulary between chapter 5 and LXX Genesis includes the words "woman" (5:25 and LXX Gen. 3:1), "all" (5:26 and LXX Gen. 3:1), "heard" (5:27 and LXX Gen. 3:8), "know/realize" (5:29, 33 and LXX Gen. 3:5), "perceive" (5:30 and LXX Gen. 3:5), "touch" (5:28, 30, 31 and LXX Gen. 3:3), "see" (5:32 and LXX Gen. 3:6), "done" (5:32 and LXX Gen. 3:13), "fear" (5:32 and LXX Gen. 3:10), "happen" (5:33 and LXX Gen. 3:22), "told" (5:33 and LXX Gen. 3:13), and "said" (5:34 and LXX Gen. 3:16).

4. Marcus, *Mark 1–8*, 358.

the opposite of what happens. In the Genesis text, Adam is passive. In the bleeding woman's story, Jesus is also passive.

As a result of all of these associations, Mark's audience assumes that Jesus will be filling the role of Adam when the stories are compared. However, when Jesus asks a question and then pronounces a blessing (instead of the expected curse), it becomes clear that he is no longer filling the role of Adam but rather the role of God, since in the Garden of Eden it is God who asks the questions and pronounces the curses. Much as with the calming of the storm, Mark began by encouraging the audience to think of Jesus in one particular narrative role but then abruptly shifted so that he was in the role of God instead. In both stories, after the transgressive touch, the woman hides from the divine presence until summoned by a question about her behavior. In the garden, God asks whether Eve has eaten; in Mark, Jesus asks who has touched him. In both stories, the focus of the passage is on the consequences of the woman's actions. But whereas Eve's choice to touch resulted in her separation from God, the bleeding woman's choice to touch resulted in her communion with Jesus and acceptance as his daughter. In Mark, the wording suggests that the woman came back when questioned, implying that she had already moved on. She had left Jesus' presence, analogous to leaving the garden and the presence of God. In other words, Jesus invited the now-healed woman back into his presence. This is in contrast to the story of Eve, where she is cast out from the presence of the Lord for her action.

The story of the Fall ends with serious consequences and curses; Mark's story ends with a blessing ("go in peace"). Genesis 3 ends with Eve's desire for her husband; the story of the bleeding woman begins with her desire for Jesus (who is in the role of Adam). The story ends with the woman assuming the role, not of wife, but of daughter; this is because Jesus' role in the story has shifted from Adam's to God's.[5]

So careful attention to the ways in which the story of the bleeding woman echoes the story of the Fall suggests that, once again, Jesus begins in one narrative role but ends in another; his final role is that of God.

Jesus Passes By

The story of Jesus walking on the sea in chapter 6 places Jesus in God's narrative role in multiple ways. First, Mark notes that Jesus intended to

---

5. Smith, "Redemptive Reading of Mark 5:25–34," 100.

"pass by" the disciples (6:48). Several biblical texts make reference to a divine "parade," in which God "passes by" a person as a way of revealing the divine presence. In the LXX, "to pass by" is "almost a technical term for a divine epiphany."[6] For example, Job 9:11 reads, "he goeth by me, and I see him not: he passeth [by] also, but I perceive him not." Not only is the divine presence "passing by" Job, but Job is unaware of it, which is also the case for the disciples in Mark's story. This text from Job may have particular resonance for Mark's story since just a few verses earlier in Job 9:8, Job described God as walking upon the sea: "thus, in Job 9 the image of God's walking on the sea is linked with a confession of God's mysterious transcendence of human comprehension: God's 'passing by' is a metaphor for our inability to grasp his power."[7] Other instances of God "passing by" humans include Exodus 33:19–34:8 and 1 Kings 19:11. If these texts are the background to Mark's story, it shifts the emphasis away from the miracle of walking on water to the manifestation of the divine. Jesus' intention was to reveal himself as a divine being by "passing them by" as he walked on the water, but his plan is foiled by his disciples' fear that they are seeing a ghost.

In 6:50, Jesus attempts to calm his disciples; he says, "I am" (KJV: "it is I"). When God appeared to Moses through the burning bush, Moses asks by what name he should refer to God. God replies, "I AM" (Ex. 3:14). Jesus uses the same words as the LXX for this title, which means that he is claiming the distinct name of God for himself. This is incredibly significant in terms of Mark's Christology. Ironically, Jesus' intention to "pass by" as a divine manifestation to the disciples is foiled by the disciples' assumption that Jesus is a ghost, but Jesus responds to their confusion and terror by revealing himself as God. The story is an excellent example of Mark's unique mixture of high and low Christology: Jesus intends to reveal himself as God but is initially thwarted in his plan (by his disciples' screaming), yet he ultimately accomplishes the revelation to the audience, if not to the disciples.

The Christological revelation of this story is even greater when it is read in the light of the previous sea crossing in Mark: in that first sea miracle, the story ended with the question "what manner of man is this, that even the wind and the sea obey him?" (4:41). This sea miracle answers that question via Jesus' announcement that he is the great "I AM." And in both cases, Jesus' control of the sea shows him exercising a power that only God was thought to possess.

---

6. Marcus, *Mark 1–8,* 426.
7. Hays, "Can the Gospels," 410.

Mark's story probably also alludes to Exodus 20:18–20. In that text, the people are aware of God's presence on the mountain, and they are afraid. They want to keep their distance, and they want Moses (and only Moses) to speak with God. Moses tells them to have courage and that God has come to them to test them. The parallels to Mark's story are instructive: Jesus too was in the mountain as the story begins, and the disciples are also afraid of him. In both cases, the message to have courage is conveyed. An allusion to the Exodus text implies that the purpose of God's presence was to test the people. Jesus' divine "passing by" and walking on the water is a test that, as Mark explains in 6:52, the disciples did not pass. There, Mark tells the audience that the disciples did not understand what was happening because they had not considered the miracles of the loaves. This suggests that there was something beyond the surface of the event to understand: that Jesus' passing by, walking on water, and "I AM" statement were supposed to be interpreted by the disciples as evidence that he is the God of the HB. The disciples were not able to understand this message because they did not consider how the feeding miracle showed Jesus to be like God, who provided manna to his people in the wilderness.

Jesus as the God Who Grants Petitions

After conversing with a Greek woman, Jesus performs an exorcism on her daughter in 7:29. Extensive parallels link the Greek woman's story and Hannah's story (see 1 Sam. 1–2). Both feature a desperate woman from the geographic periphery of her respective narrative who struggles under the weight of a problem that threatens her progeny. In both stories, the women approach the location of divine comfort (Hannah's story refers to the "house of the Lord"; Mark's text uses the same two words for "house" and "Lord" as the LXX), each with an unorthodox approach (Hannah by praying silently and the Greek woman by boldly making her request). The women are initially rebuffed by a religious leader, but both meet his rejection with kind but firm words that result in a changed approach from the male leader. They both go home with a promise of healing but without any evidence of it. Each woman is granted what she wanted. Interestingly, both texts refer to food in similar ways: Hannah does not eat for her grief, and Jesus compares the Greek woman's situation to begging for bread that she cannot have. There may also be a parallel in that Eli does not hear Hannah's silent prayer, much as Jesus does not "hear" the Greek woman's initial request until she clarifies her position. Similarly, when the women respond to the initial rebuffs, both stories use the same verb (Greek: *apokrinomai*), both have a doubled verb to introduce her response, and both responses have the woman call her conversation partner "Lord" (Greek: *kyrios*). And while the same Greek words are not used, there is a high degree of similarity to the sentiment after the woman's second statement, with both Eli and Jesus telling the women to "go"; but where Eli says, "may the God of Israel grant your petition," Jesus announces that the devil has gone out of the Syrophenician woman's daughter. At the moment when a reader alert to the allusion would expect Jesus to refer to the God of Israel, he announces on his own authority that the woman's request has been granted, aligning himself with the God of Israel. This is yet another instance in an intertextual reading when Jesus shifts from one narrative role into God's role.

Jesus Approaches the Temple

In chapter 10, Jesus, on his way to Jerusalem and the temple, converses with the rich man who asks him what he must do to have eternal life. This story likely alludes to Malachi 3. In that text, the Lord is on the way to the temple to examine its corruption, as Jesus is "on the way" to the temple to examine its corruption in Mark's text. Malachi asks who will be able to stand when the Lord comes, so the rich man's kneeling could be read as a narrative signal that the man cannot "stand" in the Lord's presence[8] (as his unwillingness to divest of his possessions will later indicate). An allusion to Malachi might help explain Jesus' puzzling objection to being called good: in Malachi, apparently innocuous questions weary the Lord (Mal. 2:17).[9] A close link between the two texts comes with Malachi 3:5, which in the LXX uses the same Greek word for "defraud" (KJV: "oppress") as is found in 10:19. Another verbal link exists with the word "observed" (10:20), which is also found in LXX Malachi 3:7 (KJV: "kept"): in Mark, the rich man insists that he has observed the commandments, but the link to the Malachi texts suggests that the Lord's complaint is that he has not in fact done so. Further, Jesus' reference to "treasures in heaven" (10:21) echoes Malachi 3:10's use of "treasure" (KJV: "storehouse") and "heaven." But the rich man rejects Jesus' offer, just as the audience rejects the Lord's offer in Malachi. The surprising reference to Jesus' love for the man echoes the "theme of God's covenantal love for unfaithful Israel [that] underlies

---

8. Hicks, "Markan Discipleship," 189.
9. Hicks, "Markan Discipleship," 190.

the entire book of Malachi."[10] These allusions to the Malachi text would once again place Jesus in the narrative role of the God of the HB.

Minor Alignments

While the above examples of Jesus in God's narrative role are well developed, there are many minor instances where Jesus occupies this role.

1. Mark 1:3 quotes Isaiah 40:3. Both the Hebrew and the LXX of Isaiah 40:3 read "our God" where Mark has "his" (referring to Jesus) in reference to the "path." The change from "God" to "his" creates a link between Jesus and God. This is particularly significant since it occurs so early in the narrative.

2. In 1:16–20, Jesus calls his disciples, but "the call of the disciples is what God does to make people prophets, not what rabbis do to make people disciples. The claim is absolute, asking what only God can ask."[11]

3. In 2:19, Jesus presents himself as the bridegroom. The HB never identifies the Messiah as the bridegroom, but does associate the God of Israel and the bridegroom (Isa. 54:5; 61:10; 62:4–5; Jer. 2:2; Ezek. 16; Hosea 2:19–20), which means that Jesus is implicitly identifying himself with the God of the HB.

4. In 3:5, Jesus tells the man with the withered hand to stretch out his hand, using the same phrase as LXX Exodus 14:16. This parallel puts the man with the withered hand in the role of Moses and Jesus in the role of the God.

5. In 3:13, Jesus calls his chosen disciples on a mountain. In the Bible, mountains are symbolic spaces where humans encounter God, most notably in the case of Moses on Mt. Sinai (Ex. 19; see also Ex. 34; Num. 27:12; and Deut. 9–10). So in Mark, God's role is filled by Jesus.

6. The exorcism of a Gentile in chapter 5 echoes Isaiah 65:1–7 through multiple shared themes. But Isaiah 65 is in the voice of God, which means that the association between the two passages emphasizes the alignment between Jesus and the God of the Bible.

7. When Jesus raises Jairus's daughter from the dead, he does so without praying; this is in contrast to raisings performed by Elijah and Elisha, which required prayer to raise the dead (1 Kgs. 16:17–24; 2 Kgs. 4:18–37). Thus, Jesus takes the role of God, not the role of a prophet, when he raises the girl.[12]

---

10. Hicks, "Markan Discipleship," 194.

11. M. Eugene Boring, "Markan Christology: God-Language for Jesus?" *New Testament Studies* 45 (October 1999): 465.

12. Ira Brent Driggers, "God as Healer of Creation in the Gospel of Mark," in *Character Studies and the Gospel of Mark*, ed. Christopher W. Skinner and Matthew Ryan Hauge (London: Bloomsbury, 2014), 87.

8. The miracles of the loaves and fishes (6:35–44; 8:1–9) echo the miracle of the manna in Numbers 11. Moses despairs of feeding the people in the wilderness without sufficient resources; his complaint mirrors that of the disciples in Mark's texts. God intervenes by showing Moses how he will be able to feed all of the people. This allusion aligns Jesus with the God of the Bible as the miraculous provider of food to those in need.

9. In 7:15, Jesus overrides the law of Moses (he does not merely reinterpret it). This places him in the role of law giver.[13]

10. In the ancient world, it was thought that in order for a temple to be destroyed, the God whom it honored would have to have abandoned it.[14] Mark's notice that Jesus has just left the temple (13:1–2) takes on an added resonance and symbolic meaning, positioning Jesus as God, when Jesus speaks of the temple's coming destruction.

Taken together, these instances combine to suggest a clearly established pattern in Mark's Gospel: Jesus is identified with the God of the HB. At this point, it is worth reconsidering the earlier materials that showed Jesus exercising God's power. While in isolation, it is possible to argue that in those instances Jesus was not being aligned with God but rather was having God's power extended to him, now that there are over a dozen instances of Jesus occupying God's role in this Gospel, there is no reason to eliminate the possibility that in those earlier examples Jesus was exercising God's unique powers.

Given the history of Christological thought, it is perhaps natural that one would at this point ponder precisely how Mark understands the relationship between Jesus and God: Are they actually one and the same, or something else? If the later, what are the precise contours of their relationship? There is evidence in Mark that they are not identical; this includes the voice from heaven at Jesus' baptism and the Transfiguration, as well as Jesus' prayers in Gethsemane and on the cross. But Mark simply does not engage the kind of intricate questions regarding the relationship between the Father and the Son that would obsess later Christians. Demanding that Mark answer questions that were not posed during Mark's lifetime is probably about as productive as trying to determine whether Joseph Smith preferred Apple or Android.

---

13. Boring, "Markan Christology," 467.
14. Kloppenborg, "*Evocatio Deorum* and the Date of Mark," 441.

MARK'S FULL CHRISTOLOGY

Mark's Christology is not one-dimensional: the high aspects mentioned above are complemented by lower aspects. Mark often paints a more human portrait of Jesus:

1. Jesus seeks out John the Baptist for baptism.

2. Jesus exhibits a variety of emotions, including compassion (1:41; 6:34; 7:29), anger (3:5), grief (3:5; 14:33–34), indignation (10:14), and distress (14:33–34). Most significant are his expressions of amazement (4:40; 6:6; 14:34) since that emotion generally requires one's expectations to be violated. Also, Jesus responds to the leper by "snorting like a horse" (1:43; KJV: "straitly charged").[15]

3. In 5:7–8, Jesus' first attempt at exorcism is not successful.

4. In 5:30, Jesus does not know who touched him.

5. In 7:24–30, Jesus changes his mind in response to the words of a gentile woman. This story also involves the use of what was probably an ethnic slur ("dogs" in 7:27).

6. In 8:22–26, Jesus does not heal the blind man on the first attempt.

7. In 13:32, Jesus explains that he does not know the timing of the return of the Son of Man.

8. Mark strongly and frequently emphasizes Jesus' sufferings. This comes through the three predictions of Jesus' suffering that structure the middle section of the text (8:31–32; 9:30–32; 10:32–34) as well as the depiction of Jesus' death on the cross, including his scream and his sense of abandonment by God (15:34–37) as well as his inability to carry his own cross (15:20).

These instances suggest a fully human presentation of Jesus in Mark and, hence, evince a lower Christology. These examples of Jesus' human nature can make some modern readers uncomfortable, but they are an important part of Mark's portrayal of Jesus: they show that Jesus was indeed fully human. The Latter-day Saint tradition provides additional evidence of Jesus' fully human condition: a comparison of Jesus' similar words in Matthew 5:48 ("be ye therefore perfect, even as your Father which is in heaven is perfect") with 3 Nephi 12:48 ("be ye therefore perfect even as I, or your Father who is in heaven is perfect") illustrates that the mortal Jesus was not perfect. Further, D&C 93:12–14 explains that Jesus "received not of the fulness at first, but received grace for grace; And he received not of the fulness at first, but continued from grace to grace, until he received a

---

15. Marcus, *Mark 1–8*, 205. See also Witherington, *Gospel of Mark*, 99.

fulness; And thus he was called the Son of God, because he received not of the fulness at the first." Given that D&C 93:17 infers that the "fulness" is "all power" and "the glory of the Father," these verses may indicate that the mortal Jesus, lacking the divine power and glory of God, learned and grew "from grace to grace" like other imperfect mortals.[16]

So Mark is neither high nor low, but full. Perhaps the best evidence for this full Christology comes from the capstone story of Mark's Gospel: the anointing of Jesus.[17] In 14:3–9, Jesus is anointed in a story that serves as the narrative and theological hinge of the text. The fact that Jesus is anointed by a woman implies a lower Christology, and yet because the anointing symbolically suggests his royal nature, it encapsulates both the high and low aspects of Mark's Christology in one—perhaps leading directly to Jesus' statement that wherever the gospel is preached throughout the whole world, this story of his anointing should be told. As Eugene Boring explains, "Narrative is capable of affirming dialectic in a way that is difficult for discursive logic. Mark exploits this capability in his presentation of Jesus."[18]

IMPLICATIONS

The position that Mark's Christology is full, rather than high or low, leads to at least three significant implications:

1. A major theme of Mark's Gospel is discipleship, so it is important to consider Mark's Christology in light of what the text has to say about the disciples. It becomes apparent that the disciples—especially the Twelve and

---

16. Given the Latter-day Saint belief that Jesus "was in all points tempted like as we are, yet without sin" (Heb. 4:15), episodes which depict a very human Jesus being angry, sarcastic, or prejudiced can be puzzling. There are several possible ways to understand these stories: (1) These stories are accurate recollections of Jesus' actions and thus were included in the Gospels. This approach may be uncomfortable for Latter-day Saint readers, who view Jesus' sinlessness as a prerequisite for his atoning sacrifice. (2) While God would have counted these actions as sinful for someone possessing perfect knowledge, in Jesus' limited mortal state he was not culpable for these actions (see D&C 82:3). (3) These actions, though they appear troubling to us from a modern perspective, may have been less problematic within Jesus' historical and cultural context. (4) These stories are imperfect recollections of Jesus' actions. More accurate descriptions of Jesus' actions in these situations would exonerate him.

17. Smith, "'She Hath Wrought a Good Work,'" 31–46.

18. Boring, "Markan Christology," 462.

most especially Peter—swing between a Christology too low and one too high. Peter's view of Jesus is far too low in the instances where he wants to manage and direct Jesus' ministry for him (1:37; 9:5) and yet far too high when he rejects Jesus' prophecies of suffering (8:32). Like the other disciples, Peter is unable to grasp a full Christology. The exception to this, as previously mentioned, is the woman who anoints Jesus, whose actions—uniquely in this Gospel—embrace a full Christological vision.

2. Generally speaking, the lower elements of Mark's Christology are apparent on the surface—they are manifest in titles applied to Jesus or in the actions of Jesus that make him seem very human—while the higher elements are found via allusion to biblical texts. This suggests that the audiences' initial impression of Mark's Gospel would probably involve a lower Christology, while deeper exposure and further consideration—particularly for that portion of the audience familiar with the HB—would have suggested a higher (and thus a fuller) Christology. Under the current model of thinking of Mark as a text primarily for oral performance, honed and maybe even composed orally, and existing fundamentally as an oral text, one can easily imagine audiences hearing the gospel more than once and being gently led from a lower to a fuller Christology as a part of that experience.

3. A close reading of Mark disputes the idea of a historical development from low to high Christology. While there was historical development in understandings of Christology, the track was not from low to high but rather from full to high. The lower elements of Markan Christology are usually elided by Matthew and Luke, and John's tradition is almost entirely lacking in these lower elements. The trajectory of the historical development of the canonized Gospels at least shows a diminished portrait of Jesus, changed from being painted with Mark's full palette to John's far more restricted one.

Appendix H:
The "Messianic Secret" in Mark

There is a most curious aspect to Mark's Gospel: Jesus frequently tells people to *not* tell others what he has done for them and sometimes he appears to try to hide his identity.[1] Scholars have offered various theories to explain this phenomenon, which came to be called the "messianic secret." The first prominent theory, advanced in the early twentieth century by William Wrede, was that the messianic secret did not originate with Jesus but rather was constructed later in the tradition in order to explain why Jesus was not perceived to be a Messiah. While this theory was popular for much of the twentieth century, it became less so in the 1970s when the argument was made that the theory did not entirely account for all of the data. Today, scholars generally recognize the tendency in Mark's Gospel for Jesus to put restrictions on the proclamation of his identity, but they no longer accept Wrede's explanation for it; not all scholars accept the idea of a messianic secret in Mark,[2] and those who do turn to other explanations for it. Some have held that secrecy was appropriate before Jesus' death because it would have been premature to declare that Jesus was the Christ before that point. A variation on this theory is that it would have been misleading for people to follow Jesus solely because he was a miracle worker, and so Jesus did not want people drawn to him for that reason.[3] Support for this theory may be found in the idea that Jesus was actually quite open when prophesying about his suffering (8:31–33).

---

1. For examples of the "messianic secret," see 1:25, 34, 43–45; 3:11–12; 5:43; 7:36; 8:26, 30; and 9:9. There is one odd exception to the general rule of secrecy: Jesus tells the man who had had a demon, a Gentile, to tell his family that Jesus had healed him (5:19).

2. Gundry, *Mark,* 1.

3. Of course, this raises the question: Why did Jesus perform miracles if it was not helpful for people to know about them?

A curious aspect about the secrecy motif is the frequency with which Mark records that it is violated; Jesus' requests for secrecy are often ignored, and Mark records the results (1:25–28, 43–45; 7:36–37). These passages cast doubt on Wrede's theory that the idea of Jesus as Messiah is a later creation because if Mark's story is that Jesus really was the Messiah and that the reason no one realized it was because Jesus told people not to tell, then it makes little sense to show Jesus' command being violated on multiple occasions. There is no current scholarly consensus regarding the messianic secret in Mark, though most experts recognize that Jesus tried to limit transmission of knowledge about his identity. Beyond that, there is no agreement regarding the purpose or parameters of the prohibition.

A few Latter-day Saint writers have weighed in on the idea of secrecy in Mark's Gospel. Daniel C. Peterson points to the existence of the messianic secret as evidence that secrecy is not foreign to Christianity in a defense of the Latter-day Saint practice of maintaining secrecy around temple rituals.[4] Daniel B. McKinlay has similarly argued that what can appear to be "the messianic secret" in Mark is not the result of Mark fabricating a practice of Jesus, but rather was the very real practice of restricting some teachings to an inner group of disciples.[5] Two objections might be raised to these interpretations: first, the material that Jesus asked the disciples to keep secret does not overlap with the material central to modern Latter-day Saint temple ritual and, second, what Jesus tried to keep secret during his ministry *was* revealed in the Gospel of Mark, suggesting that the function of secrecy is different in Mark.[6] Roger R. Keller explains the messianic secret in different terms, finding two reasons for the secret. First, the crush of people that resulted when people violated Jesus' request for secrecy (1:38, 45) made it impossible for Jesus to pursue his ministry; he had to go into the desert to avoid the crowds. Thus the purpose of the secrecy was to permit Jesus to fulfill his ministry. Second, it created a false impression of what it meant to be the Messiah when people were focused on Jesus as a miracle

---

4. See Daniel C. Peterson, *Offenders for a Word* (Provo, Utah: Foundation for Ancient Research and Mormon Studies, 1998), 108–17.

5. Daniel B. McKinlay, "Temple Imagery in the Epistle of Peter," in *Temples of the Ancient World: Ritual and Symbolism,* ed. Donald W. Parry (Salt Lake City: Deseret Book; Provo, Utah: Foundation for Ancient Research and Mormon Studies, 1994), 509.

6. For it to be parallel with modern Latter-day Saint practice, one would envision a situation where, a generation after Joseph Smith's death, Latter-day Saint writers made the contents of the temple ceremony freely available in writing.

worker and did not understand that Jesus had come to suffer and die.[7] This theory is more in line with the thinking of non–Latter-day Saint scholars on the subject.

It is difficult to draw conclusions about the messianic secret because the evidence for its existence is mixed and somewhat complicated. Perhaps it is safe to say that Mark has a general tendency to feature Jesus asking people not to publicize certain aspects of his ministry. Latter-day Saint readers would not generally be sympathetic to Wrede's argument that the idea of Jesus as Messiah originated not with Jesus but with the later church; they might find an affinity between Jesus' requests for secrecy and modern Latter-day Saint practices related to temple worship, although it must be admitted that the comparison is not precise. Jesus' requests for people to not preach about his healing miracles is most likely tied to his desire that, particularly before his death, people are not misled about what it means to be a Messiah.

---

7. Keller, "Mark and Luke," 92–107.

Appendix I:
The Joseph Smith Translation[1]

Joseph Smith believed that he was called by God to produce a new translation of the Bible (D&C 45:60–61; 76:15; 90:13; 93:53). He did not work from ancient texts but rather claimed inspiration as one of his sources. Joseph Smith and his contemporaries normally referred to his project of Bible translation as the New Translation. When excerpts of it were added to the Latter-day Saint Bible in the late twentieth century, it required a new moniker (since "NT" was already in use as the abbreviation for the New Testament), so it became known as the Joseph Smith Translation (hereafter JST); since this term is now in wide use, it is used herein despite the anachronism. (This appendix also uses the KJV versification—not the JST versification, which sometimes differs. The JST did change verse numbers, but that system is no longer in use. Where the JST versification differs from the KJV, it reflects a system adopted by the Reorganized Church of Jesus Christ of Latter Day Saints/Community of Christ. Since it is not original to the text and since it can create confusion, it is not used here, despite the fact that it is used in the Latter-day Saint Bible.)

About one-third of the JST is included in the Latter-day Saint Bible; many Latter-day Saint are unaware that not all of the JST is included. Further, what is included is not a representative sample. Robert J. Matthews describes the criteria used to determine what was included: "It was anything that was doctrinal, anything that was necessary in the Old Testament to help us understand the New Testament, anything that bore witness of Christ, anything that bore witness of the Restoration. ... Also anything

---

1. Originally published as Julie M. Smith, "Five Impulses of the Joseph Smith Translation of Mark and Their Implications for LDS Hermeneutics," *Studies in the Bible and Antiquity* 7 (2015), available at https://scholarsarchive.byu.edu/sba/vol7/iss1/2. The paper, with some changes, is reproduced here with permission.

that clarified the role of the tribe of Joseph . . . paramount to the work of the Lord in the last days. . . . There was one other item, and that is anything that was clarified in the JST which no other scripture would clarify."[2]

Latter-day Saint scholars suggest that the JST consists of several kinds of material, including restoration of the original text, inspired commentary, harmonization, simplification, and perhaps other kinds of material as well. There is no absolute way to determine which kind of material any particular JST passage is, although sometimes it is possible to rule out certain options.[3] This means that the reader cannot absolutely determine whether a particular JST restores the original text or is serving some other function. Since the guiding question of this commentary is "How would Mark's first audiences have understood this story?" and since some (perhaps many?) of the JST changes would not have been known to those audiences, the JST is not discussed in the main portion of the commentary and is instead discussed in this appendix. Not every JST change is included in the Latter-day Saint Bible; readers will want to consult Thomas Wayment's book (which, helpfully, provides the KJV and JST in side-by-side columns) for a thorough list of all of the changes.[4] This appendix focuses on the big picture by examining five impulses of the JST in Mark's Gospel. In so doing, some interpretive principles for best practices in reading scripture are suggested—these are suggestions that the commentary has tried to incorporate. In this sense, the commentary itself is imbued with the impulses of the JST even though it does not include the JST changes themselves.

THE IMPULSE TO AMPLIFY MARK'S UNIQUE TENDENCIES

There is a harmonizing impulse to the JST; this means that some of the changes made to the Gospels serve to make the Gospels more similar to each other than they are without the JST changes. This harmonizing

---

2. Quoted in Fred E. Woods, "The Latter-day Saint Edition of the King James Bible," in *The King James Bible and the Restoration,* ed. Kent P. Jackson (Provo, Utah: Religious Studies Center, Brigham Young University, 2011), 269.

3. As Kent P. Jackson wrote, "Even though I believe that the JST restores original text, it is likely that most changes have other explanations." Kent P. Jackson, "New Discoveries in the Joseph Smith Translation of the Bible," in *By Study and by Faith: Selections from the Religious Educator,* ed. Richard Neitzel Holzapfel and Kent P. Jackson (Provo, Utah: Religious Studies Center, Brigham Young University, 2009), 169–81.

4. Thomas A. Wayment, ed., *The Complete Joseph Smith Translation of the New Testament: A Side-by-side Comparison with the King James Version* (Salt Lake City: Deseret Book, 2005).

impulse is evident in both style and content. For example, JST Mark harmonizes Mark's style by changing the historical present tense to the past tense in over two dozen instances, a tendency also found in Matthew and particularly in Luke. One instance of harmonization is the shift in JST Mark from a "young man" at the tomb to "angels" (16:5).

Though beyond the scope of this appendix, this harmonizing impulse deserves more nuanced consideration because while most interpreters of the Bible—at least until very recently—have read Mark through the perspectives of Matthew and Luke, the JST sometimes reads Matthew or Luke through the lens of Mark. For example, JST Matthew 9:18 changes "dead" to "dying" and thus conforms Matthew's account to Mark's.

Despite this harmonizing tendency, the JST also makes many deharmonizing changes.[5] This is evident in the following instances, where the JST extends a theme or method that is already common in Mark:

1. *Penchant for Irony.* The JST for 7:9 adds "by the prophets whom ye have rejected" to Jesus' response and thus increases the irony of Jesus' statement.

2. *Symbolic Use of Narrative Space.* The JST adds "turned away from him" to 14:28 and "went out" to 14:72.

3. *Differing Responses to Jesus.* Mark shows that the common people supported Jesus and that it was the religious leaders who were opposed to him; this is made clearer in JST 12:37 (which adds "but the high priest and the elders were offended at him") than it is in Mark.

4. *Copious Use of the Word "Immediately."* The word "immediately" (Greek: *euthys*) is characteristic of Mark; the JST adds it to 5:17 and 9:8.

5. *Repetition.* The addition of "saying" to 9:12 creates a third verb referring to the action of speaking; this kind of duplication is very Markan.

6. *Provocative Questions and Audience Involvement.* The addition of "who art thou?" in JST 12:34 is similar to 3:4; 4:41; 8:21; and 8:29 and thus in line with Mark's penchant for allowing important questions to dangle in the minds of the audience.[6]

One of the most distinguishing features of Mark is the portrayal of the disciples: they frequently make mistakes, experience inappropriate emotions,[7]

---

5. The JST's preservation of each Gospel writer's voice is discussed in Robert L. Millet, "The JST and the Synoptic Gospels: Literary Style," in *The Joseph Smith Translation: The Restoration of Plain and Precious Truths,* ed. Monte S. Nyman and Robert L. Millet (Provo, Utah: Religious Studies Center, Brigham Young University, 1985), 147–62; and Robert J. Matthews, *"A Plainer Translation": Joseph Smith's Translation of the Bible: A History and Commentary* (Provo, Utah: Brigham Young University Press, 1975), 239.

6. Wayment, *Complete Joseph Smith Translation,* 100, 106, 112, 125, 134, 138.

7. Millet, "Literary Style," 154–55.

or say foolish things, and thus merit rebuke from Jesus (4:10–13; 6:52; 8:14–18, 32–33). The JST amplifies this portrait of the disciples in over a dozen instances. For example, after Jesus says in Mark, "But many that are first shall be last; and the last first," the JST adds "this he [Jesus] said, rebuking Peter" (JST 10:31–32). Now that Jesus' statement is labeled a rebuke of Peter, the fact that the JST also changed "many that are first" to "many who make themselves first" becomes more evidence of the disciples' flaws, since it implies that Peter had made himself first—not that he was made first by Jesus. Similarly, in the scene in Gethsemane, the JST adds that the disciples "complain[ed] in their hearts, wondering if this be the Messiah" (JST 14:32). The JST then adds a rebuke of Peter, James,[8] and John. In all four of these instances, the portrayal of the disciples in JST Mark is markedly less positive than it is in Mark. Significantly, the JST did not make changes to the parallel stories in the other Gospel accounts to match any of these instances where the disciples are presented as more flawed in Mark. Thus, Mark's portrait of the disciples is maintained and amplified.

There are other instances where the JST preserves or extends each evangelist's distinct concerns.[9] For example, the JST adds details about Jesus' childhood to Matthew (Matt. 2:22–3:1), despite the fact that Mark's text might be considered a more likely candidate for adding material on that topic since it has no discussion of Jesus' childhood. In addition, the JST adds nine quotations from the HB to Matthew but only one to Mark, which amplifies Matthew's tendency to include references to the fulfillment of prophecies.[10]

The disciples are portrayed more negatively in the following instances:

1. In the report of the disciples' ministry, the JST changes "healed them" to "they were healed" (6:13). This change shifts the credit for the healing away from the disciples and to, presumably, God (via the "divine passive").

2. By changing the third "and" to "as if he" in 6:48, the JST intimates that Jesus was not intending to pass by the disciples as he walked on the water but rather that the disciples misunderstood Jesus' intentions.

3. To the comment that Peter, James, and John accompanied Jesus up the Mount of Transfiguration, the JST adds that they "asked him many questions concerning his saying" (9:2), which implies their lack of understanding.

4. The JST adds "with great astonishment" to the disciples' response to the Transfiguration (9:8), adding emotion and probably heightening the impression of the disciples' lack of understanding.

---

8. See the Notes on 1:19.

9. Millet, "Literary Style," 147–62; Matthews, *"Plainer Translation,"* 240.

10. The JST adds five HB allusions to Luke and three to John. Matthews, *"Plainer Translation,"* 240.

5. The JST adds "being afraid" to explain the disciples' silence when Jesus asks what they were disputing about (9:34). This makes the disciples look even more timid than Mark's text does.

6. Mark 11:13 describes Jesus looking for figs; the JST adds "and as [the disciples] supposed" to suggest that the disciples thought Jesus was looking for figs when Jesus was doing something else. Once again, they do not understand Jesus.

7. In JST 14:29, Peter's denial is changed from "yet will not I" to "yet I will never be offended." This heightening of the language means that Peter's boast is all the more misguided.

8. The JST changes the scene in Gethsemane so that the disciples—not Jesus— are sore amazed and very heavy (14:33), again emphasizing their outsized emotions.

9. The JST adds "and they said unto him" to 14:38, which means that not Jesus but the disciples say, "the spirit truly is ready but the flesh is weak." This makes it sound as if the disciples are rationalizing their weakness rather than Jesus understanding it.

10. In the depiction of Peter's denial of Jesus, the JST changes "thought thereon [and] he wept" to "went out, and fell upon his face, and wept bitterly" (14:72), expanding on the picture of Peter's emotionality.

Not only is each of these changes important in its own right, but together they suggest that preserving and enhancing the unique voice of the Gospel authors was an important impulse of the JST. It was theoretically possible that Joseph Smith could have followed the harmonizing impulse of much of Christian history and produced just one Gospel. The closest the JST comes to collapsing the narratives is with the "little apocalypse" in Matthew 24/Mark 13, which are extremely similar, but even in that case—and despite the incorrect notation in the current Latter-day Saint scriptures— the text of JST Mark 13 is not identical to JST Matthew 24. Thus the JST not only preserved all four distinct accounts but also enhanced some of the unique aspects of the voice of each writer. This suggests that canonized diversity and multivocality are important.

THE IMPULSE TO FOREGROUND WOMEN

On ten occasions, JST Mark either highlights the role of women or makes a passage gender-neutral. For example, to the story of the healing of Simon's mother-in-law (1:30–31), the JST adds the words "came and" before "ministered unto them." This change initially doesn't seem to add much to the text, but it parallels Jesus' earlier action, when he "came and took her by the hand." The JST makes a similar change in 14:3–9 (see the next paragraph), which parallels a woman's actions with Jesus' actions. Thus, the JST emphasizes the woman's ministering role by paralleling it with Jesus' role, a move made in Mark's Gospel but enhanced by the JST. The JST does not add other instances of ministering, so ministering is still only done by women, angels, and Jesus (never other males) in the JST.

The changes made to 14:3–9 are extremely significant. The Joseph Smith Translation for 14:8 creates a chiasmus that is not in the KJV text:

> A she has done what she could . . . had in remembrance
>> B in generations to come
>>> C wheresoever my gospel shall be preached
>>>> D for verily she has come beforehand
>>>>> E to anoint my body to the burying
>>>> D' verily I say unto you
>>> C' wheresoever this gospel shall be preached
>> B' throughout the whole world
> A' what she hath done . . . for a memorial of her[11]

This structure adds depth to the anointing story by first clarifying that the main point of the story, the E line, is the anointing, not the objection and response. It is easy to get sidetracked into a debate regarding whether the woman exercised wise stewardship over some very expensive oil, but the real point of the story is the anointing of Jesus' body. Second, the phrase "verily I say unto you" in the D and D' lines emphasizes not only the importance of the words that follow but also the central point of the chiasmus by literally surrounding it and encourages comparing Jesus' words with the woman's actions. The theological implications of comparing her actions and his words are profound. Third, the B and B' lines are also noteworthy for explaining that "wheresoever my gospel is preached" means not just geographically but also through time. The chiastic structure emphasizes that this story is about the anointing—not the objection—and that the woman's deeds parallel Jesus' words. The mere fact that a JST version exists also suggests that this story was a focus of attention for Joseph Smith. This structure emphasizes the centrality of the anointing woman's words and thus emphasizes her role and prominence. Further, the JST changes "spoken of for a memorial" to "spoken of *also* for a memorial" (JST 14:9; italics added), which means that her story is told for reasons other than just simply to memorialize her. This further emphasizes the woman's importance.

---

11. Smith, "'She Hath Wrought a Good Work,'" 44.

In another instance, the JST changes the description of the Simon who carried Jesus' cross (15:21) so that his child is named "Alexandria" instead of "Alexander" and, thus, is a daughter and not a son. It is possible that this situation parallels that of Junia (Rom. 16:7), where discomfort regarding the important role given to a woman resulted in later scribes performing a grammatical sex change on her.[12] It is possible that something similar happened in this situation; of course, in the context of Mark's text and the JST, this is very speculative, since no role other than daughter would be occupied by Alexandria, but given that most scholars think the reason Simon's children were mentioned at all is because they were personally known to Mark's earliest audiences, it is nonetheless possible and perhaps the most likely explanation for this enigmatic change.

Other changes that highlight women include:

1. In 8:4, the JST changes the word "men" to "so great a multitude." This makes the passage gender-neutral and fits with the analysis of the passage that suggests that, unlike the first feeding miracle, women are present.

2. The word "him" becomes "the child" in JST 9:36, making it possible that the child is female, which makes sense in context since Jesus is emphasizing the low social status of the child. The JST also changes "whosoever shall receive one of such children in my name" in 9:37 to "whosoever shall humble himself like one of these children and receiveth me, ye shall receive in my name"; so if the child is imagined as female, it is significant that Jesus is inviting the audience to model the child.

3. In 11:32, the JST changes the word "men" to "people," which implies that there were females who believed that John the Baptist was a prophet and that the religious authorities feared these women.

4. In 13:3, the JST changes a reference to Peter, James, John, and Andrew to "the disciples," which, in the Markan context, almost certainly includes women (compare 3:31–35 and 15:41). This change is significant because it means that women are included in the audience for the remainder of chapter 13, which implies that these important prophecies were not restricted to a male-only audience and that women will have significant roles in the early Christian church. (And the JST reading perhaps makes better sense of 13:17 than imagining an audience of four male disciples; see below on JST 13:37, which is similarly inclusive.)

5. In 13:32, the JST changes "no man" to "no one," implying that women are included among the angels of God.

6. In 13:37, the JST adds "two shall be grinding at the mill; the one taken, and the other left." Because this would have been understood as women's work, it adds a reference to women to the text.

---

12. John Thorley, "Junia, a Woman Apostle," *Novum Testamentum* 38, no. 1 (1996): 18–29.

7. The JST changes "he" and "young man" to "angels" in 16:5 and 6, which makes the messengers at the tomb gender-neutral and, when read alongside JST 13:32, creates the possibility that the angels were female.

Unlike the dual harmonizing and deharmonizing tendencies, there is no tendency to limit women and their roles in JST Mark. The only JST change that comes close to limiting or erasing women occurs when "her branch" (referring to the fig tree of the parable) is changed to "his branches" (13:28), but this is probably not significant.

THE IMPULSE TO READ CLOSELY AND CRITICALLY

The changes that constitute JST Mark suggest that the text is expected to be read closely and with a critical eye—and was read by Joseph Smith that way. For example, 4:10 relates that Jesus was "alone" when those with him asked about his parable. But he obviously wasn't alone if there were disciples around to ask him questions! The JST changes "alone" to "alone with the twelve and they that believed in him." Similarly, on several occasions, the JST eliminates or changes the word "answered" when the statement following is not a reply to a question (JST 9:19; 10:24, 51; 11:14, 22; 12:35; 15:12). The JST also eliminates hyperbole (JST 1:5; 2:12; 5:20; 9:23). These changes suggests that neither Joseph Smith nor the JST's reader reads passively and acquiescently; rather, the text should be approached with a critical eye.

THE IMPULSE TO MODERNIZE

While quantifying the JST is more art than science, by a rough estimate about seventy-five percent of JST Mark does not change the theological meaning of the text but rather makes it easier to read by modernizing, clarifying, or simplifying the language. This figure is the result of the author's own tally and should be considered an approximation only. To arrive at this number, I counted the number of changes rather than the number of verses changed by the JST; sometimes several changes appear in one verse. (For example, JST 10:24 is counted as having three changes: "that" becomes "who," "saith" becomes "said," and "answereth" becomes "spake.") I divided these changes into three categories: (1) those that did not change the meaning of the text, (2) those that may or may not change the meaning (depending on how they are interpreted), and (3) those that clearly change the meaning of the text. The process of both counting and categorizing is rather subjective; other interpreters would surely arrive at a different number than I did. The purpose of my rough estimate is solely to give a sense of the proportion of changes that do not involve doctrinal shifts.

Instances where the JST makes the text easier to read include changing "river of Jordan" to "river Jordan" (1:15), "of the age of twelve years" to "twelve years old" (5:42), and "so shall it not be" to "shall not be so" (10:43). The word "saith" is replaced by the word "said" in three dozen instances (1:44; 2:10; 3:3, 4, 5; 4:35; 5:19, 36, 39; 6:38, 50; 7:18, 34; 8:1, 12, 17, 29; 9:19, 35; 10:11, 23, 24, 27, 42; 11:2, 21, 33; 12:16, 43; 14:27, 30, 32, 45; 63; 15:28; 16:6); other modernizations include swapping "has" for "hath" (10:52; 14:8), "knew" for "wist" (14:40; 15:25), and "two" for "twain" (10:8—twice in this verse).

THE IMPULSE TO REVISE

The idea that the JST displays an impulse to revise is so self-evident that it may not seem to deserve consideration, but this impulse merits examination both for its details and its implications.

First, some of the details of the production of the JST are suggestive. Joseph Smith began his work on the HB until he felt called to work on the NT, which he then translated before completing the HB. His new translation had included new chapter headings at first, but these were dropped after a while.[13] He and his contemporaries apparently labored under an unwarranted suspicion of italicized words. He initially had his scribes copy the entire new translation—including passages that were not changed from their KJV iteration—but then adopted a different system that involved making notations in the Bible, with only the changes copied out by hand. This system also underwent some evolution. The scribes switched from ink to pencil because the ink bled through the pages of the Bible.[14] Further, in two instances, Joseph Smith accidentally translated the same passage twice,

13. Matthews, *"Plainer Translation,"* 162.

14. Paul W. Lambert and Thomas A. Wayment, "The Nature of the Pen and Pencil Markings in the New Testament of Joseph Smith's New Translation of the Bible," *BYU Studies* 47, no. 2 (2008), 93.

apparently not realizing that he had already translated it. A comparison of the two translations shows that his changes are similar but not identical.[15] Combined, these factors support the conclusion of Robert J. Matthews, who explains, "The translation was not a simple, mechanical recording of divine dictum, but rather a study-and-thought process accompanied and prompted by revelation."[16] Apparently Joseph Smith was given general impressions that he needed to turn into words and general guidelines that he needed to execute. Joseph Smith also revised the JST during his life. All of these details of the translation process suggest to most historians and interpreters that the JST is less analogous to stone tablets carved by the finger of God and handed down from on high and more akin to the idea of learning "line upon line, precept upon precept" (D&C 98:12).

Further, it is instructive to see how Joseph Smith used the JST in his own ministry: in many instances, he would refer to the KJV, not his new translation,[17] and sometimes he would offer alterations to the KJV that were *not* included in the JST; Thomas E. Sherry and W. Jeffrey Marsh find that Joseph Smith's "sermons from 1833 to 1844 are filled with numerous interpretations about Bible verses not found in the JST."[18] This practice,

---

15. Kent P. Jackson and Peter M. Jasinski, "The Process of Inspired Translation: Two Passages Translated Twice in the Joseph Smith Translation of the Bible," *BYU Studies* 42, no. 2 (2003): 35–64.

16. Matthews, *"Plainer Translation,"* 39.

17. For example, JST Job 1:6 and 2:1 change "sons" of God to "children of God," but Joseph Smith, on at least two occasions, referred to Job's account and mentioned the "sons of God." See "Try the Spirits," *Times and Seasons* 3 (April 1, 1842): 745; and "Sons of God," *Times and Seasons* 4 (January 16, 1843): 75. Credit for this observation belongs to Rico Martinez.

18. Thomas E. Sherry and W. Jeffrey Marsh, "Precious Truths Restored: Joseph Smith Translation Changes Not Included in Our Bible," *Religious Educator* 5, no. 2 (2004): 64–65. For example, Joseph Smith later taught that priesthood keys were given to Peter, James, and John on the Mount of Transfiguration, but there is no JST reflecting this.

Additionally, Robert L. Millet explains: "The second verse of the King James Bible describes the state of things in the morning of the creation: 'And the earth was without form, and void' (Genesis 1:2). The JST of this verse is exactly the same as the KJV. In a sermon delivered on 5 January 1841 in Nauvoo, however, Joseph Smith taught that the words 'without form and void' should be translated 'empty and desolate.'" See Robert L. Millet, "Joseph Smith's Translation of the Bible: A Historical Overview," in *The Joseph Smith Translation: The Restoration of Plain and Precious Things,* ed. Monte S. Nyman and Robert L. Millet (Provo, Utah: Religious Studies Center, Brigham Young University, 1985), 33.

A third example: Grant Underwood explains: "Twice in the Book of Mormon, Nephi says the Holy Ghost descended upon Christ 'in the *form* of a dove' (1 Nephi 11:27; 2 Nephi 31:8; emphasis added), and D&C 93:15 reports that 'the Holy Ghost descended

combined with the fact that Joseph Smith later studied Hebrew and Greek, implies that he never regarded the JST as a perfected or final text and still found an important role for the original languages of the Bible, the KJV, and continuing revelation.

So in both process and product, Joseph Smith regarded the JST as subject to revision and rerevision. This impulse to revise carries important implications. First, in contrast to traditional Latter-day Saint assumptions, the JST should not be regarded as a perfect text. Sometimes the language of D&C 35:20 ("the scriptures shall be given, even as they are in mine own bosom, to the salvation of mine own elect") is used to elevate the status of the JST. But an interpretation that suggests that the JST approaches a state of perfection is not sustainable. A closer analysis of D&C 35:20 suggests the same. First, the only biblical use of the phrase "own bosom" is Psalm 35:13, where the context is that the unanswered prayer the psalmist has returned to his "own bosom." Thus when read contextually, the language of D&C 35:20 might very well imply that the perfected iteration of scripture that resides in the heavens cannot be expected to be perfectly conveyed. Second, the verses building up to D&C 35:20 present Joseph Smith as a limited, mortal messenger: D&C 35:17 speaks of his weakness, D&C 35:18 warns him that his calling is subject to his obedience, D&C 35:19 contains a command to "watch over him that his faith fail not." Combined, these three statements contextualize Joseph Smith's abilities as limited and contingent. Nonetheless, the passage assures that his work will be adequate if not inerrant. Further, it is possible that "the scriptures" that would be

---

upon him in the *form* of a dove, *and sat upon him*' (emphasis added). Subsequently, Joseph elaborated, 'The dove which sat upon Christ's shoulder was a sure testimony that he was of God. . . . Any spirit or body that is attended by a dove you may know to be a pure spirit.' This insight was given more detailed formulation two years later. 'The Holy Ghost cannot be transformed into a Dove,' Joseph reportedly explained, 'but the sign of a Dove was given to John to signify the Truth of the Deed as the Dove was an emblem or Token of Truth.'" See Grant Underwood, "Joseph Smith and the King James Bible," in *The King James Bible and the Restoration,* ed. Kent P. Jackson (Provo, Utah: Religious Studies Center, Brigham Young University, 2011), 217–18; italics in original.

And, finally, as Robert L. Millet explains: "Just five months before his death the Prophet clarified another biblical passage which had received no alteration in the JST. 'The question is frequently asked, "Can we not be saved without going through with all those ordinances?" I would answer, No, not the fulness of salvation. Jesus said, There are many mansions in my Father's house, and I will go and prepare a place for you. *House* here named should have been translated kingdom; and any person who is exalted to the highest mansion has to abide a celestial law, and the whole law too.'" Millet, "Joseph Smith's Translation," 33–34; italics in original.

given refers to other revelations, such as D&C sections.[19] Treating the JST as an indisputable solution to a problem in the text is not legitimate if it is recognized that Joseph Smith himself did not treat the new translation in a dogmatic way. The JST illustrates that inerrancy is not a reasonable expectation from scripture.

The JST shows that a text cannot be considered perfect because it must always interact with an audience and what an audience brings to the text changes over time. For example, JST 2:14 explains what it means that Levi was at the "receipt of custom," which is perhaps helpful for modern readers of the JST but would not have been necessary for Mark's earliest audiences nor for readers of modern English translations. So the ability of the text to communicate its intent is not strictly a product of some hypothetical state of perfection resident in the text itself but also of the audience's level of knowledge. In other words, a verse that might have been perfectly functional, if not inerrant, when written, is rendered in need of revision by the passage of time resulting in an unawareness of the practice mentioned in the text. Further, there is wide recognition that the JST contains a variety of material—restoration, commentary, harmonization, modernization, doctrinal correction—but the JST reader has no obvious way to distinguish between the types. This has an important effect on the audience, who must accept their inability to determine which is which. To sum, the JST provides the modern reader with a potent vein of insight that invites careful consideration. The JST makes reading the Gospel of Mark not easier but richer.

---

19. Credit for this insight belongs to Rico Martinez.

Appendix J:
Suggestions for Further Study

Despite its length, this commentary is very narrow;[1] the following volumes are recommended for further study.

For close studies of the Greek text:
> Decker, Rodney J. *Mark 1–8: A Handbook on the Greek Text*. Waco, Tex.: Baylor University Press, 2014.
> ———. *Mark 9–16: A Handbook on the Greek Text*. Waco, Tex.: Baylor University Press, 2014.

For general study and particularly for biblical allusions:
> Marcus, Joel. *Mark 1–8*. New York: Doubleday, 2002.
> ———. *Mark 8–16*. New Haven: Yale University Press, 2009.

For an overview of various approaches to interpreting Mark:
> Anderson, Janice Capel, and Stephen D. Moore, eds. *Mark and Method: New Approaches in Biblical Studies*. 2d ed. Minneapolis: Fortress Press, 2008.

For allusions to Hellenistic literature:
> Collins, Adela Yarbro. *Mark: A Commentary*. Minneapolis: Fortress Press, 2007.

For the structure of the text:
> Deppe, Dean B. *The Theological Intentions of Mark's Literary Devices: Markan Intercalations, Frames, Allusionary Repetitions, Narrative Surprises, and Three Types of Mirroring*. Eugene, Ore.: Wipf and Stock, 2015.

---

1. See the introduction for a discussion of which approaches to Mark are taken in this commentary and which are ignored.

For brief treatments of literary issues:

Rhoads, David, Joanna Dewey, and Donald Michie. *Mark As Story: An Introduction to the Narrative of a Gospel.* 3d ed. Minneapolis: Fortress Press, 2012.

Dowd, Sharyn. *Reading Mark: A Literary and Theological Commentary on the Second Gospel.* Macon, Ga.: Smyth and Helwys, 2000.

For surveys of various interpretive options for each passage:

Blight, Richard C. *An Exegetical Summary of Mark 1–8.* Dallas, Tex.: SIL International, 2012.

————. *An Exegetical Summary of Mark 9–16.* Dallas, Tex.: SIL International, 2014.

For a curmudgeonly rebuttal to various creative interpretations of the text:

Gundry, Robert H. *Mark: A Commentary on His Apology for the Cross.* Grand Rapids, Mich.: William B. Eerdmans Publishing, 1993.

For an exploration of the theme of honor and shame in Mark's Gospel:

Kinukawa, Hisako. *Women and Jesus in Mark: A Japanese Feminist Perspective.* Maryknoll, N.Y.: Orbis Books, 1994.

For a consideration of Mark as narrative:

Malbon, Elizabeth S. *Mark's Jesus: Characterization As Narrative Christology.* Waco, Tex.: Baylor University Press, 2009.

For a close look at stories about women in Mark:

Miller, Susan. *Women in Mark's Gospel.* New York: T and T Clark International, 2004.

For a focus on the political and economic dimensions of Mark:

Myers, Ched. *Binding the Strong Man: A Political Reading of Mark's Story of Jesus.* Maryknoll, N.Y.: Orbis Books, 1995.

For a focus on Mark as an oral performance:

Shiner, Whitney. *Proclaiming the Gospel: First-Century Performance of Mark.* Harrisburg, Pa.: Trinity Press International, 2003.

Bibliography

Alt, Christopher E. "The Dynamic of Humility and Wisdom: The Syrophoenician Woman and Jesus in Mark 7:24–31a." *Lumen et Vita* 2 (2012). https://ejournals.bc.edu/ojs/index.php/lumenetvita/article/view/1901.

Ambrozic, A. M. "Mark's Concept of the Parable: Mk 4, 11f. in the Context of the Second Gospel." *Catholic Biblical Quarterly* 29, no. 2 (1967): 220–27.

Anderson, Janice Capel, and Stephen D. Moore. "Introduction: The Lives of Mark." In *Mark and Method: New Approaches in Biblical Studies,* ed. Janice Capel Anderson and Stephen D. Moore, 1–27. 2d ed. Minneapolis: Fortress Press, 2008.

Austin, Michael. *Re-reading Job: Understanding the Ancient World's Greatest Poem.* Salt Lake City: Greg Kofford Books, 2014.

Bamberger, Bernard J. "Defilement by Discharge from the Sex Organs." In *The Torah: A Modern Commentary,* ed. W. Gunther Plaut, 849–55. New York: Union of American Hebrew Congregations, 1981.

Barlow, Philip L. M*ormons and the Bible: The Place of the Latter-day Saints in American Religion.* New York: Oxford University Press, 1991.

Barney, Kevin L. "The Joseph Smith Translation and Ancient Texts of the Bible." *Dialogue: A Journal of Mormon Thought* 19, no. 3 (1987): 85–102.

Barr, Steve. "The Eye of the Needle—Power and Money in the New Community: A Look at Mark 10:17–31." *Andover Newton Review* 3, no. 1 (1992): 31–44.

Barton, Stephen C. "Mark As Narrative: The Story of the Anointing Woman (Mk 14:3–9)." *Expository Times* 102, no. 8 (1990–91): 230–34.

Bauckham, Richard. *Jesus and the Eyewitnesses: The Gospels as Eyewitness Testimony.* Grand Rapids, Mich.: William B. Eerdmans Publishing, 2006.

Bauckham, Richard. "The Son of Man: 'A Man in My Position' or 'Someone'?" *Journal for the Study of the New Testament* 23 (1985): 23–33.

Beavis, Mary Ann. "The Resurrection of Jephthah's Daughter: Judges 11:34–40 and Mark 5:21–24, 35–43." *Catholic Biblical Quarterly* 72, no. 1 (2010): 46–62.

———. "Women as Models of Faith in Mark," *Biblical Theology Bulletin* 18, no. 1 (1988): 3–9.

Betz, Hans Dieter. "Jesus and the Purity of the Temple (Mark 11:15–18): A Comparative Religion Approach." *Journal of Biblical Literature* 116, no. 3 (1997): 455–72.

Blomberg, Craig L. "New Testament Miracles and Higher Criticism: Climbing Up the Slippery Slope." *Journal of the Evangelical Theological Society* 27 (December 1984): 425–38.

Blumell, Lincoln H. "A Text-Critical Comparison of the King James New Testament with Certain Modern Translations." *Studies in the Bible and Antiquity* 3 (2011): 67–126.

Bock, Darrell. "Blasphemy and the Jewish Examination of Jesus." *Bulletin for Biblical Research* 17, no. 1 (2007): 53–114.

Bokovoy, David E. *Authoring the Old Testament: Genesis–Deuteronomy.* Salt Lake City: Greg Kofford Books, 2014.

Boobyer, George H. "Mark 2:10a and the Interpretation of the Healing of the Paralytic." *Harvard Theological Review* 47 (April 1954): 115–20.

Boomershine, Thomas E. *The Messiah of Peace: A Performance-Criticism Commentary on Mark's Passion-Resurrection Narrative.* Eugene, Ore.: Cascade Books, 2015.

———— and Bartholomew, Gilbert L. "The Narrative Technique of Mark 16:8." *Journal of Biblical Literature* 100, no. 2 (1981): 213–23.

Borg, Marcus J. *Jesus: Uncovering the Life, Teachings, and Relevance of a Religious Revolutionary.* San Francisco: HarperSanFrancisco, 1989.

———— and John Dominic Crossan. *The Last Week: The Day-by-Day Account of Jesus's Final Week in Jerusalem.* San Francisco: HarperSanFrancisco, 2006.

Boring, M. Eugene. "Markan Christology: God-Language for Jesus?" *New Testament Studies* 45 (October 1999): 451–71.

Boughton, Lynne C. "'Being Shed for You/Many': Time-Sense and Consequences in the Synoptic Cup Citations." *Tyndale Bulletin* 48, no. 2 (1997): 249–70.

Bowen, Matthew L. "'Thy Will Be Done': The Savior's Use of the Divine Passive." In *The Sermon on the Mount in Latter-day Scripture: The 39th Annual BYU Sydney B. Sperry Symposium,* ed. Gaye Strathearn, Thomas A. Wayment, and Daniel L. Belnap, 230–48. Salt Lake City: Deseret Book, 2010.

Bratcher, Robert G., and Eugene A. Nida. *A Translator's Handbook on the Gospel of Mark.* Vol. 2 of Helps for Translators. Leiden: E. J. Brill, 1961.

Breed, Brennan. "The Reception of the Psalms: The Example of Psalm 91." In *The Oxford Handbook of the Psalms,* ed. William P. Brown, 297–310. Oxford: Oxford University Press, 2014.

Broadhead, Edwin K. *Teaching with Authority: Miracles and Christology in the Gospel of Mark.* Vol. 74 of Journal for the Study of the New Testament Supplement Series. Sheffield, Eng.: JSOT Press, 1992.

Brown, S. Kent. "The Testimony of Mark." In *Studies in Scripture, Volume Five: The Gospels,* ed. Kent P. Jackson and Robert L. Millet, 61–87. Salt Lake City: Deseret Book, 1986.

Burdon, Christopher. "'To the Other Side': Construction of Evil and Fear of Liberation in Mark 5.1–20." *Journal for the Study of the New Testament* 27, no. 2 (2004): 149–67.

Busch, Austin. "Questioning and Conviction: Double-Voiced Discourse in Mark 3:22–30." *Journal of Biblical Literature* 125, no. 3 (2006): 477–505.

Calpino, Teresa. "The Gerasene Demoniac (Mark 5:1–20): The Pre-Markan Function of the Pericope." *Biblical Research* 53 (2008): 15–24.

Carrington, Philip. *According to Mark: A Running Commentary on the Oldest Gospel.* Cambridge, Eng.: University Press, 1960.

Chance, J. Bradley. "The Cursing of the Temple and the Tearing of the Veil in the Gospel of Mark." *Biblical Interpretation* 15, no. 3 (2007): 268–91.

Chronis, Harry L. "The Torn Veil: Cultus and Christology in Mark 15:37–39." *Journal of Biblical Literature* 101, no. 1 (1982): 97–114.

Clark, J. Reuben, Jr. *Why the King James Version.* Salt Lake City: Deseret Book, 1956.

Collins, Adela Yarbro. *Mark: A Commentary.* Minneapolis: Fortress Press, 2007.

———. "The Apocalyptic Rhetoric of Mark 13 in Historical Context." *Biblical Research* 41 (1996): 5–36.

Collins, C. John. *Genesis 1–4: A Linguistic, Literary, and Theological Commentary.* Phillipsburg, N.J.: P and R Publishing, 2006.

Combs, Jason Robert. "A Ghost on the Water? Understanding an Absurdity in Mark 6:49–50." *Journal of Biblical Literature* 127, no. 2 (2008): 345–58.

Comfort, Philip W. *New Testament Text and Translation Commentary: Commentary on the Variant Readings of the Ancient New Testament Manuscripts and How They Relate to the Major English Translations.* Carol Stream, Ill.: Tyndale House Publishers, 2008.

Cranfield, C. E. B. *The Gospel according to St Mark.* London: Cambridge University Press, 1959.

———. "Message of Hope: Mark 4:21–32." *Interpretation: A Journal of Bible and Theology* 9, no. 2 (1955): 150–64.

Crossley, James G. "Halakah and Mark 7.4: '. . . and Beds.'" *Journal for the Study of the New Testament* 25, no. 4 (2003): 433–47.

Croy, N Clayton. "Where the Gospel Text Begins: A Non-theological Interpretation of Mark 1:1." *Novum Testamentum* 43, no. 2 (2001): 105–27.

Cutler, Ian. "A Tale of Two Cynics: The Philosophic Duel between Jesus and the Woman from Syrophoenicia." *Philosophical Forum* 41 (Winter 2010): 365–87.

Davis, Ryan Conrad, and Paul Y. Hoskisson. "Usage of the Title Elohim." *Religious Educator* 14, no. 1 (2013): 109–27.

Decker, Rodney J. *Mark 1–8: A Handbook on the Greek Text.* Waco, Tex.: Baylor University Press, 2014.

———. *Mark 9–16: A Handbook on the Greek Text.* Waco, Tex.: Baylor University Press, 2014.

Delorme, Jean. "John the Baptist's Head—the Word Perverted: A Reading of a Narrative (Mark 6:14–29)." *Semeia* 81 (1998): 115–29.

de Moor, Johannes C. "The Targumic Background of Mark 12:1–12: The Parable of the Wicked Tenants." *Journal for the Study of Judaism in the Persian, Hellenistic, and Roman Period* 29, no. 1 (1998): 63–80.

Deppe, Dean B. *The Theological Intentions of Mark's Literary Devices: Markan Intercalations, Frames, Allusionary Repetitions, Narrative Surprises, and Three Types of Mirroring.* Eugene, Ore.: Wipf and Stock, 2015.

Derrett, J. Duncan M. "Contributions to the Study of the Gerasene Demoniac." *Journal for the Study of the New Testament* 3 (1979): 2–17.

———. "Eating Up the Houses of Widows: Jesus' Comment on Lawyers?" *Novum Testamentum* 14, no. 1 (1972): 1–9.

———. "Law in the New Testament: The Syro-Phoenician Woman and the Centurion of Capernaum." *Novum Testamentum* 15, no. 3 (1973): 162–86.

———. "Mark's Technique: The Haemorrhaging Woman and Jairus' Daughter." *Biblica* 63, no. 4 (1982).

———. "No Stone upon Another: Leprosy and the Temple." *Journal for the Study of the New Testament* 30 (1987): 3–20.

———. "Trees Walking, Prophecy, and Christology." *Studia Theologica* 35 (1981): 33–54.

———. "Why and How Jesus Walked on the Sea." *Novum Testamentum* 23, no. 4 (1981): 330–48.

Dew, Sheri L. *Go Forward with Faith: The Biography of Gordon B. Hinckley.* Salt Lake City: Deseret Book, 1996.

Dewey, Joanna. "The Literary Structure of the Controversy Stories in Mark 2:1–3:6." *Journal of Biblical Literature* 92, no. 3 (1973): 394–401.

———. *The Oral Ethos of the Early Church: Speaking, Writing, and the Gospel of Mark.* Eugene, Ore.: Cascade Books, 2013.

———. "The Survival of Mark's Gospel: A Good Story?" *Journal of Biblical Literature* 123, no. 3 (2004): 495–507.

———. "Women in the Gospel of Mark." *Word & World* 26 (Winter 2006): 22–29.

Dodd, C. H. *The Parables of the Kingdom.* New York: Charles Scribner's Sons, 1961.

Donahue, John R. *Are You the Christ? The Trial Narrative in the Gospel of Mark.* Missoula, Mont.: Society of Biblical Literature, 1973.

Dowd, Sharyn Echols. *Prayer, Power, and the Problem of Suffering: Mark 11:22–25 in the Context of Markan Theology.* Atlanta, Ga.: Scholars Press, 1988.

———. *Reading Mark: A Literary and Theological Commentary on the Second Gospel.* Macon, Ga.: Smyth and Helwys, 2000.

——— and Elizabeth Struthers Malbon. "The Significance of Jesus' Death in Mark: Narrative Context and Authorial Audience." *Journal of Biblical Literature* 125, no. 2 (2006): 271–97.

Driggers, Ira Brent. "God as Healer of Creation in the Gospel of Mark." In *Character Studies and the Gospel of Mark,* ed. Christopher W. Skinner and Matthew Ryan Hauge, 81–106. London: Bloomsbury, 2014.

Duff, Paul Brooks. "The March of the Divine Warrior and the Advent of the Greco-Roman King: Mark's Account of Jesus' Entry into Jerusalem." *Journal of Biblical Literature* 111, no. 1 (1992): 55–71.

Edwards, James R. "Markan Sandwiches: The Significance of Interpolations in Markan Narratives." *Novum Testamentum* 31, no. 3 (1989): 193–216.

Ehrman, Bart D. *Jesus, Interrupted: Revealing the Hidden Contradictions in the Bible (and Why We Don't Know about Them).* New York: HarperOne, 2009.

———. "The Text of Mark in the Hands of the Orthodox." *Lutheran Quarterly,* n.s., 5, no. 2 (1991): 143–56.

Evans, Craig A. *Mark 8:27–16:20*. Nashville: Thomas Nelson Publishers, 2001.

———. "Jesus' Action in the Temple: Cleansing or Portent of Destruction?" *Catholic Biblical Quarterly* 51, no. 2 (1989): 237–70.

Farrer, Austin Marsden. *A Study in St. Mark*. London: Dacre Press, 1951.

Fields, Weston W. "'Everyone Will Be Salted with Fire' (Mark 9:49)." *Grace Theological Journal* 6, no. 2 (1985): 299–304.

Finney, Paul Corby. "The Rabbi and the Coin Portrait (Mark 12:15B, 16): Rigorism Manqué." *Journal of Biblical Literature* 112, no. 4 (1993): 629–44.

Focant, Camille. *The Gospel according to Mark: A Commentary*. Trans. Leslie Robert Keylock. Eugene, Ore.: Pickwick Publications, 2012.

Fowler, Robert M. "Reader-Response Criticism: Figuring Mark's Reader." In *Mark and Method: New Approaches in Biblical Studies,* ed. Janice Capel Anderson and Stephen D. Moore, 59–93. 2d ed. Minneapolis: Fortress Press, 2008.

France, N. T. *The Gospel of Mark: A Commentary on the Greek Text*. Grand Rapids, Mich.: William B. Eerdmans Publishing, 2002.

Funk, Robert W. "The Looking-Glass Tree Is for the Birds: Ezekiel 17:22–24; Mark 4:30–32." *Interpretation: A Journal of Bible and Theology* 27, no. 1 (1973): 3–9.

Gaiser, Frederick J. "In Touch with Jesus: Healing in Mark 5:21–43." *Word & World* 30 (Winter 2010): 5–15.

———. "'Your Sins Are Forgiven. . . . Stand Up and Walk': A Theological Reading of Mark 2:1–12 in the Light of Psalm 103." *Ex Auditu* 21 (2005): 71–87.

Garland, David E. *A Theology of Mark's Gospel: Good News about Jesus the Messiah, the Son of God*. Ed. Andreas J. Köstenberger. Grand Rapids, Mich.: Zondervan, 2015.

Garroway, Joshua. "The Invasion of a Mustard Seed: A Reading of Mark 5.1–20." *Journal for the Study of the New Testament* 32, no. 1 (2009): 57–75.

Geddert, Timothy J. "Beginning Again (Mark 16:1–8)." *Direction* 33 (Fall 2004): 150–57.

Glancey, Jennifer A. "Unveiling Masculinity: The Construction of Gender in Mark 6:17–29." *Biblical Interpretation* 2, no. 1 (1994): 34–50.

Graham, Susan Lochrie. "Silent Voices: Women in the Gospel of Mark." *Semeia* 54 (1991): 145–58.

Grey, Matthew J. "Simon Peter in Capernaum: An Archaeological Survey of the First Century Village." In *The Ministry of Peter the Chief Apostle: The 43rd Annual Brigham Young University Sperry Symposium,* ed. Frank F. Judd Jr., Eric D. Huntsman, and Shon D. Hopkin, 27–66. Provo, Utah: Religious Studies Center; Salt Lake City: Deseret Book, 2014.

Guelich, Robert A. *Mark 1–8:26*. Vol. 34a of Word Biblical Commentary. Dallas: Word Books, 1989.

Guijarro, Santiago, and Ana Rodríguez. "The 'Messianic' Anointing of Jesus." *Biblical Theology Bulletin* 41, no. 3 (2011): 132–43.

Gundry, Robert H. *Mark: A Commentary on His Apology for the Cross*. Grand Rapids, Mich.: William B. Eerdmans Publishing, 1993.

———. "Mark 10:29: Order in the List." *Catholic Biblical Quarterly* 59, no. 3 (1997): 465–75.

Gundry-Volf, Judith M. "Between the Text and Sermon: Mark 9:33–37." *Interpretation: A Journal of Bible and Theology* 53, no. 1 (1999): 57–61.

Gurtner, Daniel M. "LXX Syntax and the Identity of the NT Veil." *Novum Testamentum* 47, no. 4 (2005): 344–53.

———. "The Rending of the Veil and Markan Christology: 'Unveiling' the ΥΙΟΣ ΘΕΟΥ (Mark 15:38–39)." *Biblical Interpretation* 15, no. 3 (2007): 292–306.

Haber, Susan. "A Woman's Touch: Feminist Encounters with the Hemorrhaging Woman in Mark 5.24–34." *Journal for the Study of the New Testament* 26, no. 2 (2003): 171–92.

Hagedorn, Anselm C., and Jerome H. Neyrey. "'It Was Out of Envy That They Handed Jesus Over' (Mark 15:10): The Anatomy of Envy and the Gospel of Mark." *Journal for the Study of the New Testament* 69 (1998): 15–56.

Hamblin, William J. "Aspects of an Early Christian Initiation Ritual." In *By Study and Also By Faith: Essays in Honor of Hugh W. Nibley on the Occasion of His Eightieth Birthday, 27 March 1990*, ed. John M. Lundquist and Stephen D. Ricks, 1:202–21. Salt Lake City: Deseret Book; Provo, Utah: Foundation for Ancient Research and Mormon Studies, 1990.

Hardy, Heather. "'Saving Christianity': The Nephite Fulfillment of Jesus' Eschatological Prophecies." *Journal of Book of Mormon Studies* 23 (2014): 22–55.

Hays, Richard B. "Can the Gospels Teach Us How to Read the Old Testament?" *Pro Ecclesia* 11, no. 4 (2002): 402–18.

Heil, John Paul. *The Gospel of Mark as a Model for Action: A Reader-Response Commentary*. New York: Paulist Press, 1992.

———. "The Narrative Strategy and Pragmatics of the Temple Theme in Mark." *Catholic Biblical Quarterly* 59, no. 1 (1997): 76–100.

———. "Reader-Response and the Narrative Context of the Parables about Growing Seed in Mark 4:1–34." *Catholic Biblical Quarterly* 54, no. 2 (1992): 271–86.

Hellerman, Joseph H. "Wealth and Sacrifice in Early Christianity: Revisiting Mark's Presentation of Jesus' Encounter with the Rich Young Ruler." *Trinity Journal*, n.s., 21 (Fall 2000): 143–64.

Herzog, William R., II. "Dissembling, a Weapon of the Weak: The Case of Christ and Caesar in Mark 12:13–17 and Romans 13:1–7." *Perspectives in Religious Studies* 21, no. 4 (1994): 339–60.

Hicks, Richard. "Markan Discipleship according to Malachi: The Significance of *Me Apostereses* in the Story of the Rich Man (Mark 10:17–22)." *Journal of Biblical Literature* 132, no. 1 (2013): 179–99.

Hoffeditz, David M., and Gary E. Yates. "Femme Fatale *Redux*: Intertextual Connection to the Elijah/Jezebel Narratives in Mark 6:14-29." *Bulletin for Biblical Research* 15, no. 2 (2005): 199–221.

Horsley, Richard A. *Hearing the Whole Story: The Politics of Plot in Mark's Gospel.* Louisville, Ky.: Westminster John Knox Press, 2001.

Huntsman, Eric D. "The Accounts of Peter's Denial." In *The Ministry of Peter, the Chief Apostle: The 43rd Annual Brigham Young University Sperry Symposium*, ed. Frank F. Judd Jr., Eric D. Huntsman, and Shon D. Hopkin, 127–49. Provo, Utah: Religious Studies Center; Salt Lake City: Deseret Book, 2014.

———. *The Miracles of Jesus.* Salt Lake City: Deseret Book, 2014.

———. "The Petrine *Kērygma* and the Gospel according to Mark," in *The Ministry of Peter, the Chief Apostle: The 43rd Annual Brigham Young University Sperry Symposium,* ed. Frank F. Judd Jr., Eric D. Huntsman, and Shon D. Hopkin, 169–90. Provo, Utah: Religious Studies Center; Salt Lake City: Deseret Book, 2014.

Ilan, Tal. "'Man Born of Woman . . .' (Job 14:1): The Phenomenon of Men Bearing Metronymes at the Time of Jesus." *Novum Testamentum* 34, no. 1 (1992): 23–45.

Iverson, Kelly R. "A Centurion's 'Confession': A Performance-Critical Analysis of Mark 15:39." *Journal of Biblical Literature* 130, no. 2 (2011): 329–50.

Jackson, Kent P., and Peter M. Jasinski. "The Process of Inspired Translation: Two Passages Translated Twice in the Joseph Smith Translation of the Bible." *BYU Studies* 42, no. 2 (2003): 35–64.

Janzen, J. Gerald. "The Verb *Paradidomi* and the Last Judgment in Mark 4:29." *Encounter* 69 (Winter 2008): 25–50.

Johnson, Luke Timothy. *Hebrews: A Commentary.* Louisville, Ky.: Westminster John Knox Press, 2006.

Judd, Frank F., Jr. "Who Really Wrote the Gospels? A Study of Traditional Authorship." In *How the New Testament Came to Be: The Thirty-fifth Annual Sidney B. Sperry Symposium,* ed. Kent P. Jackson and Frank F. Judd Jr., 123–40. Provo, Utah: Religious Studies Center, Brigham Young University; Salt Lake City: Deseret Book, 2006.

Juel, Donald. *A Master of Surprise: Mark Interpreted.* Minneapolis: Fortress Press, 1994.

Kahler, Martin. *The So-called Historical Jesus and the Historic, Biblical Christ.* Philadelphia: Fortress Press, 1964.

Keck, Leander E. "Toward the Renewal of NT Christology." *New Testament Studies* 32 (1986): 362–77.

Kelber, Werner H. *Mark's Story of Jesus.* Philadelphia: Fortress Press, 1979.

Keller, Roger R. "Mark and Luke: Two Facets of a Diamond." In *Sperry Symposium Classics: The New Testament,* ed. Frank F. Judd Jr. and Gaye Strathearn, 92–107. Provo, Utah: Religious Studies Center, Brigham Young University; Salt Lake City: Deseret Book, 2006.

Kinukawa, Hisako. *Women and Jesus in Mark: A Japanese Feminist Perspective.* Maryknoll, N.Y.: Orbis Books, 1994.

Kinman, Brent. "Jesus' Royal Entry into Jerusalem." *Bulletin for Biblical Research* 15, no. 2 (2005): 223–60.

Kirk, J. R. Daniel. "Time for Figs, Temple Destruction, and Houses of Prayer in Mark 11:12–25." *Catholic Biblical Quarterly* 74, no. 3 (2012): 509–27.

Kirkland, Boyd. "Elohim and Jehovah in Mormonism and the Bible." *Dialogue* 19 (Spring 1986): 77–93.

Kirkland, J. R. "Earliest Understanding of Jesus' Use of Parables: Mark 4:10–12 in Context." *Novum Testamentum* 19, no. 1 (1977): 1–21.

Kleist, James A. "The Two False Witnesses (Mk. 14:55 ff)." *Catholic Biblical Quarterly* 9, no. 3 (1947): 321–23.

Kloppenborg, John S. "*Evocatio Deorum* and the Date of Mark." *Journal of Biblical Literature* 124, no. 3 (2005): 419–50.

———. "Self-Help or *Deus ex Machina* in Mark 12.9?" *New Testament Studies* 50, no. 4 (2004): 495–518.

Knapp, Stephen A. "He Could Do No Mighty Deed There . . . Mark 6:1–6." *Proceedings* (Grand Rapids, Mich.) 12 (1992): 155–66.

Knohl, Israel. "The Apocalyptic and Messianic Dimensions of the *Gabriel Revelation* in Their Historical Context." In *Hazon Gabriel: New Readings of the Gabriel Revelation,* ed. Matthias Henze, 39–59. Atlanta, Ga.: Society of Biblical Literature, 2011.

Kraemer, Ross S. "Implicating Herodias and Her Daughter in the Death of John the Baptizer: A (Christian) Theological Strategy?" *Journal of Biblical Literature* 125, no. 2 (2006): 321–49.

Kuruvilla, Abraham. "The Naked Runaway and the Enrobed Reporter of Mark 14 and 16: What Is the Author Doing with What He Is Saying?" *Journal of the Evangelical Theological Society* 54 (September 2011): 527–45.

Kvam, Kristen E., Linda S. Schearing, and Valarie H. Ziegler. *Eve and Adam: Jewish, Christian and Muslim Readings on Genesis and Gender.* Bloomington: Indiana University Press, 1999.

Lake, Kirsopp. "'Εμβριμησαμενος and 'Οργισθεις, Mark 1, 40–43." *Harvard Theological Review* 16, no. 2 (1923): 197–98.

Lane, William L. *The Gospel according to Mark.* Grand Rapids, Mich.: William B. Eerdmans Publishing, 1974.

Larsen, Kevin W. "A Focused Christological Reading of Mark 8:22–9:13." *Trinity Journal,* n.s., 26 (Spring 2005): 33–46.

Lauterbach, Jacob Z., trans. *Mekhilta de-Rabbi Ishmael: A Critical Edition, Based on the Manuscripts and Early Editions, with an English Translation, Introduction, and Notes.* 2d ed. 2 vols. Philadelphia: Jewish Publication Society, 2004.

Leander, Hans. "With Homi Bhabha at the Jerusalem City Gates: A Postcolonial Reading of the 'Triumphant' Entry (Mark 11.1–11)." *Journal for the Study of the New Testament* 32, no. 3 (2010): 309–35.

Levine, Amy-Jill. *The Misunderstood Jew.* San Francisco: HarperSanFrancisco, 2006.

Liddle, Stephen W., and Richard Galbraith. LDS Scripture Citation Index. http://scriptures.byu.edu.

Ludlow, Daniel H. *A Companion to Your Study of the New Testament.* Salt Lake City: Deseret Book, 1982.

———, ed. *Encyclopedia of Mormonism.* 4 vols. New York: Macmillan, 1992.

Malbon, Elizabeth Struthers. *Hearing Mark: A Listener's Guide.* Harrisburg, Pa.: Trinity Press International, 2002.

———. *Mark's Jesus: Characterization As Narrative Christology.* Waco, Tex.: Baylor University Press, 2009.

———. "Narrative Criticism: How Does the Story Mean?" In *Mark and Method: New Approaches in Biblical Studies,* ed. Janice Capel Anderson and Stephen D. Moore, 29–57. 2d ed. Minneapolis: Fortress Press, 2008.

Mann, C. S. *Mark: A New Translation with Introduction and Commentary.* Garden City, N.Y.: Doubleday, 1986.

Marcus, Joel. *Mark 1–8: A New Translation with Introduction and Commentary.* Vol. 27 of the Anchor Yale Bible. New Haven, Conn.: Yale University Press, 2005.

———. *Mark 8–16: A New Translation with Introduction and Commentary.* Vol. 27A of the Anchor Yale Bible. New Haven, Conn.: Yale University Press, 2009.

Martin, Troy W. "Watch during the Watches (Mark 13:35)." *Journal of Biblical Literature* 120, no. 4 (2001): 685–701.

Matthews, Robert J. "The JST: Retrospect and Prospect—a Panel." In *The Joseph Smith Translation: The Restoration of Plain and Precious Truths,* ed. Monte S. Nyman and Robert L. Millet, 291–305. Provo, Utah: Religious Studies Center, Brigham Young University, 1985.

———. *"A Plainer Translation": Joseph Smith's Translation of the Bible: A History and Commentary.* Provo, Utah: Brigham Young University Press, 1975.

McComiskey, Douglas S. "Exile and the Purpose of Jesus' Parables (Mark 4:10–12; Matt 13:10–17; Luke 8:9–10)." *Journal of the Evangelical Theological Society* 51 (March 2008): 59–85.

McInerny, William F. "An Unresolved Question in the Gospel Called Mark: 'Who Is This Whom Even Wind and Sea Obey?' (4:41)." *Perspectives in Religious Studies* 23, no. 3 (1996): 255–68.

Meier, John P. "The Historical Jesus and the Historical Herodians." *Journal of Biblical Literature* 119, no. 4 (2000): 740–46.

Metzger, Bruce M. *A Textual Commentary on the Greek New Testament: A Companion Volume to the United Bible Societies' Greek New Testament (Second Edition).* Stuttgart: United Bible Societies, 2001.

——— and Bart D. Ehrman. *The Text of the New Testament: Its Transmission, Corruption, and Restoration.* 4th ed. New York: Oxford University Press, 2005.

Meyer, Marvin. "Taking Up the Cross and Following Jesus: Discipleship in the Gospel of Mark." *Calvin Theological Journal* 37, no. 2 (2002): 230–38.

Miller, Susan. *Women in Mark's Gospel.* New York: T and T Clark International, 2004.

Miller, Richard C. "Mark's Empty Tomb and Other Translation Fables in Classical Antiquity." *Journal of Biblical Literature* 129, no. 4 (2010): 759–76.

Millet, Robert L. "Joseph Smith's Translation of the Bible: A Historical Overview." In *The Joseph Smith Translation: The Restoration of Plain and Precious Things,* ed. Monte S. Nyman and Robert L. Millet, 23–47. Provo, Utah: Religious Studies Center, Brigham Young University, 1985.

Mitchell, Curtis C. "The Case for Persistence in Prayer." *Journal of the Evangelical Theological Society* 27 (June 1984): 161–68.

Mitchell, Joan L. *Beyond Fear and Silence: A Feminist-Literary Approach to the Gospel of Mark.* New York: Continuum, 2001.

Moloney, Francis J. *The Gospel of Mark: A Commentary.* Peabody, Mass.: Hendrickson, 2002.

———. *Mark: Storyteller, Interpreter, Evangelist.* Peabody, Mass.: Hendrickson Publisher, 2004.

Moss, Candida R. "The Transfiguration: An Exercise in Markan Accommodation." *Biblical Interpretation* 12, no. 1 (2004): 69–89.

Mullins, Terence Y. "Papias on Mark's Gospel." *Vigiliae Christianae* 14, no. 4 (1960): 216–24.

Myers, Ched. *Binding the Strong Man: A Political Reading of Mark's Story of Jesus.* Maryknoll, N.Y.: Orbis Books, 1995.

Neyrey, Jerome H. "Questions, *Chreiai,* and Challenges to Honor: The Interface of Rhetoric and Culture in Mark's Gospel." *Catholic Biblical Quarterly* 60, no. 4 (1998): 657–81.

Oaks, Dallin H. "Scripture Reading and Revelation." *Ensign* 25 (January 1995): 6–9.

Oden, Thomas C., and Christopher A. Hall, eds. *Mark.* Vol. 2 of Ancient Christian Commentary on Scripture, New Testament. Downers Grove, Ill.: InterVarsity Press, 1998.

Ossandón, Juan Carlos. "Bartimaeus' Faith: Plot and Point of View in Mark 10,46–52." *Biblica* 93, no. 3 (2012): 377–402.

Parker, Pierson. "The Authorship of the Second Gospel." *Perspectives in Religious Studies* 5, no. 1 (1978): 4–9.

Peppard, Michael. "Torah for the Man Who Has Everything: 'Do Not Defraud' in Mark 10:19." *Journal of Biblical Literature* 134, no. 3 (2015): 595–604.

Perrin, Norman. "Creative Use of the Son of Man Traditions by Mark." *Union Seminary Quarterly Review* 23 (Summer 1968): 357–65.

Peterson, Dwight N. "Translating παραλυτικός in Mark 2:1–12: A Proposal." *Bulletin for Biblical Research* 16, no. 2 (2006): 261–72.

Pfann, Stephen J. "The Essene Yearly Renewal Ceremony and the Baptism of Repentance." In *The Provo International Conference on the Dead Sea Scrolls: Technological Innovations, New Texts, and Reformulated Issues,* ed. Donald W. Parry and Eugene Ulrich, 337–52. Leiden: Brill, 1999.

Perkins, Pheme. *Introduction to the Synoptic Gospels.* Grand Rapids, Mich.: William B. Eerdmans Publishing, 2007.

Pickett, Raymond. "Following Jesus in Galilee: Resurrection as Empowerment in the Gospel of Mark." *Currents in Theology and Mission* 32 (December 2005): 434–44.

Pitre, Brant James. "Blessing the Barren and Warning the Fecund: Jesus' Message for Women Concerning Pregnancy and Childbirth." *Journal for the Study of the New Testament* 81 (March 2001): 59–80.

Porter, Stanley E. *Linguistic Analysis of the Greek New Testament: Studies in Tools, Methods, and Practice.* Grand Rapids, Mich.: Baker Academic, 2015.

Powery, Emerson B. "The Spirit, the Scripture(s), and the Gospel of Mark: Pneumatology and Hermeneutics in Narrative Perspective." *Journal of Pentecostal Theology* 11, no. 2 (2003): 184–98.

Price, Reynolds. *Three Gospels.* New York: Touchstone, 1997.

Proctor, Mark. "'After Three Days' in Mark 8:31; 9:31; 10:34: Subordinating Jesus' Resurrection in the Second Gospel." *Perspectives in Religious Studies* 30, no. 4 (2003): 399–424.

Queller, Kurt. "'Stretch Out Your Hand!' Echo and Metalepsis in Mark's Sabbath Healing Controversy." *Journal of Biblical Literature* 129, no. 4 (2010): 737–58.

Reed, Jonathan L. *Archaeology and the Galilean Jesus: A Re-examination of the Evidence.* Harrisburg, Pa.: Trinity Press International, 2000.

Reynolds, Benjamin E. "The 'One Like a Son of Man' According to the Old Greek of Daniel 7,13–14." *Biblica* 89, no. 1 (2008): 70–80.

Reynolds, Stephen M. "Πυγμῇ (Mark 7 3) as 'Cupped Hand.'" *Journal of Biblical Literature* 85, no. 1 (1966): 87–88.

Rhoads, David M. *Reading Mark: Engaging the Gospel.* Minneapolis: Fortress Press, 2004.

———, Joanna Dewey, and Donald Michie. *Mark As Story: An Introduction to the Narrative of a Gospel.* 3d ed. Minneapolis: Fortress Press, 2012.

Richards, LeGrand. "What the Gospel Teaches." *Ensign* 12 (May 1982): 29–31.

———. "One Lord, One Faith." In *Official Report of the One Hundred Thirty-ninth Annual General Conference of The Church of Jesus Christ of Latter-day Saints,* 87–91. Salt Lake City: The Church of Jesus Christ of Latter-day Saints, 1969.

Rindge, Matthew S. "Reconfiguring the Akedah and Recasting God: Lament and Divine Abandonment in Mark." *Journal of Biblical Literature* 131, no. 4 (2012): 755–74.

Robbins, Vernon K. "The Woman Who Touched Jesus' Garment: Socio-Rhetorical Analysis of the Synoptic Accounts." *New Testament Studies* 33, no. 4 (1987): 502–15.

Rogers, T. J. "Shaking the Dust off the Markan Mission Discourse." *Journal for the Study of the New Testament* 27, no. 2 (2004): 169–92.

Ross, J. M. "Further Unnoticed Points in the Text of the New Testament." *Novum Testamentum* 45, no. 3 (2003): 209–21.

Sabin, Marie. "Women Transformed: The Ending of Mark Is the Beginning of Wisdom." *Cross Currents* 48 (Summer 1998): 149–68.

Sabin, Mary Noonan. *Reopening the Word: Reading Mark as Theology in the Context of Early Judaism.* Oxford: Oxford University Press, 2011.

Schäfer, Peter, Margarete Schlüter, and Hans Georg von Mutius, eds. *Synopse zur Hekhalot-Literatur.* Tübingen: Mohr-Siebeck, 1981.

Seeley, David. "Jesus' Temple Act." *Catholic Biblical Quarterly* 55, no. 2 (1993): 263–83.

———. "Rulership and Service in Mark 10:41–45." *Novum Testamentum* 35, no. 3 (1993): 234–50.

Shepherd, Michael B. "Daniel 7:13 and the New Testament Son of Man." *Westminster Theological Journal* 68, no. 1 (2006): 99–111.

Sherry, Thomas E., and W. Jeffrey Marsh. "Precious Truths Restored: Joseph Smith Translation Changes Not Included in Our Bible." *Religious Educator* 5, no. 2 (2004): 57–74.

Shiner, Whitney. *Proclaiming the Gospel: First-Century Performance of Mark.* Harrisburg, Pa.: Trinity Press International, 2003.

Skinner, Christopher W. "'Whom He also Names Apostles': A Textual Problem in Mark 3:14." *Bibliotheca Sacra* 161 (July–September 2004): 322–29.

Smith, Abraham. "Tyranny Exposed: Mark's Typological Characterization of Herod Antipas (Mark 6:14–29)." *Biblical Interpretation* 14, no. 3 (2006): 259–93.

Smith, Barry D. "Objections to the Authenticity of Mark 11:17 Reconsidered." *Westminster Theological Journal* 54, no. 2 (1992): 255–71.

Smith, Joseph Fielding. *Doctrines of Salvation.* Comp. Bruce R. McConkie. 3 vols. Salt Lake City: Bookcraft, 1954–56.

Smith, Julie M. "A Double Portion: An Intertextual Reading of Hannah (1 Samuel 1–2) and Mark's Greek Woman (Mark 7:24–30)." *Dialogue: A Journal of Mormon Thought* 50, no. 2 (2017): 125–38.

———. "'I Will Sing to the Lord': Women's Songs in the Scriptures." *Dialogue: A Journal of Mormon Thought* 45 (Fall 2012): 56–69.

———. "Narrative Atonement Theology in the Gospel of Mark." *BYU Studies Quarterly* 54, no. 1 (2015): 29–41.

———. "Paradoxes in Paradise." In *Fleeing the Garden: Reading Genesis 2–3,* ed. Adam S. Miller, 1–30. Proceedings of the Mormon Theology Seminar. Provo, Utah: Neal A. Maxwell Institute for Religious Scholarship, 2017.

———. "A Redemptive Reading of Mark 5:25–34." *Interpreter: A Journal of Mormon Scripture* 14 (2015): 95–105.

———. "She Hath Wrought a Good Work: The Anointing of Jesus in Mark's Gospel." *Studies in the Bible and Antiquity* 5 (2013): 31–46.

Snodgrass, Klyne. "A Hermeneutic of Hearing Informed by the Parables with Special Reference to Mark 4." *Bulletin for Biblical Research* 14, no. 1 (2004): 59–70.

———. "Recent Research on the Parable of the Wicked Tenants: An Assessment." *Bulletin for Biblical Research* 8 (1998): 187–216.

Snow, Marcellus S. "The Challenge of Theological Translation: New German Versions of the Standard Works." *Dialogue: A Journal of Mormon Thought* 17 (Summer 1984): 133–49.

Snow, Robert S. "Let the Reader Understand: Mark's Use of Jeremiah 7 in Mark 13:14." *Bulletin for Biblical Research* 21, no. 4 (2011): 467–77.

Spackman, Ben. "Why Bible Translations Differ: A Guide for the Perplexed." *Religious Educator* 15, no. 1 (2014): 30–65.

Stapley, Jonathan A., and Kristine Wright. "Female Ritual Healing in Mormonism." *Journal of Mormon History* 37 (Winter 2011): 1–85.

St. Clair, Raquel A. *Call and Consequence: A Womanist Reading of Mark.* Minneapolis: Fortress Press, 2008.

Starobinski, Jean. "An Essay in Literary Analysis—Mark 5:1–20." *Ecumenical Review* 23, no. 4 (1971): [377–97].

Stein, Robert H. "The Ending of Mark." *Bulletin for Biblical Research* 18, no. 1 (2008): 79–98.

———. *Mark.* Grand Rapids, Mich.: Baker Academic, 2008.

Story, J. Lyle. "The Parable of the Budding Fig Tree (Mark 13:28–31)." *American Theological Inquiry* 4, no. 1 (2011): 85–94.

Swanson, Richard W. "Moving Bodies and Translating Scripture: Interpretation and Incarnation." *Word and World* 31 (Summer 2011): 271–78.

Talkmon, Shemaryahu. "The 'Desert Motif' in the Bible and in Qumran Literature." In *Biblical Motifs: Origins and Transformations,* ed. Alexander Altmann, 31–63. Cambridge: Harvard University Press, 1966.

Talmage, James E. *Jesus the Christ.* Salt Lake City: Deseret Book, 1973.

Tannehill, Robert C. *The Shape of the Gospels: New Testament Essays.* Eugene, Ore.: Cascade Books, 2007.

Taylor, Joan E. "The Garden of Gethsemane: Not the Place of Jesus' Arrest." *Biblical Archaeology Review* 21 (July/August 1995): 26–35.

Thorley, John. "Junia, a Woman Apostle." *Novum Testamentum* 38, no. 1 (1996): 18–29.

Tolbert, Mary Ann. *Sowing the Gospel: Mark's World in Literary-Historical Perspective.* Minneapolis: Fortress Press, 1989.

Tvedtnes, John A. "I Have a Question." *Ensign* 15 (March 1985): 29.

Ukpong, Justin S. "Tribute to Caesar, Mark 12:13–17 (Mt 22:15–22; Lk 20:20–26)." *Neotestamentica* 33, no. 2 (1999): 433–44.

Ulansey, David. "The Heavenly Veil Torn: Mark's Cosmic *Inclusio.*" *Journal of Biblical Literature* 110, no. 1 (1991): 123–25.

Underwood, Grant. "Joseph Smith and the King James Bible." In *The King James Bible and the Restoration,* ed. Kent P. Jackson, 215–33. Provo, Utah: Religious Studies Center, Brigham Young University, 2011.

van Eck, Ernest. "The Tenants in the Vineyard (GThom 65/Mark 12:1–12): A Realistic and Social-Scientific Reading." *Hervormde Teologiese Studies* 63, no. 3 (2007): 909–36.

Waetjen, Herman C. *A Reordering of Power: A Sociopolitical Reading of Mark's Gospel.* Minneapolis: Fortress Press, 1989.

Wallace, Daniel B. "Mark 16:8 As the Conclusion to the Second Gospel." In *Perspectives on the Ending of Mark,* ed. David Alan Black, 1–39. Nashville: B&H Academic, 2008.

Wayment, Thomas A. "The Endings of Mark and Revelation." In *The King James Bible and the Restoration,* ed. Kent P. Jackson, 75–94. Provo, Utah: Religious Studies Center, Brigham Young University, 2011.

——— and Richard Neitzel Holzapfel. *Making Sense of the New Testament.* Salt Lake City: Deseret Book, 2010.

Welch, John W. "The Factor of Fear in the Trial of Jesus." In *Jesus Christ: Son of God, Savior,* ed. Paul H. Peterson, Gary L. Hatch, and Laura D. Card, 284–312. Provo, Utah: Religious Studies Center, Brigham Young University, 2002.

Wheaton, Gerald. "Thinking the Things of God? The Translation and Meaning of Mark 8:33c." *Novum Testamentum* 56 (2015): 42–56.

Widtsoe, John A. *In Search of Truth: Comments on the Gospel and Modern Thought.* Salt Lake City: Deseret Book, 1930.

Williams, Joel F. "Foreshadowing, Echoes, and the Blasphemy at the Cross (Mark 15:29)." *Journal of Biblical Literature* 132, no. 4 (2013): 913–33.

Williams, Margaret H. *Jews in a Graeco-Roman Environment.* Tübingen: Mohr Siebeck, 2013.

Wire, Antoinette Clark. *The Case for Mark Composed in Performance.* Eugene, Ore.: Cascade Books, 2011.

Witherington, Ben, III. *The Gospel of Mark: A Socio-rhetorical Commentary.* Grand Rapids, Mich.: William B. Eerdmans Publishing, 2001.

Woods, Fred E. *Water and Storm Polemics against Baalism in the Deuteronomic History.* New York: Peter Lang Publishing, 1994.

———. "The Latter-day Saint Edition of the King James Bible." In *The King James Bible and the Restoration,* ed. Kent P. Jackson, 260–80. Provo, Utah: Religious Studies Center; Salt Lake City: Deseret Book, 2011.

Wright, Addison G. "The Widow's Mites: Praise or Lament—a Matter of Context." *Catholic Biblical Quarterly* 44, no. 2 (1982): 256–65.

Wright, Mark Alan. "'According to Their Language, unto Their Understanding': The Cultural Context of Hierophanies and Theophanies in Latter-day Saint Canon." *Studies in the Bible and Antiquity* 3 (2011): 51–65.

Wright, N. T. *Simply Jesus: A New Vision of Who He Was, What He Did, and Why He Matters.* New York: HarperOne, 2011.

Zacharias, H. Daniel. "Old Greek Daniel 7:13–14 and Matthew's Son of Man." *Bulletin for Biblical Research* 21, no. 4 (2011): 453–61.

Scripture Index

This index is ordered by book under Hebrew Bible, New Testament, Book of Mormon, Pearl of Great Price, Other Ancient Sources (alphabetized), and Doctrine and Covenants.

Subject Index

money... 206, 384, 614–15, 623, 646, 647–48, 666, 708, 717, 719

Mosaic law
atonement/forgiveness and... 169, 182
blasphemy and... 162, 243, 768
cleanness and... 144–45, 148, 150, 176, 319, 342, 345, 348, 364–65, 368, 369, 370, 437–39, 444, 472. *See also* demons
divorce and... 549–51
fasting and... 182, 184, 187
forgiveness of sins and... 71
lepers and... 144–45, 148, 150
leper's house and... 676, 715
maiming and... 548
marriage and... 394, 559
miracles and... 237
plucking grain and... 190
possession and... 237
Sabbath prohibitions and... 191, 199–201, 202, 204, 206
supremacy of... 556
taxes and... 645, 646
touch and... 132
witnesses and... 764

Moses
on all people as prophets... 541–42
as author... 550
clothing and... 433
delegates leadership responsibilities... 224
despairs of feeding people... 421, 469, 887, 897
divides people into groups... 418
on God testing people... 428, 894
on hearing... 264
invites those on Lord's side to come... 249
kingdom of God and... 507–8
on Mount Sinai... 220
speaks to God in burning bush... 428, 653, 893
speaks to Pharaoh... 164
at Transfiguration... 514–16

mother... 245–46, 247, 249, 254, 442–43
motif inversion... 89, 107–8, 166, 302, 315, 347, 349, 350, 362–63, 368–69, 616, 890–91, 892
mountain... 220, 426, 513, 519, 618–20, 687, 896
Mount of Olives... 603–4, 619, 672–73
mourning... 184
multitude. *See* crowd
mustard seed... 300–302
muteness... 529
myrrh... 790–91
mystery... 270–72, 285

N

Naaman... 75
Naboth... 635
nakedness... 760–61
names
anointing and... 721, 722
give power over named... 323, 501
lack of... 721
new... 224, 226, 227–28, 231, 750
narrator... 756
Nathan... 241–42, 274
Nazareth... 87, 373, 375
Nebuchadnezzar... 301
neighbor... 657
Nephites... 668
"new." *See* "old" versus "new"
numbers, symbolism of... 16, 98, 218, 221, 231, 264, 360, 364, 469, 470, 471–72, 481, 658, 859

O

Oaks, Dallin H., on scriptural commentaries... 8
oath... 442–43, 477
Obadiah... 418
obedience... 248
offense... 280–81, 377, 542–44, 740, 741
offerings... 665–69
oil... 387, 746
ointment... 707
olive oil... 746
olive trees... 299, 488
"old" versus "new"... 104, 106, 185–86, 187–88, 196, 209
omniscience... 296, 345, 379, 414, 420, 456, 457, 486, 489
ordaining... 221
outsiders... 14, 235, 238, 246, 250, 254, 272, 285, 287, 357, 358, 726

P

palsy... 158
Papias... 841–46
parables... 238, 256–57, 264–66, 302–3, 697
children of the bridechamber... 183–85
enacted... 303, 347, 355, 358, 487, 556, 563, 613–14, 623–24, 625, 673, 722, 738, 825, 831
fig tree... 691–92, 698
foods entering don't defile... 444–47
house divided against itself... 239
kingdom divided against itself... 239
kingdom of God compared to seed/harvest... 295–300